HANDBOOK
of
PSYCHOLOGY

HANDBOOK
of
PSYCHOLOGY

VOLUME 9
HEALTH PSYCHOLOGY

Arthur M. Nezu

Christine Maguth Nezu

Pamela A. Geller

Volume Editors

Irving B. Weiner

Editor-in-Chief

John Wiley & Sons, Inc.

Copyright © 2003 by John Wiley & Sons, Inc., Hoboken, New Jersey. All rights reserved.

Published simultaneously in Canada.

Library of Congress Cataloging-in-Publication Data:

Handbook of psychology / Irving B. Weiner, editor-in-chief.
    p.   cm.
    Includes bibliographical references and indexes.
    Contents: v. 1. History of psychology / edited by Donald K. Freedheim — v. 2. Research methods in psychology / edited by John A. Schinka, Wayne F. Velicer — v. 3. Biological psychology / edited by Michela Gallagher, Randy J. Nelson — v. 4. Experimental psychology / edited by Alice F. Healy, Robert W. Proctor — v. 5. Personality and social psychology / edited by Theodore Millon, Melvin J. Lerner — v. 6. Developmental psychology / edited by Richard M. Lerner, M. Ann Easterbrooks, Jayanthi Mistry — v. 7. Educational psychology / edited by William M. Reynolds, Gloria E. Miller — v. 8. Clinical psychology / edited by George Stricker, Thomas A. Widiger — v. 9. Health psychology / edited by Arthur M. Nezu, Christine Maguth Nezu, Pamela A. Geller — v. 10. Assessment psychology / edited by John R. Graham, Jack A. Naglieri — v. 11. Forensic psychology / edited by Alan M. Goldstein — v. 12. Industrial and organizational psychology / edited by Walter C. Borman, Daniel R. Ilgen, Richard J. Klimoski.
    ISBN 0-471-17669-9 (set) — ISBN 0-471-38320-1 (cloth : alk. paper : v. 1) — ISBN 0-471-38513-1 (cloth : alk. paper : v. 2) — ISBN 0-471-38403-8 (cloth : alk. paper : v. 3) — ISBN 0-471-39262-6 (cloth : alk. paper : v. 4) — ISBN 0-471-38404-6 (cloth : alk. paper : v. 5) — ISBN 0-471-38405-4 (cloth : alk. paper : v. 6) — ISBN 0-471-38406-2 (cloth : alk. paper : v. 7) — ISBN 0-471-39263-4 (cloth : alk. paper : v. 8) — ISBN 0-471-38514-X (cloth : alk. paper : v. 9) — ISBN 0-471-38407-0 (cloth : alk. paper : v. 10) — ISBN 0-471-38321-X (cloth : alk. paper : v. 11) — ISBN 0-471-38408-9 (cloth : alk. paper : v. 12)
    1. Psychology. I. Weiner, Irving B.

BF121.H1955 2003
150—dc21

2002066380

Printed in the United States of America.

10 9 8 7 6 5 4 3 2 1

Editorial Board

Because of their undaunting spirit, this volume is dedicated to the uniformed and volunteer men and women who unselfishly offered their help to many during the aftermath of the September 11, 2001, atrocities. No doubt such care will impact greatly on the world's healing.

Handbook of Psychology Preface

Psychology at the beginning of the twenty-first century has become a highly diverse field of scientific study and applied technology. Psychologists commonly regard their discipline as the science of behavior, and the American Psychological Association has formally designated 2000 to 2010 as the "Decade of Behavior." The pursuits of behavioral scientists range from the natural sciences to the social sciences and embrace a wide variety of objects of investigation. Some psychologists have more in common with biologists than with most other psychologists, and some have more in common with sociologists than with most of their psychological colleagues. Some psychologists are interested primarily in the behavior of animals, some in the behavior of people, and others in the behavior of organizations. These and other dimensions of difference among psychological scientists are matched by equal if not greater heterogeneity among psychological practitioners, who currently apply a vast array of methods in many different settings to achieve highly varied purposes.

Psychology has been rich in comprehensive encyclopedias and in handbooks devoted to specific topics in the field. However, there has not previously been any single handbook designed to cover the broad scope of psychological science and practice. The present 12-volume *Handbook of Psychology* was conceived to occupy this place in the literature. Leading national and international scholars and practitioners have collaborated to produce 297 authoritative and detailed chapters covering all fundamental facets of the discipline, and the *Handbook* has been organized to capture the breadth and diversity of psychology and to encompass interests and concerns shared by psychologists in all branches of the field.

Two unifying threads run through the science of behavior. The first is a common history rooted in conceptual and empirical approaches to understanding the nature of behavior. The specific histories of all specialty areas in psychology trace their origins to the formulations of the classical philosophers and the methodology of the early experimentalists, and appreciation for the historical evolution of psychology in all of its variations transcends individual identities as being one kind of psychologist or another. Accordingly, Volume 1 in the *Handbook* is devoted to the history of psychology as it emerged in many areas of scientific study and applied technology.

A second unifying thread in psychology is a commitment to the development and utilization of research methods suitable for collecting and analyzing behavioral data. With attention both to specific procedures and their application in particular settings, Volume 2 addresses research methods in psychology.

Volumes 3 through 7 of the *Handbook* present the substantive content of psychological knowledge in five broad areas of study: biological psychology (Volume 3), experimental psychology (Volume 4), personality and social psychology (Volume 5), developmental psychology (Volume 6), and educational psychology (Volume 7). Volumes 8 through 12 address the application of psychological knowledge in five broad areas of professional practice: clinical psychology (Volume 8), health psychology (Volume 9), assessment psychology (Volume 10), forensic psychology (Volume 11), and industrial and organizational psychology (Volume 12). Each of these volumes reviews what is currently known in these areas of study and application and identifies pertinent sources of information in the literature. Each discusses unresolved issues and unanswered questions and proposes future directions in conceptualization, research, and practice. Each of the volumes also reflects the investment of scientific psychologists in practical applications of their findings and the attention of applied psychologists to the scientific basis of their methods.

The *Handbook of Psychology* was prepared for the purpose of educating and informing readers about the present state of psychological knowledge and about anticipated advances in behavioral science research and practice. With this purpose in mind, the individual *Handbook* volumes address the needs and interests of three groups. First, for graduate students in behavioral science, the volumes provide advanced instruction in the basic concepts and methods that define the fields they cover, together with a review of current knowledge, core literature, and likely future developments. Second, in addition to serving as graduate textbooks, the volumes offer professional psychologists an opportunity to read and contemplate the views of distinguished colleagues concerning the central thrusts of research and leading edges of practice in their respective fields. Third, for psychologists seeking to become conversant with fields outside their own specialty and for persons outside of psychology seeking information about psychological matters, the *Handbook* volumes serve as a reference source for expanding their knowledge and directing them to additional sources in the literature.

The preparation of this *Handbook* was made possible by the diligence and scholarly sophistication of the 25 volume editors and co-editors who constituted the Editorial Board. As Editor-in-Chief, I want to thank each of them for the pleasure of their collaboration in this project. I compliment them for having recruited an outstanding cast of contributors to their volumes and then working closely with these authors to achieve chapters that will stand each in their own right as

valuable contributions to the literature. I would like finally to express my appreciation to the editorial staff of John Wiley and Sons for the opportunity to share in the development of this project and its pursuit to fruition, most particularly to Jennifer Simon, Senior Editor, and her two assistants, Mary Porterfield and Isabel Pratt. Without Jennifer's vision of the *Handbook* and her keen judgment and unflagging support in producing it, the occasion to write this preface would not have arrived.

IRVING B. WEINER
Tampa, Florida

Volume Preface

When we were first asked to serve as editors of the health psychology volume for this *Handbook,* we were very excited to be part of a larger set of editors whose landmark, but daunting, task was to corral an impressive list of leading psychologists to chronicle all of psychology. Having the opportunity to invite internationally known psychologists to author specific chapters that would be both comprehensive and practical in one volume offered a tremendous and exciting challenge. We were also very pleased to have the opportunity to put together a comprehensive text on health psychology that could be useful to graduate psychology students interested in health psychology, health psychology researchers interested in having up-to-date information, clinical health psychologists working with medical patients, *and* nonpsychology professionals (e.g., physicians, nurses) who wish to learn more about psychology's contributions to health and health service delivery.

It was these four audiences that we had in mind when we developed the structure for this volume on health psychology. We cover both conceptual and professional issues (Parts One and Two, Overview and Causal and Mediating Psychosocial Factors, respectively), as well as a plethora of disease-specific chapters (Part Three, Diseases and Disorders). This latter section focuses on 14 major disease entities or medical problems and provides information concerning prevalence, psychosocial causal factors, and treatment approaches. Because we view all phenomena as taking place within varying contexts, we also believe that health and health care need to be viewed within the context of varying developmental stages, hence the inclusion of Part Four on Health Psychology across the Life Span. Last, because we believed there were additional contextual issues, such as gender (Chapter 22 on women's health issues) and cultural/ethnic background (Chapter 23 on cultural diversity issues in health), as well as emerging related issues in the field (Chapter 24 on occupational health psychology and Chapter 25 on complementary and alternative therapies), we added Part Five titled Special Topics.

Although we provided wide latitude to the various authors in terms of chapter structure and content, we insisted on comprehensive and timely coverage for each topic. We believe each set of authors did a magnificent job. We wish to thank them for their outstanding contributions. We also wish to thank Irv Weiner, Editor-in-Chief of the *Handbook,* for his indefatigable support, feedback, and advice concerning this volume. Much appreciation also should be extended to the editorial staff at Wiley, Jennifer Simon and Isabel Pratt, for their support and advice. Finally, we need to underscore the huge assistance that Marni Zwick, soon to be a clinical health psychologist in her own right, gave to this project. Without her, this book would not have come to fruition.

ARTHUR M. NEZU
CHRISTINE MAGUTH NEZU
PAMELA A. GELLER

Contents

PART FOUR
HEALTH PSYCHOLOGY ACROSS THE LIFE SPAN

PART FIVE
SPECIAL TOPICS

Contributors

Joyce Adkins, PhD (USAF)
DoD Deployment Health Center
Department of Defense
Washington, DC

Norman B. Anderson, PhD
Department of Health and Social Behavior
Harvard University
Boston, Massachusetts

Frank Andrasik, PhD
Institute for Human and Machine Cognition
University of West Florida
Pensacola, Florida

Amy M. Andrews, BSN, RN
Department of Medical and Clinical Psychology
Uniformed Services University of the Health Sciences
Bethesda, Maryland

Lamia P. Barakat, PhD
Department of Psychology
Drexel University
Philadelphia, Pennsylvania

Kim P. Baron, MA
Department of Psychology
Drexel University
Philadelphia, Pennsylvania

Edward B. Blanchard, PhD, ABPP
Center for Stress and Anxiety Disorders
State University of New York at Albany
Albany, New York

Hayden B. Bosworth, PhD
Health Services Research and Development
Durham Veteran's Administration Medical Center and
   Departments of Medicine and Psychiatry
Duke University Medical Center
Durham, North Carolina

Heather M. Burke, MA
Department of Psychology
Arizona State University
Tempe, Arizona

Michael P. Carey, PhD
Center for Health and Behavior
Syracuse University
Syracuse, New York

Rodney Clark, PhD
Department of Psychology
Wayne State University
Detroit, Michigan

Joyce A. Corsica, PhD
Department of Clinical and Health Psychology
University of Florida
Gainesville, Florida

Meagan Daley, MPs
École de Psychologie
Université Laval
Québec, Canada

Mary C. Davis, PhD
Department of Psychology
Arizona State University
Tempe, Arizona

Faith Dyson-Washington, MEd
Department of Psychology
Drexel University
Philadelphia, Pennsylvania

Timothy R. Elliott, PhD
Department of Physical Medicine and Rehabilitation
University of Alabama at Birmingham
Birmingham, Alabama

Merrill F. Elias, PhD, MPH
Department of Mathematics and Statistics,
   College of Arts and Sciences
Boston University and Boston University
   Schools of Medicine and Public Health
Boston, Massachusetts

Jonathan M. Feldman, MS
Department of Psychology
Rutgers University
New Brunswick, New Jersey

Stephanie H. Felgoise, PhD
Department of Psychology
PCOM
Philadelphia, Pennsylvania

Pamela A. Geller, PhD
Department of Psychology
Drexel University
Philadelphia, Pennsylvania

Nicholas D. Giardino, PhD
Department of Rehabilitation Medicine
University of Washington
Seattle, Washington

Ronald Glaser, PhD
Department of Molecular Virology, Immunology and
    Medical Genetics, Comprehensive Cancer Center,
    Institute for Behavioral Medicine Research
The Ohio State University
Columbus, Ohio

Maria C. Graf, MA
Department of Psychology
Drexel University
Philadelphia, Pennsylvania

Karen S. Hudmon, DrPH
Department of Clinical Pharmacy, School of Pharmacy
University of California
San Francisco, California

Leonard A. Jason, PhD
Center for Community Research
DePaul University
Chicago, Illinois

Anne E. Kazak, PhD
Departments of Pediatrics and Psychology
The Children's Hospital of Philadelphia
Philadelphia, Pennsylvania

Laurie Keefer, MA
Center for Stress and Anxiety Disorders
State University of New York at Albany
Albany, New York

Taline V. Khroyan, PhD
Center for Health Sciences
SRI International
Menlo Park, California

Janice K. Kiecolt-Glaser, PhD
Department of Psychiatry
Comprehensive Cancer Center, Institute for
    Behavioral Medicine Research
The Ohio State University
Columbus, Ohio

Charles Klunder, PhD
Behavioral Analysis Service, 59th Medical Wing (USAF)
Lackland Air Force Base, Texas

David S. Krantz, PhD
Department of Medical and Clinical Psychology
Uniformed Services University of the Health Sciences
Bethesda, Maryland

Alicia Kunin-Batson, PhD
Department of Psychology
The Children's Hospital of Philadelphia
Philadelphia, Pennsylvania

Julie Landel-Graham, PhD
Philadelphia, Pennsylvania

Paul M. Lehrer, PhD
Department of Psychiatry
UMDNJ-Robert Wood Johnson Medical School
Newark, New Jersey

Elizabeth R. Lombardo, PhD
Department of Psychology
Drexel University
Philadelphia, Pennsylvania

Sharon Manne, PhD
Division of Population Science and
    Psychooncology Program
Fox Chase Cancer Center
Philadelphia, Pennsylvania

David F. Marks, PhD
Department of Psychology
City University
London, United Kingdom

Lynanne McGuire, PhD
Department of Psychiatry
The Ohio State University
Columbus, Ohio

Jennifer M. McKinley, MSc
Department of Psychology
City University
London, United Kingdom

Charles M. Morin, PhD
École de Psychologie
Université Laval
Québec, Canada

Arthur M. Nezu, PhD, ABPP
Center for Behavioral Medicine
Departments of Psychology, Medicine, and Public Health
Drexel University
Philadelphia, Pennsylvania

Christine Maguth Nezu, PhD, ABPP
Center for Behavioral Medicine
Departments of Psychology and Medicine
Drexel University
Philadelphia, Pennsylvania

Mark O'Callahan, BS
Department of Medical and Clinical Psychology
Uniformed Services University of the Health Sciences
Bethesda, Maryland

Akiko Okifuji, PhD
Department of Anesthesiology
University of Utah
Salt Lake City, Utah

Marie-Christine Ouellet, MPs
École de Psychologie
Université Laval
Québec, Canada

Michael G. Perri, PhD, ABPP
Department of Clinical and Health Psychology
University of Florida
Gainesville, Florida

Sheridan Phillips, PhD
Department of Psychiatry
University of Maryland School of Medicine
Baltimore, Maryland

James Campbell Quick, PhD
Center for Research on Organizational
   and Managerial Excellence
The University of Texas at Arlington
Arlington, Texas

John W. Reich, PhD
Department of Psychology
Arizona State University
Tempe, Arizona

Patricia Rivera, PhD
Department of Physical Medicine and Rehabilitation
University of Alabama at Birmingham
Birmingham, Alabama

Ted Robles, BS
Department of Psychology
The Ohio State University
Columbus, Ohio

Susan R. Rudnicki, PhD
Behavioral Research Center
American Cancer Society
Atlanta, Georgia

Josée Savard, PhD
École de Psychologie
Université Laval
Québec, Canada

Karen B. Schmaling, PhD
College of Health Sciences
University of Texas at El Paso
El Paso, Texas

Amy S. Schultz, MA
Department of Psychology
Arizona State University
Tempe, Arizona

Ute Schulz
Health Psychology
Freie Universitat Berlin
Berlin, Germany

Ralf Schwarzer, PhD
Health Psychology
Freie Universitat Berlin
Berlin, Germany

Ilene C. Siegler, PhD, MPH
Behavioral Medicine Research Center and Department
   of Psychiatry and Behavioral Sciences
Duke University Medical Center
Durham, North Carolina

Jeffrey R. Stowell, PhD
Department of Psychiatry
The Ohio State University
Columbus, Ohio

Gary E. Swan, PhD
Center for Health Sciences
SRI International
Menlo Park, California

Catherine M. Sykes, MSc
Department of Psychology
City University
London, United Kingdom

Renee R. Taylor, PhD
Department of Occupational Therapy
University of Illinois at Chicago
Chicago, Illinois

Lois E. Tetrick, PhD
Department of Psychology
University of Houston
Houston, Texas

Solam Tsang, MA
Department of Psychology
Drexel University
Philadelphia, Pennsylvania

Dennis C. Turk, PhD
Department of Anesthesiology
University of Washington
Seattle, Washington

Peter A. Vanable, PhD
Center for Health and Behavior
Syracuse University
Syracuse, New York

Susan E. Walch, PhD
Department of Psychology
University of West Florida
Pensacola, Florida

Gerdi Weidner, PhD
Vice President and Director of Research, Preventive
    Medicine Research Institute
Sausalito, California

Keith E. Whitfield, PhD
Department of Biobehavioral Health
The Pennsylvania State University
University Park, Pennsylvania

Susan E. Yount, PhD
Center on Outcomes, Research, and Education
Northwestern University
Evanston, Illinois

Alex J. Zautra, PhD
Department of Psychology
Arizona State University
Tempe, Arizona

Marni L. Zwick, MA
Department of Psychology
Drexel University
Philadelphia, Pennsylvania

Introduction

The power of the imagination is a great factor in medicine.
It may produce diseases in man and in animals, and it may cure them.

PARACELSUS, SIXTEENTH CENTURY

By no means should the above observation be equated with a contemporary definition of health psychology, but in his quote, the noted reformer and physician Paracelsus argues that disease, neither in its etiology nor in its cure, can be totally understood in terms limited to the realm of the *soma*. This is the essence of the field of health psychology that disease processes cannot be understood solely in terms of biological and physiological parameters. Instead, a *biopsychosocial* model better represents a more complete picture of disease, illness, health, and wellness. Rather than underscoring the primacy of somatic variables, such a model (see Schwartz, 1982) contends that biological, psychological, and social factors all constitute important and crucial indices of a definition of disease with regard to issues of etiology, pathogenesis, course, and treatment. Recent research suggests that less than 25% of physical complaints presented to primary care physicians have known or demonstrable organic or biological etiologies, greatly highlighting the need for a more complete model (Nezu, Nezu, & Lombardo, 2001). Such a view is consistent with a *planned critical multiplism* perspective (Shadish, 1986), which is a methodological approach whereby attempts are made to minimize the biases inherent in any univariate search for knowledge. During the past two decades, efforts by a wide range of psychologists interested in disease and illness have provided varying types of support for this biopsychosocial model using this multivariate perspective.

Starting with simpler questions, such as what types of psychological processes affect illness, the field of health psychology has since expanded greatly in terms of its scope, depth, and impact. For example, Taylor's (1990) confident prediction that succinct papers reviewing the current status of health psychology would disappear due to the "diversity of issues studied and the complexity and sophistication of the models and designs used to explore them" (p. 47) appears to have been confirmed. Initially, the field was composed of researchers and practitioners with common interests in issues related to health and illness who were trained in more traditional (but varied) areas of psychology. The diversity of conceptual approaches, models, and designs brought together by these individuals have helped to establish a field that is broad in scope, eclectic, multidisciplinary, dynamic, and allowing for creative developments. Training programs in health psychology have tapped this breadth and students now have significant exposure to neurology, endocrinology, immunology, public health, epidemiology, and other medical subspecialties, in addition to a solid grounding in psychology (Brannon & Feist, 1992).

Over the past two decades, health psychologists have become more integrated into the general field of health research and intervention, and have gained job opportunities in a range of health-oriented settings (Belar & Deardorf, 1995). Although psychology has been involved with health in some capacity since early in the twentieth century, very few psychologists worked in medical settings, and more as adjuncts than as full members of multidisciplinary teams. Recent issues of the *APA Monitor*, however, now advertise a wide array of health-related positions for psychologists in settings such as universities, medical schools, hospitals, health clinics, health maintenance organizations, and private practices, highlighting the growing demand for such services. The focus of clinical health psychology on empirically supported, brief, problem-centered, cognitive-behavioral interventions and skills training has been compatible with the demands of the managed care system, which must provide authorization for treatment plans. Moreover, the large and continually growing percentage of the gross national product that Americans spend on health care, more than any other industrialized country (over 13.5% in 1998; U.S. Health Care Financing Administration, 1999), highlights the need to contain costs through early detection and disease prevention. Health psychology research focusing on the development and

1

evaluation of prevention activities intended to assist with health maintenance and improvement is more cost-efficient and can help reduce the need for high cost health care services (Taylor, 1990). Such economic factors have thus helped to facilitate the acceptance of psychologists in the health arena.

The future seems bright for continued acceptance of and opportunities for health psychologists as the field has demonstrated its value through the contributions made in supporting a biopsychosocial model, as well as with regard to their applied and clinical implications (e.g., primary, secondary, and tertiary prevention). Recent reports emanating from the U.S. Surgeon General's Office continue to highlight the causal importance of behavioral and psychological factors regarding the leading causes of mortality in the United States. For example, such reports suggest that various behavioral risk factors (e.g., substance abuse, stress, diet, tobacco use) are among the most important foci regarding health promotion and disease prevention (see also *Healthy People 2000*). As such, health psychologists are in a unique position to conduct research and develop programs geared to prevent and change unhealthy habits and behaviors, as well as to promote healthy ones.

However, despite such advances, there is still a tremendous need for work in this area. For example, although an exorbitant amount of money is spent on health care in the United States, this does not necessarily translate to high-quality care for most Americans. Comparing mortality and morbidity rates among ethnic/racial groups reveals vast differences. For example, although there has been a general decline in mortality for all groups, overall mortality was 55% greater for Blacks than for Whites in 1997 (Hoyert, Kochanek, & Murphy, 1999). There also are significant health discrepancies relating to socioeconomic status, ethnic/racial status, and even gender (e.g., National Center for Health Statistics, 1999; Rodin & Ickovics, 1990).

As such, there is a continuing need for health psychology efforts, both research and clinical, to expand in scope. Not only do we need to better understand how biological, psychological, and social factors interact with each other regarding various symptom clusters and medical disorders, but also we need to improve the manner in which health care delivery is provided. Research needs to be conducted regarding the impact of health care *policy* on health and well-being. Therefore, lest we begin to wish to sit on our laurels and believe that our job is nearly done in terms of health psychology research and clinical applications, we should remember the words of John Locke concerning overconfidence:

> He that judges without informing himself to the upmost that he is capable, cannot acquit himself of judging amiss.

This current volume should be viewed as but one major stop on a road that will continue far into the future. However, the road thus far has been very fruitful, as evidenced by the rich material contained in the various chapters in this volume. More importantly, such strides strongly justify continued travels.

REFERENCES

Belar, C. D., & Deardorff, W. W. (1995). *Clinical health psychology in medical settings: A practitioner's guidebook.* Washington, DC: American Psychological Association.

Brannon, L., & Feist, J. (1992). *Health Psychology: An introduction to behavior and health* (2nd ed.). Belmont, CA: Wadsworth Publishing.

Healthy People 2000: National health promotion and disease prevention objectives. [DHHS Publication No. (PHS) 91-50212]. Washington, DC: U.S. Government Printing Office.

Hoyert, D. L., Kochanek, K. D., & Murphy, S. L. (1999). Deaths: Final data for 1997. *National Vital Statistics Reports, 47,* 1–104.

Nezu, A. M., Nezu, C. M., & Lombardo, E. R. (2001). Cognitive-behavior therapy for medically unexplained symptoms. A critical review of the treatment literature. *Behavior Therapy, 32,* 537–583.

Rodin, J., & Ickovics, J. R. (1990). Women's health: Review and research agenda as we approach the 21st century. *American Psychologist, 45,* 1018–1034.

Schwartz, G. (1982). Testing the biopsychosocial model: The ultimate challenge facing behavioral medicine? *Journal of Consulting and Clinical Psychology, 50,* 1040–1053.

Shadish, W. R. (1986). Planned critical multiplism: Some elaborations. *Behavioral Assessment, 8,* 75–103.

Taylor, S. E. (1990). Health Psychology: The science and the field. *American Psychologist, 45,* 40–50.

U.S. Health Care Financing Administration. (1999). National health expenditures, 1998. *Health Care Financing Review, 20,* Publication 03412.

PART ONE

OVERVIEW

CHAPTER 1

Health Psychology: Overview and Professional Issues

DAVID F. MARKS, CATHERINE M. SYKES, AND JENNIFER M. McKINLEY

The importance of psychological processes in the experience of health and illness is being increasingly recognized. More and more evidence is accumulating for the role of behavior in current trends of morbidity and mortality: Certain health behaviors reduce morbidity and mortality (Breslow & Enstrom, 1980; Broome & Llewellyn, 1995; Marks, Murray, Evans, & Willig, 2000; Matarazzo, Weiss, Herd, Miller, & Weiss, 1984; Taylor, 1986). Maes and von Veldhoven (1989), reviewing all the English language handbooks on health psychology

known at that time, counted 15 published during the period 1979 to 1989. Recent developments, especially in clinical practice, have been even more encompassing, and health psychologists are in increasing demand in clinical health care and medical settings. In the United States, the single largest area of placement of psychologists in recent years has been in medical centers. Psychologists have become vital members of multidisciplinary clinical and research teams in rehabilitation, cardiology, pediatrics, oncology, anesthesiology, family practice, dentistry, and other medical fields (American Psychological Association [APA], 1996). With this increasing participation of psychologists in health services, guidelines for professional training programs and ethical practice have been developed in the United States, Europe, and elsewhere. This chapter reviews some of the professional and ethical issues that have been identified and discussed in these regions. The emphasis is on education and training.

In reviewing the field's development in the United States, Wallston (1993) states, "It is amazing to realize that formal

The authors would like to thank the members of the EFPPA Task Force on Health Psychology (convenor: David F. Marks): Carola Brucher-Albers, Berufsverband Deutscher Psychologen e.V.; Frank J. S. Donker, Nederlands Institut van Psychogen; Zenia Jepsen, Dansk Psykologforening; Jesus Rodriguez-Marin, Colegio Oficial de Psicologos; Sylvaine Sidot, Association Nationale des Organizations de Psychologues; Brit Wallin Backman, Norsk Psykologforening. Sections of this chapter are adapted from the Task Force report (Marks et al., 1998).

recognition of the field of health psychology in the United States occurred less than 20 years ago. It is no longer correct to speak of health psychology as an 'emerging' specialty within American psychology; for the last dozen or so years, health psychology has flourished as one of the most vibrant specialties within the larger discipline of psychology. Not only is it recognized as a specialty in its own right, health psychology has had a profound impact on clinical psychology, and has played a major (if not the major) role in developing and vitalizing the interdisciplinary field called 'behavioral medicine'" (p. 215). The overlap with behavioral medicine in both theory and practice has been strong and, like behavioral medicine, health psychology is really an interdisciplinary field (Marks, 1996). Because the leading causes of mortality have substantial behavioral components, behavioral risk factors (e.g., drug and alcohol use, unsafe sexual behavior, smoking, diet, a sedentary lifestyle) are the main focus of efforts in the area of health promotion and disease prevention. Behavioral methods are also playing an increasing role in treatment and rehabilitation. Beyond the clinical domain, the relevance of psychology to public health, health education and health promotion has been discussed by health psychologists (Bennett & Murphy, 1997; Winett, King, & Altman, 1989) and health promotion specialists (Macdonald, 2000).

Given its emphasis on behavior and behavioral change, psychology has a unique contribution to make to health care and public health. Health psychologists are currently conducting research on the development of healthy habits as well as the prevention or reduction of unhealthy behaviors. Both the impact of behavior on health as well as the influence of health and disease states on psychological factors are being explored. Psychosocial linkages in areas such as psychoneuroimmunology, pain, cardiovascular disorders, cancer, AIDS/HIV, and other chronic diseases are being defined. Psychosocial mediators of effective public health promotion are being identified.

The United States has produced the most influential theoretical and ideological frameworks and a large proportion of the empirical work. The Health Psychology Division of the APA (Division 38) is one of the largest and fastest growing in the association. Its journal, *Health Psychology,* has one of the largest circulations among psychology journals. However, in the 1990s, a considerable amount of research was initiated in Europe. Health psychology was no longer totally dominated by developments in the United States. The European Health Psychology Society (EHPS) has organized scientific meetings since 1986. Undoubtedly these have had an influential role in the proliferation of the European health psychology scene. Linked to the EHPS, the journal *Psychology and Health* is a respected review of health psychology and since 1985 has been the leading European journal. The establishment of the *Journal of Health Psychology* in 1996 has encouraged an interdisciplinary and international orientation to the field and created a forum for new methods and theories, discussions, and debate, including critical approaches. Another journal, *Psychology, Health & Medicine* has focused on psychological care for medical problems. Other journals that publish papers in this field are the *International Journal of Behavioural Medicine* and *Social Science & Medicine.* Several other academic journals focus on health psychology at a national level (e.g., *British Journal of Health Psychology, Gedrag & Gezondheid: Tijdschrift voor Psychologie en Gezondheid, Revista de Psicologia de la Salud, Zeitschrift far Gesundheitpsychologie*). As in the United States and Europe, psychological associations in Canada, Australia, New Zealand, and elsewhere have boards, divisions, or branches specializing in health psychology and research and professional work in the field are expanding rapidly.

In the light of these developments, it can be seen that health psychology is one of the most vibrant and dynamic fields in Western psychology. As health psychology progresses from a research field to health service delivery, it is inevitable that professional and ethical issues are at the forefront of discussion within the major psychological associations. This chapter reflects the principle focus of this discussion that is on education and training.

THE DEFINITION AND SCOPE OF HEALTH PSYCHOLOGY

The currently accepted definition of health psychology was originally proposed by Matarazzo (1982) as:

> [T]he aggregate of the specific educational, scientific, and professional contributions of the discipline of psychology to the promotion and maintenance of health, the prevention and treatment of illness, the identification of etiologic and diagnostic correlates of health and illness and related dysfunctions, and the analysis and improvement of the health care system and health policy.

Virtually every health psychology organization and textbook has adopted Matarazzo's (1982) definition without criticism, debate, or discussion. For researchers in health psychology, this definition is a very fine and appropriate one. Researchers invariably specialize and the fact that a definition of their field is a very broad one is not a problem. For practitioners, however, the breadth of the Matarazzo definition can pose some serious difficulties. In fact, at face value, the definition is quite grandiose, encompassing all of clinical psychology, counseling psychology, rehabilitation psychology, occupational psychology, and much else as well. No single health care professional can reasonably be expected to possess and practice with genuine competence in all of the areas mentioned in Matarazzo's definition and yet that is what the American, British, and most other psychological associations have agreed to.

The "official" definition of health psychology needs to be narrowed, or at least specialties within it, need to be defined (e.g., clinical health psychologist, rehabilitation health psychologist, occupational health psychologist, health promotion psychologist). Otherwise there is a risk of becoming Jacks-and-Jills-of-all-trades, and master-of-none. McDermott (2001) recently argued that the Matarazzo definition is over-inclusive, encompassing any topic connected with health, including primary, secondary, and tertiary care in their entirety. McDermott states, "The over-inclusivity is likely to prove detrimental to the long-term well-being of health psychology since such a broad definition does not allow for the subject area to distinguish itself clearly from other subdisciplines, in particular from clinical psychology and behavioral medicine" (p. 7). McDermott's solution to this problem is to replace the first Matarazzo definition with another, his definition of behavioral health:

> . . . new, interdisciplinary subspecialty . . . specifically concerned with the maintenance of health and the prevention of illness and dysfunction in currently healthy persons. (Matarazzo, 1982, p. 807, cited by McDermott, 2001)

This proposal is an elegant one. Secondary and tertiary care would thus remain the province of clinical psychology, leaving health psychology to become a true psychology of health. Correspondence suggests that Matarazzo (2001) essentially agrees with this proposal (Marks, 2002).

Another critique questions the focus on the rejection of the biomedical model and argues for a more social orientation, drawing on the knowledge base of the social sciences. The first author has argued elsewhere for a new agenda in which "health psychology should accept its interdisciplinary nature, venture more often out of the clinical arena, drop white-coated scientism, and relocate in the richer cultural, sociopolitical and community contexts of society" (Marks, 1996, p. 19). Ogden (1998) has suggested that the challenge of the biomedical model in the form of the "biopsychosocial" model is a rhetorical strategy lacking any solid theoretical foundation. A more societal emphasis in health psychology, and psychology as a whole, will encourage psychologists to make a more significant contribution in a world threatened by the sequelae of its industrial, scientific, and medical attainments but also by war, crime, and poverty.

This step broadens the agenda rather than narrows it. It is a broadening of awareness about the social context of health experience and behavior and of the social and economic determinants of health. In no way does it dilute the psychologist's ability to deliver effective approaches to health issues. Economic and political changes have considerable, long-lasting influence on human well-being. Warfare remains an intermittent threat to human security. The gap between the "haves" and the "have-nots" widens, the Western population is aging, and the impacts of learned helplessness, poverty, and social isolation are becoming increasingly salient features of society. Global warming and energy addiction remain unabated. The health and psychological impacts of these phenomena present many challenges that lead us to repeat what Taylor already wrote over 10 years ago, "The only aspect of health psychology that is more exciting than its distinguished past and its impressive present, is its promising future" (Taylor, 1986, p. 17).

As currently defined, health psychology is the application of psychological theory, methods, and research to health, physical illness, and health care. Human well-being is a complex product of genetic, developmental, and environmental influences. In accordance with the World Health Organization (WHO) definition, health is seen as well-being in its broadest sense, not simply the absence of illness. Expanding the WHO definition, well-being is the product of a complex interplay of biological, sociocultural, psychological, economic, and spiritual factors. The promotion and maintenance of health involves psychosocial processes at the interface between the individual, the health care system, and society (Marks et al., 2000).

Health psychology is concerned with the psychological aspects of the promotion, improvement, and maintenance of health. The *ecological context* of these psychological aspects of health includes the many influential social systems within which human beings exist: families, workplaces, organizations, communities, societies, and cultures (Marks, 1996; Marks et al., 2000; Whitehead, 1995). Any psychological activity, process, or intervention that enhances well-being is of interest to health psychology. Equally, any activity, process, or circumstance which has psychological components and which threatens well-being is of concern to health psychology. Interventions need to be considered in the light of the prevailing environmental conditions that contain the contextual cues for health-related behaviors. A behavioral change resulting from an intervention delivered in one specific environment (e.g., a classroom, hospital, or prison) will not necessarily transfer to other environments.

The mission of professional health psychology is to promote and maintain well-being through the application of psychological theory, methods, and research, taking into account the economic, political, social, and cultural context. The primary purpose or "vision" of professional health psychology is the employment of psychological knowledge, methods, and skills toward the promotion and maintenance of well-being. The latter extends beyond hospitals and clinics—it includes health education and promotion among the healthy population as well as among those who are already sick.

The application of psychological knowledge, methods, and skills in the promotion and maintenance of well-being is a multifaceted activity; it is not possible to define the field narrowly because of the many different settings and situations in which psychologists may have a role in promoting and maintaining human health. It also must be acknowledged that the psychologist often will be working with laypeople, many of whom are patients' relatives, acting as informal caregivers: "People are not just consumers of health care, they are the true primary care providers in the health care system. Increasing the confidence and skills of these primary care providers can make health and economic sense" (Sobell, 1995, p. 238).

Relationships with Other Professions

Health psychology is an interdisciplinary field with theoretical and practical links with many other professions (e.g., medicine, nursing, health promotion, and social work among many others). Health psychology overlaps with many other subfields or professional activities of psychology. Particular examples include subfields such as clinical psychology and activities such as psychotherapy. These overlapping subfields and activities are concerned with the independent application of psychological principles and methods to health, illness, and health care. However there are similarities and synergy between health psychology, clinical psychology, psychotherapy, and other applied psychological fields that have common foundations and overarching objectives. The primary goals are (a) the promotion and maintenance of good health and quality of life; (b) the prevention and improvement of ill health, disability, and the conditions of impairment and handicap through psychological intervention; and (c) adherence to the ethical guidelines specified by the national societies.

Health psychology is primarily concerned with physical health, illness, and health care although it is recognized that mental and physical health are highly interrelated. Clinical psychology is primarily concerned with assessing, predicting, preventing, and alleviating cognitive, emotional, and behavioral disorders and disabilities. Psychotherapy is primarily concerned with the treatment of psychological and psychologically influenced disorders by psychological means. Although it is recognized that these three fields overlap, they are independent professions of psychologists with university degrees that have their own postgraduate training needs and curricula.

Health and clinical psychologists, and those psychologists who conduct psychotherapy, work with:

1. Individuals, couples, families, groups, and communities;
2. People of all ages;
3. In institutions, organizations, and companies;
4. In the public, private, and voluntary sectors.

They undertake: (a) assessment and diagnosis; (b) intervention and treatment; (c) teaching and training; (d) supervision, counseling, and consultancy; (e) evaluation, research, and development for a range of areas of life, including promotion of well-being; prevention of deterioration of health; intervention in psychological aspects of physical health; intervention in psychological aspects of mental health; and promotion of optimum development and aging. These individuals are responsible for:

1. The delivery of good services with respect to standards of quality and control;
2. Planning of new services;
3. Informing and influencing the health care system and health policy; and
4. Contributing toward multidisciplinary working in the health care system.

Areas of overlap exist between health psychology and many other types of psychology: community psychology, organizational/occupational psychology, work psychology, rehabilitation psychology, educational psychology, and forensic psychology. To the extent that the psychology discipline is concerned with arriving at a better understanding of behavior and experience and in the improvement of well-being, *all aspects of psychology have relevance to the psychology of health in its broadest sense.*

The Clinical and Community Approaches to Health Psychology

There are two different approaches to health psychology. The first is based on the biopsychosocial model and working within the health care system. It is founded on Matarazzo's (1980) definition of health psychology. It locates professional health psychology within the clinical domain, in hospitals, and outpatient settings. The environment in which the practice occurs is the health care marketplace. Another name for it is "clinical health psychology." The second approach is community research and action. This forms a significant part of community psychology, working on health promotion and illness prevention among healthy people as members of communities and groups. This approach is consistent with Matarazzo's (1980) definition of behavioral health, but it locates behavioral health not purely within the individual but within its social, economic, and political context. A summary of the two approaches is presented in Table 1.1.

Each approach has its strengths and weaknesses. There is a need for both and they complement each other. Each requires appropriate training and education. A third hybrid approach would be to attempt to integrate the clinical and community approaches within a single profession or discipline. This is an ambitious target that may be too difficult to achieve. It would be comparable to putting clinical and public health medicine together as a single endeavor. It seems unlikely that this will happen and, sadly, the paths of the community and clinical health psychologist may be forced to diverge. The training pathways are already separate, as we shall discuss next.

Conditions That Promote and Maintain Health

Cohesion, harmony, and meaningfulness are key characteristics of psychosocial well-being; fragmentation, disharmony, and

TABLE 1.1   Two Approaches to Health Psychology: The Health Service Provider and Community Action Models

Characteristic	Health Service Provider Model	Community Action Model
Definition	"[T]he aggregate of the specific educational, scientific, and professional contributions of the discipline of psychology to the promotion and maintenance of health, the prevention and treatment of illness, the identification of etiologic and diagnostic correlates of health and illness and related dysfunctions, and the analysis and improvement of the health care system and health policy" Matarazzo (1982).	"*Advancing theory, research and social action to promote positive well-being, increase empowerment, and prevent the development of problems of communities, groups, and individuals*" Society for Community Research and Action (2001).
Theory/philosophy	Biopsychosocial model: Health and illness are: "*the product of a combination of factors including biological characteristics (e.g., genetic predisposition), behavioral factors (e.g., lifestyle, stress, health beliefs), and social conditions (e.g., cultural influences, family relationships, social support)*" APA Division 48 (2001).	Social and economic model: "*Change strategies are needed at both the individual and systems levels for effective competence promotion and problem prevention*" Society for Community Research and Action (2001).
Context	Patients within the health care system, i.e., hospitals, clinics, health centers.	Families, communities, and populations within their social, cultural, and historical context.
Focus	Physical illness and dysfunction.	Physical and mental health promotion.
Target groups	Patients in hospital and clinics.	Healthy but vulnerable and/or exploited persons and groups.
Objective	Therapeutic intervention.	Empowerment and social change.
Orientation	Top-down service delivery.	Bottom-up, working alongside.
Skills	Clinical and therapeutic.	Participatory and facilitative.
Discourse and buzz words	Evidence-based. Effective. Cost-effective. Intervention. Controls. Outcomes. Randomized controlled trials.	Empowering. Giving voice to. Diversity. Community development. Capacity building. Social capital. Inequalities.
Research methodology	Effectiveness trials, typically using quantitative or quasi-experimental methods.	Action research: Active collaboration between researchers, practitioners, and community members utilizing multiple methodologies.

meaninglessness are key characteristics of illness. Having the resources to deal effectively with life events and changing social and economic circumstances is a necessary condition for health. Resources can be classified into five main categories: biological, sociocultural, psychological, economic, and spiritual. The availability and appropriate combination of these resources creates the conditions for well-being. Their absolute or relative nonavailability, creates the conditions for ill health. A primary goal of health psychology is to establish and improve the conditions that promote and maintain the quality of life of individuals, communities, and groups.

Inalienable Right to Health and Health Care for All

All people have an inalienable right to health and health care without prejudice or discrimination with regard to gender, age, religion, ethnic grouping, social class, material circumstances, political affiliation, or sexual orientation. The Health-For-All 2000 strategy of the WHO (1985), originally formulated in Alma Ata in 1978, served as an aspirational goal for all countries. As the year 2000 approached, it was apparent that the ambitious goals of Alma Ata would not be achieved, at least, by the year 2000. In 1995, the forty-eighth World Health Assembly renewed the Health-For-All global strategy as a "timeless aspirational goal" and urged member states to "adapt the global health policy . . . into national or subnational context for implementation, selecting approaches specific to their social and economic situation and culture" (WHO, 1995). Professional psychological organizations across the globe can lend their support to the WHO's renewed strategy.

Centrality of the Scientist-Practitioner Model

The scientist-practitioner model provides the ideal model for professional training in health psychology. It is a common principle across programs in all Western countries. This accords with the position statements on health psychology training provided by an expert group working in the United States (Sheridan et al., 1988) and in Europe (Marks et al., 1998). Professional health psychologists normally require some form of practitioner skills training in health care settings in addition to research and evaluation skills. Only by demonstrating competency both in the provision of health care and in evaluation and research will professional health psychologists be able to meet the future challenges and demands of health care systems and society more generally. In the next section, we review the professional status of health psychology in the United States.

EDUCATION AND TRAINING IN THE UNITED STATES

At present, health psychologists in the United States are divided fairly evenly between academia and the health care system, some having a foot in both camps. Health psychology in the United States is being taught, researched, and practiced in two different traditions. The first tradition, which can fairly be described as the mainstream, focuses on the clinical issues of patients in the health care system. Responsibility for accrediting professional health psychology programs in the United States lies with the American Psychological Association (APA) Division 38. Division 38 employs the *biopsychosocial model* that defines health and illness as: "the product of a combination of factors including biological characteristics (e.g., genetic predisposition), behavioral factors (e.g., lifestyle, stress, health beliefs), and social conditions· (e.g., cultural influences, family relationships, social support)." We will return to this model later, but the model is an extension, rather than a replacement, of the biomedical model (Marks, 2002).

The second approach is that of community health psychology as represented by Division 27 of the APA, the Society for Community Research and Action (SCRA). The mission of the SCRA is described as follows:

> The Society is devoted to advancing theory, research, and social action to promote positive well-being, increase empowerment, and prevent the development of problems of communities, groups, and individuals. The action and research agenda of the field is guided by three broad principles. Community research and action is an active collaboration between researchers, practitioners, and community members and utilizes multiple methodologies. Human competencies and problems are best understood by viewing people within their social, cultural, and historical context. Change strategies are needed at both the individual and systems levels for effective competence promotion and problem prevention.

Membership of the SCRA includes psychologists and people from related disciplines such as psychiatry, social work, sociology, anthropology, public health, and political science, including teachers, researchers, and activists. Community psychology is concerned with healthy psychosocial development within an ecological perspective. It focuses on health promotion and disease prevention, rather than waiting for illness to develop and to diagnose and treat the symptoms.

Education and training for health psychologists in the United States is offered using both models that will be described in turn. Among clinical service providers, education and training in health psychology was first discussed in the early 1980s. A National Working Conference on Education and Training in Health Psychology at Arden House recommended that two years of postdoctoral training be mandated for licensed practitioners in health psychology. The conference proposed a three-stage continuum of education from predoctoral studies leading to the PhD through a predoctoral internship year followed by a mandatory two-year postdoctoral residency.

The predoctoral content of education is the traditional coverage of biological and social bases of behavior, individual differences, history and systems, ethics, and professional responsibility. Within this generic general psychology education, there should be a health psychology track including specific instruction in the theory and science of human physiology, pathophysiology, neuropsychology, social systems theory, psychopharmacology, human development across the life cycle, and psychopathology. Students are expected to acquire special skills during this predoctoral phase including: assessment, intervention techniques, broad consultation skills, short-term psychotherapy, family interventions, group dynamics, sensitization to group and ethnic norms, and prospective epidemiologic research training (Sheridan et al., 1988). This list of topics covers a huge range of knowledge and skills but the conference viewed these as a basic foundation for effective functioning in a general hospital setting.

A postdoctoral implementation committee, appointed at the Arden House Conference, added other areas of mastery at the postdoctoral level including:

- Coping strategies for chronic illness.
- Pain intervention techniques.
- Presurgery and postsurgery counseling.
- Compliance programs for specific illness groups.
- Stimulus reduction prevention programs and strategies.
- Counseling for parents with high-risk infants.
- Psychotherapy for persons with eating disorders.
- Programs for the chemically dependent.
- Stress reduction for cardiovascular disorders.
- Training in supervisory techniques, and
- Advanced liaison skills.

The Arden House recommendations were elaborated on in a position statement published by the postdoctoral implementation committee (Sheridan et al., 1988) who described the rationale for requiring this training, a model, and criteria for developing programs. The scientist practitioner model used in clinical psychology training was adopted and

Matarazzo's (1980) definition of health psychology was the foundation stone. The model is based on the programs that exist for medicine and dentistry and as such should be no less rigorous and quality controlled. The committee proposed a "model" of postdoctoral training with the following points:

- Candidates should possess a PhD or PsyD from an APA-approved program with a track or specialty in health psychology and have completed a formal one-year predoctoral residency.
- General hospitals and outpatient clinics are likely to be the principal setting for health psychology training and at least 50% of any postdoctoral trainee's time should be spent in such settings.
- Two years of integrated, specialty training.
- Postdoctoral faculty should be predominantly psychologists, yet interdisciplinary, with doctoral degrees, licensed, and have established expertise in the areas advertised by the programs.
- At least one supervisor per rotation.
- A resident will have a minimum of two rotations in the first year and, normally, two in the second year.
- At least six of the following techniques and skills:
  1. Relaxation therapies.
  2. Short-term individual psychotherapy.
  3. Group therapy.
  4. Family therapy.
  5. Consultation skills.
  6. Liaison skills.
  7. Assessment of specific patient populations (e.g., pain patients, spinal cord injury patients).
  8. Neuropsychological assessment.
  9. Behavior modification techniques.
  10. Biofeedback.
  11. Hypnosis.
  12. Health promotion and public education skills.
  13. Major treatment programs (e.g., chemical dependence, eating disorders).
  14. Compliance motivation.

Sheridan and coworkers (1988) conclude their report with a brief review of the key issue of funding: Who pays for health psychology training? In the late 1980s, federal funding of training posts through the NIH and Alcohol, Drug Abuse, and Mental Health Administration was under threat and it seemed likely that Medicare and Medicaid would not pick up the tab. The removal of public and private training funds meant that training providers would be forced to pass the training costs on to the trainees themselves in tuition fees. However, in spite of this changing climate, a large proportion of training places in doctoral programs have remained fully or partly funded.

The very impressive range of expertise listed by the postdoctoral implementation committee surely requires an educational program extending into a minimum of two years, and arguably, much longer. It cannot be doubted that to carry out any six of the 14 areas of competence would certainly require a minimum of two years.

Approximately 50 clinical and counseling doctoral programs in North America offer a concentration in health psychology. Another few are concerned exclusively with health psychology. Almost all of these programs require candidates to complete a one-year internship/residency before obtaining their doctorates. The *Guide to Internships in Health Psychology* developed by Division 38's Committee on Education and Training lists APA-accredited psychology internship programs at about 70 establishments in the United States and five in Canada. These internships devote a minimum of half of the intern's time to training in health psychology. Another dozen institutions offer minor rotations with less than halftime spent on health psychology. Stipends for predoctoral internships are generally in the range of $15 to $20 thousand. At postdoctoral level, there are around 30 training programs in the United States. Weiss and Buchanan (1996) published a list of international training opportunities, some of which may be substituted for an internship in the United States. Once a postdoctoral qualification has been obtained, a health psychologist in the United States can apply for a state license and be listed in the National Register of Health Service Providers.

The second training model for health psychologists exists within graduate programs in community psychology. A survey on behalf of the Council of Program Directors in Community Action and Research (CPDCRA) by Lounsbury, Skourtes, and Cantillon (1999). The survey revealed 43 programs offering graduate training in community psychology, 21 of which have a primary emphasis on community psychology. Twelve of the programs are community/clinical programs that typically have grown out of preexisting clinical psychology programs and offer doctorates. These programs accepted approximately 80 students in 1998 from a total of 1,700 applications. Health promotion, in the sense of positive well-being, is a prominent theme in these programs and the graduates. Field placements occur in a variety of settings including mental health settings. Graduates most often take clinical or community work positions. With a growing awareness of the community psychology, such programs are likely to expand.

It can be seen from this brief description that both of the approaches to health psychology described previously (see Table 1.1) are being developed in the United States.

EDUCATION AND TRAINING IN EUROPE

Professionalization of health psychology in European countries is on average 10 to 20 years behind the United States but follows a similar philosophy and rationale. In some countries (e.g., France, Portugal), it is 50 years behind, in others (e.g., Austria, Netherlands), it is not behind at all. Responsibility for policy regarding professional psychology in Europe lies with an umbrella organization called the European Federation of Professional Psychologists' Associations (EFPPA). Under the umbrella of EFPPA, national member associations operate with a mixture of national and transnational agendas and policies. Member associations balance the desirability of subscribing to pan-European principles with national priorities and interests.

A Task Force on Health Psychology was established by EFPPA in 1992 with the following objectives:

1. To define the nature and scope of health psychology and its possible future development to the year 2000.
2. To specify training needs and objectives for professional health psychologists consistent with the agreed definition.
3. To examine different models and options for the training of health psychologists and to select from among them suitable models for EFPPA countries.

The Task Force disseminated its working papers in a series of newsletter reports, conference symposia, and workshops (Donker, 1994, 1997; Marks, 1993, 1994a, 1994b, 1994c, 1994d, 1997a, 1997b; Marks, Donker, Jepsen, & Rodriguez-Marin, 1994; Marks et al., 1995a; Marks & Rodriguez-Marin, 1995; Rodriguez-Marin, 1994; Sidot, 1994; Wallin, 1994). An interim progress report was accepted by the EFPPA General Assembly in 1995 (Marks et al., 1995b). The Final Report was adopted by the General Assembly of EFPPA in Dublin in 1997 and published by Marks et al. (1998). The EFPPA approach followed the health service provider model of Table 1.1 although it addressed some issues that are amenable to the community action approach.

Rationale for Training

The rationale for developing training of health psychologists in Europe is the rapid growth of new developments in research and practice flowing out of this interdisciplinary field. At the same time, changes in health policy in many countries are generating new roles for psychologists. With a growing awareness of the importance of psychosocial factors in the promotion and maintenance of well-being, the demands for professional health psychology services within European health care systems are expected to increase. As Garcia-Barbero (1994) stated, "Health professionals clearly need more appropriate training to meet the challenges of the health for all policy, to meet the health needs of the population, to reduce health costs, to assure quality, and to permit the free movement of sufficiently qualified health professionals."

Under the national ethical codes of the psychology profession, there is an absolute responsibility to ensure that psychologists only practice in areas of competence. This principle requires that health psychologists be trained and assessed for their competence before they enter into unsupervised practice. Psychologists wishing to practice in new areas therefore have a responsibility to become appropriately trained and experienced.

Complementing Other Fields of Applied Psychology

As noted earlier, there are overlapping competencies between health psychologists and other applied psychologists working in health fields and it is likely that there will be shared, generic components of training. All psychologists working in health fields have a common foundation of basic education in psychology. Psychologists with experience and/or training in fields of applied psychology wishing to have a professional qualification in health psychology should be permitted to receive accreditation of their prior experience and/or training. The proposed training should be specifically designed to fulfill this objective of complementarity.

Professional Autonomy and Complementary Independence

The ultimate objective of training should be professional autonomy and complementary independence. The latter requires mutual respect of experience and training, without intrusions, infringements, or subordination across health care professions.

Stages of Competency

It is recognized that practitioner-training passes through stages in which a person will, at first, practice under supervision of another fully experienced practitioner. Following an appropriate level of supervised, placement experience with a range of settings and client groups, the psychologist will be competent to practice in his or her own right. However, training is never final and practitioners require continuous professional development through the acquisition of new skills and with the development of new technologies and the updating of knowledge following the advancement of research.

Training Guidelines for Professional Health Psychologists

Different educational systems and traditions affect the structure of curricula for training professional psychologists in different European countries. In several meetings, the Task Force deliberated on the idea of formulating a fixed set of minimal standards for the whole of Europe. Three case studies of training at different levels of development were analyzed in depth (training in Denmark, Germany, and Holland). Symposia and workshops were held at international conferences at which training models for different countries were compared and contrasted (Donker, 1994; Marks et al., 1995a; Rodriguez-Marin, 1994; Rumsey et al., 1994a; Sidot, 1994; Wallin, 1994). Large, possibly irreconcilable, variations are evident in the models and methods of training and in the amount of experience deemed necessary for nationally accredited recognition as professional psychologists across different countries. One country (Austria) has a law specifying the tasks to be performed by professional health psychologists. In the remainder, the tasks and responsibilities of professional health psychologists (and, for most countries, other applied psychologists as well) are dependent on a complex array of national, regional, and local agreements. Training practices are equally diverse. In a few countries, training programs are well advanced and have been implemented by national associations (e.g., Berufsverband Osterreichischer Psychologen, 1995; Dansk Psykologforening, 1996). Other associations are making progress in formulating and implementing training guidelines (e.g., British Psychological Society: Edelmann et al., 1996; Rumsey et al., 1994b; Berufsverband Deutscher Psychologen: Rielander, 1995). However, many European countries still do not yet train health psychologists in any specific and specialized manner.

If health psychology is to achieve its full potential in European health care systems, training will need to be implemented much more widely than is presently the case. This will only be possible within the particular legal and professional conditions that determine the organization of psychology and health care in different countries. A principle of subsidiarity must therefore operate. However, it will be necessary to at least have a framework for training in each country and these guidelines provide that framework.

The EFPPA task force placed the training requirements of professional health psychologists into eight categories:

1. *Academic Knowledge Base (Psychology)*. Professional health psychologists require an in-depth understanding of:
   - Lifespan perspectives and developmental processes.
   - Health-related cognitions.
   - Social factors and ethnicity.
   - Psychoneuroimmunology.
   - Psychophysiological processes.
   - Primary, secondary, and tertiary prevention in the context of health-related behavior.
   - Risk factors.
   - The health and safety of individuals in the workplace.
   - Personality, health, and disease.
   - Stress, illness, and coping.
   - Health care professional-patient communication.
   - Psychological aspects of medical procedures.
   - Coping with life events.

2. *Academic Knowledge Base (Other)*. Professional health psychologists require understanding of relevant aspects only of:
   - Epidemiology.
   - Ethics.
   - Genetics.
   - Health policy.
   - Health sociology.
   - Health economics.
   - Human biology.
   - Immunology.
   - Medical anthropology.
   - Medicine.
   - Physiology.
   - Pharmacology.
   - Neuroendocrinology.
   - Cultural and religious studies.

3. *Application of Psychological Skills to Health Care*. Professional health psychologists require a working knowledge of:
   - Communication skills.
   - Consultancy skills.
   - Counseling skills.
   - Assessment and evaluation.
   - Psychological interventions aimed at change in individuals and systems (e.g., families, groups, worksites, communities).

4. *Research Skills*. Professional health psychologists require a working knowledge of research skills in specific application to health and health care.

5. *Teaching and Training Skills*. Professional health psychologists require skills for teaching and training students and other health and social care professionals including supervisory skills.

6. *Management Skills*. Professional health psychologists require a working understanding of organizations and teams.

7. *Professional Issues*. Professional health psychologists require a working understanding of:
   - The place and status of health psychology in society.
   - Professional identity and autonomy.
   - Legal and statutory obligations and restrictions.
   - Transcultural issues.
   - International perspectives on professional health psychology.

8. *Ethical Issues*. Professional health psychologists are required to follow the ethical code of their national associations.

Implementation of Training

The future development of health psychology as a profession depends on putting theory and policy into practice through the implementation of high-quality training. Currently, there are relatively few European countries where this has yet happened. Training programs need to be introduced in all European countries within the framework of each member-country's national laws, regulations, and practices.

Section three specifies five skill areas that were seen, not as optional, but as mandatory. The assumptions of the Matarazzo definition, the biopsychosocial model, and working in clinical settings are held in Europe as strongly as in the United States. The Education and Training Committee of the EHPS has published a reference guide of graduate programs in health psychology in Europe (McIntyre, Maes, Weinman, Wrzesniewski, & Marks, 2000). There are many masters and PhD level programs but few DPsych or PsyD programs have yet been developed. The traditional PhD is an academic qualification providing little or no training in practitioner skills. With some exceptions (e.g., the Netherlands), European programs have a long way to go before they match most U.S. programs for the depth and breadth of coverage.

EDUCATION AND TRAINING IN THE UNITED KINGDOM

Responsibility for the accreditation of education and training in psychology in the United Kingdom lies with the British Psychological Society (BPS). The Society approved regulations for a full professional qualification in health psychology in 2001. This qualification is essential to all those wishing to work professionally in the health psychology field. On completion, candidates are eligible for full membership of the Division of Health Psychology permitting the member to use the title "Chartered Health Psychologist" and to have his or her name listed in the Society's Register. The training system is based on the health service provider model of Table 1.1. No programs using the community action model have yet been accredited by the BPS Health Psychology Division. In the United Kingdom, community action programs are more likely to be located in departments of geography or in health promotion units than in departments of psychology (e.g., Cave & Curtis, 2001; Lethbridge, 2001). To date, with one or two notable exceptions (e.g., Bennett & Murphy, 1997), there has been relatively little interest in the community approach within British health psychology.

Education and training of health psychologists in the United Kingdom is in three stages: (a) undergraduate, (b) postgraduate stage 1 (MSc), (c) postgraduate stage 2 (MPhil, PhD, PsychD, or DPsych). To enroll as a candidate for the stage 1 postgraduate qualification in Health Psychology, the applicant must:

1. Be a graduate member of the British Psychological Society and hold the Graduate Basis for Registration; and
2. Either hold, or be enrolled in, a postgraduate research degree relevant to health psychology and include an empirical research project, or
3. Be a chartered psychologist seeking lateral transfer from another area of psychology.

The postgraduate stage 1 is often completed as a BPS-accredited MSc degree in health psychology in any one of about 20 institutions. Otherwise candidates may take an examination set by the Board of Examiners in Health Psychology (BEHP). This examination comprises four written papers, a research project, and an oral examination on the research project. The topics covered in the written examination papers are:

- Health-related behavior: Cognitions and individual differences.
- Psychosocial processes in illness and health care delivery.
- Research and development in health psychology.
- Context and related areas.

The research dissertation must be a piece of supervised, self-selected original health-related research in accordance with the BPS ethical guidelines, and should not exceed 14,000 words.

Following successful completion of the stage 1 qualification, candidates may proceed to stage 2. To enroll as a candidate for the stage 2 qualification, the applicant must:

1. Be a graduate member of the BPS and hold Graduate Basis for Registration.
2. Hold either the stage 1 qualification in health psychology, or a postgraduate BPS accredited qualification in health psychology, or have a statement of permission to proceed to the stage 2 Qualification from the BEHP.
3. The stage 1 qualification involves the attainment of a health psychology knowledge base and postgraduate research skills. The stage 2 qualification builds on stage 1 by assessing professional level capability in research, consultancy, teaching, and training and also generic professional competence in relation to psychological practice. From September 2004, applicants for Chartered Health Psychology status who began their training after September 1, 2001, will have to demonstrate competence in 21 units—19 core units and two optional units. The 19 required units are divided into 73 specific components in four domains.

Professional Competence

Health psychologists should be able to maintain personal and professional standards in their practice and act ethically. Core competencies include:

1. Implement and maintain systems for legal, ethical, and professional standards in applied psychology—security and control of information; compliance with legal, ethical, and professional practices; procedures to ensure competence in psychological practice and research.
2. Contribute to the continuing development of self as a professional applied psychologist—process of self-development; knowledge and feedback to inform practice; access to competent consultation and advice; professional development; best practice as standard.
3. Provide psychological advice and guidance to others—assess opportunity, need, and context for giving psychological advice; provide psychological advice; evaluate advice given.
4. Provide feedback to clients—evaluate feedback requirements; preparation and structure; methods of communication; presentation of feedback.

Research Competence

Health psychologists must be capable of being independent researchers. Core competencies include:

1. Conduct systematic reviews—define topic and search parameters; employ appropriate databases and sources; summarize findings.
2. Design psychological research—identify relevant research findings; generate testable hypotheses; define resources and constraints; methodology; validation of measures; prepare, present, and revise research designs.
3. Conduct psychological research—obtain required resources and access to data and/or participants; research protocol; pilot existing methods; conduct research.
4. Analyze and evaluate psychological research data—analyze and interpret data; evaluate research findings; written account of research project; review research process; review and evaluate relationships between current issues in psychological theory and practice.
5. Initiate and develop psychological research—conduct research; monitor and evaluate research in accordance to protocols; explain and critique implications of research for practice; evaluate potential impact of research developments on health care.

Consultancy Competence

Health psychologists must be capable to apply psychological knowledge to health care and health promotion practice. Core competencies include:

1. Assessment of requests for consultancy—determine, prioritize, and confirm expectations and requisites of clients; review literature for relevant information; assess feasibility of proposal.
2. Plan consultancy—aims, objectives, and criteria; implementation plan.
3. Establish, develop, and maintain working relationships with clients—establish contact with client; contract; develop and maintain, and monitor and evaluate, working relationships with clients.
4. Conduct consultancy.
5. Monitor the implementation of consultancy—review consultancy; implement necessary changes; review client expectations and requisites; implement quality assurance.
6. Evaluate the implementation of consultancy—design and implement evaluation; assess evaluation outcomes.

Teaching and Training Competence

Health psychologists must be capable to train others to understand and apply psychological knowledge skills, practices and procedures. Core competencies include:

1. Plan and design training programs that enable students to learn about psychological knowledge, skills, and practices—assess training needs; identify training program; select methods; produce materials; employ appropriate media.
2. Deliver training programs—implement training methods; facilitate learning.
3. Plan and implement assessment of such training programs—identify assessment methods and select regime; determine availability of resources for assessment procedures; produce assessment materials; ensure fair appreciation of assessment methods; keep record of progress and outcomes.
4. Evaluate such training programs—evaluate outcomes; identify contributing factors of outcomes; identify improvements.

Optional Competences

Two of the following eight optional units of competence must also be attained:

1. Implement interventions to change health-related behavior.
2. Direct the implementation of interventions.
3. Communicate the processes and outcomes of interventions and consultancies.
4. Provide psychological advice to aid policy decision making for the implementation of psychological services.
5. Promote psychological principles, practices, services, and benefits.
6. Provide expert opinion and advice, including the preparation and presentation of evidence in formal settings.
7. Contribute to the evolution of legal, ethical, and professional standards in health and applied psychology.
8. Disseminate psychological knowledge to address current issues in society.

The trainee health psychologist undergoes a period of supervised practice equivalent to two years of full-time work (a five-day week for 46 weeks a year). This provides direct experience of professional life and facilitates the development of skills and abilities relevant to health psychology. Candidates' total work experience should encompass at least two different categories of clients and be health-related work of a psychological nature. Health-related work may include paid employment, academic work, training and development activities, and voluntary work.

Candidates must arrange supervision from an approved Chartered Health Psychologist. A contract of supervision, indicating payment, is drawn up. Candidates devise a formal supervision plan that includes a work plan outlining core competencies addressed with target dates, details of evidence that will demonstrate satisfactory completion of competencies, name of supervisor, expected date of completion of stage 2, and any additional training and development activities needed. To achieve the stage 2 qualification, candidates must demonstrate competencies in all 19 areas. No exemptions are permitted. All candidates are bound by the BPS Code of Conduct.

The role of the supervisor is to:

- Oversee the preparation and review of the supervision plan.
- Countersign the supervision plan, supervision log, and supporting evidence, and fill in the required sections of the completion forms.
- Provide information.
- Listen to the views and concerns of the candidates concerning their work in progress and advise as appropriate.
- Encourage reflection, creativity, problem solving, and the integration of theory into practice.

The examination consists of an oral examination and the submission of a portfolio of evidence of competencies. The portfolio should include a practice diary, supervision log, records of completion, supporting evidence, and any additional clarification. Candidates are enrolled for a minimum of two years, and a maximum of five years. When full membership of the Division of Health Psychology has been gained, members become Chartered Health Psychologists and they are listed in the British Psychological Society's Register.

SIMILARITIES AND DIFFERENCES BETWEEN THE U.S., EUROPEAN, AND U.K. MODELS

It is informative to compare the three health service models developed in the United States, Europe, and United Kingdom. A summary of the competencies included in the three models are presented in Table 1.2.

A Common Core

It can be seen that there is a solid core of three competencies that all three models include in one form or another:

teaching/training, consultancy, and *research.* All practicing health psychologists need to acquire these skills for their professional work whether they are working in the United States or Europe. In the United States, health psychologists are trained to carry out therapies and interventions alongside their clinical colleagues. Perhaps more than in some other areas of applied psychology, the core competencies of the health psychology practitioner in the United Kingdom show considerable overlap with those of the academic psychologist. However, this is likely to change as the profession becomes more confident about what it has to offer.

Differences between Regions or Countries and Gaps in Training

Some skills that are seen as essential in one region or country are seen as optional in others, for example, interventions aimed at change in individuals and systems, counseling, management, liaison, and health promotion skills. There are some significant omissions in training requirements that warrant further discussion by the relevant committees. For example, the BPS curriculum omits training in assessment and evaluation, communication, counseling, and management skills. The APA curriculum also omits communication, counseling, and management. Can health psychologists really practice to their maximum potential without competence in these areas? Merely having access to research information about these subjects is insufficient: Knowing *about* is not the same as knowing *how.*

Table 1.2 reveals a number of gaps in training in the United States and United Kingdom medical textbooks invariably have chapters about doctor-patient communication, comment on its deficiencies, and recommend special training on communication skills for medical doctors. Why should health psychologists be any better at communication, without special training, than physicians? Without mandatory training, these competencies are left to individual practitioners to pick up when, where, and however they can. The quality of services and health improvements may be less than optimum as a consequence. Another surprising gap is the lack of assessment and evaluation training in the U.K. training curriculum. These are basic competencies that are used everyday within clinical psychology. Assessment is a necessary stage in the choosing and tailoring interventions for individual clients. Evaluation of effectiveness is paramount to the assessment of efficacy and effectiveness.

Perhaps these differences and gaps reflect the histories and cultures of professional psychology in different regions and countries. Perhaps they reflect a desire not to encroach on other established psychological professions such as clinical,

TABLE 1.2   Health Psychology Competencies Mandated by Professional Associations in the United States, Europe, and the United Kingdom. Skills or competencies in *bold* are required. Others are optional

United States/APA (1988): At Least 6 of 14 Techniques	Europe/EFPPA (1997): 10 Competencies in 8 Domains	United Kingdom/BPS (2001): 21 Units across 4 Domains
—	**Communication skills.**	—
—	**Teaching and training skills.**	**Teaching and training competence.**
Health promotion and public education skills.	—	—
Consultation skills.	**Consultancy skills.**	**Consultancy competence.**
Assessment of specific patient populations (e.g., pain patients, spinal cord injury patients).	**Assessment and evaluation.**	—
Short-term individual psychotherapy. Group therapy. Family therapy. Relaxation therapies.	**Psychological interventions aimed at change in individuals and systems.**	Implement interventions to change health related behavior.
—	**Professional issues.**	**Professional and ethical issues.**
—	**Ethical issues.**	
—	**Counseling skills.**	—
—	**Management skills.**	—
Liaison skills. Neuropsychological assessment. Behavior modification. Biofeedback. Hypnosis. Major treatment programs (e.g., chemical dependence, eating disorders). Compliance motivation.	—	Direct the implementation of interventions. Communicate the processes and outcomes of interventions and consultancies. Provide psychological advice to aid policy decision making for the implementation of psychological services. Promote psychological principles, practices, services, and benefits. Provide expert opinion and advice, including the preparation and presentation of evidence in formal settings. Contribute to the evolution of legal, ethical, and professional standards in health and applied psychology. Disseminate psychological knowledge to address current issues in society.
Doctoral dissertation.	**Research skills.**	**Research competence.**

counseling, and occupational psychology. Perhaps they also reflect the lack of consensus about the definition of health psychology. Should it strive to become the overarching health care profession of Matarazzo's (1980) definition, or a more specialized profession focusing on the maintenance of health and prevention of illness in currently healthy persons in line with Matarazzo's (1980) definition of behavioral health, as recommended by McDermott (2001)? Only the future will tell which of these models wins the day.

CRITIQUE OF PROFESSIONALIZATION

The development of an outline of a set of core competencies for health psychologists has led to a great deal of discussion and debate. One of the main issues of concern has been whether health psychology is ready yet to become a profession, and if so, how this change in status is to be accomplished. Developing the profession too early may result in a profession with too little to deliver, a "naked emperor" (Michie, 2001). Worse, a naked emperor, or empress, might cause offense and do harm to, rather than improve, the health of his or her subjects!

The construction of a core set of competencies took the APA and EFPPA five years and the BPS six years to complete. Similar periods will, no doubt, be required for any new system to be thoroughly tried and tested. Judgments about what a health psychologist should know and be able to do are based on extant beliefs, values, and aspirations, and little else but intuition. Consequentially, committee decisions about the objectives and content of education and training are highly contentious.

Despite being a relatively new area of applied psychology, health psychology is developing at an astonishing rate. New health psychology programs are being introduced, textbooks are appearing continuously and going into second, third, and fourth editions, and the academic journals are expanding and flourishing. Health psychology has a real potential to have a positive impact on the health of society. Yet the definition of health psychology is still in contention and there are at least two quite different approaches to the field. In a recent essay, the first author suggested that four styles of working are beginning to emerge: clinical, public, community, and critical health psychology (Marks, 2002b).

In a recent debate in the BPS Division of Health Psychology's newsletter, *Health Psychology Update,* Bolam (2001) asked, "Whom does professionalization advantage, and at what cost?" Bolam suggested that any abstract attempt at a definition inevitably obscures the complex web of social, institutional, historical, and economic forces from which health psychology has emerged. He suggested that the argument that health psychologists "owe it to the public" to be professional is only part of the story. Bolam felt little confidence in the claim that health psychology has a unique set of techniques to offer the health care system. Bolam argued that professionalization is really about "self-promotion and the struggle to increase access to resources and power." What health psychologists gain comes at a cost, however, and identity is not only about claiming what health psychologists are, but also what they are not. Health psychologists should challenge the biologically reductionist tendencies and the hierarchical structures of biomedicine by introducing new discourses about people and health. Bolam suggests that "Instead of challenging the biologically reductionist tendencies and hierarchical structures of biomedicine by introducing new discourses of people and health, we replicate the very mistakes we could help to remedy, merely aspiring to be further up the table." This leads to a concern that the current mainstream training proposals in the United States, Europe, and the United Kingdom are strongly influenced by the biopsychosocial model that could stifle the development of the field.

Michie (2001), on the other hand, contra Bolam, argued that professionalization "does not just benefit health psychologists . . . but also benefits recipients of psychological services, employers, policymakers, and the public. It benefits everybody to know who we are and what we do" (p. 18). A definition, at least of the core concept, is essential for the progress of science and for strategic development of its application. Professionalization helped to ensure minimum standards of practice and accountability.

Sykes (2001) entered the debate with the thought that it was the health psychologists' responsibility to practice only in those areas where they have been trained and have a level of competence. Consumers, patients, clients, and communities need to feel confident that health psychologists have been fully trained to deliver evidence-based services. Clients have a right to know who health psychologists are and what services they are competent to deliver.

Have the current education and training proposals left unrecognized a lot of work that health psychologists do, or could do? For example, health psychologists can work not only within the health service delivery model but from a communitarian perspective, following a model of community action and research. Community action requires a unique set of skills. These include communication and negotiation skills, the art of unlearning, appropriately empowering others, flexibility, a great amount of perseverance, and a belief in a vision. Working alongside others on an equal footing is the order of the day, not offering a service, but sharing an action. This type of work is as much in need of a professional approach as any other. Thus, the debate has turned full circle and reflects the differences between the two models of training discussed earlier, the clinical treatment of illness approach versus the community health promotion approach.

Despite these differences in opinion, there is a central theme in the debate: making *health improvement* the main priority for health psychology. Such debates should be viewed positively because an applied discipline must continuously reflect and be open to change.

ETHICAL AND POLICY ISSUES

Professional health psychologists are expected to comply with the ethical codes of their national associations. However, ethics must not be viewed simply as a set of principles for dealing with special or specific circumstances when dilemmas occur. Every action, or inaction, in health care has an ethical dimension (Seedhouse, 1998). In this section, we review issues of a policy nature that highlight ethical issues for health psychologists and all other health care professionals.

Poverty and Inequality

All people have an equal right to health and health care. That contemporary societies have large health variations is readily apparent (Carroll & Davey Smith, 1997; Wilkinson, 1996). Of major significance in both developed and developing societies is poverty. In pursuit of health-for-all, the health care system must strive to equalize the opportunities of all members of society. This principle requires psychologists to provide their services (whenever possible) to all people regardless of gender, age, religion, ethnic grouping, social class, material circumstances, political affiliation, or sexual orientation. When access is low, or when there is evidence of greater needs, special efforts should be made to target services to those with the poorest access or greatest need (e.g., refugees, the homeless, lower income groups). Policy decisions concerning the allocation of resources to these needy groups both inside and outside of the health care system are about ethics as much as politics.

Economics

The demand for health care exceeds supply. This fact has economic implications for services. First, it is necessary to provide services according to the health needs of all client groups. Second, it is necessary to analyze health care economically. This means that cost-benefit analyses and evidence of cost-effectiveness should be utilized in making decisions about services. It is likely that some psychological interventions are able to provide more cost-effective options than pharmacological and medical treatments (Sobell, 1995). However, the evidence to provide definite support of this claim is often not available. If psychological interventions are to be more widely employed, it is necessary that more effort and resources be devoted to economic analyses of their cost-effectiveness. Third, whether we like it or not, health services have to be rationed. Unless we accept the philosophy that those who receive a service are those who can afford it (or the insurance premiums), the decision about who receives or does not receive a service is both political and ethical in nature. In many countries, psychology services are in short supply and among the least accessible and most rationed. Yet rationing is rarely discussed in the psychology literature.

New Technologies

New scientific and medical technologies are having dramatic effects on the cost-effectiveness, efficiency, and competence of health care (e.g., microsurgery, organ transplantation, genetic testing/screening, gene therapy, in vitro fertilization). Genetic information and its communication to individuals and families are sensitive issues that have both psychological and ethical implications (Lerman, 1997). Following the production of a sheep clone, "Dolly" (Wilmut, Schnieke, McWhir, Kind, & Campbell, 1997), the cloning of humans is likely soon to become technically possible. In spite of reassurances from a professor of fertility studies (Winston, 1997), this prospect raises profound ethical questions among health professionals, patients, and families (Human Genetics Commission, 2000).

There may be biological, psychosocial, or moral implications that have not yet been adequately conceptualized.

Not only do new technologies increase the need for public understanding and debate, they require medical scientists and health professionals to be completely open and honest about the benefits, risks, and possible sequelae of treatments and procedures. Communication, counseling, and informed consent are becoming increasingly vital elements of health care (Marteau & Richards, 1996). However, it is recognized that providing people with genetic information on risk may not increase their motivation to change behavior and in some cases may even decrease their motivation (Marteau & Lerman, 2001). In these areas, psychologists should play a major role.

The Aging Population

Demographic data show that the Western population is aging. In Europe in January 1993, there were 117 million people aged 50 years and over (32%) and nearly 75 million aged 60 and over (20%) in the 15 countries of the European Union. The latter will increase to over 25% by the year 2020. In terms of health policy, the most significant increase is in the numbers of people who are 80 years or more, particularly women, large numbers (48%) of whom live alone, especially in northern Europe (Walker & Maltby, 1997).

An increasingly prevalent combination of frailty, poverty, and social isolation is making older age a time of significantly reduced quality of life. This is particularly true for the increasing numbers of people suffering from Alzheimer's disease, or other forms of dementia, and their informal caregivers (European Alzheimer Clearing House, 1997). A report from the Eurobarometer surveys suggests that poverty, age discrimination, fear of crime, and access to health and social care are significant barriers to social integration among older people (Walker & Maltby, 1997). On the more positive side, the surveys suggest that, "Just under one-quarter of older people were very satisfied with their lives, more than half fairly satisfied and only one in five not satisfied" (p. 122). Promotion of social integration of older people, particularly those living alone, presents a major challenge for the future. Health psychologists will need to work closely with other professionals to find new ways of enhancing social integration and well-being of older members of the population and their caregivers.

CONCLUSIONS

Health psychology is a research field that entered the marketplace of health care quite recently. Competing and contrasting definitions suggest different approaches to the enterprise. The mainstream approach is modeled on health service provision similar to clinical psychology, but dealing principally with physical health and illness. It is founded on what is termed the "biopsychosocial" model. This approach is sometimes referred to as "clinical health psychology." Another approach is modeled on community action and research and deals with the promotion of well-being in its social and community context, a kind of psychological health promotion. The different approaches have different philosophies, methods of working, models of training, goals, and objectives. Up to the present, little effort has been directed toward integrating these two approaches. Perhaps they are resistant to integration.

Professionalization in health psychology is a problematic exercise. Some contend that it has occurred too soon, before there is sufficient evidence to play on the same field with the "big-hitters" of the more established health professions (medicine, nursing, dentistry). Others argue that it is necessary to credentialize practitioners as soon as possible with registration procedures following approval of their training and supervised experience. Others argue that the health service provider model limits the development of health psychology. While the debate continues, education and training programs are proceeding apace.

Training programs in the United States were established at least 10 years earlier than in most of the rest of the world. Core elements of health psychology competence agreed to by three independent panels are research, consultancy, and teaching and training. Other skills, viewed as optional by some panels and as mandatory by others, include: interventions for individuals and systems; communication skills; counseling skills; and assessment and evaluation skills. New programs are currently being developed and it would be a valuable exercise to evaluate progress in another decade's time.

REFERENCES

American Psychological Association. (1996). Division 38—Health psychology home page [Online].

Bennett, P., & Murphy, S. (1997). *Psychology and health promotion.* Buckingham, England: Open University Press.

Berufsverband Osterreichischer Psychologen. [Austrian Psychological Society]. (1995). 1090 Wien [Vienna], Garnisongasse 1/21a, Austria.

Bolam, B. (2001). The professionalisation of health psychology: Against. *Health Psychology Update, 10*(1), 16–17.

Breslow, L., & Enstrom, J. E. (1980). Persistence of health habits and their relationship to mortality. *Preventive Medicine, 9,* 469–483.

Broome, A. K., & Llewellyn, S. (1995). *Health psychology* (2nd ed.). London: Chapman & Hall.

Carroll, D., & Davey Smith, G. (Eds.). (1977). Health variations [Special section]. *Journal of Health Psychology, 2,* 275–425.

Cave, B., & Curtis, S. (2001). Developing a practical guide to assess the potential health impact of urban regeneration schemes. *Promotion and Education, 8,* 12–16.

Dansk Psykologforening. (1996). *Postbasic training in health psychology.* Copenhagen, Denmark: Stockholmsgade.

Donker, F. J. S. (1994). Health and clinical psychology in Holland. In D. F. Marks (Chair), *Psychology's contribution to health.* Symposium conducted at the 23rd International Congress of Applied Psychology, Madrid, Spain.

Donker, F. J. S. (1997). Health psychology in the Netherlands. In D. F. Marks (Chair), *Health psychology: Putting theory into practice.* Symposium conducted at the 5th European Congress of Psychology, Dublin, Ireland.

Edelmann, R., Maguire, B., Marks, D. F., Michie, S., Watts, M., Weinman, J., et al. (1996). *A framework for training in health psychology: A suggested training programme for psychology graduates wishing to become chartered health psychologists.* Leicester, England: British Psychological Society.

European Alzheimer Clearing House. (1997). Home page [Online]. Available from www.each.be

European Federation Professional Psychologists Association. (1995). *European Federation of Professional Psychologists Association's metacode of ethics.* Stockholm, Sweden: Author.

Garcia-Barbero, M. (1994). *An education and training strategy for health-for-all.* Copenhagen, Denmark: World Health Organization, Regional Office for Europe.

Human Genetics Commission. (2000). *Whose hands on your genes? A discussion document on the storage protection and use of personal health information.* London: Department of Health.

Lerman, C. (Ed.). (1997). Psychological aspects of genetic testing [Special issue]. *Health Psychology, 16*(1).

Lethbridge, J. (2001). Health promotion within the development process. *Promotion and Education, 8,* 23–28.

Lounsbury, D., Skourtes, S., & Cantillon, D. (1999). *1999 survey of graduate training programs in community psychology.* Society for Community Research and Action webpage: http://www.apa.org/divisions/div27

Macdonald, G. (2000). A new evidence framework for health promotion practice. *Health Education Journal, 59,* 3–11.

Maes, S., & van Veldhoven, M. (1989). Gezondsheidspsychologie: Van ziektegedrag tot gesondsheidgedrag (thematische bespeking van 15 belangrijke titels uit de jaren 80 op het gebied van de gezondheidspsychogie). *Gedrag & Gezondheid, 17,* 34–40.

Marks, D. F. (1993). European Federation of Professional Psychologists Association task force on health psychology, *News from EFPPA, 7*(2), 28–29.

Marks, D. F. (1994a). European Federation of Professional Psychologists. A task force on health psychology: Recommendations on training, *Health Psychology Update, 17,* 18–21.

Marks, D. F. (1994b). The training needs of professional health psychologists. *European Health Psychology Society Newsletter, 8,* 1–7.

Marks, D. F. (1994c). Psychology's contribution to health. In D. F. Marks (Chair), *Psychology's contribution to health.* Symposium conducted at the 23rd International Congress of Applied Psychology, Madrid, Spain.

Marks, D. F. (1994d). European Federation of Professional Psychologists Association Task Force on Health Psychology: Progress report. *News from EFPPA, 8*(3), 18–20.

Marks, D. F. (1996). Health psychology in context. *Journal of Health Psychology, 1,* 7–21.

Marks, D. F. (1997a). Health psychology 2000: The development of professional health psychology. *News from EFPPA, 11*(1), 3–8.

Marks, D. F. (1997b). Health psychology: Putting theory into practice. In D. F. Marks (Chair), *Health psychology: Putting theory into practice.* Symposium conducted at the 5th European Congress of Psychology, Dublin, Ireland.

Marks, D. F. (2002a). *The health psychology reader.* London: Sage.

Marks, D. F. (2002b). Freedom, responsibility, and power: Contrasting approaches to health psychology. *Journal of Health Psychology, 7,* 5–9.

Marks, D. F., Donker, F. J. S., Jepsen, Z., & Rodriguez Marin, J. (1994). *The training needs of professional health psychologists.* Round-table discussion, European Health Psychology Society conference, Alicante, Spain.

Marks, D. F., Donker, F. J. S., Jepsen, Z., Rodriguez-Marin, J., Sidot, S., & Wallin, B. (1995a). *Health psychology 2000.* Workshop, 4th European Congress of Psychology, Athens, Greece.

Marks, D. F., Donker, F. J. S., Jepsen, Z., Rodriguez Marin, J., Sidot, S., & Wallin, B. (1995b). *Health psychology 2000: The development of professional health psychology.* Progress report, EFPPA General Assembly, Athens, Greece.

Marks, D. F., Donker, F. J. S., Jepsen, Z., Rodriguez Marin, J., Sidot, S., & Wallin, B. (1998). Health psychology 2000: The development of professional health psychology. *Journal of Health Psychology, 3,* 149–160.

Marks, D. F., Murray, M., Evans, B., & Willig, C. (2000). *Health psychology. Theory, research and practice.* London: Sage.

Marks, D. F., & Rodriguez-Marin, J. (1995). European Federation of Professional Psychologists Association: La psicologia de la salud. *Papeles del Psycologo, 3*(61), 64–66.

Marteau, T. M., & Lerman, C. (2001). Genetic risk and behavioural change. *British Medical Journal, 322,* 1056–1059.

Marteau, T. M., & Richards, M. P. M. (Eds.). (1996). *The troubled helix: The social and psychological implications of the new human genetics* (pp. 82–103). Cambridge, England: Cambridge University Press.

Matarazzo, J. D. (1980). Behavioral health and behavioral medicine: Frontiers for a new health psychology. *American Psychologist, 35,* 807–817.

Matarazzo, J. D. (1982). Behavioral health's challenge to academic, scientific, and professional psychology. *American Psychologist, 37,* 1–14.

Matarazzo, J. D., Weiss, S. M., Herd, J. A., & Miller, N. E. (1984). *Behavioural health: A handbook of health enhancement and disease prevention.* New York: Wiley.

McDermott, M. (2001). Redefining health psychology: Matarazzo revisited. *Health Psychology Update, 10,* 3–10.

McIntyre, T. M., Maes, S., Weinman, J., Wrzesniewski, K., & Marks, D. F. (2000). *Postgraduate programs in health psychology in Europe: A reference guide.* Leiden, The Netherlands: European Health Psychology Society Education and Training Committee.

Michie, S. (2001). The professionalisation of health psychology: Reply to the debate. *Health Psychology Update, 10*(1), 18–19.

Ogden, J. (1997). The rhetoric and the reality of psychosocial theories of health: A challenge to biomedicine. *Journal of Health Psychology, 2,* 21–29.

Rielander, M. (1995). *Psychological health promotion for health psychologists* (German Psychologists' Academy Working Group "Further Training in Health Promotion"). Bonn, Germany: Berufsverband Deutscher Psychologen.

Rodriguez-Marin, J. (1994). Health psychology in Spain. In D. F. Marks (Chair), *Psychology's contribution to health.* Symposium conducted at the 23rd International Congress of Applied Psychology, Madrid, Spain.

Rumsey, N., Maguire, B., Marks, D. F., Watts, M., Weinman, J., & Wright, S. (1994a). Training proposals for professional health psychologists in the United Kingdom. In D. F. Marks (Chair), *Psychology's contribution to health.* Symposium conducted at the 23rd International Congress of Applied Psychology, Madrid, Spain.

Rumsey, N., Maguire, B., Marks, D. F., Watts, M., Weinman, J., & Wright, S. (1994b). Towards a core curriculum. *The Psychologist, 7*(3), 129–131.

Seedhouse, D. (1998). *Ethics. The heart of health care.* (2nd ed.) Chichester: Wiley.

Sheridan, E. P., Matarazzo, J. D., Boll, T. J., Perry, N. W., Weiss, S. M., & Belar, C. D. (1988). Postdoctoral education and training for clinical service providers in health psychology. *Health Psychology, 7*(1), 1–17.

Sidot, S. (1994). Nature, extent and prospects of psychology and health in France. In D. F. Marks (Chair), *Psychology's contribution to health.* Symposium conducted at the 23rd International Congress of Applied Psychology, Madrid, Spain.

Sobell, D. S., (1995). Rethinking medicine: Improving health outcomes with cost-effective psychosocial interventions. *Psychosomatic Medicine, 57,* 234–244.

Sykes, C. M. (2001). The professionalisation of health psychology: For. *Health Psychology Update, 10*(1), 14–15.

Taylor, S. E. (1986). *Health psychology* (3rd ed.) New York: Random House.

Walker, A., & Maltby, T. (1997). *Ageing Europe.* Buckingham, England: Open University press.

Wallace, L. M. (1998). Consultancy in health psychology to health services: An NHS CEO's views. *Health Psychology Update, 34,* 42–47.

Wallin, B. (1994). Health psychology in the Nordic countries. In D. F. Marks (Chair), *Psychology's contribution to health.* Symposium conducted at the 23rd International Congress of Applied Psychology, Madrid, Spain.

Wallston, K. E. (1993). Health psychology in the USA. In S. Maes, H. Leventhal, & M. Johnston (Eds.), *International review of health psychology* (Vol. 2, pp. 215–228). Chichester, England: Wiley.

Weiss, S. M., & Buchanan, J. (1996). *International directory of health psychology training programs.* Washington: APA Division 38 and International Affairs Office.

Whitehead, M. (1995). Tackling inequalities: A review of policy initiatives. In M. Benzeval, K. Judge, & M. Whitehead (Eds.), *Tackling inequalities in health: An agenda for action* (pp. 22–52). London: King's Fund.

Wilkinson, R. G. (1996). *Unhealthy societies: The afflictions of inequality.* London: Routledge.

Wilmut, T., Schnieke, A. K., McWhir, J., Kind, A. J., & Campbell, K. H. S. (1997). Viable offspring derived from fetal and adult mammalian cells. *Nature, 385,* 810–813.

Winett, R., King, A. C., & Altman, D. G. (1989). *Health psychology and public health.* New York: Pergamon Press.

Winston, R. (1997). The promise of cloning for human medicine: Not a moral threat but an exciting challenge. *British Medical Journal, 314,* 351–352.

World Health Organization. (1985). *Targets for health for all.* Copenhagen, Denmark: World Health Organization, Regional Office for Europe.

World Health Organization. (1995). *Renewing the health-for-all strategy: Elaboration of a policy for equity, solidarity and health.* Geneva, Switzerland: Author.

PART TWO

CAUSAL AND MEDIATING PSYCHOSOCIAL FACTORS

CHAPTER 2

Stressful Life Events

RALF SCHWARZER AND UTE SCHULZ

November 11, 2000, Salzburg, Austria: Around 170 people, mostly children and youths, are believed to have been killed when a blaze erupted on a cable train in the Austrian Alps. Rescuers at the scene of the inferno in the province of Salzburg say there is "no hope of any more survivors" after just a handful of people out of an estimated 180 passengers escaped alive. (CNN online)

The tragedy in Austria reported by CNN left behind hundreds of relatives and friends of the victims, devastated and mourning over the loss of loved ones. Some of the mourners might never fully recover from the shock and the pain, others might be able to return to the lives they were living before the event had occurred. Among those affected are also the few survivors, whose lives will probably never be the same, and the rescue personnel. Although those affected by the tragedy may have similar first responses, namely, shock, disbelief, and numbness, the specific impact on each individual may be different. Some have lost a child or spouse; others have faced death in the tunnel inferno. Unfortunately, major accidents such as fires, airplane crashes, or gas explosions, just to name

a few, happen quite frequently in industrial societies. Nevertheless, they take most people by surprise, require major readjustment efforts, and alter the course of their lives. Some experiences may have a long-lasting impact on a person's mental and physical health, while others exert only a short-term influence.

We start this chapter with a brief overview of theoretical concepts and critical issues related to stressful life event research and discuss some characteristics of major events and disasters, and the attempts to measure the unique ways people experience them. We also present some empirical findings on the relationship between specific life events and health impairments. Examples are drawn from a variety of natural and technological disasters, war, bereavement, criminal victimization, and migration. Not included in this chapter are those health effects that might be due to individual differences in personality, coping, and social support. Life events and coping are inevitably intertwined. In many studies, coping has been identified as a mediating link between stress and imminent health outcomes (see the chapter by Manne in this volume).

STRESS AND CRITICAL LIFE EVENTS: THEORETICAL PERSPECTIVES

There is no agreement among researchers about the definition of stress. In the biomedical sciences, stress is mainly understood as an organism's response to adverse stimulation. In psychology, stress is usually understood as the process where a person and the environment interact. In health psychology, joint effects of the person and environment on pathology have been the focus of research, along with mediating and moderating factors, such as coping and social support (Hobfoll, Schwarzer, & Chon, 1998). Basically, three broad perspectives can be chosen when studying stress: (a) the response-based perspective, (b) the stimulus-based perspective, and (c) the cognitive-transactional process perspective. We briefly address this distinction in order to provide a better understanding of the role of stressful life events.

The Response-Based Perspective

When people say, "I feel a lot of stress," they refer to their response to some adverse situation. The focus is on the way their organism reacts. Selye (1956) has distinguished between a stressor (the stimulus) and stress (the response). Selye was not interested in the nature of the stressor, but rather in the physiological response and the development of illness. This response to a stimulus follows the same typical three-stage pattern in humans and animals, called the general adaptation syndrome (GAS). According to GAS, the body initially defends itself against adverse circumstances by activating the sympathetic nervous system. This has been called the *alarm reaction.* It mobilizes the body for the "fight or flight" response, which can be seen phylogenetically as an adaptive short-term reaction to emergency situations. In many cases, the stress episode is mastered during the alarm reaction stage.

Often, however, stress is a longer encounter, and the organism moves on to the *resistance stage,* in which it adapts more or less successfully to the stressor. Although the person does not give the impression of being under stress, the organism does not function well and becomes ill. According to Selye, the immune system is compromised, and some typical "diseases of adaptation" develop under persistent stress, such as ulcers and cardiovascular diseases.

Finally, in the *exhaustion stage,* the organism's adaptation resources are depleted, and a breakdown occurs. This is associated with parasympathetic activation that leads to illness, burnout, depression, or even death.

This response-based perspective of stress has some merits, and it is still dominant in the biomedical sciences, but not in psychology. The main reason that it is no longer supported in psychology is that Selye has neglected the role of emotions and cognitions by focusing solely on physiological reactions in animals. Selye claimed that all these organisms show a nonspecific response to adverse stimulations, no matter what the situation looks like. In contrast, modern psychological theories highlight the individual's interpretation of the situation as a major determinant of a stressful encounter.

The Stimulus-Based Perspective

When someone says, "I have a stressful marriage," they refer to a trying situation, not to their response to that situation. The stimulus-based perspective takes this approach, paying more attention to the particular characteristics of the stressor. It is argued that each critical episode has its unique demands, be it social, physical, psychological, or intellectual, that specifically tax the individual's coping resources, thus triggering a particular stress response. The research question establishes relationships between a variety of distinct stressors and outcomes, including illness.

This line of research emerged when Holmes and Rahe (1967) attempted to measure life stress by assigning numbers, called life-change units, to 43 critical life events (see the discussion that follows). They assumed that the average amount of adaptive effort necessary to cope with an event would be a useful indicator of the severeness of such an event. A volume edited by B. S. Dohrenwend and B. P. Dohrenwend (1974) was another milestone of the stimulus-based perspective of stress. Today, research in this tradition continues, but it is often flawed by a number of problems. One basic shortcoming is the use of average weights for events, neglecting that different individuals may have a very different perception of the same kind of event. Studies rely too often on retrospective reports of previous challenges that might not be remembered well, or that are distorted as a result of defense mechanisms. In addition, coping processes and changes in social support are often insufficiently examined. The degree to which the objective nature of the stressor should be emphasized in contrast to its subjective interpretation is still undergoing debate (Hobfoll, 1998; Schwarzer, 2001).

The Cognitive-Transactional Process Perspective

Cognitive-transactional theory (Lazarus, 1966, 1991) defines stress as a particular relationship between the person and the environment that is appraised by the person as being taxing or exceeding his or her resources and endangering his or her well-being.

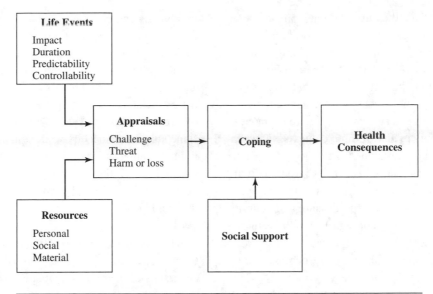

Figure 2.1   Process model of the stress/health relationship, based on the Transactional Stress Theory by Lazarus (1991).

There are three metatheoretical assumptions: *transaction, process,* and *context.* It is assumed that (a) stress occurs as a specific encounter of the person with the environment, both of them exerting a reciprocal influence on each other, (b) stress is subject to continuous change, and (c) the meaning of a particular transaction is derived from the underlying context. Research has neglected these metatheoretical assumptions in favor of unidirectional, cross-sectional, and context-free designs. Within methodologically sound empirical research, it is hardly possible to study complex phenomena such as emotions and coping without constraints. Because its complexity and transactional character lead to interdependencies between the variables involved, the metatheoretical system approach cannot be investigated and empirically tested as a whole model. Rather, it represents a heuristic framework that may serve to formulate and test hypotheses in selected subareas of the theoretical system only. Thus, in terms of the ideal research paradigm, we have to make certain concessions. Investigators have often focused on structure instead of process, measuring single states or aggregates of states. Ideally, however, stress has to be analyzed and investigated as an *active, unfolding process.*

Lazarus (1991) conceives stress as an active, unfolding process that is composed of causal antecedents, mediating processes, and effects. *Antecedents* are person variables, such as commitments or beliefs, and environmental variables, such as demands or situational constraints. *Mediating processes* refer to coping and appraisals of demands and resources. Experiencing stress and coping bring about both immediate effects, such as affect or physiological changes, and

long-term effects concerning psychological well-being, somatic health, and social functioning (see Figure 2.1).

Cognitive appraisals comprise two component processes, namely, primary (demand) appraisals and secondary (resource) appraisals. Appraisal outcomes are divided into the categories challenge, threat, and harm/loss. First, *demand appraisal* refers to the stakes a person has in a stressful encounter. A situation is appraised as challenging when it mobilizes physical and mental activity and involvement. In the evaluation of *challenge,* a person may see an opportunity to prove herself, anticipating gain, mastery, or personal growth from the venture. The situation is experienced as pleasant, exciting, and interesting, and the person feels ardent and confident in being able to meet the demands. *Threat* occurs when the individual perceives danger, expecting physical injuries or blows to his self-esteem. In the experience of *harm/loss,* damage has already occurred. This can be the injury or loss of valued persons, important objects, self-worth, or social standing.

Second, *resource appraisals* refer to our available coping options for dealing with the demands at hand. The individual evaluates his competence, social support, and material or other resources that can help to readapt to the circumstances and to reestablish equilibrium between person and environment.

Hobfoll (1988, 1998, 2001) has expanded stress and coping theory with respect to the conservation of resources as the main human motive in the struggle with stressful encounters. His conservation of resources (COR) theory provides an integrative framework for studying stress that takes environmental as well as internal processes equally into account.

COR theory follows from the basic motivational tenet that people strive to obtain, retain, protect, and foster that which they value or that serve as a means of obtaining what is valued by the individual. According to Hobfoll, such resources are objects (e.g., property, car), conditions (e.g., close friendship, marriage, job security), personal characteristics (e.g., self-esteem, mastery), or energies (e.g., money, knowledge). Stress occurs in any of three contexts: (a) when individuals' resources are threatened with loss, (b) when individuals' resources are actually lost, and (c) when individuals fail to gain resources. This loss/gain dichotomy, and in particular the resource-based loss spirals and gain spirals, shed a new light on stress and coping. The *change* of resources (more so the loss than the gain) appears to be particularly stressful, whereas the mere lack of resources or their availability seems to be less influential.

Resources were also important ingredients in Lazarus' theory. The difference between the two views lies mainly in the status of *objective* and *subjective resources*. Hobfoll, considering both objective and subjective resources as components, lends more weight to objective resources. Thus, the difference between the two theories, in this respect, is a matter of degree, not a matter of principle.

THE NATURE OF STRESSFUL LIFE EVENTS AND DISASTERS

Disasters of various kinds are widespread. About 3 million people worldwide have been killed and 800 million adversely affected by natural disasters and other calamities over the past two decades (Weisaeth, 1992). In the United States, fire, floods, hurricanes, tornadoes, severe tropical storms or windstorms, and earthquakes have left approximately 2 million households with physical damage and injuries (S. D. Solomon & Green, 1992). Injuries and damages from fires, floods, storms, and earthquakes are estimated to be experienced by 24.5 households per 1,000 (Briere & Elliot, 2000; Rossi, Wright, Weber-Burdin, & Perina, 1983).

Historically, research on health effects of stressful life events commenced with clinical records of individual reactions to war. Following the American Civil War and World War I, shell shock and battle fatigue became known as extreme reactions to this kind of stress. After World War II, studies on the long-term effects of the Holocaust and other war-related events, such as the devastation of Hiroshima, were conducted. Disasters unrelated to war have been investigated by psychologists since the 1970s. At present, a broad variety of disasters, ranging from tornadoes and floods to fire and toxic spills, are being examined for their health impact on

individuals and communities. A comprehensive overview of disaster characteristics and postdisaster response is given by Meichenbaum (1995) and Schooler (2001). A cataclysmic event qualifies as a disaster according to the amount of damage done and the amount of assistance required. The power of the event alone is inadequate: A powerful earthquake in a desert may not be considered as a disaster, whereas one of the same magnitude in a city would qualify because of the resulting substantial damage. In addition to harm sustained, considerable disruption to people's lives can also factor into the definition of disaster. Disasters represent one of the most threatening situations a person can experience (Schooler, 2001).

This section deals with distinctions that have been applied to characteristics of life events and disasters. Objective characteristics of a stressful encounter influence the way people appraise them cognitively as challenges, threat, harm, or loss. Severity, duration, and ambiguity of a stressor, among other characteristics, make a difference when it comes to appraisal, emotions, coping, and outcomes. Loss of loved ones, academic failure, injury, job loss, divorce, and disasters that affect an entire community can be categorized along a number of dimensions, including predictability, controllability, suddenness, and strength of impact, and so on. A common distinction is the one between normative and nonnormative events. Normative refers to anticipating a certain class of events that naturally happen to many individuals at certain times during their lives and are expected, for example, school transitions, marriage, childbirth, academic exams, retirement, death of parents, and others. In contrast, nonnormative events pertain to rare or unexpected events, such as disasters, accidents, or diseases. We can prepare in general for a broad array of potential harm, but we do not know when and if such events will occur.

Natural and Technological Disasters

Another common distinction is between natural and technological disasters. *Natural disasters* occur primarily without human influence. Typical examples are hurricanes, tornadoes, earthquakes, and floods, but also drought and famine. Humans may have contributed to the likelihood of certain cataclysmic events by changing the course of nature, for example by cutting down forests and allowing landscapes to erode. However, natural forces crop up suddenly and uncontrolled, take lives, and alter the environment dramatically. Predictability and impact of natural disasters vary greatly. Earthquakes, for example, are virtually unpredictable, whereas most volcanic eruptions are preceded by detectable seismic changes or fissures in the mountain wall. Hurricanes and tornadoes can be tracked long before they hit land, which allows for precaution measures. Nevertheless, the extent of physical destruction and disruption of the daily life in the aftermath of a natural disaster take many victims by surprise. When the immediate threat is over, rescue and recovery work as well as cleaning and rebuilding follow. Litigation, insurance, or general financial issues add to the difficulties that may hamper recovery and adjustment after disasters (Schooler, 2001).

Technological disasters can also be sudden and intense, creating havoc in the community. Devastating industrial, maritime, and aviation accidents may take place without warning. Examples include leaking toxic waste dumps, collapsing bridges, and dam failures, but also industrial accidents involving chemical spills or discharge of radiation. "With increasingly widespread prevalence of technological systems there will inevitably be an increase in the potential for loss of control over these systems" (Schooler, 2001, p. 3714).

Controllability

Perceived controllability is considered to be an important dimension when it comes to categorizing the characteristics of stressful life events. The feeling of being in control of something that happens to you has been shown to be important for coping with that event. Further, a sudden versus a slow onset, its duration, and its intensity are major determinants in evaluating the stress impact. Natural disasters point toward a *lack* of control over the environment, whereas technological disasters indicate a *loss* of control of what has been once under control. A major supposition underlying our dependence on technological systems is that they won't break down. That is, bridges and dams are supposed to resist all forces of nature, and airplanes and trains are not supposed to crash. Deviations from this supposition contribute to the harm experienced by victims and witnesses when disaster strikes unexpectedly and uncontrolled. "In the case of technological disasters, an implicit social contract between citizens and corporations is violated. The assumption is that corporations will not harm their customers, workers, or members of the community where they make their products. When this contract is violated, anger and rage are added to the range of emotional responses to disasters" (Schooler, 2001, p. 3715). Another way to conceptualize disasters was suggested by Green (1998), who pointed to the role of perceived intent. Natural disasters represent the low end of a continuum of intent, technological disasters the middle position, and robbery, terrorist attacks, and other acts of violence the high end.

Impact of Disasters

Responses to extreme stress vary greatly in severity and length. Some individuals and communities are paralyzed for a long time, whereas others are affected only moderately and for a very short time period. When high magnitude events occur, not only the individual, but also whole communities are challenged to cope with them. Figley, Giel, Borgo, Briggs, and Haritos-Fatouros (1995) list *five criteria* for the determination of a disaster's impact: (a) knowledge about the magnitude of loss, (b) knowledge of the hazard, (c) knowledge of recurring risk, degree of warning and preparedness at the individual as well as at the community level, (d) scope of impact to community functioning, and, finally, (e) chance of escaping during or immediately after the disaster strikes.

Victims of Disasters

Another relevant dimension pertains to the *victims of disasters*. Considerable differences in the exposure to the event (long- or short-term, first or secondhand, that is, having experienced the event themselves instead of through close friends and family) determine the individuals' responses (e.g., severity of symptoms postevent). Some victims are involved directly because the critical event happened to them, and they have suffered harm or loss. Others are involved indirectly, for example, observing a train collision or losing family members in an earthquake or plane crash. A third kind of victims are professional helpers, such as rescue workers who are involved in the cleanup and body handling after a disastrous event.

Posttraumatic Stress Disorder (PTSD)

A frequent effect of disaster experience is posttraumatic stress disorder (PTSD). It is usually defined as a pattern of symptoms following exposure to a stressful life event that sets off clinically significant distress or impairment of human functioning. The concept has been described in different terms in former times, in particular, in the context of railway accidents in the nineteenth century and as shell shock during World War I. At that time, 7% to 10% of the officers and 3% to 4% of the other ranks in the British Army were diagnosed with mental breakdowns. In World War II, mental disorder accounted for 31% of medical discharges from the British Army. Of all U.S. Vietnam War veterans, an estimated 15% (450,000) were diagnosed with PTSD (Newman, 2001).

Diagnostic criteria for PTSD are provided in the *Diagnostic and Statistical Manual of Mental Disorders* (*DSM-IV;*

American Psychiatric Association, 1994). According to this manual, PTSD may follow exposure to a traumatic event that the person experienced, witnessed, or was confronted with. Such an incident may have involved actual or threatened death or serious injury, or a threat to the physical integrity of self or others. The individual should have reacted with intense fear, helplessness, or horror. To be diagnosed as a PTSD case, the person should be persistently reexperiencing the traumatic event, such as living through repetitive and intrusive distressing recollections of the event, experiencing incessant upsetting dreams of the incident, acting or feeling as if the incident was recurring, suffering intense distress at exposure to internal or external cues that symbolize or resemble an aspect of the traumatic event, or being subjected to physiological reactivity on exposure to such cues. There should be evidence of continuing avoidance of trauma-related stimuli and numbing of general responsiveness (not present before the trauma), as indicated by three or more of the following: efforts to avoid thoughts, feelings, or conversations connected with the trauma; efforts to avoid activities, places, or people that arouse recollections of the trauma; failure to recall an important aspect of the trauma; markedly diminished interest or participation in significant activities; a feeling of detachment or estrangement from others; restricted range of emotions; or sense of a foreshortened future. There should also be at least two persistent symptoms of increased arousal (not present before the trauma), such as difficulty falling or staying asleep, irritability or outbursts of anger, difficulty concentrating, hypervigilance, or an exaggerated startle response. These symptoms should have persisted for at least one month, causing significant distress or impairment of functioning (Newman, 2001).

Several measures have been developed to quantify aspects of PTSD. The Horowitz Impact of Event Scale (Horowitz, Wilner, & Alvarez, 1979) is a 15-item self-rating scale with intrusion and avoidance as subscales. It provides a subjective estimate of the frequency of intrusive recall of a traumatic event and of attempts to avoid such recall. The inventory has been used frequently in research as a measure of postevent psychological disturbance, but it does not result in a clinical case definition according to the *DSM* standards. Closer to this aim is the scale by J. R. T. Davidson et al. (1997), who developed a 17-item self-rating scale for PTSD that was designed to measure each *DSM-IV* symptom on five-point frequency and severity scales. There also are some measures for assessing PTSD in children, such as: (a) "Darryl" (Neugebauer et al., 1999); (b) the Child Posttraumatic Stress Reaction Index (Shannon, Lonigan, Finch, & Taylor, 1994); and (c) the Post-Traumatic Stress Disorder Reaction Index-Child Version (Pynoos et al., 1987).

ASSESSMENT OF STRESSFUL LIFE EVENTS

The main practical problem with transactional theories of stress is that there is no good way of measuring stress as a process. Therefore, all common procedures to assess stress are either dominantly stimulus-based, pointing at critical events and demands, or dominantly response-based, pointing at symptoms and feelings experienced. Some procedures measure the frequency or intensity of stressors (stimuli), while others measure distress (response), sometimes called "strain." Response-based measures that are available entail symptoms, emotions, illness, and behavioral and physiological changes. Heart rate, blood pressure, immune functioning, illness records, work absentee statistics, avoidance behaviors, performance data, and self-reports are common ways to obtain stress response indicators. Some authors have developed "perceived stress scales" that ask people how "stressed" they feel. Using such measures to tap the construct of stress can be misleading because individual changes in these variables occur at later stages of a demanding episode. Thus, stress is confounded with its consequences. We cannot clearly identify whether the subjective feeling constitutes stress itself or rather the outcome of stress. This chapter is not concerned with stress as a response, and, therefore, this issue is not addressed further.

Stimulus-based instruments were developed more than 40 years ago when Hawkins, Davies, and Holmes (1957) introduced their Schedule of Recent Experiences (SRE). A more refined and better-known instrument is the Social Readjustment Rating Scale (SRRS) by Holmes and Rahe (1967), who elaborated on the SRE. The SRRS contains 43 events, ranging from 100 (death of spouse) to 11 (minor violations of the law).

Participants responding to the SRRS check the items they have experienced in the past, for example, within the last year. The life-change values of the checked items are then summed to yield a total score that indicates how much "stress" the individuals had. For example, someone who has experienced the loss of a loved one is supposed to suffer about as much stress as someone else who has married and been fired from work within the same time period. The same stress score can refer to completely different life events in different individuals, and it is questionable whether they should be regarded as psychologically equal and lumped together in the same analyzes. The stress score is usually related to mood, illness, depression, and other possible outcomes.

The underlying assumption was that the negative nature of events is not the important factor, but the amount of *change* that is required to readjust to a tolerable level of functioning. Therefore, some positive events have also been included in the checklist, such as vacation, Christmas, marriage, and pregnancy. Any change, whether desirable or not, was seen as stressful. Other researchers have eliminated the positive events in favor of more negative ones, and they have added a subjective severity rating for each event to weigh the cognitive appraisals that might differ from person to person (Sarason, Johnson, & Siegel, 1978).

There have been many debates about the usefulness and effectiveness of such an approach (Turner & Wheaton, 1995). Some find that assigning the same event weights to all individuals who check an item might not do justice to subjective feelings of stress that could differ enormously between individuals. For example, some people experience divorce as the beginning of a long period of suffering and depression, whereas for others it marks the end of marital discord and is thus a relief. Event weighting could be done either objectively or subjectively. In the case of objective weighting, an expert panel of "judges" may rate the events, or groups of victims might provide information about the seriousness or importance of events. In contrast, subjective weighting refers to individuals rating their own events. Whichever method is chosen, assigning different weights to each event has been shown to result in lower correlations with health outcomes (Turner & Wheaton, 1995).

Another suggestion was made by Lazarus and Folkman (1989) by introducing the Daily Hassles Scale and the Daily Uplift Scale. These inventories are based on the assumption that peoples' lives are more affected by the cumulation of frequent minor events than by the rare occurrence of a major event. Typical hassles are concern about body weight, health of family members, rising prices of common goods, home maintenance, misplacing or losing items, crime, physical appearance, and so on. It was found that hassles and major life events were only modestly intercorrelated, and that hassles, compared to major life events, were more closely related to illness.

The *reliability* of life event checklists are suspected to be low (Turner & Wheaton, 1995). Reporting past events requires an accurate recollection of those events. The measurement points in time and the reporting period exert one influence, among others, on how well people remember and report what has allegedly caused them stress. In a 10-month study, women were asked once every month to check all their stressful life events for that month. At the end of the study, they were asked to report once again all events for the entire 10-month period. It turned out that only 25% of the event categories appeared in both the first and the second lists, the latter containing far fewer events (Raphael, Cloitre, & Dohrenwend, 1991). Basic research on survey methods has shown that responses change with the reference periods

given (Winkielman, Knäuper, & Schwarz, 1998). Such studies have demonstrated that life event checklists often represent unreliable measures. And if they are unreliable, they cannot be valid, which means that they inaccurately predict illness. The choice of a time frame entails consideration of the particular nature of the stressors. However, since checklists contain numerous events that might have occurred at different times under diverse circumstances, any time frame implies a bias. Moreover, some events are short term, whereas others are long term. The accuracy of remembering and reporting applies to a number of events, but not to all of them. For example, loss of loved ones, divorce, or serious accidents are remembered for a lifetime. Their psychological and health consequences can also last for an extended time. Restricting the time frame of events to only one year might lead to failure to notice such previous experiences and, thus, might invalidate the research findings. This argues for the inclusion of lifetime traumas and the assessment of their duration and pervasiveness.

Interview measures that allow for qualitative probes have been used as an alternative to checklists (Wethington, Brown, & Kessler, 1995). Narrative stories can shed more light on the nature of subjective experiences (Meichenbaum, 1995). Individuals can name the events they experienced and describe their context more accurately, which would result in more meaningful scores of event significance. However, there is a price for this because interview studies entail more research resources. Moreover, quantification is sometimes difficult. Phrases such as "I am a prisoner of the past," "part of me died," or "the disaster opened a can of worms" are illustrative, but scoring them might constitute a problem. Nevertheless, in small sample studies and, in particular, in the explorative phase of research, the interview methodology can be of profound value. Several interview schedules have been published. The most widely known is the Life Events and Difficulties Schedule (LEDS) by Brown and Harris (1978). It yields a narrative story of each nominated event, which is then used by researchers to rate the significance of the event. Another method is the Standardized Event Rating System (SERATE) by B. P. Dohrenwend, Raphael, Schartz, Stueve, and Skodol (1993). This is a structured event probe and narrative rating method for measuring stressful life events that deconfounds some aspects of the narration.

In sum, a broad array of life event checklists and interview measures have been published. At least 20 critical reviews on the life event methodology are available (Turner & Wheaton, 1995) documenting the difficulties that are necessarily involved in estimating variations in stress exposure. Using a stress measure implies a particular definition of stress, which is not always transparent in the studies. Sometimes stress is not measured at all, but is merely inherent in the sample selection. For example, stress is simply implied in a sample of earthquake victims, students facing an exam, or patients undergoing surgery, since it is a common understanding that the situations chosen are very resource demanding and require adjustment. The advantage of such an approach is that all participants undergo a homogeneous class of stressors instead of having been assigned a similar "life-change score" based on an event checklist. In situations where exposure levels are given and no further assessment is needed, we still have to deal with the measurement of coping with stress, which is an equally challenging problem (Schwarzer & Schwarzer, 1996).

HEALTH OUTCOMES OF STRESSFUL LIFE EVENTS

Does stress cause illness? Individuals are confronted with a great number of taxing situations, for instance, a noisy neighborhood, difficulties at work, time pressure, problems with a romantic partner, or financial constraints. This list might seem to be an arbitrary array of situations. In fact, probably not everyone would consider these situations as being stressful or of great personal importance. However, the cumulative exposure to a number of aggravating daily hassles or situations regarded as stressful over a long time period may have detrimental health effects. In contrast, there is no doubt about the personal significance of major life events and their potential impact on health. Extreme stressors can create both acute and prolonged psychological distress and bodily ailments.

Research is inconsistent when it comes to answering the question of whether the characteristics of the event itself (e.g., injury, threat, near-death experience) or the changes that occur in its aftermath (e.g., relocation, job loss) are responsible for adjustment difficulties. How does stress cause illness? It is a general assumption that stress leads to poor health in a number of different ways. According to Selye (1956), stress operates in three phases: alarm, resistance, and exhaustion. When the organism's resistance breaks down, an ensuing long period of exhaustion can manifest itself in illness. In the 1950s, Selye did not have much evidence for his claim, but today there is a great deal of substantiation. However, a strong linear relationship cannot be expected since illness is obviously caused by many factors (stress being only one of them), contributing to pathogenesis in one way or another. Generally, correlation coefficients from .20 to .30 are found. Cohen, Kamarck, and Mermelstein (1983), for example, reported an association of only .14 between stress scores and physiological ailments in college students.

Most individuals who experience stress do not develop illness. Stressful life changes are usually temporary, whereas other risk factors for disease can be longer lasting, for example, smoking, alcohol consumption, a high-fat, low-fiber diet, and risky lifestyle in general. When comparing a single life event with those long-term behaviors, the latter seem to be more influential in developing illness. Moreover, the experience of a critical life event is related to coping and social support, whereby these two factors may moderate the stress-illness connection. How can we understand the mechanisms of the stress-illness association? There are three major pathways that link stressful life events to ill health (Figure 2.2).

The main pathway places *physiological changes* as a mediator between origin and outcome, in particular, changes of immune parameters, and endocrine and cardiovascular reactivity. Recent research, for example, in the field of psychoneuroimmunology, has documented progress in identifying bodily responses to stress that constitute precursors of disease (see Ader, 2001; Herbert & Cohen, 1993a, 1993b). Endocrine and cardiovascular reactivity, as expressed in blood pressure, heart rate, or catecholamine excretion, is considered a stress-based codeterminant of cardiovascular disease, including myocardial infarcts. The amount of reactivity is, however, not exclusively governed by the stress experience. Rather, it is moderated by genes, personality, age, and gender, as well as other factors (Weidner, 2001).

The other major pathway is represented by *health-compromising behaviors*. People under stress might want to relieve their tension by consuming more tobacco, illicit drugs, alcohol, and so on. They feel too absorbed by their stress to monitor their diets and to maintain other preventive behaviors. Adherence to routine self-care might suffer during a stress episode. Among smokers, stress may increase the number of cigarettes consumed as well as the intensity of smoking by deep inhaling. When under stress, women seem to be more likely to engage in unhealthy eating behaviors, whereas men tend to turn to drinking and illicit drug use (Brannon & Feist, 1997).

A third pathway pertains to all kinds of *negative affect* often associated with experiencing stress. Constant rumination, worrying, anxiety, pessimism, depression, and anger are health compromising in the long run. Studies have shown that optimism is related to good health, whereas depression can be a precursor of sickness (Carver, 2001). The mechanism of pathogenesis operates through physiological changes, including immune suppression and blood pressure elevations. Scheier and Bridges (1995) reviewed depression and health outcomes. Depression may be a general risk factor for premature death. The evidence for mortality effects is most compelling for cardiac disease. Studies indicate that cardiac

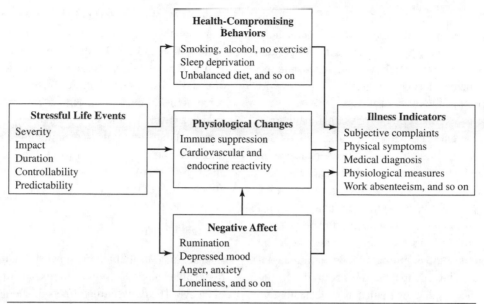

Figure 2.2 Mediators between stressful life events and ill health (excluding other major mediators such as personality, appraisals, coping, and social support).

patients who were depressed while in the hospital were more likely to die of cardiac causes than those who were not depressed. However, most research in this area fails to include control variables, such as physical illness at baseline, smoking, or alcohol abuse.

Figure 2.2 gives a simplified view of mediating effects. In addition, moderator effects can emerge, for example, a synergistic relationship between stress, risk behaviors, and ill health. Personality, appraisals, coping, and social support were not considered in the figure to reduce its complexity.

Efforts in contemporary life event research aim at a better understanding of the linkage between stress and the manifestation of illness. Research striving to identify single events as the cause of illness often fail. Ideally, finding a truly causal relationship between a specific stressor (e.g., loss of a loved person) and a specific disease (e.g., breast cancer) would be a breakthrough in this field. The onset of specific diseases has been related frequently to prior stress experience. Tension headache, for example, seems to be closely connected to daily hassles, whereas a link to major life events has not been found. Infectious diseases such as the common cold can be triggered by stress. Prospective studies have shown that people develop a cold several days after the onset of negative life events. Experimental studies with the intentional administration of cold viruses have found that persons under stress are more likely to develop a cold than if they are relaxed. In a British common cold unit, Cohen, Tyrrell, and Smith (1991) administered different stress measures, including a stressful life event index based on the past year, to about 400 healthy participants. Then they exposed them to respiratory viruses to

see whether they would come down with a cold. Within the experimental group, the number of respiratory infections and clinical colds was related to stress in a dose-response way: the more stressful life events experienced, the higher the likelihood of a cold.

Only a small number of studies focus explicitly on selected stressors in relation to a specific disease (e.g., Jacobs & Bovasso, 2000, on early loss and breast cancer; Matsunaga et al., 1999, on sexual abuse and bulimia nervosa). In most studies, either stress (often measured by a life event checklist) or health outcomes (assessed by symptom checklists) are unspecific. Moreover, methodological inequalities make it difficult to compare research findings directly. Therefore, it is not surprising that research has produced conflicting results. The following example on ulcers illustrates one of the problems, namely, the differences in the time span between stress occurrence and health impairment.

In a study by Köhler, Kuhnt, and Richter (1998), participants were asked to indicate events experienced within six months prior to gastroscopy, a screening for duodenal ulcer. Contrary to the widely assumed idea that stress triggers ulcer onset, Köhler and colleagues did not find any relationship between perceived stress or life change scores and duodenal ulcer. Their findings were corroborated in a study by Gilligan, Fung, Piper, and Tennant (1987), who conclude that acute life events do not play a role in duodenal ulcer onset or relapse. They suggest that the reason could be the transient nature of the emotional as well as humoral changes caused by the event.

Kumar, Rastogi, and Nigam (1996) came to a different conclusion by analyzing the number and severity of life events in a sample of peptic ulcer patients. Compared to matched controls, ulcer patients reported a significantly higher number of events and greater severity. It is important to note that the time span in this study was longer than in the former study. Here, the occurrence of the events reported was mostly four years prior to the onset of illness.

Studies that focus exclusively on physical health outcomes following an event are relatively scarce. This is due partly to methodological limitations of life event research. The repeated demand for prospective rather than retrospective studies can hardly be met. However, in some cases, settings allow for prospective designs. For example, in a study on the effects of job loss, researchers found an increase of rheumatoid arthritis during the time of unemployment (Cobb, 1976). There is some empirical evidence on the connection between stress and arthritis, but this is purely correlational. The problem here is that the main cause of rheumatoid arthritis remains unknown. For diseases whose origin has not been fully discovered, it is difficult to establish a causal role of stress in the pathogenesis.

It is commonly assumed that stress is detrimental to health, and different mechanisms of pathogenesis have been described earlier. But not everyone develops health problems in the face of severe stress. Other factors operate at the same time. A large body of literature is dedicated to interpersonal differences in dealing with aversive situations. In fact, it is almost impossible to examine the effects of stressful life events without considering the various ways of coping with them. As events differ in their nature and impact, so do people differ in their immediate responses to events. Since the latter belongs to the realm of coping research and is addressed elsewhere in the chapter by Manne, we will focus only on some characteristics and health effects of stressful events and the challenges they pose. In the following paragraphs, several stressful life events and their health implications are discussed.

RESEARCH EXAMPLES OF STRESSFUL LIFE EVENTS

The following examples stem from a large body of research on a variety of stressful negative life events. Starting with disasters, we briefly characterize the impact of natural and man-made disasters on individuals and communities and will present some findings regarding their health-hazard potential. Further, we move on to more individual events that are characterized by personal harm and loss, such as conjugal bereavement and criminal victimization. Finally, we discuss studies regarding the health of immigrants and refugees in Western countries. In recent years, with a continuously growing number of worldwide refugees, sojourners, and immigrants, there are increased efforts to investigate the impact of migration and acculturation on health.

The relationship between stressful life events and the individual's response is indirect in that it is mediated by the perception and evaluation of the disaster impact on the individual as well as the community level. As shown in the empirical data, attempts to examine psychological and physiological correlates of disastrous traumatic events need to allow for short-term as well as long-term analyses of the effects to cover full symptomatology.

Natural Disasters

Intense, uncontrollable, and powerful natural forces can dramatically change the lives of thousands of people in the blink of an eye. The devastating effects of sudden natural disasters, such as earthquakes, hurricanes, tornadoes, tsunamis, volcano eruptions, floods, and landslides, have been witnessed many times in recent history. One example is an earthquake in the Los Angeles area in 1994 that resulted in 72 fatalities and caused $12.5 billion in property damage (McMillen, North, & Smith, 2000; Reich, 1995).

The predictability and impact of natural disasters vary greatly. Every year, the Southeastern states of the United States and neighboring countries experience a hurricane season. People living in such areas are able to take precautions before a hurricane hits. Although such an event is predictable, neither the course of the hurricane nor its devastating effects can be influenced. In contrast, earthquakes are virtually unpredictable and take people by surprise. Often lasting only a few seconds or minutes, the destruction of property and the disruption of lives can take months or even years to restore, if at all.

Both short- and long-term psychological and physiological effects of disasters have been widely studied. Large-scale disasters leave behind at least three groups of victims: (a) individuals who have witnessed the event, (b) individuals who were absent then, but are effected by the devastation, and (c) rescue personnel confronted with the devastation. Such extreme experiences have often been studied in trauma research. Individuals who were exposed to extreme stressors are prone to develop PTSD. Very often, the onset of the disorder is delayed for years (see also Kimerling, Clum, & Wolfe, 2000).

Surprisingly, according to McMillen et al. (2000), victims of natural disasters report the lowest rates of PTSD. On the contrary, Madakasira and O'Brien (1987) found a high incidence of acute PTSD in victims of a tornado five months postdisaster. Again, methodological differences make it difficult to compare various studies, especially when short-term and long-term effects are mingled. Green (1995) found that especially one year or more after the disaster, diagnosable pathology is the exception rather than the rule. Moreover, only a systematic and detailed analysis of the individual experience (e.g., loss of family members and/or property) would help to determine under which conditions PTSD and other psychiatric symptoms are likely to occur. Nevertheless, individuals involved in other traumatic events, such as combat, criminal victimization, or technological disasters, are far more likely to witness grotesque and violent scenes, which in turn may lead to higher incidence rates of PTSD.

Low incidence rates of PTSD should not lead to the conclusion that posttraumatic stress does not exist among the survivors of natural disasters. Survivors may experience a number of PTSD-related symptoms (e.g., unwanted memories, nightmares, event amnesia, sleeping problems), but do not meet all criteria for a psychiatric diagnosis (McMillen et al., 2000). In a study by Sharan, Chauhardy, Kavethekar, and Saxena (1996), 59% of earthquake survivors in rural India received a psychiatric diagnosis that was either PTSD or depression. Here, psychiatric morbidity was associated with gender (women) and destruction of property.

Briere and Elliot (2000) give an impressive overview of a number of studies dealing with the potential effects of exposure to natural disasters (e.g., bushfires; cf. McFarlane, Clayer, & Bookless, 1997). Among the various symptoms that are likely to occur in the aftermath of a natural disaster are anxiety, PTSD, somatic complaints, and substance abuse (Adams & Adams, 1984; McFarlane, Atchison, Rafalowicz, & Papay, 1994). Escobar, Canino, Rubio-Stipec, and Bravo (1992) examined the prevalence of somatization symptoms after a natural disaster in Puerto Rico. They found higher prevalence of medically unexplained physical (e.g., gastrointestinal) and pseudoneurological symptoms (e.g., amnesia, fainting) related to disaster exposure.

In a study on the long-term sequelae of natural disasters in the general population of the United States, Briere and Elliot (2000) found that 22% of the participants had been exposed to a natural disaster (earthquake, hurricane, tornado, flood, or fire). Though the mean period from the last disaster exposure until the study took place was 13 years, researchers found current elevations on 6 of 10 scores in the Traumatic Symptom Inventory (Briere, 1995). Type of disaster did not determine the symptomatology, but the disaster characteristics, such as physical injury, fear of death, and property loss, did. Apparently, the number of characteristics people were exposed to effected the extent to which symptoms were experienced. Individuals who had suffered all (injury, fear of death, and property loss) scored at clinical levels (see also Rotton, Dubitsky, Milov, White, & Clark, 1997). As the authors conclude from their data, more research efforts should aim at the long-term effects rather than the immediate sequelae of disaster experience.

Finally, a number of studies have looked at the physiological changes that occurred in survivors of natural disaster. For example, in a longitudinal study by Trevisan et al. (1997), factory workers' uric acid levels were measured on three occasions within 12 years. In between, a major earthquake interrupted the study, so that some of the participants were measured before, others after the quake. Those workers measured after the quake had significantly lower levels of serum uric acid than those examined before. Seven years later, workers who reported suffering from the aftermath of the quake had elevated levels of uric acid compared to unaffected individuals.

Technological Disasters

Unlike natural disasters, technological disasters are caused by people. Nevertheless, their occurrence is as difficult to predict as natural forces. In modern civilization, we are surrounded by numerous potentially health-threatening technological devices. Although a large number of specific precaution measures are employed, power plants, giant dams, atomic submarines, or contemporary air traffic harbor a risk of failure with potentially disastrous effects.

Among others, the list of technological hazards includes the release of radiation (e.g., Three Mile Island, Chernobyl), leaking toxic waste dumps (e.g., Love Canal), and aviation and maritime accidents, such as the Exxon Valdez oil spill in 1989. Despite similarities between natural and technological disasters as to their unpredictability, uncontrollability, devastation, and impact for the individual and the community, considerable differences may contribute to various mental as well as physical health outcomes.

By definition, technological disasters could have been prevented. Thus, someone can be blamed for the harm and damage, and anger and frustration can be addressed to authorities, companies, or single persons. As Green (1995) argues, because of these characteristics, such events might be more difficult to process than natural disasters, which can be seen as inevitable or fate. Effects of technological catastrophes appear to be longer lasting. Support for this assumption comes from a study by Baum, Fleming, Israel, and O'Keefe (1992), who compared 23 flood victims with 27 people living near a leaking hazardous toxic waste dump and 27 control persons. Nine months postevent, those persons exposed to the hazardous material were more depressed, anxious, alienated, and aroused than those in the other two groups. Such effects have been found for technological failures as well (e.g., Bromet, Parkinson, & Dunn, 1990; L. Davidson, Fleming, & Baum, 1986).

Green (1995) studied the effects of the Buffalo Creek Disaster. In winter 1972, a dam constructed from coal mining waste collapsed, releasing millions of gallons of black water and sludge. In the community below the dam, 125 people were killed and thousands were left homeless. Typical for small communities where people know each other well, many residents lost close friends or family members. Looking at the long-term effects on adults, the results indicate a decrease in the psychopathology over one to three years. However, even 14 years later, a subset of survivors still showed continuing effects of the traumatic experience.

Arata, Picou, Johnson, and McNally (2000) examined the effects of the Exxon Valdez oil spill on commercial fishermen six years after the incident. According to their hypotheses, the fishermen had higher levels of depression, anxiety, and PTSD symptoms compared to a normative sample. One-fifth of the fishermen showed clinically significant symptoms of anxiety, and more than one-third suffered from depression and/or PTSD. Despite methodological limitations, findings are consistent with other research, suggesting chronic impairment as a result from technological disasters (Freudenburg & Jones, 1991; Green, 1995). Posttraumatic stress disorders as a consequence of toxic spills were found in several studies (e.g., Freed, Bowler, & Fleming, 1998).

War and Genocide

A section about disasters caused by humans cannot be concluded without mentioning the most terrible disasters that continue to happen daily at some place in the world, namely, war and genocide. Research on the health effects of stressful life events started with recording reactions to war experience. During the two world wars, psychiatrists examined shell shock and battle fatigue among soldiers. Long-term effects of the Holocaust and the wars in Vietnam and Korea were studied as well. Posttraumatic stress disorder is one of the most frequently addressed phenomena in this line of research. Studies focus mainly on specific aspects of the war experience rather than the event as a whole. For example, there is a large body of research literature on torture victims (Neria, Solomon, & Dekel, 2000), Holocaust survivors (e.g., Lomranz, 1995), and combat stress (e.g., Z. Solomon, 1995). There is overlap with studies on migration effects, since ethnic conflicts, combat, and political persecution are among the most common reasons for people to emigrate.

Psychological and physical impairment can transpire even decades after the traumatic experience. Landau and Litwin (2000) compared a community-based sample of Holocaust survivors at age 75 and older with control persons of a similar age and sociocultural background. The assessment of vulnerability included physical as well as mental health and PTSD. The findings suggest that extremely traumatic events have long-lasting effects on the victims. Men who survived demonstrated a higher prevalence of PTSD, whereas women reported greater health-related difficulties and poorer health (Wagner, Wolfe, Rotnitsky, Proctor, & Ericson, 2000).

In line with the former findings, Falger et al. (1992) found among 147 Dutch World War II resistance veterans the highest scores on cardiovascular disease (i.e., angina pectoris, Type A behavior, life stressors, and vital exhaustion) compared to age-matched patients with myocardial infarction and patients who underwent surgery. Moreover, veterans diagnosed with PTSD reported more risk factors.

Eberly and Engdahl (1991) analyzed medical and psychiatric data for American former prisoners of war (World War II and Korean War). In comparison with the general population, PTSD prevalence rates were greatly elevated, whereas lifetime prevalence rates of depressive disorders were only moderately increased. However, the authors did not find evidence for generally higher rates of hypertension, diabetes, myocardial infarction, alcoholism, and other psychiatric disorders. Within the study group, those former prisoners who had suffered massive weight loss demonstrated a greater number of psychiatric disorders than their comrades.

More evidence for the long-term effects of trauma comes from a study by Desivilya, Gal, and Ayalon (1996), who investigated the effects of early trauma in adolescence for victims' mental health and adaptation in later life. The critical incident took place in 1974 in a small town close to the border of Israel and Lebanon, when hundreds of hostages were taken during a terrorist attack, most of them adolescents. Participants in the study displayed significantly more health problems 17 years later than the nontraumatized individuals in the control group. Also, survivors of the early traumatic event later showed greater vulnerability to psychological difficulties when Israel was attacked by Iraqi Scud missiles in 1991 (see also Ben-Zur & Zeidner, 1991; Zeidner & Hammer, 1992). As the authors conclude, the scars of the event remained for a lifetime.

These studies, together with other empirical evidence on the effects of traumatic events, underline the importance of long-term observation of health outcomes in traumatized individuals in facilitating appropriate intervention and rehabilitation programs beyond acute needs for help.

Conjugal Loss and Bereavement

Experiencing loss is one of the major factors in the explanation of stress reactions. According to Hobfoll's (1989, 1998) conservation of resources (COR) theory, the threat or the actual loss of resources is considered to be a powerful predictor of psychological stress. This can occur in many ways: loss of health, job, property, and loved ones. For most stressful life events, loss is an inherent characteristic. This section focuses on conjugal loss and the health effects resulting from bereavement.

Loss of a spouse is regarded as the most stressful experience on the Social Readjustment Rating Scale (SRRS; Holmes & Rahe, 1967). Considering the frequency and likelihood of such an event among those who have close long-term relationships, the relevance of research in this field becomes evident. In fact, the only way to protect yourself from that experience is to die either before or at the same time as the partner.

The effects of bereavement on morbidity and mortality have been widely studied (for an overview, cf. M. Stroebe, Stroebe, & Hansson, 2000; W. Stroebe & Stroebe, 1992). In particular, gender and age differences in responding to the death of a spouse have received most attention.

A quarter of a century ago, Bartrop, Luckhurst, Lazarus, Kiloh, and Penny (1977) described immunological changes associated with conjugal loss. The death of a spouse is suspected to lead to increased mortality in response to diseases that are presumed to depress the immune function (reduced lymphoproliferative responses, impaired natural killer cell activity). It has not been demonstrated, however, that morbidity and mortality following conjugal loss are the direct results of stressor-induced changes in immune function (Ader, 2001).

Considerable differences between widowers and widows regarding the physical and psychological reactions to an event as well as the coping strategies have been found. One set of studies suggests that men suffer more after losing their partner than women, whereas others report more health complaints of bereaved women.

Miller and Wortman (in press) suggest examining the impact of loss for the spouse who is left behind. You might conclude that women should be at more of a disadvantage. Is there any evidence for such an assumption? Traditionally, women depend economically on their husbands. Although norms and values regarding self-determination and economic independence of women have greatly changed over the past decades, elderly couples are more bound to traditional roles. Therefore, in addition to the loss of the intimate partner, women also face the loss of income and financial security, which in turn could enhance the vulnerability for illness and the frequency of ailments. With increasing age, conjugal loss becomes a normative life event more often for widows, who outlive their husbands. In turn, widowers have a greater chance to engage in new romantic relationships simply because there are more potential partners available. These objective disadvantages for widows do not necessarily translate into greater health impairment. In contrast, bereaved men are at higher risk for mental health problems, morbidity, and mortality.

Can the life event of losing a spouse be so detrimental that it results in the premature death of the survivor? For decades, studies addressing this question have found, on average, that the mortality risk for widows/widowers is increased, compared to those who do not experience this loss (see M. Stroebe et al., 2000). The risk seems to be greatest for men during the first six months of bereavement. There may be several reasons for this gender difference: Men typically have a smaller social network than women, so their loss cuts more deeply into their network (Weidner, in press). Also, bereavement occurs at an older age for men than for women because men, on average, die earlier than their spouses, due to age differences in couples and biological gender differences in longevity. As a result, the death of a wife leaves a man who is older and more in need of support. Moreover, men usually confide in their spouse as their only intimate partner, whereas women cultivate a larger network of family members and friends, to whom they find it easier to turn in times of need. This higher social integration and support may buffer the stressful experience of losing their husbands.

Traumatic grief has been shown to be a risk factor for mental and physical morbidity (Miller & Wortman, in press). When widowers feel socially isolated during the grieving process, they may develop depression and loneliness, which in turn may lead to more severe consequences. In other cases, their immune system or cardiovascular reactivity may be affected, resulting in illness and eventually in death. The mechanism of pathogenesis needs to be further explored. Not only is death from all causes higher among widowers, but also specific causes of death, such as suicide. Li (1995), for example, showed a five times higher risk of suicide for elderly widowers than for married men. In contrast, the relative risk to commit suicide among the widows was near zero.

Widowed individuals show impaired psychological and social functioning. Nonetheless, frequency of sick days, use of ambulant services, and onset of illness according to medical diagnosis seem to be about the same for widowed persons and for controls. Schwarzer and Rieckmann (in press), examining the effects of social support on cardiovascular disease and mortality, found that cardiac events are more frequent among isolated and unsupported widowers. However, there is not much evidence that the onset of specific diseases, such as cancer or coronary heart disease, is actually caused or triggered by conjugal loss or a different kind of bereavement. This may be explained by the long time span of pathogenesis.

For example, it takes many years to develop chronic degenerative diseases, and other factors that contribute synergistically to illness may emerge during this time.

Miller and Wortman (in press) analyzed data from 13 studies in terms of gender differences in mortality and morbidity following conjugal bereavement. They provide evidence of greater vulnerability among bereaved men (Glick, Weiss, & Parkes, 1994; Goldman, Korenman, & Weinstein, 1995) and showed that widowers are more likely to become depressed, to become susceptible for various diseases, and to experience greater mortality than widows. These effects are more pronounced among younger men.

Some of the causes of death among widowers are alcohol-related diseases, accidents, suicide, and chronic ischemic heart disease. Miller and Wortman discuss various possible explanations for their findings. The first reason for experiencing widowhood differently may be the different marital roles. Men tend to rely solely on their spouses in many ways. Wives are often the main confidant for their husbands, but they also tend to have larger and tighter social networks that they can mobilize and rely on in taxing situations. Second, women are found to recognize themselves as support providers rather than as receivers. Until recently, women maintained the main responsibility for household and childcare. If such a strong anchor is lost, bereaved men's stress is doubled, not only by taking on new roles in the family, but also by lacking adequate support. Third, for men, widowerhood takes away a powerful agent for social control. Lack of control can translate into a higher risk for men to engage in health-compromising behavior, for example, heavy drinking or risky driving. In many marriages, women are responsible for the family's psychological and physical well-being. Wives provide care during illness, are likely to be attentive to necessary changes in health behavior (e.g., dieting), and remind their husbands of regular health check-ups or prevent them from engaging in behaviors that are hazardous to their health.

Criminal Victimization

Whenever a person becomes the victim of an intentional negative act, we speak of criminal victimization. There is an ever-growing public interest in reports on criminal offenses. So-called "reality TV" provides life coverage from crime scenes, and daily news broadcasts give an update of the latest developments and the condition of the victims. But many crimes remain undetected. Domestic violence is one of the most common crimes that is committed in silence and privacy. The number of cases reported is far lower than the actual prevalence rate. In most cases, it is women who report physical abuse by their partners. But many battered women

do not dare to seek professional help. Instead, they blame themselves for provoking the incident, or they are ashamed or threatened by their abusive partners. Physical nonsexual abuse in this context could be defined as behavior, such as hitting, biting, hitting with an object, punching, kicking, or choking.

Clements and Sawhney (2000) investigated the coping responses of women exposed to domestic violence. Almost half of the battered women reported dysphoria consistent with a clinical syndrome of depression. Abusive severity seemingly did not play a role. Feeny, Zoellner, and Foa (2000) report that 33% of the women living in the United States will experience a sexual or nonsexual assault at least once in their lifetime. Although victims of domestic violence, rape, burglary, robbery, and other severe traumatic events, such as accidents, show surprising commonality in their emotional reactions to the event (Hanson Frieze & Bookwala, 1996), the physical effects of each of these events can differ greatly. The immediate response after confronting extreme stressors may be denial, disbelief, self-blame, numbness, and disorientation. Another common outcome of exposure to unusually stressful situations is PTSD. Symptoms include, for example, reexperiencing the event, avoiding reminders, trouble with sleeping, nightmares, and chronic hyperarousal.

Traumatic events not only contribute to mental health problems, they also lead to increased physical health complaints. According to Zoellner, Goodwin, and Foa (2000), unspecific complaints, such as headaches, stomachaches, back pain, cardiac arrhythmia, and menstrual symptoms, are among the most common problems.

The question arises whether the event itself or its psychological correlates can be held responsible for somatic complaints. As discussed in the section on combat veterans, PTSD was associated with an increased risk for cardiovascular disease. To date, research on the relationship between a stressful event and physical health with PTSD as the moderating variable have remained relatively scarce.

Zoellner et al. (2000) conducted a study with 76 women who were victims of sexual assault suffering from chronic PTSD and who were seeking treatment. The results show negative life events, anger, depression, and PTSD severity related to self-reported physical symptoms. Moreover, PTSD severity predicted self-reported physical symptoms in addition to these factors.

A number of studies have explored the relationship between sexual abuse and the onset of eating disorders in later life. The contexts of these studies vary (e.g., sexual abuse as part of a torture experience versus domestic sexual abuse during childhood). For example, Matsunaga et al. (1999) explored the psychopathological characteristics of women who had recovered from bulimia and who had a history of sexual abuse. Abused persons revealed a trend toward lifetime diagnosis of PTSD and substance dependence. Judging from these findings, authors suggest a possible association between abusive experiences and psychopathogenesis of bulimia nervosa. Moret (1999) did not find differences in eating behavior and body image concerns between women with and without sexual abuse in their past. Nevertheless, sexually abused women might be prone to develop an eating disorder because they show more psychological traits commonly associated with these disorders, such as perfectionism, maturity fear, or interpersonal distrust. Teegen and Cerney-Seeler (1998) found a correlation between the severity of traumatization in victims of child sexual abuse and the frequency of eating disorder development.

Migration

Migration is increasingly becoming a typical facet of modern society. The globalization and internationalization of industries contribute to a constant flow of people from one country to another. The reasons why people migrate range from economic difficulties, civil wars, ecological disasters (e.g., repeated drought or flood), and political persecution affecting their work and study. Forceful displacement from the homeland and resettlement in a new environment cause physical as well as psychological scars. Extreme stress can occur at any point of the migration process—prior to, during, and after. Thus, exposure to a number of stressors may cumulate and be responsible for health problems long after migration. Many individuals who have escaped war, ethnic cleansing, political persecution, or famine carry into their new countries the burden of these stressful experiences.

After the Islamic revolution in Iran in 1979, for example, many political opponents of the new regime were forced into hiding with the constant threat of discovery, imprisonment, and torture. Many of those in prison had suffered extreme torture, witnessed the killing of other prisoners, and lived in constant fear for their families and friends. Moreover, escaping from the country is often not only dangerous, but also costly, sometimes exhausting the financial resources of entire families. Migrants who cannot leave their homeland legally often have to pay large sums of money to traffickers who promise to take them to the desired country. Also, the very process of migration itself can be a source of extreme stress. Thousands of illegal migrants are forced to hide, sometimes without food or water for many days, in cars or ships, or even outdoors without shelter. Finally, arriving at their destination, migrants often face new legal and personal problems. Migrants who are weakened physically and psychologically by traumatic experiences and who undergo continuous stress regarding adaptation, acculturation, and integration into the new society, are especially vulnerable to physical and mental illness.

Following Hobfoll's (1998) COR theory, migration stress can be explained by the threat of loss and actual loss of resources of any kind. The chances to compensate these losses and to restore one's resources are very limited, at least at the beginning of the adaptation process in a new country.

Living in a foreign country is inevitably associated with social and material losses as well as new challenges, regardless of the duration or purpose of the stay. To some extent, all newly arrived travelers, sojourners, immigrants, and refugees face similar challenges: different climate, new language, and unfamiliar customs, cultural norms, and values. In cases of involuntary relocation, uncertainty about the duration of the stay can contribute to elevated levels of stress. Also, the greater the cultural differences between the indigenous and host cultures, the more stress is likely to be expected.

Acculturation stress (Berry & Kim, 1988; Schwarzer, Hahn, & Schröder, 1994) often emerges in conflicting situations within an immigrant's own ethnic or cultural group and/or the dominant group of that society. Potential stressors range from everyday life with the family or at the workplace to direct effects that are associated with migration, such as status loss, discrimination, and prejudice. Acculturative stress and the behavior that results from coping with it are very likely responsible for mental health problems and somatic complaints.

Another common source of continuing stress is bad news from the home country, survivor guilt related to leaving family and friends behind, and thoughts about the duty to care for them (Graham & Khosravi, 1997; Lipson, 1993). Studies by Yee (1995) on Southeast Asians in the United States as well as Tran (1993) on Vietnamese confirmed the hypothesis that acculturation stress coupled with stressful experiences lead to poorer health. Similarly, Cheung and Spears (1995) assume a strong association between negative life events and depression among Cambodian immigrants in New Zealand. Moreover, they identified lack of acculturation, feelings of discrimination, and poor language skills as risk factors for mental disorders.

Chung and Kagawa-Singer (1993) examined predictors of psychological distress among Southeast Asian refugees. Even five years after arrival in the United States, premigration stressors, such as number of years in the refugee camp, number of traumatic events, and loss of family members, significantly predicted depression. Apart from cultural changes, living conditions for immigrants are often below average, especially for refugees from Third World countries.

Here, postmigration factors (e.g., income, work situation, language skills) also played a role in the development of mental health problems (e.g., Hyman, Vu, & Beiser, 2000). Lipson (1993) reviewed studies on Afghan refugees' mental health. Afghan refugees residing in California displayed high levels of depression and psychosomatic symptoms of stress. This is assumed to be due to family role changes and the resulting conflict in the American society. Furthermore, loneliness as well as isolation among the elderly have been linked to psychiatric morbidity.

One of the rare studies on the physical health of refugees comes from Hondius, van Willigen, Kleijn, and van der Ploeg (2000), who investigated health problems of Latin American and Middle Eastern refugees in the Netherlands, with special focus on traumatic experience and ongoing stress. Study participants, who had experienced torture, reported medical complaints. Surprisingly, PTSD was identified among few of the respondents. However, not only traumatic experience prior to migration, but also worries about current legal status, duration of stay, and family problems contributed to ill health.

These studies underline the common assumption that acute as well as chronic stressors in the larger context of migration contribute to poorer physical as well as mental health. Various factors, such as acculturation styles, education, income, or social networks moderate the relationship between migration and health. Future research should support programs tailored culturally and individually that help immigrants to recover from their traumatic experiences, restore a normal life, and find their place in the new society.

STRESSFUL LIFE EVENTS IN THE LIGHT OF INDIVIDUAL DIFFERENCES: GENDER, CULTURE, ETHNICITY, AND AGE

Health reactions in the aftermath of a disaster are largely determined by the impact of an event (e.g., number of casualties or material damage). As a consequence, if the resources we value are threatened or lost, stress occurs (Hobfoll, 1989, 2001). However, societal structures as well as cultural norms and values largely determine the way individuals respond to an incident. Although it is often believed that valuable goods or resources are the same across cultures, we can assume that the weight given to each resource varies (Hobfoll, 2001).

On the other hand, certain resources and their impact are almost universal. For instance, in all societies, the loss of a loved one is regarded as extremely stressful for the individual. Nevertheless, reactions to the loss of a family member may be multifaceted due to different cultural traditions, religious beliefs, and attitudes toward family. For example, one might assume that in large multigenerational families with close ties between individuals, family members are better able to support each other in the grief process, compared to small families where the deceased may have been the only confidant for those who are left behind.

Another example of cultural differences in response to stressful events is the diversity of attitudes toward loss and grief. Often, those attitudes are closely related to religious beliefs within each culture. Gillard and Paton (1999) examined the role of religious differences for distress following a hurricane in the Fiji Islands. They compared the impact of hurricane Nigel in 1997 on Christian Fijians, Indians following Islam, and Indians practicing Hinduism. Results indicated that religious denomination had a differential impact on vulnerability. Gillard and Paton show that one major difference between all three groups lies in the amount of assistance that was provided for the victims of the disaster. Moreover, the unfulfilled expectations of Muslims and Hindus as to support provision constitute a stressor that may increase their vulnerability.

Most widely used psychological principles and theories are derived from research that is anchored in Western scientific practices. Yet, there is an overall agreement that, for example, women and men differ in their responses to stressful events. Socioeconomic factors have been detected as being central to the way individuals cope with adverse situations.

Gender roles and economic equipment vary greatly across nations and cultures. Given the fact that gender, socioeconomic status, and culture are often intertwined, methodological problems may be one cause for the relative scarcity of research in this field. However, these differences are rich avenues for study.

Gender

There is ample evidence for gender differences in response to stressful life events. For example, Karanci, Alkan, Balta, Sucuoglu, and Aksit (1999) found greater levels of distress and more negative life events for women than for men after the 1995 earthquake in Dinal, Turkey. Ben-Zur and Zeidner (1991) found women reporting more anxiety and bodily symptoms than men, as well as higher tension, fear, and depression during the Gulf War. Bar-Tal, Lurie, and Glick (1994) came to a similar conclusion when they investigated the effects of stress on Israeli soldiers. Women soldiers' situational stress assessment as well as stress experiences were higher than those of the men.

Although women often report more distress and bodily symptoms than men, we should not conclude that women generally lack appropriate coping skills. For example, in response to the death of a spouse, women seem to be better capable than men of overcoming the loss.

Since the vast majority of research relies on self-report scales, we presuppose that women have a greater tendency to admit symptoms such as pain, depression, or negative mood. In Western societies, men are commonly expected to be psychologically and physiologically more resilient than women. Admitting pain or depression would be contradictory to the desired male picture.

Keeping that in mind, findings on the causes of death among bereaved men appear in a different light: Risk behavior that either includes or leads to an unhealthy diet or lifestyle (e.g., smoking, drinking, fast driving) is again socially more acceptable for men than for women.

Another factor that has to be taken into account is the social support system. The perception, availability, and activation of social support is a major factor in successfully dealing with stress. Women tend to have larger and tighter networks that enable them to seek support from many sources, whereas men often solely rely on their spouses as support providers (Greenglass, 1982; Hobfoll, 1986; Simon, 1995).

Striking evidence for the importance of support as a predictor of negative affect and health complaints after a stressful life event comes from a study on East German migrants (Knoll & Schwarzer, in press). Women who reported the most social support also reported the least health complaints. This effect could not be replicated for the men in the study. Again, this result could partly be due to societal constraints in two ways. First, from a more context-specific perspective, finding work in West Germany was probably more difficult for East German women than for men. The pronounced age effects among women underline this notion. Since older women in the study revealed the highest levels of health complaints and the lowest levels of support, we can assume that environmental (e.g., socioeconomic) factors have contributed to either the perception or even the actual reception of social support.

Second, as Hobfoll (1998) argues, men and women are assumed to have different experience with social support. Whereas men are supposed to be more independent and self-reliant, women are expected to seek and provide support for others. Research on gender differences in dealing with life-threatening diseases has contributed considerably to the discussion. Again, differences between men and women are primarily mediated by the social support they seek and receive.

Gender and Culture

If gender differences in response to stressful events follow from culturally defined norms, what does the picture look like in societies that foster different views of masculinity and femininity than our Western societies?

From this point of departure, Norris, Perilla, Ibañez, and Murphy (2001) conducted a study to identify the causes for higher rates of PTSD among women compared to men, as epidemiological research suggests. The authors argue that it is complicated to determine the extent to which sex differences are culturally bound if one does not include distinct societies in the research. Thus, Norris et al. picked two countries with a distinguished cultural heritage and makeup: Mexico, where traditional gender roles are fostered, and the United States, where the roles of women and men are less rigidly defined. Data were collected six months after Hurricane Paulina hit Mexico and Hurricane Andrew hit the United States.

The findings confirmed the hypothesis that women were more highly distressed by these natural disasters than men. This was especially prominent among Mexican women, who were also most likely to meet the criteria for PTSD. These findings support the hypothesis that traditional cultures amplify gender differences in response to disastrous events.

Nevertheless, other external factors may have been influential. As the authors critically state, Mexico does not have sufficient resources to provide for disaster relief, contrary to their wealthy American neighbor. According to COR Theory, resourcefulness plays the central role in dealing with stress, even long after the actual event. These findings notwithstanding, biological, feminist/psychodynamic and social cognitive perspectives cannot be excluded from the discussion. Conclusive evidence for the explanation of culturally bound gender differences is still missing.

Culture and Ethnicity

Beyond the discussion of gender differences, probably anyone would agree that cultural standards may have the potential to shape the experience of catastrophic events. In addition, cultural norms and values largely determine the needs of disaster-struck individuals. This becomes especially evident when disaster relief and aid measures are planned and administered in a culture different than those of the rescue personnel.

Since most natural disasters occur in underdeveloped countries or regions, this scenario is more the rule than the exception. Moreover, in pluralistic countries with a multicultural makeup, such as Canada, the United Kingdom or the United States, rescue personnel is challenged to be prepared for culturally tailored counseling even within their own society. Therefore, culturally sensitive methods and approaches are needed to meet the various needs of different cultural groups (Doherty, 1999).

One convenient way of studying the role of culture, ethnicity, and religion in a stressful situation is by comparing different ethnic immigrant groups regarding either the acculturation process or their responses to catastrophic events within the host country. As to the former, acculturation has been regarded a stressful encounter since newly arrived immigrants face a number of challenges. However, immigrant groups of different nationality are difficult to compare since the numerous factors that determine acculturation (e.g., socioeconomic equipment or migration history) vary greatly across immigrant groups.

The latter approach of studying ethnic differences in response to stressful events was taken by Webster, McDonald, Lewin, and Carr (1995). They conducted a study to scrutinize the effects of natural disasters on immigrants and the host population. In the aftermath of the 1989 Newcastle, Australia, earthquake, the General Health Questionnaire as well as the Impact of Event Scale for event-related psychological morbidity were administered to immigrants with a non-English background as well as to Australian-born controls. Data analyses showed greater psychological distress among the non-English group. Among those, women, older people, and those who had experienced dislocation following the earthquake were especially distressed. Other factors, such as personal history of traumatization and age upon arrival, were also found to contribute to the increased levels of psychological distress.

Age

Unfortunately, only few empirical findings are available about the influence of age in the face of aversive situations. According to theories of successful development, resources available for coping with stressful situations diminish with age. Since resources are the key to successful coping with life events, elderly people are presumably worse off than younger ones. Is that really the case?

Cwikel and Rozovski (1998) investigated the immigration process of people from the former Soviet Union to Israel. The immigrants came from republics adjacent to the Chernobyl power plant. The authors found that the "late-in-life" immigrants (Torres, 1995), those aged 65 years and older, were disadvantaged in terms of adaptation and integration. Moreover, the recovery process after the event was slower among immigrants 55 years and older compared to the younger group.

In a study on Chernobyl victims, younger adults displayed greater fears of health risks than older individuals (Muthny, Gramus, Dutton, & Stegie, 1987). In the same context, Hüppe and Janke (1994) found women and younger people (18 to 39 years old) to be more concerned than men and older individuals (40 to 59 years), respectively. On the contrary, investigations in the aftermath of natural disasters often reveal stronger concerns by elderly victims. In terms of depression, Toukmanian, Jadaa, and Lawless (2000) found older (31 to 55 years) individuals who were exposed to an earthquake scoring higher on depression scales than younger people (17 to 30 years). Also, the common gender effect of women being more highly depressed than men could be replicated.

Ben-Zur and Zeidner (1991) investigated psychological distress and health complaints under the threat of missile attacks during the Gulf War. Here, younger adults reported more anxiety, bodily symptoms, anxiety, fear, and depression compared to older adults. This finding is consistent with other results, as Milgram (1994) reports in a summary about Gulf War-related studies. Explanations of these age differences refer to the greater experience that older Israeli citizens have with war-related stressors. Moreover, older individuals' coping efforts have been proven effective in other situations.

The diversity of research findings does not allow for a final conclusion. However, the vast majority of studies have detected resources as the primary determinants of successful coping with an event, which in turn buffers the detrimental effects for the mental and physical health of the victims.

FUTURE DIRECTIONS

Stressful life events constitute an important research paradigm for health psychology. They are commonly seen as independent variables called *stressors* that lead to a number of predominantly negative outcomes. From a stress theory perspective, however, this bivariate relationship is too simplistic. Stress is a process that takes place in context, and the amount of stress actually perceived is different from the objective magnitude of a stressor. Characteristics of the taxing event, such as intensity, duration, predictability, and controllability, have some bearing on the way this actual event is cognitively appraised by individuals, along with other determinants, such as personality, social networks, and coping resources or vulnerabilities (Aldwin, Sutton, & Lachman, 1996). Research on stressful life events too often adheres to a stimulus-based view of stress, neglecting transactional processes.

This shortcoming is also reflected by the measurement of stress. One common research prototype in health psychology rests mainly on checklists or interview schedules on life events that require the respondents to review all demanding and disastrous situations in the past and to supply subjective ratings of incidence and severity. These ratings of cumulative life stress can lead to an ambiguous sum score that may obscure various exposure conditions and may mask more information than it reveals. Moreover, the rating procedure confounds the current psychological state with an accurate recollection of past events. If the research question deals with mental health effects of prior stress exposure, we can hardly arrive at meaningful conclusions by asking respondents about the severity and impact of their life events. A different common research prototype lies, for example, in sampling survivors, observers, or rescue workers of a disaster. In this situation, the stressful life event is given by definition. To yield an index of severity, predictability, controllability, or other characteristics of the event, we can ask independent judges to rate the event along a number of dimensions. This provides useful stimulus information that should be supplemented by data on victims' cognitive appraisals.

Stressful life events can shape individual lives and affect mental and physical health to a large extent, including premature death as a result of suicide or severe disease. Numerous studies have documented morbidity and mortality data as a result of stress. The relationship between stressful life events and health, however, is complex, and it requires consideration of mediators and moderators. Several pathways portray the causal mechanisms. One path refers to stress-induced physiological changes, such as the wear and tear on blood vessels, immunosuppression, or endocrine and cardiovascular reactivity. This again might not be a direct relationship, but it could be mediated by negative affects that follow stressful life events. Constant rumination, worrying, loneliness, or depression themselves generate physiological changes that produce illness in the long run. A different pathway is represented by stress-induced behaviors that impair health, such as smoking, alcohol consumption, lack of exercise, sleep deprivation, unhealthy eating, and so on. Furthermore, someone who is already ill and needy might fail to mobilize social support, seek treatment, adhere to medication, and so on, in times of severe stress.

The existence of several causal pathways in the development of poor health is intuitive, but empirical evidence is sparse. One of the reasons for this deficit lies in the difficulty in identifying synergistic effects. Moreover, we cannot discover causal links when only cross-sectional data are available. The existing state of research calls for longitudinal and prospective study designs that allow for a more detailed analysis of the stress/health association, including mediators and moderators, such as personality, coping, and social support.

Many clinical and community interventions have been initiated, mainly as debriefing and crisis counseling, but they are not well evaluated. Systematic intervention studies allow treatment effects to be examined, for example by testing coping strategies that aim at modifying certain stress/health pathways.

REFERENCES

Adams, P., & Adams, G. (1984). Mount Saint Helen's ashfall. *American Psychologist, 39,* 252–260.

Ader, R. (2001). Psychoneuroimmunology. In N. J. Smelser & P. B. Baltes (Eds.), *The international encyclopedia of the social and behavioral sciences* (Vol. 18, pp. 12422–12428). Oxford, England: Elsevier.

Aldwin, C. M., Sutton, K. J., & Lachman, M. (1996). The development of coping resources in adulthood. *Journal of Personality, 64,* 837–871.

American Psychiatric Association. (1994). *Diagnostic and statistical manual of mental disorders* (4th ed.). Washington, DC: Author.

Arata, C. M., Picou, J. S., Johnson, G. D., & McNally, T. S. (2000). Coping with technological disaster: An application of the conservation of resources model to the Exxon Valdez oil spill. *Journal of Traumatic Stress, 13,* 23–39.

Bar-Tal, Y., Lurie, O., & Glick, D. (1994). The effect of gender on the stress process of Israeli soldiers during the Gulf war. *Anxiety, Stress, and Coping, 7,* 263–276.

Bartrop, R. W., Luckhurst, E., Lazarus, L., Kiloh, L. G., & Penny, R. (1977). Depressed lymphocyte function after bereavement. *Lancet, 1,* 834–837.

Baum, A., Fleming, I., Israel, N., & O'Keefe, M. K. (1992). Symptoms of chronic stress following a natural disaster and discovery of a human-made hazard. *Environment and Behavior, 24,* 347–365.

Ben-Zur, H., & Zeidner, M. (1991). Anxiety and bodily symptoms under the threat of missile attacks: The Israeli scene. *Anxiety Research, 4,* 79–95.

Berry, J. W., & Kim, U. (1988). Acculturation and mental health. In P. R. Dasen, J. W. Berry, & N. Sartorius (Eds.), *Health and cross-cultural psychology: Toward applications* (pp. 207–236). Newbury Park, CA: Sage.

Brannon, L., & Feist, J. (1997). *Health psychology: An introduction to behavior and health.* Pacific Grove, CA: Brooks/Cole.

Briere, J. (1995). *Trauma Symptom Inventory professional manual.* Odessa, FL: Psychological Assessment Resources.

Briere, J., & Elliot, D. (2000). Prevalence, characteristics, and long-term sequelae of natural disaster exposure in the general population. *Journal of Traumatic Stress, 13,* 661–679.

Bromet, E., Parkinson, D., & Dunn, L. (1990). Long-term mental health consequences of the accident at Three Mile Island. *International Journal of Mental Health, 19,* 8–60.

Brown, G. W., & Harris, T. O. (1978). *Social origins of depression.* New York: Free Press.

Carver, C. S. (2001). Depression, hopelessness, optimism and health. In N. J. Smelser & P. B. Baltes (Eds.), *The international encyclopedia of the social and behavioral sciences* (Vol. 5, pp. 3516–3522). Oxford, England: Elsevier.

Cheung, P., & Spears, G. (1995). Psychiatric morbidity among New Zealand Cambodians: The role of psychosocial factors. *Social Psychiatry and Psychiatric Epidemiology, 30,* 92–97.

Chung, R. C., & Kagawa-Singer, M. (1993). Predictors of psychological distress among Southeast Asian refugees. *Social Science and Medicine, 36,* 631–639.

Clements, C. M., & Sawhney, D. K. (2000). Coping with domestic violence: Control attributions, dysphoria, and hopelessness. *Journal of Traumatic Stress, 13,* 219–240.

Cobb, S. (1976). Social support as a moderator of life stress. *Psychosomatic Medicine, 38,* 300–314.

Cohen, S., Kamarck, T., & Mermelstein, R. (1983). A global measure of perceived stress. *Journal of Health and Social Behavior, 24,* 385–396.

Cohen, S., Tyrrell, D. A., & Smith, A. P. (1991). Psychological stress and susceptibility to the common cold. *New England Journal of Medicine, 325,* 606–612.

Cwikel, J., & Rozovski, U. (1998). Coping with the stress of immigration among new immigrants to Israel from Commonwealth of Independent States (CIS) who were exposed to Chernobyl: The effect of age. *International Journal of Aging and Human Development, 46,* 305–318.

Davidson, J. R. T., Book, S. W., Colket, J. T., Tupler, L. A., Roth, S., David, D., et al. (1997). Assessment of a new self-rating scale for post-traumatic stress disorder. *Psychological Medicine, 27,* 153–160.

Davidson, L., Fleming, I., & Baum, A. (1986). Post-traumatic stress as a function of chronic stress and toxic exposure. In C. Figley (Ed.), *Trauma and its wake* (Vol. 2, pp. 57–77). New York: Brunner/Mazel.

Desivilya, H. S., Gal, R., & Ayalon, O. (1996). Long-term effects of trauma in adolescence: Comparison between survivors of a terrorist attack and control counterparts. *Anxiety, Stress and Coping, 9,* 135–150.

Doherty, G. W. (1999). Cross-cultural counseling in disaster settings. *Australasian Journal of Disaster and Trauma Studies, 2.* Available from www.massey.ac.nz/~trauma/issues/1999–2/doherty .htm

Dohrenwend, B. P., Raphael, K. G., Schartz, S., Stueve, A., & Skodol, A. (1993). The structured event probe and narrative rating method for measuring stressful life events. In L. Goldberg & S. Breznitz (Eds.), *Handbook of stress* (pp. 174–199). New York: Free Press.

Dohrenwend, B. S., & Dohrenwend, B. P. (Eds.). (1974). *Stressful life events: Their nature and effects.* New York: Wiley.

Eberly, R. E., & Engdahl, B. E. (1991). Prevalence of somatic and psychiatric disorders among former prisoners of war. *Hospital and Community Psychiatry, 42*(8), 807–813.

Escobar, J. I., Canino, G., Rubio-Stipec, M., & Bravo, M. (1992). Somatic symptoms after a natural disaster: A prospective study. *American Journal of Psychiatry, 149*(7), 965–967.

Falger, P. R., Op den Velde, W., Hovens, J. E., Schouten, E. G. W., DeGroen, J. H. M., & Van Duijn, H. (1992). Current posttraumatic stress disorder and cardiovascular disease risk factors in Dutch resistance veterans from World War II. *Psychotherapy and Psychosomatics, 57*(4), 164–171.

Feeny, N. C., Zoellner, L. A., & Foa, E. B. (2000). Anger, dissociation, and posttraumatic stress disorder among female assault victims. *Journal of Traumatic Stress, 13,* 89–100.

Figley, C., Giel, R., Borgo, S., Briggs, S., & Haritos-Fatouros, M. (1995). Prevention and treatment of community stress: How to be a mental health expert at the time of disaster. In S. E. Hobfoll & M. W. de Vries (Eds.), *Extreme stress and communities: Impact and intervention* (pp. 307–324). Dordrecht, The Netherlands: Kluwer Press.

Freed, D., Bowler, R., & Fleming, I. (1998). Post-traumatic stress disorder as a consequence of a toxic spill in Northern California. *Journal of Applied Social Psychology, 28*(3), 264–281.

Freudenburg, W. R., & Jones, T. R. (1991). Attitudes and stress in the presence of technological risks: Towards a sociological perspective. *Social Forces, 69,* 1143–1168.

Gillard, M., & Paton, D. (1999). Disaster stress following a hurricane: The role of religious differences in the Fijian Islands. *The Australasian Journal of Disaster and Trauma Studies, 2.* Available from www.massey.ac.nz/~trauma/issues/1999–2/gillard. htm

Gilligan, I., Fung, L., Piper, D. W., & Tennant, C. (1987). Life event stress and chronic difficulties in duodenal ulcer: A case control study. *Journal of Psychosomatic Research, 31,* 117–123.

Glick, I., Weiss, R. S., & Parkes, C. M. (1974). *The first year of bereavement.* New York: Wiley.

Goldman, N., Korenman, S., & Weinstein, R. (1995). Marital status and health among the elderly. *Social Science and Medicine, 40,* 1717–1730.

Graham, M., & Khosravi, S. (1997). Home is where you make it: Repatriation and diaspora culture among Iranians in Sweden. *Journal of Refugee Studies, 10*(2), 115–133.

Green, B. L. (1995). Long-term consequences on disaster. In S. E. Hobfoll & M. W. de Vries (Eds.), *Extreme stress and communities: Impact and intervention* (pp. 307–324). Dordrecht, The Netherlands: Kluwer Press.

Green, B. L. (1998). Psychological responses to disasters: Conceptualization and identification of high-risk survivors. *Psychiatry and Clinical Neuroscience, 52,* 57–73.

Greenglass, E. R. (1982). *A world of difference: Gender roles in perspective.* Toronto, Ontario, Canada: Wiley.

Hanson Frieze, I., & Bookwala, J. (1996). Coping with unusual stressors. Criminal victimization. In M. Zeidner & N. S. Endler (Eds.), *Handbook of coping: Theory, research and applications* (pp. 303–321). New York: Wiley.

Hawkins, N. G., Davies, R., & Holmes, T. H. (1957). Evidence of psychosocial factors in the development of pulmonary tuberculosis. *American Review of Tuberculosis and Pulmonary Diseases, 75,* 768–780.

Herbert, T. B., & Cohen, S. (1993a). Depression and immunity: A meta-analytic review. *Psychological Bulletin, 113,* 472–486.

Herbert, T. B., & Cohen, S. (1993b). Stress and immunity in humans: A meta-analytic review. *Psychosomatic Medicine, 55,* 364–379.

Hobfoll, S. E. (1986). *Stress, social support, and women.* Washington, DC: Hemisphere.

Hobfoll, S. E. (1988). *The ecology of stress.* Washington, DC: Hemisphere.

Hobfoll, S. E. (1989). Conservation of resources: A new attempt at conceptualizing stress. *American Psychologist, 44,* 513–524.

Hobfoll, S. E. (1998). *Stress, culture, and community: The psychology and philosophy of stress.* New York: Plenum Press.

Hobfoll, S. E. (2001). Social support and stress. In N. J. Smelser & P. B. Baltes (Eds.), *The international encyclopedia of the social and behavioral sciences* (Vol. 21, pp. 14461–14465). Oxford, England: Elsevier.

Hobfoll, S. E., Schwarzer, R., & Chon, K. K. (1998). Disentangling the stress labyrinth: Interpreting the meaning of the term stress as it is studied in health context. *Anxiety, Stress, and Coping, 11*(3), 181–212.

Holmes, T. H., & Rahe, R. H. (1967). The social adjustment rating scale. *Journal of Psychosomatic Research, 11,* 213–218.

Hondius, A. J. K., van Willigen, L. H. M., Kleijn, W. C., & van der Ploeg, H. M. (2000). Health problems among Latin-American and Middle-Eastern refugees in the Netherlands: Relations with violence exposure and ongoing sociopsychological strain. *Journal of Traumatic Stress, 13*(4), 619–634.

Horowitz, M. J., Wilner, N., & Alvarez, W. (1979). Impact of Event Scale: A measure of subjective stress. *Psychosomatic Medicine, 41,* 209–218.

Hüppe, M., & Janke, W. (1994). The nuclear plant accident in Chernobyl experienced by men and women of different ages: Empirical study in the years 1986–1991. *Anxiety, Stress, and Coping, 7,* 339–355.

Hyman, I., Vu, N., & Beiser, M. (2000). Post-migration stresses among Southeast Asian refuge youths in Canada: A research note. *Journal of Comparative Family Studies, 31*(2), 281–293.

Jacobs, J. R., & Bovasso, G. B. (2000). Early and chronic stress and their relation to breast cancer. *Psychological Medicine, 30*(3), 669–678.

Karanci, N. A., Alkan, N., Balta, E., Sucuoglu, H., & Aksit, B. (1999). Gender differences in psychological distress, coping, social support and related variables following the 1995 Dinal (Turkey) earthquake. *North American Journal of Psychology, 1,* 189–204.

Kimerling, R., Clum, G. A., & Wolfe, J. (2000). Relationships among trauma exposure, chronic posttraumatic stress disorder symptoms, and self-reported health in women: Replication and extension. *Journal of Traumatic Stress, 13,* 115–128.

Knoll, N., & Schwarzer, R. (in press). Gender and age differences in social support: A study on East German migrants. In M. Kopp, G. Weidner, & M. Kristenson (Eds.), *Heart disease: Environment, stress, and gender.* Amsterdam: IOS Press.

Köhler, T., Kuhnt, K., & Richter, R. (1998). The role of life event stress in the pathogenesis of duodenal ulcer. *Stress Medicine, 14*(2), 121–124.

Kumar, R., Rastogi, C. K., & Nigam, P. (1996). A study of life events in cases of peptic ulcer and controls with special reference to their temporal relationship to the onset of illness. *Indian Journal of Clinical Psychology, 23*(2), 129–134.

Landau, R., & Litwin, H. (2000). The effects of extreme early stress in very old age. *Journal of Traumatic Stress, 13*(3), 473–487.

Lazarus, R. S. (1966). *Psychological stress and the coping process.* New York: McGraw-Hill.

Lazarus, R. S. (1991). *Emotion and adaptation.* London: Oxford University Press.

Lazarus, R. S., & Folkman, S. (1989). *Hassles and Uplifts Scales.* Palo Alto, CA: Consulting Psychologists Press.

Li, G. (1995). The interaction effect of bereavement and sex on the risk of suicide in the elderly: An historical cohort study. *Social Science and Medicine, 40,* 825–828.

Lipson, J. G. (1993). Afghan refugees in California: Mental health issues. *Issues in Mental Health Nursing, 14*(4), 411–423.

Lomranz, J. (1995). Endurance and living: Long-term effects of the Holocaust. In S. E. Hobfoll & M. W. de Vries (Eds.), *Extreme stress and communities: Impact and intervention* (pp. 325–352). Dordrecht, The Netherlands: Kluwer Press.

Madakasira, S., & O'Brien, K. F. (1987). Acute posttraumatic stress disorder in victims of a natural disaster. *Journal of Nervous and Mental Disease, 175*(5), 286–290.

Matsunaga, H., Kaye, W. H., McCohaha, C., Plotnicov, K., Pollice, C., Rao, R., et al. (1999). Psychopathological characteristics of recovered bulimics who have a history of physical or sexual abuse. *Journal of Nervous and Mental Diseases, 187*(8), 472–477.

McFarlane, A. C., Atchison, M., Rafalowicz, E., & Papay, P. (1994). Physical symptoms in posttraumatic stress disorder. *Journal of Psychosomatic Research, 38,* 715–726.

McFarlane, A. C., Clayer, J. R., & Bookless, C. L. (1997). Psychiatric morbidity following a natural disaster: An Australian bushfire. *Social Psychiatry and Psychiatric Epidemiology, 32*(5), 261–268.

McMillen, J. C., North, C. S., & Smith, E. M. (2000). What parts of PTSD are normal: Intrusion, avoidance, or arousal? Data from the Northridge, California, earthquake. *Journal of Traumatic Stress, 13,* 57–75.

Meichenbaum, D. (1995). Disasters, stress, and cognition. In S. E. Hobfoll & M. W. de Vries (Eds.), *Extreme stress and communities: Impact and intervention* (pp. 33–61). Dordrecht, The Netherlands: Kluwer Press.

Milgram, N. (1994). Israel and the Gulf war: The major events and selected studies. *Anxiety, Stress, and Coping, 7,* 205–215.

Miller, E., & Wortman, C. B. (in press). Gender differences in mortality and morbidity following a major stressor: The case of conjugal bereavement. In G. Weidner, M. Kopp, & M. Kristenson (Eds.), *Heart disease: Environment, stress, and gender* (NATO Science Series. I: Life and behavioural sciences, Vol: 327). Amsterdam: IOS Press.

Moret, L. B. (1999). Eating-disordered symptomatology, body image concerns, and social support of female survivors of sexual abuse. *Dissertation Abstracts International, 60,* 4B, 1863.

Muthny, F. A., Gramus, B., Dutton, M., & Stegie, R. (1987). *Tschernobyl—Erlebte Belastung und erste Verarbeitungsversuche* [Chernobyl—experienced stress and first coping attempts]. Jahrbuch der politischen Psychologie [Yearbook of political psychology]. Weinheim, Germany: Studienverlag.

Neria, Y., Solomon, Z., & Dekel, R. (2000). Adjustment to war captivity: The role of sociodemographic background, trauma severity, and immediate responses, in the long-term mental health of Israeli ex-POWs. *Anxiety, Stress, and Coping, 13*(3), 229–240.

Neugebauer, R., Wasserman, G. A., Fisher, P. W., Kline, J., Geller, P. A., & Miller, L. S. (1999). Darryl, a cartoon-based measure of cardinal posttraumatic stress symptoms in school-age children. *American Journal of Public Health, 89*(5), 758–761.

Newman, M. (2001). Post-traumatic stress disorder. In N. J. Smelser & P. B. Baltes (Eds.), *The international encyclopedia of the social and behavioral sciences* (Vol. 17, pp. 11881–11885). Oxford, England: Elsevier.

Norris, F. H., Perilla, J. L., Ibañez, G. E., & Murphy, A. D. (2001). Sex differences in symptoms of posttraumatic stress: Does culture play a role? *Journal of Traumatic Stress, 14,* 7–28.

Pynoos, R. S., Frederick, C., Nader, K., Arroyo, W., Steinberg, A., Eth, S., et al. (1987). Life threat and posttraumatic stress in school-age children. *Archives of General Psychiatry, 44,* 1057–1063.

Raphael, K. G., Cloitre, M., & Dohrenwend, B. P. (1991). Problems of recall and misclassifications with checklist methods of measuring stressful life events. *Health Psychology, 10,* 62–74.

Reich, K. (1995, December 20). Study raises Northridge quake death toll to 72. *Los Angeles Times,* p. A1.

Rossi, P. H., Wright, J. D., Weber-Burdin, E., & Perina, J. (1983). Victimization by natural hazards in the United States, 1970–1980: Survey estimates. *International Journal of Mass Emergencies and Disasters, 1,* 467–482.

Rotton, J., Dubitsky, A. A., Milov, A., White, S. M., & Clark, M. C. (1997). Distress, elevated cortisol, cognitive deficits, and illness following a natural disaster. *Journal of Environmental Psychology, 17*(2), 85–98.

Sarason, I. G., Johnson, J. H., & Siegel, J. M. (1978). Assessing the impact of life changes: Development of the life experiences survey. *Journal of Consulting and Clinical Psychology, 46,* 932–946.

Scheier, M. F., & Bridges, M. W. (1995). Person variables and health: Personality predispositions and acute psychological states as shared determinants for disease. *Psychosomatic Medicine, 57,* 255–268.

Schooler, T. Y. (2001). Disasters, coping with. In N. J. Smelser & P. B. Baltes (Eds.), *The international encyclopedia of the social and behavioral sciences* (Vol. 6, pp. 3713–3718). Oxford, England: Elsevier.

Schwarzer, R. (2001). Stress, resources, and proactive coping. *Applied Psychology: An International Journal, 50,* 400–407.

Schwarzer, R., Hahn, A., & Schröder, H. (1994). Social integration and social support in a life crisis: Effects of macrosocial change in East Germany. *American Journal of Community Psychology, 22*(5), 685–706.

Schwarzer, R., & Rieckmann, N. (in press). Social support, cardiovascular disease, and mortality. In M. Kopp, G. Weidner, & M. Kristenson (Eds.), *Heart disease: Environment, stress, and gender.* Amsterdam: IOS Press.

Schwarzer, R., & Schwarzer, C. (1996). A critical survey of coping instruments. In M. Zeidner & N. S. Endler (Eds.), *Handbook of coping: Theory, research and applications* (pp. 107–132). New York: Wiley.

Selye, H. (1956). *The stress of life.* New York: McGraw-Hill.

Shannon, M. P., Lonigan, C. J., Finch, A. J., & Taylor, C. M. (1994). Children exposed to disaster: Epidemiology of post-traumatic symptoms and symptom profiles. *Journal of the American Academy of Child Adolescent Psychiatry, 33,* 80–93.

Sharan, P., Chauhardy, G., Kavethekar, S. A., & Saxena, S. (1996). Preliminary report of psychiatric disorders in survivors of a severe earthquake. *American Journal of Psychiatry, 153*(4), 556–558.

Simon, R. W. (1995). Gender, multiple roles, role meaning and mental health. *Journal of Health and Social Behavior, 36,* 182–194.

Solomon, S. D., & Green, B. L. (1992). Mental health effects of natural and human made disasters. *PTSD Research Quarterly, 3,* 1–8.

Solomon, Z. (1995). The pathogenic effects of war stress: The Israeli experience. In S. E. Hobfoll & M. W. de Vries (Eds.), *Extreme stress and communities: Impact and intervention* (pp. 229–246). Dordrecht, The Netherlands: Kluwer Press.

Stroebe, M., Stroebe, W., & Hansson, R. O. (Eds.). (2000). *Handbook of bereavement: Consequences, coping, and care.* New York: Cambridge University Press.

Stroebe, W., & Stroebe, M. (1992). Bereavement and health: Processes of adjusting to the loss of a partner. In L. Montada,

S.-H. Filipp, & M. J. Lerner (Eds.), *Life crisis and experience of loss in adulthood* (pp. 3–22). Hillsdale, NJ: Erlbaum.

Teegen, F., & Cerney-Seeler, B. (1998). Sexuelle Kindesmisshandlung und die Entwicklung von Essstoerungen [Sexual child abuse and the development of eating disorders]. *Zeitschrift für Klinische Psychologie, Psychopathologie und Psychotherapie, 46,* 14–28.

Torres, S. (1995). *Late in life immigrants in Sweden.* Unpublished master's thesis, Uppsala University, Department of Sociology, Uppsala, Sweden.

Toukmanian, S. G., Jadaa, D., & Lawless, D. (2000). A cross-cultural study of depression in the aftermath of a natural disaster. *Anxiety, Stress, and Coping, 13,* 289–307.

Tran, T. V. (1993). Psychological traumas and depression in a sample of Vietnamese people in the United States. *Health and Social Work, 18*(3), 184–194.

Trevisan, M., O'Leary, E., Farinaro, E., Jossa, F., Galasso, R., Celentano, E., et al. (1997). Short- and long-term association between uric acid and natural disaster. *Psychosomatic Medicine, 59,* 109–113.

Turner, R. J., & Wheaton, B. (1995). Checklist measurement of stressful life events. In S. Cohen, R. C. Kessler, & L. U. Gordon (Eds.), *Measuring stress: A guide for health and social scientists* (pp. 29–58). New York: Oxford University Press.

Wagner, A. W., Wolfe, J., Rotnitsky, A., Proctor, S., & Ericson, D. (2000). An investigation of the impact of posttraumatic stress disorder on physical health. *Journal of Traumatic Stress, 13,* 41–55.

Webster, R. A., McDonald, R., Lewin, T. J., & Carr, V. J. (1995). Effects of a natural disaster on immigrants and host population. *Journal of Nervous and Mental Diseases, 183,* 390–397.

Weidner, G. (2001). Why do men get more heart disease than women? An international perspective. *Journal of American College Health, 48,* 291–294.

Weidner, G. (in press). Gender and cardiovascular health. In N. J. Smelser & P. B. Baltes (Eds.), *The international encyclopedia of the social and behavioral sciences.* Oxford, England: Elsevier.

Weisaeth, L. (1992). Prepare and repair: Some principles in prevention of psychiatric consequences of traumatic stress. *Psychiatria Fennica, 23,* 11–18.

Wethington, E., Brown, G. W., & Kessler, R. C. (1995). Interview measurement of stressful life events. In S. Cohen, R. C. Kessler, & L. U. Gordon (Eds.), *Measuring stress: A guide for health and social scientists* (pp. 59–79). New York: Oxford University Press.

Winkielman, P., Knäuper, B., & Schwarz, N. (1998). Looking back at anger: Reference periods change the interpretation of emotion frequency questions. *Journal of Personality and Social Psychology, 75*(3), 719–728.

Yee, V. (1995). Acculturation stress, emigration stress, self-efficacy, personal mastery, depression, and somatization. A path-analytic model of mental illness in Southeast Asian Americans. *Dissertation Abstracts International, 56,* 4B, 2347.

Zeidner, M., & Hammer, A. L. (1992). Coping with missile attack: Resources, strategies, and outcomes. *Journal of Personality, 60,* 709–746.

Zoellner, L. A., Goodwin, M. L., & Foa, E. B. (2000). PTSD severity and health perceptions in female victims of sexual assault. *Journal of Traumatic Stress, 13*(4), 635–649.

CHAPTER 3

Coping and Social Support

SHARON MANNE

Coping and social support are among the most widely written about and researched topics in health psychology. Both constructs have been hypothesized as reasons why particular individuals are at increased risk for developing illnesses such as cardiovascular disease and cancer, why some individuals do not adapt well once they develop a disease, and, more recently, linked with disease course and survival once an illness is diagnosed. In this chapter, we explore the historical context of coping and social support in the context of health, as well as the empirical work examining the role of coping and social support in disease etiology, disease management, and outcomes. Each section is divided into a historical discussion, current theoretical perspectives on each construct, and descriptive studies. Key challenges and areas for future research are also discussed.

COPING

Over the past two decades, there has been a substantial amount of research devoted to understanding the role of coping in disease etiology, management of health risk, adaptation to disease, and disease outcomes. In the context of health risk and outcomes, the role of coping in psychological adaptation to disease has received the most empirical attention.

Theories of Coping

Stress and Coping Paradigm

Research on stress and coping exploded with Lazarus and Folkman's stress and coping theory (1984). They put forth the transactional stress and coping paradigm and the most widely accepted definition of coping. According to Lazarus, coping refers to cognitive and behavioral efforts to manage disruptive events that tax the person's ability to adjust (Lazarus, 1981, p. 2). According to Lazarus and Folkman, coping responses are a dynamic series of transactions between the individual and the environment, the purpose of which is to regulate internal states and/or alter person-environment relations. The theory postulates that stressful emotions and coping are due to cognitions associated with the way a person appraises or perceives his or her relationship with the environment. There are several components of the coping process. First, appraisals of the harm or loss posed by the stressor (Lazarus, 1981) are thought to be important determinants of coping. Second, appraisal of the degree of controllability of the stressor is a determinant of coping strategies selected. A third component is the person's evaluation of the outcome of their coping efforts and their expectations for future success in coping with the stressor. These evaluative judgments lead to changes in the types of coping employed. In addition, they play a role in determining psychological adaptation. Two main dimensions of coping are proposed, problem-focused and emotion-focused coping. Problem-focused coping is aimed at altering the problematic situation. These coping efforts include information seeking and planful problem solving. Emotion-focused coping is aimed at managing emotional responses to stressors. Such coping efforts include cognitive reappraisal of the stressor and minimizing the problem.

How the elements of coping unfold over time is a key theoretical issue involved in studies of coping processes. Although the theory is dynamic in nature, most of the research utilizing the stress and coping paradigm put forth by Lazarus and colleagues (1981) has relied on retrospective assessments of coping and has been cross-sectional. However, a team of researchers, including Glen Affleck, Howard Tennen, and Francis Keefe (e.g., Affleck et al., 1999) have utilized a daily diary approach to assessing coping with pain, a methodology that can examine the proposed dynamic nature of coping.

Cognitive Processing Theories

In recent years, there has been an expansion in theoretical perspectives on cognitive coping. The literature on cognitive processing of traumatic life events has provided a new direction for coping research and broadened theoretical perspectives on cognitive methods of coping with chronic illness. According to cognitive processing theory, traumatic events can challenge people's core assumptions about themselves and their world (Janoff-Bulman, 1992). For example, the unpredictable nature of many chronic illnesses, as well as the numerous social and occupational losses, can cause people to question the beliefs they hold about themselves. A diagnosis of cancer can challenge a person's assumptions about being personally invulnerable to illness and/or providing for his or her family. To the extent that a chronic illness challenges these basic assumptions, integrating the illness experience into their preexisting beliefs should promote psychological adjustment. Cognitive processing is defined as cognitive activities that help people view undesirable events in personally meaningful ways and find ways of understanding the negative aspects of the experience, and ultimately reach a state of acceptance (e.g., Greenberg, 1995). By finding meaning or positive benefit in a negative experience, individuals may be better able to accept the losses they experience. Focusing on the positive implications of the illness or finding personal significance in a situation are two ways of finding meaning. Coping activities that help individuals to find redeeming features in an event must be distinguished from the successful outcome of these attempts. For example, people may report that as a result of a serious illness, they have found a new appreciation for life or that they place greater value on relationships. Patients may also develop an explanation for the illness that is more benign (e.g., attributing it to God's will) or make sense of the illness by using their existing views of the world (e.g., assuming responsibility for the illness because of a lifestyle that caused the illness). While cognitive processing theory constructs have been applied to adjustment to losses such as bereavement (e.g., Davis, Nolen-Hoeksema, & Larson, 1998), these processes have received relatively little attention from researchers examining patients coping with chronic illness.

Another coping process that falls under the rubric of cognitive processing is social comparison (SC). Social comparison is a common cognitive process whereby individuals compare themselves to others to obtain information about themselves (Gibbons & Gerrard, 1991). According to SC theory, health problems increase uncertainty; uncertainty increases the desire for information, and creates the need for comparison. Studies of coping with chronic illness have included social comparison as a focus. A certain type of SC, downward comparison, has been the focus of empirical study among patients with chronic illnesses such as rheumatoid arthritis (RA) (Tennen & Affleck, 1997). Wills (1981) has suggested that people experiencing a loss can experience an improvement in mood if they learn about others who are worse off. Although there is little evidence that SC increases as a result of experiencing health problems, there is considerable evidence to suggest this may be the case (Kulik & Mahler, 1997). One proposed mechanism for SC is that downward comparison impacts cognitive appraisal by reducing perceived threat. When another person's situation appears significantly worse, then the appraisal of one's own illness may be reduced (Aspinwall & Taylor, 1993).

Coping Style Theories

Although the majority of coping theories focus on the transactional, dynamic aspects of coping, there remains a group of behavioral scientists who consider coping more of a disposition or trait. Although there has been some inconsistency in the use of the term, *coping style* is typically the term used to refer to characteristic methods individuals use to deal with threatening situations. Coping style theorists propose that individuals differ in a consistent and stable manner in how they respond to threatening health information and how they react to it affectively. Several coping style constructs have been explored in the health psychology literature. The *monitoring coping style construct,* which has been put forth by Miller (1980; 1987), proposes that individuals have characteristic ways of managing health threats in terms of their attentional processes. According to Monitoring Process Theory, there are two characteristic ways of dealing with health threat, monitoring, and blunting. Monitors scan for and magnify threatening cues, and blunters distract from and downgrade threatening information (Miller, 1995).

A similar coping style construct that has received theoretical and empirical attention is coping with affective responses to health threats. Two constructs, *repressive coping style* and *emotional control,* have been the most studied in the area of health psychology. Repressive coping style, a construct derived from psychoanalytic theory is based on the defense of repression (e.g., Kernberg, 1982). Repressive coping style is exhibited by individuals who believe they are not upset despite objective evidence to the contrary. Thus, it is inferred that they are consciously repressing threatening feelings and concerns. This style has been variously labeled as *attention-rejection* (Mullen & Suls, 1982) and *repression-sensitization* (Byrne, 1961). A second, but related, coping style is the construct of emotional control, which describes an individual who experiences and labels emotions, but does not express the emotional reaction (Watson & Greer, 1983). Both constructs have sparked particular interest in the area of psychosocial oncology, where investigations have focused on the role of emotional repression and suppression in cancer onset and progression (e.g., Butow, 2000; Goldstein & Antoni, 1989; Kneier & Temoshok, 1984; Kreitler, Chaitchik, & Kreitler, 1993). More recently, repressive coping has also been associated with higher risk for poor disease outcome, as physiological and immunological correlates of repressive coping have been identified, including high systolic blood pressure (Broege, James, & Peters, 1997) and reduced immunocompetence (Jamner & Leigh, 1999). In addition, repressive coping has been associated with lower ability to perceive symptoms (Lehrer, 1998). Unfortunately, measurement of this construct has been a challenge to behavioral scientists.

Although the majority of coping theories treat coping as a situational variable, a subset of investigators have conceptualized coping behaviors as having trait-like characteristics. That is, coping is viewed as largely consistent across situations because individuals have particular coping styles or ways of handling stress. In general, the contribution of trait versus states to the prediction of behavior has been a hotly debated topic in the last several decades, starting with the work of Walter Mischel (1968). One response to the trait-situation debate was the development of the interactionist position, which postulates that all behaviors are a function of both the person's traits and the situation (e.g., Endler & Hunt, 1968). Recent studies investigating coping using daily assessments suggest that coping, particularly avoidance and religious coping, has a moderate degree of consistency when multiple daily assessments are utilized (Schwartz, Neale, Marco, Schiffman, & Stone, 1999). Interestingly, these aggregated daily reports of coping activities using the Daily Coping Assessment are only moderately associated with self-report measures of trait coping (how one generally copes with stress) (Schwartz, Neale, Marco, Schiffman, & Stone, 1999).

Theories of Coping with Health Risk

One of the only health belief models that has incorporated coping is Leventhal and colleagues' self-regulatory model of illness behavior (Prohaska, Leventhal, Leventhal, & Keller, 1985). According to this model, symptoms are key factors in how health threats are perceived. Symptoms are also the main targets for coping and symptom reduction is necessary for appraising progress with mitigating health threats (Cameron, Leventhal, & Leventhal, 1993). There are multiple components to this model: First, the individual perceives a change in somatic activity or a symptom, such as pain. Next, this symptom is compared with the person's memory of prior symptoms in an attempt to evaluate the nature of the health threat. The person forms a symptom or illness representation, which has several key components: (a) identity of the health problem that includes its label and its attributes such as severity, (b) duration—an evaluation of how long it will last, (c) consequences—how much it will disrupt daily activity and anticipated long-term consequences or severity of the threat, (d) causes of the symptom, and (e) expectation about controllability of the symptom (Lau, Bernard, & Hartman, 1989). Once the person completes this evaluation then he or she decides how to cope with the symptom. Coping procedures are defined in two ways that correspond roughly to Lazarus and Folkman's emotion- and problem-focused coping. Problem-solving behaviors include seeking medical care and self-care behaviors (e.g., taking insulin for diabetes), as well as attempts to seek information. This model is innovative because care-seeking and self-care behaviors such as adherence to medical regimens for chronic illnesses are defined as coping behaviors. Thus, this model would include the study of determinants of adherence to medical regimens under the rubric of coping literature. This literature is beyond the scope of the present chapter, so we present only a brief review on this topic.

The second aspect of coping is the manner in which the person copes with the affective response to the symptom. An innovative component of the self-regulatory model is that it incorporates how people cope with emotional responses to health threats. Emotional responses such as fear can be elicited by symptom-induced pain or by an interpretation that the symptom represents a serious health threat such as cancer (Croyle & Jemmott, 1991). Coping responses to manage emotions have been evaluated in a similar way to Lazarus and colleagues; individuals are asked how they coped with the problem and responses are categorized using similar categories (e.g., direct coping such as seeking information, and passive coping such as distraction).

The Role of Coping in Health Behaviors and in the Management of Health Risk

As compared to the relatively large literature on coping with illness, there is little published on the role of coping in health behavior change and in the management of health risk. Coping with a health risk is defined as those efforts to manage the knowledge that one is at higher risk for disease because of family history of the disease or because of behavioral risk factors. To date, there have been almost no studies evaluating coping's role in managing health behaviors. Barron, Houfek, and Foxall (1997) examined the role of repressive coping style in women's practice of breast self-examination (BSE). Repressive coping resulted in less frequent BSE and less proficient performance of BSE. Individuals who exhibited repressive coping also reported more barriers and fewer benefits of BSE. Although it is generally thought that specific coping styles (e.g., monitoring) or coping strategies (e.g., denial or avoidance) would predict patients' adherence to medical regimes, the literature linking coping to medical adherence has not supported this hypothesis. General coping style has not been consistently linked to adherence (see Dunbar-Jacob et al., 2000). Other investigators have evaluated the role of specific coping responses in treatment adherence. Catz, McClure, Jones, and Brantley (1999) hypothesized that HIV-positive patients who engaged in spiritual coping may be more likely to adhere to medical regimens for HIV. However, their results did not support this hypothesis.

Coping and Health Outcomes

Whether psychological characteristics influence the development and course of disease has been a hotly debated topic in the empirical literature. This discussion of the association between coping and health outcomes is organized into two sections: first, the association between coping and disease risk; second, the relation between coping and disease progression.

Disease Risk

The most investigated topic in this area is the association between coping and risk for cancer, particularly breast cancer. Most scientists view the development of cancer as a multifactorial phenomenon involving the interaction of genetic, immunological, and environmental factors (see Levy, Herberman, Maluish, Schlien, & Lipman, 1985). The notion that psychological factors, particularly certain personality characteristics, contribute to the development of cancer, has been proposed by a number of behavioral scientists over the course of the past 30 years (e.g., Greer, Morris, & Pettingale, 1979). Strategies that individuals use to deal with stress, particularly the use of denial and repression when dealing with stressful life events, have been suggested as potential factors in the development of breast cancer (Anagnostopoulos et al., 1993; Goldstein & Antoni, 1989). Studies of women who are at-risk for breast cancer and women undergoing breast biopsy do not consistently report an association. Edwards et al. (1990) used the Ways of Coping Checklist and found no association between coping and breast cancer risk. Testing for an interaction effect, additional analyses revealed that coping did not modify the effect of life event stress on breast cancer risk, after adjusting for age and history of breast cancer. Some studies have reported counterintuitive findings. For example, Chen et al. found that women who confronted stress by working out a plan to deal with the problem were at higher risk of breast cancer, independent of life events, and adjusted for age, family history, menopausal status, personality, tobacco and alcohol use. This literature was recently subjected to a meta-analysis by McKenna and colleagues (McKenna, Zevon, Corn, & Rounds, 1999), who found a moderate effect size for denial and repressive coping style in an analysis of 17 studies. Breast cancer patients were more likely to respond to stressful life events by using repressive coping. However, such studies cannot prove causation. It is just as likely that having breast cancer may have resulted in changes in use of repressive coping. In addition, biological/immunological mechanisms to account for any association between repressive coping and the development of breast cancer have yet to be elucidated.

One study linked coping with outcomes of in vitro fertilization (IVF). Demyttenaere and colleagues (1998) examined the association between coping (active, palliative, avoidance, support seeking, depressive coping, expression of negative emotions, and comforting ideas) and the outcome of IVF. Women who had higher than median scores on a palliative coping measure had a significantly greater chance of conceiving than women who had a lower than median score on the palliative coping measure. While this is an extremely interesting finding, the underlying mechanisms were not discussed.

Disease Progression

One of the most studied areas of psychosocial factors in disease outcomes is the link between coping and HIV outcomes. The HIV to AIDS progression provides a model for studying the connection between psychological factors and immunological outcomes, as well as disease progression. The majority of studies have focused on some aspect of avoidant coping and have yielded contradictory results. Reed and colleagues (Reed, Kemeny, Taylor, Wang, & Visscher, 1994) found that realistic acceptance as a coping strategy (defined as focusing on accepting, preparing for, and ruminating about the future course of HIV infection) predicted decreased survival time among gay men who had clinical AIDS at study entry. This effect held after controlling for confounding variables such as CD4 cell counts, use of azidothymidine (AZT), and alcohol or substance abuse. These results are inconsistent with Ironson and colleagues (Ironson et al., 1994) who found that use of denial to cope with a newly learned HIV seropositive diagnosis and poorer adherence to behavioral interventions predicted lower CD4 counts one year later and a greater progression to clinical AIDS two years later. Solano et al. (1993) found that having a fighting spirit was related to less progression to HIV infection one year later, after controlling for baseline CD4 cell count. Mulder, de Vroome, van Griensven, Antoni, and Sanfort (1999) found that the degree to which men avoided problems in general was associated with less decline in CD4 cells and less progression to immonologically defined AIDS over a seven-year period. However, avoidance coping was not significantly associated with AIDS-defining clinical events (e.g., developing Kaposi's sarcoma). Contradictory findings have been reported by Leserman and colleagues (1999). They followed HIV-infected men for 7.5 years. Results indicated that men who used denial to cope with the threat of AIDS had faster disease progression. In fact, the risk of AIDS was approximately doubled for every 1.5 unit increase in denial. This relationship remained significant even after taking into account potential mediators such as age and number of biomedical and behavioral factors (e.g., smoking, use of marijuana, cocaine, and other drugs and having had unprotected intercourse). The inconsistency in findings across studies is difficult to explain. Because these studies are observational in nature, causal inferences cannot be made.

Findings from studies linking coping with cancer progression have also been contradictory. Early studies by Buddenberg and colleagues (1996) and Watson and Greer (1983) reported an association between coping style and outcome in early stage breast cancer. However, these early studies did not control for known prognostic indicators such as tumor stage, disease site, and mood. Brown and colleagues (Brown, Butow, Culjak, Coates, & Dunn, 2000) found that melanoma patients who did not use avoidance as a coping strategy experienced longer periods without relapse, after controlling for tumor thickness, disease site, metastatic status, and mood. A similar finding was reported by Epping-Jordan et al. (1999), who followed a group of cancer patients over a one-year period. Longitudinal findings revealed that, after controlling for initial disease parameters and age, avoidance predicted disease status one year later; however, neither psychological symptoms nor intrusive thoughts and emotions accounted for additional variance in disease outcomes.

Coping and Psychological Adaptation to Disease

Cross-Sectional Studies of Coping with Chronic Illness

Early studies of coping using the stress and coping paradigm were cross-sectional and used retrospective checklists such as the Ways of Coping Checklist (WOC). The earliest studies divided coping into the overly general categories of problem- and emotion-focused strategies, and focused mostly on psychological outcomes rather than pain and functional status outcomes.

Later studies have investigated specific types of coping. For example, Felton, Revenson, and Hinrichsen (1984) examined two types of coping, wish-fulfilling fantasy and information seeking, using a revision of the WOC. Wish-fulfilling fantasy was a more consistent predictor of psychological adjustment than information seeking. While information seeking was associated with higher levels of positive affect, its effects on negative affect were modest, accounting for only 4% of the variance. In a second study, Felton and Revenson (1984) examined coping of patients with arthritis, cancer, diabetes, and hypertension. Wish-fulfilling fantasy, emotional expression, and self-blame were associated with poorer adjustment, while threat minimization was associated with better adjustment. Scharloo and colleagues (1998) conducted a cross-sectional study of individuals with Chronic Obstructive Pulmonary Disease (COPD), RA, or psoriasis. Unlike the majority of studies, this study first entered illness-related variables such as time elapsed since diagnosis and the severity of the patient's medical condition into the equation predicting role and social functioning. Overall, coping was not strongly related to social and role functioning. Among patients with COPD, passive coping predicted poorer physical functioning. Among patients with RA, higher levels of passive coping predicted poorer social functioning.

Very few studies have examined coping with other chronic illnesses. Several studies have investigated the association between coping and distress among individuals with multiple sclerosis (MS). Pakenham, Stewart, and Rogers (1997) categorized coping as either emotion- or problem-focused, and found that emotion-focused coping was related to poorer adjustment, while problem-focused coping was associated with better adjustment. In contrast, Wineman and Durand (1994) found that emotion- and problem-focused coping were unrelated to distress. Mohr, Goodkin, Gatto, and Van Der Wende (1997) found that problem-solving and cognitive reframing strategies are associated with lower levels of depression, whereas avoidant strategies are associated with higher levels of depression.

As noted previously, most studies have used instructions that ask participants how they coped with the illness in general, rather than asking participants how they coped with specific stressors associated with the illness. Van Lankveld and colleagues (Van Lankveld, Van't Pad Bosch, Van De Putte, Naring, & Van Der Staak, 1994) assessed how patients cope with the most important stressors associated with arthritis. When coping with pain was considered, patients with similar degrees of pain who scored high on comforting cognitions and diverting attention scored higher on well-being, and decreased activity was associated with lower well-being. When coping with functional limitation was examined, patients who used pacing reported lower levels of well-being, and optimism was associated with higher well-being after functional capacity was controlled for in the equation. Finally, when coping with dependence was examined, only showing consideration was associated with higher well-being after functional capacity was controlled for in the equation.

Cross-Sectional Studies of Coping with Cancer

The earliest work was conducted by Weisman and Worden (1976–1977). In this study, patients were studied during the first 100 days after diagnosis. Positive reinterpretation was associated with less distress, and attempts to forget the cancer were associated with high distress. Unfortunately, this study did not evaluate the contribution of severity of disease. Dunkel-Schetter and colleagues (Dunkel-Schetter, Feinstein, Taylor, & Falke, 1992) administered the WOC Inventory, cancer specific version, to a sample of patients with varying types of cancer. Participants were asked to select a problem related to their cancer and rate coping responses to that

problem. Coping through social support, focusing on the positive, and distancing were associated with less emotional distress, whereas using cognitive and behavioral escape-avoidance was associated with more emotional distress. Although disease severity (e.g., stage) and demographic information were collected, these variables were not included in the analyses.

Manne, Alfieri, Taylor, and Dougherty (1994) also administered the WOC to women with early stage breast cancer. In this study, physical symptoms were controlled for in the analysis of associations between coping and positive and negative affect, as measured by the Profile of Mood States. Physical symptoms had a greater influence on relations between coping and negative affect than on coping and positive affect relations. Escape-avoidance coping and confrontive coping were associated with more negative affect, whereas distancing, positive appraisal, and self-controlling coping were all associated with more positive affect.

Epping-Jordan and colleagues (1999) evaluated the association between coping (assessed with the COPE) and anxiety and depressive symptoms among a sample of 80 women with all stages of breast cancer. Coping was evaluated as a mediator of the relation between optimism and distress. Optimism was predicted to predict less emotion-focused disengagement, which, in turn, predicted fewer symptoms of anxiety and depression. In addition, this study advanced the literature because cancer stage, patient age, and education were each incorporated into associations between coping and distress rather than simply partialled out of associations. In addition, cross-sectional associations at three separate points were conducted (at diagnosis, three months after diagnosis, and six months after diagnosis), which provided a picture of how coping changed over the course of treatment. At diagnosis, low optimism predicted more distress, and the relation between optimism and distress was mediated partially by emotion-focused disengagement.

Relatively few studies have evaluated coping among patients with advanced disease. Sherman, Simonton, Adams, Vural, and Hanna (2000) used the COPE to study coping by patients with late-stage cancers and found that denial, behavioral disengagement, and emotional ventilation were associated with higher distress as assessed by the Profile of Mood States.

Longitudinal Studies

Unfortunately, relatively few studies have employed longitudinal designs. Overall, passive coping strategies such as avoidance, wishful thinking, withdrawal, and self-blame have been shown to be associated with poorer psychological adjustment (e.g., Scharloo et al., 1999), and problem-focused coping efforts such as information seeking have been found to be associated with better adjustment among MS patients (e.g., Pakenham, 1999).

Two studies have used longitudinal designs to study the relation of coping to adaptation to cancer. Carver, Pozo, Harris, Noriega, Scheirer, and Robinson (1993) evaluated coping strategies used by early-stage breast cancer patients, evaluated at two time points, and found that cognitive and behavioral avoidance were detrimental to adjustment, whereas acceptance was associated with lower distress. Stanton, Danoff-Burg, Cameron, Bishop, and Collins (2000) examined emotionally expressive coping, defined as emotional processing (delving into feelings), and emotional expression (expressing emotions) among 92 women with early stage breast cancer. Women were assessed at two points, spaced three months apart. The findings revealed that coping through emotional expression was associated with decreased distress, even after accounting for the contribution of other coping strategies. In contrast, women who coped by using emotional processing became more distressed over time, but only when emotional expression was controlled for in the analysis. This finding suggests that active engagement in the attempt to talk about cancer-related feelings may be beneficial, but rumination may exacerbate distress.

Other Coping Processes: Social Comparison

Social comparison is a common but little-studied process in the context of its use among individuals dealing with a health problem. Stanton and colleagues (2000) evaluated the association between both upward and downward comparisons and affect among women with breast cancer by using an experimental manipulation. Patients listened to tapes of other breast cancer patients, which varied by level of disease prognosis and psychological adaptation. Descriptive data indicated that women extracted positive comparisons from both worse-off and better-off women, reporting gratitude in response to worse-off others and inspiration in response to better-off others. Negative affect increased and positive affect decreased after patients listened to audiotaped interviews with other patients. Those with better prognosis cancers had a greater decrement in positive mood. These findings suggest that social comparison, at least in the short term, may result in mood disruption.

Studies of Coping with Chronic Pain

The majority of these studies have used longitudinal designs. For example, Brown and Nicassio (1987) studied pain coping

strategies among RA patients and found that patients who engaged in more passive coping when experiencing more pain became more depressed six months later than did patients who engaged in these strategies less frequently. Keefe and colleagues (Keefe, Brown, Wallston, & Caldwell, 1989) conducted a six-month longitudinal study of the relationship between catastrophizing (negative thinking) and depression in RA patients. Those patients who reported high levels of catastrophizing had greater pain, disability, and depression six months later. Similar findings have been reported by other investigators (Parker et al., 1989). Overall, studies have suggested that self-blame, wishful thinking, praying, catastrophizing, and restricting activities are associated with more distress, while information seeking, cognitive restructuring, and active planning are associated with less distress.

Gil and colleagues (Gil, Abrams, Phillips, & Keefe, 1989; Gil, Abrams, Phillips, & Williams, 1992) have studied Sickle Cell Disease (SCD), which has not been given a great deal of attention by behavioral scientists. Pain is a frequent problem among SCD patients. Adults who used the cognitive coping strategy of catastrophizing reported more severe pain, less work and social activity, more health care use, and more depression and anxiety (Gil et al., 1989). SCD patients who coped with pain in an active fashion by using a variety of strategies such as distraction were more active in work and social activities. These associations were significant even after controlling for frequency of pain episodes, disease severity, and demographics. In their later studies, Gil and colleagues (Gil, Phillips, Edens, Martin, & Abrams, 1994) have incorporated laboratory methodologies to provide a better measure of pain reports.

Several recent studies have employed prospective daily study designs in which participants complete a 30-day diary for reporting each day's pain, mood, and pain coping strategies using the Daily Coping Inventory (Stone & Neale, 1984). These studies, which have been conducted with RA and OA (Osteoarthritis) patients, have shown that emotion-focused strategies, such as attempting to redefine pain to make it more bearable and expressing distressing emotions about the pain, predict increases in negative mood the day after the diary report. The daily design is a promising new method of evaluating the link between coping strategies and mood. More importantly, these studies can elucidate coping processes over time. For example, Tennen, Affleck, Armeli, and Carney (2000) found that the two functions of coping, problem- and emotion-focused, evolve in response to the outcome of the coping efforts. An increase in pain from one day to the next increased the likelihood that emotion-focused coping would follow problem-focused coping. It appeared that, when efforts to directly influence pain were not successful, participants tried to alter their cognitions rather than influence the pain.

Challenges to the Study of Coping with Chronic Illness

Recently, the general literature on coping has received a great deal of criticism from researchers (e.g., Coyne & Racioppo, 2000). The main concern voiced in reviews regards the gap between the elegant, process-oriented stress and coping theory and the inelegant, retrospective methodologies that have been used to evaluate the theory. Although the theory postulates causal relations among stress, coping, and adaptation, the correlational nature of most empirical work has been unsuitable to test causal relations. In addition, retrospective methods require people to recall how they coped with an experience, and thus are likely to be influenced by both systematic and nonsystematic sources of recall error. Coping efforts, as well as psychological outcomes such as distress, are best measured close to when they occur. Recent studies have used an approach that addresses these concerns. These studies have employed a microanalytic, process-oriented approach using daily diary assessments (e.g., Affleck et al., 1999). These time-intensive study designs allow for the tracking of changes in coping and distress close to their real time occurrence and moments of change, are less subject to recall error, and capture coping processes as they unfold over time. The daily assessment approach can also evaluate how coping changes as the individual learns more about what coping responses are effective in reducing distress and/or altering the stressor. These advances may help investigators determine whether the methods used to cope with stressors encountered in the day-to-day experience of living with a chronic disease predict long-term adaptation. Unfortunately, this approach has been used only among individuals with arthritis and has not been applied to individuals dealing with other chronic illnesses.

Another key problem with coping checklists that has been noted in a number of reviews of the coping with chronic illness literature is the instructional format. The typical instructions used (e.g., "How do you cope with RA?") are so general that it is not clear what aspect of the stressor the participant is referring to when answering questions. Thus, the source of the stress may differ across participants. There are problems even when the participant is allowed to define the stressor prior to rating the coping strategies used. The self-defined stressor may differ across participants, and thus the analyses will be conducted with different stressors being rated.

A third assessment problem is the definition of coping. While Lazarus and Folkman (1984) regard only effortful, conscious strategies as coping, other investigators have argued that less effortful, more automatic coping methods also fall under the definition of coping (Wills, 1997). Indeed, some coping responses would not necessarily be seen by the individual as choices, but rather automatic responses to stressful events. For example, wishful thinking or other types of avoidant types of coping such as sleeping or alcohol use may be categorized by researchers as a coping strategy, but not categorized as such by the individual completing the questionnaire because the individual did not engage in this as an effortful coping strategy. A related and interesting issue regards the categorization of unconscious defense mechanisms. Cramer (2000), in a recent review of defense mechanisms, distinguishes between defenses that are not conscious and unintentional and coping processes that are conscious and intentional. However, there has been an interest in repressive coping, suggesting that some researchers regard defensive strategies such as denial and repression under the rubric of coping. More clarity and consistency between investigators in the definition of coping, particularly when unintentional strategies are being evaluated, would provide more clarity for research.

A fourth assessment issue is the distinction between *problem-focused* and *emotion-focused* coping efforts. While researchers may categorize a particular coping strategy as problem-focused coping, the participant's intention may not be to alter the situation, but rather to manage an emotional reaction. For example, people may seek information about an illness as a way of coping with anxiety and altering their appraisal of a situation, rather than to engineer a change in the situation. The lack of an association between emotion-focused coping and psychological outcomes may, in part, be due to a categorization strategy that does not account for the intention of the coping. Studies using these two categories to distinguish coping dimensions may help to evaluate coping intention.

A number of additional methodological and conceptual challenges are specifically relevant to studies of coping with illness and health threats. First, relatively few studies control for disease severity in statistical analyses. Extreme pain or disability can result in both more coping attempts and more distress. Studies that do not take these variables into account may conclude mistakenly that more coping is associated with more distress. In addition, little attention has been paid to the effects of progressive impairment on the selection of coping strategies, and in the perceived effectiveness of those strategies. Chronic progressive illnesses may be expected to increase feelings of hopelessness. For example, Revenson and Felton (1989) studied changes in coping and adjustment over a six-month period and found that increases in disability were accompanied by less acceptance, more wishful thinking, and greater negative affect.

Another issue is the lack of longitudinal studies, which would help the literature in a number of ways. First, this type of design might help clarify whether coping influences distress or whether coping is merely a symptom of distress, a criticism frequently raised in critiques of coping (e.g., Coyne & Racioppo, 2000). Second, longitudinal studies may clarify the role of personality factors in coping (Zautra & Manne, 1992). While some investigators suggest that personality factors play a limited role in predicting coping, other investigators argue that coping is a personality process that reflects dispositional differences during stressful events.

Although the lack of progress in the area of coping is frequently attributed to methods of assessment and design, the relatively narrow focus on distress outcomes may also account for some of the problem, particularly when coping with chronic illness is being evaluated. Chronic illness does not ultimately lead to psychological distress for the majority of patients. Indeed, many individuals report psychological growth in the face of chronic illness, and they are able to find personal significance in terms of changes in views of themselves, their relationships with others, and their philosophy of life (Tennen, Affleck, Urrows, Higgins, & Mendola, 1992). While positive affect is included as an adaptational outcome in some studies (e.g., Bendtsen & Hornquist, 1991), the majority of studies do not include positive outcomes. Positive affect is a particularly important outcome to evaluate when positive coping processes such as cognitive reappraisal and finding meaning in the experience are examined, as these types of coping may play a stronger role in generating and maintaining positive mood than in lowering negative mood.

Relatively few studies have focused solely on coping and distress, ignoring potential moderators such as level of pain, appraisals of controllability, gender, and personality. A careful evaluation of potential moderators will provide both researchers and clinicians with information about the most effective coping strategies.

Conclusions and Directions for Future Research

As Richard Lazarus points out in his commentary in *American Psychologist,* "A premise that occurs again and again . . . is that for quite a few years research has disappointed many who had high hopes it would achieve both fundamental and practical knowledge about the coping process and its adaptational consequences. I am now heartened by positive signs that there is a growing number of sophisticated, resourceful and vigorous researchers who are dedicated to the study of coping" (Lazarus, 2000). It is clear that, despite the multiple methodological problems this area of research has faced, a heightened awareness of these limitations has led to the application of sophisticated methods that might help fulfill the high hopes for this research. If investigators in the field of coping with illnesses can adapt daily diary methods to their populations, focus on specific stressors related to the illness when instructing participants to answer coping questions, include coping appraisals and the perceived efficacy of coping efforts, and carefully delineate illness-related, contextual and dispositional moderators, the findings may lead to the development of effective interventions for clinicians hoping to improve the quality of life for these individuals.

SOCIAL SUPPORT

Introduction

The role of social support in adaptation to illness and in health outcomes is one of the most studied topics in health psychology. Social relationships have been posited to influence the maintenance of health and well-being by scientists and practitioners in both behavioral science and medical disciplines. A comprehensive review of all of the studies of the role of social relationships in health is beyond the scope of this chapter. Comprehensive reviews of specific topics such as the role of social relationships and cancer can be found in other sources (e.g., Berkman, Vaccarino, & Seeman, 1993; Helgeson, Cohen, Schulz, & Yasko, 1999). In this chapter, we review key definitions of social support and health and empirical studies linking social relationships with a variety of health outcomes.

Social Support Definitions

Paper-and-pencil, interview, and observational methods have been used to measure social support. Measurement methods are guided by the perspectives taken on understanding support mechanisms, as different types of support are hypothesized to exert their effects in different ways. The most common distinctions made in social support measurement are the distinctions between perceived support, received support, and social integration (Cassel, 1976; Cobb, 1976; Weiss, 1974). *Perceived support,* which is actually more of an appraisal than an actual support-related interaction, is the perception that specific types of social support would be available if needed. The proposed mechanism for perceived support is protection of the individual by altering his or her interpretation of the threat or harm posed by situations (Cohen & McKay, 1984). *Received support* is defined as actual supportive behaviors. The majority of investigators studying received support hypothesize that it exerts a beneficial effect because it promotes adaptive coping (Cutrona & Russell, 1990). A third method of measuring support, *social integration,* asks the individual to report how many different roles he or she has or the degree to which the individual is active in different activities (e.g., church). The proposed mechanism for this type of support is that a person who has a greater number of roles or is more active in social activities has a more differentiated identity and that stressful events in one area of life, or one role function, would be less likely to impact the individual because fewer roles and areas of life are disrupted.

Both perceived and received support have been measured by assessing the degree to which others would provide perceived support or actually provide (received support) the basic functions of social support. The key support dimensions have varied from theorist to theorist (see House, 1981; Weiss, 1974), but the majority of theories have incorporated emotional, instrumental, informational, companionship, and validation support (Argyle, 1992; House, 1981). The multidimensional nature of support measures provides a powerful tool because researchers can investigate the degree to which different functions of support are helpful for dealing with different types of stressors.

Social Support and Health Outcomes

Cardiovascular Function

The majority of studies examining the role of social support in physiological processes have focused on aspects of cardiovascular function. One reason investigators are interested in this area of research is that increased cardiovascular reactivity has been linked to the development of cardiovascular disease. Increased sympathetic nervous system (SNS) responses have been associated with a number of pathophysiological processes that may lead to coronary heart disease (see Rozanski, Blumenthal, & Kaplan, 1999). Differences between individuals in terms of their cardiovascular reactivity to stressors are assumed to be markers of increased SNS responsivity, as studies have shown that individuals who have increased reactivity to mental stress are at higher risk for hypertension (e.g., Menkes et al., 1989), arteriosclerosis (Barnett, Spence, Manuck, & Jennings, 1997), and recurrent heart attacks (Manuck, Olsson, Hjemdahl, & Rehnqvist, 1992).

A review of the more than 25 studies evaluating the association between social support and social context (e.g., marital status) and cardiovascular function is beyond the scope of this chapter (see Uchino, Cacioppo, & Kiecolt-Glaser, 1996, for a review of this topic). Overall, the majority of the studies examining the association between support and cardiovascular function indicate that social support is associated with lower blood pressure, lower systolic blood

pressure (SBP), and lower diastolic blood pressure (DBP) (e.g., Hanson, Isacsson, Janzon, Lindell, & Rastam, 1988; Janes, 1990). A small subset of studies reported no relationship between social support and cardiovascular function (e.g., Lercher, Hortnagl, & Kofler, 1993), and one study reported that social support was associated with poorer cardiovascular function (Hansell, 1985). Uchino and colleagues (1996) conducted a metaanalysis on the studies reporting a correlation between blood pressure and social support and found a small but reliable effect size across studies. Several studies have reported gender differences. Social resources are a stronger predictor of blood pressure among men, and instrumental support is a stronger predictor of blood pressure in women (see Uchino and colleagues, 1996, for a review of this topic).

Over the course of the past 10 years, researchers have begun to use laboratory studies to examine the ways that social support can influence cardiovascular reactivity. The underlying hypothesis of these studies is that higher reactivity to stressors may be one mechanism whereby cardiovascular disease develops (see Manuck, 1994, for a review of this topic). Researchers working in a laboratory setting have used two basic ways to investigate whether social support can reduce reactivity. One approach, labeled the "passive" support paradigm by Lepore (1998), compares the cardiovascular responses of a person exposed to a stressor when alone to the responses when another person is present. A second approach, labeled the "active" support paradigm by Lepore (1998), examines the effect of having another person provide different types and levels of support. Some experiments combine both types of manipulations or compare the effects of the provision of supportive feedback versus nonsupportive or evaluative feedback. One early study by Kamarck, Manuck, and Jennings (1990) compared cardiovascular reactivity during two tasks. Half of the subjects completed the tasks without social support, and half of the subjects brought a friend who provided support by touching the subject on the wrist during the task. Results indicated a significant reduction in cardiovascular response when the friend was present. Edens, Larkin, and Abel (1992) found that, during a mental arithmetic task, the presence of a friend resulted in lower heart rate (HR), SBP, and DBP than when a friend was not present during the task. A second study evaluated the potential buffering effects of social support in stress reactivity among women under conditions of high or low social threat (i.e., punitive consequences). Kamarck, Annunziato, and Amaateau (1995) found that, under conditions of low stress, the availability of social support made no difference in heart rate or blood pressure. Under conditions of high stress, the same social support reduced cardiovascular response. Similar findings have been reported by others (Gerin, Milnor, Chawla, & Pickering, 1995; Lepore, Allen, & Evans, 1993; Christenfeld et al., 1997; Gerin, Pieper, Levy, & Pickering, 1992).

Several studies have evaluated whether individual difference factors such as cynical hostility moderate the effects of social support on cardiovascular reactivity. For example, Lepore (1995) found that subjects with high scores on cynical hostility did not have lowered cardiovascular activity when provided with social support, whereas those subjects with lower scores on cynical hostility did derive benefit from social support.

Because correlational studies are limited in terms of causal inferences that can be made, intervention studies that manipulate social support may provide more insight into the relation between social support and cardiovascular function. Only a small number of studies manipulate social support. Overall, these studies found that social support interventions result in reduced blood pressure when the participants underwent a stressor challenge assessment postintervention. For example, Sallis, Grossman, Pinski, Patterson, and Nader (1987) randomly enrolled participants in a support education group (support group), relaxation training, or a multicomponent stress management intervention, and intervention or a control group. Results indicated that support education and relaxation training intervention resulted in smaller increases in DBP from preintervention to follow-up, and lower DBP levels during recovery from a cold pressure stress test, compared with the multicomponent stress management intervention. Among individuals at higher cardiovascular risk (hypertensives), studies have consistently shown that interventions focusing on increasing positive support, particularly support provided by family, result not only in short-term decreases in DBP, but also in long-term effects on blood pressure regulation (Levine et al., 1979). Indeed, a recent meta-analysis of these intervention studies suggests that social support manipulations can assist in the reduction of blood pressure (Uchino et al., 1996).

Several studies have examined the link between social support and cholesterol. Welin and colleagues (Welin, Rosengren, & Wilhelmsen, 1996) found that low serum cholesterol was associated with low social support in a study of middle-aged men. This association was also found in a study of healthy women, even after controlling for the effects of other psychosocial factors including depression and recent life events, and lifestyle factors (smoking, alcohol, obesity) (Horsten, Wamala, Vingerhoets, & Orth-Gomer, 1997). These findings are interesting from a clinical perspective, as low lipid levels have been associated with increased mortality from violent causes (Muldoon et al., 1993).

Endocrine Function

The most commonly studied endocrine measures are the catecholamines (e.g., norepinephrine [NE] and epinephrine [EPI]) and cortisol. Studies evaluating endocrine function are important because of its association with the cardiovascular and immune systems. Catecholamines play an important role in cardiovascular regulation functions such as constriction of arterial blood vessels. The association between endocrine function and social support has not been well documented. The majority of these studies have found an association between social support and catecholamine levels (e.g., Seeman, Berkman, Blazer, & Rowe, 1994; Fleming, Baum, Gisriel, & Gatchel, 1982). For example, Ely and Mostardi (1986) studied 331 men and found that high social support, defined as social resources and marital status, was associated with lower NE than low social support. However, studies of cortisol and support suggest that increasing social contact does not influence cortisol levels. One study examined the association between support from a stranger or partner and cortisol reactivity during acute psychological stress (Kirschbaum, Klauer, Filipp, & Hellhammer, 1995). The results indicated that men who received support from their partners evidenced lower cortisol levels than men who received stranger support or no support. However, women evidenced a trend toward greater cortisol response during the partner-supported conditions compared with the other two conditions. Overall, the link between social support and endocrine function has not been very consistently confirmed.

Immune Function

Studies linking social support to immune function indices suggest that higher social support is associated with better immune system function. Levy and colleagues (1990) examined the association between perceived emotional support from spouse, family member, friends, doctors, and nurses and the immune system function in women with breast cancer. The results indicated that emotional support from spouse and physician was associated with greater natural killer cell activity (NKCA). Some studies have controlled for the influence of other psychological factors, such as mood and stressful life events, that could contribute to the association between support and immune function. Baron and colleagues (Baron, Cutrona, Hicklin, Russell, & Lubaroff, 1990) evaluated the association between perceived support and immune indexes among spouses of cancer patients and found that all aspects of support were related to phytoheammagluttinin (PHA) and NKCA, even after controlling for life events and depression. Kiecolt-Glaser, Dura, and Speicher (1991) conducted a prospective longitudinal study of caregivers to individuals with Alzheimer's disease. Caregivers were assessed twice in a one-year time period. Both positive and unhelpful support were assessed. Results indicated a buffering effect for social support; caregivers low in positive support evidenced greater negative changes in immune response (Con A, PHA, and EBV) after controlling for age, income, and depression. Similar findings among caregivers were reported by Esterling and colleagues (Esterling, Kiecolt-Glaser, Bodnar, & Glaser, 1994). Persson and colleagues (Persson, Gullberg, Hanson, Moestrup, & Ostergren, 1994) reported that low social participation, low satisfaction with social participation, and low emotional support were associated with CD4+ counts compared with HIV-positive men without AIDS who scored high on these social support measures. The associations were stronger when age and length of time since treatment were taken into account. Studies of older populations have consistently found an association between support and immunity (e.g., Seeman et al., 1994; Thomas, Goodwin, & Goodwin, 1985). Finally, Ward and colleagues (1999) found an association between perceived adequacy of social support and immune parameters associated with systemic lupus erythmetosus activity (SLE). Greater SLE activity was associated with less adequate social support. However, several studies have not found an association between social support and immunological outcomes (Arnetz et al., 1987; Kiecolt-Glaser et al., 1985; Perry, Fishman, Jacobsberg, & Frances, 1992).

Social Support and Disease Recovery

Cardiac disease is the most studied disease when the role of social support is being considered. There is evidence that social support influences recovery from cardiac events. Ostergren et al. (1991) found that practical support predicted improvement in physical working capacity among a small group of 40 persons admitted with first-time myocardial infarction (MI). Yates (1995) interviewed a mixed group of patients post-MI, coronary artery bypass grafting, and/or coronary artery angioplasty. Emotional information provided during the recovery from spouse and health care provider, along with perceived physical recovery were evaluated. Results indicated that greater satisfaction with health care provider support was associated with 1-year perceived physical recovery. This study is limited because self-reported physical health was measured using a single item perceived health measure, which is quite subjective.

Hamalainen and colleagues (2000) reported a small association between support factors (defined as formal services), semi-formal assistance, and informal social support (network size, frequency of contacts, availability, and reciprocity in

relationships) and either functional capacity or working capacity (defined using a bicycle ergometer test as well as functional limitations) among 147 MI and 159 coronary artery bypass patients. High functional capacity at one year was associated with less assistance and emotional support in both patient groups. It is difficult to infer causality from these findings, as the need for assistance may be driven by poor functional capacity. However, the authors also suggest that it is possible that supportive family members may actually lead to poorer health outcomes because family members overprotect the patient during the recovery by reinforcing unhealthy sedentary behaviors.

Social support has also been investigated as a factor predicting readmissions among patients with ischemic heart disease (MI, unstable angina, stable angina). Stewart, Hirth, Klassen, Makrides, and Wolf (1997) did not find significant differences in total social support or support from different network sources that predicted readmission among patients with a history of multiple admissions.

Disease Progression and Mortality

AIDS

A relatively large literature evaluates the association between social support and human immunodeficiency virus (HIV) progression in gay and bisexual men. Theorell and colleagues (1995) evaluated the association between perceived support and CD4 T-lymphocyte levels in HIV-infected hemophiliacs, and found that lower perceived support was associated with greater declines in CD4 levels over a five-year period. Patterson and colleagues (1996) followed a large group of HIV-positive men over a five-year period, using measures of CD4+ counts, symptomatology, AIDS diagnosis, and mortality as outcome variables. Social support was assessed as received informational and emotional support, as well as network size (number of social contacts). Results indicated that a larger network size was actually associated with a shorter symptom-free period among individuals who were symptom free at baseline. After controlling for this interaction, higher ratings of informational support predicted a longer time until the onset of an AIDS-defining opportunistic infection. After controlling for depressive symptoms, the size of the social network was a predictor of mortality among individuals with symptoms at baseline. Individuals with 15 persons in their network had an 84% chance of remaining alive after 48 months, while those who listed only two people had a 44% chance. Among participants that were symptomatic at baseline, higher ratings of informational support predicted a longer survival time after controlling for depressive symptoms and network size. Overall, support played a mixed role in predicting HIV disease progression. Among participants with more advanced symptoms at baseline, longevity was positively associated with network size and informational support. Among participants with asymptomatic disease status at baseline, a large network size predicted more immediate onset of symptoms. The authors suggest that the negative influence of network size may be related to the stress of disclosure of HIV status to others or to poor health habits. Miller, Kemeny, Taylor, Cole, and Visscher (1997) conducted a three-year longitudinal study measuring the association between social integration (defined as the number of close friends), the number of family members, and the number of groups or organizations to which the participant belonged, and HIV progression (immune parameters, AIDS diagnosis, death from AIDS). Contrary to other studies, they did not find an association between social support and HIV progression.

Leserman and colleagues (1999) followed a cohort of 82 HIV-infected men without symptoms of AIDS every six months for 5.5 years. Satisfaction with social support was evaluated, as well as the number of support persons. AIDS progression was defined as the point at which the person met Center for Disease Control (CDC) AIDS surveillance case definition. Some confounding factors (age, education, race, baseline helper cells, tobacco use, and number of retroviral medications) were controlled in the analysis. For each point decrease in cumulative support satisfaction, the risk of AIDS progression increased by 2.7 times. Number of social support persons was not related to AIDS progression. Thornton and colleagues (2000) studied long-term HIV-1 infected gay men. Perceived support was measured using the Interpersonal Support Evaluation List (ISEL), and participants were followed for up to 30 months. Survival analyses indicated that social support was not related to a transition to AIDS-related complex (ARC) or AIDS.

In summary, studies linking social support to HIV progression to AIDS have shown mixed results. Social support may have a protective effect among individuals with more advanced symptoms, although findings have been inconsistent. Mechanisms for social support, including health behaviors and medical adherence, also need further study. A potential mechanism may be adherence to medical appointments. For example, Catz and colleagues (1999) found greater outpatient appointment adherence among patients with more perceived social support.

Coronary Disease

Social isolation, defined as having inadequate social support or social contact, has been implicated in decreased survival time following a myocardial infarction (MI). Studies have suggested that a lack of support places patients at increased risk for cardiac mortality after an MI (Berkman, Leo-Summers, & Horwitz, 1992; Case, 1992; Ruberman, Weinblatt, Goldberg, & Chaudhary, 1984; Welin, Lappas, & Wilhelmsen, 2000). Further evidence sustaining the link between support and cardiac mortality has been provided by interventions that provide emotional support and stress reduction. These studies have been shown to result in reduced incidence of MI recurrence over a seven-year follow-up period (Frasure-Smith & Prince, 1985).

However, a secondary analysis of data from Frasure-Smith's Canadian Signal-Averaged ECG Trial indicated that neither living alone, having close friends, nor perceived social support were significantly related to cardiac events, acute coronary syndrome recurrences, or arrhythmic events (Frasure-Smith, Lesperace, & Talajec, 1995). The authors explain the lack of a negative finding by proposing that their inclusion of a measure of negative emotions (e.g., depressive and anxiety symptoms) had a stronger relation with cardiac events, and may have accounted for much of the association between social support and cardiac events. A later study by the same team evaluated a potential moderating effect for social support on the consistent association between depressive symptoms and cardiac mortality (Frasure-Smith et al., 2000). In this study, social support was not associated with cardiac mortality. However, the interaction between depression and perceived support indicated that among patients with very low and moderate levels of perceived support, the impact of depression on a one-year prognosis was significant. For patients in the highest quartile of perceived social support, there was no depression-related increase in cardiac mortality. Further analyses evaluated whether the buffering effect of perceived support was produced by reducing depressive symptoms over time. Results supported this hypothesis: Among one-year survivors who had been depressed at baseline, higher baseline social support predicted improvements in depressive symptoms over the one-year post-MI follow-up period. Future studies should more carefully control for potential covariates as well as elucidate potential mechanisms for support's impact on prognosis after MI. Orth-Gomer and Unden (1990) have found a second potential factor that, combined with social isolation, predicts mortality among men post-MI. In their study, the combined effects of lack of social ties and the coronary-prone behavior pattern were a better predictor of mortality than social isolation alone, explaining almost 70% of the mortality.

One study has linked social support with the incidence of and death from coronary artery disease among general populations of individuals who were not previously diagnosed with coronary artery disease. Orth-Gomer, Rosengren, and Wilhelmsen (1993) measured emotional support from close relationships (labeled attachment) and social support by an extended network (labeled social integration) in a randomly selected sample of 50-year-old men in Sweden. The men were followed for six years. Both attachment and social integration were lower in men who contracted coronary artery disease, and the associations remained significant after controlling for other risk factors.

Pulmonary Disease

One study has examined the role of social support in pulmonary disease. Grodner and colleagues (1996) studied both satisfaction with support and the number of persons in the support network as predictors of forced expiratory volume (FEV), maximum oxygen uptake during a treadmill test, exercise endurance, perceived breathlessness, and perceived fatigue. Participants were enrolled in a rehabilitation program. The association of baseline social support with six-year mortality was also assessed. Results indicated that the number of network members was predictive or there was improvement in perceived breathlessness after the rehabilitation, but support satisfaction was not associated with indices of improvement. There was a difference between males and females in the association between support satisfaction and survival. For males, there was no difference in survival between the low and high social support groups. For females, survival for subjects with high social support was significantly better than for those with low social support. This study provides preliminary evidence to suggest that social support may promote morbidity and mortality among COPD patients. However, it would be helpful to understand how social support networks influence outcomes for patients with COPD. As with coronary artery disease and AIDS outcomes, affective factors such as depressive symptoms, health behaviors including nutrition and adherence to medical and rehabilitation regimens, and potential physiological components to social support and social isolation are potential mechanisms that should be investigated.

Arthritis

One very interesting study has linked marital status with progression of functional disability in patients with RA. A large cohort of 282 RA patients was followed for up to 9.5 years. Progression of RA was determined using the Health Assessment Questionnaire Index completed every six months. Over time the progression rate of disability was higher among the 94 unmarried participants, even after adjusting for socio-demographic factors. Although mechanisms for this slower progression are not determined in this study, it is possible that better nutrition, adherence to medical regimen, engagement

in correct types of physical activity, as well the instrumental assistance and emotional support may influence both disease progression and immunologic parameters contributing to RA progression. Since marital status is not the most accurate index of social support, future studies should measure support using other indicators.

Other Diseases

Relatively few studies have evaluated the link between social support and disease outcomes other than HIV, AIDS, and cardiac events. Social support has been studied in the context of end-stage renal disease (ESRD). Burton, Kline, Lindsay, and Heidenheim (1988) followed a group of 351 ESRD patients for 17 months. Perceived social support was not associated with mortality or with inability to perform home dialysis (versus returning to the clinic for dialysis).

Social Support and Psychological Outcomes

Social support has been one of the most studied predictors of psychological adaptation to health problems, particularly disabling medical problems such as arthritis or life-threatening health problems such as cancer. Studies evaluating support's role in several key diseases will be reviewed next.

Cancer

Measurement of Support

Much of the early literature on social support and psychological adaptation among individuals with cancer focused on understanding what types of responses were perceived as helpful, and what responses were perceived as unhelpful. Excellent theoretical and descriptive work was conducted by Wortman and Dunkel-Schetter (1979, 1987) and Dunkel-Schetter (1984), and later work by Dakof and Taylor (1990) and Gurowka and Lightman (1995) attempted to delineate both supportive and unsupportive responses. Dakof and Taylor (1990) categorized types of social support into three main categories: esteem/emotional support, informational support, and tangible support. Unhelpful responses were not categorized. The authors described nine unhelpful actions by others: criticisms of the patients' response to cancer, minimization of the impact of cancer on the patient, expressions of too much worry or pessimism, expressions of too little concern or empathy, avoiding social contact with the patient, rudeness, provision of incompetent medical care, acting as a poor role model, and provision of insufficient information. A recent study by Manne and Schnoll (2001) used exploratory and confirmatory factor analyzes to examine the psychometric properties of the Partner Responses to Cancer Inventory (PRCI). This inventory contained both spouse positive and negative responses, and behaviors by others that specifically encouraged particular coping efforts. Four factors emerged: emotional and instrumental support, cognitive information and guidance, encouraging distancing and self-restraint, and criticism and withdrawal.

Levels of Support

Bloom and Kessler (1994) compared perceived emotional support by patients with early stage breast cancer, patients undergoing surgery for gallbladder disease, biopsy for benign breast disease, or women who did not undergo surgery. Perceived emotional support was rated at three time points after surgery. Results indicated that, in contrast to the authors' hypothesis that breast cancer patients would experience less emotional support over time than women undergoing other types of surgery, breast cancer patients perceived more emotional support during the three months after surgery. Neuling and Winefield (1988) followed early stage breast cancer patients at the time of surgery, one month postsurgery, and three months postsurgery. Women rated the frequency of, and satisfaction with, supportive behaviors from family members, close friends, and surgeons. Empathic support and reassurance from family members and friends decreased over time, as did empathic support from the surgeon. Informational and tangible support increased over the first month postsurgery, and then decreased.

Support and Psychological Adaptation

The majority of studies investigating the role of social support in adaptation to cancer have been cross-sectional, many studies have had relatively small sample sizes. Perceived social support has been investigated in several studies, and results have been inconsistent. Ord-Lawson and Fitch (1997) investigated the relation between perceived social support, as measured by the Medical Outcomes Study social support survey and the Importance of Social Support Questionnaire (developed by the authors), and mood of 30 men diagnosed with testicular cancer within the past two months. Results indicated that there was no significant relationship between social support and mood. Komproe, Rijken, Winnubst, Ros, and Hart (1997) found that perceived available support, as rated by women who recently underwent surgery for breast cancer (84% early stage cancer), was associated with lower levels of depressive symptoms. Budin (1998) studied unmarried early stage breast cancer patients using a cross-sectional design,

and found that, after accounting for symptom distress and treatment (e.g., lumpectomy or radical mastectomy), perceived support accounted for a significant, but small (2%) variance in distress. Two prospective studies have found postsurgical perceived support from family members to be related to less distress at later time points, among women with breast cancer (Hoskins et al., 1996; Northouse, 1988). However, neither study adjusted for initial levels of psychological distress, which would have clarified whether or not perceived support predicted changes in distress. Alferi, Carver, Antoni, Weiss, and Duran (2000) examined cancer-specific distress (intrusive thoughts and avoidance symptoms) and psychological distress among 51 Hispanic women being treated for early stage breast cancer. Women were evaluated presurgery, postsurgery, and at 3-, 6-, and 12-month follow-ups. Emotional support from friends and instrumental support from the spouse at presurgery predicted lower distress postsurgery. No other prospective benefits of perceived support on distress emerged. This study evaluated the impact of distress on subsequent support from spouse, friends, and family. Distress at several time points predicted erosion of instrumental support from women in the family. Similar findings were reported by Bolger, Foster, Vinokur, and Ng (1996) in a sample of breast cancer patients followed up to 10 months postdiagnosis.

Several studies have evaluated the associations between received or enacted support and psychological adaptation among cancer patients. De Ruiter, de Haes, and Tempelaar (1993) examined the relationship between the number of positive social interactions and psychological distress among a group of cancer patients who were either in treatment or completed treatment. In this cross-sectional study, positive support was associated with distress only among patients who had completed treatment. A second cross-sectional study by Manne and colleagues (Manne, Taylor, Dougherty, & Kemeny, 1997) investigated the potential moderating role of functional impairment and gender on the relationship between spouse support and psychological distress. Spouse support was associated with lower levels of distress and higher levels of well-being for female patients, but was not associated with distress or well-being among male patients. Spouse support was associated with lower psychological distress among patients with low levels of functional impairment, whereas spouse support was not significantly associated with distress among patients with high levels of functional impairment. Similar associations were reported by Dunkel-Schetter (1984). These results suggest that the reason that the association between support and distress has not consistently been found is because support's impact may depend on contextual or demographic variables such as gender and physical disability. One of the few studies focusing on patients with late stage disease was recently conducted by Butler, Koopman, Classen, and Spiegel (1999), who studied a relatively large group of metastatic breast cancer patients. This cross-sectional study suggested that avoidance was associated with smaller emotional support networks. Unfortunately, the methodology would not allow for evaluation of causality; it is possible that patient avoidant symptoms lead them to avoid others and thus lead to a smaller group of people providing emotional support.

AIDS

Social support has been evaluated as a key determinant of psychological adaptation among individuals dealing with the myriad of both medical and social stresses associated with HIV and AIDS. In addition, the stigma associated with this disease places patients at high risk for social isolation. Friends and family members may experience helplessness or fear in response to the AIDS diagnosis, and therefore may have problems providing support (Siegel, Raveis, & Karus, 1997). Many of the early studies used cross-sectional methodologies. These studies suggested that perceived availability of support is associated with psychological distress in persons with AIDS (e.g., Hays, Chauncey, & Tobey, 1990) and in persons with asymptomatic HIV (Blaney et al., 1990; Grassi, Caloro, Zamorani, & Ramelli, 1997), and several studies found that the number of members of the support network and the satisfaction with support were associated with depressive symptoms (Ingram, Jones, Fass, Neidig, & Song, 1999). Similar findings were reported in longitudinal studies (Hays, Turner, & Coates, 1992; Nott, Vedhara, & Power, 1995). Swindells and colleagues (1999) followed 138 patients with HIV over a six-month period of time. Less satisfaction with social support at baseline was predictive of a decline in quality of life.

Studies have also investigated the possibility that different types of support are associated with distress. Satisfaction with informational support appears to be the strongest correlate of distress in persons with symptomatic HIV (Hays et al., 1990). However, this type of support is a less strong correlate of distress in persons with asymptomatic HIV (Hays et al., 1992). Studies examining potential buffering effects of social support, using both cross-sectional (Pakenham, Dadds, & Terry, 1994) and longitudinal (Siegel et al., 1997) designs, did not find evidence supporting a buffering effect of social support.

Arthritis

Rheumatoid arthritis (RA) is a chronic, unpredictable, and progressive inflammatory disease affecting primarily the joints. Osteoarthritis is a similar chronic disease that is painful, but typically less disabling and progressive in nature. Both diseases have numerous physical consequences, including pain and severe physical disability that can result in significant social and psychological impact. It is perhaps because of the chronic and disabling nature of RA that the findings regarding the role of both perceived and received social support have been consistent. Studies using measures of both perceived available support and support received (e.g., Doeglas et al., 1994), structural (e.g., Pennix et al., 1997), qualitative (e.g., Affleck, Pfeiffer, Tennen, & Fifield, 1988; Revenson, Schiaffino, Majerovitz, & Gibovsky, 1991), and quantitative (e.g., Evers, Kraaimaat, Geenen, & Bijlsma, 1997; Nicassio, Brown, Wallston, & Szydlo, 1985; Pennix et al., 1997) measures have all shown associations. Although the majority of studies have employed cross-sectional designs, several studies using longitudinal designs have also reported associations between social support and psychological distress (e.g, Evers et al., 1997).

Brown, Wallston, and Nicassio (1989) examined the longitudinal association between social support and depression and whether social support had a moderational role in the relation between arthritis-related pain and depressive symptoms in a group of 233 RA patients followed over a one-year period. The quality and number of social ties were assessed. There was no significant association between the number of close friends and relatives and depression. However, the quality of emotional support predicted later depression even after controlling for the effects of demographics, pain, and disability factors. A moderating effect for social support was not found.

Mechanisms for Social Support's Effects on Well-Being

Social support is likely to have both direct and indirect effects on psychological outcomes. There have been a number of discussions of how support may impact psychological outcomes. One potential mechanism is that advice and guidance from others may alter the threatening appraisal of a difficult situation to a more benign appraisal of a situation. For example, a breast cancer patient who is facing mastectomy may see the surgery as a threat to her body image; however, if her husband suggests that reconstructive surgery will restore her body to close to what it was prior to the surgery, her appraisal of the situation as threatening may lessen. Second, social support can function as a coping assistant; that is, supportive others may provide help in identifying adaptive coping strategies and assistance in using these strategies (Thoits, 1985). Studies of individuals with arthritis (Manne & Zautra, 1989) and cancer (Manne, Pape, Taylor, & Dougherty, 1999) have found that positive reappraisal coping mediates the relation between spousal support and psychological well-being. Third, listening, caring, and reassuring a friend or loved one that he or she is worthy and loved can directly bolster self-esteem. Druley and Townsend (1998) found that self-esteem mediated the relation between marital interactions and depressive symptoms among individuals with lupus. Although some support for the mechanisms of social support has accumulated, unfortunately these studies have been cross-sectional. Longitudinal studies may further elucidate support mechanisms.

Conclusions and Directions for Future Research

As the research reviewed indicates, social support is one of the most widely researched constructs in health psychology. The evidence linking social support to health outcomes depends on the health problem investigated. Social support has been consistently associated with cardiac outcomes: Social integration and social isolation have been linked with recovery post-MI, and the presence of a supportive other has been associated with lower cardiovascular reactivity in laboratory studies. Another widely researched area is social support and birth outcomes. The data are more mixed with regard to ARC to AIDS progression and with AIDS progression. Relatively little attention has been given to the role of social support in morbidity and mortality outcomes among individuals with other health problems.

There are several important areas for future research. First, future studies should examine the role of support in other disease outcomes. Second, it will be important for future studies to identify why support has beneficial health effects. For example, instrumental support may be associated with better birth outcomes because women receiving more assistance with daily activities have less physical strain and fatigue, or they are more compliant with prenatal care and have better nutritional practices. Key mechanisms for support's effects on health outcomes may be medical adherence or health practices that prevent disease progression, or mechanisms may be cardiovascular, endocrine, and immune changes. Few studies have evaluated potential physiological mechanisms for support's effects on health. The role of mood, particularly anxiety and depression, on the relation between support and health outcomes is also important to evaluate.

The bulk of the research on social support has evaluated support's effects on psychological outcomes among individuals dealing with illness. The majority of this research has assessed perceived support, with less research investigating support actually provided, or not provided, to the patient during the illness experience. The link between perceived available support (in particular, emotional support) and

psychological adaptation is stronger than the association between received support and adaptation. As pointed out in numerous studies, one reason for the inconsistent findings about received support is that distressed persons are more likely to seek support from others. However, it is possible that received support might result in lower distress at a later time. In the case of a chronic health problem, it is also possible that individuals who receive more support at one point may alienate support providers in the long run, as providers tire of providing support. Longitudinal studies would be more likely to unravel these complex associations.

Relatively few studies have identified what characteristics of patients may determine who benefits most from support, and even less attention has been paid to potential mechanisms for support. Does emotional support have its effect because it bolsters the patients' self-esteem or reduces isolation, alters perceptions of the illness to be less threatening, or because it assists the patient in finding benefit and meaning in the illness experience? What types of support are responsible for changes in patients' cognitive appraisals? Another methodological issue that is particularly relevant to studies of adaptation to illness is the large number of instruments used to assess illness-specific support. While measures of perceived support selected have been relatively consistent across studies, many investigators have developed their own measures specifically for their studies. This practice is problematic because it prevents comparisons across studies and because many investigators do not provide adequate psychometric information on the measures.

One limitation of the majority of studies is that the research is almost exclusively conducted on well-educated, Caucasian individuals. Recent research on social support and cancer screening is an exception. Differences in the types of support that are perceived as helpful may differ across cultures. For example, suggestions for cancer screening that are made by an individual whom the person does not perceive as credible are less likely to influence screening decisions. A second limitation is the almost exclusive focus on the patient. Since social support is obviously an exchange between recipient and provider, evaluating providers' perceptions of support given and examining the dyadic exchange between provider and recipients using observational methodologies would be important.

The study of social support's role in health outcomes has yielded a rich set of findings that has illustrated the key role that psychological factors may play in the prevention of health problems, the progression of health problems once they develop, as well as individuals' ultimate adaptation to health problems. Despite the large number of studies, a large number of unanswered questions remain.

REFERENCES

Affleck, G., Pfeiffer, C., Tennen, H., & Fifield, J. (1988). Social support and psychosocial adjustment to rheumatoid arthritis: Quantitative and qualitative findings. *Arthritis Care and Research, 1,* 71–77.

Affleck, G., Tennen, H., Keefe, F. J., Lefebrve, J. C., Kashikar-Zuck, S., & Wright, K. (1999). Everyday life with osteoarthritis or rheumatoid arthritis: Independent effects of disease and gender on daily pain, mood, and coping. *Pain, 83,* 601–609.

Alferi, S. M., Carver, C. S., Antoni, M. H., Weiss, S., & Duran, R. E. (2000). An exploratory study of social support, distress, and life disruption among low-income Hispanic women under treatment for early stage breast cancer. *Health Psychology, 20*(1), 41–46.

Anagnostopoulos, F., Vaslamatzis, G., Markidis, M., Katsovyanni, K., Vassilaros, S., & Stefanis, C. (1993). An investigation of hostile and alexithymic characteristics in breast cancer patients [Abstract]. *Psychotherapeutic Pscyhosomatics, 59*(3/4), 179–189.

Argyle, M. (1992). Benefits produced by supportive social relationships. In H. O. F. Veiel & U. Baumann (Eds.), *The meaning and measurement of social support* (pp. 13–32). New York: Hemisphere.

Arnetz, B. B., Wasserman, J., Petrini, B., Brenner, S. O., Levi, L., Eneroth, P., et al. (1987). Immune function in unemployed women. *Psychosomatic Medicine, 49,* 3–12.

Aspinwall, L. G., & Taylor, S. E. (1993). Effects of social comparison direction, threat, and self-esteem on affect, self-evaluation, and expected success. *Journal of Personality and Social Psychology, 64,* 708–722.

Barnett, P. A., Spence, J. D., Manuck, S. B., & Jennings, J. R. (1997). Psychological stress and the progression of carotid artery disease. *Journal of Hypertension, 15*(1), 49–55.

Baron, R. S., Cutrona, C. E., Hicklin, D., Russell, D. W., & Lubaroff, D. M. (1990). Social support and immune function among spouses of cancer patients. *Journal of Personality and Social Psychology, 59,* 344–352.

Barron, C. R., Houfek, J. F., & Foxall, M. J. (1997). Coping style, health beliefs, and breast self-examination. *Issues Mental Health Nursing, 18*(4), 331–350.

Bendtsen, P., & Hornquist, J. (1991). Rheumatoid arthritis, coping and well-being. *Scandinavian Journal of Social Medicine, 22,* 97–106.

Berkman, L., Leo-Summers, L., & Horwitz, R. (1992). Emotional support and survival after myocardial infarction: A prospective population based study of the elderly. *Annals of International Medicine, 117*(12), 1003–1008.

Berkman, L. F., Vaccarino, V., & Seeman, T. (1993). Gender differences in cardiovascular morbidity and mortality: The contribution of social networks and support. *Annals of Behavioral Medicine, 15,* 112–118.

Blaney, N. T., Millon, C., Morgan, R., Feaster, D., Millon, C., Szapocznik, J., et al. (1990). Emotional distress, stress-related disruption and coping among healthy HIV-positive gay males. *Psychology & Health, 4,* 259–273.

Bloom, J. R., & Kessler, L. (1994). Emotional support following cancer: A test of the stigma and social activity hypotheses. *Journal of Health and Social Behavior, 35,* 118–133.

Bolger, N., Foster, M., Vinokur, A. D., & Ng, R. (1996). Close relationships and adjustment to a life crisis: The case of breast cancer. *Journal of Personality and Social Psychology, 70*(2), 283–294.

Broege, P., James, G. D., & Peters, M. (1997). Anxiety coping style and daily blood pressure variation of female nurses. *Blood Pressure Monitoring, 2*(4), 155–159.

Brown, G., & Nicassio, P. (1987). Development of a questionnaire for the assessment of active and passive coping strategies in chronic pain patients. *Pain, 3,* 53–84.

Brown, G. K., Wallston, K. A., & Nicassio, P. (1989). Social support and depression in rheumatoid arthritis: A one-year prospective study. *Journal of Applied Social Psychology, 19*(14), 1164–1181.

Brown, J. E., Butow, P. N., Culjak, G., Coates, A. S., & Dunn, S. M. (2000). Psychosocial predictors of outcome: Time to relapse and survival in patients with early stage melanoma. *British Journal of Cancer, 83*(11), 1448–1453.

Buddenberg, C., Sieber, M., Wolf, C., Landolt-Ritter, C., Richter, D., & Steiner, R. (1996). Are coping strategies related to disease outcome in early breast cancer? *Journal of Psychosomatic Research, 40,* 255–263.

Budin, W. C. (1998). Psychosocial adjustment to breast cancer in unmarried women. *Research in Nursing and Health, 21,* 155–166.

Burton, H. J., Kline, S. A., Lindsay, R. M., & Heidenheim, P. (1988). The role of support in influencing outcome of end-stage renal disease. *General Hospital Psychiatry, 10,* 260–266.

Butler, L. D., Koopman, C., Classen, C., & Spiegel, D. (1999). Traumatic stress, life events, and emotional support in women with metastatic breast cancer: Cancer-related traumatic stress symptoms associated with past and current stressors. *Health Psychology, 18*(6), 555–560.

Butow, P. N., Hiller, J. E., Price, M. A., Thackway, S. V., Kricker, A., & Tennant, C. C. (2000). Epidemiological evidence for a relationship between life events, coping style, and personality factors in the development of breast cancer. *Journal of Psychosomatic Research, 49*(3), 169–181.

Byrne, D. (1961). The repression-sensitization scale: Rationale, reliability, and validity. *Journal of Personality, 29,* 334–349.

Cameron, L., Leventhal, E. A., & Leventhal, H. (1993). Symptom representations and affect as determinants of care seeking in a community-dwelling, adult sample population. *Health Psychology, 12*(3), 171–179.

Carver, C. S., Pozo, C., Harris, S. D., Noriega, V., Scheirer, M. F., & Robinson, D. S. (1993). How coping mediates the effect of optimism on distress. A study of women with early stage breast cancer. *Journal of Personality and Social Psychology, 65,* 375–390.

Case, R., Moss, A., Case, N., et al. (1992). Living alone after myocardial infarction: Impact on progress. *Journal of American Medical Association, 267*(4), 515–519.

Cassel, J. (1976). The contribution of the social environment to host resistance. *American Journal of Epidemiology, 104,* 107–123.

Catz, S. L., McClure, J. B., Jones, G. N., & Brantley, P. J. (1999). Predictors of outpatient medical appointment attendance among persons with HIV. *Aids Care, 11*(3), 361–373.

Chen, C. C., David, A. S., Nunnerley, H., Michell, M., Dawson, J. L., & Berry, H. (1995). Adverse life events and breast cancer: Case-control study. *British Medical Journal, 311,* 1527–1530.

Christenfeld, N., Gerin, W., Linden, W., Sanders, M., Mathur, J., & Pickering, T. G. (1997). Social support effects on cardiovascular reactivity: Is a stranger as effective as a friend? *Psychosomatic Medicine, 59,* 388–398.

Cobb, S. (1976). Social support as a moderator of life stress. *Psychosomatic Medicine, 38,* 300–314.

Cohen, S., & McKay, G. (1984). Social support, stress, and the buffering hypothesis: A theoretical analysis. In A. Baum, J. E. Singer, & S. E. Taylor (Eds.), *Handbook of psychology and health* (Vol. 4, pp. 253–267). Hillsdale, NJ: Erlbaum.

Coyne, J., & Racioppo, M. (2000). Never the twain shall meet? Closing the gap between coping research and clinical intervention research. *American Psychology, 55,* 655–664.

Cramer, P. (2000). Defense mechanisms in psychology. *Psychology Review, 3,* 357–370.

Croyle, R. T., & Jemmott, J. B. (1991). Psychological reactions to risk factor testing. In J. A. Skelton & R. T. Croyle (Eds.), *Mental representations in health and illness* (pp. 85–107). New York: Springer-Verlag.

Cutrona, C. E., & Russell, D. W. (1990). Type of social support and specific stress: Toward a theory of optimal matching. In B. R. Sarason, I. G. Sarason, & G. R. Pierce (Eds.), *Social support: An interactional view* (pp. 319–366). New York: Wiley.

Dakof, G. A., & Taylor, S. E. (1990). Victims' perceptions of social support: What is helpful from whom? *Journal of Personality and Social Psychology, 58*(1), 80–89.

Davis, C. G., Nolen-Hoeksema, S., & Larson, J. (1998). Making sense of loss and benefiting from the experience: Two construals of meaning. *Journal of Personality and Social Psychology, 75*(2), 561–574.

Demyttenaere, K., Bonte, L., Gheldof, M., Vervaeke, M., Meuleman, C., & Vanderschuerem, D. (1998). Coping style and depression level influence outcome in in vitro fertilization. *Fertility and Sterility, 69*(6), 1026–1033.

de Ruiter, J., de Haes, J., & Tempelaar, R. (1993). Cancer patients and their network: The meaning of the social network and social interactions for quality of life. *Supportive Care in Cancer, 1,* 152–155.

Doeglas, D., Suurmeijer, T., Krol, B., Sanderman, R., van Rijswijk, R., & van Leeuwen, M. (1994). Social support, social disability, and psychological well-being in rheumatoid arthritis. *Arthritis Care and Research, 7*(1), 10–15.

Druley, J. A., & Townsend, A. L. (1998). Self-esteem as a mediator between spousal support and depressive symptoms: A comparison of healthy individuals and individuals coping with arthritis. *Health Psychology, 17*(3), 255–261.

Dunbar-Jacob, J., Erlen, J. A., Schlenk, E. A., Ryan, C. M., Sereika, S. M., & Doswell, W. M. (2000). Adherence in chronic disease. *Annual Review Nursing Research, 18,* 48–90.

Dunkel-Schetter, C. (1984). Social support and cancer: Findings based on patient interviews and their implications. *Journal of Social Issues, 40,* 77–98.

Dunkel-Schetter, C., Feinstein, L. G., Taylor, S. E., & Falke, R. (1992). Patterns of coping with cancer [Lead article]. *Health Psychology, 11*(2), 79–87.

Edens, J., Larkin, K. T., & Abel, J. L. (1992). The effect of social support and physical touch on cardiovascular reactions to mental stress. *Journal of Psychosomatic Research, 36,* 371–382.

Edwards, J. R., Cooper, C. L., Pearl, S. G., de Paredes, E. S., O'Leary, T., & Wilhelm, M. C. (1990). The relationship between psychosocial factors and breast cancer: Some unexpected results. *Behavioral Medicine, 16*(1), 5–14.

Ely, D. L., & Mostardi, R. A. (1986). The effect of recent life events stress, life assets, and temperament pattern on cardiovascular risk factors for Akron City police officers. *Journal of Human Stress, 12*(2), 77–91.

Endler, N. S., & Hunt, J. M. (1968). S-R inventories of hostility and comparisons of the proportions of variance from persons, responses, and situations for hostility and anxiousness. *Journal of Personality and Social Psychology, 9*(4), 309–315.

Epping-Jordan, J. E., Compas, B. E., Osowiecki, D. M., Oppedisano, G., Gerhardt, C., Primo, K., et al. (1999). Psychological adjustment in breast cancer: Processes of emotional distress. *Health Psychology, 18*(4), 315–326.

Esterling, B. A., Kiecolt-Glaser, J. K., Bodnar, J. C., & Glaser, R. (1994). Chronic stress, social support, and persistent alterations in the natural killer cell response to cytokines in older adults. *Health Psychology, 13,* 291–299.

Evers, A. W. M., Kraaimaat, F. W., Geenen, R., & Bijlsma, J. W. (1997). Determinants of psychological distress and its course in the first year after diagnosis in rheumatoid arthritis patients. *Journal of Behavioral Medicine, 20*(5), 489–504.

Felton, B., & Revenson, T. (1984). Coping with chronic illness: A study of illness controllability and the influence of coping strategies on psychological adjustment. *Journal of Consulting and Clinical Psychology, 52*(3), 343–353.

Felton, B., Revenson, T., & Hinrichsen, G. (1984). Stress and coping in the explanation of psychological adjustment among chronically ill adults. *Social Science Medicine, 10,* 889–898.

Fleming, R., Baum, A., Gisriel, M. M., & Gatchel, R. J. (1982). Mediating influences of social support on stress at Three Mile Island. *Journal of Human Stress, 8,* 14–22.

Frasure-Smith, N., Lesperace, F., Gravel, G., Masson, A., Juneau, M., Talajic, M., et al. (2000). Social support, depression, and mortality during the first year after myocardial infarction. *Circulation, 101,* 1919–1929.

Frasure-Smith, N., Lesperace, F., & Talajec, M. (1995). Depression and 18 month prognosis following myocardial infarction. *Circulation, 91,* 999–1005.

Frasure-Smith, N., & Prince, R. (1985). The ischemic heart disease life stress monitoring program: Impact on mortality. *Psychosomatic Medicine, 47,* 431–445.

Gerin, W., Milnor, D., Chawla, S. J., & Pickering, T. J. (1995). Social support as a moderator of cardiovascular reactivity in women: A test of the direct effects and buffering hypotheses. *Psychosomatic Medicine, 57,* 16–22.

Gerin, W., Pieper, C., Levy, R., & Pickering, T. G. (1992). Social support in social interaction: A moderator of cardiovascular reactivity. *Psychosomatic Medicine, 54,* 324–336.

Gibbons, F. X., & Gerrard, M. (1991). Downward comparison and coping with threat. In J. Suls & T. Wills (Eds.), *Social comparison: Contemporary theory and research* (pp. 317–346). Hillsdale, NJ: Erlbaum.

Gil, K. M., Abrams, M. R., Phillips, G., & Keefe, F. J. (1989). Sickle cell disease pain: Relation of coping strategies to adjustment. *Journal of Consulting and Clinical Psychology, 57*(6), 725–731.

Gil, K. M., Abrams, M. R., Phillips, G., & Williams, D. A. (1992). Sickle cell disease pain-2: Predicting health care use and activity level at nine-month follow-up. *Journal of Consulting and Clinical Psychology, 60,* 267–273.

Gil, K. M., Phillips, G., Edens, J., Martin, N. J., & Abrams, M. (1994). Observation of pain behaviors during episodes of sickle cell disease pain. *Clinical Journal of Pain, 10*(2), 128–132.

Goldstein, D., & Antoni, M. H. (1989). The distribution of repressive coping styles among non-metastatic and metastatic breast cancer patients as compared to non-cancer patients. *Psychology and Health: An International Journal, 3,* 245–258.

Grassi, L., Caloro, G., Zamorani, M., & Ramelli, G. P. (1997). Psychological morbidity and psychosocial variables associated with life-threatening illness: A comparative study of patients with HIV infection or cancer. *Psychology, Health and Medicine, 2*(1), 29–39.

Greenberg, M. (1995). Cognitive processing of traumas: The role of intrusive thoughts and reappraisals. *Journal of Applied Social Psychology, 5,* 1262–1296.

Greer, S., Morris, T., & Pettingale, K. W. (1979). Psychological response to breast cancer: Effect on outcome. *Lancet, 2*(8146), 785–787.

Grodner, S., Prewitt, L., Jaworski, B., Myers, R., Kaplan, R., & Ries, A. (1996). The impact of social support on pulmonary rehabilitation of patients with chronic obstructive pulmonary disease. *Annals of Behavioral Medicine, 18,* 139–145.

Gurowka, K. J., & Lightman, E. S. (1995). Supportive and unsupportive interactions as perceived by cancer patients. *Social work in Health Care, 21*(4), 71–88.

Hamalainen, H., Smith, R., Puukka, P., Lind, J., Kallio, V., Kutilla, K., et al. (2000). Social support and physical and psychological recovery one year after myocardial infarction or coronary artery bypass surgery. *Scandinavian Journal of Public Health, 28,* 62–70.

Hansell, S. (1985). Adolescent friendship networks and distress in school. *Social Forces, 63,* 698–715.

Hanson, B. S., Isacsson, J. T., Janzon, L., Lindell, S. E., & Rastam, L. (1988). Social anchorage and blood pressure in elderly men. *Journal of Hypertension, 6,* 503–510.

Hays, R. B., Chauncey, S., & Tobey, L. A. (1990). The social support networks of gay men with AIDS. *Journal of Community Psychology, 18,* 374–385.

Hays, R. B., Turner, H., & Coates, T. J. (1992). Social support, AIDS-related symptoms, and depression among gay men. *Journal of Consulting and Clinical Psychology, 60,* 463–469.

Helgeson, V., Cohen, S., Schulz, R., & Yasko, J. (1999). *Archives of General Psychiatry, 56*(4), 340–347.

Horsten, M., Wamala, S. P., Vingerhoets, A., & Orth-Gomer, K. (1997). Depressive symptoms, social support, and lipid profile in healthy middle-aged women. *Psychosomatic Medicine, 59,* 521–552.

Hoskins, C. N., Baker, S., Sherman, D., Bohlander, J., Bookbinder, M., Budin, W., et al. (1996). Social support and patterns of adjustment to breast cancer. *Scholarly Inquiry for Nursing Practice, 10*(2), 99–123.

House, J. S. (1981). *Work stress and social support.* Reading, MA: Addison-Wesley.

Ingram, K. M., Jones, D. A., Fass, R. J., Neidig, J. L., & Song, Y. S. (1999). Social support and unsupportive social interactions: Their association with depression among people living with HIV. *AIDS CARE, 11*(3), 313–329.

Ironson, G., Friedman, A., Klimas, N., Antoni, M., Flietcher, M. A., La Perriere, A., et al. (1994). Distress, denial, and low adherence to behavioral interventions predict faster disease progression in gay men infected with human immunodeficiency virus. *International Journal of Behavioral Medicine, 1,* 90–105.

Jamner, L. D., & Leigh, H. (1999). Repressive/defensive coping, endogenous opioids and health: How a life so perfect can make you sick. *Psychiatry Research, 85*(1), 17–31.

Janes, C. R. (1990). Migration, changing gender roles and stress: The Samoan case. *Medical Anthropology, 12,* 217–248.

Janoff-Bulman, R. (1992). *Shattered assumptions: Towards a new psychology of trauma.* New York: Free Press.

Kamarck, T. W., Annunziato, B., & Amaateau, L. M. (1995). Affiliation moderates the effects of social threat on stress-related cardiovascular responses: Boundary conditions for a laboratory model of social support. *Psychosomatic Medicine, 57,* 183–194.

Kamarck, T. W., Manuck, S. D., & Jennings, J. R. (1990). Social support reduces cardiovascular reactivity to psychological challenge: A laboratory model. *Psychosomatic Medicine, 52,* 42–58.

Keefe, F. J., Brown, G. K., Wallston, K. A., & Caldwell, D. S. (1989). Coping with rheumatoid arthritis pain: Catastrophizing as a maladaptive strategy. *Pain, 37,* 51–56.

Kernberg, O. (1975). *Borderline conditions and pathological narcissism.* New York: Science House.

Kernberg, O. (1982). Self, ego, affects, and drives. *Journal of American Psychoanalytical Association, 30*(4), 893–917.

Kiecolt-Glaser, J., Glaser, R., Williger, D., Stout, J., Messick, G., Sheppard, S., et al. (1985). Psychosocial enhancement of immunocompetence in a geriatric population. *Health Psychology, 4,* 25–41.

Kiecolt-Glaser, J. K., Dura, J. R., & Speicher, C. E. (1991). Spousal caregivers of dementia victims: Longitudinal changes in immunity and health. *Psychosomatic Medicine, 53,* 345–362.

Kirschbaum, C., Klauer, T., Filipp, S. H., & Hellhammer, D. H. (1995). Sex-specific effects of social support on cortisol and subjective responses to acute psychological stress. *Psychosomatic Medicine, 57,* 23–31.

Kneier, A. W., & Temoshok, L. (1984). Repressive coping reactions in patients with malignant melanoma as compared to cardiovascular disease patients. *Journal of Psychosomatic Research, 28*(2), 145–155.

Komproe, I. H., Rijken, M., Winnubst, J. A. M., Ros, W. J. G., & Hart, H.'t. (1997). Available support and received support: Different effects under stressful circumstances. *Journal of Social and Personal Relationships, 14*(1), 59–77.

Kreitler, S., Chaitchik, S., & Kreitler, H. (1993). Repressiveness: Cause or result of cancer? *Psycho-Oncology, 2,* 43–54.

Kulik, J., & Mahler, H. (1997). Social comparison, affiliation, and coping with acute medical threats. In B. P. Buunk & F. X. Gibbons (Eds.), *Health, coping and well-being: Perspectives from social comparison theory* (pp. 227–261). Mahwah, NJ: Erlbaum.

Lau, R. R., Bernard, T. M., & Hartman, K. A. (1989). Further explorations of common sense representations of common illnesses. *Health Psychology, 8,* 167–185.

Lazarus, R. (1981). The stress and coping paradigm. In C. Eisdorfer, D. Cohen, A. Kleinman, & P. Maxim (Eds.), *Models for clinical psychopathology.* New York: Spectrum.

Lazarus, R. (2000). Toward better research on stress and coping. *American Psychologist, 55,* 775–673.

Lazarus, R., & Folkman, S. (1984). *Stress, appraisal, and coping.* New York: Springer.

Lehrer, P. M. (1998). Emotionally triggered asthma: A review of research literature and some hypotheses for self-regulation therapies. *Applied Psychophysiological Biofeedback, 23*(1), 13–41.

Lepore, S. J. (1995). Cynicism, social support, and cardiovascular reactivity. *Health Psychology, 14,* 210–216.

Lepore, S. J. (1998). Problems and prospects for the social support-reactivity hypothesis. *Annals of Behavioral Medicine, 20*(4), 257–269.

Lepore, S. J., Allen, K. A., & Evans, G. W. (1993). Social support lowers cardiovascular reactivity to an acute stressor. *Psychosomatic Medicine, 55,* 518–524.

Lercher, P., Hortnagl, J., & Kofler, W. W. (1993). Work noise annoyance and blood pressure: Combined effects with stressful working conditions. *International Archives of Occupational and Environmental Health, 65,* 23–28.

Leserman, J., Jackson, E. D., Petitto, J. M., Golden, R. N., Silva, S. G., & Perkins, D. O. (1999). Progression to AIDS: The effects of stress, depressive symptoms, and social support. *Psychosomatic Medicine, 61,* 397–406.

Levine, D. M., Green, L. W., Deeds, S. G., Chwalow, J., Russell, R. P., & Finlay, J. (1979). Health education for hypertensive patients. *Journal of the American Medical Association, 241,* 1700–1703.

Levy, S. M., Herberman, R. B., Maluish, A., Schlien, B., & Lipman, M. (1985). Prognostic risk assessment in primary breast cancer by behavioural and immunological parameters. *Health Psychology, 4,* 99–113.

Levy, S. M., Herberman, R. B., Whiteside, T., Sanzo, K., Lee, J., & Kirkwood, J. (1990). Perceived social support and tumor estrogen/progesterone receptor status as predictors of natural killer cell activity in breast cancer patients. *Psychosomatic Medicine, 51,* 73–85.

Manne, S., & Schnoll, R. (2001). Measuring supportive and unsupportive responses during cancer treatment: A factor analytic assessment of the partner responses to cancer inventory. *Journal of Behavioral Medicine, 24*(4), 297–321.

Manne, S. L., Alfieri, T., Taylor, K. L., & Dougherty, J. (1999). Spousal negative responses to cancer patients: The role of social restriction, spouse mood, and relationship satisfaction. *Journal of Consulting and Clinical Psychology, 67*(3), 352–361.

Manne, S. L., Pape, S. J., Taylor, K. L., & Dougherty, J. (1999). Spouse support, coping, and mood among individuals with cancer. *Annals Behavioral Medicine, 21*(2), 111–121.

Manne, S. L., Sabbioni, M., Bovbjerg, D. H., Jacobsen, P., Taylor, K., & Redd, W. (1994). Coping with chemotherapy for breast cancer. *Journal of Behavioral Medicine, 17*(1), 41–55.

Manne, S. L., Taylor, K. L., Dougherty, J., & Kemeny, N. (1997). Supportive and negative responses in the partner relationship: Their association with psychological adjustment among individuals with cancer. *Journal of Behavioral Medicine, 29*(2), 101–125.

Manne, S. L., & Zautra, A. (1989). Spouse criticism and support: Their association with coping and psychological adjustment among women with rheumatoid arthritis. *Journal of Personality and Social Psychology, 56,* 608–617.

Manuck, S. B. (1994). Cardiovascular reactivity in cardiovascular disease: Once more unto the breach. *International Journal of Behavioral Medicine, 1,* 4–31.

Manuck, S. B., Olsson, G., Hjemdahl, P., & Rehnqvist, N. (1992). Does cardiovascular reactivity to mental stress have prognostic value in postinfarction patients? A pilot study. *Psychosomatic Medicine, 54*(1), 102–108.

McKenna, M. C., Zevon, M. A., Corn, B., & Rounds, J. (1999). Psychosocial factors and the development of breast cancer: A meta-analysis. *Health Psycholology, 18,* 520–531.

Menkes, M. S., Matthews, K. A., Krantz, D. S., Lundberg, U., Mead, L. A., Qaqish, B., et al. (1989). Cardiovascular reactivity to the cold pressor test as a predictor of hypertension. *Hypertension, 14,* 524–530.

Miller, G. E., Kemeny, M. E., Taylor, S. E., Cole, S. W., & Visscher, B. R. (1997). Social relationships and immune processes in HIV seropositive gay and bisexual men. *Annals of Behavioral Medicine, 19,* 139–151.

Miller, S. M. (1980). When is a little information a dangerous thing? Coping with stressful events by monitoring versus blunting. In S. Levine & H. Ursin (Eds.), *Coping and health* (p. 145). New York: Plenum Press.

Miller, S. M. (1987). Monitoring and blunting: Validation of a questionnaire to access styles of information seeking under threat. *Journal of Personality and Social Psychology, 52,* 345–353.

Miller, S. M. (1995). Monitoring versus blunting styles of coping with cancer influence: The information patients want and need about their disease (implications for cancer screening and management). *Cancer, 76*(1), 167–177.

Mischel, W. (1968). *Personality and assessment.* New York: Wiley.

Mohr, D., Goodkin, D., Gatto, N., & Van Der Wende, J. (1997). Depression, coping, and level of neurological impairment in multiple sclerosis. *Multiple Sclerosis, 3,* 254–258.

Mulder, C. L., de Vroome, E. M., van Griensven, G. J., Antoni, M. H., & Sanfort, T. G. (1999). Avoidance as a predictor of the biological course of HIV infection over a 7-year period in gay men. *Health Psychology, 18*(2), 107–113.

Muldoon, M. F., Rossouw, J. E., Manuck, S. B., Glueck, C. J., Kaplan, J. R., & Kaufmann, P. G. (1993). Low or lowered cholesterol and risk of death from suicide and trauma. *Metabolism, 42*(9, Suppl. 1), 45–56.

Mullen, B., & Suls, J. (1982). The effectiveness of attention and rejection as coping styles. *Journal of Psychosomatic Research, 26,* 43–49.

Neuling, S. J., & Winefield, H. R. (1988). Social support and recovery after surgery for breast cancer: Frequency and correlates of supportive behaviors by family, friends, and surgeon. *Social Science and Medicine, 27,* 385–392.

Nicassio, P. M., Brown, G. K., Wallston, K. A., & Szydlo, W. (1985). Arthritis experience and social support as predictors of psychological dysfunction in RA. *Arthritis and Rheumatism, 28,* (Suppl. 147).

Northouse, A. L. (1988). Social support in patients' and husbands' adjustment to breast cancer. *Nursing Research, 37,* 91–95.

Nott, K. H., Vedhara, K., & Power, M. J. (1995). The role of social support in HIV infection. *Psychological Medicine, 25,* 971–983.

Ord-Lawson, S., & Fitch, M. (1997). The relationship between perceived social support and mood of testicular cancer patients. *Cancer Oncology Nursing Journal, 7*(2), 990–995.

Orth-Gomer, K., Rosengren, A., & Wilhelmsen, L. (1993). Lack of social support and incidence of coronary heart disease in middle-aged Swedish men. *Psychosomatic Medicine, 55,* 37–43.

Orth-Gomer, K., & Unden, A. (1990). Type A behavior, social support, and coronary risk: Interaction and significance for mortality in cardiac patients. *Psychosomatic Medicine, 52,* 59–72.

Ostergren, P. O., Freitag, M., Hanson, B. S., Hedin, E., Isacsson, S. O., Odeberg, H., et al. (1991). Social network and social support predict improvement of physical working capacity in rehabilitation of patients with first myocardial infarction. *Scandinavian Journal of Social Medicine, 19,* 225–234.

Pakenham, K. (1999). Adjustment to multiple sclerosis: Application of a stress and coping model. *Health Psychology, 18*(4), 383–392.

Pakenham, K., Stewart, C., & Rogers, A. (1997). The role of coping in adjustment to multiple sclerosis-related adaptive demands. *Psychology, Health and Medicine, 2,* 197–211.

Pakenham, K. L., Dadds, M. R., & Terry, D. J. (1994). Relationships between adjustment to HIV and both social support and coping. *Journal of Consulting and Clinical Psychology, 62*(6), 1194–1203.

Parker, J., Smarr, K., Buescher, K., Phillips, L. R., Frank, R. G., & Beck, N. C. (1989). Pain control and rational thinking. *Arthritis and Rheumatism, 32*(8), 984–990.

Patterson, T., Shaw, W., Semple, S. J., Cherner, M., Nannis, E., McCutchan, J. A., et al. (1996). Relationship of psychosocial factors to HIV disease progression. *Annals of Behavioral Medicine, 18*(1), 30–39.

Pennix, B. W., van Tilburg, T., Deeg, D. J., Kriegsman, D. M., Boeke, T., & van Eijk, C. (1997). Direct and buffer effects of social support and personal coping resources in individuals with arthritis. *Social Science and Medicine, 44*(3), 393–402.

Perry, S., Fishman, B., Jacobsberg, L., & Frances, A. (1992). Relationships over 1 year between lymphocyte subsets and psychosocial variables among adults with infection by human immunodeficiency virus. *Archives of General Psychiatry, 49,* 396–401.

Persson, L., Gullberg, B., Hanson, B., Moestrup, T., & Ostergren, P. (1994). HIV infection: Social network, social support, and CD4 lymphocyte values in infected homosexual men in Malmo, Sweden. *Journal of Epidemiology and Community Health, 48,* 580–585.

Prohaska, T. R., Leventhal, E. A., Leventhal, H., & Keller, M. L. (1985). Health practices and illness cognition in young, middle-aged, and elderly adults. *Journal of Gerontology, 40,* 569–578.

Reed, G. M., Kemeny, M. E., Taylor, S. E., Wang, H. Y., & Visscher, B. R. (1994). Realistic acceptance as a predictor of decreased survival time in gay men with AIDS. *Health Psychology, 13*(4), 299–307.

Revenson, T., & Felton, B. (1989). Disability and coping as predictors of psychological adjustment to rheumatoid arthritis. *Journal of Consulting and Clinical Psychology, 57,* 344–348.

Revenson, T. A., Schiaffino, K. M., Majerovitz, S. D., & Gibovsky, A. (1991). Social support as a double-edged sword: The relation of positive and problematic support to depression among rheumatoid arthritis patients. *Social Science and Medicine, 33*(7), 807–813.

Rozanski, A., Blumenthal, J. A., & Kaplan, J. (1999). Impact of psychological factors on the pathogenesis of cardiovascular disease and implications for therapy. *Circulation, 99*(16), 2192–2217. Review.

Ruberman, W., Weinblatt, E., Goldberg, J. D., & Chaudhary, J. D. (1984). Psychosocial influences on mortality after myocardial infarction. *New England Journal of Medicine, 311,* 522–559.

Sallis, J. F., Grossman, R. M., Pinski, R. B., Patterson, T. L., & Nader, P. R. (1987). The development of scales to measure social support for diet and exercise behaviors. *Preventive Medicine, 16,* 825–836.

Scharloo, M., Kaptein, A. A., Weinman, J., Hazes, J., Breedveld, F., & Rooijmans, H. (1999). Predicting functional status in patients with rheumatoid arthritis. *Journal of Rheumatology, 26,* 1686–1693.

Scharloo, M., Kaptein, A. A., Weinman, J., Hazes, J., Willems, L., Bergman, W., et al. (1998). Illness perceptions, coping and functioning in patients with rheumatoid arthritis, chronic obstructive pulmonary disease and psoriasis. *Journal of Psychosomatic Research, 44*(5), 573–585.

Schwartz, J. E., Neale, J., Marco, C., Schiffman, S. S., & Stone, A. A. (1999). Does trait coping exist? A momentary assessment approach to the evaluation of traits. *Journal of Personal and Social Psychology, 77*(2), 360–369.

Seeman, T. E., Berkman, L. F., Blazer, D., & Rowe, J. W. (1994). Social ties and support and neuroendocrine function: The MacArthur studies of successful aging. *Annals of Behavioral Medicine, 16,* 95–106.

Sherman, A. C., Simonton, S., Adams, D. C., Vural, E., & Hanna, E. (2000). Coping with head and neck cancer during different phases of treatment. *Head and Neck, 22*(8), 787–793.

Siegel, K., Raveis, V. H., & Karus, D. (1997). Illness-related support and negative network interactions: Effects on HIV-infected men's depressive symptomatology. *American Journal of Community Psychology, 25*(3), 395–420.

Solano, L., Costa, M., Salvati, S., Coda, R., Aiuti, F., Mezzaroma, I., & Bertini, M. (1993). Psychological factors and clinical evolution in HIV-1 infection: A longitudinal study. *Journal of Psychosomatic Research, 37,* 39–51.

Stanton, S. L., Danoff-Burg, S., Cameron, C. L., Bishop, M., & Collins, C. A. (2000). Emotionally expressive coping predicts psychological and physical adjustment to breast cancer. *Journal of Consulting and Clinical Psychology, 68*(5), 875–882.

Stewart, M. J., Hirth, A. M., Klassen, G., Makrides, L., & Wolf, H. (1997). Stress, coping, and social support as psychosocial factors in readmissions for ischemic heart disease. *International Nurse Student, 34*(2), 151–163.

Stone, A., & Neale, J. (1984). The effects of severe daily events on mood. *Journal of Personal and Social Psychology, 46,* 137–144.

Swindells, S., Mohr, J., Justis, J. C., Berman, S., Squier, C., Wagener, M. M., et al. (1999). Quality of life in patients with human immunodeficiency virus infection: Impact of social support, coping style and hopelessness. *Journal of STD and AIDS, 10*(6), 383–391.

Tennen, H., & Affleck, G. (1997). Social comparisons and occupational stress: The identification-contrast, model. In B. P. Buunk & F. X. Gibbons (Eds.), *Health, coping and well-being: Perspectives from social comparison theory* (pp. 359–388). Mahwah, NJ: Erlbaum.

Tennen, H., Affleck, G., Armeli, S., & Carney, M. (2000). A daily process approach to coping: Linking theory, research and practice. *American Psychologist, 55,* 626–636.

Tennen, H., Affleck, G., Urrows, S., Higgins, P., & Mendola, R. (1992). Perceiving control, construing benefits and daily processes in rheumatoid arthritis. *Canadian Journal of Behavioral Science, 24,* 186–203.

Theorell, T., Blomkvist, V., Jonsson, H., Schulman, S., Berntorp, E., & Stigenoal, L. (1995). Social support and the development of immune function in human immunodeficiency virus infection. *Psychosomatic Medicine, 57,* 32–36.

Thoits, P. (1985). Social support and psychological well-being: Theoretical possibilities. In I. Sarason & B. Sarason (Eds.), *Social support: Theory, research and applications* (pp. 51–72). Dordrecht, The Netherlands: Martinus Nijhoff.

Thomas, P. D., Goodwin, J. M., & Goodwin, J. S. (1985). Effects of social support on stress-related changes in cholesterol level, uric acid level, and immune function in an elderly sample. *American Journal of Psychiatry, 142,* 735–737.

Thornton, S., Troop, M., Burgess, A. P., Button, J., Goodall, R., Flynn, R., et al. (2000). The relationship of psychological variables and disease progression among long-term HIV-infected men. *International Journal of STD & Aids, 11,* 734–742.

Uchino, B. N., Cacioppo, J. T., & Kiecolt-Glaser, J. K. (1996). The relationship between social support and physiological processes: A review with emphasis on underlying mechanisms and implications for health. *Psychological Bulletin, 119,* 488–531.

Van Lankveld, W., van't Pad Bosch, P., van De Putte, L., Naring, G., & van Der Staak, C. (1994). Disease-specific stressors in rheumatoid arthritis: Coping and well-being. *British Journal of Rheumatology, 33,* 1067–1073.

Ward, M. M., Lotstein, D. S., Bush, T. M., Lambert, R. E., van Vollen Hoven, R., & Newelt, C. M. (1999). Psychosocial correlates of morbidity in women with systemic lupus erythematosus. *Journal of Rheumatology, 26*(10), 2153–2158.

Watson, M., & Greer, S. (1983). Development of a questionnaire measure of emotional control. *Journal of Psychosomatic Research, 27,* 299–305.

Weisman, A. D., & Worden, J. W. (1976–1977). The existential plight in significance of the first 100 days. *International Journal of Psychiatry in Medicine, 7,* 1–15.

Weiss, R. (1974). The provisions of social relationships. In A. Rubin (Ed.), *Doing unto others* (pp. 17–26). Englewood Cliffs, NJ: Prentice-Hall.

Welin, C., Lappas, G., & Wilhelmsen, L. (2000). Independent importance of psychosocial factors for prognosis after myocardial infarction. *Journal of Internal Medicine, 247*(6), 629–639.

Welin, C. L., Rosengren, A., & Wilhelmsen, L. W. (1996, April). Social relationships and myocardial infarction: A case-control study. *Journal Cardiovascular Risk, 3*(2), 183–190.

Wills, T. (1981). Downward comparison principles in social psychology. *Psychology Bulletin, 90,* 245–271.

Wills, T. (1997). Modes and families of coping. In B. P. Buunk & F. X. Gibbons (Eds.), *Health, coping and well-being: Perspectives from social comparison theory* (pp. 167–193). Mahwah, NJ: Erlbaum.

Wineman, M., & Durand, E. (1994). Examination of the factor structure of the ways of coping questionnaire with clinical populations. *Nursing Research, 43*(5), 266–273.

Wortman, C. B., & Dunkel-Schetter, C. (1979). Interpersonal relationships and cancer: A theoretical analysis. *Journal of Social Issues, 35,* 120–155.

Wortman, C. B., & Dunkel-Schetter, C. (1987). Conceptual and methodological issues in the study of social support. In A. Baum & J. Singer (Eds.), *Handbook of psychology and health* (pp. 63–108). Hillsdale, NJ: Erlbaum.

Yates, B. C. (1995). The relationships among social support and short- and long-term recovery outcomes in men with coronary heart disease. *Research in Nursing and Health, 18,* 193–203.

Zautra, A., & Manne, S. (1992). Coping with rheumatoid arthritis: A review of a decade of research. *Annals of Behavioral Medicine, 14*(1), 31–39.

CHAPTER 4

Psychoneuroimmunology

JEFFREY R. STOWELL, LYNANNE McGUIRE, TED ROBLES, RONALD GLASER, AND JANICE K. KIECOLT-GLASER

The field of psychoneuroimmunology (PNI) addresses how psychological factors influence the immune system and physical health through neural and endocrinological pathways. These relationships are especially relevant to immunologically mediated health problems, including infectious disease, cancer, autoimmunity, allergy, and wound healing. In this chapter, we briefly introduce two major physiological systems that modulate immune function and then provide evidence for stress-immune relationships. Next, we explore the psychosocial factors that may be important in moderating and mediating these relationships, including negative affect, social support, and interpersonal relationships. Finally, we review intervention strategies that may be beneficial in reducing the negative effects of stress on the immune system. For more detailed explanations of immunological terms or processes, we recommend the text by Rabin (1999).

STRESS-IMMUNE PATHWAYS

HPA Axis

Activation of the hypothalamic-pituitary-adrenal (HPA) axis by stress results in a predictable cascade of events (see Figure 4.1). Neurons in the hypothalamus release corticotropin-releasing hormone (CRH), which stimulates the anterior pituitary to release adrenocorticotropin hormone (ACTH) into the general circulation. The adrenal cortex then responds to ACTH by releasing glucocorticoids, predominantly cortisol in humans.

Some of cortisol's effects are anti-inflammatory and immunosuppressive. These immunological effects may be adaptive, as they can limit a potentially overactive immune response that could result in inflammatory or autoimmune disease (Munck & Guyre, 1991; Munck, Guyre, & Holbrook, 1984; Sternberg, 1997). Although glucocorticoids exert anti-inflammatory and immunosuppressive effects, they have a more complex role in immune modulation than originally thought. For example, glucocorticoids suppress cytokines that promote a cell-mediated TH-1 type immune response (e.g., interleukin-2 [IL-2]), but they enhance the production of cytokines that promote a humoral TH-2 type immune response (e.g., IL-4; Daynes & Araneo, 1989). Thus, there may be a shift in the type of immune defense toward an antibody-mediated response. This shift may or may not be adaptive depending on the types of pathogens that are present. Additionally, glucocorticoids induce a redistribution of immune cells from the blood to other organs or tissues (McEwen et al., 1997). Thus, a drop in peripheral blood lymphocyte counts may mistakenly be interpreted as immunosuppression when the cells may simply be migrating to other

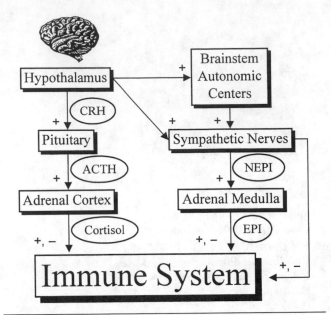

Figure 4.1 Neural and endocrine pathways that may modulate the immune system. The hypothalamic-pituitary-adrenal (HPA) and sympathoadrenomedullary (SAM) axes are represented, which influence the immune system in multiple ways.
Abbreviations:
CRH–corticotropin-releasing hormone,
ACTH–adrenocorticotropin hormone,
NEPI–norepinephrine,
EPI–epinephrine, (+) stimulation, (−) inhibition.

organs or tissues, such as the skin, where they are more likely to encounter antigens (Dhabhar & McEwen, 1997). This illustrates the complexity of understanding the pattern of changes in immune function, particularly when only one or two measures of immune function are assessed. Thus, the term *immune dysregulation* is probably a more descriptive term than *immune suppression* (or enhancement) when discussing general changes in immune function.

Although the HPA axis significantly modulates immune function, other pathways also exist, as noted when the blastogenic response to phytohemagglutinin (PHA) was still suppressed following stress, despite removal of the adrenal glands (Keller, Weiss, Schleifer, Miller, & Stein, 1983). Later studies suggested that the sympathetic nervous system is another important modulator of immune function (Felten, Felten, Carlson, Olschowka, & Livnat, 1985; Irwin, 1993).

Sympathetic Nervous System (SNS)

As with the HPA axis, the hypothalamus is centrally involved in the regulation of autonomic nervous system activity. Neurons in the hypothalamus project to autonomic centers in the lower brainstem and spinal cord, including preganglionic sympathetic neurons (Luiten, ter Horst, Kȧrst, & Steffens, 1985). During a classical "fight or flight" response,

sympathetic nerve terminals release norepinephrine into various effector organs including the adrenal medulla, which releases the catecholamines, epinephrine and norepinephrine, into the blood stream; hence the term *sympathoadrenomedullary* (SAM) axis (see Figure 4.1).

Additionally, sympathetic nerve terminals innervate primary and secondary lymphoid tissue and appose lymphocytes and macrophages in synaptic-like contacts (Felten, Ackerman, Wiegand, & Felten, 1987; Felten et al., 1985; Felten & Olschowka, 1987; Madden, Rajan, Bellinger, Felten, & Felten, 1997). Consequently, catecholamines released from either the adrenal medulla or local sympathetic nerves may influence immune function. Indeed, lymphocytes possess adrenergic receptors that induce a change in the pattern of cytokine production following stimulation. For example, adrenergic agonists decrease TH-1 cytokine production (e.g., IL-2 and IFN-γ), but have no effect on TH-2 cytokine production (e.g., IL-4; Ramer-Quinn, Baker, & Sanders, 1997; Sanders et al., 1997). In humans, catecholamine infusion increases the number of peripheral blood lymphocytes, likely due to actions at the β_2 adrenergic receptor (Schedlowski et al., 1996). Natural killer (NK) cells, thought to be important in the surveillance and elimination of tumor and virus-infected cells, appear to be especially sensitive to catecholamines, increasing in number (Crary et al., 1983) and cytotoxic ability (Nomoto, Karasawa, & Uehara, 1994).

Although the HPA axis and SNS are major pathways by which stress can influence immune function, other systems, such as the opioid system, are also involved (Rabin, 1999). Furthermore, brain-immune communication is bidirectional. A growing body of literature acknowledges that the immune system can modulate brain activity and subsequent behavior via the production of cytokines (Dantzer et al., 1998). The immune system acts as a diffuse sensory organ by providing information about antigenic challenges to the brain, which, in turn, regulates behaviors appropriate to deal with these challenges (Maier & Watkins, 1998).

ACUTE VERSUS CHRONIC STRESS

As stress-induced modulations of brain-immune relationships were discovered, multiple types of stressors that varied in duration, intensity, and controllability were studied. In comparing the effects of acute and chronic stress on immune function, different patterns have emerged depending on the model of stress being studied. Using an animal model of stress, Dhabhar and McEwen (1997) operationally defined acute stress as restraint for two hours, and chronic stress as daily restraint for three to five weeks. Exposure of humans to laboratory stressors generally falls within this definition of acute stress, while the chronic stress of long-term events such as caregiving may last for years (Heston, Mastri, Anderson, & White, 1981). The stress of major academic examinations is often preceded by a period of anxiety that varies (Bolger, 1990), and therefore, may fall somewhere along the continuum of acute and chronic stress (i.e., subacute stress). No definitive criterion has been established for classifying stressors as acute, subacute, or chronic, but the general categories of acute and chronic will be used to illustrate the complexity of the different patterns of immunological changes that occur in various models of stress.

Acute Stress

Laboratory Stress

Exposure to laboratory stressors, such as mental arithmetic and public speaking tasks that generally lasted no longer than 20 minutes, were associated with lower CD4+/CD8+ (T helper/T cytotoxic-suppressor) cell ratios, poorer blastogenic responses, and increased catecholamine release (Bachen et al., 1995; Bachen et al., 1992; Burleson et al., 1998; Cacioppo et al., 1995; Herbert et al., 1994). These same studies also revealed that peripheral NK cell number and cytotoxicity (NKCC) were consistently increased. Furthermore, these stress-induced immune changes were blocked by an adrenergic receptor blocker (Bachen et al., 1995), suggesting that these short-term immune changes were largely mediated by sympathetically activated catecholamine release.

Studies using laboratory stressors have also revealed important individual differences in physiological responses to stress. For example, subjects who showed the greatest change in sympathetic activity to laboratory mental stress also had the greatest change in HPA activity and immune function, despite reporting similar levels of stress (Cacioppo et al., 1995; Herbert et al., 1994; Matthews et al., 1995). This suggests additional psychological or genetic factors may be responsible for the observed differences in physiological reactivity to laboratory stressors, and possibly other types of stressors. These differences may be explained, in part, by psychosocial factors such as negative affect, social support, and interpersonal relationships.

Academic Examination Stress

Using academic examinations as a model of "subacute" stress, depression and loneliness in first-year medical students increased during final exams compared to the less stressful baseline period (Kiecolt-Glaser et al., 1984). In contrast to studies that used laboratory stressors, NKCC was decreased, and students who reported the highest levels of loneliness had the lowest NKCC (Kiecolt-Glaser et al., 1984). Compared to the less stressful baseline period, examination stress also impaired blastogenic responses to the mitogens PHA and concanavalin A (Con A; Glaser, Kiecolt-Glaser, Stout, et al., 1985). An inhibition of the memory immune (blastogenic) response to Epstein-Barr Virus (EBV) polypeptides was also observed (Glaser et al., 1993). Production of interferon-gamma (IFN-γ), an important antitumor and antiviral cytokine (Bloom, 1980), was decreased in leukocytes obtained at the time of exams (Glaser, Rice, Speicher, Stout, & Kiecolt-Glaser, 1986). Additional studies confirmed examination stress-induced changes in leukocyte numbers (Maes et al., 1999), serum immunoglobulin levels (Maes et al., 1997), and cytokine production (Maes et al., 1998).

Comparison of the delayed type hypersensitivity (DTH) response to acute stress in animals and humans adds complexity to the domain of acute stress. For example, stress associated with an academic examination suppressed DTH responses in subjects who reported higher levels of stress (Vedhara & Nott, 1996), while acute restraint stress in rodents during the sensitization or challenge phase enhanced DTH responses (Dhabhar & McEwen, 1997; Dhabhar, Satoskar, Bluethmann, David, & McEwen, 2000). In another study, socially inhibited individuals showed heightened DTH responses compared to controls following five weekly sessions of high-intensity social engagement (Cole, Kemeny, Weitzman, Schoen, & Anton, 1999). Further research will be required to understand these complex interactions.

The clinical importance of the immunological changes associated with examination stress is underscored by several findings. First, students who reported greater distress during exams took longer to seroconvert after inoculation with a hepatitis B vaccine (Glaser, Kiecolt-Glaser, Bonneau, Malarkey, Kennedy, et al., 1992). They also had lower antibody titers to the vaccine six months postinoculation and a less vigorous virus-specific T cell response. Furthermore, examination stress was associated with reactivation of two latent herpesviruses, EBV and herpes simplex virus type-1 (HSV-1; Glaser, Kiecolt-Glaser, Speicher, & Holliday, 1985; Glaser, Pearl, Kiecolt-Glaser, & Malarkey, 1994). Finally, examination stress prolonged the time to heal a standardized oral wound compared to a low stress period (three days or 40% longer to heal); in fact, none of the students healed as fast during exams as they did during vacation (Marucha, Kiecolt-Glaser, & Favagehi, 1998). This delay in wound healing was accompanied by a reduction in the production of the proinflammatory cytokine IL-1β, which, in addition to IL1-α, is important in the early stages of wound healing (Barbul, 1990; Lowry, 1993).

Importantly, glucocorticoids modulate processes involved in wound healing. For example, exogenously administered glucocorticoids suppressed the production of several proinflammatory cytokines, delaying wound healing (Hubner et al., 1996). Furthermore, restraint stress in mice increased corticosterone levels and prolonged wound healing, which was normalized when a glucocorticoid receptor antagonist was administered (Padgett, Marucha, & Sheridan, 1998). In a related human study, perceived stress was associated with increased salivary cortisol production and decreased mRNA levels of the cytokine IL-1α in peripheral blood leucocytes (Glaser, Kiecolt-Glaser, et al., 1999). Thus, the HPA axis appears to be an important factor in the stress-induced delay of wound healing, likely via regulation of cytokine production.

Chronic Stress

To explore the question of whether stress-induced immunological changes adapt over time and perhaps eventually return to prestress values, we studied a sample of chronically stressed caregivers of family members with progressive dementia disorders, primarily Alzheimer's disease (AD). Following disease onset, modal survival time for patients with AD is about eight years (Heston et al., 1981). Caregivers report greater distress and depression and reduced social support compared to noncaregivers (Bodnar & Kiecolt-Glaser, 1994; D. Cohen & Eisdorfer, 1988; Dura, Stukenberg, & Kiecolt-Glaser, 1990; Kiecolt-Glaser, Dura, Speicher, Trask, & Glaser, 1991; Redinbaugh, MacCallum, & Kiecolt-Glaser, 1995). Thus, caregiving has been conceptualized as a model of chronic stress.

As with short-term stress, chronic stress has significant effects on immune function. For example, caregiving was associated with lower percentages of T helper and total T cells and poorer cellular immunity against latent EBV (Kiecolt-Glaser, Glaser, et al., 1987). In a longitudinal study of spousal caregivers and community matched controls, caregivers showed greater decrements in cellular immunity over time as measured by decreased blastogenic responses to PHA and Con A (Kiecolt-Glaser et al., 1991). Additional studies have confirmed that caregiving is associated with reduced blastogenic responses (Castle, Wilkins, Heck, Tanzy, & Fahey, 1995; Glaser & Kiecolt-Glaser, 1997), decreased virus-specific-induced cytokine production (Kiecolt-Glaser, Glaser, Gravenstein, Malarkey, & Sheridan, 1996), inhibition of the NK cell response to recombinant IL-2 (rIL-2) and rIFN-γ (Esterling, Kiecolt-Glaser, & Glaser, 1996), and reduced sensitivity of lymphocytes to certain effects of glucocorticoids (Bauer et al., 2000).

Other studies have confirmed that chronic stress may have behavioral and immunological consequences. Following the nuclear reactor meltdown at Three Mile Island (TMI) in 1979, psychological assessments revealed that local TMI residents reported more symptoms of distress and intrusive thoughts and continued to have higher blood pressure, heart rate, norepinephrine, and cortisol levels than control subjects who lived 80 miles away, up to five years after the accident (Davidson & Baum, 1986). TMI residents also had fewer B lymphocytes, T-suppressor/cytotoxic lymphocytes and NK cells, as well as evidence for reactivation of latent HSV (McKinnon, Weisse, Reynolds, Bowles, & Baum, 1989). In the aftermath of the Northridge earthquake, local residents similarly showed a decrease in T cell numbers, blastogenic responses, and NKCC (Solomon, Segerstrom, Grohr, Kemeny, & Fahey, 1997).

Chronic stress can have significant clinical consequences. As previously mentioned, caregivers and TMI residents showed evidence for reactivation of latent herpes viruses (Glaser & Kiecolt-Glaser, 1997; McKinnon et al., 1989). Following influenza vaccination, caregivers were less likely to achieve a four-fold increase in antibody titers than controls (Kiecolt-Glaser, Glaser, et al., 1996; Vedhara et al., 1999), which suggests greater susceptibility or more serious illness in the event of exposure to influenza virus. Caregivers also took 24% longer to heal a standardized punch biopsy wound (Kiecolt-Glaser, Marucha, Malarkey, Mercado, & Glaser, 1995) and reported a greater number and duration of illness episodes, with more physician visits than control subjects (Kiecolt-Glaser & Glaser, 1991).

The immune dysregulation associated with caregiving may be especially relevant for older adults, as cellular immunity declines with age (Bender, Nagel, Adler, & Andres, 1986; Murasko, Weiner, & Kaye, 1987), and is associated with greater morbidity and mortality, especially due to infectious diseases (Murasko, Gold, Hessen, & Kaye, 1990; Wayne, Rhyne, Garry, & Goodwin, 1990). However, even in younger populations, longer term stress (greater than one month) has been associated with immune dysregulation and increased susceptibility to infection by a common cold virus (Cohen et al., 1998).

The studies mentioned support the argument that immunological dysregulation associated with chronic stress does not necessarily undergo habituation over time. Rather, these effects appear to be present for the duration of the stressor, and in some cases, persist even after the stressor is no longer present (Esterling, Kiecolt-Glaser, Bodnar, & Glaser, 1994).

INDIVIDUAL PSYCHOLOGICAL DIFFERENCES

Negative emotions are related to a range of diseases whose onset and course may be influenced by the immune system, particularly by inflammation resulting from the production of proinflammatory cytokines (Kiecolt-Glaser, McGuire, Robles, & Glaser, 2002). Individual differences in emotional and coping responses may account for some of the variation in neuroendocrine and immunological changes associated with stress. Currently, research is aimed at identifying the relationships among these changes and emotional traits and states, daily subclinical fluctuations in mood, bereavement, clinical disorders of major depression and anxiety, and coping strategies.

Negative and Positive Affect

Negative affect is defined as general subjective distress and includes a range of negative mood states, such as depression, anxiety, and hostility (Watson & Pennebaker, 1989). Cohen and colleagues demonstrated an association between negative affect and rates of respiratory infection and clinical colds following intentional exposure to five different respiratory viruses (S. Cohen, Tyrrell, & Smith, 1991). A dose-response relationship was found between rates of respiratory infection/ clinical colds and increased levels of a composite measure of psychological stress that included negative affect, major stressful life events, and perceived ability to cope with current stressors. In further analyses of these data, negative affect predicted the probability of developing a cold across the five different upper respiratory infection viruses independent of negative life events (S. Cohen, Tyrrell, & Smith, 1993). Furthermore, the higher illness complaints in individuals high in state negative affect were associated with increased severity of colds and influenza as seen in the amount of mucus produced (S. Cohen et al., 1995). However, negative affect was not related to the development of clinical colds among already infected individuals but rather was associated with individuals' susceptibility to infection (S. Cohen et al., 1993; Stone et al., 1992).

In another study, baseline personality variables that are thought to be characteristic of negative affect (high internalizing, neuroticism, and low self-esteem) predicted lower titers of rubella antibodies 10 weeks postvaccination in subjects who were seronegative prior to vaccination (Morag, Morag, Reichenberg, Lerer, & Yirmiya, 1999). This relationship was not found in subjects who were seropositive prior to vaccination.

Dispositional positive affect and the expectation of positive outcomes, termed optimism, have been less well studied in relation to immune variables. Davidson and colleagues (Davidson, Coe, Dolski, & Donzella, 1999) demonstrated positive relationships between NKCC and greater positive dispositional mood, defined by relative left-sided anterior brain activation. Greater relative left-sided activation was associated with higher levels of basal NKCC and with smaller declines in NKCC from a nonstress baseline to a final exam period that occurred six weeks later.

Although optimism has been related to positive physical health outcomes in surgery patients (Scheier et al., 1999), its association with immune function has been inconsistent among prospective studies of naturalistic stressors. These inconsistencies might be due to different methodology in defining optimism, different periods of follow-up for immune measures, and differences in the presence and definition of acute and chronic stress. Segerstrom, Taylor, Kemeny, and Fahey (1998) examined optimism and immune function in first-year law students before entry into the law school program and again at midsemester, two months before students' first examination period. Dispositional optimism was not related to immune measures but to higher situational optimism (defined as positive expectations specific to academic performance) and was associated with higher NKCC. This association was partially mediated by lower levels of perceived stress. In another study, healthy women were followed for three months, using daily self-reports of stressful events. In this case, dispositional optimism was associated with a greater reduction in NKCC following high stress that lasted longer than one week compared to less optimistic individuals (F. Cohen et al., 1999). Thus, optimism may have differential effects on NKCC, depending on whether situational or dispositional optimism is measured.

Daily Negative and Positive Mood

The relationships between normal daily mood fluctuations and immune variables have been evaluated by tracking subjects' naturalistic mood changes and by inducing positive and negative mood states in the laboratory. In the first case, negative mood over the course of two days was associated with reduced NKCC, but there was evidence that positive mood moderated this association (Valdimarsdottir & Bovbjerg, 1997). In the second case, studies of induced mood in the laboratory have shown transient increases in NKCC (Futterman, Kemeny, Shapiro, & Fahey, 1994; Knapp et al., 1992), but conflicting outcomes related to the lymphocyte proliferative response to PHA. Both positive and negative induced mood conditions were associated with a decreased response to PHA (Knapp et al., 1992), whereas positive induced mood was associated with an increased response to PHA and negative induced mood was associated with a decreased response to PHA (Futterman et al., 1994). The differences in immune outcomes in these two laboratory-induced mood studies may be, in part, due to different levels of arousal and physical activity during the mood induction procedure and the use of trained actors in one study (Futterman et al., 1994). Nevertheless, the different NKCC responses to mood in the naturalistic and laboratory studies parallel the different NKCC responses to stress in the acute and laboratory studies described earlier.

Bereavement

Early studies of bereavement and immune function showed reduced lymphocyte proliferation to the mitogens Con A and PHA relative to controls in bereaved spouses two months after the death of their spouse (Bartrop, Luckhurst, Lazarus, Kiloh, & Penny, 1977). In a within-subjects design, lymphocyte proliferation to Con A, PHA, and pokeweed mitogen (PWM) was decreased for two months, relative to the prebereavement response (Schleifer, Keller, Camerino, Thorton, & Stein, 1983). The severity of depressive symptoms in women experiencing bereavement or anticipating bereavement due to their husbands' diagnosis of metastatic lung cancer was negatively related to NKCC (Irwin, Daniels, Smith, Bloom, & Weiner, 1987). Conflicting immunological consequences of bereavement in HIV seropositive gay males have been reported (Kemeny et al., 1995; Kessler et al., 1991) but may be, in part, due to individuals' different coping strategies in response to bereavement (Bower, Kemeny, Taylor, & Fahey, 1998).

Studies of the immunological impact of bereavement have generally included small sample sizes and short follow-up periods. The mechanisms underlying the association between bereavement and immune changes and the time line of such changes have not been identified, but changes in mood, health behaviors, and neuroendocrine function have been proposed.

Depression

Clinical depression has been associated with reduced NKCC (Irwin, Patterson, & Smith, 1990; Irwin, Smith, & Gillin, 1987), decreased lymphocyte proliferation to mitogens (Schleifer et al., 1984), poorer specific proliferative response (memory) to varicella-zoster virus (Irwin et al., 1998), and decreased delayed-type hypersensitivity (Hickie, Hickie, Lloyd, Silove, & Wakefield, 1993). Nonmeta-analytic review studies have drawn different conclusions about the existence of an association between depression and immune function (Stein, Miller, & Trestman, 1991; Weisse, 1992); however, a meta-analytic review concluded that clinically depressed individuals, especially older and hospitalized individuals, have lower lymphocyte proliferative responses to PHA, Con A, and PWM and have lower NKCC compared to nondepressed,

healthy controls (Herbert & Cohen, 1993). A classic study by Schleifer, Keller, Bond, Cohen, and Stein (1989) most clearly showed the interactions of age, depression, and immune function; older depressed individuals had the lowest lymphocyte proliferation to mitogen compared to controls.

Mild to moderate levels of clinical depression in nonhospitalized individuals were associated with reduced lymphocyte proliferation and decreased NKCC (Miller, Cohen, & Herbert, 1999). Nonclinical depressed mood also has been reliably associated with decreased NKCC and decreased lymphocyte proliferative response to PHA, although the effect sizes of these relationships are smaller than for clinically depressed mood (Herbert & Cohen, 1993). The time course of immunological correlates in depression is not known, but individuals that recovered from depression no longer showed decreased NKCC (Irwin, Lacher, & Caldwell, 1992).

One potential pathway for the association of depression and immune function includes alterations in health behaviors, such as sleep, exercise, smoking, diet, and alcohol and drug use (Kiecolt-Glaser & Glaser, 1988). Patients with depression or alcoholism showed reduced NKCC relative to controls, and dually diagnosed patients showed even greater NKCC reductions (Irwin, Caldwell, et al., 1990). Physical activity mediated the association between mild to moderate depression and reduced proliferation to Con A and PHA in ambulatory female outpatients (Miller, Cohen, et al., 1999). Depressed men who smoked light to moderate amounts had the lowest NKCC, whereas nonsmoking depressed subjects, control smokers, and control nonsmokers did not differ from one another (Jung & Irwin, 1999). Other potential pathways include SNS and endocrine dysregulation. Although such physiological dysregulation has been shown in depression (Chrousos, Torpy, & Gold, 1998; Gold, Goodwin, & Chrousos, 1988), these pathways have not been consistently linked to alterations in immune function in depressed individuals (Miller, Cohen, et al., 1999; Schleifer, Keller, Bartlett, Eckholdt, & Delaney, 1996; Schleifer et al., 1989).

Anxiety

Higher levels of anxious mood have been related to a poorer immune response to a hepatitis B vaccination series (Glaser, Kiecolt-Glaser, Bonneau, Malarkey, & Hughes, 1992), lower proliferative responses to Con A and lower plasma levels of IL-1β (Zorrilla, Redei, & DeRubeis, 1994), decreased NKCC (Locke et al., 1984), and higher antibody titers to latent EBV (Esterling, Antoni, Kumar, & Schneiderman, 1993). Anxiety related to the anticipation of HIV serostatus notification has been associated with higher plasma cortisol levels, which were associated with lower lymphocyte proliferation to PHA

(Antoni et al., 1990) and decreased NKCC in the postacute notification period in gay males (Ironson et al., 1990). High levels of trait worry, a central feature of generalized anxiety disorder (GAD), interfered with the increase in NK cells in peripheral blood seen in individuals with a normal level of trait worry during exposure to an acute stressor (Segerstrom, Glover, Craske, & Fahey, 1999), and was associated with 25% fewer NK cells throughout a four-month follow-up period following the natural disaster of an earthquake (Segerstrom et al., 1998b).

The association between clinical diagnoses of anxiety disorders and immune function is a recent focus of investigation. Significant associations have not been found with obsessive-compulsive disorder (Maes, Meltzer, & Bosmans, 1994), and discrepant outcomes have been reported with panic disorder (Andreoli et al., 1992; Brambilla et al., 1992; Rapaport, 1998; Weizman, Laor, Wiener, Wolmer, & Bessler, 1999). More consistent immune relationships have been reported for GAD and posttraumatic stress disorder (PTSD). Patients with GAD showed changes in monocyte function and structure, reduced NKCC, reduced lymphocyte proliferation to PHA, and a poorer response to two DTH tests compared to controls (Castilla-Cortazar, Castilla, & Gurpegui, 1998), reduced IL-2 production (Koh & Lee, 1998), and lower expression of IL-2 receptors on stimulated T cells compared to controls (La Via et al., 1996). Chronic PTSD has been associated with elevated lymphocyte, total T cell, and CD4+ T cell counts in Vietnam combat veterans (Boscarino & Chang, 1999) and a higher index of lymphocyte activation in patients with a history of childhood sexual abuse (Wilson, van der Kolk, Burbridge, Fisler, & Kradin, 1999).

The outcomes of the studies that have evaluated the association of clinical anxiety disorders and immune function should be considered preliminary. The sample sizes are small and there is wide variability in the methodology and rigor of the studies. It is not yet known what aspects of clinical anxiety disorders, such as classes of symptoms, severity and time course of symptoms, arousal, or hypervigilance, are most important for immunity. The consequences of comorbid disorders, especially depression, and mixed groups of anxiety disorder patients require further evaluation.

Coping

Individual differences in appraisal and response to stressful situations have been evaluated through assessment of coping strategies. The positive or negative association of coping strategies with immune function appears to depend, to some extent, on stress levels, with active coping being significantly related to more vigorous proliferative responses to

PHA and Con A in individuals who report high stress levels, but not in those who report low stress levels (Stowell, Kiecolt-Glaser, & Glaser, 2001).

Reactivation of latent EBV in healthy college students was associated with a repressive personality style and a tendency to not disclose emotion on a laboratory task (Esterling, Antoni, Kumar, & Schneiderman, 1990) and to higher levels of defensiveness (Esterling et al., 1993). Repressive personality or coping style were not related to immune measures following an earthquake, but an appropriate psychological reaction to the realistic degree of life stress caused by the earthquake was described as least disruptive to immune measures (Solomon et al., 1997). In partners of bone marrow transplant patients, escape-avoidance coping was the strongest and most consistent variable associated with changes indicative of poorer immune function, especially during the anticipatory period prior to the initiation of the transplant (Futterman, Wellisch, Zighelboim, Luna-Raines, & Weiner, 1996). Greater denial in gay men awaiting notification of HIV seronegative status was associated with less impairment in PHA response at baseline, perhaps through a reduction in intrusive thoughts related to notification (Antoni et al., 1990).

Disease Progression

Evidence of greater risk of physical morbidity and mortality in individuals with depression (Herrmann et al., 1998; Penninx et al., 1999) suggests an important association between psychosocial factors and disease onset and progression. The association of psychosocial factors and cancer remains controversial due to conflicting study outcomes. Some prospective studies have found greater cancer-related mortality in depressed individuals (Persky, Kempthorne-Rawson, & Shekelle, 1987; Shekelle et al., 1981), while other studies have not found this relationship (Kaplan & Reynolds, 1988; Zonderman, Costa, & McCrae, 1989). The most promising psychological factors related to tumor progression include a low level of social support, hopelessness, and repression of negative emotions (see for review Garssen & Goodkin, 1999; Kiecolt-Glaser & Glaser, 1999).

Significant psychosocial associations have been found in the progression of HIV. Depression has been associated with an increased rate of CD4+ T-cell decline in HIV-seropositive men, but the relationship appears to depend on the presence of higher levels of CD4+ cells in the early stage of disease (Burack et al., 1993; Lyketsos et al., 1993). More rapid disease progression has been associated with greater concealment of homosexual identity (Cole, Kemeny, Taylor, Visscher, & Fahey, 1996), high realistic acceptance and negative expectations about future health (Reed, Kemeny, Taylor, Wang, & Visscher, 1994), attribution of negative events to the self (Segerstrom, Taylor, Kemeny, Reed, & Visscher, 1996), a passive coping style (Goodkin, Fuchs, Feaster, Leeka, & Rishel, 1992), and denial of diagnosis in seropositive gay men (Ironson et al., 1994). Alternatively, more deliberate cognitive processing about the death of a close friend or partner was associated with greater likelihood of finding positive meaning in the loss, and greater positive meaning was associated with a less rapid decline in levels of CD4+ cells over three years and lower rates of AIDS-related mortality nine years later in HIV-seropositive men (Bower et al., 1998).

From the studies reviewed, it appears that the immunological effects of stressors are influenced by affective, cognitive, behavioral, and psychosocial individual differences in appraisal and response to stressors. Through better understanding and assessment of the role of individual differences in physiological responses, we may more accurately predict immune changes in the context of stress. The physiological mechanisms that underlie the psychosocial and immune function associations are not yet fully known, but the HPA, SAM, SNS, and opioid systems are likely involved (Rabin, 1999).

SOCIAL RELATIONSHIPS AND PSYCHONEUROIMMUNOLOGY

Psychoneuroimmunology research focusing on social relationships originated from a larger literature on the relationships between social support and health. Cassel (1976) and Cobb (1976) provided important theoretical and empirical integration of social support and health research, concluding that social support was positively associated with health outcomes. Following the publication of these reviews, research on social support and health experienced "geometric growth" (House, Landis, & Umberson, 1988). In particular, epidemiological studies showed that lower social integration (lower number of social relationships and activities) was consistently associated with higher risk of mortality, independent of age, physical health, and a number of other health behavior risk factors (Berkman & Syme, 1979; House, Robbins, & Metzner, 1982; Schoenbach, Kaplan, Fredman, & Kleinbaum, 1986). In their seminal review of this work, House et al. (1988) concluded that "social relationships, or the relative lack thereof, constitute a major risk factor for health—rivaling the effects of well-established health risk factors such as cigarette smoking, blood pressure, blood lipids, obesity, and physical activity" (p. 541). The underlying theme of psychoneuroimmunology and social support research is that positive support provided by social relationships protects against susceptibility to disease by promoting immune competence. At the same time, negative qualities of social relationships may act as stressors, resulting in compromised immune function.

Social Relationships

Cross-Sectional Studies

In the first published cross-sectional study of social support and immune function, a greater number of frank and confiding relationships was associated with higher total lymphocyte counts and a greater blastogenic response to PHA in women, with smaller effects found for men (Thomas, Goodwin, & Goodwin, 1985). Subsequent studies examined these relationships in the context of stressful life events. In the context of job strain, greater social support was associated with lower levels of serum IgG, but only for persons under high job strain (Theorell, Orth-Gomer, & Eneroth, 1990). As previously discussed, in a series of studies of spousal caregivers for AD patients, lower levels of helpful emotional and tangible support in caregivers were associated with an inhibition of NK cell responses (Esterling, Kiecolt-Glaser, et al., 1994; Esterling et al., 1996). Similarly, in spouses of cancer patients, lymphocyte proliferation to PHA and NK cell activity were positively associated with perceived provision of various types of social support (Baron, Cutrona, Hicklin, Russell, & Lubaroff, 1990).

Prospective Studies

Prospective studies of social support and immune function have focused on samples undergoing both chronic and acute life events. Caregivers of AD patients reported less social support than controls, and caregivers with low social support showed a greater negative change in immune function from intake to follow-up (Kiecolt-Glaser et al., 1991). In patients undergoing an acute stress, hernia surgery, perceived social support was positively correlated with lymphocyte proliferation to mitogens both pre- and post-operation (Linn, Linn, & Klimas, 1988). Finally, in a sample of both healthy and asthmatic adolescents, social support was positively associated with CD4+/CD8+ ratios and neutrophil superoxide production at higher levels of perceived stress (Kang, Coe, Karszewski, & McCarthy, 1998).

Clinical Disease Studies

Studies of clinical disease and social support are important in psychoneuroimmunology research because they are directly relevant to clinical health outcomes. This research is especially informative to current approaches to clinical treatment of infectious disease and cancer, by suggesting that psychosocial interventions can promote lower susceptibility and increased resistance (Andersen, Kiecolt-Glaser, & Glaser, 1994; Glaser, Rabin, Chesney, Cohen, & Natelson, 1999). One of the first studies used an academic examination paradigm to investigate acute stress, social support, and immune response to hepatitis B vaccination (Glaser, Kiecolt-Glaser, Bonneau, Malarkey, & Hughes, 1992). Although no differences in seroconversion rates were found when comparing subjects on social support, social support was positively associated with the immune response to the vaccine as measured by total antibody titers and T cell responses to the vaccine antigen. Similarly, subjects with low social integration (less diverse social roles) were three times more likely to develop clinical symptoms of cold when infected with a cold virus compared to subjects with high social integration (Cohen, Doyle, Skoner, Rabin, & Gwaltney, 1997).

A large number of studies on social support have involved HIV-positive individuals who had not yet progressed to AIDS (asymptomatic). Given the positive benefits of social support on immune function, perhaps HIV-positive individuals with high social support would show a slower decline in immune competence associated with progression to AIDS. Although initial studies indicated negative findings (Goodkin, Blaney, et al., 1992; Perry, Fishman, Jacobsberg, & Frances, 1992), later studies found increased social participation and decreased loneliness to be associated with higher CD4+ counts (Persson, Gullberg, Hanson, Moestrup, & Ostergren, 1994; Straits-Troester et al., 1994). Moreover, low perceived emotional support was associated with a more rapid decline in CD4+ cells (Theorell et al., 1995).

Social Support-Immune Pathways

Considerable evidence suggests that social support contributes positively to immune function. The pathways through which social relationships can influence immune competence appear to be through primarily stress-buffering effects (Esterling, Kiecolt-Glaser, et al., 1994; Esterling et al., 1996; Goodkin, Blaney, et al., 1992; Kang et al., 1998; Kiecolt-Glaser et al., 1991; Theorell et al., 1990), although ample evidence suggests that immunological regulation is promoted by the mere presence of supportive others (S. Cohen et al., 1997; Levy et al., 1990; Linn et al., 1988; Persson et al., 1994; Theorell et al., 1995; Thomas et al., 1985). The magnitude of these effects appears to be small ($r = .21$), as shown in a meta-analysis of the literature up to 1995 (Uchino, Cacioppo, & Kiecolt-Glaser, 1996). However, these effects may have clinical relevance because social

relationships can be associated with both disease susceptibility (common cold, hepatitis B studies) and progression (breast cancer, HIV/AIDS). Moreover, this effect is impressive given the diverse conceptualizations and assessments of both social support and immune function.

Close Personal Relationships

While the previously reviewed studies explored the support relationships provided by one's social network (friends, family, coworkers, etc.), certain social relationships have greater psychological and physiological importance than others. Close personal relationships provide a unique source of social support, often encompassing all of the four general components of social support (e.g., emotional support, instrumental support, informational support, and appraisal support). Arguably, the most important close personal relationship is the marital relationship. Married persons have lower rates of morbidity and mortality compared to nonmarried persons across a variety of conditions, including cancer, myocardial infarction, and surgery (Chandra, Szklo, Goldberg, & Tonascia, 1983; Goodwin, Hunt, Key, & Samet, 1987; Gordon & Rosenthal, 1995; House et al., 1988).

Although healthy marital relationships afford health benefits, disruptions in the marital relationship are associated with health risks. Separated or divorced adults have higher rates of acute illness and physician visits compared to married persons and higher rates of mortality from infectious diseases, including pneumonia (Somers, 1979; Verbrugge, 1979, 1982). As such, PNI studies in this domain have focused on disruptive aspects of the marital relationship and their consequences for immune competence.

Marital Disruption

Initial studies of marital relationships and immune function focused on the immune consequences of separation and/or divorce (Kiecolt-Glaser, Fisher, et al., 1987; Kiecolt-Glaser et al., 1988). In these studies, married adults were compared to separated and/or divorced adults on enumerative and functional measures of immune function. Separated/divorced males and females showed higher IgG antibody titers to latent EBV, indicative of poorer immune competence in controlling the latent virus. Separated/divorced males also showed higher antibody titers to latent HSV, and separated/divorced females showed poorer blastogenic response to PHA compared to married counterparts. Poorer psychological adjustment to separation, particularly stronger feelings of attachment and shorter separation periods, were associated with increased distress, lower helper to suppressor T-cell ratios, and poorer blastogenic responses to mitogen. Subjective ratings of low marital quality, as measured by the Dyadic Adjustment Scale (Spanier, 1976), were associated with higher antibody titers to latent EBV for males and females. These findings suggest separation and divorce result in dysregulation of cell-mediated immunity, particularly for persons who have difficulty adapting.

Marital Interaction

Further studies of marital disruption focused on how behaviors exhibited during a couple's interaction were related to immune function. In the first study, we assessed autonomic, endocrine, and immune function over a 24-hour period in 90 newlywed couples who met stringent mental and physical criteria (Kiecolt-Glaser et al., 1993). Couples engaged in a 30-minute conflict resolution task in which they discussed current marital problems. Individuals who exhibited more hostile or negative behaviors during conflict showed greater decrements in functional immune measures, including decreased NK cell lysis, blastogenic response to PHA and Con A, and proliferative response to a monoclonal antibody against the T cell receptor. Notably, these declines in immune function were more likely to occur in women than men. In addition, similar to the previous findings, individuals who exhibited more negative or hostile behaviors during conflict had higher antibody titers to latent EBV. Thus, not only were negative behaviors during conflict a significant predictor of declines in marital satisfaction (Markman, 1991), but these same behaviors significantly predicted declines in immune function during a 24-hour period and in immune competence in controlling latent herpes viruses.

Older couples display less negative behavior and more affectionate behavior than younger couples during conflict (Carstensen, Levenson, & Gottman, 1995), and therefore may display a different pattern of immune changes. To explore this possibility, older couples (mean age = 67) who had been married an average of 42 years, were studied using the same paradigm as our newlywed study (Kiecolt-Glaser et al., 1997). Subjects who showed poorer responses on functional immune measures, including blastogenic responses to PHA and Con A, and antibody titers to latent EBV, engaged in more negative behavior during conflict. Moreover, these subjects characterized their typical marital disagreements as more negative than subjects with relatively better immune function. Overall, these results are particularly striking given that these couples, both young and old, had happy marriages and were mentally and physically fit. Thus, it is likely that these findings actually underestimate the physiological impact of marital strife (Kiecolt-Glaser, 1999).

Other studies of marital interaction also show that behavior during conflict is associated with immune modulation. A decrease in the blastogenic response to PHA was found in females, but not in males, in response to marital conflict, and this negative change was associated with increased hostility (Mayne, O'Leary, McCrady, Contrada, & Labouvie, 1997). Consistent with immunological changes during acute laboratory stress, marital conflict was associated with increased NK cell cytotoxicity, specific to male subjects high in hostility (Miller, Dopp, Myers, Felten, & Fahey, 1999). This is likely due to altered trafficking of specific NK cell subtypes into peripheral blood (Dopp, Miller, Myers, & Fahey, 2000).

In the context of the marital relationship, negative behaviors during an interaction are also reliably associated with endocrine changes. Newlywed couples exhibiting higher levels of hostile and negative behavior during conflict showed elevated levels of epinephrine, norepinephrine, ACTH, and growth hormone, and lower levels of prolactin (Malarkey, Kiecolt-Glaser, Pearl, & Glaser, 1994). Moreover, the association between high negative behavior and endocrine changes were stronger and more consistent for women compared to men. Higher probabilities of a husband's withdrawal in response to their wife's negative behavior were associated with higher norepinephrine and cortisol in wives. Behavior during marital conflict accounted for a significant proportion of variance in various endocrine measures, accounting for 24% to 37% of the variance over a 24-hour period (Kiecolt-Glaser, Newton, et al., 1996). Similar effects were found in older couples, with negative behaviors accounting for 16% to 21% of the variance in changes in cortisol, ACTH, and epinephrine (Kiecolt-Glaser et al., 1997). These endocrine changes may mediate the immune function changes observed during conflict.

Overall, these findings suggest that marital disruption can influence health outcomes through immunological pathways. In particular, high levels of hostile and negative behavior during marital conflict may be particularly harmful. Moreover, the endocrine and immunological changes in response to negative behavior are more readily observed in women compared to men. This suggests that the negative physiological impacts of marital discord are greater for women compared to men, though the gender discrepancy in health outcomes is less clear (Kiecolt-Glaser & Newton, 2001).

PSYCHOLOGICAL INTERVENTIONS

Evidence that psychosocial characteristics are associated with alterations in immune function suggests that psychological interventions targeting psychosocial vulnerability factors may have beneficial immune outcomes. In both healthy and ill (e.g., cancer, HIV) populations, psychological interventions, such as classical conditioning, relaxation and hypnosis, emotional disclosure, and cognitive-behavioral strategies, have been used to improve mood, coping ability, and social support in attempts to modulate immune function.

Classical Conditioning

Classical conditioning studies in rodents have demonstrated modulation of humoral, cell mediated, and nonspecific immunity with potential biological significance related to the onset and course of autoimmune diseases, morbidity, and mortality (see for review, Ader & Cohen, 1993; Ader, Felten, & Cohen, 1991). Although there have been few human studies of classical conditioning, their findings are encouraging. In one study, tuberculin DTH responses were conditioned by administering tuberculin once a month for six months. Tuberculin was drawn from a red vial and administered to one arm, while saline was drawn from a green vial and administered to the other arm. On the double blind test trial, the contents of the vials were switched. Saline did not produce a skin reaction on the arm that had previously received tuberculin, but the reaction to tuberculin was diminished on the arm that normally received saline (Smith & McDaniels, 1983).

In a second study, conditioning in a naturalistic setting was observed in women undergoing chemotherapy for ovarian cancer. Following repeated pairing of immunosuppressive chemotherapy with hospital stimuli, the hospital stimuli alone produced a suppression of lymphocyte proliferation to PHA and Con A (Bovbjerg et al., 1990). In a case study of pediatric lupus, neutral stimuli (a taste and a smell) were paired with a toxic immunosuppressive medication (cyclophosphamide). Following monthly conditioning trials, the patient showed clinical improvement and required only one-half the cumulative typical dose of medication (Olness & Ader, 1992). Additional studies have shown enhanced NKCC activity in response to neutral stimuli after they were paired with injections of epinephrine (Buske-Kirschbaum, Kirschbaum, Stierle, Jabaij, & Hellhammer, 1994; Buske-Kirschbaum, Kirschbaum, Stierle, Lehnert, & Hellhammer, 1992).

Relaxation and Hypnosis

A relaxation study with older adults in independent living facilities showed significant increases in NKCC and better control of latent HSV following one month, three times weekly, of progressive muscle relaxation training with guided imagery, compared to social contact and no intervention (Kiecolt-Glaser et al., 1985). These benefits were maintained at one-month follow-up. In a subsequent study, relaxation intervention with medical students prior to exams did not significantly alter stress-induced changes in immune function in the group as a whole. However, students who practiced relaxation more frequently had higher helper T-lymphocyte percentages during examinations, after controlling for baseline levels (Kiecolt-Glaser et al., 1986). Varied methods of relaxation and guided imagery intervention have been associated with increased lymphocyte proliferation to mitogens (McGrady et al., 1992), increased NKCC (Zachariae et al., 1990), increased plasma IL-1 (Keppel, Regan, Heffeneider, & McCoy, 1993), and enhanced neutrophil phagocytic activity (Peavey, Lawlis, & Goven, 1986).

Hypnosis studies using the "double arm" technique have evaluated whether individuals can intentionally modify their immunological response, such as immediate and delayed hypersensitivity. In these studies, the same allergic substance is injected into both arms of a subject and hypnotic suggestions are made about inflammatory response changes (e.g., itching, wheal, erythema) in one arm and no changes in the other arm. Differences in the responses of both arms have been found in several studies (Black, 1963; Black & Friedman, 1965; Black, Humphrey, & Niven, 1963; Zachariae & Bjerring, 1990; Zachariae, Bjerring, & Arendt-Nielsen, 1989), but not in others (Beahrs, Harris, & Hilgard, 1970; Locke et al., 1987).

Whether the hypersensitivity changes found in some studies are due to immune function changes or only skin surface changes remains to be determined. However, high hypnotizable individuals do produce greater immune changes than low hypnotizable subjects (Gregerson, Roberts, & Amiri, 1996; Ruzyla-Smith, Barabasz, Barabasz, & Warner, 1995; Zachariae, Jorgensen, Christensen, & Bjerring, 1997; Zachariae, Oster, & Bjerring, 1994).

Emotional Disclosure

Negative life events can have psychological impact for many years (Tait & Silver, 1989) and can result in persistent elevation of stress hormones (Baum, Cohen, & Hall, 1993). There is evidence that social constraints to emotional expression and discussion of negative events are associated with negative emotional (Lepore & Helgeson, 1998) and physiological (Helgeson, 1991) outcomes, including increased intrusive thoughts, more avoidant coping, and greater depression and anxiety. Emotional disclosure interventions, to the extent that they increase cognitive processing, alter appraisals, reduce intrusive thoughts, and reduce negative mental health consequences of negative events, have been related to positive alterations in immune function. These immune changes are found typically weeks to months postintervention. For example, healthy college students who wrote about personal, traumatic experiences showed increased lymphocyte proliferation to PHA and fewer health center visits at the six-week follow-up, and this effect was strongest for those who wrote about experiences they had not previously shared (Pennebaker, Kiecolt-Glaser, & Glaser, 1988). In another study, medical students who wrote about a highly traumatic personal event generated higher antibody titers to a hepatitis vaccination given on the last day of writing by four- and six-month follow-up than did control subjects who wrote about trivial topics (Petrie, Booth, Pennebaker, Davison, & Thomas, 1995). Four months following a written emotional disclosure intervention, asthma patients experienced improved lung function and rheumatoid arthritis patients had clinically significant improvements in overall disease activity, compared to controls (Smyth, Stone, Hurewitz, & Kaell, 1999). Finally, the extent to which individuals became emotionally and cognitively involved in the disclosure process, reorganized the meaning of the traumatic event, and reduced avoidance of the topic was correlated with the degree of change in antibody titers to latent EBV (Esterling, Antoni, Fletcher, Margulies, & Schneiderman, 1994; Lutgendorf, Antoni, Kumar, & Schneiderman, 1994).

Cancer

A classic, well-controlled study of the impact of a psychological intervention on immune function and progression of cancer involved Stage I and II malignant melanoma patients. A six-week structured group intervention included stress management, relaxation, support, health education, and problem-solving skills related to participants' illness (Fawzy et al., 1990). The patients who received the intervention had reduced psychological distress, increased percentage of NK cells, increased IFN-α augmented NKCC, and a small reduction in the percentage of helper T cells by six-month follow-up. Decreased depression and anxiety symptoms and increased assertiveness and defiance were related to increased NKCC. At the six-year follow-up, there was a trend for fewer recurrences and significantly lower mortality in the intervention subjects, even after controlling for the size of the initial malignant melanoma (Fawzy et al., 1993). In a study of breast cancer patients, a six-month intervention, including relaxation, guided imagery, and biofeedback, was associated with greater NKCC, lymphocyte proliferative response to Con A, and mixed lymphocyte responsiveness in women post radical mastectomy for stage 1 breast cancer (Gruber et al., 1993).

Another relaxation intervention study was targeted at altering conditioned anticipatory immune suppression in women receiving chemotherapy for ovarian cancer. The intervention included progressive muscle, release-only, and cue-controlled relaxation techniques and was practiced daily for more than four weeks. Training began the day before the start of the first course of chemotherapy. In this case, the relaxation intervention was not associated with reliable changes in NKCC or lymphocyte proliferation to Con A measured prior to subsequent courses of chemotherapy (Lekander, Furst, Rotstein, Hursti, & Fredrikson, 1997). Difficulties in interpreting the outcomes of cancer-related intervention studies stem from such methodological differences as method of assignment of subjects to control and intervention conditions, control for type and stage of disease, variable outcome measures, and different follow-up periods.

HIV

Several intervention studies involving HIV seropositive and seronegative gay men have found some positive effects of intervention on immune function. In the first of these studies, exercise interventions protected asymptomatic seropositive gay men from depression, anxiety, and a decrease in NK cell numbers that was observed in seropositive control subjects following notification of serostatus (LaPerriere et al., 1990). Similarly, a comprehensive 10-week cognitive-behavioral stress management intervention, which included relaxation training, cognitive restructuring, assertiveness training, anger management, and social support, was associated with significant increases in CD4+ and NK cell counts from 72 hours before to one week after HIV-positive serostatus notification in healthy, asymptomatic gay men (Antoni et al., 1991). Cognitive-behavioral and exercise interventions were also associated with better cellular immunity to the latent herpesviruses, EBV, and human herpes virus type-6 in asymptomatic seropositive gay men (Esterling et al., 1992), and HSV-2 in symptomatic gay men (Lutgendorf et al., 1997). Greater practice of relaxation (Antoni et al., 1991; Lutgendorf et al., 1997) and greater adherence to the intervention protocols (Ironson et al., 1994) were significant predictors of less distress and disease progression. In one other intervention study, progressive muscle relaxation and guided imagery were both associated with decreased depression in HIV seropositive individuals, but only progressive muscle relaxation was associated with a significant increase in CD4+ cell counts compared to controls (Eller, 1995).

Psychosocial factors may play a role in HIV progression because there is great variability among individuals in the length of time to develop clinical symptoms and in the severity of illness at different stages of AIDS. However, not all studies have shown significant relationships between psychosocial measures and immune variables in HIV-1 seropositive individuals (Perry et al., 1992; Rabkin et al., 1991) or between psychological intervention and immune changes (Coates, McKusick, Kuno, & Stites, 1989; Mulder et al., 1995). Such negative findings indicate the need for theoretically driven models of association between psychosocial and immune or health outcomes, controls for health behaviors, inclusion of a broad range of immune measures, and control for stage of disease (Goodkin et al., 1994).

Psychological interventions that show evidence of immune function modulation likely have their effects through alterations of appraisal, coping, or mood, which in turn affect health behaviors, endocrine activity, and immune function. The importance of intervention effects on negative emotions is demonstrated by studies showing covariation in immunological changes and reduced negative emotion (Antoni et al., 1991; Fawzy et al., 1990; Lutgendorf et al., 1997). The potential health outcomes of immunological changes that follow psychological interventions remain to be determined. Further studies are needed that more directly assess changes in disease incidence, severity, and duration, as well as studies that include immune measures in therapy outcome studies. Finally, in evaluating psychological intervention studies, it is important to remember that it may not be possible or desirable to enhance immune function (e.g., autoimmune disease) if the immune system is already functioning at normal levels. There is greater likelihood of positive intervention effects when participants show some degree of dysregulation in immune function relative to their demographically matched peers.

Health impact will likely depend on the type, intensity, and duration of intervention, the extent and duration of immune alteration, and prior immunological and health status (Kiecolt-Glaser & Glaser, 1992). Potential benefits of psychological interventions on immunity may be particularly relevant for wound healing and surgical recovery. In particular, interventions that target fear and distress before surgery and pain management following surgery may improve postoperative outcomes and recovery through modulation of endocrine and immune systems (Kiecolt-Glaser, Page, Marucha, MacCallum, & Glaser, 1998).

CONCLUSIONS

Basic and applied PNI research studies have provided an encouraging foundation for characterizing the links between psychosocial and immunological factors. The current knowledge of PNI with respect to individual psychological differences, emotions, coping strategies, and interpersonal relationships has already had a significant impact on understanding the contribution that the psychosocial context has on immune function, health, and disease. Further understanding of the bidirectional relationships between brain, behavior, and immunity will be attained with theoretical and methodological refinements. In addition to these refinements, the next wave of PNI research will expand our knowledge of psychosocial factors and their role in the progression of immunologically mediated conditions, including HIV/AIDS, rheumatoid arthritis, certain cancers, and surgical recovery. From this knowledge, we can devise and implement effective interventions to enhance quality of life and improve health. Indeed, PNI embodies the biopsychosocial approach (Engel, 1977) that has come to define health psychology.

REFERENCES

Ader, R., & Cohen, N. (1993). Psychoneuroimmunology: Conditioning and stress. *Annual Review of Psychology, 44,* 53–85.

Ader, R., Felten, D. L., & Cohen, N. (Eds.). (1991). *Psychoneuroimmunology.* New York: Academic Press.

Andersen, B. L., Kiecolt-Glaser, J. K., & Glaser, R. (1994). A biobehavioral model of cancer stress and disease course. *American Psychologist, 49,* 389–404.

Andreoli, A., Keller, S. E., Rabaeus, M., Zaugg, L., Garrone, G., & Taban, C. (1992). Immunity, major depression, and panic disorder comorbidity. *Biological Psychiatry, 31*(9), 896–908.

Antoni, M. H., August, B. A., LaPerriere, A. R., Baggett, H. I., Klimas, N. G., Ironson, G., et al. (1990). Psychological and neuroendocrine measures related to functional immune changes in anticipation of HIV-1 serostatus notification. *Psychosomatic Medicine, 52,* 496–510.

Antoni, M. H., Baggett, L., Ironson, G., August, S., LaPerriere, A. R., Klimas, N. G., et al. (1991). Cognitive-behavioral stress management intervention buffers distress responses and elevates immunologic markers following notification of HIV-1 seropositivity. *Journal of Consulting and Clinical Psychology, 59,* 906–915.

Bachen, E. A., Manuck, S. B., Cohen, S., Muldoon, M. F., Raible, R., Herbert, T. B., et al. (1995). Adrenergic blockade ameliorates cellular immune responses to mental stress in humans. *Psychosomatic Medicine, 57*(4), 366–372.

Bachen, E. A., Manuck, S. B., Marsland, A. L., Cohen, S., Malkoff, S. B., Muldoon, M. F., et al. (1992). Lymphocyte subset and cellular immune responses to a brief experimental stressor. *Psychosomatic Medicine, 54*(6), 673–679.

Barbul, A. (1990). Immune aspects of wound repair. *Clinics in Plastic Surgery, 17*(3), 433–442.

Baron, R. S., Cutrona, C. E., Hicklin, D., Russell, D. W., & Lubaroff, D. M. (1990). Social support and immune function among spouses of cancer patients. *Journal of Personality and Social Psychology, 59,* 344–352.

Bartrop, R., Luckhurst, E., Lazarus, L., Kiloh, L. G., & Penny, R. (1977). Depressed lymphocyte function after bereavement. *Lancet, 1*, 374–377.

Bauer, M. E., Vedhara, K., Perks, P., Wilcock, G. K., Lightman, S. L., & Shanks, N. (2000). Chronic stress in caregivers of dementia patients is associated with reduced lymphocyte sensitivity to glucocorticoids. *Journal of Neuroimmunology, 103*(1), 84–92.

Baum, A., Cohen, L., & Hall, M. (1993). Control and intrusive memories as possible determinants of chronic stress. *Psychosomatic Medicine, 55*, 274–286.

Beahrs, J. O., Harris, D. R., & Hilgard, E. R. (1970). Failure to alter skin inflammation by hypnotic suggestion in five subjects with normal skin reactivity. *Psychosomatic Medicine, 32*, 627–631.

Bender, B. S., Nagel, J. E., Adler, W. H., & Andres, R. (1986). Absolute peripheral blood lymphocyte count and subsequent mortality of elderly men. The Baltimore Longitudinal Study of Aging. *Journal of the American Geriatrics Society, 34*(9), 649–654.

Berkman, L. F., & Syme, S. L. (1979). Social networks, host resistance, and mortality: A nine-year follow-up study of Alameda County residents. *American Journal of Epidemiology, 109*, 186–204.

Black, S. (1963). Inhibition of immediate-type hypersensitivity response by direct suggestion under hypnosis. *British Medical Journal, 1*, 925–929.

Black, S., & Friedman, M. (1965). Adrenal function and the inhibition of allergic responses under hypnosis. *British Medical Journal, 1*, 562–567.

Black, S., Humphrey, J. H., & Niven, J. S. (1963). Inhibition of mantoux reaction by direct suggestion under hypnosis. *British Medical Journal, 1*, 1649–1652.

Bloom, B. R. (1980). Interferons and the immune system. *Nature, 284*(5757), 593–595.

Bodnar, J. C., & Kiecolt-Glaser, J. K. (1994). Caregiver depression after bereavement: Chronic stress isn't over when it's over. *Psychology and Aging, 9*(3), 372–380.

Bolger, N. (1990). Coping as a personality process: A prospective study. *Journal of Personality and Social Psychology, 59*(3), 525–537.

Boscarino, J. A., & Chang, J. (1999). Higher abnormal leukocyte and lymphocyte counts 20 years after exposure to severe stress: Research and clinical implications. *Psychosomatic Medicine, 61*(3), 378–386.

Bovbjerg, D. H., Redd, W. H., Maier, L. A., Holland, J. C., Lesko, L. M., Niedzwiecki, D., et al. (1990). Anticipatory immune suppression and nausea in women receiving cyclic chemotherapy for ovarian cancer. *Journal of Consulting and Clinical Psychology, 58*, 153–157.

Bower, J. E., Kemeny, M. E., Taylor, S. E., & Fahey, J. L. (1998). Cognitive processing, discovery of meaning, CD4 decline, and AIDS-related mortality among bereaved HIV-seropositive men. *Journal of Consulting and Clinical Psychology, 66*, 979–986.

Brambilla, F., Bellodi, L., Perna, G., Battaglia, M., Sciuto, G., Diaferia, G., et al. (1992). Psychoimmunoendocrine aspects of panic disorder. *Neuropsychobiology, 26*(1/2), 12–22.

Burack, J., Barrett, D. C., Stall, R. D., Chesney, M. A., Ekstrand, M. L., & Coates, T. J. (1993). Depressive symptoms and CD4 lymphocyte decline among HIV-infected men. *Journal of American Medicine Association, 270*, 2568–2573.

Burleson, M. H., Malarkey, W. B., Cacioppo, J. T., Poehlmann, K. M., Kiecolt-Glaser, J. K., Berntson, G. G., et al. (1998). Postmenopausal hormone replacement: Effects on autonomic, neuroendocrine, and immune reactivity to brief psychological stressors. *Psychosomatic Medicine, 60*(1), 17–25.

Buske-Kirschbaum, A., Kirschbaum, C., Stierle, H., Jabaij, L., & Hellhammer, D. (1994). Conditioned manipulation of natural killer (NK) cells in humans using a discriminative learning protocol. *Biological Psychology, 38*, 143–155.

Buske-Kirschbaum, A., Kirschbaum, C., Stierle, H., Lehnert, H., & Hellhammer, D. (1992). Conditioned increase of natural killer cell activity (NKCA) in humans. *Psychosomatic Medicine, 54*, 123–132.

Cacioppo, J. T., Malarkey, W. B., Kiecolt-Glaser, J. K., Uchino, B. N., Sgoutas-Emch, S. A., Sheridan, J. F., et al. (1995). Heterogeneity in neuroendocrine and immune responses to brief psychological stressors as a function of autonomic cardiac activation. *Psychosomatic Medicine, 57*(2), 154–164.

Carstensen, L. L., Levenson, R. W., & Gottman, J. M. (1995). Emotional behavior in long-term marriage. *Psychology of Aging, 10*, 140–149.

Cassel, J. (1976). The contribution of the social environment to host resistance. *American Journal of Epidemiology, 104*, 107–123.

Castilla-Cortazar, I., Castilla, A., & Gurpegui, M. (1998). Opioid peptides and immunodysfunction in patients with major depression and anxiety disorders. *Journal of Physiology and Biochemistry, 54*(4), 203–215.

Castle, S., Wilkins, S., Heck, E., Tanzy, K., & Fahey, J. (1995). Depression in caregivers of demented patients is associated with altered immunity: Impaired proliferative capacity, increased CD8+, and a decline in lymphocytes with surface signal transduction molecules (CD38+) and a cytotoxicity marker (CD56+ CD8+). *Clinical and Experimental Immunology, 101*(3), 487–493.

Chandra, V., Szklo, M., Goldberg, R., & Tonascia, J. (1983). The impact of marital status on survival after an acute myocardial infarction: A population-based study. *American Journal of Epidemiology, 117*, 320–325.

Chrousos, G. P., Torpy, D. J., & Gold, P. W. (1998). Interactions between the hypothalamic-pituitary-adrenal axis and the female reproductive system: Clinical implications. *Annals of Internal Medicine, 129*, 229–240.

Coates, T. J., McKusick, L., Kuno, R., & Stites, D. P. (1989). Stress reduction training changed number of sexual partners but no immune function in men with HIV. *American Journal of Public Health, 79*, 885–887.

Cobb, S. (1976). Social support as a moderator of life stress. *Psychosomatic Medicine, 38,* 300–314.

Cohen, D., & Eisdorfer, C. (1988). Depression in family members caring for a relative with Alzheimer's disease. *Journal of the American Geriatrics Society, 36*(10), 885–889.

Cohen, F., Kearney, K. A., Zegans, L. S., Kemeny, M. E., Neuhaus, J. M., & Stites, D. P. (1999). Differential immune system changes with acute and persistent stress for optimists vs. pessimists. *Brain, Behavior, and Immunity, 13,* 155–174.

Cohen, S., Doyle, W. J., Skoner, D. P., Fireman, P., Gwaltney, J. M., Jr., & Newsom, J. T. (1995). State and trait negative affect as predictors of objective and subjective symptoms of respiratory viral infections. *Journal of Personality and Social Psychology, 68*(1), 159–169.

Cohen, S., Doyle, W. J., Skoner, D. P., Rabin, B. S., & Gwaltney, J. M. (1997). Social ties and susceptibility to the common cold. *Journal of the American Medical Association, 277,* 1940–1944.

Cohen, S., Frank, E., Doyle, W. J., Skoner, D. P., Rabin, B. S., & Gwaltney, J. M., Jr. (1998). Types of stressors that increase susceptibility to the common cold in healthy adults. *Health Psychology, 17*(3), 214–223.

Cohen, S., Tyrrell, D. A., & Smith, A. P. (1991). Psychological stress and susceptibility to the common cold. *New England Journal of Medicine, 325*(9), 606–612.

Cohen, S., Tyrrell, D. A., & Smith, A. P. (1993). Negative life events, perceived stress, negative affect, and susceptibility to the common cold. *Journal of Personality and Social Psychology, 64,* 131–140.

Cole, S. W., Kemeny, M. E., Taylor, S. E., Visscher, B. R., & Fahey, J. L. (1996). Accelerated course of human immunodeficiency virus infection in gay men who conceal their homosexual identity. *Psychosomatic Medicine, 58,* 1–13.

Cole, S. W., Kemeny, M. E., Weitzman, O. B., Schoen, M., & Anton, P. A. (1999). Socially inhibited individuals show heightened DTH response during intense social engagement. *Brain, Behavior, and Immunity, 13*(2), 187–200.

Crary, B., Hauser, S. L., Borysenko, M., Kutz, I., Hoban, C., Ault, K. A., Weiner, H. L., et al. (1983). Epinephrine-induced changes in the distribution of lymphocyte subsets in peripheral blood of humans. *Journal of Immunology, 131*(3), 1178–1181.

Dantzer, R., Bluthe, R. M., Laye, S., Bret-Dibat, J. L., Parnet, P., & Kelley, K. W. (1998). Cytokines and sickness behavior. *Annals of the New York Academy of Sciences, 840,* 586–590.

Davidson, L. M., & Baum, A. (1986). Chronic stress and posttraumatic stress disorders. *Journal of Consulting and Clinical Psychology, 54*(3), 303–308.

Davidson, R. J., Coe, C. C., Dolski, I., & Donzella, B. (1999). Individual differences in prefrontal activation asymmetry predict natural killer cell activity at rest and in response to challenge. *Brain, Behavior, and Immunity, 13*(2), 93–108.

Daynes, R. A., & Araneo, B. A. (1989). Contrasting effects of glucocorticoids on the capacity of T cells to produce the growth factors interleukin 2 and interleukin 4. *European Journal of Immunology, 19*(12), 2319–2325.

Dhabhar, F. S., & McEwen, B. S. (1997). Acute stress enhances while chronic stress suppresses cell-mediated immunity in vivo: A potential role for leukocyte trafficking. *Brain, Behavior, and Immunity, 11*(4), 286–306.

Dhabhar, F. S., Satoskar, A. R., Bluethmann, H., David, J. R., & McEwen, B. S. (2000). Stress-induced enhancement of skin immune function: A role for gamma interferon. *Proceedings of the National Academy of Sciences of the United States of America, 97*(6), 2846–2851.

Dopp, J. M., Miller, G. E., Myers, H. F., & Fahey, J. L. (2000). Increased natural killer-cell mobilization and cytotoxicity during marital conflict. *Brain, Behavior, and Immunity, 14,* 10–26.

Dura, J. R., Stukenberg, K. W., & Kiecolt-Glaser, J. K. (1990). Chronic stress and depressive disorders in older adults. *Journal of Abnormal Psychology, 99*(3), 284–290.

Eller, L. S. (1995). Effects of two cognitive-behavioral interventions on immunity and symptoms in persons with HIV. *Annals of Behavioral Medicine, 17,* 339–348.

Engel, G. L. (1977). The need for a new medical model: A challenge for biomedicine. *Science, 196*(4286), 129–136.

Esterling, B. A., Antoni, M. H., Fletcher, M. A., Margulies, S., & Schneiderman, N. (1994). Emotional disclosure through writing or speaking modulates latent Epstein-Barr virus antibody titers. *Journal of Consulting and Clinical Psychology, 62*(1), 130–140.

Esterling, B. A., Antoni, M. H., Kumar, M., & Schneiderman, N. (1990). Emotional repression, stress disclosure responses, and Epstein-Barr viral capsid antigen titers. *Psychosomatic Medicine, 52,* 397–410.

Esterling, B. A., Antoni, M. H., Kumar, M., & Schneiderman, N. (1993). Defensiveness, trait anxiety, and Epstein-Barr viral capsid antigen antibody titers in healthy college students. *Health Psychology, 12*(2), 132–139.

Esterling, B. A., Antoni, M. H., Schneiderman, N., Carver, C. S., LaPerriere, A. R., Ironson, G., et al. (1992). Psychosocial modulation of antibody to Epstein-Barr viral capsid antigen and human herpes virus type-6 in HIV-1-infected and at-risk gay men. *Psychosomatic Medicine, 54,* 354–371.

Esterling, B. A., Kiecolt-Glaser, J. K., Bodnar, J. C., & Glaser, R. (1994). Chronic stress, social support, and persistent alterations in the natural killer cell response to cytokines in older adults. *Health Psychology, 13*(4), 291–298.

Esterling, B. A., Kiecolt-Glaser, J. K., & Glaser, R. (1996). Psychosocial modulation of cytokine-induced natural killer cell activity in older adults. *Psychosomatic Medicine, 58*(3), 264–272.

Fawzy, F. I., Fawzy, N. W., Hyun, C. S., Elashoff, R., Guthrie, D., Fahey, J. L., et al. (1993). Malignant melanoma: Effects of an early structured psychiatric intervention, coping, and affective state on recurrence and survival 6 years later. *Archives of General Psychiatry, 50,* 681–689.

Fawzy, F. I., Kemeny, M. E., Fawzy, N. W., Elashoff, R., Morton, D., Cousins, N., et al. (1990). A structured psychiatric intervention for cancer patients. *Archives of General Psychiatry, 47,* 729–735.

Felten, D. L., Ackerman, K. D., Wiegand, S. J., & Felten, S. Y. (1987). Noradrenergic sympathetic innervation of the spleen: I. Nerve fibers associate with lymphocytes and macrophages in specific compartments of the splenic white pulp. *Journal of Neuroscience Research, 18*(1), 28–36.

Felten, D. L., Felten, S. Y., Carlson, S. L., Olschowka, J. A., & Livnat, S. (1985). Noradrenergic and peptidergic innervation of lymphoid tissue. *Journal of Immunology, 135*(Suppl. 2), 755–765.

Felten, S. Y., & Olschowka, J. A. (1987). Noradrenergic sympathetic innervation of the spleen: II. Tyrosine hydroxylase (TH)-positive nerve terminals form synapticlike contacts on lymphocytes in the splenic white pulp. *Journal of Neuroscience Research, 18*(1), 37–48.

Futterman, A. D., Kemeny, M. E., Shapiro, D., & Fahey, J. L. (1994). Immunological and physiological changes associated with induced positive and negative mood. *Psychosomatic Medicine, 56,* 499–511.

Futterman, A. D., Wellisch, D. K., Zighelboim, J., Luna-Raines, M., & Weiner, H. (1996). Psychological and immunological reactions of family members to patients undergoing bone marrow transplantation. *Psychosomatic Medicine, 58*(5), 472–480.

Garssen, B., & Goodkin, K. (1999). On the role of immunological factors as mediators between psychosocial factors and cancer progression. *Psychiatry Research, 85*(1), 51–61.

Glaser, R., & Kiecolt-Glaser, J. K. (1997). Chronic stress modulates the virus-specific immune response to latent herpes simplex virus type 1. *Annals of Behavioral Medicine, 19*(2), 78–82.

Glaser, R., Kiecolt-Glaser, J. K., Bonneau, R. H., Malarkey, W. B., & Hughes, J. (1992). Stress-induced modulation of the immune response to recombinant hepatitis B vaccine. *Psychosomatic Medicine, 54,* 22–29.

Glaser, R., Kiecolt-Glaser, J. K., Bonneau, R. H., Malarkey, W. B., Kennedy, S., & Hughes, J. (1992). Stress-induced modulation of the immune response to recombinant hepatitis B vaccine. *Psychosomatic Medicine, 54*(1), 22–29.

Glaser, R., Kiecolt-Glaser, J. K., Marucha, P. T., MacCallum, R. C., Laskowski, B. F., & Malarkey, W. B. (1999). Stress-related changes in proinflammatory cytokine production in wounds. *Archives of General Psychiatry, 56*(5), 450–456.

Glaser, R., Kiecolt-Glaser, J. K., Speicher, C. E., & Holliday, J. E. (1985). Stress, loneliness, and changes in herpes virus latency. *Journal of Behavioral Medicine, 8*(3), 249–260.

Glaser, R., Kiecolt-Glaser, J. K., Stout, J. C., Tarr, K. L., Speicher, C. E., & Holliday, J. E. (1985). Stress-related impairments in cellular immunity. *Psychiatry Research, 16*(3), 233–239.

Glaser, R., Pearl, D. K., Kiecolt-Glaser, J. K., & Malarkey, W. B. (1994). Plasma cortisol levels and reactivation of latent Epstein-Barr virus in response to examination stress. *Psychoneuroendocrinology, 19*(8), 765–772.

Glaser, R., Pearson, G. R., Bonneau, R. H., Esterling, B. A., Atkinson, C., & Kiecolt-Glaser, J. K. (1993). Stress and the memory T-cell response to the Epstein-Barr virus in healthy medical students. *Health Psychology, 12*(6), 435–442.

Glaser, R., Rabin, B., Chesney, M., Cohen, S., & Natelson, B. (1999). Stress-induced immunomodulation: Implications for infectious diseases? *Journal of the American Medical Association, 281,* 2268–2270.

Glaser, R., Rice, J., Speicher, C. E., Stout, J. C., & Kiecolt-Glaser, J. K. (1986). Stress depresses interferon production by leukocytes concomitant with a decrease in natural killer cell activity. *Behavioral Neuroscience, 100*(5), 675–678.

Gold, P. W., Goodwin, F. K., & Chrousos, G. P. (1988). Clinical and biochemical manifestations of depression: Relation to the neurobiology of stress (1). *New England Journal of Medicine, 319*(6), 348–353.

Goodkin, K., Blaney, N. T., Feaster, D., Fletcher, M. A., Baum, M. K., Mantero-Atienza, E., et al. (1992). Active coping style is associated with natural killer cell cytotoxicity in asymptomatic HIV-1 seropositive homosexual men. *Journal of Psychosomatic Research, 36,* 635–650.

Goodkin, K., Fuchs, I., Feaster, D., Leeka, J., & Rishel, D. D. (1992). Life stressors and coping style are associated with immune measures in HIV-1 infection: A preliminary report. *International Journal of Psychiatry in Medicine, 22*(2), 155–172.

Goodkin, K., Mulder, C. L., Blaney, N., Ironson, G., Kumar, M., & Fletcher, M. A. (1994). Psychoneuroimmunology and human immunodeficiency virus type 1 infection revisited. *Archives of General Psychiatry, 51,* 246–247.

Goodwin, J. S., Hunt, W. C., Key, C. R., & Samet, J. M. (1987). The effect of marital status on stage, treatment, and survival of cancer patients. *Journal of the American Medical Association, 34,* 20–26.

Gordon, H. S., & Rosenthal, G. E. (1995). Impact of marital status on outcomes in hospitalized patients. *Archives of Internal Medicine, 155,* 2465–2471.

Gregerson, M. B., Roberts, I. M., & Amiri, M. M. (1996). Adsorption and imagery locate immune responses in the body. *Biofeedback and Self-Regulation, 21,* 149–165.

Gruber, B. L., Hersh, S. P., Hall, N. R. S., Walerzky, L. R., Kunz, J. F., Carpenter, J. K., et al. (1993). Immunological responses of breast cancer patients to behavioral interventions. *Biofeedback and Self-Regulation, 18,* 1–22.

Helgeson, V. S. (1991). The effects of masculinity and social support on recovery from myocardial infraction. *Psychosomatic Medicine, 53,* 621–633.

Herbert, T. B., & Cohen, S. (1993). Depression and immunity: A meta-analytic review. *Psychological Bulletin, 113,* 472–486.

Herbert, T. B., Cohen, S., Marsland, A. L., Bachen, E. A., Rubin, B. S., Muldoon, M. F., et al. (1994). Cardiovascular reactivity and the course of immune response to an acute psychological stressor. *Psychosomatic Medicine, 56*(4), 337–344.

Herrmann, C., Brand-Driehorst, S., Kaminsky, B., Leibing, E., Staats, H., & Ruger, U. (1998). Diagnostic groups and depressed mood as predictors of 22-month mortality in medical inpatients. *Psychosomatic Medicine, 60*, 570–577.

Heston, L. L., Mastri, A. R., Anderson, V. E., & White, J. (1981). Dementia of the Alzheimer type: Clinical genetics, natural history, and associated conditions. *Archives of General Psychiatry, 38*(10), 1085–1090.

Hickie, I., Hickie, C., Lloyd, A., Silove, D., & Wakefield, D. (1993). Impaired in vivo immune responses in patients with melancholia. *British Journal of Psychiatry, 162*, 651–657.

House, J. S., Landis, K. R., & Umberson, D. (1988). Social relationships and health. *Science, 241*, 540–545.

House, J. S., Robbins, C., & Metzner, H. L. (1982). The association of social relationships and activities with mortality: Prospective evidence from the Tecumseh Community Health Study. *American Journal of Epidemiology, 116*, 123–140.

Hubner, G., Brauchle, M., Smola, H., Madlener, M., Fassler, R., & Werner, S. (1996). Differential regulation of pro-inflammatory cytokines during wound healing in normal and glucocorticoid-treated mice. *Cytokine, 8*(7), 548–556.

Ironson, G., Friedman, A., Klimas, N. G., Antoni, M. H., Fletcher, M. A., LaPerriere, A. R., et al. (1994). Distress, denial, and low adherence to behavioral interventions predict faster disease progression in gay men infected with human immunodeficiency virus. *International Journal of Behavioral Medicine, 1*, 90–105.

Ironson, G., LaPerriere, A. R., Antoni, M. H., O'Hearn, P., Schneiderman, N., Klimas, N. G., et al. (1990). Changes in immune and psychological measures as a function of anticipation and reaction of news of HIV-1 antibody status. *Psychosomatic Medicine, 52*, 247–270.

Irwin, M. (1993). Stress-induced immune suppression: Role of the autonomic nervous system. *Annals of the New York Academy of Sciences, 697*, 203–218.

Irwin, M., Caldwell, C., Smith, T. L., Brown, S., Schuckit, M. A., & Gillin, J. C. (1990). Major depressive disorder, alcoholism, and reduced natural killer cell cytotoxicity. *Archives of General Psychiatry, 47*, 713–719.

Irwin, M., Costlow, C., Williams, H., Artin, K. H., Chan, C. Y., Stinson, D. L., et al. (1998). Cellular immunity to varicella-zoster virus in patients with major depression. *Journal of Infectious Diseases, 178*(Suppl. 1), 104–108.

Irwin, M., Daniels, M., Smith, T. L., Bloom, E., & Weiner, H. (1987). Impaired natural killer cell activity during bereavement. *Brain, Behavior, and Immunity, 1*, 98–104.

Irwin, M., Lacher, U., & Caldwell, C. (1992). Depression and reduced natural killer cytotoxicity: A longitudinal study of depressed patients and control subjects. *Psychological Medicine, 22*, 1045–1050.

Irwin, M., Patterson, T., & Smith, T. L. (1990). Reduction of immune function in life stress and depression. *Biological Psychiatry, 27*, 22–30.

Irwin, M., Smith, T. L., & Gillin, J. C. (1987). Low natural killer cytotoxicity in major depression. *Life Sciences, 41*, 2127–2133.

Jung, W., & Irwin, M. (1999). Reduction of natural killer cytotoxic activity in major depression: Interaction between depression and cigarette smoking. *Psychosomatic Medicine, 61*(3), 263–270.

Kang, D., Coe, C. L., Karszewski, J., & McCarthy, D. O. (1998). Relationship of social support to stress responses and immune function in healthy and asthmatic adolescents. *Research in Nursing and Health, 21*, 117–128.

Kaplan, G. A., & Reynolds, P. (1988). Depression and cancer mortality and morbidity: Prospective evidence from the Alameda County study. *Journal of Behavioral Medicine, 11*, 1–13.

Keller, S. E., Weiss, J. M., Schleifer, S. J., Miller, N. E., & Stein, M. (1983). Stress-induced suppression of immunity in adrenalectomized rats. *Science, 221*(4617), 1301–1304.

Kemeny, M. E., Weiner, H., Duran, R., Taylor, S. E., Visscher, B., & Fahey, J. L. (1995). Immune system changes after the death of a partner in HIV-positive gay men. *Psychosomatic Medicine, 57*, 547–554.

Keppel, W. H., Regan, D. H., Heffeneider, S. H., & McCoy, S. (1993). Effects of behavioral stimuli on plasma interleukin-1 activity in humans at rest. *Journal of Clinical Psychology, 49*, 777–789.

Kessler, R. C., Foster, C., Joseph, J., Ostrow, D., Wortman, C., Phair, J., et al. (1991). Stressful life events and symptom onset in HIV infection. *American Journal of Psychiatry, 148*(6), 733–738.

Kiecolt-Glaser, J. K. (1999). Stress, personal relationships, and immune function: Health implications. *Brain, Behavior, and Immunity, 13*, 61–72.

Kiecolt-Glaser, J. K., Dura, J. R., Speicher, C. E., Trask, O. J., & Glaser, R. (1991). Spousal caregivers of dementia victims: Longitudinal changes in immunity and health. *Psychosomatic Medicine, 53*(4), 345–362.

Kiecolt-Glaser, J. K., Fisher, L., Ogrocki, P., Stout, J. C., Speicher, C. E., & Glaser, R. (1987). Marital quality, marital disruption, and immune function. *Psychosomatic Medicine, 49*, 31–34.

Kiecolt-Glaser, J. K., Garner, W., Speicher, C., Penn, G. M., Holliday, J., & Glaser, R. (1984). Psychosocial modifiers of immunocompetence in medical students. *Psychosomatic Medicine, 46*(1), 7–14.

Kiecolt-Glaser, J. K., & Glaser, R. (1988). Methodological issues in behavioral immunology research with humans. *Brain, Behavior, and Immunity, 2*, 67–78.

Kiecolt-Glaser, J. K., & Glaser, R. (1991). Stress and the immune system: Human studies. In A. Tasman & M. B. Riba (Eds.), *Annual review of psychiatry* (Vol. 11, pp. 169–180). Washington, DC: American Psychiatric Press.

Kiecolt-Glaser, J. K., & Glaser, R. (1992). Psychoneuroimmunology: Can psychological interventions modulate immunity? *Journal of Consulting and Clinical Psychology, 60,* 569–575.

Kiecolt-Glaser, J. K., & Glaser, R. (1999). Psychoneuroimmunology and cancer: Fact or fiction? *European Journal of Cancer, 11,* 1603–1607.

Kiecolt-Glaser, J. K., Glaser, R., Cacioppo, J. T., MacCallum, R. C., Snydersmith, M., Kim, C., et al. (1997). Marital conflict in older adults: Endocrinological and immunological correlates. *Psychosomatic Medicine, 59*(4), 339–349.

Kiecolt-Glaser, J. K., Glaser, R., Gravenstein, S., Malarkey, W. B., & Sheridan, J. (1996). Chronic stress alters the immune response to influenza virus vaccine in older adults. *Proceedings of the National Academy of Sciences of the United States of America, 93*(7), 3043–3047.

Kiecolt-Glaser, J. K., Glaser, R., Shuttleworth, E. C., Dyer, C. S., Ogrocki, P., & Speicher, C. E. (1987). Chronic stress and immunity in family caregivers of Alzheimer's disease victims. *Psychosomatic Medicine, 49*(5), 523–535.

Kiecolt-Glaser, J. K., Glaser, R., Strain, E. C., Stout, J. C., Tarr, K., Holliday, J., et al. (1986). Modulation of cellular immunity in medical students. *Journal of Behavioral Medicine, 9,* 311–320.

Kiecolt-Glaser, J. K., Glaser, R., Williger, D., Stout, J., Messick, G., Sheppard, S., et al. (1985). Psychosocial enhancement of immunocompetence in a geriatric population. *Health Psychology, 4*(1), 25–41.

Kiecolt-Glaser, J. K., Kennedy, S., Malkoff, S., Fisher, L., Speicher, C. E., & Glaser, R. (1988). Marital discord and immunity in males. *Psychosomatic Medicine, 50,* 213–229.

Kiecolt-Glaser, J. K., Malarkey, W. B., Chee, M., Newton, T., Cacioppo, J. T., Mao, H., et al. (1993). Negative behavior during marital conflict is associated with immunological downregulation. *Psychosomatic Medicine, 55,* 395–409.

Kiecolt-Glaser, J. K., Marucha, P. T., Malarkey, W. B., Mercado, A. M., & Glaser, R. (1995). Slowing of wound healing by psychological stress. *Lancet, 346*(8984), 1194–1196.

Kiecolt-Glaser, J. K., McGuire, L., Robles, T. F., & Glaser, R. (2002). Emotions, morbidity, and mortality: New perspectives from psychoneuroimmunology. *Annual Review of Psychology, 53,* 83–107.

Kiecolt-Glaser, J. K., & Newton, T. (2001). Marriage and health: His and hers. *Psychological Bulletin, 127*(4), 472–503.

Kiecolt-Glaser, J. K., Newton, T., Cacioppo, J. T., MacCallum, R. C., Glaser, R., & Malarkey, W. B. (1996). Marital conflict and endocrine function: Are men really more physiologically affected than women? *Journal of Consulting and Clinical Psychology, 64,* 324–332.

Kiecolt-Glaser, J. K., Page, G. G., Marucha, P. T., MacCallum, R. C., & Glaser, R. (1998). Psychological influences on surgical recovery perspectives from psychoneuroimmunology. *American Psychologist, 53*(11), 1209–1218.

Knapp, P. H., Levy, E., Giorgi, R. G., Black, P. H., Fox, B. H., & Herren, T. C. (1992). Short-term immunological effects of induced emotion. *Psychosomatic Medicine, 54,* 133–148.

Koh, K. B., & Lee, B. K. (1998). Reduced lymphocyte proliferation and interleukin-2 production in anxiety disorders. *Psychosomatic Medicine, 60*(4), 479–483.

LaPerriere, A. R., Antoni, M. H., Schneiderman, N., Ironson, G., Klimas, N. G., Caralis, P., et al. (1990). Exercise intervention attenuates emotional distress and natural killer cell decrements following notification of positive serologic status for HIV-1. *Biofeedback and Self-Regulation, 15,* 229–242.

La Via, M. F., Munno, I., Lydiard, R. B., Workman, E. W., Hubbard, J. R., Michel, Y., et al. (1996). The influence of stress intrusion on immunodepression in generalized anxiety disorders patients and controls. *Psychosomatic Medicine, 58,* 138–142.

Lekander, M., Furst, C. J., Rotstein, S., Hursti, T. J., & Fredrikson, M. (1997). Immune effects of relaxation during chemotherapy for ovarian cancer. *Psychotherapy and Psychosomatics, 66*(4), 185–191.

Lepore, S. J., & Helgeson, V. S. (1998). Social constraints, intrusive thoughts, and mental health after prostate cancer. *Journal of Social and Clinical Psychology, 17*(1), 89–106.

Levy, S. M., Herberman, R. B., Whiteside, T., Sanzo, K., Lee, J., & Kirkwood, J. (1990). Perceived social support and tumor estrogen/progesterone receptor status as predictors of natural killer cell activity in breast cancer patients. *Psychosomatic Medicine, 52,* 73–85.

Linn, B. S., Linn, M. W., & Klimas, N. G. (1988). Effects of psychophysical stress on surgical outcomes. *Psychosomatic Medicine, 50,* 230–244.

Locke, S. E., Kraus, L., Leserman, J., Hurst, M. W., Heisel, J. S., & Williams, R. M. (1984). Life change stress, psychiatric symptoms, and natural killer cell activity. *Psychosomatic Medicine, 46*(5), 441–453.

Locke, S. E., Ransil, B. J., Covino, N. A., Toczydlowski, J., Lohse, C. M., Dvorak, H. F., et al. (1987). Failure of hypnotic suggestion to alter immune response to delayed-type hypersensitivity antigens. *Annals of the New York Academy of Science, 496,* 745–749.

Lowry, S. F. (1993). Cytokine mediators of immunity and inflammation. *Archives of Surgery, 28,* 1235–1241.

Luiten, P. G., ter Horst, G. J., Karst, H., & Steffens, A. B. (1985). The course of paraventricular hypothalamic efferents to autonomic structures in medulla and spinal cord. *Brain Research, 329*(1/2), 374–378.

Lutgendorf, S. K., Antoni, M. H., Ironson, G., Klimas, N. G., McCabe, P., Cleven, K., et al. (1997). Cognitive-behavioral stress management decreases dysphoric mood and herpes simplex virus-type 2 antibody titers in symptomatic HIV-seropositive gay men. *Journal of Consulting and Clinical Psychology, 65,* 31–43.

Lutgendorf, S. K., Antoni, M. H., Kumar, M., & Schneiderman, N. (1994). Changes in cognitive coping strategies predict EBV-antibody titre change following a stressor disclosure induction. *Journal of Psychosomatic Research, 38*, 63–78.

Lyketsos, C. G., Hoover, D. R., Guccione, M., Senterfitt, W., Dew, M. A., Wesch, J., et al. (1993). Depressive symptoms as predictors of medical outcomes in HIV infection. Multicenter AIDS Cohort Study. *Journal of the American Medical Association, 270*(21), 2563–2567.

Madden, K. S., Rajan, S., Bellinger, D. L., Felten, S. Y., & Felten, D. L. (1997). Age-associated alterations in sympathetic neural interactions with the immune system. *Developmental and Comparative Immunology, 21*(6), 479–486.

Maes, M., Hendriks, D., Van Gastel, A., Demedts, P., Wauters, A., Neels, H., et al. (1997). Effects of psychological stress on serum immunoglobulin, complement and acute phase protein concentrations in normal volunteers. *Psychoneuroendocrinology, 22*(6), 397–409.

Maes, M., Meltzer, H. Y., & Bosmans, E. (1994). Psychoimmune investigation in obsessive-compulsive disorder: Assays of plasma transferrin, IL-2 and IL-6 receptor, and IL-1 beta and IL-6 concentrations. *Neuropsychobiology, 30*(2/3), 57–60.

Maes, M., Song, C., Lin, A., De Jongh, R., Van Gastel, A., Kenis, G., et al. (1998). The effects of psychological stress on humans: Increased production of pro-inflammatory cytokines and a Th1-like response in stress-induced anxiety. *Cytokine, 10*(4), 313–318.

Maes, M., Van Bockstaele, D. R., Van Gastel, A., Song, C., Schotte, C., Neels, H., et al. (1999). The effects of psychological stress on leukocyte subset distribution in humans: Evidence of immune activation. *Neuropsychobiology, 39*(1), 1–9.

Maier, S. F., & Watkins, L. R. (1998). Cytokines for psychologists: Implications of bidirectional immune-to-brain communication for understanding behavior, mood, and cognition. *Psychological Review, 105*(1), 83–107.

Malarkey, W. B., Kiecolt-Glaser, J. K., Pearl, D., & Glaser, R. (1994). Hostile behavior during marital conflict alters pituitary and adrenal hormones. *Psychosomatic Medicine, 56*(1), 41–51.

Markman, H. J. (1991). Constructive marital conflict is not an oxymoron. *Behavioral Assessment, 13*, 83–96.

Marucha, P. T., Kiecolt-Glaser, J. K., & Favagehi, M. (1998). Mucosal wound healing is impaired by examination stress. *Psychosomatic Medicine, 60*(3), 362–365.

Matthews, K. A., Caggiula, A. R., McAllister, C. G., Berga, S. L., Owens, J. F., Flory, J. D., et al. (1995). Sympathetic reactivity to acute stress and immune response in women. *Psychosomatic Medicine, 57*(6), 564–571.

Mayne, T. J., O'Leary, A., McCrady, B., Contrada, R., & Labouvie, E. (1997). The differential effects of acute marital distress on emotional, physiological and immune functions in maritally distressed men and women. *Psychology and Health, 12*, 277–288.

McEwen, B. S., Biron, C. A., Brunson, K. W., Bulloch, K., Chambers, W. H., Dhabhar, F. S., et al. (1997). The role of adrenocorticoids as modulators of immune function in health

and disease: Neural, endocrine and immune interactions. *Brain Research, Brain Research Reviews, 23*(1/2), 79–133.

McGrady, A., Conran, P., Dickey, D., Garman, D., Farris, E., & Schumann-Brzezinski, C. (1992). The effects of biofeedback-assisted relaxation on cell mediated immunity, cortisol, and white blood cell count in healthy adult subjects. *Journal of Behavioral Medicine, 15*, 343–354.

McKinnon, W., Weisse, C. S., Reynolds, C. P., Bowles, C. A., & Baum, A. (1989). Chronic stress, leukocyte subpopulations, and humoral response to latent viruses. *Health Psychology, 8*(4), 389–402.

Miller, G. E., Cohen, S., & Herbert, T. B. (1999). Pathways linking major depression and immunity in ambulatory female patients. *Psychosomatic Medicine, 61*(6), 850–860.

Miller, G. E., Dopp, J. M., Myers, H. F., Felten, S. Y., & Fahey, J. L. (1999). Psychosocial predictors of natural killer cell mobilization during marital conflict. *Health Psychology, 18*, 262–271.

Morag, M., Morag, A., Reichenberg, A., Lerer, B., & Yirmiya, R. (1999). Psychological variables as predictors of rubella antibody titers and fatigue: A prospective, double blind study. *Journal of Psychiatric Research, 33*, 389–395.

Mulder, C. L., Antoni, M. H., Emmelkamp, P. M., Veugelers, P. J., Sandfort, T. G., van de Vijver, F. A., et al. (1995). Psychosocial group intervention and the rate of decline of immunological parameters in asymptomatic HIV-infected homosexual men. *Psychotherapy and Psychosomatics, 63*(3/4), 185–192.

Munck, A., & Guyre, P. M. (1991). Glucocorticoids and immune function. In R. Ader, D. L. Felten, & N. Cohen (Eds.), *Psychoneuroimmunology* (2nd ed., pp. 447–473). San Diego, CA: Academic Press.

Munck, A., Guyre, P. M., & Holbrook, N. J. (1984). Physiological functions of glucocorticoids in stress and their relation to pharmacological actions. *Endocrine Reviews, 5*(1), 25–44.

Murasko, D. M., Gold, M. J., Hessen, M. T., & Kaye, D. (1990). Immune reactivity, morbidity, and mortality of elderly humans. *Aging Immunology and Infectious Disease, 2*(3), 171–180.

Murasko, D. M., Weiner, P., & Kaye, D. (1987). Decline in mitogen induced proliferation of lymphocytes with increasing age. *Clinical and Experimental Immunology, 70*(2), 440–448.

Nomoto, Y., Karasawa, S., & Uehara, K. (1994). Effects of hydrocortisone and adrenaline on natural killer cell activity. *British Journal of Anaesthesia, 73*(3), 318–321.

Olness, K., & Ader, R. (1992). Conditioning as an adjunct in the pharmacotherapy of lupus erythematosus. *Journal of Developmental and Behavioral Pediatrics, 13*, 124–125.

Padgett, D. A., Marucha, P. T., & Sheridan, J. F. (1998). Restraint stress slows cutaneous wound healing in mice. *Brain, Behavior, and Immunity, 12*(1), 64–73.

Peavey, B. S., Lawlis, G. F., & Goven, A. (1986). Biofeedback-assisted relaxation: Effects on phagocytic capacity. *Biofeedback and Self Regulation, 10*, 33–47.

Pennebaker, J. W., Kiecolt-Glaser, J. K., & Glaser, R. (1988). Disclosure of trauma and immune function: Health implications for psychotherapy. *Journal of Consulting and Clinical Psychology, 56*, 239–245.

Penninx, B. W. J. H., Geerlings, S. W., Deeg, D. J. H., van Eijk, J. T. M., van Tilburg, W., & Beekman, A. T. F. (1999). Minor and major depression and the risk of death in older persons. *Archives of General Psychiatry, 56*, 889–895.

Perry, S., Fishman, B., Jacobsberg, L., & Frances, A. (1992). Relationship over 1 year between lymphocyte subsets and psychosocial variables among adults with infection by human immunodeficiency virus. *Archives of General Psychiatry, 49*, 396–401.

Persky, V. W., Kempthorne-Rawson, J., & Shekelle, R. B. (1987). Personality and risk of cancer: 20-year follow-up of the western electric study. *Psychosomatic Medicine, 49*, 435–449.

Persson, L., Gullberg, B., Hanson, B. S., Moestrup, T., & Ostergren, P. O. (1994). HIV infection: Social network, social support, and CD4 lymphocyte values in infected homosexual men in Malmo, Sweden. *Journal of Epidemiology and Community Health, 48*, 580–585.

Petrie, K. J., Booth, R. J., Pennebaker, J. W., Davison, K. P., & Thomas, M. G. (1995). Disclosure of trauma and immune response to a hepatitis B vaccination program. *Journal of Consulting and Clinical Psychology, 63*, 787–792.

Rabin, B. S. (1999). *Stress, immune function, and health: The connection.* New York: Wiley.

Rabkin, J. G., Williams, J. G. W., Remien, R. H., Goetz, R. R., Kertzner, R., & Gorman, J. M. (1991). Depression, lymphocyte subsets, and human immunodeficiency virus symptoms on two occasions in HIV-positive homosexual men. *Archives of General Psychiatry, 48*, 111–119.

Ramer-Quinn, D. S., Baker, R. A., & Sanders, V. M. (1997). Activated T helper 1 and T helper 2 cells differentially express the beta-2-adrenergic receptor: A mechanism for selective modulation of T helper 1 cell cytokine production. *Journal of Immunology, 159*(10), 4857–4867.

Rapaport, M. H. (1998). Circulating lymphocyte phenotypic surface markers in anxiety disorder patients and normal volunteers. *Biological Psychiatry, 43*(6), 458–463.

Redinbaugh, E. M., MacCallum, R. C., & Kiecolt-Glaser, J. K. (1995). Recurrent syndromal depression in caregivers. *Psychology and Aging, 10*(3), 358–368.

Reed, G. M., Kemeny, M. E., Taylor, S. E., Wang, H. Y. J., & Visscher, B. R. (1994). Realistic acceptance as a predictor of decreased survival time in gay men with AIDS. *Health Psychology, 13*, 299–307.

Ruzyla-Smith, P., Barabasz, A., Barabasz, M., & Warner, D. (1995). Effects of hypnosis on the immune response: B-cells, T-cells, helper and suppressor cells. *American Journal of Clinical Hypnosis, 38*, 71–79.

Sanders, V. M., Baker, R. A., Ramer-Quinn, D. S., Kasprowicz, D. J., Fuchs, B. A., & Street, N. E. (1997). Differential expression of the beta2-adrenergic receptor by Th1 and Th2 clones:

Implications for cytokine production and B cell help. *Journal of Immunology, 158*(9), 4200–4210.

Schedlowski, M., Hosch, W., Oberbeck, R., Benschop, R. J., Jacobs, R., Raab, H. R., et al. (1996). Catecholamines modulate human NK cell circulation and function via spleen-independent beta 2-adrenergic mechanisms. *Journal of Immunology, 156*(1), 93–99.

Scheier, M. F., Matthews, K. A., Owens, J. F., Schulz, R., Bridges, M. W., Magovern, G. J., et al. (1999). Optimism and rehospitalization after coronary artery bypass graft surgery. *Archives of Internal Medicine, 159*, 829–835.

Schleifer, S. J., Keller, S. E., Bartlett, J. A., Eckholdt, H. M., & Delaney, B. R. (1996). Immunity in young adults with major depressive disorder. *American Journal of Psychiatry, 153*, 477–482.

Schleifer, S. J., Keller, S. E., Bond, R. N., Cohen, J., & Stein, M. (1989). Depression and immunity: Role of age, sex, and severity. *Archives of General Psychiatry, 46*, 81–87.

Schleifer, S. J., Keller, S. E., Camerino, M., Thorton, J. C., & Stein, M. (1983). Suppression of lymphocyte stimulation following bereavement. *Journal of the American Medical Association, 250*, 374–377.

Schleifer, S. J., Keller, S. E., Heyerson, A. T., Raskin, M. J., Davis, K. L., & Stein, M. (1984). Lymphocyte function in major depressive disorder. *Archives of General Psychiatry, 41*, 484–486.

Schoenbach, V. J., Kaplan, B. H., Fredman, L., & Kleinbaum, D. G. (1986). Social ties and mortality in Evans County, Georgia. *American Journal of Epidemiology, 123*, 577–591.

Segerstrom, S. C., Glover, D. A., Craske, M. G., & Fahey, J. L. (1999). Worry affects the immune response to phobic fear. *Brain, Behavior, and Immunity, 13*(2), 80–92.

Segerstrom, S. C., Taylor, S. E., Kemeny, M. E., & Fahey, J. L. (1998). Optimism is associated with mood, coping, and immune change in response to stress. *Journal of Personality and Social Psychology, 74*(6), 1646–1655.

Segerstrom, S. C., Taylor, S. E., Kemeny, M. E., Reed, G. M., & Visscher, B. R. (1996). Causal attributions predict rate of immune decline in HIV-seropositive gay men. *Health Psychology, 15*, 485–493.

Shekelle, R. B., Raynor, W. J., Ostfeld, A. M., Garron, D. C., Bieliauskas, L. A., Liv, S. C., et al. (1981). Psychological depression and the 17-year risk of death from cancer. *Psychosomatic Medicine, 43*, 117–125.

Smith, G. R., & McDaniels, S. M. (1983). Psychologically mediated effect on the delayed hypersensitivity reaction to tuberculin in humans. *Psychosomatic Medicine, 45*, 65–70.

Smyth, J. M., Stone, A. A., Hurewitz, A., & Kaell, A. (1999). Effects of writing about stressful experiences on symptom reduction in patients with asthma or rheumatoid arthritis: A randomized trial. *Journal of the American Medical Association, 281*(14), 1304–1309.

Solomon, G. F., Segerstrom, S. C., Grohr, P., Kemeny, M. E., & Fahey, J. (1997). Shaking up immunity: Psychological and

Immunologic changes after a natural disaster. *Psychosomatic Medicine, 59*(2), 114–127.

Somers, A. R. (1979). Marital status, health, and use of health services. *Journal of the American Medical Association, 241,* 1818–1822.

Spanier, G. B. (1976). Measuring dyadic adjustment: New scales for assessing the quality of marriage and similar dyads. *Journal of Marriage and the Family, 38,* 15–28.

Stein, M. S., Miller, A. H., & Trestman, R. L. (1991). Depression, the immune system, and health and illness. *Archives of General Psychiatry, 48,* 171–177.

Sternberg, E. M. (1997). Neural-immune interactions in health and disease. *Journal of Clinical Investigation, 100*(11), 2641–2647.

Stone, A. A., Bovbjerg, D. H., Neale, J. M., Napoli, A., Valdimarsdottir, H., Cox, D., et al. (1992). Development of common cold symptoms following experimental rhinovirus infection is related to prior stressful life events. *Behavioral Medicine, 18,* 115–120.

Stowell, J. R., Kiecolt-Glaser, J. K., & Glaser, R. (2001). Perceived stress and cellular immunity: When coping counts. *Journal of Behavioral Medicine, 24*(4), 323–339.

Straits-Troester, K. A., Patterson, T. L., Semple, S. J., Temoshok, L., Roth, P. G., McCutchan, J. A., et al. (1994). The relationship between loneliness, interpersonal competence, and immunologic status in HIV-infected men. *Psychology and Health, 9,* 205–219.

Tait, R., & Silver, R. C. (1989). Coming to terms with major negative life events. In J. S. Uleman & J. A. Bargh (Eds.), *Unintended thought* (pp. 351–382). New York: Guilford Press.

Theorell, T., Blomkvist, V., Jonsson, H., Schulman, S., Berntorp, E., & Stigendel, L. (1995). Social support and the development of immune function in human immunodeficiency virus infection. *Psychosomatic Medicine, 57,* 32–36.

Theorell, T., Orth-Gomer, K., & Eneroth, P. (1990). Slow-reacting immunoglobin in relation to social support and changes in job strain: A preliminary note. *Psychosomatic Medicine, 52,* 511–516.

Thomas, P. D., Goodwin, J. M., & Goodwin, J. S. (1985). Effects of social support on stress-related changes in cholesterol level, uric acid level, and immune function in an elderly sample. *American Journal of Psychiatry, 142,* 735–737.

Uchino, B. N., Cacioppo, J. T., & Kiecolt-Glaser, J. K. (1996). The relationship between social support and physiological processes: A review with emphasis on underlying mechanisms and implications for health. *Psychological Bulletin, 119,* 488–531.

Valdimarsdottir, H. B., & Bovbjerg, D. H. (1997). Positive and negative mood: Association with natural killer cell activity. *Psychology and Health, 12,* 319–327.

Vedhara, K., Cox, N. K., Wilcock, G. K., Perks, P., Hunt, M., Anderson, S., et al. (1999). Chronic stress in elderly carers of dementia patients and antibody response to influenza vaccination. *Lancet, 353*(9153), 627–631.

Vedhara, K., & Nott, K. (1996). The assessment of the emotional and immunological consequences of examination stress. *Journal of Behavioral Medicine, 19*(5), 467–478.

Verbrugge, L. M. (1979). Marital status and health. *Journal of Marriage and the Family, 41,* 267–285.

Verbrugge, L. M. (1982). Sex differentials in health. *Public Health Reports, 97,* 417–437.

Watson, D., & Pennebaker, J. (1989). Health complaints, stress, and distress: Exploring the central role of negative affectivity. *Psychological Review, 96,* 234–254.

Wayne, S. J., Rhyne, R. L., Garry, P. J., & Goodwin, J. S. (1990). Cell-mediated immunity as a predictor of morbidity and mortality in subjects over 60. *Journal of Gerontology, 45*(2), M45–M48.

Weisse, C. S. (1992). Depression and immunocompetence: A review of the literature. *Psychological Bulletin, 111,* 475–489.

Weizman, R., Laor, N., Wiener, Z., Wolmer, L., & Bessler, H. (1999). Cytokine production in panic disorder patients. *Clinical Neuropharmacology, 22*(2), 107–109.

Wilson, S. N., van der Kolk, B. A., Burbridge, J., Fisler, R., & Kradin, R. (1999). Phenotype of blood lymphocytes in PTSD suggests chronic immune activation. *Psychosomatics, 40,* 222–225.

Zachariae, R., & Bjerring, P. (1990). The effect of hypnotically induced analgesia on flare reaction of the cutaneous histamine prick test. *Archives of Dermatological Research, 282,* 539–543.

Zachariae, R., Bjerring, P., & Arendt-Nielsen, L. (1989). Modulation of Type I immediate and Type IV delayed immunoreactivity using direct suggestion and guided imagery during hypnosis. *Allergy, 44,* 537–542.

Zachariae, R., Jorgensen, M. M., Christensen, S., & Bjerring, P. (1997). Effects of relaxation on the delayed-type hypersensitivity (DTH) reaction to diphenylcyclopropenone (DCP). *Allergy, 52,* 760–764.

Zachariae, R., Kristensen, J. S., Hokland, P., Ellegaard, J., Metze, E., & Hokland, M. (1990). Effect of psychological intervention in the form of relaxation and guided imagery on cellular immune function in normal healthy subjects: An overview. *Psychotherapy and Psychosomatics, 54,* 32–39.

Zachariae, R., Oster, H., & Bjerring, P. (1994). Effects of hypnotic suggestions on ultraviolet B radiation-induced erythema and skin blood flow. *Photodermatology, Photoimmunology, and Photomedicine, 10,* 154–156.

Zonderman, A. B., Costa, P. T., Jr., & McCrae, R. R. (1989). Depression as a risk for cancer morbidity and mortality in a nationally representative sample. *Journal of the American Medical Association, 262*(9), 1191–1195.

Zorrilla, E. P., Redei, E., & DeRubeis, R. J. (1994). Reduced cytokine levels and T-cell function in healthy males: Relation to individual differences in subclinical anxiety. *Brain, Behavior, and Immunity, 8*(4), 293–312.

PART THREE

DISEASES AND DISORDERS

CHAPTER 5

Asthma

KAREN B. SCHMALING, PAUL M. LEHRER, JONATHAN M. FELDMAN, AND NICHOLAS D. GIARDINO

This chapter reviews the application of psychological theories to the understanding of asthma; the effects of stress and mood states on asthma; and the prevalence of psychiatric disorders among persons with asthma and the effects of co-occurring psychiatric disorders and asthma on patient morbidity. We also provide an overview of medical treatments for asthma and the challenge of adherence with those treatments, with an examination of the role of psychological variables in adherence. The research on psychological variables associated with outcomes, such as medical utilization, also are summarized. Behavioral and other psychological interventions are reviewed that directly or indirectly affect asthma. We conclude with suggestions for future research needs and directions.

Asthma is a common condition characterized by reversible airway obstruction, airway inflammation, and increased bronchial responsiveness to a variety of stimuli, ranging from allergens and other irritants to strong emotions (National Heart Lung and Blood Institute, 1997). In particular, the role of inflammation in asthma has been recognized as crucial and has received increasing attention in the past decade. The central role of inflammation has implications for treatment, and for pathways by which psychosocial factors may affect asthma. Symptoms of cough, wheezing, and shortness of breath are commonly associated with an asthma exacerbation. An asthma attack may be characterized by hypercapnia (excessive carbon dioxide) and hypoxia (lack of oxygen), which may partially account for the high prevalence of anxiety disorders among persons with asthma. We will examine these issues later in this chapter.

Asthma and allergies co-occur frequently; allergies are a common trigger for an asthma exacerbation. About 60% of persons with asthma are allergic (Ford, 1983); the development of asthma and allergies may occur early in childhood as a common outcome of immune system development (see Wright, Rodriguez, & Cohen, 1998, for a review). Some genetic predisposition is probably necessary to develop asthma, but not all persons who are predisposed will develop asthma; family stress seems to be implicated in its development in childhood (Mrazek, Klinnert, Mrazek, & Macey, 1991; Wright, Weiss, & Cohen, 1996). Asthma is a condition worthy of the attention and efforts of behavioral scientists:

psychosocial variables may be implicated in the initiation, course (exacerbations versus quiescence) and outcomes (morbidity, mortality) of asthma; psychological interventions have a role in the treatment of asthma as a complement to the use of medications.

EPIDEMIOLOGY AND HEALTH CARE COSTS RELATED TO ASTHMA

Approximately 7.5% of the U.S. population reports having asthma, or about 17 million persons (Centers for Disease Control, 2001). (The estimated lifetime rate for asthma is 10.5%.) Approximately one third of persons with asthma are children under the age of 18. Although most but not all asthma is identified in childhood, asthma does not resolve in puberty or adulthood for the majority of cases. Asthma has been reported to be more common among women (9.1% versus 5.1% among men), persons with less family income (9.8% among persons with family incomes of less than $15,000 per year versus 3.9% among those with more than $75,000 per year), and among persons of African American ethnicity (8.5% versus 7.1% for Whites and 5.6% for persons of other racial/ethnic backgrounds) (Centers for Disease Control and Prevention, 2001). The cause for gender differences in self-reported asthma is unknown; greater body mass (Camargo, Weiss, Zhang, Willett, & Speizer, 1999) and/or use of exogenous hormones (Troisi, Speizer, Willett, Trichopoulos, & Rosner, 1995) may contribute to higher rates of asthma among women.

Prevalence and mortality rates have been steadily increasing in recent decades. According to the National Health Interview Survey the age-specific prevalence rate for self-reported asthma increased 58.6% between 1982 and 1996. In particular, the prevalence rate increased 123.4% during these 14 years (1982–1996) for young adults aged 18 to 44 years (American Lung Association, 2001). The age-adjusted death rate for asthma increased 55% between 1979 and 1998, totaling over 5,400 persons per year in 1998 (American Lung Association, 2001), although such figures based on reviews of death certificates may underestimate the actual mortality attributable to asthma (Hunt et al., 1993). Environmental factors such as pollution only partially explain the increase in asthma prevalence and mortality. Of interest is the psychosocial factors that may contribute directly or indirectly to the increasing prevalence and mortality related to asthma. Purely biological explanations are believed to be insufficient to explain asthma onset, exacerbation, or its rising prevalence, as a "paradigm shift" (Wright et al., 1998). A conceptualization of asthma as having emotional and psychosocial components is not novel,

however. From the early twentieth century, asthma was considered a prototypical "psychosomatic" disease (Groddeck, 1928). Developments in psychoneuroimmunology may be contributing to a new synthesis and appreciation for how biological and psychological systems interact to produce and maintain asthma.

Asthma is costly. In 2000, U.S. asthma care totaled $12.7 billion in direct and indirect costs, including costs associated with premature death and time away from work because of asthma (see http://www.lungusa.org/data/asthma/ASTHMA1.pdf). In the United States, approximately 3 million days of work and 10.1 million days of school are lost each year due to asthma. Of particular interest to persons interested in psychosocial factors associated with asthma might be the costs associated with adherence and nonadherence to self-care regimens (we address psychosocial factors associated with adherence in a later section). For example, persons who are adherent with their medication regimens may incur more direct costs in medications and scheduled outpatient office visits. By contrast, persons who are less adherent with their medication regimens may incur less direct costs for medications and outpatient office visits, but incur more costly occasional unscheduled visits, such as urgent care or emergency room visits. While we are unaware of data that report costs associated with groups of patients differentiated by their behavior, psychiatric comorbidities, or other variables of interest, the financial (and other) effects of optimal and nonoptimal behavioral self-management is an issue worthy of further exploration (and a potential source of information that would motivate patients to be more adherent with their medications).

EVIDENCE BASIS FOR PSYCHOLOGICAL THEORIES APPLIED TO MECHANISMS INVOLVED IN ASTHMA

Classical and Operant Conditioning

It would be possible for asthma to be a classically conditioned response if allergens and irritants that caused bronchoconstriction were repeatedly linked to a novel stimulus, thereby creating a conditioned stimulus. There are case studies in the literature that describe conditioned visual stimuli (E. Dekker & Groen, 1956) and other stimuli (the experimental setting: a provocative inhaled substance given in the experimental setting produced asthma, the substance was omitted in subsequent experimental trials) (E. Dekker, Pelser, & Groen, 1957) that provoke asthma attacks in participants with asthma. Respiratory resistance has been classically conditioned in participants without asthma. For example, mental arithmetic, a task that can elicit increased respiratory resistance (although note that Lehrer, Hochron, Carr, et al., 1996, found mental arithmetic to decrease respiratory resistance), was preceded by the display of a specific color and a different color preceded the appearance of a clear slide (i.e., no demand for mental arithmetic); increased respiratory resistance was demonstrated in response to the specific color (D. Miller & Kotses, 1995). In their debriefing, 90% of participants recalled correctly which color preceded the arithmetic, but only 17% guessed correctly that the purpose of the experiment was to examine changes in breathing in anticipation of performing mental arithmetic, suggesting that conditioning occurred without subjects' awareness.

Rietveld, van Beest, and Everaerd (2000) exposed adolescents with asthma to placebo, citric acid at levels that induced cough, or citric acid at 50% of cough-inducing levels. The purpose of their experiment was to examine the role of expectations: some participants were led to believe the experiment was about asthma, others were told the experiment was about evaluating flavors. Cough frequency was greater among participants who were told the experiment was about asthma than among those who were told the experiment was about evaluating flavors. Expectancies are important variables in cognitive explanatory models, and the results of this study suggest that expectancies about the research topic may influence symptom perception and reporting. An additional interpretation of the results is in terms of classical conditioned effects. It is likely that cough has a conditioned association with the presence of asthma; a focus on asthma may make cough more likely, and persons with asthma are more likely to label cough as indicative of asthma than are persons without asthma. These studies suggest that the unintended development of classically conditioned precipitants should be considered among persons with unexplained triggers for their asthma.

In contrast to classical conditioning, operant conditioning has received little attention as a potentiating or maintenance mechanism for asthma. The role of operant conditioning is perhaps more prominent in medically unexplained conditions such as chronic pain (Romano et al., 1992) or chronic fatigue syndrome (Schmaling, Smith, & Buchwald, 2000). The illness-related behavior of patients with medically unexplained conditions may be shaped more by the reactions and consequences in their environment than is the behavior of patients with physiologically well-characterized conditions for which effective treatments exist, such as asthma. Nonetheless, it is likely that consequences in patients' environments shape patients' self-management behavior (e.g., medication use), thereby exerting indirect effects on asthma. These processes await examination in future research.

Cognitive and Perceptual Processes

A model of cognitive processes in asthma would posit that perceptions, attitudes, and beliefs about asthma can affect symptom report, medical utilization, and so forth. Several areas of research inform our understanding of cognitive and perceptual processes in asthma, including research on the effects of suggestion on pulmonary function, and comparisons of perceived with objective measures of pulmonary function.

Effects of Suggestion on Pulmonary Function

The usual method for examining the effects of suggestion on pulmonary function is to create an expectation for bronchoconstriction by telling participants that they will inhale a substance that causes bronchoconstriction, when the actual substance is saline. Isenberg, Lehrer, and Hochron (1992a) provided a comprehensive review of this literature. Their summary of the 23 studies (19 used adult participants, 4 used children) in the literature at that time found that 36% of 427 participants demonstrated objective bronchoconstriction to suggestion. The typical although not uniform criterion for bronchoconstriction was a 20% decrement in pulmonary function. An examination of participant characteristics (asthma severity, intrinsic versus extrinsic disease, age) potentially related to the likelihood of response to suggestion did not reveal clear patterns, although more equivocal results for gender differences were noted, with two of three studies reporting women to be more responsive to suggestion than men.

A search for studies on response to suggestion not included in the Isenberg et al. (1992a) publication revealed one additional study (Isenberg, Lehrer, & Hochron, 1992b). Of 33 participants, none showed changes in pulmonary function as a result of suggestion, which was not consistent with earlier research. The authors suggested that their use of room air, compared to the use of saline (which has a slight bronchoconstrictive effect) in the previous studies, could account for the divergent results. Suggestion resulted in changes in perceived airflow, but again, not in actual airflow. Certainly an interesting area for further research would be the identification of individual variables that predict who is likely to respond to suggestion. If, as Isenberg et al. (1992a) suggest, similar proportions of persons respond to suggestion and to emotions with bronchoconstriction, might the same persons respond to both, suggesting a common pathway or mechanism? If a cognitive-emotional pathway to the airways was identified, cognitive-behavioral interventions to optimize patient functioning could be developed.

Perceived versus Objective Pulmonary Function

Good self-management is crucial to optimal asthma care; self-management skills include adherence with medications, which typically involves using as-needed medications based on perceptions of need by self-monitoring or awareness of possible exposure to triggers (e.g., pretreatment before exercise). From this perspective, it is clear that patients' perceptions are the foundations for optimal asthma control. But, how ably can patients with asthma accurately perceive their respiratory status?

The process of detection, perception, and response to objectively demonstrable changes in airflow seems subject to a good deal of personal variation, perhaps akin to the experience of and response to pain. In terms of patients' abilities to perceive changes in airflow, many studies have shown a poor correspondence between symptoms and airflow among the majority of individuals. One study reported that only a quarter of patients demonstrated a statistically significant association between PEFR and symptoms (Apter et al., 1997), and these correlations, while statistically significant, were of questionable clinical significance (e.g., coefficients ranged from $-.25$ to $-.39$, leaving at least 80% of the variability in PEFR unaccounted for by symptom report). Similarly, Kendrick, Higgs, Whitfield, and Laszlo (1993) found statistically significant correlations between PEFR and symptoms in only 40% of patients. A series of studies by Reitveld and colleagues (reviewed next) showed poor correspondence between subjective symptom report and objective pulmonary function; they suggest that symptom perception is largely attributable to mood. However, other studies have reported much stronger associations between perceived breathlessness and lung function (e.g., $r = 0.88$ by Burdon, Juniper, Killian, Hargreave, & Campbell, 1982). While correlations reflect the relative association of two variables, they do not reflect other important information for asthma management (e.g., how frequently can a patient detect when his/her airflow has diminished significantly), to the point at which medications should be used? Finally, behavioral follow-through—actually using medications when the need to do so is identified—is yet another independent step in appropriate self-management. There are alarming reports of significant delays in seeking treatment, despite patients' reported awareness of decreased respiratory function in the 24 to 48 hours prior to obtaining treatment (e.g., Molfino, Nannini, Martelli, & Slutsky, 1991).

In a subset of persons with severe asthma, the inability to perceive changes in airflow may be life threatening or fatal. For example, a comparison of patients who had near fatal asthma attacks, patients with asthma without near-fatal attacks, and a group of participants without asthma revealed that patients who had a near fatal attack had a blunted respiratory response to hypoxia generated by rebreathing (breathing within a confined space, resulting in gradually increasing carbon dioxide as the available air is recycled), and their perception of dyspnea was lower than participants without asthma (Kikuchi et al., 1994). Inaccurate perception of respiratory status has been associated with repressive-defensive coping (see also next section) (Isenberg, Lehrer, & Hochron, 1997; Steiner, Higgs, & Fritz, 1987).

Timely and accurate perception of your respiratory status is central to appropriate asthma self-management, but research suggests a good deal of variability among patients' perceptual abilities that may have life-threatening consequences.

Psychoanalytic Theory

From the psychoanalytic perspective, asthma has been posited to develop in response to repressed emotions and emotional expression, such as repressed crying (Alexander, 1955). This perspective views asthma as a psychosomatic illness, suggesting direct causal links between psychological factors and disease. The psychoanalytically-informed literature related to asthma is largely limited to case studies and other clinical materials (e.g., Levitan, 1985). Two areas of empirical research, however, may have been influenced by these early psychoanalytic formulations, namely, research on alexithymia and the repressive-defensive coping style.

Alexithymia

Difficulty in labeling and expressing emotions has been termed *alexithymia* (Nemiah, 1996). Several decades ago, a group of researchers developed a measure of alexithymia as a subscale of the MMPI (Kleiger & Kinsman, 1980) and used it in a series of studies of patients with asthma. They found that alexithymic patients were more likely to be rehospitalized and had longer lengths of stay than did non-alexithymic patients (Dirks, Robinson, & Dirks, 1981); these differences were not attributable to underlying asthma severity. More recently, it has been shown that difficulty distinguishing between feelings and bodily sensations, as measured by the Toronto Alexithymia Scale, is related to greater report of asthma symptomatology, but not objective measures of pulmonary function (Feldman, Lehrer, Carr, & Hochron, 1998). One possible interpretation of these results is that asthma symptom complaints may be more accessible (to the patient) and socially acceptable ways to communicate distress than are emotions among patients who may be characterized as alexithymic. Helping such patients identify emotions, cope with emotional arousal, and discriminate emotional reactions from asthma symptoms could lead to more appropriate utilization of medical resources.

Repressive-Defensive Coping Style

More recently, the repressive-defensive coping style has received attention in relationship to persons with asthma and other chronic medical conditions. This style is characterized by the co-occurrence of low levels of self-reported distress, high levels of self-reported defensiveness, and high levels of objectively measured arousal and physiological reactivity. In adults, repressive-defensive coping has been associated with immune system down-regulation (Jamner, Schwartz, & Leigh, 1988). Among persons with asthma, immune system down-regulation could increase risk for respiratory infections, which are known to exacerbate asthma through several possible mechanisms (Wright et al., 1998). Adults with asthma who display the repressive-defensive coping style were found to display a decline in pulmonary function after exposure to laboratory tasks (e.g., reaction time, distressing films) and their autonomic nervous system was characterized by sympathetic hypoarousal and parasympathetic hyperarousal during these tasks (Feldman, Lehrer, & Hochron, in press). However, among samples of children with asthma, repressive-defensive coping style was not characteristic of a majority of children, was not associated with more physiological reactivity under stress (Nassau, Fritz, & McQuaid, 2000), and was associated with more accurate symptom perception (Fritz, McQuaid, Spirito, & Klein, 1996), which would not be predicted by a psychosomatic model.

Alexithymia and the repressive-defensive coping style appear to be the most well-operationalized concepts that have roots in psychoanalytic theory and have been implicated among persons with asthma. However, the utility of these constructs in explaining important asthma-related processes such as symptom onset, expression, variability, course, and outcomes, is limited based on current research. Despite the data on repressive-defensive coping among children with asthma not providing robust support for predicted results, research on repressive-defensive coping among adults is warranted since adults' styles may be more polarized and may exert a stronger influence on self-management behavior than

among children, who share self-management responsibilities with parents and other responsible adults.

Family Systems Theory

Family systems models have been explored in relationship to children and adolescents with asthma, and will be mentioned only briefly here. The classic systemic view of family dynamics that creates and perpetuates a "psychosomatic" illness such as asthma was outlined by Minuchin, Rosman, and Baker (1978). These dysfunctional dynamics include rigidity, overprotectiveness, enmeshment, and lack of conflict resolution. In the systemic view, the function of the illness is to diffuse conflict and maintain homeostasis in the family (e.g., escalating tension between the parents may prompt an asthma attack in the child, which distracts the parents from continuing conflict). Akin to the status of support for psychoanalytic theories related to asthma, evidence to corroborate a systemic view is largely based on clinical anecdotes, although a few attempts to operationalize and assess key family dynamics exist. Families with and without a child with asthma engaged in a decision-making task (Di Blasio, Molinari, Peri, & Taverna, 1990). Families with a child with asthma were characterized by protracted decision-making times, chaotic responses, lack of agreement, and acquiescence to the child's wishes, which may reflect an overprotective stance and difficulties with conflict resolution, as would be suggested by systems theory.

Observational studies have found mothers of children with asthma to be more critical of their children than mothers of healthy children (Hermanns, Florin, Dietrich, Rieger, & Hahlweg, 1989; F. Wamboldt, Wamboldt, Gavin, Roesler, & Brugman, 1995). These communication patterns would seem inconsistent with the hypothesized characteristic of overprotectiveness in such families, although they may reflect a tendency toward lack of conflict resolution, which would be consistent with systemic hypotheses. An observational study of couples and children with and without asthma (Northey, Griffin, & Krainz, 1998) examined base rates of specific behaviors (e.g., agree, disagree) and sequences of behavior hypothesized to be more characteristic of psychosomatic families based on the Minuchin et al. (1978) model, such as recruitment or solicitation of child input after a parental position statement. Couples with a child with asthma were less likely to agree with one another, and were more likely to solicit the child's input. Couples with a child with asthma who were unsatisfied with their marriage were about half as likely to disagree with one another than were couples without a child with asthma. Relative avoidance of disagreement in the face of relationship distress may preclude problem solving about the source of the disagreement, and the subsequent possibility of improvement in relationship satisfaction with problem resolution. The authors suggest that parental recruitment of child input among families with a child with asthma could indicate compensatory attempts to involve an ill child in family activities. The family systems model, on the other hand, would posit that the focus on the child deflects attention from the parents' marital distress: Parental solicitousness toward the child functions to avoid conflict in the marital dyad so the child's illness is "protective" and maintains homeostasis in the family.

There are several questionnaires such as the Family Environment Scale (Moos & Moos, 1986), the Family Adaptability and Cohesion Scale (Olson, Portner, & Laree, 1985), and the Family Assessment Device (Epstein, Baldwin, & Bishop, 1983) that are scored to reflect systemic constructs of rigidity, cohesion, conflict, and so forth. These questionnaires have been used to characterize the environment and dynamics of the families of children with asthma on a limited basis (e.g., Bender, Milgrom, Rand, & Ackerson, 1998). As yet, however, research informed by family systems theory that focuses on adults with asthma is lacking.

PSYCHOLOGICAL FACTORS ASSOCIATED WITH ASTHMA

Effects of Stress and Emotions on Asthma

Patients with asthma often believe that stress and emotions can trigger or exacerbate asthma (e.g., Rumbak, Kelso, Arheart, & Self, 1993). The association between emotions and airflow has been examined empirically through laboratory-based experiments and studies of the covariation of airflow and emotions in naturalistic conditions.

Laboratory Studies

Isenberg et al. (1992a), in addition to reviewing response to suggestion, also reviewed studies that examined individuals' responses to emotional provocation. Across the seven studies reviewed that involved the induction of emotions in the laboratory, 31 of 77 (40%) participants showed significant airway constriction in response to emotion. In addition, a trend toward greater likelihood of reacting to emotions among adult versus child participants was found. Isenberg et al. (1992) note that the proportion of participants who respond to suggestion and to emotion are similar, but studies have not tested directly if participants who respond to suggestion also are likely to respond to emotion. It also is possible that

bronchoconstrictive responses to emotion may occur via the effects of expectation and suggestion, that is, if patients believe that emotions trigger their asthma, then they also are likely to believe that participating in a study on the effects of emotional arousal on asthma will indeed trigger their asthma.

Since the Isenberg et al. (1992a) review, a number of other laboratory studies have been conducted to examine the effects of emotion induction on symptom perception (e.g., breathlessness) and objective measures of pulmonary function. Emotional imagery during asthma attacks diminished accurate symptom perception and enhanced sensations of breathlessness among adolescents with asthma (Rietveld, Everaerd, & van Beest, 2000), but breathlessness was not associated with objective measures of lung function. The induction of negative emotions followed by exercise increased subjective asthma symptom report (e.g., breathlessness), which was not associated with objective measures of pulmonary function (Rietveld & Prins, 1998). Similarly, the induction of stress and negative emotions resulted in increased breathlessness, but not airways obstruction, among adolescents with asthma; the sensations of breathlessness were stronger during the stress induction paradigm than during the induction of actual airway obstruction through a bronchial provocation procedure (Rietveld, van Beest, & Everaerd, 1999).

This series of studies by Rietveld and colleagues provide important information about the role of stress and negative emotions in subjective and objective asthma symptoms. These studies utilize adolescents, and as such, the generalizability of the results to adults warrants examination in future studies. For example, to the extent that emotion regulation and chronic illness self-management are both processes that tend to improve with experience, maturity, and so forth, the results of these studies may overestimate the extent to which emotion induction results in subjective reports of asthma reports in adults. Physiologically, to the extent that hormonal responses to stress differ in adolescents versus adults, the relative activation of the HPA axis may result in cortisol release or attenuation, and anti- versus pro-inflammatory effects, with consequences for airflow.

Other laboratory studies have found more support for an association between stress and emotional arousal, and objective changes in pulmonary function. Ritz, Steptoe, DeWilde, and Costa (2000) asked adults with and without asthma to view seven film clips designed to elicit specific emotional states, to engage in mental arithmetic (designed to elicit active coping), and to view graphic medical photographs (designed to elicit passive coping). The emotion induction procedure resulted in significant increases in respiratory resistance among the participants with asthma for all emotional conditions compared to the neutral condition, but this effect did not occur significantly more strongly among subjects with asthma compared to those without. However, participants with asthma had significantly more shortness of breath, minute ventilation, arousal, and depression during the medical photographs than during the mental arithmetic, as compared to participants without asthma. These results are similar to those of Rietveld and colleagues, suggesting that stressful tasks (especially tasks during which only passive coping was likely) increased asthma and emotional symptoms among adults with asthma. Although objective changes in pulmonary function (i.e., respiratory resistance) were observed, these changes were not specific to, nor more pronounced among, participants with asthma.

Finally, two additional studies were performed in the laboratory that used a personally relevant stressor paradigm to enhance ecological validity. In this paradigm, the patient with asthma and their intimate partner discussed two topics: a problem in their relationship and an asthma attack that occurred when the partner was present. Mood and pulmonary function (peak expiratory flow rate, PEFR) were recorded before, in the midst of, and after the discussions, which were videotaped and behaviorally coded. The first study involved six individuals with severe asthma and their partners (Schmaling et al., 1996). PEFR improved for two patients and deteriorated for four patients over 30 minutes of interaction with an average magnitude of about one standard deviation. Across patients, more hostile and depressed moods were associated with decrements in PEFR. The second study involved 50 patients with mild-to-moderate asthma and their partners (Schmaling, Afari, Hops, Barnhart, & Buchwald, submitted). On average, pulmonary function (PEFR) decreased one-third of a standard deviation, and self-reported anxiety was related to decrements in pulmonary function. Variability in pulmonary function was associated with more aversive behavior, less problem-solving behavior, and less self-reported anxiety. Interactions with a significant other appeared to result in more change in pulmonary function among participants in the first study with more severe asthma (average baseline FEV_1 was 56% of predicted), than among participants in the second study with asthma of mild-to-moderate severity (average baseline PEFR was 78% of predicted), and could not be explained by differences in global relationship satisfaction between the two samples, which were comparable. Decrements in pulmonary function were associated with depression and hostility in the first study, and anxiety in the second study. Participants in the two studies had similar average levels of observed behavior and self-reported depression and hostility, but among the sample with severe asthma, self-reported anxiety was nearly three times that of the sample with asthma of mild-to-moderate severity.

More marked anxiety may be related to the larger magnitude of change in pulmonary function among participants with severe asthma, even though anxiety was not related to changes in pulmonary function in this group, potentially due to the small sample size, and ceiling effects and limited variability in the anxiety measure in the sample with severe asthma.

Taken together, stressful laboratory tasks are associated with changes in subjective asthma symptoms. Studies of adults suggest that stressful tasks also are associated with changes in objective measures of pulmonary function, but since not all studies included a healthy control group (Ritz et al., 2000, being an exception), we cannot say that stress-induced changes in pulmonary function are specific to or more pronounced among persons with asthma.

Studies in the Natural Environment

Several studies have measured the covariation of asthma symptoms and/or measures of airflow with mood states, using daily or more frequent monitoring of patients with asthma. Hyland and colleagues have published several case reports and multiple case series that examine the association between mood states and peak flow. Among 10 adults with asthma who completed measures of mood state (positive and negative affect) and peak flow in the morning and evening, three showed significant correlations of mood state with PEFR over 15 days (rs $\geq$ ~.50): more positive mood states were associated with higher PEFR (Hyland, 1990). These relationships were more robust in the evening than the morning. One study (Browne & Hyland, 1992) examined the association between mood states and peak flow in a single case before and during the initiation of medical treatment. They reported robust correlations averaging .55 before treatment, and .77 during the initiation of treatment, with more positive mood states being related to higher PEFR.

Apter and colleagues (1997) had 21 adults with asthma rate mood states and measure PEFR for 21 days, three times a day. The data were pooled across subjects and observations and revealed multiple associations between mood states and PEFR, after controlling for symptom ratings. Positive mood states (pleasant, active) were concurrently associated with greater PEFR; unpleasant and passive mood states were associated with lower PEFR. An examination of lagged associations showed that pleasant mood states predicted subsequent higher PEFR, but PEFR did not predict subsequent mood states. In another study by this group (Affleck et al., 2000), 48 adults with moderate to severe asthma collected mood states and PEFR data thrice daily for 21 days. Between-subjects associations of PEFR and mood state revealed no statistically significant associations. Four percent of within-subjects variability in PEFR was associated with more active and aroused mood states. This study sought to differentiate mood states' arousal levels from their hedonic valence, and generally found that arousal levels were more strongly associated with PEFR than hedonic valence. This approach represents an important step toward reducing error in the measurement of mood.

In a sample of 32 adults who rated moods and stressors and measured PEFR for an average of 140 days, once a day, 50% of participants had one or more significant mood or stress predictors of PEFR (Schmaling, McKnight, & Afari, in press). Patients' characteristics were examined in an attempt to identify variables that were related to an association between mood and PEFR. Lower global relationship satisfaction tended to characterize participants for whom PEFR was associated with relationship stress on a day-to-day basis, and the presence of an anxiety disorder tended to be related to a greater day-to-day covariation of anxiety and PEFR.

Another study demonstrated strong associations between moods and stressors and PEFR among 20 adults who monitored psychosocial variables and peak flow five times a day for 10 days (Smyth, Soefer, Hurewitz, Kliment, & Stone, 1999). Moods and stressors accounted for 17% of the variance in peak flow; positive moods were associated with increased peak flow, and negative moods and stressors were associated with peak flow decrements.

Steptoe and Holmes (1985) asked 14 men (half of whom had asthma) to monitor mood and PEFR four times a day for 24 days. Six of the seven participants with asthma, but only three of the seven participants without asthma, demonstrated significant within-subject associations between mood and PEFR. Fatigue was the sole mood state that demonstrated an association for all three participants without asthma. For participants with asthma, which moods were associated with asthma varied by person.

Summary

In their review, Rietveld, Everaerd, and Creer (2000) state, "it remains unclear whether stress-induced airways obstruction really exists." Their critiques of the methodological issues with the studies in this area are worthy of note. For example, PEFR and spirometry are dependent on effort, and spurious associations between mood and asthma could result if the measure of asthma is dependent on effort and influenced by mood. Their conclusions are based on classic research assumptions that for an effect to be observed reliably, it should be repeatedly demonstrable in studies with sufficient sample sizes utilizing between-subjects designs. Thus, one possible

interpretation of the research to date is that the association between stress and asthma is weak. Another interpretation is that the possible mechanisms involved in an association between stress and asthma are multifaceted and complex, probably involving endocrine, immune, and autonomic pathways. It is a thorny issue to reveal simultaneously the mechanism and the effect, since significant error may be introduced by inadvertently covarying factors that may affect the observed association between stress and asthma. With the likelihood that multiple, complex paths are involved, let us suggest that the association between stress and asthma is *idiographic*, that is, to be determined on an individual basis and influenced by an as-yet not fully characterized set of variables that convey or protect against the risk for an association between stress and asthma. An idiographic approach also is consistent with the results of existing studies that have examined the association between stress and asthma on an individual-by-individual basis and found that some but not all individuals demonstrate an association, and that different emotions may be associated with change in pulmonary function for different individuals.

Future research in this area should systematically examine data resulting from laboratory versus naturalistic sources of emotions; consider a parsimonious set of interaction effects such as the interaction of emotion induction and suggestion, or emotion induction in various environments (e.g., with or without the presence of a supportive significant other); examine the effects of emotions with positive versus negative valences; consider the role of emotional intensity; and examine these relationships in well characterized subgroups of patients for differences by gender, age group (adults versus adolescents), asthma severity, and so forth. In addition, the type of stressor and the potential coping methods available for the participants' use is worthy of further study. Potentially, the trend toward different results obtained in laboratory situations using contrived tasks and in naturalistic studies may be attributable to differences in the ability to engage in active or passive coping, as the former has been associated with bronchodilation and the latter with bronchoconstriction (Lehrer, 1998; Lehrer et al., 1996).

Comorbid Psychiatric Disorders: Prevalence and Effects

Panic Disorder

Panic disorder occurs among patients with asthma at a rate several times greater than has been reported in the population. For example, the National Comorbidity Survey (Kessler et al., 1994) reported the lifetime prevalence of panic disorder to be 3.5%. By comparison, the prevalence of panic disorder among samples of patients with asthma has been reported to be 24% (Yellowlees, Alpers, Bowden, Bryant, & Ruffin, 1987), 12% (Yellowlees, Haynes, Potts, & Ruffin, 1988), 10% (Carr, Lehrer, Rausch, & Hochron, 1994), 9% (van Peski-Oosterbaan, Spinhoven, van der Does, Willems, & Sterk, 1996), and 10% (Afari, Schmaling, Barnhart, & Buchwald, 2001). The reasons for this increased co-occurrence are not known, but there are several possible contributing factors: Patients with each condition experience similar symptoms (Schmaling & Bell, 1997), and consequences, such as avoidance of situations where previous attacks have occurred, or situations that bear similarities to the venues of previous attacks. Anxiety-related hyperventilation may exacerbate asthma through cooling of the airways, and asthma may increase susceptibility to panic through hypercapnia, and the anxiogenic side effects of beta-agonist medications. See Carr (1999) for a recent review on other potential associations between asthma and panic.

Mood Disorders

As with other chronic medical conditions, asthma also is associated with a greater prevalence of mood disorders than in the general population. Among samples of patients with asthma, lifetime diagnoses of major depression or dysthymia were found among 16% (Yellowlees et al., 1987) and 40% (Afari et al., 2001) of persons, which can be compared to 17% in the National Comorbidity Study (Kessler et al., 1994). The cross-sectional association of several conditions including asthma and major depression among young adults in a population-based study was done to investigate the hypothesis that inflammation-associated activation of the HPA axis results from dysfunctional responses to stress (Hurwitz & Morgenstern, 1999). This study found that persons with asthma were approximately twice as likely as persons without asthma to have had an episode of major depression in the past year. A study of twins found evidence for a genetic contribution to the association of allergies and depression (M. Wamboldt et al., 2000). As noted previously, allergies frequently co-occur with asthma, leading to evidence for a genetic contribution to the association between asthma and depression. Hypothesized links between the mechanisms involved in depression and allergies (and by association, asthma) have been suggested previously (Marshall, 1993).

Previously, we noted that respiratory drive and the ability to perceive dyspnea were impaired among patients with a near-fatal asthma attack. Depression has been postulated to be associated with these impairments (Allen, Hickie, Gandevia, & McKenzie, 1994); and others have suggested that depression is an important risk factor for fatal asthma (B. Miller, 1987).

In contrast with studies that have found an increased incidence of psychiatric disorders among patients with asthma, other studies have found anxiety and depressive symptoms to be strongly related to respiratory symptoms, but not a diagnosis of asthma (Janson, Bjornsson, Hetta, & Boman, 1994).

There is significant variability in the sampling and measurement methodology used by the studies in this area, and the effects of such methodological variations should be considered when attempting to draw conclusions about the state of knowledge in this area. For example, Janson et al. (1994) accrued a random population sample, then assessed those respondents who endorsed breathing symptoms more fully to confirm a diagnosis of asthma. But most other studies used nonrandom samples of convenience, such as hospitalized patients with asthma, or patients from a respiratory clinic. The source of subjects and sampling methods likely result in differences that may affect rates of psychiatric symptoms and disorders. For example, a population-based sample will probably have a smaller proportion of patients with moderate and severe asthma than does a sample of hospitalized patients, based on the distribution of asthma severity in the population.

Measurement variability also can result in different estimates of psychiatric disorders. While measures of symptom severity convey dimensional information more readily amenable to robust parametric statistical techniques than the current psychiatric diagnostic nomenclature, the classification-based diagnostic systems are the gold standard, and symptom measures only estimate the presence or absence of a given diagnosis. Unfortunately, the relative contributions of sampling and measurement variability to divergent results are difficult to untangle as self-reported symptom measures are more practical and therefore often used in population-based studies whereas more labor-intensive diagnostic interviews are more likely to be utilized in smaller clinical samples.

Functional Status

Population-based studies such as the Medical Outcomes Study demonstrate that individually, psychiatric conditions and chronic medical conditions are associated with poorer functional status (e.g., Hays, Wells, Sherbourne, Rogers, & Spritzer, 1995). Asthma is associated with a lower quality of life (Quirk & Jones, 1990), is the third leading cause of lost time from work, behind two categories of back problems (Blanc, Jones, Besson, Katz, & Yelin, 1993); and generally, has a negative effect on functional status (Bousquet et al., 1994; Ried, Nau, & Grainger-Rousseau, 1999). In particular, patients with asthma *and* depression or anxiety had significantly worse physical functioning and health perceptions than patients with asthma but without depression or anxiety (Afari et al., 2001).

Autonomic Nervous System and Inflammatory Processes in Stress and Asthma: Possible Connections

As noted, a reasonable conclusion regarding the effects of stress and emotions on asthma is that *some* persons with asthma demonstrate stress- or emotion-linked changes in pulmonary function. Given that stress results in sympathetic activation and the release of sympathomimetics (cortisol, epinephrine), which are known to relax airway smooth muscles, one would expect stress to be associated with bronchodilation. What physiological mechanisms might explain the seemingly paradoxical association of stress with bronchoconstriction, including the contemporary emphasis on the role of inflammation in asthma? Here we summarize briefly the common elements of several thoughtful review articles that suggest potential pathways by which stress and emotions may affect pulmonary function (Lehrer, Isenberg, & Hochron, 1993; Rietveld, Everaerd, & Creer, 2000; Wright et al., 1998).

The immune, endocrine, and autonomic nervous system may contribute to airway variability and interact in complex ways to help explain stress-related changes in airway function. Stress increases vulnerability to infection; upper respiratory infections are frequently associated with asthma exacerbations. Stress affects immune function, changes in immune function may include inflammatory responses, including airway inflammation, and individual differences in changes in immune function in response to stress may partially explain idiographic variability in the response to stress. Bronchoconstriction may result from vagal reactivity in response to stress, reflecting contributions of the autonomic nervous system to airway control. It is important to consider the baseline level of stress in a given individual, and the results of possible interactions of different levels of acute and chronic stress. Chronic stress may result in a hyporesponsive HPA axis with attenuated cortisol secretion under added acute stress (perhaps compounded by chronic daily use of beta-agonist medications), suggesting a partial explanation of the seemingly paradoxical response of bronchoconstriction when stressed among some patients with asthma. Other contributing factors include immune system down-regulation and the increased risk of infection when stressed (Cohen, Tyrrell, & Smith, 1991); infections in turn cause inflammation and increase susceptibility to asthma exacerbations. The effects of chronic and acute stress on immune-mediated changes in pulmonary function await investigation in future research.

MEDICAL TREATMENTS FOR ASTHMA

The 1997 expert panel recommendations (National Heart Lung and Blood Institute, 1997) are considered the gold standard of current practice guidelines. These recommendations define four levels of asthma severity (mild-intermittent, mild-persistent, moderate-persistent, and severe-persistent) defined by a combination of factors of lung function, nocturnal symptom frequency, and daytime symptom frequency. Treatment recommendations are matched to the level of severity, resulting in a stepped-care model wherein treatment guidelines are yoked to severity step.

Medications to treat asthma typically fall into two categories: *controller* and *reliever* medications. Consistent with the emphasis on the inflammatory processes involved in asthma, controller medications exert anti-inflammatory effects, and include long-term inhaled (e.g., flunisolide) or oral (e.g., prednisone) forms. Reliever medications reverse acute bronchoconstriction through relaxing the smooth muscles; examples include short-acting beta-2 agonists (e.g., albuterol). Mild-intermittent asthma may be controlled through the as-needed use of reliever medications. Severe-persistent asthma requires the consistent use of reliever medications and both oral and inhaled controller medications. Common side effects of reliever medications include nervousness, rapid heartbeat, trembling, and headaches. More common side effects of inhaled controller medications include hoarseness and sore or dry mouth and throat, whereas oral controller medications (corticosteroids) are most commonly associated with increased appetite, and nervousness or restlessness. Patients may confuse corticosteroids prescribed for their asthma with anabolic steroids (often used illegally to enhance muscle mass with significant iatrogenic effects). Although the chronic use of oral corticosteroids for asthma control can be associated with significant side effects, patients may need to be reassured that their asthma medications are of a different class of medications that anabolic steroids. Erroneous and dysfunctional beliefs about asthma and asthma medications may impede adherence with asthma self-care recommendations. Adherence with recommended medication regimens for asthma is a knotty issue, as we discuss in the next section.

The Expert Panel Report emphasizes the role of patient self-management in optimal asthma care. We review components of asthma self-management next.

ADHERENCE

The lack of adherence to prescribed medication regimens is thought to explain significant proportions of morbidity, mortality, and urgent/emergent medical care. There are different methods to describe adherence: in terms of the overall percentage of prescribed medication that is taken, or as a percentage of a sample that takes an adequate amount of medication, with a criterion for adequacy defined as a proportion of the total prescribed (e.g., 70%). Using the former method, a recent review estimated that patients take about 50% of prescribed medication (Bender, Milgrom, & Rand, 1997), but single studies suggest that the problem with nonadherence may be even more significant. For example, one study reported that 30% of their participants took 50% of more of prescribed medications (F. Dekker, Dieleman, Kapstein, & Mulder, 1993). Adherence with reliever medications is typically better than with controller medications (e.g., Kelloway, Wyatt, DeMarco, & Adlis, 2000). There are a number of reasons why patient use of reliever medications is more than controller medications, such as the fast-acting effects of the former being more reinforcing than the use of the latter, despite the greater importance of controller medications in ongoing asthma management.

Researchers have cast a broad net in their efforts to understand adherence difficulties and identify predictors of nonadherence. There are methodological challenges inherent in the study of adherence, ranging from the evidence that such research is reactive (that participants change their medication-taking behavior when they know it is monitored), that assays for levels of common asthma medications in body fluids (serum, urine, saliva, etc.) do not exist, to ethical considerations in the covert monitoring of medication use (with covert monitoring methodology, deception may be involved in which participants do not receive full disclosure regarding the purposes of the research: see Levine, 1994). Recent efforts to understand better the perspective of the patient through qualitative research (Adams, Pill, & Jones, 1997) and the development of self-report measures to assess patients' reasons for and against taking their asthma medications as prescribed (Schmaling, Afari, & Blume, 2000) may lead to effective patient-centered interventions to improve adherence. For example, a pilot trial with patients with asthma comparing education with education plus a single session of motivational enhancement therapy (MET) (W. Miller & Rollnick, 1991), a structured client-centered psychotherapy, found that MET improved attitudes toward taking medications among patients initially unwilling to or ambivalent about taking medications as prescribed (Schmaling, Blume, & Afari, 2001).

Research on predictors of adherence has revealed that specific sociodemographic variables are linked to adherence, including age and gender. Older age (Bosley, Fosbury, & Cochrane, 1995; Laird, Chamberlain, & Spicer, 1994; Schmaling, Afari, & Blume, 1998), female gender (Gray et al., 1996; Jones, Jones, &

Katz, 1987), more education (Apter, Reisine, Affleck, Barrows, & ZuWallack, 1998), Caucasian ethnicity (Apter et al., 1998), and higher socioeconomic status (Apter et al., 1998) have been associated with better adherence to medication regimens among patients with asthma.

Adherence with medications is only one component of treatment adherence. Research has yet to focus on other components of treatment adherence, such as adherence with allergen avoidance and environmental control. Indeed, a prerequisite for patient adherence with such measures would be receiving information and education on allergen avoidance and environmental control from providers. Yet, despite practice guidelines that mandate allergy evaluations, provider adherence is low—among 6,703 patients with moderate or severe asthma across the United States, less than two-thirds of patients reported ever having had an allergy evaluation (Meng, Leung, Berkbigler, Halbert, & Legorreta, 1999). There may be a number of pragmatic barriers to the consistent implementation of practice guidelines. For example, with increasing pressure for treatment providers to see more patients in less time, relatively time-consuming interventions (such as education) may be curtailed or skipped. In a managed care setting, referrals for allergy evaluations may be avoided for financial reasons. Or, limited dissemination may result in some treatment providers being unaware of current practice guidelines. Patients who receive their asthma care from a specialist rather than a general practitioner have self-care practices more consistent with treatment guidelines (Legoretta et al., 1998; Meng et al., 1999; Vollmer et al., 1997). The extent to which practitioners' behavior is consistent with practice guidelines should be determined before assessing patients' behavior; patients should not be considered nonadherent if the appropriate evaluations and treatments have not been first established by the practitioner. However, these steps have not been taken consistently in the studies to date. Investigations on factors associated with atopic patients' adherence with allergen avoidance or control (e.g., regular cleaning and washing to decrease dust mite exposure) would be a useful area for future research.

PSYCHOSOCIAL FACTORS ASSOCIATED WITH MEDICAL TREATMENTS AND OUTCOMES

Psychiatric Disorders

Psychiatric disorders impede the ability of patients with asthma to perceive accurately their pulmonary status, and to respond appropriately. Both poor perceivers, whose perceived breathlessness is less than actual airflow limitation, and "exaggerated perceivers," whose perceived breathlessness is greater than actual airflow limitation, were five and seven times, respectively, more likely to have psychiatric disorders than were more accurate perceivers (Rushford, Tiller, & Pain, 1998). The mechanism by which airflow perception is affected by psychiatric disorders is unknown. There are several possible explanations involving psychological influences on symptom perception (Rietveld, 1998). First, poor perception may be a consequence of psychiatric disorders by creating difficulties with concentration because of the distracting and disabling emotional symptoms. Second, asthma symptoms may be similar to symptoms of certain psychiatric disorders, leading to confusion about the source of the symptoms among patients with both types of disorders. For example, shortness of breath is a symptom of asthma and of panic disorder. Errors in discrimination and attribution, such as taking an anxiolytic in response to a supposed panic attack, would delay appropriate treatment if the symptoms actually reflected an exacerbation of asthma. Third, poor perception and psychiatric disorders may reflect a common pathway, such as priming or kindling effects for emotional and somatic sensations. Asthma occurring in the context of a comorbid psychiatric disorder should cue providers to assess patients' perceptual accuracy regarding their pulmonary status, for example, by comparing perceptions of dyspnea with peak expiratory flow.

Other Psychological Variables and Their Associations with Self-Care and Medical Utilization

Apart from categories of psychiatric diagnoses, certain psychosocial characteristics have been reliably linked to nonoptimal self-care and medical utilization. We will examine two characteristics in terms of their associations with self-care and medical utilization behaviors, the tendency to respond to asthma with panic-fear and social relationships.

Panic-Fear

Research on the role of panic-fear in asthma has focused on generalized panic-fear and asthma-specific panic-fear. Generalized tendencies toward panic-fear reactions have been measured using a subscale of the MMPI, and tendencies for panicky and fearful responses specifically to asthma symptoms have been measured using a subscale of the Asthma Symptom Checklist (Kinsman, Luparello, O'Banion, & Spector, 1973). Independent of objective asthma severity, both high generalized and asthma-specific panic-fear have been associated with more medical utilization

(Dahlem, Kinsman, & Horton, 1977; Dirks, Kinsman, et al., 1977; Hyland, Kenyon, Taylor, & Morice, 1993; Kinsman, Dahlem, Spector, & Staudenmayer, 1977; Nouwen, Freeston, Labbe, & Boulet, 1999). However, generalized panic-fear may be a better predictor of asthma-related morbidity than asthma-specific panic-fear (Dirks, Fross, & Evans, 1977). Greater generalized panic-fear has been associated with *higher* rehospitalization rates (Dirks, Kinsman, Horton, Fross, & Jones, 1978) whereas greater illness-specific panic-fear has been associated with *lower* rehospitalization rates (Staudenmeyer, Kinsman, Dirks, Spector, & Wangaard, 1979). High asthma-specific panic-fear is accompanied by more catastrophic cognitions (Carr, Lehrer, & Hochron, 1995), particularly among patients who also meet criteria for panic disorder (Carr et al., 1994), suggesting that cognitive interventions are indicated for patients with co-morbid asthma and panic disorder. Persons with high generalized panic-fear may not be able to determine the seriousness of a threat, and determine onset and offset of those threats, leading to a generally heightened reactivity. Moderate levels of asthma-specific panic-fear is optimal, signaling the need for vigilance and action (e.g., increased self-monitoring, taking appropriate medications) by the patient. By contrast, patients with low asthma-specific panic-fear may ignore early symptoms that signal the need for more medication, possibly leading to the need for (potentially avertable) high-intensity intervention to reverse the airflow obstruction. Taken together, some asthma-specific panic-fear is adaptive but high levels of generalized panic-fear is maladaptive for optimal self-management of asthma.

Social Relationships

Social relationships can decrease or buffer the effects of stress on illness, or be another source of stress. An early study showed that patients with asthma who were high in psychosocial assets (a construct that included familial and interpersonal relationships) required a lower average steroid dose than those who were low in psychosocial assets (De Araujo, van Arsdel, Holmes, & Dudley, 1973). More intimate relationship satisfaction was associated with more medication use, after accounting for the effects of disease severity, suggesting that patients in more satisfied relationships may be more adherent (Schmaling, Afari, Barnhart, & Buchwald, 1997). Patients with intimate relationships were 1.5 times more likely to evidence satisfactory adherence with their medications than single patients (Rand, Nides, Cowles, Wise, & Connett, 1995). Although this study was conducted with a large sample of patients with chronic obstructive pulmonary disease (COPD), the results are relevant because inhaled medications are a cornerstone of COPD treatment, as they are for asthma. It appears, then, that the presence of an intimate partner and satisfaction with close relationships may be associated with more appropriate medication utilization (more adherent use of medications; less necessity for oral steroids suggesting better disease control through inhaled medications), perhaps resulting in less morbidity due to asthma.

As mentioned, patients with a tendency toward generalized fearful, catastrophizing reactions have more medical utilization. How might fearful reactions and social relationships interact in patients with asthma? Two models are relevant: first, the concept of the safety signal, which was developed based on persons with panic disorder. Safety signals are items (e.g., medications) or people associated with feelings of security and relief (Rachman, 1984). Among patients with asthma, the presence of the significant other may be hypothesized to decrease fearful cognitions, and be associated with lesser reports of asthma symptoms. An alternate hypothesis comes from kindling-sensitization models that posit that over time, increasingly lower levels of stimuli are needed to prompt the occurrence of the target symptoms (Post, Rubinow, & Ballenger, 1986). Extending this model to asthma, to the extent that the significant other is a source of stress, the significant other may be associated with increasing discomfort and greater reports of asthma symptoms over time. Theory-driven examinations of the role of the significant other and the moderating effects of relationship satisfaction await future research efforts.

PSYCHOLOGICAL INTERVENTIONS FOR ASTHMA

Asthma Education

Self-care for asthma involves a number of rather complex behaviors. The patient must be able to identify asthma symptoms, measure his/her peak flow at home; calculate whether pulmonary function is low enough to require action; take various kinds of medications, each with different purposes, effects, and side effects; avoid certain asthma triggers; and visit a doctor regularly.

The NHLBI-sponsored Expert Panel Report (1997) has recommended that each asthma patient should have a written action plan. The asthma action plan instructs the patient to take medication and to contact health care providers according to the patient's asthma severity. Severity is portrayed as a traffic light. Three zones are based on signs, symptoms, and peak flow values. When in the green zone (no symptoms, relatively normal pulmonary function), the patient continues taking his or her regular dose of "controller" medication (anti-inflammatory medication, usually inhaled steroids and/or leukotreine inhibitors, sometimes along with a long-acting beta-2 agonist) at the current dose. When in the yellow zone, the patient takes "reliever" or emergency medication (bronchodilator, usually albuterol) and may increase the dose of controller medication. If yellow zone symptomatology does not resolve within a specific time frame, the patient is instructed to contact his or her asthma physician. The red zone describes a severe asthma exacerbation. The patient is instructed to take more medication (sometimes including oral steroid medication), contact the physician, and, in some cases, proceed to an emergency room.

The following components are included in asthma education: instructing the patient about basic facts of asthma and the various asthma medications, teaching techniques for using inhalers and avoiding allergens, devising a daily self-management plan, and completing an asthma diary for self-monitoring.

Asthma education programs have been shown to be cost effective for both children (Greineder, Loane, & Parks, 1999) and adults (Taitel, Kotses, Bernstein, Bernstein, & Creer, 1995). Studies of these programs have demonstrated improvements on measures such as frequency of asthma attacks and symptoms, medication consumption, and self-management skills (Kotses et al., 1995; Wilson et al., 1996). More research, though, is needed to determine which specific components of the interventions (e.g., environmental control, peak flow monitoring) are effective.

Psychotherapy

Sommaruga and colleagues (1995) combined an asthma education program with three sessions of cognitive-behavioral therapy (CBT) focusing on areas that may interfere with proper medical management. However, few significant between-group differences on measures of anxiety, depression, and asthma morbidity (e.g., missed school/work days) emerged between the control group receiving medical treatment alone and the CBT group. In an uncontrolled study, Park, Sawyer, and Glaun (1996) applied principles of CBT for panic disorder to children with asthma reporting greater subjective complaints and consuming medication in excess of the level warranted by their pulmonary impairment. In the 12 months following treatment, the rate of hospitalization for asthma decreased, but other measures of clinical outcome were not analyzed. We have recently combined components of asthma education and CBT for panic disorder to develop a treatment protocol appropriate for adults with asthma and panic disorder (Feldman, Giardino, & Lehrer, 2000). The treatment includes components on education about asthma and panic, asthma self-management, anxiety management, instruction on distinguishing asthma attacks from panic attacks, exposure and problem-solving therapy, and finally, relapse prevention. This treatment is currently being empirically tested. The NHLBI guidelines for asthma treatment recommend referral to mental health professionals when stress appears to interfere with medical management of asthma (NHLBI, 1997).

Written Emotional Expression Exercises

Persons with asthma, and especially children with asthma, are more likely to experience negative emotions than are healthy individuals, but may be less likely to express them (Hollaender & Florin, 1983; Lehrer et al., 1993; Silverglade, Tosi, Wise, & D'Costa, 1994). However, empirical data as to whether and how negative emotions precipitate or exacerbate asthma attacks are mixed (Lehrer, 1998).

Smyth, Stone, Hurewitz, and Kaell (1999) asked participating subjects to write an essay expressing their thoughts and feelings about a traumatic experience. They demonstrated generally improved health outcomes. Among participants with asthma, the authors reported a clinically significant improvement in FEV_1 after a four-month follow-up, with no improvement noted in a control group who wrote on innocuous topics.

Other Psychosocial Interventions

Castés et al. (1999) provided children with asthma a six-month program that included cognitive stress-management therapy, a self-esteem workshop, and relaxation/guided imagery. Improvement occurred both in clinical measures of asthma and in asthma-related immune-system measures. The treatment group, but not the control group, significantly decreased their use of beta-2 agonist medications, showed improvements in FEV_1, and, at the end of treatment, no longer showed a response to bronchodilators (consistent with improvement in asthma). Basal FEV_1 improved to normal levels in the treatment group after six months of treatment. Children in the treatment group showed increased natural killer cell activity and a significantly augmented expression of the T-cell receptor for IL-2, along with a significantly decreased count of leukocytes with low affinity receptors for IgE. The results suggest that, over the long-term, stress management methods may have important preventive effects on asthma, and may affect the basic inflammatory mechanisms that underlie this disease.

Direct Effects of Psychological Treatments on the Pathophysiology of Asthma

Relaxation Training

In an earlier review (Lehrer, Sargunaraj, & Hochron, 1992), we concluded that relaxation training often has statistically significant but small and inconsistent effects on asthma. More recent studies have yielded a similar pattern (Henry, de Rivera, Gonzales-Martin, Abreu, 1993; Lehrer et al., 1994; Lehrer, Hochron, et al., 1997; Loew, Siegfried, Martus, Trill, & Hahn, 1996; Smyth, Stone, et al., 1999; Vazquez & Buceta, 1993a, 1993b, 1993c). Outcome measures, populations, and relaxation procedures differ across studies, and may explain some of the inconsistencies. Although clinically significant relaxation-induced changes in pulmonary function have been noted in asthma, they do not occur consistently. It is possible that relaxation training may have an important effect only among people with emotional asthma triggers, or that the pre-existing effects of asthma medication attenuated the effects of relaxation training in these studies.

Data from our laboratory suggest that the immediate effects of relaxation on asthma may differ from the longer term effects (Lehrer et al., 1994; Lehrer, Hochron, et al., 1997). We found that pulmonary function *decreased* between the beginning and end of specific relaxation sessions, and that these decreases were correlated with evidence of increased parasympathetic tone. Such "parasympathetic rebound" effects are commonly seen during the practice of relaxation. A small *improvement* in pulmonary function was observed over six weeks of treatment, showing that the immediate effects of relaxation may differ from the longer term effects. We have hypothesized that this improvement results from a general decrease in autonomic reactivity. Gellhorn (1958) hypothesized that this is a general effect of relaxation methods, mediated by decreased sympathetic arousal, and consequent downregulation of homeostatic parasympathetic reflexes. More recent literature confirms this hypothesis (Lehrer, 1978, 1996). Therefore, when assessing the impact of interventions that are directed at reducing autonomic arousal or reactivity, it may be important not only to measure physiological changes over the course of multiple sessions, but also to be aware that measures taken immediately following the termination of a session of relaxation training may reflect to observe any therapeutic benefits that may be produced.

Vazquez and Buceta (1993a, 1993b, 1993c) studied the effects of an asthma education program, both alone and combined with progressive relaxation instruction. They found evidence for relaxation-induced therapeutic effects on duration of asthma attacks only among children with a history of emotional triggers. Participants without emotional triggers showed greater changes on this measure without relaxation instruction. At a borderline significant level, participants given relaxation training showed a greater decrease in consumption of beta-2 adrenergic stimulant (rescue) medications than those not given relaxation training. However, on measures of pulmonary function, participants with emotional asthma triggers benefited significantly from asthma education *without* relaxation, but *not* with it. The authors hypothesized these subjects may have put less emphasis on proper medical management of asthma. Thus, relaxation training may only be beneficial for asthma patients with emotionally-triggered symptoms.

Biofeedback Techniques

EMG Biofeedback

Kotses and his colleagues (Glaus & Kotses, 1983; Kotses et al., 1991) hypothesized that changes in facial muscle tension directly produce respiratory impedance through a trigeminal-vagal reflex pathway (such that tensing these muscles produces bronchoconstriction, while relaxing them produces bronchodilation). They tested the model using frontal EMG biofeedback to increase and decrease tension in the facial muscles. Frontal EMG relaxation training was found to decrease facial muscle tension and to produce improvements in pulmonary function, while training to increase tension in this area had the opposite effect. EMG biofeedback training to the forearm muscles had no effects. Several studies from other laboratories have failed to replicate these findings, however (Lehrer et al., 1994, 1996; Lehrer, Generelli, & Hochron, 1997; Mass, Wais, Ramm, & Richter, 1992; Ritz, Dahme, & Wagner, 1998).

Another biofeedback strategy, suggested by Peper and his colleagues, linked pulmonary function with tension in the skeletal muscles of the neck and thorax (Peper & Tibbetts, 1992). (Tension in this area often is produced by a pattern of thoracic breathing.) They used EMG biofeedback training to teach participants to relax these muscles, while simultaneously increasing volume and smoothness of breathing. This training was done in the context of a multi-component treatment that included desensitization to asthma sensations and training in slow diaphragmatic breathing. The latter training was carried out by a biofeedback procedure using an incentive inspirometer. At the follow-up, all subjects significantly reduced their EMG tension levels while simultaneously increasing their inhalation volumes. Subjects reported reductions in their asthma symptoms, medication use, emergency room visits, and breathless episodes. A small study from our laboratory did not show significant effects for this method

(Lehrer, Carr, et al., 1997), but this study lacked power to determine whether some trends in the data were significant. More research on this method is warranted.

Respiratory Resistance Biofeedback

Mass and his colleagues (1991) attempted to train subjects to decrease respiratory resistance by providing continuous biofeedback of this measure, using the forced oscillation method. In an uncontrolled trial, this feedback technique decreased average respiratory resistance within sessions but not between sessions (Mass, Dahme, & Richter, 1993). It did not increase FEV_1 (Mass, Richter, & Dahme, 1996). They concluded that this type of biofeedback is not an effective technique for the treatment of bronchial asthma in adults.

Respiratory Sinus Arrhythmia (RSA) Biofeedback

More recently, a novel biofeedback approach that utilizes the phenomenon of respiratory sinus arrhythmia (RSA) has been used to improve pulmonary function in asthma patients (Lehrer, Carr, et al., 1997; Lehrer, Smetankin, & Potapova, 2000). In RSA, the increase and decrease in heart rate with inspiration and expiration, is mediated by vagal outflow at the sino-atrial node. Normally, the magnitude of heart rate variability at respiratory frequency is directly associated with efferent vagal activity and may also be related to autonomic regulatory control. A detailed manual for conducting this procedure has been published (Lehrer, Vaschillo, & Vaschillo, 2000). In brief, patients utilize slow (approximately six breaths per minute), abdominal, pursed-lips breathing to increase the magnitude of RSA at their own particular optimal respiratory frequency. Multiple case studies from clinics in Russia support the hypothesis that RSA biofeedback training is an effective treatment for various neurotic and stress-related physical disorders (Chernigovskaya, Vaschillo, Petrash, & Rusanovskii, 1990; Chernigovskaya, Vaschillo, Rusanovskii, & Kashkarova, 1990; Pichugin, Strelakov, & Zakharevich, 1993; Vaschillo, Zingerman, Konstantinov, & Menitsky, 1983), and asthma (Lehrer, Smetankin, et al., 2000). Larger scale, controlled clinical trials are currently underway to further assess the effectiveness and therapeutic mechanisms of this intervention.

Other Self-Regulation Methods

Yoga

Two studies of yoga among asthmatics found improvement in asthma symptoms, as well as a more positive attitude, feelings of well-being, and fewer symptoms of panic. One was an uncontrolled trial (Jain et al., 1991), while the other had a no-treatment control condition (Vedanthan et al., 1998). These studies suggested that yoga may have greater effects on the subjective symptoms of asthma than on physiological function. However, these conclusions remain tentative because of the small amount of research on this topic, and the wide variety of yoga methods used throughout the world.

Hypnosis

In a controlled study of hypnosis as a treatment of asthma among children, Kohen (1995) noted improvement in asthma symptoms, but not in pulmonary function, compared with no treatment and waking suggestion groups. A greater decrease in emergency room visits and missed days in school also were found in the hypnosis group. These data suggest that hypnotic interventions may improve asthma quality of life, but not pulmonary function. Further evaluation of these effects is warranted. Similar findings were obtained in a later uncontrolled study among preschool children (Kohen & Wynne, 1997) for parental reports of asthma symptoms, but not pulmonary function.

Discussion

Asthma education programs that emphasize asthma self-care have become standard components in the accepted protocol for treating asthma and are of proven effectiveness in reducing general asthma morbidity. However, these interventions are complex, and the task of component analysis has just begun to determine which aspects of these programs are most effective, and the particular population to whom each should be directed. Also, the possibly independent effects of these interventions on pulmonary function and asthma quality of life deserve further evaluation.

In addition, future research may identify more exactly the individuals for whom stress-management interventions (such as relaxation therapies) should be targeted (e.g., people who frequently experience stress-induced asthma exacerbations), and the magnitude of this effect. The overall effects of these methods appear to be small, but studies of more finely targeted populations may show greater results. Finally, the effects of these interventions on mediating immune and inflammatory processes have not yet been investigated, so the pathway of their effects has not yet been established.

Other promising new interventions for asthma include biofeedback training to increase the amplitude of respiratory sinus arrhythmia, practice in slow breathing, and training to improve accuracy of perceiving airway obstruction (Harver, 1994; Stout, Kotses, & Creer, 1997) to increase patients' abilities to respond appropriately and in a timely fashion to asthma symptoms.

CONCLUSIONS, UNANSWERED QUESTIONS, AND FUTURE DIRECTIONS

Asthma is a common and costly chronic illness associated with significant morbidity and mortality, which have increased in recent years despite advances in knowledge about asthma and its treatment.

A review of the application of major psychological theories to asthma research revealed that there is some support for the roles of classical conditioning of respiratory resistance and asthma symptoms (e.g., cough), and cognitive processes including suggestion and other perceptual processes in asthma. By contrast, research informed by other theories is appealing but relatively unexplored. Future research could examine the contributions of operant conditioning (e.g., to what extent is self-management behavior shaped by consequences in patients' environments?), questionnaire or observational research of key constructs from family systems theories, and covariates of repressive-defensive coping among adults with asthma.

Our review of the associations of asthma with stress or emotions suggested that few general statements can be made across persons: Stress or emotions are associated with pulmonary function among some but not all persons with asthma, and furthermore, emotions associated with asthma may vary from person to person. Despite the methodological challenges inherent in this area of research, an appropriate conclusion appears to be that stress or certain emotions are salient covariates of pulmonary function for some persons and that this association should be determined on a personal, or idiographic, basis.

Behavioral scientists interested in asthma will find many other fertile areas for research and treatment development, including psychosocial variables affecting adherence with treatment recommendations and self-management practices, new behavioral interventions for asthma, and identifying the characteristics of persons who would most benefit from these interventions. A focus on behavior, to characterize pathological processes and develop relevant behavioral interventions, is crucial to reverse the disturbing trend of increasing morbidity and mortality among persons with asthma.

REFERENCES

Adams, S., Pill, R., & Jones, A. (1997). Medication, chronic illness and identity: The perspective of people with asthma. *Social Science and Medicine, 45,* 189–201.

Afari, N., Schmaling, K. B., Barnhart, S., & Buchwald, D. (2001). Psychiatric comorbidity and functional status in adult patients with asthma. *Journal of Clinical Psychology in Medical Settings, 8,* 245–252.

Affleck, G., Apter, A., Tennen, H., Reisine, S., Barrows, E., Willard, A., et al. (2000). Mood states associated with transitory changes in asthma symptoms and peak expiratory flow. *Psychosomatic Medicine, 62,* 61–68.

Alexander, F. (1955). *Psychosomatic medicine: Its principles and applications.* New York: Norton.

Allen, G. M., Hickie, I., Gandevia, S. C., & McKenzie, D. K. (1994). Impaired voluntary drive to breathe: A possible link between depression and unexplained ventilatory failure in asthmatic patients. *Thorax, 49,* 881–884.

American Lung Association, Epidemiology and Statistics Unit. (January, 2001). *Trends in asthma morbidity and mortality* [online]. Available: www.lungusa.org/data/asthma/ASTHMA1.pdf

Apter, A. J., Affleck, G., Reisine, S. T., Tennen, H. A., Barrows, E., Wells, M., et al. (1997). Perception of airway obstruction in asthma: Sequential daily analysis of symptoms, peak expiratory flow rate, and mood. *Journal of Allergy and Clinical Immunology, 99,* 605–612.

Apter, A. J., Reisine, S. T., Affleck, G., Barrows, E., & ZuWallack, R. L. (1998). Adherence with twice-daily dosing of inhaled steroids: Socioeconomic and health-belief differences. *American Journal of Respiratory and Critical Care Medicine, 157,* 1810–1817.

Bender, B., Milgrom, H., & Rand, C. (1997). Nonadherence in asthmatic patients: Is there a solution to the problem? *Annuals of Allergy, Asthma, and Immunology, 79,* 177–185.

Bender, B., Milgrom, H., Rand, C., & Ackerson, L. (1998). Psychological factors associated with medication nonadherence in asthmatic children. *Journal of Asthma, 35,* 347–353.

Blanc, P. D., Jones, M., Besson, C., Katz, P., & Yelin, E. (1993). Work disability among adults with asthma. *Chest, 104,* 1371–1377.

Bosley, C. M., Fosbury, J. A., & Cochrane, G. M. (1995). The psychological factors associated with poor compliance with treatment in asthma. *European Respiratory Journal, 8,* 899–904.

Bousquet, J., Knani, J., Dhivert, H., Richard, A., Chicoye, A., Ware, J. E., et al. (1994). Quality of life in asthma: I. Internal consistency and validity of the SF-36 questionnaire. *American Journal of Respiratory and Critical Care Medicine, 149,* 371–375.

Browne, S., & Hyland, M. E. (1992). Mood and peak flow in asthma. *Lancet, 339,* 118–119.

Burdon, J. G. W., Juniper, E. F., Killian, K. J., Hargreave, F. E., & Campbell, E. J. M. (1982). The perception of breathlessness in asthma. *American Review of Respiratory Disease, 126,* 825–828.

Camargo, C. A., Weiss, S. T., Zhang, S., Willett, W. C., & Speizer F. E. (1999). Prospective study of body mass index, weight change and risk of adult-onset asthma in women. *Archives of Internal Medicine, 159,* 2582–2588.

Carr, R. E. (1999). Panic disorder and asthma. *Journal of Asthma, 36,* 143–152.

Carr, R. E., Lehrer, P. M., & Hochron, S. M. (1995). Predictors of panic-fear in asthma. *Health Psychology, 14,* 421–426.

Carr, R. E., Lehrer, P. M., Rausch, L. L., & Hochron, S. M. (1994). Anxiety sensitivity and panic attacks in an asthmatic population. *Behavioral Research and Therapy, 32,* 411–418.

Castés, M., Hager, I., Palenque, M., Canelones, P., Corao, A., & Lynch, N. (1999). Immunology changes associated with clinical improvement of asthmatic children subjected to psychosocial intervention. *Brain, Behavior, and Immunity, 13,* 1–13.

Centers for Disease Control. (1992). Asthma—United States, 1980–1990. *Morbidity and Mortality Weekly Reports, 41,* 733–735.

Centers for Disease Control. (1995). Asthma—United States, 1982–1992. *Morbidity and Mortality Weekly Reports, 43,* 952–955.

Centers for Disease Control. (1996). Asthma surveillance programs in public health departments—United States. *Morbidity and Mortality Weekly Reports, 45,* 802–804.

Centers for Disease Control. (2001). Self-reported asthma prevalence among adults—United States, 2000. *Morbidity and Mortality Weekly Reports, 50,* 682–686.

Chernigovskaya, N. V., Vaschillo, E. G., Petrash, V. V., & Rusanovskii, V. V. (1990). Voluntary regulation of the heart rate as a method of functional condition correction in neurotics. *Human Physiology, 16,* 58–64.

Chernigovskaya, N. V., Vaschillo, E. G., Rusanovskii, V. V., & Kashkarova, O. E. (1990). Instrumental autotraining of mechanisms for cardiovascular function regulation in treatment of neurotics. *The SS Korsakov's Journal of Neuropathology and Psychiatry, 90,* 24–28.

Cohen, S., Tyrrell, D. A., & Smith, A. P. (1991). Psychological stress and susceptibility to the common cold. *New England Journal of Medicine, 325*(9), 606–612.

Dahlem, N. W., Kinsman, R. A., & Horton, D. J. (1977). Panic-fear in asthma: Requests for as-needed medications in relation to pulmonary function measurements. *Journal of Allergy and Clinical Immunology, 60,* 295–300.

De Araujo, G., van Arsdel, P. P., Holmes, T. H., & Dudley, D. L. (1973). Life change, coping ability and chronic intrinsic asthma. *Journal of Psychosomatic Research, 17,* 359–363.

Dekker, E., & Groen, J. (1956). Reproducible psychogenic attacks of asthma. *Journal of Psychosomatic Research, 1,* 58–67.

Dekker, E., Pelser, H. E., & Groen, J. (1957). Conditioning as a cause of asthma attacks. *Journal of Psychosomatic Medicine, 2,* 97–108.

Dekker, F. W., Dieleman, F. E., Kapstein, A. A., & Mulder, J. D. (1993). Compliance with pulmonary medication in general practice. *European Respiratory Journal, 6,* 886–890.

Di Blasio, P., Molinari, E., Peri, G., & Taverna, A. (1990). Family competency and childhood asthma: A preliminary study. *Family Systems Medicine, 8,* 145–149.

Dirks, J. F., Fross, K. H., & Evans, N. W. (1977). Panic-fear in asthma: Generalized personality trait vs. specific situational state. *Journal of Asthma, 14,* 161–167.

Dirks, J. F., Kinsman, R. A., Horton, D. J., Fross, K. H., & Jones, N. F. (1978). Panic-fear in asthma: Rehospitalization following intensive long-term treatment. *Psychosomatic Medicine, 40,* 5–13.

Dirks, J. F., Kinsman, R. A., Jones, N. F., Spector, S. L., Davidson, P. T., & Evans, N. W. (1977). Panic-fear: A personality dimension related to length of hospitalization in respiratory illness. *Journal of Asthma Research, 14,* 61–71.

Dirks, J. F., Robinson, S. K., & Dirks, D. I. (1981). Alexithymia and the psychomaintenance of bronchial asthma. *Psychotherapy and Psychosomatics, 36,* 63–71.

Epstein, N. B., Baldwin, L. M., & Bishop, D. S. (1983). The McMaster Family Assessment Device. *Journal of Marital and Family Therapy, 9,* 171–180.

Feldman, J. M., Giardino, N. D., & Lehrer, P. M. (2000). Asthma and panic disorder. In D. I. Mostofsky & D. H. Barlow (Eds.), *The management of stress and anxiety in medical disorders* (pp. 220–239). Needham Heights, MA: Allyn & Bacon.

Feldman, J. M., Lehrer, P. M., Carr, R. E., & Hochron, S. M. (1998, April). *The relationship between alexithymia factor scores and asthma severity.* Poster presented at the meeting of the Association for Applied Psychophysiology and Biofeedback, Orlando, FL.

Feldman, J. M., Lehrer, P. M., & Hochron, S. M. (in press). Defensiveness and individual response stereotype in asthma. *Psychosomatic Medicine.*

Ford, R. M. (1983). Etiology of asthma: A continuing review (8071 cases seen from 1970–1980). *Annuals of Allergy, 50,* 47–50.

Fritz, G. K., McQuaid, E. L., Spirito, A., & Klein, R. B. (1996). Symptom perception in pediatric asthma: Relationship to functional morbidity and psychological factors. *Journal of the American Academy of Child and Adolescent Psychiatry, 35,* 1033–1041.

Gellhorn, E. (1958). The physiological basis of neuromuscular relaxation. *Archives of Internal Medicine, 102,* 392–399.

Glaus, K. D., & Kotses, H. (1983). Facial muscle tension influences lung airway resistance: Limb muscle tension does not. *Biological Psychology, 17,* 105–120.

Gray, S. L., Williams, D. M., Pulliam, C. C., Sirgo, M. A., Bishop, A. L., & Donohue, J. F. (1996). Characteristics predicting incorrect metered-dose inhaler technique in older subjects. *Archives of Internal Medicine, 156,* 984–988.

Greineder, D. K., Loane, K. C., & Parks, P. (1999). A randomized controlled trial of a pediatric asthma outreach program. *Journal of Allergy and Clinical Immunology, 103,* 436–440.

Groddeck, G. (1928). *The book of the it.* New York: Nervous and Mental Diseases.

Harver, A. (1994). Effects of feedback on the ability of asthmatic subjects to detect increases in the flow-resistive component to breathing. *Health Psychology, 13,* 52–62.

Hays, R. D., Wells, K. B., Sherbourne, C. D., Rogers, W., & Spritzer, K. (1995). Functioning and well-being outcomes of patients with depression compared with chronic general medical illnesses. *Archives of General Psychiatry, 52,* 11–19.

Henry, M., de Rivera, J. L. G., Gonzalez-Martin, I. J., & Abreu, J. (1993). Improvement of respiratory function in chronic asthmatic patients with autogenic therapy. *Journal of Psychosomatic Research, 37,* 265–270.

Hermanns, J., Florin, I., Dietrich, M., Rieger, C., & Hahlweg, K. (1989). Maternal criticism, mother-child interaction, and bronchial asthma. *Journal of Psychosomatic Research, 33,* 469–476.

Hollaender, J., & Florin, I. (1983). Expressed emotion and airway conductance in children with bronchial asthma. *Journal of Psychosomatic Research, 27,* 307–311.

Hunt, L. W., Silverstein, M. D., Reed, C. E., O'Connell, E. J., O'Fallon, W. M., & Yunginger, J. W. (1993). Accuracy of the death certificate in a population-based study of asthmatic patients. *Journal of the American Medical Association, 269,* 1947–1952.

Hurwitz, E. L., & Morgenstern, H. (1999). Cross-sectional associations of asthma, hay fever, and other allergies with major depression and low-back pain among adults aged 20–39 years in the United States. *American Journal of Epidemiology, 150,* 1107–1116.

Hyland, M. E. (1990). The mood-peak flow relationship in adult asthmatics: A pilot study of individual differences and direction of causality. *British Journal of Medical Psychology, 63,* 379–384.

Hyland, M. E., Kenyon, C. A. P., Taylor, M., & Morice, A. H. (1993). Steroid prescribing for asthmatics: Relationship with Asthma Symptom Checklist and Living with Asthma Questionnaire. *British Journal of Clinical Psychology, 32,* 505–511.

Isenberg, S. A., Lehrer, P. M., & Hochron, S. M. (1992a). The effects of suggestion and emotional arousal on pulmonary function in asthma: A review and a hypothesis regarding vagal mediation. *Psychosomatic Medicine, 54,* 192–216.

Isenberg, S. A., Lehrer, P. M., & Hochron, S. M. (1992b). The effects of suggestion on airways of asthmatic subjects breathing room air as a suggested bronchoconstrictor and bronchodilator. *Journal of Psychosomatic Research, 36,* 769–776.

Isenberg, S. A., Lehrer, P. M., & Hochron, S. M. (1997). Defensiveness and perception of external inspiratory resistive loads in asthma. *Journal of Behavioral Medicine, 20,* 461–472.

Jain, S. C., Rai, L., Valecha, A., Jha, U. K., Bhatnagar, S. O. D., & Ram, K. (1991). Effect of yoga training in exercise tolerance in adolescents with childhood asthma. *Journal of Asthma, 28,* 437–442.

Jamner, L. D., Schwartz, G. E., & Leigh, H. (1988). The relationship between repressive and defensive coping styles and monocyte, eosinophile, and serum glucose levels: Support for the opioid peptide hypothesis of repression. *Psychosomatic Medicine, 50,* 567–575.

Janson, C., Bjornsson, E., Hetta, J., & Boman, G. (1994). Anxiety and depression in relation to respiratory symptoms and asthma.

American Journal of Respiratory and Critical Care Medicine, 149, 930–934.

Jones, P. K., Jones, S. L., & Katz, J. (1987). Improving compliance for asthmatic patients visiting the emergency department using a health belief model intervention. *Journal of Asthma, 24,* 199–206.

Kelloway, J. S., Wyatt, R., DeMarco, J., & Adlis, S. (2000). Effect of salmeterol on patients' adherence to their prescribed refills for inhaled corticosteroids. *Annals of Allergy, Asthma, and Immunology, 84,* 324–328.

Kendrick, A. H., Higgs, C. M. B., Whitfield, M. J., & Laszlo, G. (1993). Accuracy of perception of severity of asthma: Patients treated in general practice. *British Medical Journal, 307,* 422–424.

Kessler, R. C., McGonagle, K. A., Zhao, S., Nelson, C. B., Hughes, M., Eshleman, S., et al. (1994). Lifetime and 12-month prevalence of *DSM-III-R* psychiatric disorders in the United States. *Archives of General Psychiatry, 51,* 8–19.

Kikuchi, Y., Okabe, S., Tamura, G., Hida, W., Homma, M., Shirato, K., et al. (1994). Chemosensitivity and perception of dyspnea in patients with a history of near-fatal asthma. *New England Journal of Medicine, 330,* 1329–1334.

Kinsman, R. A., Dahlem, N. W., Spector, S., & Staudenmayer, H. (1977). Observations on subjective symptomatology, coping behavior, and medical decisions in asthma. *Psychosomatic Medicine, 39,* 102–119.

Kinsman, R. A., Luparello, T., O'Banion, K., & Spector, S. (1973). Multidimensional analysis of the subjective symptomatology of asthma. *Psychosomatic Medicine, 35,* 250–267.

Kleiger, J. H., & Kinsman, R. A. (1980). The development of an MMPI alexithymia scale. *Psychotherapy and Psychosomatics, 34,* 17–24.

Kohen, D. P. (1995). Applications of relaxation/mental imagery (self-hypnosis) to the management of childhood asthma: behavioral outcomes of a controlled study. *Hypnosis: Journal of the European Society of Hypnosis in Psychotherapy and Psychosomatic Medicine, 22,* 132–144.

Kohen, D. P., & Wynne, E. (1997). Applying hypnosis in a preschool family asthma education program: Uses of storytelling, imagery, and relaxation. *American Journal of Clinical Hypnosis, 39,* 169–181.

Kotses, H., Bernstein, I. L., Bernstein, D. I., Reynolds, R. V. C., Korbee, L., Wigal, J. K., et al. (1995). A self-management program for adult asthma. Part I: development and evaluation. *Journal of Allergy and Clinical Immunology, 95,* 529–540.

Kotses, H., Harver, A., Segreto, J., Glaus, K. D., Creer, T. L., & Young, G. A. (1991). Long-term effects of biofeedback-induced facial relaxation on measures of asthma severity in children. *Biofeedback and Self Regulation, 16,* 1–21.

Laird, R., Chamberlain, K., & Spicer, J. (1994). Self management practices in adult asthmatics. *New Zealand Medical Journal, 107,* 73–75.

Legoretta, A. P., Christian-Herman, J., O'Connor, R. D., Hasan, M. M., Evans, R., & Leung, K. M. (1998). Compliance with national asthma management guidelines and specialty care: A health maintenance organization experience. *Archives of Internal Medicine, 158,* 457–464.

Lehrer, P. M. (1978). Psychophysiological effects of progressive relaxation in anxiety neurotic patients and of progressive relaxation and alpha feedback in nonpatients. *Journal of Consulting and Clinical Psychology, 46,* 389–404.

Lehrer, P. M. (1996). Varieties of relaxation methods and their unique effects. *International Journal of Stress Management, 3,* 1–15.

Lehrer, P. M. (1998). Emotionally triggered asthma: A review of research literature and some hypotheses for self-regulation therapies. *Applied Psychophysiology and Biofeedback, 23,* 13–41.

Lehrer, P. M., Carr, R. E., Smetankine, A., Vaschillo, E. G., Peper, E., Porges, S., et al. (1997). Respiratory sinus arrhythmia versus neck/trapezius EMG and incentive spirometry biofeedback for asthma: A pilot study. *Applied Psychophysiology and Biofeedback, 22,* 95–109.

Lehrer, P. M., Generelli, P., & Hochron, S. M. (1997). The effect of facial and trapezius muscle tension on respiratory impedance in asthma. *Applied Psychophysiology and Biofeedback, 22,* 43–54.

Lehrer, P. M., Hochron, S. M., Carr, R. E., Edelberg, R., Hamer, R., Jackson, A., et al. (1996). Behavioral task-induced bronchodilation in asthma during active and passive tasks: A possible cholinergic link to psychologically induced airway changes. *Psychosomatic Medicine, 58,* 113–122.

Lehrer, P. M., Hochron, S. M., Mayne, T., Isenberg, S. A., Carlson, V., Lasoski, A. M., et al. (1994). Relaxation and music therapies for asthma among patients prestabilized on asthma medication. *Journal of Behavioral Medicine, 17,* 1–24.

Lehrer, P. M., Hochron, S. M., Mayne, T., Isenberg, S. A., Lasoski, A. M., Carlson, V., et al. (1997). Relationship between changes in EMG and respiratory sinus arrhythmia in a study of relaxation therapy for asthma. *Applied Psychophysiology and Biofeedback, 22,* 183–191.

Lehrer, P. M., Isenberg, S. A., & Hochron, S. M. (1993). Asthma and emotion: A review. *Journal of Asthma, 30,* 5–21.

Lehrer, P. M., Sargunaraj, D., & Hochron, S. M. (1992). Psychological approaches to the treatment of asthma. *Journal of Consulting and Clinical Psychology, 60,* 639–643.

Lehrer, P. M., Smetankin, A., & Potapova, T. (2000). Respiratory sinus arrhythmia biofeedback therapy for asthma: A report of 20 unmedicated pediatric cases using the Smetankin method. *Applied Psychophysiology and Biofeedback, 25,* 193–200.

Lehrer, P. M., Vaschillo, E. G., & Vaschillo, B. (2000). Resonant frequency biofeedback training to increase cardiac variability: Rationale and manual for training. *Applied Psychophysiology and Biofeedback, 25,* 177–191.

Levine, R. J. (1994). Monitoring for adherence: Ethical consideration. *American Journal of Respiratory and Critical Care Medicine, 149,* 287–288.

Levitan, H. (1985). Onset of asthma during intense mourning. *Psychosomatics, 26,* 939–941.

Loew, T. H., Siegfried, W., Martus, P., Trill, K., & Hahn, E. G. (1996). Functional relaxation reduces acute airway obstruction in asthmatics as effectively as inhaled terbutaline. *Psychotherapy and Psychosomatics, 65,* 124–128.

Marshall, P. (1993). Allergy and depression: A neurochemical threshold model of the relation between the illnesses. *Psychological Bulletin, 113,* 23–43.

Mass, R., Dahme, B., & Richter, R. (1993). Clinical evaluation of a respiratory resistance biofeedback training. *Biofeedback and Self Regulation, 18,* 211–223.

Mass, R., Harden, H., Leplow, B., Wessel, M., Richter, R., & Dahme, B. (1991). A device for functional residual capacity controlled biofeedback of respiratory resistance. *Biomedizinische Technik-Biomedical Engineering, 36,* 78–85.

Mass, R., Richter, R., & Dahme, B. (1996). Biofeedback-induced voluntary reduction of respiratory resistance in severe bronchial asthma. *Behaviour Research and Therapy, 34,* 815–819.

Mass, R., Wais, R., Ramm, M., & Richter, R. (1992). Frontal muscles activity: A mediator in operant reduction of respiratory resistance? *Journal of Psychophysiology, 6,* 167–174.

Meng, Y., Leung, K., Berkbigler, D., Halbert, R. J., & Legorreta, A. (1999). Compliance with U.S. asthma management guidelines and specialty care: A regional variation or national concern? *Journal of Evaluation in Clinical Practice, 5,* 213–221.

Miller, B. (1987). Depression and asthma: A potentially lethal mixture. *Journal of Allergy and Clinical Immunology, 80,* 481–486.

Miller, D. J., & Kotses, H. (1995). Classical conditioning of total respiratory resistance in humans. *Psychosomatic Medicine, 57,* 148–153.

Miller, W. R., & Rollnick, S. (1991). *Motivational interviewing: Preparing people to change addictive behavior.* New York: Guilford Press.

Minuchin, S., Rosman, S., & Baker, L. (1978). *Psychosomatic families.* Boston: Harvard University Press.

Molfino, N. A., Nannini, L. J., Martelli, A. N., & Slutsky, A. S. (1991). Respiratory arrest in near-fatal asthma. *New England Journal of Medicine, 324,* 285–288.

Moos, R. H., & Moos, B. S. (1986). *Family Environment Scale manual.* Palo Alto, CA: Consulting Psychologists Press.

Mrazek, D. A., Klinnert, M. D., Mrazek, P. J., & Macey, T. (1991). Early asthma onset: Consideration of parenting issues. *Journal of the American Academy of Child and Adolescent Psychiatry, 30,* 277–282.

Nassau, J. H., Fritz, G. K., & McQuaid, E. (2000). Repressive-defensive style and physiological reactivity among children and adolescents with asthma. *Journal of Psychosomatic Research, 48,* 133–140.

National Heart Lung and Blood Institute. (1997, July). *National asthma education program expert panel report 2: Guidelines for the diagnosis and management of asthma* (NIH Publication No. 97–4051). Bethesda, MD: Author.

Nemiah, J. (1996). Alexithymia: Present, past—and future? *Psychosomatic Medicine, 58,* 217–218.

Northey, S., Griffin, W. A., & Krainz, S. (1998). A partial test of the psychosomatic family model: Marital interaction patterns in asthma and nonasthma families. *Journal of Family Psychology, 12,* 220–233.

Nouwen, A., Freeston, M. H., Labbe, R., & Boulet, L. P. (1999). Psychological factors associated with emergency room visits among asthmatic patients. *Behavior Modification, 23,* 217–233.

Olson, D., Portner, J., & Laree, Y. (1985). *FACES III.* St. Paul: University of Minnesota.

Park, S. J., Sawyer, S. M., & Glaun, D. E. (1996). Childhood asthma complicated by anxiety: An application of cognitive behavioural therapy. *Journal of Paediatrics and Child Health, 32,* 183–187.

Peper, E., & Tibbetts, V. (1992). Fifteen-month follow-up with asthmatics utilizing EMG/incentive inspirometer feedback. *Biofeedback and Self-Regulation, 17,* 143–151.

Pichugin, V. I., Strelakov, S. A., & Zakharevich, A. S. (1993). Usage of a portable device with ECG biofeedback ("Cardiosignalizer") to reduce psychoemotional stress level. In A. Smetankine (Ed.), *Biofeedback: Visceral training in clinics* (pp. 149–159). St. Petersburg, Russia: Biosvaz.

Post, R. M., Rubinow, D. R., & Ballenger, J. C. (1986). Conditioning and sensitization in the longitudinal course of affective illness. *British Journal of Psychiatry, 149,* 191–201.

Quirk, F. H., & Jones, P. W. (1990). Patients' perceptions of distress due to symptoms and effects of asthma on daily living and an investigation of possible influential factors. *Clinical Science, 79,* 17–21.

Rachman, S. (1984). Agoraphobia: A safety-signal perspective. *Behaviour Research and Therapy, 22,* 59–70.

Rand, C. S., Nides, M., Cowles, M. K., Wise, R. A., & Connett, J. (1995). Long-term metered-dose inhaler adherence in a clinical trial: The Lung Health Study Research Group. *American Journal of Respiratory and Critical Care Medicine, 152,* 580–588.

Ried, L. D., Nau, D. P., & Grainger-Rousseau, T. J. (1999). Evaluation of patients health-related quality of life using a modified and shortened version of the Living with Asthma Questionnaire (ms-LWAQ) and the medical outcomes study, Short-Form 36 (SF-36). *Quality of Life Research, 8,* 491–499.

Rietveld, S. (1998). Symptoms perception in asthma: A multidisciplinary review. *Journal of Asthma, 35,* 137–146.

Rietveld, S., Everaerd, W., & Creer, T. (2000). Stress-induced asthma: A review of research and potential mechanisms. *Clinical and Experimental Allergy, 30,* 1058–1066.

Rietveld, S., Everaerd, W., & van Beest, I. (2000). Excessive breathlessness through emotional imagery in asthma. *Behavior Research and Therapy, 38,* 1005–1014.

Rietveld, S., & Prins, P. J. (1998). The relationship between negative emotions and acute subjective and objective symptoms of childhood asthma. *Psychological Medicine, 28,* 407–415.

Rietveld, S., van Beest, I., & Everaerd, W. (1999). Stress-induced breathlessness in asthma. *Psychological Medicine, 29,* 1359–1366.

Rietveld, S., van Beest, I., & Everaerd, W. (2000). Psychological confounds in medical research: The example of excessive cough in asthma. *Behavior Research and Therapy, 38,* 791–800.

Ritz, T., Dahme, B., & Wagner, C. (1998). Effects of static forehead and forearm muscle tension on total respiratory resistance in healthy and asthmatic participants. *Psychophysiology, 35,* 549–562.

Ritz, T., Steptoe, A., DeWilde, S., & Costa, M. (2000). Emotions and stress increase respiratory resistance in asthma. *Psychosomatic Medicine, 62,* 401–412.

Romano, J. M., Turner, J. A., Friedman, L. S., Bulcroft, R. A., Jensen, M. P., Hops, H., et al. (1992). Sequential analysis of chronic pain behavioral and spouse responses. *Journal of Consulting and Clinical Psychology, 60,* 777–782.

Rumbak, M. J., Kelso, T. M., Arheart, K. L., & Self, T. H. (1993). Perception of anxiety as a contributing factor of asthma: Indigent versus nonindigent. *Journal of Asthma, 30,* 165–169.

Rushford, N., Tiller, J. W., & Pain, M. C. (1998). Perception of natural fluctuations in peak flow in asthma: Clinical severity and psychological correlates. *Journal of Asthma, 35,* 251–259

Schmaling, K. B., Afari, N., Barnhart, S., & Buchwald, D. S. (1997). The association of disease severity, functioning status, and medical utilization with relationship satisfaction among asthma patients and their partners. *Journal of Clinical Psychology in Medical Settings, 4,* 373–382.

Schmaling, K. B., Afari, N., & Blume, A. W. (1998). Predictors of treatment adherence among asthma patients in the emergency department. *Journal of Asthma, 35,* 631–636.

Schmaling, K. B., Afari, N., & Blume, A. W. (2000). Assessment of psychological factors associated with adherence to medication regimens among adult patients with asthma. *Journal of Asthma, 37,* 335–343.

Schmaling, K. B., Afari, N., Hops, H., Barnhart, S., & Buchwald, D. S. (submitted). *The effects of couple interaction on pulmonary function among patients with asthma.* Manuscript submitted for publication.

Schmaling, K. B., & Bell, J. (1997). Asthma and panic disorder. *Archives of Family Medicine, 6,* 20–23.

Schmaling, K. B., Blume, A. W., & Afari, N. (2001). A randomized controlled trial of motivational interviewing to change attitudes about adherence to medications for asthma. *Journal of Clinical Psychology in Medical Settings, 8,* 167–172.

Schmaling, K. B., McKnight, P., & Afari, N. (in press). A prospective study of the relationship of mood and stress to pulmonary function in asthma. *Journal of Asthma.*

Schmaling, K. B., Smith, W. R., & Buchwald, D. B. (2000). Significant other responses are associated with fatigue and functional status among patients with chronic fatigue syndrome. *Psychosomatic Medicine, 62,* 444–450.

Schmaling, K. B., Wamboldt, F., Telford, L., Newman, K. B., Hops, H., & Eddy, J. M. (1996). Interaction of asthmatics and their spouses: A preliminary study of individual differences. *Journal of Clinical Psychology in Medical Settings, 3,* 211–218.

Silverglade, L., Tosi, D. J., Wise, P. S., & D'Costa, A. (1994). Irrational beliefs and emotionality in adolescents with and without bronchial asthma. *Journal of General Psychology, 121,* 199–207.

Smyth, J. M., Soefer, M. H., Hurewitz, A., Kliment, A., & Stone, A. A. (1999). Daily psychosocial factors predict levels and diurnal cycles of asthma symptomatology and peak flow. *Journal of Behavioral Medicine, 22,* 179–193.

Smyth, J. M., Stone, A. A., Hurewitz, A., & Kaell, A. (1999). Effects of writing about stressful experiences on symptom reduction in patients with asthma or rheumatoid arthritis: A randomized trial. *Journal of the American Medical Association, 281,* 1304–1309.

Sommaruga, M., Spanevello, A., Migliori, G. B., Neri, M., Callegari, S., & Majani, G. (1995). The effects of a cognitive behavioral intervention in asthmatic patients. *Monaldi Archives of Chest Disease, 50,* 398–402.

Staudenmeyer, H., Kinsman, R. A., Dirks, J. F., Spector, S. L., & Wangaard, C. (1979). Medical outcome in asthmatic patients: Effects of airways hyperreactivity and symptom-focused anxiety. *Psychosomatic Medicine, 41,* 109–118

Steiner, H., Higgs, C., & Fritz, G. K. (1987). Defense style and the perception of asthma. *Psychosomatic Medicine, 49,* 34–44.

Steptoe, A., & Holmes, R. (1985). Mood and pulmonary function in adult asthmatics: A pilot self-monitoring study. *British Journal of Medical Psychology, 58,* 87–94.

Stout, C., Kotses, H., & Creer, T. L. (1997). Improving perception of airflow obstruction in asthma patients. *Psychosomatic Medicine, 59,* 201–206.

Taitel, M. A., Kotses, H., Bernstein, I. L., Bernstein, D. I., & Creer, T. L. (1995). A self-management program for adult asthma. Part II: Cost-benefit analysis. *Journal of Allergy and Clinical Immunology, 95,* 672–676.

Troisi, R. J., Speizer, F. E., Willett, W. C., Trichopoulos, D., & Rosner, B. (1995). Menopause, postmenopausal estrogen preparations, and the risk of adult-onset asthma: A prospective cohort study. *American Journal of Respiratory and Critical Care Medicine, 152,* 1183–1188.

van Peski-Oosterbaan, A. S., Spinhoven, P., van der Does, A. J. W., Willems, L. N. A., & Sterk, P. J. (1996). Is there a specific relationship between asthma and panic disorder? *Behavior Research and Therapy, 34,* 333–340.

Vaschillo, E. G., Zingerman, A. M., Konstantinov, M. A., & Menitsky, D. N. (1983). Research of the resonance characteristics for cardiovascular system. *Human Psychology, 9,* 257–265.

Vazquez, M. I., & Buceta, J. M. (1993a). Effectiveness of self-management programmes and relaxation training in the treatment of bronchial asthma: Relationships with trait anxiety and emotional attack triggers. *Journal of Psychosomatic Research, 37,* 71–81.

Vazquez, M. I., & Buceta, J. M. (1993b). Psychological treatment of asthma: Effectiveness of a self-management program with and without relaxation training. *Journal of Asthma, 30,* 171–183.

Vazquez, M. I., & Buceta, J. M. (1993c). Relaxation therapy in the treatment of bronchial asthma: Effects on basal spirometric values. *Psychotherapy and Psychosomatics, 60,* 106–112.

Vedanthan, P. K., Kesavalu, L. N., Murthy, K. C., Duvall, K., Hall, M. J., Baker, S., et al. (1998). Clinical study of yoga techniques in university students with asthma: A controlled study. *Allergy and Asthma Proceedings, 19,* 3–9.

Vollmer, W. M., O'Hollaren, M., Ettinger, K. M., Stibolt, T., Wilkins, J., Buist, A. S., et al. (1997). Specialty differences in the management of asthma: A cross-sectional assessment of allergists' patients and generalists' patients in a large HMO. *Archives of Internal Medicine, 157,* 1207–1208.

Wamboldt, F. S., Wamboldt, M. Z., Gavin, L. A., Roesler, T. A., & Brugman, S. M. (1995). Parental criticism and treatment outcome in adolescents hospitalized for severe, chronic asthma. *Journal of Psychosomatic Research, 39,* 995–1005.

Wamboldt, M. Z., Hewitt, J. K., Schmitz, S., Wamboldt, F. S., Rasanen, M., Koskenvuo, M., et al. (2000). Familial association between allergic disorders and depression in adult Finnish twins. *American Journal of Medical Genetics, 96,* 146–153.

Wilson, S. R., Latini, D., Starr, N. J., Fish, L., Loes, L. M., Page, A., et al. (1996). Education of parents of infants and very young children with asthma: A developmental evaluation of the wee wheezers program. *Journal of Asthma, 33,* 239–254.

Wright, R. J., Rodriguez, M., & Cohen, S. (1998). Review of psychosocial stress and asthma: An integrated biopsychosocial approach. *Thorax, 53,* 1066–1074.

Wright, R. J., Weiss, S. T., & Cohen, S. (1996). Life events, perceived stress, home characteristics and wheeze in asthmatic/allergic families. *American Journal of Respiratory and Critical Care Medicine, 153,* A420.

Yellowlees, P. M., Alpers, J. H., Bowden, J. J., Bryant, G. D., & Ruffin, R. E. (1987). Psychiatric morbidity in patients with chronic airflow obstruction. *Medical Journal of Australia, 146,* 305–307.

Yellowlees, P. M., Haynes, S., Potts, N., & Ruffin, R. E. (1988). Psychiatric morbidity in patients with life-threatening asthma: Initial report of a controlled study. *Medical Journal of Australia, 149,* 246–249.

CHAPTER 6

Obesity

JOYCE A. CORSICA AND MICHAEL G. PERRI

Over the past two decades, the prevalence of overweight and obesity in the United States has increased dramatically (Flegal, Carroll, Kuczmarski, & Johnson, 1998). More than half of all Americans are now overweight or obese (Mokdad et al., 1999), and the trend toward increasing prevalence has not abated (Mokdad et al., 2000). Concern about this epidemiclike trend stems from an overwhelming body of evidence demonstrating the negative health consequences associated with increased body weight. Being overweight or obese substantially raises the risk for a variety of illnesses, and excess weight is associated with increased all-cause mortality (Pi-Sunyer, 1999). Consequently, millions of Americans stand poised to develop weight-related illnesses such as cardiovascular disease, hypertension, diabetes mellitus, and osteoarthritis. As the second leading contributor to preventable death in the United States (McGinnis & Foege, 1993), obesity constitutes a major threat to public health and a significant challenge to health care professionals.

In this chapter, we provide a review of research related to understanding and managing obesity. We begin with the assessment and classification of obesity, and we describe the epidemiology of body weight in the United States. We summarize the physical, psychosocial, and economic consequences associated with excess body weight, and we examine prominent biological and environmental contributors to obesity. Next we describe current treatments of obesity, including behavioral (lifestyle) interventions, pharmacotherapy, and bariatric surgery; we give special attention to what may be the most problematic aspect of obesity treatment, the maintenance of lost weight. We conclude our review by discussing recommendations for the management and prevention of obesity.

CLASSIFICATION OF OBESITY

Obesity is defined as an excessive accumulation of body fat—excessive to the extent that it is associated with negative health consequences. An individual is considered obese when body fat content equals or exceeds 30% to 35% in women or 20% to 25% in men (Lohman, 2002). However, this deceptively simple definition obscures the complexities involved in the measurement and classification of body composition. Direct measurement of body fat can be accomplished through a variety of methods, including hydrostatic (underwater) weighing, skinfold measurement, bioelectrical impedance, dual energy x-ray absorptiometry (DEXA), and computerized tomography (CT). Direct measurement is typically either expensive (as is the case with DEXA and CT) or inconvenient (as is the case with hydrostatic weighing and skinfold measures). Consequently, for practical purposes, overweight and obesity often have been defined in terms of the relation of body weight to height.

"Ideal" Weight

Actuarial data from insurance companies have provided tables of "ideal" weights for mortality rates (Metropolitan Life Insurance Company, 1983). For many years, 20% or more over ideal weight for height was commonly used as the definition of obesity (National Institutes of Health [NIH] Consensus Development Panel on the Health Implications of Obesity, 1985). In recent years, however, the limitations of this approach have become increasingly apparent. For example, insurance company data are not representative of the U.S. population, particularly for women and minorities (Foreyt, 1987). In addition, alternative weight-to-height indices have shown greater correspondence to direct measures of body fat and to the negative health consequences of obesity (L. Sjöstrom, Narbro, & Sjöstrom, 1995).

Body Mass Index

Body Mass Index (BMI), also known as Quetelet's Index, is an alternative weight-to-height ratio that has gained general acceptance as the preferred method for gauging overweight. BMI is calculated by dividing weight in kilograms by the square of height in meters (kg/m^2). BMI can also be calculated without metric conversions by use of the following formula: $pounds/inches^2 \times 704.5$. BMI is not encumbered by the problems inherent in defining "ideal weight," and it corresponds more closely to direct measures of body fat than alternative weight-to-height ratios (Keys, Fidanza, Karvonen, Kimura, & Taylor, 1972; L. Sjöstrom et al., 1995).

While BMI provides an "acceptable approximation of total body fat for the majority of patients" (National Heart, Lung, and Blood Institute [NHLBI], 1998 p. xix), it does not discriminate between weight associated with fat versus

TABLE 6.1 Body Mass Index

Height	Body Mass Index				
	18.5	25	30	35	40
	Body Weight				
58	89	119	143	167	191
59	92	124	149	174	198
60	95	128	153	179	204
61	99	132	158	185	211
62	100	136	164	191	218
63	104	141	169	197	225
64	108	145	174	204	232
65	111	150	180	210	240
66	115	155	186	216	247
67	118	159	191	223	255
68	122	164	197	230	262
69	125	169	203	236	270
70	130	174	207	243	278
71	133	179	215	250	286
72	136	184	221	258	294
73	139	189	227	265	302
74	144	195	234	273	312

weight associated with muscle. For example, an athlete may have a high BMI as a result of the higher body weight associated with greater levels of muscle mass rather than excess fat. In addition, because one can be *overfat,* even in the context of a healthy BMI, other measures such as waist measurement should be used concurrently for a comprehensive assessment of a person's "risk due to weight" status.

Table 6.1 presents body weights (in pounds) by height (in inches) that correspond to BMI values of 18.5, 25, 30, 35, and 40. These selected values correspond to the various cut points used by the World Health Organization (WHO) system to categorize overweight and obesity.

The WHO Classification System

The WHO (1998) has developed a graded classification system for categorizing overweight and obesity in adults according to BMI. In the WHO system, overweight is defined as a BMI $\geq$ 25, and obesity is defined as a BMI $\geq$ 30. The WHO system, which has also been accepted by NIH (NHLBI, 1998), employs six categories based on the known risk of comorbid conditions associated with different BMI levels (see Table 6.2). For example, the risk of comorbid conditions is considered "average" in the normal weight category and "very severe" in the obese class III category. Thus, the WHO classification system facilitates the identification of individuals and groups at increased risk of morbidity and mortality, and it allows for meaningful comparisons of weight status within and between populations.

TABLE 6.2   World Health Organization Classification of Overweight According to BMI and Risk of Comorbidities

Category	BMI (kg/m²)	Disease Risk
Underweight	<18.5	Low*
Normal weight	18.5–24.9	Average
Overweight	≥25.0	
Pre-obese	25.0–29.9	Increased
Obese Class I	30.0–34.9	Moderate
Obese Class II	35.0–39.9	Severe
Obesity Class III	≥40.0	Very severe

*There is an increased risk of other clinical problems (e.g., anorexia nervosa).

Measurement of Abdominal Fat

The health risks associated with obesity vary significantly according to the distribution of body fat (WHO, 1998). Upper body (abdominal) fatness is more closely associated with abnormalities of blood pressure, glucose tolerance, and serum cholesterol levels than is lower body obesity (Pouliot et al., 1994). Consequently, individuals with abdominal obesity incur increased risk for heart disease and for type 2 diabetes mellitus. Because abdominal fatness can vary substantially within a narrow range of BMI, it is important in clinical settings to include a measure of abdominal obesity (James, 1996). For example, the waist-hip ratio (WHR) represents one method of identifying individuals with potentially health-compromising abdominal fat accumulation. A high WHR (defined as >1.0 in men and >.85 in women) reflects increased risk for obesity-related diseases (James, 1996). Evidence, however, suggests that a simple measure of waist circumference may provide a better indicator of abdominal adiposity and the likelihood of detrimental health consequences than does the WHR (James, 1996; Thomas, 1995). A waist circumference measurement greater than 40 inches in men and greater than 35 inches in women confers increased risk for morbidity and mortality (James, 1996; NHLBI, 1998; Pouliot et al., 1994).

EPIDEMIOLOGY OF OBESITY

Data from recent population surveys (Flegal et al., 1998; Kuczmarski, Carrol, Flegal, & Troiano, 1997) indicate that 19.9% of the men and 24.9% of the women in the United States are obese (i.e., BMI > 30). An additional 39.4% of men and 24.7% of women are overweight (i.e., BMI of 25.0 to 29.9). Collectively, the data show that the majority (54.9%) of adults in the United States, approximately 97 million people between the ages of 20 to 74, are overweight or obese. The rates of obesity are highest among African American

TABLE 6.3   Prevalence of Overweight and Obesity by Gender and Race/Ethnicity

Gender, Race/Ethnicity	25.0–29.9 (Overweight) %	≥30.0 (Obese) %	≥25.0 (Overweight or Obese) %
Women			
White	23.1	22.4	45.5
African American	29.1	37.4	66.5
Mexican American	33.4	34.2	67.6
All	24.7	24.9	49.6
Men			
White	39.6	20.0	59.6
African American	36.2	21.3	57.5
Mexican American	44.0	23.1	67.1
All	39.4	19.9	59.3

Source: Data from NHANES III (Flegal et al., 1998).

women (37.4%) and Mexican American women (34.2%), and additional percentages of each of these groups (29.1% and 33.4%, respectively) are overweight (Flegal et al., 1998). Table 6.3 presents the current prevalence rates of overweight and obesity by gender and by race/ethnicity.

Socioeconomic and age-related differences in obesity rates are also evident in the population surveys. Women with lower income or lower levels of education are more likely to be obese than those of higher socioeconomic status, and obesity rates generally increase with age across all groups. Current rates of obesity by age group for men and women are shown in Figure 6.1. Note that the obesity prevalence peaks at ages 50 to 59 for both men and women.

Dating back to 1960, national surveys have assessed height and weight in large representative samples of the U.S. population. These data, from the National Health Examination Survey (NHES; Kuczmarski, Flegal, Campbell, & Johnson, 1994) and the National Health and

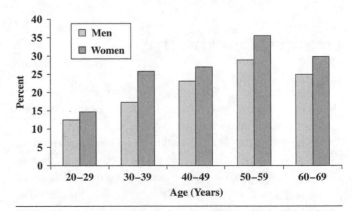

Figure 6.1   Current prevalence of obesity (BMI ≥ 30) in United States. *Source:* Data from NHANES III; Flegal et al., 1998.

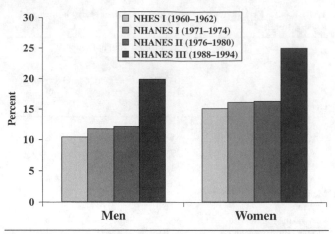

Figure 6.2 Prevalence of obesity (BMI ≥ 30) in United States. *Source:* Data from NHANES I, II, and III; Flegal et al., 1998.

Nutrition Examination Surveys I, II, III (NHANES I-III; Flegal et al., 1998; Kuczmarski et al., 1994) allow a comprehensive examination of the changing rates of overweight and obesity over the past four decades. NHES evaluated data collected from 1960 to 1962 and reported an overweight prevalence of 43.3% in adults. Nearly a decade later, the data from NHANES I, conducted in 1971 to 1974, indicated an overall prevalence of 46.1%, a level which remained relatively constant during the next decade, as reflected in the 46.0% prevalence observed in NHANES II, conducted in 1976 to 1980. However, the results of NHANES III, conducted in 1988 to 1994, revealed an alarming increase in the prevalence of overweight individuals to 54.9%. Particularly disturbing were the rates of obesity (BMI > 30), which increased 10% among women and 8% among men during the 14 years between NHANES II-III (Leigh, Fries, & Hubert, 1992). Figure 6.2 presents the prevalence rates of obesity from the four population surveys conducted between 1960 and 1994.

CONSEQUENCES OF OBESITY

Impact on Morbidity

Obesity has a substantial adverse impact on health via its association with a number of serious illnesses and risk factors for disease. Obesity-related conditions include hypertension, dyslipidemia, type 2 diabetes mellitus, coronary heart disease (CHD), stroke, gallbladder disease, osteoarthritis, sleep apnea, respiratory problems, and cancers of the endometrium, breast, prostate and colon.

Some of the more prominent comorbidities of obesity are described next.

- *Hypertension.* The prevalence of high blood pressure in adults is twice as high for individuals with BMI > 30 than for those with normal weight (Dyer & Elliott, 1989; Pi-Sunyer, 1999). Mechanisms for increased blood pressure appear to be related to increases in blood volume, vascular resistance, and cardiac output. Hypertension is a risk factor for both CHD and stroke (Havlik, Hubert, Fabsitz, & Feinleib, 1983).

- *Dyslipidemia.* Obesity is associated with lipid profiles that increase risk for CHD, including elevated levels of total cholesterol, triglycerides, and low-density lipoprotein ("bad") cholesterol, as well as low levels of high-density lipoprotein ("good") cholesterol (Allison & Saunders, 2000).

- *Type 2 Diabetes Mellitus.* Data from international studies consistently show that obesity is a robust predictor of the development of diabetes (Folsom et al., 2000; Hodge, Dowse, Zimmet, & Collins, 1995; NHLBI, 1998). A 14-year prospective study concluded that obese women were at 40 times greater risk for developing diabetes than normal-weight, age-matched counterparts (Colditz et al., 1990). Current estimates suggest that 27% of new cases of type 2 diabetes are attributable to weight gain of 5 kg or more in adulthood (Ford, Williamson, & Liu, 1997). Moreover, abdominal obesity is a specific major risk factor for type 2 diabetes (Chan, Rimm, Colditz, Stampfer, & Willett, 1994).

- *Coronary Heart Disease.* Overweight, obesity, and abdominal adiposity are associated with increased morbidity and mortality due to CHD. These conditions are directly related to elevated levels of cholesterol, blood pressure, and insulin, all of which are specific risk factors for cardiovascular disease. Recent studies suggest that, compared to a BMI in the normal range, the relative risk for CHD is twice as high at a BMI of 25 to 29, and three times as high for BMI > 29 (Willett et al., 1995). Moreover, a weight gain of 5 to 8 kg increases CHD risk by 25% (NHLBI, 1998; Willett et al., 1995).

- *Stroke.* The Framingham Heart Study (Hubert, Feinleib, McNamara, & Castelli, 1983) suggested that overweight may contribute to stroke risk, independent of hypertension and diabetes. Later research established that the relationship between obesity and stroke is clearer for ischemic stroke versus hemorrhagic stroke (Rexrode et al., 1997). Recent prospective studies show a graduated increase in risk for ischemic stroke with increasing BMI (i.e., risk is

75% higher with BMIs > 27; 137% higher with BMIs > 32) (Rexrode et al., 1997).

- *Gallstones.* Obesity is a risk factor across both age and ethnicity for gallbladder disease. The risk of gallstones is 4 to 6 times higher for women with BMIs > 40 compared to women with BMIs < 24 (Stampfer, Maclure, Colditz, Manson, & Willett, 1992).

- *Sleep Apnea.* Sleep apnea is a serious and potentially life-threatening breathing disorder, characterized by repeated arousal from sleep due to temporary cessation of breathing. Both the presence and severity of sleep apnea, is associated with obesity, and sleep apnea occurs disproportionately in people with BMIs > 30 (Loube, Loube, & Miller, 1994). Large neck circumference (≥ 17 inches in men and ≥ 16 inches in women) is highly predictive of sleep apnea (Davies & Stradling, 1990).

- *Women's Reproductive Health.* Menstrual irregularity and amenorrhea are observed with greater frequency in overweight and obese women (Hartz, Barboriak, Wong, Katayama, & Rimm, 1979). Polycystic ovary syndrome, which often includes infertility, menstrual disturbances, hirsutism, and anovulation, is associated with abdominal obesity, hyperinsulinemia, and insulin resistance (Dunaif, 1992; Goudas & Dumesic, 1997).

Impact on Mortality

Not only does obesity aggravate the onset and progression of some illnesses, it also shortens life (Allison, Fontaine, Manson, Stevens, & Van Itallie, 1999). Studies show that all-cause mortality rates increase by 50% to 100% when BMI is equal to or greater than 30 as compared with BMIs in the normal range (Troiano, Frongillo, Sobal, & Levitsky, 1996). Indeed, more than 300,000 deaths per year in the United States are attributable to obesity-related causes (Allison et al., 1999).

Psychosocial Consequences

Many obese people experience social discrimination and psychological distress as a consequence of their weight. The social consequences associated with obesity include bias, stigmatization, and discrimination—consequences that can be highly detrimental to psychological well-being (Stunkard & Sobal, 1995). Social bias results from the widespread, but mistaken, belief that overweight people lack self-control. Negative attitudes toward obese people, which are pervasive in our society, have been reported in children as well as adults, in health care professionals as well as the general public, and in overweight individuals themselves (Crandall &

Biernat, 1990; Rand & Macgregor, 1990). An obese person is less likely to get into a prestigious college, to get a job, to marry, and to be treated respectfully by a physician than is his or her nonobese counterpart (Gortmaker, Must, Perrin, Sobol, & Dietz, 1993; Pingitore, Dugoni, Tindale, & Spring, 1994). Indeed, obesity may well be the last socially acceptable object of prejudice and discrimination in our country.

Despite the negative social consequences of overweight, most early studies have reported similar rates of psychopathology in obese and nonobese individuals. However, these studies suffered from a number of limitations, for example, failing to account for gender effects (Wadden, Womble, Stunkard, & Anderson, 2002). More recent studies have attempted to rectify this. A large-scale, general population study (Carpenter, Hasin, Allison, & Faith, 2000) recently showed that obesity was associated with a 37% greater risk of major depressive disorder, as well as increased suicidal ideation and suicide attempts among women but interestingly, not among men, for whom obesity was associated with a reduced risk of major depression. A consistent finding is the higher levels of body image dissatisfaction that are widely reported by obese individuals. Body image dissatisfaction is particularly elevated in women with higher socioeconomic status, those who were overweight as children, and binge eaters (French, Jeffery, Sherwood, & Neumark-Sztainer, 1999; Grilo, Wilfley, Brownell, & Rodin, 1994). In contrast, members of certain minority groups, particularly, Hispanic and African Americans, are less likely to display disparaging attitudes toward obesity in either themselves or others (Crandall & Martinez, 1996; Kumanyika, 1987; Rucker & Cash, 1992). In fact, Black women often ascribe positive attributes such as stamina and authority to being large (Rosen & Gross, 1987).

In contrast to studies of obese persons in the general population, research on psychological disturbance in people presenting for treatment at obesity clinics shows a clear pattern of results. Obese help-seekers display higher rates of psychological distress and binge eating when compared to normal-weight individuals and to obese persons who are not seeking help (Fitzgibbon, Stolley, & Kirschenbaum, 1993; Spitzer et al., 1993).

Economic Costs of Obesity

The economic impact of obesity is enormous. In 1995, the total costs attributable to obesity amounted to $99.2 billion (Wolf & Colditz, 1998). This total can be further viewed in terms of direct and indirect costs. Direct costs (i.e., dollars expended in medical care due to obesity) amount to approximately $51.6 billion and represent 5.7% of national health expenditures in the United States. The indirect costs (i.e., lost productivity due to morbidity and mortality from diseases associated with obesity) amount to an additional $47.6 billion. In addition, consumers spend in excess of $33 billion annually for weight-loss interventions, exercise programs, weight-control books, and diet foods and beverages (Thomas, 1995). Researchers estimate that the overall economic impact of obesity is similar to that of cigarette smoking (NHLBI, 1998; Wolf & Colditz, 1998).

CONTRIBUTORS TO OBESITY

Given the prevalence and seriousness of obesity, it is essential that we understand its etiology. Understanding the factors that contribute to the development of obesity may lead to effective interventions for its control and prevention. In this section, we address genetic and environmental contributors to overweight and obesity.

Genetic Contributors

In the past decade, there has been great enthusiasm about the prospects of identifying the biological causes of obesity. A body of research showing that obesity tends to run in families spurred the search for the genetic basis of obesity. For example, familial studies consistently have shown that BMI is highly correlated among first-degree relatives (Bouchard, Perusse, Leblanc, Tremblay, & Theriault, 1988), and investigations of identical twins reared apart have suggested that the genetic contribution to BMI may be as high as 70% (Stunkard, Harris, Pedersen, & McClearn, 1990). Such findings have led researchers to suspect that a single major, but as yet unidentified, recessive gene accounts for a significant proportion of the variance in body mass (Bouchard, Perusse, Rice, & Rao, 1998). In addition, researchers also believe that body-fat distribution, resting metabolic rate, and weight gain in response to overconsumption are each controlled by genetic factors that may interact to predispose certain individuals to obesity (Chagnon et al., 2000; Feitosa et al., 2000; Levin, 2000).

Among the first genetic defects linked to obesity was the discovery of the ob gene and its protein product leptin (Zhang et al., 1994). Leptin, a hormone produced by fat cells, influences hypothalamic regulation of energy intake and expenditure. Laboratory mice that fail to produce leptin due to a genetic defect become obese as the result of excess energy intake and physical inactivity (Zhang et al., 1994). Moreover, the administration of recombinant leptin in such animals decreases food intake, increases physical activity, and reduces body weight (Campfield, Smith, Guisez, Devos, & Burn, 1995). In humans, however, only a very small percentage of obese individuals have leptin deficiencies (Montague et al., 1997). Most obese individuals actually have *higher* rather than lower levels of leptin due to their higher levels of adipose tissue (Considine et al., 1996). Thus, some researchers (Ahima & Flier, 2000) have suggested that obese persons may become leptin "resistant" similar to the way obese persons with type 2 diabetes become insulin resistant. Trials of recombinant leptin as treatment for obesity have yielded modest results. High doses of leptin (administered via daily subcutaneous injections) have produced reductions in body weight of about 8%—a decrease equivalent to what is typically accomplished in lifestyle interventions (Heymsfield et al., 1999).

Several other single-gene defects have been discovered that contribute to obesity in animals (Collier et al., 2000; Levin, 2000). However, only one of these mutations appears to be a frequent contributor to human obesity. Investigators (Farooqi et al., 2000; Vaisse et al., 2000) have found that 4% of morbidly obese individuals display a genetic mutation in the melanocortin-4 receptor (MC4), which plays a key role in the hypothalamic control of food intake. Thus, research into the MC4 receptor and other potential genetic causes of obesity continues at a rapid pace (Comuzzie & Allison, 1998).

Environmental Contributors

Poston and Foreyt (1999) have recently argued that "genes are not the answer" to understanding the development of obesity (p. 201). They maintain that animal models of obesity are severely limited in their generalizability to humans. Moreover, they contend that several sources of information indicate that environmental factors are the primary determinants of human obesity.

For example, the influence of sociocultural factors on the development of obesity can be seen in preindustrialized societies that undergo a transition to modernization (i.e., Westernization). In a classic study of the association between obesity and modernization in Polynesia, Prior (1971) found that the prevalence of obesity in the highly Westernized region of Maori was more than double the rate of obesity on the more traditional island of Pakupaku (i.e., 35% versus 15%, respectively). Similarly, the influence of environmental factors can be seen in a comparison of groups that share the same genetic heritage but live in environments that support very different lifestyles. For example, the Pima Indians of Arizona, who live in a "modern" environment, have the highest prevalence of obesity of any ethnic/racial group in the United States (Krosnick, 2000). However, the prevalence of obesity in the Pima Indians of rural Mexico is less than half that of their Arizona counterparts. Although the two groups share the same genetic makeup, they differ dramatically in their lifestyles. The Pimas in rural Mexico consume a diet with less animal fat and more complex carbohydrates, and they expend a greater amount of energy in physical labor than do their cousins in Arizona (Ravussin, Valencia, Esparza, Bennett, & Schultz, 1994). Thus, environments that foster appropriate food consumption and energy expenditure can limit the development of obesity even in the presence of a strong genetic predisposition.

Alternatively, environments that offer unlimited access to high-calorie foods and simultaneously support low levels of physical activity can promote obesity even in the absence of a specific genetic predisposition. As several authors (Hill & Peters, 1998; Poston & Foreyt, 1999) have noted, the human gene pool has not changed in the past quarter century. Consequently, the increased prevalence of obesity in the United States and other Western countries must be due to the influence of environmental factors on energy consumption and/or energy expenditure.

Are Americans eating more food and taking in more calories? Research on the trends in energy intake has been inconclusive (Ernst, Sempos, Briefel, & Clark, 1997; Nestle & Woteki, 1999). Some surveys (e.g., Norris et al., 1997) show that energy intake has been declining, whereas others (e.g., Centers for Disease Control and Prevention, 1994) suggest that energy intake has been rising. Because surveys of self-reported food consumption are susceptible to response biases, alternative methods of gauging population trend in energy intake are worth examining. The data from food supply and disappearance studies show a consistent pattern. Between 1970 and 1994, per capita energy availability increased by 15% (Harnack, Jeffery, & Boutelle, 2000), an amount sufficient to help explain the increased prevalence of overweight in the United States.

Americans are surrounded by a "toxic" environment that promotes the overconsumption of energy-dense, nutrient-poor food (Battle & Brownell, 1996; Kant, 2000). The temptation to eat is virtually everywhere. Tasty, low-cost, high-calorie items are readily available not only at fast-food restaurants, but also in supermarkets, food courts, vending machines, and even 24-hour service stations. In addition, larger portion sizes, "supersizing," "value meals," and "2-for-1" deals, all provide increased opportunities for excess consumption. Americans are eating more meals outside the home and in doing so they are consuming larger portions of food. In the early 1970s, about 20% of the household food dollar was spent on food outside the home but by 1995 that amount had doubled to 40% (Putnam &

Allshouse, 1996). Importantly, eating away from home, particularly at fast-food restaurants, is associated with higher energy intake and with higher fat intake (French, Harnack, & Jeffery, 2000). Thus, it is not surprising that studies have shown "eating out" to be a significant contributor to weight gain and the increasing prevalence of overweight (Binkley, Eales, & Jekanowski, 2000; McCrory et al., 1999).

Physical inactivity also appears to be a significant contributor to overweight and obesity. Few occupations now require vigorous levels of physical activity. Moreover, labor-saving devices such as cars, elevators, escalators, motorized walkways, and remote controls, have had a significant cumulative impact in decreasing daily energy expenditure (Hill, Wyatt, & Melanson, 2000; James, 1995). In addition, energy expended in leisure-time activities has decreased as people spend more time sitting passively in front of televisions, VCRs/DVD players, and computers rather than participating in physical activities that require movement and greater amounts of energy expenditure. According the Surgeon General (U.S. Department of Health and Human Services, 1996), 54% of the U.S. population engages in little or no leisure-time physical activities and fewer than 10% of Americans regularly participate in vigorous physical activity.

Cross-sectional population studies typically show an inverse relationship between physical activity and body weight (DiPietro, 1995). Lower body weights and lower BMIs are associated with higher levels of self-reported physical activity. The findings appear strongest for high-intensity physical activities (presumably due to more accurate reporting of vigorous activities such as jogging). However, in cross-sectional studies, it is sometimes difficult to determine the direction of cause-and-effect relationships. While physical activity may affect body weight, it is also likely that body weight impacts physical activity via increased discomfort associated with higher body weight, including higher levels of breathlessness and sweating, and general difficulty in negotiating body movement. Many obese individuals also report embarrassment at being seen exercising (Ball, Crawford, & Owen, 2000).

Longitudinal cohort studies may provide a better perspective on the cause-and-effect relationship between physical activity and body weight. For example, in the Male Health Professionals Study, Coakley et al. (1998) examined the impact of changes in activity on body weight in a prospective cohort study of 19,478 men. The researchers found that over the course of a four-year period, vigorous activity was associated with weight reduction, whereas sedentary behavior (TV/VCR viewing) and eating between meals were associated with weight gain. Men who increased their exercise, decreased TV viewing, and stopped eating between meals, lost an average weight of 1.4 kg compared to a weight gain of

1.4 kg among the overall population. Furthermore, the prevalence of obesity was lowest among men who maintained a relatively high level of vigorous physical activity, compared to those who were relatively sedentary. These data show that increased physical activity may prevent weight gain.

By fostering decreased energy expenditure and increased energy consumption, modern environments have promoted increases in body weights and in the prevalence of obesity. Eaton and Konner (1985) have noted that there is a significant mismatch between modern lifestyle and the lifestyles for which humans (and our genes) evolved over tens of thousands of years. This discordance has produced "diseases of civilization" as typified by the current epidemic of obesity. Prior to the past century, periodic shortages of food plagued most societies, and obesity was rarely a problem. From an evolutionary perspective, the scarcity of food acted as an agent of natural selection. Because body fat serves primarily as a reserve source of energy, genetic traits that contribute to the accumulation of fat stores served an adaptive role by enhancing the chances of survival in times of scarcity. In modern societies, there are no intervals of scarcity to periodically reduce the buildup of body fat. As a result, the constant and abundant supply of food, coupled with lower levels of physical activity and energy expenditure, has led to dramatic increases in the prevalence of overweight and obesity.

TREATMENT OF OBESITY

National surveys indicate that substantial numbers of Americans are trying to lose weight. Recent data show that about 44% of women and 29% of men report that they are currently dieting to lose weight (Serdula et al., 1999). Most people try to lose weight on their own (Jeffery, Adlis, & Forster, 1991). Those who seek professional treatment exhibit higher levels of distress and are more likely to be binge eaters than obese persons in the general population (Fitzgibbon et al., 1993). The options commonly available for professional treatment of obesity include lifestyle interventions (typically a combination of behavior therapy, low-calorie diet, and exercise) and more aggressive interventions including pharmacotherapy and surgery.

Lifestyle Interventions

Behavior modification procedures have become the foundation of lifestyle interventions for weight loss (Wadden & Foster, 1992). Participants in behavioral treatment are taught to modify their eating and exercise habits so as to produce weight loss through a negative energy balance. The key components typically used in behavioral interventions include: (a) goal setting and daily self-monitoring of eating and physical activity; (b) nutritional training aimed at the consumption of a balanced low-calorie diet sufficient to produce a weight loss of 0.5 kg per week; (c) increased physical activity through the development of a walking program and/or increased lifestyle activities; (d) arrangement of environmental cues and behavioral reinforcers to support changes in eating and exercise behaviors; (e) cognitive restructuring techniques to identify and change negative thoughts and feelings that interfere with weight-loss progress; and (f) training in problem solving or relapse prevention procedures to enhance coping with setbacks and obstacles to progress.

More than 150 studies have examined the effects of behavioral treatment of obesity. Reviews of randomized trials conducted since 1985 (Jeffery et al., 2000; NHLBI, 1998; Perri & Fuller, 1995; Wadden, Sarwer, & Berkowitz, 1999) show consistent findings. Behavioral treatments (typically delivered in 15 to 26 weekly group sessions) produce mean weight losses of approximately 8.5 kg and 9% reductions in body weight. Attrition rates are relatively low, averaging about 20% over six months. Negative side effects are uncommon, and participants typically report decreases in depressive symptoms. In addition, beneficial changes in blood pressure, glucose tolerance, and lipid profiles typically accompany weight reductions of the magnitude produced by behavioral treatment (NHLBI, 1998; Pi-Sunyer, 1999). Thus, lifestyle interventions are recommended as the first-line of professional intervention in a stepped-care approach to the management of overweight and obesity (NHLBI, 1998).

The long-term effectiveness of lifestyle interventions has remained an area of considerable concern. During the year following behavioral treatment, participants typically regain 30% to 40% of their lost weight (Jeffery et al., 2000; Wadden & Foster, 2000). Perri and Corsica (2002) summarized the results of behavioral treatment studies with follow-ups of two or more years and found a reliable pattern of gradual weight regain during the years following behavioral treatment. Nonetheless, the data show a mean weight loss of 1.8 kg from baseline to follow-ups conducted on average 4.3 years after treatment.

Several considerations must be taken into account in evaluating the long-term results of weight-loss interventions. Findings of small net losses or a return to baseline weights at long-term follow-up need to be viewed in the context of what might have happened had the obese individual never entered treatment. Secular trends clearly show that the natural course of obesity in untreated adults entails steady weight gain (Shah, Hannan, & Jeffery, 1991). Hence, long-term findings that show the maintenance of small amounts of weight loss may represent relatively favorable outcomes. In addition, mean weight changes provide only a partial view of long-term outcome. A fuller perspective may be gleaned from an examination of categories of partial success. For example, Kramer, Jeffery, Forster, and Snell (1989) reported an overall mean weight loss of 2.7 kg at 4.5-year follow-up. However, an analysis by categories of relative success revealed that approximately 20% of the subjects maintained losses of 5 kg or more, suggesting a notable degree of success for a significant number of individuals.

Pharmacotherapy

Four types of medications have been used to treat obesity. These include (a) noradrenergic agents, (b) serotoninergic agents, (c) combined noradrenergic and serotoninergic agents, and (d) lipase inhibitors. Recent years have witnessed major changes in the medications available for weight loss. The serotoninergic drugs, fenfluramine (Pondimin) and dexfenfluramine (Redux), were withdrawn in 1997 due to their association with occurrence of heart valve disease (Connolly et al., 1997), and in 2000, the over-the-counter weight-loss products, Accutrim and Dexatrim, which contain the noradrenergic ingredient phenylpropanolamine, were withdrawn due to concerns about increased risk of stroke (FDA, Nov. 6, 2000). Since 1997, the Food and Drug Administration has approved two new anti-obesity agents, sibutramine (Meridia; Knoll Pharmaceutical Company) and orlistat (Xenical; Roche Pharmaceutical Company). Table 6.4 summarizes the current status of drugs used to treat obesity. In the following section, we describe sibutramine and orlistat, the two newest ant-obesity agents.

Sibutramine is a combined serotonin and noradrenaline reuptake inhibitor. Rather than decreasing appetite, sibutramine works by increasing satiety after the onset of eating. Sibutramine may also produce a small increase in basal metabolic rate (Hansen, Toubro, Stock, Macdonald, & Astrup, 1998). In controlled trials lasting 6 to 12 months, sibutramine (15 mg per day) produced mean body weight reductions of 6% to 7%, compared to 1% to 2% for placebo (Bray et al., 1999; Jones, Smith, Kelly, & Gray, 1995). Weight loss occurs in the first six months of use and tends to plateau thereafter.

Sibutramine may also enhance the effects of intensive dieting. For example, Apfelbaum et al. (1999) showed that subjects who initially lost 6 or more kg through four weeks of very low calorie dieting increased their weight losses by an additional 5.2 kg through the use of sibutramine, whereas subjects on placebo gained 0.5 kg.

The major drawback of sibutramine lies in its effect on blood pressure. Sibutramine produces a modest mean increase in blood pressure (about 2-mm Hg systolic and diastolic at the 15-mg dose). However, some people (approximately 17%) who take sibutramine experience an increase of 10-mm Hg or more in diastolic systolic blood pressure (compared to 7% of subjects taking placebo). A 2-mm rise in diastolic blood pressure increases the risk of coronary heart disease by 6% and increases the risk of stroke by 15% (Cook, Cohen, Hebert, Taylor, & Hennekens, 1995). Therefore, patients with a history of heart disease, stroke, hypertension, or other risk factors for heart disease should not take sibutramine, and those on sibutramine must have their blood pressure monitored frequently (Hensrud, 2000; Knoll Pharmaceutical Co., 2000). Other less serious side effects of sibutramine include headache, dry mouth, anorexia, constipation, and insomnia.

Orlistat is a gastric and pancreatic lipase inhibitor (Roche Laboratories, 2000). Rather than suppressing appetite or increasing satiety, orlistat works by preventing the digestion and absorption of up to 30% of fat intake. In a large-scale, randomized controlled trial (Davidson et al., 1999), treatment with diet plus orlistat (120 mg, 3 times a day) for two years produced a 7.6% weight loss while treatment with diet plus placebo resulted in a 4.2% reduction. Maximum weight loss with orlistat typically occurs after 8 to 12 months of treatment, and 25% to 30% of the weight lost during the first year is regained during the following year, despite continued treatment (Davidson et al., 1999; L. Sjöstrom et al., 1998). Nonetheless, weight loss after two years of treatment with diet plus orlistat remains significantly greater than treatment

TABLE 6.4   Current Status of Drugs Used to Treat Obesity

Type of Agent	Generic Name	Trade Name	Current Status
Noradrenergic	Benzphetamine	Didrex	Available
	Diethylproprion	Tenuate, Tepanil	Available
	Mazindol	Mazanor, Sanorex	Available
	Phendimetrazine	Anorex, Obalan, Wehless	Available
	Phentermine	Adipex-P, Fastin, Ionamin	Available
	Phenylpropanolamine	Accutrim, Dexatrim	Withdrawn
Serotoninergic	Dexfenfluramine	Redux	Withdrawn
	Fenfluramine	Pondimin	Withdrawn
	Fluoxetine	Prozac, Lovan	Not approved
Combined noradrenergic + serotoninergic	Sibutramine	Meridia	Available
Lipase inhibitor	Orlistat	Xenical	Available

with diet plus placebo (Davidson et al., 1999). When used *following* a period of low-calorie dieting, orlistat reduces the regaining of weight lost (Hill et al., 1999).

The major side effects of orlistat include oily spotting, abdominal pain, flatus with discharge, fecal urgency, oily stools, increased defecation, and fecal incontinence. Side effects are reported by 20% to 50% of users (Roche Laboratories, 2000). The consumption of excessive quantities of fat increases the risk of side effects. Thus, in addition to inhibiting fat absorption, the aversive consequences of consuming fats while taking orlistat may condition patients to limit their intakes of dietary fats.

The rates of attrition in drug treatment studies have often been quite high. For example, in the clinical trial of orlistat by Davidson et al. (1999), more than half the patients in both the drug (54%) and placebo (57%) conditions dropped out prior to the final evaluation. Moreover, adverse side effects led to a significantly higher drop out rate among subjects on orlistat (9%) than on placebo (4%), whereas a lack of treatment effectiveness produced greater attrition among subjects on placebo (5%) than on orlistat (1%). The combination of a high attrition rate and differential reasons for subjects dropping out are often not taken into account in analyzing the results in drug studies. As a consequence, the benefits of drug treatment may be overstated (Williamson, 1999).

An additional concern centers about the use of drugs to treat obesity independent of significant lifestyle changes. Many patients, and some practitioners, may rely on medication as the "magic bullet" or sole element of obesity management (Kushner, 1997). Such an approach is likely to result in a disappointing outcome. The benefits of weight-loss medications can be enhanced when drug treatment serves as one component in a comprehensive treatment regimen that includes lifestyle modification (Wadden, Berkowitz, Sarwer, Prus-Wisniewski, & Steinberg, 2001).

Bariatric Surgery

Class III or morbid obesity (BMI > 40) confers an extremely high risk for morbidity and decreased longevity. With a prevalence of 3.9% among women and 1.8% among men, morbid obesity affects approximately 12 million Americans (Flegal et al., 1998). Because lifestyle and pharmacological interventions produce very limited benefits for morbidly obese patients, bariatric surgery represents the treatment of choice for such individuals (Albrecht & Pories, 1999).

Gastroplasty and gastric bypass are the two major types of bariatric surgery currently available for morbidly obese individuals and for persons with BMIs > 35 who have obesity-related comorbid conditions. In vertical banded gastroplasty, the stomach is stapled so as create a small vertical pouch. This gastric pouch limits the amount of food that can be ingested in a single eating period to about 15 ml. A ring with a diameter of 9 to 10 mm is placed at the outlet of the pouch to slow the rate at which food passes through the remainder of the stomach and into the duodenum and jejunum (small intestine). Gastroplasty exerts a regulatory effect on eating behavior through aversive conditioning. Eating more than the small amount of solid food that the stomach pouch can accommodate typically results in regurgitation. Fear of vomiting provides a disincentive for overeating, and the perception of fullness associated with the distention of the stomach pouch serves as a cue to stop eating. Unfortunately, gastroplasty does not limit the consumption of high-calorie liquids or soft foods. As a result, poor outcome attributable to "soft calorie syndrome" may be as high as 30% (Kral, 1989). An additional problem with gastroplasty is that over time the size of the pouch may expand, thereby limiting its long-term effectiveness.

In gastric bypass procedures, such as the Roux-en-Y, a small gastric pouch is created via stapling, and a limb of the jejunum is attached directly to the pouch. Ingested food bypasses 90% of the stomach, the duodenum, and a small portion of the proximal jejunum (Kral, 1995). The surgery facilitates weight loss in three ways. First, the pouch can only hold a small amount of food (15 ml), and over-filling the pouch results in regurgitation. Second, the emptying of partially digested food from the pouch into the small intestine results in malabsorption, such that a portion of nutrients (and calories) consumed are not absorbed. Third, the consumption of sweets and foods containing refined sugar produces aversive consequences (i.e., the "dumping syndrome) including nausea, light-headedness, sweating, palpitations, and gastrointestinal distress.

Because it produces superior weight-loss outcome, gastric bypass has replaced gastroplasty as the preferred type of bariatric surgery (Balsiger, Murr, Poggio, & Sarr, 2000). For example, Glenny and colleagues (Glenny, O'Meara, Melville, Sheldon, & Wilson, 1997) reviewed seven studies that compared gastric bypass with gastroplasty. Six of the seven showed significantly greater weight losses favoring the gastric bypass procedure. Typical weight losses one year after gastric bypass ranged from 45 to 65 kg compared to 30 to 35 kg after gastroplasty. Similar findings have been obtained a large-scale trial of bariatric surgery in Sweden (C. Sjöstrom, Lissner, Wedel, & Sjöstrom, 1999). Patients who received gastric bypass had a 33% reduction in body weight at two years compared to 23% for patients with gastroplasty. Long-term studies show some regaining of weight (e.g., 5 to 7 kg over five years) but gastric bypass patients commonly maintain 80% to 90% of their initial (i.e., first year) weight losses (Balsiger et al., 2000).

Bariatric surgery entails both greater risks and greater benefits than alternative treatments of obesity. The risks associated with surgery can include postoperative complications, micronutrient deficiencies, and late postoperative depression (National Institutes of Health, 1992). Among surgeons and centers experienced in these surgical procedures, mortality associated with bariatric surgery is approximately 0.5% (L. Sjöstrom et al., 1995). These risks should be considered in light of the documented benefits of bariatric surgery.

Gastric bypass reduces or eliminates the major comorbid conditions experienced by severely obese patients. Significant improvements in hypertension, diabetes, dyslipidemia, asthma, and sleep apnea are seen in the majority of patients affected by these conditions (Kral, 1995; Long et al., 1994; NIH, 1992). Moreover, a nonrandomized study showed a significantly lower mortality rate among morbidly obese diabetic patients who underwent gastric bypass surgery compared to a matched group who did not (MacDonald et al., 1997). Bariatric surgery also appears to prevent the *development* of serious diseases that commonly occur in morbidly obese patients. L. Sjöstrom et al. (1995) documented a three to fourfold reduction in risk for hypertension and a 14-fold reduction in the risk for diabetes. Finally, it should be noted that significant improvements in quality of life routinely accompany the large weight losses achieved by bariatric surgery patients (NIH, 1992).

STRATEGIES TO IMPROVE LONG-TERM OUTCOME

With the exception of surgery, virtually all treatments for obesity show limited long-term effectiveness. Indeed, after reviewing the outcome of all nonsurgical treatments of obesity, the Institute of Medicine (Thomas, 1995) concluded that ". . . those who complete weight-loss programs lose approximately 10% of their body weight, only to regain two thirds of it back within one year and almost all of it back within 5 years" (p. 1).

What accounts for such disappointing outcomes? Poor maintenance of weight loss seems to stem from a complex interaction of physiological, environmental, and psychological factors. Physiological factors, such as reduced metabolic rate (Dulloo & Jacquet, 1998; Ravussin & Swinburn, 1993), adaptive thermogenesis (Leibel, Rosenbaum, & Hirsch, 1995; Stock, 1999), and increased adipose tissue lipoprotein lipase activity (Kern, 1997; Kern, Ong, Saffari, & Carty,

1990), prime the dieter to regain lost weight. Continuous exposure to an environment rich in tasty high-fat, high-calorie foods (Hill & Peters, 1998), combined with a dieting-induced heightened sensitivity to palatable foods (Rodin, Schank, & Striegel-Moore, 1989), further predisposes the individual to setbacks in dietary control.

This challenging combination of physiological and environmental barriers makes long-term success a very difficult proposition. Thus, it is not surprising that most overweight individuals experience difficulties after the completion of weight-loss treatment. In addition, from the patient's viewpoint, the most satisfying aspect of treatment, weight loss, usually ends with the termination of intervention. As a result, many perceive a high behavioral "cost" associated with continued efforts at weight control precisely at the same time they are experiencing diminished "benefits" in terms of little or no additional weight loss. A regaining of weight often leads to attributions of personal ineffectiveness that can trigger negative emotions, a sense of hopelessness, and an abandonment of the weight-control effort (Goodrick, Raynaud, Pace, & Foreyt, 1992; Jeffery, French, & Schmid, 1990).

Over the past 15 years, researchers have examined a wide array of strategies with the goal of improving long-term outcome in obesity treatment. These include very low-calorie diets, extended treatment, skills training, monetary incentives, food provision, peer support, exercise/physical activity, and multicomponent posttreatment programs (see Table 6.5). In the following sections, we review the effectiveness of these approaches to improving long-term outcome.

Very Low-Calorie Diets

If obese patients lose larger amounts of weight during initial treatment, will they keep off more weight in the long run? Investigations of very low-calorie-diets (VLCDs) provide a partial answer to this question. VLCDs are portion-controlled, very low energy (<800 kcal/day), high protein diets, often delivered in liquid form. Losses of 20 to 25 kg (approximately 20% of initial body weight) are usually incurred following use of VLCD. A review of seven studies comparing VLCDs with lifestyle interventions (using 1200 to 1500 kcal/day diets) showed that participants treated with a VLCD *initially* lost nearly twice as much weight as those in lifestyle interventions (Wadden & Foster, 2000). However, at the conclusion of VLCD treatment, a rapid regaining of weight usually occurs such that the long-term weight losses produced by VLCDs are no greater than those obtained by lifestyle interventions (e.g., Wadden, Foster, & Letizia, 1994).

TABLE 6.5   Effects of Strategies Designed to Improve Long-Term Outcome

	Beneficial Effect Observed	
	Beneficial Effect	Beneficial Effect
Strategy	6 to 12 Months after Initial Treatment	13 or More Months after Initial Treatment
Very-low calorie diets	Yes	No
Continued therapy		
Extended therapy (continued weekly or biweekly group sessions up to one year)	Yes	Yes
Therapist contact by mail + phone	Yes	Unknown
Telephone prompts by nontherapists	No	Unknown
Skills training		
Relapse prevention training during initial treatment	No	Unlikely
Relapse prevention training combined with posttreatment therapist contacts	Yes	Unknown
Portion-controlled meals		
Provision of portion-controlled meals	Yes	No
Optional purchase of portion-controlled meals	No	Unlikely
Financial incentives		
Financial incentives for weight loss	No	No
Financial incentives for exercise	No	No
Physical activity		
Supervised exercise	No	No
Use of personal trainers	No	No
Home-based exercise	Yes	Unknown
Short-bout exercise + home exercise equipment	Yes	Unknown
Social support training		
Peer support training	No	Unlikely
Social support training for clients recruited with friends or relatives	Yes	Unknown
Multicomponent programs		
Therapist contact + increased exercise	Yes	Yes
Therapist contact + social support	Yes	Yes
Therapist contact + increased exercise + social support	Yes	Yes

Source: Data from Perri (2002).

Extended Treatment

Improving the long-term effects of treatment involves finding ways to assist clients in sustaining key changes in the behaviors that regulate energy balance and weight loss. Extending the length of treatment may offer the opportunity for continued reinforcement of adherence to the behaviors needed for negative energy balance. Perri, Nezu, Patti, and McCann (1989) tested whether extending treatment would improve adherence and weight loss by comparing a standard 20-week program with an extended 40-week program. The results showed that the extended program significantly improved outcome compared to the standard treatment. During the period from Week 20 to Week 40, participants in extended treatment increased their weight losses by 35% while those in the standard length treatment gained a small amount of weight. Moreover, both weight loss and adherence data supported the hypothesis that the longer patients are in treatment the longer they adhere to the behaviors necessary for weight loss.

Perri and Corsica (2002) reviewed the results of 13 studies in which behavioral treatment was extended beyond six months through the use of weekly or biweekly treatment sessions. On average, treatment in the extended-intervention groups in these 13 studies included 41 sessions over the course of 54 weeks. One year after the initiation of treatment, those groups that received behavior therapy with extended contact succeeded in maintaining 96.3% of their initial losses. The inclusion of a control group (i.e., behavioral treatment without extended contact) in three of the studies permits a rough comparison of the groups with and without extended treatment (see Figure 6.2). The groups without extended contact maintained about two-thirds (66.5%) of their initial weight reductions. Judging the effects of the extended-treatments by comparison with the

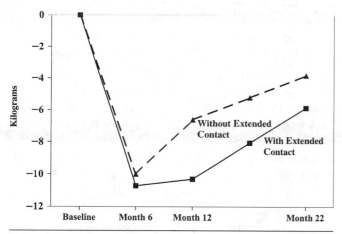

Figure 6.3   Long-term weight losses in behavioral treatments and with extended therapist contacts.   *Source:* Data from Perri and Corsica, 2002.

standard-length groups suggests a beneficial impact for extended contact (i.e., 96.3% versus 66.5% of initial loss maintained). Furthermore, the results of additional follow-up visits conducted on average of 22 months after the initiation of treatment showed that the extended treatment groups maintained 65.8% of their initial reductions. In contrast, the three groups without extended contact maintained only 38.3% of their initial reductions. Collectively, the data in Figure 6.3 suggest that extended treatment improves long-term outcome.

Relapse Prevention Training

Relapse prevention training (RPT) involves teaching participants how to avoid or cope with slips and relapses (Marlatt & Gordon, 1985). Studies of the effectiveness of RPT on long-term weight management have revealed mixed results. Perri, Shapiro, Ludwig, Twentyman, and McAdoo (1984) found that the inclusion of RPT during initial treatment was not effective, but combining RPT with a posttreatment program of client-therapist contacts by mail and telephone significantly improved the maintenance of weight loss. Similarly, Baum, Clark, and Sandler (1991) showed that participants who received RPT combined with posttreatment therapist contacts maintained their end of treatment losses better than did participants in a minimal contact condition. Recently, however, Perri and colleagues (Perri, Nezu, et al., 2001) compared RPT and problem-solving therapy (PST) as year-long extended treatments for weight loss. PST showed better long-term outcome than the control group, but RPT did not. RPT in this study was administered as a standardized didactic program; it may be more effective when applied as an individualized therapy (Marlatt & George, 1998).

Telephone Prompts

Providing patients with additional face-to-face treatment sessions entails considerable time and effort. Therefore, it is reasonable to consider whether telephone contact might be used as a more efficient means of long-term care. Wing, Jeffery, Hellerstedt, and Burton (1996) examined the impact of weekly posttreatment calls designed to prompt self-monitoring of body weight and food intake. The interviewers, who were not the participants' therapists, offered no counseling or guidance. Participation in the telephone contacts was associated with better long-term outcome, but it did not enhance maintenance of weight loss compared to a no-contact control condition. In contrast, Perri, McAdoo, Spevak, and Newlin (1984) found that client-therapist contacts by telephone and mail significantly improved the maintenance of lost weight. In this study, the participants' therapists actually made the phone call and provided counseling, whereas in the Wing study, the contacts were made by callers who were unknown to the clients and who did not offer advice.

Food Provision/Monetary Incentives

Can manipulation of the antecedents and consequences of key behaviors improve long-term weight-loss outcome? Jeffery and his colleagues (1993) addressed this question in a study of the effects of food provision and monetary incentives on weight loss. During initial treatment and the year following initial treatment, participants were provided with prepackaged, portion-controlled meals (10 per week at no cost) or with monetary incentives for weight loss or with both. The monetary incentives did not influence progress, but the portion-controlled meals resulted in significantly greater weight losses, compared to standard behavioral treatment. The findings of an additional 12-month follow-up showed a significant regaining of weight in all conditions (Jeffery & Wing, 1995). A subsequent study (Wing et al., 1996) indicated that providing participants with the "opportunity" to purchase and use portion-controlled meals as a maintenance strategy was ineffective, largely because participants did not purchase the prepackaged meals.

Peer Support

Can social support be utilized to improve long-term outcome? The benefits of a peer support maintenance program were investigated by Perri et al. (1987). After completing standard behavioral treatment, participants were taught how to run their own peer group support meetings. A meeting place equipped with a scale was provided to the group, and biweekly meetings were scheduled over a seven-month pe-riod. Although attendance at the peer group meetings was high (67%), no advantage was observed in terms of adher-ence or weight change during the maintenance period com-pared to a control condition. The results of a long-term follow-up showed a trend toward better maintenance of weight lost in the peer support group compared to the control condition. Wing and Jeffery (1999) recently tested the effects of recruiting participants alone or with three friends or family members. The researchers used a partially randomized study in assigning subjects (recruited alone versus with friends) to receive either standard behavior therapy or behavior therapy with social support training. The results of a six-month follow-up showed that participants who were recruited with friends *and* were provided social support training maintained 66% of their initial weight losses. In contrast, the individuals who entered the study alone and received standard treatment maintained only 24% of their initial losses.

Exercise/Physical Activity

The association between long-term weight loss and increased physical activity is a common finding in correlational studies (e.g., Harris, French, Jeffery, McGovern, & Wing, 1994; McGuire, Wing, Klem, Lang, & Hill, 1999; Sherwood, Jeffery, & Wing, 1999). Nonetheless, an important question remains as to whether the addition of exercise or physical activity can improve long-term outcome in the treatment of obesity (Garrow, 1995). Wing (1999) recently reviewed the results of randomized controlled trials of exercise in the treat-ment of obesity. Wing found that only 2 of 13 studies showed significantly greater initial weight losses for the combination of diet plus exercise versus diet alone, and only 2 of 6 studies with follow-ups of one or more years showed significantly better maintenance of lost weight for diet plus exercise versus diet alone. However, in all the studies reviewed, the direction of the findings favored treatment that included exercise. Wing noted that the short duration of treatments and the rela-tively low levels of exercise prescribed in many of the stud-ies may have accounted for the modest effects of exercise on weight loss.

In addition, treatment integrity represents an important problem in controlled trials of exercise. Participants assigned to exercise conditions often vary greatly in their adherence to their exercise prescriptions, and subjects assigned to "diet only" conditions sometimes initiate exercise on their own. Compromises in treatment integrity can obscure the effects of exercise interventions. For example, Wadden and his col-leagues (1997) investigated the impact of adding aerobic ex-ercise, strength training, and their combination, to a 48-week behavioral treatment program. None of the exercise additions improved weight loss or weight-loss maintenance, compared to behavior therapy with diet only. Across all conditions, ad-herence to exercise assignments was highly variable, espe-cially during follow-up. Nonetheless, the researchers found a significant positive association between exercise and long-term weight loss. Participants who indicated that they "exer-cised regularly" had long-term weight losses (12.1 kg) nearly twice as large as those who described themselves as "non-exercisers" (6.1 kg).

Given the potential benefits of exercise for long-term management of weight, how can adherence to physical activ-ity regimens be improved? The various strategies that have been examined include: home-based exercise, the use of short bouts of exercise, the provision of home exercise equip-ment, monetary incentives for exercise, and posttreatment programs focused exclusively on exercise.

Home-Based Exercise

Although group-based exercise programs offer the opportu-nity for enhanced social support, over the long run such benefits may be limited by potential barriers that one must overcome in meeting with others to exercise at a designated time and location. In contrast, home-based exercise offers a greater degree of flexibility and fewer obstacles. Perri, Martin, Leermakers, Sears, and Notelovitz (1997) investigated the use of home-based versus supervised group-based exercise pro-grams in the treatment of obesity. After six months, both approaches resulted in significant improvements in exercise participation, cardiorespiratory fitness, eating patterns, and weight loss. However, over the next six months, participants in the home-based condition completed a significantly higher percentage of prescribed exercise sessions than subjects in the group program (83.3% versus 62.1%, respectively). More-over, at long-term follow-up, the participants in the home-based program displayed significantly better maintenance of lost weight, compared to subjects in the group-based program.

Personal Trainers/Financial Incentives

The use of personal trainers and financial incentives have been tested as strategies to improve exercise adherence and long-term weight loss (Jeffery, Wing, Thorson, & Burton, 1998). Personal trainers exercised with participants and made phone calls reminding them to exercise. In addition, participants could earn $1 to $3 per bout of walking. The use of personal trainers and financial incentives both increased attendance at supervised exercise sessions, but neither improved weight loss. In fact, participants in the control condition, which received a home based exercise regimen, showed superior maintenance of weight loss at follow-up compared to all other conditions. These results corroborate the findings of Perri et al. (1997) regarding the benefits of home-based exercise in the management of obesity.

Short Bouts and Home Exercise Equipment

Jakicic, Winters, Lang, and Wing (1999) showed that the benefits of home exercise may be enhanced by providing participants with exercise equipment and by allowing them to exercise in brief bouts. Jakicic et al. tested the effects of intermittent exercise (i.e., four 10-min bouts per day versus one 40-min bout per day) and the use of home exercise equipment on adherence and weight loss, and fitness. The researchers provided half of the subjects in the short-bout condition with motorized treadmills for home use. The benefits from exercise in short or long bouts were equivalent. However, participants *with* the home exercise equipment maintained significantly higher levels of long term exercise adherence and weight loss compared to subjects *without* exercise equipment.

Exercise-Focused Maintenance Program

Finally, Leermakers, Perri, Shigaki, and Fuller (1999) examined whether a posttreatment program focused exclusively on exercise might improve long-term outcome in obesity treatment. These researcher compared the effects of exercise-focused and weight-focused posttreatment programs. The components of exercise-focused program included supervised exercise, incentives for exercise completion, and relapse prevention training aimed at the maintenance of exercise. The weight-focused maintenance program included problem solving of barriers to weight-loss progress. The results of a long-term follow-up showed that participants in the weight-focused program had significantly greater decreases in fat intake and significantly better maintenance of lost weight, compared to subjects in the exercise-focused condition. These results highlight the necessity of focusing on dietary intake as well exercise in the long-term management of obesity.

Multicomponent Posttreatment Programs

A number of investigations have studied the impact of posttreatment programs with multiple components. Perri, McAdoo, et al. (1984) tested the effects of a multicomponent program that included peer group meetings combined with ongoing client-therapist contacts by mail and telephone. The multicomponent program produced significantly better maintenance of weight loss, compared to a control group. These findings were replicated in a later study (Perri, McAdoo, McAllister, Lauer, & Yancey, 1986) that employed a longer initial treatment (20 rather than 14 weeks), included aerobic exercise, and achieved larger weight losses at posttreatment and at follow-ups.

Finally, Perri and colleagues (1988) examined the effects of adding increased exercise and a social influence program (or both) to a posttreatment therapist contact program consisting of 26 biweekly group sessions. Compared to a control condition that received behavioral therapy without posttreatment contact, all four posttreatment programs produced significantly greater weight losses at an 18-month follow-up evaluation. The four maintenance groups succeeded in sustaining on average 83% of their initial weight losses, compared to 33% for the group without a posttreatment program.

Summary

A review of strategies designed to improve long-term outcome in obesity treatment reveals an interesting pattern of findings. The use of VLCDs, relapse prevention training, peer group meetings, telephone prompts by nontherapists, monetary incentives for weight loss, supervised group exercise, the assistance of personal trainers, and the availability of portion-controlled meals do not appear effective in improving long-term outcome. On the other hand, there is evidence suggesting that extending treatment beyond six months through the use of weekly or biweekly sessions and providing multicomponent programs with ongoing patient-therapist contact improves the maintenance of lost weight. In addition, home-based exercise programs and the use of home exercise equipment may enhance adherence and may contribute to improved long-term outcome.

FUTURE RESEARCH DIRECTIONS

Several areas for clinical research appear promising. Some of these are discussed next.

Address Unrealistic Weight-Loss Expectations

Most obese clients enter weight-loss treatment with unrealistically high expectations about the amount of weight loss they can reasonably achieve (Foster, Wadden, Vogt, & Brewer, 1997). The discrepancy between clients' expectations and actual outcome may cause them to discount the beneficial impact of modest weight losses and lead ultimately to demoralization and difficulty maintaining the behavior changes needed to sustain weight loss (Foster et al., 1997). Addressing unrealistic weight-loss expectations at treatment outset may improve clients' satisfaction with the outcome of weight-loss therapy and thereby increase the likelihood of maintenance of weight lost.

Match Treatments to Clients

Matching long-term care to the specific needs of particular subgroups of obese persons may be fostered by the development of an empirical database (Brownell & Wadden, 1991). Such a database might include the clinical markers known to be associated with poor response to treatment (e.g. binge eating, depression, significant life stress, and minimal weight loss in the first month of treatment; Wadden & Letizia, 1992). This database might also help to identify persons for whom successful maintenance of weight lost might require combined behavioral plus pharmacological treatment versus those for whom behavioral management alone provides a satisfactory outcome. In addition, the interaction of genetic and environmental contributors to success and failure in the long-term management of obesity requires investigation (Campfield, Smith, Guisez, Devos, & Burn, 1995). For example, leptin as an obesity treatment appears promising, and clinical trials have yielded a positive dose-response effect on weight loss in both obese and normal weight subjects (Heymsfield et al., 1999). Findings such as these may contribute significantly to treatment matching in patients with a potential biological disposition for obesity.

Test Innovative Models

Cooper and Fairburn (2001) have suggested that innovative cognitive-behavioral interventions based on a newer conceptualization of the "maintenance problem" may improve long-term results. These authors argue that the absence of training in weight stabilization may hinder long-term success. They recommend that after an active period of weight loss, it is essential to provide patients with training in the maintenance of a stable body weight. These authors are currently conducting a randomized clinical trial to test the effects of this promising cognitive-behavioral model.

Examine Schedules of Follow-Up Care

Research has shown that greater frequency of follow-up contacts improves the success of weight loss treatment. What is unknown is the specific frequency and timing of professional contacts that are needed to sustain progress during follow-up care. It will be important to determine the minimal and optimal frequency of contacts needed for maintenance of

treatment effects. Importantly, the schedule in which follow-up is generally conducted (intervals determined in advance by the experimenters) may not provide patients with assistance at critical junctures (e.g., when facing a significant stressor or after experiencing a weight gain). Whether follow-up care should be tailored to each patient's progress rather than a fixed interval schedule, and whether a more open format or drop-in approach may prove more useful for clients should be investigated. Finally, the decline in attendance at long-term follow-up sessions has proven a formidable obstacle to successful maintenance treatment. Thus, we need to develop ways to keep patients actively involved in the long-term management of their obesity.

IMPROVING THE MANAGEMENT AND PREVENTION OF OBESITY

In this section, we offer two sets of recommendations. The first set entails suggestions to health professionals about ways to improve the care of the obese patient. The second set includes suggestions for the prevention of obesity.

Managing Obesity

Guidelines for a stepped-care approach for matching treatments to patients based on the severity of obesity and previous response to weight-loss treatment have been described in the recent report of the NIH (NHLBI, 1998). We offer several additional recommendations to health care professionals who treat obese patients.

1. *Begin with a comprehensive assessment.* An effective treatment plan should begin with a comprehensive assessment of the effects of obesity on the individual's health and emotional well-being (Beliard, Kirschenbaum, & Fitzgibbon, 1992). In addition to determining BMI and waist circumference, the evaluation should include an assessment of the impact of body weight on the obese person's current health and risk for future disease. The presence of significant co-morbidities may justify consideration of pharmacotherapy in patients with BMIs as low as 27 and bariatric surgery in patients with BMIs as low as 35. The obese person should receive a thorough physical examination that specifically assesses risk for diabetes, dyslipidemia, and hypertension—conditions that are very common yet often go undetected among obese individuals. The initial assessment should also include an assessment of "behavioral" risk factors, including sedentary lifestyle, consumption of a high-fat diet, and binge eating. Quality of life indicators including social adjustment, body image satisfaction, and

emotional status (i.e., the presence of anxiety and depressive symptomatology) ought to be included as well. A careful individualized assessment will often reveal important behavioral and psychological targets for intervention such as binge eating, body image disparagement, anxiety, depression, or poor social adjustment—problems that need to be addressed regardless of whether weight loss itself becomes an objective of treatment (Perri, Nezu, & Viegener, 1992; Wadden & Foster, 1992).

2. *Discuss treatment expectations.* Virtually all obese clients begin weight-loss therapy with unrealistically high expectations about the amount of weight loss they can achieve (Foster et al., 1997). These faulty expectations may lead patients to discount the beneficial impact of modest weight losses. Treatment of faulty weight-loss expectations may improve the patient's satisfaction with the outcome of weight-loss therapy and thereby foster better maintenance of weight loss. In some situations, it may be particularly important to address the internalized aesthetic standards that produce faulty weight-loss expectations. Teaching patients to resist the social pressure to achieve an "ideal" body, to adopt nonderogatory self-statements about large body size, and to uncouple the association between body weight and self-esteem should represent significant objectives for therapy (Foster & Kendall, 1994).

3. *Focus on behavior change.* Obese persons do not have direct control over how much weight they lose. Therefore, treatment goals should be framed in terms of behaviors that they can control, such as the quantity and quality of food they consume and the amounts and types of physical activity they perform. Moreover, obese persons should be informed that significant health benefits can be derived from even modest weight losses of 5% to 10%. The maintenance of stable weight and the prevention of weight gain should be recognized as a legitimate treatment option for some obese persons, particularly since the natural course of obesity entails weight gain.

4. *Include multiple indicators of "success."* Successful outcome in the care of the obese person should not be viewed solely in terms of weight change. Beneficial changes in risk factors for disease and improvements in quality of life (Atkinson, 1993) represent important indicators of success. Improvements in the quality of diet should be a component of care independent of whether weight reduction is an identified objective of care (Hill, Drougas, & Peters, 1993). Reductions in amounts of dietary fats, particularly saturated fats, can improve health as well as assist in weight loss (Insull et al., 1990). Similarly, increased physical activity and a decrease in sedentary lifestyle can represent beneficial components of long-term care irrespective of the

impact of exercise on weight loss (Lee, Blair, & Jackson, 1999; Leermakers, Dunn, & Blair, 2000; Paffenbarger & Lee, 1996). Finally, self-acceptance, independent of weight body, may also be a significant indicator of success (Wilson, 1996).

5. *Adopt a lifelong perspective.* We believe that obesity should be viewed as a chronic condition requiring long-term, if not lifelong, care. The clinical challenge is not to convince the obese person that they need to be in treatment forever. Rather the challenge is to convince the overweight person that successful management of weight will require constant vigilance and ongoing efforts at self-management of eating and exercise behaviors. Although weight management may become somewhat easier over time, it is always likely to entail conscious efforts to maintain behavioral control of one's energy balance. In a compassionate manner, health providers must communicate to their obese patients not merely a recognition of the chronicity of problem, but also an empathic understanding of the emotional aspects of what it means to be obese in a culture that values thinness. Finally, clinicians need to assure obese patients of their ready availability to assist in the long-term management of weight and related issues.

Prevention of Obesity

Clinical treatment of obesity will not resolve the current epidemic of overweight in the United States. Serious public health efforts are needed to counter the ominous trend of increasing body weights in our country. Accordingly, a number of far-reaching initiatives are warranted. We describe four sets of recommendations:

1. *Develop a national plan to prevent and treat obesity.* The increasing prevalence of obesity and obesity-related disorders demands serious attention from policymakers as well as the general public. As Mokdad and colleagues (2000) have noted, "The time has come to develop a national, comprehensive plan to prevent and treat the obesity epidemic" (p. 1650). The overarching objective of such a plan would be to identify and implement effective educational, behavioral, and environmental approaches to control and prevent obesity. The development of a national plan would require the collaborative efforts of both the public and the private sectors including scientists, physicians, public health officials, educators, and leaders from the agricultural and food industries (Nestle & Jacobson, 2000).

2. *Intervene in the schools.* Schools are in a unique position to support the promotion of healthy lifestyles. Interventions in the school environment can result in beneficial changes in both diet and physical activity (Sallis et al.,

1997). School-based physical activity programs that provide for enjoyable and regular exercise participation for all students are a must. In addition, schools should promote healthy eating patterns by ensuring that cafeterias and vending machines offer a variety of low-cost, nutritious foods and snacks. Alternatively, it is not too soon to begin a prohibition against two disturbing trends, specifically, the establishment of fast-food operations on school premises, and contracts with soft-drink companies that provide financial incentives based on student consumption of products with "empty calories." We need to decrease access to high-calorie, nutritionally poor foods and provide greater opportunities for students to select healthy foods. An effective school-based intervention may require multiple components including a behavioral curriculum, parental involvement, changes in the school food program, and support from the food industry (Story et al., 2000).

3. *Regulate advertising of junk foods.* In the course of a typical year, the average child sees more than 9,500 TV commercials advertising fast food, soft drinks, candy, and sugared cereals. Moreover, restaurant, soft drink, and candy companies spend more than $400 billion per year to advertise their products, often targeting their messages to young people. In contrast, very little is spent on advertising to promote healthy dietary practices. For example, the National Cancer Institute's entire annual budget for the "5 a Day" campaign to increase fruit and vegetable consumption is a relatively paltry $1 million (Battle & Brownell, 1996). This dramatic inequity requires attention, and more stringent regulation is needed to decrease the advertising of unhealthy foods, particularly during children's shows. Moreover, it may be helpful to require TV commercials to disclose prominently the nutrient values (e.g., calories, calories from fats, per serving) of advertised products, particularly snack foods.

4. *Impose a "fat tax."* Brownell and his colleagues (Brownell, 1994; Jacobson & Brownell, 2000) have suggested a controversial approach toward modifying the environmental factors that promote weight gain. They recommend adoption of a tax on unhealthy foods with the revenues from such a tax used to fund public health initiatives to promote healthy eating and exercise habits. Brownell (1994) originally advocated a steep tax to serve as a deterrent to unhealthy food purchases. Such an approach is unlikely to gain general acceptance. A more modest tax such as one penny per 12-oz soft drink or per pound of snack foods could go toward subsidizing healthier food choices, such as fruits and vegetables (or underwriting the cost of a national campaign to improve the nation's eating habits). Small-scale studies have shown that the consumption of healthy foods can be increased by lowering their costs (e.g., French, Jeffery, Story, Hanna, & Snyder, 1997). In addition, a recent national survey showed that 45% of adults would support a penny tax if the revenues were used to fund health education programs (Center for Science in the Public Interest, 1999).

CONCLUSION

Over the past two decades, the rates of overweight and obesity in the United States have increased at an alarming pace. Obesity constitutes a major public health problem because it confers increased risk for morbidity and mortality on the majority of the adult population. Understanding the factors that contribute to obesity may help in its control. Although genetics predispose some individuals to obesity, environmental factors are the major contributors to the current epidemic of overweight. Continuous exposure to an overabundance of high-calorie and high-fat foods, coupled with decreased occupational and leisure-time physical activity, has produced the significant increases in body weights observed over the past two decades. Weight loss can reverse many of the disadvantages associated with obesity, and progress has been made in the development of weight-loss treatments. Behavioral (lifestyle) interventions can produce weight reductions of sufficient magnitude to decrease the risk for many diseases, and new drug treatments can enhance the effectiveness of lifestyle interventions. Furthermore, gastric bypass surgery now provides a viable treatment option for the very severely obese. Nonetheless, with the exception of surgery, all weight-loss interventions suffer from the problem of poor long-term maintenance. Providing obese patients with extended treatment and long-term care has shown some benefits in this regard, but more research on the long-term management of obesity is clearly needed. Moreover, reversing the epidemic of obesity will require a major public health initiative aimed at identifying and implementing effective behavioral, educational, and environmental strategies for the prevention and control of obesity.

REFERENCES

Ahima, R. S., & Flier, J. S. (2000). Leptin. *Annual Review of Physiology, 62,* 413–437.

Albrecht, R. J., & Pories, W. J. (1999). Surgical intervention for the severely obese. *Baillieres Best Practice in Research and Clinical Endocrinology and Metabolism, 13,* 149–172.

Allison, D. B., Fontaine, K. R., Manson, J. E., Stevens, J., & Van Itallie, T. B. (1999). Annual deaths attributable to obesity in the

United States. *Journal of the American Medical Association, 282,* 1530–1538.

Allison, D. B., & Saunders, S. E. (2000). Obesity in North America: An overview. *Medical Clinics of North America, 84,* 305–332.

Apfelbaum, M., Vague, P., Ziegler, O., Hanotin, C., Thomas, F., & Leutenegger, E. (1999). Long term maintenance of weight loss after a very-low-calorie-diet: A randomized blinded trial of the efficacy and tolerability of sibutramine. *American Journal of Medicine, 106,* 179.

Atkinson, R. L. (1993). Proposed standards for judging the success of the treatment of obesity. *Annals of Internal Medicine, 119,* 677–680.

Ball, K., Crawford, D., & Owen, N. (2000). Too fat to exercise? Obesity as a barrier to physical activity. *Australia and New Zealand Journal of Public Health, 24,* 331–333.

Balsiger, B. M., Murr, M. M., Poggio, J. L., & Sarr, M. G. (2000). Bariatric surgery: Surgery for weight control in patients with morbid obesity. *Medical Clinics of North America, 84,* 477–489.

Battle, E. K., & Brownell, K. D. (1996). Confronting a rising tide of eating disorders and obesity: Treatment vs. prevention and policy. *Addictive Behaviors, 21,* 755–765.

Baum, J. G., Clark, H. B., & Sandler, J. (1991). Preventing relapse in obesity through posttreatment maintenance systems: Comparing the relative efficacy of two levels of therapist support. *Journal of Behavioral Medicine, 14,* 287–302.

Beliard, D., Kirschenbaum, D. S., & Fitzgibbon, M. L. (1992). Evaluation of an intensive weight control program using a priori criteria to determine outcome. *International Journal of Obesity, 16,* 505–517.

Binkley, J. K., Eales, J., & Jekanowski, M. (2000). The relation between dietary change and rising U.S. obesity. *International Journal of Obesity, 24,* 1032–1039.

Bouchard, C., Perusse, L., Leblanc, C., Tremblay, A., & Theriault, G. (1988). Inheritance of the amount and distribution of human body fat. *International Journal of Obesity, 12,* 205–215.

Bouchard, C., Perusse, L., Rice, T., & Rao, D. C. (1998). The genetics of human obesity. In G. A. Bray, C. Bouchard, & W. P. T. James (Eds.), *Handbook of Obesity* (pp. 157–190). New York: Marcel Dekker.

Bray, G. A., Blackburn, G. L., Ferguson, J. M., Greenway, F. L., Jain, A. K., Mendel, C. M., et al. (1999). Sibutramine produces dose-related weight loss. *Obesity Research, 7,* 189–198.

Brownell, K. D. (1994, December 15). Get slim with higher taxes. *New York Times,* p. A29.

Brownell, K. D., & Wadden, T. A. (1991). The heterogeneity of obesity: Fitting treatments to individuals. *Behavior Therapy, 22,* 153–177.

Campfield, L. A., Smith, F. J., & Burn, P. (1998). Strategies and potential molecular targets for obesity treatment. *Science, 280,* 1383–1387.

Campfield, L. A., Smith, F. J., Guisez, Y., Devos, R., & Burn, P. (1995). Recombinant mouse OB protein: Evidence for peripheral signal linking adiposity and central neural networks. *Science, 269,* 475–476.

Carpenter, K. M., Hasin, D. S., Allison, D. B., & Faith, M. S. (2000). Relationship between obesity and *DSM-IV* major depressive disorder, suicide ideation, and suicide attempts: Results from a general population study. *American Journal of Public Health, 90,* 251–257.

Centers for Disease Control and Prevention. (1994). From the Centers for Disease Control and Prevention. Daily dietary fat and total food-energy intakes-NHANES III, Phase 1, 1988–1991. *Journal of the American Medical Association, 271,* 1309.

Center for Science in the Public Interest. (1999). *Bruskin-Goldring Research Telephone Survey.* Washington, DC: Author.

Chagnon, Y. C., Perusse, L., Weisnagel, S. J., Rankinen, T., & Bouchard, C. (2000). The human obesity gene map: The 1999 update. *Obesity Research, 8,* 89–117.

Chan, J. M., Rimm, E. B., Colditz, G. A., Stampfer, M. J., & Willett, W. C. (1994). Obesity, fat distribution, and weight gain as risk factors for clinical diabetes in men. *Diabetes Care, 17,* 961–969.

Coakley, E. H., Kawachi, I., Manson, J. E., Speizer, F. E., Willet, W. C., & Colditz, G. A. (1998). Lower levels of physical functioning are associated with higher body weight among middle-aged and older women. *International Journal of Obesity, 22,* 958–965.

Colditz, G. A., Willett, W. C., Stampfer, M. J., Manson, J. E., Hennekens, C. H., Arky, R. A., et al. (1990). Weight as a risk factor for clinical diabetes in women. *American Journal of Epidemiology, 132,* 501–513.

Collier, G. R., McMillan, J. S., Windmill, K., Walder, K., Tenne-Brown, J., de Silva, A., et al. (2000). Beacon: A novel gene involved in the regulation of energy balance. *Diabetes, 49,* 1766–1771.

Comuzzie, A. G., & Allison, D. B. (1998). The search for human obesity genes. *Science, 280,* 1374–1377.

Connolly, H. M., Crary, J. L., McGoon, M. D., Hensrud, D. D., Edwards, B. S., Edwards, W. D., et al. (1997). Valvular heart disease associated with fenfluramine-phentermine. *New England Journal of Medicine, 337,* 581–588.

Considine, R. V., Sinha, M. K., Heiman, M. L., Kriauciunas, A., Stephens, T. W., Nyce, M. R., et al. (1996). Serum immunoreactive-leptin concentrations in normal weight and obese humans. *New England Journal of Medicine, 334,* 292–295.

Cook, N. R., Cohen, J., Hebert, P. R., Taylor, J. O., & Hennekens, C. H. (1995). Implications of small reductions in diastolic blood pressure for primary prevention. *Archives of Internal Medicine, 155,* 701–709.

Cooper, Z., & Fairburn, C. G. (2001). A new cognitive behavioral approach to the treatment of obesity. *Behavior Research and Therapy, 39,* 499–511.

Crandall, C. S., & Biernat M. (1990). The ideology of antifat attitudes. *Journal of Applied Social Psychology, 20,* 227–243.

Crandall, C. S., & Martinez, R. (1996). Culture, ideology, and antifat attitudes. *Personality and Social Psychology Bulletin, 22,* 1165–1176.

Davidson, M. H., Hauptman, J., DiGirolamo, M., Foreyt, J. P., Halsted, C. H., Heber, D., et al. (1999). Weight control and risk factor reduction in obese subjects treated for 2 years with orlistat: A randomized controlled trial. *Journal of the American Medical Association, 281,* 235–242.

Davies, R. J., & Stradling, J. R. (1990). The relationship between neck circumference, radiographic pharyngeal anatomy, and the obstructive sleep apnoea syndrome. *European Respiratory Journal, 3,* 509–514.

DiPietro, L. (1995). Physical activity, body weight, and adiposity: An epidemiologic perspective. *Exercise Sport Science Review, 23,* 275–303.

Dulloo, A. G., & Jacquet, J. (1998). Adaptive reduction in basal metabolic rate in response to food deprivation in humans: A role for feedback signals from fat stores. *American Journal of Clinical Nutrition, 68,* 599–606.

Dunaif, A. (1992). *Polycystic ovary syndrome.* Boston: Blackwell Scientific.

Dyer, A. R., & Elliott, P. (1989). The INTERSALT study: Relations of body mass index to blood pressure: INTERSALT Cooperative Research Group. *Journal of Human Hypertension, 3,* 299–308.

Eaton, S. B., & Konner, M. (1985). Paleolithic nutrition: A consideration of its nature and current implications. *New England Journal of Medicine, 312,* 283–289.

Ernst, N. D., Sempos, C. T., Briefel, R. R., & Clark, M. B. (1997). Consistency between U.S. dietary fat intake and serum total cholesterol concentrations: The National Health and Nutrition Examination Survey. *American Journal of Clinical Nutrition, 66,* 965S–972S.

Farooqi, I. S., Yeo, G. S. H., Keogh, J. M., Aminian, S., Jebb, S. A., Butler, G., et al. (2000). Dominant and recessive inheritance of morbid obesity associated with melanocortin 4 receptor deficiency. *Journal of Clinical Investigation, 106,* 271–279.

Feitosa, M. F., Borecki, I., Hunt, S. C., Arnett, D. K., Rao, D. C., & Province, M. (2000). Inheritance of the waist to hip ratio in the National Heart Lung, and Blood Institute Family Heart Study. *Obesity Research, 8,* 294–301.

Fitzgibbon, M. L., Stolley, M. R., & Kirschenbaum, D. S. (1993). Obese people who seek treatment have different characteristics than those who do not seek treatment. *Health Psychology, 12,* 342–345.

Flegal, K. M., Carroll, M. D., Kuczmarski, R. J., & Johnson, C. L. (1998). Overweight and obesity in the United States: Prevalence and trends, 1960–1994. *International Journal of Obesity, 22,* 39–47.

Folsom, A. R., Kushi, L. H., Anderson, K. E., Mink, P. J., Olson, J. E., Hong, C. P., et al. (2000). Associations of general and abdominal obesity with multiple health outcomes in older women: The Iowa Women's Health Study. *Archives of Internal Medicine, 160,* 2117–2128.

Food and Drug Administration. (2000, November 6). *Public health advisory. Subject: Safety of Phenylpropanolamine.* Retrieved from http://www.fda.gov/cder/drug/infopage/ppa/advisory.htm.

Ford, E. S., Williamson, D. F., & Liu, S. (1997). Weight change and diabetes incidence: Findings from a national cohort of U.S. adults. *American Journal of Epidemiology, 146,* 214–222.

Foreyt, J. P. (1987). Issues in the assessment and treatment of obesity. *Journal of Consulting and Clinical Psychology, 55,* 677–684.

Foster, G. D., & Kendall, P. C. (1994). The realistic treatment of obesity: Changing the scales of success. *Clinical Psychology Review, 14,* 701–736.

Foster, G. D., Wadden, T. A., Vogt, R. A., & Brewer, G. (1997). What is a reasonable weight loss? Patients' expectations and evaluations of obesity treatment outcomes. *Journal of Consulting and Clinical Psychology, 65,* 79–85.

French, S. A., Harnack, L., & Jeffery, R. W. (2000). Fast food restaurant use among women in the Pound of Prevention study: Dietary, behavioral and demographic correlates. *International Journal of Obesity, 24,* 1353–1359.

French, S., Jeffery, R., Sherwood, N., & Neumark-Sztainer, D. (1999). Prevalence and correlates of binge eating in a nonclinical sample of women enrolled in a weight gain prevention program. *International Journal of Obesity, 23,* 555–585.

French, S. A., Jeffery, R. W., Story, M., Hannan, P., & Snyder, P. (1997). A pricing strategy to promote low-fat snacks through vending machines. *American Journal of Public Health, 87,* 849–851.

Garrow, J. S. (1995). Exercise in the treatment of obesity: A marginal contribution. *International Journal of Obesity, 19*(Suppl. 4), S126–S129.

Glenny, A. M., O'Meara, S., Melville, A., Sheldon, T. A., & Wilson, C. (1997). The treatment and prevention of obesity: A systematic review of the literature. *International Journal of Obesity, 21,* 715–737.

Goodrick, G. K., Raynaud, A. S., Pace, P. W., & Foreyt, J. P. (1992). Outcome attribution in a very low calorie diet program. *International Journal of Eating Disorders, 12,* 117–120.

Gortmaker, S. L., Must, A., Perrin, J. M., Sobol, A. M., & Dietz, W. H. (1993). Social and economic consequences of overweight in adolescence and young adulthood. *New England Journal of Medicine, 329,* 1008–1012.

Goudas, V. T., & Dumesic, D. A. (1997). Polycystic ovary syndrome. *Endocrinology and Metabolism Clinics of North America, 26,* 893–912.

Grilo, C. M., Wilfley, D. E., Brownell, K. D., & Rodin, J. (1994). Teasing, body image, and self-esteem in a clinical sample of obese women. *Addictive Behaviors, 19,* 443–450.

Hansen, D. L., Toubro, S., Stock, M. J., Macdonald, I. A., & Astrup, A. (1998). Thermogenic effects of sibutramine in humans. *American Journal of Clinical Nutrition, 68,* 1180–1186.

Harnack, L. J., Jeffery, R. W., & Boutelle, K. N. (2000). Temporal trends in energy intake in the United States: An ecologic perspective. *American Journal of Clinical Nutrition, 71,* 1478–1484.

Harris, J. K., French, S. A., Jeffery, R. W., McGovern, P. G., & Wing, R. R. (1994). Dietary and physical activity correlates of long-term weight loss. *Obesity Research, 2,* 307–313.

Hartz, A. J., Barboriak, P. N., Wong, A., Katayama, K. P., & Rimm, A. A. (1979). The association of obesity with infertility and related menstrual abnormalities in women. *International Journal of Obesity, 3,* 57–73.

Havlik, R. J., Hubert, H. B., Fabsitz, R. R., & Feinleib, M. (1983). Weight and hypertension. *Annals of Internal Medicine, 98,* 855–859.

Hensrud, D. D. (2000). Pharmacotherapy for obesity. *Medical Clinics of North America, 84,* 463–476.

Heymsfield, S. B., Greenberg, A. S., Fujioka, K., Dixon, R. M., Kushner, R., Hunt, T., et al. (1999). Recombinant leptin for weight loss in obese and lean adults: A randomized, controlled, dose-escalation trial. *Journal of the American Medical Association, 282,* 1568–1575.

Hill, J. O., Drougas, H., & Peters, J. C. (1993). Obesity treatment: Can diet composition play a role? *Annals of Internal Medicine, 119,* 694–697.

Hill, J. O., Hauptman, J., Anderson, J. W., Fujioka, K., O'Neil, P. M., Smith, D. K., et al. (1999). Orlistat, a lipase inhibitor, for weight maintenance after conventional dieting: A 1-year study. *American Journal of Clinical Nutrition, 69,* 1108–1116.

Hill, J. O., & Peters, J. C. (1998). Environmental contributions to the obesity epidemic. *Science, 280,* 1371–1374.

Hill, J. O., Wyatt, H. R., & Melanson, E. L. (2000). Genetic and environmental contributions to obesity. *Medical Clinics of North America, 84,* 333–346.

Hodge, A. M., Dowse, G. K., Zimmet, P. Z., & Collins, V. R. (1995). Prevalence and secular trends in obesity in Pacific and Indian Ocean island populations. *Obesity Research, 3*(Suppl. 2), S77–S87.

Hubert, H. B., Feinleib, M., McNamara, P. M., & Castelli, W. P. (1983). Obesity as an independent risk factor for cardiovascular disease: A 26-year follow-up of participants in the Framingham Heart Study. *Circulation, 67,* 968–977.

Insull, W., Henderson, M., Prentice, R., Thompson, D. J., Moskowitz, M., & Gorbach, S. (1990). Results of a feasibility study of a low-fat diet. *Archives of Internal Medicine, 150,* 421–427.

Jacobson, M. F., & Brownell, K. D. (2000). Small taxes on soft drinks and snack foods to promote health. *American Journal of Public Health, 90,* 854–857.

Jakicic, J. M., Winters, C., Lang, W., & Wing, R. R. (1999). Effects of intermittent exercise and use of home exercise equipment on adherence, weight loss, and fitness in overweight women: A randomized trial. *Journal of the American Medical Association, 282,* 1554–1560.

James, W. P. T. (1995). A public health approach to the problem of obesity. *International Journal of Obesity, 19,* S37–S45.

James, W. P. T. (1996). The epidemiology of obesity. In D. J. Chadwick & G. C. Cardew (Eds.), *The origins and consequences of obesity* (pp. 1–16). Chichester, England: Wiley.

Jeffery, R. W., Adlis, S. A., & Forster, J. L. (1991). Prevalence of dieting among working men and women: The healthy worker project. *Health Psychology, 10,* 274–281.

Jeffery, R. W., Drewnowski, A., Epstein, L. H., Stunkard, A. J., Wilson, G. T., Wing, R. R., et al. (2000). Long-term maintenance of weight loss: Current status. *Health Psychology, 19*(Suppl. 1), 5–16.

Jeffery, R. W., French, S. A., & Schmid, T. L. (1990). Attributions for dietary failures: Problems reported by participants in the Hypertension Prevention Trial. *Health Psychology, 9,* 315–329.

Jeffery, R. W., & Wing, R. R. (1995). Long-term effects of interventions for weight loss using food provision and monetary incentives. *Journal of Consulting and Clinical Psychology, 63,* 793–796.

Jeffery, R. W., Wing, R. R., Thorson, C., & Burton, L. R. (1998). Use of personal trainers and financial incentives to increase exercise in a behavioral weight-loss program. *Journal of Consulting and Clinical Psychology, 66,* 777–783.

Jeffery, R. W., Wing, R. R., Thorson, C., Burton, L. R., Raether, C., Harvey, J., et al. (1993). Strengthening behavioral interventions for weight loss: A randomized trial of food provision and monetary incentives. *Journal of Consulting and Clinical Psychology, 61,* 1038–1045.

Jones, S. P., Smith, I. G., Kelly, F., & Gray, J. A. (1995). Long term weight loss with sibutramine. *International Journal of Obesity, 19*(Suppl. 2), 41.

Kant, A. K. (2000). Consumption of energy-dense, nutrient-poor foods by adult Americans: Nutritional and health implications. The third National Health and Nutrition Examination Survey, 1988–1994. *American Journal of Clinical Nutrition, 72,* 929–936.

Kern, P. A. (1997). Potential role of TNFalpha and lipoprotein lipase as candidate genes for obesity. *Journal of Nutrition, 127,* 1917S–1922S.

Kern, P. A., Ong, J. M., Saffari, B., & Carty, J. (1990). The effects of weight loss on the activity and expression of adipose-tissue lipoprotein lipase in very obese humans. *New England Journal of Medicine, 322,* 1053–1059.

Keys, A., Fidanza, F., Karvonen, M. J., Kimura, N., & Taylor, H. (1972). Indices of relative weight and obesity. *Journal of Chronic Diseases, 25,* 329–343.

Knoll Pharmaceutical Co. (2000). Meridia (sibutramine hydrochloride monohydrate): Prescribing information. In *Physician's desk reference* (pp. 1509–1513). Montvale, NJ: Drug Information Services Group.

Kral, J. G. (1989). Surgical treatment of obesity. *Medical Clinics of North America, 73,* 251–269.

Kral, J. G. (1995). Surgical interventions for obesity. In K. D. Brownell & C. G. Fairburn (Eds.), *Eating disorders and obesity: A comprehensive handbook* (pp. 510–515). New York: Guilford Press.

Kramer, F. M., Jeffery, R. W., Forster, J. L., & Snell, M. K. (1989). Long-term follow-up of behavioral treatment for obesity:

Patterns of weight gain among men and women. *International Journal of Obesity, 13,* 124–136.

Krosnick, A. (2000). The diabetes and obesity epidemic among the Pima Indians. *New England Journal of Medicine, 97*(8), 31–37.

Kuczmarski, R. J., Carrol, M. D., Flegal, K. M., & Troiano, R. P. (1997). Varying body mass index cutoff points to describe overweight prevalence among U.S. adults: NHANES III (1988–1994). *Obesity Research, 5,* 542–548.

Kuczmarski, R. J., Flegal, K. M., Campbell, S. M., & Johnson, C. L. (1994). Increasing prevalence of overweight among U.S. adults. The National Health and Nutrition Examination Surveys, 1960 to 1991. *Journal of the American Medical Association, 272,* 205–211.

Kumanyika, S. (1987). Obesity in Black women. *Epidemiology Review, 9,* 31–50.

Kushner, R. (1997). The treatment of obesity. A call for prudence and professionalism. *Archives of Internal Medicine, 157,* 602–604.

Lee, C. D., Blair, S. N., & Jackson, A. S. (1999). Cardiorespiratory fitness, body composition, and all-cause and cardiovascular disease mortality in men. *American Journal of Clinical Nutrition, 69,* 373–380.

Leermakers, E. A., Dunn, A. L., & Blair, S. N. (2000). Exercise management of obesity. *Medical Clinics of North America, 84,* 419–440.

Leermakers, E. A., Perri, M. G., Shigaki, C. L., & Fuller, P. R. (1999). Effects of exercise-focused versus weight-focused maintenance programs on the management of obesity. *Addictive Behaviors, 24,* 219–227.

Leibel, R. L., Rosenbaum, M., & Hirsch, J. (1995). Changes in energy expenditure resulting from altered body weight. *New England Journal of Medicine, 332,* 673–674.

Leigh, J. P., Fries, J. F., & Hubert, H. B. (1992). Gender and race differences in the correlation between body mass and education in the 1971–1975 NHANES I. *Journal of Epidemiology and Community Health, 46,* 191–196.

Levin, B. E. (2000). The obesity epidemic: Metabolic imprinting on genetically susceptible neural circuits. *Obesity Research, 8,* 342–347.

Lohman, T. G. (2002). Body Composition. In K. D. Brownell & C. G. Fairburn (Eds.), *Eating disorders and obesity: A comprehensive handbook* (2nd ed., pp. 62–66). New York: Guilford Press.

Long, S. D., O'Brien, K., MacDonald, K. G., Jr., Leggett-Frazier, N., Swanson, M. S., Pories W. J., et al. (1994). Weight loss in severely obese subjects prevents the progression of impaired glucose tolerance to type-II diabetes: A longitudinal intervention study. *Diabetes Care, 17,* 372–375.

Loube, D. I., Loube, A. A., & Milter, M. M. (1994). Weight loss for obstructive sleep apnea: The optimal therapy for obese patients. *Journal of the American Dietetic Association, 94,* 1291–1295.

MacDonald, K. G., Jr., Long, S. D., Swanson, M. S., Brown, B. M., Morris, P., Dohm, G. L., et al. (1997). The gastric bypass operation reduces the progression and mortality of noninsulin-dependent diabetes mellitus. *Journal of Gastrointestinal Surgery, 1,* 213–220.

Marlatt, G. A., & George, W. H. (1998). Relapse prevention and the maintenance of optimal health. In S. A. Shumaker, E. B. Schron, J. K. Ockene, & W. L. McBee (Eds.), *The handbook of health behavior change* (2nd ed., pp. 33–58). New York: Springer.

Marlatt, G. A., & Gordon, J. R. (1985). *Relapse prevention: Maintenance strategies in the treatment of addictive behaviors.* New York: Guilford Press.

McCrory, M. A., Fuss, P. J., Hays, N. P., Vinken, A. G., Greenberg, A. S., & Roberts, S. B. (1999). Overeating in America: Association between restaurant food consumption and body fatness in healthy adult men and women ages 19 to 80. *Obesity Research, 7,* 564–571.

McGinnis, J. M., & Foege, W. H. (1993). Actual causes of death in the United States. *Journal of the American Medical Association, 270,* 2207–2212.

McGuire, M., Wing, R., Klem, M., Lang, W., & Hill, J. (1999). What predicts weight regain in a group of successful weight losers? *Journal of Consulting and Clinical Psychology, 67,* 177–185.

Metropolitan Life Insurance Company. (1983). Metropolitan height and weight tables. *Statistic Bulletin of the Metropolitan Life Foundation, 64,* 3–9.

Mokdad, A. H., Serdula, M. K., Dietz, W. H., Bowman, B. A., Marks, J. S., & Koplan, J. P. (1999). The spread of the obesity epidemic in the United States. *Journal of the American Medical Association, 282,* 1519–1522.

Mokdad, A. H., Serdula, M. K., Dietz, W. H., Bowman, B. A., Marks, J. S., & Koplan, J. P. (2000). The continuing epidemic of obesity in the United States. *Journal of the American Medical Association, 284,* 1650–1651.

Montague, C. T., Farooqi, I. S., Whitehead, J. P., Soos, M. A., Rau, H., Wareham, N. J., et al. (1997). Congenital leptin deficiency is associated with severe early-onset obesity in humans. *Nature, 387,* 903–908.

National Heart, Lung, and Blood Institute. (1998). Obesity education initiative expert panel on the identification, evaluation, and treatment of overweight and obesity in adults. *Obesity Research, 6*(Suppl. 2).

National Institutes of Health. (1992). Gastrointestinal surgery for severe obesity. Proceedings of a National Institutes of Health Consensus Development Conference. *American Journal of Clinical Nutrition, 55,* S487–S619.

National Institutes of Health Consensus Development Panel on the Health Implications of Obesity. (1985). Health implications of obesity. *Annals of Internal Medicine, 103,* 147–151.

Nestle, M., & Jacobson, M. F. (2000). Halting the obesity epidemic: A public health policy approach. *Public Health Report, 115,* 12–24.

Nestle, M., & Woteki, C. (1999). Interpretation of dietary change in the United States: Fat as an indicator. *Appetite, 32,* 107–112.

Norris, J., Harnack, L., Carmichael, S., Pouane, T., Wakimoto, P., & Block, G. (1997). U.S. trends in nutrient intake: The 1987 and 1992 National Health Interview Surveys. *American Journal of Public Health, 87,* 740–746.

Paffenbarger, R. S., & Lee, I. M. (1996). Physical activity and fitness for health and longevity. *Research Quarterly for Exercise and Sport, 67,* 11–28.

Perri, M. G. (2002). Improving maintenance in behavioral treatment. In K. D. Brownell & C. G. Fairburn (Eds.), *Eating disorders and obesity: A comprehensive handbook* (2nd ed., pp. 593–598). New York: Guilford Press.

Perri, M. G., & Corsica, J. A. (2002). Improving the maintenance of weight lost in behavioral treatment of obesity. In T. A. Wadden & A. J. Stunkard (Eds.), *Obesity handbook* (pp. 357–379). New York: Guilford Press.

Perri, M. G., & Fuller, P. R. (1995). Success and failure in the treatment of obesity: Where do we go from here? *Medicine, Exercise, Nutrition and Health, 4,* 255–272.

Perri, M. G., Martin, A. D., Leermakers, E. A., Sears, S. F., & Notelovitz, M. (1997). Effects of group- versus home-based exercise in the treatment of obesity. *Journal of Consulting and Clinical Psychology, 65,* 278–285.

Perri, M. G., McAdoo, W. G., McAllister, D. A., Lauer, J. B., Jordan, R. C., Yancey, D. Z., et al. (1987). Effects of peer support and therapist contact on long-term weight loss. *Journal of Consulting and Clinical Psychology, 55,* 615–617.

Perri, M. G., McAdoo, W. G., McAllister, D. A., Lauer, J. B., & Yancey, D. Z. (1986). Enhancing the efficacy of behavior therapy for obesity: Effects of aerobic exercise and a multicomponent maintenance program. *Journal of Consulting and Clinical Psychology, 54,* 670–675.

Perri, M. G., McAdoo, W. G., Spevak, P. A., & Newlin, D. B. (1984). Effect of a multi-component maintenance program on long-term weight loss. *Journal of Consulting and Clinical Psychology, 52,* 480–481.

Perri, M. G., McAllister, D. A., Gange, J. J., Jordan, R. C., McAdoo, W. G., & Nezu, A. M. (1988). Effects of four maintenance programs on the long-term management of obesity. *Journal of Consulting and Clinical Psychology, 56,* 529–534.

Perri, M. G., Nezu, A. M., McKelvey, W. F., Shermer, R. L., Renjilian, D. A., & Viegener, B. J. (2001). Relapse prevention training and problem-solving therapy in the long-term management of obesity. *Journal of Consulting and Clinical Psychology, 69,* 722–726.

Perri, M. G., Nezu, A. M., Patti, E. T., & McCann, K. L. (1989). Effect of length of treatment on weight loss. *Journal of Consulting and Clinical Psychology, 57,* 450–452.

Perri, M. G., Nezu, A. M., & Viegener, B. J. (1992). *Improving the long-term management of obesity: Theory, research, and clinical guidelines.* New York: Wiley.

Perri, M. G., Shapiro, R. M., Ludwig, W. W., Twentyman, C. T., & McAdoo, W. G. (1984). Maintenance strategies for the treatment of obesity: An evaluation of relapse prevention training and post-treatment contact by mail and telephone. *Journal of Consulting and Clinical Psychology, 52,* 404–413.

Pingitore, R., Dugoni, B. L., Tindale, R. S., & Spring, B. (1994). Bias against overweight job applicants in a simulated employment interview. *Journal of Applied Psychology, 79,* 909–917.

Pi-Sunyer, F. X. (1999). Co-morbidities of overweight and obesity: Current evidence and research issues. *Medicine and Science in Sports and Exercise, 31*(Suppl. 11), S602–S608.

Poston, W. S., & Foreyt, J. P. (1999). Obesity is an environmental issue. *Atherosclerosis, 146,* 201–209.

Pouliot, M. C., Despres, J. P., Lemieux, S., Moorjani, S., Bouchard, C., Tremblay, A., et al. (1994). Waist circumference and abdominal sagittal diameter: Best simple anthropometric indexes of abdominal visceral adipose tissue accumulation and related cardiovascular risk in men and women. *American Journal of Cardiology, 73,* 460–488.

Prior, I. A. (1971). The price of civilization. *Nutrition Today, 6,* 2–11.

Putnam, J. J., & Allshouse, J. E. (1996). Food consumption, prices, and expenditures, 1970–1994. Washington, DC: U.S. Department of Agriculture.

Rand, C. S., & Macgregor, A. M. (1990). Morbidly obese patients perceptions of social discrimination before and after surgery for obesity. *Southern Medical Journal, 83,* 1390–1395.

Ravussin, E., & Swinburn, B. A. (1993). Energy metabolism. In143 A. J. Stunkard & T. A. Wadden (Eds.), *Obesity: Theory and therapy* (2nd ed., pp. 97–124). New York: Raven.

Ravussin, E., Valencia, M. E., Esparza, J., Bennett, P. H., & Schultz, L. O. (1994). Effects of a traditional lifestyle on obesity in Pima Indians. *Diabetes Care, 17,* 1067–1074.

Rexrode, K. M., Hennekens, C. H., Willett, W. C., Colditz, G. A., Stampfer, M. J., Rich-Edwards, J. W., et al. (1997). A prospective study of body mass index, weight change, and risk of stroke in women. *Journal of the American Medical Association, 277,* 1539–1545.

Roche Laboratories. (1999–2000). Xenical (orlistat): Prescribing information. In *Physician's desk reference* (pp. 2693–2696). Montvale, NJ: Drug Information Services Group.

Rodin, J., Schank, D., & Striegel-Moore, R. (1989). Psychological features of obesity. *Medical Clinics of North America, 73,* 47–66.

Rosen, J. C., & Gross, J. (1987). Prevalence of weight reducing and weight gaining in adolescent girls and boys. *Health Psychology, 6,* 131–147.

Rucker, C. E., & Cash, T. F. (1992). Body images, body-size perceptions, and eating behaviors among African-American and White college women. *International Journal of Eating Disorders, 12,* 291–299.

Sallis, J. F., McKenzie, T. L., Alcaraz, J. E., Kolody, B., Faucette, N., & Hovell, M. F. (1997). The effects of a 2-year physical education program (SPARK) on physical activity and fitness in elementary school students. Sports, Play and Active Recreation for Kids. *American Journal of Public Health, 87,* 1328–1334.

Serdula, M. K., Mokdad, A. H., Williamson, D. F., Galuska, D. A., Medlein, J. M., & Heath, G. W. (1999). Prevalence of attempting weight loss and strategies for controlling weight. *Journal of the American Medical Association, 282,* 1353–1358.

Shah, M., Hannan, P. J., & Jeffery, R. W. (1991). Secular trends in body mass index in the adult population of three communities from the upper mid-western part of the USA: the Minnesota Heart Health Program. *International Journal of Obesity, 15,* 499–503.

Sherwood, N. E., Jeffery, R. W., & Wing, R. R. (1999). Binge status as a predictor of weight loss treatment outcome. *International Journal of Obesity, 23,* 485–493.

Sjöstrom, C. D., Lissner, L., Wedel, H., & Sjöstrom, L. (1999). Reduction in incidence of diabetes, hypertension and lipid disturbances intentional weight loss induced by bariatric surgery: The SOS Intervention Study. *Obesity Research, 7,* 477–484.

Sjöstrom, L., Narbro, K., & Sjöstrom, D. (1995). Costs and benefits when treating obesity. *International Journal of Obesity, 19*(Suppl. 6), S9–S12.

Sjöstrom, L., Rissanen, A., Andersen, T., Boldrin, M., Golay, A., Koppeschaar, H. P., et al. (1998). Randomised placebo-controlled trial of orlistat for weight loss and prevention of weight regain in obese patients. European Multicentre Orlistat Study Group. *Lancet, 352,* 167–172.

Smith, D. E., & Wing, R. R. (1991). Diminished weight loss and behavioral compliance using repeated diets in obese women with Type II diabetes. *Health Psychology, 10,* 378–383.

Spitzer, R. L., Yanovski, S., Wadden, T., Wing, R., Marcus, M. D., Stunkard, A., et al. (1993). Binge eating disorder: Its further validation in a multisite study. *International Journal of Eating Disorders, 13,* 137–153.

Stampfer, M. J., Maclure, K. M., Colditz, G. A., Manson, J. E., & Willett, W. C. (1992). Risk of symptomatic gallstones in women with obesity. *American Journal of Clinical Nutrition, 55,* 652–658.

Stock, M. J. (1999). Gluttony and thermogenesis revisited. *International Journal of Obesity, 23,* 1105–1117.

Story, M., Mays, R. W., Bishop, D. B., Perry, C. L., Taylor, G., Smyth, M., et al. (2000). 5-A-Day Power Plus: Process evaluation of a multicomponent elementary school program to increase fruit and vegetable consumption. *Health Education Behavior, 27,* 187–200.

Stunkard, A. J., Harris, J. R., Pedersen, N. L., & McClearn, G. E. (1990). The body mass index of twins who have been reared apart. *New England Journal of Medicine, 322,* 1483–1487.

Stunkard, A. J., & Sobal, J. (1995). Psychosocial consequences of obesity. In K. D. Brownell & C. G. Fairburn (Eds.), *Eating disorders and obesity: A comprehensive handbook* (pp. 417–421). New York: Guilford Press.

Thomas, P. R. (Ed.). (1995). *Weighing the options: Criteria for evaluating weight management programs.* Washington, DC: National Academy Press.

Troiano, R. P., Frongillo, E. A., Sobal, J., & Levitsky, D. A. (1996). The relationship between body weight and mortality: A quantitative analysis of combined information from existing studies. *International Journal of Obesity, 20,* 63–75.

U.S. Department of Health and Human Services. (1996). *Physical activity and health: A report of the surgeon general.* Atlanta, GA: International Medical.

Vaisse, C., Clement, K., Durand, E., Hercberg, S., Guy-Grand, B., & Froguel, P. (2000). Melanocortin-4 receptor mutations are a frequent and heterogeneous cause of morbid obesity. *Journal of Clinical Investigation, 106,* 253–262.

Wadden, T. A., Berkowitz, R. I., Sarwer, D. B., Prus-Wisniewski, R., & Steinberg, C. M. (2001). Benefits of lifestyle modification in the pharmacologic treatment of obesity: A randomized trial. *Archives of Internal Medicine, 161,* 218–227.

Wadden, T. A., & Foster, G. D. (1992). Behavioral assessment and treatment of markedly obese patients. In T. A. Wadden & T. B. Van Itallie (Eds.), *Treatment of the seriously obese patient* (pp. 290–330). New York: Guilford Press.

Wadden, T. A., & Foster, G. D. (2000). Behavioral treatment of obesity. *Medical Clinics of North America, 84,* 441–461.

Wadden, T. A., Foster, G. D., & Letizia, K. A. (1994). One-year behavioral treatment of obesity: Comparison of moderate and severe caloric restriction and the effects of weight maintenance therapy. *Journal of Consulting and Clinical Psychology, 62,* 165–171.

Wadden, T. A., & Letizia, K. A. (1992). Predictors of attrition and weight loss in patients treated by moderate and severe caloric restriction. In T. A. Wadden & T. B. Van Itallie (Eds.), *Treatment of the seriously obese patient* (pp. 383–410). New York: Guilford Press.

Wadden, T. A., Sarwer, D. B., & Berkowitz, R. I. (1999). Behavioral treatment of the overweight patient. *Bailliere's Best Practice and Research in Clinical Endocrinology and Metabolism, 13,* 93–107.

Wadden, T. A., Vogt, R. A., Andersen, R. E., Barlett, S. J., Foster, G. D., Kuehnel, R. H., et al. (1997). Exercise in the treatment of obesity: Effects of four interventions on body composition, resting energy expenditure, appetite, and mood. *Journal of Consulting and Clinical Psychology, 65,* 269–277.

Wadden, T. A., Womble, L. G., Stunkard, A. J., & Anderson, D. A. (2002). Psychosocial consequences of obesity and weight loss. In T. A. Wadden & A. J. Stunkard (Eds.), *Obesity Handbook* (pp. 144–169). New York: Guilford Press.

Willett, W. C., Manson, J. E., Stampfer, M. J., Colditz, G. A., Rosner, B., Speizer, F. E., et al. (1995). Weight, weight change, and coronary heart disease in women: Risk within the "normal" weight range. *Journal of the American Medical Association, 273,* 461–465.

Williamson, D. F. (1999). Pharmacotherapy for obesity. *Journal of the American Medical Association, 281,* 278–280.

Wilson, G. T. (1996). Acceptance and change in the treatment of eating disorders and obesity. *Behavior Therapy, 27,* 417–439.

Wing, R. R. (1999). Physical activity in the treatment of the adulthood overweight and obesity: Current evidence and research issues. *Medicine and Science in Sports and Exercise, 31,* S547–S552.

Wing, R. R., & Jeffery, R. W. (1999). Benefits of recruiting participants with friends and increasing social support for weight loss and maintenance. *Journal of Consulting and Clinical Psychology, 67,* 132–138.

Wing, R. R., Jeffery, R. W., Hellerstedt, W. L., & Burton, L. R. (1996). Effect of frequent phone contacts and optional food provision on maintenance of weight loss. *Annals of Behavioral Medicine, 18,* 172–176.

Wolf, A. M., & Colditz, G. A. (1998). Current estimates of the economic costs of obesity in the United States. *Obesity Research, 6,* 97–106.

World Health Organization. (1998). *Obesity: Preventing and managing the global epidemic. Report of a WHO Consultation on Obesity.* Geneva: Author.

Zhang, Y., Proenca, R., Maffei, M., Barone, M., Leopold, L., & Friedman, J. M. (1994). Positional cloning of the mouse obese gene and its human homologue. *Nature, 372,* 425–432.

CHAPTER 7

Tobacco Dependence

GARY E. SWAN, KAREN S. HUDMON, AND TALINE V. KHROYAN

Tobacco dependence is determined by psychosocial, environmental, and biological factors. Individual differences in exposure to various environmental risk factors influence susceptibility to become addicted to nicotine initially just as do differences in a multitude of biological and physiological characteristics. Moreover, the extent to which the various risk factors interact with each other within and across these broad sources of individual variation provide additional sources of influence that can determine an individual's likelihood of becoming addicted to nicotine once exposed. Smoking behavior can be viewed as a sequence of specific components that vary across the life-cycle. Thus, just as biological and environmental factors can exert main and interactive effects to determine susceptibility, so too can they influence the likeli-

Preparation of this chapter was supported in part by grants from the Tobacco-Related Disease Research Program, University of California (7PT2000), the National Cancer Institute (CA71358), and the National Institute on Drug Abuse (DA11170). The authors wish to thank Ms. Kymberli Hemberger for her assistance with the preparation of this manuscript.

hood of maintaining tobacco dependence once it is established, response to treatment for tobacco dependence, and the likelihood of relapse following treatment. This chapter reviews state-of-the-art findings and poses questions in need of further investigation.

Tobacco smoke, inhaled either directly or as second-hand smoke, contains more than 4,000 different compounds, many of which are proven carcinogens (Roberts, 1988). There is substantial evidence suggesting that nicotine plays a pivotal role in mediating the addictive nature of tobacco in humans U.S. Department of Health and Human Services ([USDHHS], 1988). Nicotine is readily absorbed across the respiratory tract epithelium, buccal mucosa (cheek), and skin. Systemic bioavailability through the gastrointestinal tract is limited because of first-pass liver metabolism. After inhalation, nicotine reaches the brain in approximately 10 to 19 seconds (Benowitz, Porchet, Sheiner, & Jacob, 1988), resulting in rapid onset of behaviorally reinforcing effects on the nervous system, including pleasure, relief of anxiety, improved task performance, improved memory, mood modulation, and skeletal muscle relaxation (Benowitz, 1999). These positive effects, mediated by alterations in neurotransmitter levels, give way to negative, withdrawal effects in the absence of nicotine among dependent tobacco users. Withdrawal symptoms include anger/irritability, anxiety, difficulty concentrating, drowsiness, fatigue, hunger/weight gain, impatience, and restlessness (Hughes, Gust, Skoog, Keenan, & Fenwick, 1991). These symptoms tend to manifest in the first 24 hours, peak in the first 1 to 2 weeks, and generally resolve within 30 days after quitting. Although many patients report cravings for cigarettes many months or years after quitting.

An estimated 47.2 million Americans smoke (Centers for Disease Control and Prevention, 2000); 70% want to quit completely (Centers for Disease Control and Prevention, 1994); and each year, approximately 17 million adult smokers in the United States make a serious attempt to quit. Despite decades of research into improving methods for attaining cessation, smoking quit rates remain low—annually, only an estimated 2.5% are able to quit permanently (Centers for Disease Control and Prevention, 1993). Economically, the burden of smoking is enormous, costing the United States an estimated $72 billion annually in lost productivity and medical care (Horgan, Marsden, & Larson, 1993).

Figure 7.1, a summary of numerous studies (Chassin, Presson, Sherman, & Edwards, 1990; Choi, Pierce, Gilpin, Farkas, & Berry, 1997; Flay, 1999; Gilpin, Lee, Evans, & Pierce, 1994; Gritz et al., 1998; Jessor & Jessor, 1977; Johnston, O'Malley, & Bachman, 1991, 1995; Kendler, 1999), illustrates the development of tobacco dependence. Tobacco dependence consists of several identifiable phases when viewed from a developmental perspective.

Following initial exposure to tobacco, an individual will experiment with it and, assuming that the consequences of experimentation have provided more positive than negative consequences, that individual will acquire regular tobacco use as a feature of his or her behavioral repertoire. To the extent that tobacco use itself acquires an instrumental component (e.g., helping the individual to cope with stress, manage weight, regulate affect), it will be maintained and, depending on the person and environmental conditions, perhaps even strengthen over time (increase in cigarettes smoked per day, for example). There is the possibility that tobacco use will lessen (smoking fewer cigarettes or "lighter" cigarettes) and perhaps extinguish altogether. For many people desiring to quit, however, there begins a process of cessation-reacquisition-relapse that commonly is repeated many times.

BASIC MECHANISMS OF NICOTINE ADDICTION

The diverse effects of nicotine on brain function are mediated by activating nicotinic acetylcholine receptors (nACHRs). The nACHRs are formed by the combination of five α and/or β subunits. Thus far, 11 subunits have been identified in different neuronal populations, those being $\alpha 2$ to $\alpha 9$ and $\beta 2$ to $\beta 4$. In the brain, nACHRs can be divided into two subfamilies: homoligomeric receptors that are composed of identical subunits ($\alpha 7$, $\alpha 8$, or $\alpha 9$ subunits); and heteromeric receptors that are composed of varying combinations of $\alpha 2$, $\alpha 3$, $\alpha 4$, and $\alpha 6$ with either $\beta 2$ or $\beta 4$ and in some cases also with $\alpha 5$ or $\beta 3$ subunits (Clementi, Fornasari, & Gotti, 2000; Paterson & Nordberg, 2000). The nACHRs are found on the cell body

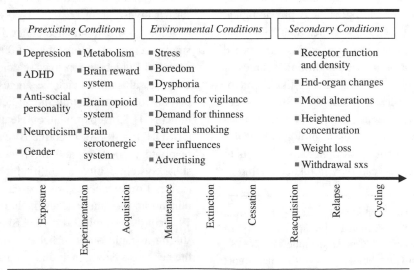

Figure 7.1 A working model of genetic and environmental factors in the developmental span of smoking.

region and axons of many important neurotransmitter systems; stimulation of these receptors can influence the release of other neurotransmitters such as dopamine, norepinephrine, acetylcholine, GABA, and glutamate, leading to behavioral changes associated with arousal, mood, and cognition function (for review, see Clementi et al., 2000; Paterson & Nordberg, 2000).

Similar to other drugs of abuse, nicotine is hypothesized to produce its reinforcing effects by activating the mesocorticolimbic dopamine system (for reviews, see Di Chiara, 2000; Stolerman & Shoaib, 1991; Watkins, Koob, & Markou, 2000). This pathway originates in the ventral tegmental area (VTA) and projects to the nucleus accumbens (NAc) and other cortical target areas. Nicotine depolarizes dopaminergic neurons in the VTA *in vitro,* and stimulates the release of dopamine in the NAc *in vivo* (Calabresi, Lacey, & North, 1989; Imperato, Mulas, & Di Chiara, 1986). In humans, functional magnetic resonance imaging reveals that an acute nicotine injection results in an increase in neuronal activity in limbic and cortical brain regions such as the amygdala, NAc, cingulate, and frontal cortical lobes (Stein et al., 1998). This increase is accompanied by increases in behavioral measures of feelings such as "rush," "high," and drug liking (Stein et al., 1998). In animals, intravenous (i.v.) nicotine self-administration in the rat produces regional brain activation in the NAc, medial prefrontal cortex, and medial caudate area, as assessed by c-Fos and Fos-related protein expression (Pagliusi, Tessari, DeVevey, Chiamulera, & Pich, 1996; Pich et al., 1997).

Variability in the metabolism of nicotine across individuals might contribute to nicotine's addictive potential. For example, "slow" metabolizers of nicotine may be more subject to the aversive properties of nicotine because of the higher levels of untransformed nicotine per unit time and, consequently, may use less tobacco. Conversely, "fast" metabolizers of nicotine may be less subject to nicotine toxicity because of lower levels of nicotine and, consequently, need to use more tobacco per unit time to maintain sufficient levels of nicotine. It has been suggested that the nicotine metabolism pathway may be altered via genetic polymorphisms (Idle, 1990). Studies have examined genetic variation of enzymes involved in the metabolism of nicotine, however, the outcomes are not conclusive and warrant further investigation. Understanding of individual differences in nicotine metabolism and their relationship to susceptibility for becoming and/or remaining a regular tobacco user is in the early stages. Increased information is needed on the full array of genes involved in the various metabolic processes, the extent of individual variation in the genetic substrate, along with a better appreciation of how these differences influence susceptibility to become addicted to nicotine.

ANIMAL MODELS OF NICOTINE ADDICTION

Animal models examining the reinforcing effects of nicotine have been used to assess the various contributing factors of tobacco dependence as observed in the human population. The extent to which animal models can be used to interpret the underlying nature of dependence in humans depends mainly on the validity of the model. Animal models have been evaluated based on predictive, face, and construct validity (Willner, 1991). Predictive validity of an animal model is defined as "performance in the test predicts performance in the condition being modeled." For example, valid animal models of drug reward can differentiate between drugs that are abused by humans and those that are not and can therefore be used to evaluate whether a novel drug possesses abuse liability as well as to detect potential candidate medications for prevention of drug addiction. Face validity is an indication of whether the "behavioral and pharmacological qualities" of an animal model are similar in nature to those seen in the human condition. Construct validity is assessed by determining whether there is a "sound theoretical rationale" between the animal model and the human condition being modeled (Willner, 1991). Table 7.1 addresses the questions that assess the validity of each animal model discussed next as related to nicotine addiction.

Several animal models have been used to examine the reinforcing effects of nicotine. In the following paragraphs, we discuss methodology, findings directly related to nicotine addiction, and validity (see Table 7.1) of two frequently used animal models, the self-administration and the place-conditioning paradigms.

Self-Administration

The self-administration (SA) paradigm provides a measure of the reinforcing effects of drugs. The animal learns the relationship of its behavior such as pressing a lever or a nosepoke and a reinforcer such as an i.v. injection of a drug. If the relationship between the animal's behavior and the response is reinforcing, the probability of the animal continuing the behavior is increased. It has taken 10 to 15 years of research with animals to map out the conditions that will support reliable SA of nicotine. Nicotine SA has been demonstrated in nonhuman primates (Goldberg, Spealman, & Goldberg, 1981), rats (Corrigall & Coen, 1989; Donny, Caggiula, Knopf, & Brown, 1995), and mice (Picciotto et al., 1998; Stolerman, Naylor, Elmer, & Goldberg, 1999). The role of the mesocorticolimbic dopamine system in mediating nicotine SA has also been examined. For example, lesions of dopaminergic neurons in the NAc, and administration of

TABLE 7.1 Validity of Animal Models as Related to Human Tobacco Dependence

Animal model	Predictive Validity	Face Validity	Construct Validity
	"Does the animal model provide a valid measure of the reinforcing effects of nicotine?"	"Does the animal model have phenomenological similarities with human smoking behavior?"	"Is the theoretical premise underlying the animal model similar to that for tobacco dependence in humans?" and "Is there evidence for the role of dopamine in modulating the effects of nicotine?"
Self-administration (SA)	*Moderate-High:* Animals will self-administer nicotine, *however,* under limited experimental conditions.	*High:* • Animals have control over nicotine delivery. • SA paradigm provides a measure of compulsive nicotine-taking behavior. • The intravenous route of SA is used, providing a route allowing rapid absorption.	*High:* • SA provides a good measure of reinforcement since primary reinforcers (such as food and water) are also self-administered. • Studies have examined the importance of the dopamine system in mediating nicotine SA.
Place-conditioning (PC)	*Moderate-High:* Nicotine can produce PC, *however,* nicotine PC has been difficult to establish.	*Moderate:* • Unlike human nicotine consumption, nicotine delivery is passive with the PC animal model. *But:* • Intravenous route of administration can be used (rapid absorption). • Animals receive repeated injections of nicotine over many days. • Animals "seek" nicotine similar to humans. • The environment paired with nicotine produces a conditioned response (similar to humans).	*Moderate-High:* • PC paradigm provides a valid measure of both nicotine-induced reward and aversion (at higher doses). PC is a valid model of incentive motivation. • Neurochemical evidence is sparse. Only one reported study of the importance of dopamine in acquisition of nicotine PC.

antagonists systemically and directly into the VTA produces dose-related decreases in nicotine SA (Corrigall & Coen, 1991; Corrigall, Coen, & Adamson, 1994; Corrigall, Franklin, Coen, & Clarke, 1992). Further evidence for possible long-term adaptations in the mesocorticolimbic system stems from research examining activation of immediate early genes such as the transcription factor c-Fos induced in neurons following various environmental and pharmacological manipulations. Nicotine SA increases c-Fos-related antigens expressed in the NAc as well as other regions similar to that seen with cocaine SA (Pagliusi et al., 1996; Pich et al., 1997). Thus, nicotine self-administration can result from an action of nicotine on nAChRs that activate the mesocorticolimbic dopamine system.

The SA paradigm has high predictive validity since compounds that are deemed addictive in humans will also support SA. For example, similar to other drugs of abuse such as cocaine and morphine, animals will self-administer nicotine (see above). The SA paradigm also possesses a high degree of face validity. First, similar to human drug intake, animals are given control over the drug administration and they perform a required schedule of responses to obtain the drug. Second, because the current smoking epidemic involves routes of administration that allow rapid distribution to brain tissue, the i.v. route often used in animal SA studies is a route that closely mimics human drug intake. The degree of construct validity associated with the SA paradigm is high. In humans, nicotine becomes addictive in nature partially because it produces reinforcing interoceptive stimuli or positive subjective effects. Similarly, a drug is said to maintain SA behavior in animals because it acts as a positive reinforcer. Thus, the addictive nature of smoking in humans is assumed to be the same as that measured by the SA paradigm. With regard to construct validity, the SA paradigm also provides evidence for the role of dopamine in mediating the reinforcing effects of nicotine. The various aspects of validity of the SA model as a measure for nicotine addiction are summarized in Table 7.1.

The Place-Conditioning Paradigm

The place-conditioning (PC) paradigm has also been used to measure the rewarding as well as the aversive properties of drugs of abuse. The PC paradigm measures the incentive motivational properties of stimuli that become associated with drug effects through classical conditioning. The drug is administered in a distinct environment. After several pairings, the environment becomes associated with the effects of the drug, thereby acquiring incentive-motivational properties. Thus, the environment provides cues eliciting either

approach (i.e., conditioned place preference, CPP) or avoidance (i.e., conditioned place aversion, CPA) behaviors depending on whether rewarding or aversive properties of the drug have been conditioned, respectively.

Nicotine-induced PC has been examined in rodents; however, similar to nicotine SA, nicotine-induced PC has been difficult to establish (Clarke & Fibiger, 1987). Nicotine-induced CPP and CPA have been shown in a variety of strains of rats and mice (Acquas, Carboni, Leone, & Di Chiara, 1989; Calcagnetti & Schechter, 1994; Fudala, Teoh, & Iwamoto, 1985; Martin & Itzhak, 2000; Schechter, Meehan, & Schechter, 1995). The role of dopamine in mediating nicotine-induced CPP has not been extensively studied. In one published study, a dopamine receptor antagonist, SCH23390, prevents acquisition of nicotine-induced CPP (Acquas et al., 1989). Further studies are needed to clarify the role of dopamine in mediating the rewarding/aversive effects of nicotine as measured by the PC paradigm.

The PC paradigm is considered to have a high degree of predictive validity since drugs that are addictive in humans also produce CPP in animals. On the other hand, the PC paradigm is thought to possess a low degree of face validity relative to the SA paradigm in regard to the method of drug delivery. In the PC paradigm, nicotine delivery is passive and does not depend on the animal's behavior, whereas with the SA paradigm the animal actively self-administers nicotine. However, the PC paradigm possesses a certain level of face validity since the environment that is paired with effects of nicotine acquires the status of a conditioned stimulus. Thus, when the animal is given access to both compartments, and the resulting effect is a CPP, the environment is said to have elicited a conditioned response. Conditioned responses also play an important role in human smoking behavior. Previous research has shown that drug-associated environments as well as paraphernalia associated with drug taking (the conditioned stimuli) can evoke both physiological and psychological drug-related responses (Ehrman, Robbins, Childress, & O'Brien, 1992). This parallel seen with human smoking behavior and the PC paradigm provides evidence for some degree of face validity with this animal model. The PC paradigm possesses a high degree of construct validity since it measures drug-induced reinforcement or incentive motivation. These theoretical constructs play a fundamental role in addiction theory (T. Robinson & Berridge, 1993). Similar to the SA paradigm, findings using the PC paradigm also support the dopamine hypothesis of addiction. Evidence supporting the latter is sparse in regard to nicotine-induced PC since only one published experiment has examined the effects of a dopamine antagonist (see Acquas et al., 1989). However, previous research has thoroughly examined the effects of dopamine in mediating CPP induced by other drugs of abuse such as cocaine, amphetamine, and morphine (Hoffman, 1989; Schechter & Calcagnetti, 1993). Various aspects of validity as related to the PC paradigm are summarized in Table 7.1.

Preclinical Genetic Models: Insights into Individual Differences in Nicotine-Induced Behavior

Animal studies using inbred strains have indicated that there are potential strain differences providing some insight as to why there are individual differences in the development of nicotine addiction in humans. Indeed, when inbred strains of mice are provided with a choice of nicotine or vehicle solutions, the strains differ dramatically in their self-selection of nicotine (Crawley et al., 1997; Meliska, Bartke, McGlacken, & Jensen, 1995; S. Robinson, Marks, & Collins, 1996). Across the different strains, the higher the preference for the nicotine solution, the lower the sensitivity to nicotine-induced seizures (S. Robinson et al., 1996). Thus, the negative toxic actions of nicotine limit nicotine consumption in mice. There are also differences in SA of nicotine by inbred strains of mice, where nicotine can serve as a positive reinforcer in c75BL/6 mice but not in DBA/2 mice (Stolerman et al., 1999).

Genetically altered mice with certain targeted gene mutations are also becoming important tools in studying the molecular nature of nicotine addiction (Mohammed, 2000; Picciotto et al., 1998). These "knock out" mice are mutant mice lacking genetic information encoding specific nACHR subunits. Because the β2 subunit is widely expressed in the central nervous system and is found in the mesocorticolimbic dopamine system, the reinforcing effects of nicotine have been examined in β2-knockout mice (Picciotto et al., 1998). Picciotto et al. (1998) report that nicotine-induced dopamine release in the ventral striatum is only observed in wild-type mice and not in β2-knockout mice. Furthermore, mesencephalic dopamine neurons are no longer responsive in β2-knockout mice. Similar to their wild-type counterparts, β2-knockout mice learned to self-administer cocaine. However, when nicotine was substituted for cocaine, nicotine SA was attenuated in the β2-knockout mice relative to wild-types. These findings suggest that the β2 receptor subtype plays a crucial role in the reinforcing effects of nicotine. Studies using mutant mice provide some insight as to individual differences in tobacco smoking. For example, different expression of nACHR subtypes (i.e., by knocking out various nACHR subunits in animals) can partially account for differences in nicotine effects. Although genetic knockout mice are a powerful tool, research using this technique has not yet reached its full potential. Thus far, the gene of interest is knocked out prior to birth, possibly resulting in compensatory changes in the developing central nervous system of the animal. For a finer assessment of the role of various nACHR subtypes, mutant mice that undergo gene-specific mutations in certain brain regions at a precise time in their adult life are needed. Eventually, this line of research will provide identification of molecular sites that modulate nicotine addiction facilitating medication development for the treatment of tobacco dependence in human smokers.

Relevance of Preclinical Studies to Understanding Tobacco Dependence

Animal models, such as the SA and PC paradigms (discussed previously), provide a unique contribution toward our understanding of tobacco dependence in humans. These models allow the examination of the reinforcing effects of nicotine that are highly relevant to tobacco dependence in humans, and that cannot be easily studied in human subjects mainly for ethical reasons. In animals, potential behavioral effects of pharmacological agents can be more fully characterized. Furthermore, these animal models allow the investigation of the basic underlying neurochemical mechanisms that are relevant to nicotine addiction.

Animal models also can be used to study environmental factors in initiation and maintenance of nicotine addiction. Smokers report that environmental factors such as stress induce smoking behavior and that smoking helps to alleviate stress (McKennell, 1970; USDHHS, 1988). Preclinical studies have shown that environmental stressors can increase corticosterone levels and in turn can alter behavioral responses to administration of drugs of abuse. For example, prenatal stress (Deminiere et al., 1992), isolation (Alexander, Coambs, & Hadaway, 1978; Schenk, Lacelle, Gorman, & Amit, 1987), foot-shocks (Goeders & Guerin, 1994), and exposure to social defeat stress (Miczek & Mutschler, 1996) can activate as well as facilitate SA of psychomotor stimulants and opioids. In addition, exposure to intermittent foot-shock can reinstate heroin (Shaham & Stewart, 1995), cocaine (Ahmed & Koob, 1997; Erb, Shaham, & Stewart, 1996), alcohol (Lê et al., 1998), and nicotine (Buczek, Lê, Stewart, & Shaham, 1999) drug-seeking behavior following extinction and an extended period of abstinence. However, the role of environmental stressors in eliciting nicotine reinforcement using animal models has not been characterized thoroughly. These experiments will lead to the development of animal models of gene-environment interactions in nicotine addiction. Future experiments will provide us with clues as to whether the interactions can be demonstrated, the magnitude of their effect, and the conditions under which the interactions vary in strength.

Next, we present an overview of several of the psychological and social and environmental factors known or suspected to enhance the likelihood of initiation and/or maintenance of regular tobacco use in humans.

SOCIAL AND PSYCHOLOGICAL RISK FACTORS FOR INITIATION AND MAINTENANCE OF TOBACCO USE

Gender and Ethnic Differences

It has been estimated that every day approximately 5,500 youth experiment with cigarettes for the first time and nearly 3,000 young people transition to daily smoking (Gilpin, Choi, Berry, & Pierce, 1999). The factors involved in the initiation of smoking are numerous, and indeed, there are several important studies involving careful longitudinal assessment of environmental, social, and contextual smoking initiation among adolescents (Chassin, Presson, Pitts, & Sherman, 2000; Colder et al., 2001; Duncan, Tildesley, Duncan, & Hops, 1995). Giovino (1999) provides a thorough review of the current state of knowledge of the epidemiology of tobacco use and concludes that male and female adolescents are equally as likely to smoke cigarettes with approximately 20% of persons aged 12 to 17 years in the United States having smoked within the past 30 days. The prevalence of smoking varies as a function of ethnicity. Among male high school seniors, 41% of American Indian/Alaska Natives, 33% of Whites, 29% of Hispanics, 21% for Asian Americans/Pacific Islanders, and 12% of African Americans are current smokers. Among female high school seniors, corresponding prevalence estimates of current smoking for each of the ethnic groups mentioned earlier are 39%, 33%, 19%, 14%, and 9%, respectively. The ethnic differences that exist in smoking prevalence have attracted recent attention. Great interest exists, for example, in understanding the apparent susceptibility among White adolescents to social influences to smoke, while African American youth appear to be comparatively resistant to these influences to smoke. Mermelstein (1999), in a review of the literature, concludes that the source of these ethnic differences in smoking may generate from the differential role that parental and family factors or youth ability to cope with negative affect play across the various ethnicities.

Cognitive Effects of Smoking

Individual differences in cognitive assets and liabilities may also play a role in susceptibility to tobacco dependence. There is substantial evidence to suggest that nicotine plays a role in attention, learning, and memory. In humans, a wide variety of studies have reported the positive effects of nicotine on cognitive function (Heishman, 1999; Levin & Rezvani, 2000). However, in most of these studies, certain methodological issues cloud the conclusions that can be drawn. For example, the majority of the earlier studies examined cognitive effects in cigarette smokers. Nicotine administration can produce a marked improvement in vigilance, rapid information processing, and short-term verbal recall and reduces time to name a color on the Stroop test (Hatsukami, Fletcher, Morgan, Keenan, & Amble, 1989; Warburton, 1992; Warburton & Wesnes, 1984). Some studies have not found this positive effect on memory. In a nicotine-dependent population, it is difficult to determine whether enhancement in cognitive function is due to relief of attentional deficits mediated by nicotine withdrawal. If smokers are deprived of nicotine, cognition is impaired and these deficits can be reversed once the individual is re-exposed to nicotine (Hatsukami et al., 1989; Parrott & Roberts, 1991; Snyder & Henningfield, 1989). To try to rule out the effects of nicotine on withdrawal versus cognitive performance, experiments have examined the effects of nicotine on attention in normal nonsmoking adults. For example, in a computerized test of attention, nicotine can significantly reduce errors in normal nonsmoking adults (Levin et al., 1998). However, even though examination of the effects of nicotine in nonsmoking adults provides a reasonable baseline, it is still difficult to compare these findings directly to those seen in smokers since smokers may differ from nonsmokers on a variety of different factors including genetic, environmental, and psychological factors (Gilbert, 1995).

Psychiatric Comorbidity and Tobacco Dependence

Attention-deficit hyperactivity disorder (ADHD) is characterized by an increase in inactivity, an inability to retain attention for any length in time, and increased impulsivity. Previous research has indicated that a possible cause could be due to impairment in the functioning of the dopamine system (Barkley, 1990). In children, the prevalence of ADHD ranges from 2% to 8% and is seen more frequently in boys relative to girls (Barkley, 1990). In the adult population with ADHD, 40% are smokers compared to 26% in the general population (Pomerleau, Downey, Stelson, & Pomerleau, 1995). Since smoking and nicotine administration has been shown to increase attention (see earlier discussion), it is possible that adults with ADHD are nicotine users because it helps alleviate some of the symptoms associated with their psychiatric condition. In fact, Levin et al. (1996) have shown that nicotine transdermal patches ameliorate inattention. This effect also was observed in nonsmoking adults without ADHD (Levin et al., 1998). The positive effects of nicotine on the symptoms of ADHD could be due to the modulatory role of the nACHR system on dopaminergic neurons (Wonnacott, Irons, Rapier, Thorne, & Lunt, 1989).

As with ADHD patients, the incidence of smoking in patients with schizophrenia is 40% to 100% higher than in patients with other psychiatric disorders and about three times more prevalent than levels seen in the general population (Goff, Henderson, & Amico, 1992; Hughes, Hatsukami, Mitchell, & Dahlgren, 1986). Some authors have suggested that patients with schizophrenia smoke to alleviate possible medication-induced side effects (Goff et al., 1992; Jarvik, 1991; O'Farrell, Connors, & Upper, 1983). However, it also is possible that these patients use nicotine as a form of self-medication and to ameliorate certain symptoms associated with the disease (Goff et al., 1992; Mihailescu & Drucker-Colín, 2000). For example, patients with schizophrenia have abnormalities in sensory-gating, which can be improved following nicotine administration (Adler, Hoffer, Wiser, & Freedman, 1993). It has been hypothesized that nicotine can improve some of the negative symptoms of schizophrenia by increasing dopaminergic activity in the mesocorticolimbic pathway (Glassman, 1993). Thus, the ability of nicotine to enhance dopamine release could provide a possible explanation for the high frequency of smoking seen in patients with schizophrenia.

In a similar vein, there is a higher incidence of smoking in people who suffer from depression (Balfour & Ridley, 2000; Breslau, Kilbey, & Andreski, 1993; Choi et al., 1997; Covey, Glassman, & Stetner, 1998; Kelder et al., 2001). High levels of depression are associated with higher dependency on smoking (Breslau et al., 1993). Similar to ADHD and schizophrenia, it is possible that depressed individuals are self-medicating to alleviate the symptoms of depression and this behavior could be an important factor for tobacco dependence. However, another explanation could be that there might be a common genetic basis for the association of the two disease states (Breslau et al., 1993; Kendler et al., 1993).

ENVIRONMENTAL RISK FACTORS FOR INITIATION

Tobacco Advertising and Promotions

A significant amount of research over the past few decades has been devoted to examining the relationship between mass media advertising and tobacco sales. Tobacco companies spend nearly half of their marketing dollars on point-of-purchase promotions in retail stores; this proportion has increased substantially over the past 15 years (Federal Trade Commission, 2001). In a study based in California, retail outlets display an average of 17 tobacco advertising materials, and 94% of retail outlets display at least some advertising (Feighery, Ribisl, Schleicher, Lee, & Halvorson, 2001). In addition, tobacco is marketed through other venues such as magazines, newspapers, clothing and gear, and outdoor advertising (e.g., billboards).

Despite significant public and scientific concern over whether tobacco advertising promotes youth smoking, the available evidence was deemed inconclusive in a recent review article on the topic (Lantz et al., 2000). Furthermore, the extent to which tobacco advertising bans impact youth smoking is not clear (Lantz et al., 2000). Saffer and Chaloupka (2000), in an analysis of the effects of tobacco advertising in 22 countries across the time period 1970 to 1992, concluded that tobacco advertising increased tobacco consumption, and a comprehensive set of advertising bans, in fact, reduced tobacco consumption. It is projected that the 1999 ban on outdoor advertising, as part of the U.S. tobacco industry settlement, will have little effect on tobacco consumption because other forms of advertising (print, point-of-purchase, and sponsorship) have not been banned; thus, these forms will be the focus of heightened tobacco promotion (Saffer & Chaloupka, 2000).

Effects of Pricing and Tobacco Control Policies

Although cigarettes have been subjected to federal taxes since the Civil War and state taxes since the 1920s, it wasn't until 1964 when the Surgeon General's report was released that states began to increase taxes to deter smoking (Warner, 1981). In four states (California, Massachusetts, Michigan, and Arizona), voters have approved tobacco tax increases, with portions of the revenues being earmarked for tobacco control activities. Based on econometric studies, researchers cite evidence suggesting that higher cigarette prices are associated with reductions in cigarette smoking in general (National Cancer Institute, 1993) and in youths, in particular, who may be especially sensitive to tobacco pricing (Chaloupka & Wechsler, 1997; Lewit, Coate, & Grossman, 1981; National Cancer Institute, 1993). However, the fact that several studies have failed to identify an association between cigarette prices and smoking among adolescents (Chaloupka, 1991; Wasserman, Manning, Newhouse, & Winkler, 1991) has led some investigators to examine whether the price-versus-consumption relationship differs as a function of key factors such as age (Chaloupka & Pacula, 1999; Gruber & Zinman, 2000), ethnicity (Chaloupka & Pacula, 1999), and stage of adoption of tobacco use (Emery, White, & Pierce, 2001). It was determined in these studies that higher cigarette prices differentially affect older adolescents (Gruber & Zinman, 2000), young males (as opposed to young women; Chaloupka & Pacula, 1999) and young Black men (compared to young White men; Chaloupka & Pacula, 1999). In addition, increased prices may deter rate of adoption of regular smoking among current smokers (Emery et al., 2001). Conversely, cigarette pricing is unrelated to experimentation for adolescents of all ages, probably because this stage is characterized by very low consumption, and cigarettes often are obtained from friends (Emery et al., 2001). Thus, it appears as though "cigarette prices are a critically important policy tool in reducing adolescent smoking beyond experimentation" (Emery et al., 2001, p. 269).

Youth Access to Tobacco

It has been estimated that more than 947 million packages of cigarettes and 26 million cans of chewing tobacco are purchased each year by American youth (USDHHS, 1994). Although laws exist to limit youth access to tobacco, research has shown that the laws are not heavily enforced (DiFranza, Norwood, Garner, & Tye, 1987; Forster & Wolfson, 1998; Jacobson, Wasserman, & Anderson, 1997). Johnston et al. (1999) reported that in a survey conducted in 1998, approximately 90% of adolescents aged 15 to 16 described obtaining cigarettes as "fairly easy" or "very easy." In a survey conducted in 1997 (Centers for Disease Control and Prevention, 1998), 30% of high school smokers reported having purchased cigarettes in the previous month; of these, fewer than one-third were asked to provide proof of age.

In a comprehensive review of the literature, Stead and Lancaster (2000) summarized the effects of interventions for preventing tobacco sales to minors. Minimal interventions such as providing retailers with information about the law have been shown to be largely ineffective. Retailer participation in voluntary compliance programs, in general, is low (DiFranza & Brown, 1992; DiFranza, Savageau, & Aisquith, 1996), and while there is evidence that interventions to educate retailers can improve compliance, more effective interventions require application of multiple strategies simultaneously, such as personal visits to retailers and education of the community (Altman, Wheelis, McFarlane, Lee, & Fortmann, 1999). High levels of commercial retailer compliance, combined with community participation, may be necessary if adolescent smoking is to be reduced.

PREVENTION AND TREATMENT OF TOBACCO DEPENDENCE

Although smoking rates among adolescents rose during most of the 1990s (Johnston, O'Malley, & Bachman, 1999), results of the 2000 Monitoring the Future Study suggest that there has been a modest decline, particularly among twelfth graders, who evidenced a 3.2 percentage-point drop in 2000 (Lantz et al., 2000). Despite this decline, smoking persists as a significant public health problem, particularly among school absentees, dropouts, and other high-risk youth for whom smoking rates are appreciably higher (de Moor et al., 1994; Glynn, Anderson, & Schwarz, 1991; Grunbaum & Basen-Engquist, 1993; Karle et al., 1994).

Because 89% of adult current smokers began smoking before their nineteenth birthday, and a substantial proportion of adolescents experiment with smoking before entering high school (USDHHS, 1994), tobacco prevention efforts generally have been concentrated on elementary and middle school years. However, if early smoking prevention lessons are not reinforced and repeated in high school, smoking rates return to levels comparable to those seen in the general high school population (Bell, Ellickson, & Harrison, 1993; Ellickson, Bell, & McGuigan, 1993; Flay, 1985). The United States has evidenced an alarming rise in smoking prevalence among college students. Although this trend is thought to reflect the increase in smoking initiation from the early 1990s (Wechsler, Rigotti, Gledhill-Hoyt, & Lee, 1998), initiation among young adults may be playing a role (Lantz et al., 2000). As smoking in younger cohorts (youth, young adults) continues to rise, heightened prevention efforts are needed. Promising prevention strategies include aggressive antitobacco media campaigns, increased cigarette prices, school and community interventions, and environmental changes, such as increased emphasis on reducing adult smoking (thereby reducing the number of smoking adult role models), expanded clean indoor air laws, and enforcement of laws against sales of tobacco to minors (Lantz et al., 2000).

Cessation Methods

Pharmaceutical Aids for Cessation

Since 1984, five pharmaceutical products (nicotine gum, patch, spray, inhaler, and sustained release [SR] bupropion) have been approved by the U.S. Food and Drug Administration (FDA) as aids for smoking cessation, and research has demonstrated that use of these agents significantly increases the likelihood of successful quitting. In addition, the effects of pharmaceutical agents are substantially increased when coupled with behavioral interventions. When feasible and not medically contraindicated, it is recommended that tobacco cessation interventions include at least one FDA-approved pharmaceutical aid for cessation in parallel with tobacco dependence counseling (Fiore et al., 2000).

In a systematic review of relevant studies (Silagy, Mant, Fowler, & Lancaster, 2000), meta-analyzes of outcomes related to nicotine replacement therapies (all dosage forms combined) revealed an odds ratio for abstinence of 1.7, compared with control. The odds of abstinence for the four different forms of nicotine replacement therapy that currently are available in the United States were 1.6, 1.8, 2.3, and 2.1 for the gum, transdermal patch, nasal spray, and inhaler, respectively. The nicotine sublingual tablet also has been investigated (Molander, Lunell, & Fagerström, 2000; Wallstrom, Nilsson, & Hirsch, 2000); this has been approved for use in Europe but not in the United States (odds ratio for quitting, 1.7).

Bupropion SR was the first nonnicotine pharmaceutical product approved for smoking cessation. The mechanism of action of this medication, originally marketed as an antidepressant, is not fully understood although it is hypothesized to promote smoking cessation through its capacity to block neural re-uptake of the neurotransmitters dopamine and norepinephrine, reducing cravings for nicotine and symptoms of withdrawal (Fiore et al., 2000). The first four published placebo-controlled trials of bupropion for smoking cessation demonstrated increased odds of quitting, compared to placebo (Ferry & Burchette, 1994; Ferry, Robbins, & Scariati, 1992; Hurt et al., 1997; Jorenby et al., 1999). Pooling the 12-month continuous abstinence rates for the four trials provides an odds ratio estimate of 2.7 (Hughes, Stead, & Lancaster, 2001).

Currently, insufficient data are available to rank-order the effectiveness of the different cessation agents (Fiore et al., 2000). Most clinical trials have examined the use of a single agent. More recently, however, investigators have reported enhancements in cessation rates when agents are used in combination. For example, there is evidence that concurrent use of two forms of nicotine replacement therapy, whereby one form provides steady levels of nicotine in the body and the second form is used as needed to control cravings, suppress nicotine withdrawal symptoms (Fagerström, 1994; Fagerström, Schneider, & Lunell, 1993) and increase ability to quit compared to monotherapy (Blondal, Gudmundsson, Olafsdottir, Gustavsson, & Westin, 1999; Kornitzer, Bousten, Dramaix, Thijs, & Gustavsson, 1995; Puska et al., 1995). Dual nicotine replacement therapy, however, is recommended only for use with patients who are unable to quit

using monotherapy, because of the inherent increased risk of nicotine overdose (Fiore et al., 2000). Use of bupropion SR in combination with the nicotine patch has been shown to increase cessation rates 5.2 percentage points over bupropion SR alone, from 30.3% to 35.5%, although this increase was not statistically significant (Jorenby et al., 1999). Thus, despite the small number of trials that have examined combination therapy versus monotherapy, the results appear promising and may be particularly applicable to refractory patients who have been unable to quit using single agents. Additional research is needed to delineate more clearly the value-added effects of combination therapy, to compare the relative effects of the different constellations of agents, and to examine the comparative side effect profiles and toxicities associated with combination therapy.

Despite the fact that several different classes of drugs have been examined in recent years for their effectiveness in promoting smoking cessation, quit rates remain low, with fewer than one third of patients being abstinent at five or more months posttreatment. Furthermore, because few studies extend beyond one year, it is not known whether cessation is maintained long term. Although the nicotine transdermal patch and nicotine gum now are available without a prescription, it is not clear whether this increased access compromises efficacy because patients can now self-prescribe and self-treat their tobacco dependence without the proven positive effects of intervention from a health professional.

Nonpharmaceutical Methods for Cessation

Of smokers attempting to quit, many give up smoking on their own, without assistance of any kind. A variety of self-help materials are available; in general, these materials are just marginally more effective than no intervention, although tailored materials tend to have a greater impact than do nontailored materials (Lancaster & Stead, 2000). Social support, other than that provided by cessation counselors, has been shown to increase the likelihood of quitting by approximately 50% (Fiore et al., 2000). When feasible, smoking cessation treatment should involve some form of tobacco dependence counseling. In a meta-analysis of trials assessing the effects of cessation advice from medical practitioners (Silagy & Stead, 2001), it was determined that brief advice is associated with an increased likelihood of quitting versus no advice (odds ratio, 1.7); in addition, more intensive advice leads to a higher likelihood of quitting when compared to more minimal advice (odds ratio, 1.4). Although tobacco is the leading cause of morbidity and premature mortality in the United States, allied health professionals generally do not receive adequate tobacco cessation training. The vast majority of medical schools, for example, do not provide comprehensive tobacco cessation training to medical students (Ferry, Grissino, & Runfola, 1999). Receiving specialized training, however, has been shown to lead to increased delivery of smoking cessation counseling among health care professionals (Lancaster, Silagy, & Fowler, 2000; Sinclair et al., 1998). According to the "Clinical Practice Guideline for Treating Tobacco Use and Dependence," which summarizes the results of more than 6,000 published articles, five key components of tobacco cessation counseling are: (a) ask patients whether they use tobacco, (b) advise tobacco users to quit, (c) assess patients' interest in quitting, (d) assist patients with quitting, and (e) arrange follow-up care (Fiore et al., 2000).

Although physicians are aware of the health consequences of using tobacco (Wechsler, Levine, Idelson, Schor, & Coakley, 1996), smoking status is assessed in only about one-half two-thirds of patient clinic visits, and cessation assistance is provided in only about one-fifth of smokers' visits (Goldstein et al., 1997; Thorndike, Rigotti, Stafford, & Singer, 1998).

Group cessation programs offer an alternative to individual counseling. In a meta-analysis of 13 studies comparing group programs to self-help programs (Stead & Lancaster, 2000), group program participants were significantly more likely to have quit for six or more months (odds ratio 2.1). Group therapy exhibited similar efficacy as similar-intensity individual counseling. A principal drawback of group programs is their limited reach, because participation rates tend to be low (Stead & Lancaster, 2000). Smokers must be motivated not only to attempt to stop, but also to commit the time and effort required to attend group meetings.

Although data indicate that quit rates are enhanced with more intensive group programs or counseling, smokers tend to prefer less intense, briefer forms of self-help counseling (Fiore, Smith, Jorenby, & Baker, 1994; Hughes, 1993). Mandatory counseling, such as that required by many health insurers if a patient is to receive cessation medications at no cost or at a reduced price (co-pay), may act as a barrier to patients' quitting (Fiore et al., 1994). Thus, from a health policy standpoint, it will be important to weigh the costs/benefits of offering a brief, less intense, and less effective treatment to more potential quitters versus the costs/benefits of offering a more intense, more effective treatment to fewer potential quitters.

Future Directions

The market for smoking cessation aids is relatively small but growing. Based on available sales data from drug manufacturers, the current worldwide market for pharmaceutical aids for cessation is estimated to be $670 million ($505 million nonprescription products + $165 million, bupropion SR). Sales of nonprescription NRT products appear to be enjoying continued growth while that of bupropion SR appears to be leveling off or even declining in some market segments (Through the Loop Consulting. Corporate Focus: Health care, January, 2000 see http://www.throughtheloop.com/focus; also GlaxoSmithKline Financial Report, 2000; GlaxoSmithKline Annual Report, 2000 see http://corp.gsk.com/financial/reports/ar/report/op_finrev_prosp/op_finrev_prosp.html). It is clear that improved methods of promoting cessation are needed; this might include new medications (Centers for Disease Control and Prevention, 2000), new indications for existing medications, combination therapy, new or improved behavioral approaches, and/or increased knowledge for effective methods of matching medications and behavioral approaches to individual patients. In addition, research is needed to examine the safety and efficacy of different medications for use in special populations, such as adolescents, pregnant women, patients with depression, and smokeless tobacco users (Fiore et al., 2000).

While risk factors for relapse following treatment with pharmacological and nonpharmacological cessation approaches have been identified, relatively little work has been done to identify which smokers should receive which treatments. One reason for this is that the typical analytic approach used to identify risk factors (e.g., multiple, logistic, or Cox regression) lends itself to identification of risk factors and not necessarily the nature of smokers most or least at risk. For example, it is incorrect to assume that because all women, who have been shown to be at higher risk for relapse than men by conventional statistical methods, require the same treatment approach. In fact, it can be shown with appropriate analytic tools, that some women do very well in response to treatment. Previous research has identified subgroups of smokers with wide variation in responsiveness to both pharmacological (Swan, Jack, Niaura, Borrelli, & Spring, 1999; Swan, Jack, & Ward, 1997) and nonpharmacological (Swan, Ward, Carmelli, & Jack, 1993) treatments. One of the keys to the future of matching treatments to individual smokers will be consistent attention to and analysis of individual differences in treatment responsiveness.

EVIDENCE FOR GENETIC INFLUENCE ON TOBACCO USE IN HUMANS

In humans, as more is learned about the genetic basis of tobacco dependence, the chronic use of tobacco is increasingly appreciated as a complex genetic trait and is likely influenced by gene-environment interactions (Khoury, Beaty, & Cohen, 1993). While no one has yet demonstrated the presence of specific gene-environment interactions on tobacco use in humans, because of insufficient study sample sizes, interactions have been demonstrated in biometric models of twin similarity for alcohol use (Koopmans, Heath, Neale, & Boomsma, 1997). It has been speculated that if such interactions exist, they could emerge as potentially powerful determinants of susceptibility and maintenance of tobacco dependence (Kendler, 1999; Swan, 1999).

Definition of Phenotypes

In most behavior genetic and genetic epidemiologic studies, "smoking" has been assessed as a static phenotype (i.e., as if the behavior is a trait that remains constant over time). (See next section for a review of these studies.) However, a variety of studies from the developmental, epidemiologic, psychiatric, and smoking literature suggest that smoking in general, and the consumption of nicotine on a regular basis specifically, is tremendously more complex than a simple trait perspective (Swan, 1999b). Not only do reasons and motivations for smoking vary across individuals, it is likely that motivations (biological, social, and psychological individually and in combination with each other) vary within an individual across time and situations (Hiatt & Rimer, 1999; Petraitis, Flay, & Miller, 1995; USDHHS, 1994).

In the field of psychiatric genetics, an area fraught with numerous examples of nonreplication (Kendler, 1999), some investigators believe that more detailed measures of phenotypes, relying on actual measurements of behavior, physiological responses, or biological characteristics such as brain structure from imaging studies, will provide more replicable associations with genetic markers than have more general summary measures (Gelernter, 1997; Kendler, 1999). In the field of tobacco use, numerous possibilities exist in which the relationships of phenotypes to genetic factors may actually be larger should the full range of phenotypes be explored.

We have developed a classification of possible phenotypes (referred to as endophenotypes by Kendler, 1999) to organize phenotype selection for genetic investigations of tobacco use (see Table 7.2); we make use of this classification in our review of existing genetic studies that follows.

Evidence for a Genetic Basis to a Variety of Smoking-Related Phenotypes

Extensive literature studying twins reared together and apart supports the conclusion that genetic influences underlie the

TABLE 7.2   Proposed Tobacco and Nicotine Phenotype Classification System

Phenotype	Characteristics
Class I	Relatively crude, broad summary or cross-sectional measures of smoking behavior, such as ever/never-smoker, current/former/never-smoker, age at smoking initiation, and average number of cigarettes smoked per day. The majority of genetic studies, to date, have involved only this level of phenotypic description.
Class II	Measures or indicators of tobacco dependence, such as the Fagerström Tolerance Questionnaire and its more recent variant, the Fagerström Test for Nicotine Dependence, time to first cigarette in the morning, and number of quit attempts, or psychiatric-type classifications based on the *DSM IV* system.
Class III	Longitudinal assessments that emphasize the *process of,* or *progression toward* the development of regular smoking or tobacco dependence. Although class III phenotypes can be "summarized" to create a class I or II phenotype, class III is differentiated by the nature of the data, whereby class III retains its longitudinal properties and is presented as a trajectory. As an illustration, two individuals both might be classified as ever-smokers, having smoked 100 or more cigarettes in their life, yet their smoking topography may differ dramatically—for example, one person might have taken years to develop into a daily smoker, whereas the other might have converged rapidly on daily smoking (and thus have a much steeper "slope" or "trajectory" for the development of daily smoking).
Class IV	Nicotine pharmacokinetic parameters (the effects of the body on the drug, i.e., nicotine absorption, distribution, metabolism, and excretion rates; and pharmaco-dynamic effects (the effects of the drug on the body, including physiologic responses such as mood alteration, heightened concentration, and changes in receptor function and density).

initiation and lifetime use of tobacco as well as several indirect measures of tobacco dependence (including amount smoked and persistence; for reviews, see Heath & Madden, 1995; Sullivan & Kendler, 1999; Swan, 1999a; Swan & Carmelli, 1997). Pooled analyzes of the results from these studies lead to the conclusion that 56% of smoking initiation is attributable to genetic factors (44% to environmental sources), while 67% of variance in indirect measures of tobacco dependence can be attributed to genetic factors (33% to environmental sources; Sullivan & Kendler, 1999). The vast majority of the studies conducted thus far have examined genetic influences on class I phenotypes.

Several studies have discovered that different genetic and environmental influences play a role at different stages in the development of smoking. Heath and Martin (1993) found that the best-fitting genetic model was one that incorporated separate but correlated genetic sources of variation for each phase of the natural history of smoking. At least three subsequent twin studies have supported the presence of separate but correlated sources of genetic and environmental sources of variation in smoking initiation and persistence and/or dependence (Koopmans et al., 1997; True et al., 1997). Of these papers, only Kendler et al. (1999) utilized a direct measure of dependence, a factor derived from the FTQ, a class II phenotype according to our classification scheme. (See following discussion of the genetics of dependence.)

The appreciation of smoking behavior as multidimensional in behavior genetic studies is relatively recent and parallels similar work being conducted in the areas of alcohol and substance use. Along with the genetic models applied by Heath and Martin (1993) to smoking initiation and persistence, Koopmans et al. (1997) also examined the goodness-of-fit of a combined liability model first developed by Heath, Meyer, Jardine, and Martin (1991) and found it to provide the best fit to adolescent twin covariance for smoking initiation and amount smoked. Their analysis provided results similar to that found by Kendler et al. (1999): separate genetic liabilities for initiation and quantity were present, accounting for 39% of initiation and 86% in amount smoked. Heath, Kirk, Meyer, and Martin (1999) also provide evidence that different genetic and environmental factors are present for risk of initiation (11%–74% genetic) and for the age at onset (50%–60% genetic) of smoking, with shared environmental effects playing a larger role in initiation than in the age at onset of smoking. Madden et al. (1999) provide further evidence of the dimensionality of smoking behavior by using a correlated liability dimensions model to determine that less than 40% of the total genetic variance in smoking persistence was accounted for by the same genetic factors that increased risk of smoking initiation, a percentage that decreased with the age of the twins under study. It is important to remember that these investigations based their findings on differing combinations of class I phenotypes determined from survey-type questionnaires.

In a study of direct relevance to the present chapter, Stallings, Hewitt, Beresford, Heath, and Eaves (1999) examined the contribution of genetic and environmental influences to age at onset and, for the first time of which we are aware, the *time* in years between first use and regular use of tobacco and alcohol. The latency in progression to regular use qualifies as a class III phenotype according to our system, and represents an advance in the use of more descriptive tobacco-related phenotypes. These investigators found little evidence for genetic involvement in several milestones (age at first use, age at daily use of at least one cigarette per day, age at daily use of at least 10 cigarettes per day, all class I phenotypes). In contrast, 37% of the variation in the speed with which twins progressed from first use to regular smoking of at least 10 cigarettes per day could be attributed to genetic factors.

With regard to existing molecular genetic literature involving smoking-related phenotypes, most reported studies examined class I, and occasionally class II, phenotypes measured retrospectively (Bierut et al., 2000; Boustead, Taber, Idle, & Cholerton, 1997; Cholerton, Boustead, Taber, Arpanahi, & Idle, 1996; Comings et al., 1996; Lerman et al., 1998, 1999; Noble et al., 1994; Pianezza, Sellers, & Tyndale, 1998; Sabol et al., 1999; Shields et al., 1998). For example, Spitz et al. (1998) report an association between the dopamine d2 receptor, DRD2, alleles and likelihood of being a smoker based on assessments of self-reported smoking behavior that was assessed years, or even decades, after the onset of smoking. Nicotine dependence also was assessed retrospectively; as such, subjects (former smokers) were asked to recall specifics about their smoking behavior, in an attempt to answer items from the FTQ. Retrospective case-control designs are subject to limitations of recall bias. Many of these studies have not yet received independent confirmation.

While the existing behavioral genetic and genetic epidemiologic literature has just begun to scratch the surface of the developmental aspect of smoking behavior by using class III phenotypes (Stallings et al., 1999), the few studies that have been reported suggest that not only do different developmental phases of smoking have identifiable genetic sources of variance (Carmelli, Swan, Robinette, & Fabsitz, 1992; Heath & Martin, 1993; Swan, Reed, & Carmelli, 2000) but that the underlying genetic factors involved in each may be different (Heath & Martin, 1993; Kendler et al., 1999; Koopmans et al., 1997; Madden et al., 1999; Swan et al., 2000; True et al., 1997). Therefore, it is within the realm of possibility that molecular genetic investigations of adult smokers that identify associations between the likelihood of being a smoker (as assessed by single-point measures) while perhaps being of relevance to understanding factors involved in the maintenance of smoking, are *less relevant* to the understanding of genetic factors in the acquisition, cessation, and relapse phases of smoking.

Tobacco Dependence: A Construct in Need of Refinement

The definition and measurement of tobacco dependence continues to represent a challenge to the field. While it was pointed out early (Hughes, 1985; also Lombardo, Hughes, & Fross, 1988) that dependence has several dimensions including physical, behavioral, and psychological components, the assessment of tobacco dependence has relied largely on the Fagerström Tolerance Questionnaire

(FTQ; Fagerström, 1978) and its more recent variant, the Fagerström Test for Nicotine Dependence (FTND; Heatherton, Kozlowski, Frecker, & Fagerström, 1991), or the *DSM* criteria, an approach deriving from the need to include tobacco dependence in psychiatric nomenclature and classification and which attempts to adhere to classic definitions of drug dependence (American Psychiatric Association, 1994; Robins, Helzer, Cottler, & Goldring, 1988). Although both paper-and-pencil and psychiatric diagnostic approaches have provided reliable definitions for use in many different types of studies, neither of the current existing approaches relied on test development approaches well grounded in psychometric theory. Moreover, even though dependence may consist of several components (Lombardo et al., 1988), factor analyses of the FTQ consistently result in one large factor marked primarily by the number of cigarettes smoked per day (Kendler et al., 1999; Lichtenstein & Mermelstein, 1986). More recently, we (Hudmon, Marks, Pomerleau, Brigham, & Swan 2000; Shiffman, Hickcoz, Gnys, Paty, & Kassel, 1995) presented multidimensional scales for assessing tobacco dependence; however, these measures have not yet been published. While several twin studies claim to have identified a heritable component to dependence, they have relied on indirect measures such as continued smoking after becoming a regular smoker (Heath & Martin, 1993; Madden et al., 1999; True et al., 1997) or amount smoked (Koopmans et al., 1997; Swan, Carmelli, & Cardon, 1996, 1997). The few genetic analyzes involving the FTQ (Kendler et al., 1999; Straub et al., 1999) of which we are aware have identified a heritable component for "dependence" (Kendler et al., 1999) as well as tentative linkage with regions on six different chromosomes (Straub et al., 1999), while leaving the question of *which* components of tobacco dependence have the most or least genetic influence unresolved.

The Potential Importance of Gene-Behavior-Environment Interactions in Tobacco Dependence

A second feature of Figure 7.1 presented at the beginning of this chapter that needs further investigation concerns the plethora of environmental conditions that are recognized to play a role in the acquisition, maintenance, cessation, and relapse of smoking (USDHHS, 1994). Simply put, previous genetic investigations of smoking have not adequately incorporated environmental measures into their study designs. Often overlooked is the fact that behavior genetic studies, while consistently finding that about 60% of variation in smoking is attributable to genetic sources, *have also found that the remaining 40% is due to environmental influences*

(Sullivan & Kendler, 1999). Despite the importance of environmental influences in explaining variation in smoking, invariably, genetic investigations can only speculate as to the specific environmental sources of variation because they were not assessed. Evidence has been obtained for a role for gene-environment interactions in alcoholism and conduct disorder, supporting the notion that the coupling of a genetic susceptibility with a high-risk environment increases risk for pathology to a greater extent than would be expected in the presence of either factor alone or in additive combination (Legrand, McGue, & Iacono, 1999). Religious upbringing, for example, was recently identified as a significant mediating factor reducing the risk for initiation of alcohol use (Koopmans et al., 1997).

A final feature of Figure 7.1 concerns preexisting conditions or comorbidities. As described earlier, it is known that certain individual characteristics increase the likelihood of becoming, remaining, or becoming again a smoker. Factors such as depression, attention deficit disorder, and schizophrenia may well map into and contribute to a number of lifetime tobacco use milestones, trajectories, and/or dimensions of tobacco dependence (Hughes, 1999). While each of these comorbidities may have heritable components (Heath & Madden, 1995), we are only at the beginning of our understanding of the extent to which they share a genetic correlation with tobacco dependence phenotypes. Although Kendler and colleagues (1993) identified a common genetic substrate to depression and smoking in female twins, we need to know more about the specifics of this relationship before this information can inform prevention and treatment efforts. For example, of the possible tobacco dependence dimensions, which ones are most strongly associated with depression? What are the genetic correlations between depression and specific dimensions of dependence?

PUBLIC HEALTH IMPERATIVE FOR COLLABORATIVE, TRANSDISCIPLINARY RESEARCH

More integration of the psychosocial and biogenetic lines of research is needed because tobacco dependence is a complex genetic trait. In this context, we use the term *complexity* as defined by the field of genetic epidemiology (Lander & Schork, 1994; Ottman, 1990, 1995, 1996). A complex trait has the following features: (a) it has reduced penetrance (i.e., not everyone with a susceptibility gene(s) will become dependent on tobacco); (b) genetic heterogeneity is involved (i.e., a different set of susceptibility genes may contribute to the likelihood of becoming a smoker in different people);

(c) pleitropy is involved (i.e., the same genetic risk factors may lead to different addictions such as alcoholism in addition to tobacco dependence in different people); (d) epistasis refers to the situation in which a genetic risk factor modifies the expression of another genetic risk factor to produce tobacco dependence; and, (e) the interaction of the environment with a gene can produce an increased likelihood of becoming dependent on tobacco.

It is important to use lessons from other areas of biomedical research on complex genetic traits to inform the tobacco dependence community about problems and pitfalls that should be avoided over the next decade of research. Initially, obesity was thought to be a simple characteristic to measure, but now it is known to be quite complex with many different endophenotypes. At least four genetic linkage or association designs have been used in obesity research over the past decade resulting in the identification of more than 17 candidate markers. Linkage has been reported for more than 20 genes or markers. Currently there are at least six independent genome scanning efforts being conducted around the world. Unfortunately, there has been no overall coordination of these efforts. Because obesity has been linked to many markers with small effect sizes (a plausible situation for tobacco dependence), researchers have recently recognized the need to pool their data across studies to have sufficiently powerful tests. However, because barriers to collaboration exist (e.g., dissimilar measures) and the research environment is highly competitive, the pooling of the data may take longer than it should. Meanwhile, in spite of the progress on the genetic front, the obesity rates in the U.S. population continue to rise (Comuzzie & Allison, 1998). Similarly, the tobacco-related death toll continues to rise.

The public health challenge of tobacco dependence makes it fundamentally different from obesity. Three thousand new smokers per day and over 430,000 premature deaths annually provide an urgency to conduct a coordinated, large multidisciplinary effort to identify both main and interactive effects for genetic and environmental risk factors as quickly as possible so that effective and more powerful preventive efforts can begin to offset the highly addictive nature of nicotine.

Ethical Considerations

As described previously, genetic influences consistently account, at least partially, for twin and family similarity in smoking. Recent findings point to specific molecular genetic markers that suggest increased susceptibility for smoking. The implications of such research and its use in clinical practice, in health promotion and disease prevention, and for health policy decision making are highly significant and very broad (Parker, 1995; Plomin & Rutter, 1998; Quaid, Dinwiddie, Conneally, & Nurnberger, 1996).

Currently, although genetic markers for tobacco use have been identified, there is no clear scientific understanding of how these markers influence smoking initiation and tobacco dependence nor is there any understanding of the *degree* to which they influence smoking behavior. Although research into the genetic bases for behavior could yield enormous benefit for those suffering from addictions, such research also creates a danger of reduction, that is, that complex multifactorial behavior could be perceived to be genetic or biological alone (Annas, 1998; Philpott, 1996). At the same time, concerted efforts at tobacco control have arrived at a multipronged approach that includes "denormalization" of smoking by changing social norms and tolerance for smoking by nonsmokers.

Research efforts on both of these fronts are making progress toward a comprehensive and integrative understanding of tobacco dependence, in terms of biological and social factors. However, it is entirely possible that advances in both arenas may converge to have undesirable or unintended effects on the individuals with tobacco dependence, their families, their employment, and their access to health care and insurance (American Society of Human Genetics and the American College of Medical Genetics, 1995; Annas, Glantz, & Roche, 1995).

SUMMARY

This chapter emphasizes the importance of a multidisciplinary approach to understanding the problem of tobacco dependence. Findings from preclinical animal studies examining the neurobiology of nicotine and the reinforcing effects of nicotine have been integrated with human clinical and population studies examining sex and ethnic differences, cognitive effects, various environmental risk factors, complex genetic traits, and prevention and cessation methods for tobacco dependence. In many respects, examination of social, behavioral, and genetic risk factors in humans has developed independently from basic animal research. Fortunately, there has been a greater collaboration and exchange of findings between the human and animal fields of research, prompted mainly by significant progress at the molecular genetic level. For example, present and future research is addressing the following important issues: the study of nicotine pharmacokinetics and gene-environment interactions in families as they relate to tobacco dependence; the examination of gene-environment interactions in the development and maintenance of nicotine addiction in well-controlled conditions using animal models; and the extent to which genetic variation influences response to treatment for tobacco dependence. These previously disparate lines of research, which are beginning to converge through multidisciplinary, collaborative research efforts, will lead to an improved understanding of the complexities of tobacco dependence and will provide key information to the development of medications and behavioral treatments for curtailing tobacco dependence worldwide.

REFERENCES

Acquas, E., Carboni, E., Leone, P., & Di Chiara, G. (1989). SCH 23390 blocks drug-conditioned place-preference and place-aversion: Anhedonia (lack of reward) or apathy (lack of motivation) after dopamine-receptor blockade? *Psychopharmacology, 99*(2), 151–155.

Adler, L. E., Hoffer, L. D., Wiser, A., & Freedman, R. (1993). Normalization of auditory physiology by cigarette smoking in schizophrenic patients. *American Journal of Psychiatry, 150*(12), 1856–1861.

Ahmed, S. H., & Koob, G. F. (1997). Cocaine- but not food-seeking behavior is reinstated by stress after extinction. *Psychopharmacology, 132*(3), 289–295.

Alexander, B. K., Coambs, R. B., & Hadaway, P. F. (1978). The effect of housing and gender on morphine self-administration in rats. *Psychopharmacology, 58*(2), 175–179.

Altman, D. G., Wheelis, A. Y., McFarlane, M., Lee, H., & Fortmann, S. P. (1999). The relationship between tobacco access and use among adolescents: A four community study. *Social Science and Medicine, 48*(6), 759–775.

American Psychiatric Association. (1994). *Diagnostic and statistical manual of mental disorders* (4th ed.). Washington, DC: American Psychiatric Association.

American Society of Human Genetics and the American College of Medical Genetics. (1995). Points to consider: Ethical, legal, and psychosocial implications of genetic testing in children and adolescents. American Society of Human Genetics Board of Directors, American College of Medical Genetics Board of Directors. *American Journal of Human Genetics, 57*(5), 1233–1241.

Annas, G. J. (1998). *Some choice: Law, medicine, and the market.* New York: Oxford University Press.

Annas, G. J., Glantz, L. H., & Roche, P. A. (1995). Drafting the Genetic Privacy Act: Science, policy, and practical considerations. *Journal of Law and Medical Ethics, 23*(4), 360–366.

Balfour, D. J., & Ridley, D. L. (2000). The effects of nicotine on neural pathways implicated in depression: A factor in nicotine addiction? *Pharmacology, Biochemistry, and Behavior, 66*(1), 79–85.

Barkley, R. A. (1990). *Attention-deficit hyperactivity disorder: A handbook for diagnosis and treatment* (pp. 1–10). New York: Guilford Press.

Bell, R. M., Ellickson, P. L., & Harrison, E. R. (1993). Do drug prevention effects persist into high school? How project ALERT did with ninth graders. *Preventive Medicine, 22*(4), 463–483.

Benowitz, N. L. (1999). Nicotine addiction. *Primary Care, 26*(3), 611–631.

Benowitz, N. L., Porchet, H., Sheiner, L., & Jacob, P., III. (1988). Nicotine absorption and cardiovascular effects with smokeless tobacco use: Comparison with cigarettes and nicotine gum. *Clinical Pharmacology Therapy, 44*(1), 23–28.

Bierut, L. J., Rice, J. P., Edenberg, H. J., Goate, A., Foroud, T., Cloninger, C. R., et al. (2000). Family-based study of the association of the dopamine D2 receptor gene (DRD2) with habitual smoking. *American Journal of Medical Genetics, 90*(4), 299–302.

Blondal, T., Gudmundsson, L. J., Olafsdottir, I., Gustavsson, G., & Westin, A. (1999). Nicotine nasal spray with nicotine patch for smoking cessation: Randomised trial with six year follow up. *British Medical Journal, 318*(7179), 285–288.

Boustead, C., Taber, H., Idle, J. R., & Cholerton, S. (1997). CYP2D6 genotype and smoking behaviour in cigarette smokers. *Pharmacogenetics, 7*(5), 411–414.

Breslau, N., Kilbey, M. M., & Andreski, P. (1993). Nicotine dependence and major depression. New evidence from a prospective investigation. *Archives of General Psychiatry, 50*(1), 31–35.

Buczek, Y., Lê, A. D., Stewart, J., & Shaham, Y. (1999). Stress reinstates nicotine seeking but not sucrose solution seeking in rats. *Psychopharmacology, 144*(2), 183–188.

Calabresi, P., Lacey, M. G., & North, R. A. (1989). Nicotinic excitation of rat ventral tegmental neurones in vitro studied by intracellular recording. *British Journal of Pharmacology, 98*(1), 135–140.

Calcagnetti, D. J., & Schechter, M. D. (1994). Nicotine place preference using the biased method of conditioning. *Progress in Neuro-psychopharmacology and Biological Psychiatry, 18*(5), 925–933.

Carmelli, D., Swan, G. E., Robinette, D., & Fabsitz, R. (1992). Genetic influence on smoking: A study of male twins [see comments]. *New England Journal of Medicine, 327*(12), 829–833.

Centers for Disease Control and Prevention. (1993). Smoking cessation during previous year among adults—United States, 1990 and 1991. *Morbidity and Mortality Weekly Report, 42*(46), 504–507.

Centers for Disease Control and Prevention. (1994). Health objectives for the nation: Cigarette smoking among adults—United States, 1993. *Morbidity and Mortality Weekly Report, 43*(50), 925–930.

Centers for Disease Control and Prevention. (1998). Youth risk behavior surveillance United States, 1997. *Morbidity and Mortality Weekly Report, 47*(SS-3), 1–90.

Centers for Disease Control and Prevention. (2000). Cigarette smoking among adults—United States, 1998. *Morbidity and Mortality Weekly Report, 49*(39), 881–884.

Chaloupka, F. J. (1991). Rational addictive behavior and cigarette smoking. *Journal of Political Economy, 99*(4), 722–742.

Chaloupka, F. J., & Pacula, R. L. (1999). Sex and race differences in young people's responsiveness to price and tobacco control policies. *Tobacco Control, 8*(4), 373–377.

Chaloupka, F. J., & Wechsler, H. (1997, June). Price, tobacco control policies and smoking among young adults. *Journal of Health Economics, 16*(3), 359–373.

Chassin, L., Presson, C. C., Pitts, S. C., & Sherman, S. J. (2000). The natural history of cigarette smoking from adolescence to adulthood in a midwestern community sample: Multiple trajectories and their psychosocial correlates. *Health Psychology, 19*(3), 223–231.

Chassin, L., Presson, C. C., Sherman, S. J., & Edwards, D. A. (1990). The natural history of cigarette smoking: Predicting young-adult smoking outcomes from adolescent smoking patterns. *Health Psychology, 9*(6), 701–716.

Choi, W. S., Pierce, J. P., Gilpin, E. A., Farkas, A. J., & Berry, C. C. (1997). Which adolescent experimenters progress to established smoking in the United States. *American Journal of Preventive Medicine, 13*(5), 385–391.

Cholerton, S., Boustead, C., Taber, H., Arpanahi, A., & Idle, J. R. (1996). CYP2D6 genotypes in cigarette smokers and non-tobacco users. *Pharmacogenetics, 6*(3), 261–263.

Clarke, P. B., & Fibiger, H. C. (1987). Apparent absence of nicotine-induced conditioned place preference in rats. *Psychopharmacology, 92*(1), 84–88.

Clementi, F., Fornasari, D., & Gotti, C. (2000). Neuronal nicotinic receptors, important new players in brain function. *European Journal of Pharmacology, 393*(1/3), 3–10.

Colder, C. R., Mehta, P., Balanda, K., Campbell, R. T., Mayhew, K. P., Stanton, W. R., et al. (2001). Identifying trajectories of adolescent smoking: An application of latent growth mixture modeling. *Health Psychology, 20*(2), 127–135.

Comings, D. E., Ferry, L., Bradshaw-Robinson, S., Burchette, R., Chiu, C., & Muhleman, D. (1996). The dopamine D2 receptor (DRD2) gene: A genetic risk factor in smoking. *Pharmacogenetics, 6*(1), 73–79.

Comuzzie, A. G., & Allison, D. B. (1998). The search for human obesity genes. *Science, 280*(5368), 1374–1377.

Corrigall, W. A., & Coen, K. M. (1989). Nicotine maintains robust self-administration in rats on a limited-access schedule. *Psychopharmacology, 99*(4), 473–478.

Corrigall, W. A., & Coen, K. M. (1991). Selective dopamine antagonists reduce nicotine self-administration. *Psychopharmacology, 104*(2), 171–176.

Corrigall, W. A., Coen, K. M., & Adamson, K. L. (1994). Self-administered nicotine activates the mesolimbic dopamine system through the ventral tegmental area. *Brain Research, 653*(1/2), 278–284.

Corrigall, W. A., Franklin, K. B., Coen, K. M., & Clarke, P. B. (1992). The mesolimbic dopaminergic system is implicated in the reinforcing effects of nicotine. *Psychopharmacology, 107*(2/3), 285–289.

Covey, L. S., Glassman, A. H., & Stetner, F. (1998). Cigarette smoking and major depression. *Journal of Addictive Diseases, 17*(1), 35–46.

Crawley, J. N., Belknap, J. K., Collins, A., Crabbe, J. C., Frankel, W., Henderson, N., et al. (1997). Behavioral phenotypes of inbred mouse strains: Implications and recommendations for molecular studies. *Psychopharmacology, 132*(2), 107–124.

Deminiere, J. M., Piazza, P. V., Guegan, G., Abrous, N., Maccari, S., Le Moal, M., et al. (1992). Increased locomotor response to novelty and propensity to intravenous amphetamine self-administration in adult offspring of stressed mothers. *Brain Research, 586*(1), 135–139.

de Moor, C., Johnston, D. A., Werden, D. L., Elder, J. P., Senn, K., & Whitehorse, L. (1994). Patterns and correlates of smoking and smokeless tobacco use among continuation high school students. *Addictive Behaviors, 19*(2), 175–184.

Di Chiara, G. (2000). Role of dopamine in the behavioural actions of nicotine related to addiction. *European Journal of Pharmacology, 393*(1/3), 295–314.

DiFranza, J. R., & Brown, L. J. (1992). The tobacco institute's "it's the law" campaign: Has it halted illegal sales of tobacco to children? *American Journal of Public Health, 82*(9), 1271–1273.

DiFranza, J. R., Norwood, B. D., Garner, D. W., & Tye, J. B. (1987). Legislative efforts to protect children from tobacco. *Journal of the American Medical Association, 257*(24), 3387–3389.

DiFranza, J. R., Savageau, J. A., & Aisquith, B. F. (1996). Youth access to tobacco: The effects of age, gender, vending machine locks, and "it's the law" programs. *American Journal of Public Health, 86*(2), 221–224.

Donny, E. C., Caggiula, A. R., Knopf, S., & Brown, C. (1995). Nicotine self-administration in rats. *Psychopharmacology, 122*(4), 390–394.

Duncan, T. E., Tildesley, E., Duncan, S. C., & Hops, H. (1995). The consistency of family and peer influences on the development of substance use in adolescence. *Addiction, 90*(12), 1647–1660.

Ehrman, R. N., Robbins, S. J., Childress, A. R., & O'Brien, C. P. (1992). Conditioned responses to cocaine-related stimuli in cocaine abuse patients. *Psychopharmacology, 107*(4), 523–529.

Ellickson, P. L., Bell, R. M., & McGuigan, K. (1993). Preventing adolescent drug use: Long-term results of a junior high program. *American Journal of Public Health, 83*(6), 856–861.

Emery, S., White, M. M., & Pierce, J. P. (2001). Does cigarette price influence adolescent experimentation? *Journal of Health Economics, 20*(2), 261–270.

Erb, S., Shaham, Y., & Stewart, J. (1996). Stress reinstates cocaine-seeking behavior after prolonged extinction and a drug-free period. *Psychopharmacology, 128*(4), 408–412.

Fagerström, K. O. (1978). Measuring degree of physical dependence to tobacco smoking with reference to individualization of treatment. *Addictive Behaviors, 3*(3/4), 235–241.

Fagerström, K. O. (1994). Combined use of nicotine replacement therapies. *Health Values, 18*(3), 15–20.

Fagerström, K. O., Schneider, N. G., & Lunell, E. (1993). Effectiveness of nicotine patch and nicotine gum as individual versus combined treatments for tobacco withdrawal symptoms. *Psychopharmacology, 111*(3), 271–277.

Federal Trade Commission. (2001). *Report to congress for 1999 pursuant to the federal cigarette labeling and advertising act.* Washington, DC: Author.

Feighery, E. C., Ribisl, K. M., Schleicher, N., Lee, R. E., & Halvorson, S. (2001). Cigarette advertising and promotional strategies in retail outlets: Results of a statewide survey in California. *Tobacco Control, 10*(2), 184–188.

Ferry, L. H., & Burchette, R. J. (1994). Efficacy of bupropion for smoking cessation in non depressed smokers [Abstract]. *Journal of Addictive Diseases, 13*(4), 249.

Ferry, L. H., Grissino, L. M., & Runfola, P. S. (1999). Tobacco dependence curricula in U.S. undergraduate medical education. *Journal of the American Medical Association, 282*(9), 825–829.

Ferry, L. H., Robbins, A. S., & Scariati, P. D. (1992). Enhancement of smoking cessation using the antidepressant bupropion hydrochloride [Abstract 2670]. *Circulation, 86*(4, Suppl. 1), 1–671.

Fiore, M. C., Bailey, W. C., Cohen, S. J., Dorfman, S. F., Fox, B. J., Goldstein, M. G., et al. (2000). *Treating tobacco use and dependence: Clinical practice guideline.* Rockville, MD: U.S. Department of Health and Human Service.

Fiore, M. C., Smith, S. S., Jorenby, D. E., & Baker, T. B. (1994). The effectiveness of the nicotine patch for smoking cessation: A meta-analysis. *Journal of the American Medical Association, 271*(24), 1940–1947.

Flay, B. R. (1985). Psychosocial approaches to smoking prevention: A review of findings. *Health Psychology, 4*(5), 449–488.

Flay, B. R. (1999). Understanding environmental, situational, and intrapersonal risk and protective factors for youth tobacco use: The theory of triadic influence. *Nicotine & Tobacco Research, 1,* S111–S114.

Forster, J. L., & Wolfson, M. (1998). Youth access to tobacco: Policies and politics. *Annual Review of Public Health, 19,* 203–235.

Fudala, P. J., Teoh, K. W., & Iwamoto, E. T. (1985). Pharmacologic characterization of nicotine-induced conditioned place preference. *Pharmacology, Biochemistry, and Behavior, 22*(2), 237–241.

Gelernter, J. (1997). Genetic association studies in psychiatry: Recent history. In K. Blum & E. P. Noble (Eds.), *Handbook of psychiatric genetics* (pp. 25–46). New York: CRC Press.

Gilbert, D. G. (1995). *Smoking: Individual difference, psychopathology, and emotion.* Washington, DC: Taylor & Francis.

Gilpin, E. A., Choi, W. S., Berry, C., & Pierce, J. P. (1999). How many adolescents start smoking each day in the United States? *Journal of Adolescent Health Care, 25*(4), 248–255.

Gilpin, E. A., Lee, L., Evans, N., & Pierce, J. P. (1994). Smoking initiation rates in adults and minors: United States, 1944–1988. *American Journal of Epidemiology, 140*(6), 535–543.

Giovino, G. A. (1999). Epidemiology of tobacco use among U.S. adolescents. *Nicotine & Tobacco Research, 40,* S31–S40.

Glassman, A. H. (1993). Cigarette smoking: Implications for psychiatric illness. *American Journal of Psychiatry, 150*(4), 546–553.

Glynn, T. J., Anderson, D. M., & Schwarz, L. (1991). Tobacco-use reduction among high-risk youth: Recommendations of a National Cancer Institute Expert Advisory Panel. *Preventive Medicine, 20*(2), 279–291.

Goeders, N. E., & Guerin, G. F. (1994). Non-contingent electric footshock facilitates the acquisition of intravenous cocaine self-administration in rats. *Psychopharmacology, 114*(1), 63–70.

Goff, D. C., Henderson, D. C., & Amico, E. (1992). Cigarette smoking in schizophrenia: Relationship to psychopathology and medication side effects. *American Journal of Psychiatry, 149*(9), 1189–1194.

Goldberg, S. R., Spealman, R. D., & Goldberg, D. M. (1981). Persistent behavior at high rates maintained by intravenous self-administration of nicotine. *Science, 214*(4520), 573–575.

Goldstein, M. G., Niaura, R., Willey-Lessne, C., DePue, J., Eaton, C., Rakowski, W., et al. (1997). Physicians counseling smokers: A population-based survey of patients' perceptions of health care provider-delivered smoking cessation interventions. *Archives of Internal Medicine, 157*(12), 1313–1319.

Gritz, E. R., Prokhorov, A. V., Hudmon, K. S., Chamberlain, R. M., Taylor, W. C., DiClemente, C. C., et al. (1998). Cigarette smoking in a multiethnic population of youth: Methods and baseline findings. *Preventive Medicine, 27*(3), 365–384.

Gruber, J., & Zinman, J. (2000). *Youth smoking in the U.S.: Evidence and implications* (Vol. W7780). Cambridge, MA: National Bureau of Economic Research Working Paper.

Grunbaum, J. A., & Basen-Engquist, K. (1993). Comparison of health risk behaviors between students in a regular high school and students in an alternative high school. *The Journal of School Health, 63*(10), 421–425.

Hatsukami, D., Fletcher, L., Morgan, S., Keenan, R., & Amble, P. (1989). The effects of varying cigarette deprivation duration on cognitive and performance tasks. *Journal of Substance Abuse, 1*(4), 407–416.

Heath, A. C., Kirk, K. M., Meyer, J. M., & Martin, N. G. (1999). Genetic and social determinants of initiation and age at onset of smoking in Australian twins. *Behavior Genetics, 29*(6), 395–407.

Heath, A. C., & Madden, P. A. (1995). Genetic influences on smoking behavior. In J. R. Turner & L. R. Cardon (Eds.), *Behavior genetic approaches in behavior medicine* (pp. 45–66). New York: Plenum Press.

Heath, A. C., & Martin, N. G. (1993). Genetic models for the natural history of smoking: Evidence for a genetic influence on smoking persistence. *Addictive Behaviors, 18,* 19–34.

Heath, A. C., Meyer, J. M., Jardine, R., & Martin, N. G. (1991). The inheritance of alcohol consumption patterns in a general population twin sample. II: Determinants of consumption frequency and quantity consumed. *Journal of Studies on Alcohol, 52*(5), 425–433.

Heatherton, T. F., Kozlowski, L. T., Frecker, R. C., & Fagerström, K. O. (1991). The Fagerström Test for Nicotine Dependence: A revision of the Fagerström Tolerance Questionnaire. *British Journal of Addiction, 86*(9), 1119–1127.

Heishman, S. J. (1999). Behavioral and cognitive effects of smoking: Relationship to nicotine addiction. *Nicotine & Tobacco Research, 1,* S143–S147.

Hiatt, R. A., & Rimer, B. K. (1999). A new strategy for cancer control research. *Cancer Epidemiology, Biomarkers, and Prevention, 8*(11), 957–964.

Hoffman, D. C. (1989). The use of place conditioning in studying the neuropharmacology of drug reinforcement. *Brain Research, 23,* 373–387.

Horgan, C., Marsden, M. E., & Larson, M. J. (1993). *Substance abuse: The nation's number one health problem.* Princeton, NJ: Robert Wood Johnson Foundation.

Hudmon, K. S., Marks, J. L., Pomerleau, C. S., Brigham, J., & Swan, G. E. (2000, February 18–20). *A multi-dimensional approach to measuring nicotine dependence.* Poster presented at the Society for Research on Nicotine and Tobacco annual meeting, Arlington, VA.

Hughes, J. R. (1985). Identification of the dependent smoker: Validity and clinical utility. *Behavioral Medicine Abstracts, 5,* 202–204.

Hughes, J. R. (1993). Transdermal nicotine: Clarifications, side effects, and funding [letter; comment]. *Journal of the American Medical Association, 269*(15), 1939–1940.

Hughes, J. R. (1999). Comorbidity and smoking. *Nicotine & Tobacco Research, 1,* S149–S152.

Hughes, J. R., Gust, S. W., Skoog, K., Keenan, R. M., & Fenwick, J. W. (1991). Symptoms of tobacco withdrawal: A replication and extension. *Archives of General Psychiatry, 48*(1), 52–59.

Hughes, J. R., Hatsukami, D. K., Mitchell, J. E., & Dahlgren, L. A. (1986). Prevalence of smoking among psychiatric outpatients. *American Journal of Psychiatry, 143*(8), 993–997.

Hughes, J. R., Stead, L. F., & Lancaster, T. (2001). Antidepressants for smoking cessation. *Cochrane Database of Systematic Reviews, 2,* CD000031.

Hurt, R. D., Sachs, D. P., Glover, E. D., Offord, K. P., Johnston, J. A., Dale, L. C., et al. (1997). A comparison of sustained-release bupropion and placebo for smoking cessation. *New England Journal of Medicine, 337*(17), 1195–1202.

Idle, J. R. (1990). Titrating exposure to tobacco smoke using cotinine: A minefield of misunderstandings. *Journal of Clinical Epidemiology, 43*(4), 313–317.

Imperato, A., Mulas, A., & Di Chiara, G. (1986). Nicotine preferentially stimulates dopamine release in the limbic system of freely moving rats. *European Journal of Pharmacology, 132*(2/3), 337–338.

Jacobson, P. D., Wasserman, J., & Anderson, J. R. (1997). Historical overview of tobacco legislation and regulation. *Journal of Social Issues, 53*(1), 75–95.

Jarvik, M. E. (1991). Beneficial effects of nicotine. *British Journal of Addiction, 86*(5), 571–575.

Jessor, R., & Jessor, S. L. (1977). *Problem behavior and psychosocial development: A longitudinal study of youth.* New York: Academic Press.

Johnston, L. D., O'Malley, P. M., & Bachman, J. G. (1991). *Drug use among American high school seniors, college students and young adults, 1975–1990.* Rockville, MD: National Institute on Drug Abuse.

Johnston, L. D., O'Malley, P. M., & Bachman, J. G. (1992). *Smoking, drinking and illicit drug use among American secondary school students, college students, and young adults, 1975–1991* (NIH Publication No. 93–3480). Rockville, MD: National Institute on Drug Abuse.

Johnston, L. D., O'Malley, P. M., & Bachman, J. G. (1995). *National survey results on drug use from the Monitoring the Future study, 1975–1994: Vol. 1. Secondary school students* (NIH Publication No. 95–4026): Rockville, MD: National Institute on Drug Abuse.

Johnston, L. D., O'Malley, P. M., & Bachman, J. G. (1999). *National survey results on drug use from the Monitoring the Future study, 1975–1998: Vol. 1. Secondary school students* (NIH Publication No. 99–4660). Rockville, MD: National Institute on Drug Abuse.

Jorenby, D. E., Leischow, S. J., Nides, M. A., Rennard, S. I., Johnston, J. A., Hughes, J. R., et al. (1999). A controlled trial of sustained-release bupropion, a nicotine patch, or both for smoking cessation. *New England Journal of Medicine, 340*(9), 685–691.

Karle, H., Shenassa, E., Edwards, C., Werden, D. L., Elder, J. P., & Whitehorse, L. (1994). Tobacco control for high risk youth: Tracking and evaluation issues. *Family Community Health, 16,* 10–17.

Kelder, S. H., Murray, N. G., Orpinas, P., Prokhorov, A., McReynolds, L., Zhang, Q., et al. (2001). Depression and substance use in minority middle-school students. *American Journal of Public Health, 91*(5), 761–766.

Kendler, K. S. (1999). Preparing for gene discovery: A further agenda for psychiatry. *Archives of General Psychiatry, 56*(6), 554–555.

Kendler, K. S., Neale, M. C., MacLean, C. J., Heath, A. C., Eaves, L. J., & Kessler, R. C. (1993). Smoking and major depression. A causal analysis. *Archives of General Psychiatry, 50*(1), 36–43.

Kendler, K. S., Neale, M. C., Sullivan, P., Corey, L. A., Gardner, C. O., & Prescott, C. A. (1999). A population-based twin study in women of smoking initiation and nicotine dependence. *Psychological Medicine, 29*(2), 299–308.

Khoury, M. J., Beaty, T. H., & Cohen, B. H. (1993). *Fundamentals of genetic epidemiology.* New York: Oxford Press.

Koopmans, J. R., Heath, A. C., Neale, M. C., & Boomsma, D. I. (1997). The genetics of initiation and quantity of alcohol and tobacco use. In J. R. Koopmans (Ed.), *The genetics of health-related behaviors* (pp. 90–108). Amsterdam: Print Partners Ipskamp.

Kornitzer, M., Boutsen, M., Dramaix, M., Thijs, J., & Gustavsson, G. (1995). Combined use of nicotine patch and gum in smoking cessation: A placebo controlled clinical trial. *Preventive Medicine, 24*(1), 41–47.

Lancaster, T., Silagy, C., & Fowler, G. (2000). Training health professionals in smoking cessation. *Cochrane Database of Systematic Reviews, 3,* CD000214.

Lancaster, T., & Stead, L. F. (2000). Self-help interventions for smoking cessation. *Cochrane Database of Systematic Reviews, 2,* CD001118.

Lander, E. S., & Schork, N. J. (1994). Genetic dissection of complex traits. *Science, 265*(5181), 2037–2048.

Lantz, P. M., Jacobson, P. D., Warner, K. E., Wasserman, J., Pollack, H. A., Berson, J., et al. (2000). Investing in youth tobacco control: A review of smoking prevention and control strategies. *Tobacco Control, 9*(1), 47–63.

Lê, A. D., Quan, B., Juzystch, W., Fletcher, P. J., Joharchi, N., & Shaham, Y. (1998). Reinstatement of alcohol-seeking by priming injections of alcohol and exposure to stress in rats. *Psychopharmacology, 135,* 169–174.

Legrand, L. N., McGue, M., & Iacono, W. G. (1999). Searching for interactive effects in the etiology of early-onset substance use. *Behavior Genetics, 29*(6), 433–444.

Lerman, C., Caporaso, N. E., Audrain, J., Main, D., Bowman, E. D., Lockshin, B., et al. (1999). Evidence suggesting the role of specific genetic factors in cigarette smoking. *Health Psychology, 18*(1), 14–20.

Lerman, C., Caporaso, N. E., Main, D., Audrain, J., Boyd, N. R., Bowman, E. D., et al. (1998). Depression and self-medication with nicotine: The modifying influence of the dopamine D4 receptor gene. *Health Psychology, 17*(1), 56–62.

Levin, E. D., Conners, C. K., Silva, D., Hinton, S. C., Meck, W. H., March, J., et al. (1998). Transdermal nicotine effects on attention. *Psychopharmacology, 140*(2), 135–141.

Levin, E. D., Conners, C. K., Sparrow, E., Hinton, S. C., Erhardt, D., Meck, W. H., et al. (1996). Nicotine effects on adults with attention-deficit/hyperactivity disorder. *Psychopharmacology, 123*(1), 55–63.

Levin, E. D., & Rezvani, A. H. (2000). Development of nicotinic drug therapy for cognitive disorders. *European Journal of Pharmacology, 393*(1/3), 141–146.

Lewit, E. M., Coate, D., & Grossman, M. (1981). The effects of government regulations on teenage smoking. *Journal of Law Economics, 24,* 545–569.

Lichtenstein, E., & Mermelstein, R. J. (1986). Some methodological cautions in the use of the Tolerance Questionnaire. *Addictive Behaviors, 11*(4), 439–442.

Lombardo, T. W., Hughes, J. R., & Fross, J. D. (1988). Failure to support the validity of the Fagerström Tolerance Questionnaire as a measure of physiological tolerance to nicotine. *Addictive Behaviors, 13*(1), 87–90.

Madden, P. A., Heath, A. C., Pedersen, N. L., Kaprio, J., Koskenvuo, M. J., & Martin, N. G. (1999). The genetics of smoking persistence in men and women: A multicultural study. *Behavior Genetics, 29*(6), 423–431.

Martin, J. L., & Itzhak, Y. (2000). 7-Nitroindazole blocks nicotine-induced conditioned place preference but not LiCl-induced conditioned place aversion. *Neuroreport, 11*(5), 947–949.

McKennell, A. C. (1970). Smoking motivation factors. *The British Journal of Social and Clinical Psychology, 9*(1), 8–22.

Meliska, C. J., Bartke, A., McGlacken, G., & Jensen, R. A. (1995). Ethanol, nicotine, amphetamine, and aspartame consumption and preferences in C57BL/6 and DBA/2 mice. *Pharmacology Biochemistry, and Behavior, 50*(4), 619–626.

Mermelstein, R. (1999). Explanations of ethnic and gender differences in youth smoking: A multi-site, qualitative investigation. The Tobacco Control Network Writing Group. *Nicotine & Tobacco Research, 8,* S91–S98.

Miczek, K. A., & Mutschler, N. H. (1996). Activational effects of social stress on IV cocaine self-administration in rats. *Psychopharmacology, 128*(3), 256–264.

Mihailescu, S., & Drucker-Colín, R. (2000). Nicotine and brain disorders. *Acta Pharmacologica Sinica, 21,* 97–104.

Mohammed, A. H. (2000). Genetic dissection of nicotine-related behaviour: A review of animal studies. *Behavioural Brain Research, 113*(1/2), 35–41.

Molander, L., Lunell, E., & Fagerström, K. O. (2000). Reduction of tobacco withdrawal symptoms with a sublingual nicotine tablet: A placebo controlled study. *Nicotine & Tobacco Research, 2*(2), 187–191.

National Cancer Institute. (1993). *The impact of cigarette excise taxes on smoking among children and adults: Summary report of a National Cancer Institute Expert Panel.* Washington, DC: Author.

Noble, E. P., St. Jeor, S. T., Ritchie, T., Syndulko, K., St. Jeor, S. C., Fitch, R. J., et al. (1994). D2 dopamine receptor gene and cigarette smoking: A reward gene? *Medical Hypotheses, 42*(4), 257–260.

O'Farrell, T. J., Connors, G. J., & Upper, D. (1983). Addictive behaviors among hospitalized psychiatric patients. *Addictive Behaviors, 8*(4), 329–333.

Ottman, R. (1990). An epidemiologic approach to gene-environment interaction. *Genetic Epidemiology, 7*(3), 177–185.

Ottman, R. (1995). Gene-environment interaction and public health. *American Journal of Human Genetics, 56*(4), 821–823.

Ottman, R. (1996). Gene-environment interaction: Definitions and study designs. *Preventive Medicine, 25*(6), 761–770.

Pagliusi, S. R., Tessari, M., DeVevey, S., Chiamulera, C., & Pich, E. M. (1996). The reinforcing properties of nicotine are associated with a specific patterning of c-fos expression in the rat brain. *European Journal of Neuroscience, 8*(11), 2247–2256.

Parker, L. S. (1995). Ethical concerns in the research and treatment of complex disease. *Trends in Genetics, 11*(12), 520–523.

Parrott, A. C., & Roberts, G. (1991). Smoking deprivation and cigarette reinstatement: Effects upon visual attention. *Journal of Psychopharmacology, 5,* 404–409.

Paterson, D., & Nordberg, A. (2000). Neuronal nicotinic receptors in the human brain. *Progress in Neurobiology, 61*(1), 75–111.

Petraitis, J., Flay, B. R., & Miller, T. Q. (1995). Reviewing theories of adolescent substance use: Organizing pieces in the puzzle. *Psychological Bulletin, 117*(1), 67–86.

Philpott, M. (1996). Not guilty, by reason of genetic determinism. In H. Tam (Ed.), *Punishment, excuses and moral development* (pp. 95–112). Aldershot, England: Avebury.

Pianezza, M. L., Sellers, E. M., & Tyndale, R. F. (1998). Nicotine metabolism defect reduces smoking. *Nature, 393*(6687), 750.

Picciotto, M. R., Zoli, M., Rimondini, R., Lena, C., Marubio, L. M., Pich, E. M., et al. (1998). Acetylcholine receptors containing the beta2 subunit are involved in the reinforcing properties of nicotine. *Nature, 391*(6663), 173–177.

Pich, E. M., Pagliusi, S. R., Tessari, M., Talabot-Ayer, D., Hooft van Huijsduijnen, R., & Chiamulera, C. (1997). Common neural substrates for the addictive properties of nicotine and cocaine. *Science, 275*(5296), 83–86.

Plomin, R., & Rutter, M. (1998). Child development, molecular genetics, and what to do with genes once they are found. *Child Development, 69*(4), 1223–1242.

Pomerleau, O. F., Downey, K. K., Stelson, F. W., & Pomerleau, C. S. (1995). Cigarette smoking in adult patients diagnosed with attention deficit hyperactivity disorder. *Journal of Substance Abuse, 7*(3), 373–378.

Puska, P., Korhonen, H., Vartiainen, E., Urjanheimo, E. L., Gustavsson, G., & Westin, A. (1995). Combined use of nicotine patch and gum compared with gum alone in smoking cessation: A clinical trial in North Karelia. *Tobacco Control, 4,* 231–235.

Quaid, K. A., Dinwiddie, H., Conneally, P. M., & Nurnberger, J. I., Jr. (1996). Issues in genetic testing for susceptibility to alcoholism: Lessons from Alzheimer's disease and Huntington's disease. *Alcoholism: Clinical and Experimental Research, 20*(8), 1430–1437.

Roberts, D. L. (1988). Natural tobacco flavor. *Recent Advances in Tobacco Science, 14,* 49–113.

Robins, L., Helzer, J., Cottler, L., & Goldring, E. (1988). *NIMH Diagnostic Interview Scheduled Version III (DIS-III-R).* St Louis, MO: Washington University Medical School, Department of Psychiatry.

Robinson, S. F., Marks, M. J., & Collins, A. C. (1996). Inbred mouse strains vary in oral self-selection of nicotine. *Psychopharmacology, 124*(4), 332–339.

Robinson, T. E., & Berridge, K. C. (1993). The neural basis of drug craving: An incentive-sensitization theory of addiction. *Brain Research. Brain Research Reviews, 18*(3), 247–291.

Sabol, S. Z., Nelson, M. L., Fisher, C., Gunzerath, L., Brody, C. L., Hu, S., et al. (1999). A genetic association for cigarette smoking behavior. *Health Psychology, 18*(1), 7–13.

Saffer, H., & Chaloupka, F. (2000). The effect of tobacco advertising bans on tobacco consumption. *Journal of Health Economics, 19*(6), 1117–1137.

Schechter, M. D., & Calcagnetti, D. J. (1993). Trends in place preference conditioning with a cross-indexed bibliography: 1957–1991. *Neuroscience and Biobehavioral Reviews, 17*(1), 21–41.

Schechter, M. D., Meehan, S. M., & Schechter, J. B. (1995). Genetic selection for nicotine activity in mice correlates with conditioned place preference. *European Journal of Pharmacology, 279*(1), 59–64.

Schenk, S., Lacelle, G., Gorman, K., & Amit, Z. (1987). Cocaine self-administration in rats influenced by environmental conditions: Implications for the etiology of drug abuse. *Neuroscience Letters, 81*(1/2), 227–231.

Shaham, Y., & Stewart, J. (1995). Stress reinstates heroin-seeking in drug-free animals: An effect mimicking heroin, not withdrawal. *Psychopharmacology, 119*(3), 334–341.

Shields, P. G., Lerman, C., Audrain, J., Bowman, E. D., Main, D., Boyd, N. R., et al. (1998). Dopamine D4 receptors and the risk of cigarette smoking in African-Americans and Caucasians. *Cancer Epidemiology, Biomarkers, and Prevention, 7*(6), 453–458.

Shiffman, S., Hickcoz, M., Gnys, M., Paty, J. A., & Kassel, J. R. (1995, March). *The nicotine dependence syndrome scale: Development of a new measure.* Poster presented at the first annual meeting of the Society for Research on Nicotine and Tobacco, San Diego, CA.

Silagy, C., Mant, D., Fowler, G., & Lancaster, T. (2000). Nicotine replacement therapy for smoking cessation. *Cochrane Database of Systematic Reviews, 2,* CD000146.

Silagy, C., & Stead, L. F. (2001). Physician advice for smoking cessation (Cochrane Review). *Cochrane Database of Systematic Reviews, 2,* CD000165.

Sinclair, H. K., Bond, C. M., Lennox, A. S., Silcock, J., Winfield, A. J., & Donnan, P. T. (1998). Training pharmacists and pharmacy assistants in the stage-of-change model of smoking cessation: A randomised controlled trial in Scotland. *Tobacco Control, 7*(3), 253–261.

Snyder, F. R., & Henningfield, J. E. (1989). Effects of nicotine administration following 12 h of tobacco deprivation: Assessment on computerized performance tasks. *Psychopharmacology, 97*(1), 17–22.

Spitz, M. R., Shi, H., Yang, F., Hudmon, K. S., Jiang, H., Chamberlain, R. M., et al. (1998). Case-control study of the D2 dopamine receptor gene and smoking status in lung cancer patients. *Journal of the National Cancer Institute, 90*(5), 358–363.

Stallings, M. C., Hewitt, J. K., Beresford, T., Heath, A. C., & Eaves, L. J. (1999). A twin study of drinking and smoking onset and latencies from first use to regular use. *Behavior Genetics, 29*(6), 409–421.

Stead, L. F., & Lancaster, T. (2000). Group behaviour therapy programmes for smoking cessation. *Cochrane Database of Systematic Reviews, 2,* CD001007.

Stein, E. A., Pankiewicz, J., Harsch, H. H., Cho, J. K., Fuller, S. A., Hoffmann, R. G., et al. (1998). Nicotine-induced limbic cortical activation in the human brain: A functional MRI study. *American Journal of Psychiatry, 155*(8), 1009–1015.

Stolerman, I. P., Naylor, C., Elmer, G. I., & Goldberg, S. R. (1999). Discrimination and self-administration of nicotine by inbred strains of mice. *Psychopharmacology, 141*(3), 297–306.

Stolerman, I. P., & Shoaib, M. (1991). The neurobiology of tobacco addiction. *Trends in Pharmacological Sciences, 12*(12), 467–473.

Straub, R. E., Sullivan, P. F., Ma, Y., Myakishev, M. V., Harris-Kerr, C., Wormley, B., et al. (1999). Susceptibility genes for nicotine dependence: A genome scan and followup in an independent sample suggest that regions on chromosomes 2, 4, 10, 16, 17 and 18 merit further study. *Molecular Psychiatry, 4*(2), 129–144.

Sullivan, P. F., & Kendler, K. S. (1999). The genetic epidemiology of smoking. *Nicotine & Tobacco Research, 1,* S51–S57.

Swan, G. E. (1999a). Implications of genetic epidemiology for the prevention of tobacco use. *Nicotine & Tobacco Research, 56,* S49–S56.

Swan, G. E. (1999b). Tobacco smoking as a complex genetic trait. *Nicotine & Tobacco Research, 1*(2), 182–183.

Swan, G. E., & Carmelli, D. (1997). Behavior genetic investigations of cigarette smoking and related issues. In E. P. Noble & K. Blum (Eds.), *Handbook of psychiatric genetics* (pp. 379–398). Boca Raton, FL: CRC Press.

Swan, G. E., Carmelli, D., & Cardon, L. R. (1996). The consumption of tobacco, alcohol, and coffee in Caucasian male twins: A multivariate genetic analysis. *Journal of Substance Abuse, 8*(1), 19–31.

Swan, G. E., Carmelli, D., & Cardon, L. R. (1997). Heavy consumption of cigarettes, alcohol and coffee in male twins. *Journal of Studies on Alcohol, 58*(2), 182–190.

Swan, G. E., Jack, L. M., Niaura, R., Borrelli, B., & Spring, B. (1999). *Subgroups of smokers with different success rates after treatment with fluoxetine for smoking cessation.* Paper presented to the 5th annual meeting of the Society for Research on Nicotine and Tobacco, San Diego, CA.

Swan, G. E., Jack, L. M., & Ward, M. M. (1997). Subgroups of smokers with different success rates after use of transdermal nicotine. *Addiction, 92*(2), 207–217.

Swan, G. E., Reed, T., & Carmelli, D. (2000). Maximum number of cigarettes ever smoked and age of quitting in 1140 twin pairs from the NAS/NRC WWII twin registry [Abstract]. *Nicotine & Tobacco Research, 2,* 307.

Swan, G. E., Ward, M. M., Carmelli, D., & Jack, L. M. (1993). Differential rates of relapse in subgroups of male and female smokers. *Journal of Clinical Epidemiology, 46*(9), 1041–1053.

Thorndike, A. N., Rigotti, N. A., Stafford, R. S., & Singer, D. E. (1998). National patterns in the treatment of smokers by physicians. *Journal of the American Medical Association, 279*(8), 604–608.

True, W. R., Heath, A. C., Scherrer, J. F., Waterman, B., Goldberg, J., Lin, N., et al. (1997). Genetic and environmental contributions to smoking. *Addiction, 92*(10), 1277–1287.

U.S. Department of Health and Human Services. (1988). *The health consequences of smoking: Nicotine addiction. A report of the Surgeon General.* (DHHS Publication No. (PHS) (CDC) 88-8406). Washington, DC: U.S. Department of Health and Human Services, Public Health Service, Centers for Disease Control, Center for Health Promotion and Education, Office on Smoking and Health.

U.S. Department of Health and Human Services. (1994). *Preventing tobacco use among young people: A report of the Surgeon General.* Atlanta, GA: U.S. Department of Health and Human Services, Public Health Service, Centers for Disease Control and Prevention, National Center for Chronic Disease Prevention and Health Promotion, Office on Smoking and Health.

Wallstrom, M., Nilsson, F., & Hirsch, J. M. (2000). A randomized, double-blind, placebo-controlled clinical evaluation of a nicotine sublingual tablet in smoking cessation. *Addiction, 95*(8), 1161–1171.

Warburton, D. M. (1992). Nicotine as a cognitive enhancer. *Progress in Neuro-psychopharmacology and Biological Psychiatry, 16*(2), 181–191.

Warburton, D. M., & Wesnes, K. (1984). Mechanisms for habitual substance use: Food, alcohol and cigarettes. In A. Ale & J. A. Edwards (Eds.), *Physiological correlates of human behaviour: Basic issues* (Vol. 1, pp. 277–297). London: Academic Press.

Warner, K. E. (1981). State legislation on smoking and health: A comparison of two policies. *Policy Sciences, 13,* 139–152.

Wasserman, J., Manning, W. G., Newhouse, J. P., & Winkler, J. D. (1991). The effects of excise taxes and regulations on cigarette smoking. *Journal of Health Economics, 10*(1), 43–64.

Watkins, S. S., Koob, G. F., & Markou, A. (2000). Neural mechanisms underlying nicotine addiction: Acute positive reinforcement and withdrawal. *Nicotine & Tobacco Research, 2*(1), 19–37.

Wechsler, H., Levine, S., Idelson, R. K., Schor, E. L., & Coakley, E. (1996). The physician's role in health promotion revisited—a survey of primary care practitioners. *New England Journal of Medicine, 334*(15), 996–998.

Wechsler, H., Rigotti, N. A., Gledhill-Hoyt, J., & Lee, H. (1998). Increased levels of cigarette use among college students: A cause for national concern. *Journal of the American Medical Association, 280*(19), 1673–1678.

Willner, P. (1991). Methods for assessing the validity of animal - models of human psychopathology. In A. Boulton, G. Baker, & M. Martin-Iverson (Eds.), *Neuromethods: Animal models in psychiatry I* (Vol. 18, pp. 1–23). Clifton, NJ: Humana Press.

Wonnacott, S., Irons, J., Rapier, C., Thorne, B., & Lunt, G. G. (1989). Presynaptic modulation of transmitter release by nicotinic receptors. *Progress in Brain Research, 79,* 157–163.

CHAPTER 8

Arthritis and Musculoskeletal Conditions

HEATHER M. BURKE, ALEX J. ZAUTRA, MARY C. DAVIS, AMY S. SCHULTZ, AND JOHN W. REICH

While the diseases discussed in other chapters of this volume are most striking in their threats to survival, arthritis and musculoskeletal conditions are notable due to the profound disability they create. Arthritis and other musculoskeletal conditions collectively represent the most common cause of disability in the United States. Currently, more than 40 million Americans suffer from some form of arthritis (Lawrence et al., 1998). The widespread prevalence and disability associated with these conditions emphasize the importance of identifying mechanisms that affect arthritis onset, course, and outcome. Traditionally, researchers attempting to understand these chronic diseases have focused on indices of disease activity to evaluate the effectiveness of treatment. However, the lack of a one-to-one correspondence between objective disease activity and subjective suffering underscores the futility of applying a strict biomedical model to these conditions. Instead, consideration of psychosocial in addition to traditional biomedical factors may yield more accurate predictions of treatment outcomes. Engel's (1977) biopsychosocial model offers a broader view in urging simultaneous consideration of the role of biological, psychological, and social factors in the health and well-being of individuals.

One extension of the biopsychosocial model is its distinction between illness and health. According to the traditional medical model, "health" refers to the absence of disease.

However, according to the biopsychosocial model, "health" refers to overall biological, psychological, and social well-being. This feature of the biopsychosocial model may be especially salient to musculoskeletal conditions, since these are diseases that are currently not medically curable. Thus, approaches to treatment that focus on strictly medical outcomes, such as objective disease activity, yet overlook the well-being and psychosocial adaptation of an individual are shortsighted. In this chapter, we present evidence that a diagnosis of a musculoskeletal condition does not necessarily translate into a lifetime of disability and despair. Instead, there are psychological and social factors that influence the course and prognosis of these challenging conditions.

Just how do biopsychosocial factors influence disease onset, course, and outcome in musculoskeletal conditions? The stress-diathesis approach, although initially developed in studies of schizophrenia, has recently been applied to better understand the complex mechanisms underlying other disorders such as depression and chronic pain (Banks & Kerns, 1996; Monroe & Simons, 1991). According to this approach, a predisposing vulnerability (e.g., diathesis) and a precipitating environmental agent (e.g., stress) interact to produce disease. Traditionally, diathesis factors have been considered to be sources of vulnerability that interact with stress to produce negative outcomes. However, just as there exist predisposing sources of *vulnerability,* there may exist predisposing sources of *resilience* to stress. These resilience factors may either serve to buffer, or protect against, the negative effects of stress, or to interact with stress to produce positive outcomes. We propose that health psychology researchers and practitioners

This research was supported by grants from the National Institute on Aging, 1 F31 AG05850–01 (Heather M. Burke, Predoctoral Fellow) and the Arthritis Foundation (Alex J. Zautra, Principal Investigator).

should devote balanced attention to these dual influences. Thus, in this chapter, we review the biological, psychological, and social sources of vulnerability and resilience in the most common forms of arthritis in the United States: rheumatoid arthritis (RA), osteoarthritis (OA), and fibromyalgia (FM).

DIATHESIS

According to the diathesis-stress model, the process of adaptation and its health consequences are dependent on an individual's vulnerability and resistance to the threats to psychological and physical well-being posed by stressful circumstances. There exist individual differences in biological, psychological, and social sources of vulnerability and resilience, which ultimately interact with stress factors to produce outcomes. Individuals with musculoskeletal conditions confronted with the stress of chronic pain react differently according to their relative balance of vulnerability and resilience, so that identical stressors do not produce identical outcomes across individuals. Furthermore, despite the fact that RA, OA, and FM have many symptoms in common and are often treated within the same medical specialty, each disorder varies in composition of biological, psychological, and social factors. Thus, there are individual and disease-specific sources of variability in biopsychosocial diathesis factors. In this section, we describe the biological and epidemiological features of each disorder and identify psychological and social sources of vulnerability and resilience to stress.

Biological Diathesis Factors

Rheumatoid Arthritis

Currently, more than two million Americans suffer from either juvenile or adult RA (Lawrence et al., 1998). RA differs from OA and FM in several important ways (see Table 8.1). First, RA is an autoimmune disease characterized by systemic attacks by immune cells on the synovial tissue lining the joints of the body. As a result of chronic inflammation, the synovial lining of affected joints becomes saturated with lymphocytes, cytokines, and other pro-inflammatory cells. These cells in turn release substances that sustain the inflammatory responses. The inflammation at affected joints typically causes swelling and tenderness. Over time, the chronic inflammation eventually erodes the surrounding cartilage, bone, and ligaments, resulting in loss of function in the affected joint (Harris, 1993).

In RA, disease sequelae often directly produce the most common symptoms. Aside from the joint swelling and tenderness characteristic of inflammation, other common symptoms of RA include pain, morning stiffness, and fatigue (Harris, 1993). Joints most commonly affected in RA are the proximal interphalangeal (PIP), metacarpophalangeal (MCP), and wrist joints. As the disease progresses, larger joints become more symptomatic. Another defining feature of RA is the widespread, symmetric involvement of joint inflammation. Although joint tenderness and swelling may initially appear asymmetric, more symmetric involvement occurs as the disease progresses (Harris, 1993).

TABLE 8.1   Characteristics of RA, OA, and FM

	RA	OA	FM
Pathology	Autoimmune disease: Inflammation of synovial lining of joints leads to destruction of joint.	Imbalance of cartilage destruction and repair.	Unknown: Possible CNS dysregulation of neurohormonal or pain-transmitting substances.
Inflammation	Systemic.	Local.	Not present.
Distribution	Widespread and usually symmetric.	Localized, usually weight-bearing joints affected first.	Widespread and symmetric.
Areas commonly affected	Proximal interphalangeal (PIP), metacarpophalangeal (MCP), and wrist joints.	Hips, knees, spine, hands, and feet.	Tender points.
Genetic component	Present.	Present.	Present.
Lab measures	Radiographic and immune markers of inflammation.	Radiographic.	Tender point exam.
Epidemiology	More prevalent in women; increases with age.	Hand, knee, and generalized OA more common in women; hip OA more common in men; increases with age.	More prevalent in women; increases with age.

Several forms of onset have been described for RA. Most commonly, symptoms develop insidiously over weeks or months, although a small percentage of patients may experience an acute onset of symptoms (Harris, 1993). As many as 56% of RA patients may experience a course with partial remissions, but many (44%) experience a progressive decline (Eberhardt & Fex, 1998). Due to improvements in pharmaceutical technology, the prognosis for RA is considerably more favorable today than in the past. However, despite these medical advances, RA remains a progressive disease resulting in functional decline and a shortened lifespan (Harris, 1993).

Several demographic and clinical variables have been associated with poor prognosis in RA. Women appear to be at particular risk, as RA affects women 2 to 3 times more than men (Lawrence et al., 1998). Age is also a source of vulnerability. Although incidence of RA increases with age, there is evidence that an early onset, particularly before age 60, is associated with more aggressive disease (Harris, 1993). Furthermore, younger patients with RA are more vulnerable to developing depression, which itself is a disabling condition (Wright et al., 1998). Duration of disease is another risk factor for poor prognosis, as the first two years of disease activity appear to be the most amenable to treatment effects (J. Anderson, Wells, Verhoeven, & Felson, 2000). Thus, female gender, younger age at onset, and longer duration of disease activity serve as epidemiological and clinical diathesis factors contributing to course and prognosis in individuals with RA. Conversely, male gender, older age at onset, and recent diagnosis serve to benefit RA progression and outcome.

Besides epidemiological and clinical sources of vulnerability, there exist genetic predispositions to developing RA. For instance, some studies have demonstrated a fourfold increase in risk for developing severe RA in first-degree relatives of individuals with RA (Aho, Koskenvuo, Tuominen, & Kaprio, 1986). Other genetic studies have found heritability of RA as high as 65% (MacGregor et al., 2000). Genetics have been hypothesized to influence RA disease initiation and progression via immunological and hormonal processes. First, due to the autoimmune nature of RA, much genetic research has focused on the specific structure of immune cells in RA patients. One model is that RA patients inherit genes that produce immune cells that have a structure very similar to that of infectious agents such as viruses or bacteria (for review, see Harris, 1993). As long as the individual is not exposed to the infectious agent, the autoimmune response is not generated. However, once an infection occurs, the individual's immune system mounts an attack against the infectious agent but also mistakenly attacks its own immune cells, particularly the ones that line the synovial joints. The result is full-blown RA. Another genetic model of RA development suggests that individuals with RA inherit genes that produce abnormal hypothalamic-pituitary-adrenal axis (HPA) responses to stress and inflammation (Sternberg et al., 1989). As HPA responses typically inhibit inflammation, hypoactivity of the HPA axis may fail to control inflammation. Thus, when an individual with this genetic HPA vulnerability experiences inflammation in the initial stages of RA, his or her HPA responses are insufficient to suppress the RA disease process. It should be clear from both of these models that, although genetics play a role in establishing vulnerability to developing RA, genetic influences alone are insufficient to produce RA. Instead, these genetic models illustrate the utility of applying a diathesis-stress approach to understanding RA.

Osteoarthritis

OA is the most prevalent form of arthritis in the United States, affecting approximately 20.7 million Americans (Lawrence et al., 1998). Because the prevalence of this condition increases linearly with age, the number of OA cases is expected to rise considerably as the American population matures (Mankin, 1993). Although the precise etiology of OA is currently unknown, the pathogenesis is primarily characterized by cartilage destruction and bone erosions (Kraus, 1997). In individuals without arthritis, the processes of cartilage and bone synthesis and destruction operate in concert. In contrast, in individuals with OA, cartilage repair does not keep pace with cartilage destruction and bone synthesis. The levels of enzymes that promote cartilage destruction are elevated relative to those that promote cartilage synthesis in individuals with OA. The net result of the imbalance of cartilage destruction and synthesis is a reduction in overall cartilage in affected joints. Further complicating the process, bone synthesis continues and eventually encroaches into the joint space once occupied by cartilage (Kraus, 1997). Eventually, due to the contact of bone on bone, movement becomes limited and pain ensues in affected joints.

As in RA, common symptoms of OA are pain and inflammation, limited range of motion, and morning stiffness (Kraus, 1997). Furthermore, as disease activity progresses, joint deformity may develop (Mankin, 1993). However, in contrast to the widespread, symmetrical joint involvement characteristic of RA, joint swelling and tenderness in OA are localized to specific joints. The weight-bearing joints of the body, such as hip, knee, and spinal column joints, are those at most risk of developing OA. In addition, the hand joints are also affected in OA, particularly in women (Kraus, 1997).

Onset of OA is usually insidious, with disease slowly progressing over a period of years. However, although OA is a progressive condition, there remains great variability in the subjective experience of the disease. Some patients with radiographically confirmed advanced disease report few symptoms, whereas some patients with mild but detectable disease activity report a great deal of pain and activity limitation (Pincus et al., 1984). Thus, the biopsychosocial diathesis factors discussed in this chapter may serve as moderators of the relationship between radiographic evidence of joint damage and the person's experience.

As in RA, there exist many epidemiological and clinical risk factors for the development and prognosis of OA. First, the prevalence of OA increases dramatically with age (Lawrence et al., 1998). However, there is evidence that younger individuals with OA suffer from more psychological disability and pain, whereas older individuals experience more physical disability (Weinberger, Tierney, Booher, & Hiner, 1990). This finding underscores the importance of considering psychosocial in addition to biological factors when evaluating OA prognosis. Second, although women are at greater overall risk, men and women are vulnerable to different forms of OA. For instance, women tend to develop knee and hand OA whereas men are more likely to develop hip OA (Lawrence et al., 1998; Mankin, 1993). Furthermore, women are more likely than men to develop generalized OA, which is a more widespread form of OA. Thus, gender appears to affect the clinical presentation of OA.

In addition to epidemiological risk factors, there also exist clinical risk factors for OA. Among these are skeletal structure abnormalities and obesity (Kraus, 1997). The role of these risk factors for development of OA is best understood with a diathesis-stress approach. For instance, neither skeletal structure abnormalities nor obesity alone is sufficient for development of OA. Instead, these clinical risk factors may interact with one another to produce OA. For example, an individual with a congenital skeletal structural abnormality may not develop OA unless he or she experiences an injury or stresses a structurally vulnerable joint with a lifetime of excess weight.

Genetic influences are not limited to RA. In OA, genetics have been hypothesized to influence different aspects of the disease process. For instance, results of some studies indicate that individuals with OA inherit genes that either change the consistency of the cartilage (thus making it more vulnerable to destruction) or produce greater levels of cartilage-destroying enzymes (for review, see Kraus, 1997). Additionally, there appear to be genetic influences on the type of OA that individuals develop. There is strong evidence for a genetic influence on development of hand, spine, and generalized OA (Bijkerk et al., 1999; Felson et al., 1998). However, while genetics may increase the risk of developing OA, these genetic risk factors alone are not sufficient to produce OA.

Fibromyalgia

FM is a chronic pain syndrome of unknown origin that currently affects an estimated 3.7 million Americans. In contrast to the physical evidence of disease processes in RA and OA, individuals with FM experience chronic musculoskeletal pain with no identifiable site of pathology. Despite the lack of identifiable pathology, numerous researchers have attempted to understand the biological processes in FM. One of the most viable models for FM is a dysregulation of neurohormonal and pain-transmitting substances in the central nervous system (CNS) (for a review, see Bennett, 1999). An imbalance of crucial pain-transmitting chemicals such as substance P (Russell et al., 1994) and dysregulation of HPA axis activity have been documented in patients with FM (Adler, Kinsley, Hurwitz, Mossey, & Goldenberg, 1999; Bennett, 1999; Catley, Kaell, Kirschbaum, & Stone, 2000; Clauw & Chrousos, 1997). The finding that the majority of individuals with FM report nonrefreshing sleep provides further evidence for CNS dysregulation in FM (Bennett, 1993). In healthy individuals, stage 3 and 4 sleep is characterized by delta-wave activity. However, results of early studies on sleep patterns in FM patients revealed that the delta-wave activity of stages 3 and 4 sleep were consistently interrupted by the alpha waves normally found in stage 1 and stage 2 (Moldofsky, Scarisbrick, England, & Smythe, 1975). Furthermore, when healthy individuals were selectively deprived of stage 4 sleep for several days, they began to complain of musculoskeletal pain and fatigue (Moldofsky & Scarisbrick, 1976). Although the alpha-delta sleep abnormality is not specific to FM, as it has been observed in individuals without FM, it may represent a source of vulnerability to development of FM under favorable circumstances, especially considering that stage 4 sleep is a time of neurohormonal and neurotransmitter restoration (Bennett, 1993).

Unlike OA and RA, which are diseases that affect the joints, FM is characterized by widespread pain in soft tissue. Pain appears to be particularly noxious at specific "tender points" distributed throughout the body. To receive a diagnosis of FM, an individual must experience widespread pain in all four quadrants of the body and especially pronounced pain in at least 11 of 18 "tender point" spots (Wolfe et al., 1990). Other common symptoms of FM include fatigue, stiffness, and depression (Bennett, 1993; Wolfe et al., 1990).

There remains considerable controversy surrounding the course and prognosis for this condition. Although FM symptoms tend to be chronic, there is substantial individual variability in the course of the illness. Studies of clinic samples of individuals with FM have demonstrated continued presence of symptoms for most patients 10 years after symptom onset (Kennedy & Felson, 1996; Wigers, 1996). However, other investigators using community samples have uncovered better recovery rates. For example, in a community-based, longitudinal study of individuals with chronic widespread pain, 35% still had widespread pain, 50% had regional pain, and 15% had no pain at a two-year follow-up, suggesting improvement in 65% of the sample (MacFarlane et al., 1996). Those with FM who do not recover tend to be older, have less education, and have more symptoms for a longer period of time.

As in RA and OA, women are at particular risk for developing FM. Approximately 85% of FM patients are women (Lawrence et al., 1998). Furthermore, the prevalence of FM increases with age, and in many cases is secondary to other chronic pain conditions, such as OA, which occur most frequently among older adults (Lawrence et al., 1998).

Despite the lack of definitive pathology in FM, investigators have attempted to identify the role of genetic influences in FM. Specifically, researchers have hypothesized that if FM is indeed a disorder of neurohormone or pain-transmission dysregulation, there may exist a genetic vulnerability for this dysregulation (Clauw & Chrousos, 1997). Consistent with this hypothesis, there is evidence of familial predisposition to FM (Pellegrino, Waylonis, & Sommer, 1989; Stormorken & Brosstad, 1992). Furthermore, results of a recent study demonstrated that individuals with FM were more likely to have a specific genotype of the serotonin-transporter gene than healthy individuals (Offenbacher et al., 1999). In addition, among individuals with FM, those who had this genotype displayed greater amounts psychological distress than those without this genotype (Offenbacher et al., 1999). These results are underscored by the fact that serotonin regulates mood, sleep, and pain, which are disturbed in FM (Schwarz et al., 1999). Although preliminary, collectively these results suggest that genetics may play a role in the development of FM.

Psychological Diathesis Factors

Biological factors play a prominent role as diatheses for pain and disability in musculoskeletal conditions. We next turn our attention to the psychological sources of vulnerability and resilience that may affect adjustment to these conditions. Among the psychological features that have been the focus of empirical research are factors such as neuroticism, low self-efficacy, locus of control, depression, somatization, and low levels of positive affect.

Neuroticism

Personality has long been thought to play a role in the development of and adaptation to a host of chronic illnesses, including arthritis-related conditions (Affleck, Tennen, Urrows, & Higgins, 1992). Early empirical work aimed at determining whether certain personality attributes were more prevalent among individuals with particular medical disorders relative to other groups. In contrast, more recent research has focused on identifying individual differences in personality within diagnostic groups that contribute to disease course. One personality characteristic that has particular relevance for a biopsychosocial understanding of adaptation among those with chronic pain is neuroticism, or the dispositional tendency to experience negative emotions. Because individuals high in neuroticism report an increased frequency of stressful experiences (Bolger & Schilling, 1991), and because the experience of stress may enhance disease activity and symptoms of chronic pain (Zautra, Burleson, Matt, Roth, & Borrows, 1994), neuroticism may be especially problematic for those with a musculoskeletal condition. In fact, among individuals with RA, neuroticism has been associated with poor self-rated functional status (Radanov, Schwarz, & Frost, 1997), more intense pain (Affleck et al., 1992), and mental health problems (Fyrand, Wichstrom, Moum, Glennas, & Kvien, 1997). A neurotic disposition is also likely to play a role in adaptation to OA and FM, and although few studies have investigated it, the available data do point to this possibility. For instance, patients with FM who score high in neuroticism are more frustrated with their physicians than those low in neuroticism (Walker et al., 1997). Moreover, in one of the few studies investigating the role of neuroticism in adaptation to OA, neuroticism at baseline predicted pain up to 20 years later (Turk-Charles, Gatz, Pedersen, & Dahlberg, 1999). The existing data suggest that identifying subsets of pain patients with certain personality attributes, particularly neuroticism, may enhance our accuracy in the prediction of clinical outcomes in chronic pain.

Self-Efficacy and Control

One of the most well-researched individual difference variables in health psychology is that of self-efficacy or, a related concept, locus of control. Both concepts refer to an individual's belief in being capable of achieving desired goals. Research over many years has shown that having such a belief system is strongly related to health maintenance and recovery from health stressors. Certainly, chronic illnesses such as arthritis and FM are major challenges to freedom of action and general well-being. Thus, developing and enhancing a person's beliefs in self-efficacy and control are major goals in the treatment of an individual with a musculoskeletal condition.

The bulk of the extant research literature on these variables is both consistent with and encouraging of future developments. Patients with higher self-efficacy beliefs report less arthritis pain (Buckelew, Murray, Hewett, Johnson, & Huyser, 1995; Keefe, Lefebvre, Maixner, Salley, & Caldwell, 1997) and show greater flexibility and movement capacity (Rejeski, Craven, Ettinger, McFarlane, & Shumaker, 1996). While these results come from cross-sectional studies, similar results have been found in longitudinal studies. For instance, Lefebvre et al. (1999) have shown that self-efficacy beliefs predict outcome even after controlling for medical status variables.

In spite of the consistency and reliability of results such as these, questions remain. For instance, the mechanisms whereby these effects hold true need further investigation. Self-efficacy may influence an individual's stress response because feeling confident in his or her abilities to cope may lead an individual to be less likely to appraise situations as stressful than an individual who does not have beliefs in self-competence. This would suggest an underlying cognitive mechanism behind efficacy/control beliefs (Lazarus & Folkman, 1984). In that sense, self-efficacy beliefs may not only affect stress responses, but may also affect coping responses themselves. More indirectly, low beliefs in self-efficacy and control may be indicants of depression and helplessness, which themselves predict poorer health.

Like self-efficacy, locus of control has also been associated with health outcomes in individuals with arthritis-related conditions. Whereas self-efficacy refers to an individual difference variable related to the achievement of specific goals, the locus of control construct is thought of as a stable personality disposition. Despite this difference, it is noteworthy that the locus of control and health literature is nevertheless relatively consistent with the self-efficacy literature. Greater sense of control is associated with higher levels of health, health behaviors, and health beliefs (Thompson & Spacapan, 1991). Although there are some differences between OA, RA, and FM samples, there has been a relative lack of research cross-comparing those illnesses on locus of control scales. As might be expected, attributing causes of ill health to external forces such as chance is associated with poorer coping strategies, higher depression, and higher anxiety in chronic pain patients (Crisson & Keefe, 1988). Similarly, low internal control is correlated with high impairment in performing activities of daily living (Nicassio, Wallston, Callahan, Herbert, & Pincus, 1985). Some data indicate that FM patients report more intense pain and are more external in

their sense of control than RA patients (Pastor et al., 1993); however, Nicassio, Schuman, Radojevic, and Weisman (1999) were not able to detect the same pattern in their sample of FM patients. Overall, these results suggest that those patients who perceive themselves as having higher levels of dispositional control report less pain and better adjustment to their illness. Thus, having a high locus of control may serve as a source of resilience to the effects of stress.

Depression

Any discussion of chronic pain must necessarily include elaboration of the role of depression. In fact, the clear and consistent relationship between chronic pain and depression serves to convincingly illustrate how pain consists not only of biological, but also psychological and social factors (for reviews, see Banks & Kerns, 1996; Romano & Turner, 1985). There is a high prevalence of clinical depression in both RA (Creed, Murphy, & Jayson, 1990) and FM patient populations (Aaron et al., 1996; Hudson, Hudson, Pliner, & Goldenberg, 1985). Cross-sectional data gleaned from RA patients show a significant positive relationship between clinical depression and pain (Parker & Wright, 1995), as well as an association between depressive symptoms and pain (Affleck, Tennen, Urrows, & Higgins, 1991; Ferguson & Cotton, 1996). A key question remains unanswered, however: Does the experience of chronic pain precede or follow the development of depression? While not definitive, some longitudinal data provide evidence that pain precedes clinical depression (Morrow, Parker, & Russell, 1994) and depressive symptoms (Brown, 1990) in individuals with RA.

Because chronic pain and depression are so strongly related, and because FM lacks any clear etiology or identifiable biological markers, some investigators have proposed that FM be considered an "affective spectrum disorder" (Hudson & Pope, 1989). Support for this hypothesis would include demonstration of a higher prevalence of affective disorders among FM patients and their relatives, compared with other chronic pain patients. Some studies have demonstrated that FM patients, in fact, do score higher on measures of psychological distress (Uveges et al., 1990) and depressive symptoms (Alfici, Sigal, & Landau, 1989), report higher lifetime prevalence of affective disorder (Walker et al., 1997), and have a higher familial prevalence of major affective disorder (Hudson et al., 1985) than their RA counterparts. FM patients also experience significantly more depressive symptoms than patients with other forms of musculoskeletal pain, including low back pain and lumbar herniation (Krag, Norregaard, Larsen, & Danneskiold-Samsoe, 1994). In contrast, some findings have indicated that there is no difference in current or lifetime history of major depressive disorder between patient populations with FM and those with RA (Ahles, Khan, Yunus, Spiegel, & Masi, 1991). Thus, there is accumulating evidence that depression may be an inherent part of FM and other pain disorders of unknown origin.

Positive Affect

It is important to keep in mind that *depression* is a term that stands for a heterogeneous set of disturbances of affect and cognition. Under its umbrella may be found the workings of two major affect systems: a positive one, characterized by active, approach behaviors, optimistic expectancies, and positive emotions, and a negative one, characterized by high levels of avoidance and retreat behaviors, highly pessimistic expectancies, and considerable negative emotion. Although these systems typically operate independently of one another, they both contribute to our understanding of depression. Both loss of the capacity for pleasure and sustained elevations in feeling downhearted and "blue" define depressive disorders. Both of these affect systems may influence and are influenced by the chronic pain and disability of musculoskeletal conditions in distinct ways. In an examination of data from three large community studies of RA patients, Zautra, Burleson, Smith, et al. (1995) found that these two affect systems were differentially associated with RA symptoms. RA pain was strongly associated with higher levels of negative affect, but was not associated with less positive affect. Disability, however, was most strongly associated with low levels of positive affect, and not high levels of negative affect. These two affects also appeared to be linked with different forms of coping. Those RA patients who coped actively with the challenges of their illness were more likely to show high levels of positive affect. Those who used avoidant and other more passive strategies tended to experience more negative affect. How depression plays a role in RA then is best understood by asking two questions: Does the person experience a relative deficit in the positive affective system and/or an abnormally high level of negative affectivity?

These distinctions may also be useful in specifying the affective conditions underlying the different forms of chronic pain. Zautra, Hamilton, and Burke (1999) have provided evidence to suggest that when pain levels are controlled, FM patients do not differ in level of negative affective responses from RA and OA patient groups. However, they do appear to evidence greater deficits in positive affects than either RA or OA groups. During stressful times, these affective conditions may be particularly important. Zautra, Hamilton, and Yocum (2000) provide evidence that improvement in positive affect can reduce disease activity among patients with RA, and

Zautra and Smith (2001) provide further evidence that positive events may diminish stress-reactive disease processes for RA patients. Further, Davis, Zautra, and Reich (2001) have shown that the absence of positive affect is associated with greater increases in FM pain following the administration of a laboratory stressor. OA patients did not show the same patterns as the FM subjects, suggesting that affective conditions are associated with illness symptoms in different ways for OA and FM patients. Thus, positive affect may serve as a source of resilience to the effects of stress.

Somatization

Besides depression, chronic pain patients have also been documented to experience many symptoms of somatization (Bacon et al., 1994). Somatization is characterized by excessive preoccupation with somatic symptoms and health care seeking for symptoms with no known cause (American Psychiatric Association, 1994). Somatization disorder has been associated with chronic pain in general (Wilson, Dworkin, Whitney, & LeResche, 1994). For instance, somatization behavior has been demonstrated in diverse chronic pain conditions such as low back pain (Bacon et al., 1994) and irritable bowel syndrome (Chang, Mayer, Johnson, Fitzgerald, & Naliboff, 2000). Thus, it appears that there is only weak evidence of comorbid somatization disorder in musculoskeletal conditions, and only in FM patients (Kirmayer, Robbins, & Kapusta, 1988; Wolfe & Hawley, 1999). However, one major limitation to distinguishing FM symptoms from somatization behavior is that they share one defining feature: widespread bodily symptoms with no clear physical evidence of a pathological problem.

Social Diathesis Factors

Our discussion to this point has highlighted the biological and psychological sources of vulnerability and resilience in adaptation to musculoskeletal conditions. But life experiences, including pain and other symptoms, occur in a social context. This has profound implications for adaptation and quality of life. Two important social factors that influence the functioning of individuals with chronic pain include social support, a source of resilience, and stigmatization, a source of vulnerability.

Social Support

Supportive social relationships represent one of the most influential social factors that sustain physical health (Sarason, Sarason, & Gurung, 1997). Supportive social relationships are related to positive health outcomes via at least two possible paths. One path involves a direct link between support and positive health outcomes, such that the benefits of support are experienced under all circumstances. The second path is a moderated one, such that the benefits of support are experienced only during times of high stress. The second path may be particularly important for individuals with musculoskeletal conditions, because individuals with chronic pain and disability may be especially vulnerable to the effects of stress. Thus, social support may be a key factor influencing adaptation to chronic pain. In fact, there is evidence to suggest that social support exerts a stress-buffering effect in individuals with arthritis and musculoskeletal conditions (Affleck, Pfeiffer, Tennen, & Fifield, 1988; for review, see Manne & Zautra, 1992). Moreover, the quality of close relationships has also been associated with greater pain medication effectiveness (Radanov, Frost, Schwarz, & Augustiny, 1996), less disability (Weinberger et al., 1990), and lower levels of depression (Nicassio, Radojevic, Schoenfeld-Smith, & Dwyer, 1995) among arthritis pain patients.

The detrimental health effects of a lack of supportive social ties during stress in individuals with chronic illness is also apparent and may be compounded by depression, poor coping responses, and other psychological factors. For instance, the tendency of individuals with FM to cope with pain by withdrawing from personal relationships may make them more vulnerable to the negative effects of stress (Zautra et al., 1999).

Stigma

Along with the benefits of social relationships, some individuals with chronic pain may also experience stresses and strains from their social ties through stigmatization. Individuals with chronic pain of unknown etiology are particularly likely to feel stigmatized and think that others are attributing their symptoms to personality problems, compared to people with pain from an identifiable cause (Lennon, Link, Marback, & Dohrenwend, 1989). Moreover, a brief perusal of recent research suggests that the perception of pain patients that they are stigmatized is warranted. For example, both the early investigations of RA and more recent studies of FM have focused on identifying personality attributes that distinguish pain patients from healthy individuals, in part to identify a psychological explanation for the experience of these pain conditions. Although it may be an accurate perception, perceived stigmatization is problematic because it appears to promote use of maladaptive coping strategies. For instance, common responses to perceived stigma among those with chronic pain include withdrawal from personal

relationships (Osborn & Smith, 1998) and increasing frequency of medical consultations (Lennon et al., 1989). Although no data are yet available for FM, some evidence suggests that stigma may be a common source of social stress in FM patients: They have a condition of unknown etiology, tend to withdraw from social relationships (Zautra et al., 1999), and have high medical utilization rates (Kirmayer et al., 1988). Furthermore, the perception of being stigmatized is quite likely to extend beyond those with FM. As one example, RA patients may feel stigmatized by the physical disfigurement that typically marks the later stages of RA. Given the pronounced effect of the experience of stigmatization on adaptation, greater attention to vulnerability to stigmatization in arthritis and musculoskeletal conditions is warranted.

STRESS

According to the diathesis-stress model, stressors in life are seen as provoking agents that challenge adaptation for all, but only harm those who are vulnerable (Banks & Kerns, 1996; Monroe & Simons, 1991). Before discussing the biopsychosocial aspects of stress in RA, OA, and FM, it is important to first describe how stress is defined in this chapter. Stress may be defined as a physiological, emotional, or behavioral response to an event, or stressor, that is perceived as threatening or beyond one's ability to cope (Lazarus & Folkman, 1984). Individual differences in appraisal of a stressor may determine the degree of perceived stress experienced and how an individual copes with this perceived stress. Thus, biopsychosocial influences may affect exposure to, appraisal of, and reaction to stressful events. In this section, we discuss the biological, psychological, and social contributions to stress in RA, OA, and FM.

Biological Stress Systems

Since the pioneering work of Cannon (1932) and Seyle (1956), the most extensively studied physiological stress systems have been the hypothalamic-pituitary-adrenal axis (HPA) and the sympathetic-adrenal-medullary axis (SAM). In addition, other aspects of the CNS, hypothalamic-pituitary-gonadal axis (HPG; i.e., reproductive system), and immune systems appear to be activated under stressful conditions. We briefly describe each of these stress systems, and then present evidence for the intrinsic involvement of these systems in musculoskeletal conditions.

The interrelationships between the endocrine and nervous systems have evolved to maintain biological equilibrium, or homeostasis, in the face of an ever-changing environment.

Through positive and negative feedback of hormone levels, up- and down-regulation of postsynaptic receptors, and activation and inhibition of the immune system, the body is able to recover homeostasis during and after stressful perturbations. However, when dysregulation of any of these mechanisms occurs, homeostasis is more difficult to sustain, recovery of the balance of physiological processes takes longer, and disease may result. Thus, biological stress systems are crucial components of the diathesis-stress model; individuals with a preexisting weakness at any point in the stress system may experience inadequate or interminable responses to stress. Moreover, stress response dysregulation appears to be a shared feature of many chronic illnesses.

HPA Axis

A significant body of research on the biological aspects of stress has focused on the HPA axis and its role in suppression of immune function. Stress activates the CNS, causing the release of corticotropin-releasing hormone (CRH) from the hypothalamus. CRH then stimulates the release of adrenal corticotrophic hormone (ACTH) from the anterior pituitary, which in turn triggers release of cortisol from the adrenal cortex (Figure 8.1). In the healthy individual, cortisol is believed

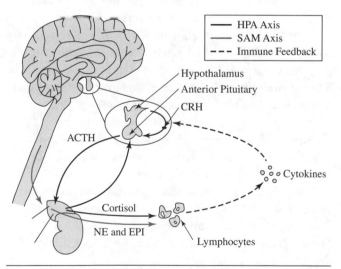

Figure 8.1 *Hypothalamic-Pituitary-Adrenal (HPA) Axis:* Stress activates the CNS, causing the release of corticotropin-releasing hormone (CRH) from the hypothalamus. CRH then stimulates the release of adrenal corticotrophic hormone (ACTH) from the anterior pituitary, which in turn triggers release of cortisol from the adrenal cortex. Cortisol then suppresses lymphocyte production. Cortisol also feeds back to the anterior pituitary, suppressing the release of more ACTH.

Sympathetic-Adrenal-Medullary (SAM) Axis: In the SAM axis, stress stimulates nerves that directly innervate the adrenal medulla, which in turn releases norepinephrine (NE) and epinephrine (EPI) into the bloodstream. The SAM axis promotes lymphocyte proliferation.

Immune Feedback: The immune system also feeds back onto the HPA axis. Cytokines stimulate the HPA axis.

to reduce inflammation by suppressing cellular immune function. Thus, via cortisol secretion, stress serves an anti-inflammatory purpose.

The anti-inflammatory effects of cortisol have led investigators to believe that HPA axis dysregulation could be a source of the inflammation observed in RA. There is a growing body of evidence to suggest that RA is the endpoint of a continuum of psychological, endocrine, and immune dysregulation (Chrousos & Gold, 1992). The hormonal responses intrinsic to psychological stress are thought to trigger a cascade of dysregulated endocrine and immune activity that ultimately results in the inflammation seen in RA.

Given the extreme inflammation seen in RA, we would expect that either the inflammation in RA is a result of low cortisol levels or, alternatively, that cortisol levels are ineffectively compensating for the degree of inflammation. Consistent with these expectations, some studies have revealed blunted cortisol responses to stimulation and decreased cortisol secretion associated with a disease flare (van den Brink, Blankenstein, Koppeschaar, & Bijlsma, 1993). Yet, while some studies have found blunted cortisol responses, others have demonstrated relatively normal cortisol levels in response to stress in RA patients (Huyser & Parker, 1998; Neeck, Federlin, Graef, Rusch, & Schmidt, 1990). However, as cortisol serves an anti-inflammatory purpose, normal cortisol levels in an inflammatory disease such as RA may not be adaptive. These findings have led investigators to hypothesize that the magnitude of cortisol responses may not be proportional to the stimulation of inflammatory processes in RA patients. The lack of a dose-dependent cortisol response to inflammation may be due to feedback failure at several levels (Templ et al., 1996). In other words, after chronically elevated circulating levels of cortisol are stimulated by the inflammatory process, target organs may downregulate cortisol receptor density to compensate. As a result, the same level of cortisol may not be as effective as it once was. This is analogous to insulin-resistant diabetes, in which chronically elevated insulin levels cause down-regulation of insulin receptors. There is evidence to support this decreased cortisol sensitivity hypothesis in RA. For instance, researchers have documented decreased cortisol receptor densities on peripheral blood mononuclear cells in patients with RA (Morand, Jefferiss, Dixey, Mitra, & Goulding, 1994).

HPA dysregulation has also been hypothesized to be associated with FM symptoms. Some investigators have found evidence for HPA hyperactivity in FM patients. For instance, one study found a trend toward increased cortisol in FM patients compared to RA and low back pain patients in response to dexamethasone administration (Ferraccioli et al., 1990). However, in another study, although both FM and RA patients had higher cortisol levels than a healthy control group, there were no differences in cortisol reactivity to acute stressors between the FM and RA groups (Catley et al., 2000).

While some studies have found trends toward cortisol hypersecretion in FM patients, others have instead found hypersecretion of ACTH, with no dose-dependent increase in cortisol (Crofford et al., 1994; Griep, Boersma, & deKloet, 1993). These results suggest a decreased responsiveness of the adrenal cortex to ACTH, possibly as a result of down-regulation of ACTH receptors. Furthermore, there is evidence of a flattened diurnal pattern of cortisol secretion in FM patients compared to RA patients (Crofford et al., 1994). Another recent study found reduced ACTH responses to hypoglycemic stress in FM patients, suggesting hypoactivity of the HPA axis (Adler et al., 1999). Thus, as in RA, there is conflicting evidence for HPA dysregulation in RA and FM patients.

In RA and FM, different neuroendocrine processes may produce the cortisol hyposecretion common to both disorders. For instance, in RA patients, cortisol may have been chronically secreted due to the chronic inflammatory process of RA. To compensate for these chronically elevated cortisol levels, other systems, including those that regulate the immune system, may become increasingly less sensitive to cortisol through down-regulation of cortisol receptors. The net result would be normal or relatively low cortisol levels for a given level of inflammation. In contrast, depression is not only associated with elevated cortisol levels (Deuschle, Weber, Colla, Depner, & Heuser, 1998), but is often comorbid with FM. As a result, of the chronically elevated levels of cortisol associated with depression in FM, glucocorticoid receptors may have down-regulated. Thus, patients with RA and FM may both have cortisol hyposecretion, but from different causes.

SAM Axis

Stress can affect health via pathways other than the HPA axis. The SAM axis is part of the sympathetic nervous system and is responsible for initiating the "fight-or-flight" response (Cannon, 1932). Whereas the HPA axis is primarily an endocrine system (i.e., hormones travel through the bloodstream), the SAM axis is neuroendocrine, consisting of both neural and endocrine tissues. In the SAM axis, stress stimulates nerves that directly innervate the adrenal medulla, which in turn releases norepinephrine (NE) and epinephrine (EPI) into the bloodstream (Figure 8.1). Like the HPA axis, the SAM axis has immunomodulating effects. Whereas the HPA axis inhibits the inflammatory response, the SAM axis activates it (Madden & Livnat, 1991). As nervous impulses

directly stimulate the adrenal medulla, the SAM axis has much faster and more immediate effects than the slower acting HPA axis.

There is some evidence for SAM dysregulation in RA. Some investigators believe that the cycle of inflammation in RA reflects hypersecretion of pro-inflammatory hormones with the SAM axis serving an immunostimulating function (Madden & Livnat, 1991). Indeed, results of some studies suggest SAM hyperactivity in RA. For instance, one study found that RA patients had higher plasma NE and EPI levels than healthy controls (Lechin et al., 1994). Another study found down-regulation of beta-2 receptor density on peripheral blood mononuclear cells in RA, which may be a result of chronically elevated sympathetic activity (Baerwald, Graefe, Muhl, von Wichert, & Krause, 1992).

As with HPA axis dysregulation, evidence of SAM dysregulation in RA is far from conclusive. Just as results of several studies have suggested SAM hyperactivity, still others have presented evidence for SAM hypoactivity in RA. Although not exclusively due to SAM activity, blood pressure and heart rate are often used as indices of SAM activity. For instance, in a study of recently diagnosed RA patients, Geenan, Godaert, Jacobs, Peters, and Bijlsma (1996) found that blood pressure was negatively related to pain severity. In another study, compared to healthy controls, RA patients had lower heart rate and blood pressure responses to a cognitive stress test, although levels still fell within normal limits (Geenan et al., 1998). The authors of those studies suggest that, since the SAM axis stimulates the immune system, SAM hypoactivity may have developed over time as a means to minimize the inflammation present in RA.

Investigators have also begun to examine the role of SAM activity in FM (Mengshoel, Saugen, Forre, & Vollestad, 1995; van Denderen, Boersma, Zeinstra, Hollander, & van Neerbos, 1992). The few preliminary investigations of cross-sectional differences between urinary catecholamine secretion in FM and healthy controls (with no stress conditions) have suggested a trend toward increased NE in FM patients (Yunus, Dailey, Aldag, Masi, & Jobe, 1992).

Reproductive System

The greater prevalence of arthritis and other musculoskeletal conditions in women than men has led investigators to hypothesize a role of reproductive hormones in these disorders. Although men also experience hormonal changes with aging, women endure a dramatic decrease in reproductive hormones such as estrogen, progesterone, and gonadotropins such as follicle-stimulating hormone and luteinizing hormone. This decline in reproductive hormone levels coincides with an increased risk of developing arthritis and musculoskeletal conditions.

Besides the epidemiological data, there is considerable evidence to support a role of reproductive hormones in the development of RA (for review, see Grossman, Roselle, & Mendenhall, 1991). Early observations of pregnant women with RA revealed that the women typically developed remission of RA activity during the third trimester, only to experience relapses postpartum (Hazes, 1991; Persellin, 1977). Other research has demonstrated that nulliparious women are at greater risk for developing RA (Hazes, 1991). Finally, reproductive hormones have been found to have immune stimulating and suppressing effects. For instance, the reproductive hormones prolactin and estrogen are presumed to have immunoenhancing effects (Jorgensen & Sany, 1994). Furthermore, prolactin suppresses cortisol secretion (Jorgensen & Sany, 1994). The immunostimulatory effects of prolactin coupled with suppressed cortisol may partially explain the relapse of RA postpartum, when prolactin levels are elevated. Thus, there may exist an association between reproductive hormones and arthritis activity via the effects on the immune system. Despite the promise of this hypothesis, few studies have investigated the relationship. However, one study found that, when confronted with interpersonal stressors, women with RA displayed greater increases in immunostimulatory hormones such as prolactin and estrogen than women with OA (Zautra et al., 1994). Furthermore, these increases in prolactin and estrogen were associated with clinicians' ratings of arthritis disease activity. Overall, these results support a central role of reproductive hormones in the RA disease activity.

Fewer studies have investigated the role of reproductive hormones in OA. However, the established protective effect of osteoporosis (which is associated with low estrogen levels) on development of OA suggests that there may exist a link between reproductive hormones and OA (for review, see Sambrook & Naganathan, 1997). However, it is also feasible the negative association between osteoporosis and OA is due to a spurious variable such as body mass; women with osteoporosis tend to weigh less, whereas OA is associated with obesity.

As in RA and OA, there is also preliminary evidence to suggest a relationship between FM and reproductive hormones. The greater prevalence of FM in women than men supports a role of female reproductive hormones in the development of FM (Lawrence et al., 1998). In addition, like RA, there is evidence that FM symptoms worsen during the third trimester of pregnancy and the postpartum period (Ostensen, Rugelsjoen, & Wigers, 1997). Furthermore, in one study, investigators compared the prevalence of FM in women with clinically high

levels of prolactin to women with normal levels of prolactin (Buskila et al., 1993). Results revealed that 71% of the women with elevated prolactin levels met diagnostic criteria for FM, whereas less than 5% of the women with normal prolactin levels met this criteria. Finally, results of some studies revealed elevated basal prolactin levels (Griep et al., 1994) and exaggerated prolactin responses to hormonal challenges in women with FM compared to healthy women, although not all studies demonstrated these differences (Korszun et al., 2000). Overall, these results suggest that, as in individuals with RA, individuals with FM may have elevated levels of prolactin. As prolactin promotes inflammatory processes, these results imply an inflammatory process in FM. However, since there is currently no direct evidence of inflammation in FM, this conclusion is putative.

The Immune System

Although we have discussed the indirect effects of stress on immunity via the endocrine and nervous systems, the immune system reciprocally affects the endocrine and nervous systems. When the immune system is activated, a cell-mediated immune response ensues to activate T cells that attack "foreign" cells. Activated T cells also release a series of chemical mediators to stimulate more T cell, B cell, and macrophage activity. Activated macrophages then release a series of chemicals called interleukins, which are also called cytokines. Although there are many interleukins, for the purposes of this chapter we primarily focus on interleukin-1 (Il-1), interleukin-2 (Il-2), and interleukin-6 (Il-6). These cytokines in turn stimulate further inflammatory processes.

Autoimmunity occurs when the body's immune system mistakes its own tissue as foreign (i.e., an antigen) and initiates an immune response to destroy it. In the case of RA, the immune system attacks the synovial lining of the joints. Investigators have identified at least one mechanism by which this process occurs. In some RA patients, an acute infection causes the immunoglobulin-G (IgG) antibody to mutate. The immune system then mistakes this mutated antibody for an antigen and mounts an attack against it (for review, see Mageed, Borretzen, Moyes, Thompson, & Natvig, 1997). During this attack, immunoglobulin-M (IgM) antibody binds to the mutated IgG antibody, creating a bound complex commonly referred to as rheumatoid factor (RF; Mageed et al., 1997). Although RF is not found in all RA patients, there is some evidence that RF-positive and RF-negative RA patients may differ in degree of life stress. For instance, Stewart, Knight, Pakmer, and Highton (1994) found that RF-negative RA patients experienced more life stress prior to onset of RA symptoms than their RF-positive counterparts.

There is evidence that in RA, both the T cells and cytokines are integrally involved in disease activity (for review, Smolen et al., 1996). Compared to healthy controls, RA patients have increased Il-1 levels in sera (Symons, Wood, DiGiovine, & Duff, 1988) and increased levels of soluble Il-2 receptors (sIL-2R) in sera and synovial fluid (Keystone et al., 1988). In addition, compared to OA patients, RA patients have higher sera and synovial levels of Il-6 (Okamoto et al., 1997). Besides evidence for elevated cytokine levels in RA patients, some researchers have found a positive relationship between sIL-2R levels and disease activity (Harrington et al., 1993; Wood, Symons, & Duff, 1988). Furthermore, although few studies have investigated the role of cytokine activity in FM, there is preliminary evidence suggesting elevated soluble IL-6 receptor (sIL-6R) and soluble IL-1 receptor (sIL-1R) levels in FM patients, and in depressed patients (Maes et al., 1999).

As mentioned previously, cytokines play a feedback role on the stress systems of the body. For example, in samples of RA patients, there is evidence that cytokines activate the HPA axis, stimulating release of cortisol, perhaps in an effort to suppress inflammation (Geenan et al., 1998; Neeck et al., 1990). Furthermore, in a sample of FM patients, cytokine infusion led to exaggerated SAM responses, which stimulate the immune system (Torpy et al., 2000). These results suggest that understanding the immune-endocrine relationship may be key to understanding the physiological mechanisms that underlie stress-related illness activity in RA and possibly FM.

The Pain System

From the previous discussion, it should be clear that although RA, OA, and FM differ from one another they also have many things in common. Not only are they often treated within the same medical specialty, but they also share common symptoms. These disorders are inherently associated with chronic pain, chronic pain, which may serve as the common denominator for each of these conditions. Defined by the International Association of the Study of Pain as "an unpleasant sensory and emotional experience associated with actual or potential tissue damage" (Merskey & Bogduk, 1994), pain is best understood by considering biopsychosocial factors within a diathesis-stress model. In this section, we describe the gate control theory of pain, and its relevance to RA, OA, and FM.

Although both the HPA and SAM originate in the CNS, their target organs lie outside the CNS. However, there is also evidence of stress-related changes within the CNS that directly affect pain perception, or nociception, a common symptom to all arthritis-related conditions. One model that describes the role of the CNS in nociception is the gate control theory of pain. Developed by Melzack and Wall (1965), the gate control theory of pain represents an attempt to consider the sensory, affective, and evaluative components of pain within an integrated neurophysiological framework. The crux of the gate control theory of pain is that both ascending (i.e., input to brain) and descending (i.e. output from brain) factors affect the "opening" and "closing" of a pain gate located in the dorsal horn of the spinal cord (Figure 8.2). Pain promoting, or nocioceptive, signals open the gate to pain perception at the brain level, whereas antinociceptive, or pain inhibiting, signals close the gate to pain perception. Nociceptive and antinociceptive signals may originate either at the brain or spinal cord level. Therefore, both the brain and spinal cord act in concert to either open or close the gate. Thus, due to its emphasis on the important roles of biological, psychological, and social factors, the gate control theory of pain is a biopsychosocial formulation of pain systems.

Pain signals are usually transmitted from the site of injury to the spinal cord via A-delta and C-fibers (Melzack & Wall, 1965). A-delta fibers are characteristically small and have myelinated axons, a feature that accelerates the rate of transmission to the spinal cord. As a result, A-delta fibers tend to

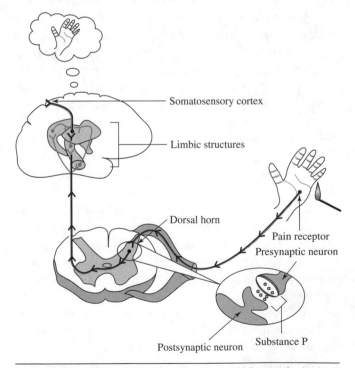

Figure 8.2 Pain elicits a signal in a pain receptor, which transmits the signal to the dorsal horn of the spinal cord. The pre-synaptic neuron releases substance P into the synapse, which excites the post-synaptic neuron. The post-synaptic neuron then sends the painful signal to the somatosensory cortex via two different pathways: (1) directly through the thalamus, or (2) through the thalamus after processing by the limbic structures. In the somatosensory cortex, the pain sensation is consciously experienced.

quickly transmit sharp pain signals. In contrast, C-fibers are not myelinated. Thus, their signals are sent more slowly than the A-delta fibers, and transmit dull and aching pain signals. When either the A-delta or C-fibers are activated and synapse at the spinal cord, substance P is released, which in turn stimulates the ascending nerve to send the pain signal to the brain (Figure 8.2). Thus, substance P appears to be crucial to the transmission of pain signals from the peripheral nervous system to the CNS. After the signal ascends, it may take at least two different pathways. The acute pain pathway synapses in the somatosensory cortex directly via the thalamus. Another, less direct pathway is to first pass through synaptic connections in the brain stem, thalamus, hypothalamus, and other limbic structures before synapsing at the thalamus. The latter pathway, which is associated with more chronic forms of pain, is noteworthy because it travels through the so-called emotion-centered (limbic) parts of the brain. Thus, indirect processing via the limbic structures provides a physiological substrate to the affective components of pain.

Pain signals are also regulated by descending pathways. The brain has evolved to release several neurotransmitters to inhibit pain perception. Among these transmitters are endogenous opioids and serotonin. Endogenous opioids such as beta-endorphins are characterized by pain-relieving properties. Endogenous opioids are also intrinsically related to the HPA axis, as CRH stimulates their release. Like endogenous opioids, serotonin, a neurotransmitter also involved in mood regulation, serves to close the pain gate (Basbaum & Fields, 1984).

The example just described illustrates how tissue injury such as in RA and OA causes pain perception. However, what about conditions like FM in which there is no discernable tissue damage yet considerable perceived pain? Melzack and Wall (1965) proposed an explanation for that scenario as well. They observed the "wind-up" phenomenon in which repetitive stimulation of nociceptive fibers resulted in greater stimulation of the dorsal horn neurons (Melzack & Wall, 1965; cited in Bennett, 1999). Over time, these dorsal horn neurons require less and less actual stimulation to become activated. Eventually, nonnociceptive sensory stimuli can activate the nociceptive neurons of the dorsal horn, creating pain impulses (Kramis, Roberts, & Gillette, 1996). One of the neuropeptides that mediates this process is substance P (Clauw & Chrousos, 1997). The production of pain sensation from nonnociceptive stimuli is referred to as *allodynia,* and the process that produces allodynia is called *central sensitization* (Bennett, 1999). Bennett refers to central sensitization process as "an increased excitability of spinal and supraspinal neural circuits." Thus, with the central sensitization process, not only does nonnociceptive stimuli produce

pain sensations, but the total area of the body initially considered painful widens. Central sensitization may explain why regional pain syndromes often become widespread. Another quality of central sensitization relevant to arthritis and musculoskeletal conditions is that central sensitization is more likely to occur in muscle fibers than in skin fibers (Wall & Woolf, 1984). Thus, individuals with musculoskeletal pain are at an increased risk for the sequelae of central sensitization.

The stress response is intrinsically linked to nociception. What is particularly noteworthy about the descending pathway in the context of this chapter is that the transmitters involved are stimulated by acute stress. Stress-induced analgesia occurs when the release of these transmitters, particularly the endogenous opioids, inhibits pain perception (Fields & Basbaum, 1994; Lewis, Terman, Sharit, Nelson, & Liebeskind, 1984). Acute stress also stimulates the release of other substances, such as serotonin, NE, and CRH (Clauw & Chrousos, 1997). Likewise, release of beta endorphin during acute stress may suppress immune responses and therefore pain (Akil et al., 1984). Under acutely stressful experiences, these substances serve to close the pain gate.

Other nociceptive substances besides substance P can serve to open the pain gate. For instance, bradykinin is a substance that produces pain by stimulating production of histamine and prostaglandins and exciting nociceptive neurons (Marieb, 1993). Furthermore, disease processes associated with inflammation can open the pain gate. For instance, Il-6, which is released during inflammation, is also intrinsically involved in nociception (Arruda, Colburn, Rickman, Rutkowski, & DeLeo, 1998).

There are several reasons why the CNS has been hypothesized to play a role in RA disease activity. First, the widespread symmetric pattern of joint inflammation and the proximal joint involvement suggests that a CNS abnormality may underlie RA disease activity. There is evidence to support this observation. First, patients with RA who have suffered paralysis no longer experience RA disease activity on the paralyzed side (Glick, 1967). There is also evidence that substance P may play a role in RA disease activity. For instance, substance P stimulates lymphocyte proliferation and other inflammatory responses (Felten, Felten, Bellinger, & Lorton, 1992). Also, results of one study suggest a positive correlation between substance P fiber innervation and arthritis inflammation (Levine, Coberre, Helms, & Basbaum, 1988). These observations indicate that the CNS is involved in RA flare-ups.

CNS involvement may also influence OA. For instance, the common transition from localized to the widespread pain that occurs in many individuals with OA may reflect a central sensitization process. Furthermore, as the OA disease process progresses, inflammation of the affected joints may trigger substance P secretion, which in turn should produce more pain. Thus, although few studies have investigated the role of the CNS in OA, its role is plausible.

Although an etiological mechanism for the pain of FM is unknown, CNS involvement is likely. Substance P has also been suggested to play a role in FM. There is preliminary evidence for elevated levels of substance P and substance P agonists in FM patients (Giovengo, Russell, & Larson, 1999; Russell et al., 1994), although not every study found such effects (Reynolds, Chiu, & Inman, 1988).

Due to the high prevalence of mood disorders and severity of pain in individuals with FM, some investigators have hypothesized that there may be low levels of serotonin in FM. Although some researchers have demonstrated an inverse relationship between serotonin levels and pain in individuals with FM (Russell et al., 1992), others have found no group differences in platelet serotonin levels between FM, RA, and low back pain patients (Krag et al., 1995). However, results of some studies have revealed high levels of antibodies to serotonin in individuals with FM and depression, suggesting a possible autoimmune basis for these disorders (Klein & Berg, 1995; Samborski et al., 1998). Results of these studies illustrate the need for further research in this area.

Psychological Stress Factors

From the previous discussion it should be clear that the biological aspects of the stress response are intrinsically involved in musculoskeletal disease processes. However, there also exist psychological factors that moderate the amount of perceived stress experienced. Among these psychological factors are those that affect the appraisal of the stressor and those that influence coping responses.

Appraisal

There are several psychological qualities of stressful situations that influence the degree of perceived stress experienced. For instance, situations that are perceived as uncontrollable, unpredictable, or ambiguous are perceived as more stressful than situations that are perceived as controllable, predictable, or unambiguous (Glass & Singer, 1972). These influences on perceived stress have implications for RA, OA, and FM. First, the chronic pain associated with each of these conditions coupled with the lack of complete symptom relief from traditional pharmacological treatment may classify chronic pain as an uncontrollable stressor. However, while uncontrollable chronic pain may be common to RA, OA, and

FM, its predictability may vary across disorders. Whereas the pain of OA is usually exacerbated by activity, the pain of RA and FM does not necessarily follow a predictable pattern. This increase in pain unpredictability may affect the degree of perceived stress experienced by individuals with RA and FM. Furthermore, the pain of RA, OA, and FM may differ in terms of ambiguity. For instance, while the pain of RA and OA stem from identifiable disease processes, the pain of FM has no known cause. This ambiguity may be a source of increased perceived stress in individuals with FM. Thus, not only do individuals differ in their appraisal of stressful events, there may be disease-specific effects on appraisal as well. Pain sensations have evolved to allow individuals to take notice of harm and reduce activity in order to heal. In the context of RA and OA, which involve identifiable disease processes, this is an adaptive response. However, in FM, there is a paradox; pain messages signal that something is wrong and that the individual should reduce activity, yet the pain is of benign origin. As a result, individuals with FM experience a discrepancy between an experience of chronic pain and the fact that the pain symptoms do not represent an underlying tissue pathology. This discrepancy may be partially responsible for the "doctor shopping" commonly exhibited in this group, as individuals with FM attempt to find a physician who will acknowledge their experience of pain. It is also possible that individuals differ in their appraisal of the discrepancy. Whereas some individuals may experience reassurance when told that their pain is of benign origin, others may interpret this message as either a dismissal of their subjective experience or an oversight of some underlying disease process. Thus, appraisal factors may interact with pain symptoms to produce several of the behaviors observed in individuals with FM.

Coping

The adaptiveness of specific coping strategies may also be context- and disease-specific (for review, see Manne & Zautra, 1992). There is evidence that those with RA and OA who use active coping strategies have more favorable outcomes than those who use passive coping strategies, which involve retreat in the face of a stressor. In individuals with RA and OA, passive coping, but not active coping, is related to reduced functional status (Affleck et al., 1992; Zautra et al., 1995). In addition, coping strategies such as wishful thinking and catastrophizing account for a significant amount of variability in physical disability, pain, and depression in individuals with RA and OA (Beckham, Keefe, Caldwell, & Roodman, 1991). There is some evidence that individuals with FM cope differently than those with OA or RA. For example, Zautra et al. (1999) found that FM patients used more avoidant strategies than their OA counterparts. Despite the evidence for an association between active coping and favorable outcomes in individuals with RA and OA, studies focusing on individuals with FM have yielded conflicting results. In individuals with FM, increases in both passive and active coping have been associated with depression (Nicassio, Schoenfeld-Smith, Radojevic, & Schuman, 1995), and more coping effort was associated with increased physical disability, although less psychological disability (Martin et al., 1996). These results suggest that coping responses which may be adaptive in some conditions (RA and OA) may actually be maladaptive in another (FM). For instance, in conditions such as OA, where pain is somewhat predictable and controllable, active coping processes may reduce pain symptoms. As a result, an individual may experience increased feelings of self-esteem and self-efficacy, and subsequently less depression. In contrast, when pain is experienced in spite of active coping responses, as in FM, these coping responses may be interpreted as failures to affect pain, resulting in decreased self-efficacy and increased feelings of helplessness and depression. Thus, the adaptiveness of specific coping responses may be influenced by symptom characteristics unique to each disorder.

Social Stress Factors

In addition to the data highlighting the psychological aspects of stress, there is mounting evidence that social stressors are particularly stressful for patients coping with chronic illnesses. Family conflict has been associated with poor psychological adjustment to RA (Manne & Zautra, 1989). Indeed, patients with chronic illness may be more sensitive than their healthy counterparts to interpersonal conflict with individuals who are major sources of support, such as family and close friends (Revenson, Schiaffino, Majerovitz, & Gibofsky, 1991). Since chronic illness often leads to severe limitation in the capacity to function independently, a disturbance in supportive relationships threatens to further isolate the patients and thus may increase anxiety and depression.

IMPLICATIONS FOR TREATMENT

The goals of controlling disease activity and reducing disease symptoms have been the typical targets for conventional biomedical treatment of arthritis and musculoskeletal conditions. Within pharmacological interventions, a disease-specific methodology has prevailed, so that drugs used to treat RA, OA, or FM disease activity are not always identical.

In contrast to the specific nature of conventional biomedical treatment, psychosocial interventions have typically been based on the idea that one general strategy is adequate to treat all of the diseases, thus ignoring specific needs or issues unique to each disease. Although some interventions have included a more holistic combination of biological and psychological factors, the two components have not always been utilized in a coordinated fashion.

Biological Treatment

Traditional pharamacological approaches to treating RA have followed a "pyramidal strategy" of aiming to minimize harm by prescribing steroid and nonsteroidal anti-inflammatory drugs (NSAIDS) in attempts to control inflammation and other disease symptoms (McCracken, 1991). Unfortunately, the progressive nature of RA, left unchecked, often causes significant disability and mortality (Harris, 1993). As a result, physicians changed their strategy, attempting to "turn the pyramid upside down" by prescribing an aggressive arsenal of pharmaceutical treatments in the earlier stages of the disease (Fries, 1990; Harris, 1993). This included disease-modifying drugs and biologic response modifiers, as well as the more traditional medications that reduce symptom and physical impairment, such as NSAIDS, salicylates, and prednisone (Harris, 1993).

Given that OA has no known cure, symptom relief is targeted as the primary goal of treatment. Such treatment includes pharmacological agents such as NSAIDS, analgesics, and topical ointments (Brandt, 1993). Surgical replacement of joints, although usually viewed as a last-resort option, is often utilized for severe OA and RA (Brandt, 1993).

As in OA, treatment for FM focuses on symptom management. Thus, far, optimal treatment strategies are far from clear, as both pharmacological and psychological interventions have yielded conflicting results. In contrast to RA and OA, FM does not involve an inflammatory process, so treatment with NSAIDs and corticosteroids is usually ineffective (Bennett, 1993). Tricyclic antidepressants, taken at lower doses than required for the treatment of depression, are one common form of pharmacological treatment. In addition, the newer class of selective serotonin-reuptake inhibitors (SSRIs) is used widely in the treatment of FM pain. In addition to pain relief, these substances also promote slow-wave sleep, something that has often been demonstrated to be deficient in patients with FM (Moldofsky et al., 1975). Unfortunately, because of the fear of dependence and addiction, medications such as narcotic analgesics have been avoided, even when their use may have been greatly beneficial. While effective pharmacological treatment of the pain associated with FM remains elusive, a recent metaanalysis of common treatments for FM demonstrated that nonpharmacological interventions are often more efficacious than pharmacological treatments at treating the pain of FM (Rossy et al., 1999).

Psychosocial Treatment

Given that biological, psychological, and social factors all contribute to the experience of RA, OA, and FM, numerous psychosocial interventions have been developed. Cognitive-behavioral therapy (CBT) has emerged as one of the most common forms of psychosocial treatment. Common elements of CBT include biofeedback, relaxation exercises, education, mastery, modeling, and cognitive appraisal (for reviews, see K. Anderson, Bradley, Young, McDaniel, & Wise, 1988; Nicassio & Greenberg, 2001). CBT is directed toward the goal of improving targeted aspects of health status such as pain tolerance, mobility, self-management, and self-efficacy. In the treatment of RA, CBT has been found to decrease pain, lower disease activity, decrease depression, and reduce health care utilization (K. Anderson et al., 1988; McCracken, 1991; Nicassio & Greenberg, 2001). Other common components of CBT therapy, recently researched in OA patients, include exercise treatments (Rejeski, Ettinger, Martin, & Morgan, 1998) and enhancing coping skills and spousal support (Keefe et al., 1987). These studies found significant improvements in health status and enhancement of self-efficacy. Interventions that succeeded in increasing self-efficacy and the health of individuals with RA and OA have also been studied in samples of FM patients (Burckhardt & Bjelle, 1994). These interventions utilized elements such as graded exercise programs and cognitive-based psychoeducation. Furthermore, these techniques have been shown to increase self-esteem and various aspects of health in individuals with FM (Gowans, deHueck, Voss, & Richardson, 1999).

Self-help groups have also been shown to effectively increase arthritis knowledge, improve compliance with health behaviors, increase self-efficacy, and reduce pain and health care utilization in individuals with RA and OA (Nicassio & Greenberg, 2001). For example, the Arthritis Self-Management Program has traditionally focused on improving knowledge and increasing health behaviors in individuals with arthritis and musculoskeletal conditions (Lorig, Gonzalez, Laurent, Morgan, & Laris, 1998). In addition, these programs increase self-efficacy by including experiences of mastery (successfully controlling psychological or physiological responses), modeling (observing others succeed), and cognitive appraisal (reducing negative thoughts) (for review, see Nicassio & Greenberg, 2001). While self-help management programs have recently been applied to FM patients, further research is needed to demonstrate the effectiveness of these programs in FM.

FUTURE DIRECTIONS

The unique contributions from biological, psychological, and social factors have been illustrated separately for RA, OA, and FM. However, despite the unique experience of these factors in each disorder, psychosocial treatment has yet to be individualized to address the different needs of people with various forms of chronic pain. Future treatments of these conditions must consider the specific biopsychosocial qualities unique to each condition. For example, RA is a condition with many known pathophysiological features and some effective pharmacological treatments. As a result, psychosocial interventions that influence biological processes that underlie RA may be especially effective. It may also be helpful to research the psychosocial factors that influence compliance with pharmacological treatment. Furthermore, interventions that utilize existing social systems (i.e., family, peers, and health care providers) to address barriers to compliance may be especially beneficial.

Although new pharmacological treatments of OA (e.g., Celebrex, Vioxx) have been developed, many treatments of OA are not pharmacological. Furthermore, the fact that many treatments of FM do not involve medications underscores the importance of compliance with nonpharmacological treatment recommendations. For example, the development of OA is often dependent on preventable factors such as exercise and obesity. Therefore, treatments addressing compliance with exercise regimens would be especially useful in this population. Similarly, compliance with lifestyle changes would also be a useful target for FM interventions. Interventions promoting exercise initiation in individuals with FM must recognize the specific need for close supervision by trained health care professionals with this population.

Future treatments should also consider how each condition may engender unique sources of stress. For instance, we have reviewed how unpredictable and uncontrollable events are perceived as the most stressful. OA, characterized by relatively predictable symptom exacerbation from variables such as overexertion and climate changes, may be less stressful than FM and RA, which are known for unpredictable exacerbations. Similarly, FM's relative lack of symptom relief may be an additional source of stress that might not be as pronounced as in OA, where pharmacological agents provide some relief. Thus, treatments may maximize their effectiveness by considering the controllability and predictability of stressors and devising ways to affect these qualities.

Another promising treatment, mindfulness meditation, trains attention deployment and promotes nonjudgmental acceptance of all life conditions, whether positive or negative (Kabat-Zinn, 1990). Preliminary studies on the effects of mindfulness meditation in FM populations (Kaplan, Goldenberg, & Galvin-Nadeau, 1993; Singh, Berman, Hadhazy, & Creamer, 1998) have shown it to be effective in decreasing pain and fatigue as well as improving quality of sleep. The use of mindfulness meditation with people suffering from arthritis and musculoskeletal conditions is likely to increase as more professionals become aware of its efficacy in enhancing holistic well-being.

Due to the fact that the effects of arthritis and musculoskeletal conditions are not limited to the individual afflicted with the disease, the social aspect of each condition may be a particularly important component to target, with significant implications for quality of life. We have reviewed evidence that interpersonal stress is particularly damaging to the health of individuals with RA. Therefore, interventions that seek to improve the quality of relationships between people with RA and their family members and/or spouses by eliciting family participation may yield more powerful effects. Relatedly, targeting improvements in the social environment of individuals with OA may assist individuals in adopting lifestyle changes (e.g., exercise, weight management) important in the prevention and treatment of OA. In addition, we have illustrated how individuals with FM often feel misunderstood by their health care providers and react to stress by withdrawing from social relationships. Thus, interventions that encourage spouses and family members of individuals with FM to continue to engage them in their social activities may improve the outcome of these patients. Furthermore, "doctor-shopping" among patients with FM may be reduced by teaching health care professionals to be aware of stigmatization factors and highlighting the importance of effective communication with their patients.

This discussion emphasized that RA, OA, and FM are distinct conditions, despite the fact that they share many common symptoms and forms of treatment. More comprehensive models and efficacious treatments for these chronic conditions will result from careful consideration of their unique biological, psychological, and social factors.

REFERENCES

Aaron, L. A., Bradley, L. A., Alarcon, G. S., Alexander, R. W., Triana-Alexander, M., Martin, M. Y., et al. (1996). Psychiatric diagnoses in patients with fibromyalgia are related to health-care seeking behavior rather than to illness. *Arthritis and Rheumatism, 39*(3), 436–445.

Adler, G. K., Kinsley, B. T., Hurwitz, S., Mossey, C. J., & Goldenberg, D. L. (1999). Reduced hypothalamic-pituitary and sympathoadrenal responses to hypoglycemia in women with fibromyalgia syndrome. *American Journal of Medicine, 106,* 534–543.

Affleck, G., Pfeiffer, C., Tennen, H., & Fifield, J. (1988). Social support and psychosocial adjustment to rheumatoid arthritis: Quantitative and qualitative findings. *Arthritis Care and Research, 1*(2), 71–77.

Affleck, G., Tennen, H., Urrows, S., & Higgins, P. (1991). Individual differences in the day to day experience of chronic pain: A prospective daily study of rheumatoid arthritis patients. *Health Psychology, 10*(6), 419–426.

Affleck, G., Tennen, H., Urrows, S., & Higgins, P. (1992). Neuroticism and the pain-mood relation in rheumatoid arthritis: Insights from a prospective daily study. *Journal of Consulting and Clinical Psychology, 60*(1), 119–126.

Ahles, T. A., Khan, S. A., Yunus, M. B., Spiegel, D. A., & Masi, A. T. (1991). Psychiatric status of patients with primary fibromyalgia, patients with rheumatoid arthritis, and subjects without pain: A blind comparison of *DSM-III* diagnoses. *American Journal of Psychiatry, 148*(12), 1721–1726.

Aho, K., Koskenvuo, M., Tuominen, J., & Kaprio, J. (1986). Occurrence of rheumatoid arthritis in a nation-wide series of twins. *Journal of Rheumatology, 13,* 899–902.

Akil, H., Watson, S. J., Young, E., Lewis, M. E., Khachaturden, H., & Walker, J. M. (1984). Endogenous opioids: Biology and function. *Annual Review of Neuroscience, 7,* 223–255.

Alfici, S., Sigal, M., & Landau, M. (1989). Primary fibromyalgia syndrome: A variant of depressive disorder? *Psychotherapy and Psychosomatics, 51*(3), 156–161.

American Psychiatric Association. (1994). *Diagnostic and statistical manual of mental disorders* (4th ed.). Washington, DC: Author.

Anderson, J. J., Wells, G., Verhoeven, A. C., & Felson, D. T. (2000). Factors predicting response to treatment in rheumatoid arthritis: The importance of disease duration. *Arthritis and Rheumatism, 43*(1), 22–29.

Anderson, K. O., Bradley, L. A., Young, L. D., McDaniel, L. K., & Wise, C. M. (1988). Rheumatoid arthritis: Review of psychological factors related to etiology, effects, and treatment. *Psychological Bulletin, 98*(2), 358–387.

Arruda, J. L., Colburn, R. W., Rickman, A. J., Rutowski, M. D., & DeLeo, J. A. (1998). Increase of interleukin-6 mRNA in the spinal cord following peripheral nerve injury in the rat: Potential role of IL-6 in neuropathic pain. *Brain Research and Molecular Brain Research, 62*(2), 228–235.

Bacon, N. M., Bacon, S. F., Atkinson, J. H., Slater, M. A., Patterson, T. L., Grant, I., et al. (1994). Somatization symptoms in chronic low back pain patients. *Psychosomatic Medicine, 56*(2), 118–127.

Baerwald, C., Graefe, C., Muhl, C., von Wichert, P., & Krause, A. (1992). Beta 2-adrenergic receptors on peripheral blood mononuclear cells in patients with rheumatic diseases. *European Journal of Clinical Investigations, 1,* 42–46.

Banks, S. M., & Kerns, R. D. (1996). Explaining high rates of depression in chronic pain: A diathesis stress framework. *Psychological Bulletin, 119*(1), 95–110.

Basbaum, A. I., & Fields, H. L. (1984). Endogenous pain control systems: Brainstem spinal pathways and endorphin circuitry. *Annual Review of Neuroscience, 7,* 309–338.

Beckham, J. C., Keefe, F. J., Caldwell, D. S., & Roodman, A. A. (1991). Pain coping strategies in rheumatoid arthritis: Relationships to pain, disability, depression and daily hassles. *Behavior Therapy, 22*(1), 113–124.

Bennett, R. M. (1993). The fibromyalgia syndrome: Myofascial pain and the chronic fatigue syndrome. In W. N. Kelley, E. D. Harris, Jr., S. Ruddy, & C. B. Sledge (Eds.), *Textbook of rheumatology* (4th ed., pp. 471–483). Philadelphia: Saunders.

Bennett, R. M. (1999). Emerging concepts in the neurobiology of chronic pain: Evidence of abnormal sensory processing in fibromyalgia. *Mayo Clinic Proceedings, 74,* 385–398.

Bijkerk, C., Houwing-Duistermaat, J. J., Valkenburg, H. A., Meulenbelt, I., Hofman, A., Breedveld, F. C., et al. (1999). Heritabilities of radiologic osteoarthritis in peripheral joints and of disc degeneration of the spine. *Arthritis and Rheumatism, 42*(8), 1729–1735.

Bolger, N., & Schilling, E. A. (1991). Personality and the problems of everyday life: The role of neuroticism in exposure and reactivity to daily stressors. *Journal of Personality, 59*(3), 355–386.

Brandt, K. D. (1993). Management of osteoarthritis. In W. N. Kelley, E. D. Harris, S. Ruddy, & C. B. Sledge (Eds.), *Textbook of rheumatology* (4th ed., pp. 1385–1399). Philadelphia: Saunders.

Brown, G. K. (1990). A causal analysis of chronic pain and depression. *Journal of Abnormal Psychology, 22,* 127–137.

Buckelew, S. P., Murray, S. E., Hewett, J. E., Johnson, J., & Huyser, B. (1995). Self-efficacy, pain, and physical activity among fibromyalgia subjects. *Arthritis Care and Research, 8*(1), 43–50.

Burckhardt, C. S., & Bjelle, A. (1994). Perceived control: A comparison of women with fibromyalgia, rheumatoid arthritis, and systemic lupus erythematosus using a Swedish version of the Rheumatology Attitudes Index. *Scandinavian Journal of Rheumatology, 25,* 300–306.

Buskila, D., Fefer, P., Harman-Boehm, I., Press, J., Neumann, L., Lunenfeld, E., et al. (1993). Assessment of nonarticular tenderness and prevalence of fibromyalgia in hyperprolactinemic women. *Journal of Rheumatology, 20*(12), 2112–2115.

Cannon, W. B. (1932). *The wisdom of the body.* New York: Norton.

Catley, D., Kaell, A. T., Kirschbaum, C., & Stone, A. A. (2000). Naturalistic evaluation of cortisol secretion in persons with fibromyalgia and rheumatoid arthritis. *Arthritis Care and Research, 13*(1), 51–61.

Chang, L., Mayer, E. A., Johnson, T., Fitzgerald, L. Z., & Naliboff, B. (2000). Differences in somatic perception in female patients with irritable bowel syndrome with and without fibromyalgia. *Pain, 84*(2/3), 297–307.

Chrousos, G. P., & Gold, P. W. (1992). The concepts of stress and stress system disorders. Overview of physical and behavioral homeostasis. *Journal of the American Medical Association, 267*(9), 1244–1252.

Clauw, D. J., & Chrousos, G. P. (1997). Chronic pain and fatigue syndromes: Overlapping clinical and neuroendocrine features and potential pathogenic mechanisms. *Neuroimmunomodulation, 4,* 134–153.

Creed, F., Murphy, S., & Jayson, M. V. (1990). Measurement of psychiatric disorder in rheumatoid arthritis. *Journal of Psychosomatic Research, 34*(1), 79–87.

Crisson, J. E., & Keefe, F. J. (1988). The relationship of locus of control to pain coping strategies and psychological distress in chronic pain patients. *Pain, 35*(2), 147–154.

Crofford, L. J., Pillemer, S. R., Kalogeras, K. T., Cash, J. M., Michelson, D., Kling, M. A., et al. (1994). Hypothalamic-pituitary-adrenal axis perturbations in patients with fibromyalgia. *Arthritis and Rheumatism, 37*(11), 1583–1592.

Davis, M. C., Zautra, A. J., & Reich, J. W. (2001). Vulnerability to stress among women in chronic pain from fibromyalgia and osteoarthritis. *Annals of Behavioral Medicine, 23*(3), 215–226.

Deuschle, M., Weber, B., Colla, M., Depner, M., & Heuser, I. (1998). Effects of major depression, aging, and gender upon calculated diurnal free plasma cortisol concentrations: A re-evaluation study. *Stress, 2*(4), 281–287.

Eberhardt, K., & Fex, E. (1998). Clinical course and remission rate in patients with early rheumatoid arthritis: Relationship to outcome after 5 years. *British Journal of Rheumatology, 37*(12), 1324–1329.

Engel, G. L. (1977). The need for a new medical model: A challenge for biomedicine. *Science, 196,* 129–136.

Felson, D. T., Couropmitree, N. N., Chaisson, C. E., Hannan, M. T., Zhang, Y., McAlindon, T. E., et al. (1998). Evidence for a Mendelian gene in a segregation analysis of generalized radiographic osteoarthritis: The Framingham Study. *Arthritis and Rheumatism, 41*(6), 1064–1071.

Felten, D. L., Felten, S. Y., Bellinger, D. L., & Lorton, D. (1992). Noradrenergic and peptidergic innervation of secondary lymphoid organs: Role in experimental rheumatoid arthritis. *European Journal of Clinical Investigations, 1,* 37–41.

Ferguson, S. J., & Cotton, S. (1996). Broken sleep, pain, disability, social activity, and depressive symptoms in rheumatoid arthritis. *Australian Journal of Psychology, 48*(1), 9–14.

Ferraccioli, G., Cavalieri, F., Salaffi, F., Fontana, S., Scita, F., Nolli, M., et al. (1990). Neuroendocrinologic findings in primary fibromyalgia and in other chronic rheumatic conditions. *Journal of Rheumatology, 17*(7), 869–873.

Fields, H. L., & Basbaum, A. I. (1994). Central nervous system mechanisms of pain modulation. In P. D. Wall & R. Melzack (Eds.), *Textbook of pain* (3rd ed., pp. 245–257). Edinburgh, Scotland: Churchill Livingstone.

Fries, J. F. (1990). Reevaluating the therapeutic approach to rheumatoid arthritis: The "sawtooth" strategy. *Journal of Rheumatology, 17*(22), 12–15.

Fyrand, L., Wichstrom, L., Moum, T., Glennas, A., & Kvien, T. K. (1997). The impact of personality and social support on mental health for female patients with rheumatoid arthritis. *Social Indicators Research, 40*(3), 285–298.

Geenan, R., Godaert, G. L. R., Heijnen, C. J., Vianen, M. E., Wenting, M. L. G., Nederoff, M. G. J., et al. (1998). Experimentally induced stress in rheumatoid arthritis of recent onset: Effects on peripheral blood lymphocytes. *Clinical and Experimental Rheumatology, 16*, 553–559.

Geenan, R., Godaert, G. L. R., Jacobs, J. W. G., Peters, M. L., & Bijlsma, J. W. J. (1996). Diminished autonomic nervous system responsiveness in rheumatoid arthritis of recent onset. *Journal of Rheumatology, 23*(2), 258–264.

Giovengo, S. L., Russell, I. J., & Larson, A. A. (1999). Increased concentrations of nerve growth factor in cerebrospinal fluid of patients with fibromyalgia. *Journal of Rheumatology, 26*(7), 1564–1569.

Glass, D. C., & Singer, J. E. (1972). *Urban stress.* New York: Academic Press.

Glick, E. N. (1967). Asymmetrical rheumatoid arthritis after poliomyelitis. *British Medical Journal, 3*, 26–28.

Gowans, S. E., deHueck, A., Voss, S., & Richardson, M. (1999). A randomized, controlled trial of exercise and education for individuals with fibromyalgia. *Arthritis Care and Research, 12*(2), 120–128.

Griep, E. N., Boersma, J. W., & deKloet, E. R. (1993). Altered reactivity of the hypothalamic-pituitary-adrenal axis in the primary fibromyalgia syndrome. *Journal of Rheumatology, 20*, 469–474.

Grossman, C. J., Roselle, G. A., & Mendenhall, C. L. (1991). Sex steroid regulation of autoimmunity. *Journal of Steroid Chemistry and Molecular Biology, 40*, 649–659.

Harrington, L., Affleck, G., Urrows, S., Tennen, H., Higgins, P., Zautra, A., et al. (1993). Temporal covariation of soluble interleukin-2 receptor levels, daily stress, and disease activity in rheumatoid arthritis. *Arthritis and Rheumatism, 36*(2), 199–203.

Harris, E. D. (1993). Clinical features of rheumatoid arthritis. In W. N. Kelley, E. D. Harris, Jr., S. Ruddy, & C. B. Sledge (Eds.), *Textbook of rheumatology* (4th ed., pp. 874–911). Philadelphia: Saunders. .

Hazes, J. M. W. (1991). Pregnancy and its effect on the risk of developing rheumatoid arthritis. *Annals of Rheumatic Disease, 50*, 71–72.

Hudson, J. I., Hudson, M. S., Pliner, L. F., & Goldenberg, D. L. (1985). Fibromyalgia and major affective disorder: A controlled phenomenology and family history study. *American Journal of Psychiatry, 142*(4), 441–446.

Hudson, J. I., & Pope, H. G., Jr. (1989). Is fibromyalgia a form of "affective spectrum disorder?" *Journal of Rheumatology, 19*, 15–22.

Huyser, B., & Parker, J. C. (1998). Stress and rheumatoid arthritis: An integrative review. *Arthritis Care and Research, 11*(2), 135–145.

Jorgensen, C., & Sany, J. (1994). Modulation of the immune response by the neuro-endocrine axis in rheumatoid arthritis. *Clinical and Experimental Rheumatology, 12*, 435–441.

Kabat-Zinn, J. (1990). *Full catastrophe living.* New York: Delacorte.

Kaplan, K. H., Goldenberg, D. L., & Galvin-Nadeau, M. (1993). The impact of a meditation-based stress reduction program on fibromyalgia. *General Hospital Psychiatry, 15*(5), 284–289.

Keefe, F. J., Caldwell, D. S., Queen, K. T., Gil, K. M., Martinez, S., Crisson, J. E., et al. (1987). Pain coping strategies in osteoarthritis patients. *Journal of Consulting and Clinical Psychology, 55*(2), 208–212.

Keefe, F. J., Lefebvre, J. C., Maixner, W., Salley, A. N., & Caldwell, D. S. (1997). Self-efficacy for arthritis pain: Relationship to perception of thermal laboratory pain stimuli. *Arthritis Care and Research, 10*(3), 177–184.

Kennedy, M. F., & Felson, D. T. (1996). A prospective long term study of fibromyalgia syndrome. *Arthritis and Rheumatism, 39*(4), 682–685.

Keystone, E. C., Snow, K. M., Bombardier, C., Chang, C. H., Nelson, D. L., & Rubin, L. A. (1988). Elevated soluble interleukin-2 receptor levels in the sera and synovial fluids of patients with rheumatoid arthritis. *Arthritis and Rheumatism, 31*(7), 844–849.

Kirmayer, L. J., Robbins, J. M., & Kapusta, M. A. (1988). Somatization and depression in fibromyalgia syndrome. *American Journal of Psychiatry, 145*(8), 950–954.

Klein, R., & Berg, P. A. (1995). High incidence of antibodies to 5-hydroxytryptamine, gangliosides, and phospholipids in patients with chronic fatigue syndrome and fibromyalgia syndrome and their relatives: Evidence for a clinical entity of both disorders. *European Journal of Medical Research, 1*(1), 21–26.

Korszun, A., Young, E. A., Engleberg, N. C., Masterson, L., Dawson, E. C., Spindler, K., et al. (2000, June). Follicular phase hypothalamic-pituitary-gonadal axis function in women with fibromyalgia and chronic fatigue syndrome. *Journal of Rheumatology, 27*(6), 1526–1530.

Krag, N. J., Norregaard, J., Larsen, J. K., & Danneskiold-Samsoe, B. (1994). A blinded, controlled evaluation of anxiety and depressive symptoms in patients with fibromyalgia, as measured by standardized psychometric interview scales. *Acta Psychiatrica Scandinavica, 89*(6), 370–375.

Kramis, R. C., Roberts, W. J., & Gillette, R. G. (1996). Nonnociceptive aspects of persistent musculoskeletal pain. *Journal of Orthopedic, Sports, and Physical Therapy, 24*(4), 255–267.

Kraus, V. B. (1997). Pathogenesis and treatment of osteoarthritis. *Advances in Rheumatology, 81*(1), 85–104.

Lawrence, R. C., Helmick, C. G., Arnett, F. C., Deyo, R. A., Felson, D. T., Giannini, E. H., et al. (1998). Estimates of the prevalence of arthritis and selected musculoskeletal disorders in the United States. *Arthritis and Rheumatism, 41*(5), 778–799.

Lazarus, R. S., & Folkman, S. (1984). *Stress, appraisal, and coping.* New York: Springer.

Lechin, F., van der Dijs, B., Lechin, A., Orozco, B., Lechin, M., Baez, S., et al. (1994). Plasma neurotransmitters and cortisol in chronic illness: Role of stress. *Journal of Medicine, 25*(3/4), 181–192.

Lefebvre, J. C., Keefe, F. J., Affleck, G., Raezer, L. B., Starr, K., Caldwell, D. S., et al. (1999). The relationship of arthritis self-efficacy to daily pain, daily mood, and daily pain coping in rheumatoid arthritis patients. *Pain, 80*(1/2), 425–435.

Lennon, M. C., Link, B. G., Marback, J. J., & Dohrenwend, B. P. (1989). The stigma of chronic facial pain and its impact on social relationships. *Social Problems, 36*(2), 117–134.

Levine, J. D., Coderre, T. J., Helms, C., & Basbaum, A. I. (1988). Beta 2-adrenergic mechanisms in experimental arthritis. *Proceedings of the National Academy of Science, 85*(12), 4553–4556.

Lewis, J. W., Terman, S. W., Sharit, Y., Nelson, L. R., & Liebeskind, J. C. (1984). Neural, neurochemical, and hormonal bases of stress-induced analgesia. In L. Kruger & J. C. Liebeskind (Eds.), *Advances in pain research and therapy* (Vol. 6, pp. 277–288). New York: Raven Press.

Lorig, K., Gonzalez, V. M., Laurent, D. D., Morgan, L., & Laris, B. A. (1998). Arthritis self-management program variations: Three studies. *Arthritis Care and Research, 11*(6), 448–454.

MacFarlane, G. J., Thomas, E., Papageogiou, A. C., Schollum, J., Croft, P. R., & Silman, A. J. (1996). The natural history of chronic pain in the community: A better prognosis than in the clinic? *Journal of Rheumatology, 23,* 1617–1620.

MacGregor, A. J., Snieder, H., Rigby, A. S., Koskenvuo, M., Kaprio, J., Aho, K., et al. (2000). Characterizing the quantitative genetic contribution to rheumatoid arthritis using data from twins. *Arthritis and Rheumatism, 43*(1), 30–37.

Madden, K. S., & Livnat, S. (1991). Catecholamine action and immunologic reactivity. In R. Ader, D. I. Felten, & N. Cohen, (Eds.), *Psychoneuroimmunology* (2nd ed., p. 283). New York: Academic Press.

Maes, M., Libbrecht, I., Van Hunsel, F., Lin, A. H., De Clerck, L., Stevens, W., et al. (1999). The immune-inflammatory pathophysiology of fibromyalgia: Increased serum soluble gp130, the common signal transducer protein of various neurotrophic cytokines. *Psychoneuroendocrinology, 24*(4), 371–383.

Mageed, R. A., Borretzen, M., Moyes, S. P., Thompson, K. M., & Natvig, J. B. (1997). Rheumatoid factor autoantibodies in health and disease. *Annals of the New York Academy of Sciences, 815,* 296–311.

Mankin, H. J. (1993). Clinical features of osteoarthritis. In W. N. Kelley, E. D. Harris, Jr., S. Ruddy, & C. B. Sledge (Eds.), *Textbook of rheumatology* (4th ed., pp. 1374–1384). Philadelphia: Saunders.

Manne, S. L., & Zautra, A. J. (1989). Spouse criticism and support: Their association with coping and psychological adjustment among women with rheumatoid arthritis. *Journal of Personality and Social Psychology, 56*(4), 608–617.

Manne, S. L., & Zautra, A. J. (1992). Coping with arthritis. *Arthritis and Rheumatism, 35,* 1273–1280.

Marieb, E. N. (1993). *Human anatomy and physiology* (2nd ed.). New York: Benjamin Cummings.

Martin, M. Y., Bradley, L. A., Alexander, R. W., Alarcon, G. S., Triana-Alexander, M., Aaron, L. A., et al. (1996). Coping strategies predict disability in patients with primary fibromyalgia. *Pain, 68*(1), 45–53.

McCracken, L. M. (1991). Cognitive behavioral treatment of rheumatoid arthritis: A preliminary review of efficacy and methodology. *Annals of Behavioral Medicine, 13*(2), 57–65.

Melzack, R., & Wall, P. D. (1965). Pain mechanisms: A new theory. *Science, 150,* 971–979.

Mengshoel, A. M., Saugen, E., Forre, O., & Vollestad, N. K. (1995). Muscle fatigue in early fibromyalgia. *Journal of Rheumatology, 22*(1), 143–150.

Merskey, H., & Bogduk, N. (1994). *Classification of chronic pain: Descriptions of chronic pain syndromes and definitions of pain terms.* Seattle, WA: IASP Press.

Moldofsky, H., & Scarisbrick, P. (1976). Induction of neurasthenic musculoskeletal pain syndrome by selective sleep deprivation. *Psychosomatic Medicine, 38,* 35–44.

Moldofsky, H., Scarisbrick, P., England, R., & Smythe, H. (1975). Musculoskeletal symptoms and non-REM sleep disturbance in patients with "fibrositis syndrome" and healthy subjects. *Psychosomatic Medicine, 37,* 341–351.

Monroe, S. M., & Simons, A. D. (1991). Diathesis-stress theories in the context of life stress research: Implications for the depressive disorders. *Psychological Bulletin, 110*(3), 406–425.

Morand, E. F., Jefferiss, C. M., Dixey, J., Mitra, D., & Goulding, N. J. (1994). Impaired glucocorticoid induction of mononuclear leukocyte lipocortin-1 in rheumatoid arthritis. *Arthritis and Rheumatism, 37*(2), 207–211.

Morrow, K. A., Parker, J. C., & Russell, J. L. (1994). Clinical implications of depression in rheumatoid arthritis. *Arthritis Care and Research, 7*(2), 58–63.

Neeck, G., Federlin, K., Graef, V., Rusch, D., & Schmidt, K. L. (1990). Adrenal secretion of cortisol in patients with rheumatoid arthritis. *Journal of Rheumatology, 17*(1), 24–29.

Nicassio, P. M., & Greenberg, M. A. (2001). The effectiveness of cognitive-behavioral and psychoeducational interventions in the management of arthritis. In M. H. Weisman & J. Louie (Eds.), *Treatment of the rheumatic diseases* (2nd ed., pp. 147–161). Orlando, FL: William Saunders.

Nicassio, P. M., Radojevic, V., Schoenfeld-Smith, K., & Dwyer, K. (1995). The contribution of family cohesion and the pain coping process to depressive symptoms in fibromyalgia. *Annals of Behavioral Medicine, 17*(4), 349–356.

Nicassio, P. M., Schoenfeld-Smith, K., Radojevic, V., & Schuman, C. (1995). Pain coping mechanisms in fibromyalgia: Relationship to pain and functional outcomes. *Journal of Rheumatology, 22*(8), 1552–1558.

Nicassio, P. M., Schuman, C., Radojevic, V., & Weisman, M. H. (1999). Helplessness as a mediator of health status in fibromyalgia. *Cognitive Therapy and Research, 23*(2), 181–196.

Nicassio, P. M., Wallston, K. A., Callahan, L. F., Herbert, M., & Pincus, T. (1985). The measurement of helplessness in rheumatoid arthritis: The development of the Arthritis Helplessness Index. *Journal of Rheumatology, 12*(3), 462–467.

Offenbaecher, M., Bondy, B., de Jonge, S., Glatzeder, K., Kruger, M., Schopeps, P., et al. (1999). Possible association of fibromyalgia with a polymorphism in the serotonin transporter gene regulatory region. *Arthritis and Rheumatism, 42*(11), 2482–2488.

Okamoto, H., Yamamura, M., Morita, Y., Harada, S., Makino, H., & Ota, Z. (1997). The synovial expression and serum levels of interleukin-6, interleukin-11, leukemia inhibitory factor, and oncostatin M in rheumatoid arthritis. *Arthritis and Rheumatism, 40*(6), 1096–1105.

Osborn, M., & Smith, J. A. (1998). The personal experience of chronic benign lower back pain: An interpretative phenomenological analysis. *British Journal of Health Psychology, 3*(1), 65–83.

Ostensen, M., Rugelsjoen, A., & Wigers, S. H. (1997). The effect of reproductive events and alterations of sex hormone levels on the symptoms of fibromyalgia. *Scandinavian Journal of Rheumatology, 26*(5), 355–360.

Parker, J. C., & Wright, G. E. (1995). The implications of depression for pain and disability in rheumatoid arthritis. *Arthritis Care and Research, 8*(4), 279–283.

Pastor, M. A., Salas, E., Lopez, S., Rodriguez, J., Sanchez, S., & Pascual, E. (1993). Patients' beliefs about their lack of pain control in primary fibromyalgia syndrome. *British Journal of Rheumatology, 32*(6), 484–489.

Pellegrino, M. J., Waylonis, G. W., & Sommer, A. (1989). Familial occurrence of primary fibromyalgia. *Archives of Physical Medicine and Rehabilitation, 70*, 61–63.

Persellin, R. H. (1977). The effect of pregnancy on rheumatoid arthritis. *Bulletin of Rheumatic Diseases, 27*, 922–927.

Pincus, T., Callahan, L., Sale, W., Brooks, A., Psyne, L., & Vaughn, W. (1984). Severe functional declines, work disability, and increased mortality in seventy-five rheumatoid arthritis patients studies over nine years. *Arthritis and Rheumatism, 27*(8), 864–872.

Radanov, B. P., Frost, S. A., Schwarz, H. A., & Augustiny, K. F. (1996). Experience of pain in rheumatoid arthritis: An empirical evaluation of the contribution of developmental psychosocial stress. *Acta Psychiatrica Scandinavica, 93*(6), 482–488.

Radanov, B. P., Schwarz, H. A., & Frost, S. A. (1997). Determination of future health status expectation in rheumatoid arthritis. *Journal of Psychosomatic Research, 42*(4), 403–406.

Rejeski, W. J., Craven, T., Ettinger, W. H., McFarlane, M., & Shumaker, S. (1996). Self-efficacy and pain in disability with osteoarthritis of the knee. *Journal of Gerontology, 51*, 24–29.

Rejeski, W. J., Ettinger, W. H., Martin, K., & Morgan, T. (1998). Treating disability in knee osteoarthritis with exercise therapy: A central role for self-efficacy and pain. *Arthritis Care and Research, 11*(2), 94–101.

Revenson, T. A., Schiaffino, K. M., Majerovitz, S. D., & Gibofsky, A. (1991). Social support as a double-edged sword: The relation of positive and problematic support to depression among rheumatoid arthritis patients. *Social Science and Medicine, 33*(7), 807–813.

Reynolds, W. J., Chiu, B., & Inman, R. D. (1988). Plasma substance P levels in fibrositis. *Journal of Rheumatology, 15*(12), 1802–1803.

Romano, J. M., & Turner, J. A. (1985). Chronic pain and depression: Does the evidence support a relationship? *Psychological Bulletin, 97*(1), 18–34.

Rossy, L. A., Buckelew, S. P., Dorr, N., Hagglund, K. J., Thayer, J. F., McIntosh, M. J., et al. (1999). A meta-analysis of fibromyalgia treatment interventions. *Annals of Behavioral Medicine, 21*(2), 180–191.

Russell, I. J., Michalek, J. E., Vipraio, G. A., Fletcher, E. M., Javors, M. A., & Bowden, C. A. (1992). Platelet 3H-imipramine uptake receptor density and serum serotonin levels in patients with fibromyalgia/fibrositis syndrome. *Journal of Rheumatology, 19*(1), 104–109.

Russell, I. J., Orr, M. D., Littman, B., Vipraio, G. A., Alboukrek, D., Michalek, J. E., et al. (1994). Elevated cerebrospinal fluid levels of substance P in patients with the fibromyalgia syndrome. *Arthritis and Rheumatism, 37*(11), 1593–1601.

Samborski, W., Sluzewska, A., Lacki, J. K., Sobieska, M., Klein, R., & Mackiewicz, S. (1998). Antibodies against serotonin and gangliosides in patients with fibromyalgia and major depression [Letter]. *Human Psychopharmacology, 13*, 137–138.

Sambrook, P., & Naganathan, V. (1997). What is the relationship between osteoarthritis and osteoporosis? *Baillieres of Clinical Rheumatology, 11*(4), 695–710.

Sarason, B. R., Sarason, I. G., & Gurung, R. A. R. (1997). Close personal relationships and health outcomes: A key to the role of social support. In S. Duck (Ed.), *Handbook of personal relationships* (pp. 547–573). New York: Wiley.

Schwarz, M. J., Spath, M., Muller-Bardoff, H., Pongratz, D. E., Bondy, B., & Ackenheil, M. (1999). Relationship of substance P, 5-hydroxyindole acetic acid and tryptophan in serum of fibromyalgia patients. *Neuroscience Letters, 259*(3), 196–198.

Selye, H. (1956). *The stress of life.* New York: McGraw-Hill.

Singh, B. B., Berman, M. B., Hadhazy, V. A., & Creamer, P. (1998). A pilot study of cognitive behavioral therapy in fibromyalgia. *Alternative Therapies, 4*(2), 67–70.

Smolen, J. S., Tohidast-Akrad, G. A., Kunaver, M., Eberl, G., Zenz, P., Falus, A., et al. (1996). The role of T-lymphocytes and cytokines in rheumatoid arthritis. *Scandinavian Journal of Rheumatology, 25*, 1–4.

Sternberg, E. M., Young, W. S., II, Bernardini, R., Calogero, A. E., Chrousos, G. P., Gold, P. W., et al. (1989). A central nervous system defect in biosynthesis of corticotropin-releasing hormone is associated with susceptibility to streptococcal cell wall-induced arthritis in Lewis rats. *Proceedings of the National Academy of Science, 86,* 4771–4775.

Stewart, M. W., Knight, R. G., Palmer, D. G., & Highton, J. (1994). Differential relationships between stress and disease activity for immunologically distinct subgroups of people with rheumatoid arthritis. *Journal of Abnormal Psychology, 103*(2), 251–258.

Stormorken, H., & Brosstad, F. (1992). Fibromyalgia: Family clustering and sensory urgency with early onset indicate genetic predisposition and thus a "true" disease. *Scandinavian Journal of Rheumatology, 21,* 207.

Symons, J. A., Wood, N. C., DiGiovine, F. S., & Duff, G. W. (1988). Soluble IL-2 receptor in rheumatoid arthritis. *Journal of Immunology, 141*(8), 2612–2618.

Templ, E., Koeller, M., Riedl, M., Wagner, O., Graninger, W., & Luger, A. (1996). Anterior pituitary function in patients with newly diagnosed rheumatoid arthritis. *British Journal of Rheumatology, 35*(4), 350–356.

Thompson, S. C., & Spacapan, S. (1991). Perceptions of control in vulnerable populations. *Journal of Social Issues, 47,* 1–22.

Torpy, D. J., Papanicolaou, D. A., Lotsikas, A. J., Wilder, R. L., Chrousos, G. P., & Pillemer, S. R. (2000). Responses of the sympathetic nervous system and the hypothalamic-pituitary-adrenal axis to interleukin-6: A pilot study in fibromyalgia. *Arthritis and Rheumatism, 43*(4), 872–880.

Turk-Charles, S., Gatz, M., Pedersen, N. L., & Dahlberg, L. (1999). Genetic and behavioral risk factors for self-reported joint pain among a population-based sample of Swedish twins. *Health Psychology, 18*(6), 644–654.

Uveges, K. M., Parker, J. C., Smarr, K. L., McGowan, J. F., Lyon, M. G., Irvin, W. S., et al. (1990). Psychological symptoms in primary fibromyalgia syndrome: Relationship to pain, life stress, and sleep disturbance. *Arthritis and Rheumatism, 33*(8), 1279–1283.

van den Brink, H. R., Blankenstein, M. A., Koppeschaar, H. P., & Bijlsma, J. W. (1993). Influence of disease activity on steroid hormone levels in peripheral blood of patients with rheumatoid arthritis. *Clinical and Experimental Rheumatology, 11*(6), 649–652.

van Denderen, J. C., Boersma, J. W., Zeinstra, P., Hollander, A. P., & van Neerbos, B. R. (1992). Physiological effects of exhaustive physical exercise in primary fibromyalgia syndrome (PFS): Is PFS a disorder of neuroendocrine reactivity? *Scandinavian Journal of Rheumatology, 21*(1), 35–37.

Walker, E. A., Keegan, D., Gardner, G., Sullivan, M., Katon, W. J., & Bernstein, D. (1997). Psychosocial factors in fibromyalgia compared with rheumatoid arthritis: I. Psychiatric diagnoses and functional disability. *Psychosomatic Medicine, 59,* 565–571.

Wall, P. D., & Woolf, C. J. (1984). Muscle but not cutaneous C-afferent input produces prolonged increases in the excitabiliy of the flexion reflex in the rat. *Journal of Physiology, 356,* 443–458.

Weinberger, M., Tierney, W. M., Booher, P., & Hiner, S. L. (1990). Social support, stress and functional status in patients with osteoarthritis. *Social Science and Medicine, 30*(4), 503–508.

Wigers, S. H. (1996). Fibromyalgia outcome: The predictive values of symptom duration, physical activity, disability pension, and critical life events: A 4.5-year prospective study. *Journal of Psychosomatic Research, 41*(3), 235–243.

Wilson, L., Dworkin, S. F., Whitney, C., & LeResche, L. (1994). Somatization and pain dispersion in chronic temporomandibular disorder pain. *Pain, 57*(1), 55–61.

Wolfe, F., & Hawley, D. J. (1999). Evidence of disordered symptom appraisal in fibromyalgia: Increased rates of reported comorbidity and comorbidity severity. *Clinical and Experimental Rheumatology, 17*(3), 297–303.

Wolfe, F., Smythe, H. A., Yunus, M. B., Bennett, R. M., Bombardier, C., Goldenberg, D. L., et al. (1990). The American College of Rheumatology 1990 criteria for the classification of fibromyalgia. *Arthritis and Rheumatism, 33*(2), 160–172.

Wood, N. C., Symons, J. A., & Duff, G. W. (1988). Serum interleukin-2-receptor in rheumatoid arthritis: A prognostic indicator of disease activity? *Journal of Autoimmunity, 1,* 353–361.

Wright, G. E., Parker, J. C., Smarr, K. L., Johnson, J. C., Hewett, J. E., & Walker, S. E. (1998). Age, depressive symptoms, and rheumatoid arthritis. *Arthritis and Rheumatism, 41*(2), 298–305.

Yunus, M. B., Dailey, J. W., Aldag, J. C., Masi, A. T., & Jobe, P. C. (1992). Plasma tryptophan and other amino acids in primary fibromyalgia: A controlled study. *Journal of Rheumatology, 19*(1), 90–94.

Zautra, A. J., Burleson, M. H., Matt, K. S., Roth, S., & Burrows, L. (1994). Interpersonal stress, depression, and disease activity in rheumatoid arthritis and osteoarthritis patients. *Health Psychology, 13*(2), 139–148.

Zautra, A. J., Burleson, M. H., Smith, C. A., Blalock, S. J., Wallston, K. A., Devellis, R. F., et al. (1995). Arthritis and perceptions of quality of life: An examination of positive and negative affect in rheumatoid arthritis patients. *Health Psychology, 14,* 399–408.

Zautra, A. J., Hamilton, N., & Burke, H. M. (1999). Comparison of stress responses in women with two types of chronic pain: Fibromyalgia and osteoarthritis. *Cognitive Therapy and Research, 23,* 209–230.

Zautra, A. J., Hamilton, N., & Yocum, D. (2000). Patterns of positive social engagement among women with rheumatoid arthritis. *Occupational Therapy Journal of Research, 20,* 1–20.

Zautra, A. J., & Smith, B. W. (2001). Depression and reactivity to stress in older women with rheumatoid arthritis and osteoarthritis. *Psychosomatic Medicine, 63*(4), 687–696.

CHAPTER 9

Diabetes Mellitus

JULIE LANDEL-GRAHAM, SUSAN E. YOUNT, AND SUSAN R. RUDNICKI

Diabetes mellitus represents a group of metabolic disorders of varying etiologies that are all characterized by hyperglycemia (i.e., high blood sugar levels). Across all subtypes of diabetes, this chronic hyperglycemia is associated with acute symptoms as well as a variety of serious long-term medical complications, including retinopathy, peripheral and autonomic neuropathies, nephropathy, and cardiovascular disease. Diabetes is the leading cause of blindness, amputations, and kidney transplants.

Diabetes occurs in approximately 15.7 million people in the United States, with 5.4 million of these persons undiagnosed and approximately 800,000 additional new cases diagnosed per year (Centers for Disease Control and Prevention [CDC], 1998). Importantly, recent research indicates that the prevalence of diabetes continues to increase rapidly in the United States, rising by 33% between 1990 and 1998 (Mokdad et al., 2000). These authors suggest that diabetes will become even more common in subsequent years because of the increasing prevalence of obesity. Diabetes is more frequent in the elderly and certain racial and ethnic groups (e.g., African Americans, Hispanic/Latino Americans, American Indians) and is the seventh leading cause of death in the United States (CDC, 1998). The annual costs of diabetes, including both direct medical costs and indirect costs due to disability, work loss, and premature mortality, were estimated to be $98 billion in 1997 (American Diabetes Association [ADA], 1998). Because of its increasing prevalence, disease burden on the individual, and economic costs to the nation,

diabetes should be seen as a prominent public health problem (Glasgow, Wagner, et al., 1999).

The Expert Committee on the Diagnosis and Classification of Diabetes Mellitus (2000) presented a revised diabetes classification system that differentiates four types of diabetes on the basis of etiology and pathogenesis: type 1, type 2, gestational diabetes, and other specific types. Most patients have either type 1 diabetes (historically referred to as insulin-dependent diabetes mellitus or juvenile onset diabetes) or type 2 diabetes (historically referred to as noninsulin-dependent diabetes mellitus or adult onset diabetes). Thus, the material in this chapter focuses on adults with type 1 or type 2 diabetes.

The Expert Committee on the Diagnosis and Classification of Diabetes Mellitus (2000) provides a thorough discussion of the types of diabetes, their etiologies, and pathogenesis. A brief review of this information is provided here for type 1 and type 2 diabetes. Type 1 diabetes, which accounts for approximately 5% to 10% of cases of diabetes, occurs as a result of the gradual destruction of the insulin-producing beta cells in the pancreas. In most patients, this destruction is caused by an identifiable autoimmune process, which leads to an absolute deficiency of endogenous insulin. Thus, use of exogenous insulin is required for survival to prevent the development of diabetic ketoacidosis (a life-threatening metabolic imbalance), coma, and death. It appears that genetic influences, as well as environmental factors, may play a role in the pathogenesis of type 1 diabetes. Although the majority of patients with type 1 diabetes are diagnosed in childhood or adolescence, type 1 diabetes may develop and be diagnosed at any age. Because markers of the autoimmune destruction of the pancreatic beta cells are now understood, major clinical trials are underway to intervene with patients at risk for developing type 1 diabetes. A variety of treatments are being used in an attempt to delay or prevent the development of overt type 1 diabetes.

Type 2 diabetes is the most prevalent form of diabetes, encompassing approximately 90% of cases. Type 2 diabetes results from insulin resistance (i.e., low cellular sensitivity to insulin) and/or a defect in insulin secretion that results in relative (as opposed to absolute) insulin deficiency. Most, but not all, patients with type 2 diabetes are obese, which tends to increase insulin resistance. Because the level of hyperglycemia develops gradually and may be less severe, up to 50% of type 2 patients are undiagnosed (Expert Committee on the Diagnosis and Classification of Diabetes Mellitus, 2000). Thus, the hyperglycemia may be "silently" causing end organ complications. Risk factors for type 2 diabetes include older age, obesity, lack of physical activity, family history of diabetes, prior history of gestational diabetes, impaired glucose tolerance, and race/ethnicity (CDC, 1998). There is also a strong, but poorly understood, genetic component to type 2 diabetes.

From a physiological perspective, the successful management of diabetes is operationally defined as the patient's level of glycemic (i.e., blood glucose) control. This is most commonly measured using glycosylated hemoglobin (GHb) assays (also referred to as glycohemoglobin, glycated hemoglobin, HBA_{1c}, or HbA_1). GHb levels yield an estimate of average blood glucose (BG) levels over the previous two to three months (ADA, 2000b). GHb assays are routinely performed as part of standard diabetes care and are commonly used as outcome measures in research. In addition, the data provided by patients' records of their self-monitored BG levels are important indicators of daily BG levels and variability.

The goal of treatment for all diabetes patients is to achieve normal or as near normal as possible BG levels. The importance of this goal has been firmly established for type 1 patients by the Diabetes Control and Complications Trial Research Group (DCCT, 1993) and for type 2 patients by the United Kingdom Prospective Diabetes Study Group (UKPDS, 1998). Both of these randomized clinical trials determined that patients on intensive treatment regimens were able to achieve better glycemic control and significantly reduce their risk for diabetes complications. For example, the DCCT found a 50% to 75% risk reduction for the development or progression of retinopathy, nephropathy, and neuropathy in the intensive treatment group.

To achieve these important risk reductions in diabetes complications, there has been renewed clinical effort to work effectively with patients to achieve the tightest glycemic control feasible for a given patient's circumstances. For most patients, these goals can be achieved only through an intensive treatment regimen that places a strong emphasis on self-management. As reviewed by the ADA (2000a), the treatment components for type 1 and type 2 patients include medical nutrition therapy; self-monitoring of BG (SMBG); regular physical activity; physiologically based insulin regimens when needed; oral glucose-lowering agents when needed; and regular medical care to modify treatment, screen for complications, and provide education and support. The selection of regimen components and their intensity are individualized for each patient's particular needs, resulting in great variability in treatment both between patients and within a patient over time. For example, patients may be either prescribed insulin or not, and those on insulin may perform between one and four injections per day or use a continuous infusion insulin pump. The treatment of diabetes is not static: The patient is required to balance these multiple treatment components in everyday life, adjusting for a myriad of factors that affect BG throughout the day. Thus, diabetes is truly a chronic disease that can be effectively treated only through a combination of skilled medical care and optimal self-management.

ADHERENCE IN DIABETES

The daily treatment regimen for diabetes is complex, demanding, and necessitates not only knowledge and technical skills, but also the ability to modify the treatment components as needed to achieve optimal glycemic control. Given the complexity of this regimen and the fact that it is required on a daily basis for the rest of the patient's life, it is not surprising that many type 1 and type 2 diabetes patients (40% to 90%) have difficulty following treatment recommendations (McNabb, 1997).

Adherence is commonly referred to as the extent to which a person's behavior (in terms of taking medications, following diets, or executing lifestyle changes) coincides with medical advice (Haynes, 1979). As McNabb (1997) pointed out, the definition of adherence can be expanded to include important patient-centered notions—the degree to which a patient follows a predetermined set of behaviors or actions (established cooperatively by the patient and provider) to care for diabetes on a daily basis. It is in this spirit that the term *adherence* is used throughout the remainder of this chapter.

Several measurement considerations limit the study of adherence and its relationship to health outcomes. McNabb (1997) and Johnson (1992) provide excellent reviews of these methodological difficulties in adherence research. The first difficulty is in defining the set of behaviors involved in the treatment regimen because of the wide variability in types and intensities of treatment regimens, the lack of explicit recommendations in medical charts, and/or the inability of patients to recall recommendations. In addition, adherence to one aspect of the regimen is relatively independent of adherence to other aspects of the regimen (Glasgow, McCaul, & Schafer, 1987), with adherence to medications the highest while adherence to behaviors necessitating greater lifestyle change (e.g., diet, exercise) is lower (Johnson, 1992). Thus, global rating systems and judgments of patients as *adherent* versus *nonadherent* are inappropriate.

As reviewed by Johnson (1992), methods used to evaluate diabetes patients' adherence levels include physiological outcomes (e.g., GHb), physician ratings, collateral reports, measurement of permanent products (e.g., number of pills consumed, data stored in memory BG meters), and patient self-reports. There is no widely accepted, reliable measure of adherence or approach to quantifying the level of adherence at present (McNabb, 1997). Each method of assessment has its advantages as well as its limitations. Despite reliability and validity concerns, self-report measures are the most commonly used measures of adherence. A variety of psychometrically sound questionnaires (e.g., the Summary of Diabetes Self-Care Activities; Toobert, Hampson, & Glasgow, 2000); self-monitoring diaries (e.g., Glasgow et al., 1987); and interviews (e.g., 24 Hour Recall Interview; Johnson, Silverstein, Rosenbloom, Carter, & Cunningham, 1986) have been developed. Given the difficulties in each of the measurement methods, Johnson and McNabb recommend selecting instruments carefully, using a multicomponent measurement strategy, and measuring adherence across time and within a time period consistent with other measures of constructs to which the researcher is seeking to relate adherence. Once measured, however, decisions about how to evaluate the obtained adherence levels must be made. Without a known standard of adherence, researchers and practitioners are left without clear guidelines for qualifying levels of behavior that fall below this elusive standard (McNabb, 1997).

Adherence as a construct is important because of its presumed link with glycemic control and thus indirectly its link to diabetes complications. Despite the clear logic of this relationship, research has been inconsistent in its ability to find a direct link between patient adherence and metabolic control in diabetes. This may be because of the multidetermined nature of glycemic control, the limitations of GHb as a measure of glycemia, methodological problems in adherence measurement and analysis, and the potential for an idiosyncratic effect of adherence on glycemic control between individuals (Johnson, 1992; McNabb, 1997).

PSYCHOSOCIAL FACTORS IN DIABETES MANAGEMENT

Despite the difficulties in its conceptualization, accurate measurement, interpretation, and relationship to glycemic control, adherence continues to be the focus of research efforts and clinical interventions. Research, reviewed next, has sought to (a) identify the factors associated with either the promotion or suppression of adherence levels and (b) develop effective interventions to enhance adherence levels and subsequent health outcomes. This chapter focuses on six such variables: patient knowledge, stress, depression, social support, patient practitioner relationships, and perceived barriers and coping styles. The selection of these six factors was based on the amount of research conducted with the variable as the focus, the availability of empirically tested interventions focusing on the factor, and clinical relevancy.

Knowledge

The increasing complexity of the diabetes regimen and emphasis on self-management (M. Williams, Baker, Parker, & Nurss, 1998) has placed higher educational demands on patients (ADA, 1996). Education may facilitate patients' acceptance of their diagnosis, engagement in the behavioral changes necessary for their active participation (M. Williams et al., 1998), and ability to lead normal, productive lives (Garrard et al., 1987).

Diabetes Education Programs

In the late 1970s, diabetes education programs were initiated to ensure that patients had sufficient knowledge and understanding of their disease (Beeney, Dunn, & Welch, 1994). The need to evaluate these programs led to the development of tests of diabetes knowledge (e.g., Garrard et al., 1987; Hess & Davis, 1983; Miller, Goldstein, & Nicolaisen, 1978). Diabetes education has historically had as its objective the didactic transmission of facts about diabetes, based on the assumption that increasing knowledge of the "facts" of diabetes would improve BG control and, ultimately, reduce the incidence and severity of complications (Beeney et al., 1994). The traditional patient education has relied primarily on written material about the disease process, medical management, and self-care instructions. Despite decades of effort, gaps remain in the number of diabetes patients who have access to or take advantage of education (Coonrod, Betschart, & Harris, 1994), the amount of knowledge achieved (McCaul, Glasgow, & Schafer, 1987), and the diabetes-related information disseminated or acquired by patients (Dunn, Beeney, Hoskins, & Turtle, 1990). Early diabetes education programs demonstrated increases in knowledge that did not translate into improvements in glycemic control or other health outcomes (Watts, 1980), although good measures of glycemic control, for example GHb, were not available then. More recent studies have also failed to find a link between knowledge and glycemic control (Peyrot & Rubin, 1994), but some have found improvements that were maintained up to 12 months (Rubin, Peyrot, & Saudek, 1991).

A number of researchers have recognized that education through information transfer alone, without attention to other aspects of diabetes care, has limited impact on BG control (Dunn et al., 1990; Rubin, Peyrot, & Saudek, 1989). Patient education has been influenced by the growing awareness that psychosocial factors such as motivation, health beliefs, coping strategies, and self-efficacy contribute significantly to behavior and health outcomes and are amenable to change (Beeney et al., 1994). Thus, more recent educational efforts have gone beyond didactic presentation of facts and have adopted a more pragmatic approach by teaching self-care skills and strategies to facilitate lifestyle change, with positive (Clement, 1995), and sometimes long-term, (Rubin et al., 1991) results.

Other studies have sought to disaggregate the components of diabetes education in an attempt to understand the mechanisms by which the programs achieve their outcomes. Some have proposed that it may be important to distinguish between self-regulation behaviors (e.g., SMBG, insulin adjustments) and self-care activities (e.g., diet, exercise). Self-care activities have been shown to be more resistant to improvement (Rubin et al., 1991), possibly because they are more rooted in a person's lifestyle and take more time to accomplish. Another study demonstrated the additive effect of three aspects of diabetes behaviors: insulin administration, self-monitoring, and exercise (Peyrot & Rubin, 1994). Additionally, physician factors have been shown to play a role in the success of diabetes patient education. A study that incorporated education and training for both the patient (e.g., target behaviors) and resident physician (e.g., attitudes, beliefs) accomplished greater improvements in health outcomes than the education of either participant alone (Vinicor et al., 1987). Finally, because of the demands of the regimen for newly diagnosed insulin-requiring diabetes patients, Jacobson (1996) suggested that an

incremental approach to education be undertaken, starting with information and skill building, with the immediate goal of stabilizing metabolism, followed by more in-depth education once the patient and family have made an "emotional adjustment" to the disease. Other recommendations for components of a diabetes education program include use of the patient's primary language (Martinez, 1993); accommodation of the patient's literacy level, a model that involves two-way communication between patient and provider (Glasgow, Fisher, et al., 1999); and recognition of the dynamic nature of the diabetic regimen (Glasgow & Anderson, 1999).

A goal of *Healthy People 2000* (U.S. Department of Health and Human Services, 1991) is to have 75% of people with diabetes receive education. Toward that end and toward the goal of continuing to improve the effectiveness of diabetes education, a number of recent models for diabetes patient education have been proposed (e.g., Glasgow, 1995) and guidelines established (Funnell & Haas, 1995). Common themes include the consideration of individual patient characteristics (e.g., attitudes & beliefs, cultural influences, psychological status, literacy, age), process skills (e.g., coping, self-efficacy, problem solving), attitudes and beliefs, patient-provider outcomes, behavioral orientation, ongoing support and evaluation, improved access, and examination of cost effectiveness.

Summary

Diabetes education has had positive effects on a number of aspects of diabetes management. Despite attempts to broaden the access and scope of diabetes education, many diabetic individuals have never had the opportunity to participate in and benefit from diabetes education. This remains especially problematic for subgroups of diabetic patients, such as those of lower socioeconomic status, those who do not speak English, those who do not require insulin, and/or those with a high prevalence of the disease. Diabetes management is complex and involves multiple behaviors and components, and effective diabetes education is likely to be similarly complex and multifactorial. We already know that optimal programs will include multiple options to accommodate individualized modes of learning, knowledgeable and trained instructors, integration with clinical services, a behavioral/interactive approach, culturally relevant and linguistically appropriate content and process, ongoing support, and program evaluation. Future studies will further enhance our understanding of the process by continuing to test models for diabetes education and examining what components of a program are responsible for the positive effects.

Stress

Since the seventeenth century, psychological stress has been suspected to be a psychosomatic factor involved in diabetes. In the twentieth century, clinical observation and anecdotal evidence gave way as Walter Cannon (1941) introduced the experimental study of the effects of stress on diabetes with his research on stress-induced hyperglycemia in normal cats. A detailed review of the literature on stress and diabetes is beyond the scope of this chapter (see Evans, 1985; Surwit & Williams, 1996); however, we include a brief review of the research linking stress and the development and management of type 1 and type 2 diabetes.

Stress in the Etiology of Diabetes

The underlying assumption in type 1 diabetes is that the stress response in some way disrupts the immune system of genetically susceptible individuals, making pancreatic beta cells more vulnerable to autoimmune destruction (Cox & Gonder-Frederick, 1991). Only 50% of identical twins are concordant for type 1 diabetes, suggesting that an environmental stimulus may be required for expression of the disease, although evidence for this mechanism is lacking (Surwit & Schneider, 1993). There are numerous reports of the development of type 1 diabetes following major stressful life events, particularly losses (Robinson & Fuller, 1985). However, studies of life events have been criticized methodologically for lack of controls, small sample sizes, and retrospective recall of events (Surwit, Schneider, & Feinglos, 1992). Animal research has provided limited and mixed evidence of an effect for stress in the onset of type 1 diabetes (Surwit & Schneider, 1993). Surgically pancreatized animals have been shown to develop either transient or permanent diabetes after restraint stress (Capponi, Kawada, Varela, & Vargas, 1980). Studies using another animal model of type 1 diabetes, the diabetes-prone BB Wistar rat, have shown that the combined effects of behavioral stressors, such as restraint and crowding, lower the age of diabetes onset (Carter, Herman, Stokes, & Cox, 1987) and increase the percentage of animals that became diabetic compared to nonstressed controls (Lehman, Rodin, McEwen, & Brunton, 1991). However, because of other endocrine abnormalities in these animals, generalizability of these findings to humans is limited (Surwit & Schneider, 1993).

Because type 2 diabetes has a concordance rate of almost 100% among identical twins (Sperling, 1988), there is theoretically less of an opportunity for stress to play an etiological role in the incidence of this diabetes type. Retrospective case studies suggest that stress acts as a triggering factor in the development of type 2 diabetes (Cox & Gonder-Frederick, 1991). However, there are no controlled studies of the possible role of stress in the onset of type 2 diabetes in humans. In the past 20 years, increasing evidence suggests that the autonomic nervous system is involved in the pathophysiology of type 2 diabetes (Surwit & Feinglos, 1988). Exaggerated glycemic reactivity to stress appears to be characteristic of some humans who are predisposed to developing type 2 diabetes, such as the Pima Indians (Spraul & Anderson, 1992; Surwit, McCubbin, Feinglos, Esposito-Del Puente, & Lillioja, 1990), as well as some animal models of type 2 diabetes (Mikat, Hackel, Cruz, & Lebovitz, 1972; Surwit, Feinglos, Livingston, Kuhn, & McCubbin, 1984). The data argue that expression of hyperglycemia in these genetic animal models is dependent on exposure to stressful stimuli. However, there is little evidence to suggest that stress is associated with the onset of type 2 diabetes de novo (Wales, 1995).

Stress and Glycemic Control

It has been hypothesized that stress has both direct and indirect effects on BG control in type 1 diabetes. A direct influence implies that the stress response results in direct hormonal/neurological effects that can, in turn, affect BG level. The stress hormones epinephrine, cortisol, and growth hormones are all believed to raise BG levels (Cox & Gonder-Frederick, 1991), and it is widely reported that patients with type 1 diabetes believe that stress affects BG (Cox et al., 1984). Some human studies have attempted to model the effects of stress by infusing stress hormones and measuring glucose metabolism. The data from these studies are fairly consistent in supporting the notion of a direct and acute connection between stress and BG (Kramer, Ledolter, Manos, & Bayless, 2000; Sherwin, Shamoon, Jacob, & Sacca, 1984). However, the infusion paradigm only partially mimics the complexity of bodily reactions.

Studies involving laboratory stressors with type 1 diabetes have been less consistent in demonstrating a stress-glycemic control relationship (e.g., Gonder-Frederick, Carter, Cox, & Clarke, 1990; Kemmer et al., 1986). Methodological factors may partially explain the contradictory data, including lack of control for the prestress metabolic status of the individual (Cox, Gonder-Frederick, Clarke, & Carter, 1988). Caution is also warranted in the potential lack of generalizability between relatively short-lived laboratory stressors that, in general, induce only modest physiological changes, and real-world stressors that may be profoundly different in terms of magnitude, duration, and spectrum (Kemmer et al., 1986).

Both human (Gonder-Frederick et al., 1990) and animal (Lee, Konarska, & McCarty, 1989) studies have demonstrated that stress has idiosyncratic effects on BG, which are manifest in two ways: Different stressors may have different effects on BG, and different individuals may respond to the same stressor in different ways. Further, these individual response differences appear to be stable over time (Gonder-Frederick et al., 1990). This line of research has prompted an exploration into the role of individual differences. Stabler et al. (1987) found that the glucose response to experimental stress was related to a Type A behavior pattern, but this finding has not been replicated in other studies (Aikens, Wallander, Bell, & McNorton, 1994).

Life events have also been implicated in glycemic control and symptomatology (Lloyd et al., 1999), although the association tends to be weak (Cox et al., 1984). In contrast with major life events, the role of daily stress variability has been shown to provide more convincing data on a link between stress and somatic health (Aikens, Wallander, Bell, & Cole, 1992).

Because relaxation techniques have been shown to decrease adrenocortical activity (DeGood & Redgate, 1982) and circulating levels of catecholamines (Mathew, Ho, Kralik, Taylor, & Claghorn, 1980), this intervention has been proposed as a means of moderating the negative effects of the stress response on glycemic control in diabetes. Relaxation interventions with type 1 patients have produced mixed results (e.g., Feinglos, Hastedt, & Surwit, 1987; McGrady, Bailey, & Good, 1991). This may be caused by heterogeneous glucose responses to stress in type 1 diabetes and/or more labile glycemic control resulting from diet, insulin, exercise, and illness (Feinglos et al., 1987).

Alternatively or concurrently, stress may also relate to diabetes management through the indirect effects on treatment adherence (Peyrot & McMurray, 1985). This is particularly relevant to individuals with type 1 diabetes or those requiring insulin, since self-management in these patients is more complex. Stress can disrupt self-care by promoting inappropriate behaviors (e.g., drinking alcohol, binge eating) or by upsetting normal routine behaviors (Cox & Gonder-Frederick, 1991).

Finally, BG fluctuations can indirectly affect stress levels through neuroendocrine changes that are subjectively perceived as stress or mood states (Grandinetti, Kaholokula, & Chang, 2000). At extreme BG levels, mental confusion, disorientation, and coma can result. Diabetes is the leading cause of adult blindness, lower extremity amputations, kidney disease, and impotence (Glasgow, Fisher, et al., 1999). Thus, glucose may also be responsible for indirectly inducing stress secondary to the requirement for aversive therapeutic interventions (Bernbaum, Albert, & Duckro, 1988).

A modest literature has developed over the past 20 years on the effects of stress on control of type 2 diabetes. Studies have demonstrated a relationship between life events and diabetic symptomatology, although the association is sometimes weak (Grant, Kyle, Teichman, & Mendels, 1974) or absent (Inui et al., 1998). To explain the conflicting results, Bradley (1979) suggested that type 2 patients may have some degree of endogenous homeostatic control of their glucose levels, making them less likely to experience disruption in response to stress.

Physical stressors, such as elective surgery and anesthesia (McClesky, Lewis, & Woodruff, 1978), as well as laboratory stressors (Goetsch, Wiebe, Veltum, & Van Dorsten, 1990), affect BG. Although the mechanisms for the metabolic response to stress in type 2 diabetes are unknown, there is some evidence for an altered adrenergic sensitivity and responsivity in type 2 diabetic humans and animal models, as supported by studies examining the role of alpha-adrenergic blockades in altering glucose-stimulated insulin secretion (e.g., Kashiwagi et al., 1986).

Some researchers propose that environmental stress, which activates the sympathetic nervous system, may be particularly deleterious to patients with type 2; therefore, methods to reduce the effects of stress are believed to have some clinical utility in this disease (Surwit et al., 1992). With some exceptions (Lane, McCaskill, Ross, Feinglos, & Surwit, 1993), well-controlled group studies have demonstrated that relaxation training can have a significant positive impact on BG level or range with type 2 patients (Lammers, Naliboff, & Straatmeyer, 1984; Surwit & Feinglos, 1983). There is also evidence that anxiolytic pharmacotherapy effectively attenuates the effects of stress on hyperglycemia in animals (Surwit & Williams, 1996) and humans (Surwit, McCasKill, Ross, & Feinglos, 1991).

Summary

Speculation regarding the role of stress in the development and course of diabetes has continued for more than 300 years. Only limited evidence supports the notion that stress is involved in the onset of type 1 diabetes. The literature on the effects of stress on the course of type 1 diabetes in experimental and clinical settings is complicated by a variety of methodological limitations and issues. Importantly, less than half of individuals with type 1 diabetes may manifest a relationship between stress and BG control (Kramer et al., 2000), and individuals who are "stress reactors" may respond idiosyncratically (Goetsch et al., 1990; Riazi, Pickup, & Bradley, 1996). Evidence that stress reduction strategies are effective in type 1 diabetes is limited and inconclusive. The literature on the effects of stress on type 2 diabetes is somewhat more consistent in both animal and human studies. Stress and stress hormones have been more consistently shown to produce hyperglycemic effects in type 2 diabetes. Animal and human studies provide evidence of autonomic nervous system abnormalities in the etiology of type 2 diabetes, with exaggerated sympathetic nervous system activity affecting glucose metabolism. Although additional evidence is needed, the effects of stress management techniques appear to have more beneficial effects in type 2 diabetes.

Depression in Diabetes

Substantial research indicates that depression is three to four times more prevalent among adults with diabetes than among the general population, affecting one in every five patients (Lustman, Griffith, & Clouse, 1988). In addition, evidence suggests that in both types of diabetes depressive episodes tend to last longer in comparison to individuals without diabetes (Talbot & Nouwen, 2000). The effects of depression on diabetes management, its etiology, assessment, and treatment are reviewed in the next section.

Etiology

The etiology of depression in diabetes is not yet fully understood. However, an increasing number of studies have investigated potential causal mechanisms underlying these coexisting conditions. A thorough review (Talbot & Nouwen, 2000) attempted to identify support for two dominant hypotheses linking depression and diabetes: (a) depression results from biochemical changes directly due to the illness or its treatment, and (b) depression results from the psychosocial burden of having a chronic medical condition, not from the disease itself. Instead of evidence in support of these hypotheses, the findings support a relationship between the presence of major depressive disorder (MDD) or depressive symptomatology and increased risk of developing type 2 diabetes and diabetes-related complications. Thus, in accordance with a diathesis-stress framework, metabolic changes (e.g., insulin resistance) resulting from MDD may trigger an individual's biological vulnerability to developing type 2 diabetes (e.g., Winokur, Maislin, Phillips, & Amsterdam, 1988). Patterns regarding causality of MDD are less clear for type 1 diabetes (Talbot & Nouwen, 2000). There is speculation that MDD is a consequence of having type 1 diabetes, since the first episode of MDD generally follows the diagnosis of diabetes. Future prospective studies with type 1 diabetes patients, their self-care regimen, and adherence level should help clarify this issue.

Impact of Depression in Diabetes

The comorbidity of depression and diabetes can have substantial and debilitating effects on patients' health. This may occur either directly via physiological routes or indirectly through alterations in self-care. Lustman, Griffith, and Clouse (1997) developed an empirically based model in which depression has direct and indirect links to glucose dysregulation and risk of diabetes complications. In this model, depression is directly associated with obesity, physical inactivity, and treatment noncompliance. These factors lead to the risk of diabetes complications. Depression is also directly related to diabetes complications as well as to specific behavioral factors, such as smoking and substance abuse, that have been found to increase the risk of disease complications. According to this model, smoking cessation treatment and weight loss programs would aid in the reduction of diabetes complications. Unfortunately, however, depressed patients are generally more resistant to such treatment approaches and thus continue to compromise their diabetes management. In further support of the mechanisms inherent in this model, the presence of concomitant depressive symptoms among older diabetic Mexican Americans was found to be associated with significantly increased health burden (e.g., myocardial infarction, increased health service use; Black, 1999). Thus, treating depression in patients with diabetes is particularly important in preventing or delaying diabetes complications, stabilizing metabolic control, and decreasing health service utilization.

Other studies have focused on the relationship between depressive symptoms and medical outcomes. Results of a meta-analysis including 24 studies in which research participants had either type 1 or type 2 diabetes indicate that depression is significantly associated with hyperglycemia (Lustman, Anderson, et al., 2000). Similar effect sizes were found in studies of patients with both types of diabetes. However, results differed depending on the assessment methods utilized. To elucidate, larger effect sizes were found when standardized interviews and diagnostic criteria were employed to assess depression in comparison to self-report questionnaires (e.g., BDI; Beck, Ward, & Mendelson, 1961). According to the authors, it is possible that one of the reasons for these results is the decreased specificity of self-report measures that capture not only depression but also anxiety, general emotional distress, or medical illness. Nonetheless, the authors assert that future research is needed to determine the cause and effect relationship between depression and hyperglycemia as well as the effect of depression treatment on glycemic control and the continuous course of diabetes. In addition, Gary, Crum, Cooper-Patrick,

Ford, & Brancati (2000) reported a significant graded relationship between greater depressive symptoms and higher serum levels of cholesterol and triglycerides in African American patients with diabetes. Similar to the aforementioned study, the temporal relationship between depression and metabolic control is unknown. Despite this limitation, such an association emphasizes the importance and benefit of providing depression treatment for individuals with diabetes to improve health outcomes.

Assessment

Identifying depression in diabetes can be problematic since somatic symptoms of depression usually included in assessment scales are often similar to the somatic symptoms of diabetes (Bradley, 2000). Thus, this commonality of symptoms could potentially compromise the sensitivity and specificity of psychiatric diagnosis, leading to overdiagnosis of depression (Lustman, Clouse, Griffith, Carney, & Freedland, 1997). Current psychodiagnostic procedures, as specified in the *Diagnostic and Statistical Manual of Mental Disorders, Fourth Edition* (*DSM-IV;* American Psychiatric Association [APA], 1994), account for this symptom overlap when determining the diagnosis of depression by excluding depression symptoms resulting from a medical condition. Self-report measures have also successfully identified depression in diabetes patients. For example, the Beck Depression Inventory (Beck et al., 1961; Lustman, Clouse, et al., 1997) was found to effectively differentiate depressed diabetes patients from nondepressed patients by using the 21-item BDI as well as the cognitive and somatic items alone.

Treatment

Similar to the general population, the most common treatments for depression in diabetic patients involve psychotherapy and medication. Lustman, Freedland, Griffith, and Clouse (1998) conducted the first randomized, controlled trial of the efficacy of cognitive-behavioral therapy (CBT) for major depression in diabetes. The cognitive-behavioral strategies included encouraging patients to reengage in enjoyable social and physical activities, employing problem-solving skills to cope with environmental stressors, and restructuring cognitive distortions by replacing them with more rational and functional thought processes. The outcome of their 10-week study suggests that CBT in combination with a diabetes education program is more effective in treating depression than diabetes education alone in the short and long term. Moreover, although there were no differences between groups immediately after treatment, HbA$_{1c}$ levels at

the six-month follow-up were significantly better in the CBT group as compared to the control group. Higher HbA$_{1c}$, lower SMBG compliance, and higher weight were related to failure to achieve full remission of depression in the overall sample (Lustman et al., 1998). Thus, the authors propose that patients who exhibit poor compliance with SMBG may be less likely to benefit from CBT, a type of therapy that involves the use of self-management skills.

Studies investigating the efficacy of pharmacological treatment for diabetes patients suffering from depression are scarce. Lustman, Freedland, Griffith, and Clouse (2000) conducted a randomized placebo-controlled double-blind trial employing fluoxetine with 60 type 1 and type 2 diabetes patients. Results pointed toward the effectiveness of reducing depression with patients treated with fluoxetine as compared to placebo. Moreover, although not statistically significant, patients in the experimental group showed greater improvements in mean HbA$_{1c}$ levels after eight weeks of treatment.

These more recent studies suggest the burgeoning of treatments that aid diabetes patients in managing their depression. Thus, it is incumbent upon health practitioners to select interventions that specifically match patients' needs (Lustman, Griffith, Clouse, Freedland, et al., 1997). To further clarify, pharmacological treatment may be most effective for patients lacking self-management skills or for those who exhibit somatic complaints, whereas psychotherapy may be most conducive for patients experiencing interpersonal difficulties or cognitive distortions. Nonetheless, empirical support for depression management in diabetes is clearly lacking, and controlled studies are needed to elucidate the most effective strategies to reduce depression and improve BG control in diabetes patients.

Summary

It is well-known that depression is highly prevalent in the diabetes population. However, the etiology of depression in diabetes remains speculative, with a less clear understanding of the patterns of causality for type 1 diabetes. Such uncertainty highlights the need for future empirical studies to examine the causal relationship between depression and diabetes. Other primary areas of empirical investigations have included uncovering factors that prevent diabetes complications or affect health behaviors and outcomes within a depressed diabetes population. Positive outcomes of preliminary treatment studies involving cognitive-behavioral strategies and pharmacological management are providing practitioners with more effective intervention strategies to lower depressive symptomatology as well as to enhance metabolic control in depressed patients with diabetes.

Social Support

There is a general consensus that social support mediates health-related behaviors and outcomes. Two widely accepted models by which social support may influence health outcomes have been proposed: a main effect model and a buffering model (see Cohen & Wills, 1985). The main effect model postulates that social support has a beneficial effect on health or well-being regardless of whether individuals are under stress. The buffering model proposes that social support lessens the impact of stress on well-being when high levels of stress are experienced but does not affect health/well-being in the absence of stress. Social support may insulate patients from adverse physiologic and behavioral consequences of stress by modifying their perception of a stressor, thereby providing them with additional coping resources, or by modifying the physiological reaction to the stressor, thereby diminishing the pathological outcome of the stressor.

Social support may play a particularly influential role in a chronic, demanding disease such as diabetes. Because of the many self-care behaviors involved in diabetes management, patients with diabetes may be in special need of both instrumental and emotional support to allow them to maintain appropriate levels of adherence and psychological adjustment. The family environment may be especially important in this patient population. In fact, the family unit has been described as "the environment in which diabetes management and coping occur" (Newbrough, Simpkins, & Maurer, 1985). A relationship between family support, regimen adherence, and metabolic control seems intuitive for two reasons: (a) family members are often asked to share in the responsibility for implementation of the diabetic regimen, and (b) family routines can be disrupted by the diabetes self-care regimen (B. Anderson & Auslander, 1980; Wishner & O'Brien, 1978).

Impact on Adherence

Research has focused on the role of social support as a determinant of self-care behaviors and/or metabolic control. Links between social support and regimen adherence have been documented in adults with diabetes, and some studies have defended social support's role in buffering the negative effects of stress (Glasgow & Toobert, 1988; Schafer, McCaul, & Glasgow, 1986). Studies have also suggested that diabetes regimen-specific measures of family support may be more efficacious in predicting adherence than general support measures (Glasgow & Toobert, 1988; W. Wilson et al., 1986). Research has also focused on specific aspects of the social and family environment that are related to regimen adherence, including support ratio (ratio of received to desired amount of support; Boehm, Schlenk, Funnell, Powers, & Ronis, 1997), the influence of negative versus positive family interactions (Schafer et al., 1986), aspects of the regimen that are benefited (e.g., diet, medication, exercise; W. Wilson et al., 1986), and gender differences in the effects of support on adherence (Goodall & Halford, 1991).

Impact on Metabolic Control

The impact of social support on metabolic control has also been investigated, with mixed results. Direct, main effects of support on glycemic control have infrequently been studied (Klemp & LaGreca, 1987). Of those studies that have examined the relationship between social support and both adherence and glycemic control, findings have been both positive (Hanson, Schinkel, DeGuire, & Kolterman, 1995; Schwartz, Russell, Toovy, Lyons, & Flaherty, 1991) and negative (Griffith, Field, & Lustman, 1990; Trief, Grant, Elbert, & Weinstock, 1998). Again, some findings support a stress-buffering role for social support (Griffith et al., 1990). It has been suggested that negative findings of a relationship between social support and glycemic control should not be surprising, given that psychosocial and behavioral variables are more strongly related to behavioral variables, such as self-care, than multidetermined physiologic variables, such as glycemic control (Wilson et al., 1986).

Social Support Interventions

Recent studies have explored the potential role for technology-based interventions in helping to educate and provide support to individuals with diabetes. Interventions such as computer/Internet support groups have reportedly been well received, actively used, and associated with positive effects. One professionally moderated Internet support group for diabetes patients and their families provided educational and emotional support to more than 47,000 users over a 21-month period, with 79% of respondents rating their participation as having a positive effect on coping with diabetes (Zrebiec & Jacobson, 2001). Other studies using the Internet have focused on both broad populations of patients with diabetes (McKay, Feil, Glasgow, & Brown, 1998) and specific diabetic populations, such as rural women (Smith & Weinert, 2000) in providing education, social support, and other types of information, with similarly high rates of satisfaction and utilization.

Summary

Although the mixed research findings to date suggest that the influence of family and social environment on behaviors of adults with diabetes warrants further investigation, the existing literature has provided a basis for Anderson (1996) and others to offer preliminary guidelines for clinical interactions with patients and their support systems: (a) Social support should be individually defined for each patient within each family system; (b) support is dynamic and changes over time as the patient and family grow and change; (c) at times, it must be recognized that in families with dysfunctional interaction patterns, successful family involvement may not be feasible; and (d) assistance should be provided to patients in determining the amount and types of social support that would be beneficial to them (Boehm et al., 1997). Systematic empirical treatment efficacy studies focusing on social support in adults are needed.

Research has highlighted the importance of social—and especially family—support in the management of diabetes. Also apparent are the complexities involved in the relationship between social support and a person's ability to adjust to and live with this disease, including the impact of age, gender, race, family developmental stage, and type of diabetes regimen (e.g., insulin- vs. noninsulin-requiring). More traditional interventions, such as individual, couples, and family therapy, have proven to be beneficial in assisting individuals with communication, assertiveness, and problem-solving skills. The potential role of multidisciplinary health care interventions with both individuals and families and the use of technology-based interventions remain to be more fully and rigorously explored in future studies.

Patient-Practitioner Interactions

The traditional biomedical model of care, in which the practitioner is seen as the expert who sets treatment goals and standards, is inappropriate for the demands of daily diabetes care (R. Anderson, 1995). Optimal disease management can be achieved only through the partnership and active participation of a knowledgeable, motivated patient and staff. Research regarding several aspects of the patient practitioner relationship and their relationships to adherence and health outcomes are reviewed in the following section.

Patient Participation

In accordance with findings in other chronic illness populations (Garrity, 1981), it has been suggested that by increasing patients' participation and responsibility in their care, motivation for adherence and disease management may be enhanced (Greenfield, Kaplan, Ware, Yano, & Frank, 1988). Several studies have sought to empirically examine the effects of the patients' level of involvement in the patient-practitioner

relationship on diabetes outcomes such as adherence and metabolic control. It should be noted, however, that playing an active role in medical encounters and decision making may not be easily achieved for all patients (e.g., Greenfield et al., 1988).

Poorer metabolic control has been associated with less patient involvement, less effective information-seeking behavior, and less exchange of opinions during office visits (Kaplan, Greenfield, & Ware, 1989). Physicians' provision of autonomy support (i.e., providing choice to the patients, giving information, acknowledging emotions, and providing minimal pressure for patients to behave a certain way) has been related to better glycemic control, perceived competence, and autonomous motivation for adherence (G. Williams, Freedman, & Deci, 1988). Randomized studies have found that interventions designed to increase patient participation in medical encounters lead to behavioral changes in the interactions with practitioners, fewer physical limitations, and improved glycemic control (Greenfield et al., 1988; Rost, Flavin, Cole, & McGill, 1991). Greenfield and colleagues (1988) developed an intervention consisting of two brief sessions in which patients were taught communication skills pertaining to information seeking, negotiation, focused question asking, and asserting control. Patients' medical charts were reviewed with them, and any perceived barriers to active participation were discussed and coping strategies suggested. The patients who were randomized to the intervention group were twice as effective at eliciting information from the physician and were more active in the patient practitioner interaction. Importantly, these patients reported fewer functional limitations and better glycemic control at follow-up. The authors state that further research is needed to determine whether the noted improvements are related to increased information that patients obtained in the visit or to the increased involvement. Rost et al. (1991) investigated whether similar improvements could be achieved by adding a patient activation component to an inpatient diabetes education program. Patient activation training involved reviewing their medical charts and obstacles to active involvement, writing down questions for practitioners, and improving communication. Patients who were randomized to the activation condition were more active in their discharge visit and showed a trend for increased decision-making behaviors. This group reported fewer physical limitations in activities of daily living four months later and some improvements in metabolic control. Importantly, the physicians' satisfaction was not negatively affected by the interaction. The active role and personal responsibility of patients are major tenets of patient empowerment programs (R. Anderson et al., 1995). R. Anderson and colleagues found that patients in an empowerment program had improved self-efficacy, diabetes attitudes, and glycemic control at the six-week follow-up.

Many of the studies reviewed have not evaluated the mediating role that adherence may play in the demonstrated outcome improvements (R. Anderson et al., 1995; Greenfield et al., 1988; Kaplan et al., 1989; Rost et al., 1991). The effects of patient participation on adherence may be seen through several routes: a direct effect on adherence, an indirect effect on adherence by increasing the understanding of the regimen and the appropriateness of the regimen, and/or an indirect negative effect on adherence by decreasing satisfaction with the relationship when there is a discrepancy between a patient's desired role and what is possible (Golin, DiMatteo, & Gelberg, 1996). Future empirical research in this area needs to incorporate measures of adherence to fully evaluate and understand the effects of patient activation interventions on outcomes.

Patient Satisfaction

Satisfaction with care appears to be more heavily influenced by such factors as information giving, the meeting of patient expectations, and expressions of empathy than by variables related to the technical competence of the physician or cost of care (Golin et al., 1996). Patient satisfaction has been linked to higher adherence rates in various chronic illness populations (Sherbourne, Hays, Ordway, DiMatteo, & Kravitz, 1992) and to better adherence (Landel, Delamater, Barza, Schneiderman, & Skyler, 1995) and health outcomes (Landel et al., 1995; Viinamaki, Niskanen, Korhonen, & Tahka, 1993) in diabetes populations specifically.

Psychometrically sound measures of patient satisfaction are available for the general population (e.g., Marshall, Hays, Sherbourne, & Wells, 1993), as well as for diabetes treatment, including the Diabetes Clinic Satisfaction Questionnaire (A. Wilson & Home, 1993) and the Patient Practitioner Relationship Questionnaire (Landel, 1995). Other diabetes satisfaction scales examine specific types of satisfaction, for example, satisfaction with diabetes management programs (Paddock, Veloski, Chatterton, Gevirtz, & Nash, 2000).

Clinical Suggestions for Enhancing the Relationship

Based on the research findings described and on clinical experiences, a number of suggestions for enhancing the quality of the patient-practitioner relationship are relevant for a variety of practitioners working with diabetes patients. The establishment of a caring, empathetic, and nonjudgmental partnership between practitioner and patient is seen as integral

(Glasgow, 1995). Through collaborative goal setting and contracting, expectations on each party's part may be made explicit. In addition, such interactions allow the patient to voice concerns, other competing demands, desires for involvement in diabetes care, and lifestyle factors that may influence the fit of the proposed regimen to the person's lifestyle at that time. Glasgow provides pointers for low-cost systemwide interventions to promote better diabetes management, such as paying attention to the patient's past medical care experiences, reducing the number of treatment goals per visit (focusing on one or two key behaviors), providing adherence prompts to patients, and distributing appropriate written materials. For patients in need of further intervention, Glasgow (1995) suggests preparing patients before medical appointments by reviewing their medical charts with them, doing relapse-prevention training, having more frequent follow-up appointments scheduled, providing further education as needed, and using visual displays and analyses of their SMBG data.

Clinical recommendations for achieving long-term behavioral change and health benefits in patients with diabetes may also be garnered from the experiences of the DCCT (Lorenz et al., 1996). The particular behavioral strategies used by the practitioners and patients involved in the DCCT were not standardized or specifically measured; rather, behavioral strategies were individualized according to the needs of particular centers and patients. Lorenz and colleagues (1996) summarized the types of strategies commonly used and emphasized the importance of a collaborative style of interaction and the support provided for the patients involved in the intensive treatment. Further research is needed to systematically evaluate these strategies for enhancing patient adherence and outcomes in heterogeneous samples of diabetes patients.

Summary

As medicine becomes more patient-centered, it is increasingly recognized that successful management of diabetes is predicated upon a partnership between the person with diabetes and his or her medical team. Through such a partnership, the individual may establish self-care behaviors that optimize metabolic control. However, the quality and characteristics of such relationships vary widely, both between and within individuals. Research indicates that several characteristics of the patient-practitioner relationship are related to health outcomes. Persons who take an active role in their care, assuming appropriate levels of personal responsibility, are able to achieve better metabolic control. In addition, individuals achieve better outcomes when their physicians have congruent diabetes beliefs and specific interests in diabetes, and when they are more generally satisfied with their care. Suggestions on how to establish a collaborative, supportive relationship have been developed. In addition, some interventions have begun to be evaluated for their effects on adherence and health outcomes. As this important moderator of outcomes receives more attention, additional research should seek to develop and empirically evaluate interventions to promote effective patient-physician partnerships. The effect of such interventions on levels of self-care, psychosocial factors (e.g., adaptive coping, perceptions of social support), and health outcomes needs to be examined. Individual differences in factors such as desire for an active role in care and communication style should also be studied for their effects on such interventions.

Barriers to Adherence, Coping, and Problem Solving

Barriers to Adherence

Glasgow, Hampson, Strycker, and Ruggiero (1997) have proposed two specific categories of barriers that impede daily diabetes self-care: personal and social-environmental. The personal model includes patients' cognitions about the disease including health beliefs (e.g., vulnerability to negative outcomes), emotions, knowledge, and experiences. Such perceptions affect the implementation of specific health behaviors including disease management and patient-practitioner interactions. Social-environmental factors include barriers to self-care (e.g., weather), social support from family or peers, interactions with health care providers, and community resources and services (Glasgow, 1994). Gaining awareness of patients' social contexts provides clinically relevant information on how patients live and cope with their diabetes on a daily basis.

Research indicates that diabetes patients experience the greatest number of barriers to diet and exercise, a moderate amount of barriers to glucose testing, and the fewest barriers to insulin injections and medication-taking (Glasgow, Hampson, et al., 1997; Glasgow, McCaul, & Schafer, 1986). Each of the several components of the diabetes regimen can have its own set of personal and social-environmental barriers (Glasgow, 1994). For example, dietary planning has been shown to be influenced by personal factors (e.g., motivation, emotions, food selection knowledge, understanding of meal plans; El-Kebbi et al., 1996; Travis, 1997), social-environmental factors (e.g., holidays; Travis, 1997), and lack of family support (e.g., pressure to deviate from dietary guidelines; El-Kebbi et al., 1996).

To quantify particular barriers to diabetes self-care, researchers have developed psychometrically sound self-report scales that encompass multiple components of diabetes self-care such as the Barriers to Adherence Questionnaire (Glasgow et al., 1986). Other barriers scales have focused specifically on one aspect of diabetes management. For example, the Hypoglycemic Fear Survey (Cox, Irvine, Gonder-Frederick, Nowacek, & Butterfield, 1987) was designed to evaluate four aspects of fear related to hypoglycemia, including events precipitating fear, the phenomenological experience of the fear response, adaptive and maladaptive reactions to hypoglycemia, and physiological outcomes. In addition to empirical utility, both of these scales have been shown to be clinically useful tools for the purpose of assessing and facilitating treatment adherence and glycemic control, respectively.

Coping and Problem Solving

Knowing the barriers that diabetes patients encounter is particularly important since their ability to cope with such barriers will impact regimen adherence (Glasgow, Hampson, et al., 1997) and possibly metabolic control (Spiess et al., 1994). A dearth of research, however, examines the coping abilities of adult diabetes patients. The limited research indicates that active or problem-solving coping is related to positive disease-related outcome and well-being, whereas avoidant, passive, or emotion-focused coping is associated with less favorable psychological and health outcomes (e.g., Smári & Valtysdóttir, 1997). Thus, problem-solving skills seem particularly relevant to diabetes self-care, enabling patients to be more effective and flexible in coping with the variety of barriers they encounter in treatment (Glasgow, Toobert, Hampson, & Wilson, 1995). To date, the Diabetes Problem-Solving Interview (Toobert & Glasgow, 1991) is the only diabetes-specific problem-solving measure. The interview presents a variety of situations to elicit specific problem-solving strategies that patients would employ in attempts to adhere to their treatment regimen. Preliminary results indicate that this measure significantly and uniquely predicts levels of dietary and exercise self-care behaviors in the long term.

Interventions to Cope with Barriers to Care

Behavioral intervention research on diabetes self-care management with adults has focused primarily on problem-solving interventions (Glasgow et al., 1995). For example, training in problem-solving skills has produced favorable behavioral and metabolic outcomes in studies of older adults with 102 type 2 diabetes (Glasgow et al., 1992). The intervention, entitled the "Sixty Something . . ." program, included the following treatment components: (a) modifying dietary behaviors to decrease caloric intake and consumption of fats, and to increase intake of dietary fiber, (b) engaging in low-impact exercise such as walking, (c) using problem-solving skills to overcome barriers to adherence and consequently developing adaptive coping strategies, (d) establishing weekly personal goals, (e) increasing enjoyable social interaction, and (f) discussing strategies to prevent relapse. Participants who received the immediate intervention condition showed significantly greater reductions in caloric and fat intake and weight as well as increases in the frequency of blood glucose monitoring as compared to the control group. These results were maintained at the six-month follow-up and were quite similar to the delayed intervention group.

Glasgow, Toobert, and Hampson (1996) also conducted a cost-effective medical office-based intervention versus standard care, which included computer assessments to provide immediate feedback on key barriers to dietary self-management, goal-setting, and problem-solving assistance and follow-up contact to review progress and facilitate problem solving to barriers. At the three-month follow-up, participants experienced greater improvements in percent of calories from fat, kilocalories consumed per day, overall eating habits and behaviors, serum cholesterol levels, and patient satisfaction (Glasgow et al., 1996). Improvements in percent of calories from fat, serum cholesterol levels, and patient satisfaction were maintained at the 12-month follow-up (Glasgow, La Chance, et al., 1997). Patient empowerment programs seek to aid patients with goal setting, problem solving, stress management, self-awareness, effective coping strategies, and motivation (R. Anderson et al., 1995). Findings from the study conducted by R. Anderson and colleagues suggest that patients who received the intervention were more self-efficacious and had a more positive attitude toward their quality of life with diabetes. In addition, HbA_{1c} levels were lower in the intervention group as compared to the control group.

Summary

Although it appears that the research on barriers to care, coping, and problem solving continues to be scarce, preliminary evidence points toward the importance of assessing and identifying personal and social-environmental barriers to diabetes self-care. The continued use of available assessment tools that incorporate multiple or specific components of diabetes care, as well as the proliferation of other scales, will greatly improve the current level of understanding barriers to care and its impact on diabetes self-management. The intervention studies reviewed demonstrate the importance of including problem-solving skills to produce favorable psychosocial and physiological outcomes. Therefore, future research should include the continuous development of interventions that incorporate active patient participation programs in efforts to empower patients, optimize diabetes self-care, and facilitate mental and physical health.

SPECIAL ISSUES IN DIABETES

Sexual Dysfunction

Sexual dysfunctions in men and women are characterized by disturbances in sexual desire and in the psychophysiological components of the sexual response cycle (e.g., desire, arousal, orgasm, resolution; Fugl-Meyer, Lodnert, Branholm, & Fugl-Meyer, 1997). Sexual functioning is a complex phenomenon that is best viewed from a biopsychosocial perspective (Enzlin, Mathieu, Vanderschueren, & Demyttenaere, 1998; Spector, Leiblum, Carey, & Rosen, 1993). Sexual dysfunctions are widely believed to be multicausal and multidimensional. It is difficult to identify cases with a purely organic or purely psychogenic etiology, in part, because sexual dysfunction is often developed and maintained by a reciprocal process in which organic factors (e.g., diabetes) lead to psychological distress, which in turn exacerbates the organic problems (Schiavi & Hogan, 1979).

Sexual Dysfunction in Men with Diabetes

The consequences of diabetes on sexual functioning in men are well documented. Although disorders of all phases of the sexual cycle have been reported in diabetic men (Jensen, 1981), erectile dysfunction (ED) has received the most attention. An estimated 35% to 70% of men will experience ED at some time during the course of diabetes, either intermittently or persistently (Spector et al., 1993), and the prevalence may be three times that found in the general population (Feldman, Goldstein, Hatzichristou, Krane, & McKinlay, 1994). Possible etiologic factors include peripheral neuropathy, peripheral vascular disease, and psychological factors (Rendell, Rajfer, Wicker, & Smith, 1999). The severity of ED may also be related to both severity (Metro & Broderick, 1998) and duration (McCulloch, Campbell, Wu, Prescott, & Clarke, 1980) of diabetes. Although psychogenic factors, such as performance anxiety, can contribute to the etiology of ED (Whitehead, 1987), organic factors are believed to be the predominant etiology in diabetic men (Saenz de Tejada & Goldstein, 1988).

Autonomic neuropathy is considered to be the main etiological factor in diabetic impotence due to damage both to parasympathetic and sympathetic innervation of the corpora cavernosa (Watkins & Thomas, 1998). Penile erection, a vascular event under neurogenic control, is dependent on relaxation of the smooth muscle cells and arteries of the corpus cavernosum (Bloomgarden, 1998). Animal research with male Wistar rats has demonstrated that GHb impairs corpora cavernosal smooth muscle relaxation, and this effect is dose dependent (Cartledge, Eardley, & Morrison, 2000), suggesting a role for hyperglycemia in ED. Sexually dysfunctional diabetic men may also experience reduced tactile sensitivity and altered perception of stimulation (Morrissette, Goldstein, Raskin, & Rowland, 1999).

No studies have focused exclusively on the role of glycemic control in the risk of developing sexual complications in diabetes (Herter, 1998). However, the relationship between glycemic control and risk of neuropathy is clearly established for type 1 diabetes (DCCT, 1993) and has been suggested in type 2 diabetes as well (Toyry, Niskanen, Mantysaari, Lansimies, & Uusitupa, 1996). Thus, if neuropathy can be prevented by glycemic control, sexual dysfunction, mediated by hyperglycemia in diabetes mellitus, may also be prevented (Herter, 1998).

Treatment options include both invasive (e.g., penile prosthesis implants, intracavernous injection therapy) and noninvasive (e.g., vacuum device) medical and psychosocial interventions (e.g., sex therapy; Watkins & Thomas, 1998). More recently, oral agents such as sildenafil citrate have been introduced with success in men with types 1 and 2 diabetes, regardless of age, duration of ED, and duration of diabetes (Rendell et al., 1999).

Sexual Dysfunction in Women with Diabetes

The research on sexual dysfunction in women with diabetes is limited and lags behind that of male sexuality. The existing research is characterized by methodological limitations and variations and contradictory results, which makes it difficult to interpret the findings.

Findings on the prevalence and correlates of sexual desire in these women range from no difference in the number of complaints between diabetes patients and healthy controls (Kolodny, 1971) to significantly decreased desire (Schreiner-Engel, Schiavi, Vietorisz, Eichel, & Smith, 1985). Some have found sexual desire deficits limited to women with neuropathy (Leedom, Feldman, Procci, & Zeidler, 1991) or type 2 diabetes (Schreiner-Engel, Schiavi, Vietorisz, & Smith, 1987). Thus, it is not clear that women with diabetes experience difficulties with sexual desire at rates dissimilar from the general population. The objective assessment of arousal is more difficult in women (Enzlin et al., 1998); therefore,

studies have used questionnaires or self-reported subjective arousal, and these findings suggest that arousal may be a concern for women with diabetes (Schreiner-Engel et al., 1985). Because of a weak correlation between genital and subjective arousal, recent studies have included objective assessments of arousal such as labiothermometry or vaginal plethysmography (Enzlin et al., 1998; Spector et al., 1993), but these findings are also equivocal (Wincze, Albert, & Bansal, 1993). With respect to the orgasm phase, research findings are again contradictory and range from significantly reduced orgasmic responses in women with diabetes compared to controls (Schreiner-Engel et al., 1987), no decrease (Montenero, Donatoni, & Magi, 1973), or failure to specify orgasmic difficulties as a concern (Jensen, 1981). Rates of dyspareunia, a recurrent or persistent genital pain with sexual intercourse, appear similar to those found in the general population (Spector et al., 1993). However, Schreiner-Engel et al. (1985) found higher rates in women with type 2 diabetes than in controls.

In women, the role of organic etiologic factors is not as clear or well understood as in men (Cox, Gonder-Frederick, & Saunders, 1991). Although diabetic autonomic neuropathy is believed to be a major cause of organic impotence in men, evidence for a relationship between neuropathy and sexual dysfunction in women is unclear (Spector et al., 1993). Based on the limited research to date, microvascular disease, nephropathy, retinopathy, macrovascular disease, age of onset, duration, and glycemic control tend not to be associated with sexual dysfunction in female diabetes patients (Campbell, Redelman, Borkman, McLay, & Chisholm, 1989; Jensen, 1986). The few studies that included psychosocial factors, such as marital satisfaction (Schreiner-Engel et al., 1985), disease acceptance (Jensen, 1986), and depression (Leedom et al., 1991), have found relationships between poorer psychosocial adjustment and sexual functioning in these women. In one of the few studies comparing types of diabetes, type 2 diabetes was predictive of sexual dysfunction (Schreiner-Engel et al., 1987), which the authors attribute to the later age of onset of this type of diabetes. Treatment of sexual dysfunction in women has also received little recognition in the literature. Interventions typically focus on difficulties with arousal and lubrication, with recommendations of diversification of sexual behaviors/positions and use of lubricating products.

Summary

The research on sexual dysfunction in diabetes has focused predominantly on men and has supported an organic etiology (autonomic neuropathy) for the primary form of dysfunction,

ED. In women, the incidence, prevalence, etiology, and treatment options are much less clear. Studies of sexual dysfunction in diabetic women, although still lagging behind studies in men, have improved methodologically over the past 20 years and have provided strong evidence for the presence of sexual problems in women. Psychosocial factors may be more strongly related to sexual dysfunction in women than in men, but this conclusion remains tentative and may be, in part, linked to the lack of a consistent etiologic factor in women. Future studies should include longitudinal designs, larger sample sizes, and control groups; studies in women should incorporate factors such as diabetes type, menopausal status, and obesity/body image concerns. Given that sexual functioning is an important part of life, sexual dysfunction is integral to the challenge of improving quality of life in individuals with diabetes.

Hypoglycemia

With the recognition that tight glycemic control can reduce the risk of complications associated with diabetes (DCCT, 1993; UKPDS, 1998), intensified treatment regimens (e.g., multiple daily insulin injections, subcutaneous insulin pumps) have been increasingly important in diabetes management. One well-documented side effect of such tight glycemic control is hypoglycemia (Cryer, 1994). Hypoglycemia (BG levels <70 mg/dl) has been estimated to occur three times more often in patients on intensive insulin regimens (DCCT, 1993) and is more common in patients with a history of hypoglycemia and lower BG levels (Gonder-Frederick, Clarke, & Cox, 1997). Hypoglycemia is designated as either mild or severe depending on whether the person is able to treat his or her BG, loses consciousness, and/or experiences seizures. However, mild hypoglycemia is associated with serious physical, emotional, and social consequences (Gonder-Frederick, Clarke, et al., 1997).

Consequences of Hypoglycemia

Hypoglycemia, if undetected and thus untreated, can progress to loss of consciousness, coma, and death. Severe hypoglycemia is the fourth leading cause of mortality in type 1 diabetes (Gonder-Frederick, Cox, & Clarke, 1996). Hypoglycemia is also associated with a variety of physical symptoms as well as behavioral, emotional, and social consequences that may affect patients' quality of life. The symptoms of hypoglycemia stem from the autonomic nervous system's release of counter-regulatory hormones (such as epinephrine) to raise BG levels and from neuroglycopenia (when the brain is not receiving sufficient glucose for normal functioning). As reviewed by Gonder-Frederick et al. (1996), there are many autonomic (e.g., tachycardia, sweating, shaking) and neuroglycopenic (e.g., difficulty concentrating, lightheadedness, lack of coordination) symptoms stemming from these physiological changes. Task performance may therefore decline with hypoglycemia, with obvious implications for occupational and educational functioning (Cox, Gonder-Frederick, & Clarke, 1996). The emotional sequelae of hypoglycemia may include transient mood changes (e.g., irritability, tension) due to neuroglycopenia (Gonder-Frederick, Clarke, et al., 1997), as well as specific anxiety surrounding the occurrence of hypoglycemia (Cox et al., 1987). The Hypoglycemia Fear Survey (Cox et al., 1987) can be effectively used with patients or family members to ascertain the degree of worry regarding hypoglycemia and the behavioral consequences of their fear. In addition, Gonder-Frederick et al. (1996) have provided useful clinical guidelines regarding such assessment. The social consequences of hypoglycemia may include embarrassment when hypoglycemia occurs in public, work-related problems, and interpersonal problems (e.g., conflict both during hypoglycemia and afterwards; Gonder-Frederick, Clarke, et al., 1997). The long-term effects of repeated hypoglycemia on relationship dynamics and satisfaction is a fruitful area for future research.

Detection of Hypoglycemia

Importantly, the symptoms of hypoglycemia and the threshold for their occurrence differ both between persons and within individuals over time and situations. In fact, patients may fail to detect hypoglycemia half of the time that it occurs (Clarke et al., 1995), possibly due to inattentiveness (e.g., being distracted by competing demands); inaccurate symptom beliefs (e.g., using unreliable or inaccurate symptoms to detect hypoglycemia); and/or misattribution of symptoms (e.g., misattributing symptoms of actual hypoglycemia to another cause). All of these factors may be readily assessed and used as a focus of treatment in diabetes patients.

To enhance patients' awareness and use of appropriate corrective actions to treat the hypoglycemia, Cox and colleagues have developed a manualized behavioral group treatment program, Blood Glucose Awareness Training (BGAT; Cox, Carter, Gonder-Frederick, Clarke, & Pohl, 1988). The intervention program is designed to teach persons with diabetes to anticipate when hypoglycemia may occur, to prevent its occurrence when possible, to be aware of their symptoms of hypoglycemia, and to engage in appropriate corrective actions to treat hypoglycemia when it occurs. To do this, the program involves an individualized educational component on peaks in insulin action, carbohydrate metabolism, and the impact of changes in physical activity and other aspects of self-care on BG levels. Through educational materials and homework exercises, people are taught to identify their unique sensitive and specific cues for hypoglycemia using a BG diary in which they record symptoms, estimate their BG level, then actually perform SMBG and record their BG. Errors in estimation and unrecognized hypoglycemia are identified and discussed. Appropriate corrective actions for treating hypoglycemia are also introduced. Cox and colleagues have recently revised their program (BGAT II) to include updated information and more attention to external cues for hypoglycemia (e.g., changes in self-care behaviors that influence BG levels). BGAT and BGAT II have been shown to increase BG estimation accuracy and decrease episodes of hypoglycemia (e.g., Cox et al., 1995; ter Braak et al., 2000) in persons with type 1 diabetes. Long-term follow-up of patients who underwent BGAT training indicated fewer automobile crashes and continued improvements in glycemic control (Cox, Gonder-Frederick, Julian, & Clarke, 1994). Booster sessions administered to persons who previously underwent BGAT seem to improve detection of low BG events (Cox et al., 1994). Importantly, these improvements occurred without decrements in metabolic control. For clinicians working with an individual patient with repeated hypoglycemia or reduced awareness of hypoglycemia, Cox and colleagues (1996) have published very useful and specific clinical recommendations for the prevention of hypoglycemia, the recognition of low BG, and treating low BG. This chapter also provides a copy of the BG diary, described previously, that the authors developed for the BGAT program.

Severe Hypoglycemia

Given the dangers associated with severe hypoglycemia, patients with such a history have been the focus of research to identify the correlates of risk for severe hypoglycemic episodes. Cox and colleagues have developed a biopsychobehavioral model of severe hypoglycemia (Cox et al., 1999; Gonder-Frederick, Cox, Kovatchev, Schlundt, & Clarke, 1997) in which physiological, psychological, and behavioral factors are taken into account. Cox et al. (1999), using this model, identified several differences between those with and without a history of severe hypoglycemia. Specifically, patients with a history of severe hypoglycemia engaged in more risky and fewer preventative behaviors. They were less likely to recognize neuroglycopenic symptoms as indicative of hypoglycemia and engage in appropriate treatment of low BG, even when aware of their BG level. Thus, interventions

that have a strong focus on such neuroglycopenic symptom detection and appropriate behavioral responses to low BG may be especially fruitful for reducing repeated severe hypoglycemic episodes in these patients.

Summary

Hypoglycemia is a common side effect of intensive diabetes management. Importantly, it is associated with serious physical, behavioral, emotional, and social consequences. Thus, persons must be able to prevent, detect, and effectively treat hypoglycemic episodes. Randomized clinical investigations of a systemic intervention with these targets developed by Cox and colleagues at the University of Virginia (BGAT and BGAT II) indicate that persons who participate in the intervention program show improvements in various areas related to hypoglycemia (e.g., decrease in episodes of hypoglycemia, improvement in detection of low BG) without decrements in metabolic control. Persons with severe hypoglycemia may particularly benefit from such treatment. Future research is needed to expand such treatment to more heterogeneous patient groups, identify which components of this package intervention are the most effective in leading to the noted improvements, and determine characteristics of individuals that predict successful outcomes following such an intervention program.

Weight Management

Obesity is strongly related to type 2 diabetes, with as many as 90% of those who develop type 2 diabetes being obese (Wing, Marcus, Epstein, & Jawad, 1991). Independently, obesity can lead to cardiovascular disease, hypertension, hyperglycemia, hyperinsulinemia, dyslipidemia, and hypertriglyceridemia (Albu, Konnarides, & Pi-Sunyer, 1995). The coexistence of obesity and diabetes heightens the risk for developing these associated medical conditions, hence increasing morbidity and mortality (Wing, 1991).

Benefits of Weight Loss

Weight loss continues to be the cornerstone of treatment for obese individuals with type 2 diabetes (Wing, 1991). Because type 2 diabetes accounts for the largest proportion of individuals with diabetes, weight loss interventions continue to receive significant empirical attention. Weight loss is associated with multiple health benefits, including improved glycemic control, increased insulin sensitivity, decreased risk of coronary heart disease, reduction in medication utilization and cost, and enhanced mood (Butler & Wing, 1995; Maggio &

Pi Sunyer, 1997). Even mild to modest weight losses (5 to 10 kg/10 to 20 pounds) greatly enhances physical status and improves metabolic control (ADA, 1997b). Thus, obese individuals with type 2 diabetes do not need to reach ideal weight to experience the benefits from weight loss (Redmon et al., 1999). Weight loss treatment also helps in the prevention of diabetes in those with impaired glucose tolerance, as well as in the treatment of weight gain in patients with type 1 diabetes who are using intensive insulin therapy (Wing, 1996).

Weight Loss Interventions

The research on weight loss in diabetes reflects patterns of findings in the general population, namely, that behavioral weight management programs lead to modest weight losses, and interventions should be tailored to the specific needs of the individual (Ruggiero, 1998). Findings of a recent study employing obese women with type 2 diabetes indicate that combining a 16-week standard behavioral treatment program with a motivational interviewing component (e.g., personalizing goals) enhances adherence to program recommendations and glycemic control (D. Smith, Heckemeyer, Kratt, & Mason, 1997). Overall, the results of behavioral research with obese individuals with type 2 diabetes emphasize dietary and exercise behaviors as important factors in improved weight loss (Wing, 1993). Traditionally, diets have been identified as the treatment of choice in obese patients with type 2 diabetes (Maggio & Pi-Sunyer, 1997), but several studies have found little or no benefit to dieting (e.g., Milne, Mann, Chisolm, & Williams, 1994), perhaps because of failure to adhere to dietary recommendations. Additionally, physiological changes occur with dieting (e.g., increased activity of the fat storage enzyme lipoprotein lipase; Eckel & Yost, 1987), which may impede weight loss.

Very low calorie diets (VLCD) have been found to be a safe method of attaining greater and more rapid weight losses than traditional standard low calorie diets (e.g., Maggio & Pi-Sunyer, 1997). In obese patients with type 2 diabetes, VLCD treatments have been generally associated with large improvements in major metabolic control variables (e.g., Brown, Upchurch, Anding, Winter, & Ramirez, 1996; Wing, Marcus, Salata, et al., 1991). Findings from another study that randomized 93 obese type 2 diabetes patients to different levels of caloric restriction (400 versus 1,000 kcal/day) suggest that caloric restriction rather than actual weight loss contributes to the initial, rapid change in metabolic control (Wing et al., 1994). Furthermore, the group that initiated the treatment program with 1,000 kcal/day and maintained this caloric intake for 15 weeks experienced further improvements in blood glucose and insulin sensitivity. In contrast, the group that increased caloric intake from 400 to 1,000 kcal/day throughout the study had worse fasting glycemic control despite their continued weight loss. These findings suggest that the amount of calorie restriction and weight loss have differential effects on improvements in metabolic control and insulin sensitivity.

Dietary interventions have not been effective in achieving long-term weight loss to date. The ADA (1997b) proposes that emphasis be placed instead on glucose and lipid goals as opposed to traditional weight loss goals. Individuals with type 2 diabetes who follow the ADA dietary guidelines experience significant improvements in glycemic control and cardiovascular risk factors (Pi-Sunyer et al., 1999). In addition to a nutritionally adequate diet, ideal metabolic goals can also be achieved by exercise and/or using medication (ADA, 1997a).

Exercise is also a key ingredient in the management of diabetes and should be used as an adjunct to nutrition and/or drug therapy (ADA, 1997a). The benefits of exercise in type 2 diabetes patients are extensive and include improved insulin sensitivity and action (Wing, 1991), glycemic control (Blake, 1992), cardiovascular benefits (Schneider, Khachadurian, Amorosa, Clemow, & Ruderman, 1992), short- and long-term weight loss (Wing, 1993), reduced need for insulin and/or hypoglycemic agents (Marrero & Sizemore, 1996), and psychological benefits including improvements in mood, self-esteem, well-being, and quality of life (Rodin & Plante, 1989). In addition, exercise has been found to increase muscle mass, leading to improvements in insulin and glucose levels (Schneider et al., 1992). Outcomes of studies have also revealed the protective benefit of exercise against developing type 2 diabetes (Pan et al., 1997). Unfortunately, nonadherence is common and naturally limits the degree to which individuals may benefit from exercise (Marcus et al., 2000). Thus, a prominent role for the health care team is to motivate patients and personalize goals that incorporate patients' specific physical activity needs while accounting for their tolerable level of strength and aerobic capacity.

The use of medication is considered an adjunct to diet and exercise treatment approaches particularly for obese individuals with type 2 diabetes who have been unable to achieve and maintain weight loss (North American Association for the Study of Obesity, 1995). Similar to other weight loss approaches, individuals tend to gain weight once the medication is discontinued (National Task Force on the Prevention and Treatment of Obesity, 1996), thus, negatively affecting glycemic control (Wing, 1995). Catecholaminergic agents (e.g., phentermine) have been shown to effect greater weight losses than placebo groups but with no improvement in glycemic control (e.g., Crommelin, 1974). Results of double-blind trials with serotoninergic agents (fenfluramine, dexfenfluramine) in patients with type 2 diabetes have suggested that these agents directly improve glycemic control, irrespective of effects of food intake and body weight (e.g., Willey, Molyneaux, & Yue, 1994). The effects of fenfluramine and phentermine, in combination with 12 months of intensive nutrition counseling, an exercise prescription, and instruction in behavior modification, resulted in significant reductions in body weight, BMI, and HbA_{1c} throughout the six months of treatment in addition to decreases in diabetes medications, fasting plasma glucose, and triglycerides (Redmon et al., 1999). Although fenfluramine was withdrawn from the market in 1997 (mid-study), it is promising to note that other drug therapies such as sibutramine, a serotonin reuptake inhibitor (Meridia; Bray et al., 1996), have been recently FDA approved and continue to be evaluated (Jeffrey et al., 2000).

Several studies have evaluated the effects of social support, typically from spouses or significant others, as a method for enhancing motivation for weight loss (Jeffrey et al., 2000). Wing, Marcus, Epstein, et al. (1991) did not find any weight loss differences between patients treated alone and together at posttreatment or at one-year follow-up. However, gender differences emerged with respect to the effects of support on weight loss such that women lost more weight when treated with their spouses and men lost more weight when treated alone. The authors proposed that involving husbands in a weight loss program allows women to be more conscientious of food preparation and purchase for both herself and her husband, whereas men tend to allow their wives to establish their eating patterns and are less involved in the weight monitoring process. Gender differences have also been found with respect to the effects of support on glycemic control, with women achieving better control and men achieving poorer control (Heitzman & Kaplan, 1984). Other weight loss studies have indicated the positive effects of group support strategies (e.g., Wing & Jeffrey, 1999) as well as maintenance support contact (Perri et al., 1988) on weight loss. Specific contributions of group or individual support (e.g., enhanced motivation) appear to be valuable factors in weight loss treatment. However, maintenance of behavioral changes that produce positive results for patients again become problematic following treatment.

Maintenance of Weight Loss

As reviewed previously, sustained weight loss on a long-term basis is one of the greatest challenges for obese individuals with diabetes, as with obese patients in general (Jeffrey et al., 2000). One reason for this struggle is that there may be different behavioral, cognitive, and psychological mechanisms inherent in weight loss maintenance in contrast to initial weight loss. Continued research efforts that focus on intensifying and lengthening treatment may help to delineate factors responsible for success in weight loss maintenance and improved health outcomes for obese individuals (Jeffrey et al., 2000). Researchers continue to propose lifestyle modification strategies that seem to effectuate weight loss maintenance and improve health status. Specific strategies include implementing dietary practices, professional contact, behavior modification, social support strategies, and exercise on an ongoing basis (Perri, Sears, & Clark, 1993). Thus, educating obese individuals with diabetes on how to incorporate various long-term treatment components into their daily lives may aid them in the difficult task of maintaining treatment gains.

Summary

Because of the increased risk of medical problems associated with the coexistence of obesity and type 2 diabetes, weight loss continues to be the golden standard of treatment for obese individuals with type 2 diabetes. A wealth of empirical research has delineated specific behavioral strategies (e.g., exercise, diet), adjunctive pharmacological agents, and social support and contingency maintenance programs that facilitate short-term weight loss. Similar to diabetes, obesity is a chronic medical condition that warrants continuous health care and lifestyle changes to maintain treatment gains and positive behavioral patterns. As such, the challenge for researchers and clinicians is to continue developing differential intervention strategies that meet patients' complex biopsychosocial needs and will contribute to long-term modifications of health behaviors and weight loss maintenance in type 2 diabetes patients.

ROLE OF HEALTH PSYCHOLOGY IN DIABETES MELLITUS

As illustrated in the preceding literature review, health psychologists can play an invaluable role in enhancing the emotional and physical well-being of persons with diabetes. Ideally, health psychologists function as part of the treatment team, helping to provide comprehensive diabetes care to all patients, not solely to those already distressed. As a member of the treatment team, the psychologist is able to provide both preventative services as well as problem-focused interventions when needed. In addition, membership on the team facilitates the ongoing exchange of mutual feedback between the psychologist and others on the medical team. When such an arrangement is not possible, consultation and referral to outside health psychologists is another option.

A role for health psychology is clearly justified by several factors. First, the prevalence of psychological problems (e.g., major depression) in patients with diabetes suggests that health psychology could have a prominent role with these patients. The experience of multiple losses may be characteristic of a chronic illness such as diabetes. Patients face not only the loss of their previously healthy body, but also potential losses of function, self-esteem, and freedom as diabetic complications develop. Second, the literature has demonstrated that the majority of patients find it difficult to follow the recommendations for self-care. The diabetes treatment regimen clearly presents multiple, ongoing challenges and demands. Adherence problems appear to be most difficult for those components of the diabetes regimen that require lifestyle changes (e.g., diet, exercise), which all patients with diabetes are prescribed. Health psychologists are well-suited to assess and treat these difficulties and to facilitate the behavioral changes needed for optimal outcomes. In addition, health psychologists as researchers have a role in advancing our understanding of psychosocial factors associated with adjustment to, and coping with, diabetes, the link between physiological and psychosocial factors in diabetes, and interventions to address the psychosocial challenges inherent in a chronic disease such as diabetes.

Assessment of diabetes patients should occur on an ongoing basis, starting at the time of diagnosis. Throughout the natural history of diabetes, there will be times that present challenges to both emotional and physical well-being. For example, at diagnosis, patients are faced with issues of loss while attempting to assimilate a large amount of novel information and new skills for disease management. However, the need for health psychologists is not limited to this early contact. Other times of need may be when complications develop, physical status worsens, or the treatment regimen changes. By having the psychologist readily available and familiar, patients may be more apt to avail themselves of needed psychological services. In the clinical setting, health psychologists are likely to use a combination of clinical interviewing, along with self-report questionnaires, in a comprehensive assessment. Varieties of diabetes-specific, as well as general assessment, instruments have been reviewed briefly. Assessment of diabetes patients should be dictated by the referral question or presenting problem. However, common targets of assessment include affect (e.g., depression, anxiety), current and past stressors, coping styles, resources available to the person (e.g., social support from natural support network as well as medical team), and levels of self-care.

By adopting an empathetic, nonjudgmental stance, health psychologists may build rapport with patients, delineate the nature of the presenting problem, and jointly determine treatment goals with the patients.

The goal of psychological treatment with diabetes patients is to maximize psychological well-being as well as glycemic control. The provision of psychological services can also positively affect the use of medical services (e.g., distressed patients will use more medical services; psychological interventions can reduce medical utilization). Treatment may occur in a variety of modalities (e.g., group, individual, marital, and family therapy) according to the needs and desires of the patient. As part of a multidisciplinary treatment team, the health psychologist can work together with other professionals (e.g., diabetes educators, nutritionists) to achieve treatment goals with patients and their families. Clinician researchers have begun to establish an empirical foundation for particular interventions with diabetes patients. Behavioral treatment appears to be particularly well-suited for many of the presenting problems (e.g., adherence, stress management). As described next, research is needed to further delineate effective treatments that can be individualized for particular patients' needs.

CONCLUSIONS AND FUTURE DIRECTIONS

Given the recent landmark findings of the DCCT (1993) and UKDPS (1998), there has been increased emphasis on achieving optimal management of diabetes mellitus. Persons with diabetes are faced with a rigorous treatment regimen, which relies heavily on self-management to attain the tight glycemic control that was fundamental to the decreases in complications found in these clinical trials. Thus, research into factors that either facilitate or suppress optimal disease management is even more crucial at this time. Studies have indicated the difficulties that diabetes patients have in following treatment recommendations, even when these recommendations are not as complex or demanding as the management strategies that are typically recommended today. The preceding review has highlighted empirical findings on the relationship between several psychosocial factors and both adherence levels and physiological outcomes. Importantly, behavioral researchers have begun to develop and evaluate the efficacy of various treatment programs designed to modify these psychosocial variables and thereby enhance patients' psychosocial and physical outcomes.

Rubin and Peyrot (1992) have reviewed the need for improvements in the intervention work being conducted. These authors note that, historically, intervention studies have used small sample sizes, which were either not representative of the larger diabetes population or were inappropriate in the sense that the participants reported low levels of concern with the factor on which the treatment was focused. In addition, Rubin and Peyrot (1992) raise other methodological limitations of previous research, such as the use of poor quality outcomes measures; flawed designs (e.g., no control groups used, no follow-up period); and comprehensive "shotgun" interventions that included a variety of medical and psychosocial components, which precluded the identification of the effective treatment components. Future treatment outcome studies may benefit from increased attention to these points as well as to long-term follow-up of patients, the clinical significance of obtained changes (Goodall & Halford, 1991), issues of cost containment and cost effectiveness (Glasgow, Fisher, et al., 1999), and the maintenance of behavior change as a separate construct from initial behavior change (Wing, 2000).

In addition to these improvements in intervention methodology, future research should also address more thoroughly individual differences in psychosocial factors and their modification. Little research exists on the specific needs of racial and cultural minorities with diabetes. This is especially noteworthy given the facts that in racial/ethnic minorities (a) diabetes is more common (CDC, 1998) and (b) metabolic control and complications are worse (see review by Weller et al., 1999). Similarly, the unique management issues relevant to women with diabetes also deserve increased attention. Although there has been some research in areas of women's health such as diabetes in pregnancy and weight management, there is a dearth of studies on the effects of diabetes on other aspects of women's reproductive health (e.g., fertility, contraception choices), the influence of hormonal changes (e.g., menopause) on diabetes management, eating disorders, female sexual dysfunction, and the course and management of depression in women with diabetes (Butler & Wing, 1995; Ruggiero, 1998). Research into such dimensions of individual differences will ultimately facilitate the identification of patients to be targeted for intervention by health psychologists and what intervention techniques may be most helpful for certain patients.

Diabetes research also needs to be increasingly directed by comprehensive theoretical models of patient outcomes. Such models would specify the interrelationships among psychosocial factors and adherence and would detail how such factors both influence (and are influenced by) physiological outcomes. For example, models would capture the dynamic and complex relationship between such factors as stress and outcomes by specifying how stress may affect BG directly through physiological mechanisms; how stress may affect BG indirectly through disruptions in self-care; and how physiological status (e.g., level of BG control, development of complications) may affect an individual's stress levels. Obviously, evaluating such comprehensive models would require large sample sizes of diverse patients and sophisticated statistical methodologies. Health psychologists, with their expertise in theory-based behavior change strategies and treatment efficacy research, are well-positioned to advance the field in this next era of diabetes management.

REFERENCES

Aikens, J. E., Wallander, J. L., Bell, D. S. H., & Cole, J. A. (1992). Daily stress variability, learned resourcefulness, regimen adherence, and metabolic control in Type I diabetes mellitus: Evaluation of a path model. *Journal of Consulting and Clinical Psychology, 60*(1), 113–118.

Aikens, J. E., Wallander, J. L., Bell, D. S. H., & McNorton, A. (1994). A nomothetic-idiographic study of daily psychological stress and blood glucose in women with Type I diabetes mellitus. *Journal of Behavioral Medicine, 17,* 535–548.

Albu, J., Konnarides, C., & Pi-Sunyer, F. X. (1995). Weight control: Metabolic and cardiovascular effects. *Diabetes Review, 3,* 335–347.

American Diabetes Association. (1996). National standards for diabetes self-management education programs and American Diabetes Association review criteria. *Diabetes Care, 19,* S114–S118.

American Diabetes Association. (1997a). Diabetes mellitus and exercise. *Diabetes Care, 20,* S51.

American Diabetes Association. (1997b). Nutrition recommendations and principles for people with diabetes mellitus. *Diabetes Care, 20,* S14–S17.

American Diabetes Association. (1998). Economic consequences of diabetes mellitus in the U.S. in 1997. *Diabetes Care, 21,* 196–309.

American Diabetes Association. (2000a). Standards of medical care for patients with diabetes mellitus (Position Statement). *Diabetes Care, 23*(Suppl. 1), S32–S42.

American Diabetes Association. (2000b). Tests of glycemia in diabetes (Position statement). *Diabetes Care, 23*(Suppl. 1), S80–S82.

American Psychiatric Association. (1994). *Diagnostic and statistical manual of mental disorders* (4th ed.). Washington, DC: Author.

Anderson, B. J. (1996). Involving family members in diabetes treatment. In B. J. Anderson & R. R. Rubin (Eds.), *Practical psychology for diabetes clinicians* (pp. 43–52). Alexandria, VA: American Diabetes Association.

Anderson, B. J., & Auslander, W. (1980). Research on diabetes management and the family: A critique. *Diabetes Care, 3,* 696–702.

Anderson, R. M. (1995). Patient empowerment and the traditional medical model: A case of irreconcilable differences? *Diabetes Care, 18,* 412–415.

Anderson, R. M., Funnell, M. M., Butler, P. M., Arnold, M. S., Fitzgerald, J. T., & Feste, C. C. (1995). Patient empowerment: Results of a randomized controlled trial. *Diabetes Care, 18,* 943–949.

Beck, A. T., Ward, C. H., & Mendelson, M. (1961). An inventory for measuring depression. *Archives of General Psychiatry, 4,* 561–571.

Beeney, L., Dunn, S. M., & Welch, G. (1994). Measurement of diabetes knowledge: The development of the DKN scales. In C. Bradley (Ed.), *Handbook of psychology and diabetes: A guide to psychological measurement in diabetes research and practice* (pp. 159–189). Chur, Switzerland: Harwood Academic.

Bernbaum, M., Albert, S. G., & Duckro, P. N. (1988). Psychosocial profiles in patients with vision impairment due to diabetic retinopathy. *Diabetes Care, 11,* 551–557.

Black, S. (1999). Increased health burden associated with comorbid depression in older diabetic Mexican Americans: Results from the Hispanic established populations for the epidemiologic study of the elderly survey. *Diabetes Care, 22,* 56–64.

Blake, G. H. (1992). Control of type II diabetes: Reaping the rewards of exercise and weight loss. *Postgraduate Medicine, 92,* 129–137.

Bloomgarden, Z. T. (1998). American Diabetes Association annual meeting, 1997: Endothelial dysfunction, neuropathy and the diabetic foot, diabetic mastopathy, and erectile dysfunction. *Diabetes Care, 21*(1), 183–189.

Boehm, S., Schlenk, E. A., Funnell, M. M., Powers, H., & Ronis, D. L. (1997). Predictors of adherence to nutrition recommendations in people with non-insulin dependent diabetes mellitus. *Diabetes Educator, 23*(2), 157–165.

Bradley, C. (1979). Life events and the control of diabetes mellitus. *Journal of Psychosomatic Research, 23,* 159–162.

Bradley, C. (2000). The 12-item Well-Being Questionnaire: Origins, current stage of development, and availability. *Diabetes Care, 23,* 865.

Bray, G. A., Ryan, D. H., Gordon, D., Heidingsfelder, S., Cerise, F., & Wilson, K. (1996). A double-bind randomized placebo-controlled trial of sibutramine. *Obesity Research, 4,* 263–270.

Brown, S. A., Upchurch, S., Anding, R., Winter, M., & Ramirez, G. (1996). Promoting weight loss in type II diabetes. *Diabetes Care, 19,* 613–624.

Butler, B., & Wing, R. (1995). Women with diabetes: A lifestyle perspective focusing on eating disorders, pregnancy, and weight control. In A. Stanton & S. Gallant (Eds.), *The psychology of women's health: Progress and challenges in research and application* (pp. 85–116). Hillsdale, NJ: Erlbaum.

Campbell, L. V., Redelman, M. J., Borkman, M., McLay, J. G., & Chisholm, D. J. (1989). Factors in sexual dysfunction in diabetic female volunteer subjects. *Medical Journal of Australia, 151*(10), 550–552.

Cannon, W. B. (1941). *Bodily changes in pain, hunger, fear and rage.* New York: Macmillan.

Capponi, R., Kawada, M. E., Varela, C., & Vargas, L. (1980). Diabetes mellitus by repeated stress in rats bearing chemical diabetes. *Hormone and Metabolic Research, 12,* 411–412.

Carter, W. R., Herman, J., Stokes, K., & Cox, D. J. (1987). Promotion of diabetes onset by stress in BB rat. *Diabetologia, 30,* 674–675.

Cartledge, J. J., Eardley, I., & Morrison, J. F. B. (2000). Impairment of corpus cavernosal smooth muscle relaxation by glycosylated human haemoglobin. *British Journal Urology International, 85,* 735–741.

Centers for Disease Control and Prevention. (1998). *National Diabetes Fact Sheet: National estimates and general information on diabetes in the United States* (Rev. ed.). Atlanta, GA: Author.

Clarke, W. L., Cox, D. J., Gonder-Frederick, L. A., Julian, D., Schlundt, D., & Polonsky, W. (1995). Reduced awareness of hypoglycemia in adults with IDDM: A prospective study of hypoglycemic frequency and associated symptoms. *Diabetes Care, 18,* 517–522.

Clement, C. (1995). Diabetes self-management education. *Diabetes Care, 18,* 1204–1214.

Cohen, S., & Wills, T. A. (1985). Stress, social support, and the buffering hypothesis. *Psychological Bulletin, 52,* 55–86.

Coonrod, B. A., Betschart, J., & Harris, M. I. (1994). Frequency and determinants of diabetes patient education among adults in the U.S. population. *Diabetes Care, 17*(8), 852–858.

Cox, D. J., Carter, W. R., Gonder-Frederick, L., Clarke, W. L., & Pohl, S. (1988). Blood glucose discrimination training in IDDM patients. *Biofeedback and Self Regulation, 13,* 210–217.

Cox, D. J., & Gonder-Frederick, L. A. (1991). The role of stress in diabetes mellitus. In P. M. McCabe & N. Schneiderman (Eds.), *Stress, coping, and disease* (pp. 119–134). Hillsdale, NJ: Erlbaum.

Cox, D. J., Gonder-Frederick, L. A., & Clarke, W. L. (1996). Helping patients reduce severe hypoglycemia. In B. J. Anderson & R. R. Rubin (Eds.), *Practical psychology for diabetes clinicians* (pp. 93–102). Alexandria, VA: American Diabetes Association.

Cox, D. J., Gonder-Frederick, L. A., Clarke, W. L., & Carter, W. R. (1988). *Effects of acute experimental stressors on insulin-dependent diabetes mellitus.* New Orleans, LA: American Diabetes Association.

Cox, D. J., Gonder-Frederick, L. A., Julian, D. M., & Clarke, W. L. (1994). Long-term follow-up evaluation of blood glucose awareness training. *Diabetes Care, 17,* 1–5.

Cox, D. J., Gonder-Frederick, L. A., Kovatchev, B. P., Young-Hyman, D., Donner, T. W., Julian, D. M., et al. (1999). Biopsychobehavioral model of severe hypoglycemia II: Understanding the risk of severe hypoglycemia. *Diabetes Care, 22,* 2018–2025.

Cox, D. J., Gonder-Frederick, L. A., Polonsky, W., Schlundt, D., Julian, D. M., & Clarke, W. L. (1995). A multicenter evaluation of blood glucose awareness training-II. *Diabetes Care, 18,* 523–528.

Cox, D. J., Gonder-Frederick, L. A., & Saunders, J. T. (1991). Diabetes: Clinical issues and management. In J. Sweet, R. Rozensky, & S. Tovian (Eds.), *Handbook of clinical psychology in medical settings* (pp. 473–495). New York: Plenum Press.

Cox, D. J., Irvine, A., Gonder-Frederick, L. A., Nowacek, G., & Butterfield, J. (1987). Fear of hypoglycemia: Quantification, validation, and utilization. *Diabetes Care, 10,* 617–621.

Cox, D. J., Taylor, A., Nowacek, G., Holley-Wilcox, P., Pohl, S., & Guthro, E. (1984). The relationship between psychological stress and insulin-dependent diabetic blood glucose control: Preliminary investigations. *Health Psychology, 3,* 63–75.

Crommelin, R. M. (1974). Nonamphetamine, anorectic medication for obese diabetic patients: Controlled and open investigations of mazindol. *Clinical Medicine, 81,* 20–24.

Cryer, P. (1994). Hypoglycemia: The limiting factor in the management of IDDM. *Diabetes, 43,* 1378–1389.

DeGood, D. E., & Redgate, E. S. (1982). Interrelationship of plasma cortisol and other activation indexes during EMG biofeedback training. *Journal of Behavioral Medicine, 5,* 213–224.

Diabetes Control and Complications Trial Research Group. (1993). The effect of intensive treatment of diabetes on the development and progression of long-term complications in insulin-dependent diabetes mellitus. *New England Journal of Medicine, 329,* 977–986.

Dunn, S., Beeney, L., Hoskins, P., & Turtle, J. (1990). Knowledge and attitude change as predictors of metabolic improvement in diabetes education. *Social Science and Medicine, 31,* 1135–1141.

Eckel, R. H., & Yost, T. J. (1987). Weight reduction increases adipose tissue lipoprotein lipase responsiveness in obese women. *Journal of Clinical Investigation, 80,* 992–997.

El-Kebbi, I., Bacha, G., Ziemer, D., Musey, V., Gallina, D., Dunbar, V., et al. (1996). Diabetes in urban African Americans: Use of discussion groups to identify barriers to dietary therapy among low-income individuals with non-insulin-dependent diabetes mellitus. *Diabetes Educator, 22,* 488–492.

Enzlin, P., Mathieu, C., Vanderschueren, D., & Demyttenaere, K. (1998). Diabetes mellitus and female sexuality: A review of 25 years' research. *Diabetic Medicine, 15,* 809–815.

Evans, M. (1985). Emotional stress and diabetic control: A postulated model for the effect of emotional distress upon intermediary metabolism in the diabetic. *Biofeedback and Self-Regulation, 10,* 241–254.

Expert Committee on the Diagnosis and Classification of Diabetes Mellitus. (2000). Report of the expert committee on the diagnosis and classification of diabetes mellitus. *Diabetes Care, 23*(Suppl. 1), S4–S19.

Feinglos, M. N., Hastedt, P., & Surwit, R. S. (1987). Effects of relaxation therapy on patients with Type I diabetes mellitus. *Diabetes Care, 10*(1), 72–75.

Feldman, H. A., Goldstein, I., Hatzichristou, D. G., Krane, R. J., & McKinlay, J. B. (1994). Impotence and its medical and psychosocial correlates: Results of the Massachusetts Male Aging Study. *Journal of Urology, 151,* 54–61.

Fugl-Meyer, A. R., Lodnert, G., Branholm, I. B., & Fugl-Meyer, K. S. (1997). On life satisfaction in male erectile dysfunction. *International Journal of Impotence Research, 9,* 141–148.

Funnell, M. M., & Haas, L. B. (1995). National standards for diabetes self-management education programs. *Diabetes Care, 18*(1), 100–116.

Garrard, J., Ostrom Joynes, J., Mullen, L., McNeil, L., Mensing, C., Feste, C., et al. (1987). Psychometric study of Patient Knowledge Test. *Diabetes Care, 10*(4), 500–509.

Garrity, T. (1981). Medical compliance and the clinician-patient relationship: A review. *Social Science and Medicine, 15,* 215–222.

Gary, T. L., Crum, R. M., Cooper-Patrick, L., Ford, D., & Brancati, F. L. (2000). Depressive symptoms and metabolic control in African-Americans with type 2 diabetes. *Diabetes Care, 23,* 23–29.

Glasgow, R. E. (1994). Social-environmental factors in diabetes: Barriers to diabetes self-care. In C. Bradley (Ed.), *Handbook of psychology and diabetes: A guide to psychological measurement in diabetes research and practice* (pp. 335–349). Chur, Switzerland: Harwood Academic.

Glasgow, R. E. (1995). A practical model of diabetes management and education. *Diabetes Care, 18,* 117–126.

Glasgow, R. E., & Anderson, R. (1999). In diabetes care, moving from compliance to adherence is not enough: Something entirely different is needed. *Diabetes Care, 22,* 2090–2091.

Glasgow, R. E., Fisher, E. B., Anderson, B. J., LaGreca, A. M., Marrero, D., Johnson, S. B., et al. (1999). Behavioral science in diabetes: Contributions and opportunities. *Diabetes Care, 22,* 832–843.

Glasgow, R. E., Hampson, S. E., Strycker, L. A., & Ruggiero, L. (1997). Personal-model beliefs and social-environmental barriers related to diabetes self-management. *Diabetes Care, 20,* 556–561.

Glasgow, R. E., La Chance, P.-A., Toobert, D. J., Brown, J., Hampson, S. E., & Riddle, M. C. (1997). Long term effects and costs of brief behavioural dietary intervention for patients with diabetes delivered from the medical office. *Patient Education and Counseling, 32,* 175–184.

Glasgow, R. E., McCaul, K. D., & Schafer, L. C. (1986). Barriers to regimen adherence among persons with insulin-dependent diabetes. *Journal of Behavioral Medicine, 9,* 65–77.

Glasgow, R. E., McCaul, K. D., & Schafer, L. C. (1987). Self-Care behaviors and glycemic control in type I diabetes. *Journal of Chronic Disease, 40,* 399–412.

Glasgow, R. E., & Toobert, D. J. (1988). Social environment and regimen adherence among Type II diabetic patients. *Diabetes Care, 11*(5), 377–386.

Glasgow, R. E., Toobert, D. J., & Hampson, S. E. (1996). Effects of a brief office-based intervention to facilitate diabetes dietary self-management. *Diabetes Care, 19,* 835–842.

Glasgow, R. E., Toobert, D. J., Hampson, S. E., Brown, J. E., Lewinsohn, P., & Donnelly, J. (1992). Improving self-care among older patients with type II diabetes: The "sixty-something . . ." study. *Patient Education and Counseling, 19,* 61–74.

Glasgow, R. E., Toobert, D. J., Hampson, S. E., & Wilson, W. (1995). Behavioral research on diabetes at the Oregon Research Institute. *Annals of Behavioral Medicine, 17,* 32–40.

Glasgow, R. E., Wagner, E., Kaplan, R., Vinicor, F., Smith, L., & Norman, J. (1999). If diabetes is a public health problem, why not treat it as one? A population-based approach to chronic illness. *Annals of Behavioral Medicine, 21,* 159–170.

Goetsch, V. L., Wiebe, D. J., Veltum, L. G., & Van Dorsten, B. (1990). Stress and blood glucose in Type II diabetes mellitus. *Behavior Research and Therapy, 28,* 531–537.

Golin, C., DiMatteo, M. R., & Gelberg, L. (1996). The role of patient participation in the doctor visit: Implications for adherence to diabetes care. *Diabetes Care, 19,* 1153–1164.

Gonder-Frederick, L. A., Carter, W. R., Cox, D. J., & Clarke, W. L. (1990). Environmental stress and blood glucose change in insulin-dependent diabetes mellitus. *Health Psychology, 9,* 503–515.

Gonder-Frederick, L. A., Clarke, W. L., & Cox, D. J. (1997). The emotional, social, and behavioral implications of insulin-induced hypoglycemia. *Seminars in Clinical Neuropsychiatry, 2,* 57–65.

Gonder-Frederick, L. A., Cox, D. J., & Clarke W. L. (1996). Helping patients understand and recognize hypoglycemia. In B. J. Anderson & R. R. Rubin (Eds.), *Practical psychology for diabetes clinicians* (pp. 83–92). Alexandria, VA: American Diabetes Association

Gonder-Frederick, L. A., Cox, D. J., Kovatchev, B. P., Schlundt, D., & Clarke, W. L. (1997). A bio-psycho-behavioral model of the risk of severe hypoglycemia. *Diabetes Care, 20,* 661–669.

Goodall, R. A., & Halford, W. K. (1991). Self-management of diabetes mellitus: A critical review. *Health Psychology, 10*(1), 1–8.

Grandinetti, A., Kaholokula, J. K., & Chang, H. K. (2000). Delineating the relationship between stress, depressive symptoms, and glucose intolerance. *Diabetes Care, 23,* 1443–1444.

Grant, I., Kyle, G. C., Teichman, A., & Mendels, J. (1974). Recent life events and diabetes in adults. *Psychosomatic Medicine, 36,* 121–128.

Greenfield, S., Kaplan, S., Ware, J., Yano, E., & Frank, H. (1988). Patients' participation in medical care: Effects on blood sugar control and quality of life in diabetes. *Journal of General Internal Medicine, 3,* 448–457.

Griffith, L. S., Field, B. J., & Lustman, P. J. (1990). Life stress and social support in diabetes: Association with glycemic control. *International Journal of Psychiatry in Medicine, 20*(4), 365–372.

Hanson, C. L., Schinkel, A. M., DeGuire, M. J., & Kolterman, O. G. (1995). Empirical validation for a family-centered model of care. *Diabetes Care, 18*(10), 1347–1356.

Haynes, R. (1979). Introduction. In R. Haynes, D. Taylor, & D. Sackett (Eds.), *Compliance in health care* (pp. 1–7). Baltimore: Johns Hopkins University Press.

Heitzman, C. A., & Kaplan, R. M. (1984). Interaction between sex and social support in the control of type II diabetes mellitus. *Journal of Consulting and Clinical Psychology, 52,* 1087–1089.

Herter, C. D. (1998). Sexual dysfunction in patients with diabetes. *Journal of the American Board of Family Practice, 11,* 327–330.

Hess, G. E., & Davis, W. K. (1983). The validation of a diabetes patient knowledge test. *Diabetes Care, 6*(6), 591–596.

Inui, A., Kitoaka, H., Majima, M., Takamiya, S., Uemoto, M., Yonenaga, C., et al. (1998). Effect of the Kobe earthquake on stress and glycemic control in patients with diabetes mellitus. *Archives of Internal Medicine, 158,* 274–278.

Jacobson, A. M. (1996). Current concepts: The psychological care of patients with insulin-dependent diabetes mellitus. *New England Journal of Medicine, 334,* 1249–1253.

Jeffrey, R. W., Epstein, L. H., Wilson, G. T., Drewnowski, A., Stunkard, A. J., Wing, R. R., et al. (2000). Long-term maintenance of weight loss: Current status. *Health Psychology, 19,* 5–16.

Jensen, S. B. (1981). Diabetic sexual dysfunction: A comparison study of 160 insulin-treated diabetic men and women and an age-matched control group. *Archives of Sexual Behavior, 10,* 493–504.

Jensen, S. B. (1986). Sexual dysfunction in insulin-treated diabetics: A six-year follow-up study of 101 patients. *Archives of Sexual Behavior, 15,* 271–283.

Johnson, S. B. (1992). Methodological issues in diabetes research: Measuring adherence. *Diabetes Care, 15,* 1658–1667.

Johnson, S. B., Silverstein, J., Rosenbloom, A., Carter, R., & Cunningham, W. (1986). Assessing daily management in childhood diabetes. *Health Psychology, 5,* 545–564.

Kaplan, S., Greenfield, S., & Ware, J. (1989). Assessing the effects of physician-patient interactions on the outcomes of chronic disease. *Medical Care, 27,* S110–S127.

Kashiwagi, A., Harano, Y., Suzuki, M., Kojima, H., Harada, M., Nisho, Y., et al. (1986). New a2-adrenergic blocker (DG-5128) improves insulin secretion and in vivo glucose disposal in NIDDM patients. *Diabetes, 35,* 1085–1089.

Kemmer, F. W., Bisping, R., Steingruber, H. J., Baar, H., Hardtmann, F., Schlaghecke, R., et al. (1986). Psychological stress and metabolic control in patients with Type I diabetes mellitus. *New England Journal of Medicine, 314*(17), 1078–1084.

Klemp, S. B., & LaGreca, A. M. (1987). Adolescents with IDDM: The role of family cohesion and conflict. *Diabetes, 36*(Suppl. 1), 18A.

Kolodny, R. C. (1971). Sexual dysfunction in diabetic females. *Diabetes, 20*(8), 557–559.

Kramer, J. R., Ledolter, J., Manos, G. N., & Bayless, M. L. (2000). Stress and metabolic control in diabetes mellitus: Methodological issues and an illustrative analysis. *Annals of Behavioral Medicine, 22*(1), 17–28.

Lammers, C. A., Naliboff, B. D., & Straatmeyer, A. J. (1984). The effects of progressive relaxation on stress and diabetic control. *Behavior Research and Therapy, 22,* 641–650.

Landel, J. (1995). *A model of pregnancy outcome in gestational diabetes mellitus: The roles of psychosocial and behavioral factors.* Unpublished doctoral dissertation, University of Miami, FL.

Landel, J., Delamater, A., Barza, L., Schneiderman, N., & Skyler, J. (1995). Correlates of regimen adherence in minority women with gestational diabetes mellitus. *Annals of Behavioral Medicine, 17,* S70.

Lane, J. D., McCaskill, C. C., Ross, S. L., Feinglos, M. N., & Surwit, R. S. (1993). Relaxation training for NIDDM: Predicting who may benefit. *Diabetes Care, 16,* 1087–1094.

Lee, J. H., Konorska, M., & McCarty, R. (1989). Physiological responses to acute stress in alloxan and streptozotocin diabetic rats. *Physiology & Behavior, 45,* 483–489.

Leedom, L., Feldman, M., Procci, W., & Zeidler, A. (1991). Symptoms of sexual dysfunction and depression in diabetic women. *Journal of Diabetic Complications, 5,* 38–41.

Lehman, C. D., Rodin, J., McEwen, B., & Brunton, R. (1991). Impact of environmental stress on the expression of insulin-dependent diabetes mellitus. *Behavioral Neuroscience, 105,* 241–245.

Lloyd, C. E., Dyer, P. H., Lancashire, R. J., Harris, T., Daniels, J., & Barnett, A. (1999). Association between stress and glycemic control in adult with Type I (insulin-dependent) diabetes. *Diabetes Care, 22*(8), 1278–1283.

Lorenz, R., Bubb, J., Davis, D., Jacobson, A., Jannasch, K., Kramer, J., et al. (1996). Changing behavior: Practical lessons for the Diabetes Control and Complications Trial. *Diabetes Care, 19,* 648–652.

Lustman, P., Anderson, R., Freedland, K., De Groot, M., Carney, R., & Clouse, R. (2000). Depression and poor glycemic control: A meta-analytic review of the literature. *Diabetes Care, 23,* 934–942.

Lustman, P., Clouse, R., Griffith, L., Carney, R., & Freedland, K. (1997). Screening for depression in diabetes using the Beck Depression Inventory. *Psychosomatic Medicine, 59,* 24–31.

Lustman, P., Freedland, K. E., Griffith, L. S., & Clouse, R. E. (1998). Predicting response to cognitive behavior therapy of depression in type 2 diabetes. *General Hospital Psychiatry, 20,* 302–306.

Lustman, P., Freedland, K. E., Griffith, L. S., & Clouse, R. E. (2000). Fluoxetine for depression in diabetes: A randomized double-blind placebo-controlled trial. *Diabetes Care, 23,* 618–623.

Lustman, P., Griffith, L. S., & Clouse, R. E. (1988). Depression in adults with diabetes: Results of 5-yr follow-up study. *Diabetes Care, 11,* 605–612.

Lustman, P., Griffith, L. S., & Clouse, R. E. (1997). Depression in adults with diabetes. *Seminars in Clinical Neuropsychiatry, 2,* 15–23.

Lustman, P., Griffith, L. S., Clouse, R. E., Freedland, K. E., Eisen, S. A., Rubin, E. H., et al. (1997). Effects of nortriptyline on depression and glycemic control in diabetes: Results of a double-blind, placebo-controlled trial. *Psychosomatic Medicine, 59,* 241–250.

Maggio, C. A., & Pi-Sunyer, F. X. (1997). The prevention and treatment of obesity: Application to type 2 diabetes. *Diabetes Care, 20,* 1744–1766.

Marcus, B. H., Forsyth, L. H., Stone, E. J., Dubbert, P. M., McKenzie, T. L., Dunn, A. L., et al. (2000). Physical activity behavior change: Issues in adoption and maintenance. *Health Psychology, 19,* 32–41.

Marrero, D. G., & Sizemore, J. M. (1996). Motivating patients with diabetes to exercise. In B. J. Anderson & R. R. Rubin (Eds.), *Practical psychology for diabetes clinicians: How to deal with key behavioral issues faced by patients and health care teams* (pp. 73–81). Alexandria, VA: American Diabetes Association.

Marshall, G., Hays, R., Sherbourne, C., & Wells, K. (1993). The structure of patient satisfaction with outpatient medical care. *Psychological Assessment, 5,* 477–483.

Martinez, N. C. (1993). Diabetes and minority populations: Focus on Mexican Americans. *Diabetes, 28*(1), 87–95.

Mathew, R. J., Ho, B. T., Kralik, P., Taylor, D., & Claghorn, J. L. (1980). Catecholamines and migraine: Evidence based on biofeedback-induced changes. *Headache, 20,* 247–252.

McCaul, K. D., Glasgow, R. E., & Schafer, L. C. (1987). Diabetes regimen behaviors: Predicting adherence. *Medical Care, 25*(9), 868–881.

McClesky, C. H., Lewis, S. B., & Woodruff, R. E. (1978). Glucagon levels during anesthesia and surgery in normal and diabetic patients. *Diabetes, 27,* 492A.

McCulloch, D. K., Campbell, I. W., Wu, F. C., Prescott, R. J., & Clarke, B. F. (1980). The prevalence of diabetic impotence. *Diabetologia, 18,* 279–283.

McKay, H. G., Feil, E. G., Glasgow, R. E., & Brown, J. E. (1998). Feasibility and use of an internet support service for diabetes self-management. *Diabetes Educator, 24*(2), 174–179.

McNabb, W. (1997). Adherence in diabetes: Can we define it and can we measure it? *Diabetes Care, 20,* 215–218.

Metro, M. J., & Broderick, G. A. (1998). Diabetes and vascular impotence: Does insulin dependence increase the severity? *International Journal of Impotence Research, 10,* A42.

Mikat, E. M., Hackel, D. B., Cruz, P. T., & Lebovitz, H. E. (1972). Lowered glucose tolerance in the sand rat (psammonys obesus) resulting from esophageal intubation. *Proceedings of the Society for Experimental Biology and Medicine, 139,* 1390–1391.

Miller, L. V., Goldstein, J., & Nicolaisen, G. (1978). Evaluation of patients' knowledge of diabetes self-care. *Diabetes Care, 1*(5), 275–280.

Milne, R. M., Mann, J. I., Chisolm, A. W., & Williams, S. M. (1994). Long-term comparison of three dietary prescriptions in the treatment of NIDDM. *Diabetes Care, 17,* 74–80.

Mokdad, A., Ford, E., Bowman, B., Nelson, D., Engelgau, M., & Marks, V. (2000). Diabetes trends in the U.S.: 1990–1998. *Diabetes Care, 23,* 1278–1283.

Montenero, P., Donatoni, E., & Magi, D. (1973). Diabete et activite sexuelle chez la femme. *Annuelles Diabetologie de L'Hotel-Dieu, 11,* 91–103.

Morrissette, D. L., Goldstein, M. K., Raskin, D. B., & Rowland, D. L. (1999). Finger and penile tactile sensitivity in sexually functional and dysfunctional diabetic men. *Diabetologia, 42,* 336–342.

National Task Force on the Prevention and Treatment of Obesity. (1996). Long-term pharmacotherapy in the management of obesity. *Journal of the American Medical Association, 276,* 1907–1915.

Newbrough, J. R., Simpkins, C. G., & Maurer, H. (1985). A family development approach to studying factors in the management and control of childhood diabetes. *Diabetes Care, 8,* 83–92.

North American Association for the Study of Obesity. (1995). Guidelines for the approval and use of drugs to treat obesity: A position paper of the North American Association for the Study of Obesity. *Obesity Research, 3,* 473–478.

Paddock, L., Veloski, J., Chatterton, M. L., Gevirtz, F., & Nash, D. (2000). Development and validation of a questionnaire to evaluate patient satisfaction with diabetes disease management. *Diabetes Care, 23,* 951–956.

Pan, X., Li, G., Hu, Y., Wang, J., Yang, W., An, Z., et al. (1997). Effects of diet and exercise in preventing NIDDM in people with impaired glucose tolerance: The Da Qing IGT and diabetes study. *Diabetes Care, 20,* 537–544.

Perri, M., McAllister, D., Gange, J., Jordan, R., McAdoo, W., & Nezu, A. (1988). Effects of four maintenance programs on the long-term management of obesity. *Journal of Consulting and Clinical Psychology, 56,* 529–534.

Perri, M., Sears, S., & Clark, J. (1993). Strategies for improving maintenance of weight loss: Toward a continuous care model of obesity management. *Diabetes Care, 16,* 200–209.

Peyrot, M., & McMurray, J. (1985). Psychosocial factors in diabetes control: Adjustment of insulin-treated adults. *Psychosomatic Medicine, 47,* 542–557.

Peyrot, M., & Rubin, R. (1994). Modeling the effect of diabetes education on glycemic control. *Diabetes Educator, 20*(2), 143–148.

Pi-Sunyer, F., Maggio, C., McCarron, D., Reusser, M., Stern, J., Haynes, R., et al. (1999). Multicenter randomized trial of a comprehensive prepared meal program in Type 2 diabetes. *Diabetes Care, 22,* 191–197.

Redmon, J., Raatz, S., Kwong, C., Swanson, J. E., Thomas, W., & Bantle, J. P. (1999). Pharmacologic induction of weight loss to treat type 2 diabetes. *Diabetes Care, 22,* 896–903.

Rendell, M., Rajfer, J., Wicker, P., & Smith, M. (1999). Sildenafil for treatment of erectile dysfunction in men with diabetes: A randomized controlled trial. *Journal of the American Medical Association, 281*(5), 421–426.

Riazi, A., Pickup, J., & Bradley, C. (1996). Blood glucose reactivity to stress: Individual differences in magnitude, timing, and direction of responses. *Diabetic Medicine, 13*(Suppl. 7), S5–S6.

Robinson, N., & Fuller, J. (1985). Role of life events and difficulties in the onset of diabetes mellitus. *Journal of Psychosomatic Research, 29,* 583–591.

Rodin, J., & Plante, T. (1989). The psychological effects of exercise. In R. S. Williams & A. G. Wallace (Eds.), *Biological effects of physical activity* (pp. 127–138). Champaign, IL: Human Kinetics Books.

Rost, K., Flavin, K., Cole, K., & McGill, J. (1991). Change in metabolic control and functional status after hospitalization: Impact of patient activation intervention in diabetic patients. *Diabetes Care, 14,* 881–889.

Rubin, R., & Peyrot, M. (1992). Psychosocial problems and interventions in diabetes: A review of the literature. *Diabetes Care, 15,* 1640–1657.

Rubin, R., Peyrot, M., & Saudek, C. (1989). Effect of diabetes education on self-care, metabolic control, and emotional well-being. *Diabetes Care, 12*(10), 673–679.

Rubin, R., Peyrot, M., & Saudek, C. (1991). Differential effect of diabetes education on self-regulation and life-style behaviors. *Diabetes Care, 14*(4), 335–338.

Ruggiero, L. (1998). Diabetes: Biopsychosocial aspects. In E. Blechman & K. Brownell (Eds.), *Behavioral medicine and women: A comprehensive handbook* (pp. 615–622). Hillsdale, NJ: Erlbaum.

Saenz de Tejada, I., & Goldstein, I. (1988). Diabetic penile neuropathy. *Urology Clinics of North America, 15,* 17–22.

Schafer, L., McCaul, K., & Glasgow, R. (1986). Supportive and nonsupportive family behaviors. Relationships to adherence and metabolic control in persons with Type I diabetes. *Diabetes Care, 9*(2), 179–185.

Schiavi, P., & Hogan, B. (1979). Sexual problems in diabetes mellitus: Psychological aspects. *Diabetes Care, 2,* 9–17.

Schneider, S., Khachadurian, A., Amorosa, L., Clemow, L., & Ruderman, N. (1992). Ten-year experience with an exercise-based outpatient life-style modification program in the treatment of diabetes mellitus. *Diabetes Care, 15,* 1800–1810.

Schreiner-Engel, P., Schiavi, R., Vietorisz, D., Eichel, J., & Smith, H. (1985). Diabetes and female sexuality: A comparative study of women in relationships. *Journal of Sex and Marital Therapy, 11,* 165–175.

Schreiner-Engel, P., Schiavi, R., Vietorisz, D., & Smith, H. (1987). The differential impact of diabetic type on female sexuality. *Journal of Psychosomatic Research, 31,* 23–33.

Schwartz, L., Russell, L., Toovy, D., Lyons, J., & Flaherty, J. (1991). A biopsychosocial treatment approach to the management of diabetes mellitus. *General Hospital Psychiatry, 13,* 19–26.

Sherbourne, C., Hays, R., Ordway, L., DiMatteo, M., & Kravitz, R. (1992). Antecedents of adherence to medical recommendations: Results from the medical outcomes study. *Journal of Behavioral Medicine, 15,* 447–468.

Sherwin, R., Shamoon, H., Jacob, R., & Sacca, L. (1984). Role of counterregulatory hormones in the metabolic response to stress in normal and diabetic humans. In N. Melchionda, D. L.

Horwitz, & D. S. Schade (Eds.), *Recent advances in obesity and diabetes research* (pp. 327–344). New York: Raven Press.

Smári, J., & Valtysdóttir, H. (1997). Dispositional coping, psychological distress and disease-control in diabetes. *Personality and Individual Differences, 22,* 151–156.

Smith, D., Heckemeyer, C., Kratt, P., & Mason, D. (1997). Motivational interviewing to improve adherence to a behavioral weight-control program for older obese women with NIDDM: A pilot study. *Diabetes Care, 20,* 52–54.

Smith, L., & Weinert, C. (2000). Telecommunication support for rural women with diabetes. *Diabetes Educator, 26,* 645–655.

Spector, I., Leiblum, S., Carey, M., & Rosen, R. (1993). Diabetes and female sexual function: A critical review. *Annals of Behavioral Medicine, 15*(4), 257–264.

Sperling, M. (Ed.). (1988). *Physician's guide to insulin-dependent (Type I) diabetes: Diagnosis and treatment.* Alexandria, VA: American Diabetes Association.

Spiess, K., Sachs, G., Moser, G., Pietschmann, P., Schernthaner, G., & Prager, R. (1994). Psychological moderator variables and metabolic control in recent onset type 1 diabetic patients: A two year longitudinal study. *Journal of Psychosomatic Research, 38,* 249–258.

Spraul, M., & Anderson, E. A. (1992). Baseline and oral glucose stimulated muscle sympathetic nerve activity in Pima Indians and Caucasians. *Diabetes, 41*(Suppl. 1), 189A.

Stabler, B., Surwit, R., Lane, J., Morris, M., Litton, J., & Feinglos, M. (1987). Type A behavior pattern and blood glucose control in diabetic children. *Psychosomatic Medicine, 49,* 313–316.

Surwit, R., & Feinglos, M. (1983). The effects of relaxation on glucose tolerance in non-insulin dependent diabetes mellitus. *Diabetes Care, 6,* 176–179.

Surwit, R., & Feinglos, M. (1988). Stress and autonomic nervous system in type II diabetes: A hypothesis. *Diabetes Care, 11,* 83–85.

Surwit, R., Feinglos, M., Livingston, E., Kuhn, C., & McCubbin, J. (1984). Behavioral manipulation of the diabetic phenotype in *ob/ob* mice. *Diabetes, 33,* 616–618.

Surwit, R., McCasKill, C., Ross, S., & Feinglos, M. (1991). *Behavioral and pharmacologic manipulation of glucose tolerance.* Proceedings of the 14th International Diabetes Federation Congress, Washington, DC.

Surwit, R., McCubbin, J., Feinglos, M., Esposito-Del Puente, A., & Lillioja, S. (1990). Glycemic reactivity to stress: A biologic marker for development of type 2 diabetes. *Diabetes, 39*(Suppl. 1), 8A.

Surwit, R., & Schneider, M. (1993). Role of stress in the etiology and treatment of diabetes mellitus. *Psychosomatic Medicine, 55,* 380–393.

Surwit, R., Schneider, M., & Feinglos, M. (1992). Stress and diabetes mellitus. *Diabetes Care, 15*(10), 1413–1422.

Surwit, R., & Williams, P. (1996). Animal models provide insight into psychosomatic factors in diabetes. *Psychosomatic Medicine, 58,* 582–589.

Talbot, F., & Nouwen, A. (2000). A review of the relationship between depression and diabetes in adults: Is there a link? *Diabetes Care, 23,* 1556–1562.

ter Braak, E., de Valk, H., de la Bije, Y., van der Laak, M., van Haeften, T., & Erkelens, D. (2000). Response to training in blood glucose awareness is related to absence of previous hypoglycemic coma. *Diabetes Care, 23,* 1199–1200.

Toobert, D., & Glasgow, R. (1991). Problem solving and diabetes self-care. *Journal of Behavioral Medicine, 14,* 71–86.

Toobert, D., Hampson, S., & Glasgow, R. (2000). The Summary of Diabetes Self-Care Activities measure: Results from 7 studies and a revised scale. *Diabetes Care, 23,* 943–950.

Toyry, J., Niskanen, L., Mantysaari, M., Lansimies, E., & Uusitupa, M. (1996). Occurrence, predictors, and clinical significance of autonomic neuropathy in NIDDM: Ten-year follow-up from the diagnosis. *Diabetes, 45,* 308–315.

Travis, T. (1997). Patient perceptions of factors that affect adherence to dietary regimens for diabetes mellitus. *Diabetes Educator, 23,* 152–156.

Trief, P., Grant, W., Elbert, K., & Weinstock, R. (1998). Family environment, glycemic control, and the psychosocial adaptation of adults with diabetes. *Diabetes Care, 21,* 241–245.

UK Prospective Diabetes Study Group. (1998). Intensive blood glucose control with sulphonylureas or insulin compared with conventional treatment and risk of complications in patients with type 2 diabetes (UKPDS 33). *Lancet, 352,* 837–853.

U.S. Department of Health and Human Services. (1991). *Healthy People 2000 National Health Promotion and Disease Prevention Objectives.* (DHHS Publication No. PHS91–50212). Washington, DC: U.S. Government Printing Office.

Viinamaki, H., Niskanen, L., Korhonen, T., & Tahka, B. (1993). The patient-doctor relationship and metabolic control in patients with type 1 (insulin-dependent) diabetes mellitus. *International Journal of Psychiatry in Medicine, 23,* 265–274.

Vinicor, F., Cohen, S., Mazzuca, S., Moorman, N., Wheeler, M., Kuebler, T., et al. (1987). DIABEDS: A randomized clinical trial of the effects of physician and/or patient education on diabetes patient outcomes. *Journal of Chronic Diseases, 40*(4), 345–356.

Wales, J. (1995). Does psychological stress cause diabetes? *Diabetic Medicine, 12,* 109–112.

Watkins, P., & Thomas, P. (1998). Diabetes mellitus and the nervous system. *Journal of Neurology, Neurosurgery, and Psychiatry, 65,* 620–632.

Watts, F. (1980). Behavioral aspects of the management of diabetes mellitus: Education, self-care and metabolic control. *Behavioral Research and Therapy, 18,* 171–180.

Weller, S., Baer, R., Pachter, L., Trotter, R., Glazer, M., Garcia de Alba Garcia, J., et al. (1999). Latino beliefs about diabetes. *Diabetes Care, 22,* 722–728.

Whitehead, E. D. (1987). Diabetes-related impotence and its treatment in the middle-aged and elderly: Part II. *Geriatrics, 42,* 77–80.

Willey, K., Molyneaux, L., & Yue, D. (1994). Obese patients with type 2 diabetes poorly controlled by insulin and metformin: Effects of adjunctive dexfenfluramine therapy on glycaemic control. *Diabetes Medicine, 11,* 701–704.

Williams, G., Freedman, Z., & Deci, E. (1998). Supporting autonomy to motivate patients with diabetes for glucose control. *Diabetes Care, 21,* 1644–1651.

Williams, M., Baker, D., Parker, R., & Nurss, J. (1998). Relationship of functional health literacy to patients' knowledge of their chronic disease. *Archives of Internal Medicine, 158,* 166–172.

Wilson, A., & Home, P. (1993). A dataset to allow exchange of information for monitoring continuing diabetes care. *Diabetic Medicine, 10,* 378–390.

Wilson, W., Ary, D., Biglan, A., Glasgow, R., Toobert, D., & Campbell, D. (1986). Psychosocial predictors of self-care behaviors (compliance) and glycemic control in non-insulin dependent diabetes mellitus. *Diabetes Care, 9,* 614–622.

Wincze, J., Albert, A., & Bansal, S. (1993). Sexual arousal in diabetic females: Physiological and self-report measures. *Archives of Sexual Behavior, 22,* 587–601.

Wing, R. (1991). Behavioral weight control for obese patients with Type II diabetes. In P. McCabe, N. Schneiderman, T. Field, & J. Skyler (Eds.), *Stress, coping, and disease* (pp. 147–167). Hillsdale, NJ: Erlbaum.

Wing, R. (1993). Behavioral treatment of obesity: Its application to Type II diabetes. *Diabetes Care, 16,* 193–199.

Wing, R. (1995). Promoting adherence to weight-loss regimens. *Diabetes Review, 3,* 354–365.

Wing, R. (1996). Improving weight loss and maintenance in patients with diabetes. In B. J. Anderson & R. R. Rubin (Eds.), *Practical psychology for diabetes clinicians: How to deal with key behavioral issues faced by patients and health care teams* (pp. 113–118). Alexandria, VA: American Diabetes Association.

Wing, R. (2000). Cross-cutting themes in maintenance of behavior change. *Health Psychology, 19,* 84–88.

Wing, R., Blair, E., Bononi, P., Marcus, M., Watanabe, R., & Bergman, R. (1994). Caloric restriction per se is a significant factor in improvements in glycemic control and insulin sensitivity during weight loss in obese NIDDM patients. *Diabetes Care, 17,* 30–36.

Wing, R., & Jeffrey, R. (1999). Benefits of recruiting participants with friends and increasing social support for weight loss and maintenance. *Journal of Consulting and Clinical Psychology, 67,* 132–138.

Wing, R., Marcus, M., Epstein, L., & Jawad, A. (1991). A "family-based" approach to the treatment of obese Type II diabetic patients. *Journal of Consulting and Clinical Psychology, 59,* 156–162.

Wing, R., Marcus, M., Salata, R., Epstein, L., Miaskiewicz, S., & Blair, E. (1991). Effects of a very low-low-calorie diet on long-term glycemic control in obese Type 2 diabetic subjects. *Archives of Internal Medicine, 151,* 1334–1340.

Winokur, A., Maislin, G., Phillips, J., & Amsterdam, J. (1988). Insulin resistance after oral glucose tolerance testing in patients with major depression. *American Journal of Psychiatry, 145,* 325–330.

Wishner, W., & O'Brien, M. (1978). Diabetes and the family. *Medical Clinics of North America, 62*(4), 849–856.

Zrebiec, J. F., & Jacobson, A. M. (2001). What attracts patients with diabetes to an internet support group? A 21-month longitudinal website study. *Diabetic Medicine, 18*(2), 154–158.

CHAPTER 10

AIDS/HIV

MICHAEL P. CAREY AND PETER A. VANABLE

In the 1970s and early 1980s, health psychologists suggested that we could turn our full attention to the chronic illnesses because the infectious diseases that had plagued human existence for millennia had been conquered. Within a few short years of such optimistic (and perhaps somewhat naïve) statements, however, the human immunodeficiency virus (HIV) and the resulting acquired immunodeficiency syndrome (AIDS) was identified and a pandemic of historic proportions began to unfold. Indeed, in some African countries, life expectancy has dropped to levels not seen since the Middle Ages; for example, in Botswana, life expectancy is expected to drop from 66 to 33 years (Brown, 2000). Today, HIV/AIDS is recognized as one of the most important health threats we face.

Health psychologists have and will continue to play many important roles in efforts to prevent HIV infection, facilitate adjustment to HIV disease, and treat AIDS. Therefore, in this chapter, we review basic information about HIV disease including its epidemiology, transmission, natural course, treatment, and psychosocial and economic effects. Although health psychologists have conducted extensive *basic* research regarding psychosocial aspects of HIV/AIDS (e.g., the effects of stigmatization and prejudice; Herek, 1999), we devote our chapter to reviewing *applied* research. First, we review primary prevention interventions that have been implemented to reduce transmission of HIV. Our review focuses on research conducted in the United States, but includes findings from international trials where available. Second, we review secondary prevention approaches designed to help already infected persons cope with the psychosocial challenges that HIV disease brings, adhere to treatment regimens, and avoid reinfection with HIV. Finally, we conclude the chapter by identifying important research needs and outline our expectations regarding future developments. We hope that this information helps health psychologists continue to make important contributions to the prevention and treatment of HIV.

BASIC INFORMATION ABOUT HIV DISEASE

In this section, we provide basic information about the epidemiology, transmission, natural course, treatment, and psychosocial and economic effects of HIV disease.

Epidemiology

HIV/AIDS no longer occupies the public consciousness in the United States the way it did in the mid-1980s, but it continues to threaten public health in historical proportion. In the United States, 733,374 cases of AIDS have been reported to the Centers for Disease Control and Prevention (CDC) by the end of 1999. The majority (82%) of the cases have been among men. Nearly one-half (47%) of AIDS cases have been among men who have sex with men (MSM), 25% in injection drug users, 10% in persons infected heterosexually, and 2% in persons infected through blood or blood products. Although the epidemic began among MSM, it has spread to men and women regardless of sexual orientation. AIDS cases are disproportionately seen among economically disadvantaged persons in urban settings, especially among ethnic and racial minorities. African Americans have been particularly vulnerable to HIV; during 1998, they represented 48% of all reported AIDS cases even though they constitute only 13% of the general population.

In the United States, AIDS has been identified as a leading cause of death among young adults (men and women aged 25 to 44 years). This age group accounts for about 70% of all deaths from HIV infection. During 1994 and 1995, HIV was the leading cause of death among persons 25 to 44 years old; during 1995, HIV caused almost 31,000 deaths—19% of the total in this age group. Subsequent improvements in the treatment of AIDS have extended life such that, by 1998, AIDS has become the fifth leading cause of death among young adults, causing about 8,500 deaths, or 7% of the total.

Globally, the Joint United Nations Program on HIV/AIDS (2000) estimates that 34.3 million people are now living with HIV/AIDS (http://www.unaids.org). The total number of deaths since the beginning of the epidemic is estimated at nearly 19 million with 2.8 million people having died from AIDS during 1999. The epidemic does not appear to have slowed: It is estimated that 5.4 million people acquired HIV in 1999. The primary mode of transmission is believed to be heterosexual intercourse. Consistent with this hypothesis, women account for 46% of AIDS cases worldwide. The overwhelming majority of people with HIV live in the developing world, with nearly 24.5 million cases on the continent of Africa, 5.6 million cases in south and southeast Asia, and 1.3 million cases in Latin America.

Transmission and Natural Course

HIV is a fluid-borne agent. For HIV transmission to occur, an infected person's blood, semen, vaginal secretions, or breast milk must enter the blood stream of another person. In the industrialized world, the most common routes of transmission are: (a) unprotected sexual intercourse (anal, vaginal, or oral) with an infected partner; and (b) sharing unsterilized needles (most commonly in the context of recreational drugs) with an infected person. Maternal-child transmission (e.g., infection from an infected mother through the placenta before birth or through breast-feeding after birth) remains a problem in the developing world (due to poverty, lack of clean water, inadequate food supplies, and limited access to AZT and other medications), but has become less of a problem in developed

nations. Similarly, transmission through blood transfusions (when receiving but not when giving blood) and through a variety of accidental exposures (e.g., occupational needlesticks) are relatively rare in the developed world but continue to be a problem in countries in the developing world.

Once a person is infected with HIV, the course of the disease is well known. Following initial infection, there is a window period ranging from three to four weeks to as long as several months in which a person is infectious to others but has yet to develop HIV antibodies. It is during this window period that many individuals react with symptoms of acute primary infection. Symptoms of primary infection often include fever, rash, lethargy, headache, and sore throat. Once the symptoms of primary infection subside and HIV antibodies are produced, individuals usually enter an asymptomatic period in which they look and feel healthy despite the fact that continuous viral replication is occurring. The time between HIV infection and progression to AIDS varies as a function of treatment availability and response. Without treatment, most patients experience a progression from HIV to AIDS within 7 to 10 years of initial infection (Lui, Darrow, & Rutherford, 1988; Moss & Bacchetti, 1989). Left untreated, most people with AIDS die within a year of diagnosis.

Psychosocial and Economic Impact

There is no doubt that HIV disease continues to be a devastating illness. Infection with HIV continues to be most common among adolescents and young adults. These persons would be expected to live for 40 to 50 more years if not for HIV; once infected with HIV, young people face a much foreshortened and, typically, lowered quality of life. They will need to receive burdensome treatments that are inconvenient and accompanied by side effects that hamper quality of life. Besides the direct effects of HIV on those who are infected, indirect effects extend to friends and family members, especially young children, who must cope with the premature loss of their parents. It is difficult to truly appreciate the magnitude of human suffering that results from a disease such as HIV.

The economic costs associated with HIV are also extraordinary. The cost of medical treatments are prohibitive, and out of reach for all but the best insured or most affluent. The estimated lifetime cost of medical care from the time of infection until death is $214,707 in discounted 1997 dollars (Holtgrave & Pinkerton, 1997). In the United States, where 40,000 people are infected annually, we face an annualized cost of more than $6 billion each year (CDC, 2000). To arrive at a total cost, it would also be necessary to add in the lost economic opportunities associated with young workers.

Summary

HIV disease is now considered a worldwide pandemic. Transmission of HIV through transfer of infected blood, semen, vaginal secretions, and breast milk is well-understood, and the path from infection with HIV to diagnosis with AIDS follows a known pathophysiological course. The psychosocial impact of HIV/AIDS is difficult to overstate, with dramatic implications for the infected person and her or his loved ones. Because HIV is disproportionately a disease of young adults, its economic impact includes lessened productivity and increased child care costs as well as costs associated with medical care.

PRIMARY PREVENTION

Primary prevention refers to the protection of health by personal as well as community-wide efforts (Last, 1995). A comprehensive approach to the primary prevention of HIV disease requires biological, psychological, and social interventions. As depicted in Figure 10.1, complementary interventions would direct disease prevention efforts toward different targets, such as the cell or other biological systems, the individual or couple, or communities or larger social structures that influence the likelihood of disease transmission. Psychologists will remain active in most of these levels of prevention. For example, when a vaccine is developed, psychologists will play an important role in developing delivery and adherence strategies to facilitate the vaccine's rapid, safe, and effective deployment (Hays & Kegeles, 1999; Koblin et al., 1998). However, because a vaccine is not yet available—and one may not be ready for many years—prevention of new infections through behavior change provides the most prudent, practical, and affordable public health strategy. Therefore, in this section, we review interventions that have been implemented to reduce the risk of HIV transmission through changes in sexual behavior or drug use. We focus on important early studies, and recent studies that illustrate promising developments.

The literature on primary prevention interventions can be organized in several ways. First, we might organize it based on whether the intervention is designed to reduce HIV transmission through sexual behavior change or through reduction of needle sharing. Sometimes, however, these two intervention targets overlap, as with risk reduction efforts among sexually active, injection drug users. Second, prevention interventions might be distinguished by demographic, developmental, or behavioral characteristics of the population being served (e.g., men or women, adolescents or adults, gay or straight).

A third way to distinguish prevention interventions is with respect to the setting in which they occur. In this chapter, we use McKinlay's (1995) conceptual framework, which

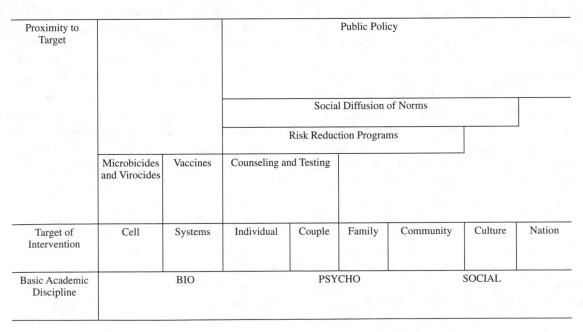

Figure 10.1   Complementary foci for HIV prevention.

identifies "downstream," "midstream," and "upstream" behavioral approaches to prevention. *Downstream* approaches are those interventions that are targeted toward persons who already exhibit high-risk behavior or who have already contracted HIV or another sexually transmitted disease. *Midstream* approaches refer to interventions targeted toward defined populations for the purpose of changing and/or preventing risk-behavior; midstream interventions tend to involve structured organizations (e.g., school, community-based organizations) as well as entire communities. *Upstream* approaches are larger, macrolevel public policy interventions designed to influence social norms and support health promoting behaviors. They tend to be more "universal," targeting entire populations rather than just groups engaged in high-risk activities. Most downstream and midstream approaches have been face-to-face interventions. Some midstream and most upstream interventions target communities or larger social units.

Downstream Approaches

Downstream interventions target populations engaging in "high risk" behavior. Thus, prevention programs delivered in settings that provide sexual health or drug abuse services provide interventionists with access to individuals who are likely to be at the highest risk for acquiring HIV. Such sites afford "teaching moments" for individuals who could benefit greatly from HIV risk reduction programs.

Sexual Health Settings

Settings that provide HIV counseling and testing (C&T), family planning, or sexually transmitted disease (STD) treatment all serve clients who are likely to have engaged in behaviors that confer high risk for HIV infection. Such sexual health settings, where it is normative to discuss sexual behavior and encourage risk reduction, is an ideal place for sexual behavior change interventions.

HIV C&T is the most heavily funded prevention activity in the United States, and research to determine whether it reduces risky sexual behavior has been abundant. Our group completed a meta-analysis of the studies completed through 1997 (Weinhardt, Carey, Johnson, & Bickham, 1999), and learned that C&T did *not* alter risky sexual behavior among those participants who tested *negative;* however, C&T was associated with risk reduction among those who tested positive and with sero-discordant couples (i.e., couples in which one partner is infected but the other partner is not). Thus, HIV C&T provides an effective behavior change strategy for HIV-positive individuals and sero-discordant couples. A criticism of many of

the early HIV C&T studies is the C&T was not guided by a sophisticated model of behavior change. The implicit model seemed to be based on the notion that knowing more about HIV would lead to behavior change, a purely educational approach. Since the completion of our meta-analysis, however, HIV C&T has been influenced more by psychological theory. In addition, recent interventions have recognized that a single counseling session may not be sufficient to prompt behavior change among individuals who test negative.

The "Voluntary HIV-1 Counseling and Testing Efficacy Study" (2000) was conducted in Kenya, Tanzania, and Trinidad. This randomized controlled trial (RCT) enrolled 3,120 individuals and 586 couples and assigned these participants to either a counseling group or to a health information (control) group. In contrast to earlier approaches that relied on education and persuasive presentations, the intervention used a client-centered approach, including a personalized risk assessment and the development of a personal risk reduction plan. This approach was designed to be sensitive to each client's emotional reactions, interpersonal situation, social and cultural context, specific risk behavior, and readiness-to-change risk behavior, consistent with a more psychological (rather than purely educational) approach. Evaluations occurred 7 and 14 months after the counseling. At the initial (7-month) follow-up, STDs were diagnosed and treated, and participants in *both* groups were retested for HIV and received the client-centered counseling. At the second (14-month) follow-up, risk behavior was assessed and additional client-centered counseling and testing were provided. The results indicated that the proportion of individuals reporting unprotected intercourse with nonprimary partners declined more for those receiving C&T than for controls. These results were maintained at the second follow-up. Consistent with Weinhardt et al.'s meta-analysis, HIV-positive men were more likely than HIV-negative men to reduce unprotected intercourse with primary and nonprimary partners, whereas infected women were more likely than uninfected women to reduce unprotected intercourse but only with primary partners. These results among HIV-positive patients were replicated among those who tested positive at the first follow-up session. Couples assigned C&T reduced unprotected intercourse with their primary partners more than control couples, but no differences were found in unprotected intercourse with other partners. For those who are interested in using the intervention manual or assessment measures from this study, these materials are available to download from http://www.caps .ucsf.edu/capsweb/projects/c&tindex.html.

In the United States, Project Respect compared the efficacy of two C&T interventions guided more explicitly by social-cognitive theory, and using the CDC's revised counseling recommendations (Kamb et al., 1998). Both interventions were implemented with adults during interactive, one-on-one sessions at five public STD clinics; the *enhanced* intervention involved four sessions whereas the *brief* intervention involved only two. Both interventions were compared to a standard care (didactic messages only) control group. The sample consisted of 5,758 heterosexual, HIV-negative patients. Evaluations at 3, 6, 9, and 12 months assessed self-reported condom use; the evaluations at 6 and 12 months also assessed new diagnoses of STDs with laboratory tests. The findings revealed that, at the 3- and 6-month follow-ups, condom use was higher in both the enhanced and brief counseling groups compared with participants in the control group. At the 6-month interval, new STDs were less common in both the enhanced (7%) and brief counseling (7%) arms compared with those in the control group (10%). This finding was replicated at the 12-month assessment. This study lends support to the notion that brief, theoretically based counseling that uses personalized action plans can increase condom use and prevent new STDs even in busy public STD clinics. Because there was not a pattern favoring the enhanced intervention, these results suggest that even a two-session counseling intervention could lead to risk reduction in downstream settings. Materials from this study are also available at http://www.cdc.gov/hiv /projects/respect/.

Downstream interventions in STD clinics have also been evaluated with adolescents. Metzler, Biglan, Noell, Ary, and Ochs (2000) recruited 339 adolescents, aged 15 to 19 years, from public STD clinics. They implemented and evaluated a five-session intervention to reduce sexual risk behavior using a RCT. Their intervention, which was influenced by social cognitive theory (Bandura, 1986) and the Information-Motivation-Behavioral Skills model (Fisher & Fisher, 1992), targeted (a) decision making about safer sex goals, (b) social skills for achieving safer sex, and (c) acceptance of negative thoughts and feelings, and was compared to a standard care control condition. Results at the 6-month follow-up indicated that adolescents who received the behavioral intervention reported fewer sexual partners, fewer nonmonogamous partners, and fewer sexual contacts with new or anonymous partners in the past 3 months, and less use of marijuana before or during sex. Treated adolescents also performed better on a role-play assessment of skill in handling difficult sexual situations.

Overall, the results from downstream settings suggests that interventions guided by theory reduce risk behavior and incident STDs, especially among patients who test positive for HIV. Encouraging findings have been obtained in one or two sessions with adults, and with longer interventions with adolescents. Continued development of such interventions

to enhance the magnitude of the behavior change, and to facilitate their incorporation into busy settings will be needed. Also needed is work demonstrating the effectiveness of such programs in family planning/pregnancy prevention programs.

Drug Abuse Treatment Settings

Because HIV is often transmitted through sharing of injection equipment, sites that provide treatment for injection drug users (IDUs) provide another excellent opportunity to prevent HIV transmission. (Later in this chapter, we discuss other approaches to HIV risk-reduction strategies for drug-using populations including community-based outreach and network approaches, as well as needle exchange programs (Needle, Coyle, Normand, Lambert, & Cesari, 1998).

Drug abuse treatment can reduce HIV risk behavior both directly and indirectly. Direct effects can result from treatment components that target HIV risk behavior, including both risky sex and IDU. Indirect benefits might result from reducing drug use, which leads to a reduction in sexual risk behavior. A recent review examined the associations among treatment participation, HIV risk reduction, and HIV infection and concluded that IDUs who are in treatment demonstrate lower rates of drug use and related risk behaviors (Metzger, Navaline, & Woody, 1998). An illustrative study was reported by Avins et al. (1997). They conducted a prospective cohort study of 700 alcoholics recruited from five public alcohol treatment centers, all of which included HIV risk-reduction counseling. At the time of entry to alcohol treatment program and again about one year later, the patients received an HIV antibody test and took part in an interviewer-administered questionnaire. Compared to baseline, at follow-up there was a 26% reduction in having sex with an IDU partner and a 58% reduction in the use of injection drugs. Respondents also showed a 77% improvement in consistent condom use with multiple sexual partners and a 23% improvement in "partner screening." Not surprisingly, patients who remained abstinent showed greater improvement than those who continued to drink. Other studies conducted in drug abuse treatment settings confirm that needle use risk behaviors tend to decrease following treatment; however, changes in sexual risk behavior are less consistently observed (Metzger et al., 1998).

The overall effect of various downstream preventive interventions targeting IDUs on HIV prevalence was the focus of a study reported by Des Jarlais et al. (2000). They accumulated a sample of more than 5,000 IDUs from two locations in New York City, a drug detoxification program or a storefront in a high drug-use area; and analyzed trends in HIV risk behaviors over the period 1990 to 1997. Their results indicated that injection and sexual risk behaviors declined significantly over time, and argued that these results mark a "declining phase" in the HIV epidemic among IDUs, at least in New York. Replication of these findings in other major urban settings is needed; nevertheless, the findings are quite encouraging regarding the modification of risk behavior among what many people would assume is the most difficult and hard-to-reach population of IDUs.

Midstream Approaches

Interventions targeted toward defined populations for the purpose of reducing risk behavior, typically in natural environments or preexisting organizations, constitute midstream approaches. Midstream approaches target people who may be engaging in the risk behavior as well as people who have not yet begun the risk behavior in an effort to prevent the behavior. Midstream approaches are often implemented in schools, primary care health clinics, and community-based settings.

School-Based Programs

Reviews of the school-based education programs indicate that one-half of these programs effectively reduce unprotected intercourse (Kirby & DiClemente, 1994). Effective programs tend to be guided by social learning theories, focus on specific strategies to reduce risk behavior, use active learning methods of instruction, address social and media influences and pressures to have sex, reinforce values against unprotected sex, and provide modeling and practice of communication or negotiation skills.

Before the AIDS pandemic, preventionists often found it challenging to secure the support of parent organizations and school boards for programs involving discussion of sexual or drug use behavior. Recently, however, a number of school districts have approved HIV prevention programs, especially in urban settings where HIV is more widely seen as a health threat. For example, in an inner-city school system in New York City, Walter and Vaughan (1993) evaluated a teacher-delivered curriculum with high school students. Their program, based on social cognitive theory, resulted in modest improvements in HIV-related knowledge and self-efficacy, and reduced sexual risk behavior. The effectiveness of this curriculum, which was accepted following meetings with all key constituent groups, demonstrates the feasibility of such an approach in school-based settings.

Increasingly, acceptance of school-based programs is occurring in nonepicenters as well. For example, in California and Texas, K. Coyle et al. (1999) are currently evaluating the effectiveness of "Safer Choices," a multicomponent HIV,

STD, and pregnancy prevention program for 9th and 10th grade students. The intervention draws upon social-cognitive theory (Bandura, 1986), social influence theory (Fisher, 1988), and models of school change, and includes a skills-based classroom curriculum for students, formation of a team of peer educators to conduct out-of-classroom activities, parent education activities and newsletters, and improvement of the schools' linkages with community resources. This innovative study is a RCT involving 3,869 students from 20 schools. In an initial report, using data from students who completed both the baseline and the initial follow-up (at 7 months), the results have been promising: The intervention enhanced 9 of 13 psychosocial variables including knowledge, self-efficacy for condom use, normative beliefs and attitudes regarding condom use, perceived barriers to condom use, risk perceptions, and parent-child communication. The program also reduced the frequency of intercourse without a condom in the three months prior to the survey and increased use of condoms at last intercourse and the use of contraceptives at last intercourse. (The latter outcome has less value for HIV prevention but does help to reduce unintended pregnancies.)

Although increased acceptance of sexual health programs in U.S. schools promises to reduce HIV transmission domestically, it can be argued that the greatest need for education and risk reduction programs is in countries where HIV and AIDS are most prevalent. Klepp, Ndeki, Leshabari, Hannan, and Lyimo (1997) described a study that tested the effects of the "Ngao" (Swahili for "shield") education program in Tanzania. The program, influenced by the theory of reasoned action (Fishbein & Middlestadt, 1989) and social learning theory (Bandura, 1986), was designed to reduce children's risk of infection and to improve their tolerance of and care for people with AIDS. This RCT (baseline, intervention, 12-month follow-up) was conducted through public primary schools in two regions of Tanzania. The schools were stratified according to location and randomly assigned to intervention or comparison conditions. The results revealed that the intervention group exhibited improved knowledge and more tolerant attitudes toward people with AIDS. Fewer students from the intervention schools (7%) than from the comparison schools (17%) had had their sexual debut during the follow-up interval.

Schools provide an ideal venue for the promotion of healthy behavior because they allow access to young people before they establish risky habits. Moreover, in countries where education is mandatory, schools can reach the vast majority of older children and adolescents without additional outreach expense. Continuing controversy exists regarding whether sex education should occur in the school or in the home, and whether abstinence is the only appropriate outcome, continues to challenge the routine integration of effective sex education and HIV risk reduction programs in many schools.

Clinic-Based Programs

Primary care settings afford a unique opportunity to reach the *general* population with HIV-risk reduction programs. Gerbert, Bronstone, McPhee, Pantilat, and Allerton (1998) developed a brief screening instrument for use in primary medical care settings. Their measure (the HIV-Risk Screening Instrument, or HSI), contains 10 items (e.g., number of sexual partners, condom use, STD history); the HSI is reliable, valid, and can be administered quickly, even by busy physicians. Patients who participated in their studies report that they felt it was important that their physician know this information about them, and that they wished to discuss their answers with their physician. This screen can serve to "break the ice" for health care providers who might otherwise find it difficult to inquire about socially sensitive behaviors. We have also found that screening can be achieved easily in mental health settings (Carey et al., 1999, 2001). Given that screening instruments can be used during the routine intake assessments, it is feasible to identify risk behavior in practice and to implement targeted interventions for patients identified as being at elevated risk for HIV.

Primary (Medical) Care Setting. Several interventions have been tested in primary care settings. For example, Kelly et al. (1994) evaluated the effectiveness of an HIV intervention group for *women* in urban clinics. Women who engaged in high risk behavior ($N = 197$) were recruited and assigned to either an HIV-risk reduction group or a health promotion comparison group. The HIV-risk reduction intervention was modeled after Kelly's (1995) successful group-based program, initially developed in community samples of gay men (described later in the chapter), and was implemented in five small-group sessions. Key intervention components involved HIV education; training in condom use, sexual assertiveness, problem-solving, and self-management skills; and peer support. At a 3-month follow-up, HIV group participants increased their sexual communication and negotiation skills as well as their condom use (from 26% to 56%) while reducing occasions of unprotected sexual intercourse.

The value of Kelly's (1995) model has also been demonstrated with *men* in primary care settings. The NIMH Multisite HIV Prevention Trial (1998) targeted 3,706 high-risk men and women at 37 clinics (mostly primary care but also some STD clinics) across the United States. This ambitious study evaluated the efficacy of an intervention based on Kelly et al.'s approach when administered to small groups during seven sessions. Participants who received the intervention reported fewer unprotected sexual acts, had higher levels of condom use, and were more likely to use condoms consistently over a 12-month follow-up period. Although clinic records revealed no difference in overall STD reinfection rate between participants in the intervention and control conditions, men recruited from STD clinics who received the intervention had a gonorrhea incidence rate that was one-half that of the control group. Participants who received the intervention also reported fewer STD symptoms over the 12-month follow-up period.

Boekeloo et al. (1999) drew on social-cognitive theory and the theory of reasoned action to develop an office-based intervention for *adolescents* seen in primary care settings. They evaluated the intervention with 12- to 15-year-old patients ($N = 215$; 81% ethnic minorities) who were receiving a general health examination in a managed care setting. Both the risk behavior and the educational intervention were administered with a private audiotape. This intervention occurred during the course of a normal office visit. One promising finding was that sexually active adolescents in the intervention group were more likely to report condom use at 3 months compared to control participants. Also, at the 9-month follow-up, there were more signs of STD reported by the controls (7/103) than the intervention group (0/94). This clever intervention approach affords an attractive and private option, especially for teens. It may also facilitate discussion of sexual health issues between teens and their health care providers.

Mental Health Care Clinics. Evidence indicating that men and women who are receiving treatment for a severe mental illness (SMI) are at elevated risk for infection with HIV (Carey, Weinhardt, & Carey, 1995; Carey, Carey, & Kalichman, 1997) has lead to the development of risk reduction programs that are tailored for this population. One of our studies examined whether training women with a SMI to be assertive in sexual situations would decrease their risk for HIV infection (Weinhardt, Carey, Carey, & Verdecias, 1998). Twenty female outpatients received either a 10-session assertiveness intervention or a control condition. All women completed measures of HIV-related information, motivation, skills, and sexual risk behavior pre- and postintervention and at two follow-ups. Compared with controls, women in the intervention group increased their assertiveness skill, HIV knowledge, and frequency of protected intercourse. Other studies have also provided evidence that cognitive-behavioral interventions facilitate risk reduction in this population (e.g., Kalichman, Sikkema, Kelly, & Bulto, 1995; Kelly, McAuliffe, et al., 1997).

Community-Based Programs

Community-based interventions have attempted to reduce risky behavior in a variety of populations, including adolescents, men who have sex with men (MSM), and urban women. Participants are typically recruited through impressive outreach efforts to social service, recreational, and business settings. The interventions may be organized into small group approaches, community-wide interventions, or media approaches.

Small Group Approaches. Perhaps the most influential approach to HIV prevention is the behavioral skills approach, initially developed by Kelly and his colleagues. After several successful evaluations of his approach, Kelly (1995) subsequently published a detailed manual that describes how to implement his approach. The key components of the intervention are: risk education and sensitization (e.g., improving recognition of their vulnerability to HIV), self-management training (e.g., having condoms available, reducing alcohol and drug use before sexual behavior, enhancing awareness of mood states that might lead to risky behavior), sexual assertion training (e.g., how to negotiate with partners for safer sex, how to refuse unsafe sex), and developing social support networks. Kelly's intervention also identifies when safer sex is not necessary, and seeks to promote pride, self-esteem, and empowerment, especially among traditionally disenfranchised groups such as gay men and ethnic minorities.

In an initial evaluation of the effectiveness of this approach, Kelly, St. Lawrence, Hood, and Brasfield (1989) recruited 104 gay men with a history of frequent HIV-risk behavior and then randomly assigned them to the skill-based behavioral intervention or to a control group. All participants completed self-report, self-monitoring, and behavioral measures related to HIV-risk at several assessment occasions pre- and postintervention. The results demonstrated that participants who received the skills intervention increased their knowledge and behavioral skills for refusing sexual coercion; they also reduced the frequency of high-risk sexual practices. These changes were maintained at the 8-month follow-up.

The small group approach developed by Kelly has been replicated with other populations in a variety of settings (e.g., Kelly et al., 1994; St. Lawrence et al., 1995), and has been the object of extensive research. For example, Kalichman,

Rompa, and Coley (1996) conducted an experimental component analysis to examine the separate and combined effects of sexual communication and self-management skills training. Low-income women were randomly assigned to one of four small-group interventions: (a) sexual communication skills training, (b) self-management skills training, (c) both sexual communication and self-management skills, or (d) HIV education and risk sensitization. Women in all four intervention conditions increased their knowledge and intentions to reduce risk behaviors, but only those in the communication skills training reported higher rates of risk reduction conversations and risk refusals. Perhaps most important, those in the combined skills training condition showed the lowest rates of unprotected sexual intercourse at the 3-month follow-up.

Based on theoretical developments in health psychology, which recognized that individuals differ in their "readiness-to-change," and that action-oriented skills programs may not be optimal for precontemplators (Prochaska, DiClemente, & Norcross, 1992), we sought to strengthen the motivational component of existing skills-based approaches to HIV risk reduction. We reasoned that a motivationally enriched intervention would be more attractive to individuals with lower initial interest due to competing life concerns, and that a motivational component may help such persons to understand the implications of HIV for other life goals and allow them to benefit from skills-oriented components. This approach was also consistent with the information-motivation-behavioral skills model of HIV risk reduction (Fisher & Fisher, 1992).

Our initial project evaluated the motivational intervention with 102 low-income women in a RCT (Carey, Maisto, et al., 1997). Women were recruited using street outreach, and invited to attend four, 90-minute group sessions. During the first two sessions, they received personalized feedback regarding their HIV-related knowledge, risk perceptions, and sexual behavior; viewed a motivational videotape of an HIV-infected woman from the community; participated in exercises to clarify the pros and cons of risky sex; and discussed HIV relative to other concerns. The final two sessions were devoted to the development of personalized action plans, education, and skills training. Results indicated that treated women increased their knowledge and risk awareness, strengthened their intentions to practice safer sex, communicated their intentions to partners, reduced substance use proximal to sexual activities, and engaged in fewer acts of unprotected vaginal intercourse. These effects were observed immediately and most were maintained at the follow-up. Comparison of these results with those obtained in similar trials suggested that the motivational approach yielded a larger effect size relative to skills-based approaches. In a second RCT (Carey et al., 2000), we strengthened our earlier design by including a health-promotion control group, and partially replicated the results. Taken together, findings from these studies demonstrate the effectiveness of an intervention that targets HIV-related *motivation* as well as behavioral skills. Subsequently, Belcher et al. (1998) have demonstrated the effectiveness of a single-session, motivational and skills-based intervention for 68 women in a community setting.

Jemmott and colleagues (Jemmott, Jemmott, & Fong, 1992, 1998) have developed risk reduction programs specifically for inner-city minority youth. In an important early study, Jemmott et al. (1992) assigned 157 African American male adolescents to receive an intervention, based on the theory of reasoned action, and aimed at increasing AIDS-related knowledge and weakening problematic attitudes toward risky sexual behavior, or to receive a control intervention on career opportunities. They found that the adolescents who received the AIDS intervention increased their knowledge, reported less favorable attitudes toward risky sexual behavior and lower intentions to engage in risky behavior, compared to control participants. Follow-up data collected three months later revealed that the adolescents who had received the AIDS intervention reported fewer occasions of vaginal intercourse, fewer partners, greater use of condoms, and a lower incidence of heterosexual anal intercourse than did the other adolescents.

In a second study, Jemmott et al. (1998) evaluated the effects of two community-based HIV prevention programs. One program was abstinence-oriented whereas the second was a safer-sex program; both were compared to a health promotion control group using a RCT with 3-, 6-, and 12-month follow-ups. The interventions took place during eight, one-hour meetings that were facilitated by adults or peer cofacilitators. The abstinence intervention stressed delaying intercourse whereas the safer-sex intervention stressed condom use. The sample, 659 inner-city African American adolescents, was recruited from three middle schools serving low-income communities in Philadelphia. The results were quite interesting. At the 3-month follow-up, abstinence intervention participants were less likely to report having sexual intercourse than were control group participants, but this effect weakened at the follow-ups. Participants in the safer-sex intervention reported more consistent condom use than did control group participants at 3 months and higher frequency of condom use at all follow-ups. Among adolescents who reported sexual experience at baseline, the safer-sex intervention group reported less sexual intercourse at 6- and 12-month follow-ups than did the control and abstinence intervention and less unprotected intercourse at all follow-ups than did control group. The results indicate that both abstinence and safer-sex interventions reduced HIV sexual risk behaviors, but that safer-sex interventions may be more effective with sexually experienced adolescents, and that they may have longer-lasting effects.

Stanton et al. (1996) focused their efforts on *naturally formed peer groups*. In a RCT, they studied 76 groups consisting of 383 (206 intervention and 177 control) African American youths aged 9 to 15. The intervention was based on protection motivation theory (R. W. Rogers, 1983). The assessment focused on perceptions, intentions, and sexual behavior; it was administered to all adolescents at preintervention, and at 6- and 12-month follow-ups. The results indicated that condom use was higher among intervention than control youths (85% vs. 61%) at the 6-month follow-up. The intervention impact at 6 months was strongest among boys and early teens. However, by 12 months, condom use was no longer higher among intervention youths. Intentions to use condoms also increased among intervention youths at 6 months but not at 12 months. Some perceptions were positively affected at 6 months, but the change did not persist at 12 months. The attenuated effects seen at the follow-up are consistent with results from other studies.

Community-Wide Approaches. Kelly is also responsible for a second influential approach to HIV risk reduction, namely the popular opinion leader (POL) or social diffusion model. This approach draws on the diffusion of innovation/social influence principles (E. M. Rogers, 1983), and posits that innovations often result from the efforts of a relatively small segment of "opinion leaders" who initially adopt a new practice and subsequently encourage its adoption by others. Gradually, the initial adoption, modeling, and encouragement by POLs results in the diffusion of innovations throughout a population.

Kelly et al.'s initial study (1991) took place in three small cities in the southern United States. Two cities served as controls and one city served as the intervention city. Across the three cities, a total of 659 gay men completed surveys at two baseline periods. The intervention involved identifying 43 popular opinion leaders in gay bars, training these men in HIV risk education and skills training, and contracting with them to endorse behavior change to their peers while in the bar settings. At the postintervention assessment, 608 men completed surveys. In the intervention city, the proportion of men who engaged in unprotected anal intercourse over a 2-month period decreased from 37% to 27%. Relative to baseline levels, there was a 16% increase in condom use during anal intercourse and an 18% decrease in the proportion of men with more than one sexual partner. In contrast, there was little change in risk behavior among men in the comparison cities. A second study replicated the effectiveness of the POL model in three cities (Kelly et al., 1992), and a third project has extended the initial findings to four more cities (Kelly, Murphy, Sikkema, et al., 1997). Subsequent extensions of the POL model to younger gay men (Kegeles, Hays, & Coates,

1996) and to women living in 18 low-income housing developments (Sikkema et al., 2000) have been reported. This model has proven to be so successful that it serves as the conceptual basis for an ongoing, NIMH-sponsored multisite international study.

Two approaches to HIV risk-reduction strategies for *drug-using populations* can be considered midstream approaches: community-based outreach and network approaches. Community-based outreach typically targets out-of-treatment injection drug users (IDUs), and provides risk reduction messages, condoms, bleach and needle disinfecting supplies, encouragement to seek HIV C&T, and referrals to drug abuse treatment. A recent review of 36 single group and quasi-experimental studies indicated that two-thirds of the outreach efforts resulted in subsequent HIV C&T and IDUs reduced baseline levels of drug-related and sex-related risk behaviors following their participation in a outreach intervention (S. Coyle, Needle, & Normand, 1998). This review also concluded that, following involvement in outreach programs, IDUs reduce drug injection behavior and are less likely to reuse syringes, needles, and other injection equipment (e.g., cookers, cotton). Outreach interventions have resulted in greater use of needle disinfection and an increased likelihood of entry into drug treatment (S. Coyle et al., 1998). One quasi-experimental study found reduced HIV seroincidence among outreach participants (Wiebel et al., 1996). The effects of outreach efforts on sex-related risks are less impressive; there has been increased condom use but the majority still practice unsafe sex.

Network approaches targeted toward drug users seek to change community based norms and patterns of risk among network members and to enhance readiness to enter drug abuse treatment. These approaches represent a shift in focus from the individual to transactions among individuals and to the context in which drugs are procured and used (Needle et al., 1998). Latkin (1998) compared a network with a standard intervention; the network approach was similar to the POL implemented in Kelly et al. (1992) in that peer leaders were identified and they participated in a 10-session training program. They were then encouraged to contact their drug using peers and provide outreach. Pretest and posttest surveys found that IDU opinion leaders were able to reach 78% of their peers. Contact with opinion leaders was associated with increased condom use, and increased use of bleach to clean needles; peers in the network were less likely to use unbleached needles.

Media Approaches.   Many preventionists recognize that intensive, individual and small group approaches work well, but they reach a relatively small segment of the community. Mass media, such as television, radio, and print publications,

afford the potential for greater "reach." Use of the media as a primary prevention strategy in the United States has not been widely implemented. One notable exception is the "Condom Campaign," which occurred in three urban Washington communities (Alstead et al., 1999). This quasi-experimental program targeted urban adolescents in areas known for high rates of adolescent STDs, and sought to overcome two widely cited obstacles to condom use among adolescents: negative attitudes and difficult access. Campaign leaders first formed an advisory board; next, they secured pro bono services from a local advertising agency to donate advertising expertise. Then, working with the advisory board and ad agency, they developed a three-pronged approach to improve condom attitudes and use: (a) secure support through outreach efforts to community-based leaders and organizations, (b) develop and distribute procondom messages through the media (e.g., radio, billboards, bus signs, and brochures); and (c) make condoms available through free or low-cost distribution in easily accessed public settings (e.g., condom bins and vending machines in dressing rooms, restrooms and other private settings accessible to teens). Pilot evaluation indicated that 73% of the target youth reported exposure to the campaign and radio influenced the largest number of adolescents. Unfortunately, evaluation of the risk reduction effects of the campaign was meager, and did not reveal risk reduction over the study interval.

Although media programs have a larger reach, we would expect individual and small group approaches to result in larger effects. As suggested earlier in this chapter (Figure 10.1), complementary prevention initiatives across multiple target points are needed over a sustained period of time. Such approaches require a large commitment of resources to implement, and would be very challenging to evaluate. From a theoretical perspective, however, such an approach would appear to be the most effective. A recent study illustrates how we might begin such a challenging task.

Celentano et al. (2000) report the results of a study that sought to evaluate the effectiveness of both a small group and social diffusion intervention. Their small group intervention was designed to encourage condom use, reduce alcohol consumption and brothel use, and enhance sexual negotiation and condom skills. Three group were formed for the study. Group 1 ($n = 450$) received the small group intervention. Group 2 ($n = 681$) lived in near-by barracks at the same military base but did not receive the intervention; this was the diffusion group. Group 3 ($n = 414$) were in distant camps (controls). Outcome measures included testing for HIV infection as well as behavioral measures. The intervention was applied for 15 months, and men were followed up at 6-month intervals (with repeated HIV and STD testing). The results were rather stunning. The intervention decreased incident

HIV infections by 50% in the intervention group. Moreover, after adjusting for baseline risk factors, incident STDs were seven times less frequent among men assigned to the intervention than the combined controls; however, contrary to earlier findings (e.g., Kelly, Murphy, Sikkema, et al., 1997), there was no diffusion of the intervention to adjacent barracks.

Summary

Three midstream approaches have been evaluated to date: individual and small group approaches, communitywide approaches, and media campaigns. Individual and small group approaches are often guided by social-cognitive theoretical frameworks and emphasize education; skills training (e.g., observation, modeling, rehearsal, feedback, reinforcement); cognitive modification (e.g., outcome expectancies, self-efficacy beliefs); and social reinforcement for instituting behavior changes. Consistent with a meta-analytic integration of this literature (Kalichman, Carey, & Johnson, 1996), our observation is that such interventions consistently reduce short-term risk behavior and, in a few studies, are also associated with a lowered incidence of new STDs. Evidence of the long-term effectiveness of these interventions is needed, and the potential reach of such programs is limited due to their cost.

A second midstream approach involves community-based interventions, often influenced by social diffusion theory. Fewer studies of this approach have been completed, but these also provide evidence of reductions in risk behavior at the community level. As with small group approaches, the effect sizes from these studies tend to be modest. Finally, media approaches have the widest reach but might be expected to have the least short-term impact. However, media approaches promise to prime communities and individuals for more intensive risk-reduction efforts, can create social norms that are supportive of risk reduction, and might serve as background "boosters" of more intensive risk-reduction strategies. Indeed, several upstream approaches completed in smaller countries demonstrate the value of combining face-to-face interventions, with media and policy changes.

Upstream Approaches

Public policy interventions including governmental, institutional, and organizational actions directed at entire populations rarely have been implemented in the United States. One upstream approach that has been evaluated is needle exchange programs, which is regarded as a "population-level" approach (Des Jarlais, 2000). The results from needle exchange programs has been mixed. Three studies conducted in Canada and the Netherlands have reported that needle exchange has no effect on HIV incidence (Bruneau et al., 1997; Strathdee et al., 1997; van Ameijden, van den Hoek, van Haastrecht, & Coutinho, 1992) but two U.S. studies have found that HIV incidence is reduced by needle exchange programs (Des Jarlais et al., 1996; Heimer, Kaplan, Khoshnood, Jariwala, & Cadman, 1993). Interpreting these mixed findings is challenging, but most experts agree that (a) measuring the effects of needle exchange on HIV incidence is complicated, (b) needle exchange programs do serve as a link to drug treatment and as platforms for the delivery of other needed clinical services, and (c) needle exchange programs are not enough but can serve as one part of a useful comprehensive approach to risk reduction for IDUs (Des Jarlais, 2000; Vlahov, 2000). There is no evidence that needle exchange programs lead to increased drug use, a concern that has been expressed.

Other countries have implemented and evaluated large national HIV prevention programs. For example, Nelson et al. (1996) evaluated Thailand's "100% Condom Program," a policy started in response to the high seroprevalence of HIV among sex workers. This program began in 1990 and mandated condom use during commercial sex. Nelson et al. followed cohorts of young men who were conscripted into the army in 1991, 1993, and 1995. In the 1991 and 1993 cohorts, the prevalence of HIV infection was 10% to 12% but by 1995, it had decreased to 7%. Over the study period, the proportion of men who reported having sexual relations with a sex worker also declined from 82% to 64%. From 1991 to 1995, condom use during the most recent sexual contacts with sex workers increased from 61% to 92%; and in 1995, 15% percent of men had a history of a STD, as compared with 42% in 1991. Subsequent reports from this research group have documented the dramatic decrease in the incidence rates of STDs, including HIV infection, among young men in military service in Thailand (Celentano et al., 1998). Such programs could be implemented by other countries experiencing epidemics of heterosexually transmitted HIV and are likely to decrease the spread of the epidemic.

Switzerland provides an example of a national AIDS prevention strategy in the developed world (Dubois-Arber, Jeannin, Konings, & Paccaud, 1997; Dubois-Arber, Jeannin, & Spencer, 1999). The intervention strategy involved three components: (a) a general publication education campaign that used the national media (print, TV, radio, posters) and public relations events to provide accurate information, to promote condom use outside of stable monogamous relationships, to encourage monogamy, and to promote tolerance regarding infected persons; and (b) risk reduction programs targeted toward suspected high risk "groups" of IDUs, adolescents, and gay men; and (c) intensive risk reduction counseling through traditional clinical and educational channels. Beginning in 1987, this strategy has been subject to a continuous process of both qualitative and quantitative evaluation (Dubois-Arber et al., 1999). For example, Dubois-Arber et al. (1997) reported that, although there had been no changes in level of sexual activity, condom use with a new steady partner increased between 1988 and 1994 from 40% to 64% among 17- to 30-year-olds, and from 57% to 72% among those aged 31 to 45. Systematic condom use with casual partners increased from 8% to 56% between 1987 and 1994 among 17- to 30-year-olds, and from 22% to 42% between 1989 and 1994 among those aged 31 to 45. As one would hope, condom use was higher among those with multiple partners. Based on these ongoing evaluations, recommendations have been formulated by investigators, and used by policymakers. Dubois-Arber et al. (1999) note that the cost of such evaluation is low relative to the amount of information provided, and that this project has also contributed to the development of a culture of evaluation in Switzerland.

Upstream approaches have much to recommend them, and often involve integration of downstream and midstream approaches. Thus, far, they have been most successful in smaller countries.

SECONDARY PREVENTION

Thus far, we have considered the progress that has been made in the development of primary prevention interventions to reduce the transmission of new HIV infections. We now consider the contributions of health psychology research in the area of HIV secondary prevention. In the present context, secondary prevention refers broadly to interventions designed to reduce adverse health, behavioral, and psychological outcomes among men and women living with HIV disease. Treatment gains brought about by the availability of highly-active antiretroviral therapies (HAART) have renewed hope for many persons living with HIV/AIDS. However, many do not experience lasting benefits from HAART, and those who do respond face many long-term stressors and behavioral demands. The availability of improved treatments raises a number of new priorities for health psychologists in their work with persons living with HIV. After providing an overview of recent advances in HIV medical care, we focus on three critical issues in secondary prevention: (a) coping and psychological intervention needs among people living with HIV, (b) adherence to complex drug regimens, and (c) sexual and drug use risk-reduction needs among persons living with HIV.

Historical and Psychosocial Context of HIV Medical Care

Nearly 20 years have passed since the first cases of AIDS were described in the scientific literature and HIV was found to be the causal agent in AIDS (Barre-Sinoussi et al., 1983; Gallo et al., 1984). Early in the epidemic, the only treatments that were available were palliative efforts to forestall AIDS-related opportunistic infections. Indeed, thousands of people lost their lives well before a diagnostic test was available to identify HIV infection. The early years of the epidemic were characterized by an atmosphere of alarm, fear, and mistrust, as many people sought to distance themselves from (and often sought to blame) stigmatized groups of gay men, Haitians, injection drug users, and hemophiliacs who were identified initially as carriers of a new and mysterious infectious disease (Kobayashi, 1997). Those who developed AIDS often died quickly and in isolation, leaving loved ones in a state of fear and disbelief, mourning a sudden loss while worrying that contact with the infected person may have infected others with the disease. Meanwhile, with no understanding of disease pathogenesis or transmission routes, the number of new cases of HIV rose steadily.

In 1985, the ability to detect HIV antibodies represented a crucial first step for the initiation of drug trials, and was of obvious importance for prevention efforts. By confirming that many who were infected with HIV looked and felt "perfectly healthy," HIV testing provided the early framework for prevention work emphasizing the need for safer sex with all partners of unknown serostatus. Further, HIV testing dispelled the myth that HIV could be transmitted through casual contact, allowing people to feel more comfortable interacting, supporting, and providing treatment for those who were infected. For many, however, the availability of HIV testing raised more concerns and questions than it answered (Kobayashi, 1997). The lack of treatment options, high levels of stigma and discrimination associated with HIV, and heightened anxiety associated with what was correctly perceived as a virtual "death sentence," led many at-risk men and women to question the utility of HIV testing.

The first major treatment milestone came in 1987 when the antiretroviral therapy zidovudine (AZT) became widely available to persons living with HIV. Clinical trials demonstrating that AZT treatment led to increased T-helper lymphocytes, reduced frequency of opportunistic infections, and prolonged survival time (Fischl et al., 1987) provided some cause for optimism. However, for most patients, long-term benefits from AZT proved to be elusive, in part because of the ability of HIV to develop resistance to individual antiretroviral agents (Larder & Kemp, 1989). Further, the use of AZT was frequently associated with dose-limiting side effects such as anemia (Richman et al., 1987), and in many patients its prolonged use was not well-tolerated. In subsequent years, the efficacy of sequencing AZT monotherapy with additional drug agents was explored. With aggressive early HIV management, patients who had already received AZT and were later switched to other antiretrovirals were shown to experience better clinical outcomes (Hammer et al., 1997). This monotherapy approach to treatment remained the standard of care up until the mid-1990s, but typically provided only transient benefits, along with a host of toxic side effects.

It was within the context of limited treatment options and bleak health prospects that two nearly simultaneous medical breakthroughs occurred. The first was the development of a diagnostic test to quantify levels of HIV RNA or "viral load" in the blood plasma of infected individuals. Although CD4 counts provided useful information about the impact of HIV on immune functioning, the ability to measure viral load provided a more precise tool for tracking progression of viral replication and assessing the impact of therapeutic medications, and led to a greater appreciation of the high HIV burden in infected persons from the onset of the illness (Ho et al., 1995). The second major breakthrough was the discovery of *protease inhibitors,* a new class of drugs that, when used in combination with two or more new or existing antiretrovirals, could target HIV at multiple points in the replication cycle. Initial clinical trials showed that many patients treated with combinations of HAART experienced reduced viral load to undetectable levels, fewer opportunistic infections, and increased life expectancies (Collier et al., 1996; Gulick et al., 1997). As a result, HIV combination therapies became the standard of care.

The availability of HIV treatments affected disease course where new treatments were available. Data from the United States indicated a 44% drop in AIDS-related deaths between 1996 and 1997 (CDC, 1997), a decline attributable to the use of combination HIV therapies (Palella et al., 1998). Many people have experienced miraculous turnarounds and sustained HIV viral suppression as a result of the newer therapies; unfortunately, however, treatment benefits are not shared equally by all persons living with HIV disease. A substantial minority of patients treated with combination therapies do not achieve or sustain lasting benefits from the newer HIV therapies. Estimates of treatment failures—stemming from drug discontinuation due to intolerable side effects, poor medication adherence, or multidrug resistant strains of HIV (Hecht et al., 1998)—range from 15% to 25% in RCTs

(Gulick et al., 1997) and are as high as 60% in uncontrolled community-based samples (Fatkenheuer et al., 1997).

In addition, access to treatment is limited to only the wealthiest of nations. It has been estimated that as few as 10% of patients worldwide have access to therapy. Even within the United States, there are disparities in treatment access (Shapiro et al., 1999). Mirroring overall seroprevalence patterns, the urban poor, ethnic minorities, women, and other the disenfranchised groups have reduced access to the new treatments (Andersen et al., 2000). Indeed, there is increasing fear that disparities in treatment access and variable treatment response may lead to two classes of persons living with HIV disease, with more favorable outcomes occurring among those with higher socioeconomic status (Rapiti, Porta, Forastiere, Fusco, & Perucci, 2000). Thus, although it was hoped that HIV might soon resemble a serious but chronic health condition, disparities in treatment access and wide variability in treatment response suggest that it is too premature to describe HIV as a manageable disease. Talk of a "cure" has therefore been replaced by a mood of guarded optimism within the HIV care community.

Critical Issues in Secondary Prevention

With this background, we now consider the important role of health psychology research and practice in improving medical outcomes and quality of life among persons living with HIV. Interventions to improve quality of life and medical management of HIV disease often must include psychosocial support and treatment to addresses the long-term adjustment and coping challenges that confront patients living with HIV. In addition, favorable treatment outcomes depend not just on access to new medications, but on patients' ability to consistently adhere to complex medication regimens. Finally, longer term treatment success also may hinge on the ability of patients' to maintain protective health behaviors to avoid re-infection with a drug resistant HIV strain.

Psychological Intervention Needs among People Living with HIV

For much of the history of the epidemic, mental health research involving HIV-positive men and women focused on the psychosocial impact of an incurable, progressively worsening health condition. Not surprisingly, studies conducted prior to the advent of HAART suggest that HIV-positive men and women were at considerable risk for Axis I mood and adjustment disorders (Rabkin, Wagener, & Rabkin, 1996). Although there is some evidence pointing to a recent decline in the prevalence of depressive disorders among some populations of HIV-positive persons because of improved treatment options (Low-Beer et al., 2000; Rabkin, Ferrando, Lin, Sewell, & McElhiney, 2000), HIV disease triggers a host of powerful stressors. Treatment and support for individuals experiencing adjustment difficulties not only can improve mental health functioning and quality of life, but also may have direct effects on disease progression. In this section, we briefly consider the range of stressors that confront persons living with HIV disease, the impact these stressors have on disease progression, and several exemplar studies suggesting promising intervention approaches to improve coping and psychological adaptation among persons living with HIV.

HIV-Related Stressors.   Persons living with HIV experience a wide range of stressors throughout the course of their illness. Although the nature and severity of psychological distress and coping difficulties vary from person to person, several distinct phases of the illness are commonly associated with increased anxiety and depressive symptoms (Kalichman, 1998). Receipt of a positive test result, even if it was expected, is described by many as being among the most challenging and stressful periods of adaptation faced during the course of the illness. Individuals often experience a mixture of shock, denial, guilt and fear, as well as concerns about whether to disclose the illness to others (Ostrow et al., 1989). During this initial phase, patients must also consider a bewildering array of options with regard to the initiation of treatment, including the difficult issue of when to start HAART. Emotional distress is often most intense during the first months of HIV infection, but prospective studies indicate that symptoms of depression and anxiety often decline in the months following HIV test notification (Rabkin et al., 1991). Distress during the asymptomatic phase of HIV disease often results from the multiple uncertainties of future health decline, impaired occupational functioning, high costs of medical care, and declining social supports.

The first signs and symptoms of HIV disease progression often lead to a resurgence of more extreme anxiety and depressive symptoms that can often persist indefinitely as patients cope with the uncertainties associated with potential progression to AIDS. Finally, the actual diagnosis of AIDS is often experienced as being very traumatic, because it can signify the "beginning of the end" for patients facing likely death. Severe distress associated with an AIDS diagnoses is often short-lived (Rabkin et al., 1997), suggesting that many people with AIDS show an extraordinary capacity to adapt to advancing disease. Regardless of disease stage, other stressors commonly experienced by persons living with HIV include the challenge of accessing and paying for medical care, experiences of stigmatization, and bereavement associated with the loss of other loved ones to AIDS (for a review, see Kalichman & Catz, 2000).

Although many of the coping challenges experienced by patients today are similar to those experienced prior to the advent of combination therapies, a number of new challenges have emerged following the advent of HAART (Kelly, Otto-Salaj, Sikkema, Pinkerton, & Bloom, 1998; Catz & Kelly, 2001). On an individual level, many patients have experienced a rapid turn-around in health status as a result of combination therapies. Improvements in health outlook, described by some as a "second life" (Rabkin & Ferrando, 1997), have led to considerable relief for those experiencing the benefits; however, this second life also gives birth to new stressors. Many who had previously anticipated the prospect of debilitating illness and early death now must adapt to the uncertain possibility of remaining in good health for many years to come. Although clearly good news, anticipation of prolonged periods of good health forces individuals to confront difficult choices concerning matters such as whether to give up disability benefits and return to work, and the initiation of new relationships. Patients who succeed with combination therapies must also cope with the lifelong need to adhere to exceedingly complex HAART regimens. In stark contrast to individuals who respond well to HAART, those who have not responded well frequently experience a profound sense of disappointment, often blaming themselves for "treatment failure" (Bogart et al., 2000). Failure to respond to combination therapies may result in a sense of injustice that the best available treatment are not personally effective, as well as fatalism about the future (Rabkin & Ferrando, 1997). Repeated treatment failure may ultimately precipitate the onset of more serious major mood disorders requiring psychological or pharmacological treatment.

Coping Interventions and Health.   There has been considerable interest in understanding whether psychosocial factors such as depression, anxiety, and coping style influence HIV disease progression. Studies linking psychosocial variables longitudinally with disease progression in HIV have yielded somewhat contradictory results, but nonetheless provide some evidence to suggest that positive psychological adjustment can be associated with improved clinical outcomes. For example, several studies report a positive association between HIV disease progression and depressive symptoms (Burack et al., 1993; Leserman et al., 1999), measures of interpersonal sensitivity (Cole, Kemeny, & Taylor, 1997), AIDS-related bereavement (Kemeny et al., 1995), and negative HIV-specific expectancies (Reed, Kemeny, Taylor, & Visscher, 1999). However, other studies have failed to find an association between stress and HIV disease progression (Coates, McKusick, Kuno, & Stites, 1989; Rabkin et al., 1991).

Drawing on research suggesting the benefits of positive psychological adjustment to HIV disease, a number of investigators have sought to evaluate the impact of stress-reduction interventions on mental health functioning and, in some instances, HIV disease course. For example, Folkman and Chesney (1991) developed an intensive coping intervention for HIV-positive individuals called Coping Effectiveness Training (CET). The CET intervention consists of 10 group-based training sessions designed to improve coping skills through the use of cognitive behavioral strategies and enhancement of social support. An RCT involving 128 HIV-positive gay men with some depressive symptoms (Chesney, Folkman, & Chambers, 1996) showed promising results for CET. Subjects were assigned to either CET or to an HIV education support group. Those receiving the CET intervention showed a significant increase in self-efficacy, and decreased distress compared to participants in the information only group. However, no differences were found between the CET and control group on CD4 cell counts or HIV-related symptoms.

A multifaceted cognitive behavioral stress management program (CBSM) developed by Antoni et al. (1991) has shown even greater promise as an approach to reducing psychological distress and improved health-related outcomes among persons living with HIV. The CBSM is a 10-week group-based intervention that includes techniques for building awareness of stress and negative thoughts, cognitive restructuring techniques, relaxation and imagery techniques, coping skills training, interpersonal skills training, and methods for enhancing social support. In one of the earliest studies involving CBSM, asymptomatic gay and bisexual men newly diagnosed with HIV and who received the CBSM experienced improvement in immune functioning in the form of increased CD4 counts relative to participants assigned to a control condition. Somewhat surprisingly, however, participants in the CBSM group showed no improvements in mood-related symptoms (Antoni et al., 1991).

Other studies provide more direct evidence of the potential utility of cognitive behavior interventions to ameliorate psychological distress and improve health outcomes. Antoni et al. (2000) tested the effects of CBSM among symptomatic HIV-positive gay men. Seventy-three men were randomized to the intervention or a wait-list control (WLC) condition. Men assigned to CBSM showed lower posttreatment levels of self-reported anxiety, anger, total mood disturbance, and perceived stress. In addition, men receiving the CBSM demonstrated less norepinephrine output as compared with men in the WLC group. Even more noteworthy were findings concerning long-term immune functioning. Significantly greater numbers of T-cell lymphocytes were found 6 to 12 months later in those assigned to CBSM relative to those in the control group, suggesting that the intervention resulted in lasting improvement in immune functioning.

Research is needed to clarify whether psychological interventions improve health outcomes among diverse populations of HIV-positive men and women. These studies, along with findings from studies involving the use of support groups (Kelly et al., 1993), nonetheless provide evidence that group-based stress management and supportive interventions can reduce distress and contribute to improved quality of life for people living with HIV. As the number of people living with HIV disease continues to rise, it will become increasingly important to incorporate promising research-based coping interventions into standard care.

Medication Adherence

Successful treatment with combination therapy results in almost total suppression of HIV viral load. Failure to achieve sustained suppression of HIV viral load can lead to the development of multidrug resistant strains of the virus and, ultimately, poor clinical outcomes (Mayer, 1999). Several biomedical factors, including prior experience with antiretroviral medications, disease stage, and the timing of the initiation of combination therapies can contribute to poor treatment response (Hatkenheuer et al., 1997). Also important to the sustained success of HIV combination therapies is patient adherence. Indeed, the critical importance of adherence has led to calls for behavioral research on the dynamics of medication adherence as a means of improving HIV medical care (Chesney, Ickovics, Hecht, Sikipa, & Rabkin, 1999; Kelly, Otto-Salaj, et al., 1998; Rabkin & Ferrando, 1997). Because research on adherence to HIV medications is just beginning to appear in the scientific literature, our focus here is to describe the nature and scope of the adherence challenge, and to identify promising directions for interventions to improve adherence.

Nature and Scope of the Problem. Combination therapy regimens have been described as being perhaps the most rigorous, demanding, and unforgiving of any outpatient oral treatments ever introduced (Rabkin & Chesney, 1999). Combination therapy regimens typically require patients to take a protease inhibitor and two or more antiretroviral therapies throughout the day and night, often at varying time intervals. Some treatments must be taken on an empty stomach, whereas others are to be taken with food. To complicate matters further, some medications must be kept in refrigeration whereas others do not. Together with other medications prescribed as a prophylactic (i.e., to prevent opportunistic infections or illnesses) or for symptomatic illnesses, patients are sometimes required to take as many as 20 pills per day. Although efforts are underway to develop simplified treatment regimens (Cohen, Hellinger, & Norris, 2000), treatments will continue to be complex, requiring considerable patient effort and tracking.

Treatment adherence is a common concern for all areas of medicine, but it takes on increasing importance in the area of HIV care because of the severe consequences associated with even modest deviations from prescribed regimens. Several studies document a strong association between poor adherence and failure to suppress viral load (Montaner et al., 1998; Paterson et al., 2000). For example, Paterson et al. (2000) report that failure to maintain viral suppression to undetectable levels was documented in 22% of patients with adherence of 95% or greater, whereas nearly two-thirds of patients with adherence rates ranging from 80% to 94% experienced virologic failure. Patients with less than 80% adherence faired even worse, with only 20% of those patients avoiding drug failure. Moreover, patients with adherence of 95% or greater had fewer days in the hospital than those with less than 95% adherence, and experienced no opportunistic infections or deaths. These dramatic findings are particularly noteworthy given that in other areas of medicine, acceptable adherence levels are often considered to be in the 80% to 90% range (Haynes, McKibbon, & Kanani, 1996), and underscore the long-term self-management challenges faced by HIV-positive patients.

The unforgiving nature of combination therapy treatments suggests that many patients who initiate combination therapies have a time-limited opportunity to succeed with treatment. Even brief drug holidays can lead to rapid viral replication, drug resistance, and (ultimately) failure to respond to other combination therapies. Further, patients initiating combination therapy treatments face what may well be a lifetime of intensive pill taking, given the inevitability of rapid viral "rebound" among patients who discontinue therapy (Dornadula et al., 1999). The complexity of the drug regimen is not the only factor rendering treatment adherence a challenge. Under even the best of circumstances, combination therapy can cause a host of unpleasant and sometimes severe side effects including fatigue, nausea, vomiting, and diarrhea, as well as longer term side effects (i.e., oral numbness, metallic taste, lipodystrophy, and peripheral neuropathy; Rabkin & Chesney, 1999).

Several studies provide estimates of the prevalence of therapy adherence problems involving HIV-positive persons. Among patients recruited from an infectious disease clinic, 17% reported missing one or more doses in the last two days, and 31% of respondents reported missing one or more doses of combination therapy in the last five days (Catz, Kelly, Bogart, Benotsch, & McAuliffe, 2000). Similar estimates of poor adherence were reported in a study involving partici-

pants in a multisite HIV treatment trial (Chesney et al., 2000), and in a community sample of predominately African American men and women (Kalichman, Ramachandran, & Catz, 1999). Adherence based on self-report may underestimate the frequency of missed dosages. A study comparing the use of self-report, unannounced pill counts, and electronic pill cap monitoring found that median adherence was 89%, 73%, and 67% by self-report, pill count, and electronic medication monitor, respectively (Bangsberg et al., 2000).

Interventions to Promote Adherence. Research investigating correlates and barriers to HIV treatment adherence point to the challenges that lie ahead in designing effective behavioral interventions to improve adherence. Risk factors that characterize individuals who are at elevated risk for contracting HIV, including poverty, social marginilization, substance abuse, and mental illness, are also likely to serve as barriers to HIV treatment adherence. Qualitative research summarized by Rabkin and Chesney (1999) identified several obstacles faced by individuals who lack adequate economic resources when they try to adhere to their HIV medications. Patients who are at elevated risk for substance use disorders (e.g., Malow et al., 1998) and psychiatric illness (e.g., Stein et al., 2000) are also less likely to adhere to their medication regimen. These findings highlight the dilemma faced by many physicians when working with individuals whose life circumstances make adequate treatment adherence unlikely. Indeed, some physicians argue that because of the risks of developing multidrug resistance from poor adherence, some newly diagnosed patients may be served best by delaying initiation of combination therapies in favor of first treating acute illnesses and resolving other basic psychosocial issues such as substance abuse, housing, and health insurance (Bangsberg, Tulsky, Hecht, & Moss, 1997).

Psychosocial factors, including social support, psychological distress, and self-efficacy beliefs also appear to be important factors contributing to combination therapy adherence (Catz, et al., 2000; Mostashari, Riley, Selwyn, & Altice, 1998). In an effort to identify other patient factors that could help to account for missed dosages, several recent studies also report on open-ended responses provided by patients concerning reasons for missed dosages (see Catz et al., 2000; Chesney et al., 2000; Weidle et al., 1999). "Simply forgetting" and confusion about the treatment regimen are cited commonly as reasons for missed dosages, as are concerns over side effects, and difficulties in fitting complicated pill-taking regimens into a daily routine. Many patients also raise concerns about the psychological impact of being reminded frequently of one's disease, and fear that others will find out that they are HIV-positive.

Finally, aspects of the treatment itself, including patients' knowledge about treatments and their experience with medications influence adherence. Chesney et al. (2000) found that patients who did not understand the relationship between missed doses and the development of drug resistance were more likely to report poor adherence. Confusion regarding treatment doses may be particularly common among patients with limited education and low rates of health literacy. For example, findings from a community sample of persons living with HIV revealed that low health literacy was a stronger predictor of poor adherence than was substance use, depression, and attitudes toward health care providers (Kalichman et al., 1999). Consistent with earlier studies of adherence prior to the advent of protease inhibitors, multiple side effects also play an important role in missed dosages or drug discontinuation (Catz et al., 2000), as do patient beliefs regarding perceived efficacy of treatments (e.g., Aversa & Kimberlin, 1996).

Clearly, there is still much to learn about the dynamics of treatment adherence. Nonetheless, it is crucial that health behavior researchers and medical treatment teams proceed with innovative approaches to improving HIV treatment adherence. Although there are no published findings concerning the comparative effectiveness of different approaches to improving treatment adherence in HIV disease, approaches to HIV treatment adherence can be informed by previous research in other areas of behavioral medicine (Sikkema & Kelly, 1996). These include intervention directed both toward individual patients, as well as interventions directed toward health care providers. Although adherence interventions might occur within a variety of settings, the integration of adherence interventions within health care and social service settings already serving people with HIV is likely to have the broadest patient impact (Kelly, Otto-Salaj, et al., 1998).

In other areas of medicine, a common approach to improving patient adherence is to provide targeted interventions to patients who are at greatest risk for adherence problems. In HIV care settings, it may be most prudent to assume that *all* patients are vulnerable to adherence problems. Because of the complexities of combination therapy regimens and because many patients come from disadvantaged educational backgrounds, health education strategies should start at the onset of treatment (Wainberg & Cournos, 2000). Health care providers need to supply information about the nature of HIV treatment and its side effects, as well as both oral and written directions concerning daily pill taking schedules. In addition, providers should provide information about treatment efficacy, and a clear description of the potentially dire consequences of poor adherence (Laws, Wilson, Bowser, & Kerr, 2000).

Educational strategies alone are unlikely to be sufficient for most patients. Many HIV-infected individuals live in chaotic environments involving multiple stressors, including substance abuse, mental illness, or poverty. These multiple stressors, taken together with the demanding nature of HIV treatment regimens, suggest that a multimodal approach to adherence may be most appropriate. Behavioral strategies, including multiple reminders (e.g., daily pill boxes, daily checklists, watch alarms), self-management skills training, identification of common relapse triggers, and problem solving to facilitate integration of medication regimens into daily activities, are components that are likely to be useful when developing individually tailored adherence interventions (Rabkin & Chesney, 1999). Interventions should also help patients to use social support networks and to strengthen self-efficacy for following treatment plans because these factors have been identified as correlates of improved adherence (e.g., Catz et al., 2000).

Treatment adherence may be improved by training providers in effective communication skills to improve adherence; developing integrative teams of care providers that are accessible to patients; and encouraging providers (e.g., physicians, pharmacists) to provide flexible patient scheduling and easier access to prescriptions (see Kelly, Otto-Salaj, et al., 1998). Many persons living with HIV require care for other life circumstances. Providers must be trained to recognize and address life-circumstances that can interfere with adherence. Providing support and appropriate referral services for patients struggling with problems such as substance abuse or recurring psychiatric illness, as well as more basic needs concerning housing, child care, or financial problems, can reduce barriers to good treatment adherence and serve to strengthen patient provider relationships. Unfortunately, the provision of multidisciplinary care services to promote adherence may only be feasible in large, well-funded HIV care centers.

Risk-Reduction among Persons Living with HIV

Improvements in HIV care have led to a decline in AIDS-related deaths, but rates of new infections have remained stable in recent years. As the population of HIV-positive men and women grows, and as some with HIV disease continue to experience improvements in health, attention must increasingly be directed toward the sexual behavior and drug use practices among infected persons. Although many persons living with HIV do practice safer sex and refrain from risky sexual behaviors, studies of gay men (Kalichman, Kelly, & Rompa, 1997; Vanable, Ostrow, McKirnan, Taywaditep, & Hope, 2000), injection drug users (Bluthenthal, Kral, Gee,

Erringer, & Edlin, 2000), and patients recruited through HIV clinics (De Rosa & Marks, 1998) indicate that at least 30% of persons living with HIV engage in risky behaviors.

Sexual risk behavior among persons living with HIV are of obvious public health concern in terms of the risks such behavior poses to people who are not yet infected. An increasing concern, however, is that HIV-infected patients, especially those who develop multiple drug resistances to HIV combination therapies, may then transmit drug-resistant HIV strains to others through unprotected sex or needle sharing. Transmission of treatment resistant strains of HIV through sexual or drug use behaviors is still the subject of ongoing study, but initial reports suggests such transmission is possible (Hecht, 1998). Besides posing an alarming risk to uninfected partners, the possibility of drug resistant strains of HIV being transmitted through sexual or drug use practices is also of concern for HIV-positive individuals, in that HIV "reinfection" with a treatment resistant strain of HIV would likely contribute to poor treatment outcomes.

Paradoxically, the availability of improved HIV treatments may actually be eroding commitment to safer sex due to the belief that AIDS is no longer the dire health threat it had been (Kelly, Hoffmann, Rompa, & Gray, 1998). Such concerns may be particularly relevant to persons living with HIV because they have had more direct experience with the newer therapies. In a study involving HIV-positive and HIV-negative gay men in Chicago (Vanable et al., 2000), a full 27% of respondents endorsed agreement with one or more items reflecting reduced concern about HIV due to new treatments. In addition, respondents perceived the risk of HIV transmission as lower in hypothetical scenarios describing unprotected sex with an HIV-positive partner with undetectable viral loads, relative to scenarios in which a seropositive partner had not been taking combination treatments. More important in terms of prevention implications, reduced HIV concern was associated most strongly with sexual risk taking (unprotected anal sex) among HIV-positive participants, suggesting that the availability of combination treatments has had a greater impact on the sexual behavior of men living with HIV.

Such overly optimistic beliefs regarding the effectiveness of new treatments, coupled with the prospect of behaviorally transmitted drug-resistant strains of HIV and more general concern for reducing HIV transmission behaviors to uninfected men and women, point to the urgent need for HIV risk reduction interventions for persons living with HIV. To date, however, HIV risk-reduction interventions involving persons living with HIV have been quite limited. Research on HIV counseling and testing suggests that posttest counseling promotes short-term reductions in HIV risk behavior among newly infected men and women (Weinhardt et al., 1999), but other research reveals continued high risk behavior among persons with HIV (Kalichman, 2000). Taken together, these findings suggest that posttest counseling is not enough.

Given the importance of sexual and drug use practices among HIV-positive persons, it is surprising to note the relative paucity of intervention research involving persons living with HIV. Our review of the literature identified only one RCT designed to test specifically the effectiveness of a risk reduction intervention for HIV-positive men and women. This RCT involved 271 HIV-positive blood donors from New York City and tested the effectiveness of providing risk reduction information and emotional support (Cleary et al., 1995). Results indicated a general decline in sexual risk taking among all participants, but no clear advantage of the risk reduction intervention over the gains observed among control patients who were randomized to a community referral source.

Perhaps the most informative research on approaches to interventions for persons living with HIV comes from work originally developed to assist people with emotional adjustment and coping with HIV infection. For example, researchers in San Francisco conducted a stress management program for HIV-positive men in San Francisco that included relaxation training, systematic desensitization, physical exercise, and self-management training (Coates et al., 1989). Although risk reduction was not a primary goal of the intervention, participation in the program was associated with a reduction in participants' number of partners. Kelly et al. (1993) found similar effects in a support group study of depressed HIV-positive men. Participants were randomized to either an eight-session support group, an eight-session cognitive-behavioral intervention group, or a wait-list control group. The results indicated that participants who received the social support intervention reduced their frequency of unprotected receptive anal intercourse, relative to the other two groups. Taken together, these findings raise the possibility that HIV risk reduction counseling might be most beneficial if it is included within a broader array of mental health and psychosocial services for persons living with HIV.

In summary, continued high-risk sexual and drug use behavior among HIV-positive persons poses enormous health risks for uninfected men and women, as well as for those already infected with HIV. Because all new HIV infections originate with a person who is HIV-positive, the development of effective risk-reduction interventions for HIV-positive persons is arguably an extremely efficient means of reducing the occurrence of new infections. Risk-reduction interventions would also provide considerable benefits to those living with HIV by reducing the likelihood of contracting drug-resistant strains of HIV (as well as reducing the likelihood of coinfection with other STDs). Although physicians are likely to spend considerable time discussing the importance of consistent medication adherence, care providers should arguably direct equal attention to encouraging patients to avoid high-risk sexual and drug use practices. Likewise, behavioral scientists must devote increasing attention to the development and dissemination of empirically validated risk reduction interventions for HIV-infected persons. Multicomponent interventions that meld psychosocial support, adherence, and sexual risk reduction within HIV care settings may be a particularly promising direction for future research.

FUTURE DIRECTIONS

The past decade has seen tremendous activity for health psychologists who have conducted basic qualitative and correlational research; developed and refined theoretical models of risk behavior; and implemented and evaluated individual, small group, and community-level interventions. In this chapter, we focused our attention on applied research, specifically on research evaluating behavioral interventions for the primary and secondary prevention of HIV disease.

The intervention research has evaluated the effectiveness of a variety of theory-based interventions with a wide range of populations, including hard-to-access groups such as homeless adults, runaway youth, IDUs, and the severely mentally ill. Many large RCTs have been completed, and allow for strong inferences as they control for many threats to the internal validity of intervention studies. These RCTs have included multisite and international projects, which enhance the external validity of the findings. Methodologically, the field of psychosocial HIV/AIDS has advanced very quickly. Moreover, the research that has been completed has included unprecedented collaboration among patients, community-based advocates, and biomedical and social scientists.

Continuing Challenges and Future Directions

We expect that the impressive behavioral science commitment to HIV/AIDS that we have witnessed in the past decade will continue as health psychologists address a series of continuing challenges in research and practice. In this concluding section, we identify and discuss briefly the continuing challenges and future directions for research and practice related to HIV disease.

Integration of Biopsychosocial Approaches

We expect continued research to develop safe and effective vaccines and microbicides to prevent infection. This research

and the deployment of such biological prevention strategies will benefit from involvement of health psychologists to develop acceptable distribution and adherence strategies, and address beliefs and fears regarding the common perception that governments and scientists cannot be trusted. We also expect continued collaboration among biomedical and behavioral scientists and practitioners in the prevention and treatment of HIV disease.

We expect that greater use will be made of the teachable moments that occur in HIV C&T, STD, and primary care settings. In such settings, we expect increased use of brief screening measures (e.g., Gerbert et al., 1998) and time-limited interventions (Boekeloo et al., 1999; Kalichman, 1996). Advances in computer technology will make it easier for practitioners to offer such screening, and to make available brief, office-based interventions that require little professional time (through videotape, CD-ROM, DVD, and emerging technologies). Screening will also identify persons at high risk who are most likely to benefit from more intensive, face-to-face interventions that can be delivered by peer educators and health care providers. Such a system will be more accessible, affordable, and confidential, and increase the reach of such down- and midstream approaches.

Continued Collaboration with Community Leaders

The involvement of community leaders has been essential to the development and implementation of HIV interventions. Collaboration among community groups, practitioners, and scientists will continue. Community-based and other "grass roots" groups will increasingly demand a more powerful voice in planning and decision making regarding prevention and treatment trials. Community-based groups and health professionals need to continue what has been a productive and mutually rewarding relationship to disseminate effective interventions to community-based organizations (i.e., "technology transfer"). Health psychologists will seek to develop more effective and efficient methods of technology transfer (Kelly, Sogolow, & Neumann, 2000). There will be increased study of the problem of retaining participants in interventions without the use of incentives.

Development of New Intervention Models

We expect to see continued development of new intervention models, including brief interventions that target the theorized determinants of risk behavior change in the most direct and efficient manner. We also anticipate the development and refinement of theoretical models of HIV-related risk behaviors that attend more to interpersonal relationships, human sexuality, and intimacy. Such models will also reflect greater sensitivity to developmental, gender, and cultural considerations, and will guide the development of new intervention approaches.

Refined Assessment and Data Analysis

A continuing challenge will be how to *measure* risk behavior because self-report can be compromised by memory problems and demand characteristics. Investigators will need to refine existing measures, and identify a "gold standard" to establish the accuracy of self-report measures. For example, future efforts will likely try to demonstrate an empirical link between self-reported behavior change and appropriate biological markers (e.g., incident STDs). We also expect greater use of biological markers to determine the effectiveness of prevention programs. Also, because sexual and drug use behavior are notoriously difficult to *analyze,* health psychologists, working with behavioral- and biostatisticians, will develop and use data analytic approaches that are more appropriate to highly skewed count data that are common in risk behavior research (Schroder, Carey, & Vanable, in press).

Increased Use of Technology

Prevention programs will benefit from technological advances. As mentioned earlier, technology will be used to enhance efficiencies in traditional health care settings through computer-assisted screening, assessment, and patient education. The internet will be used to enhance access to HIV-related educational materials, social support, and medical care, especially to persons who have traditionally been isolated from such resources. We expect this to occur among geographically isolated persons but we also hope that this extends to the urban poor and to persons living in the developing world.

Sophisticated School-Based Programs

Given the rising salience of sexuality in all media (e.g., music television, motion pictures) and increasing reliance on science to guide policy making, we anticipate greater acceptance of science-based, sexual health curricula in public schools. We expect that this development will reduce the incidence of unintended pregnancies, HIV, and other STDs among adolescents and young adults.

Evaluation Will Improve

Although most published studies of prevention trials in top-tier journals have used control groups, often these have been "no-treatment" or "standard care" controls. We anticipate the use of stronger control groups (e.g., alternative HIV prevention programs), and greater use of components-analyzes and other fine-grained approaches to identify the most important components of effective interventions. Intervention research is also likely to employ longer follow-up evaluations, and to develop strategies that facilitate the long-term maintenance of the gains resulting from intensive risk reduction programs. The value of booster sessions, supplemental interventions, and media campaigns to establish norms supportive of behavior change will be studied further.

We expect that the reporting of intervention trials will continue to improve. For example, investigators will be required to report effect sizes as well as inferential statistics to gauge the magnitude of change and to reflect "clinical" as well as statistical significance. There will be increasing attention paid to the cost-effectiveness of interventions (e.g., Holtgrave, 1998).

HIV-Positive Persons Will Receive Greater Attention

There will be efforts to develop more effective secondary prevention programs for HIV-positive persons. As the number of persons living with HIV continues to grow, there will be tremendous opportunities for health psychologists to play an important role in improving the lives of persons living with HIV. Within HIV care settings, health psychologists will increasingly be called upon to provide direct services and consultation directed toward improving patient adherence to complex treatment regimens and helping patients to adapt to the many stressors associated with HIV disease. Behavioral scientists will also increasingly be called upon to provide effective interventions to reduce high-risk sexual and drug use practices among HIV-infected men and women. Secondary prevention research has been slow to develop relative to the advances seen in the area of HIV primary prevention. Nonetheless, the need for empirically validated intervention approaches for HIV-positive individuals must be balanced with the immediate urgency of implementing clinic-based interventions with HIV-positive individuals already in treatment and known to be struggling with behavioral issues such as adherence or sexual risk. With increasing research funding now being directed toward the development of innovative behavioral intervention approaches for HIV-positive men and women, we are optimistic that many innovations in secondary prevention will be reported and disseminated in the very near future.

Upstream Interventions Will Become More Common

An important challenge, especially for primary prevention, is the need to develop, implement, and evaluate upstream interventions. We expect to see more research on interventions that have a wider reach (e.g., media, internet) and, proportionately, less research on face-to-face interventions delivered to individuals or small groups. Because HIV disease occurs disproportionately among the economically disadvantaged, including racial and ethnic minorities, we expect that media efforts will be implemented widely in low-income communities.

Greater International Involvement

Health psychologists will continue their involvement in research and practice in the developing world (e.g., Gibney, DiClemente, & Vermund, 1999; Hearst, Mandel, & Coates, 1995; Kalichman, Kelly, et al., 2000). Increasingly, health psychologists and other behavioral scientists will serve as consultants and collaborators to national and international health agencies, nongovernmental organizations, foreign governments, or other organizations that work to reduce the risk of HIV infection, or improve the lives of HIV-infected persons outside of the United States, western Europe, and Australia.

CLOSING COMMENTS

How among us could have imagined the devastation that HIV has caused in the years between 1981 and 2000. That nearly 500,000 Americans and 19 million people worldwide would die, and 11 million children would become orphans because of AIDS—a disease that was not even recognized in 1980—would be unthinkable, except that these events have occurred.

From this sobering look at recent history, however, we look ahead with cautious optimism. This optimism is based on the unrelenting advocacy of concerned persons; the scientific community's commitment and creativity; and the unprecedented cooperation among patients, advocates, practitioners, and scientists—within and across national boundaries. Due to these contributions, we have witnessed remarkable advances in the primary and secondary prevention of HIV and AIDS during the past decade. Health psychologists have contributed generously to these advances, and we believe that they will continue to contribute in the future. Much work remains to be done, and much remains at stake.

REFERENCES

Alstead, M., Campsmith, M., Halley, C. S., Hartfield, K., Goldbaum, G., & Wood, R. W. (1999). Developing, implementing, and evaluating a condom promotion program targeting sexually active adolescents. *AIDS Education and Prevention, 11,* 497–512.

Andersen, R., Bozzette, S., Shapiro, M., St. Clair, P., Morton, S., Crystal, S., et al. (2000). Access of vulnerable groups to antiretroviral therapy among persons in care for HIV disease in the United States. *Health Services Research, 35,* 389–416.

Antoni, M. H., Baggett, L., Ironson, G., LaPerriere, A., August, S., Klimas, N., et al. (1991). Cognitive-behavioral stress management intervention buffers distress responses and immunologic changes following notification of HIV-1 seropositivity. *Journal of Consulting and Clinical Psychology, 59,* 906–915.

Antoni, M. H., Cruess, D. G., Cruess, S., Lutgendorf, S., Kumar, M., Ironson, G., et al. (2000). Cognitive-behavioral stress management intervention effects on anxiety, 24-hr urinary norepinephrine output, and T-cytotoxic/suppressor cells over time among symptomatic HIV-infected gay men. *Journal of Consulting and Clinical Psychology, 68,* 31–45.

Aversa, S. L., & Kimberlin, C. (1996). Psychosocial aspects of antiretroviral medication use among HIV patients. *Patient Education and Counseling, 29,* 207–219.

Avins, A. L., Lindan, C. P., Woods, W. J., Hudes, E. S., Boscarino, J. A., Kay, J., et al. (1997). Changes in HIV-related behaviors among heterosexual alcoholics following addiction treatment. *Drug and Alcohol Dependence, 10,* 47–55.

Bandura, A. (1986). *Social foundations of thought and action.* Englewood Cliffs, NJ: Prentice-Hall.

Bangsberg, D. R., Hecht, F. M., Charlebois, E. D., Zolopa, A. R., Holodniy, M., Sheiner, L., et al. (2000). Adherence to protease inhibitors, HIV-1 viral load, and development of drug resistance in an indigent population. *AIDS, 14,* 357–366.

Bangsberg, D. R., Tulsky, J. P., Hecht, F. M., & Moss, A. R. (1997). Protease inhibitors in the homeless. *Journal of the American Medical Association, 278,* 63–65.

Barre-Sinoussi, F., Chermann, J. C., Rey, F., Nugeyre, M. T., Chamaret, S., Gruest, J., et al. (1983). Isolation of a T-lymphotropic retrovirus from a patient at risk for acquired immune deficiency syndrome (AIDS). *Science, 220,* 868–871.

Belcher, L., Kalichman, S., Topping, M., Smith, S., Emshoff, J., Norris, F., et al. (1998). A randomized trial of a brief HIV risk reduction counseling intervention for women. *Journal of Consulting and Clinical Psychology, 66,* 856–861.

Bluthenthal, R. N., Kral, A. H., Gee, L., Erringer, E. A., & Edlin, B. R. (2000). The effect of syringe exchange use on high-risk injection drug users: A cohort study. *AIDS, 14,* 605–611.

Boekeloo, B. O., Schamus, L. A., Simmens, S. J., Cheng, T. L., O'Connor, K., & D'Angelo, L. J. (1999). A STD/HIV prevention trial among adolescents in managed care. *Pediatrics, 103,* 107–115.

Bogart, L. M., Catz, S., Kelly, J. A., Gray-Bernhardt, M. L., Hartmann, B. R., Otto-Salaj, L. L., et al. (2000). Psychosocial issues in the era of new AIDS treatments from the perspective of persons living with HIV. *Journal of Health Psychology, 5,* 489–507.

Brown, L. R. (2000, October). *HIV epidemic restructuring Africa's population.* Washington, DC: Worldwatch Institute (www.worldwatch.org).

Bruneau, J., Lamothe, F., Franco, E., Lachance, N., Desy, M., Soto, J., et al. (1997). High rates of HIV infection among injection drug users participating in needle exchange programs in Montreal: Results of a cohort study. *American Journal of Epidemiology, 146,* 994–1002.

Burack, J. H., Barrett, D. C., Stall, R. D., Chesney, M. A., Ekstrand, M. L., & Coates, T. J. (1993). Depressive symptoms and CD4 lymphocyte decline among HIV-infected men. *Journal of the American Medical Association, 270,* 2568–2573.

Carey, M. P., Braaten, L. S., Maisto, S. A., Gleason, J. R., Forsyth, A. D., Durant, L. E., et al. (2000). Using information, motivational enhancement, and skills training to reduce the risk of HIV infection for low-income urban women: A second randomized clinical trial. *Health Psychology, 19,* 3–11.

Carey, M. P., Carey, K. B., & Kalichman, S. C. (1997). Risk for human immunodeficiency virus (HIV) infection among adults with a severe mental disorder. *Clinical Psychology Review, 17,* 271–291.

Carey, M. P., Carey, K. B., Maisto, S. A., Gleason, J. R., Gordon, C. M., & Brewer, K. K. (1999). HIV-risk behavior among outpatients at a state psychiatric hospital: Prevalence and risk modeling. *Behavior Therapy, 30,* 389–406.

Carey, M. P., Carey, K. B., Maisto, S. A., Gordon, C. M., & Vanable, P. A. (2001). Prevalence and correlates of sexual activity and HIV-related risk behavior among psychiatric outpatients. *Journal of Consulting and Clinical Psychology, 69,* 846–850.

Carey, M. P., Maisto, S. A., Kalichman, S. C., Forsyth, A. D., Wright, E. M., & Johnson, B. T. (1997). Enhancing motivation to reduce the risk of HIV infection for economically disadvantaged urban women. *Journal of Consulting and Clinical Psychology, 65,* 531–541.

Carey, M. P., Weinhardt, L. S., & Carey, K. B. (1995). Prevalence of infection with HIV among the seriously mentally ill: Review of the research and implications for practice. *Professional Psychology: Research and Practice, 26,* 262–268.

Catz, S. L., & Kelly, J. A. (2001). Living with HIV disease. In A. Baum & J. Singer (Eds.), *Handbook of health psychology* (pp. 841–850). Hillsdale, NJ: Erlbaum.

Catz, S. L., Kelly, J. A., Bogart, L. M., Benotsch, E. G., & McAuliffe, T. L. (2000). Patterns, correlates, and barriers to medication adherence among persons prescribed new treatments for HIV disease. *Health Psychology, 19,* 124–133.

Celentano, D. D., Bond, K. C., Lyles, C. M., Eiumtrakul, S., Go, V. F., Beyrer, C., et al. (2000). Preventive intervention to reduce sexually transmitted infections: A field trial in the Royal Thai Army. *Archives of Internal Medicine, 160,* 535–540.

Celentano, D. D., Nelson, K. E., Lyles, C. M., Beyrer, C., Eiumtrakul, S., Go, V. F., et al. (1998). Decreasing incidence of HIV and sexually transmitted diseases in young Thai men: Evidence for success of the HIV/AIDS control and prevention program. *AIDS, 12,* F29–F36.

Centers for Disease Control and Prevention. (1997). *HIV/AIDS Surveillance Report, 9.* Atlanta, GA: Author.

Centers for Disease Control and Prevention. (1999). U.S. HIV and AIDS cases reported through June 1999. *HIV/AIDS Surveillance Report, 11.* Atlanta, GA: Author.

Centers for Disease Control and Prevention. (2000). *HIV prevention strategic plan through 2005.* Atlanta, GA: Author.

Chesney, M. A., Folkman, S., & Chambers, D. (1996). Coping effectiveness training for men living with HIV: Preliminary findings. *International Journal of STDs and AIDS, 7*(Suppl. 2), 75–82.

Chesney, M. A., Ickovics, J. R., Chambers, D. B., Gifford, A. L., Neidig, J., Zwickl, B., et al. (2000). Self-reported adherence to antiretroviral medications among participants in HIV clinical trials: The AACTG adherence instruments. *AIDS Care, 12,* 255–266.

Chesney, M. A., Ickovics, J., Hecht, F. M., Sikipa, G., & Rabkin, J. (1999). Adherence: A necessity for successful HIV combination therapy. *AIDS, 13,* S271–S278.

Cleary, P. D., Van Devanter, N., Steilen, M., Stuart, A., Shipton-Levy, R., McMullen, W., et al. (1995). A randomized trial of an education and support program for HIV-infected individuals. *AIDS, 9,* 1271–1278.

Coates, T. J., McKusick, L., Kuno, R., & Stites, D. P. (1989). Stress reduction training changed number of sexual partners but not immune function in men with HIV. *American Journal of Public Health, 79,* 885–887.

Cohen, C. J., Hellinger, J., & Norris, D. (2000). Evaluation of simplified protease inhibitor dosing regimens for the treatment of HIV infection. *AIDS Reader, 10,* 296–313.

Cole, S. W., Kemeny, M. E., & Taylor, S. E. (1997). Social identity and physical health: Accelerated HIV progression in rejection-sensitive gay men. *Journal of Personality and Social Psychology, 72,* 320–335.

Collier, A. C., Coombs, R. W., Schoenfeld, D. A., Bassett, R. L., Timpone, J., Baruch, A., et al. (1996). Treatment of human immunodeficiency virus infection with saquinavir, zidovudine, and zalcitabine. *New England Journal of Medicine, 334,* 1011–1017.

Coyle, K., Basen-Engquist, K., Kirby, D., Parcel, G., Banspach, S., Harrist, R., et al. (1999). Short-term impact of safer choices: A multicomponent, school-based HIV, other STD, and pregnancy prevention program. *Journal of School Health, 69,* 181–188.

Coyle, S. L., Needle, R. H., & Normand, J. (1998). Outreach-based HIV prevention for injecting drug users: A review of published outcome data. *Public Health Reports, 113*(Suppl. 1), 19–30.

De Rosa, C. J., & Marks, G. (1998). Preventive counseling of HIV-positive men and self-disclosure of serostatus to sex partners: New opportunities for prevention. *Health Psychology, 17,* 224–231.

Des Jarlais, D. C. (2000). Research, politics, and needle exchange. *American Journal of Public Health, 90,* 1392–1394.

Des Jarlais, D. C., Marmor, M., Paone, D., Titus, S., Shi, Q., Perlis, T., et al. (1996). HIV incidence among injecting drug users in New York City syringe-exchange programmes. *Lancet, 348,* 987–991.

Des Jarlais, D. C., Perlis, T., Friedman, S. R., Chapman, T., Kwok, J., Rockwell, R., et al. (2000). Behavioral risk reduction in a declining HIV epidemic: Injection drug users in New York City, 1990–1997. *American Journal of Public Health, 90,* 1112–1116.

Dornadula, G., Zhang, H., VanUitert, B., Stern, J., Livornese, L., Jr., Ingerman, M. J., et al. (1999). Residual HIV-1 RNA in blood plasma of patients taking suppressive highly active antiretroviral therapy. *Journal of the American Medical Association, 282,* 1627–1632.

Dubois-Arber, F., Jeannin, A., Konings, E., & Paccaud, F. (1997). Increased condom use without other major changes in sexual behavior among the general population in Switzerland. *American Journal of Public Health, 87,* 558–566.

Dubois-Arber, F., Jeannin, A., & Spencer, B. (1999). Long term global evaluation of a national AIDS prevention strategy: The case of Switzerland. *AIDS, 13,* 2571–2582.

Fatkenheuer, G., Theisen, A., Rockstroh, J., Grabow, T., Wicke, C., Becker, K., et al. (1997). Virological treatment failure of protease inhibitor therapy in an unselected cohort of HIV-infected patients. *AIDS, 11,* F113–F116.

Fischl, M. A., Richman, D. D., Grieco, M. H., Gottlieb, M. S., Volberding, P. A., Laskin, O. L., et al. (1987). The efficacy of azidothymidine (AZT) in the treatment of patients with AIDS and AIDS-related complex: A double-blind, placebo-controlled trial. *New England Journal of Medicine, 317,* 185–191.

Fishbein, M., & Middlestadt, S. E. (1989). Using the Theory of Reasoned Action as a framework for understanding and changing AIDS-related behaviors. In V. M. Mays, G. W. Albee, & S. F. Schneider (Eds.), *Primary prevention of AIDS: Psychological approaches* (pp. 93–110). Newbury Park, CA: Sage.

Fisher, J. D. (1988). Possible effects of reference group based social influence on AIDS-risk behaviors and AIDS. *American Psychologist, 43,* 914–920.

Fisher, J. D., & Fisher, W. A. (1992). Changing AIDS-risk behavior. *Psychological Bulletin, 111,* 455–474.

Folkman, S., & Chesney, M. (1991). Translating coping theory into intervention. In J. Eckenrode (Ed.), *The social context of stress* (pp. 239–260). New York: Plenum Press.

Gallo, R. C., Salahuddin, S. Z., Popovic, M., Shearer, G. M., Kaplan, M., Haynes, B. F., et al. (1984). Frequent detection and isolation of cytopathic retroviruses (HTLV-III) from patients with AIDS and at risk for AIDS. *Science, 224,* 500–503.

Gerbert, B., Bronstone, A., McPhee, S., Pantilat, S., & Allerton, M. (1998). Development and testing of an HIV-risk screening instrument for use in health care settings. *American Journal of Preventive Medicine, 15,* 103–113.

Gibney, L., DiClemente, R. J., & Vermund, S. H. (Eds.). (1999). *Preventing HIV in developing countries: Biomedical and behavioral approaches.* New York: Kluwer Academic/Plenum Press.

Gulick, R. M., Mellors, J. W., Havlir, D., Eron, J. J., Gonzalez, C., McMahon, D., et al. (1997). Treatment with indinavir, zidovudine, and lamivudine in adults with human immunodeficiency virus infection and prior antiretroviral therapy. *New England Journal of Medicine, 337,* 734–739.

Hammer, S. M., Squires, K. E., Hughes, M. D., Grimes, J. M., Demeter, L. M., Currier, J. S., et al. (1997). A controlled trial of two nucleoside analogues plus indinavir in persons with human immunodeficiency virus infection and CD4 cell counts of 200 per cubic millimeter or less. *New England Journal of Medicine, 337,* 725–733.

Haynes, R. B., McKibbon, K. A., & Kanani, R. (1996). Systematic review of randomized trials of interventions to assist patients to follow prescriptions for medications. *Lancet, 348,* 383–386.

Hays, R. B., & Kegeles, S. M. (1999). Factors related to the willingness of young gay men to participate in preventive HIV vaccine trials. *Journal of Acquired Immune Deficiency Syndrome and Human Retrovirology, 20,* 164–171.

Hearst, N., Mandel, J. S., & Coates, T. J. (1995). Collaborative AIDS prevention research in the developing world: The CAPS experience. *AIDS, 9*(Suppl. 1), S1–S5.

Hecht, F. M., Grant, R. M., Petropoulos, C. J., Dillon, B., Chesney, M. A., Tian, H., et al. (1998). Sexual transmission of an HIV-1 variant resistant to multiple reverse-transcriptase and protease inhibitors. *New England Journal of Medicine, 339,* 307–311.

Heimer, R., Kaplan, E. H., Khoshnood, K., Jariwala, B., & Cadman, E. C. (1993). Needle exchange decreases the prevalence of HIV-1 proviral DNA in returned syringes in New Haven, Connecticut. *American Journal of Medicine, 95,* 14–20.

Herek, G. M. (1999). AIDS and stigma. *American Behavioral Scientist, 42,* 1106–1116.

Ho, D. D., Neumann, A. U., Perelson, A. S., Chen, W., Leonard, J. M., & Markowitz, M. (1995). Rapid turnover of plasma virions and CD4 lymphocytes in HIV-1 infection. *Nature, 373,* 123–126.

Holtgrave, D. R. (Ed.). (1998). *Handbook of economic evaluation of HIV prevention programs.* New York: Plenum Press.

Holtgrave, D. R., & Pinkerton, S. D. (1997). Updates of cost of illness and quality of life estimates for use in economic evaluations of HIV prevention programs. *Journal of Acquired Immune Deficiency Syndromes, 16,* 54–62.

Jemmott, J. B., Jemmott, L. S., & Fong, G. T. (1992). Reductions in HIV risk-associated sexual behaviors among Black male adolescents: Effects of an AIDS prevention intervention. *American Journal of Public Health, 82,* 372–377.

Jemmott, J. B., Jemmott, L. S., & Fong, G. T. (1998). Abstinence and safer sex HIV risk-reduction interventions for African American adolescents: A randomized controlled trial. *Journal of the American Medical Association, 279,* 1529–1536.

Kalichman, S. C. (1996). HIV-AIDS prevention videotapes: A review of empirical findings. *Journal of Primary Prevention, 17,* 259–279.

Kalichman, S. C. (1998). *Understanding AIDS.* Washington, DC: American Psychological Association.

Kalichman, S. C. (2000). HIV transmission risk behaviors of men and women living with HIV-AIDS: Prevalence, predictors, and emerging clinical interventions. *Clinical Psychology: Science and Practice, 7,* 32–47.

Kalichman, S. C., Carey, M. P., & Johnson, B. T. (1996). Prevention of sexually transmitted HIV infection: A meta-analytic review of the behavioral outcome literature. *Annals of Behavioral Medicine, 18,* 6–15.

Kalichman, S. C., & Catz, S. L. (2000). Stressors in HIV infection. In K. H. Nott & K. Vedhara (Eds.), *Psychosocial and biomedical interactions in HIV infection: HIV infection and stress* (pp. 31–60). New York: Harwood.

Kalichman, S. C., Kelly, J. A., & Rompa, D. (1997). Continued high-risk sex among HIV seropositive gay and bisexual men seeking HIV prevention services. *Health Psychology, 16,* 369–373.

Kalichman, S. C., Kelly, J. A., Sikkema, K. J., Koslov, A. P., Shaboltas, A., & Granskaya, J. (2000). The emerging AIDS crisis in Russia: Review of enabling factors and prevention needs. *International Journal of STDs and AIDS, 11,* 71–75.

Kalichman, S. C., Ramachandran, B., & Catz, S. (1999). Adherence to combination antiretroviral therapies in HIV patients of low health literacy. *Journal of General Internal Medicine, 14,* 267–273.

Kalichman, S. C., Rompa, D., & Coley, B. (1996). Experimental component analysis of a behavioral HIV-AIDS prevention intervention for inner-city women. *Journal of Consulting and Clinical Psychology, 64,* 687–693.

Kalichman, S. C., Sikkema, K. J., Kelly, J. A., & Bulto, M. (1995). Use of a brief behavioral skills intervention to prevent HIV infection among chronic mentally ill adults. *Psychiatric Services, 46,* 275–280.

Kamb, M. L., Fishbein, M., Douglas, J. M., Rhodes, F., Rogers, J., Bolan, G., et al. (1998). Efficacy of risk-reduction counseling to prevent human immunodeficiency virus and sexually transmitted diseases—a randomized controlled trial. *Journal of the American Medical Association, 280,* 1161–1167.

Kegeles, S. M., Hays, R. B., & Coates, T. J. (1996). The Mpowerment Project: A community-level HIV prevention intervention for young gay men. *American Journal of Public Health, 86,* 1129–1136.

Kelly, J. A. (1995). *Changing HIV risk behavior: Practical strategies.* New York: Guilford.

Kelly, J. A., Hoffmann, R. G., Rompa, D., & Gray, M. (1998). Protease inhibitor combination therapies and perceptions gay men regarding AIDS severity and the need to maintain safer sex. *AIDS, 12,* F91–F95.

Kelly, J. A., McAuliffe, T. L., Sikkema, K. J., Murphy, D. A., Somlai, A. M., Mulry, G., et al. (1997). Reduction in risk behavior among adults with severe mental illness who learned to advocate for HIV prevention. *Psychiatric Services, 48,* 1283–1288.

Kelly, J. A., Murphy, D. A., Bahr, G. R., Kalichman, S. C., Morgan, M. G., Stevenson, L. Y., et al. (1993). Outcome of cognitive-behavioral and support group brief therapies for depressed, HIV-infected persons. *American Journal of Psychiatry, 150,* 1679–1686.

Kelly, J. A., Murphy, D. A., Sikkema, K. J., McAuliffe, T. L., Roffman, R. A., Solomon, L. J., et al. (1997). Randomised, controlled, community-level HIV-prevention intervention for sex-risk behaviour among homosexual men in US cities. *Lancet, 350,* 1500–1506.

Kelly, J. A., Murphy, D. A., Washington, C. D., Wilson, T. S., Koob, J. J., Davis, D. R., et al. (1994). The effects of HIV/AIDS intervention groups for high-risk women in urban clinics. *American Journal of Public health, 84,* 1918–1922.

Kelly, J. A., Otto-Salaj, L. L., Sikkema, K. J., Pinkerton, S. D., & Bloom, F. R. (1998). Implications of HIV treatment advances for behavioral research on AIDS: Protease inhibitors and new challenges in HIV secondary prevention. *Health Psychology, 17,* 310–319.

Kelly, J. A., St. Lawrence, J. S., Diaz, Y. E., Stevenson, L. Y., Hauth, A. C., Brasfield, T. L., Kalichman, S. C., et al. (1991). HIV risk behavior reduction following intervention with key opinion leaders of population: An experimental analysis. *American Journal of Public Health, 81,* 168–171.

Kelly, J. A., St. Lawrence, J. S., Hood, H. V., & Brasfield, T. L. (1989). Behavioral intervention to reduce AIDS risk activities. *Journal of Consulting and Clinical Psychology, 57,* 60–67.

Kelly, J. A., St. Lawrence, J. S., Stevenson, L. Y., Hauth, A. C., Kalichman, S. C., Diaz, Y. E., et al. (1992). Community AIDS/HIV risk reduction: The effects of endorsements by popular people in three cities. *American Journal of Public Health, 82,* 1483–1489.

Kelly, J. A., Sogolow, E. D., & Neumann, M. S. (2000). Future directions and emerging issues in technology transfer between HIV prevention researchers and community-based service providers. *AIDS Education and Prevention, 12,* 126–141.

Kemeny, M. E., Weiner, H., Duran, R., Taylor, S. E., Visscher, B., & Fahey, J. L. (1995). Immune system changes after the death of a partner in HIV-positive gay men. *Psychosomatic Medicine, 57,* 547–554.

Kirby, D., & DiClemente, R. J. (1994). School-based interventions to prevent unprotected sex and HIV among adolescents. In R. J. DiClemente & J. L. Peterson (Eds.), *Preventing AIDS: Theories and methods of behavioral interventions* (pp. 117–139). New York: Plenum Press.

Klepp, K. I., Ndeki, S. S., Leshabari, M. T., Hannan, P. J., & Lyimo, B. A. (1997). AIDS education in Tanzania: Promoting risk reduction among primary school children. *American Journal of Public Health, 87,* 1931–1936.

Kobayashi, J. S. (1997). The evolution of adjustment issues in HIV/AIDS. *Bulletin of the Menninger Clinic, 61,* 146–188.

Koblin, B. A., Heagerty, P., Sheon, A., Buchbinder, S., Celum, C., Douglas, J. M., et al. (1998). Readiness of high-risk populations in the HIV Network for Prevention Trials to participate in HIV vaccine efficacy trials in the United States. *AIDS, 12,* 785–793.

Larder, B. A., & Kemp, S. D. (1989). Multiple mutations in HIV-1 reverse transcriptase confer high-level resistance to zidovudine (AZT). *Science, 246,* 1155–1158.

Last, J. M. (1995). *A dictionary of epidemiology* (3rd ed.). New York: Oxford University.

Latkin, C. A. (1998). Outreach in natural settings: The use of peer leaders for HIV prevention among injecting drug users' networks. *Public Health Reports, 113*(Suppl. 1), 151–159.

Laws, M. B., Wilson, I. B., Bowser, D. M., & Kerr, S. E. (2000). Taking antiretroviral therapies for HIV infection: Learning from patient's stories. *Journal of General Internal Medicine, 15,* 848–858.

Leserman, J., Jackson, E. D., Petitto, J. M., Golden, R. N., Silva, S. G., Perkins, D. O., et al. (1999). Progression to AIDS: The effects of stress, depressive symptoms, and social support. *Psychosomatic Medicine, 61,* 397–406.

Low-Beer, S., Chan, K., Yip, B., Wood, E., Montaner, J. S., O'Shaughnessy, M. V., et al. (2000). Depressive symptoms decline among persons on HIV protease inhibitors. *Journal of Acquired Immune Deficiency Syndromes, 23,* 295–301.

Lui, K. J., Darrow, W. W., & Rutherford, G. W. D. (1988). A model-based estimate of the mean incubation period for AIDS in homosexual men. *Science, 240,* 1333–1335.

Malow, R. M., Baker, S. M., Klimas, N., Antoni, M. H., Schneiderman, N., Penedo, F. J., et al. (1998). Adherence to complex combination antiretroviral therapies by HIV-positive drug abusers. *Psychiatric Services, 49,* 1021–1024.

Mayer, K. H. (1999). Combination antiretroviral chemotherapy: Shifting paradigms and evolving praxis. In D. G. Ostrow & S. C. Kalichman (Eds.), *Psychosocial and public health impacts of new HIV therapies* (pp. 1–26). New York: Kluwer Academic/Plenum Press.

McKinlay, J. B. (1995). The new public health approach to improving physical activity and autonomy in older populations. In E. Heikkinen, J. Kuusinen, & I. Ruoppila (Eds.), *Preparation for aging* (pp. 87–103). New York: Plenum Press.

Metzger, D. S., Navaline, H., & Woody, G. E. (1998). Drug abuse treatment as AIDS prevention. *Public Health Reports, 113*(Suppl. 1), 97–106.

Metzler, C. W., Biglan, A., Noell, J., Ary, D. V., & Ochs, L. (2000). A randomized controlled trial of a behavioral intervention to reduce high-risk sexual behavior among adolescents in STD clinics. *Behavior Therapy, 31,* 27–54.

Montaner, J. S., Reiss, P., Cooper, D., Vella, S., Harris, M., Conway, B., et al. (1998). A randomized, double-blind trial comparing combinations of nevirapine, didanosine, and zidovudine for HIV-infected patients. *Journal of the American Medical Association, 279,* 930–937.

Moss, A. R., & Bacchetti, P. (1989). Natural history of HIV infection. *AIDS, 3,* 55–61.

Mostashari, F., Riley, E., Selwyn, P. A., & Altice, F. L. (1998). Acceptance and adherence with antiretroviral therapy among HIV-infected women in a correctional facility. *Journal of Acquired Immune Deficiency Syndromes and Human Retrovirology, 18,* 341–348.

National Institute of Mental Health. (1998). The NIMH Multisite HIV Prevention Trial: Reducing HIV sexual risk behavior. *Science, 280,* 1889–1894.

Needle, R. H., Coyle, S. L., Normand, J., Lambert, E., & Cesari, H. (1998). HIV prevention with drug-using populations: Current status and future prospects: Introduction and overview. *Public Health Reports, 113*(Suppl. 1), 4–15.

Nelson, K. E., Celentano, D. D., Eiumtrakol, S., Hoover, D. R., Beyrer, C., Suprasert, S., et al. (1996). Changes in sexual behavior and a decline in HIV infection among young men in Thailand. *New England Journal of Medicine, 335,* 297–303.

Ostrow, D. G., Joseph, J. G., Kessler, R., Soucy, J., Tal, M., Eller, M., et al. (1989). Disclosure of HIV antibody status: Behavioral and mental health correlates. *AIDS Education and Prevention, 1,* 1–11.

Palella, F. J., Jr., Delaney, K. M., Moorman, A. C., Loveless, M. O., Fuhrer, J., Satten, G. A., et al. (1998). Declining morbidity and mortality among patients with advanced human immunodeficiency virus infection. HIV Outpatient Study Investigators. *New England Journal of Medicine, 338,* 853–860.

Paterson, D. L., Swindells, S., Mohr, J., Brester, M., Vergis, E. N., Squier, C., et al. (2000). Adherence to protease inhibitor therapy and outcomes in patients with HIV infection. *Annals of Internal Medicine, 133,* 21–30.

Prochaska, J. O., DiClemente, C. C., & Norcross, J. C. (1992). In search of how people change: Applications to addictive behaviors. *American Psychologist, 47,* 1102–1114.

Rabkin, J. G., & Chesney, M. (1999). Treatment adherence to HIV medications: The achilles heel of the new therapies. In D. G. Ostrow & S. C. Kalichman (Eds.), *Psychosocial and public health impacts of new HIV therapies* (pp. 61–79). New York: Kluwer Academic/Plenum.

Rabkin, J. G., & Ferrando, S. J. (1997). A "second life" agenda: Psychiatric research issues raised by protease inhibitor treatments for people with the human immunodeficiency virus or the acquired immunodeficiency syndrome. *Archives of General Psychiatry, 54,* 1049–1053.

Rabkin, J. G., Ferrando, S. J., Lin, S. H., Sewell, M., & McElhiney, M. (2000). Psychological effects of HAART: A 2-year study. *Psychosomatic Medicine, 62,* 413–422.

Rabkin, J. G., Goetz, R. R., Remien, R. H., Williams, J. B., Todak, G., & Gorman, J. M. (1997). Stability of mood despite HIV illness progression in a group of homosexual men. *American Journal of Psychiatry, 154,* 231–238.

Rabkin, J. G., Wagener, G., & Rabkin, R. (1996). Treatment of depression in HIV+ men: Literature review and report of an ongoing study of testosterone replacement therapy. *Annals of Behavioral Medicine, 18,* 24–29.

Rabkin, J. G., Williams, J. B., Remien, R. H., Goetz, R., Kertzner, R., & Gorman, J. M. (1991). Depression, distress, lymphocyte subsets, and human immunodeficiency virus symptoms on two occasions in HIV-positive homosexual men. *Archives of General Psychiatry, 48,* 111–119.

Rapiti, E., Porta, D., Forastiere, F., Fusco, D., & Perucci, C. A. (2000). Socioeconomic status and survival of persons with AIDS before and after the introduction of highly active antiretroviral therapy. *Epidemiology, 11,* 496–501.

Reed, G. M., Kemeny, M. E., Taylor, S. E., & Visscher, B. R. (1999). Negative HIV-specific expectancies and AIDS-related bereavement as predictors of symptom onset in asymptomatic HIV-positive gay men. *Health Psychology, 18,* 354–363.

Richman, D. D., Fischl, M. A., Grieco, M. H., Gottlieb, M. S., Volberding, P. A., Laskin, O. L., et al. (1987). The toxicity of azidothymidine (AZT) in the treatment of patients with AIDS and AIDS-related complex: A double-blind, placebo-controlled trial. *New England Journal of Medicine, 317,* 192–197.

Rogers, E. M. (1983). *Diffusion of innovations* (3rd ed.). New York: Free Press.

Rogers, R. W. (1983). Cognitive and physiological processes in fear appeals and attitude change: A revised theory of protection motivation. In J. T. Cacioppo & R. E. Petty (Eds.), *Social psychology* (pp. 153–176). New York: Guilford Press.

Schroder, K. E. E., Carey, M. P., & Vanable, P. A. (in press). Methodological issues in the assessment and analysis of sexual risk behavior. I: Item content and scaling. *Annals of Behavioral Medicine,* 10–56.

Shapiro, M. F., Morton, S. C., McCaffrey, D. F., Senterfitt, J. W., Fleishman, J. A., Perlman, J. F., et al. (1999). Variations in the care of HIV-infected adults in the United States: Results from the HIV Cost and Services Utilization Study. *Journal of the American Medical Association, 281,* 2305–2315.

Sikkema, K. J., & Kelly, J. A. (1996). Behavioral medicine interventions can improve the quality-of-life and health of persons with HIV disease. *Annals of Behavioral Medicine 18,* 40–48.

Sikkema, K. J., Kelly, J. A., Winett, R. A., Solomon, L. J., Cargill, V. A., Roffman, R. A., et al. (2000). Outcomes of a randomized community-level HIV prevention intervention for women living in 18 low-income housing developments. *American Journal of Public Health, 90,* 57–63.

St. Lawrence, J. S., Brasfield, T. L., Jefferson, K. W., Alleyne, E., O'Bannon, R. E., & Shirley, A. (1995). Cognitive-behavioral intervention to reduce African American adolescents' risk for HIV infection. *Journal of Consulting and Clinical Psychology, 63,* 221–237.

Stanton, B. F., Li, X., Ricardo, I., Galbraith, J., Feigelman, S., & Kaljee, L. (1996). A randomized, controlled effectiveness trial of an AIDS prevention program for low-income African-American youths. *Archives of Pediatrics and Adolescent Medicine, 150,* 363–372.

Stein, M. D., Rich, J. D., Maksad, J., Chen, M. H., Hu, P., Sobota, M., et al. (2000). Adherence to antiretroviral therapy among HIV-infected methadone patients: Effect of ongoing illicit drug use. *American Journal of Drug and Alcohol Abuse, 26,* 195–205.

Strathdee, S. A., Patrick, D. M., Currie, S. L., Cornelisse, P. G., Rekart, M. L., Montaner, J. S., et al. (1997). Needle exchange is not enough: Lessons from the Vancouver injecting drug use study. *AIDS, 11,* F59–F65.

Vanable, P. A., Ostrow, D. G., McKirnan, D. J., Taywaditep, K. J., & Hope, B. A. (2000). Impact of combination therapies on HIV risk perceptions and sexual risk among HIV-positive and HIV-negative gay and bisexual men. *Health Psychology, 19,* 134–145.

van Ameijden, E. J., van den Hoek, J. A., van Haastrecht, H. J., & Coutinho, R. A. (1992). The harm reduction approach and risk factors for human immunodeficiency virus (HIV) seroconversion in injecting drug users, Amsterdam. *American Journal of Epidemioliology, 15,* 236–243.

Vlahov, D. (2000). The role of epidemiology in needle exchange programs. *American Journal of Public Health, 90,* 1395–1396.

Voluntary HIV-1 Counselling and Testing Efficacy Study Group. (2000). Efficacy of voluntary HIV-1 counselling and testing in individuals and couples in Kenya, Tanzania, and Trinidad: A randomized trial. *Lancet, 356,* 103–112.

Wainberg, M. L., & Cournos, F. (2000). Adherence to treatment. In F. Cournos & M. Forstein (Eds.), *New directions for mental health services* (pp. 85–93). San Francisco: Jossey-Bass.

Walter, H. J., & Vaughan, R. D. (1993). AIDS risk reduction among a multiethnic sample of urban high school students. *Journal of the American Medical Association, 270,* 725–730.

Weidle, P. J., Ganera, C. E., Irwin, K. L., McGowan, J. P., Ernst, J. A., Olivo, N., et al. (1999). Adherence to antiretroviral medications in an inner-city population. *Journal of Acquired Immune Deficiency Syndromes, 22,* 498–502.

Weinhardt, L. S., Carey, M. P., Carey, K. B., & Verdecias, R. N. (1998). Increasing assertiveness skills to reduce HIV risk among women living with a severe and persistent mental illness. *Journal of Consulting and Clinical Psychology, 66,* 680–684.

Weinhardt, L. S., Carey, M. P., Johnson, B. T., & Bickham, N. L. (1999). Effects of HIV counseling and testing on sexual risk behavior: A meta-analytic review of the published research, 1985–1997. *American Journal of Public Health, 89,* 1397–1405.

Wiebel, W. W., Jimenez, A., Johnson, W., Ouellet, L., Jovanovic, B., Lampinen, T., et al. (1996). Risk behavior and HIV seroincidence among out-of-treatment injection drug users: A four-year prospective study. *Journal of Acquired Immune Deficiency Syndrome and Human Retroviruses, 12,* 282–289.

CHAPTER 11

Headaches

FRANK ANDRASIK AND SUSAN E. WALCH

Headache is a clinical syndrome affecting over 90% of the population at some time during their life, resulting in it being considered a major public health issue (Mannix, 2001). It is the seventh leading presenting complaint in ambulatory care in the United States, accounting for about 18 million office visits a year (Barrett, 1996). The impact of headache is considerable. For example, it accounts for over 100 million bedridden days per year, costs U.S. employers over $13 billion per year, and significantly decreases quality of life, much more so than many other chronic illnesses (Mannix, 2001). Although most headaches are relatively benign, for 1% to 3% of patients the etiology can be life-threatening (Evans, 2001). Consequently, nonphysician practitioners are urged to refer all headache patients to a physician who is experienced with evaluating headache and then to maintain a close collaboration during treatment as necessary. Even after arranging a medical evaluation, the nonphysician therapist must be continually alert for evidence of a developing underlying physical problem. Table 11.1 lists some "danger signs" that may suggest a need for immediate referral to a physician.

This chapter focuses chiefly on the two headache types most likely to be seen by nonmedical practitioners—migraine, experienced by about 18% of females and 7% of males, and tension-type headache, experienced by about 40% of the population (Mannix, 2001), but provides brief attention to other forms of headache likely to be encountered in practice. We first address classification and diagnosis, as well as pertinent measurement issues. The remainder of the chapter is devoted to treatment, both pharmacological and behavioral. Behavioral treatment begins with a brief overview of the biobehavioral model of headache. It then focuses on the most common approaches (relaxation, biofeedback, and cognitive behavioral therapy) and factors to consider when planning and administering treatment. The chapter closes with a brief summary and identification of directions for further study.

HEADACHE CLASSIFICATION AND DIAGNOSIS

Classification and diagnosis are important for guiding treatment (particularly medical), identifying subtypes that present special challenges or that should be referred for care elsewhere, and characterizing client samples clearly for research investigations (one of the efficacy criteria established by the initial task force on empirically validated/supported treatments) (Task Force on Promotion and Dissemination of Psychological Procedures, 1995).

In 1985, the International Headache Society (IHS) assembled headache experts from around the world to enumerate the various types and subtypes of headache and to develop explicit inclusion and exclusion diagnostic criteria (as the

TABLE 11.1 "Danger Signs" in Headache Pain Patients That May Suggest the Need for Immediate Referral to a Physician

1. Headache is a new symptom for the individual in the past three months, or the nature of the headache has changed markedly in the past three months.
2. Presence of any sensory or motor deficits preceding or accompanying headache other than the typical visual prodromata of migraine with aura. Examples include weakness or numbness in an extremity, twitching of the hands or feet, aphasia, or slurred speech.
3. Headache is one sided and has always been on the same side of the head.
4. Headache is due to trauma, especially if it follows a period of unconsciousness (even if only momentary).
5. Headache is constant and unremitting.
6. For a patient reporting tension-type headache-like symptoms:
   a. Pain intensity has been steadily increasing over a period of weeks to months with little or no relief.
   b. Headache is worse in the morning and becomes less severe during the day.
   c. Headache is accompanied by vomiting.
7. Patient has been treated for any kind of cancer and now has a complaint of headache.
8. Patient or significant other reports a noticeable change in personality or behavior or a notable decrease in memory or other intellectual functioning.
9. The patient is over 60 years of age, and the headache is a relatively new complaint.
10. Pain onset is sudden and occurs during conditions of exertion (such as lifting heavy objects), sexual intercourse, or "heated" interpersonal situation.
11. Patient's family has a history of cerebral aneurysm, other vascular anomalies, or polycystic kidneys.

Source: From Andrasik and Baskin (1987), page 327. Copyright 1987 Plenum Press. Reprinted by permission. List developed in consultation with Lawrence D. Rodichok, M.D. Diagnoses have been modified to be compatible with the classification system developed by the International Headache Society (IHS) Headache Classification Committee (1988).

TABLE 11.2 Classification of Headache

1. Migraine.
   1.1 Migraine without aura.
   1.2 Migraine with aura.
   1.3 Childhood periodic syndromes that may be precursors to or associated with migraine.
2. Tension-type headache.
   2.1 Episodic tension-type headache.
      2.1.1 Episodic tension-type headache associated with disorder of pericranial muscles.
      2.1.2 Episodic tension-type-headache unassociated with disorder of pericranial muscles.
   2.2 Chronic tension-type headache.
      2.2.1 Chronic tension-type headache associated with disorder of pericranial muscles.
      2.2.2 Chronic tension-type headache unassociated with disorder of pericranial muscles.
3. Cluster headache and chronic paroxysmal hemicrania.
   3.1 Cluster headache.
      3.1.1 Cluster headache periodicity undetermined.
      3.1.2 Episodic cluster headache.
      3.1.3 Chronic cluster headache.
4. Miscellaneous headaches unassociated with structural lesion.
5. Headache associated with head trauma.
   5.1 Acute posttraumatic headache.
      5.1.1 with significant head trauma and/or confirmatory signs.
      5.1.2 with minor head trauma and no confirmatory signs.
   5.2 Chronic posttraumatic headache.
      5.2.1 with significant head trauma and/or confirmatory signs.
      5.2.2 with minor head trauma and/or confirmatory signs.
6. Headache associated with vascular disorders.
7. Headache associated with nonvascular intracranial disorder.
8. Headache associated with substances or their withdrawal.
   8.1 Headache induced by acute substance use or exposure.
      8.1.1 Nitrate/nitrite-induced headache.
      8.1.2 Monosodium glutamate-induced headache.
      8.1.3 Carbon monoxide-induced headache.
      8.1.4 Alcohol-induced headache.
      8.1.5 Other substances.
   8.2 Headache induced by chronic substance use or exposure.
      8.2.1 Ergotamine induced headache.
      8.2.2 Analgesics abuse headache.
      8.2.3 Other substances.
   8.3 Headache from substance withdrawal (acute use).
      8.3.1 Alcohol withdrawal headache (hangover).
      8.3.2 Other substances.
   8.4 Headache from substance withdrawal (chronic use).
      8.4.1 Ergotamine withdrawal headache.
      8.4.2 Caffeine withdrawal headache.
      8.4.3 Narcotics abstinence headache.
      8.4.4 Other substances.
   8.5 Headache associated with substances but with uncertain mechanism.
      8.5.1 Birth control pills or estrogens.
      8.5.2 Other substances.
9. Headache associated with noncephalic infection.
10. Headache associated with metabolic disorder.
11. Headache or facial pain associated with disorder of cranium, neck, eyes, ears, nose, sinuses, teeth, mouth, or other facial or cranial structures.
12. Cranial neuralgias, nerve trunk pain, and deafferentation pain.
13. Headache nonclassifiable.

Source: From the International Headache Society (IHS) Headache Classification Committee (1988), pp. 13–17. The Norwegian University Press.

prior system was inexplicit and outdated). Their recommendations were published in 1988 (International Headache Society Headache Classification Committee), and have since been endorsed by all national headache societies within IHS, the World Federation of Neurology, and the World Health Organization for inclusion in *ICD-10* (see Olesen, 2000, for further discussion). Thirteen different categories resulted (see Table 11.2), with categories 1, 2, 3 (termed primary headache disorders), 5 and 8 (termed secondary headaches) being the most likely to present for treatment to behaviorally oriented pain specialists. Diagnostic criteria for these five categories are listed in Table 11.3 (International Headache Society Headache Classification Committee, 1988). It is not uncommon for migraine and tension-type headache to coexist within the same individual and to warrant separate diagnoses (which in the past had been termed variously mixed headache, tension-vascular headache, or combination headache).

Migraine has been found to be much more complex and multidetermined than previously thought. In addition to the

TABLE 11.3 Headache Diagnostic Criteria

1.0 Migraine.

1.1 Migraine without aura.
  A. At least 5 attacks fulfilling B–D.
  B. Headache attacks lasting 4–72 hours (2–48 hours for children below age 15), untreated or unsuccessfully treated.
  C. Headache has at least two of the following characteristics:
    1. Unilateral location.
    2. Pulsating quality.
    3. Moderate or severe intensity (inhibits or prohibits daily activities).
    4. Aggravation by walking stairs or similar routine physical activity.
  D. During headache at least one of the following:
    1. Nausea and/or vomiting.
    2. Photophobia and phonophobia.
  E. At least one of the following:
    1. History, physical, and neurological examinations do not suggest one of the disorders listed in groups 5–11 (see Table 11.2).
    2. History and/or physical, and/or neurological examinations do suggest such disorder, but is ruled out by appropriate investigations.
    3. Such disorder is present, but migraine attacks do not occur for the first time in close temporal relation to the disorder.

1.2 Migraine with aura.
  A. At least two attacks fulfilling B.
  B. At least three of the following four characteristics:
    1. One or more fully reversible aura symptoms indicating focal cerebral cortical and/or brain stem dysfunction.
    2. At least one aura symptom develops gradually over more than 4 minutes or two or more symptoms occur in succession.
    3. No aura symptom lasts more than 60 minutes. If more than one aura symptom is present, accepted duration is proportionally increased.
    4. Headache follows with a free interval of less than 60 minutes. It may also begin before or simultaneously with the aura.
  C. Same as Migraine without aura, criteria E.

2.0 Tension-Type.

2.1 Episodic tension-type headache.
  A. At least 10 previous headache episodes fulfilling criteria B–D. Number of days with such headache < 180/year (< 15/month).
  B. Headache lasting from 30 minutes to 7 days.
  C. At least two of the following pain characteristics:
    1. Pressing/tightening (nonpulsating) quality.
    2. Mild or moderate intensity (may inhibit, but does not prohibit activities).
    3. Bilateral location.
    4. No aggravation by walking stairs or similar routine physical activity.
  D. Both of the following:
    1. No nausea or vomiting (anorexia may occur).
    2. Photophobia and phonophobia are absent, or one but not the other is present.
  E. Same as Migraine without aura, criteria E.

2.1.1 Episodic tension-type headache associated with disorder of pericranial muscles.
  A. Fulfills criteria for 2.1.
  B. At least one of the following:
    1. Increased tenderness of pericranial muscles demonstrated by manual palpation or pressure algometer.
    2. Increased EMG level of pericranial muscles at rest or during physiological tests.

2.1.2 Episodic tension-type headache unassociated with disorder of pericranial muscles.
  A. Fulfills criteria for 2.1.
  B. No increased tenderness of pericranial muscles. If studied, EMG of pericranial muscles shows normal levels of activity.

2.2 Chronic tension-type headache.
  A. Average headache frequency ≥15 days/month (180 days/year) for ≥6 months fulfilling criteria B–D listed below.

B. Same as criteria B, episodic tension type headache.
C. Both of the following:
  1. No vomiting.
  2. No more than one of the following: nausea, photophobia, or phonophobia.
D. Same as Migraine without aura, criteria E.

2.2.1 Chronic tension-type headache associated with disorder of pericranial muscles.
  A. Fulfills criteria for 2.2.
  B. Same as criteria B for 2.1.1.

2.2.2 Chronic tension-type headache unassociated with disorder of pericranial muscles.
  A. Fulfills criteria for 2.2.
  B. Same as criteria B for 2.1.2.

3.1 Cluster headache.
  A. At least five attacks fulfilling B–D.
  B. Severe unilateral orbital, supraorbital, and/or temporal pain lasting 15–180 minutes untreated.
  C. Headache is associated with at least one of the following signs which have to be present on the pain-side:
    1. Conjunctival injection.
    2. Lacrimation.
    3. Nasal congestion.
    4. Rhinorrhea.
    5. Forehead and facial sweating.
    6. Miosis.
    7. Ptosis.
    8. Eyelid edema.
  D. Frequency of attacks from one every other day to eight per day.
  E. Same as criteria E for 1.1.

5.2 Chronic posttraumatic headache
5.2.1 With significant head trauma and/or confirmatory signs.
  A. Significance of head trauma documented by at least one of the following:
    1. Loss of consciousness
    2. Posttraumatic amnesia lasting more than 10 minutes.
    3. At least two of the following exhibit relevant abnormality: clinical neurological examination, x-ray of skull, neuroimaging, evoked potentials, spinal fluid examination, vestibular function test, neuropsychological testing.
  B. Headache occurs less than 14 days after regaining consciousness (or after trauma, if there has been no loss of consciousness). Headache continues more than 8 weeks after regaining consciousness (or after trauma, if there has been no loss of consciousness).

5.2.2 With minor head trauma and no confirmatory signs.
  A. Head trauma that does not satisfy 5.2.1.A.
  B. Headache occurs less than 14 days after injury.
  C. Headache continues more than 8 weeks after injury.

8.2 Headache induced by chronic substance use or exposure.
  A. Occurs after daily doses of a substance for ≥ 3 months.
  B. A certain required minimum dose should be indicated.
  C. Headache is chronic (15 days or more a month).
  D. Headache disappears within 1 month after withdrawal of the substance.

8.2.1 Ergotamine-induced headache.
  A. Is preceded by daily ergotamine intake (oral ≥ 2 mg, rectal ≥ 1 mg).
  B. Is diffuse, pulsating, or distinguished from migraine by absent attack patterns and/or absent associated symptoms.

8.2.2 Analgesics abuse headache.
  A. One or more of the following:
    1. ≥50 g aspirin a month or equivalent of other mild analgesics.
    2. ≥100 tablets a month of analgesics combined with barbiturates or other nonnarcotic compounds.
    3. One or more narcotic analgesics.

Source: From the International Headache Society (IHS) Headache Classification Committee (1988). The Norwegian University Press.

peripheral vascular abnormalities once thought to be the key causal factor, research has shown that biochemical imbalances, neurotransmitter/receptor dysfunction, and neuronal suppression play pivotal roles as well (Olesen & Goadsby, 2000).

Tension-type headache has received a number of labels over the years (muscle contraction headache, psychogenic headache, depression headache, stress headache, conversion headache, psychomyogenic headache, and the like), which reflect the varied views and confusion about its etiology. The IHS classification committee proposed a four-group scheme to help investigators and clinicians sort out the role of various causative factors. Tension-type sufferers are now grouped on the basis of chronicity (episodic versus chronic), as this has been found to have a direct bearing on outcome, and the presence of identifiable muscle involvement (evidence of pericranial muscle tenderness upon palpation or elevated electromyographic readings versus the absence of this evidence), as the role of muscle contraction in this headache type has been questioned, resulting in a 2 × 2 classification table. This more expanded coding format asks diagnosticians to identify the most likely causative factors by specifying whether one or more of the following factors are present: oromandibular dysfunction, psychosocial stress, anxiety, depression, delusion, muscular stress, drug overuse, or other headache condition. Unfortunately, researchers have rarely used this level of precision when investigating pathophysiology of tension-type headache so progress has been slow at partialing out the role of the numerous suspected causes.

A new diagnostic entity that had not been formally recognized previously concerns "headaches associated with substances or their withdrawal." Although it had long been suspected that two types of medication commonly prescribed for headache patients, namely analgesics and ergotamine preparations, could lead to "rebound" headaches if overused (Horton & Macy, 1946), it was not until the 1980s that researchers began to take serious note of this fact (Kudrow, 1982; Saper, 1987). The term *rebound* refers both to the gradual worsening of the headache as the medication wears off and the extreme exacerbation that often accompanies abrupt discontinuation of the medication (withdrawal-like phenomenon). This sequence "seduces" patients into taking ever-increasing amounts of medication, establishing a vicious cycle (Saper, 1987).

Kudrow (1982) first described this condition for tension-type headache patients. He noted that such patients gradually take increasing amounts of analgesics, which subsequently increase pain symptomatology and then renders the headache refractory to treatments that formerly would have been of benefit. Kudrow conducted one of the few empirical tests of this concept by assigning analgesic abusers to one of four conditions. Patients were either withdrawn from or allowed to continue analgesics and simultaneously were assigned either to placebo or amitriptyline (the most commonly prescribed prophylactic drug for this form of headache at that time). He found that mere withdrawal from analgesics led to measurable improvement (approximately 40%), withdrawal combined with a proven medication led to the greatest improvement (nearly 75%), and, perhaps most importantly, that allowing patients to continue analgesics at an abusively high level markedly interfered with the effectiveness of the medication (effectiveness was reduced by approximately two-thirds, or from 72% to 30%). More recent research has confirmed these findings regarding medication overuse and its interference potential (Blanchard, Taylor, & Dentinger, 1992; Mathew, Kurman, & Perez, 1990; Michultka, Blanchard, Appelbaum, Jaccard, & Dentinger, 1989).

Clinicians working with headache patients need to be familiar with criteria for medication abuse, to inquire carefully about current and past medication consumption, and to arrange, in close collaboration with a physician, a medication reduction/detoxification plan for patients suspected of experiencing medication rebound headache. Ergotamine withdrawal can be especially difficult to accomplish on an outpatient basis and may require a brief hospital stay. Saper (1987) reports that within 72 hours of ergotamine withdrawal patients may experience their most intense headache, which may last up to 72 hours (often necessitating a 6 to 7 day hospital stay). Saper believes that dosage days per week are the more critical variable in determining if ergotamine is being abused. He suggests that any patient consuming ergotamine on more than two days per week should be considered as a candidate for medication withdrawal (when taking ergotamine three or more days per week, significant enough amounts remain in the body to perpetuate the problem). More recent criteria for diagnosing drug-induced headache give primary emphasis to days of consumption, rather than quantity of consumption (Diener & Wilkinson, 1988). Lake (2001) identifies a number of behavioral patterns to look for that are suggestive of drug misuse and abuse.

Patients often find it difficult to discontinue the offending medications. Kudrow (1982) required his patients to withdraw abruptly on their own and encountered high rates of dropout in the process. Regular therapist contact and support, concurrent provision of appropriate prophylactic medication as necessary, and beginning instruction in behavioral coping skills may help patients to be more successful in completing a needed medication washout period (Worz, 1983). Grazzi et al. (2001) found it necessary to hospitalize a group of refractory drug-induced headache patients in order to withdraw them from their offending medications and to start them on an appropriate prophylactic course. Some of the patients received behavioral treatment in addition to detoxification. At the first planned follow-up, both groups revealed similar levels of improvement. However, at the three-year follow-up, patients receiving the combined treatment showed greater improvement on two of three measures collected prospectively and lower rates of relapse. Additional discussion of abuse and abuse-proneness may be found in Saper and Sheftell (2000).

Treating patients who have cluster headache chiefly by nonpharmacological treatments has met with limited success (Blanchard, Andrasik, Jurish, & Teders, 1982). Nonpharmacological approaches may still be of value to some cluster sufferers, however, in helping them cope more effectively with the at times overwhelming distress that may result from having to endure repeated, intense attacks of these types of headache. Similarly, patients whose headaches occur following trauma typically experience a multitude of problems that make treatment particularly difficult (Andrasik & Wincze, 1994; Ramadan & Keidel, 2000). A coordinated, interdisciplinary approach, similar to that found in place at most comprehensive pain centers, is typically required (Duckro, Tait, Margolis, & Silvermintz, 1985; Medina, 1992). Inpatient headache specialty units have sprouted across the country to handle complicated cases; headaches that are prolonged, unrelenting, and intractable; are caused or exacerbated by substances; are accompanied by significant medical disease; or require complicated copharmacy (Freitag, 1992). Intensive multidisciplinary headache treatment programs (day and inpatient), modeled after those in place at chronic pain centers, have shown great value with patients who are particularly difficult to treat (e.g., Saper, Lake, Madden, & Kreeger, 1999).

Despite their best efforts to identify, characterize, and define all forms of headache, some headache types have not been addressed adequately by the IHS. The first of these is daily or near daily headache, which is widespread, particularly in pain specialty clinics. Studies have shown that a sizeable number of people presenting with chronic daily headache cannot be classified according to the IHS criteria (Silberstein, Lipton, Solomon, & Mathew, 1994). The diagnostic challenge is distinguishing between a migraineous headache that has been "transformed" to a continuous presentation (first discussed by Mathew, Reuveni, & Perez, 1987), from a chronic form of tension-type headache, that is due in part to medication rebound, and other rare forms of short-duration daily pain (Guitera, Muñoz, Castillo, & Pascual, 1999). This distinction (migraine versus other) is especially important when pursuing pharmacological treatment.

Although a sizeable number of females experience all of a portion of their migraine symptoms during a menstrual cycle, little attention has been given to the study of such headaches (MacGregor, 1997; Massiou & Bousser, 2000). Indeed, the IHS did not list menstrual migraine as a diagnostic entity, leaving those who have investigated this topic to develop their own criteria. Early investigations suggested that headaches linked to the menstrual cycle were not as responsive to behavioral treatment as were those migraines that occurred at other times. More recent research has begun to question this notion (Holroyd & Lipchik, 1997). Clearly, further study of this headache type is warranted.

MEASUREMENT OF HEADACHE PAIN

Headache Diary

Pain is a private event and no method yet exists that can reliably objectify any headache parameters. By default, subjective diary-based ratings have come to be regarded as the "gold standard." In early research on headache (Budzynski, Stoyva, Adler, & Mullaney, 1973), patients were asked to rate pain intensity on an hour-by-hour, day-by-day basis on recording grids reproduced on pocket-sized cards. Medication consumption was monitored as well. Because change in headache could occur along varied dimensions, several different indices were examined: frequency, duration, severity (peak or mean level), and Headache Index/Activity, a composite or derived measure that incorporated all dimensions (calculated by summing all intensity values during which a headache was present). This latter measure was believed to reflect the total burden or suffering of patients.

In behavioral treatment studies, the composite diary measure has been utilized most consistently. However, committees recently charged by the IHS to develop guidelines for conducting and evaluating pharmacological agents have recommended that composite measures no longer be used (International Headache Society, 1999a, 1999b). This index is seen as weighting severity and duration in an arbitrary manner, which renders it of little value when conducting comparisons across subjects. Further, the clinical meaning of changes is noted to be unclear. Rather, these committees recommend that the following serve as the primary diary-based measures of headache pain:

1. Number of days with headache in a four-week period (see Blanchard, Hillhouse, Appelbaum, & Jaccard, 1987, for a contrasting opinion about the desired length of the measurement interval).

2. Severity of attacks, rated on either (a) a 4-point scale, where 0 = no headache, 1 = mild headache (allowing normal activity), 2 = moderate headache (disturbing but not prohibiting normal activity, bed rest is not necessary), and 3 = severe headache (normal activity has to be discontinued, bed rest may be necessary) or (b) a visual analogue scale, wherein one end is anchored as "none" and the other as "very severe."

3. Headache duration in hours.

4. Responder rate—the number or percentage of patients achieving a reduction in headache days or headache duration per day that is equal to or greater than 50%. (This is in accord with the recommendations of Blanchard & Schwarz, 1988.)

Several modifications to the intensive, hourly recording format have been proposed in order to improve adherence and accuracy. Epstein and Abel (1977) directly observed inpatients and noticed that most did not record continuously; rather, they periodically omitted recordings and completed them later by recall. Their modified procedure asked patients to make ratings only four times per day: wakeup/breakfast, lunch, evening meal, and bedtime. These events tend to occur at fairly regular times that are easily discriminated.

Although a time-sampling format (such as four times per day) is less demanding for patients and is likely to yield more reliable and valid data, it has certain shortcomings. In this approach, it is not possible to obtain true measures for headache frequency and duration. Chronic or unwavering pain lends itself quite nicely to either format, but the clinician might want to make alterations for people with infrequent, but discrete, prolonged migraine attacks. In the latter case, the patient could make ratings repeatedly throughout an attack or, alternatively, could note the time of onset and offset and then perform a single rating of peak headache intensity. This would allow the therapist to keep track of all key parameters. We have used this procedure successfully with pediatric migraineurs (Andrasik, Burke, Attanasio, & Rosenblum, 1985). If patients resist recording on multiple occasions throughout the day, then a single recording at the end of the day is most advisable. Occasionally a patient's symptoms will display "reactivity" when being recorded systematically and worsen because of this increased symptom focus. These reactions are typically shortlived.

A critical concern with any type of daily monitoring record is the level of patient adherence. In an analog sample of college students, approximately 40% of subjects evidenced some degree of nonadherence. The most common form of noncompliance involved subjects recalling and completing ratings at a later time (Collins & Thompson, 1979). Review-

ing pain records regularly, socially praising efforts to comply (yet refraining from punishing noncompliance), anticipating problem areas, and having the patient mail records to the office when gaps between appointments are large may help emphasize the importance of and facilitate accurate record keeping (Lake, 2001).

It is common for clinicians to have their patients monitor headaches on a systematic basis during treatment but to conduct follow-up evaluations by interview or questionnaire completion. Several studies have examined correspondence between these two approaches: prospective, daily monitoring versus retrospective, global determinations (Andrasik & Holroyd, 1980a; Andrasik et al., 1985; Cahn & Cram, 1980). Very different results emerge, with the latter believed to yield biased overestimates of improvement. Clinicians and researchers alike need to be aware of the potential for bias when it is necessary to alter measures midstream and not be lulled into uncritical acceptance of global reports of benefit that might be inflated.

Supplementary Approaches

A number of supplementary and alternative approaches have been developed to assess headaches, and these are reviewed in greater depth in Andrasik (2001a). Four approaches may be easily adopted by practitioners and researchers:

1. Measurement of multiple aspects of pain, specifically affective/reactive as well as sensory/intensity.

2. Social validation of patient improvement.

3. Measurement of pain behavior or behavior motivated by pain, including medication consumption.

4. Impact on other aspects of functioning, such as general health or overall quality of life, physical functioning, emotional functioning, cognitive functioning, role functioning, and social well-being (see Andrasik, 2001a, 2001b; Holroyd, in press).

HEADACHE TREATMENT

Pharmacological Treatment

Most individuals will experience a headache from time to time, yet few of these individuals seek regular treatment from a health care provider, even when headaches are severe and disabling (Mannix, 2001; Michel, 2000). More typically, headaches are tolerated, treated symptomatically with over-the-counter analgesics, or managed by "borrowing" prescribed medications from friends and family members. When recurrent headache sufferers do present to a health care practitioner, their headaches are most commonly managed with a combination of medication and advice from the treating clinician. In fact, among primary care headache patients, over 80% reported the use of over-the-counter medications and over 75% reported the use of some form of prescription-only medications for the management of their headaches (Von Korff, Galer, & Stang, 1995). A number of effective pharmacologic options are available to treat headaches and these may be categorized into three broad classes: symptomatic, abortive, and prophylactic medications.

Symptomatic Medications

Symptomatic medications are pharmacologic agents with analgesic or pain relieving effects. These include over-the-counter analgesics (i.e., aspirin, acetaminophen), nonsteroidal anti-inflammatory agents (i.e., ibuprofen), opioid analgesics, muscle relaxants, and sedative/hypnotic agents, which are consumed during the occurrence of headache to provide relief from pain. Von Korff et al. (1995) found that ibuprofen accounted for 84% of all use of nonsteroidal anti-inflammatory consumption in a sample of over 600 primary care headache patients. The most commonly consumed opioid analgesics were acetaminophen with codeine (33%), meperdine (also known as Demerol; 21%), and percocet (15%). Midrin (33%), cyclobenzaprine (28%), and methocarbonal (10%) were the most commonly consumed sedative/hypnotic medications.

Abortive Medications

Abortive medications are pharmacologic agents that are consumed at the onset of a migraine headache, in an effort to terminate or markedly lessen an attack. Ergotamine tartrate preparations were the mainstays of abortive care until the early 1990s when triptans, designed to act on specific serotonin receptor subtypes, were introduced. Multiple triptan formulations are now available, differing with respect to potency, delivery mode (oral vs. other, for patients likely to vomit during attacks), time of peak onset, duration of sustained headache relief, rate of headache recurrence, improvement in associated symptoms, safety, and tolerability (Rapoport & Tepper, 2001; Tepper, 2001). Evidence supporting efficacy is mounting but, as pointed out by Rapoport and Tepper, nonindustry sponsored research is lacking. We are unaware of research comparing triptans to behavioral approaches. Comparison of a combined behavioral treatment (relaxation + thermal biofeedback) to ergotamine tartrate for migraine and migraine combined with tension-type headache revealed similar levels of treatment response. Improvements

for the medication group were evident quicker (within the first month), whereas improvements for the behavioral group did not occur until the second month of treatment. Only the behavioral group showed reductions in analgesic usage, however (Holroyd et al., 1988).

Prophylactic Medications

Prophylactic medications are consumed daily in an effort to prevent headaches or reduce the occurrence of attacks in the chronic sufferer. Beta blockers, calcium channel blockers, and antidepressants (e.g., tricyclics, serotonin-specific reuptake inhibitors) are used most frequently as prophylactic medications for migraine headache (Tfelt-Hansen & Welch, 2000a, 2000b). Recent metaanalyzes comparing various prophylactic agents, conducted with child as well as adult patients, have shown them to be superior to varied control conditions (waiting list, medication placebo, etc.) (Hermann, Kim, & Blanchard, 1995; Holroyd, Penzien, & Cordingley, 1991). One of these analyzes (Hermann et al., 1995), along with an additional metaanalysis (Holroyd & Penzien, 1990), found various behavioral treatments achieved outcomes similar to those for varied prophylactic medications.

For tension-type headache, the most commonly administered medications include tricyclic and other antidepressants, muscle relaxants, nonsteroidal anti-inflammatory agents, and miscellaneous drugs (Mathew & Bendtsen, 2000). A recent, large-scale randomized controlled trial found stress management and drug prophylaxis to be equivalent in effectiveness (although time of response was quicker for medication). The combination of the two treatments was more effective than either treatment by itself (Holroyd et al., 2001). Combined care is probably the most common treatment in clinical practice.

While a number of medications are effective in the treatment of recurring headache, concern exists regarding the risks of frequent, long-term use of certain medications. Major risks associated with pharmacological management of recurrent headache disorders include the potential for misuse and dependency (Mathew, 1987), as discussed previously. Several other risks may be associated with chronic/frequent use of headache medications, including the potential for rebound headache, the possibility of drug-induced chronic headache, reduced efficacy of prophylactic headache medications, potential side effects, and acute symptoms associated with the cessation of headache medication (such as increased headache, nausea, cramping, gastrointestinal distress, sleep disturbance, and emotional distress).

Unfortunately, chronic/frequent use of prescription-only medication has been reported by 10% of primary care headache patients and chronic/frequent use of over-the-counter medications has been reported by almost 20% of primary care headache patients (Von Korff et al., 1995). These potential risks, combined with the growing interest in self management and alternative approaches, warrant the consideration of nonpharmacological treatments. Fortunately, a number of such treatments have been systematically evaluated and have been found to demonstrate therapeutic efficacy.

Nonpharmacological Treatments for Headache

There are three basic approaches to nonpharmacological treatments for recurrent headache disorders. These approaches are designed (a) to promote general overall relaxation either by therapist instruction alone (e.g., progressive muscle relaxation, autogenic training, meditation) or therapist instruction augmented by feedback of various physiological parameters indicative of autonomic arousal or muscle tension to help fine tune relaxation (e.g., temperature, electromyographic, or electrodermal biofeedback); (b) to control, in more direct fashion, those physiological parameters assumed to underlie headache (e.g., blood flow and electroencephalographic biofeedback); and (c) to enhance abilities to manage stressors and stress reactions to headache (e.g., cognitive and cognitive behavior therapy).

Investigations of these treatments are extensive and too numerous to review study by study. This has led recent reviewers to examine efficacy by the quantitative procedure of metaanalyzes. The metaanalyzes conducted to date are summarized in Table 11.4. Early metaanalyzes excluded very few of the available studies, including poorly designed studies along with expertly designed studies (the main entrance criterion was a minimal sample size). More recent analyzes have been much more selective about the studies permitted to enter analysis. For example, the AHCPR metaanalysis (Goslin et al., 1999) located 355 behavioral and physical treatment (acupuncture, TENS, occlusal adjustment, cervical manipulation, and hyperbaric oxygen) articles, 70 of which consisted of controlled trials of behavioral treatments for migraine. Only 39 of these trials met criteria for inclusion in the analysis. Findings from the most recent metaanalyzes should be considered as providing lower bound estimates of effectiveness, under very tightly controlled conditions.

TABLE 11.4   Average Improvement Rates from Separate Metaanalyzes

A. Tension-Type Headache

	EMG	REL	EMG + REL	BFCT	COG	PHARM	OTHER	PTCT	MDCT	WTLT
Blanchard, Andrasik, Ahles, Teders, and O'Keefe (1980)	61	59	59					35	35	−5
Holroyd and Penzien (1986)	46	45	57	15						−4
Bogaards and ter Kuile (1994)	47	36	56		53	39	38	20		−5
McCrory, Penzien, Hasselblad, and Gray (2001)	48	38	51		40	35*		17		3

B. Migraine Headache

	ATFB	THBF	REL	VMBF	THBF + REL	EMG	COG	COG + BF	PTCT	MDCT	WTLT
Blanchard et al. (1980)	65	52	53							17	
Holroyd, Penzien, Holm, and Hursey (1984)		28	44	31	57						11
Blanchard and Andrasik (1987)	49	27	48	43		29			26	13	
Goslin et al. (1999)			37	32	33	40	49	35	9		5

EMG = Electromyographic biofeedback, generally provided from the frontal/forehead muscles.
REL = Relaxation therapy, generally of the muscle tensing and relaxing variety.
BFCT = Biofeedback control procedure, generally false or noncontingent biofeedback.
COG = Cognitive therapy, stress coping training, or problem-solving therapy.
BF = EMG or thermal biofeedback.
PHARM = Various medications, ranging from aspirin and nonsteroidal inflammatories to prophylactics to narcotics.
OTHER = Various approaches, other than BF, REL, or COG.
PTCT = Psychological or pseudotherapy control procedure.
MDCT = Medication control procedure; results taken from double blind placebo controlled medication trials.
WTLT = Waiting list control procedure; no treatment.
ATFB = Thermal biofeedback augmented by components of autogenic training, as developed at the Menninger Clinic.
THBF = Thermal biofeedback by itself.
VMBF = Vasomotor biofeedback provided from the temporal artery.
*Amitriptyline alone.

In addition to meta-analytic approaches, various groups have assembled panels to conduct evidence-based reviews, wherein rigorous methodological criteria are used to evaluate every study under consideration. Evidence-based analyzes have been performed by the Division 12 Task Force, the U.S. Headache Consortium (composed of the American Academy of Family Physicians, American Academy of Neurology, American Headache Society, American College of Emergency Physicians, American College of Physicians-American Society of Internal Medicine, American Osteopathic Association, and National Headache Foundation) (Campbell, Penzien, & Wall, 2000), and the Task Force of the Society of Pediatric Psychology (Holden, Deichmann, & Levy, 1999).

Consideration of the findings from these studies leads to the following conclusions. First, relaxation, biofeedback, and cognitive therapy lead to significant reductions in headache activity, ranging from 30% to 60%. Second, conversely, there are a fair number of patients who are nonresponders or partial responders (approximately 40% to 70%). Prediction of treatment response and careful treatment planning become particularly important when attempting to improve on this outcome. Upon their extensive review, the U.S. Headache Consortium concluded that behavioral treatments may be particularly well suited for patients having one or more of the following characteristics: The patient prefers such an approach; Pharmacological treatment cannot be tolerated or is medically contraindicated; The response to pharmacological treatment is absent or minimal; The patient is pregnant, has plans to become pregnant, or is nursing; The patient has a long-standing history of frequent or excessive use of analgesic or acute medications that can aggravate headache; or The patient is faced with significant stressors or has deficient stress-coping skills. More is said about treatment prediction later. Third, improvements exceed those obtained for various control conditions. Fourth, nonpharmacological treatments produce benefits similar to those obtained for pharmacological treatments. Fifth, combining treatments often increments effectiveness, especially so for nonpharmacological and pharmacological. However, the net gain of adding a second treatment modality beyond a single treatment sometimes is relatively small. This again stresses the importance of finding the "right" therapy or combination of therapies for an individual patient. Research into the prediction of treatment response may elucidate some of this and allow clinicians to maximize therapeutic gains. Sixth, most studies of nonpharmacological interventions have included subjects that continued their consumption of any number of pharmacological agents while undergoing nonpharmacological interventions. Only a very few studies have systematically isolated pure treatments (e.g., Holroyd et al., 1988, 1995, 2001; Mathew, 1981; Reich, 1989).

There is also a fair amount of evidence to suggest that the effects of these types of therapies are durable. A number of studies have found substantial maintenance of treatment gains, at least among those who respond initially, for periods of up to seven years posttreatment (see Blanchard, 1992), and that these effects maintain whether further contact is provided (booster sessions) or not (Andrasik, Blanchard, Neff, & Rodichok, 1984). For example, in a prospective follow-up, Blanchard, Appelbaum, Guarnieri, Morrill, and Dentinger (1987) found that 78% of tension headache sufferers and 91% of migraine headache sufferers remained significantly improved (as assessed by headache diary) five years following completion of relaxation training and/or biofeedback training. In a retrospective four-year follow-up study of almost 400 headache patients who had completed a comprehensive clinical program including several types of biofeedback and relaxation training, Diamond and Montrose (1984) found that 65% reported maintenance of treatment gains. While this latter study is retrospective, the results are encouraging because of the very large sample size and the fact that the data were collected from patients enrolled in a clinical program (as opposed to a research program). As such, these data may provide information about follow-up with "naturalistic" or "real life" clinical programs.

BEHAVIORAL TREATMENT

A Biobehavioral Model of Headache

The biobehavioral model, which guides treatment of headache, states that the likelihood of any individual experiencing headache depends on the specific pathophysiological mechanisms that are "triggered" by the interplay of the individual's physiological status (e.g., level of autonomic arousal), environmental factors (e.g., stressful circumstances, certain foods, alcohol, toxins, hormonal fluctuations), the individual's ability to cope with these factors (both cognitively and behaviorally), and consequential factors that may serve to reinforce, and thus increase, the person's chances of reporting head pain (Martin, 1993; Waggoner & Andrasik, 1990). The main determinant for the resulting headache is the pathophysiological biological response system that is activated. Psychological and behavioral factors do not play a causal role per se. Rather, they contribute to headache as factors that (a) trigger, (b) maintain, or (c) exacerbate headache, or (d) as sequelae to continued head pain that subsequently disrupt overall functioning.

The prolonged presence of headache begins to exert a psychological toll on the patient over time, such that the patient becomes "sick and tired of feeling sick and tired." The negative thoughts and emotions arising from the repeated experience of headache thus can become further stressors or trigger factors in and of themselves (referred to as "headache-related distress"), serving at that point both to help maintain the disorder and to increase the severity and likelihood of future attacks. Pointing out the direct and indirect psychological influences on headache may make it easier for the patient to understand and accept the role of psychological factors and can often facilitate referral for adjunctive psychological/psychiatric care when needed (to illustrate, ask the patient which is worse, onset of a headache when the patient is refreshed and rested or when work and family frustrations are at a peak). This model points out the various areas to address when interviewing headache patients.

Implementation

Appropriate treatment implementation assumes adequate expertise in the application of the interventions selected. Because this chapter is intended for nonmedical practitioners, the following sections will address the application and implementation of nonpharmacological, behavioral and cognitive behavioral, interventions that have garnered empirical support to date. As previous sections have indicated, appropriate medical evaluation cannot be overlooked and pharmacological therapy may be the treatment of choice or a necessary component. When pharmacotherapy is used, ongoing medical assessment and collaboration with a qualified medical provider is critical (Blanchard & Diamond, 1996).

A common element among all therapies is patient education, which begins at the onset and continues throughout treatment. Research by Packard (1987) reveals that information about headache is one of the top needs of patients when they come for treatment. Each of the following treatments begins with an educational component that typically includes information on the etiology of headache, the rationale for treatment, and an explanation of what is involved with the particular treatment, as well as encouragement of active participation on the part of the patient (Andrasik, 1986, 1990; Holroyd & Andrasik, 1982). Therapists are encouraged to discuss the aforementioned biobehavioral model of headache in clear, nontechnical terms.

In the initial session emphasis is placed on the importance of collaboration between the therapist and patient and of regular home practice to facilitate skill acquisition (Holroyd & Andrasik, 1982; Martin, 1993). Although strongly encouraged, the role of home practice has received inconsistent support in the research literature. In clinical practice, the importance of home practice is emphasized, even though this may often be an unexamined assumption (Blanchard, Nicholson, Radnitz, et al., 1991; Blanchard, Nicholson, Taylor, et al., 1991).

Relaxation Training

Relaxation training for recurrent headache disorders may take a variety of forms. Two forms in particular have been widely applied in the treatment of recurrent headache disorders: progressive muscle relaxation (e.g., Cox, Freundlich, & Meyer, 1975) and autogenic training (e.g., Sargent, Green, & Walters, 1973). Transcendental Meditation (Benson, Klemchuk, & Graham, 1974) and self-hypnosis (ter Kuile, Spinhoven, Linssen, & van Houwelingen, 1995) have also been applied, but not extensively.

Progressive muscle relaxation training as applied to recurrent headache disorders is most often based upon the work of Jacobson (1938) or Bernstein and Borkovec's (1973) abbreviated adaptation of Jacobson's procedures. Progressive muscle relaxation may be used alone or in conjunction with biofeedback. Typically applied during 10 sessions over the course of eight weeks, the procedure involves therapist-guided training of patients to alternately tense and relax target muscle groups. Patients are instructed to tense the target muscle group for five to ten seconds, focusing on the sensations that result from the tension. Following the tension phase, patients are instructed to release the tension and relax the muscle for 20 to 30 seconds, again focusing on the sensations associated with the release of tension. The tense/relax cycle instructions are repeated two to three times for each muscle group. As the patient becomes proficient at tensing and relaxing muscle groups, training proceeds to consolidate muscle groups, facilitate the deepening of relaxation, enhance abilities to discriminate among various levels of relaxation, and induce relaxation by recall. Patients are typically instructed to practice their relaxation exercises once or twice daily for 20 minutes. Table 11.5 from Andrasik (1986) and Tables 11.6 and 11.7 contain a summary of a typical protocol.

Autogenic training was first applied to headache disorders (typically migraine) by Sargent et al. (1973). Autogenic training (Schultz & Luthe, 1969) involves focusing on a set of phrases specifically designed to promote a desired physiologic state. Autogenic training for headache treatment utilizes phrases intended to elicit sensations of relaxation, heaviness, and warmth in the entire body (face/head, trunk, and extremities) with a particular emphasis placed on warming of the hands. Autogenic training is often employed in conjunction

TABLE 11.5 Outline of Progressive Muscle Relaxation Training Program

Week	Session	Introduction and Treatment Rationale	Number of Muscle Groups	Deepening Exercises	Breathing Exercises	Relaxing Imagery	Muscle Discrimination Training	Relaxation by Recall	Cue-Controlled Relaxation
1	1	X	14	X	X				
	2		14	X	X		X		
2	3		14	X	X	X	X		
	4		14	X	X	X	X		
3	5		8	X	X	X	X		
	6		8	X	X	X	X	X	
4	7		4	X	X	X	X	X	
5	8		4	X	X	X	X	X	X
6	9		4	X	X	X	X	X	X
7	none								
8	10		4	X	X	X	X	X	X

Source: Andrasik (1986).

with thermal biofeedback, which also places an emphasis on warming of the hands, leading to a treatment termed "autogenic feedback" by Sargent et al. (1973). Autogenic training involves the verbatim repetition of the selected phrases, first demonstrated by the therapist. Tape recordings of sessions or printed copies of verbatim scripts may be helpful until patients learn the phrases and their sequence as well as the ability to elicit the desired sensations.

TABLE 11.6 Fourteen Initial Muscle Groups and Procedures for Tensing in 18 Steps

1. Right hand and lower arm (have client make fist, simultaneously tense lower arm).
2. Left hand and lower arm.
3. Both hands and lower arms.
4. Right upper arm (have client bring his or her hand to the shoulder and tense biceps).
5. Left upper arm.
6. Both upper arms.
7. Right lower leg and foot (have client point his or her toe while tensing the calf muscles).
8. Left lower leg and foot.
9. Both lower legs and feet.
10. Both thighs (have client press his or her knees and thighs tightly together).
11. Abdomen (have client draw abdominal muscles in tightly, as if bracing to receive a punch).
12. Chest (have client take a deep breath and hold it).
13. Shoulders and lower neck (have client "hunch" his or her shoulders or draw his or her shoulders up toward the ears).
14. Back of the neck (have the client press head backward against headrest or chair).
15. Lips/mouth (have client press lips together tightly, but not so tight as to clench teeth; or have client place the tip of the tongue on the roof of the mouth behind upper front teeth).
16. Eyes (have client close the eyes tightly).
17. Lower forehead (have client frown and draw the eyebrows together).
18. Upper forehead (have client wrinkle the forehead area or raise the eyebrows).

Biofeedback

A number of biofeedback interventions have been applied to recurrent headache disorders, including: EMG, thermal, electrodermal, cephalic vasomotor, transcranial doppler, and EEG biofeedback (see Andrasik, 2000). EMG biofeedback and thermal biofeedback are described here, as these have the most empirical support and they are the biofeedback approaches most widely used in clinical practice (they are the "workhorses" of the biofeedback "general practitioner"). The other approaches require more specialized training and equipment.

EMG and thermal biofeedback interventions are commonly employed in conjunction with relaxation training and/or autogenic training. As with relaxation training and autogenic training, a rationale for efficacy is provided to the patient at the start of biofeedback treatment (see Andrasik, 1986, and Blanchard & Andrasik, 1985, for verbatim explanations). The therapist will often be present and active in "coaching"

TABLE 11.7 Abbreviated Muscle Groups

Eight Muscle Groups
1. Both hands and lower arms.
2. Both legs and thighs.
3. Abdomen.
4. Chest.
5. Shoulders.
6. Back of neck.
7. Eyes.
8. Forehead.

Four Muscle Groups
1. Arms.
2. Chest.
3. Neck.
4. Face (with a particular focus on the eyes and forehead).

the patient in early sessions of biofeedback but it has been suggested that the therapist's presence, particularly if overly active or intrusive, can become a distraction and interfere with the training (Borgeat, Hade, Larouche, & Bedwani, 1980). Hence, biofeedback training is designed to be therapist-guided in the initial phases, with an effort to move in the direction of increased self-regulation on the part of the patient as training proceeds.

For both types of biofeedback training described next, 8 to 16 sessions of training are usually provided, typically between 20 and 40 minutes in duration (or long enough for training to be effective but brief enough to minimize the likelihood of fatigue). Instead of a universal prescriptive for the length of treatment, the number of sessions is more usefully determined by the individual patient's response to treatment. Training may be discontinued when maximum benefit has been achieved, as in a significant reduction in headache activity or when the reduction in headache activity plateaus or stabilizes. In some cases, a reduction of headache activity may not have occurred. In these cases, it may be useful to determine whether the patient has achieved sufficient skill at physiological self-regulation of the target response. If the patient has achieved sufficient skill and is able to apply these skills in real-life settings but has not experienced a reduction in headache activity, other treatment options may be indicated.

EMG biofeedback is relatively straightforward and can be performed both in the clinic and at home with portable devices. The aim of EMG biofeedback training is to decrease muscle tension (as evidenced by electrical activity) of the frontal muscles of the forehead (e.g., Budzynski et al., 1973), although other muscles may be targeted in a similar fashion if these muscles appear to play an important role in the individual's headache activity. To achieve these aims, patients are encouraged to experiment with a variety of methods of physiological self-control (such as relaxation exercises, imagery exercises, or breathing exercises) while receiving feedback about their performance via an EMG device. Often, the training portions of the biofeedback sessions proceed in brief intervals of 1 to 5 minutes in length, interspersed with brief pauses that provide an opportunity for rest periods and discussion with the therapist. Across sessions, patients are encouraged to further increase and refine their self-regulatory skills in this manner.

Thermal biofeedback also generally aims to increase physiological self-regulation. Specifically, the aim is to increase peripheral body temperature or a hand-warming response. To achieve these aims, patients are encouraged to experiment with a variety of methods of physiological self-control (such as relaxation exercises, imagery exercises, or breathing exercises) while receiving feedback about their finger tempera-

ture. Relaxation may be induced by recall prior to start of biofeedback session. Often, autogenic phrases or imagery are used during thermal biofeedback training sessions as a means of raising peripheral body temperature. An adaptation phase and baseline period are often used to note baseline temperature, followed by training phases that proceed in short intervals characterized by voluntary efforts to warm the hands. Some have suggested that it may be beneficial for patients to achieve a certain criterion level during training (e.g., be able to increase finger temperature to a certain temperature value within a specified period or for a specified length; Fahrion, Norris, Green, Green, & Snarr, 1986). Although this makes sense from a clinical perspective, there is minimal data to support this notion.

The mechanisms of action for these therapies are not fully clear, as the data suggest that the direction of change in EMG level and finger temperature and extent of physiological control achieved are not predictive of outcome. Similarly, comparisons of relaxation therapies and biofeedback interventions often find equivalence, suggesting that the effects are not specific to the type of therapy employed but rather due to nonspecific effects that may have an underlying relaxation mechanism (Cohen, McArthur, & Rickles, 1980; Primavera & Kaiser, 1992). It is possible that a generalized relaxation response or physiological self-control is the common denominator and active ingredient in these therapies, rather than the directional change in a specific physiological process. Alternative explanations of the mechanism of action of these therapies have included alteration of cognitive and behavioral responses to stress and improved coping (Andrasik & Holroyd, 1980b) and cognitive changes such as an increased sense of perceived control and mastery (Cohen et al., 1980). Cognitive changes that may underlie the effectiveness of biofeedback may be mediated by performance feedback that suggests "success" (Holroyd, Penzien, Hursey, et al., 1984), allowing for increased perceptions of control and mastery. In short, research into the psychophysiological mechanisms of biofeedback has led to the suggestion that cognitive factors may play an important role in the efficacy of behavioral and physiological self-regulation interventions; however, our understanding of these mechanisms remains "rudimentary" (Gauthier, Ivers, & Carrier, 1996).

Cognitive Behavioral Interventions

This type of therapy has been labeled variously as cognitive behavior therapy, cognitive stress coping therapy, cognitive therapy, stress management, or other terms. In addition to the evidence from biofeedback studies that suggests that cognitive factors play a role in the treatment of recurrent headache disorders, there is also evidence to suggest that stress, appraisal of stress, and coping play a significant role in recurrent headache disorders (Holm, Holroyd, Hursey, & Penzien, 1986; Lake, 2001). Theoretically, cognitive behavioral therapies may work by altering cognitive appraisals/ expectancies, stress responses, or cognitive/behavioral coping responses, although the specific causal relationships between stress and headaches and cognitive therapies and headaches remain unclear (Morley, 1986).

Much of the empirical study of cognitive behavioral interventions for recurrent headache disorders have adapted the traditional cognitive behavioral framework of Meichenbaum's stress inoculation training as applied to pain (Meichenbaum, 1977; Turk, Meichenbaum, & Genest, 1983) or Beck's cognitive therapy (Beck, Emery, & Greenberg, 1985; Beck, Rush, Shaw, & Emery, 1979). These traditional cognitive-behavioral therapies have been adapted specifically for the treatment of recurrent headache disorders by Holroyd and Andrasik (1982) and Holroyd, Andrasik, and Westbrook (1977). It should be kept in mind that cognitive behavioral therapies for headache are most often applied in the form of a "treatment package" that may include a number of the other approaches discussed previously.

In CBT patients are taught a rationale that suggests that learning to identify and modify cognitions will mediate the stress headache relationship. Unfortunately, empirical investigation of these assumptions is very limited, as are data to support the validity of these assumptions. This led Morley (1986) to conclude that "this approach to treatment is open to the criticism that the therapy works because of a convincing rationale and not because the rationale is essentially correct" (p. 317). This conclusion still applies. Although CBT has been shown to be superior to no treatment and to be as good as (if not superior to) other effective treatments for headache, it is also unclear whether CBT is superior to a credible attention placebo (Blanchard, 1992). While it is clear that much more investigation is required before this rationale can be claimed as validated, the data are also clear that cognitive behavioral therapies possess efficacy in the treatment of recurrent headache disorders, even if the mechanisms of action are poorly understood.

Holroyd and Andrasik (1982) identify three general phases of CBT for headache disorders, including: education, self-monitoring, and problem-solving or coping skills training. For the most part, cognitive behavioral approaches to headache disorders are fairly consistent in their emphasis on education and self-monitoring. It is within the last phase that much of the variability exists.

Once the rationale has been explained in sufficient detail, CBT for headache disorders moves quickly into a very detailed form of self-monitoring. Patients are taught to monitor and record the factors that precede, accompany, and follow stressful situations and headaches. Patients are taught to monitor their thoughts (cognitions), feelings (emotions), behaviors, and sensations. This functional analysis of antecedents, concomitants, and consequences is intended as a means of identifying modifiable aspects of headache and stress. Emphasis is often placed on the antecedents and concomitants of headache and stress, particularly cognitive and behavioral antecedents and concomitants because of the assumption that these may be amenable to modification.

The remainder of cognitive behavioral therapy focuses on modifying those factors that appear to be related to headache activity and stress. This phase of the therapy may vary substantially. A number of strategies and techniques may be used to modify the factors that were identified through self-monitoring. Some of the most common cognitive strategies applied include cognitive restructuring and reappraisal (in the tradition of the Cognitive Therapy of Beck or Rational Emotive Therapy of Ellis) and the use of coping self-statements (in the tradition of Meichenbaum's Stress Inoculation Training). Common to each of these approaches is the identification and revision of maladaptive cognitions. Using any of these approaches, the therapist assists the patient in the review of self-monitoring data by helping the client identify maladaptive cognitions and challenge them effectively. Therapists may also assist in the identification of maladaptive behavioral responses to stress and provide training and support in the use of problem solving strategies to identify more adaptive behavioral responses to stress and headache.

BEHAVIORAL TREATMENT PLANNING

The empirical treatment outcome literature, pharmacological and nonpharmacological, provides a useful starting point for treatment planning with an individual patient. In addition to reporting on the overall efficacy of various treatments, this literature also offers some insights into individual factors that increase or decrease the likelihood of a clinically significant treatment response. Unlike treatment outcome studies that are confined by the restraints of empirical rigor for the purpose of hypothesis testing and maintenance of internal validity, clinical treatment of patients presenting with recurrent headache disorders must rely on sound clinical judgment and careful selection of interventions that are most likely to provide the best treatment outcome for the individual. Whereas treatment outcome studies utilize a somewhat standardized approach, optimal clinical treatment is not always suited by a "one-size-fits-all" stance. The following sections describe some of the individual factors that have been found to be related to treatment outcome and that can be useful in determining which of the numerous options for treatment might be particularly useful for an individual patient. These factors include: headache type, frequency, and chronicity; age and gender; comorbid psychological disorder or distress; environmental factors; and treatment history. Other factors, such as patient preference and cost effectiveness, have not received as much empirical attention, but these are nonetheless important when considering treatment options. While much of the empirical literature has examined "intensive" individual therapy formats (typically 8 to 12 sessions), other methods of treatment delivery merit consideration, including reduced therapist contact and group treatments.

Headache Type, Frequency, and Chronicity

Both tension-type and migraine headache respond well to pharmacological and nonpharmacological treatments. With regard to nonpharmacological interventions, both headache types benefit from relaxation training and cognitive behavioral interventions. Although thermal biofeedback is more widely applied to migraine headache and EMG biofeedback is more widely applied to tension-type headache, there is evidence to suggest that EMG biofeedback is also useful for migraine headache. Patients with mixed migraine and tension-type headaches also respond to the treatments discussed above, although typically not as well as those with "pure" migraine or tension-type headaches. Cluster headache does not appear to respond as well to behavioral treatments. Data are less clear for headaches that are associated with menses. Headaches resulting from trauma require intensive, multicomponent treatment.

Patients with chronic daily or near daily, high intensity headache do not respond well to behavioral interventions alone (Blanchard, Appelbaum, Radnitz, Jaccard, & Dentinger, 1989). However, chronic daily headache has been found to be unrelated or positively related to the use of abortive and prophylactic medications (Holroyd et al., 1988). These data suggest that medications may be the first-line treatment for patients with chronic/daily or almost continuous headache.

Age and Gender

Young adults generally respond better to nonpharmacological interventions than older adults and women generally respond better than men (Diamond, Medina, Diamond-Falk, & DeVeno, 1979; Diamond & Montrose, 1984). Geriatric headache patients have been found to be less responsive to standard behavioral treatment protocols (Holroyd & Penzien, 1986). When protocols are adjusted to compensate for any age-related declines in information processing capabilities, however, outcomes become much more favorable (e.g., Arena, Hannah, Bruno, & Meador, 1991; Arena, Hightower, & Chong, 1988; Nicholson & Blanchard, 1993).

Behavioral treatments have been found to be especially effective for pediatric headache sufferers (Attanasio, Andrasik, Burke, Blake, Kabela, & McCarran, 1985; Hermann, Blanchard, & Flor, 1997; Hermann et al., 1995; Holden et al., 1999). Although no direct comparisons of child and adult headache patients have been conducted within a single study, a recent metaanalyzes, drawing on nearly 60 existing separate child and adult studies, revealed that children improved at a much greater level when treated in a similar fashion with either temperature or EMG biofeedback (Sarafino & Goehring, 2000).

Treatment History

Patients who have a history of habituation to medication, consume large amounts of medication, are suffering from drug-induced headaches, or are particularly refractory tend to respond less well to behavioral interventions (see earlier sections). In these situations, detoxification may need to be accomplished before nonpharmacological intervention; some have suggested that nonpharmacological interventions be implemented during a gradual reduction and discontinuation of the offending medication in an effort to reduce the high dropout rates associated with drug withdrawal procedures (Gauthier et al., 1996; Grazzi et al., 2001). In these cases, previous treatment provides clear contraindications for specific pharmacological interventions and begins to suggest alternate strategies that may be helpful to refractory patients.

Blanchard, Andrasik, Neff, et al. (1982) examined a stepped-approach to treating diverse headache patients. Initially, all subjects (tension-type, migraine, or both combined) were treated with relaxation training, resulting in a substantial reduction in headache for all three headache types but particularly for tension-type headache sufferers. Those subjects who did not respond well to relaxation training were subsequently treated with biofeedback (thermal for pure migraine or combined headache; EMG for tension-type). The subsequent biofeedback treatment resulted in further significant reductions, particularly for combined headache patients. These findings suggest that relaxation training is useful for all three types of headaches but also emphasize the value of biofeedback for those who do not respond initially to relaxation training (especially those with migraine or mixed headaches). These results further suggest that relaxation and biofeedback may not work through a common mechanism, at least for a subset of patients.

Comorbid Psychological Distress or Disorder

The psychological status of the patient deserves special attention in order to identify conditions (mood and anxiety disorders, formal thought disorder, certain personality disorders) that might interfere with treatment and that need to be handled prior to or concurrent with treatment of the headache (see Holroyd, Lipchik, & Penzien, 1998; Lake, 2001; Merikangas & Stevens, 1997; Radat et al., 1999; see also the chapter by O'Callahan, Andrews, & Krantz in this volume; and the chapter by Jason & Taylor in this volume). These authors speculate that attention to comorbid conditions may be crucial to the success of *both* pharmacologic and nonpharmacologic therapies for certain patients. This conclusion is based on studies revealing the following:

1. The risk for major depression and anxiety disorders is higher for migraineurs than for nonmigraineous controls.
2. This influence is bi-directional. Migraine increases the risk of a subsequent episode of major depression (adjusted relative risk = 4.8), and major depression increases the risk of subsequent migraine (adjusted relative risk = 3.3).
3. Comorbid anxiety and depression lead to increases in disability and contribute to headaches becoming intractable.
4. Psychological distress is greater in headaches that are more frequent and chronic.
5. Depression is implicated in the transformation of episodic to chronic tension-type headache.
6. Certain personality disorders reveal a higher incidence of headache than otherwise would be expected.

Further evidence for the importance of considering psychological factors is obtained from research that has attempted to identify variables associated with outcome. For example, studies have consistently shown that patients displaying only minor elevations on a scale commonly used to assess depression (Beck Depression Inventory) have a diminished response to self-regulatory treatments (Blanchard et al., 1985; Jacob, Turner, Szekely, & Eidelman, 1983) and even abortive medication (Holroyd et al., 1988). Other variables (anxiety, scales 1, 2, and 3 of the MMPI) have been suggested as predictive of response to behavioral treatments as well (Blanchard et al., 1985; Werder, Sargent, & Coyne, 1981).

Holroyd et al. (1988) found that patients who were high in trait anger, and to a lesser extent, depressive symptoms, were less likely to respond to abortive pharmacological agents for migraine headache but these variables were uncorrelated

with response to a combination of relaxation training and thermal biofeedback, suggesting that the presence of the trait anger or depression could indicate nonpharmacological interventions as a first line treatment. Jacob et al. (1983) found that headache patients without significant depressive symptomatology responded better to relaxation training than those with depressive symptomatology. These data suggest that a combination of pharmacological and nonpharmacological interventions may be useful, such as nonpharmacological management of headache combined with pharmacological management of depression. CBT, which has received extensive support for treating anxiety and depression, may be more useful when comorbid conditions are present. Finally, significant reductions in anxiety and depression typically occur following behavioral treatment, regardless of the headache type or the extent of headache relief (Blanchard et al., 1986; Blanchard, Steffek, Jaccard, & Nicholson, 1991).

Environmental Factors

It is also important to be mindful of environmental factors/consequences that may be serving to maintain pain, as pointed out long ago by Fordyce (1976). Fowler (1975) has applied this perspective to headache patients. A patient is most likely to "learn" pain behavior when (a) pain behavior is positively reinforced or rewarded, or (b) "well" behavior is insufficiently reinforced, punished, or aversive. Therapists can unwittingly become a part of the learned pain behavior process in several different ways. Attention from others is a near universal reinforcer; the sympathetic ear of a therapist can be especially powerful. Medication prescribing practices can foster untoward learning effects as well. Palliative medications are often prescribed on an "as-needed" basis, accompanied by the caution, "Take this only when you really need it; it is powerful and may be addicting." When instructed in this manner, many patients will delay taking the medication until their pain becomes barely tolerable or near maximum level. If the medication effectively relieves the headache, medication-taking behavior has become strongly reinforced and is likely to become more frequent in the future (based on principles of learning theory). Similar factors come into play when treating patients whose headache severity has markedly compromised their day-to-day functioning (a common occurrence with post-traumatic headache). Such patients are typically instructed, "Do only what you can" or continue activities "until the pain becomes unbearable." The patient begins an activity, experiences increased pain, and then stops. Stopping the activity reduces discomfort and makes the patient less likely to engage in activity in the future. Consequently, therapists need to probe for environmental conditions, including familial factors, which might be serving to maintain headache pain behavior and to be aware of how he or she may subtly begin to contribute to the headache problem itself.

When such environmental factors are in evidence, therapists are urged to lessen (gradually) attention given to pain symptoms, encourage and reinforce efforts to cope with head pain (ask, "How are you trying to manage your headaches?" rather than, "How is your headache today?"), encourage the inactive patient to set daily goals and stick to them despite the pain level, and arrange for needed analgesic medications to be taken on a time-contingent, as opposed to a pain-contingent, basis. Fordyce (1976) presents a detailed format for questions to ask of patients and family members being treated for chronic pain, which are also appropriate to consider when evaluating headache patients. In the only examination of its type, Allen and Shriver (1998) found that adding parent training in pain behavior management to standard biofeedback treatment significantly incremented effectiveness over biofeedback alone for adolescent migraineurs.

Patient Preference and Cost Effectiveness

To date, there are no clear empirical data to suggest whether patient preference is predictive of treatment outcome. Nonetheless, this factor should always be considered when providing clinical treatments or interventions to individual patients. As a matter of course, compliance and cooperation are likely to be influenced by patient preference for treatment type; to ignore this would be a serious error.

Treatment Algorithms

Holroyd et al. (1998) provide treatment algorithms for the integration of behavioral and pharmacological therapies for recurrent migraine and tension-type headache that clinicians and researchers may find useful. While these algorithms have not been empirically tested, they are based on the extensive empirical literature previously described and represent a set of empirically supported decision-making guidelines.

These authors suggest the use of both pharmacological and nonpharmacological treatments for migraines that are frequent and/or severe. For migraine headaches that are less frequent and unaccompanied by psychological problems, factors such as patient preference, previous treatment experience/outcome, and cost may be used to select either pharmacological or nonpharmacological methods of treatment as a first line treatment. Should the initial choice fail to result in a satisfactory outcome, the alternate strategies may then be used as a supplement or second-line treatment.

For tension-type headaches, Holroyd et al. (1998) consider behavioral interventions to be the treatment of choice. However, if the headaches are unremitting or complicated by significant psychological disturbance, the use of antidepressant medication should be considered early. Minimal therapist contact interventions (see next) may be tried initially, with more intensive treatments applied if initial efforts are unsuccessful. If the addition of other behavioral and cognitive behavioral interventions fails to result in a satisfactory outcome, then prophylactic medications should be considered.

Treatment Format and Delivery

In addition to individual characteristics of patients that may predict response to treatment and aid in the selection of appropriate intervention(s), treatment planning also involves decisions about treatment format and delivery. Practical factors, such as limited patient and/or therapist time, cost prohibitions, and limited geographical access, may preclude intensive individual therapies (Rowan & Andrasik, 1996). This has led researchers to explore more economical alternatives.

Minimal Therapist Contact Interventions

The main alternate delivery approach investigated to date retains a 1:1 focus, but markedly reduces clinician contact by supplementing treatment with instructional manuals and cassettes that subjects utilize on their own at home or at work. The "prototypical" minimal therapist contact intervention includes an initial in-office session, a mid-treatment office session, and a final session with the therapist over the course of eight weeks or so, plus the use of two to three telephone contacts in between. These intermittent visits and calls are designed to keep patients engaged in treatment and to offset the high dropout rates that have occurred with entirely self-help approaches (Rowan & Andrasik, 1996). Thus, while time spent at the office and with the therapist is significantly reduced (as are costs), time investments by the patient are still extensive.

There is a substantial body of literature to suggest that nonpharmacological interventions may be effectively applied in cost-effective, minimal therapist contact formats and that these formats rival more "intensive" interventions, with both adults and children (Haddock et al., 1997; Rowan & Andrasik, 1996). Furthermore, the benefits appear to be well maintained over time (Blanchard et al., 1988). Minimal therapist contact interventions have been found to have attrition rates similar to more intensive therapies and to produce two to six times more headache reduction per therapist hour than more intensive therapies (thus affirming their cost-effectiveness). Factors that predict response to such minimal contact interventions are less clear than those that have been previously discussed for more "intensive" treatments.

Minimal therapist contact interventions have both advantages and disadvantages. Some of the advantages include reduced therapist time and costs to the patient, expanded accessibility of treatment, reduced scheduling demand, and reduced patient apprehension. Disadvantages include an increase in the time commitment and possibly a need for greater motivation on the part of the patient (Andrasik, 1996).

Researchers have begun to explore the feasibility of administering behavioral treatments to large numbers of patients, via mass media and the Internet. Researchers in the Netherlands (de Bruin-Kofman, van de Wiel, Groenman, Sorbi, & Klip, 1997) used television and radio instruction to supplement home-study material on headache management. Favorable results were obtained for the small sample ($n = 271$) that was available to participate in the outcome analysis, however this was just a fraction of the people who purchased the self-help program (approximately 15,000). The first Internet-based study was centered at the worksite and was implemented via computer kiosks (Schneider, Furth, Blalock, & Sherrill, 1999). In the second study, patients accessed the Web from terminals at home (Ström, Pettersson, & Andersson, 2000). Modest improvements occurred, but attrition was considerable (greater than 50%) in both investigations.

Group Treatment

Napier, Miller, and Andrasik (1997–1998), upon examining the limited investigations of behavioral and cognitive behavioral group interventions for recurrent headache, offered the following conclusions. Although only one study directly compared individual versus group delivery (Johnson & Thorn, 1989), the clinical outcomes for group treatment appeared to rival those reported for individually administered treatments. Subject retention rates were similar as well. Time devoted to group treatment varied considerably, ranging from a low of 270 minutes (or 4.5 hours) for a minimal contact approach to 900 minutes (or 15 hours) for an intensive, interdisciplinary approach. Group sizes ranged from 2 to 15 participants and utilized 1 to 2 therapists. The only study that directly investigated the role of therapist experience found it was significantly related to clinical outcome (Holroyd & Andrasik, 1978). These limited data suggest that group treatment is as effective as individual treatment for recurrent headache disorders. Once again, group treatment may be less expensive than individual therapy. However, group treatment also requires greater scheduling demands and may pose some of the same disadvantages as individual treatment, such as demands on patient and/or therapist time, cost prohibitions, and limited geographical access.

SUMMARY AND FUTURE DIRECTIONS

Individual studies, metaanalytic analyzes, and task force reviews have shown that a number of behavioral treatments (relaxation, biofeedback, and CBT) are efficacious for uncomplicated forms of migraine and tension-type headache, that improvement rates appear to rival those for pharmacological treatments, and that certain treatment combinations can be more efficacious than single modality approaches. Researchers continue to explore the boundary dimensions for who is and who is not an ideal candidate for behavioral treatment. People experiencing cluster, menstrual, posttraumatic, drug-induced, or daily, unremitting headaches or certain comorbid conditions present special challenges that can require integrative, multidisciplinary, and intensive treatment approaches. Although much has been accomplished since behavioral researchers entered the headache arena approximately 30 years ago, the battle has only begun. Much additional research is needed, and we conclude the chapter with brief mention of likely directions this research will take.

Researchers have just begun to realize the advantages of computers and the Web for facilitating both assessment and treatment. Pocket computers make it possible to monitor when ratings are actually made, administer prompts when data are incomplete, collect volumes of data in a relatively easy and efficient manner, transmit data directly to the research/clinic site, and communicate interactively with the therapist or researcher (Holroyd, in press). Web- and CD-Rom-administered treatments have the potential to reach patients that heretofore could not or would not seek treatment. Folen, James, Earles, and Andrasik (2001) have shown that it is possible to use the Internet to transport biofeedback treatment to remote sites that lack the needed expertise. Particular challenges in these approaches will be ensuring adequate medical evaluation and follow-up, dealing with emergencies and crises, and resolving issues related to practicing across state-licensing boundaries.

Although it is clear that certain behavioral treatments are efficacious, the mechanisms by which they operate are not well understood. This is not so surprising, considering that the etiologies of headache were not all that clear until recently. Accounts of pathophysiology for both of the major forms of headache have shifted from peripheral and vascular models to models that focus on central nervous system dysfunction (central sensitization for tension-type headache and central excitability for migraine). Recognition of this will certainly lead to development of new psychophysiological assessment approaches, investigation of biochemical changes that result from treatment (e.g., Olness, Hall, Rozneicki, Schmidt, & Theoharidies, 1999), and further development of treatments that are more directly tied to the underlying etiology (such as EEG biofeedback).

Researchers are only beginning to address the all-important issues of treatment selection, treatment sequencing, and patient selection. This is a daunting task that will require large samples and much effort. Most of the research to date has been conducted in specialized research or treatment centers, with patients who have been highly selected. The majority of patients who seek treatment are not seen in these settings. Importing treatments to the settings where they are most needed (primary care) and investigating parameters for optimizing success will occupy much research time in the near term. Finally, it is expected that future research may identify certain headache types or situations that are uniquely suited for behavioral interventions, such as during pregnancy when women are advised to be very cautious about use of certain medications (e.g., Marcus, Scharff, & Turk, 1995).

REFERENCES

Allen, K. D., & Shriver, M. D. (1998). Role of parent-mediated pain behavior management strategies in biofeedback treatment of childhood migraines. *Behavior Therapy, 29,* 477–490.

Andrasik, F. (1986). Relaxation and biofeedback for chronic headaches. In A. D. Holzman & D. C. Turk (Eds.), *Pain management: A handbook of psychological treatment approaches* (pp. 213–329). New York: Pergamon Press.

Andrasik, F. (1990). Psychologic and behavioral aspects of chronic headache. *Neurologic Clinics, 8,* 961–976.

Andrasik, F. (1996). Behavioral management of migraine. *Biomedicine and Pharmacotherapy, 50,* 52–57.

Andrasik, F. (2000). Biofeedback. In D. I. Mostofsky & D. H. Barlow (Eds.), *The management of stress and anxiety in medical disorders* (pp. 66–83). Boston: Allyn & Bacon.

Andrasik, F. (2001a). Assessment of patients with headache. In D. C. Turk & R. Melzack (Eds.), *Handbook of pain assessment* (2nd ed., pp. 454–474). New York: Guilford Press.

Andrasik, F. (2001b). Migraine and quality of life: Psychological considerations. *Journal of Headache and Pain, 2*(Suppl. 1), S1–S9.

Andrasik, F., & Baskin, S. (1987). Headache. In R. L. Morrison & A. S. Bellack (Eds.), *Medical factors and psychological disorders: A handbook for psychologists* (pp. 325–349). New York: Plenum Press.

Andrasik, F., Blanchard, E. B., Neff, D. F., & Rodichok, L. D. (1984). Biofeedback and relaxation training for chronic headache: A controlled comparison of booster treatments and regular contacts for long-term maintenance. *Journal of Consulting and Clinical Psychology, 52,* 609–615.

Andrasik, F., Burke, E. J., Attanasio, V., & Rosenblum, E. L. (1985). Child, parent, and physician reports of a child's headache pain: Relationships prior to and following treatment. *Headaches, 25,* 421–425.

Andrasik, F., & Holroyd, K. A. (1980a). Reliability and concurrent validity of headache questionnaire data. *Headache, 20,* 44–46.

Andrasik, F., & Holroyd, K. A. (1980b). A test of specific and nonspecific effects in the biofeedback treatment of tension headache. *Journal of Consulting and Clinical Psychology, 48,* 575–586.

Andrasik, F., & Wincze, J. P. (1994). Emotional and psychological aspects of mild head injury. *Seminars in Neurology, 14,* 60–66.

Arena, J. G., Hannah, S. L., Bruno, G. M., & Meador, K. J. (1991). Electromyographic biofeedback training for tension headache in the elderly: A prospective study. *Biofeedback and Self-Regulation, 16,* 379–390.

Arena, J. G., Hightower, N. E., & Chong, G. C. (1988). Relaxation therapy for tension headache in the elderly: A prospective study. *Psychology and Aging, 3,* 96–98.

Attanasio, V., Andrasik, F., Burke, E. J., Blake, D. D., Kabela, E., & McCarran, M. S. (1985). Clinical issues in utilizing biofeedback with children. *Clinical Biofeedback and Health, 8,* 134–141.

Barrett, E. J. (1996). Primary care for women: Assessment and management of headache. *Nurse Midwifery, 41,* 117–124.

Beck, A. T., Emery, G., & Greenberg, R. L. (1985). *Anxiety disorders and phobias: A cognitive perspective.* New York: Basic Books.

Beck, A. T., Rush, A. J., Shaw, B. F., & Emery, G. (1979). *Cognitive therapy of depression.* New York: Guilford Press.

Benson, H., Klemchuk, H. P., & Graham, J. R. (1974). The usefulness of the relaxation response in the therapy of headache. *Headache, 14,* 49–52.

Bernstein, D. A., & Borkovec, T. D. (1973). *Progressive relaxation training.* Champaign, IL: Research Press.

Blanchard, E. B. (1992). Psychological treatment of benign headache disorders. *Journal of Consulting and Clinical Psychology, 60,* 537–551.

Blanchard, E. B., & Andrasik, F. (1985). *Management of chronic headaches: A psychological approach.* New York: Pergamon Press.

Blanchard, E. B., & Andrasik, F. (1987). Biofeedback treatment of vascular headache. In J. P. Hatch, J. G. Fisher, & J. D. Rugh (Eds.), *Biofeedback: Studies in clinical efficacy* (pp. 1–79). New York: Plenum Press.

Blanchard, E. B., Andrasik, F., Ahles, T. A., Teders, S. J., & O'Keefe, D. (1980). Migraine and tension headache: A meta-analytic review. *Behavior Therapy, 14,* 613–631.

Blanchard, E. B., Andrasik, F., Appelbaum, K. A., Evans, D. D., Jurish, S. E., Teders, S. J., et al. (1985). The efficacy and cost-effectiveness of minimal-therapist-contact, non-drug treatments of chronic migraine and tension headache. *Headache, 25,* 214–220.

Blanchard, E. B., Andrasik, F., Appelbaum, K. A., Evans, D. D., Myers, P., & Barron, K. D. (1986). Three studies of psychologic changes in chronic headache patients associated with biofeedback and relaxation therapies. *Psychosomatic Medicine, 48,* 73–83.

Blanchard, E. B., Andrasik, F., Jurish, S. E., & Teders, S. J. (1982). The treatment of cluster headache with relaxation and thermal biofeedback. *Biofeedback and Self-Regulation, 7,* 185–191.

Blanchard, E. B., Andrasik, F., Neff, D. F., Arena, J. G., Ahles, T. A., Jurish, S. E., et al. (1982). Biofeedback and relaxation training with three kinds of headache: Treatment effects and their prediction. *Journal of Consulting and Clinical Psychology, 50,* 562–575.

Blanchard, E. B., Appelbaum, K. A., Guarnieri, P., Morrill, B., & Dentinger, M. P. (1987). Five year prospective follow-up on the treatment of chronic headache with biofeedback and/or relaxation. *Headache, 27,* 580–583.

Blanchard, E. B., Appelbaum, K. A., Guarnieri, P., Neff, D. F., Andrasik F., Jaccard, J., et al. (1988). Two studies of the long-term follow-up of minimal therapist contact treatments of vascular and tension headache. *Journal of Consulting and Clinical Psychology, 56,* 427–432.

Blanchard, E. B., Appelbaum, K. A., Radnitz, C. L., Jaccard, J., & Dentinger, M. P. (1989). The refractory headache patient. I: Chronic daily, high intensity headache. *Behaviour Research and Therapy, 27,* 403–410.

Blanchard, E. B., & Diamond, S. (1996). Psychological treatment of benign headache disorders. *Professional Psychology: Research and Practice, 27,* 541–547.

Blanchard, E. B., Hillhouse, J., Appelbaum, K. A., & Jaccard, J. (1987). What is an adequate length of baseline in research and clinical practice with chronic headache? *Biofeedback and Self-Regulation, 12,* 323–329.

Blanchard, E. B., Nicholson, N. L., Radnitz, C. L., Steffek, B. D., Appelbaum, K. A., & Dentinger, M. P. (1991). The role of home practice in thermal biofeedback. *Journal of Consulting and Clinical Psychology, 59,* 507–512.

Blanchard, E. B., Nicholson, N. L., Taylor, A. E., Steffek, B. D., Radnitz, C. L., & Appelbaum, K. A. (1991). The role of regular home practice in the relaxation treatment of tension headache. *Journal of Consulting and Clinical Psychology, 59,* 467–470.

Blanchard, E. B., & Schwarz, S. P. (1988). Clinically significant changes in behavioral medicine. *Behavioral Assessment, 10,* 171–188.

Blanchard, E. B., Steffek, B. D., Jaccard, J., & Nicholson, N. L. (1991). Psychological changes accompanying non-pharmacological treatment of chronic headache: The effects of outcome. *Headache, 31,* 249–254.

Blanchard, E. B., Taylor, A. E., & Dentinger, M. P. (1992). Preliminary results from the self-regulatory treatment of high medication consumption headache. *Biofeedback and Self-Regulation, 17,* 179–202.

Bogaards, M. C., & ter Kuile, M. M. (1994). Treatment of recurrent tension headache: A Meta-analytic review. *Clinical Journal of Pain, 10,* 174–190.

Borgeat, F., Hade, B., Larouche, L. N., & Bedwani, C. N. (1980). Effects of therapist active presence on EMG biofeedback training of headache patients. *Biofeedback and Self-Regulation, 5,* 275–282.

Budzynski, T. H., Stoyva, J. M., Adler, C. S., & Mullaney, D. J. (1973). EMG biofeedback and tension headache: A controlled outcome study. *Psychosomatic Medicine, 35,* 484–496.

Cahn, T., & Cram, J. R. (1980). Changing measurement instrument at follow-up: A potential source of error. *Biofeedback and Self-Regulation, 5,* 265–273.

Campbell, J. K., Penzien, D. B., & Wall, E. M. (2000). *Evidence-based guidelines for migraine headaches: Behavioral and physical treatments.* Retrieved October 2000, from www.aan.com/public/practiceguidelines/headache_g1.htm

Cohen, M. J., McArthur, D. L., & Rickles, W. H. (1980). Comparison of four biofeedback treatments for migraine headache: Physiological and headache variables. *Psychosomatic Medicine, 42,* 463–480.

Collins, F. L., & Thompson, J. K. (1979). Reliability and standardization in the assessment of self-reported headache pain. *Journal of Behavioral Assessment, 1,* 73–86.

Cox, D. J., Freundlich, A., & Meyer, R. G. (1975). Differential effectiveness of electromyograph feedback, verbal relaxation instructions, and medication placebo with tension headaches. *Journal of Consulting and Clinical Psychology, 43,* 892–898.

de Bruin-Kofman, A. T., van de Wiel, H., Groenman, N. H., Sorbi, M. J., & Klip, E. (1997). Effects of a mass media behavioral treatment for chronic headache: A pilot study. *Headache, 37,* 415–420.

Diamond, S., Medina, J., Diamond-Falk, J., & DeVeno, T. (1979). The value of biofeedback in the treatment of chronic headache: A five-year retrospective study. *Headache, 19,* 90–96.

Diamond, S., & Montrose, D. (1984). The value of biofeedback in the treatment of chronic headache: A four-year retrospective study. *Headache, 24,* 5–18.

Diener, H. C., & Wilkinson, M. (Eds.). (1988). *Drug-induced headache.* Berlin, Germany: Springer-Verlag.

Duckro, P. N., Tait, R., Margolis, R. B., & Silvermintz, S. (1985). Behavioral treatment of headache following occupational trauma. *Headache, 25,* 328–331.

Epstein, L. H., & Abel, G. G. (1977). An analysis of biofeedback training effects for tension headache patients. *Behavior Therapy, 8,* 37–47.

Evans, R. W. (2001). Diagnostic testing for headache. *Medical Clinics of North America, 85,* 865–886.

Fahrion, S., Norris, P., Green, A., Green, E., & Snarr, C. (1986). Biobehavioral a treatment of essential hypertension: A group outcome study. *Biofeedback and Self-Regulation, 11,* 257–277.

Folen, R. A., James, L. C., Earles, J. E., & Andrasik, F. (2001). Biofeedback via telehealth: A new frontier for applied psychophysiology. *Applied Psychophysiology and Biofeedback, 26,* 195–204.

Fordyce, W. E. (1976). *Behavioral methods for chronic pain and illness.* St. Louis, MO: Mosby.

Fowler, R. S. (1975). Operant therapy for headaches. *Headache, 15,* 1–6.

Freitag, F. G. (1992). Headache clinics and inpatient units for treatment of headache. In S. Diamond & D. J. Dalessio (Eds.), *The practicing physician's approach to headache* (5th ed., pp. 270–280). Baltimore: Williams & Wilkins.

Gauthier, J. G., Ivers, H., & Carrier, S. (1996). Nonpharmacological approaches in the management of recurrent headache disorders and their comparison and combination with pharmacotherapy. *Clinical Psychology Review, 15,* 543–571.

Goslin, R. E., Gray, R. N., McCrory, D. C., Penzien, D. B., Rains, J. C., & Hasselblad, V. (1999, February). *Behavioral physical treatments for migraine headache: Technical review 2.2* (Prepared for the Agency for Health Care Policy and Research under Contract No. 290–94-2025). (Available from the National Technical Information Service; NTIS Accession No. 127946)

Grazzi, L., Andrasik, F., D'Amico, D., Leone, M., Usai, S., Kass, S. J., et al. (2001). *Behavioral and pharmacological treatment of drug-induced daily headache: Outcome at three years.* Manuscript submitted for publication.

Guitera, V., Muñoz, P., Castillo, J., & Pascual, J. (1999). Transformed migraine: A proposal for the modification of its diagnostic criteria based on recent epidemiological data. *Cephalalgia, 19,* 847–850.

Haddock, C. K., Rowan, A. B., Andrasik, F., Wilson, P. G., Talcott, G. W., & Stein, R. J. (1997). Home-based behavioral treatments for chronic benign headache: A meta-analysis of controlled trials. *Cephalalgia, 17,* 113–118.

Hermann, C., Blanchard, E. B., & Flor, H. (1997). Biofeedback treatment for pediatric migraine: Prediction of treatment outcome. *Journal of Consulting and Clinical Psychology, 65,* 611–616.

Hermann, C., Kim, M., & Blanchard, E. B. (1995). Behavioral and prophylactic pharmacological intervention studies of pediatric migraine: An exploratory meta-analysis. *Pain, 60,* 239–256.

Holden, E. W., Deichmann, M. M., & Levy, J. D. (1999). Empirically supported treatments in pediatric psychology: Recurrent pediatric headache. *Journal of Pediatric Psychology, 24,* 91–109.

Holm, J. E., Holroyd, K. A., Hursey, K. G., & Penzien, D. B. (1986). The role of stress in recurrent tension headache. *Headache, 26,* 160–167.

Holroyd, K. A. (in press). Assessment and psychological management of recurrent headache disorders. *Journal of Consulting and Clinical Psychology.*

Holroyd, K. A., & Andrasik, F. (1978). Coping and the self-control of chronic tension headache. *Journal of Consulting and Clinical Psychology, 46,* 1036–1045.

Holroyd, K. A., & Andrasik, F. (1982). A cognitive-behavioral approach to recurrent tension and migraine headache. In P. C. Kendall (Ed.), *Advances in cognitive-behavioral research and therapy* (Vol. 1, pp. 275–320). New York: Academic Press.

Holroyd, K. A., Andrasik, F., & Westbrook, T. (1977). Cognitive control of tension headache. *Cognitive Therapy and Research, 1,* 121–133.

Holroyd, K. A., France, J. L., Cordingley, G. E., Rokicki, L. A., Kvaal, S. A., Lipchik, G. L., et al. (1995). Enhancing the effectiveness of relaxation-thermal biofeedback training with propanolol hydrochloride. *Journal of Consulting and Clinical Psychology, 63*(2), 327–330.

Holroyd, K. A., Holm, J. E., Hursey, K. G., Penzien, D. B., Cordingley, G. E., Theofanous, A. G., et al. (1988). Recurrent vascular headache: Home-based behavioral treatment versus abortive pharmacological treatment. *Journal of Consulting and Clinical Psychology, 56,* 218–223.

Holroyd, K. A., & Lipchik, G. L. (1997). Recurrent headache disorders. In S. J. Gallant, G. P. Keita, & R. Royak-Schaler (Eds.), *Health care for women: Psychological, social, and behavioral influences* (pp. 365–384). Washington, DC: American Psychological Association.

Holroyd, K. A., Lipchik, G. L., & Penzien, D. B. (1998). Psychological management of recurrent headache disorders: Empirical basis for clinical practice. In K. S. Dobson & K. D. Craig (Eds.), *Empirically supported therapies* (pp. 187–236). Thousand Oaks, CA: Sage.

Holroyd, K. A., O'Donnell, F. J., Stensland, M., Lipchik, G. L., Cordingley, G. E., & Carlson, B. W. (2001). Management of chronic tension-type headache with tricyclic antidepressant medication, stress management therapy, and their combination. *Journal of the American Medical Association, 285,* 2208–2215.

Holroyd, K. A., & Penzien, D. B. (1986). Client variables and the behavioral treatment of recurrent tension headache: A meta-analytic review. *Journal of Behavioral Medicine, 9,* 515–536.

Holroyd, K. A., & Penzien, D. B. (1990). Pharmacological versus non-pharmacological prophylaxis of recurrent migraine headache: A meta-analytic review of clinical trials. *Pain, 42,* 1–13.

Holroyd, K. A., Penzien, D. B., & Cordingley, G. E. (1991). Propanolol in the management of recurrent migraine: A meta-analytic review. *Headache, 31,* 333–340.

Holroyd, K. A., Penzien, D. B., Holm, J. E., & Hursey, K. G. (1984, June). *Behavioral treatment of recurrent headache: What does the literature say?* Paper presented at the American Association for the Study of Headache, San Francisco.

Holroyd, K. A., Penzien, D. B., Hursey, K. G., Tobin, D. L., Rogers, L., Holm, J. E., et al. (1984). Change mechanisms in EMG biofeedback training: Cognitive changes underlying improvements in tension headache. *Journal of Consulting and Clinical Psychology, 52,* 1039–1053.

Horton, B. T., & Macy, D., Jr. (1946). Treatment of headache. *Medical Clinics of North America, 30,* 811–831.

International Headache Society. (1999a). Guidelines for controlled trials of drugs in migraine. In P. Tfelt-Hansen (Chair), *Members' handbook 2000* (2nd ed., pp. 111–133). Oslo, Norway: Scandinavian University Press.

International Headache Society. (1999b). Guidelines for trials of drug treatments in tension-type headache. In J. Schoenen (Chair), *Members' handbook 2000* (pp. 134–160). Oslo, Norway: Scandinavian University Press.

International Headache Society Headache Classification Committee. (1988). Classification and diagnostic criteria for headache disorders, cranial neuralagias, and facial pain. *Cephalalgia, 8*(Suppl. 7), 1–96.

Jacob, R. G., Turner, S. M., Szekely, B. C., & Eidelmen, B. H. (1983). Predicting outcome of relaxation therapy in headaches: The role of "depression." *Behavior Therapy, 14,* 457–465.

Jacobson, E. (1938). *Progressive relaxation.* Chicago: University of Chicago Press.

Johnson, P. R., & Thorn, B. E. (1989). Cognitive behavioral treatment of intractable headache. *Headache, 29,* 358–365.

Kudrow, L. (1982). Paradoxical effects of frequent analgesic use. In M. Critchley, A. Friedman, S. Gorini, & F. Sicuteri (Eds.), *Headache: Physiopathological and clinical concepts, Advances in neurology* (Vol. 33, pp. 335–341). New York: Raven Press.

Lake, A. E., IV. (2001). Behavioral and nonpharmacological treatments of headache. *Medical Clinics of North America, 85,* 1055–1075.

MacGregor, E. A. (1997). Menstruation, sex hormones, and migraine. *Neurologic Clinics, 15,* 125–141.

Mannix, L. K. (2001). Epidemiology and impact of primary headache disorders. *Medical Clinics of North America, 85,* 887–895.

Marcus, D. A., Scharff, L., & Turk, D. C. (1995). Nonpharmacological management of headache during pregnancy. *Psychosomatic Medicine, 57,* 527–535.

Martin, P. R. (1993). *Psychological management of chronic headaches.* New York: Guilford Press.

Massiou, H., & Bousser, M. G. (2000). Influence of female hormones on migraine. In J. Olesen, P. Tfelt-Hansen, & K. M. A. Welch (Eds.), *The headaches* (2nd ed., pp. 261–267). Philadelphia: Lippincott, Williams, & Wilkins.

Mathew, N. T. (1981). Prophylaxis of migraine and mixed headache: A randomized controlled study. *Headache, 21,* 105–109.

Mathew, N. T. (1987). Drugs and headache: Misuse and dependency. In C. S. Adler, S. M. Adler, & R. C. Packard (Eds.), *Psychiatric aspects of headache* (pp. 289–297). Baltimore: Williams & Wilkins.

Mathew, N. T., & Bendtsen, L. (2000). Prophylactic pharmacotherapy of tension-type headache. In J. Olesen, P. Tfelt-Hansen, & K. M. A. Welch (Eds.), *The headaches* (2nd ed., pp. 667–673). Philadelphia: Lippincott, Williams, & Wilkins.

Mathew, N. T., Kurman, R., & Perez, F. (1990). Drug induced refractory headache-Clinical features and management. *Headache, 30,* 634–638.

Mathew, N. T., Reuveni, U., & Perez, F. (1987). Transformed or evolutive migraine. *Headache, 27,* 102–106.

McCrory, D. C., Penzien, D. B., Hasselblad, V., & Gray, R. N. (2001). *Evidence report: Behavioral and physical treatments for tension-type and cervicogenic headache* (Product No. 2085). Des Moines, IA: Foundation for Chiropractic Education and Research.

Medina, J. L. (1992). Efficacy of an individualized outpatient program in treatment of chronic post-traumatic headache. *Headache, 32,* 180–183.

Meichenbaum, D. H. (1977). *Cognitive-behavior modification: An integrative approach.* New York: Plenum Press.

Merikangas, K. R., & Stevens, D. E. (1997). Comorbidity of migraine and psychiatric disorders. *Neurologic Clinics, 15,* 115–123.

Michel, P. (2000). Socioeconomic costs of headache. In J. Olesen, P. Tfelt-Hansen, & K. M. A. Welch (Eds.), *The headaches* (2nd ed., pp. 33–40). Philadelphia: Lippincott, Williams, & Wilkins.

Michultka, D. M., Blanchard, E. B., Appelbaum, K. A., Jaccard, J., & Dentinger, M. P. (1989). The refractory headache patient. II: High medication consumption (analgesic rebound) headache. *Behaviour Research and Therapy, 27,* 411–420.

Morley, S. (1986). Cognitive approaches to the treatment of chronic benign headache: A review and critique. *Behavioral Psychotherapy, 14,* 310–325.

Napier, D. A., Miller, C. M., & Andrasik, F. (1997–1998). Group treatment for recurrent headache. *Advances in Medical Psychotherapy, 9,* 21–31.

Nicholson, N. L., & Blanchard, E. B. (1993). A controlled evaluation of behavioral treatment of chronic headache in the elderly. *Behavior Therapy, 24,* 395–408.

Olesen, J. (2000). Classification of headache. In J. Olesen, P. Tfelt-Hansen, & K. M. A. Welch (Eds.), *The headaches* (2nd ed., pp. 9–15). Philadelphia: Lippincott, Williams, & Wilkins.

Olesen, J., & Goadsby, P. J. (2000). Synthesis of migraine mechanisms. In J. Olesen, P. Tfelt-Hansen, & K. M. A. Welch (Eds.), *The headaches* (2nd ed., pp. 331–336). Philadelphia: Lippincott, Williams, & Wilkins.

Olness, K., Hall, H., Rozneicki, J., Schmidt, W., & Theoharidies, T. C. (1999). Mast cell activation in children with migraine before and after training in self-regulation. *Headache, 39,* 101–107.

Packard, R. C. (1987). Differing expectations of headache patients and their physicians. In C. S. Adler, S. M. Adler, & R. C. Packard

(Eds.), *Psychiatric aspects of headache* (pp. 29–33). Baltimore: Williams & Wilkins.

Primavera, J. P., & Kaiser, R. S. (1992). Non-pharmacological treatment of headache: Is less more? *Headache, 32,* 393–395.

Radat, F., Sakh, D., Lutz, G., El Amrani, M., Ferreri, M., & Bousser, M.-G. (1999). Psychiatric comorbidity is related to headache induced by chronic substance use in migraineurs. *Headache, 39,* 477–480.

Ramadan, N. M., & Keidel, M. (2000). Chronic posttraumatic headache. In J. Olesen, P. Tfelt-Hansen, & K. M. A. Welch (Eds.), *The headaches* (2nd ed., pp. 771–780). Philadelphia: Lippincott, Williams, & Wilkins.

Rapoport, A. M., & Tepper, S. J. (2001). All triptans are not the same. *Journal of Headache and Pain, 2*(Suppl. 1), S87–S92.

Reich, B. A. (1989). Non-invasive treatment of vascular and muscle contraction headache: A comparative longitudinal study. *Headache, 29,* 34–41.

Rowan, A. B., & Andrasik, F. (1996). Efficacy and cost-effectiveness of minimal therapist contact treatments of chronic headaches: A review. *Behavior Therapy, 27,* 207–234.

Saper, J. R. (1987). Ergotamine dependency: A review. *Headache, 27,* 435–438.

Saper, J. R., Lake, A. E., III, Madden, S. F., & Kreeger, C. (1999). Comprehensive/tertiary care for headache: A 6-month outcome study. *Headache, 39,* 249–263.

Saper, J. R., & Sheftell, F. D. (2000). Headache in the abuse-prone individual. In J. Olesen, P. Tfelt-Hansen, & K. M. A. Welch (Eds.), *The headaches* (2nd ed., pp. 953–958). Philadelphia: Lippincott, Williams, & Wilkins.

Sarafino, E. P., & Goehring, P. (2000). Age comparisons in acquiring biofeedback control and success in reducing headache pain. *Annals of Behavioral Medicine, 22,* 10–16.

Sargent, J. D., Green, E. E., & Walters, E. D. (1973). Preliminary report on the use of autogenic feedback training in the treatment of migraine and tension headaches. *Psychosomatic Medicine, 35,* 129–135.

Schneider, W. J., Furth, P. A., Blalock, T. H., & Sherrill, T. A. (1999). A pilot study of a headache program in the workplace. *Journal of Occupational and Environmental Medicine, 41,* 868–871.

Schultz, J. H., & Luthe, W. (1969). *Autogenic training* (Vol. 1). New York: Grune & Stratton.

Silberstein, S. D., Lipton, R. B., Solomon, S., & Mathew, N. T. (1994). Classification of daily and near-daily headaches: Proposed revisions to the IHS criteria. *Headache, 34,* 1–7.

Ström, L., Pettersson, R., & Andersson, G. (2000). A controlled trial of self-help treatment of recurrent headache conducted via the Internet. *Journal of Consulting and Clinical Psychology, 68,* 722–727.

Task Force on Promotion and Dissemination of Psychological Procedures. (1995). Training in and dissemination of empirically-validated psychological treatments: Report and recommendations. *Clinical Psychologist, 48,* 3–23.

Tepper, S. J. (2001). Safety and rational use of the triptans. *Medical Clinics of North America, 85,* 959–970.

ter Kuile, M. M., Spinhoven, P., Linssen, A. C. G., & van Houwelingen, H. C. (1995). Cognitive coping and appraisal processes in the treatment of chronic headaches. *Pain, 64,* 257–264.

Tfelt-Hansen, P., & Welch, K. M. A. (2000a). General principles of pharmacological treatment of migraine. In J. Olesen, P. Tfelt-Hansen, & K. M. A. Welch (Eds.), *The headaches* (2nd ed., pp. 385–389). Philadelphia: Lippincott, Williams, & Wilkins.

Tfelt-Hansen, P., & Welch, K. M. A. (2000b). Prioritizing prophylactic treatment of migraine. In J. Olesen, P. Tfelt-Hansen, & K. M. A. Welch (Eds.), *The headaches* (2nd ed., pp. 499–500). Philadelphia: Lippincott, Williams, & Wilkins.

Turk, D. C., Meichenbaum, D., & Genest, M. (1983). *Pain and behavioral medicine: A cognitive-behavioral perspective.* New York: Guilford Press.

Von Korff, M., Galer, B. S., & Stang, P. (1995). Chronic use of symptomatic headache medications. *Pain, 62,* 179–186.

Waggoner, C. D., & Andrasik, F. (1990). Behavioral assessment and treatment of recurrent headache. In T. W. Miller (Ed.), *Chronic pain* (Vol. 1, pp. 319–361). Madison, CT: International Universities Press.

Werder, D. S., Sargent, J. D., & Coyne, L. (1981). MMPI profiles of headache patients using self-regulation to control headache activity. *Headache, 21,* 164–169.

Worz, R. (1983). Analgesic withdrawal in chronic pain treatment. In K. A. Holroyd, B. Schlote, & H. Zenz (Eds.), *Perspectives in research on headache* (pp. 137–144). Toronto, Ontario, Canada: Hogrefe.

CHAPTER 12

Psychosocial Oncology

ARTHUR M. NEZU, CHRISTINE MAGUTH NEZU, STEPHANIE H. FELGOISE, AND MARNI L. ZWICK

Like most wars, the "war on cancer" leaves casualties, scars, and lives in need of healing in its wake. It has only been recently that the community of health and mental health professionals has focused on the psychosocial needs of cancer patients and their families. An increasing awareness of the significant emotional, interpersonal, family, vocational, and functional problems experienced by such individuals, and how these problems potentially impact on their overall health quality of life and even health outcome, has led to the creation of the field of *psychosocial oncology* or *psycho-oncology*. According to Holland (1990), the two major areas of interest characterizing this cancer subspecialty involve: "(a) the impact of cancer on the psychological function of the patient, the patient's family, and staff; and (b) the role that psychological and behavioral variables may have in cancer

risk and survival" (p. 11). In addition, an important outgrowth of these areas of scientific inquiry involves developing and evaluating the efficacy of psychosocial interventions geared to improve a cancer patient's quality of life (Baum & Andersen, 2001; A. Nezu, Nezu, Freidman, Faddis, & Houts, 1998). This chapter provides an overview of this field, beginning with a brief description of cancer itself.

CANCER: A BASIC PRIMER

The word *cancer* was first used to describe various types of tumors by the Greek physician, Hippocrates. In Greek, words such as *carcinos* and *carcinoma* refer to a crab and initially described tumors that were probably due to the finger-like projections from a cancer that is reminiscent of a crab.

Although cancer is often thought of as being a single disease, it is actually a term used to describe in excess of 200 different diseases. The differing types of cancers can be classified into five major groups: *carcinoma* (a cancerous tumor, or malignant neoplasm, that originates in the surface tissue of body organs), *sarcoma* (a cancerous tumor originating in the bone, cartilage, muscle, fibrous connective tissue, or fatty tissue); *myeloma* (a malignant neoplasm originating in the plasma cells of the bone marrow), *lymphoma* (a cancerous tumor originating in the lymph system), and *leukemia* (cancer originating in the blood-forming tissue).

All types of cancer have one characteristic in common—the uncontrollable growth and accumulation of abnormal cells. Normal cells behave according to preprogrammed genetic rules unique to a particular cell type (e.g., skin, blood, brain). They divide, mature, die, and are replaced according to this systematic plan. Cancer cells, on the other hand, do not follow biological rules—they divide more rapidly than usual, grow in a disorderly fashion, and do not properly mature.

Immortal cells are those cancer cells that are not "programmed" to know when to stop dividing or die. They can destroy normal surrounding tissue and have a propensity to spread throughout the body. This abnormal process of malignancy leads to the accumulation of cancer cells that eventually form a mass or tumor. If the proliferation of this cancerous growth is not halted, the abnormal cells can extend to surrounding areas and metastasize or spread to form tumors in other parts of the body. Eventually, the organs and body systems that are affected cannot perform their proper functions which can lead to death.

Cancer Statistics

All of the statistics provided in this section were obtained from the American Cancer Society (2000) and Greenlee, Murray, Bolden, and Wingo (2000). During the year 2000, over 1.2 million new cases of invasive cancer are expected to have been diagnosed in the United States. This estimate does not include noninvasive cancers such as basal and squamous cell skin cancers, of which 1.3 million new cases will be diagnosed during this year. Since 1990, approximately 13 million new cancer cases have been diagnosed. More than 1,500 people are expected to die each day from cancer this year. It is the second leading cause of death in the United States, surpassed only by heart disease—1 of every 4 deaths in the United States is cancer-related.

Gender

Rates for the year 2000 indicate similar levels of incidence for men and women across all cancer types, the major difference being the incidence of breast cancer. For men, the most common cancers are expected to be cancers of the prostate, lung and bronchus, and colon and rectum. Accounting for 29% of the new cancer cases (i.e., 180,400 new cases), prostate cancer is the leading site for cancer incidence among men.

Among women, the three most commonly diagnosed cancers are breast, lung and bronchus, and colon and rectum. Collectively, these three sites will account for over 50% of all new cases of cancer in women. However, by itself, breast cancer is expected to account for over 180,000 new cancer cases (30%) in the year 2000.

Race

The incidence of cancer varies widely among differing racial and ethnic groups in the United States. In general, cancer incidence rates are highest among African Americans. For example, they are approximately 60% more likely to develop cancer as compared to Hispanics and Asian Americans/Pacific Islanders and twice as likely to develop cancer than among American Indians. African American men are also about 33% more likely to die from cancer than are Whites and twice as likely to die of cancer as compared to Asian Americans/Pacific Islanders, Hispanics, and American Indians.

The incidence of female breast cancer is highest among White women and lowest among American Indian women. However, African American women are more likely to die of breast cancer (as well as colon and rectum cancer) than are women of any other racial and ethnic group.

Improvement in Survival Rates

Approximately 8.4 million Americans who have a history of cancer are alive today. Some of these individuals are considered to be "cured," whereas the others continue to show evidence of cancer. Although there has been an increase in the mortality rates in the United States during the second half of the twentieth century, this is largely due to the increase in lung cancer. When deaths attributed to this cancer type are excluded, cancer mortality actually shows a decrease of approximately 16% since 1950.

More important as an indicator that there is significant progress in the "war on cancer" is the improvement in survival rates. Early in the twentieth century, few patients diagnosed with cancer were expected to live. In the 1930s, the survival rate was about 1 in 4. The five-year survival rate has improved during the past 60+ years—approximately 4 in 10 cancer patients are expected to be alive five years after they are diagnosed. The five-year relative survival rate for all cancers combined is approximately 59%.

Staging Cancer

Staging is the process of defining the extent or seriousness of a given cancer type, as well as a means to denote the degree of spread of the cancer cells from the origin of site to other parts of the body. The American Joint Commission on Cancer developed a classification system that incorporates three related variables: T (tumor); N (nodes); and M (metastasis). The T relates to the size of the primary tumor and whether it has invaded nearby tissues and structures. The N involves the degree to which lymph nodes have been affected by the primary tumor. When there is lymph node involvement, this means that the cancer has likely spread from the primary site and is more likely to spread to other sites. Last, M refers to whether the cancer has actually spread to other organs and the degree to which it has metastasized.

Cancers are then classified according to stages as a means of determining how far a cancer has progressed and whether and where it has spread. Labeled 0 to IV, there are five cancer stages. In addition, depending on the type of cancer, stages are sometimes subdivided (e.g., IIA, IIB). The higher the stage, the more advanced the cancer. Practically, a cancer in the early stage will likely be small and confined to a primary site. Advanced-stage cancers will likely be large and have spread to lymph nodes or other structures.

Cancer Treatment

Cancer treatment varies and includes surgery, radiation, chemotherapy, immunotherapy, and bone marrow transplantation. Any of these can be used as a primary treatment, which is the major intervention for a particular cancer type. Adjuvant therapy is given after the primary treatment has been implemented as part of a comprehensive treatment protocol. For example, a woman may have surgery to remove a breast tumor (primary treatment), followed by chemotherapy (adjuvant therapy). Adjuvant therapy eliminates those cancer cells not possible to remove during surgery. Neo-adjuvant therapy occurs prior to the primary treatment in order to control known or potential sites of metastasis. Prophylactic treatment is targeted to a site where a high risk for cancer development exists. For example, because small cell carcinoma of the lung has a high propensity for metastasis to the brain, prophylactic radiotherapy can be used to prevent such metastasis.

Surgery

Surgery is the oldest and most common form of cancer treatment, resulting in the removal of a primary tumor, the surrounding tissue, and affected lymph nodes. Surgery is also performed to remove tumors that are metastatic, recurrent, or residual. Surgery can also be prophylactic, for example, a woman who has had breast cancer may have her second breast removed to reduce the risk of cancer recurrence.

Chemotherapy

This approach is used for the treatment of hematological tumors and for solid tumors that have metastasized to other areas. Chemotherapy is a systemic intervention that alters the cancer cell life processes. The drug, or antineoplastic agent, does not have the ability to select only the malignant cells, however, so both normal and malignant cells are damaged. Side effects occur from the damage to rapidly dividing cells. Some agents damage other cells, such as renal cells, because of the agents' biochemical effects.

Radiation

High-energy waves or particles during radiation damage the DNA molecules in cancer cells, resulting in their eventual death. Normal cells within the field of treatment are also killed by radiation therapy which can lead to side effects. However, normal cells have the capacity to repair themselves, while the cancer cells do not. Side effects of radiation, unlike chemotherapy, are accumulative. Acute effects occur within the first six months of treatment. Chronic effects occur after the first six months. Nausea, vomiting, diarrhea, hair loss, and anemia can result from radiation therapy depending on the site of the treatment. These side effects generally resolve after the cells have had time to repair and resume normal function. The most common side effect of radiation therapy is fatigue. Long-term effects of radiation therapy are usually the result of permanent cell damage in the area receiving the therapy. Examples of chronic side effects are pulmonary pneumonitis, fibrosis (pulmonary and bladder), and sterility.

Immunotherapy

The use of biological response modifiers (BRMs) to treat cancer is a newer treatment that uses the individual's own immune system to fight the tumor cells in order to engender a therapeutic response. It is used for particular tumors such as hairy cell leukemia, melanoma, and renal cell carcinoma. The use of this treatment is somewhat problematic in that the immune system does not always treat cancer cells as foreign. Cancer cells have the ability to alter the cell membrane such that the immune system does not "read" it as abnormal. The three most commonly known BRMs are interferon (INF), interleukin-2 (IL-2), and colony stimulating factors (CSF). These are highly purified proteins that are administered to activate, modify, enhance, or restore the immune system. The CSFs are used to treat the reduced white cell count associated with chemotherapy. The most common side effect of this treatment is a flu-like syndrome consisting of headaches, fever, chills, and muscle and joint aches and pains.

Bone Marrow Transplantation

Advances in laboratory techniques have made bone marrow transplantation (BMT) a viable treatment option for a select group of patients. For some disease entities, a BMT can extend life or even cure a hematologic malignancy. However, for many solid tumors, BMT remains experimental. Diagnoses for which BMT may be a treatment option include aplastic anemia, leukemias, lymphomas, Hodgkin's disease, breast cancer, and multiple myeloma. Bone marrow is located in the iliac crest, sternum, long bones, and ribs. The marrow contains the blood-forming components that manufacture red cells, white cells, and platelets. In the marrow and circulating blood (peripheral), an immature cell, called a stem cell, exists that is the "parent" cell for the development of red cells, white cells, and platelets. If the marrow becomes malignant (i.e., leukemia), the blood-forming process is altered and results in a life-threatening situation. The individual then becomes at risk for lethal infections or hemorrhage. If the marrow can be destroyed and replaced with normal marrow free from the malignant cells, the malignancy can be potentially cured.

BEHAVIORAL RISK FACTORS

Only about 5% to 10% of all cancers are clearly hereditary. The remaining cancers are caused by mutations resulting from various internal (e.g., hormones) or external factors (e.g., sunlight). Behavioral risk factors refer to those lifestyle activities that increase the likelihood that a person will develop cancer. Such factors include tobacco, alcohol, diet, and exposure to sun. Additional psychosocial variables that have been investigated regarding their causal link to cancer include socioeconomic status and personality.

Smoking

According to the American Cancer Society (2000), smokers have a 10-fold relative risk of developing lung cancer compared with nonsmokers. With regard to mortality rates, cigarette smoking accounts for approximately 30% of total cancer deaths and 87% of all lung cancer deaths (Cinciripini, Gritz, Tsoh, & Skaar, 1998). Overall, smokers have an increased risk for developing a wide range of cancers, including lung, oral cavity, pharynx, larynx, esophageal, pancreatic, head and neck, and renal cancer. Ceasing tobacco use has been found to be beneficial with regard to cancer risk. For example, after 10 years of nonsmoking, the risk for lung cancer mortality decreases between 30% to 50%. Moreover, a 50% reduction in cancer risk of the esophagus and oral cavity has been found after only five years of smoking cessation (U.S. Department of Health and Human Services, 1990).

Alcohol

Although the specific biological underpinnings linking alcohol and increased risk for cancer are unclear at present, studies have clearly shown a definite association. For example, the American Cancer Society (2000) recommends that decreased alcohol consumption can decrease a person's risk for head, neck, and liver cancer. Recently, a study in Canada (Rohan, Jain, Howe, & Miller, 2000) found that women who drank more than 50 grams per day of alcohol (the equivalent of about 4 to 5 beers) were almost twice more likely to develop breast cancer than those who did not use alcohol.

Diet

A link between diet and cancer has been demonstrated in a wide variety of investigations. For example, population studies have shown that excessive fat intake (i.e., greater than 20% of total calories) is strongly associated with an increased incidence of colon, breast, prostate, and possibly pancreatic cancer (Winters, 1998). Increased cancer risk has also been found to be linked to various dietary deficiencies, such as low intake of fruits and vegetables, fiber, and micronutrients (e.g., riboflavin, iron). In addition, excessive pickling, smoking, and salting of foods has been found to be associated with increased cancer risk. Modification of diets has also been found to have a profound effect on cancer incidence (see chapter on obesity this volume).

Sun Exposure

Ultraviolet radiation from the sun, in particular UVB (radiation lying between 280 and 320 nanometers of the solar spectrum), has been linked to increased risk for skin cancer (melanomas and nonmelanomas). In addition to being carcinogenic, UVB is an immunosuppressor, potentially leading to DNA damage. UVA radiation, which is between 320 and 400 nanometers of the solar spectrum, because it was thought to be noncarcinogenic, is the basis for commercial tanning salon sun lamps. Recent studies, however, demonstrate that individuals who use suntanning beds had a 39% higher risk of melanoma (Westerdahl, Olsson, & Ingvar, 1994). In addition, sunscreen lotions that block UVB, but not UVA, may also be linked to increased melanoma rates.

Socioeconomic Status

Research that cuts across many varying populations around the world provides the following conclusions: (a) depending on the specific cancer site, in general, a direct and inverse relationship exists between socioeconomic status (SES) and cancer incidence; and (b) across cancer sites, the relationship between SES and cancer *survival* is positive, that is, as SES decreases, so does the rate of cancer survival (Balfour & Kaplan, 1998). It is likely that SES impacts on cancer incidence and survival rates by influencing various lifestyle activities, health behaviors, and access to health care, rather than on any endogenous pathways (e.g., immune system) themselves.

Personality

A cancer-prone personality, Type C, has been described by Morris and Greer (1980) as being characterized by behavior that is appeasing, unassertive, unexpressive of negative emotions (particularly anger), and socially compliant. Although some research suggests that such a set of personality characteristics is frequently observed among cancer patients, there is no clear evidence that this, or any other, personality type has a causal role in cancer (Watson & Greer, 1998).

Summary

Only a small percentage of cancers are known to have a genetic etiology. Certain lifestyle activities, such as smoking, drinking alcohol, diet, and exposure to the sun, places an individual at substantial risk for developing cancer and thus underscores the major role that psychosocial and behavioral factors serve in the etiopathogenesis of cancer. More importantly, the causal role that such behaviors play suggests many cancers might be preventable.

Research that has focused on a causal link between a particular personality type and cancer, similar to the association

identified between Type A personality characteristics and heart disease (see chapter by O'Callahan, Andrews, and Krantz in this volume), has not been fruitful. Specifically, a Type C personality has not been proven to be premorbidly predictive of cancer incidence.

PSYCHOSOCIAL EFFECTS OF CANCER

Considerable medical progress has been made in treating this set of diseases. Many forms are curable and there is a sustained decline in the overall death rate from cancer when you focus on the impact on the *total* population (Murphy, Morris, & Lange, 1997). Because of improvements in medical science, more people are living with cancer than ever before. Although the extensive medical needs of such patients may be well attended to, psychosocial and emotional needs are often overlooked (Houts, Yasko, Kahn, Schelzel, & Marconi, 1986). Almost every aspect of a person's life can be affected, as cancer engenders many stressors and can lead to a significantly compromised quality of life. Even for people who historically have coped well with major negative life events, cancer and its treatment greatly increases the stressful nature of even routine daily tasks. Weisman and Worden (1976–1977) refer to this situation for cancer patients as an "existential plight," where a person's very existence may be endangered. Recognizably, not every individual diagnosed with cancer will experience a plethora of problems, but most patients do report significant difficulties.

Prevalence of Psychiatric Disorders

Estimates of the prevalence of psychological difficulties range between 23% and 66% across cancer populations (Telch & Telch, 1985). In a study of 215 cancer patients with mixed diagnoses (Massie & Holland, 1987), 53% of the cancer patients evaluated were found to be adjusting normally to stress; however, nearly half (47%) had clinically apparent psychiatric disorders. Over two thirds (68%) had reactive anxiety and depression (adjustment disorders with depressed or anxious mood), 13% had major depression, 8% had an organic mental disorder, 7% had personality disorders, and 4% had anxiety disorders. In addition, of the psychiatric disorders observed in this population, 90% were reactions to or manifestations of the disease or treatment itself.

The prevalence of psychiatric disorders is especially high in patients experiencing pain as a result of cancer and its treatment. In the Psychosocial Collaborative Oncology Group study (Derogatis, Morrow, & Fetting, 1983), 39% of those who received a diagnosis of a psychiatric disorder were experiencing significant pain. The psychiatric diagnosis of such patients was predominantly adjustment disorder with depressed mood (69%), and 15% of the patients with significant pain had symptoms of major depression (Derogatis et al., 1983; Massie & Popkin, 1998).

Depression

Depression is a common experience among cancer patients. Studies utilizing both self-report and clinical observations suggest that major depression affects approximately 25% of cancer patients (Bukberg, Penman, & Holland, 1984; Massie & Holland, 1987). However, the variability in the incidence of depression among cancer patient samples has been found to vary from 1% to 53% (DeFlorio & Massie, 1995). It is likely that this large variability is a function of the lack of standardization in measurement and diagnostic criteria, suggesting the need for improvement in methodological rigor to more accurately determine depression prevalence rates.

Depression is also responsible for the largest percentage of psychiatric consultations for cancer patients. For example, Massie and Holland (1987) found that among 546 patients referred for consultation due to emotional distress, 54% had diagnoses of adjustment disorder with depressed mood and another 9% had diagnoses of major depressive disorder. In another study by Breitbart (1987) of a sample of cancer patients referred for suicide risk evaluation, one-third of the suicidal patients had major depression, with over half having an adjustment disorder. In addition, Mermelstein and Lesko (1992) found a fourfold increase in the rate of depression among oncology patients as compared to the general population, underscoring the seriousness of the problem.

Factors associated with greater prevalence of depression are a higher level of physical disability, advanced disease stage, and the presence of pain (Williamson & Schulz, 1995). Also, higher rates of depression have been associated with the side effects of medications and treatment for cancer. Chemotherapy and oncological surgical procedures are a source of possible iatrogenically-induced depression in cancer patients because of the negative side effects that may include body image disturbances and physical symptoms (Newport & Nemeroff, 1998). For example, McCabe (1991) estimates that 40% to 60% of patients' emotional distress is directly attributable to the cancer treatment itself.

Numerous studies have also investigated various psychosocial risk factors for developing depression among cancer patients. Some of the risks identified are premorbid coping skills, social isolation, first-degree relatives with a history of cancer and depression, a personal history of depression, a personal history of alcohol or other substance abuse, and socioeconomic pressures (Newport & Nemeroff, 1998; Weissman & Worden, 1976–1977).

Anxiety

Oncology patients often experience anxiety, for example, while waiting to hear their diagnosis, before procedures, treatment and diagnostic tests, and while waiting for test results (Jenkins, May, & Hughes, 1991). In addition, cancer treatments themselves can be anxiety provoking and may contribute to the actual psychological morbidity of patients with cancer (Carey & Burish, 1988). Studies indicate that anxiety increases during certain periods of the disease, such as the discovery of the tumor, then peaks during surgery and remains high until a year subsequent when it begins to decline (Jenkins et al., 1991). For some patients, anxiety can become so severe that they may be unable to adhere adequately to their medical treatment and seek to avoid fear-provoking procedures (Patenaude, 1990).

Anxiety disorders appear to be more common in persons with cancer than controls or other chronic illnesses in the general population. Maguire, Lee, and Bevington (1978), for example, found moderate to severe anxiety in 27% of a sample of breast cancer patients as compared to 14% in a control sample. In addition, Brandenberg, Bolund, and Sigurdardottir (1992) identified 28% of advanced melanoma patients as having anxiety compared to 15% of familial melanoma patients with no diseases. Massie and Holland (1987) reported that anxiety accounted for 16% of requests for psychiatric consultations among inpatients (after depression and organic mental disorder).

Some researchers have suggested that cancer survivors may respond to the psychological distress and uncertainty about the future by displaying posttraumatic stress disorder (PTSD) with symptoms similar to those experienced by victims of war or environmental disasters (Dow, 1991; Henderson, 1997). Some of these symptoms have been reported as somatic vigilance and recurrent recollection of illness-related events, as well as symptomatology around anniversary dates. However, these symptoms appear to dissipate over time as the fear of recurrence lessens (Henderson, 1997). Other studies have reported symptoms characteristic of stress or trauma symptoms in survivors of cancer, such as avoidant behaviors, intrusive thoughts, and heightened arousability (Alter, Pelcovitz, & Axelrod, 1996). A small number of studies have found that compared to controls or community samples, cancer patients have experienced increased PTSD (Cella, 1987; Cella & Tross, 1986). However, much of the research has focused more on the symptoms of

PTSD (i.e., avoidant symptoms, intrusive symptoms), rather than on the diagnosis of PTSD per se.

Suicide

Reports of suicide in cancer patients vary widely (Breitbart & Krivo, 1998), ranging from estimates suggesting that it is similar to the general population (Fox, Stanek, Boyd, & Flannery, 1982) to estimates indicating that it is 2 to 10 times greater (e.g., Whitlock, 1978). Holland (1982) suggests that reports of suicide in cancer patients are probably greatly underestimated because of the family's reluctance to report death by suicide.

The risk for suicide may be greater in the advanced stages of the illness (Chochinov, Wilson, Enns, & Lander, 1998) and with patients experiencing significant fatigue (Breitbart, 1987). Some evidence indicates that suicide is also more prevalent among patients with oral, pharyngeal, and lung cancers (e.g., Valente, Saunders, & Cohen, 1994). There are also periods during the course of the disease when patients may be at an increased risk for suicide. These include periods of hospitalization, immediately after discharge, and at the time of recurrence and/or treatment failure (Passik & Breitbart, 1996). However, it is important to recognize that suicide risk in patients with cancer may be at its highest after successful treatment or as a person's depression lifts. As depression and hopelessness have been found to be causally linked to suicide (Beck, Kovacs, & Weissman, 1975), the degree to which cancer patients experience such feelings may increase their vulnerability to suicide. In fact, hopelessness has been found to be a better predictor of completed suicide than depression alone (Beck et al., 1975). In addition, the fear of death or of recurrence of cancer may develop into suicidal ideation (Valente et al., 1994).

Delirium

Delirium is a common psychiatric problem among cancer patients because of the direct effects of cancer on the central nervous system (CNS) and the indirect CNS complications of the disease and medical treatment. Delirium can often go unrecognized because it mimics depression (Massie & Holland, 1987). Symptoms consist of agitation, impaired cognitive function, altered attention span, and a fluctuating level of consciousness. Delirium can be attributed to medications, electrolyte imbalance, failure of a vital organ or system, nutritional state, infections, vascular complications, or hormone-producing tumors (Breitbart & Cohen, 1998). Estimates of the prevalence of delirium in cancer patients range from 8% to 40% (Derogatis et al., 1983). Those at an increased

risk for delirium are in-patients, elderly patients, and those with an advanced or terminal disease (Massie, Holland, & Glass, 1983).

Body Image Problems

Body image is one of the most profound psychological consequences from cancer treatments affecting patients with a variety of disease sites. The scars and physical disfigurement serve as reminders of the painful experience of cancer and its treatment. The stress and depression that may be a result of body image concerns can further impact other areas of the patient's and family's life, such as sexual intimacy, psychological disorders, and self-esteem.

In women who have had breast surgery, concerns range from distress over scars to feelings of decreased sexual attractiveness and restrictions of use of certain items of clothing. In a study with women who had breast-conserving surgery, 25% had serious body image problems (Sneeuw et al., 1992). Even patients with cancer who have no outward changes in appearance can experience difficulty with body image. For example, among a sample of Hodgkin's survivors, 26% felt their physical attractiveness had decreased as a consequence of cancer (Fobair et al., 1986). Moreover, these perceived changes attenuated their level of energy and frequency of sexual activities, and increased feelings of depression. A sample of leukemia patients was also found to have poorer body image than those of a healthy control group (Mumma, Mashberg, & Lesko, 1992).

Sexual Functioning Difficulties

Estimates of sexual functioning problems vary depending on the type of cancer, but appear to be common across cancer sites. For example, approximately 18% to 25% of Hodgkin's disease patients experienced decreased sexual interest and activity or poorer sexual functioning as a result of having been treated for cancer (Fobair et al., 1986). In a study of cancer patients undergoing a BMT, 47% were found to have a global sexual dysfunction and 60% had abnormalities of at least one parameter of sexual dysfunction (Marks, Crilley, Nezu, & Nezu, 1996). Common sexual functioning problems among cancer patients include loss of sexual desire in both men and women, erectile dysfunction in men, and dyspareunia (painful intercourse) in women. Studies suggest that sexual dysfunctions continue 1 to 2 years posttreatment, indicating a large impact on a patient's quality of life (Ganz, Rowland, Desmond, Meyerowitz, & Wyatt, 1998; Marks, Friedman, DelliCarpini, Nezu, & Nezu, 1997). In addition, research has shown that a positive self-schema among women (i.e., whether they regard their sexuality in a positive light) is a significant predictor of sexual adjustment after cancer, whereas women with a negative self-schema were less likely to resume sex or have good sexual functioning after treatment for gynecologic cancer (Anderson, Woods, & Copeland, 1997).

Physical factors from the cancer treatment itself can contribute greatly to the patient's sexual dysfunctions. Chemotherapy, radiation, surgery, opiate and pain medications, antidepressant or antipsychotic medications can cause sexual dysfunctions, as well as infertility, in patients. For example, in men receiving prostatectomies, 85% to 90% experience erectile impotence (von Eschenbach, 1986). Loss of sexual desire may be a result of fatigue, pain, or weakness secondary to the cancer treatment, depression, body image concerns, and feelings of guilt or misbeliefs about the development and spread of cancer (Schover, 1997).

Psychological Issues among Terminal Patients

Cancer patients in the terminal phases of illness are especially vulnerable to both psychiatric and physical complications. Suicide is also more prevalent during such advanced stages. For example, Farberow, Schneidman, and Leonard (1963) found that out of several hundred suicides studied, 86% occurred in the preterminal or terminal stages of illness. Persistent pain and terminal illness were also the most requested reasons for wanting physician-assisted euthanasia (Helig, 1988).

Patients may go through a grieving process as they face their own mortality and the impact of their death on family and friends. Some patients may experience emotional distress including symptoms of guilt, anger, depression, and anxiety. It appears to be the process of dying, more than death itself, that is feared most by the cancer patient (Cramond, 1970). Fear may prevent patients from discussing these concerns with their physicians or others. Weisman and Worden (1976–1977) have found that terminal patients with cancer who survived longer are those who believed that death was not inevitable and refused to "let others pull away from them." Those with shorter survival, on the other hand, expressed suicidal ideation and often wanted to die.

Psychological Responses to Specific Cancer Treatments

Although the medical recovery from cancer during the past several decades has improved, treatments for cancer still engender a significant amount of psychological distress. In fact, oncology patients often describe medical treatment for cancer (i.e., surgery, BMT, radiation, chemotherapy) as "worse than the disease itself." In addition to the physical side effects specific to the treatments, the psychological consequences are taxing. The uncertainty after diagnosis and before treatment is stressful, as well as the fact that treatments are costly, time-consuming, and impact negatively on the patient and his or her family's quality of life. For example, cancer treatments may dictate when patients have to be admitted to the hospital or they may require frequent outpatient visits. While in the hospital, patients have schedules dictating when they can eat, shower, take medications, or have visitors. Thus, it is not uncommon for patients with cancer to experience a loss of personal control.

The impact of cancer treatments has long-term consequences as well. Individuals may experience adverse side effects many years after the treatment. These include organ dysfunction or failure, infection, bone deterioration, cataracts, or even a secondary diagnosis of cancer (Knobf, Pasacreta, Valentine, & McCorkle, 1998). For example, Byrd (1983) found that as a result of certain treatments being carcinogenic, the incidence of developing a second malignancy 20 years after treatment is approximately 17%, about 20 times that of the general population. Common psychosocial consequences related to various cancer treatments are discussed next.

Surgery

Surgery can be very stressful for the patient and family because of the diagnostic and prognostic information that follows most procedures. Also, surgery can result in scarring or tenderness in the site of operation, impeding functioning as well as patients' appraisal of their attractiveness (Jacobsen, Roth, & Holland, 1998). Strain and Grossman (1975) identified several patient concerns that can be elicited before surgery—threats to your sense of personal invulnerability, concerns about entrusting your life to strangers, fears about separating from home and family members, fears of loss of control or death while under anesthesia, fears of being partially awake during surgery, and fears of damage to body parts.

There are often psychological reactions related to the site of surgery or to the loss of a particular function, such as bowel function as a result of a colostomy. Often these negative emotional reactions arise from the significance of the loss, especially when involving the face, genitals, breast, or colon. For example, research suggests that women receiving a mastectomy are likely to suffer from body image disturbance and sexual and marital disruptions (Mock, 1993). In addition, patients undergoing head and neck surgery must cope with subsequent speech, taste, sight, and smell impairments. The more severe the structural and functional loss, the slower the recovery, the more prolonged the isolation, the lower the self-esteem, and the more pronounced the postoperative depression (Krouse, Krouse, & Fabian, 1989).

Chemotherapy

Along with physical side effects, such as nausea, diarrhea, fatigue, cognitive changes or anorexia, chemotherapy treatments can result in time lost from work, family disruption, and depressed mood. The end of treatment also signifies a loss for the patient because of the decreased medical surveillance and the loss of support and communication with the medical personnel (Hart, McQuellon, & Barrett, 1994). Approximately 45% of adult cancer patients experience nausea, vomiting, or both in the 24 hours preceding their chemotherapy (Burish & Carey, 1986). Anticipatory nausea and vomiting is a psychological consequence resulting from an associative learning process (i.e., classical conditioning) within the context of the chemotherapy treatment. These symptoms are often embarrassing for patients and can lead to discontinuation of treatment, resulting in more detrimental conditions (Carey & Burish, 1988). After treatment, these symptoms can persist and may actually generalize to other situations (Andrykowski, Redd, & Hatfield, 1985).

Radiation Therapy

Similar to patients experiencing chemotherapy, patients' receiving radiotherapy may become anxious. Some reports indicate that the waiting room experience triggers anticipatory anxiety. Women also fear recurrence after treatment because of the decreased medical attention from the radiotherapy staff (Greenberg, 1998). Radiation often arouses associations in individuals with an atomic bomb, nuclear accidents, radiation sickness, and ionizing radiation in the atmosphere. Patients can also experience claustrophobia, fear that the machine will not release the appropriate amount of radiation, and fear of burns to the skin. Greenberg (1998) found that 26% of a sample of oncology patients undergoing radiation treatment experienced significant apprehension and anticipation due to the fear that radiation may damage their bodies. The acute physical side effects of radiotherapy depend on the site, dose, and volume of treatment. However, anticipatory or conditioned nausea is prevalent in 60% of cases (Greenberg, 1998). Dry skin, desquamation, and darkening as a result of the treatment, may cause body image concerns in patients. Other side effects impacting the patients' quality of life include fatigue, sore throat, anorexia, and diarrhea.

Bone Marrow Transplantation

Bone marrow transplantation (BMT) is a physically and emotionally taxing procedure for both the patient and family. Patients undergoing a BMT are often treated for an extended time at a major medical center, which for many, may be a distance from home. This often creates monetary and transportation problems. Waiting for a donor, fearing relapse, the threat of infection in the isolated rooms, as well as the threat of death can also produce anxiety (Wochna, 1997). Neurocognitive symptoms are likely to appear during hospitalization, resulting in hallucinations or delirium. Even after discharge, the uncertainty of recurrence, the absence of medical care, and the pressure to engage in self-care behaviors to protect against infections can be distressing. Patients may be physically compromised by fatigue and weakness that may persist for 6 to 12 months post-BMT (Patenaude, 1990). This results in functional limitations impeding the patient's quality of life.

Summary

The psychosocial sequella of cancer can be devastating. Whereas not all oncology patients go on to experience clinically significant levels of psychopathology, estimates of general prevalence suggest that individuals with cancer are likely to undergo higher rates of psychological distress than the general population. Such psychological reactions include depression, anxiety, suicide, delirium, body image problems, and sexual dysfunctions.

Although the research generally documents an increased cancer-related risk for psychological distress, estimates of incidence and prevalence often vary significantly from study to study. In large part this variability is due to the methodological variations characteristic of these investigations. More specifically, these studies use different measures of distress, vary in their sample selection process, and employ varying diagnostic criteria. Future research should attempt to develop consensual methodologies to better estimate prevalence rates of emotional distress and psychopathology among oncology populations.

In addition to the general emotional distress that oncology patients may experience, cancer treatment itself can engender additional problems. Cancer patients often describe the treatment as worse than the disease. For example, a common problem experienced by cancer patients undergoing chemotherapy is *anticipatory* nausea and vomiting, whereby the nausea is classically conditioned to the antineoplastic protocol, leading to patients experiencing such problems prior to the next chemotherapy appointment.

Collectively, research has underscored the significant negative impact of having cancer and being treated for it. However, not all oncology patients experience severe and long-lasting psychological difficulties. Similar to other major stressful events, the negative effects of cancer can be attenuated as a function of various psychosocial factors. In the next section, the stress-buffering roles of coping and social support regarding cancer are reviewed.

PSYCHOSOCIAL FACTORS INFLUENCING THE IMPACT OF CANCER

Coping

Although the type of tumor, treatment, diagnosis, and prior quality of life greatly determine the course of the disease, there are certain coping responses that significantly influence the adaptation process (Burgess, Morris, & Pettingale, 1988; A. Nezu, Nezu, Houts, Friedman, & Faddis, 1999). When facing a stressful life event, such as cancer, various coping skills and styles are valuable in maintaining adequate functioning and can actually moderate the negative impact of such traumatic events on physical, social, and emotional functioning (Billings & Moos, 1981; Moyer & Salovey, 1996).

According to Lazarus and Folkman (1984), the term *coping* refers to the cognitive and behavioral activities by which a person attempts to manage a potentially stressful situation (see also chapter by Manne in this volume). Researchers have investigated the association between various coping styles and psychological adaptation and health outcome among oncology patients. Such variables include avoidance/denial, fighting spirit/optimism, problem solving, and health information.

Avoidance/Denial

In the psychosocial oncology literature, denial generally is defined by constructs such as avoidance, distancing, and emotional suppression (Moyer & Levine, 1998). In general, research has yielded conflicting results regarding the impact of denial on adjustment. For example, Watson, Greer, Blake, and Shrapnell (1984) interviewed cancer patients after surgery and found that those who initially denied the seriousness of the illness reported less mood disturbance as compared to those patients who initially accepted the implications of the disease and admitted fears of death. Other studies further suggest that avoidance acts as an escape from the stressful situation or as a positive short-term coping mechanism for avoiding the overwhelming problems associated with the

diagnosis of cancer (Barraclough, 1994; Moyer & Levine, 1998). However, Carver et al. (1993) found avoidance coping to be positively correlated with emotional distress. In addition, Penman (1982) found that oncology patients who reported using avoidance coping also reported poorer adaptation to the cancer experience. More recently, C. M. Nezu et al. (1999) found that avoidance coping was strongly correlated with increased levels of anxiety, depression, and more frequent cancer-related problems.

Fighting Spirit/Optimism

Individuals with cancer who demonstrate more of a confrontational coping style, optimism, and a "fighting spirit" have been found to have a more positive psychological adjustment compared to those with passive acceptance, helplessness, anxious preoccupation, avoidance, and denial (Greer, Morris, & Pettingale; 1979; van't Spijker, Trijsburg, & Duivenvoorden, 1997). In general, the construct of optimism has been associated with less distress in individuals facing a diagnosis of cancer. For example, Carver et al. (1993) studied optimism in breast cancer patients for a year postsurgery and found this construct to be positively associated with higher levels of acceptance, use of humor as a coping tactic, and positive reframing of the experience, particularly in the early stages following surgery. Furthermore, Weisman and Worden (1976–1977) found that persons with cancer who experienced high levels of emotional distress were found to be pessimistic, tending to give up easily and to expect little support. Such individuals were found to have more interpersonal and intrapersonal difficulties prior to the diagnosis of cancer, and, during the course of treatment, perceived more health concerns, doubts, and a worse prognosis. Further, C. M. Nezu et al. (1999) found a positive orientation toward coping with stress to be negatively correlated with emotional distress among adult cancer patients.

Problem Solving

Problem solving in real-life situations (referred to as "social problem solving" see A. Nezu et al., 1998) is defined as "a general coping approach that can help people manage or adapt to any stressful situation, thereby enhancing their flexibility and perceived control and minimizing their emotional distress even in situations that cannot be changed for the better" (p. 10, A. Nezu et al., 1999). Deficits in problem-solving ability have also been found to be associated with psychological distress in patients with cancer. For example, C. M. Nezu et al. (1999) reported that a sample of adult cancer patients who were characterized by less effective problem-solving ability were also found to report higher levels of depressive and anxiety symptomatology, as well as more frequent cancer-related problems. Furthermore, poorer problem-solving ability was also found to predict emotional distress among a sample of breast cancer survivors who had undergone surgery between 1 and 13.3 years previously. In addition, the quality and effectiveness of a person's problem-solving skills appear to be important in determining adjustment to a sexual relationship, such as sexual satisfaction or dysfunction after a BMT. More specifically, A. Nezu and Nezu (1998) conducted a study with 30 participants who underwent a BMT and found that problem solving significantly predicted post-BMT sexual dysfunction.

A. Nezu, Nezu, Faddis, DelliCarpini, and Houts (1995) reported a study that included 134 adult cancer patients whereby problem-solving ability was found to moderate the effects of cancer-related stress. Specifically, under similar levels of high cancer-related stress, persons with cancer characterized by poor problem-solving ability reported significantly higher levels of depressive and anxiety symptomatology than oncology patients characterized by more effective problem solving.

Monitoring and Blunting

Miller and her colleagues (e.g., Miller, Fang, Diefenbach, & Bales, 2001) have developed a cognitive-social health information processing model that outlines how two types of coping styles—monitoring and blunting—predict reactions to a cancer diagnosis. Individuals who dispositionally scan for threatening cancer cues or information are considered "monitors," whereas "blunters" are individuals who dispositionally attempt to distract themselves from and minimize threatening cancer-related information. Monitors are characterized by greater perceptions of threat, lower self-efficacy expectations, and greater cancer-related distress. The importance of attempting to identify such coping styles lies in the manner in which information should be provided to the differing "types" of patients. For example, framing cancer-related information in a less negative, nonthreatening manner can lead to reduced distress among monitors.

Coping and Improved Survival Rates

Psychosocial functioning and coping have also been found to be related to length of survival and decreased mortality rates. Early research in the 1950s first suggested that cancer patients' psychological characteristics were systematically related to length of survival. For example, individuals whose disease had progressed for the worse were described as polite, cooperative, and unable to express negative affects, particularly hostility, whereas longer survivors were described as emotionally expressive (Royak-Schaler, 1991). Studies conducted at the Faith Courtauld Research Unit of King's College in London with 160 women with breast cancer found that suppression of anger and passive, stoic response styles were associated with poorer disease outcomes, especially in women under the age of 50 (Royak-Schaler, 1991). Furthermore, a 10-year prospective study continued to show higher survival rates (55%) for women with a fighting spirit versus 22% survival among women who responded with stoic acceptance or helplessness/hopelessness (Greer et al., 1979). A similar positive association has been found between fighting spirit and good health outcome by Fawzy et al. (1993), whereas anxious preoccupation (Greer, Morris, Pettingale, & Haybittle, 1990), hopelessness (Morris, Pettingale, & Haybittle, 1992), and a stoic acceptance style (Weissman & Worden 1976–1977) have all been found to be strongly associated with poor health and disease outcome.

Pessimism has also been found to be linked to cancer survival. For example, Schulz, Bookwala, Knapp, Scheier, & Williamson (1996) followed a group of cancer patients for a period of eight months, at the end of which one-third had died. Beyond site of cancer and levels of symptoms at baseline, a measure of pessimism obtained earlier significantly predicted mortality rates, that is, people with a pessimistic orientation were less likely to be alive at the eight-month follow-up.

Social Support

The difference in the level of social support or the perception of support can have an important impact on patients' sense of well-being when confronting the stress of cancer and its treatments. Social supports are the resources provided by those people in an individual's social network, such as spouses, family members, friends, coworkers, fellow patients, or professionals. These resources are helpful in times of stress (e.g., dealing with an illness) and may consist of instrumental aid, expressive or emotional aid, and informational aid. The beneficial effects of social support can be both direct (i.e., positive social interactions can directly increase positive cognitions, emotions, and behaviors), and indirect (i.e., as a stress buffer through the provision of various coping resources, such as emotional or practical support) (Helgelson, Cohen, & Fritz, 1998).

According to Bloom (1982), it is the perception of social support, measured by family cohesiveness and the frequency of social contact, that is the strongest predictor of healthy coping responses. However, some research suggests that this relationship appears to be stronger for patients with a good cancer prognosis as opposed to a poor prognosis (Dunkel-Schetter, 1984). Despite the strong importance of social support in the lives of breast cancer patients, approximately 33% of them do not feel they have adequate social support (Peters-Golden, 1982). In studies with breast cancer patients, social support has been found to be related to psychological, social, and physical benefits (Moyer & Salovey, 1996; Royak-Schaler, 1991; Stanton & Snider, 1993). Specifically, communication and shared decision making with the person's spouse enhance adjustment to mastectomy, including the sexual relationship (Royak-Schaler, 1991; Wortman & Dunkel-Schetter, 1979).

The physical benefits of social support have been noted in the research literature as well. These benefits have even been identified at the cellular level in a sample of breast cancer patients. For example, patients' perceptions of the quality of emotional support provided by significant others were the most important predictors of natural killer cell activity, an immunological defense against neoplastic cells (Moyer & Salovey, 1996). Studies with adult cancer patients suggest that those who are unmarried have a decreased overall survival because they seek help later and at a more advanced disease stage. In addition, they have a higher likelihood of being untreated for cancer. After adjustment for both factors, there remains a poorer treatment response by unmarried individuals (Anderson, 1994). Therefore, it appears that social support can act as a moderator in the relationship between stress and health outcomes in cancer patients (Helgelson et al., 1998).

Summary

Although cancer can be a potentially devastating experience, research has identified various coping variables to be significantly associated with positive psychological adaptation. Such factors include a fighting spirit or optimism and effective problem-solving ability. Conversely, avoidance and denial have been found to be correlated with poor psychological outcome, although the findings regarding denial are somewhat equivocal. In addition, research has focused on the manner in which a person seeks cancer-related information and its relationship to distress. Of great significance are the findings that link various coping reactions to improved health and disease outcome.

Social support has also been a major focus of research with specific regard to its role as a buffer of the negative effects of the cancer experience, both in terms of psychological adaptation, as well as actual health outcome. The latter has included studies focusing on overall treatment response, as well as on the cellular level regarding immunological variables.

Thus far, this overview of the field of psychosocial oncology has focused on the etiological role that various lifestyle activities play regarding cancer development, as well as the psychosocial impact of cancer and its treatment. The following section focuses on the next logical step: psychosocial interventions that address this negative impact.

PSYCHOSOCIAL INTERVENTIONS FOR CANCER PATIENTS

Given the previous description of the literature documenting the negative psychosocial consequences of cancer, the importance of developing effective interventions to improve the quality of life of cancer patients appears obvious. In fact, Redd (1995) suggests that an important factor responsible in part for the birth of psychosocial oncology as a field was the publishing of certain studies that underscored the successful use of behavioral procedures to control the anticipatory side effects of cancer chemotherapy, such as nausea and vomiting (e.g., Morrow & Morrell, 1982). Moreover, during the past two decades, a sufficiently large number of intervention studies have been conducted engendering a number of qualitative and quantitative review articles (e.g., Andersen, 1992; Dreher, 1997; Fawzy, Fawzy, Arndt, & Pasnau, 1995; Meyer & Mark, 1995; Trijsburg, van Knippenberg, & Rijpma, 1992). The general conclusion that the majority of these reviews reached underscores the efficacy of a wide variety of psychosocial interventions geared to improve the quality of life of adult cancer patients. For example, Meyer and Mark (1995) conducted a meta-analysis of 62 treatment-control comparisons and found the beneficial and significant effect size ds were .24 for emotional adjustment measures, .19 for functional adjustment measures, .26 for measures of treatment- and disease-related symptoms, and .28 for compound and global measures. However, similar to a qualitative literature review regarding earlier published studies (Watson, 1983), significant differences among varying types of treatment approaches (e.g., behavioral versus supportive group therapy) were not found.

Because a comprehensive review of the treatment outcome literature for cancer patients is beyond the scope of this chapter, the reader is directed to the listed review articles. However, in this section, we present a brief overview of this literature to illustrate the type and variety of interventions investigated.

Educational Interventions

The goal of educational interventions is to reduce cancer patients' distress and improve their sense of control that may be undermined by lack of knowledge and feelings of uncertainty. For example, Messerli, Garamendi, and Romano (1980) argued that a patient's fear, anxiety, and distress would decrease as a function of increased medical knowledge and information accessibility. With these types of interventions, patient education has involved a variety of venues, including written materials, films, audiotapes, videotapes, and lectures. The protocols studied included topics covering technical aspects of the disease and its treatment, potential side effects, navigating the medical system, and the physician-patient relationship.

An early study investigating the benefits of an educational approach was conducted by Jacobs, Ross, Walker, and Stockdale (1983). Patients with Hodgkin's disease participating in the education sample were mailed a 27-page booklet that included disease-related information. Three months later, compared to a no-education control, these individuals were found to show a decrease in depressive and anxiety symptoms, as well as an increase in their knowledge about Hodgkin's disease.

Focusing on a population of Egyptian patients diagnosed with bladder cancer, Ali and Khalil (1989) also found a reduction in anxiety symptoms as a function of a psychoeducational intervention. More specifically, compared to a control group, patients receiving the education protocol were found to be significantly less anxious three days after surgery and prior to discharge.

Pruitt et al. (1992) focused on a group of newly diagnosed cancer patients undergoing radiation treatment in order to assess the effects of a three-session (1 hour each) education intervention. Their protocol involved information about radiation therapy and cancer, coping strategies, and communication skills. Patients receiving this intervention, as compared to a control condition, were found three months subsequent to show lower levels of depression, although no differences between groups were found regarding level of knowledge.

More recently, Hack et al. (1999) conducted a multicenter study whereby patients were provided the choice to receive an audiotape of the initial consultation session with their oncologist. Such an approach was hypothesized to impact positively on the physician-patient relationship, as well as to provide the cancer patient with the opportunity to review the information discussed during the consultation. Although a trend was observed regarding a decrease in anxiety for patients who chose to receive the audiotape, this change was not statistically significant. However, at a six-week follow-up assessment, patients receiving the tape recalled significantly more information and were found to report a higher degree of satisfaction with the physician-patient relationship.

Cognitive-Behavioral Interventions

A. Nezu, Nezu, Friedman, and Haynes (1997) defined cognitive-behavior therapy (CBT) as an empirical approach to clinical case formulation, intervention, and evaluation that focuses on the manner in which behavior, thoughts, emotions, and biological events interact with each other regarding the process of symptom, disorder, and disease development and maintenance. As such, CBT, as applied to psychosocial oncology, incorporates a wide array of intervention strategies that focus on identifying and changing those behavioral, cognitive, and affective variables that mediate the negative effects of cancer and its treatment. Many strategies under the CBT rubric are theoretically based on principles of respondent and operant conditioning, such as contingency management, biofeedback, relaxation training, and systematic desensitization, whereas other strategies are more cognitive in nature, based on information-processing models, and include techniques such as cognitive distraction, cognitive restructuring, guided imagery, and problem-solving therapy. Applications of CBT for cancer patients have addressed both specific negative symptoms (e.g., anticipatory nausea, pain), as well as overall distress and quality of life.

CBT for Anticipatory Nausea

Clinically, a negative side effect of emetogenic chemotherapy is anticipatory nausea and vomiting. From a respondent conditioning conceptualization, this occurs when previously neutral stimuli (e.g., colors and sounds associated with the treatment room) acquire nausea-eliciting properties due to repeated association with chemotherapy treatments and its negative aftereffects. Investigations conducted in the early 1980s by Burish and Lyles (1981; Lyles, Burish, Krozely, & Oldham, 1982) found progressive muscle relaxation combined with guided imagery to be effective in reducing anticipatory nausea and vomiting among samples of patients already experiencing such symptoms. Morrow and Morrell (1982) further found systematic desensitization to be another effective CBT approach for these symptoms. Further, in a subsequent study, Morrow and Morrell (1982) replicated their earlier findings and also observed no differences in the magnitude of the effects of systematic desensitization as a function of what type of professional delivered the intervention (i.e., psychologist, nurse, or physician). Research also has indicated that conducting CBT *prior* to receiving chemotherapy may prevent anticipatory nausea and vomiting, as well as fostering improved posttreatment emotional well-being (Burish, Carey, Krozely, & Greco, 1987).

CBT for Pain

CBT strategies that have been suggested as being potentially effective clinically for the reduction of cancer-related pain include relaxation, guided imagery and distraction, and cognitive coping and restructuring (Breitbart & Payne, 1998). However, actual investigations assessing their efficacy have been few and provide somewhat conflicting results. The first study to empirically evaluate CBT for cancer-related pain focused on oral mucositis pain related to the chemotherapy treatment a group of patients received prior to a bone marrow transplantation (Syrjala, Cummings, & Donaldson, 1992). CBT (which in this study included relaxation training, cognitive restructuring, and cognitive coping training) was not effective in reducing pain as compared to control participants, whereas patients receiving hypnosis did report significantly less pain. However, in a subsequent study conducted by this same group of investigators, CBT was found to be effective in reducing cancer-related pain (Syrjala, Donaldson, Davis, Kippes, & Carr, 1995). More recently, Liossi and Hatira (1999) compared the effects of hypnosis and CBT as pain management interventions for pediatric cancer patients undergoing bone marrow aspirations. Their results indicated that both treatment conditions, as compared to a no-treatment control condition, were effective in reducing pain and pain-related anxiety.

CBT for Emotional Distress

CBT protocols have also been increasingly implemented as a means to decrease cancer patients' psychological distress (e.g., depression, anxiety) and to improve their overall emotional well-being and quality of life. This trend began with a landmark study conducted by Worden and Weisman (1984). Two interventions were evaluated, both focused on the development of problem-solving skills as a means to promote effective coping and adaptation among newly diagnosed cancer patients. One condition involved discussing the problems a specific cancer patient was experiencing without teaching specific skills, whereas the second focused on fostering general problem-solving skills and also included relaxation training. Both conditions were found to engender decreases in psychological distress as compared to a *nonrandomized* control condition. Despite this methodological limitation, their study did have a major impact on the field of psychosocial oncology (Jacobsen & Hann, 1998).

Behavioral stress management strategies (e.g., relaxation, guided imagery) have been found to be especially effective in reducing emotional distress and improving cancer patients' quality of life (e.g., Baider, Uziely, & De-Nour, 1994; Bridge,

Benson, Pietroni, & Priest, 1988; Decker, Cline-Elsen, & Gallagher, 1992; Gruber et al., 1993). Multicomponent CBT protocols have also been found to be effective. For example, Telch and Telch (1986) evaluated the differential effects of a group-administered, multicomponent CBT coping skills training protocol, as compared to a supportive group therapy condition, and a no-treatment control. Their coping skills training included instruction in (a) relaxation and stress management, (b) assertive communication, (c) cognitive restructuring and problem solving, (d) management of emotions, and (e) planning pleasant activities. Results indicated that patients receiving the CBT protocol consistently fared significantly better than participants in the other two conditions. In fact, patients in the supportive group therapy condition evidenced little improvement, whereas untreated patients demonstrated significant deterioration in their overall psychological adjustment.

Another multicomponent CBT-based investigation included patients who were newly diagnosed with malignant melanoma (Fawzy, Cousins, et al., 1990; Fawzy, Kemeny, et al., 1990). The cancer patients were assigned to one of two conditions: a structured group intervention and a no-treatment control. The six-week CBT-oriented intervention was comprised of four components: health education, stress management, problem-solving training, and group support. At the end of the six weeks, patients receiving the structured intervention began showing reductions in psychological distress as compared to the control patients. However, six months posttreatment, such group differences were very pronounced. More impressively, five years following the intervention, treated patients continued to show significantly lower levels of anxiety, depression, and total mood disturbance (Fawzy, Fawzy, & Canada, 2001). Their intervention was later adapted to be applied to a Japanese population and found to be effective for Japanese women with breast cancer (Hosaka, 1996).

Greer et al. (1992) evaluated the effectiveness of an individually administered CBT intervention geared to improve emotional well-being. Their protocol included coping skills training, cognitive restructuring, and relaxation training. At a four-month follow-up assessment point, CBT participants were found to be experiencing less emotional distress than patients in the no-treatment control condition. Such beneficial treatment effects were further found to be evident at a one-year follow-up point (Moorey et al., 1994).

Problem-Solving Therapy (PST) for Cancer Patients

Although training individuals to be more effective problem solvers to improve their ability to cope with stressful life events and difficult problems, such as cancer, has been included as part of various multicomponent CBT treatment packages (e.g., Fawzy, Cousins, et al., 1990; Telch & Telch, 1986), it has never been empirically evaluated as a sole intervention. As such, A. Nezu, Nezu, Felgoise, et al. (2001; see also A. Nezu et al., 1998), based on previous research that highlighted the efficacy of PST for major depression (e.g., A. Nezu, 1986; A. Nezu & Perri, 1989) conducted a study whereby adult cancer patients who were experiencing significant distress (e.g., depression) were randomly assigned to one of three conditions: (a) ten 1.5 hr sessions of individual PST; (b) ten 1.5 hr sessions of PST provided simultaneously to both the patient and his or her designated significant other (e.g., spouse, family member); and (c) waiting-list control. The condition that involved a significant other was included to assess the enhanced effects of "formalizing" a social support system where the role of the significant other was conceptualized as a "problem-solving coach." Results at posttreatment across self-report, clinician-ratings, and ratings by the significant other provided evidence in support of the efficacy of PST for decreasing emotional distress and improving the overall quality of life of patients with cancer. Specifically, patients in both treatment conditions were found to evidence significant improvement as compared to individuals in the wait-list control—no differences were found between these two conditions. However, at a six-month follow-up assessment, on approximately half of the measures assessed, patients who received PST along with a significant other continued to improve significantly beyond those individuals receiving PST by themselves.

Group Therapy Approaches

The potential strengths of group psychotherapy for cancer patients are threefold: (a) it can provide for a milieu in which people with similar experiences can provide emotional support to each other, (b) it is cost-effective for the patient, and (c) it is time-efficient for the mental health professional (Spira, 1998). However, research evaluating these approaches provides limited evidence for their efficacy to reduce distress and improve psychological adjustment (Helgelson & Cohen, 1996). Further, the empirical literature suggests that group therapy protocols that focus primarily on providing peer support and emphasize the shared expression of emotions are less effective than either educational protocols (e.g., Helgelson, Cohen, Schulz, & Yasko, 1999) or programs teaching coping skills (Edelman, Craig, & Kidman, 2000).

One study that is often cited as underscoring the efficacy of a "supportive-expressive" group therapy protocol was conducted by Spiegel, Bloom, and Yalom (1981). Their

investigation included 86 women with metastatic breast cancer who were randomly assigned to one of two conditions: a weekly group therapy program or a no-treatment control. The group therapy program included supportive interaction among the participants, encouragement to express one's emotions, and discussion of cancer-related problems. At 100 and 200 days after entry into the protocol, trends were observed regarding improvements in mood only for the treated patients. However, at a 300-day evaluation, treated patients reported significantly less anxiety, depression, confusion, and fatigue, as well as fewer phobias and less maladaptive coping responses as compared to the control group. Despite these positive results, concerns about a high drop-out rate (i.e., at 300 days, only 16 women remained in the therapy condition and 14 women remained in the control condition) point to the tentative nature of these findings (e.g., Edelman et al., 2000; Fox, 1998). On the other hand, Spiegel et al. (1999) published another study that does supports the efficacy of this approach, as well as highlighting the feasibility of implementing such a protocol in community settings across the United States.

Telephone Counseling

Despite the literature documenting the efficacy of psychosocial interventions for cancer patients, a major obstacle to the potential utilization of such protocols is accessibility. In response to such barriers, various programs using the telephone as a communication tool have been developed to provide health education, referral information, counseling, and group support (Bucher, Houts, Glajchen, & Blum, 1998). Few studies, however, have been reported in the literature that have empirically evaluated the efficacy of such approaches, although at present, two different studies are underway, one assessing the effects of a multicomponent CBT intervention (Marcus et al., 1998), and the second evaluating interpersonal psychotherapy (which focuses on role transitions, interpersonal conflicts, and grief precipitated by cancer) for breast cancer patients (Donnelly et al., 2000). In addition, a recently completed investigation evaluating the effects of a combined face-to-face (two sessions) and telephone (four sessions) problem-solving-based intervention provides support for its efficacy in reducing cancer-related difficulties for young breast cancer patients (Allen et al., 2001).

Effects of Psychosocial Interventions on Health Outcome

This review strongly underscores the efficacy of a variety of psychosocial interventions for cancer patients with specific regard to reducing specific psychological (e.g., depression, anxiety) and physical (e.g., anticipatory nausea and vomiting; pain) cancer-related symptoms, as well as improving their overall adjustment and emotional well-being. A logical next question is: Do psychosocial interventions have any impact on health outcome? For example, do they actually affect the course or prognosis of the disease? As noted earlier, various psychosocial variables have been found to be associated with survival, such as coping and social support. Moreover, as more research highlights the interplay between psychological and medical symptoms (e.g., A. Nezu, Nezu, & Lombardo, 2001), such a question appears both legitimate and imperative. For example, psychosocial treatments may affect the course of cancer by (a) improving patient self-care (e.g., reduce behavioral risk factors), (b) increasing patients' compliance with medical treatment, or (c) influencing disease resistance regarding certain biological pathways, such as the immune system (Classen, Sephton, Diamond, & Spiegel, 1998).

To date, the literature providing answers to this question remains equivocal, that is, three studies provide data supporting the notion that psychosocial interventions extend the life of cancer patients, whereas three investigations lacked an effect on survival. With regard to the first group of studies, the investigation described by Spiegel et al. (1981) evaluating the effects of supportive-expressive group therapy was not originally designed to evaluate survival effects. However, 10 years after their study was completed, these authors collected survival data for all participants (Spiegel, Bloom, Kraemer, & Gottheil, 1989). To their admitted surprise, women receiving the group therapy program lived an average of 36.6 months from time of initial randomization as compared to the control patients who lived an average of 18.9 months. This difference was found to be both statistically and clinically significant.

Similar to the Spiegel et al. (1981) study, the investigation also previously described (Fawzy et al., 1993) with malignant melanoma patients, was also not originally designed to specifically assess differences in survival rates as a function of the differing experimental conditions. However, they did find six years later that the treatment group experienced longer survival as compared to control participants, as well as a trend for a longer period to recurrence for the treated patients (Fawzy et al., 1993).

Richardson, Shelton, Krailo, and Levine (1990) reported on the effects of three treatment approaches geared to improve treatment compliance for patients newly diagnosed with hematologic malignancies: (a) education and a home visit by a nurse; (b) education and a shaping program designed to foster better adherence in taking medication; and (c) education, shaping, and a home visit. With regard to survival rates, these researchers found that assignment to *any* of these treatment conditions, as compared to a control group, significantly predicted survival.

The three studies that found no difference on survival as a function of participating in a psychosocial intervention include (a) a study that provided intensive individual supportive counseling to men in a Veterans Administration hospital with tumors across several sites (Linn, Lin, & Harris, 1982); (b) an investigation that included 34 women with breast cancer who participated in a program that provided individual counseling, peer support, family therapy, and stress management training (Gellert, Maxwell, & Siegel, 1993); and (c) a study that focused on the effects of three different supportive group therapy conditions (Ilnyckyj, Farber, Cheang, & Weinerman, 1994).

In summary, whereas three studies provide no evidence to support the enhanced survival rates for cancer patients receiving psychosocial treatment, three studies, in fact, do offer such data. However, methodological issues across all these investigations further add to the tentativeness of any firm conclusions (Classen et al., 1998).

Effects of Psychosocial Interventions on Immune Functioning

One possible mediator of the positive effects of psychosocial interventions on improved health, as well as emotional well-being, is the immune system. In part, support for this hypothesis emanates from research indicating alterations regarding certain measures of immune functioning in humans experiencing stressful events (Herbert & Cohen, 1993), as well as studies demonstrating changes in immune functioning as a result of receiving psychosocial treatment. For example, the study described earlier by Fawzy, Kemeny and colleagues (1990) indicated that at the end of the six-week intervention, patients receiving the treatment evidenced significant increases in the percentage of large granular lymphocytes. Six months posttreatment, this increase in granular lymphocytes continued and increases in natural killer cells were also evident. Relaxation training has also been found to lead to higher lymphocyte counts and higher white blood cell numbers even in cancer patients receiving myelosuppressive therapy (Lekander, Furst, Rotstein, Hursti, & Fredrikson, 1997). Although research investigating the link between immunologic parameters and psychosocial variables in cancer patients is in its nascent stage and, therefore, can only be viewed as suggestive at this time (see Bovbjerg & Valdimarsdottir, 1998), such a framework provides an exciting area for future research and a possible means of explaining one pathway between behavioral factors and cancer-related health outcome.

Prevention Issues

All of the interventions discussed so far are geared to impact on health and mental health parameters *after* a person is diagnosed with cancer. However, treatment strategies can also affect behavioral risk factors, thus attempting to *prevent* cancer to some extent. Some of the behavioral risk factors mentioned earlier include smoking, alcohol, diet, and sun exposure. Reviews of the relevant treatment literature bases concerning some of these behaviors is contained in other chapters of this volume, and therefore will not be repeated here. With regard to sun exposure, some interventions have led to increased knowledge of skin cancer and awareness of protective measures; however, programs have had only limited success with increasing preventive behaviors in at-risk groups (Cohen & Baum, 2001).

Prevention strategies are also important for individuals considered at high risk due to genetic and familial factors. For example, a positive family history of breast cancer is an important risk factor for breast cancer in women (Slattery & Kerber, 1993). As such, first-degree relatives of women with breast cancer may also be at risk for psychological distress. With this in mind, Kash, Holland, Osborne, and Miller (1995) evaluated the efficacy of a group psychoeducational intervention for women at high risk for breast cancer. Their protocol included breast cancer education and risk communication, coping skills training, and group social support. As compared to no-treatment control participants, patients undergoing the group therapy program exhibited significant improvements in knowledge and risk comprehension and a significant decrease in perceived barriers to mammography. More importantly, group therapy participants increased having mammograms, clinical breast examinations, and breast self-examinations during the year following treatment as compared to the control subjects.

Schwartz et al. (1998) evaluated a brief PST intervention as a means to reduce distress among women with a first-degree relative recently diagnosed with breast cancer. Results indicated that whereas patients in both the PST and an educational control group exhibited significant decreases in psychological distress, such differences did not differ as a function of treatment condition. However, for participants in the PST condition who were found to regularly practice the PST techniques, differences in decreased cancer-specific distress were significantly greater as compared to control

participants and those PST subjects only infrequently using the problem-solving skills.

Summary

Overall, research has amply demonstrated that a variety of psychosocial interventions are effective in reducing specific cancer-related physical (e.g., pain, nausea, and vomiting) and emotional (e.g., depression, anxiety) symptoms, as well as enhancing the overall quality of life of cancer patients. Such treatment programs include educational interventions, a wide array of cognitive-behavioral interventions, and group psychotherapy protocols. Using the telephone to increase accessibility to such programs has also begun to show promise. Among these various approaches, CBT interventions have been more often the focus of empirical investigations, and thus, have tended to emerge as the more effective and versatile overall therapeutic model.

In addition to improving cancer patients' emotional well-being, data suggests that psychosocial interventions can also lead to improved survival by affecting the course of the cancer itself. One biological pathway that has been identified as a potential mechanism by which this can occur is the immune system. However, additional studies have noted a lack of an affect on survival rates as a function of participating in psychosocial treatment. Moreover, the literature providing evidence to support a link between behavioral variables and health outcome as mediated by the immune system is only in its infancy with regard to cancer. Therefore, substantial additional research is necessary before the nature of these relationships can be clearly elucidated.

Psychosocial interventions have also been developed for at-risk groups (e.g., first-degree relative of women with breast cancer) or people engaging in risky cancer-engendering behaviors (e.g., excessive sun exposure) as a means of reducing risk and preventing cancer.

FAMILY AND CAREGIVER ISSUES

In addition to the effects on patients themselves, the experience of cancer and its treatment can change the lives of family members, and in particular, the primary caregiver (e.g., spouse). With shifts in health care economics, especially during the end of the twentieth century, more care and recovery of cancer patients takes place at home, therefore, having a potentially greater impact on the roles and responsibilities of family members (Houts, Nezu, Nezu, & Bucher, 1996; Laizner, Yost, Barg, & McCorkle, 1993). This shift in caretaking has also increased professionals' attention to the vital roles, participation, and impact the experience of cancer has on families and caregivers as they become the extension of the health care team (Friedman, 1999).

Impact of Cancer on Caregivers

The potential demands and subsequent burden on caregivers is significant. For example, in a study by Barg et al. (1998), 61% of a sample of 750 caregivers reported that caregiving was the center of their activities. In addition, 58% of this sample indicated that to provide care, caregivers were required to give up many other activities. For the majority of caregivers (62%), their responsibilities to the patient warranted 24-hour-per-day availability, whereas 42% of the sample provided 6 to 40 hours of care per week.

Because caregivers are laypersons who usually have not had professional training in preparation for caring for an individual with cancer, such demands and responsibilities can lead to significant distress. For example, in the Barg et al. (1998) sample, 89% of the caregivers reported feeling "stressed" by their responsibilities. In addition, the caregivers who experienced more stress also reported significantly lowered self-esteem, less family support, more negative impact on their schedules, more negative impact on their physical health, and more caregiving demands than nonstressed caregivers.

Psychological Distress

In a study conducted by Kelly et al. (1999), 67% percent of a sample of caregivers of spouses with various cancer diagnoses reported "high to very high" illness-related distress levels. In general, studies of spouses of cancer patients, many in the terminal stage of care, have reported eating disorders, sleep disturbances, anxiety, and depression due to the stresses of caregiving (Kristjanson & Aschercraft, 1994).

Impact on Health

The stress of caregiving has also been shown to have negative biological (immunologic, cardiovascular, metabolic) consequences for family caregivers (Vitaliano, 1997). For example, 62% of a sample of 465 caregivers reported declines in health resulting from their caregiving experiences (Barg et al., 1998). Whereas some research (e.g., Hinds, 1985; Oberst, Thomas, Gass, & Ward, 1989) has identified significant relationships between patients' and caregivers' physical health, as well as patients' physical health and caregivers' emotional reactions, other studies have found that the physical health of the cancer patients across varying cancer diagnoses and stages did not directly impact the health of the caregiver. In fact, the patients' *emotional* well-being has been found to be a better predictor of caregiver distress. For example, in a study of 196 patient-caregiver dyads, patient depression, and not the patient's medical status, mediated the relationship between patient dependencies, symptom distress, and patient immobility on caregivers' physical health (Given et al., 1993).

Unmet Caregivers' Needs

In addition to the impact on their psychological and physical health, caregivers have also reported that many of their needs as caregivers continue to go unmet (Houts et al., 1986). For example, Hinds (1985) interviewed 83 family caregivers and found that 53% of this sample identified several areas of unresolved psychosocial needs. In a different sample, 16% of 45 caregivers reported serious unmet needs, where 49% considered unmet informational needs to be a significant problem (Wright & Dyck, 1984). Interestingly, Sales, Schulz, and Biegel (1992) found that younger caregivers reported more psychological and personal needs than older caregivers.

Psychosocial Interventions for Caregivers

As a function of the increased vulnerability to negative psychological and physical effects of the cancer-related caregiving role, various intervention strategies have been developed to help these individuals. Such strategies include both psychoeducational and problem-solving approaches.

Psychoeducational Interventions

Derdiarian (1989) evaluated a psychoeducational intervention that provided medical, counseling, and referral information to caregivers. This was followed by two telephone calls to check the adequacy of the information. This protocol was compared to "standard care." The aim was to measure the caregivers' satisfaction with the information received and their perceived coping with the consequences of the diagnosis (i.e., behaviors indicating problem solving and emotional regulation). The results of this investigation showed significant decreases in perceived need for information and increases in satisfaction and coping as a function of participating in the experimental intervention.

Problem-Solving Approaches

Several problem-solving interventions have been developed for caregivers of persons with cancer. For example, using a randomized design, Toseland, Blanchard, and McCallion (1995) evaluated a protocol including six individual counseling sessions that included both support and training in problem-solving and coping skills. Caregivers in a control group received standard medical care. Initial overall results comparing the intervention to usual treatment showed no difference on a wide range of measures. However, posthoc analyses evaluating the interaction of distressed and moderately burdened caregivers by condition showed favorable outcomes for patients in the treatment condition. Specifically, distressed caregivers who participated in the intervention reported significant improvement in their physical role and social functioning. In addition, burdened caregivers significantly improved their ability to cope with pressing problems.

Houts et al. (1996) and Bucher, Houts, Nezu, and Nezu (1999) described a problem-solving approach to family caregiver education entitled the *Prepared Family Caregiver Course* that was adapted from the D'Zurilla and Nezu (1999; A. Nezu et al., 1998) problem-solving therapy model. The course was taught over three two-hour group sessions and included prepared instructional videotapes to guide interactive practice exercises along with an instructor's manual (Bucher et al., 1999). The *Home Care Guide for Cancer* (Houts, Nezu, Nezu, Bucher, & Lipton, 1994), an informational resource consistent with this model, was also a key element to this training.

The premise for the problem-solving approach was based on the idea that successfully solving problems increases a person's sense of mastery or control, which, in turn, contributes to positive mental health. Further, information, and a framework in which to gather additional information and solve problems, can allay the uncertainty caregivers often feel (i.e., Have I done everything that I can do?) (Houts et al., 1996). Caregivers are provided with information about a series of medical (e.g., fatigue, hair loss) and psychosocial (e.g., depression, loneliness) problems, and are trained to (a) better define the problem; (b) know when to obtain professional help; (c) learn to deal with, as well as prevent, a problem; (d) identify obstacles when they arise and plan to overcome them; and (e) effectively implement a problem-solving plan and adjust it if the initial attempts are not successful. Results from a program evaluation study including a sample of 41 caregivers indicated that 78% of these participants reported an improvement in their feelings of burden and stress (Houts et al., 1996). In addition, 48% and 58%, respectively, reported using their plans for tiredness and depression in their caregiving. Further program evaluation investigations of the *Prepared Family Caregiver Course* reveal a generally high level of satisfaction with and interest in using the information and problem-solving skills taught to family caregivers, hospice volunteers, home health aides, nurses, and people with cancer (Bucher et al., 1999). Well-controlled studies are necessary prior to making definitive conclusions about the potential efficacy of such an approach. However, preliminary results provide promising support.

Summary

Cancer and its treatment can have a profound impact on family members. Due to recent changes in health care delivery and economics, there has been a significant shift in caregiving responsibility from the professional health care team to family caregivers, such as the patient's spouse. This shift increases the potential demands and responsibilities for such individuals. As such, caregivers experience an increased vulnerability to both psychological and medical difficulties. In response to these problems, researchers have begun to develop and evaluate psychosocial interventions geared to improve the caregiving skills of such individuals, as well as decrease their burden and improve their quality of life. Because such research is in its nascent stage, increased attempts to develop efficacious programs are particularly needed.

SUMMARY AND FUTURE DIRECTIONS

Cancer is the second leading cause of death in the United States, surpassed only by heart disease. Despite its prevalence as a medical disease, only about 5% to 10% of all cancers are clearly hereditary. A variety of lifestyle activities have been identified as potential risks for cancer, such as smoking, alcohol abuse, diet, and excessive exposure to the sun. Because such factors are behavioral in nature, the relevance of psychology for the field of psychosocial oncology is clear. Not only is this emerging subfield of oncology concerned with the role of cancer-related behavioral risk factors, but also the identification of efficacious means to reduce such risk factors, as well as to better understand and impact positively on the negative psychosocial consequences of cancer, such as emotional distress and decreased quality of life. The past few decades have seen an increase in interest by psychologists in this field and the development of effective strategies of meeting these goals.

Based on our review of the literature, we offer several recommendations for future research that are focused mainly on intervention studies:

1. *More research should be conducted regarding efficacious interventions to improve the quality of life of cancer patients and their families.* Although a substantial body of

research already exists, we need to know more about what types of treatment approaches are effective for what types of patients as a function of type of cancer, stage of cancer, SES, ethnic background, level of stress experienced, and other important patient-relevant psychosocial variables. Because of the significant personal, medical, and economic impact cancer and its treatment represents, more research evaluating the efficacy of a wide range of psychosocial strategies should be conducted in the future.

2. *More research should be conducted regarding the effects of psychosocial interventions on health outcome (i.e., prolonged survival).* Currently, the literature is equivocal in its ability to indicate whether psychosocial treatments can have an impact on health outcome, particularly with regard to prolonging the life of a cancer patient. As mentioned earlier, many of the studies that either provide support for or against such a hypothesis were not designed to specifically address this question. Well-controlled investigations capable of addressing such a question requires extensive resources. However, preliminary results suggest that such efforts may be worthwhile.

3. *Improve the methodological rigor of the research.* Because a thorough critical analysis of the reviewed literature was beyond the scope of this chapter, we did not document the many methodological limitations identified across the studies. We will not belabor the point, except to list specific recommendations: (a) include adequate control groups; (b) use manualized protocols; (c) include treatment integrity (i.e., therapist adherence and competence) measures; and (d) use more multimodal assessment procedures (e.g., multitrait, multimethod approaches) for outcome measurement. In addition, special care needs to be taken in describing each population under study in detail to better allow for meaningful comparisons across studies.

4. *Conduct component analyzes of the intervention studies.* The majority of the randomized outcome studies reviewed simply compared an intervention to either an alternative treatment approach (e.g., education) or a control condition (e.g., waiting-list). Additional research strategies should be implemented to help answer the question: "Which treatment components are responsible for the actual improvement in symptoms?" Future research needs to be more explicit in delineating specific treatment strategies and provide for an assessment of the specific impact of a particular intervention on a given hypothesized mechanism of action and its resulting impact on changes of interest. In that manner, a more comprehensive and microanalytic understanding of cause-effect relationships can

be obtained. Such research strategies include dismantling, constructive, and parametric approaches. In addition, matching studies (i.e., matching treatment strategies with identified patient vulnerabilities, for example, problem-solving therapy for the depressed cancer patient with identified problem-solving deficits) also fall in this category.

5. *Identify important moderators of treatment efficacy.* Identification of important moderator variables (e.g., race, age, gender, cultural background, severity of symptoms, number of symptoms) can potentially lead to better matching of a given treatment for a particular patient, as well as the development of more effective interventions per se.

6. *Identify important mechanisms of action.* Future research should also address the relationship between outcome (e.g., psychological well-being, improved health) and a variety of variables (e.g., cognitive, emotional, behavioral, immune system) hypothesized to contribute to the etiopathogenesis and course of that outcome. In this manner, salient treatment targets can be identified and more empirically-based decisions about treatment design can be made.

7. *Improve treatment implementation and access.* Related to the issue of health economics, future research should also attempt to save costs directly related to implementing psychosocial interventions. Having a doctoral-level psychologist, for example, providing individual or group therapy to cancer patients and their families is likely to be viewed as having too high a price to the health care delivery system. As such, studies geared to assess alternative means of conducting psychosocial interventions should be conducted in the future. For example, additional methods exist to conduct such treatment approaches besides the traditional use of a single therapist in face-to-face situations. Use of videos, computers, the Internet, or telemedicine support systems represent further possibilities regarding ways to cut costs, as well as to increase accessibility to patients not living close to a major medical center.

REFERENCES

Ali, N., & Khalil, H. (1989). Effects of psychoeducational intervention on anxiety among Egyptian bladder cancer patients. *Cancer Nursing, 12,* 236–242.

Allen, S. M., Shah, A. C., Nezu, A. M., Nezu, C. M., Mor, V., Ciambrone, D., et al. (2001). *A problem-solving approach to stress reduction among younger women with breast cancer: A randomized controlled trial.* Providence, RI: Brown University.

Alter, C. L., Pelcovitz, D., & Axelrod, A. (1996). Identification of PTSD in cancer survivors. *Psychosomatics, 37,* 137–143.

American Cancer Society. (2000). *Cancer facts and figures.* American Cancer Society.

Andersen, B. L. (1992). Psychological interventions for cancer patients to enhance the quality of life. *Journal of Consulting and Clinical Psychology, 60,* 552–568.

Anderson, B. L. (1994). Surviving cancer. *Cancer Supplement, 74,* 1484–1494.

Anderson, B. L., Woods, X. A., & Copeland, L. J. (1997). Sexual self-schema and sexual morbidity among gynecologic cancer survivors. *Journal of Consulting and Clinical Psychology, 65,* 221–229.

Andrykowski, M. A., Redd, W. H., & Hatfield, A. K. (1985). Development of anticipatory nausea: A prospective analysis. *Journal of Consulting and Clinical Psychology, 53,* 447–454.

Baider, L., Uziely, B., & De-Nour, A. K. (1994). Progressive muscle relaxation and guided imagery in cancer patients. *General Hospital Psychiatry, 16,* 340–347.

Balfour, J. L., & Kaplan, G. A. (1998). Social class/socioeconomic factors. In J. C. Holland (Ed.), *Psycho-oncology* (pp. 78–90). New York: Oxford University Press.

Barg, F. K., Pasacreta, J. V., Nuamah, I. F., Robinson, K. D., Angeletti, K., Yasko, J. M., et al. (1998). A description of a psychoeducational intervention for family caregivers of cancer patients. *Journal of Family Nursing, 4,* 394–414.

Barraclough, J. (1994). *Cancer and emotion.* New York: Wiley.

Baum, A., & Andersen, B. L. (Eds.). (2001). *Psychosocial interventions for cancer.* Washington, DC: American Psychological Association.

Beck, A. T., Kovacs, M., & Weissman, A. (1975). Hopelessness and suicidal behavior: An overview. *Journal of the American Medical Association, 234,* 1146–1149.

Billings, A. G., & Moos, R. H. (1981). The role of coping responses and social resources in attenuating the stress of life events. *Journal of Behavioral Medicine, 4,* 139–157.

Bloom, J. R. (1982). Social support, accommodation to stress and adjustment to breast cancer. *Social Science and Medicine, 16,* 1329–1338.

Bovbjerg, D. H., & Valdimarsdottir, H. B. (1998). Psychoneuroimmunology: Implications for psycho-oncology. In J. C. Holland (Ed.), *Psycho-oncology* (pp. 125–134). New York: Oxford University Press.

Brandenberg, Y., Bolund, C., & Sigurdardottir, V. (1992). Anxiety and depressive symptoms at different stages of malignant melanoma. *Psycho-oncology, 1,* 71–78.

Breitbart, W. (1987). Suicide in cancer patients. *Oncology, 1,* 49–53.

Breitbart, W., & Cohen, K. R. (1998). Delirium. In J. C. Holland (Ed.), *Psycho-oncology* (pp. 564–576). New York: Oxford University Press.

Breitbart, W., & Krivo, S. (1998). Suicide. In J. C. Holland (Ed.), *Psycho-oncology* (pp. 541–547). New York: Oxford University Press.

Breitbart, W., & Payne, D. K. (1998). Pain. In J. C. Holland (Ed.), *Psycho-oncology* (pp. 450–467). New York: Oxford University Press.

Bridge, L. R., Benson, P., Pietroni, P. C., & Priest, R. G. (1988). Relaxation and imagery in the treatment of breast cancer. *British Medical Journal, 297,* 1169–1172.

Bucher, J. A., Houts, P. S., Glajchen, M., & Blum, D. (1998). Telephone counseling. In J. C. Holland (Ed.), *Psycho-oncology* (pp. 758–766). New York: Oxford University Press.

Bucher, J. A., Houts, P. S., Nezu, C. M., & Nezu, A. M. (1999). Improving problem-solving skills of family caregivers through group education. *Journal of Psychosocial Oncology, 16,* 73–84.

Bukberg, J. B., Penman, D. T., & Holland, J. C. (1984). Depression in hospitalized cancer patients. *Psychosomatic Medicine, 46,* 199–212.

Burgess, C., Morris, T., & Pettingale, K. W. (1988). Psychological response to cancer diagnosis. II: Evidence for coping styles (coping styles and cancer diagnosis). *Journal of Psychosomatic Research, 32,* 263–272.

Burish, T. G., & Carey, M. P. (1986). Conditioned aversive responses in cancer chemotherapy patients: Theoretical and developmental analysis. *Journal of Consulting and Clinical Psychology, 54,* 593–600.

Burish, T. G., Carey, M. P., Krozely, M. K., & Greco, F. A. (1987). Conditioned side effects induced by cancer chemotherapy: Prevention through behavioral treatment. *Journal of Consulting and Clinical Psychology, 55,* 42–48.

Burish, T. G., & Lyles, J. N. (1981). Effectiveness of relaxation training in reducing adverse reactions to cancer chemotherapy. *Journal of Behavioral Medicine, 4,* 65–78.

Byrd, B. L. (1983). Late effects of treatment of cancer in children. *Pediatric Annals, 12,* 450–460.

Carey, M. P., & Burish, T. G. (1988). Psychological side effects in chemotherapy patients. *Psychological Bulletin, 104,* 307–325.

Carver, C. S., Pozo, C., Harris, S. D., Noriega, V., Scheier, M. F., Robinson, D. S., et al. (1993). How coping mediates the effect of optimism on distress: A study of women with early stage breast cancer. *Journal of Personality and Social Psychology, 65,* 375–390.

Cella, D. F. (1987). Cancer survival: Psychosocial and public issues. *Cancer Investigation, 5,* 59–67.

Cella, D. F., & Tross, S. (1986). Psychological adjustment to survival from Hodgkin's disease. *Journal of Consulting and Clinical Psychology, 54,* 616–622.

Chochinov, H. M., Wilson, K. G., Enns, M., & Lander, S. (1998). Depression, hopelessness, and suicidal ideation in the terminally ill. *Psychosomatics, 39,* 366–370.

Cinciripini, P. M., Gritz, E. R., Tsoh, J. Y., & Skaar, K. L. (1998). Smoking cessation and cancer prevention. In J. C. Holland (Ed.), *Psycho-oncology* (pp. 27–44). New York: Oxford University Press.

Classen, C., Sephton, S. E., Diamond, S., & Spiegel, D. (1998). Studies of life-extending psychosocial interventions. In J. C. Holland (Ed.), *Psycho-oncology* (pp. 730–742). New York: Oxford University Press.

Cohen, L., & Baum, A. (2001). Targets for interventions to reduce cancer morbidity. In A. Baum & B. L. Anderson (Eds.), *Psychosocial interventions for cancer* (pp. 321–342). Washington, DC: American Psychological Association.

Cramond, W. A. (1970). Psychotherapy of the dying patient. *British Medical Journal, 3,* 389–393.

Decker, T., Cline-Elsen, J., & Gallagher, M. (1992). Relaxation therapy as an adjunct in radiation oncology. *Journal of Clinical Psychology, 48,* 388–393.

DeFlorio, M., & Massie, M. J. (1995). Review of depression in cancer: Gender differences. *Depression, 3,* 66–80.

Derdiarian, A. K. (1989). Effects of information on recently diagnosed cancer patients' and spouses' satisfaction with care. *Cancer Nursing, 12,* 285–292.

Derogatis, L. R., Morrow, G. R., & Fetting, J. (1983). The prevalence of psychiatric disorders among cancer patients. *Journal of the American Medical Association, 249,* 751–757.

Donnelly, J. M., Kornblith, A. B., Fleishman, S., Zuckerman, E., Raptis, G., Hudis, C. A., et al. (2000). A pilot study of interpersonal psychotherapy by telephone with cancer patients and their partners. *Psycho-oncology, 9,* 44–56.

Dow, K. H. (1991). The growing phenomenon of cancer survivorship. *Journal of Professional Nursing, 7,* 54–61.

Dreher, H. (1997). The scientific and moral imperative for broad-based psychosocial interventions for cancer. *Advances: Journal of Mind-Body Health, 13,* 38–49.

Dunkel-Schetter, C. (1984). Social support and cancer: Findings based on patient interviews and their implications. *Journal of Social Issues, 40,* 77–79.

D'Zurilla, T. J., & Nezu, A. M. (1999). *Problem-solving therapy: A social competence approach to clinical intervention* (2nd ed.). New York: Springer.

Edelman, S., Craig, A., & Kidman, A. D. (2000). Group interventions with cancer patients: Efficacy of psychoeducational versus supportive groups. *Journal of Psychosocial Oncology, 18,* 67–85.

Farberow, N. L., Schneidman, E. S., & Leonard, V. V. (1963). Suicide among general medical and surgical hospital patients with malignant neoplasm. *Medical Bulletin, 9.* Washington, DC: U.S. Veterans Administration.

Fawzy, F. I., Cousins, N., Fawzy, N. W., Kemeny, M. E., Elashoff, R., & Morton, D. (1990). A structured psychiatric intervention for cancer patients: I. Changes over time in methods of coping and affective disturbance. *Archives of General Psychiatry, 47,* 720–725.

Fawzy, F. I., Fawzy, N. W., Arndt, L. A., & Pasnau, R. O. (1995). Critical review of psychosocial interventions in cancer care. *Archives of General Psychiatry, 52,* 100–113.

Fawzy, F. I., Fawzy, N. W., & Canada, A. L. (2001). Psychoeducational intervention programs for patients with cancer. In A. Baum & B. L. Anderson (Eds.), *Psychosocial interventions for cancer* (pp. 235–267). Washington, DC: American Psychological Association.

Fawzy, F. I., Fawzy, N. W., Hyun, C. S., Guthrie, D., Fahey, J. L., & Morton, D. L. (1993). Malignant melanoma: Effects of an early structured psychiatric intervention, coping and affective state on recurrence and survival 6 years later. *Archives of General Psychiatry, 50,* 681–689.

Fawzy, F. I., Kemeny, M. E., Fawzy, N. W., Elashoff, R., Morton, D., Cousins, N., et al. (1990). A structured psychiatric intervention for cancer patients. II: Changes over time in immunologic measures. *Archives of General Psychiatry, 47,* 729–735.

Fobair, P., Hoppe, R. T., Bloom, J., Cox, R., Varghese, A., & Spiegel, D. (1986). Psychosocial problems among survivors of Hodgkin's disease. *Journal of Clinical Oncology, 4,* 805–814.

Fox, B. H. (1998). A hypothesis about Spiegel et al.'s 1989 paper on psychosocial intervention and breast cancer survival. *Psycho-Oncology, 6,* 279–289.

Fox, B. H., Stanek, E. J., Boyd, S. C., & Flannery, J. T. (1982). Suicide rates among cancer patients in Connecticut. *Journal of Chronic Diseases, 35,* 85–100.

Friedman, S. H. (1999, August). Behavioral-analytic model of test construction: A measure of caregivers' cancer knowledge. *Dissertation Abstracts International, 60*(02), 0869B.

Ganz, P. A., Rowland, J. H., Desmond, K., Meyerowitz, B. E., & Wyatt, G. E. (1998). Life after breast cancer: Understanding women's health-related quality of life and sexual functioning. *Journal of Clinical Oncology, 16,* 501–514.

Gellert, G. A., Maxwell, R. M., & Siegel, B. S. (1993). Survival of breast cancer patients receiving adjunctive psychosocial support therapy: A 10-year follow-up study. *Journal of Clinical Oncology, 11,* 66–69.

Given, C. W., Stommel, M., Given, B., Osuch, J., Kurtz, M., & Kurtz, J. C. (1993). The influence of cancer patients' symptoms and functional states on patients' depression and family caregivers' reaction and depression. *Health Psychology, 12,* 277–285.

Greenberg, D. B. (1998). Radiotherapy. In J. C. Holland (Ed.), *Psycho-oncology* (pp. 269–277). New York: Oxford University Press.

Greenlee, R. T., Murray, T., Bolden, S., & Wingo, P. A. (2000). Cancer statistics, 2000. *CA: A Cancer Journal for Clinicians, 50,* 7–33.

Greer, S., Moorey, S., Baruch, J. D. R., Watson, M., Robertson, B. M., Mason, A., et al. (1992). Adjuvant psychological therapy for patients with cancer: A prospective randomized trial. *British Medical Journal, 304,* 675–680.

Greer, S., Morris, T., & Pettingale, K. W. (1979). Psychological response to breast cancer: Effect on outcome. *Lancet, 13,* 785–787.

Greer, S., Morris, T., Pettingale, K. W., & Haybittle, J. (1990). Psychological response to breast cancer and 15 year outcome. *Lancet, 24,* 49–50.

Gruber, B. L., Hersh, S. P., Hall, N. R. S., Walerzky, L. R., Kunz, J. F., Carpenter, J. K., et al. (1993). Immunological responses of breast cancer patients to behavioral interventions. *Biofeedback and Self-Regulation, 18,* 1–21.

Hack, T. F., Pickles, T., Bultz, B. D., Degner, L. F., Katz, A., & Davison, B. J. (1999). Feasibility of an audiotape intervention for patients with cancer: A multicenter, randomized controlled pilot study. *Journal of Psychosocial Oncology, 17,* 1–15.

Hart, G. J., McQuellon, R. P., & Barrett, R. J. (1994). After treatment ends. *Cancer Practice, 2,* 417–420.

Helgelson, V. S., & Cohen, S. (1996). Relation of social support to adjustment to cancer: Reconciling descriptive, correlational, and intervention research. *Health Psychology, 15,* 135–148.

Helgelson, V. S., Cohen, S., & Fritz, H. L. (1998). Social ties and cancer. In J. C. Holland (Ed.), *Psycho-oncology* (pp. 99–109). New York: Oxford University Press.

Helgelson, V. S., Cohen, S., Schulz, R., & Yasko, J. (1999). Education and peer discussion group interventions and adjustment to breast cancer. *Archives of General Psychiatry, 56,* 340–347.

Helig, S. (1988). The San Francisco Medical Society euthanasia survey: Results and analysis. *San Francisco Medicine, 61,* 24–34.

Henderson, P. (1997). Psychosocial adjustment of adult cancer survivors: Their needs and counselor interventions. *Journal of Counseling and Development, 75,* 188–194.

Herbert, T. B., & Cohen, S. (1993). Stress and immunity in humans: A meta-analytic review. *Psychosomatic Medicine, 55,* 364–379.

Hinds, C. (1985). The needs of families who care for patients with cancer at home: Are we meeting them? *Journal of Advanced Nursing, 10,* 575–581.

Holland, J. C. (1982). Psychological aspects of cancer. In J. F. Holland & E. Frei III (Eds.), *Cancer medicine* (pp. 1175–1203). New York: Oxford University Press.

Holland, J. C. (1990). Historical overview. In J. C. Holland & J. H. Rowland (Eds.), *Handbook of psychooncology* (pp. 3–12). New York, Oxford University Press.

Hosaka, T. (1996). A pilot study of a structured psychiatric intervention for Japanese women with breast cancer. *Psycho-Oncology, 5,* 59–65.

Houts, P. S., Nezu, A. M., Nezu, C. M., & Bucher, J. A. (1996). A problem-solving model of family caregiving for cancer patients. *Patient Education and Counseling, 27,* 63–73.

Houts, P. S., Nezu, A. M., Nezu, C. M., Bucher, J. A., & Lipton, A. (Eds.). (1994). *Homecare guide for cancer.* Philadelphia: American College of Physicians.

Houts, P. S., Yasko, J., Kahn, S. B., Schelzel, G., & Marconi, K. (1986). Unmet psychological, social and economic needs of persons with cancer in Pennsylvania. *Cancer, 58,* 2355–2361.

Ilnyckyj, A., Farber, J., Cheang, M. C., & Weinerman, B. F. (1994). A randomized controlled trial of psychotherapeutic intervention in cancer patients. *Annuals of the Royal College of Physicians and Surgeons of Canada, 27,* 93–96.

Jacobs, C., Ross, R. D., Walker, I. M., & Stockdale, F. E. (1983). Behavior of cancer patients: A randomized study of the effects of education and peer support groups. *Journal of Clinical Oncology, 6,* 347–350.

Jacobsen, P. B., & Hann, D. M. (1998). Cognitive-behavioral interventions. In J. C. Holland (Ed.), *Psycho-oncology* (pp. 717–729). New York: Oxford University Press.

Jacobsen, P. B., Roth, A. J., & Holland, J. C. (1998). Surgery. In J. C. Holland (Ed.), *Psycho-oncology* (pp. 257–269). New York: Oxford University Press.

Jenkins, P. L., May, V. E., & Hughes, L. E. (1991). Psychological morbidity associated with local recurrence of breast cancer. *International Journal of Psychiatry in Medicine, 21,* 149–155.

Kash, K. M., Holland, J. C., Osborne, M. P., & Miller, D. G. (1995). Psychological counseling strategies for women at risk for breast cancer. *Journal of the National Cancer Institute Monographs, 17,* 73–80.

Kelly, B., Edwards, P., Synott, R., Neil, C., Baillie, R., & Battistutta, D. (1999). Predictors of bereavement outcome for family caregivers of cancer patients. *Psycho-oncology, 8,* 237–249.

Knobf, M. T., Pasacreta, J. V., Valentine, A., & McCorkle, R. (1998). Chemotherapy, hormonal therapy, and immunotherapy. In J. C. Holland (Ed.), *Psycho-oncology* (pp. 277–289). New York: Oxford University Press.

Kristjanson, L. J., & Aschercraft, T. (1994). The family's cancer journey: A literature review. *Cancer Nursing, 17,* 1–17.

Krouse, J. H., Krouse, H. J., & Fabian, R. L. (1989). Adaptation to surgery for head and neck cancer. *Laryngoscope, 99,* 789–794.

Laizner, A. M., Yost, L. M., Barg, F. K., & McCorkle, R. (1993). Needs of family caregivers of persons with cancer: A review. *Seminars in Oncology Nursing, 9,* 114–120.

Lazarus, R. S., & Folkman, S. (1984). *Stress, appraisal, and coping.* New York: Springer.

Lekander, M., Furst, C. J., Rotstein, S., Hursti, T. J., & Fredrikson, M. (1997). Immune effects of relaxation during chemotherapy for ovarian cancer. *Psychotherapy and Psychosomatics, 66,* 185–191.

Linn, M. W., Lin, B. S., & Harris, R. (1982). Effects of counseling for late stage cancer patients. *Cancer, 49,* 1048–1055.

Liossi, C., & Hatira, P. (1999). Clinical hypnosis versus cognitive behavioral training for pain management with pediatric cancer patients undergoing bone marrow aspirations. International *Journal of Clinical and Experimental Hypnosis, 47,* 104–116.

Lyles, J. N., Burish, T. J., Krozely, M. G., & Oldham, R. K. (1982). Efficacy of relaxation training and guided imagery in reducing the aversiveness of cancer chemotherapy. *Journal of Consulting and Clinical Psychology, 50,* 509–524.

Maguire, G. P., Lee, E. G., & Bevington, D. J. (1978). Psychiatric problems in the first year after mastectomy. *British Journal of Medicine, 1,* 963–965.

Marcus, A. C., Garrett, K. M., Cella, D., Wenzel, L. B., Brady, M. J., Crane, L. A., et al. (1998). Telephone counseling of breast cancer patients after treatment: A description of a randomized clinical trial. *Psycho-oncology, 7,* 470–482.

Marks, D. I., Crilley, P., Nezu, C. M., & Nezu, A. M. (1996). Sexual dysfunction prior to high-dose chemotherapy and bone marrow transplantation. *Bone Marrow Transplantation, 17,* 595–599.

Marks, D. I., Friedman, S. H., DelliCarpini, L., Nezu, C. M., & Nezu, A. M. (1997). A prospective study of the effects of high dose chemotherapy and bone marrow transplantation on sexual function in the first year after transplant. *Bone Marrow Transplantation, 19,* 819–822.

Massie, M. J., & Holland, J. C. (1987). The cancer patient with pain: Psychiatric complications and their management. *Medical Clinics of North America, 71,* 243–257.

Massie, M. J., Holland, J. C., & Glass, E. (1983). Delirium in terminally ill cancer patients. *American Journal of Psychiatry, 140,* 1048–1050.

Massie, M. J., & Popkin, M. (1998). Depressive disorders. In J. C. Holland (Ed.), *Psycho-oncology* (pp. 518–541). New York: Oxford University Press.

McCabe, M. S. (1991). Psychological support for the patient on chemotherapy. *Oncology, 5,* 91-103.

Mermelstein, H. T., & Lesko, L. (1992). Depression in patients with cancer. *Psycho-oncology, 1,* 199–225.

Messerli, M. L., Garamendi, C., & Romano, J. (1980). Breast cancer: Information as a technique of crisis intervention. *American Journal of Orthopsychiatry, 50,* 728–731.

Meyer, T. J., & Mark, M. M. (1995). Effects of psychosocial interventions with adult cancer patients: A meta-analysis of randomized experiments. *Health Psychology, 14,* 101–108.

Miller, S. M., Fang, C. Y., Diefenbach, M. A., & Bales, C. B. (2001). Tailoring psychosocial interventions to the individual's health information-processing style. In A. Baum & B. L. Andersen (Eds.), *Psychosocial interventions for cancer* (pp. 343–362). Washington, DC: American Psychological Association.

Mock, V. (1993). Body image in women treated for breast cancer. *Nursing Research, 42,* 153–157.

Moorey, S., Greer, S., Watson, M., Baruch, J. D. R., Robertson, B. M., Mason, A., et al. (1994). Adjuvant psychological therapy for patients with cancer: Outcome at one year. *Psycho-Oncology, 3,* 39–46.

Morris, T., & Greer, S. (1980). A "type C" for cancer? Low trait anxiety in the pathogenesis of breast cancer. *Cancer Detection and Prevention, 3,* 102.

Morris, T., Pettingale, K. W., & Haybittle, J. (1992). Psychological response to cancer diagnosis and disease outcome in patients with breast cancer and lymphoma. *Psycho-oncology, 1,* 105–114.

Morrow, G. R., & Morrell, B. S. (1982). Behavioral treatment for the anticipatory nausea and vomiting induced by cancer chemotherapy. *New England Journal of Medicine, 307,* 1476–1480.

Moyer, A., & Levine, E. (1998). Clarification of the conceptualization and measurement of denial in psychosocial oncology research. *Annals of Behavioral Medicine, 20,* 149–158.

Moyer, A., & Salovey, P. (1996). Psychosocial sequelae of breast cancer and its treatment. *Annals of Behavioral Medicine, 18,* 110–125.

Mumma, G. H., Mashberg, D., & Lesko, L. M. (1992). Long-term psychosexual adjustment of acute leukemia survivors: Impact of marrow transplantation versus conventional chemotherapy. *General Hospital Psychiatry, 14,* 43–55.

Murphy, G. P., Morris, L. B., & Lange, D. (1997). *Informed decisions: The complete book of cancer diagnosis, treatment, and recovery.* New York: Viking.

Newport, D., & Nemeroff, C. (1998). Assessment and treatment of depression in the cancer patient. *Journal of Psychosomatic Research, 45,* 215–237.

Nezu, A. M. (1986). Efficacy of a social problem-solving therapy approach for unipolar depression. *Journal of Consulting and Clinical Psychology, 54,* 196–202.

Nezu, A. M., & Nezu, C. M. (1998, February). *Problem solving, distress, and sexual difficulties among cancer patients.* Paper presented at the 8th International Congress on Anti-Cancer Treatment, Paris.

Nezu, A. M., Nezu, C. M., Faddis, S., DelliCarpini, L. A., & Houts, P. S. (1995, November). *Social problem solving as a moderator of cancer-related stress.* Paper presented to the Association for Advancement of Behavior Therapy, Washington, DC.

Nezu, A. M., Nezu, C. M., Felgoise, S. H., McClure, K. S., & Houts, P. S. (2001). *The effects of problem-solving therapy for reducing psychological distress of adult cancer patients.* Philadelphia: MCP Hahnemann University.

Nezu, A. M., Nezu, C. M., Friedman, S. H., Faddis, S., & Houts, P. S. (1998). *A problem-solving approach: Helping cancer patients cope.* Washington, DC: American Psychological Association.

Nezu, A. M., Nezu, C. M., Friedman, S. H., & Haynes, S. N. (1997). Case formulation in behavior therapy: Problem-solving and functional analytic strategies. In T. D. Eells (Ed.), *Handbook of psychotherapy case formulation* (pp. 368–401). New York: Guilford Press.

Nezu, A. M., Nezu, C. M., Houts, P. S., Friedman, S. H., & Faddis, S. (1999). Relevance of problem-solving therapy to psychosocial oncology. *Journal of Psychosocial Oncology, 16,* 5–26.

Nezu, A. M., Nezu, C. M., & Lombardo, E. A. (2001). Cognitive-behavior therapy for medically unexplained symptoms: A critical review of the treatment literature. *Behavior Therapy, 32,* 537–583.

Nezu, A. M., & Perri, M. G. (1989). Problem-solving therapy for unipolar depression: An initial dismantling investigation. *Journal of Consulting and Clinical Psychology, 57,* 408–413.

Nezu, C. M., Nezu, A. M., Friedman, S. H., Houts, P. S., DelliCarpini, L. A., Nemeth, C. B., et al. (1999). Cancer and psychological distress: Two investigations regarding the role of problem solving. *Journal of Psychosocial Oncology, 16,* 27–40.

Oberst, M. T., Thomas, S. E., Gass, M. A., & Ward, S. E. (1989). Caregiving demands and appraisal of stress among family caregivers. *Cancer Nursing, 12,* 209–215.

Passik, S. D., & Breitbart, W. S. (1996). Depression in patients with pancreatic cancer. *Cancer Supplement, 78,* 615–626.

Patenaude, A. F. (1990). Psychological impact of bone marrow transplantation: Current perspectives. *Yale Journal of Biology and Medicine, 63,* 515–519.

Penman, D. T. (1982). Coping strategies in adaptation to mastectomy. *Psychosomatic Medicine, 44,* 117.

Peters-Golden, H. (1982). Breast cancer: Varied perceptions of social support in the illness experience. *Social Science and Medicine, 16,* 483–491.

Pruitt, B. T., Waligora-Serafin, B., McMahon, T., Byrd, G., Besselman, L., Kelly, G. M., et al. (1992). An educational intervention for newly diagnosed cancer patients undergoing radiotherapy. *Psycho-Oncology, 2,* 55–62.

Redd, W. H. (1995). Behavioral research in cancer as a model for health psychology. *Health Psychology, 14,* 99–100.

Richardson, J. L., Shelton, D. R., Krailo, M., & Levine, A. M. (1990). The effect of compliance with treatment on survival among patients with hematologic malignancies. *Journal of Clinical Oncology, 8,* 356–364.

Rohan, T. E., Jain, M., Howe, G. R., & Miller, A. B. (2000). Alcohol consumption and risk of breast cancer: A cohort study. *Cancer Causes and Control, 11,* 239–247.

Royak-Schaler, R. (1991). Psychological processes in breast cancer: A review of selected research. *Journal of Psychosocial Oncology, 9,* 71–89.

Sales, E., Schulz, R., & Biegel, D. (1992). Predictors of strain in families of cancer patients: A review of the literature. *Journal of Psychosocial Oncology, 10,* 1–26.

Schover, L. R. (1997). *Sexuality and fertility after cancer.* New York: Wiley.

Schulz, R., Bookwala, J., Knapp, J. E., Scheier, M. F., & Williamson, G. M. (1996). Pessimism, age, and cancer mortality. *Psychology and Aging, 11,* 304–309.

Schwartz, M. D., Lerman, C., Audrian, J., Cella, D., Garber, J., Rimer, B., et al. (1998). The impact of a brief problem-solving training intervention for relatives of recently diagnosed breast cancer patients. *Annals of Behavioral Medicine, 20,* 7–12.

Slattery, M. L., & Kerber, R. A. (1993). A comprehensive evaluation of family history and breast cancer risk: The Utah population database. *Journal of the American Medical Association, 270,* 1563–1568.

Sneeuw, K. C., Aaronson, N. K., Yarnold, J. R., Broderick, M., Regan, J., Ross, G., et al. (1992). Cosmetic and functional outcomes of breast conserving treatment for early stage breast cancer. II: Relationship with psychosocial functioning. *Radiotherapy Oncology, 25,* 160–166.

Spiegel, D., Bloom, J. R., Kraemer, H. C., & Gottheil, E. (1989). Effect of psychosocial treatment on survival of patients with metastatic breast cancer. *Lancet, 2,* 888–891.

Spiegel, D., Bloom, J. R., & Yalom, I. D. (1981). Group support for patients with metastatic cancer: A randomized prospective outcome study. *Archives of General Psychiatry, 38,* 527–533.

Spiegel, D., Morrow, G. R., Classen, C., Raubertas, R., Stott, P. B., Mudaliar, N., et al. (1999). Group psychotherapy for recently diagnosed breast cancer patients: A multicenter feasibility study. *Psycho-oncology, 8,* 482–493.

Spira, J. L. (1998). Group therapies. In J. C. Holland (Ed.), *Psycho-oncology* (pp. 701–716). New York: Oxford University Press.

Stanton, A. L., & Snider, P. R. (1993). Coping with a breast cancer diagnosis: A prospective study. *Health Psychology, 12,* 16–23.

Strain, J. J., & Grossman, S. (1975). *Psychological care of the medically ill.* New York: Appleton-Century-Crofts.

Syrjala, K. L., Cummings, C., & Donaldson, G. (1992). Hypnosis or cognitive-behavioral training for the reduction of pain and nausea during cancer treatment: A controlled clinical trial. *Pain, 48,* 137–146.

Syrjala, K. L., Donaldson, G. W., Davis, M. W., Kippes, M. E., & Carr, J. E. (1995). Relaxation and imagery and cognitive-behavioral training reduce pain during cancer treatment: A controlled clinical trial. *Pain, 63,* 189–198.

Telch, C. F., & Telch, M. J. (1985). Psychological approaches for enhancing coping among cancer patients: A review. *Clinical Psychology Review, 5,* 325–344.

Telch, C. F., & Telch, M. J. (1986). Group coping skills instruction and supportive group therapy for cancer patients: A comparison of strategies. *Journal of Consulting and Clinical Psychology, 54,* 802–808.

Toseland, R. W., Blanchard, C. G., & McCallion, P. (1995). A problem solving intervention for caregivers of cancer patients. *Social Science and Medicine, 40,* 517–528.

Trijsburg, R. W., van Knippenberg, F. C. E., & Rijpma, S. E. (1992). Effects of psychological treatment on cancer patients: A critical review. *Psychosomatic Medicine, 54,* 489–517.

U.S. Department of Health and Human Services. (1990). *The heath benefits of smoking cessation: A report of the surgeon general.* Washington, DC: U.S. Department of Health of Human Services.

Valente, S., Saunders, J., & Cohen, M. (1994). Evaluating depression among patients with cancer. *Cancer Practice, 2,* 65–71.

van't Spijker, A., Trijsburg, R. W., & Duivenvoorden, H. J. (1997). Psychological sequelae of cancer diagnosis: A meta-analytical review of 58 studies after 1980. *Psychosomatic Medicine, 59,* 280–293.

Vitaliano, P. P. (1997). Physiological and physical concomitants of caregiving: Introduction to special issue. *Annals of Behavioral Medicine, 19,* 75–77.

von Eschenbach, A. C. (1986). Sexual dysfunction following therapy for cancer of the prostate, testis, and penis. In J. M. Vaeth (Ed.), *Body image, self-esteem, and sexuality in cancer patients* (pp. 48–57). San Francisco: Karger.

Watson, M. (1983). Psychosocial intervention with cancer patients: A review. *Psychological Medicine, 13,* 839–846.

Watson, M., & Greer, S. (1998). Personality and coping. In J. C. Holland (Ed.), *Psycho-oncology* (pp. 91–98). New York: Oxford University Press.

Watson, M., Greer, S., Blake, S., & Shrapnell, K. (1984). Reaction to a diagnosis of breast cancer: Relationship between denial, delay, and rates of psychological morbidity. *Cancer, 53,* 2008–2012.

Weisman, A. D., & Worden, J. W. (1976–1977). The existential plight in cancer: Significance of the first 100 days. *International Journal of Psychiatric Medicine, 7,* 1–15.

Westerdahl, J., Olsson, H., & Ingvar, C. (1994). At what age do sunburn episodes play a crucial role for the development of malignant melanoma? *European Journal of Cancer, 30A,* 1647–1654.

Whitlock, F. A. (1978). Suicide, cancer, and depression. *British Journal of Psychiatry, 132,* 269–274.

Williamson, G., & Schulz, R. (1995). Activity restriction mediates the association between pain and depressed affect: A study of younger and older adult cancer patients. *Psychology and Aging, 10,* 369–378.

Winters, B. L. (1998). Diet and cancer. In J. C. Holland (Ed.), *Psycho-oncology* (pp. 49–57). New York: Oxford University Press.

Wochna, V. (1997). Anxiety, needs, and coping in family members of the bone marrow transplant patient. *Cancer Nursing, 20,* 244–250.

Worden, J. W., & Weisman, A. D. (1984). Preventive psychosocial intervention with newly diagnosed cancer patients. *General Hospital Psychiatry, 6,* 243–249.

Wortman, C., & Dunkel-Schetter, C. (1979). Interpersonal relationships and cancer. *Journal of Social Issues, 35,* 120–129.

Wright, K., & Dyck, S. (1984). Expressed concerns of adult cancer patient's family members. *Cancer Nursing, 7,* 371–374.

CHAPTER 13

Pain Management

DENNIS C. TURK AND AKIKO OKIFUJI

People are capable of perceiving pain at least from the time of birth. From our earliest experiences, we all become familiar with the pain of a cut, sunburn, or a bruised knee. In these instances, the pain is *acute*. That is, it is self-limiting and will remit on its own or with use of over-the-counter analgesic medication in a reasonably short period of time (usually hours, days, or a few weeks). Rarely are there any long-term consequences following acute pain episodes.

In acute pain, *nociception* (activation of sensory conduction in nerve fibers that transmit information about tissue damage from the affected peripheral area to brain via the spinal cord) has a definite purpose. It acts as a warning signal directing concentration and demanding immediate attention to prevent further damage and to expedite the healing process. For example, when we place a hand on a hot stove, we quickly remove it to avoid being burned. Pain also signals that an injury or disease state is present as in the case of a

broken leg or inflamed appendix. In these instances, pain serves an important, protective function informing us that we should take steps to prevent additional problems and, if necessary, seek medical attention.

There is another type of pain problem that does not fit nicely or adhere to the characteristics of acute pain. There are a number of pain diagnoses and syndromes (e.g., migraine, rheumatoid arthritis, tic doloureux) in which intense pain episodes recur over time, often in an unpredictable fashion. Although each episode tends to last for a relatively brief duration, pain may start any time often without an identifiable provocation. For example, a migraine is a particularly severe form of headache that may last for several hours and then remit without any treatment. The migraine sufferer may be headache-free for days or weeks and then have another migraine episode. After the headache has run its course, the person is headache free until stricken by yet another episode. Thus, the person with migraines has repeated bouts of acute pain. Migraine and conditions with similar episodic characteristics may be viewed as *recurrent acute pain* characterized by pain-free periods punctuated by pain episodes. In the case of recurrent acute pain, the role of pain is unclear because there is no protective action that can be taken, nor is there necessarily any identifiable tissue damage that might cause the

---

Support for the preparation of this manuscript was provided in part by grants from the National Institute of Arthritis and Musculoskeletal and Skin Diseases (AR44724, AR47298) and the National Institute of Child Health and Human Development (HD33989) awarded to the first author and National Institutes of Health/Shannon Director's Award (R55 AR44230) awarded to the second author.

episode. Thus, in both recurrent acute pain and chronic pain the symptom may appear to serve no useful purpose.

Chronic pain persists and can last for months, years, and even decades beyond any period for which healing of the initial injury is expected. There have been some suggestions regarding plasticity within the nervous system where prolonged pain leads to neurophysiological changes and increased sensitization within the central nervous system (CNS) that perpetuate the experience of pain even when the initial cause has resolved (Coderre, Katz, Vaccarino, & Melzack 1993). The average duration of pain noted for patients treated at specialized clinics typically exceeds seven years (Flor, Fydrich, & Turk, 1992).

As is the case in recurrent acute pain, in chronic pain syndromes (e.g., spinal stenosis, osteoarthritis), the pain does not appear to have any obvious useful function. Pain that is chronic or recurrent can significantly compromise quality of life and, if unremitting, may actually produce physical harm by suppressing the body's immune system. Because of significant psychological contributions, we focus on chronic pain in this chapter.

UNIDIMENSIONAL CONCEPTUALIZATIONS OF CHRONIC PAIN

We contrast two types of models or conceptualizations of pain: *unidimensional* ones that focus on single causes of the symptoms reported and *multidimensional* ones that emphasize the contributions of a range of factors that influence patients' experiences and reports of pain.

Biomedical Model of Chronic Pain

The traditional biomedical view of pain is reductionistic. It assumes that reports of pain must be associated, in a proportionate manner, with a specific physical cause. As a consequence, the extent of pain should be directly related to the amount of detectable neurophysiological perturbations. Health care providers often undertake Herculean efforts (at great expense) attempting to establish the specific link between tissue damage and the severity of pain. The expectation is that once *the* physical cause has been identified, appropriate treatment will follow. Treatment will then focus on eliminating the putative cause(s) of the pain or chemically (e.g., oral medication, regional anesthesia, implantable drug delivery systems), surgically (e.g., laminectomy), or electrically (e.g., spinal cord stimulation) blocking the pain pathways.

There are several perplexing features of chronic pain that do not fit neatly within the traditional biomedical model, with its suggestion of an isomorphic relationship between pathology and symptoms. For example, pain may be reported even in the absence of an identified pathological process. It is estimated that one-third to one-half of all visits to primary care physicians are prompted by symptoms for which no biomedical causes can be detected (Kroenke & Mangelsdorff, 1989). In 80% to 85% of the cases, the cause of back pain is unknown (Deyo, 1986). The postulated neural plasticity—central sensitization explanation for these findings—has only been support in acute, animal pain models and has yet to be confirmed for chronic pain.

Conversely, imaging studies using computed tomography (CT) scans and magnetic resonance imaging (MRIs) have noted the presence of significant pathology in up to 35% of *asymptomatic* people (e.g., M. Jensen, Brant-Zawadzki, Obuchowski, Modic, & Malkasian Ross, 1994; Wiesel, Tsourmas, Feffer, Citrin, & Patronas, 1984). Similarly, asymptomatic individuals may have significant degrees of degeneration, and more importantly, a similar prevalence of disk herniation that is comparable to symptomatic people with back pain (Boos et al., 1995). Yet, they do not appear to experience any pain. Thus, those who report severe pain with *no* identifiable pathology, and those with demonstrable pathology may *not* report pain.

Not all people experiencing pain seek medical care. There are large numbers of people with recurrent and chronic pain problems who do not seek medical attention. For example, Brattberg, Thorslund, and Wikman (1989) observed that up to 40% of the adult population sampled reported considerable pain lasting longer than six months, yet the majority did not seek any medical care. Similarly, in a survey of nurses, Linton and Buer (1995) found that the majority reported moderate to severe pain *often* or *always* but they indicated that they had not missed a single day of work due to pain.

Psychogenic Model of Chronic Pain

As is frequently the case in medicine, when physical explanations seem inadequate or when the results of treatment are inconsistent, psychological alternatives are proposed as causal explanations. Moreover, if the report of pain is recalcitrant to *appropriate* treatment that should eliminate or alleviate the pain, it is assumed that psychological processes are involved. The Psychogenic view is the opposite side of the coin of the biomedical model. If the pain reported is deemed to be *disproportionate*—based on the subjective opinion of the health care provider—to any objectively determined pathological process, it may be attributed to psychological causes and thus are psychogenic.

Assessment based on the psychogenic perspective is directed toward identifying the personality factors or psychopathological tendencies that instigate and maintain the reported pain. Traditional psychological measures such as the Minnesota Multiphasic Personality Inventory (MMPI) and the Symptom Checklist-90 (SCL90) are commonly used to evaluate chronic pain patients (Piotrowski, 1997). High scores in these instruments are considered to support the notion of psychogenic pain. It is assumed that reports of pain will cease once the psychological problems are managed. Treatment is geared toward helping the patient gain *insight* into the underlying maladaptive, predisposing psychological factors (e.g., Beutler, Engle, Oro'-Beutler, Daldrup, & Meredith 1986; Grzesiak, Ury, & Dworkin, 1996).

Although the psychogenic pain notion is ubiquitous, empirical evidence supporting it is scarce. A substantial number of chronic pain patients do not exhibit significant psychopathology. Moreover, studies suggest that in the majority of cases the emotional distress observed in these patients occurs in response to persistence of pain and not as a causal agent (e.g., Okifuji, Turk, & Sherman, 2000; Rudy, Kerns, & Turk, 1988) and may resolve once pain is adequately treated (Wallis, Lord, & Bogduk, 1997). Not surprisingly, insight-oriented therapy has not been shown to be effective in reducing symptoms for the majority of patients with chronic pain. There are, however, some patients for whom such insight is essential before they are able to engage successfully in rehabilitation (Grzesiak et al., 1996).

Secondary-Gain Model of Chronic Pain

The secondary-gain model is an alternative to the psychogenic model. From this perspective, reports of pain in the absence of or in excess of physical pathology are attributed to the desire of the patient to obtain some benefit such as attention, time off from undesirable activities, or financial compensation—*secondary gains.* In contrast to the psychogenic model, in the secondary-gain view, the assumption is that the patient is *consciously* attempting to acquire a desirable outcome. Simply put, the report of pain in the absence of a pathological process is regarded as fraudulent (Bayer, 1984).

Assessment of patients from the secondary-gain model focuses on identifying discrepancies between what patients say they are capable of doing and what they actually can do or from facial expressions that deviate from norm-based expectations (Craig, Hyde, & Patrick, 1991). A high degree of discrepancy between what patients say about their pain and physical capacity and performance on more objective assessment of physical functioning and facial expressions are believed to be evidence that patients are exaggerating or fabricating their symptoms to obtain a desired outcome. Thus, repeated performance of functional capacity testing that identifies discrepancies (sometimes referred to as the *index of congruence*) in performance has been used to label patients as symptom magnifiers at best or malingerers at worst. Surveillance is also used, again seeking discrepancies between the patient's reports of activity and objective performance. Thus, a patient who states that he cannot lift weights over 10 pounds might and who refuses to attempt to lift during a functional capacity evaluation might be observed or even videotaped lifting groceries out of his car. The ability to lift the bags of groceries is taken as evidence that the patient is capable of lifting. Thus, the report of the inability to lift, in light of the lifting of groceries, is viewed as proof of dissimulation. Inconsistency in reported ability and actual performance fails to consider the limited ability of people to accurately estimate the capacity and the refusal to perform associated with fear of injury, reinjury, or exacerbation of pain (e.g., Lenthem, Slade, Troup, & Bentley, 1983; Vlaeyen, Kole-Snijders, Boeren, & van Eek, 1995).

The treatment of pain from the secondary-gain perspective is simple, denial of disability payments. The assumption being that denial of disability will lead inevitably to prompt resolution of the reported symptoms. Although this view is prevalent, especially among third-party payers, there is little evidence of dramatic cure of pain following denial of disability.

Behavioral Conceptualizations

Pain is an unavoidable part of human life. No learning is required to activate nociceptive receptors. However, pain is a potent and salient experience for all sentient organisms (animals including humans). Beyond mere reflexive actions, all must learn to avoid, modify, or cope with noxious stimulation. There are three major principles of behavioral learning that help us understand acquisition of adaptive as well as dysfunctional behaviors associated with pain.

Classical (Respondent) Conditioning

In his classic experiment, Pavlov found that a dog could be taught, or *conditioned,* to salivate at the sound of a bell by pairing the sound with food presented to a hungry dog. Salivation of dogs in response to food is natural; however, by preceding the feeding with the sound of a bell, Pavlov's dogs learned to associate the sound of the bell with an imminent feeding. Once this association was learned, or conditioned, the dogs were found to salivate at the mere sound of a bell *even in the absence of the food.* That is, the dogs were conditioned to anticipate food at the sound of a bell.

The influence of classical conditioning can be observed in pain patients as well. Consider physical therapy, a mainstay of treatments for chronic pain patients, where treatment may evoke a conditioned fear response in patients. A patient, for example, who experienced increased pain following physical therapy may become conditioned and experience a negative emotional response to the presence of the physical therapist, to the treatment room, and to any contextual cues associated with the nociceptive stimulus. The negative emotional reaction may lead to tensing of muscles and this in turn may exacerbate pain and, thereby, strengthen the association between the presence of the physical therapist and pain.

Once a pain problem persists, fear of motor activities may become increasingly conditioned, resulting in avoidance of activity. Avoidance of pain is a powerful rationale for reduction of activity, where muscle soreness associated with exercise functions as a justification for further avoidance. Thus, although it may be useful to reduce movement in the acute pain stage, limitation of activities can be chronically maintained not only by pain but also by *anticipatory* fear that has been acquired through the mechanism of classical conditioning. Here we can note how cognitive processes may interact with pure conditioning. It is the anticipation that motivates a conscious decision to avoid specific behaviors or stimuli.

In chronic pain, many activities that are neutral or even pleasurable may come to elicit or exacerbate pain. As a consequence, they are experienced as aversive and actively avoided. Over time, more and more stimuli (e.g., activities and exercises) may be expected to elicit or exacerbate pain and will be avoided. This process is referred to as *stimulus generalization*. Thus, the anticipatory fear of pain and restriction of activity, and not just the actual nociception, may contribute to disability. Anticipatory fear also can elicit physiological reactivity that may aggravate pain. In this way, conditioning may directly increase nociceptive stimulation and pain.

The conviction that patients hold that they must remain inactive is difficult to modify, as long as activity-avoidance succeeds in preventing aggravation of pain. By contrast, repeatedly engaging in behavior—*exposure*—that produces progressively less pain than was predicted (corrective feedback) will be followed by reductions in anticipatory fear and anxiety associated with the activity (Fordyce, Shelton, & Dundore, 1982; Vlaeyen et al., 1995). Such transformations add support to the importance of a quota-based physical exercise programs, with patients progressively increasing their activity levels despite fear of injury and discomfort associated with the use of deconditioned muscles (Dolce, Crocker, Moletteire, & Doleys, 1986).

Operant Conditioning—Contingencies of Reinforcement

The effects of environmental factors in shaping the experience of people suffering with pain was acknowledged long ago (Collie, 1913). A new era in thinking about pain began with Fordyce's (1976) extension of *operant conditioning* to chronic pain. The main focus of operant learning is modification in frequency of a given behavior. The fundamental principle is that if the consequence of a given behavior is rewarding, its occurrence increases; whereas if the consequence is aversive, the likelihood of its occurrence decreases.

When a person is exposed to a stimulus that causes tissue damage, the immediate behavioral response is withdrawal in an attempt to escape from noxious sensations. Such reflexive behaviors are adaptive and appropriate. Behaviors associated with pain, such as limping and moaning, are called *pain behaviors*. Pain behaviors include overt expressions of pain, distress, and suffering. According to Fordyce (1976), these behaviors can become subjected to the principles of operant conditioning. These behaviors may be positively reinforced directly, for example, by attention from a family member, acquaintance, or health care provider. The principles of operant learning suggest that behaviors that are positively reinforced will be reported more frequently. Pain behaviors may also be maintained by the escape from noxious stimulation by the use of drugs or rest, or the avoidance of undesirable activities. In addition *well behaviors* (e.g., activity, working) may not be positively reinforced, and the more rewarded pain behaviors may therefore be maintained.

The following example illustrates the role of operant conditioning: When back pain flares up, the sufferer may lie down and hold her back. Her husband may observe her behavior and infer that she is experiencing pain. He may respond by offering to rub her back. This response may positively reward the woman and her pain behaviors (i.e., lying down) may be repeated even in the absence of pain. In other words, her pain behaviors are being maintained by the learned consequences.

The woman's pain behaviors are reinforced by allowing the person to avoid undesirable activities. When observing his wife lying on the floor, her husband may suggest that they cancel the evening plans with his brother, an activity that she may have preferred to avoid anyway. In this situation, her

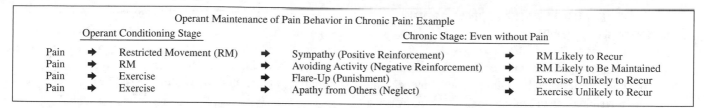

Operant Maintenance of Pain Behavior in Chronic Pain: Example		
Operant Conditioning Stage		Chronic Stage: Even without Pain
Pain ➡ Restricted Movement (RM)	➡ Sympathy (Positive Reinforcement)	➡ RM Likely to Recur
Pain ➡ RM	➡ Avoiding Activity (Negative Reinforcement)	➡ RM Likely to Be Maintained
Pain ➡ Exercise	➡ Flare-Up (Punishment)	➡ Exercise Unlikely to Recur
Pain ➡ Exercise	➡ Apathy from Others (Neglect)	➡ Exercise Unlikely to Recur

Figure 13.1 Operant conditioning in chronic pain.

husband provided extra attention, comfort, and the opportunity to avoid an undesirable social obligation. Therefore, her pain behaviors were rewarded.

Figure 13.1 describes examples of basic operant principles in chronic pain. The operant learning paradigm does not uncover the etiology of pain but focuses primarily on the maintenance of pain behaviors and deficiency in well behaviors. Adjustment of reinforcement schedules will likely modify the probability of recurrence of pain behaviors and well behaviors.

Pain sufferers *do not intentionally* communicate pain to obtain attention or avoid undesirable activities. It is more likely to be the result of a gradual process of the shaping of behavior that neither the sufferer nor her comforter (i.e., husband) recognizes. Thus, a person's response to life stressors as well as how others respond can influence the experience of pain in many ways, but are not the cause of the pain condition.

It is important not to make the mistake of viewing pain behaviors as being synonymous with *malingering*. Malingering involves the patient consciously and purposely faking a symptom such as pain for some gain, usually financial. As we noted earlier, in the case of pain behaviors, there is no suggestion of conscious deception but rather the unintended performance of pain behaviors resulting from environmental reinforcement contingencies. The patient is typically not aware that these behaviors are being displayed, nor is he or she consciously intending to obtain a positive reinforcement from the behaviors. Contrary to the beliefs of many third-party payers, there is little support for the contention that outright faking of pain for financial gain is prevalent (e.g., Craig, Hill, & McMurtry, 1999).

Social Learning Processes

Social learning has received some attention in acute pain and in the development and maintenance of chronic pain states. From this perspective, the acquisition of pain behaviors may occur by means of *observational learning* and *modeling* processes. That is, people can acquire behavioral responses

that were not previously in their repertoire by the observation of others.

Children develop attitudes about health and health care, and the perception and interpretation of symptoms and physiological processes from their parents and social environment. They learn appropriate and inappropriate responses to injury and disease and thus may be more or less likely to ignore or overrespond to symptoms they experience based on behaviors modeled in childhood. The culturally acquired perception and interpretation of symptoms determines how people deal with disease states. The observation of others in pain is an event that captivates attention. This attention may have survival value, may help to avoid experiencing more pain, and may help us to learn what to do about acute pain.

There is ample evidence of the role of social learning from controlled laboratory pain studies and from some evidence based on observations of people's behaviors in naturalistic and clinical settings. For example, children of chronic pain patients may make more pain-related responses during stressful times than would children with healthy parents. These children tend to exhibit greater illness behaviors (e.g., complaining, days absent, visit to school nurse) than children of healthy parents (Richard, 1988). Models can influence the expression, localization, and methods of coping with pain (Craig, 1986). Physiological responses may be conditioned during observation of others in pain (Vaughan & Lanzetta, 1980). Expectancies and actual behavioral responses to nociceptive stimulation are based, at least partially, on prior social learning history. This may, along with classical conditioning and operant learning history, contribute to the marked variability in response to objectively similar degrees of physical pathology noted by health care providers.

The biomedical, psychogenic, secondary-gain, and behavioral views are unidimensional. Reports of pain are ascribed to *either* physical *or* psychological factors. Rather than being categorical, either somatogenic or psychogenic, both physical and psychological components may interact to create and influence the experience of pain. Several efforts have been made to integrate physical, psychosocial, and behavioral factors within multidimensional models.

INTEGRATIVE, MULTIDIMENSIONAL MODEL— GATE CONTROL THEORY

The first attempt to develop an integrative model designed to address the problems created by unidimensional models and to integrate physiological and psychological factors was the gate control theory (GCT) proposed by Melzack and Wall (1965). Perhaps the most important contribution of the GCT is the way it changed thinking about pain perception. In this model, three systems are postulated to be related to the processing of nociceptive stimulation—sensory-discriminative, motivational-affective, and cognitive-evaluative—all of which contribute to the subjective experience of pain. Melzack and Wall emphasized the central nervous system mechanisms and provided a physiological basis for the role of psychological factors in chronic pain.

The GCT proposes that a process in the dorsal horn substantia gelatinosa of the spinal cord acts as a gating mechanism that inhibits or facilitates transmission of nerve impulses on the basis of the diameters of the active peripheral fibers as well as the dynamic action of brain processes. Melzack and Wall (1965) postulated that the spinal gating mechanism was influenced by the relative amount of excitatory activity in afferent, large-diameter (myelinated) and small-diameter (unmyelinated nociceptors) fibers converging in the dorsal horns. They also proposed that activity in A-beta (large-diameter) fibers tends to inhibit transmission of nociceptive signals ("closes the gate") while activity in A-delta and c (small-diameter) fibers tends to facilitate transmission ("open the gate"). The hypothetical gate in the dorsal horn modulates the sensory input by the balance of activity of small diameter (A-delta and c) and large-diameter (A-beta) fibers (see Figure 13.2).

As an important innovation, Melzack and Wall (1965) postulated further that the spinal gating mechanism is influenced not only by peripheral afferent activity but also by efferent neural impulses that *descend from the brain*. They suggested that a specialized system of large-diameter, rapidly conducting fibers (the central control trigger) activate selective cognitive processes that then influence, by way of descending fibers, the modulating properties of the spinal gating mechanism. Melzack and Wall speculated that the brain stem reticular formation functions as a central biasing mechanism, inhibiting the transmission of pain signals at multiple synaptic levels of the somatosensory system.

The GCT maintains that loss of sensory input to this complex neural system, such as occurs in neuropathies, causalgia, and phantom limb pain, tends to weaken inhibition and lead to persistent pain. Herniated disc material, tumors, and other factors that exert pressure on these neural structures may operate through such losses of sensory input. Emotional stress and medication may also alter the biasing mechanisms and thus intensity of pain.

From the GCT perspective, the experience of pain is an ongoing sequence of activities, largely reflexive in nature at the outset, but modifiable even in the earliest stages by a variety of excitatory and inhibitory influences, and by the integration of ascending and descending nervous system activity. The process results in overt expressions communicating pain and strategies to terminate the pain. In addition, considerable potential for shaping of the pain experience is implied because the GCT invokes continuous interaction of multiple systems (sensory-physiological, affect, cognition, and, ultimately, behavior).

The GCT describes the integration of peripheral stimuli with cortical states, such as anxiety, in the perception of pain. This model contradicts the notion that pain is either somatic or psychogenic and instead postulates that both factors have either potentiating or moderating effects on pain perception. In this model, for example, pain is not understood to be the result of depression or vice versa, but rather the two are seen as evolving simultaneously. Any significant change in mood or pain will necessarily alter the others.

The GCT's emphasis on the modulation of inputs in the dorsal horns and the dynamic role of the brain in pain processes resulted in the integration of psychological variables such as past experience, attention, and other cognitive activities into research and therapy on pain. Prior to this formulation, psychological processes were largely dismissed as reactions to pain. This new model suggested that cutting nerves and pathways was inadequate because a host of other factors modulated the input. Perhaps the major contribution of the GCT was that it highlighted the central nervous system as an essential component in pain processes and perception.

The physiological details of the GCT have been challenged, and it has been suggested that the model is incomplete. As

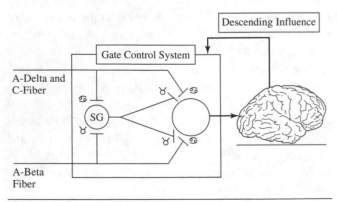

Figure 13.2   Gate control model of pain.

additional knowledge has been gathered since the original formulation, specific points of posited mechanisms have been disputed and have required revision and reformulation. Overall, however, the GCT has proved remarkably resilient and flexible in the face of accumulating scientific data and challenges. It still provides a powerful summary of the phenomena observed in the spinal cord and brain, and this model has the capacity to explain many of the most mysterious and puzzling problems encountered in the clinic. The GCT has had enormous heuristic value in stimulating further research in the basic science of pain mechanisms. The GCT can also be credited as a source of inspiration for diverse clinical applications to control or manage pain, including neurophysiologically based procedures (for example, neural stimulation techniques, from peripheral nerves and collateral processes in the dorsal columns of the spinal cord), pharmacological advances, behavioral treatments, and those interventions targeting modification of attentional and perceptual processes involved in the pain experience. After the GCT was first described in 1965, no one could try to explain pain exclusively in terms of peripheral factors.

A number of authors have extended the GCT to integrate more detailed psychological contributions has lead to the presentation of biopsychosocial or biobehavioral models of pain (e.g., Turk 1996; Turk & Flor, 1999). These conceptual models emphasize the important contributions, mediating, and modulation role of a range of cognitive, affective, and behavioral variables. Before describing these models, it is important to focus on the psychology of pain.

PSYCHOLOGY OF PAIN

For the person experiencing pain, particularly chronic pain, there is a continuing quest for relief that remains elusive and leads to feelings of frustration, anxiety, demoralization, and depression, compromising the quality of all aspects of their lives. People with chronic pain confront not only the stress of pain but also a cascade of ongoing problems (e.g., financial, familial). Moreover, the experience of "medical limbo" (i.e., the presence of a painful condition that eludes diagnosis and that carries the implication of either psychiatric causation or malingering on the one hand, or an undiagnosed potentially disabling condition on the other) is itself the source of significant stress and can initiate psychological distress.

Biomedical factors, in the majority of cases, appear to instigate the initial report of pain. Over time, however, psychosocial and behavioral factors may serve to maintain and exacerbate the level of pain, influence adjustment, and contribute to excessive disability. Following from this view, pain that persists over time should not be viewed as solely physical or solely psychological; the experience of pain is maintained by an interdependent set of biomedical, psychosocial, and behavioral factors.

Consider the following scenario: A person with chronic pain becomes inactive, leading to preoccupation with his or her body and pain, and these cognitive-attentional changes increase the likelihood of amplifying and distorting pain symptoms. This person may then perceive himself or herself as disabled. At the same time, due to fear, the pain sufferer limits his or her opportunities to build flexibility, endurance, and strength without the risk of pain or injury. To the pain sufferer, hurt is viewed as synonymous with harm. Thus, if an activity produces an increase in pain, the sufferer terminates the activity and avoids similar activities in the future. Chronic pain sufferers often develop negative expectations about their own ability to exert any control over their pain. The negative expectations lead to feelings of frustration and demoralization when *uncontrollable* pain interferes with participation in physical and social activities.

Pain sufferers frequently terminate active efforts to manage pain and, instead, turn to passive coping strategies such as inactivity, medication, or alcohol to reduce emotional distress and pain. They also absolve themselves of personal responsibility for managing their pain and, instead, rely on family and health care providers. The thinking of chronic pain patients has been shown to contribute to the exacerbation, attenuation, and maintenance of pain, pain behaviors, affective distress, adjustment to chronic pain, health care seeking, and response to treatment (e.g., Council, Ahern, Follick, & Cline, 1988; Flor & Turk, 1988).

In the case of chronic pain, health care providers need to consider not only the physical basis of pain but also patients' moods, fears, expectancies, coping resources, coping efforts, and response of significant others, including themselves. Regardless of whether there is an identifiable physical basis for the reported pain, psychosocial and behavioral factors interact to influence the nature, severity, and persistence of pain and disability. In particular, behavioral, emotional, and cognitive variables should be addressed. We have already described the important role of environmental contingencies of reinforcement in chronic pain (e.g., Fordyce, 1976). We now turn to the range of affective and cognitive factors that play an equally important role.

Affective Factors

Pain is ultimately a subjective, private experience, but it is invariably described in terms of sensory and affective properties. As defined by the International Association for the Study of Pain: "[Pain] is unquestionably a sensation in a part or parts of the body but it is also always unpleasant and therefore also an emotional experience" (Merskey, 1986). The central and interactive roles of sensory information and affective state are supported by an overwhelming amount of evidence (Fernandez & Turk, 1992). The affective components of pain include many different emotions, but they are primarily negative emotions. Depression and anxiety have received the greatest amount of attention in chronic pain patients; however, anger has recently received considerable interest as an important emotion in chronic pain patients.

Depression

Clinical data suggest that from 40% to 50% of chronic pain patients suffer from significant depression (Banks & Kerns, 1996). In the majority of cases, depression appears to be reactions, although some have suggested that chronic pain is a form of "masked depression," whereby patients use pain to express their depressed mood because they feel it is more acceptable to report pain than to acknowledge depression. Although this may be true in a small number of cases, the research on this topic does not suggest that depression precedes the development of chronic pain (Turk & Salovey, 1984).

It is not surprising that a large number of chronic pain patients are depressed. It is interesting to ponder the other side of the coin. Given the nature of the symptom and the problems created by chronic pain, why is it that all such patients are *not* depressed? We (Okifuji et al., 2000; Turk, Okifuji, & Scharff, 1995) examined this question and determined that patients' appraisals of the effects of the pain on their lives and of their ability to exert any control over the pain and their lives mediated the pain-depression link. That is, those patients who believed that they could continue to function despite their pain, and who believed that they could maintain control despite their pain, did not become depressed.

Anger

Anger has been widely observed in people with chronic pain (Schwartz, Slater, Birchler, & Atkinson, 1991). Pilowsky and Spence (1976) reported "bottled-up anger" in 53% of chronic pain patients. Kerns, Rosenberg, and Jacob (1994) noted that the internalization of angry feelings was strongly related to measures of pain intensity, perceived interference, and reported frequency of pain behaviors. Summers and colleagues (Summers, Rapoff, Varghess, Porter, & Palmer, 1991) examined patients with spinal cord injuries and found that anger and hostility were powerful predictors of pain severity.

Moreover, even though chronic pain patients in psychotherapy might present an image of themselves as even-tempered, 88% of the patients treated acknowledged their feelings of anger when these were explicitly sought (Corbishley, Hendrickson, Beutler, & Engle, 1990).

Frustrations related to persistence of symptoms, limited information on etiology, and repeated treatment failures along with anger toward employers, the insurance, the health care system, family members, and themselves, all contribute to the general dysphoric mood of these patients. The effects of anger and frustration on exacerbation of pain and treatment acceptance has not received much attention, but it would be reasonable to expect that the presence of anger may serve as a complicating factor, increasing autonomic arousal and blocking motivation and acceptance of treatments oriented toward rehabilitation and disability management rather than cure, which are often the only treatments available for chronic pain (Fernandez & Turk, 1995).

It is important to be aware of the central role of negative mood in chronic pain patients because it is likely to affect treatment motivation and compliance with treatment recommendations. For example, patients who are anxious may fear engaging in what they perceive as demanding activities; patients who are depressed and who feel helpless may have little initiative to comply; and patients who are angry with the health care system are not likely to be motivated to respond to recommendations from yet another health care professional.

Cognitive Factors

A great deal of research has been directed toward identifying cognitive factors that contribute to pain and disability. These studies have consistently demonstrated that patients attitudes, beliefs, and expectancies about their plight, themselves, their coping resources, and the health care system affect reports of pain, activity, disability, and response to treatment.

Beliefs about Pain

People respond to medical conditions in part based on their subjective ideas about illness and their symptoms. Health care providers working with chronic pain patients are aware that patients having similar pain histories and reports of pain may differ greatly in their beliefs about their pain. Behavior and emotions are influenced by interpretations of events and expectations, rather than solely by objective characteristics of the event itself. Thus, pain, when interpreted as signifying ongoing tissue damage or a progressive disease, is likely to produce considerably more suffering and behavioral dysfunction than if it is viewed as being the result of a stable problem that is expected to improve.

People build fairly elaborate views of their physical states and these views or representations provide the basis for action plans and coping. Beliefs about the meaning of pain and their ability to function despite discomfort are important aspects of expectations about pain. For example, a cognitive representation that you have a very serious, debilitating condition, that disability is a necessary aspect of pain, that activity is dangerous, and that pain is an acceptable excuse for neglecting responsibilities will likely result in maladaptive responses.

Chronic pain patients often demonstrate poor behavioral persistence in exercise tasks. Their performance on these tasks may not be independent of physical exertion or actual self-reports of pain, but rather be related to *previous* pain reports or fear of injury, reinjury, or exacerbation of their pain (Vlaeyen et al., 1995). These people appear to have a negative view of their abilities and expect increased pain if they performed physical exercises. The rationale for their avoidance of exercise was not the presence of pain but their *learned expectation* of heightened pain and accompanying physical arousal that might exacerbate pain and reinforce patients' beliefs regarding the pervasiveness of their disability. If people view disability as a necessary reaction to their pain, that activity is dangerous, and that pain is an acceptable excuse for neglecting their responsibilities, they are likely to experience greater disability. Pain sufferers' negative perceptions of their capabilities for physical performance form a vicious circle, with the failure to perform activities reinforcing the perception of helplessness and incapacity. Once again we can see how behavioral (conditioning) factors interact with cognitive processes.

To illustrate the important role of cognitive processes in affective and behavior related to noxious sensations, consider the case of a person who wakes up one morning with a headache. Very different responses would be expected depending on whether he attributed the headache to excessive alcohol intake or a brain tumor. Thus, although the amount of nociceptive input in the two cases may be equivalent, the emotional and behavioral responses would vary in nature and intensity. If the interpretation is that the headache is related to excessive alcohol, there might be little emotional arousal. He might take some over-the-counter analgesics, a hot shower, and take it easy for a few hours. On the other hand, interpretation of the headache as indicating a brain tumor is likely to create significant worry and might result in a call to a neurologist.

Certain beliefs may lead to maladaptive coping, increased suffering, and greater disability. People who believe their pain will persist may be passive in their coping and fail to make use of strategies to deal with pain. People who consider their pain to be an unexplainable mystery may negatively evaluate their own abilities to control or decrease pain, and are less likely to rate their coping strategies as effective in controlling and decreasing pain (Williams & Thorn, 1989). People's beliefs, appraisals, and expectancies regarding the consequences of an event and their ability to cope with it are hypothesized to effect functioning in two ways. They may have a direct influence on physiological arousal and mood and an indirect one through their effects on coping efforts (Flor & Turk, 1988; 1989).

Once beliefs and expectancies are formed, they become stable and are very difficult to modify. As we noted, pain sufferers tend to avoid experiences that could invalidate their beliefs and guide their behavior in accordance with these beliefs, even in situations where these beliefs are no longer valid. Consequently, they do not obtain corrective feedback.

It is essential for people with chronic pain to develop adaptive beliefs about the relation among impairment, pain, suffering, and disability, and to de-emphasize the role of experienced pain in their regulation of functioning. In fact, results from numerous treatment outcome studies have shown that changes in pain level do not parallel changes in activity level, medication use, return to work, rated ability to cope with pain, and pursuit of further treatment. If health care providers hope to achieve better outcomes and to reduce their frustration from patients' lack of adherence to their advice, they need to learn about and to address patients' concerns within this therapeutic context.

Self-Efficacy

Self-efficacy is a personal expectation that is particularly important in patients with chronic pain. A self-efficacy expectation is defined as a personal conviction that you can successfully execute a course of action (perform required behaviors) to produce a desired outcome in a given situation. Self-efficacy is a major mediator of therapeutic change. Given sufficient motivation to engage in a behavior, it is a person's self-efficacy beliefs that determine the choice of activities that the he or she will initiate, the amount of effort that will be expended, and how long the individual will persist in the face of obstacles and aversive experiences. Efficacy judgments are based on four sources of information regarding capabilities, listed in descending order of effects:

1. Past performance at the task or similar tasks.
2. The performance accomplishments of others who are perceived to be similar.

3. Verbal persuasion by others.
4. Perception of a state of physiological arousal, which is in turn partly determined by prior efficacy estimation.

Performance mastery experience can be created by encouraging patients to undertake subtasks that are initially attainable but become increasingly difficult, and subsequently approaching the desired level of performance (Dolce et al., 1986). In a quota-based physical therapy system, the initial goal is set below initial performance to increase performance mastery. It is important to remember that coping behaviors are influenced by the person's beliefs that the demands of a situation do not exceed their resources. For example, Council et al. (1988) asked patients to rate their self-efficacy as well as expectancy of pain related to performance during movement tasks. Patients' performance levels were highly related to their self-efficacy expectations, which in turn appeared to be determined by their expectancies regarding levels of pain that would be experienced.

Catastrophic Thinking

Catastrophizing—experiencing extremely negative thoughts about your plight and interpreting even minor problems as major catastrophes—appears to be a particularly potent way of thinking that greatly influences pain and disability. Several lines of research have indicated that catastrophizing and adaptive coping strategies are important in determining a person's reaction to pain (Sullivan et al., 2001). People who spontaneously used more catastrophizing thoughts reported more pain than those who did not catastrophize in several acute and chronic pain studies.

Coping

Self-regulation of pain and its effects depends on the individual's specific ways of dealing with pain, adjusting to pain, and reducing or minimizing pain and distress caused by pain; in other words, their coping strategies (DeGood & Tait, 2001). Coping is assumed to be implemented by spontaneously employed purposeful and intentional acts, and it can be assessed in terms of overt and covert behaviors. Overt, behavioral coping strategies include rest, medication, and use of relaxation. Covert coping strategies include various means of distracting yourself from pain, reassuring yourself that the pain will diminish, seeking information, and problem solving. Coping strategies act to alter both the perception of intensity of pain and your ability to manage or tolerate pain and to continue everyday activities.

Studies have found active coping strategies (efforts to function in spite of pain or to distract oneself from pain, such as activity, or ignoring pain) to be associated with adaptive functioning, and passive coping strategies (depending on others for help in pain control and restricted activities) to be related to greater pain and depression (Boothby, Thorn, Stroud, & Jensen, 1999). However, beyond this, there is no evidence supporting the greater effectiveness of any one active coping strategy compared to any other (Turk, Meichenbaum, & Genest, 1983). It seems more likely that different strategies will be more effective than others for some people at some times but not necessarily for all people all of the time.

A number of studies have been demonstrated that if patients are instructed in the use of adaptive coping strategies, their rating of intensity of pain decreases and tolerance of pain increases (Boothby et al., 1999). The most important factor in poor coping appears to be the presence of catastrophic thinking, not the nature of specific adaptive coping strategies (Sullivan et al., 2001).

Given our discussion of the psychological factors that play a role in pain, we can now consider how these factors can be integrated within a multidimensional model of pain. Pain is a complex subjective phenomenon comprising a range of factors, each of which contributes to the interpretation of nociception as pain. Thus, each person uniquely experiences pain. A significant factor contributing to the current situation relates to diagnostic uncertainty. The diagnosis of pain is not an exact science. A major problem in understanding pain is that it is a subjective (internal) state. There is no *pain thermometer* that can accurately measure the amount of pain a person feels or should be experiencing.

An integrative model of chronic pain and acute recurrent pain needs to incorporate the mutual interrelationships among physical, psychosocial, and behavioral factors and the changes that occur among these relationships over time. A model that focuses on only one of these sets of factors will inevitably be incomplete. The physiological model proposed by Melzack and Wall (1965) can be contrasted with the more psychological, cognitive-behavioral (biobehavioral) model that Turk and colleagues (Turk, 1996; Turk & Flor, 1999) have proposed. Melzack and Wall focus primarily on the basic anatomy and physiology of pain; whereas, Turk and colleagues have emphasized the influence of psychological processes on physical factors underlying the experience of pain. Yet both incorporate physical and psychological factors to account for the experience of pain.

The biopsychosocial model presumes some form of physical pathology or at least physical changes in the muscles, joints, or nerves that generate nociceptive input to the brain. At the periphery, nociceptive fibers transmit sensations that may or may not be interpreted as pain. Such sensation is not yet considered pain until subjected to higher order psychological and mental processing that involve perception, appraisal, and behavior. Perception involve the interpretation of nociceptive input and identifies the type of pain (i.e., sharp, burning, and punishing). Appraisal involves the meaning that is attributed to the pain and influences subsequent behaviors. A person may choose to ignore the pain and continue working, walking, socializing, and engaging in previous levels of activity or may choose to leave work, refrain from all activity, and assume the sick role (Linton & Buer, 1995). In turn, this interpersonal role is shaped by responses from significant others that may promote either the healthy response or the sick role.

AN INTEGRATED, MULTIDIMENSIONAL MODEL

Based on what we have just described, we suggest an integrative, multidimensional model of pain. Between the stimulus of tissue injury and the subjective experience of pain is a series of complex electrical and chemical events. Four distinct physiological processes have been identified in pain: transduction, transmission, modulation, and perception.

Transduction, or receptor, activation is the process where one form of energy (chemical, mechanical, or thermal) is converted into another, in this case, the electrochemical nerve impulse in the primary afferents. Noxious stimuli lead to electrical activity in the appropriate sensory nerve endings.

Transmission refers to the process by which coded information is relayed to those structures of the CNS whose activity produces the sensation of pain. The first stage of transmission is the conduction of impulses in primary afferents to the spinal cord. At the spinal cord, activity in the primary afferents activates spinal neurons that relay the nociceptive message to the brain. This message elicits a variety of responses ranging from withdrawal reflexes to the subjective perceptual events. In addition, the responses of CNS neurons to noxious stimuli are variable because they are subject to inhibitory influences elicited by peripheral stimulation or originating within the brain itself.

Modulation refers to the neural activity leading to control of the nociceptive transmission pathway. The activity of this modulatory system is one reason why people with apparently severe injuries may deny significant levels of pain.

Although we are far from understanding all the complexities of the human brain, we know that there are specific pathways in the CNS that control pain transmission, and there is evidence that these pathways can be activated by the psychological factors described earlier.

The final process involved with pain is *perception*. Somehow, the neural activity of the nociceptive transmission neurons induces a subjective experience. How this comes about is obscure, and it is not even clear in which brain structures

the activity occurs that produces the perceptual event. The question remains, "How do objectively observable neural events produce subjective experience?" Since pain is fundamentally a subjective experience, there are inherent limitations to understanding it.

There are several reasons for the variability in people's responses to nociceptive stimuli. There may be an injury to the nociceptive transmission system or to the activity of the modulatory system that lower pain intensity. There may be abnormal neural activity that may produce hypersensitivity that can result from self-sustaining processes set in motion by an injury but that may persist beyond the time it takes for the original injury to heal. This self-sustaining process may even create a situation where pain is experienced without the noxious stimulus produced by an active tissue damaging process (e.g., neuropathic pain). Finally, the psychological processes and factors described above may affect normal pain intensity creating unpredictable responses.

From an integrative biopsychosocial perspective, pain is viewed as a subjective perception that results from the transduction, transmission, and modulation of sensory input filtered through a person's genetic composition, and prior learning history, and modulated further by their current physiological state, idiosyncratic appraisals, expectations, present mood state, and sociocultural environment.

ASSESSMENT

To understand and appropriately treat a patient whose primary symptom is pain begins with a comprehensive history and physical examination. Patients are usually asked to describe the characteristics (e.g., stabbing, burning), location, and severity of their pain. Physical examination procedures and sophisticated laboratory and imaging techniques are readily available for use in detecting organic pathology. Although the assessment of pain may at first seem to be quite an easy task, this assessment is complicated by the unique psychological, social, and behavioral characteristics of the person. Thus, in addition to this standard medical approach, an adequate pain assessment also requires evaluation of the myriad psychosocial and behavioral factors that influence the subjective report.

Quantifying the Pain Severity

The response to the apparently simple question of "How much does it hurt?" is more complex than it may at first appear. Pain resides within an individual and there is currently no pain thermometer that provides an objective quantification of the amount or severity of pain experienced by a person.

Thus, it can only be assessed indirectly based on a patient's overt communication, both verbal and behavioral.

Pain is a complex, subjective phenomenon comprised of a range of factors and is uniquely experienced by each person. Wide variability in pain severity, quality, and impact may be noted in reports of patients attempting to describe what appear to be objectively identical phenomena. In addition, patients have a different frame of reference from that of the caregiver. These unique views may complicate communication between patient and caregiver and prevent direct comparisons among patients from different backgrounds and with different experiences. Patient's descriptions of pain are also colored by cultural and sociological influences. It is the unique experiences of each patient that make assessment of pain so difficult.

Physical and Laboratory Factors

Difficulties in assessing the physical contributions to chronic pain are well recognized. There are no universal criteria for scoring the presence or importance of a particular sign (e.g., positive radiographs, limitation of spinal mobility), quantifying the degree of disability, or establishing the association of these findings with treatment outcome. Interpretation of biomedical findings relies on clinical judgments and medical consensus based on a physician's experience and in some instances quasi-standardized criteria. There remains a good deal of subjectivity both in the manner in which physical examinations are performed and diagnostic findings are interpreted.

The inherent subjectivity of physical examination is most evident when it is noted that agreement between physicians is better for items of patient history than for some items of the physical examination. The reproducibility of physical evaluation findings, even among experienced physicians, is low. For example, multiple observer agreement in physical examination of spinal motion and muscle strength, even when using standard mechanical assessment devices such as dynamometers, can be surprisingly poor (Hunt et al., in press).

The discriminative power of common objective signs of pathology determined during physical examination has also been questioned. Physical and laboratory abnormalities correlate poorly with reports of pain severity. There is no direct linear relationship between the amount of detectable physical pathology and the intensity of the pain reported.

Some of the variability in results may be associated with the patient's behavior during the examination. Measures of flexibility or strength often reflect nonphysical subjective state as much as actual physical capabilities. Thus, although physical examination is more objective that patient reports, patient motivation, efforts, and psychological state influence it.

For significant numbers of patients, no physical pathology can be identified using plain radiographs, CAT (Computed Axial Tomography) scans, or electromyography to validate the report of pain severity. Even with sophisticated advances in imaging technology, there continues to be a less-than-perfect correlation between identifiable pathology and reported pain as we noted earlier. In sum, routine clinical assessment of chronic pain patients is frequently subjective and often unreliable. It is often not possible to make any precise pathological diagnosis or even to identify an adequate anatomical origin for the pain. Despite these limitations, the patient's history and physical examination remain the basis of medical diagnosis and may be the best defense against over-interpreting results from sophisticated imaging procedures.

Physicians must be cautious not to over-interpret either the presence or absence of objective findings. An extensive literature is available focusing on physical assessment, radiographic, and laboratory assessment procedures to determine the physical basis of pain and the extent of impairments in adults. For a recent discussion of some of the complexities involved see Turk and Melzack (1992, 2001).

Psychosocial Contributions

Any physical abnormalities that are identified may be modified by coexisting psychosocial influences. The complexity of pain is especially evident when it persists over time as a range of psychological, social, and economic factors interact with physical pathology to modulate patients' reports of pain and the impact of pain on their lives. In the case of chronic pain, health care providers need to search not only for the physical source of the pain through examination and diagnostic tests but also the patient's mood, fears, expectancies, coping efforts, resources, responses of significant others, and the impact of pain on the patients' lives. In short, the health care provider must evaluate the whole patient not just the cause of the pain. Regardless of whether an organic basis for the pain can be documented or whether psychosocial problems preceded or resulted from the pain, the evaluation process can be helpful in identifying how biomedical, psychosocial, and behavioral factors interact to influence the nature, severity, and persistence of pain and disability.

We (Turk & Okifuji, 1999) have suggested that three central questions should guide assessment of people who report pain:

1. What is the extent of the patient's disease or injury (physical impairment)?

2. What is the magnitude of the illness? That is, to what extent is the patient suffering, disabled, and unable to enjoy usual activities?

3. Does the individual's behavior seem appropriate to the disease or injury or is there any evidence of amplification of symptoms for any of a variety of psychological or social reasons or purposes?

We will focus on the next two questions, specifically, the extent of the patient's disability and behavioral influences on the patient pain, distress, and suffering.

Interview

When conducting an interview with chronic pain patients, the health care professional should focus not simply on factual information but on patients' and significant others' specific thoughts and feelings and they should observe specific behaviors. During an interview, it is important to adopt the patient's perspective. Pain sufferers' beliefs about the cause of symptoms, their trajectory, and beneficial treatments will have important influences on emotional adjustment and adherence to therapeutic interventions. A habitual pattern of maladaptive thoughts may contribute to a sense of hopelessness, dysphoria, and unwillingness to engage in activity. The interviewer should determine both the patient's and the spouse's expectancies and goals for treatment.

Attention should focus on the patient's reports of specific thoughts, behaviors, emotions, and physiological responses that precede, accompany, and follow pain episodes or exacerbation, as well as the environmental conditions and consequences associated with cognitive, emotional, and behavioral responses in these situations. During the interview, the clinician should attend to the temporal association of these cognitive, affective, and behavioral events; their specificity versus generality across situations; and the frequency of their occurrence, to establish salient features of the target situations, including the controlling variables. The interviewer seeks information that will assist in the development of potential alternate responses, appropriate goals for the patient, and possible reinforcers for these alternatives.

The health care provider should be alert for *red flags* that may serve as an impetus for more through evaluation by pain specialists. Table 13.1 contains a list of 20 issues that can be stated as questions worthy of considering with patients who report persistent or recurring pain. The positive responses to any one or a small number of these questions should not be viewed as sufficient to make a referral for more extensive evaluation, but when a preponderance of them are, referral should be considered. Generally, a referral for evaluation

TABLE 13.1 Screening Questions

Clinical Issues

- Has the pain persisted for three months or longer despite appropriate interventions and in the absence of progressive disease?
- Does the patient report nonanatomical changes in sensation (e.g., glove anesthesia)?
- Does the patient seem to have unrealistic expectations of the health care provider or treatment offered?
- Does the patient complain vociferously about treatments received from previous health care providers?
- Does the patient have a history of previous painful or disabling medical problems?
- Does the patient have a history of substance abuse?
- Does the patient display many pain behaviors (e.g., grimacing, moving in a rigid and guarded fashion)?

Legal and Occupational Issues

- Is litigation pending?
- Is the patient receiving disability compensation?
- Was the patient employed prior to pain onset?
- Was the patient injured on the job?
- Does the patient have a job to which he or she can return?
- Does the patient have a history of frequent changing of jobs?

Psychological Issues

- Does the patient report any major stressful life events just prior to the onset or exacerbation of pain?
- Does the patient demonstrate inappropriate or excessive depressed or elevated mood?
- Has the patient given up many activities (social, recreational, sexual, occupational, physical) because of pain?
- Is there a high level of marital or family conflict?
- Do the patient's significant others provide positive attention to pain behaviors (e.g., take over their chores, rub their back)?
- Is there anyone in the patient's family who has chronic pain?
- Does the patient have plans for increased or renewed activities if their pain is reduced?

may be indicated where disability greatly exceeds what would be expected based on physical findings alone, when patients make excessive demands on the health care system, when the patient persists in seeking medical tests and treatments when these are not indicated, when patients display significant psychological distress (e.g., depression or anxiety), or when the patient displays evidence of addictive behaviors such as continual nonadherence to the prescribed regimen.

In addition to interviews, a number of assessment instruments designed to evaluate patients' attitudes, beliefs, and expectancies about themselves, their symptoms, and the health care system have been developed. Standardized assessment instruments have advantages over semistructured and unstructured interviews. They are easy to administer, require less time, and most importantly, they can be submitted to analyzes that permit determination of their reliability and validity. These standardized instruments should not be viewed as alternatives to interviews but rather that they may suggest issues to be addressed in more depth during an interview.

Several assessment instruments are described below (for comprehensive reviews see Turk and Melzack, 1992, 2001).

Self-Report Measurement of Pain

Often patients are asked to quantify their pain by providing a single, general rating of pain: "Is your usual level of pain 'mild,' 'moderate,' or 'severe?'" or "Rate your typical pain on a scale from 0 to 10 where 0 equals no pain and 10 is the worst pain you can imagine." More valid information may be obtained by asking about *current* level of pain or pain over the past week and by having patients maintain regular diaries of pain intensity with ratings recorded several times each day (for example, at meals and bedtime) for several days or weeks. There are a number of simple methods that can be used to evaluate current pain intensity—numerical scale, descriptive ratings scales, visual analog scales, and box scales.

One of the most frequently used pain assessment instruments is the McGill Pain Questionnaire (MPQ) (Melzack, 1975). This instrument consists of several parts including a descriptive scale (Present Pain Intensity) with numbers assigned to each of five adjectives (namely, 1 = mild, 2 = discomforting, 3 = distressing, 4 = horrible, and 5 = excruciating). A second part includes the front and back of a drawing of a human figure on which patients indicate the location of their pain. Finally, a pain-rating index is derived based on patients' selection of adjectives listed in 20 separate categories reflecting sensory, affective, and cognitive components of pain. The MPQ provides a great deal of information; however, it takes much longer to complete than simple ratings of pain severity. The MPQ may be inappropriate for use when frequent ratings of pain are required, for example, hourly following surgery. A short form of the MPQ scale consisting of 15 adjectival descriptors representing the sensory and affective dimensions of the pain experience each of which is rated on a 4-point scale (0 = none, 1 = mild, 2 = moderate, and 3 = severe) may be more efficient (Melzack, 1987).

Assessment of Functional Activities

Physical and laboratory diagnostic measures are useful primarily to the degree that they correlated with symptoms and functional ability. However, the traditional measures of function performed as part of the physical examination are not direct measures of symptoms or function, but are only approximations that may be influenced by patient motivation and desire to convey the extend of their pain, distress, and suffering to the physician. Commonly used physical examination maneuvers such as muscular strength and ranges of motion are only weakly correlated with actual functional

activities. Similarly, radiographic indicators have been shown to have little predictive value for the long-term functional capacity of a patient.

Poor reliability and questionable validity of physical examination measures has led to the development of self-report functional status measures that seek to quantify symptoms, function, and behavior directly, rather than inferring them. Self-report measures have been developed to assess peoples' reports of their abilities to engage in a range of functional activities such as the ability to walk up stairs, to sit for specific periods of time, the ability to lift specific weights, performance of activities of daily living, as well as the severity of the pain experienced during the performance of these activities have been developed.

Some of the commonly used functional assessment scales include the Roland-Morris Disability Scale (1983), the Sickness Impact Profile (Bergner, Bobbitt, Carter, & Gilson, 1981) and the Oswestry Disability Scale (Fairbank, Couper, Davies, & O'Brien, 1980). These scales ask patients to report on their ability to engage in specific activities such as sitting, standing, and walking. The items tend to be quite specific. For example, one item from the Oswestry Disability Scale asks patients to indicate whether their pain prevents them from "sitting at all, from sitting more than 10 minutes, sitting more than $\frac{1}{2}$ hour, or sitting more than hour, or whether they are able to sit for as long as they like."

Despite the obvious limitations of self-report instruments, they have several advantages. They are economical, efficient, enable the assessment of a wide range of behaviors that are relevant to the patient, some of which may be private (sexual relations) or unobservable (thoughts, emotional arousal). Although the validity of such self-reports of the ability to perform functional activities is often questioned, studies have revealed fairly high correspondence among self-reports, disease characteristics, physicians' or physical therapists' ratings of functional abilities, and objective functional performance.

A more extensive instrument, the Sickness Impact Profile (SIP; Bergner et al., 1981) examines a range of physical activities and psychological features. The SIP covers the areas of ambulation, mobility, body care, social interaction, communication, alertness, sleep and rest, eating, work, home management, recreation and pastime activities, and emotional behavior. In addition to a total score, the SIP provides subscores on the impact on physical activities and the psychological impact. There are several limitations to the SIP. It is lengthy, including over 150 questions, and it is designed to be administered in an interview format. This can be contrasted with measures such as the Oswestry Disability Questionnaire (Fairbank et al., 1980) that only includes 10 questions and the Roland-Morris Scale (1983) that includes 20 questions. As a preliminary screening, the briefer measures may provide a reasonable and adequate overview of functional limitations.

Assessment of Coping and Psychosocial Adaptation to Pain

Historically, *traditional* psychological measures that are designed to evaluate psychopathological tendencies have been used to identify specific individual differences associated with reports of pain, even though these measures were usually not developed for, or standardized on, samples of medical patients. Thus, it is possible that responses by medical patients may be distorted as a function of the disease or the medications that they take. For example, common measures of depression ask patients about their appetites, sleep patterns, and fatigue. Similarly, the commonly used MMPI includes items related to physical symptoms such as the presence of pain in the back of the neck, the ability to work, feelings of weakness, beliefs regarding health status in comparison with friends. Since disease status and medication can affect responses to such items, patients' scores may be elevated distorting the meaning of the responses.

More recently, a number of assessment instruments have been developed for use specifically with pain patients. Instruments have been developed to assess psychological distress; the impact of pain on patients' lives; feeling of control; coping behaviors; and attitudes about disease, pain, and health care providers and the patient's plight (Turk & Melzack, 1992, 2001).

A sample of an instrument developed to assess both psychosocial and behavioral factors associated with chronic pain is the West Haven-Yale Multidimensional Pain Inventory (MPI) (Kerns, Turk, & Rudy, 1985). This 60-item questionnaire is divided into three sections with the first assessing the patients' perception of pain severity, the impact of pain on their life, affective distress, feelings of control, and support from significant people in their lives. The second section assesses the patients' perceptions of the responses of significant people to their complaints of pain. The third section examines the change in patients' performance of common activities such as household chores and socializing. The MPI and many other assessment measures are reviewed and critiqued in Turk and Melzack (1992, 2001).

For many patients, there are no objective physical findings to support the complaints of pain. In other instances, the reports of pain severity seem excessive in light of physical findings. The difficult task is to know how to evaluate these patients in a comprehensive fashion. In instances where pain persists beyond the expected period of healing of an injury or where pain is associated with a progressive disease, it may be appropriate to refer patients for assessment to psychologists or psychiatrists who specialize in the evaluation of chronic pain patients.

Because of the subjectivity inherent in pain, suffering and disability are difficult to prove, disprove, or quantify in a completely satisfactory fashion. As discussed, response to the question, "How much does it hurt?" is far from simple. The experience and report of pain are influenced by multiple factors such as cultural conditioning, expectancies, current social contingencies, mood state, and perceptions of control. Physical pathology and the resulting nociception are important, albeit, not the sole contributors to the experience of pain. It is important to acknowledge the central importance of patients' self-reports along with their behavior in pain assessment. It is highly unlikely that we will ever be able to evaluate pain without reliance on the person's perceptions. The central point to keep in mind is that it is the *patient* who reports pain and not the pain itself that is being evaluated.

Assessment of Overt Expressions of Pain

Patients display a broad range of responses that communicate to others that they are experiencing pain, distress, and suffering—pain behaviors. Some of these may be controllable by the person whereas others are not. For example, in the acute pain state autonomic activity such as perspiring may indicate the presence of pain. Over time, however, these physiological signs habituate and their absence cannot be taken as an indication of the nonexistence of pain or significant pain reduction.

Pain behaviors include verbal reports, paralinguistic vocalizations (for example, sighs, moans), motor activity, facial expressions, body postures and gesturing (for example, limping, rubbing a painful body part, grimacing), functional limitations (reclining for extensive periods of time), and behaviors designed to reduce pain (for example, taking medication, use of the health care system). Although there is no one-to-one relationship between these pain behaviors and self-report of pain, they are at least modestly correlated.

A number of different observational procedures have been developed to quantify pain behaviors. Several investigators using the Pain Behavior Checklist (Turk, Wack, & Kerns, 1985) have found a significant association between these self-reports and behavioral observations. Behavioral observations scales can be used by patients' significant others as well. Health care providers can use observational methods to systematically quantify various pain behaviors and note the factors that increase or decrease them. For example, observing the patient in the waiting room, while being interviewed, or during a structured series of physical tasks.

Use of the health care system and analgesic medication are other ways to assess pain behaviors. Patients can record the times when they take medication over a specified interval such as a week. Diaries not only provide information about the frequency and quantity of medication but may also permit identification of the antecedent and consequent events of medication use. For example, a patient might note that he took medication after an argument with his wife and that when she saw him taking the medication she expressed sympathy. Antecedent events might include stress, boredom, or activity. Examination of antecedent is useful in identifying patterns of medication use that may be associated with factors other than pain per se. Similarly, patterns of response to the use of analgesics may be identified. Does the patient receive attention and sympathy whenever he or she is observed by significant others taking medication? That is, do significant others provide positive reinforcement for the taking of analgesic medication and thereby unwittingly increase medication use?

COGNITIVE-BEHAVIORAL MODEL FOR THE TREATMENT OF CHRONIC PAIN

The cognitive-behavioral model (CBM) has become the most commonly accepted psychological treatment choice of chronic pain patients (Morley, Eccleston, & Williams, 1999). The CBM perspective suggests that behaviors and emotions are influenced by interpretations of events, rather than solely by the objective characteristics of an event itself. Rather than focusing on the contribution of cognitive and emotional factors to the perception of a set of symptoms in a static fashion, emphasis is placed on the reciprocal relationships among physical, cognitive, affective, and behavioral factors.

CBM incorporates many of the psychological variables described, namely, anticipation, avoidance, and contingencies of reinforcement, but suggests that cognitive factors, in particular, expectations rather than conditioning factors are central. The CBM approach suggests that conditioned reactions are largely self-activated on the basis of learned expectations rather than automatically evoked. The critical factor for CBM, therefore, is not that events occur together in time but that people learn to predict them and to summon appropriate reactions. It is the person's processing of information that results in anticipatory anxiety and avoidance.

According to the CBM approach, it is peoples' idiosyncratic attitudes, beliefs, and unique representations that filter and interact reciprocally with emotional factors, social influences, behavioral responses, and sensory phenomena. Moreover, peoples' behaviors elicit responses from significant others that can reinforce both adaptive and maladaptive modes of thinking, feeling, and behaving. Thus, a reciprocal and synergistic model is proposed. One effective CB interviewing and intervention technique is the introduction of self-monitoring records of symptoms, feelings, thoughts, and actions. Such daily diaries are useful diagnostically and clinically. They have the potential of demonstrating to the clinician and the patients the patterns of maladaptive thinking and pain behaviors that may be contributing to their pain experience. Self-monitoring records can be used for many purposes, such as allowing the therapist to know when flare-ups occur; identifying the precedents and antecedents of painful episodes; and determining target behaviors, thoughts, and feelings that should be addressed during therapy sessions.

There are five central assumptions that characterize the CB approach (summarized in Table 13.2). The first assumption is that all people are active processors of information rather than passive reactors to environmental contingencies. People attempt to make sense of the stimuli from the external environment by filtering information through organizing attitudes derived from their prior learning histories and by general strategies that guide the processing of information. People's responses (overt as well as covert) are based on these appraisals and subsequent expectations and are not totally dependent on the actual consequences of their behaviors (i.e., positive and negative reinforcements and punishments). From this perspective, anticipated consequences are as important in guiding behavior as are the actual consequences.

A second assumption of the CB approach is that one's thoughts (e.g., appraisals, attributions, and expectations) can elicit or modulate affect and physiological arousal, both of which may serve as impetuses for behavior. Conversely, affect, physiology, and behavior can instigate or influence thinking processes. Thus, the causal priority depends on where in the cycle the person chooses to begin. Causal priority may be

TABLE 13.2 Assumptions of Cognitive-Behavioral Perspective

1. People are active processors of information rather than passive reactors to environmental contingencies.
2. Thoughts (for example, appraisals, attributions, expectancies) can elicit or modulate affect and physiological arousal, both of which may serve as impetuses for behavior. Conversely, affect, physiology, and behavior can instigate or influence a person's thinking processes.
3. Behavior is reciprocally determined by both the environment and the individual.
4. If people have learned maladaptive ways of thinking, feeling, and responding, then successful interventions designed to alter behavior should focus on each of these maladaptive thoughts, feelings, physiology, as well as behaviors and not one to the exclusion of the others.
5. In the same way as people are instrumental in the development and maintenance of maladaptive thoughts, feelings, and behaviors, they can, are, and should be considered active agents of change of their maladaptive modes of responding.

less of a concern than the view of an interactive process that extends over time with the interaction of thoughts, feelings, physiological activity, and behavior.

The CB perspectives is unique in that it emphasizes the reciprocal effects of the person on the environment and the influence of environment on the person and his or her behavior. The third assumption of the CB perspective, therefore, is that behavior is reciprocally determined by both the environment and the person. People not only passively respond to their environment but also elicit environmental responses by their behavior. In a very real sense, people create their environments. The person who becomes aware of a physical event (symptoms) and decides the symptom requires attention from a health care provider initiates a differing set of circumstances than a person with the same symptom who chooses to self-medicate or to ignore the symptoms.

A fourth assumption is that if people have learned maladaptive ways of thinking, feeling, and responding, then successful interventions designed to alter behavior should focus on these maladaptive thoughts, feelings, physiology, as well as behaviors and not on one to the exclusion of the others. There is no expectancy that changing only thoughts, or feelings, or behaviors will necessarily result in changes in the other two areas.

The final assumption is that in the same way as people are instrumental in the development and maintenance of maladaptive thoughts, feelings, and behaviors; they can, are, and should be considered active agents of change of their maladaptive modes of responding. Chronic pain sufferers, no matter how severe, despite common beliefs to the contrary, are not helpless pawns of fate. They can and should become instrumental in learning and carrying out more effective modes of responding to their environment and their plight.

From the CB perspective, people with pain are viewed as having negative expectations about their own ability to control certain motor skills without pain. Moreover, pain patients tend to believe they have limited ability to exert any control over their pain. Such negative, maladaptive appraisals about the situation and personal efficacy may reinforce the experience of demoralization, inactivity, and overreaction to nociceptive stimulation. These cognitive appraisals and expectations are postulated as having an effect on behavior leading to reduced efforts and activity, which may contribute to increased psychological distress (helplessness) and subsequent physical limitations. If we accept that pain is a complex, subjective phenomenon that is uniquely experienced by each person, then knowledge about idiosyncratic beliefs, appraisals, and coping repertoires becomes critical for optimal treatment planning and for accurately evaluating treatment outcome.

Pain sufferers' beliefs, appraisals, and expectations about pain, their ability to cope, social supports, their disorder, the medicolegal system, the health care system, and their employers are all important because they may facilitate or disrupt the sufferer's sense of control. These factors also influence patients' investment in treatment, acceptance of responsibility, perceptions of disability, adherence to treatment recommendations, support they seek from significant others, expectancies for treatment, and acceptance of treatment rationale.

Cognitive interpretations also affect how patients present symptoms to others, including health care providers. Overt communication of pain, suffering, and distress will enlist responses that may reinforce pain behaviors and impressions about the seriousness, severity, and uncontrollability of pain. That is, complaints of pain may induce physicians to prescribe more potent medications, order additional diagnostic tests, and, in some cases perform invasive procedures (Turk & Okifuji, 1997). Significant others may express sympathy, excuse the patient from responsibilities, and encourage passivity, thereby fostering further physical deconditioning. The CB perspective integrates the operant conditioning emphasis on external reinforcement and respondent view of conditioned avoidance within the framework of information processing.

People with persistent pain often have negative expectations about their own ability and responsibility to exert any control over their pain. Moreover, they often view themselves as helpless. Such negative, maladaptive appraisals about their condition, situation, and their personal efficacy in controlling their pain and problems associated with pain reinforce their experience of demoralization, inactivity, and overreaction to nociceptive stimulation. These cognitive appraisals are posited as having an effect on behavior, leading to reduced effort, reduce perseverance in the face of difficulty, and reduced activity and increased psychological distress.

The CB perspective on pain management focuses on providing the patients with techniques to help them gain a sense of control over the effects of pain on their life as well as actually modifying the affective, behavioral, cognitive, and sensory facets of the experience. Behavioral experiences help to show pain sufferers' that they are capable of more than they assumed, increasing their sense of personal competence. Cognitive techniques (for example, self-monitoring to identify relationship among thoughts, mood, and behavior, distraction using imagery, and problem solving) help to place affective, behavioral, cognitive, and sensory responses under the person's control.

The assumption is that long-term maintenance of behavioral changes will occur only if the pain sufferer has learned to attribute success to his or her own efforts. There are suggestions that these treatments can result in changes of beliefs about pain, coping style, and reported pain severity, as well as direct behavior changes. Further, treatment that results in increases in perceived control over pain and decreased catastrophizing also results in decreases in pain severity and functional disability. When successful rehabilitation occurs, there is a major cognitive shift from beliefs about helplessness and passivity to resourcefulness and ability to function regardless of pain, and from an illness conviction to a rehabilitation conviction (M. P. Jensen, Turner, & Romano, 1994; Tota-Faucette, Gil, Williams, Keefe, & Goli, 1993).

The complexity of chronic pain that we have described suggests that no single health care professional or discipline is likely to prove effective for a large number of patients by itself. Over the past 30 years, this observation has resulted in the development of multidisciplinary pain rehabilitation programs (MPRP) designed to deal with the complexities.

PATIENT-UNIFORMITY MYTH

There are a number of chronic pain syndromes (e.g., low back pain, fibromyalgia syndrome, temporomandibular disorders, migraine, pelvic pain). These disorders do not have known pathology and commonly they are defined by vague and often exclusionary criteria. Despite unknown pathology, these pain syndromes create a great deal of suffering and disability. The lack of understanding of the underlying mechanisms of the chronic pain syndromes has not inhibited attempts to treat patients with quite diverse modalities. Yet, to date, these syndromes remain largely recalcitrant to all treatments.

What is quite evident is the fact that the treatment of many chronic pain syndromes has been based on the traditional model where the intervention is matched to symptoms and medical diagnoses even when crudely defined. Prescribing treatment based on medical diagnoses is logical when there is a known etiology, but this approach has no basis when the causes are unknown. When there is no consensus regarding what treatment should be prescribed, the choice becomes empirical, delivered on a trial-and-error basis and at times motivated by pecuniary interests. This may explain why so many treatments have been applied to patients with identical diagnoses. Chronic pain patients have tended to be treated as a homogeneous group for whom a common treatment is deemed appropriate.

Few attempts have been made to individualize treatments matched to unique patient characteristics. It is common to see patients with a wide range of diagnoses and locations of pain, not to mention demographics, and psychosocial differences treated with the identical treatments (e.g., pain rehabilitation). In short, we have adopted the *patient uniformity myth* where all patients with the same diagnosis, no matter how vague, are treated in a similar fashion.

We need to develop a broader conceptualization of chronic pain patients in order to develop a more effective approach to treating them. It has become apparent that simply identifying physical factors and arriving at a diagnosis, and subsequently prescribing somatic treatments, will not ameliorate symptoms for a significant number of patients with prevalent pain syndromes. Variability in treatment outcome is understandable when we consider that pain is a personal experience influenced by attention, anxiety, prior learning history, meaning of the situation, reinforcement contingencies, and other psychosocial variables. The wisdom of treating the person with the symptom or disease and not just the symptom or disease seems particularly apt.

There is a great deal of published data suggesting that attention needs to be given to identifying the characteristics of patients who improve and those who fail to improve (Turk, 1990). Treatment should be prescribed only for those patients who are likely to derive significant benefit. The ability to identify characteristics of patients who do *not* benefit from a specific treatment should facilitate the development of innovative treatment approaches tailored to the needs of those patients.

Identifying responses to treatment by groups of patients with different characteristics (e.g., demographics and personality) has a long tradition in pain treatment outcome research. Many individual difference and demographic variables have been examined to determine who benefits from treatment. The results have not consistently identified specific demographic, disease status, pain history, prior treatments, litigation/compensation, or psychological features that consistently predict successful treatment outcome.

Attempts to identify subgroups of chronic pain patients have tended to focus on single factors such as signs and symptoms, demographics, psychopathology, idiosyncratic thinking patterns, and behavioral expression. Rehabilitative outcomes, however, are likely to be determined by the interactive effects of multiple factors; single factors may not be adequate to account for a statistically significant or clinically meaningful proportion of the variance in outcome. The delineation of homogeneous subgroups among pain patients would provide a framework for the development of specific, optimal treatment regimens for specific pain-patient subgroups when treatment can be matched to assessment or relevant variables areas: (a) that are reasonably distinct and not highly correlated, (b) when valid measures of these response classes are available, and (c) when treatments that affect these response classes are available. Although patient subgroups have been identified, few attempts have been made to evaluate the differential efficacy of treatments customized to patient subgroup characteristics.

As chronic pain involves both physical and psychosocial-behavioral factors, we have argued that it might be most appropriate to consider a *dual-diagnosis* for chronic pain patients—one based on physical mechanisms and a second on patients' unique set of psychological and behavioral features (Turk, 1990). The results of several studies conducted by Turk and Rudy (1988, 1990) and confirmed by other investigators in different countries demonstrate that psychological assessment data that incorporate cognitive, affective, and behavioral information can be integrated using empirical taxometric methods. These data and methods can serve as the basis for a classification system of chronic pain patients along relevant dimensions or axes—physical-symptomatic and psychosocial-behavioral.

Using empirical methods, Turk and Rudy (1988, 1990) have been able to identify group patients based on their:

1. Reports of pain severity and suffering.
2. Perceptions of how pain interferes with their lives, including interference with family and marital functioning, work, and social and recreational activities.
3. Dissatisfaction with present levels of functioning in family, marriage, work, and social life.
4. Appraisals of support received from significant others.
5. Life control incorporating perceived ability to solve problems and feelings of personal mastery and competence.
6. Affective distress including depressed mood, irritability, and tension.
7. Activity levels.

They identified three distinct patient profiles:

1. Dysfunctional (DYS) patients, who perceived the severity of their pain to be high, reported that pain interfered with much of their lives, reported a higher degree of psychological distress due to pain, and reported low levels of activity.
2. Interpersonally Distressed (ID) patients, with a common perception that significant others were not very supportive of their plight.
3. Adaptive Copers (AC) patients, who reported high levels of social support, relatively low levels of pain and perceived interference, and relatively high levels of activity (Turk & Rudy, 1988).

The classification system has been replicated in several studies, with different pain syndromes (Turk, Okifuji, Sinclair,

& Starz, 1998; Turk & Rudy, 1990), and in different countries. Turk and colleagues (1990; Turk et al., 1998) found that the psychosocial-behavioral subgroups are independent on demographic, disease status, and physical pathology.

The results alluded to above support the recommendation for a dual-diagnostic approach. Further the data suggest that, although different physical diagnostic groups may require common biomedical treatments, targeting the pathophysiological mechanisms underlying each disorder; they may also benefit from specific psychosocial interventions tailored to their psychosocial-behavioral characteristics.

As a preliminary step to evaluate the differential treatment response by patient subgroups, Turk and colleagues (Turk, Rudy, Kubinski, Zaki, & Greco, 1996; Turk et al., 1998) examined the outcomes of fibromyalgia syndrome and temporomandibular pain dysfunction syndrome patients to common treatments. Although as a group, both diagnostic sets of patients responded to common treatments, examination of the treatment outcomes by the psychosocial-behavioral subgroups revealed that these subgroups did not each have the same response. The results of these studies provide data supporting the existence of different psychosocial-behavioral subgroups of pain patients and the potential for treatment matching. Moreover, the outcomes suggest that treating all patients the same may dilute the efficacy of various treatments. The same logic and methodology that we have used to identify psychological subgroups can be adopted to identify physical-symptom-based subgroups. Specific interventions may have their greatest utility when matched to both dimensions—physical and psychological with particular subgroups of patients.

To date, there have been few attempts to customize treatment so as to match them to patient characteristics. Clinical investigations should, therefore, be conducted to determine the relative utility of different treatment modalities based on the match of treatment to patient characteristics, and to predict which patients are most likely to benefit from what combination of therapeutic modalities. Rather than accepting the *pain-patient homogeneity myth,* the field might be advanced by asking: "What treatment, provided by whom, in what way, is most effective for which patients, with what specific problem, and under which set of circumstances?"

The identification of subgroups, regardless of the methods used, does not mean that the resulting classification will incorporate all important features of the patients. Subgroups should be viewed as prototypes, with significant room for individual variability with a subgroup. Thus, matching treatment to subgroup characteristics will also need to consider and address unique characteristics of the individual patient. The subgroup customization should fit somewhere between the *idiographic* approach and the generic *nomothetic* approach that has characterized much of the pain treatment outcome studies. At this point, whether treatment tailoring will produce greater therapeutic effects than providing completely idiographic or generic treatments can only be viewed as a reasonable hypothesis. The fact that significant proportions of chronic pain patients are not successfully treated by generic approaches makes investigation of treatment matching of particular relevance.

MULTIDISCIPLINARY PAIN REHABILITATION PROGRAMS (MPRP)

In MPRPs, patients are usually treated in groups. Patients work on at least four generic issues simultaneously: physical, pharmacological, psychological, and vocational. Programs usually emphasize gaining knowledge about pain and how the body functions, physical conditioning, medication management, and acquisition of coping and vocational skills. Individual and group counseling address patient needs. The emphasis is on what the patient accomplishes, not on what the provider accomplishes. The providers envision themselves as teachers, coaches, and sources of information and support.

MPR requires the collaborative efforts of many health care providers, including, but not limited to, physicians, nurses, psychologists, physical therapists, occupational therapists, vocational counselors, and social workers. The health care providers must act as a team, with extensive interactions among the team members.

For many chronic pain patients, the factors that lead patients to report persistent pain remain obscure. Traditional diagnostic processes have failed to identify a remediable cause of pain. These patients require treatment because of the disruption of their life that they ascribe to pain. Indeed, their health care providers must feel comfortable abandoning the search for a cure and, instead, accept palliation and rehabilitation as a viable outcomes. The goal is to improve the patient's ability to function, not to cure the disease that has led to pain. Hence, the diagnostic process must identify the areas of functional impairment and disability, and treatment must address all of the factors that contribute to disability. In contrast to traditional medical therapy, patients cannot be passive recipients of the ministrations of providers. Patients must accept responsibility and work to achieve the benefits of treatment.

The effects of an MPRP are greater than the sum of its parts. Common features of all programs include physical therapy, medication management, education about how the body functions, psychological treatments (e.g., coping skills learning, problem solving, communication skills training),

vocational assessment, and therapies aimed at improving function and the likelihood of return to work. MPRPs usually have a standard daily and weekly format that providers can tailor to individual patient needs. The overall length of a program depends in part on unique patient requirements. The goals of MPRPs should be specific, definable, operationalizable, and realistic in nature.

As they have evolved, MPRP have become performance based, goal-directed, and outcome driven. Integration of outcomes related to patients' pain and functional limitation due to pain; how these behaviors influence patients' physical capacity; how others respond to the patient; the influence of psychosocial factors that contribute directly and indirectly to patients' physical and emotional status, and the potential for rehabilitation are essential. The treatment team must build an alliance with patients to instill acceptance of self-management.

Psychological strategies generally target alteration of behavior rather than the patient's personality (Turk, 1997). Patients learn coping skills because this is frequently a deficiency in either knowledge or implementation that has led to the patients' many difficulties. Issues that patients raise receive attention in either the group format or in individual therapy, as needed. As depression is so often a component of the chronic pain problem, it may warrant both psychological as well as pharmacological interventions. Psychologists provide relaxation and consolidation sessions that allow the patients to work on newly acquired skills and explore educational topics and new psychological skills.

Given constraints on health care resources, there is a growing interest in accountability and evidence-based treatment outcome data. All components of health care delivery are under scrutiny to determine whether they are not only clinically effective but also cost effective. The effectiveness of pain treatment facilities and, in particular, multidisciplinary pain rehabilitation treatment have been debated and singled out by some third-party payers for special criticism (Federico, 1996). Often the debates have been acrimonious, centering on anecdotal information and hearsay. Surprisingly, the dialog largely ignores the growing body of outcomes research published over the past quarter century. Referring physicians and third-party payers tend to rely on salient cases, usually failures, treating them as representative and relying upon them as the basis for criticizing MPRPs. Conversely, MPRPs often respond based on their clinical experience and the recall of particular successes that are viewed as representative of the outcomes from their facility, rather than systematically collected empirical data. There are, however, a growing number of studies, reviews, and meta-analyzes that support the clinical success of MPRPs (Cutler et al., 1994; Flor et al., 1992; Morley et al., 1999).

Despite the recalcitrance of the pain problems of the patients treated, they generally support the efficacy of MPRPs on multiple outcome criteria including reductions in pain reduction, medication consumption, health care utilization, and emotional distress, increases in activity and return to work, and closure of disability claims (e.g., Turk & Okifuji, 1998a, 1998b). Moreover, examining the available outcome data, we (Turk & Okifuji, 1998a, 1998b) concluded that the outcomes for MRPs are more clinically effective, more cost effective, and with fewer iatrogenic complications than alternatives such as surgery, spinal cord stimulation, and conventional medical care.

CONCLUDING COMMENTS

Pain is not a monolithic entity. Pain is, rather, a concept used to focus and label a group of behaviors, thoughts, and emotions. Pain has many dimensions, including sensory and affective components, location, intensity, time course and the memories, meaning, and anticipated consequences that it elicits. It has become abundantly clear that no isomorphic relationships exist among tissue damage, nociception, and pain report. The more recent conceptualizations discussed view pain as a perceptual process resulting from the nociceptive input, which is modulated on a number of different levels in the CNS. In this chapter, we presented conceptual models to explain the subjective experience of pain.

As was noted, the current state of knowledge suggests that pain must be viewed as a complex phenomenon that incorporates physical, psychosocial, and behavioral factors. Failure to incorporate each of these factors will lead to an incomplete understanding. It is wise to recall John Bonica's comment in the preface to the first edition (1953, 1990) of his volume, *The Management of Pain,* and repeated in the second edition some 36 years later:

> The crucial role of psychological and environmental factors in causing pain in a significant number of patients only recently received attention. As a consequence, there has emerged a sketch plan of pain apparatus with its receptors, conducting fibers, and its standard function that is to be applicable to all circumstances. But . . . in so doing, medicine has overlooked the fact that the activity of this apparatus is subject to a constantly changing influence of the mind. (p. 12)

REFERENCES

Banks, S. M., & Kerns, R. D. (1996). Explaining high rates of depression in chronic pain: A diathesis-stress framework. *Psychological Bulletin, 119,* 95–110.

Bayer, T. (1984). Weaving a tangled web: The psychology of deception in psychogenic pain. *Social Science and Medicine, 20,* 517–527.

Bergner, M., Bobbitt, R., Carter, W., & Gilson, B. (1981). The Sickness Impact Profile: Development and final revision of a health status measure. *Medical Care, 19,* 787–805.

Beutler, L., Engle, D., Oro'-Beutler, M., Daldrup, R., & Meredith, K. (1986). Inability to express intense affect: A common link between depression and pain? *Journal of Counseling and Clinical Psychology, 54,* 752–759.

Bonica, J. J. (1954). *The management of pain.* Philadelphia: Lea & Febiger.

Bonica, J. J. (1990). *The management of pain* (2nd ed.). Philadelphia: Lea & Febiger.

Boos, N., Rieder, R., Schade, V., Spratt, K. F., Semmer, N., & Aebi, M. (1995). The diagnostic accuracy of magnetic resonance imaging, work perception, and psychosocial factors in identifying symptomatic disc herniations. *Spine, 20,* 2613–2625.

Boothby, J. L., Thorn, B. E., Stroud, M. W., & Jensen, M. P. (1999). Coping with pain. In R. J. Gatchel & D. C. Turk (Eds.), *Psychosocial factors in pain: Critical perspectives* (pp. 243–259). New York: Guilford Press.

Brattberg, G., Thorslund, M., & Wikman, A. (1989). Prevalence of pain in a general population: The results of a postal survey in a county in Sweden. *Pain, 37,* 205–222.

Coderre, T. J., Katz, J., Vaccarino, A. L., & Melzack, R. (1993). Contribution of central neuroplasticity to pathological pain: Review of clinical and experimental evidence. *Pain, 52,* 259–285.

Collie, J. (1913). *Malingering and feigned sickness.* London: Edward Arnold.

Corbishley, M., Hendrickson, R., Beutler, L., & Engle, D. (1990). Behavior, affect, and cognition among psychogenic pain patients in group expressive psychotherapy. *Journal of Pain and Symptom Management, 5,* 241–248.

Council, J., Ahern, D., Follick, M., & Cline, C. L. (1988). Expectancies and functional impairment in chronic low back pain. *Pain 33,* 323–331.

Craig, K. D. (1986). Social modeling influences: Pain in context. In R. A. Sternbach (Ed.), *The psychology of pain* (2nd ed., pp. 67–95). New York: Raven Press.

Craig, K. D., Hill, M. L., & McMurtry, B. W. (1999). Detecting deception and malingering. In A. R. Block, E. F. Kremer, & E. Fernandez (Eds.), *Handbook of pain syndromes* (pp. 41–58). Mahwah, NJ: Erlbaum.

Craig, K. D., Hyde, S., & Patrick, C. J. (1991). Genuine, suppressed, and faked facial behavior during exacerbation of chronic low back pain. *Pain, 46,* 161–172.

Cutler, R. B., Fishbain, D. A., Rosomoff, H. L., Abdel-Moty, E., Khalil, T. M., & Rosomoff, R. S. (1994). Does nonsurgical pain center treatment of chronic pain return patients to work? A review and meta-analysis of the literature. *Spine, 19,* 643–652.

DeGood, D. E., & Tait, R. (2001). Assessment of pain beliefs, coping, and self-efficacy. In D. C. Turk & R. Melzack (Eds.), *Handbook of pain assessment* (2nd ed., pp. 320–345). New York: Guilford Press.

Deyo, R. A. (1986). Early diagnostic evaluation of low back pain. *Journal of General Internal Medicine, 1,* 328–338.

Dolce, J. J., Crocker, M. F., Moletteire, C., & Doleys, D. M. (1986). Exercise quotas, anticipatory concern, and self-efficacy expectations in chronic pain: A preliminary report. *Pain, 24,* 365–372.

Fairbank, J. C., Couper, J., Davies, J. B., & O'Brien, J. P. (1980). The Oswestry Low Back Pain Disability Questionnaire. *Physiotherapy, 66,* 271–273.

Federico, J. (1996). The cost of pain centers: Where is the return? In M. Cohen & J. Campbell (Eds.), *Pain treatment centers at a crossroads: A practical and conceptual reappraisal* (pp. 249–256). Seattle, WA: IASP Press.

Fernandez, E., & Turk, D. C. (1992). Sensory and affective components of pain: Separation and synthesis. *Psychological Bulletin, 112,* 205–217.

Fernandez, E., & Turk, D. C. (1995). The scope and significance of anger in the experience of chronic pain. *Pain, 61,* 165–175.

Flor, H., Fydrich, T., & Turk, D. C. (1992). Efficacy of multidisciplinary pain treatment centers: A meta-analytic review. *Pain, 49,* 221–230.

Flor, H., & Turk, D. C. (1988). Chronic pain and rheumatoid arthritis: Predicting pain and disability from cognitive variables. *Journal of Behavioral Medicine, 11,* 251–265.

Flor, H., & Turk D. C. (1989). The psychophysiology of chronic pain: Do chronic pain patients exhibit site-specific psychophysiological responses? *Psychological Bulletin, 105,* 215–259.

Fordyce, W. E. (1976). *Behavioral methods in chronic pain and illness.* St. Louis, MO: Mosby.

Fordyce, W. E., Shelton, J. L., & Dundore, D. E. (1982). The modification of avoidance learning in pain behaviors. *Journal of Behavioral Medicine, 5,* 405–414.

Grzesiak, R. C., Ury, G. M., & Dworkin, R. H. (1996). Psychodynamic psychotherapy with chronic pain patients. In R. J. Gatchel & D. C. Turk (Eds.), *Psychological approaches to pain management: A practitioner's handbook* (pp. 148–178). New York: Guilford Press.

Hunt, D. G., Zuberbier, O. A., Kozlowski, A. J., Robinson, J. P., Berkowitz, J., Milner, R. A., et al. (in press). Reliability of the lumbar flexion, lumbar extension, and passive straight leg raise test in normal populations embedded with a complex physical examination. *Spine.*

Jensen, M. P., Brant-Zawadzki, M., Obuchowski, N., Modic, M. T., & Malkasian Ross, J. S. (1994). Magnetic resonance imaging of the lumbar spine in people without back pain. *New England Journal of Medicine, 331,* 69–73.

Jensen, M. P., Turner, J. A., & Romano, J. M. (1994). Correlates of improvement in multidisciplinary treatment of chronic pain. *Journal of Consulting and Clinical Psychology, 62,* 172–179.

Kerns, R. D., Rosenberg, R., & Jacob, M. (1994). Anger expression and chronic pain. *Journal of Behavioral Medicine, 17,* 57–67.

Kerns, R. D., Turk, D. C., & Rudy, T. E. (1985). The West Haven-Yale Multidimensional Pain Inventory (WHYMPI). *Pain, 23,* 345–356.

Kroenke, K., & Mangelsdorff, A. (1989). Common symptoms in ambulatory care: Incidence, evaluation, therapy, and outcome. *American Journal of Medicine, 86,* 262–266.

Lenthem, J., Slade, P. O., Troup, J. P. G., & Bentley, G. (1983). Outline of a fear-avoidance model of exaggerated pain perception. *Behaviour Research and Therapy, 21,* 401–408.

Linton, S. J., & Buer, N. (1995). Working despite pain: Factors associated with work attendance versus dysfunction. *International Journal of Behavioral Medicine, 2,* 252–262.

Melzack, R. (1975). The McGill Pain Questionnaire: Major properties and scoring methods. *Pain, 1,* 277–299.

Melzack, R. (1987). The short-form McGill Pain Questionnaire. *Pain, 30,* 191–197.

Melzack, R., & Wall, P. D. (1965). Pain mechanisms: A new theory. *Science, 150,* 971–979.

Merskey, H. (1986). International Association for the Study of Pain: Classification of chronic pain. Descriptions of chronic pain syndromes and definitions of pain terms. *Pain, 3,* S1–S226.

Morley, S., Eccleston, C., & Williams, A. (1999). Systematic review and meta-analysis of randomized controlled trials of cognitive-behaviour therapy and behavior therapy for chronic pain in adults, excluding headache. *Pain, 80,* 1–13.

Okifuji, A., Turk, D. C., & Sherman, J. J. (2000). Evaluation of the relationship between depression and fibromyalgia syndrome: Why aren't all patients depressed? *Journal of Rheumatology, 27,* 212–219.

Pilowsky, I., & Spence, N. (1976). Pain, anger, and illness behaviour. *Journal of Psychosomatic Research, 20,* 411–416.

Piotrowski, C. (1997). Assessment of pain: A survey of practicing clinicians. *Perceptual and Motor Skills, 86,* 181–182.

Richard, K. (1988). The occurrence of maladaptive health-related behaviors and teacher-related conduct problems in children of chronic low back pain patients. *Journal of Behavioral Medicine, 11,* 107–116.

Roland, M., & Morris, R. (1983). A study of the natural history of back pain. Part I: Development of a reliable and sensitive measure of disability in low-back pain. *Spine, 8,* 141–144.

Rudy, T. E., Kerns, R. D., & Turk, D. C. (1988). Chronic pain and depression: Toward a cognitive-behavioral mediational model. *Pain, 35,* 129–140.

Schwartz, L., Slater, M., Birchler, G., & Atkinson, J. H. (1991). Depression in spouses of chronic pain patients: The role of patient pain and anger, and marital satisfaction. *Pain, 44,* 61–67.

Sullivan, M. J. L., Thorn, B., Haythornthwaite, J. A., Keefe, F., Martin, M., Bradley, L. A., et al. (2001). Theoretical perspectives on the relation between catastrophizing and pain. *Clinical Journal of Pain, 15,* 52–64.

Summers, J. D., Rapoff, M. A., Varghese, G., Porter, K., & Palmer, R. E. (1991). Psychosocial factors in chronic spinal cord injury pain. *Pain, 47,* 183–189.

Tota-Faucette, M. E., Gil, K. M., Williams, D. A., Keefe, F. J., & Goli, V. (1993). Predictors of response to pain management treatment: The role of family environment and changes in cognitive processes. *Clinical Journal of Pain, 9,* 115–123.

Turk, D. C. (1990). Customizing treatment for chronic pain patients: Who, what, and why. *Clinical Journal of Pain, 6,* 255–270.

Turk, D. C. (1996). Biopsychosocial perspective on chronic pain. In R. J. Gatchel & D. C. Turk (Eds.), *Psychological approaches to pain management: A practitioner's handbook* (pp. 3–30). New York: Guilford Press.

Turk, D. C. (1997). Psychological aspects of pain. In P. Bakule (Ed.), *Expert pain management* (pp. 124–178). Springhouse, PA: Springhouse.

Turk, D. C., & Flor, H. (1999). Chronic pain: A biobehavioral perspective. In R. J. Gatchel & D. C. Turk (Eds.), *Psychosocial factors in pain: Critical perspectives* (pp. 18–34). New York: Guilford Press.

Turk, D. C., Meichenbaum, D., & Genest, M. (1983). *Pain and behavioral medicine: A cognitive-behavioral perspective.* New York: Guilford Press.

Turk, D. C., & Melzack, R. (1992). *Handbook of pain assessment.* New York: Guilford Press.

Turk, D. C., & Melzack, R. (2001). *Handbook of pain assessment* (2nd ed.). New York: Guilford Press.

Turk, D. C., & Okifuji, A. (1997). What factors affect physicians' decisions to prescribe opioids for chronic non-cancer pain patients? *Clinical Journal of Pain, 13,* 330–336.

Turk, D. C., & Okifuji, A. (1998a). Efficacy of multidisciplinary pain centers: An antidote for anecdotes. *Balliere's Clinical Anesthesiology, 12,* 103–119.

Turk, D. C., & Okifuji, A. (1998b). Treatment of chronic pain patients: Clinical outcomes, cost-effectiveness and cost-benefits of multidisciplinary pain centers. *Critical Reviews in Physical Medicine and Rehabilitation, 10,* 181–208.

Turk, D. C., & Okifuji, A. (1999). A cognitive-behavioral approach to pain management. In P. D. Wall & R. Melzack (Eds.), *Textbook of pain* (4th ed., pp. 1431–1445). New York: Churchill-Livingstone.

Turk, D. C., Okifuji, A., & Scharff, L. (1995). Chronic pain and depression: Role of perceived impact and perceived control in different age cohorts. *Pain, 61,* 93–101.

Turk, D. C., Okifuji, A., Sinclair, J. D., & Starz, T. W. (1998). Differential responses by psychosocial subgroups of fibromyalgia syndrome patients to an interdisciplinary treatment. *Arthritis Care and Research, 11,* 297–404.

Turk, D. C., & Rudy, T. E. (1988). Toward and empirically-derived taxonomy of chronic pain patients: Integration of psychological assessment data. *Journal of Consulting and Clinical Psychology, 56,* 223–238.

Turk, D. C., & Rudy, T. E. (1990). The robustness of an empirically derived taxonomy of chronic pain patients. *Pain, 42,* 27–35.

Turk, D. C., Rudy, T. E., Kubinski, J. A., Zaki, H. S., & Greco, C. M. (1996). Dysfunctional TMD patients: Evaluating the efficacy of a tailored treatment protocol. *Journal of Consulting and Clinical Psychology, 64,* 139–146.

Turk, D. C., & Salovey, P. (1984). Chronic pain as a variant of depressive disease: A critical reappraisal. *Journal of Nervous and Mental Diseases, 172,* 398–404.

Turk, D. C., Wack, J. T., & Kerns, R. D. (1985). An empirical examination of the "pain behavior" construct. *Journal of Behavioral Medicine, 9,* 119–130.

Vaughan, K. B., & Lanzetta, J. T. (1980). Vicarious instigation and conditioning of facial expressive and autonomic responses to a model's expressive display of pain. *Journal of Personality and Social Psychology, 38,* 909–923.

Vlaeyen, J. W., Kole-Snijders, A. M., Boeren, R. B., & van Eek, H. (1995). Fear of movement/(re)injury in chronic low back pain and its relation to behavioral performance. *Pain, 62,* 363–372.

Wallis, B. J., Lord, S. M., & Bogduk, N. (1997). Resolution of psychological distress of whiplash patients following treatment by radiofrequency neurotomy: A randomised, double-blind, placebo-controlled trial. *Pain, 73,* 15–22.

Wiesel, S. W., Tsourmas, N., Feffer, H. L., Citrin, C. M., & Patronas, N. (1984). A study of computer-assisted tomography. I: The incidence of positive CAT scans in an asymptomatic group of patients. *Spine, 9,* 549–551.

Williams, D. A., & Thorn, B. E. (1989). An empirical assessment of pain beliefs. *Pain, 36,* 351–358.

CHAPTER 14

Insomnia

CHARLES M. MORIN, JOSÉE SAVARD, MARIE-CHRISTINE OUELLET, AND MEAGAN DALEY

Getting a good night's sleep is very much dependent on good psychological and physical health. Stress, anxiety, and depression almost inevitably interfere with sleep, as do pain and other medical problems. Chronic sleep disturbances can also increase the risk for major depression and can lower immune function. Conversely, sleep may play a protective role against infectious diseases and may even speed up recovery from some illnesses. These observations highlight the multiple links between sleep and health and illustrate why sleep has become a subject of great interest to both scientists and the lay public. Sleep clinics are now present in most major medical centers and there is a new behavioral sleep medicine specialty currently emerging. This chapter is about sleep, and more specifically about insomnia, which is the most prevalent of all sleep disorders and one of the most frequent health complaints brought to the attention of health care practitioners. After presenting an overview of some basic facts about sleep, the epidemiology of insomnia is summarized, including its main correlates and risk factors, followed by a

description of validated assessment and treatment methods for the clinical management of insomnia.

THE BASICS OF SLEEP

There are two types of sleep: nonrapid-eye-movement (NREM) and rapid-eye-movement (REM). Brain activity in NREM sleep, as measured by an electroencephalogram (EEG), is subdivided into four distinct stages, simply labeled stages 1, 2, 3, and 4. From a state of drowsiness, the individual slips into stage 1, then progresses sequentially through the other stages of NREM sleep. Of short duration (about 5 minutes), stage 1 is a transitional phase between wakefulness and more definite sleep. During this light sleep, the arousal threshold is low, and the brain wave signal is characterized by low-amplitude and high frequency waves. Progressively, the amplitude of the signal increases and its frequency decreases as the individual enters subsequent NREM stages. Stage 2 generally lasts 10 to 15 minutes and, for most people, corresponds to the phenomenological experience of falling asleep (Hauri & Olmstead, 1983). Stages 3 and 4 are considered the deepest stages of sleep and together last between 20 to 40 minutes in the first sleep cycle. They are often referred to as

---

Preparation of this chapter was supported in part by grants from the National Institute of Mental Health (MH55469) and by the Medical Research Council of Canada (MT-14039).

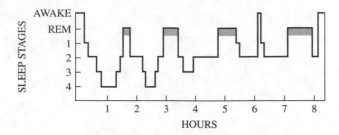

Figure 14.1 A sleep histogram illustrating the sequence of sleep stages for a good nights' sleep in a young adult. *Source:* C. Morin (1993). Copyright 1993 by Guilford Press. Reprinted by permission of the publisher and author.

"delta," or "slow-wave sleep" because of the presence of slow EEG waves of high amplitude called delta waves. After reaching stage 4, the EEG pattern reverses through stage 3, stage 2, and finally gives place to the first REM sleep episode.

In REM sleep, the EEG pattern is very similar to that observed in stage 1. Brain waves of low-amplitude and high frequency are, however, accompanied by rapid movements of the eyes under the lids. The REM stage is often referred to as "paradoxical sleep" because it is characterized by a loss of core muscle tone while the activity in the brain and in the autonomic system are at a level similar to that seen in wakefulness. Apart from occasional muscle twitches, the body is essentially paralyzed during this stage. The most vivid dreams occur during REM sleep, even though dreamlike activity may also be recalled when subjects are woken from the NREM stages.

In healthy adults with a regular sleep schedule, the proportion of time spent in REM sleep is about 25% and in NREM sleep 75%. NREM Stage 1 represents about 5%, Stage 2 another 50%, and Stages 3 to 4 about 20%. The distribution of these stages follows a very organized sequence (see Figure 14.1), with slow-wave sleep occurring mainly in the first third of the night and REM sleep becoming more prominent and more intense in the latter part of the night or early morning hours.

Biopsychosocial Determinants of Sleep

Circadian and Homeostatic Factors

The propensity to sleep and the type of sleep experienced are very dependent on circadian factors. Sleep is just one of many biological (e.g., body temperature, growth hormone secretion) and behavioral functions (e.g., meal schedules, social interactions) that are regulated by circadian rhythms. Internal brain-based mechanisms (located in the hypothala-

mus), or biological clocks, regulate this alternation between different states while interacting closely with time cues provided by the environment. The light-dark cycle is the most important of these cues (Parkes, 1985). Social interactions, work schedules, and meal times are other extrinsic time cues that also contribute to regulating our sleep-wake cycles. Homeostatic factors can also impact significantly on sleep. For instance, the time to fall asleep is inversely related to the duration of the previous period of wakefulness. With prolonged sleep deprivation, there is an increasing drive to sleep. Upon recovery, there is a rebound effect producing a shorter sleep latency, increased total sleep time, and a larger proportion of deep sleep (Webb & Agnew, 1974).

Daily variations in core body temperature, which are also controlled by circadian factors, are closely tied to sleep-wake patterns. At its lowest point in the early hours of the day (e.g., 3:00 to 5:00 A.M.), body temperature starts to increase near the time of awakening and peaks in the evening. Alertness is at its maximum during the ascending slope of the body temperature curve. In contrast, sleepiness and sleep itself occur as temperature decreases. In the absence of time cues or any constraint, individuals tend to choose a bedtime that is closely linked to a decrease in body temperature, while awakening occurs shortly after it begins to rise again (Monk & Moline, 1989).

These basic facts about homeostatic and circadian principles have important implications for understanding problems sleeping as well as problems staying awake. For night-shift workers, even those who sleep well during the day, it is often very difficult to stay alert around 3:00 or 4:00 A.M. because of decreased body temperature at that time. For the same reason, truck accidents on the road are proportionally more frequent during early morning hours, despite less dense traffic during these hours. Conversely, for insomniacs, their body temperature tends to remain elevated throughout the night, explaining partly why they have difficulties sleeping.

Age and Maturation

Important changes in the pattern of sleep accompany the natural maturation process that occurs throughout the life span. Newborns sleep about 16 to 18 hours in short episodes distributed throughout the day and the night, with REM sleep occupying more than 50% of total sleep time. From early childhood to late adolescence, the sleep architecture becomes progressively more organized into a single nocturnal phase. Total sleep time decreases gradually to level off in early adulthood at an average of 7 to 9 hours per night. There are individual differences in sleep needs, probably determined genetically, with the average being around 8 hours. Sleep changes occur very gradually during adulthood, with a decrease in the amount of stages 3 and 4 sleep and an increase in the number of awakenings. These changes become more noticeable when individuals reach their forties. In late life, nocturnal sleep is diminished, but daytime naps often maintain the total sleep time at about 7 hours. Nonetheless, sleep quality is diminished with aging, as there is a marked reduction of deep sleep and an increase of time spent in stage 1. Older adults experience more frequent and prolonged awakenings, which may explain the increased incidence of sleep complaints in this population (Webb & Campbell, 1980).

Medical Conditions and Drugs

Sleep is vulnerable to medical illnesses. A variety of endocrine, cardiovascular, and pulmonary diseases can disrupt sleep-wake functions. Neurological disorders such as epilepsy, dementias, or brain injury may also induce significant changes in sleep patterns. Sleep disturbances very frequently accompany any type of medical condition producing pain (i.e., arthritis, cancer, and chronic pain syndrome). Indeed, pain conditions have been associated with frequent intrusions of wakefulness into NREM sleep, a condition called alpha-delta sleep (Moldofsky, 1989).

Numerous prescribed and over-the-counter drugs can alter sleep patterns. Some medications prescribed for medical conditions may cause insomnia (bronchodilators, steroids) and others may produce sleepiness (antihistamines). Most psychotropic medications have a marked impact on sleep. Sedative-hypnotics induce sleep, but they also alter the underlying sleep stages. Benzodiazepines increase time in stages 1 and 2 and decrease time in stages 3 and 4 sleep. Some antidepressant medications (e.g., amitryptiline) have sedating properties, while others (e.g., fluoxetine) have a more energizing effect and produce insomnia, and still others (e.g., tricyclics) selectively suppress REM sleep. The time of administration of these pharmacological agents is often critical in determining how they will affect sleep.

Psychosocial Stressors

Sleep is very sensitive to stress and emotional distress. Major life events (e.g., divorce, death of a loved one) and more minor but daily stressors (e.g., interpersonal difficulties, pressure at work) can affect sleep patterns by heightening arousal before falling asleep and during nocturnal awakenings. Although sleep usually returns to normal once the acute stressful situation has resolved, sleep disturbances may become chronic due to a variety of perpetuating factors (Morin, 1993). There is also a clear association between sleep disturbances and psychopathology (discussed later).

Lifestyle and Environmental Factors

Many lifestyle factors have noticeable repercussions on sleep patterns including diet, exercise, sleep schedules, and environmental conditions. For example, the ingestion of heavy meals late in the evening can disrupt sleep. Social drugs such as caffeine, nicotine, and alcohol can alter sleep when ingested too close to bedtime. Physical exercise can either promote or interfere with sleep, depending on its timing, intensity, and regularity, as well as on the physical fitness of an individual. Daytime naps, particularly late in the day, will delay sleep onset the following night. Long naps may produce deep sleep, which will be proportionally reduced during the next sleep episode. Environmental factors such as noise, temperature, light, and sleeping conditions (e.g., mattress quality) can also impact on sleep. Noise from traffic or from a snoring bed partner can lead to more disrupted sleep.

The Role of Sleep and the Consequences of Sleep Deprivation

Animals totally deprived of sleep during a prolonged period eventually die, suggesting that sleep serves a critical function in humans and animals (Rechtschaffen, Gilliland, Bergmann, & Winter, 1983). However, research has not yet provided a satisfying answer to the question: Why do we sleep? Several hypotheses have been put forward. Adaptive theories suggest that sleep has evolved as a protective mechanism to keep the organism out of danger during periods of inactivity. Proponents of a recuperative theory postulate that sleep serves a "maintenance" role through which the integrity of organic tissues and of psychic functions is restored. Still, other theories have suggested a role of sleep in processes such as energy conservation, the regulation of body temperature, and of immune functions. No single theory can account for the diversity and complexity of the processes that occur during sleep (Horne, 1988). Evidence from sleep deprivation studies suggests that NREM sleep, particularly Stages 3 and 4 sleep, is involved in restoration of physical energy, while REM sleep, aside from its presumed role in the resolution of emotional conflicts, has an important function in the consolidation of newly acquired memories.

Several studies have examined the effects of total or partial sleep deprivation on physiological (e.g., sleepiness), psychological (e.g., mood, personality), and cognitive functioning (e.g., memory, reaction time, vigilance). While studies performed on rodents have shown that death occurs within three weeks of total sleep deprivation, if the animals are "rescued in extremis," many recover and appear normal, suggesting that no permanent damage is induced by prolonged sleep deprivation (Rechtschaffen et al., 1983). In humans, there is little evidence that total sleep loss, even for several days, produces any permanent or severe physical or psychological dysfunction (Horne, 1986). The most prominent effect of sleep deprivation is an increased feeling of sleepiness and desire for sleep. After one or two nights without sleep, most individuals will show microsleep episodes intruding into wakefulness, which will produce lapses of attention. These cognitive impairments are found mainly on tasks requiring sustained attention and rapid reaction time. Processes involved in safe and vigilant driving are particularly sensitive to sleep deprivation. Executive functions such as judgment, creativity, and mental flexibility are also altered after prolonged sleep loss (Horne, 1988; Johnson, 1982; Parkes, 1985). Changes in mood have been noted after as little as one night of total sleep deprivation. Individuals tend to be more irritable, and show less motivation, interest, and initiative. Conversely, acute sleep deprivation may have a transient antidepressant effect in persons with major depression (Gillin, 1983); this effect is very short-lived as mood returns to baseline after the first sleep episode. The few reports of personality changes or psychotic-like behaviors after prolonged sleep loss have been related to special contexts such as in combat situations (Horne, 1988; Parkes, 1985).

Although total sleep deprivation for more than one night is relatively rare, partial sleep loss is far more common. Individuals with sleep disorders usually experience partial sleep deprivation. For example, insomnia sufferers can experience partial sleep loss for years before consulting a professional. Patients with sleep apnea (a sleep-related breathing disorder) or with medical conditions producing chronic pain often show sleep fragmentation and frequent awakenings, which are followed by severe daytime sleepiness. The consequences of prolonged sleep deprivation, even partial, can be very serious with regard to performance, quality of life, and public health safety. For example, in situations where sustained attention is needed, while driving or while operating heavy industrial machinery, sleep-deprived individuals may put themselves and others at great risk. Several major accidents have been linked to fatigue and sleep deprivation (Mitler et al., 1988).

INSOMNIA: SCOPE OF THE PROBLEM

Insomnia entails a spectrum of complaints which reflect dissatisfaction with the quality, duration, or efficiency of sleep. These complaints can involve problems falling asleep, maintaining sleep throughout the night, or early morning wakening, either alone, or in combination. Individuals complaining

of insomnia may also describe their sleep as light and nonrestorative. Insomnia is almost always accompanied by reports of daytime fatigue, mood disturbances (e.g., irritability, dysphoria), and impairments in social and occupational functioning. Other prominent clinical features are the extensive night-to-night variability in sleep patterns and the discrepancy that is often present between the subjective complaint of insomnia and objective measures of sleep (Morin, 1993).

As virtually everyone experiences an occasional poor night's sleep at one time or another, it is important to consider the frequency, intensity, and duration of sleep difficulties to determine their clinical significance. Several criteria are used to operationalize insomnia complaints in outcome research. These include a sleep-onset latency and/or wake-after-sleep onset greater than 30 minutes, a sleep efficiency (ratio of total sleep time to time spent in bed) lower than 85%; and sleep difficulties that are present three or more nights per week (Morin, 1993). Insomnia is situational if it lasts less than one month, subacute if it lasts between one and six months, and chronic when it persists for more than six months. Because of individual differences in sleep needs, total sleep time is not a good marker of insomnia when considered alone.

According to the *International Classification of Sleep Disorders* (ICSD; American Sleep Disorders Association [ASDA], 1997), there are several broad classes of sleep-wake disorders including the insomnias, hypersomnias, parasomnias, and sleep-wake schedule disorders. Within the insomnia category, an essential distinction is made in both the *Diagnostic and Statistical Manual of Mental Disorders* (4th ed., *DSM-IV;* American Psychiatric Association [APA], 1994) and the *ICSD* between primary and secondary insomnias: the former represents an independent disorder unrelated to any other co-existing condition, while the latter encompasses sleep disturbances etiologically linked to another mental or physical problem. Table 14.1 depicts a modified and updated

TABLE 14.1 Primary and Secondary Insomnia Subtypes according to the *ICSD*

Primary insomnias.
  Psychophysiological insomnia.
  Subjective insomnia (sleep state misperception).
  Idiopathic insomnia (childhood onset).
Secondary insomnias.
  Insomnia associated with psychiatric disorders.
  Insomnia associated with medical or central nervous system disorders.
  Insomnia associated with alcohol or drug dependency.
  Insomnia associated with environmental factors.
  Insomnia associated with sleep-induced respiratory impairment.
  Insomnia associated with movement disorders.
  Insomnia associated with sleep-wake schedule disorders.
  Insomnia associated with parasomnias.

version of the insomnia subtypes as outlined in the ICSD (ASDA, 1997).

·The diagnosis of primary insomnia is often made by exclusion (i.e., after ruling out several other conditions); in addition, it is often based exclusively on the subjective complaint of an individual, which can be problematic because there may be significant discrepancies between subjective reports and objective recordings of sleep. According to the *ICSD,* there are three subtypes of primary insomnia, including psychophysiological insomnia, sleep state misperception, and idiopathic insomnia. Psychophysiological insomnia is the most classic form of insomnia. It is a type of conditioned or learned insomnia that is derived from two sources and whose symptoms can be measured objectively using polysomnography. The first involves the conditioning of sleep-preventing habits in which repeated pairing of sleeplessness and situational (bed/bedroom), temporal (bedtime), or behavioral (bedtime ritual) stimuli normally associated with sleep leads to conditioned arousal that impairs sleep. The second involves somatized tension believed to result from the internalization of psychological conflicts, dysfunctional beliefs and attitudes about sleep, and performance anxiety, all of which are incompatible with sleep (Kales & Kales, 1984; Morin, 1993).

In sleep state misperception, also referred to as subjective insomnia, the subjective complaint of sleep disturbance is not corroborated by polysomnographic recording. Although pure forms of sleep state misperception are rare, most insomniacs tend to overestimate the time it takes them to fall asleep and to underestimate their total sleep time. This condition is present in the absence of malingering or any other psychiatric disorder. It is unclear whether this phenomenon is due to a lack of sensitivity of EEG measures, the influence of information processing variables during the early stages of sleep (Borkovec, Lane, & Van Oot, 1981; Coates et al., 1983), or that it simply represents the far end of a continuum of individual differences in sleep perception. Interestingly, individuals with subjective insomnia report greater disruption of daily functioning than those with psychophysiological insomnia (Sugarman, Stern, & Walsh, 1985).

Idiopathic insomnia is a condition with an insidious childhood onset that develops in the absence of medical or psychological trauma. It is a persistent, lifelong, disturbance of sleep which can be objectively corroborated with polysomnography (Hauri & Olmstead, 1980). The underlying cause is suspected to be of a neurological nature as it often presents in conjunction with other neurologically based disorders such as attention deficit hyperactivity disorder. Despite the presence of daytime sequelae (e.g., memory, concentration, and motivational difficulties), and a more marked sleep disturbance than that observed in psychophysiological insomnia, individuals with idiopathic insomnia often experience less emotional distress than those with the psychophysiological subtype, perhaps due to coping mechanisms they have developed over their lifetime.

The secondary insomnias are considered to be a consequence of or concurrent with another problem. As discussed in detail later, sleep difficulties are frequently seen in individuals diagnosed with psychiatric disorders or health problems. In addition, some individuals experience sleep impairment as a result of tolerance to or sudden withdrawal from hypnotics. Either of these situations may lead to a return to or an increase in medication intake and the perpetuation of a vicious cycle. Environmental factors can also lead to insomnia. Examples of disruptive environmental sources are light, noise, temperature, uncomfortable sleeping quarters, disruptive movements of a bed partner, or the need to remain alert to danger or the needs of a dependent other (e.g., baby, elderly parent). In these cases, the cause is considered to be predominantly environmental, although psychological repercussions are no doubt also present.

Several additional sleep disorders can lead to a subjective complaint of insomnia (see Table 14.1). Polysomnographic recordings are usually required to corroborate their presence. These include sleep apnea, a breathing disorder in which breathing is impaired during sleep, but remains normal during wakefulness; restless legs syndrome, a disorder characterized by discomfort and aching in the calves, and the irresistible urge to move the legs; periodic limb movements, characterized by brief, repetitive, and stereotyped limb movement during sleep; circadian rhythm disorders, often associated with jet lag, shift work, and phase-delay and phase-advance syndromes; and parasomnias, or disorders of arousal involving an excessively active central nervous system and provoking episodes of somnambulism and night terrors. The diverse nature of sleep disturbances makes careful diagnosis essential, as treatment varies considerably depending on the characteristics of the disorder.

Prevalence

Insomnia is the most common of all sleep disorders. Prevalence rates vary considerably across surveys due to differences in methodology and definitions of insomnia. The best estimates available indicate that about one-third of the adult population report some problems falling or staying asleep or are dissatisfied with their sleep during the course of a year; about one-third of those, or approximately 10% of the adult population, complain of persistent and severe insomnia (Ford & Kamerow, 1989; Mellinger, Balter, & Uhlenhuth,

1985; Ohayon & Caulet, 1996). Epidemiological data indicate that between 7% (Mellinger et al., 1985) and 10% (Ohayon & Caulet, 1996) of the population use a sleep-promoting drug. Other estimates indicate that 20% of individuals with insomnia have used a sleep medication in the past and that 40% have used alcohol as a sleep aid (Gallup, 1991). Studies of insomnia complaints in general medical practice reveal even higher prevalence rates. For example, one survey found that more than 30% of medical patients had either moderate or severe insomnia, and that almost one quarter of those regularly used prescribed hypnotics (Hohagen et al., 1993). The prevalence of hypnotic use is systematically higher among older adults, women, and individuals with chronic health problems (Ohayon & Caulet, 1996). More than 40% of hypnotic drugs are prescribed for older adults, although this segment of the population represents only about 13% of the population.

Correlates and Risk Factors

Several demographic, psychosocial, and health variables have been associated with insomnia complaints. Surveys have consistently found higher rates of insomnia complaints among women, older adults, and individuals who are unemployed, separated or widowed, living alone and/or homemakers (Ford & Kamerow, 1989; Mellinger et al., 1985). Women are twice as likely as men to report insomnia; however, it is unclear whether this higher rate is accurate or reflects gender differences in reporting or sleep perception. In addition, between 25% and 40% of individuals over the age of 60 complain of sleep difficulties, with about half of these individuals reporting serious insomnia (Foley, Monjan, Izmirlian, Hays, & Blazer, 1999; Mellinger et al., 1985; National Institutes of Health, 1994). These figures remain fairly stable even after controlling for the presence of comorbid medical problems (Bliwise, King, Harris, & Haskell, 1992). Some evidence also indicates that insomnia episodes are predictive of future insomnia episodes (Breslau, Roth, Rosenthal, & Andreski, 1996; Klink, Quan, Kaltenborn, & Lebowitz, 1992) and that a positive family history of insomnia may also increase the risk for future insomnia (Bastien & Morin, 2000).

There has been no longitudinal study of psychosocial risk factors for insomnia. However, several studies have provided indirect evidence that stress may increase the vulnerability to develop insomnia. In a retrospective study, 74% of poor sleepers recalled specific stressful life events associated with the onset of their insomnia, and the frequency of such events was greater during the year the sleep problem began than in either the previous or subsequent years (Healy et al., 1981). Significant losses through separation, divorce, or the death of a loved one were the most common precipitants. In another study, individuals with insomnia reported a greater frequency of negative life events (mostly related to interpersonal relationships) and diminished coping skills relative to normal controls during the year preceding the onset of their insomnia (Vollrath, Wicki, & Angst, 1989). The rate of reported sleep disturbances among residents of Israel was also higher during rather than before or after the Gulf War (Askenasy & Lewin, 1996). Another study (Morin, Rodrigue, & Ivers, under review) found that it was the daily hassles, rather than major live events, that placed individuals at greater risk for sleep disturbances. Research about personality factors and cognitive styles has repeatedly found that individuals with insomnia are more likely, relative to good sleepers, to display anxious profiles and engage in excessive worrying, obsessive ruminations, and internalization of psychological conflicts (Edinger, Stout, & Hoelscher, 1988; A. Kales, Caldwell, Soldatos, Bixler, & Kales, 1983).

Sleep and Psychopathology

Epidemiological, cross-sectional, and longitudinal data indicate a high rate of comorbidity between sleep disturbances and psychopathology (for a review, see Morin & Ware, 1996). This is no surprise given that sleep disturbance is a diagnostic criterion or a clinical feature in several psychiatric disorders, particularly anxiety (e.g., generalized anxiety disorder) and affective disorders (e.g., major depression). The first line of evidence supporting a link between insomnia and psychopathology comes from epidemiological surveys. About 40% of randomly selected community residents with insomnia complaints also experience significant psychological symptoms, relative to base rates of about 15% among respondents without sleep complaints (Ford & Kamerow, 1989; Mellinger et al., 1985). Surveys of psychiatric outpatients indicate that 50% to 80% have sleep complaints and over 75% present significant sleep disturbances during the acute phase of their illness (Sweetwood, Grant, Kripke, Gerst, & Yager, 1980).

Several cross-sectional studies have found a higher prevalence of psychiatric disorders among poor sleepers than among good sleepers. Although specific estimates vary greatly depending on the criteria and the samples selected, estimates from clinical case series of patients consulting for insomnia at sleep disorder clinics indicate that about 35% to 40% of those patients have at least one comorbid psychiatric disorder (Buysse et al., 1994; Morin, Stone, McDonald, & Jones, 1994). The most prevalent Axis I conditions include depression (major depression and dysthymia), anxiety (e.g., generalized anxiety disorder), and substance abuse disorders. In major depression, sleep disturbances often persist even after the depression has lifted, while in older adults, persistence of sleep disturbances may prevent or delay recovery from depression (Kennedy, Kelman, & Thomas, 1991).

Finally, there is evidence that depression can be both a risk factor for insomnia and a potential consequence of chronic insomnia. Vollrath et al. (1989) found that 46% of subjects suffering from periodic or chronic insomnia reported experiencing depression and anxiety in the year prior to interview. Conversely, two other studies have shown that chronic insomnia increases the risk of developing major depression (Breslau et al., 1996; Ford & Kamerow, 1989).

Sleep and Health

There is extensive evidence showing that sleep and health are related. On the one hand, health problems can be a risk factor for insomnia; while on the other hand, poor sleep may have a negative impact on immune function and on recovery from physical illness. Individuals with insomnia report a higher frequency of health problems, medical consultations, and hospitalizations relative to good sleepers (Gislason & Almqvist, 1987; Kales et al., 1984; Mellinger et al., 1985; Simon & VonKorff, 1997). Physical complaints most frequently reported by individuals with insomnia include gastrointestinal problems, respiratory problems, as well as headaches and nonspecific aches and pain (Kales et al., 1984; Vollrath et al., 1989). Chronic conditions such as cardiopulmonary disease, painful musculoskeletal diseases, and back problems have also been observed more frequently in patients with insomnia than in good sleepers (Gislason & Almqvist, 1987; Katz & McHorney, 1998). Surveys of patients with various medical conditions have also yielded very high rates of insomnia complaints. For example, patients with neurological (e.g., Parkinson's disease, multiple sclerosis, Alzheimer's disease), gastrointestinal, renal, and cardiopulmonary diseases (e.g., asthma) all seem at higher risk for secondary sleep disorders, including insomnia (Pressman, Gollomp, Benz, & Peterson, 1997; Walsleben, 1997). Research conducted with an elderly sample has shown that poor physical health was the strongest risk factor for insomnia, even though mental health factors were also related to poor sleep (Morgan & Clarke, 1997).

In a recent study conducted by our team, 51% of women who had been treated for nonmetastatic breast cancer reported insomnia symptoms (Savard, Simard, Blanchet, Ivers, & Morin, 2001). This finding was consistent with results obtained in patients with other types of cancer, in which prevalence rates of insomnia symptoms ranged from 30% to 50% (Savard & Morin, 2001). In a comparative study, 40% of cancer patients (mixed diagnoses) reported sleep difficulties compared to only 15% of control participants with no severe illness (Malone, Harris, & Luscombe, 1994), suggesting that insomnia is much more prevalent in cancer patients than in the general population. As in other medical conditions, factors that may produce sleep disturbances include the direct physiological effects of the illness, the side effects of cancer treatment (e.g., hot flashes associated with chemotherapy and hormone therapy), pain, and the psychological reaction to the cancer diagnosis and treatment. Although the cross-sectional nature of these data precludes any conclusion about causality, these findings still suggest a very high rate of comorbidity between sleep and health problems.

Insomnia and Longevity

Further evidence for a link between insomnia and health is provided by data from prospective epidemiological surveys indicating that sleep disturbance is associated with increased mortality. Individuals who reported sleeping less than 4 (Kripke, Simons, Garfinkel, & Hammond, 1979) or 6 (Wingard & Berkman, 1983) hours per night had a mortality rate (all causes combined) 1.5 to 2.8 times higher six and nine years later compared to individuals sleeping between 7 to 8 hours each night. Longer sleep durations (i.e., more than 9 or 10 hours of sleep per night), as well as the long-term use of sleep medications, were also associated with higher mortality rates (Kripke et al., 1979; Wingard & Berkman, 1983). In another study, Enstrom (1989) observed a very low risk of mortality (including mortality due to cancer) in Mormon high priests, a church promoting good health practices. This effect was most evident in those who exercised regularly, obtained proper sleep (generally 7 to 8 hours each night), and who had never smoked cigarettes, as assessed eight years earlier.

Although sleep duration seems to be related to longevity, insomnia per se is a condition characterized by several symptoms other than a shorter sleep duration (e.g., emotional distress). As such, these findings may not generalize to insomnia. Such a cautious interpretation is warranted since subjective sleep difficulties have not been found to be as strong a predictor of mortality as total sleep time (Kripke et al., 1979; Wingard & Berkman, 1983). More importantly, these studies did not control for potential confounding variables such as the presence of preexisting medical conditions. For example, it is likely that individuals who sleep for a longer period of time do so because they already have a major medical illness.

Insomnia and Immunity

Another potential effect of insomnia on health is immune down-regulation. Although some studies have shown a deleterious effect of experimental sleep deprivation on immune functioning (Dinges, Douglas, Hamarman, Zaugg, &

Kapoor, 1995; Everson, 1997), evidence for a relationship between naturalistic sleep loss (i.e., clinical insomnia) on immunity are much more sparse. One sleep laboratory experiment (Irwin, Smith, & Gillin, 1992) has shown that total duration of sleep, sleep efficiency, and duration of NREM sleep were positively correlated with natural killer (NK) cell activity, both in depressed and nondepressed individuals. NK cells are believed to provide defense against cancer and virus-infected cells. Cover and Irwin (1994) found that initial insomnia was one of only two symptoms measured by the Hamilton Depression Rating Scale that were significantly associated with NK cell activity. Similar results were obtained in a sample of women at risk for cervical cancer (Savard et al., 1999). Higher sleep satisfaction was associated with a higher concentration of helper T cells in circulating blood, a T-lymphocyte subset that carries the CD4 marker; these cells have several functions (e.g., activate B cells to generate antibodies, activate cytotoxic T cells) and would be especially relevant for the progression of cervical cancer. This effect was still present, even after controlling for the variance explained by depression. Collectively, these studies suggest that insomnia may have an immunosuppressive effect. However, the cross-sectional nature of these data precludes any conclusion about a causal relationship. Additional experimental studies are needed to examine more rigorously the effect of insomnia on immunity, and the extent to which immune alterations are clinically significant in terms of their influence on health status.

Overall, given the reciprocal relationship between stress, somatic/health factors and sleep, as well as the cross-sectional nature of much of insomnia research, additional longitudinal investigations are necessary to better understand the clinical correlates and risk factors of insomnia.

The Impact of Insomnia

Insomnia is associated with significant consequences in one or more of the following areas: health, quality of life, social and occupational functioning, economics, and public safety. The most immediate and direct consequences of insomnia involve daytime fatigue, attention and concentration problems, reduced motivation, and mood disturbances (irritability, dysphoria) (Zammit, Weiner, Damato, Sillup, & McMillan, 1999). While these effects are fairly self-limited when sleep difficulties are situational, persistent insomnia can reduce quality of life, cause emotional distress, and even increase the risk of major depression (Breslau et al., 1996; Ford & Kamerow, 1989). There are also significant functional impairments (e.g., work absenteeism and diminished productivity) that have been linked to insomnia (Simon & VonKorff, 1997). Attention problems and reduced vigilance also can

contribute to accidents on the road or at work. Individuals with insomnia are more than twice as likely as good sleepers to report fatigue as having been a factor in their motor vehicle accident (5% versus 2%; Gallup, 1991). More than 50% of night workers acknowledged having fallen asleep on the job at least once. Sleepiness has also been implicated in several major industrial accidents (e.g., Chernobyl nuclear accident), all occurring in the middle of the night. Although these accidents are probably related more to sleep deprivation than insomnia per se, it does highlight the potential impact of lack of sleep on public health safety.

The prevalence of insomnia and the apparent chronicity and morbidity of this condition lead to the important question: What are the costs associated with this condition? Direct costs include the cost of all products used (prescription, over-the-counter, natural, etc.) and consultations for insomnia symptoms. Indirect costs of insomnia include those related to work absenteeism, low productivity, poor job performance, and accidents. Individuals with insomnia complaints report greater functional impairments, take more frequent sick leaves, and utilize health services more frequently (Leigh, 1991; Mellinger et al., 1985; Simon & VonKorff, 1997) than those without sleep complaints. The total cost for substances used in the United States in 1995 to treat insomnia was estimated at $1.97 billion (less than half of this was for prescription medication), the total of all direct costs being estimated at $13.9 billion. If indirect and associated (e.g. accidents) expenses are included, the total cost of insomnia in the United States is estimated as between $30 and $35 billion (Walsh & Engelhard, 1999). These figures are very approximate because they are usually based on retrospective estimates or on available databases (see Chilcott & Shapiro, 1996; Leger, Levey, & Paillard, 1999). Prospective and longitudinal studies are needed to measure more accurately the costs of insomnia.

EVALUATION OF SLEEP COMPLAINTS/DISORDERS

It is a common mistake to view insomnia as a simple symptomatic problem for which a simple diagnostic procedure can be used and an all-purpose intervention applied. Because of the heterogeneous nature of insomnia, a thorough evaluation of medical, psychological, pharmacological, and environmental factors is essential to make an accurate diagnosis and design an appropriate treatment. Ideally, the evaluation should be multifocused and include complementary assessment methods such as a clinical interview, daily self-monitoring of sleep habits, and self-report measures. A sleep laboratory evaluation can also be useful to corroborate the subjective complaints and to rule out the presence of other sleep disorders. Table 14.2 presents a list of insomnia measures with their respective advantages and limitations.

Clinical Interview

The clinical interview is the most important component of insomnia assessment. It elicits detailed information about the nature of the complaint, its severity, course, potential causes, and symptoms, as well as evidence of other sleep disorders, exacerbating and alleviating factors, and previous treatments including medication (Morin & Edinger, 1997; Spielman & Glovinsky, 1997). A functional analysis aims to identify predisposing, precipitating, and perpetuating factors of insomnia. It is important to inquire about life events, psychological disorders, substance use, and medical illnesses at the time of onset of the sleep problem to help establish etiology. Of particular importance for treatment planning is the identification of factors that contribute to perpetuating sleep difficulties, such as maladaptive sleep habits (e.g., spending too much

time in bed) and dysfunctional cognitions (e.g., worrying excessively about the consequences of insomnia).

Two interviews available to gather this type of information in a structured format are the Structured Interview for Sleep Disorders (Schramm et al., 1993), which is helpful in establishing a preliminary differential diagnosis among the different sleep disorders, and the Insomnia Interview Schedule (IIS; Morin, 1993), which is more specifically designed for patients with a suspected diagnosis of primary or secondary insomnia. The IIS gathers a wide range of information about the nature and severity of the sleep problem, and the current sleep/wake schedule, which includes information such as typical bedtime and arising times, time of the last awakening in the morning, frequency and duration of daytime naps, frequency of difficulties sleeping, time taken to fall asleep, number and duration of awakenings per night, and total duration of sleep. The IIS also assesses the onset (e.g., gradual or sudden, precipitating events), course (e.g., persistent, episodic, seasonal), and duration of insomnia, past and current use of sleeping aids (i.e., prescribed and over-the-counter medications, alcohol), as well as health habits

TABLE 14.2   Summary of Advantages and Limitations of Different Sleep Assessment Modalities

Assessment Modality	Instruments	Advantages	Limitations
Semistructured Interviews	• Insomnia Interview Schedule (Morin, 1993). • Structured Interview for Sleep Disorders (Schramm et al., 1993).	Provides detailed information about the nature, course, and severity of the sleep disturbance and associated aspects. Allows a functional analysis and differential diagnosis.	Requires substantial knowledge of the sleep disorders spectrum and interviewer training. Time consuming.
Sleep Diary		Assesses nightly variations in the nature, frequency, and severity of sleep difficulties, and some maladaptive behaviors. Flexible. Good ecological validity. Allows prospective evaluation over extensive periods of time. Excellent outcome measure. Economical.	Significant discrepancies with polysomnography. Reactivity and noncompliance in some individuals.
Self-Report Measures	• Sleep Impairment Index (Morin, 1993). • Pittsburgh Sleep Quality Index (Buysse et al., 1989). • Dysfunctional Beliefs and Attitudes about Sleep Scale (Morin, 1994).	Practical and economical. No need for trained staff. Can be administered repeatedly and used as an outcome measure.	Retrospective and global assessment. Risk of overestimation of sleep difficulties. Most instruments not fully validated.
Mechanical Devices	• Wrist actigraphy. • Sleep assessment device. • Switch-activated clock.	Self-administered. No need for a trained technician. Economical. Unobtrusive. Ecological validity.	Does not measure sleep stages. Convergent validity with polysomnography needs to be studied further.
Laboratory polysomnography		The "gold standard" for the evaluation and diagnosis of all sleep disorders. Provides objective measures for the entire range of sleep parameters, including sleep stages.	Expensive. Trained technician needed throughout the night and to score data. Relatively invasive. Low ecological validity. Need for repeated measures to reliability assess insomnia. "First-night effect."
Portable polysomnography		Same advantages as laboratory polysomnography. Ecological validity. Reduction of the "first-night effect."	Higher risk of artifacts and invalidation. Lack of behavioral observations.

that might influence sleep (i.e., exercise, caffeine intake, smoking, alcohol use). Information is also gathered about environmental factors (e.g., bed partner, mattress, noise level, temperature), sleep habits (e.g., watching TV in the bedroom, staying in bed when awake) and other factors (e.g., stress, vacation) that impair/facilitate sleep. In addition, the IIS assesses the impact of insomnia on daytime functioning and quality of life. Finally, symptoms of other sleep disorders and psychiatric disorders are evaluated for differential diagnosis.

A detailed clinical interview is important for differential diagnosis between insomnia and other sleep pathologies. Several of these disorders can produce a subjective complaint of insomnia, including sleep apnea, periodic limb movements, restless legs syndrome, circadian rhythm disorders, and parasomnias. Although a thorough clinical interview can help the clinician to detect the presence of such disorders, polysomnography is almost always necessary to confirm the diagnosis.

Sleep Diary Monitoring

Self-monitoring of sleep-related variables in a daily diary is the most widely used method for assessing insomnia. A typical sleep diary has entries for bedtime, arising time, naps, medication intake, and for estimates of several sleep parameters (time to fall asleep, number and duration of awakenings) and indices of sleep quality and daytime functioning. The diary can be simplified or adapted to an individual's specific needs. It is important to review the sleep diary with the patient and provide corrective feedback, particularly during the first few days of recording. Because of inevitable discrepancies between subjective estimates of sleep parameters and objective EEG recording, it is important to point out that only estimates of sleep parameters are expected.

The use of a daily sleep diary has also become a standard assessment measure in insomnia outcome research. Although it is subject to some reactivity in the initial phase of use, sleep diary monitoring has the advantage of providing a prospective evaluation of an individual's sleep pattern over an extended period of time in the home environment. As such, it may yield a more representative sample of that person's sleep than a single night of sleep laboratory assessment. While they do not reflect absolute values obtained from polysomnography, daily estimates of specific sleep parameters yield a reliable and valid relative index of insomnia (Coates et al., 1982). Specifically, sleep diary data provide very useful information on the nature, frequency, and intensity of insomnia, as well as nightly variations of sleep difficulties, and the presence of certain perpetuating factors (e.g., naps, spending too much time in bed). This practical and economical method is extremely helpful both for initial assessment and for monitoring treatment progress.

Polysomnography

A polysomnographic evaluation involves all-night sleep monitoring as measured by electroencephalography (EEG), electrooculography (EOG), and electromyography (EMG). These three parameters provide the necessary information to distinguish sleep from wake and to determine the specific sleep stages. Although these three types of recording are generally sufficient for monitoring and scoring sleep patterns, additional parameters (e.g., respiration, electrocardiogram, oxygen saturation, leg movements) are often assessed, at least during the first night, to detect the presence and severity of sleep pathologies other than insomnia such as sleep apnea or periodic limb movement.

Polysomnography provides the most comprehensive assessment of sleep. It is the only method that allows quantification of sleep stages and that can confirm or rule out the presence of another sleep pathology. For insomnia sufferers, a laboratory evaluation may be helpful for assessing the nature and severity of the sleep problem and to provide data on the full range of sleep variables from sleep-onset latency to proportion of time spent in various sleep stages. It is also useful for determining the level of discrepancy between the subjective complaints and actual sleep disturbances. Polysomnography may also play a therapeutic role in some cases by showing a patient that he or she is getting more sleep than actually perceived. Although laboratory polysomnography is recognized as the "gold standard," it is not without limitations. Because it requires sophisticated equipment and the presence of a trained technician throughout the night, nocturnal polysomnography is expensive, precluding its routine use. In addition, laboratory polysomnography is a fairly invasive assessment method that may disrupt sleep. Because individuals are not in their natural environment, they may sleep differently in the laboratory, especially the first night (the "first-night effect"). In insomnia outcome research, it is a standard practice to conduct recordings for two or three consecutive nights and to discard data from the first night because of this reactivity effect. The use of polysomnography in the assessment of insomnia is still controversial (Edinger et al., 1989; Jacobs, Reynolds, Kupfer, Lovin, & Ehrenpreis, 1988). A recent practice parameter paper concluded that it was generally not indicated for the routine evaluation of insomnia and that it should be limited to patients for whom the presence of another sleep disorder is suspected (Sateia, Doghramji, Hauri, & Morin, 2000).

Several ambulatory monitoring devices have been commercialized for conducting polysomnographic evaluations in the patient's home, thereby increasing ecological validity and reducing the "first-night effect." The typical portable recorder is self-contained and allows data storage throughout the night. Data are then transferred to a computer for scoring and analysis. Although a high concordance has been found between laboratory and home-based polysomnographic data (Ancoli-Israel, 1997; Edinger et al., 1989), most validation studies have focused on the diagnosis of sleep-related respiratory disorders. Hence, the validity of home-based polysomnography in the assessment of insomnia has yet to be demonstrated. Despite certain advantages with home-based polysomnography, there are other disadvantages such as the risk of artifacts and the invalidation of records (there is no technician to correct problems that may arise during the night) and the lack of behavioral observations from technicians (making interpretation more difficult in some cases).

Self-Report Measures

There is a wide variety of self-report questionnaires that are available to assess insomnia. Some of these instruments are designed as general screening measures of sleep quality or sleep satisfaction, others are intended to evaluate the severity/impact of insomnia, and still others focus on presumed mediating factors of insomnia. Because of the large number of such measures, only a sample of those most widely used in research and clinical practice is described here.

The Pittsburgh Sleep Quality Index (PSQI)

The PSQI (Buysse, Reynolds, Monk, Berman, & Kupfer, 1989) is a self-rating scale frequently used to assess general sleep disturbances. The PSQI is composed of 19 self-rated items assessing sleep quality and disturbances over a one-month interval. It covers subjective sleep quality, sleep latency, sleep duration, sleep efficiency, sleep disturbances, use of sleeping medication, and daytime dysfunction. A summation of these seven component scores yields a global score of sleep quality ranging from 0 to 21. The first four items are open-ended questions, while the remaining items are rated on a Likert scale ranging from 0 to 3.

The Sleep Impairment Index (SII)

The SII (Morin, 1993) yields a quantitative index of insomnia severity. The SII is composed of seven items assessing, on a five-point scale, the perceived severity of problems with sleep onset, sleep maintenance, and early morning awakenings, the satisfaction with the current sleep pattern, the degree of interference with daily functioning, the noticeability of impairment due to the sleep disturbance, and the degree of worry or concern caused by the sleep

problem. The total SII score, obtained by summing the seven ratings, ranges from 0 to 28. A higher score indicates more severe insomnia. The SII takes less than five minutes to complete and score. Two parallel versions, provided by a clinician and a significant other (e.g., spouse, roommate), are available to provide collateral validation of patients' perceptions of their sleep difficulties (Bastien, Vallières, Morin, 2001).

The Dysfunctional Beliefs and Attitudes about Sleep Scale (DBAS)

The DBAS (Morin, 1994) is a 30-item self-report scale designed to assess sleep-related beliefs and attitudes that are believed to be instrumental in maintaining sleep difficulties (Morin, 1993). The patient indicates the extent of agreement or disagreement with each statement on a visual analogue scale ranging from 0 (strongly disagree) to 100 (strongly agree). Ratings are summed to yield a total score; a higher score suggests more dysfunctional beliefs and attitudes about sleep. The content of the items reflects several themes such as faulty causal attributions (e.g., "I feel that insomnia is basically the result of aging"), amplification of the perceived consequences of insomnia (e.g., "I am concerned that chronic insomnia may have serious consequences for my physical health"), unrealistic sleep expectations (e.g., "I need eight hours of sleep to feel refreshed and function well during the day"), diminished perception of control and predictability of sleep (e.g., "I am worried that I may lose control over my abilities to sleep"), and faulty beliefs about sleep-promoting practices (e.g., "When I have trouble getting to sleep, I should stay in bed and try harder"). The DBAS is particularly useful for clinicians in identifying relevant targets for cognitive therapy.

Self-report measures offer several practical and economical advantages. They can easily be used in a variety of contexts to provide a global assessment of sleep difficulties, and they can be administered repeatedly to measure therapeutic changes. The main limitation is their retrospective nature and the associated risk of recall biases. Typically, insomnia is present only some nights in a given week, even in individuals with chronic insomnia. Also, the severity of sleep difficulties can vary considerably from night to night, which makes it difficult for the individual to retrospectively give precise information on these variables. Because individuals with insomnia are often distressed by their sleep difficulties, they tend to recall and generalize from those nights that were most disturbed, resulting in an overestimation of insomnia. Despite these limitations, self-report scales remain very cost-effective methods for initial assessment and treatment outcome evaluation.

Behavioral Assessment Devices

Several behavioral assessment devices are increasingly used to monitor sleep-wake patterns. These devices include a switch-activated clock, a voice-activated recording system, and wrist actigraphy. The first two devices use a timer (activated by a handheld switch or by a vocal response to a periodic tone) to measure the time required to fall asleep. Wrist actigraphy is currently the most widely used device for ambulatory data collection. This activity-based monitoring system uses a microprocessor to record and store wrist activity along with the actual clock time. Data are processed through microcomputer software, and an algorithm is used to estimate sleep and wake based on wrist activity. The presence of motor activity is interpreted as wakefulness and the absence of activity is interpreted as sleep. This device, as well as other behavioral assessment devices, does not measure sleep stages. Despite these limitations, wrist actigraphy is a useful complementary method for assessing insomnia and certain circadian rhythm sleep disorders (Sadeh, Hauri, Kripke, & Lavie, 1995).

The Role of Psychological Evaluation

Because sleep disturbances often co-exist with psychopathology, a psychological evaluation should be an integral component of insomnia assessment. This assessment is necessary to determine whether insomnia represents a primary disorder or a disorder secondary to psychological disturbances. In the latter case, treatment should initially target the underlying psychological condition rather than the sleep problem. Also, although most patients with insomnia do not meet diagnostic criteria for serious psychiatric disorders (e.g., major depression, generalized anxiety disorder), almost all of them display some psychological distress (i.e., depressed and anxious mood) concurrent to their sleep difficulties. It is important to quantify and monitor exacerbation or improvement of this symptomatology during the course of treatment.

The most reliable strategy to determine the presence of psychopathology is to incorporate into the clinical interview key questions from the Structured Clinical Interview for DSM (Spitzer, Williams, Gibbon, & First, 1990), along with questions about past psychiatric history and treatment. This is the most appropriate assessment modality when major psychopathology is suspected. However, a more cost-effective approach is to use brief screening instruments that target specific psychological features (e.g., emotional distress, anxiety, depression) most commonly associated with insomnia complaints. Instruments such as the Brief Symptom Inventory (Derogatis & Melisaratos, 1983), the Beck Depression Inventory (Beck, Ward, Mendelson, Mock, & Erbaugh, 1961), and the State-Trait Anxiety Inventory (Spielberger, 1983) can yield valuable screening data about psychological symptoms, although none of these self-report measures should be used alone to make a diagnosis. Psychometric screening should always be complemented by a clinical interview.

Evaluation of Daytime Sleepiness

Assessment of daytime sleepiness is essential when daytime vigilance is compromised by a sleep disorder. The "gold standard" for this evaluation is the Multiple Sleep Latency Test (MSLT), a laboratory-based procedure conducted during daytime. It involves measuring the latency to sleep onset at five 20-minute nap opportunities occurring at two-hour intervals throughout the day. Latency to sleep onset provides an objective measure of sleepiness. A mean sleep latency of less than 5 minutes is considered pathological. In comparison, (well rested) individuals without sleep disorders usually take 10 minutes or more to fall asleep or do not fall asleep at all. Although individuals with insomnia often complain about fatigue, they do not show significant sleepiness on the MSLT, most likely because of their underlying hyperarousal state both at night and during the day. The MSLT is used mostly with patients who suffer from other sleep disorders such as narcolepsy and sleep apnea. It is an excellent measure to determine functional impairments due to excessive daytime sleepiness.

Self-report questionnaires are also used to obtain subjective measures of daytime sleepiness. The Epworth Sleepiness Scale (Johns, 1991) is an eight-item global and retrospective measure assessing the likelihood of falling asleep in several situations (e.g., watching TV, driving). It is also possible to assess subjective sleepiness at a specific moment in time using the Stanford Sleepiness Scale, a 7-point Likert scale (1 = "feeling alert; wide awake" 7 = "sleep onset soon; lost struggle to remain awake") reflecting increasing levels of sleepiness (Hoddes, Zarcone Smythe, Phillips, & Dement, 1973).

In this section, several methods of sleep assessment were described with their relative strengths and weaknesses. The choice of assessment strategies depends on the goal of the evaluation. A multifaceted assessment combining a clinical interview with the use of objective (e.g., polysomnography) and subjective (e.g., sleep diary, self-report scales) measures is ideal. However, polysomnography is not always necessary, especially when the clinician has no suspicion about the presence of an underlying sleep disorder such as sleep apnea.

TREATMENTS

Despite its high prevalence and negative impact, insomnia remains for the most part untreated. Estimates from the

National Institute of Mental Health survey of psychotherapeutic drug use indicate that only 15% of those reporting serious insomnia had used either a prescribed or over-the-counter sleep aid within the previous year (Mellinger et al., 1985). The average insomnia duration before seeking professional treatment often exceeds 10 years. When individuals with persistent insomnia are asked about the types of methods they have used to cope with insomnia, the majority report passive strategies such as reading, listening to the radio or watching TV, trying to relax or, simply doing nothing.

The first line of active treatment usually involves self-help remedies such as alcohol, over-the-counter products (Sominex, Unisom, Nytol), or herbal/dietary supplements such as melatonin or valerian. When all of these strategies have failed, some individuals may seek professional help. As for other health conditions (e.g., pain), most individuals with insomnia typically seek treatment, not from a psychologist, but from a primary care physician, and treatment usually involves drug therapy. Nearly 50% of patients consulting for insomnia in medical practice are prescribed a hypnotic medication and the majority of those continue using their medications almost daily for more than one year (Hohagen et al., 1993; Ohayon & Caulet, 1996).

Help-Seeking Determinants

There is little information about the natural history of insomnia and related help-seeking determinants. Nonetheless, several factors, other than socioeconomic ones, may regulate health-seeking behaviors in the context of insomnia. Patients seeking treatment for insomnia in primary care medicine often present more co-existing medical and psychological problems than untreated individuals or those attempting to treat their sleep difficulties on their own. Likewise, those who seek treatment in sleep disorder clinics display more emotional distress than those who do not seek treatment, although the severity of sleep disturbances is comparable for these two groups (Stepanski et al., 1989). The speed of onset of insomnia may also influence help-seeking behaviors. Acute insomnia is often associated with a major stressful life event (e.g., death of a loved one, medical illness, separation) and is more likely to be brought to the attention of a physician and to receive clinical attention. Conversely, when insomnia evolves gradually and is tolerated for prolonged periods of time, it is less likely to be brought to clinical attention and, perhaps, less likely to be taken seriously. Another important determinant is the degree of acceptability of sleep medications. Many insomniacs may not consult their physicians for sleep because they are concerned that they may not be taken seriously or that a sleeping pill prescription will be the only

recommended treatment. Survey data show that very few individuals with chronic insomnia (<10%) seek treatment specifically for this condition (Mellinger et al., 1985); however, many more mention it in the context of a visit for another medical condition, and even more report sleep problems when specifically asked about their sleep patterns.

Barriers to Treatment

There are several barriers to insomnia treatment, particularly to psychological therapies. Among these are the lack of recognition of insomnia by health care practitioners, inadequate dissemination of knowledge about validated interventions, and the costs and limited availability of these treatments (National Institutes of Health, 1996). Although nondrug interventions for insomnia are generally well accepted by patients (Morin, Gaulier, Barry, & Kowatch, 1992) and physicians, specific behavioral interventions, other than general sleep hygiene recommendations (e.g., reduce caffeine, increased exercise) are not well known and are infrequently used in clinical practice (Rothenberg, 1992). For these reasons, drug therapy remains the mainstream of insomnia treatments.

Benefits and Limitations of Sleep Medications

Several classes of medications are used for treating insomnia, including benzodiazepines, nonbenzodiazepine hypnotics, antidepressants, and antihistamines. The most frequently prescribed hypnotics include benzodiazepines (e.g., flurazepam, temazepam, lorazepam, triazolam, nitrazepam) and newer agents (e.g., zolpidem, zopiclone, zelaplon) with more selective/specific hypnotic actions. Some antidepressants (e.g., trazodone, amitriptyline, doxepin) are also prescribed for sleep problems because of their sedative properties, but this practice is controversial and not supported by empirical evidence.

Most over-the-counter medicines advertised as sleep aids (e.g., Sominex, Nytol, Sleep-Eze, Unisom) contain a sedative antihistamine such as diphenhydramine. Although these agents produce drowsiness, there is limited evidence that they are efficacious in the treatment of insomnia (Monti & Monti, 2000). Melatonin, a naturally occurring hormone produced by the pineal gland at night, is increasingly used as a sleep aid. Although it may be useful for some forms of circadian sleep disturbances associated with shift-work and jet-lag, the benefits of melatonin for insomnia are equivocal and the adverse effects associated with long-term usage are unknown (Mendelson, 1997). Valerian, which is extracted from a plant of the same name, produces a mild hypnotic effect but additional studies are needed to evaluate its therapeutic benefits for clinical insomnia. Because melatonin and valerian are not regulated by the Food and Drug Administration, an important concern surrounds the lack of information available to the consumer about the substances used to in their preparation. The remainder of this section focuses on benzodiazepines and newer hypnotic drugs.

Evidence for Efficacy

Placebo-controlled clinical studies have documented the acute effects of benzodiazepine-receptor agents on sleep (Holbrook, Crowther, Lotter, Cheng, & King, 2000; Nowell et al., 1997). Hypnotic medications improve sleep continuity and efficiency through a reduction of sleep onset latency and time awake after sleep onset. They also increase total sleep time and reduce the number of awakenings and stage shifts through the night. Their effects on sleep stages vary with the specific class of medications. All benzodiazepine-receptor agents increase stage 1 and stage 2 sleep and reduce REM and slow-wave (stages 3 and 4) sleep. These latter changes are less pronounced with the newer hypnotics (e.g., zolpidem, zopiclone). In a recent meta-analysis of 22 placebo-controlled trials ($n = 1894$), benzodiazepines and zolpidem were found to produce reliable improvements of sleep-onset latency (mean effect size of 0.56), number of awakenings (0.65), total sleep time (0.71), and sleep quality (0.62) (Nowell et al., 1997). Thus, hypnotic medications are efficacious for the acute and short-term management of insomnia. However, because the median treatment duration in controlled studies is only one week (range of 4 to 35 days), and follow-ups are virtually absent, the long-term efficacy of hypnotic medications remains unknown.

Risks and Limitations

The main limitations of hypnotic medications are their residual effects (e.g., daytime sedation, cognitive and psychomotor impairments, anterograde amnesia), which are more pronounced with long-acting agents (e.g., flurazepam, quazepam) and in older adults (Monti & Monti, 1995). The use of long-acting benzodiazepines is associated with an increased rate of falls and hip fractures (Ray, 1992) and motor vehicle accidents in the elderly (Hemmelgarn, Suissa, Huang, Boivin, & Pinard, 1997). When used on a prolonged basis, hypnotics may lead to tolerance and it may be necessary to increase the dosage to maintain therapeutic effects. This tolerance effect, however, varies across agents and individuals and some people may remain on the same dosage for prolonged periods of time. Whether this prolonged usage is a sign of continued effectiveness or of fear of discontinuing the medication

is unclear. Rebound insomnia is a common problem associated with discontinuation of benzodiazepine-hypnotics; it is more pronounced with short-acting drugs and can be attenuated with a gradual tapering regimen. Zolpidem and zopiclone may produce less rebound insomnia upon discontinuation (Monti & Monti, 1995; Wadworth & McTavish, 1993). Finally, prolonged usage of sleep-promoting medications, prescribed or over-the-counter, carry some risk of dependence (APA, 1990); this dependency is often more psychological than physical (Morin, 1993). Psychological interventions have been found effective in assisting prolonged users of benzodiazepines to discontinue their drugs (Morin et al., 1998).

In summary, hypnotic medications are effective for the short-term treatment of insomnia; they produce rapid benefits which last several nights and, in some cases, up to a few weeks. There is, however, little evidence of sustained benefits upon drug discontinuation or of continued efficacy with prolonged usage. In addition, all hypnotics carry some risk of dependence, particularly with prolonged usage. The primary indication for hypnotic medications is for situational sleep difficulties; their role in the clinical management of recurrent or chronic insomnia is still controversial.

Psychological Therapies

More than a dozen psychological interventions (mostly cognitive-behavioral in content) have been used for treating insomnia. Treatment modalities that have been adequately evaluated in controlled clinical trials include stimulus control therapy, sleep restriction, relaxation-based interventions, cognitive therapy, and sleep hygiene education. The main focus of these treatments is to alter the presumed perpetuating factors of chronic insomnia. As such, they seek to modify maladaptive sleep habits, reduce autonomic and cognitive arousal, alter dysfunctional beliefs and attitudes about sleep, and educate patients about healthier sleep practices (see Table 14.3). As for most cognitive-behavioral interventions, the format of insomnia treatment is structured, short-term, and sleep-focused. Treatment duration typically lasts 4 to 6 hours and is implemented over a period of 4 to 8 weeks. A summary of these treatments is provided below; more extensive descriptions are available in other sources (Espie, 1991; Hauri, 1991; Lichstein & Morin, 2000; Morin, 1993).

Relaxation-Based Interventions

Relaxation is the most commonly used nondrug therapy for insomnia. Among the available relaxation-based interventions, some methods (e.g., progressive-muscle relaxation, autogenic training, biofeedback) focus primarily on reducing somatic

TABLE 14.3   Cognitive-Behavioral Treatments for Insomnia

Therapy	Description
Stimulus control therapy	Go to bed only when sleepy; get out of bed when unable to sleep; use the bed/bedroom for sleep only (no reading, watching TV, etc.); arise at the same time every morning; no napping.
Sleep restriction	Curtail time in bed to the actual sleep time, thereby creating mild sleep deprivation, which results in more consolidated and more efficient sleep.
Relaxation training	Methods aimed at reducing somatic tension (e.g., progressive muscle relaxation, autogenic training, biofeedback) or intrusive thoughts (e.g., imagery training, hypnosis, thought stopping) interfering with sleep.
Cognitive therapy	Psychotherapeutic method aimed at changing dysfunctional beliefs and attitudes about sleep and insomnia (e.g., unrealistic sleep expectations; fear of the consequences of insomnia).
Sleep hygiene	Avoid stimulants (e.g., caffeine and nicotine) and alcohol around bedtime; do not eat heavy or spicy meals too close to bedtime; exercise regularly but not too late in the evening; maintain a dark, quiet, and comfortable sleep environment.

arousal (e.g., muscle tension), whereas attention-focusing procedures (e.g., imagery training, meditation, thought stopping) target mental arousal in the form of worries, intrusive thoughts, or a racing mind. Biofeedback is designed to train a patient to control some physiological parameters (e.g., frontalis EMG tension) through visual or auditory feedback.

Stimulus Control Therapy

Chronic insomniacs often become apprehensive around bedtime and associate the bed/bedroom with frustration and arousal. This conditioning process may take place over several weeks or even months, without the patient's awareness. Stimulus control therapy consists of a set of instructions designed to reassociate temporal (bedtime) and environmental (bed and bedroom) stimuli with rapid sleep onset. This is accomplished by postponing bedtime until sleep is imminent, getting out of bed when unable to sleep, and curtailing sleep-incompatible activities (overt and covert). The second objective of stimulus control is to establish a regular circadian sleep-wake rhythm by enforcing a strict adherence to a regular arising time and by avoidance of daytime naps (Bootzin, Epstein, & Wood, 1991).

Sleep Restriction

Poor sleepers often increase their time in bed in a misguided effort to provide more opportunity for sleep, a strategy that is more likely to result in fragmented and poor quality of sleep. Sleep restriction therapy consists of curtailing the amount of time spent in bed to the actual amount of time asleep (Spielman, Saskin, & Thorpy, 1987). Time in bed is subsequently adjusted based on sleep efficiency (SE; ratio of total sleep/time in bed X 100%) for a given period of time (usually a week). For example, if a person reports sleeping an average of 6 hours per night out of 8 hours spent in bed, the initial prescribed sleep window (i.e., from initial bedtime to final arising time) would be 6 hours. The subsequent allowable time in bed is increased by about 20 minutes for a given week when SE exceeds 85%, decreased by the same amount of time when SE is lower than 80%, and kept stable when SE falls between 80% and 85%. Adjustments are made weekly until an optimal sleep duration is achieved. Sleep restriction produces a mild state of sleep deprivation and may also alleviate sleep anticipatory anxiety. To prevent excessive daytime sleepiness, time in bed should not be restricted to less than 5 hours per night.

Cognitive Therapy

Cognitive therapy seeks to alter dysfunctional sleep cognitions (e.g., beliefs, attitudes, expectations, attributions). The basic premise of this approach is that appraisal of a given situation (sleeplessness) can trigger negative emotions (fear, anxiety) that are incompatible with sleep. For example, when a person is unable to sleep at night and begins thinking about the possible consequences of sleep loss on the next day's performance, this can set off a spiral reaction and feed into the vicious cycle of insomnia, emotional distress, and more sleep disturbances. Cognitive therapy is designed to identify dysfunctional cognitions and reframe them into more adaptive substitutes in order to short-circuit the self-fulfilling nature of this vicious cycle. Specific treatment targets include unrealistic expectations ("I must get my 8 hours of sleep every night"), faulty causal attributions ("My insomnia is entirely due to a biochemical imbalance"), amplification of the consequences of insomnia ("Insomnia may have serious consequences on my health"), and misconceptions about healthy sleep practices (Morin, 1993; Morin, Savard, & Blais, 2000). These factors play an important mediating role in insomnia, particularly in exacerbating emotional arousal, anxiety, and learned helplessness as related to sleeplessness.

Sleep Hygiene Education

Sleep hygiene education is concerned with health practices (e.g., diet, exercise, caffeine use) and environmental factors (e.g., light, noise, temperature) that may interfere with sleep

(Hauri, 1991). Although these factors are rarely of sufficient severity to be the primary cause of insomnia, they may potentiate sleep difficulties caused by other factors. Sleep hygiene is typically incorporated with other interventions to minimize interference from poor sleep hygiene practices. Basic recommendations involve avoidance of stimulants (e.g., caffeine, nicotine) and alcohol, exercising regularly, and minimizing noise, light, and excessive temperature. It may also include advice about maintaining a regular sleep schedule and avoiding napping, although these instructions are part of the standard stimulus control therapy.

Additional nondrug interventions are available for treating insomnia including paradoxical intention, hypnosis, acupuncture, ocular relaxation, and electro-sleep therapy. Those methods have not yet received adequate empirical validation in controlled studies. Psychotherapy may also be useful to address predisposing factors to insomnia, but there has been no controlled evaluation of its efficacy.

Summary of Outcome Evidence

Evidence for Efficacy

Two meta-analyses recently summarized the findings of more than 50 clinical studies (involving over 2,000 patients) of nonpharmacological interventions for insomnia (Morin, Culbert, & Schwartz, 1994; Murtagh & Greenwood, 1995). The data indicate that behavioral treatment (lasting an average of 4 to 6 weeks) produces reliable changes in several sleep parameters of individuals with primary insomnia. Almost identical effect sizes, 0.87 and 0.88, have been reported in both meta-analyses for sleep-onset latency, the main target symptom in studies of sleep-onset insomnia. An effect size of this magnitude indicates that, on average, insomnia patients are better off (fall asleep faster) after treatment than about 80% of untreated control subjects. Reliable effect sizes, falling in what is conventionally defined as moderate to large, have also been reported for other sleep parameters, including total sleep time (0.42–0.49), number of awakenings (0.53–0.63), duration of awakenings (0.65), and sleep quality ratings (0.94). These effect sizes are comparable to those reported with benzodiazepines and zolpidem (Nowell et al., 1997). In terms of absolute changes, sleep-onset latency is reduced from an average of 60 to 65 minutes at baseline to about 35 minutes at posttreatment. The duration of awakenings is similarly decreased from an average of 70 minutes at baseline to about 38 minutes following treatment. Total sleep time is increased by a modest 30 minutes, from 6 hours to 6.5 hours after treatment, but perceived sleep quality is significantly enhanced with treatment. Overall, the magnitude of these changes indicate that between 70% to 80% of treated patients benefit from treatment. These results represent conservative estimates of efficacy because they are based on average effect sizes computed across all treatment modalities.

Comparative studies of different psychological treatments have generally, but not always, shown stimulus control therapy and sleep restriction to be the most effective single treatment modalities. As psychological interventions are not incompatible with each other, they can be effectively combined. Multifaceted interventions that incorporate behavioral, educational, and cognitive components often produce the best outcome.

Durability and Generalizability of Changes

Cognitive-behavior therapy for insomnia produces stable changes over time. Improvements of sleep parameters and satisfaction with those changes are well maintained up to 24 months after treatment. While increases in total sleep time are fairly modest during the initial treatment period, these gains are typically enhanced at follow-up, with total sleep time often exceeding 6.5 hours. Although promising, these data must be interpreted cautiously because less than 50% of studies report long-term follow-up and, among those that do, attrition rates increase substantially over time.

The large majority of behavioral and pharmacological treatment studies have focused on primary insomnia in otherwise healthy and medication-free patients. Thus, an important question is whether the findings obtained in these research studies generalize to patients typically seen in clinical practice, patients who often present with comorbid medical and psychiatric disorders. Preliminary findings from uncontrolled clinical case series (Chambers & Alexander, 1992; Dashevsky & Kramer, 1998; Jacobs, Benson, & Friedman, 1996; Morin, Stone et al., 1994) have yielded promising results suggesting that patients with medical and psychiatric conditions, or even those using hypnotic medications can benefit from behavioral treatment for sleep disturbances. Because these studies have a more naturalistic focus and are not as rigorously controlled as randomized controlled trials, these conclusions are only tentative at this time (Currie, Wilson, & Pontefract, 2000).

In summary, behavioral treatment produces reliable and durable sleep improvements in primary insomnia. The majority (70% to 80%) of treated patients benefit from treatment, but only a minority become good sleepers and a small proportion of patients do not respond at all to treatment. Behavioral treatment often leads to a greater sense of personal control over sleep and reduces the need for hypnotic medications. Behavioral interventions require more time to improve sleep patterns relative to drug therapy, but these changes are fairly durable over time.

Combined Psychological and Pharmacological Treatments

Only five studies have directly evaluated the combined or differential effects of behavioral and drug treatment modalities. Three of those studies compared triazolam to relaxation (McClusky, Milby, Switzer, Williams, & Wooten, 1991; Milby et al., 1993) or sleep hygiene (Hauri, 1997), one compared estazolam with and without relaxation (Rosen, Lewin, Goldberg, & Woolfolk, 2000), and the other one (Morin, Colecchi, Stone, Sood, & Brink, 1999) compared cognitive-behavior therapy to temazepam. Collectively, these studies indicate that both treatment modalities are effective in the short term. Drug therapy produces quicker and slightly better results in the acute phase (first week) of treatment, whereas behavioral and drug therapies are equally effective in the short-term interval (4 to 8 weeks). Combined interventions appear to have a slight advantage over a single treatment modality during the initial course of treatment. Furthermore, long-term effects have been fairly consistent for the single treatment modalities but more equivocal for the combined approach. For instance, sleep improvements are well sustained after behavioral treatment while those obtained with hypnotic drugs are quickly lost after discontinuation of the medication. Combined biobehavioral interventions may yield a slightly better outcome during initial treatment, but long-term effects are more equivocal. Studies with short-term follow-ups (<1 month) indicate that a combined intervention (i.e., triazolam plus relaxation) produces more sustained benefits than drug therapy alone (McClusky et al., 1991; Milby et al., 1993). The only two investigations with follow-ups exceeding six months in duration report more variable long-term outcomes among patients receiving a combined intervention relative to those treated with behavioral treatment alone (Hauri, 1997; Morin et al., 1999). Some of these patients retained their initial improvements whereas others returned to their baseline values.

Combined biobehavioral treatments should theoretically optimize outcome by capitalizing on the more immediate and potent effects of drug therapy and the more sustained effects of psychological interventions. In practice, however, the limited evidence is not clear as to whether a combined intervention has an additive or subtractive effect on long-term outcome (Kendall & Lipman, 1991; Morin, 1996). In light of the mediating role of psychological factors in chronic insomnia, behavioral and attitudinal changes may be essential to sustain improvements in sleep patterns. When combining behavioral and drug therapies, patients' attributions of the initial benefits may be critical in determining long-term outcomes. Attribution of therapeutic benefits to the drug alone, without integration of self-management skills, may place a person at greater risk for relapse once the drug is discontinued. Also, the literature on state-dependent learning suggests that self-management skills learned while taking hypnotics may not generalize after drug discontinuation. Thus, it is not entirely clear when, how, and for whom it is indicated to combine behavioral and drug treatments for insomnia.

CONCLUSIONS AND DIRECTIONS FOR FUTURE RESEARCH

Sleep is a critical component of health and, as such, insomnia can either be a cause or a consequence of health problems. Significant advances have been made in the past two decades in the treatment of insomnia and in our understanding of the relationships between sleep and psychological and physical health. Despite these advances, a great deal more research is still needed to address critical issues regarding the nature, epidemiology, and treatment of insomnia.

There is a need for more basic studies of psychological and biological factors that are presumed to contribute to the etiology of insomnia. For example, the role of cognitive factors (e.g., intrusive thoughts, faulty beliefs), attention, and information processing variables needs further investigation to refine and validate our current conceptual model of insomnia. New assessment technologies (e.g., spectral analysis) should also be used to gain a better understanding of the etiological mechanisms and phenomenological experience underlying insomnia complaints.

Because we know very little about the natural history of insomnia, longitudinal studies are needed to document the course, evolution, early precursors, and risk factors of the disorder. Likewise, since only a small proportion of individuals with insomnia actually seek treatment, it is important to examine help-seeking determinants among this population. This longitudinal line of research should also evaluate the long-term consequences of insomnia on psychological (e.g., depression) and physical health (e.g., immune function). The direct and indirect costs associated with insomnia should also be more fully documented.

Although significant progress has been made in the management of insomnia, only a small proportion of treated individuals achieve complete remission. Additional clinical trials are warranted to examine what parameters could optimize the outcome of psychological therapies. Research is also needed to evaluate the effects of single and combined behavioral and pharmacological treatments for insomnia and to examine potential mechanisms of changes mediating short- and long-term outcomes. Several studies are currently in progress to evaluate such issues as whether it is preferable to implement behavioral and pharmacological treatments concurrently or sequentially, what the optimal treatment dosage is in terms of frequency, timing, and duration of consultation sessions, and whether the addition of maintenance therapies enhances long-term outcome. The efficacy of behavioral interventions in facilitating benzodiazepine discontinuation among long-term users is also being examined, as is the relative cost-effectiveness of different methods for treatment delivery (e.g., brief consultation, group therapy, self-help treatment).

Finally, clinical studies are needed to further validate current treatment models for implementation in primary care medicine. This type of research is essential because the large majority of individuals with insomnia who seek treatment do so from their primary care physicians, not from psychologists. The design and dissemination of large-scale community-based sleep education/prevention programs is also needed in order to reach a larger number of individuals with insomnia complaints and, ideally, to prevent the development of more severe and persistent forms of insomnia.

REFERENCES

American Psychiatric Association. (1990). *Benzodiazepine dependence, toxicity, and abuse: A task force report of the American Psychiatric Association.* Washington, DC: Author.

American Psychiatric Association. (1994). *Diagnostic and statistical manual of mental disorders* (4th ed.). Washington, DC: Author.

American Sleep Disorders Association. (1997). *The international classification of sleep disorders: Diagnostic and coding manual.* Rochester, MN: Author.

Ancoli-Israel, S. (1997). The polysomnogram. In M. R. Pressman & W. Orr (Eds.), *Understanding sleep: The evaluation and treatment of sleep disorders* (Vol. 1, pp. 177–191). Washington, DC: American Psychological Association.

Askenasy, J. J. M., & Lewin, I. (1996). The impact of missile warfare on self-reported sleep quality. *Sleep, 19,* 47–51.

Bastien, C., & Morin, C. M. (2000). Familial incidence of insomnia. *Journal of Sleep Research, 9,* 1–6.

Bastien, C., Vallières, A., & Morin, C. M. (2001). Validation of the Sleep Impairment Index as an outcome measure for insomnia research. *Sleep Medicine, 2,* 297–307.

Beck, A. T., Ward, C. E., Mendelson, M., Mock, J. E., & Erbaugh, J. K. (1961). An inventory for measuring depression. *Archives of General Psychiatry, 4,* 561–571.

Bliwise, D. L., King, A. C., Harris, R., & Haskell, W. (1992). Prevalence of self-reported poor sleep in a healthy population aged 50–65. *Social Sciences and Medicine, 34,* 49–55.

Bootzin, R. R., Epstein, D., & Wood, J. M. (1991). Stimulus control instructions. In P. Hauri (Ed.), *Case studies in insomnia* (pp. 19–28). New York: Plenum Press.

Borkovec, T. D., Lane, T. W., & Van Oot, P. H. (1981). Phenomenology of sleep among insomniacs and good sleepers: Wakefulness experience when cortically asleep. *Journal of Abnormal Psychology, 90,* 607–609.

Breslau, N., Roth, T., Rosenthal, L., & Andreski, P. (1996). Sleep disturbance and psychiatric disorders: A longitudinal epidemiological study of young adults. *Biological Psychiatry, 39,* 411–418.

Buysse, D. J., Reynolds, C. F., Monk, T. H., Berman, S. R., & Kupfer, D. J. (1989). The Pittsburgh Sleep Quality Index: A new instrument for psychiatric practice and research. *Psychiatry Research, 28,* 193–213.

Buysse, D. J., Reynolds, C. F., Kupfer, D. J., Thorpy, M. J., Bixler, E., Manfredi, R., et al. (1994). Clinical diagnoses in 216 insomnia patients using the international classification of sleep disorders (ICSD), *DSM-IV* and ICD-10 categories: A report from the APANIMH *DSM-IV* field trial. *Sleep, 17,* 630–637.

Chambers, M. J., & Alexander, S. D. (1992). Assessment and prediction of outcome for a brief behavioral insomnia treatment program. *Journal of Therapy and Experimental Psychiatry, 23,* 289–297.

Chilcott, L. A., & Shapiro, C. M. (1996). The socioeconomic impact of insomnia: An overview. *Pharmacoeconomics, 10,* 1–14.

Coates, T. J., Killen, J. D., George, J., Marchini, E., Silverman, S., & Thoresen, C. (1982). Estimating sleep parameters: A multitrait-multimethod analysis. *Journal of Consulting and Clinical Psychology, 50,* 345–352.

Coates, T. J., Killen, J. D., Silverman, S., George, J., Marchini, E., Hamilton, S., et al. (1983). Cognitive activity, sleep disturbance, and stage specific differences between recorded and reported sleep. *Psychophysiology, 20,* 243–250.

Cover, H., & Irwin, M. (1994). Immunity and depression: Insomnia, retardation, and reduction of natural killer cell activity. *Journal of Behavioral Medicine, 17,* 217–223.

Currie, S. R., Wilson, K. G., & Pontefract, A. J. (2000). Cognitive-behavioral treatment of insomnia secondary to chronic pain. *Journal of Consulting and Clinical Psychology, 68,* 407–416.

Dashevsky, B., & Kramer, M. (1998). Behavioral treatment of chronic insomnia in psychiatrically ill patients. *Journal of Clinical Psychiatry, 59,* 693–699.

Derogatis, L. R., & Melisaratos, N. (1983). The Brief Symptom Inventory: An introductory report. *Psychological Medicine, 13,* 595–605.

Dinges, D. F., Douglas, S. D., Hamarman, S., Zaugg, L., & Kapoor, S. (1995). Sleep deprivation and human immune function. *Advances in Neuroimmunology, 5,* 97–110.

Edinger, J. D., Hoelscher, T. J., Webb, M. D., Marsh, G. R., Radtke, R. A., & Erwin, C. W. (1989). Polysomnographic assessment of DIMS: Empirical evaluation of its diagnostic value. *Sleep, 12,* 315–322.

Edinger, J. D., Stout, A. L., & Hoelscher, T. J. (1988). Cluster analysis of insomniacs' MMPI profiles: Relation of subtypes to sleep history and treatment outcome. *Psychosomatic Medicine, 50,* 77–87.

Enstrom, J. E. (1989). Health practices and cancer mortality among active California Mormons. *Journal of the National Cancer Institute, 81,* 1807–1814.

Espie, C. A. (1991). *The psychological treatment of insomnia.* Chichester, England: Wiley.

Everson, C. A. (1997). Sleep deprivation and the immune system. In M. R. Pressman & W. C. Orr (Eds.), *Understanding sleep: The evaluation and treatment of sleep disorders* (pp. 401–424). Washington, DC: American Psychological Association.

Foley, D. J., Monjan, A. A., Izmirlian, G., Hays, J. C., & Blazer, D. G. (1999). Incidence and remission of insomnia among elderly adults in a biracial cohort. *Sleep, 22,* S373–S378.

Ford, D. E., & Kamerow, D. B. (1989). Epidemiologic study of sleep disturbances and psychiatric disorders: An opportunity for prevention? *Journal of the American Medical Association, 262,* 1479–1484.

Gallup Organization. (1991). *Sleep in America.* Princeton, NJ: Author.

Gillin, J. C. (1983). The sleep therapies of depression. *Progress in Neuropsychopharmacology and Biological Psychiatry, 7,* 351–364.

Gislason, T., & Almqvist, M. (1987). Somatic diseases and sleep complaints: An epidemiological study of 3201 Swedish men. *Acta Medica Scandinavica, 221,* 475–481.

Hauri, P. J. (Ed.). (1991). *Case studies in insomnia.* New York: Plenum Press.

Hauri, P. J. (1997). Insomnia: Can we mix behavioral therapy with hypnotics when treating insomniacs? *Sleep, 20,* 1111–1118.

Hauri, P. J., & Olmstead, E. M. (1980). Childhood-onset insomnia. *Sleep, 3,* 59–65.

Hauri, P. J., & Olmstead, E. M. (1983). What is the moment of sleep onset for insomniacs? *Sleep, 6,* 10–15.

Healy, E. S., Kales, A., Monroe, L. J., Bixler, E. O., Chamberlin, K., & Soldatos, C. R. (1981). Onset of insomnia: Role of life-stress events. *Psychosomatic Medicine, 43,* 439–451.

Hemmelgarn, B., Suissa, S., Huang, A., Boivin, J. F., & Pinard, G. (1997). Benzodiazepine use and the risk of motor vehicle crash in the elderly. *Journal of the American Medical Association, 278,* 27–31.

Hoddes, E., Zarcone, V., Smythe, H., Phillips, R., & Dement, W. (1973). Quantification of sleepiness: A new approach. *Psychophysiology, 10,* 431–436.

Hohagen, F., Rink, K., Kappler, C., Schramm, E., Riemann, D., Weyerer, S., et al. (1993). Prevalence and treatment of insomnia in general practice: A longitudinal study. *European Archives of Psychiatry and Clinical Neurosciences, 242,* 329–336.

Holbrook, A. M., Crowther, R., Lotter, A., Cheng, C., & King, D. (2000). Meta-analysis of benzodiazepine use for insomnia. *Canadian Medical Association Journal, 162,* 225–233.

Horne, J. A. (1986). Human slow wave sleep. *European Neurology, 25,* 18–21.

Horne, J. A. (1988). Sleep loss and "divergent" thinking ability. *Sleep, 11,* 528–536.

Irwin, M., Smith, T. L., & Gillin, J. C. (1992). Electroencephalographic sleep and natural killer activity in depressed patients and control subjects. *Psychosomatic Medicine, 54,* 10–21.

Jacobs, E. A., Reynolds, C. F., Kupfer, D. J., Lovin, P. A., & Ehrenpreis, A. B. (1988). The role of polysomnography in the differential diagnosis of chronic insomnia. *American Journal of Psychiatry, 145*(3), 346–349.

Jacobs, G. D., Benson, H., & Friedman, R. (1996). Perceived benefits in behavioral-medicine insomnia program: A clinical report. *American Journal of Medicine, 100,* 212–216.

Johns, M. (1991). A new method for measuring daytime sleepiness: The Epworth Sleepiness Scale. *Sleep, 14,* 540–545.

Johnson, L. C. (1982). Sleep deprivation and performance. In W. B. Webb (Ed.), *Biological rhythms, sleep, and performance* (pp. 111–141). New York: Wiley.

Kales, A., Caldwell, A. B., Soldatos, C. R., Bixler, E. O., & Kales, J. D. (1983). Biopsychobehavioral correlates of insomnia. II: Pattern specificity and consistency with the Minnesota Multiphasic Personality Inventory. *Psychosomatic Medicine, 45*(4), 341–356.

Kales, A., & Kales, J. D. (1984). *Evaluation and treatment of insomnia.* New York: Oxford University Press.

Kales, J. D., Kales, A., Bixler, E. O., Soldatos, C. R., Cadieux, R. J., Kashurba, G. J., et al. (1984). Biopsychobehavioral correlates of insomnia. V: Clinical characteristics and behavioral correlates. *American Journal of Psychiatry, 141*(11), 1371–1376.

Katz, D. A., & McHorney, C. A. (1998). Clinical correlates of insomnia in patients with chronic illness. *Archives of International Medicine, 158*(10), 1099–1107.

Kendall, P. C., & Lipman, A. J. (1991). Psychological and pharmacological therapy: Methods and modes for comparative outcome research. *Journal of Consulting and Clinical Psychology, 59,* 78–87.

Kennedy, G. J., Kelman, H. R., & Thomas, C. (1991). Persistence and remission of depressive symptoms in late life. *American Journal of Psychiatry, 148,* 174–178.

Klink, M. E., Quan, S. F., Kaltenborn, W. T., & Lebowitz, M. D. (1992). Risk factors associated with complaints of insomnia in a general adult population: Influence of previous complaints of insomnia. *Archives of Internal Medicine, 152,* 1572–1575.

Kripke, D. F., Simons, R. N., Garfinkel, L., & Hammond, E. C. (1979). Short and long sleep and sleeping pills: Is increased mortality associated? *Archives of General Psychiatry, 36,* 102–116.

Leger, D., Levey, E., & Paillard, M. (1999). The direct costs of insomnia in France. *Sleep, 22,* S394–S401.

Leigh, J. P. (1991). Employee and job attributes as predictors of absenteeism in a national sample of workers: The importance of health and dangerous conditions. *Social Science Medicine, 33,* 127–137.

Lichstein, K. L., & Morin, C. M. (2000). *Treatment of late-life insomnia.* Thousand Oaks, CA: Sage.

Malone, M., Harris, A. L., & Luscombe, D. K. (1994). Assessment of the impact of cancer on work, recreation, home, management and sleep using a general health status measure. *Journal of the Royal Society of Medicine, 87,* 386–389.

McClusky, H. Y., Milby, J. B., Switzer, P. K., Williams, V., & Wooten, V. (1991). Efficacy of behavioral versus triazolam treatment in persistent sleep-onset insomnia. *American Journal of Psychiatry, 148,* 121–126.

Mellinger, G. D., Balter, M. B., & Uhlenhuth, E. H. (1985). Insomnia and its treatment: Prevalence and correlates. *Archives of General Psychiatry, 42,* 225–232.

Mendelson, W. B. (1997). A critical evaluation of the hypnotic efficacy of melatonin. *Sleep, 20,* 916–919.

Milby, J. B., Williams, V., Hall, J. N., Khuder, S., McGill, T., & Wooten, V. (1993). Effectiveness of combined triazolam-behavioral therapy for primary insomnia. *American Journal of Psychiatry, 150,* 1259–1260.

Mitler, M., Carskadon, M. A., Czeisler, C. A., Dement, W. C., Dinges, D. F., & Graeber, R. C. (1988). Catastrophes, sleep and public policy: Consensus report. *Sleep, 11,* 100–109.

Moldofsky, H. (1989). Sleep-wake mechanisms in fibrositis. *Journal of Rheumatology, 16,* 47–48.

Monk, T. H., & Moline, M. L. (1989). The timing of bedtime and waketime decisions in free-running subjects. *Psychophysiology, 26,* 304–310.

Monti, J. M., & Monti, D. (1995). Pharmacological treatment of chronic insomnia. *CNS Drugs, 4,* 182–194.

Monti, J. M., & Monti, D. (2000). Histamine H1 receptor antagonists in the treatment of insomnia: Is there a rational basis for use. *CNS Drugs, 13,* 87–96.

Morgan, K., & Clarke, D. (1997). Risk factors for late-life insomnia in a representative general practice sample. *British Journal of General Practice, 47,* 166–169.

Morin, C. M. (1993). *Insomnia: Psychological assessment and management.* New York: Guilford Press.

Morin, C. M. (1994). Dysfunctional beliefs and attitudes about sleep: Preliminary scale development and description. *Behavior Therapist,* 163–164.

Morin, C. M. (1996). Introduction: Psychosocial and pharmacological treatments in behavioral medicine. *Clinical Psychology Review, 16,* 453–456.

Morin, C. M., Bastien, C., Radouco-Thomas, M., Guay, B., Leblanc, S., Blais, F., et al. (1998). Late-life insomnia and chronic use of benzodiazepines: Medication tapering with and without behavioral interventions. *Sleep, 21*(Suppl.), 99.

Morin, C. M., Colecchi, C. A., Stone, J., Sood, R., & Brink, D. (1999). Behavioral and pharmacological therapies for late-life insomnia: A randomized clinical trial. *Journal of the American Medical Association, 281,* 991–999.

Morin, C. M., Culbert, J. P., & Schwartz, S. M. (1994). Nonpharmacological interventions for insomnia: A meta-analysis of treatment efficacy. *American Journal of Psychiatry, 151,* 1172–1180.

Morin, C. M., & Edinger, J. D. (1997). Sleep disorders: Evaluation and diagnosis. In S. M. Turner & M. Hersen (Eds.), *Adult psychopathology and diagnosis* (3rd ed., pp. 483–507). New York: Wiley.

Morin, C. M., Gaulier, B., Barry, T., & Kowatch, R. (1992). Patient's acceptance of psychological and pharmacological therapies for insomnia. *Sleep, 15,* 302–305.

Morin, C. M., Rodrigue, S., & Ivers, H. (under review). Insomnia, stress, and coping skills. Manuscript under review.

Morin, C. M., Savard, J., & Blais, F. C. (2000). Cognitive therapy. In K. L. Lichstein & C. M. Morin (Eds.), *Treatment of late-life insomnia* (pp. 207–230). Thousand Oaks: Sage.

Morin, C. M., Stone, J., McDonald, K., & Jones, S. (1994). Psychological management of insomnia: A clinical replication series with 100 patients. *Behavior Therapy, 25,* 291–309.

Morin, C. M., & Ware, C. (1996). Sleep and psychopathology. *Applied and Preventive Psychology, 5,* 211–224.

Murtagh, D. R. R., & Greenwood, K. M. (1995). Identifying effective psychological treatments for insomnia: A meta-analysis. *Journal of Consulting and Clinical Psychology, 63,* 79–89.

National Institutes of Health. (1994). Wake up America: A national sleep alert. *Report of the national commission on sleep disorders research* (Vol. 2, Working groups reports). Washington, DC: U.S. Government Printing Office.

National Institutes of Health. (1996). NIH releases statement on behavioral and relaxation approaches for chronic pain and insomnia. *American Family Physician, 53,* 1877–1880.

Nowell, P. D., Mazumdar, S., Buysse, D. J., Dew, M. A., Reynolds, C. F., & Kupfer, D. J. (1997). Benzodiazepines and zolpidem for chronic insomnia: A meta-analysis of treatment efficacy. *Journal of the American Medical Association, 278,* 2170–2177.

Ohayon, M., & Caulet, M. (1996). Psychotropic medication and insomnia complaints in two epidemiological studies. *Canadian Journal of Psychiatry, 41,* 457–464.

Parkes, J. D. (1985). *Sleep and its disorders.* Philadelphia: Saunders.

Pressman, M. R., Gollomp, S., Benz, R. L., & Peterson, D. D. (1997). Sleep and sleep disorders in non-cardiopulmonary diseases. In M. R. Pressman & W. C. Orr (Eds.), *Understanding sleep: The evaluation and treatment of sleep disorders* (pp. 371–384). Washington, DC: American Psychological Association.

Ray, W. A. (1992). Psychotropic drugs and injuries among the elderly: A review. *Journal of Clinical Psychopharmacology, 12,* 386–396.

Rechtschaffen, A., Gilliland, M. A., Bergmann, B. M., & Winter, J. B. (1983). Physiological correlates of prolonged sleep deprivation in rats. *Science, 221,* 182–184.

Rosen, R. C., Lewin, D. S., Goldberg, L., & Woolfolk, R. I. (2000). Psychophysiological insomnia: Combined effects of pharmacotherapy and relaxation-based treatments. *Sleep Medicine, 1,* 279–288.

Rothenberg, S. A. (1992). A pilot survey in the medical community on the use of behavioral treatment for insomnia. *Sleep Research, 21,* 355.

Sadeh, A., Hauri, P. J., Kripke, D. F., & Lavie, P. (1995). The role of actigraphy in the evaluation of sleep disorders. *Sleep, 18*(4), 288–302.

Sateia, M. J., Doghramji, K., Hauri, P. J., & Morin, C. M. (2000). Evaluation of chronic insomnia. *Sleep, 23,* 243–308.

Savard, J., Miller, S. M., Mills, M., O'Leary, A., Harding, H., Douglas, S. D., et al. (1999). Association between subjective sleep quality and depression on immunocompetence in low-income women at risk for cervical cancer. *Psychosomatic Medicine, 61,* 496–507.

Savard, J., & Morin, C. M. (2001). Insomnia in the context of cancer: A review of a neglected problem. *Journal of Clinical Oncology, 19,* 895–908.

Savard, J., Simard, S., Blanchet, J., Ivers, H., & Morin, C. M. (2001). Prevalence, clinical characteristics, and risk factors for insomnia in the context of breast cancer. *Sleep, 24,* 583–589.

Schramm, E., Hohagen, F., Grasshoff, U., Riemann, D., Hujak, G., Weeb, H. G., et al. (1993). Test-retest reliability and validity of the structured interview for sleep disorders according to *DSM-III-R. American Journal of Psychiatry, 150,* 867–872.

Simon, G. E., & VonKorff, M. (1997). Prevalence, burden, and treatment of insomnia in primary care. *American Journal of Psychiatry, 154*(10), 1417–1423.

Spielberger, C. D. (1983). *Manual for the State-Trait Anxiety Inventory* [Form Y]. Palo Alto, CA: Consulting Psychologists Press.

Spielman, A. J., & Glovinsky, P. B. (1997). The diagnostic interview and differential diagnosis for complaints of insomnia. In M. R. Pressman & W. C. Orr (Eds.), *Understanding sleep: The evaluation and treatment of sleep disorders* (pp. 125–160). Washington, DC: American Psychological Association.

Spielman, A. J., Saskin, P., & Thorpy, M. J. (1987). Treatment of chronic insomnia by restriction of time in bed. *Sleep, 10,* 45–56.

Spitzer, R. L., Williams, J. B. W., Gibbon, M., & First, M. B. (1990). *Structured Clinical Interview for DSM-III-R.* Washington, DC: American Psychiatric Press.

Stepanski, E., Koshorek, G., Zorick, F., Glinn, M., Roehrs, T., & Roth, T. E. (1989). Characteristics of individuals who do or do not seek treatment for chronic insomnia. *Psychosomatics, 30,* 421–427.

Sugarman, J. L., Stern, J. A., & Walsh, J. K. (1985). Daytime alertness in subjective and objective insomnia: Some preliminary findings. *Biological Psychiatry, 20,* 741–750.

Sweetwood, H., Grant, I., Kripke, D. F., Gerst, M. S., & Yager, J. (1980). Sleep disorder over time: Psychiatric correlates among males. *British Journal of Psychiatry, 136,* 456–462.

Vollrath, M., Wicki, W., & Angst, J. (1989). The Zurich study. VIII: Insomnia: Association with depression, anxiety, somatic syndromes, and course of insomnia. *European Archives of Psychiatry and Neurological Sciences, 23*(9), 113–124.

Wadworth, A. N., & McTavish, D. (1993). Zopiclone: A review of its pharmacological properties and therapeutic efficacy as an hypnotic. *Drugs and Aging, 3,* 441–459.

Walsh, J. K., & Engelhardt, C. L. (1999). The direct economic costs of insomnia in the U.S. for 1995. *Sleep, 22,* S386–S393.

Walsleben, J. A. (1997). Sleep and sleep disorders in cardiopulmonary diseases. In M. R. Pressman & W. C. Orr (Eds.), *Understanding sleep: The evaluation and treatment of sleep disorders* (pp. 359–370). Washington, DC: American Psychological Association.

Webb, W. B., & Agnew, H. W. (1974). The effects of chronic limitation of sleep length. *Psychophysiology, 11,* 265–274.

Webb, W. B., & Campbell, S. S. (1980). Awakenings and the return to sleep in an older population. *Sleep, 3,* 41–46.

Wingard, D. L., & Berkman, L. F. (1983). Mortality risk associated with sleeping patterns among adults. *Sleep, 6*(2), 102–107.

Zammit, G. K., Weiner, J., Damato, N., Sillup, G. P., & McMillan, C. A. (1999). Quality of life in people with insomnia. *Sleep, 22*(Suppl. 2), S379–S385.

CHAPTER 15

Coronary Heart Disease and Hypertension

MARK O'CALLAHAN, AMY M. ANDREWS, AND DAVID S. KRANTZ

Chronic diseases of the cardiovascular system, which include coronary heart disease (CHD), high blood pressure, and stroke, constitute a major public health problem and the leading cause of death in Western countries (American Heart Association, 1999). Many physiological, environmental, and behavioral variables interact in the development of these disorders. For example, many of the causal agents for CHD can be modified, relate to habits of living, and are under the control of the individual. Therefore, coronary heart disease can be thought of as a disorder that is a result of the individual's lifestyle, and it is not surprising that cardiovascular diseases have been among the most widely studied topics in health psychology (see for example, Baum, Gatchel, & Krantz, 1997; Krantz, Grunberg, & Baum, 1985).

In the United States, CHD continues to be a leading cause of morbidity and mortality. The Center for Disease Control (1996) reports one in five deaths are attributed to this disease process with more men than women and more African Americans than any other group dying from CHD. It is the leading cause of death for men by the age of 45 and for women by the age of 65. The specifics of the relationship between gender, race, and CHD will be discussed in greater detail later in the chapter.

A dramatic decline in mortality from CHD has been seen in the last 40 years. Since 1960, CHD mortality has declined 2% a year in this country. Both lifestyle changes, including diet and exercise, and improvements in the management of the disease medically, such as drug treatment and technology, are responsible for this decline. The epidemiologic literature estimates that greater than half (54%) of the decline between 1960 and 1985 is attributed to lifestyle changes, specifically reductions in cholesterol intake and levels (30%) and cessation of cigarette smoking (24%) (Goldman & Cook, 1984, 1988). The WHO-Monica study (Tunstall-Pedoe, 2000) examined mortality from CHD in diverse populations and found declines attributed both to secondary prevention and advances in treatment, supporting the important link between lifestyle and risk of developing CHD.

This chapter provides a selective overview of behavioral science contributions to understanding the etiology and treatment of two of the major cardiovascular disorders, coronary heart disease and essential hypertension. For comprehensive reviews of various aspects of this vast literature, see Allan and Scheidt (1996), Ockene and Ockene (1992), Rozanski, Blumenthal, and Kaplan (1999), Shumaker and Czajkowski (1994), Dubbert (1995), and Julius and Bassett (1987).

The opinions and the assertions contained herein are those of the authors and are not to be construed as those of USUHS, the U.S. Department of Defense, or the NIH. Preparation of this chapter was supported by grants from the NIH (HL47337) and USUHS (G172CK). Portions of this chapters were adapted from "Cardiovascular Disorders" in D. S. Krantz and N. R. Lundgren, *Comprehensive Clinical Psychology*. Alan S. Bellack and Michel Hersen, eds. New York: Pergamon, 1998.

CORONARY HEART DISEASE

Coronary heart disease, also called coronary artery or ischemic heart disease, is a condition that develops when the coronary arteries supplying blood to the cardiac, or myocardial, tissue become narrowed with fatty plaque deposits, a process called atherosclerosis. Myocardial ischemia, an inadequate supply of blood to the cardiac tissue, results from this coronary artery narrowing and many times is accompanied by chest pain called angina pectoris. Myocardial infarction (death of cardiac tissue), commonly called a heart attack, occurs when the supply of blood flow is stopped due to a complete blockage of the artery from unstable plaque or ischemia that is severe or prolonged. With ischemia and/or infarction, the electrical system of the heart is predisposed to disturbances that can develop into irregular cardiac rhythms, called arrhythmias. Many of these arrhythmias are life-threatening and can cause sudden cardiac death.

Risk Factors for CHD

Coronary heart disease results from many interacting causal factors. Studies, like the Framingham Heart Study (Wilson et al., 1998) show the major risk factors for CHD are additive in predictive power. The risk of an individual can be determined by totaling the risk imparted by each of the major risk factors. Many of these risk factors overlap making CHD a multifactorial disease. The most widely accepted risk factors include high blood pressure, cigarette smoking, increasing age, gender issues, family history, diabetes mellitus, sedentary lifestyle, obesity, stress, personality, and abnormal cholesterol levels.

Certain risk factors are nonmodifiable. These include age, gender, and family history. With aging, risk of developing CHD increases. Nearly half of all coronary victims are over the age of 65. Women develop heart disease at a later age, generally 10 years after men. This is thought to be due to the cardioprotective nature of estrogen before menopause (Saliba, 2000). A positive family history of CHD poses a significant risk factor for the development of heart disease independent of other risk factors. Studies have shown that a family history of CHD particularly creates risk for females and for early onset heart disease (Dzau, 1994; Pohjola-Sintonen, Rissaness, Liskola, & Luomanmaki, 1998). Individuals with various nonmodifiable risk factors such as family history can still decrease their risk by altering other risk factors that are modifiable.

Cigarette smoking, obesity, sedentary lifestyle, high blood pressure, diabetes, and elevated cholesterol levels can be modified—or at least controlled—through medication or behavioral changes, thereby decreasing CHD risk. For example, the Nurse's Health Study (Stampfer, Hu, Manson, Rimm, & Willett, 2000) showed that those individuals who smoked greater than 15 cigarettes a day were at the greatest risk for the development of CHD but, even those who smoked 1 to 14 cigarettes a day tripled their risk over those who did not smoke. There is a direct dose-response relationship of CHD and smoking and a large number of case-controlled and observational studies demonstrate that cigarette smoking doubles the incidence of CHD and increases mortality by 70% (Hennekens, 1998). Although high cholesterol level can be inherited, it is also to some extent related to diet and can be modified. There are several components to blood cholesterol that can be measured including elevated total cholesterol level, elevated low-density lipoprotein cholesterol (LDL), and low high-density lipoprotein (HDL) (Grundy, Pasternak, Greenland, Smith, & Fuster, 1999). Evidence suggests that the ratio of total cholesterol to HDL cholesterol provides the best measure of CHD risk (NCEP, 1993), and a 1% decrease in total cholesterol level is shown to produce a 2% to 3% decreased risk of CHD (La Rosa et al., 1990). Hypertension, diabetes mellitus, and obesity are also often genetically influenced but, like cholesterol levels, can be controlled with lifestyle changes and/or medication. Studies including the Nurse's Health Study (Hu et al., 1997) and the Framingham Heart Study (Wilson, 1994) show a two to threefold risk of CHD in the obese over a healthy weight population. Obesity and lack of physical activity worsen other factors including hypertension, high cholesterol, and diabetes (Hennekens, 1998).

Despite the aforementioned evidence, controversy remains regarding the importance of some of the standard risk factors and the role diet and exercise play in the development of coronary disease. Additionally, there are new findings suggesting that additional risk factors may be important. For example, an increased risk of CHD has been associated with elevated plasma homocysteine levels (Malinow, Bostrum, & Krauss, 1999). The most widely accepted CHD risk factors continue to be smoking, cholesterol levels, and high blood pressure.

Psychosocial Risk Factors

There is increasing recognition that, in addition to so-called standard CHD risk factors, additional variables in the behavioral and psychosocial domain may also contribute to the development and progression of coronary heart disease and are important to consider in efforts at treatment. These variables include aspects of personality, acute and chronic stress, and aspects of the social environment.

Acute Stress and Anger

Research has begun to focus on the role that acute stress and anger may play as triggers for the development of coronary artery disease (CAD; see Krantz, Kop, Santiago, et al., 1996). Previous studies have observed that stressful life events, such as the death of a spouse, often occurred within the 24 hours preceding death among patients who died suddenly from coronary disease (e.g., Cottington, Matthews, Talbott, & Kuller, 1980; Myers & Dewar, 1975). Another study of 95,647 individuals followed up for 4 to 5 years showed the highest relative mortality occurred immediately after bereavement, with a twofold increase in risk for men and a threefold increase in risk for women (Kaprio, Koskenvuo, & Rita, 1987).

The occurrence of natural disasters and personal traumas has also been correlated with an increase in cardiac events. During the Gulf War in 1991, there was a significant increase in fatal and nonfatal cardiac events among populations living close to Tel Aviv, where missile attacks were heaviest (Meisel et al., 1991). During a one-week period following intense missile attacks (January 17–25, 1991), the number of cases of acute MI treated in the intensive care unit of a Tel Aviv hospital was significantly greater than those treated the week prior to the attack and to an index period corresponding to the same week a year earlier. There was also an increase in the sudden death rate during January 1991 as compared to the same period one year earlier. Similarly, the number of sudden cardiac deaths rose sharply, from a daily average of 4.6 in the preceding week to 24 on the day a massive earthquake rocked Los Angeles in 1994 (Leor, Poole, & Kloner, 1996).

Mittleman et al. (1995) compared patients' activities immediately before the occurrence of an MI with their usual levels of activity to assess the immediate physical and mental triggers of onset of MI. In the study, patients were interviewed a median of four days post-MI and 2.4% reported an episode of anger prior to onset of MI. Following these anger episodes, the risk of MI following further episodes of anger was more than twice as high (Figure 15.1).

Researchers have studied the effects of acute stressors on cardiac events in a laboratory setting. Using modeled forms of stress (e.g., mental arithmetic and speaking tasks) and sensitive imaging techniques, researchers were able to induce myocardial ischemia in 30% to 60% of patients with CAD (Krantz, Kop, Santiago, et al., 1996). This mental-stress induced ischemia was observed reliably and frequently in the laboratory in patients with CAD (e.g., Rozanski et al., 1988),

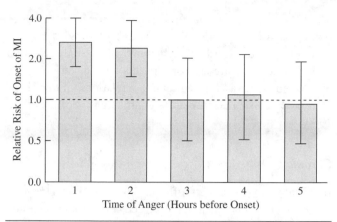

Figure 15.1 Episodes of anger and the relative risk of MI. Reprinted with permission from Mittleman et al. (1995). *Circulation, 92,* 1720–1725.

and was also studied during daily life activities (e.g., Gabbay et al., 1996; Gullette et al., 1997), using ambulatory monitoring devices in conjunction with structured diaries. Researchers have observed behaviors and/or acute stressors that trigger these ischemic episodes or other cardiac events (Kop, 1999). For example, Gabbay et al. (1996) studied 63 CAD patients with evidence of out-of-hospital ischemia by using a structured diary to assess physical and mental activities and psychological states while they underwent ambulatory electrocardiographic monitoring for 24 to 48 hours. Ischemia occurred most often during times of moderately intense physical and mental activities. The emotional state of anger was found to be an especially potent ischemic trigger, and heart rates at onset of ischemia increased with the intensity of anger experienced.

Several research teams studied the possible physiological mechanisms by which acute stress may trigger coronary events. It was found that acute psychological risk factors may result in impaired dilation of the coronary vessels in coronary patients (Howell et al., 1997), decreases in plasma volume (Patterson, Gottdiener, Hecht, Vargot, & Krantz, 1993), and increased platelet activity and blood clotting tendency (Patterson et al., 1995). These responses may result in an imbalance between cardiac demand and decreased coronary blood supply and may lead to cardiac ischemia (Kop, 1999).

Finally, acute psychological factors may also elicit electrical instability of the myocardium and cause life-threatening arrhythmias (Verrier & Mittleman, 1996). Lown (1987) proposed that ventricular arrhythmias occur in presence of three factors: myocardial electrical instability, an acute triggering event (frequently related to mental stress), and a chronic and intense psychological state. Although there is accumulating evidence that psychological factors can trigger malignant arrhythmias (Lampert, Jain, Burg, Batsford, &

McPherson, 2000), some studies have shown no evidence linking occurrence of arrhythmias with psychological factors. For example, the Cardiac Arrhythmia Pilot Study assessed various questionnaire-assessed psychological variables for 353 patients over a year and found no relationship to rates of increased ventricular premature contractions (Follick et al., 1990).

Chronic Stress

In addition to the effects of acute or short-term stressors, the possible pathophysiologic effects of chronic stressors were studied in conjunction with CHD risk. Among the more widely studied variables are occupational stress, low social support, and low SES.

Occupational Stress.   Work-related stress is the most widely studied form of chronic stress. Research has sought to elicit which occupations are most stressful and which characteristics of particular occupations lead to an increased likelihood of developing CAD (Karasek & Theorell, 1990). Several factors were determined to contribute to the amount of stress one experiences on the job. The psychological demands of the job refer to stresses that interfere or tax a worker and make him or her unable to perform at optimal levels. Level of job autonomy or control refers to the ability of the person to influence his or her working conditions, including the nature, speed, and conditions of the work. Job satisfaction includes how many of the worker's needs are met and the level of gratification attained from the overall work experience (Wells, 1985).

Karasek and colleagues (e.g., Karasek & Theorell, 1990) proposed a job demand/control hypothesis in which occupations with high work demands combined with few opportunities to control the work or make decisions (low decision latitudes) are associated with increased coronary disease risk. One prospective study of 1,928 male workers followed for 6 years showed a fourfold increase in risk of cardiovascular system-related death associated with job strain (Karasek, Baker, Marxer, Ahlbom, & Theorell, 1981). Subsequent studies replicated these findings supporting a link between job strain and CAD risk (Theorell et al., 1998) while others found negative relationships between measured job strain and outcomes in cardiac patients (Hlatky et al., 1995). These negative findings may be in part due to the population tested, most of whom (including the controls) were symptomatic, so job strain may have been obscured in such a population (Pickering, 1996).

Other models linking occupational stress to CAD development have been formulated. One such model proposes that work stress is the result of an imbalance between high work demand and low reward (Siegrist, Peter, Junge, Cremer, & Seidel, 1990). This demand-reward imbalance was associated with a 2.15-fold increase in risk for the development of new CAD. This same study, which included 6,895 working men and 3,413 working women aged 35 to 55 years, showed a nearly twofold increase in new CAD cases as a result of low job control (Bosma, Peter, Siegrist, & Marmot, 1998). Peter and Siegrist (2000) found odds-ratios ranging from 1.2 to 5.0 with respect to job strain and CAD, and odds-ratios from 1.5 to 6.1 with respect to effort-reward imbalance. These associations cannot be explained by behavioral or biomedical risk factors, nor by physical and chemical work hazards. Rather they define new, independent occupational risk conditions. This and other new models comparing work stress and subsequent CAD development have been largely positive, suggesting a strong causal relationship between occupational stress and the development of CAD.

Low Levels of Social Support/Isolation/Low SES. Certain chronic aspects of the social environment, including isolation, low social support, and lack of economic and social resources, can increase an individual's risk of developing CAD (Shumaker et al., 1994). Social support refers to the instrumental (i.e., tangible), informational, and emotional support obtained from a person's social ties and community (Cohen & Wills, 1985). In early studies, so-called "social networks" were measured quantitatively by assessing factors such as the extent of one's participation in group and organizational activities or the number of family members or friends present (Rozanski et al., 1999). Some researchers evaluated the role of living arrangements (alone, married, marital disruption), while others focused on instrumental support such as access to community services and activities. It was shown that a small social network confers a two- to threefold increase in the likelihood of developing CAD over time. It is also imperative to look at the qualitative nature of social support (i.e., amount of perceived emotional support). Low levels of perceived emotional support were shown to confer greater than a threefold increase in the risk of future cardiac events (Blazer, 1982). Furthermore, Berkman, Leo-Summers, and Horwitz (1992) showed a threefold increase in future cardiac events in post-MI patients who reported low levels of emotional support, while R. Williams et al. (1992) observed a threefold increase in mortality over a five-year period among CAD patients who were unmarried or had no major confidant in their life.

Other evidence also supports the positive association between social factors and the development of CAD. Cultural and familial support are critical aspects on one's overall social support. One study of 3,809 Japanese Americans living in California classified subjects according to the degree to which they retained their traditional Japanese values and culture (Marmot & Syme, 1976). The group with the highest level of cultural retention were found to develop the same amount of CAD as observed in Japan, while the most acculturated group had a three- to fivefold increase in CAD prevalence. Major CAD risk factors were not able to account for these differences. In 1992, Egolf, Lasker, Wolf, and Potvin published their findings of a 50-year comparison of CAD mortality rates in Roseto, Pennsylvania, and a neighboring town. Initially Roseto was a homogeneous community of three-generation households with lower incidence levels of CAD than the neighboring town despite shared medical resources. Over time, Roseto's homogeneous social structure disappeared while its incidence of CAD increased.

Within industrialized societies, cardiac morbidity and mortality are inversely related to socioeconomic status (SES) with disease rates highest among the poorest individuals. Initially, it was assumed that this disparity was due to differences in medical care and standard risk factors such as smoking and high blood pressure, but evidence shows these are only partly to blame (Luepker et al., 1993). This relationship between cardiac outcome and socioeconomic status is observable whether measured by education, income, or occupation. One study (Ruberman, Weinblatt, Goldberg, & Chaudhary, 1984) found that low-SES men were more likely to experience isolation and life stress. These men were also found to have a mortality rate twice as high as their more educated counterparts. It was also found that low SES is associated with increased levels of high-risk behaviors (Winkleby, Fortmann, & Barrett, 1990) and psychosocial risk factors (Barefoot et al., 1991).

The reasons for the differences between SES groups in CAD development are complex and need to be studied more extensively. Some studies have suggested that there may be a fetal origin to the development of CAD. These studies have hypothesized that individuals with a low birth weight have a tendency later in life to respond adversely to CAD risk factors, thus putting them at higher risk for developing the disease. Since babies born into low SES families are more prone to lower birth weights relative to their higher SES peers, it is possible that the adverse effects of low SES on the development of CAD begin at a very early age and are cumulative throughout life (Eriksson et al., 1999). Since the disparity between different SES groups is high with regard to risk of CAD development, it remains a major public health challenge to bring mortality rates of lower SES groups down to the level of their higher SES peers.

Gender and Race

Coronary artery disease remains the leading cause of death in the United States. This relationship remains among men and women and among both Caucasians and African Americans. Moreover, African Americans are at an increased risk of developing premature CAD, and the proportion of African Americans that die from CAD is at least as large as their Caucasian counterparts (American Heart Association, 1997). Among women, the onset of disease is usually later (postmenopause), but once CAD develops the case-fatality rate is higher than for men (Douglas, 1997). While both of these groups make up a large portion of the population suffering from cardiovascular disease, research and treatment has historically catered to the needs of Caucasian males. The psychosocial risk factors that affect minorities and women is discussed in this section.

It was once thought that women were spared from developing CAD, atherosclerosis, and other cardiovascular disorders relative to their male counterparts. Although studies have shown that while most premenopausal women are somewhat protected from developing CAD, postmenopausal women develop the disease at a much faster rate, with the overall incidence curve for women lagging about 10 years behind that for males (Higgins & Thom, 1993). The majority of this protective effect has been attributed to estrogen. In fact, the provision of estrogen replacement to initially healthy postmenopausal women has been associated with a significant reduction in the risk of CAD development (Manson, 1994). However, since CAD and atherosclerosis develop over decades, it is likely that clinical events occurring in postmenopausal women have their origins in the premenopausal years. This hypothesis is supported by a study that found extensive atherosclerosis in many premenopausal women (Sutton-Tyrrell et al., 1998). Another possibility is that women with ovarian abnormalities or failure have reduced amounts of endogenous estrogen, leaving them more susceptible to CAD development in later years (Rozanski et al., 1999).

In addition to possible gender differences in CAD pathophysiology, women also are less likely to get revascularization procedures and cardiac catheterizations while hospitalized, and also are prescribed fewer standard cardiac medications such as beta-blockers and nitroglycerin (Stone et al., 1996). Historically, CAD has been less studied in women, leaving physicians with fewer diagnostic strategies and treatment criteria for properly treating women. Another possibility is that there are either subtle or overt gender biases that drive the differences in care between men and women. For example, physicians may be influenced by stereotypes of gender behavior, which could have a profound effect on their decision making, diagnosis, and treatment of CAD (American Medical Association, 1991).

In addition to standard risk factors, psychosocial factors also contribute extensively to a woman's risk of developing CAD. The Framingham Heart Study longitudinally followed participants for 20 years and assessed CAD risk factors specific to women. After controlling for standard biological risk factors, the researchers found that among all women tension and infrequent vacations (once every six years or less) were independent predictors of coronary death. Among homemakers (the group most likely to be effected by psychosocial risk factors), loneliness, infrequent vacations, and the belief that one is more prone to heart disease were all predictors of the development of heart disease. The researchers argue that these findings reflect a coronary-prone situation in which women may feel isolated and lacking control, rather than a coronary-prone personality as is often believed (Eaker, Pinsky, & Castelli, 1992).

Similarly, there are also disparities in the treatment and care of African American cardiac patients in comparison to their Caucasian counterparts. Oberman and Cutter (1984) found that African American patients were less likely to undergo cardiac catheterization or bypass surgery than Caucasian patients, while Haywood (1984) found that African Americans enrolled in a beta-blocker trial had higher long-term mortality rates than Caucasians. These studies were notable because the investigators were able to control for disease burden in their analyses, thus refuting the idea that racial cardiac care differences could be largely attributed to differences in disease severity. However, a more recent study found that the lower number of cardiac catheterizations among African Americans was a reflection of overuse in the Caucasian population (Ferguson, Adams, & Weinberger, 1998). Another study, which controlled for the "appropriateness" of surgery, demonstrated that racial disparities in CABG rates are independent of available clinical factors (Laouri et al., 1997). One possible reason for these disparities may be the difference in anatomic manifestations of coronary disease between African Americans and Caucasians. It is known that the prevalence of cardiac risk factors (diabetes, hypertension, etc.) and the clustering of several risk factors for a single patient are higher in African American patients, yet despite this higher risk profile, they are diagnosed with less extensive diseases at time of catheterization (Peniston, Lu, Papademetriou, & Fletcher, 2000). Furthermore, these researchers also found that African Americans were less likely to be treated with beta-blockers at the time of catheterization. If this trend were to persist on a long-term basis, African Americans would be more likely to have negative prognoses in the future.

Socioeconomic status may also contribute to cardiac treatment and outcome. An important study by Wenneker and Epstein (1989) used zip codes to provide an estimate of individual income. After controlling for income in this way and for other clinical and demographic variables, they found that African Americans still received significantly fewer cardiac catheterizations and CABG surgeries. Another study in New York state that also used zip code-based income estimates found race to independently predict use of catheterization and CABG (Hannan, Kilburn, O'Donnell, Lukacik, & Shields, 1991). Geography and/or distance from the hospital may also play a role in coronary care disparity among African Americans and Caucasians. While Taylor, Meyers, Morse, and Pearson (1997) found that controlling for distance to the hospital did little to negate racial differences in procedure rates, others studies showed opposing results (Blustein & Weitzman, 1995; Goldberg, Hartz, Jacobsen, Krakauer, & Rimm, 1992). Goldberg et al. also found that extent of disparity in CABG use among different races varied geographically, with the greatest disparity in the rural southeast. Differences in health insurance status may also contribute to African American/Caucasian differences in cardiac care. Studies in Massachusetts, New York state, and Los Angeles County all controlled for insurance status still found race differences in cardiac procedures to persist (Carlisle, Leake, & Shapiro, 1997; Hannan et al., 1991; Wenneker et al., 1989). Two large studies of the Veterans Administration hospital system, which provides nearly identical coverage to all eligible veterans, found that racial differences still existed (Peterson, Wright, Daley, & Thibault, 1994; Whittle, Conigliaro, Good, & Lofgren, 1993). It should be noted that other studies have found little evidence of race differences based on health insurance status (Daumit, Hermann, Coresh, & Powe, 1999; Taylor et al., 1997).

Also among the psychological variables currently being studied is the influence of patient preferences and physician decision making. One study found a strong trend toward an independent association between race and likelihood of undergoing cardiac catheterization (Schecter et al., 1996). Whittle, Conigliaro, Good, and Joswiak (1997) found that 52% of African Americans would accept their physician's recommendation for PTCA (percutaneous transluminal coronary angiography) while 70% of Caucasians would accept the decision. The reasons behind these disparities are surely multifaceted and may include trust in the medical system and cultural/religious beliefs (Sheifer, Escarce, & Schulman, 2000). Physician decision making also appears to play a role in race differences in cardiac care, with conscious or subconscious racial biases possibly influencing the decision-making process (Thomson, 1997). Schulman et al. (1999) assessed physician management of hypothetical patients with chest pain. Physicians were given six experimental factors (race, gender, age, type of chest pain, coronary risk factors, and thallium stress test results) and asked whether they recommend a cardiac catheterization for each patient. The investigators found race was an independent predictor of catheterization referral. A physician's subconscious bias may cause this disparity, thus it is important to train physicians on issues such as racial stereotypes and how they effect diagnoses and referrals.

Summary

There is evidence that both acute and chronic stress may either promote the development of or trigger CHD events. Key chronic risk factors include job strain, low social support, and lack of economic resources (i.e., low socioeconomic status). Recent evidence also suggests that anger is an emotion that may potentially trigger cardiac events such as myocardial infarction and ischemia. Two other very important variables, race and gender, have gained much attention as data mounts that both may play complex roles in the development of cardiac disease.

Individual Characteristics as CAD Risk Factors

In addition to environmental and social variables, several specific individual behavioral traits have been studied as possible CHD risk factors. These include hostility and Type A behavior, and depression and related traits.

Type A Behavior: Current Status

In 1959, cardiologists Friedman and Rosenman identified a "coronary-prone" personality type characterized by hostility, an overly competitive drive, impatience, and vigorous speech characteristics. They termed this Type A behavior pattern (as opposed to Type B, a behavior pattern with a relatively easy-going style of coping). Friedman and Rosenman (1974) developed a structured interview to measure Type A behavior based on observable behaviors and the manner in which subjects responded to questions. This objective interview showed a stronger relationship to risk of developing coronary disease as opposed to previously used scales which relied heavily on a subjects' self-report of their own behavior (Matthews & Haynes, 1986).

Interest in Type A behavior accelerated after the Western Collaborative Group Study (WCGS), which tracked over 3,000 men for 8.5 years (Rosenman et al., 1975). The researchers found that Type A behavior was associated with a twofold increased risk of developing CAD and a fivefold increased risk of recurrent MI. In the 1980 Framingham Heart Study, Haynes, Feinleib, and Kannel (1980) found Type A behavior to be a predictor of coronary disease among men in white collar occupations and in women working outside of the home.

Since the 1980s, however, most studies have not been able to verify a relationship between Type A behavior and CAD risk. The Multiple Risk Factor Intervention Trial (MRFIT) was primarily designed to assess whether interventions to modify coronary risk factors such as high cholesterol levels, smoking, and high blood pressure in high-risk men would reduce the likelihood of coronary disease in these individuals. Type A behavior was measured in over 3,000 of the participants who were then followed for seven years. The researchers found no relationships between the behavior pattern and incidence of a first heart attack (Shekelle, Hulley, & Neaton, 1985), which has clearly cast doubt on the validity of initial studies that found positive relationship between Type A behavior and coronary disease. Many researchers now believe that not all components of Type A behavior are pathogenic, but rather specific personality traits such as hostility and anger may be associated with coronary disease.

Anger and Hostility

Research suggests that hostility and anger, which are both major components of Type A behavior that have been frequently correlated with coronary disease risk. A reanalysis of data from the WCGS described earlier showed that "potential for hostility," vigorous speech, and reports of frequent anger and irritation were the strongest predictors of coronary disease (Matthews, Glass, Rosenman, & Bortner, 1977). Likewise, the MRFIT study, which did not find that Type A behavior was predictive of coronary disease, found an association of hostility with coronary disease risk (Dembroski, MacDougall, Costa, & Grandits, 1989).

Hostility is a broad concept that encompasses traits such as anger (an emotion), and cynicism and mistrust (attitudes). It is also important to note the difference between the experience of hostility, a subjective process including angry feelings or cynical thoughts, and the expression of hostility, a more observable component which includes acts of verbal or physical aggression (Siegman, 1994). These overt, expressive aspects of hostility have generally been found to have a greater correlation with coronary heart disease, including confirmed myocardial infarction (Miller, Smith, Turner, Guijarro, & Hallet, 1996) even after controlling for other risk factors.

The Cook and Medley Hostility Inventory (Cook & Medley, 1954), which measures hostile attitudes such as cynicism and mistrust of others, was shown to be related to occurrence of coronary disease (Barefoot & Lipkus, 1994). One study involved a 25-year follow-up of physicians who completed the Minnesota Multiphasic Personality Inventory (MMPI; a precursor to the Cook-Medley scale) while in medical school. High scores on the MMPI predicted incidence of coronary disease and mortality from all causes, independent of smoking, age, high blood pressure, and other risk factors (Barefoot, Dahlstrom, & Williams, 1983). Another study has shown evidence that low hostility scores are associated with decreased death rates during a 20-year follow-up of nearly 1,900 subjects in the Western Electric Study (Shekelle, Gale, Ostfeld, & Paul, 1983). Later research indicated that hostility scores on the Cook-Medley are higher among certain groups, particularly men and non-Caucasians in the United States, and are positively correlated to smoking prevalence (Siegler, 1994). These findings make it possible to hypothesize that hostility may account for some of the gender and socioeconomic differences in mortality rates from cardiovascular diseases (Stoney & Engebretson, 1994).

Presence of the emotional trait of anger has also been studied as a possible risk factor for coronary disease. One study used various scales tailored specifically to anger traits and found a significant gradient between anger levels and the frequency of subsequent cardiac events (Kawachi, Sparrow, Spiro, Vokonas, & Weiss, 1996). More recently, researchers studied nearly 13,000 individuals (including African American and Caucasian individuals of either gender) and measured anger using the Speilberger Trait Anger Scale. Each individual was classified as either having high, middle, or low anger traits, with high scorers tending to be slightly younger males. Individuals who were the most anger-prone were 2.7 times more likely to have MI than those with the lowest anger ratings (J. Williams et al., 2000).

Clinical and Subclinical Depression

Approximately one in five cardiac patients can be diagnosed with the signs and symptoms of clinical depression. Depressive symptoms (not limited to major depression) following MI has been associated with a three- to fourfold increase in risk of cardiac mortality (Frasure-Smith, Lesperance, & Talajic, 1993). These and other findings have enabled the medical community to label depression as the most prevalent and epidemiologically relevant psychosocial risk factor for cardiovascular disease (Wulsin, Vaillant, & Wells, 1999).

Clinical depression can be diagnosed if a patient experiences sadness or loss of interest or pleasure in most usual activities that often interferes with his or her personal, occupational, or social activities. Other symptoms such as sleep difficulties, loss of appetite or weight, fatigue, and thoughts of suicide or death

are often present as well (APA, 1994). Depression that coexists with cardiac disease is often hard to diagnose, for patients often attribute their symptoms, such as fatigue and other unexplained somatic symptoms, to their heart disease. Also, cardiac patients often replace typical symptoms such as sadness and guilt with less typical symptoms such as irritability and anxiety (Fava, Abraham, Pava, Shuster, & Rosenbaum, 1996). In addition, studies suggest that symptoms that fall short of frank clinical depression may also confer increased risk of poor outcomes in CAD patients (Anda et al., 1993; Hans, Carney, Freedland, & Skala, 1996; Schliefer, Macari-Hinson, & Coyle, 1989).

The presence of a major depressive episode in coronary patients is associated with poor psychosocial rehabilitation and increased medical morbidity (Carney, Freedland, Rich, & Jaffe, 1995). Several studies have followed the clinical course of depressed versus nondepressed cardiac patients and have found an increase in events and lower mortality rates associated with depression. Frasure-Smith et al. (1993) prospectively followed 222 post-MI patients and found that a diagnosis of major depression has a strong association with mortality in the six months following hospital discharge. Another study followed patients for one year and found diagnosis of major depressive disorder at the time of angiography to be the best predictor of a significant cardiac event, including such things as death, reinfarction, and bypass (Carney et al., 1987). Schleifer, Keller, Bond, Cohen, and Stein (1989) found that depressed patients had higher rates of rehospitalization and reinfarction than their nondepressed peers. More recently, two studies reported that initially healthy populations who begin to experience a major depressive episode (Pratt et al., 1996) or worsening of depressive symptoms (Wassertheil-Smoller et al., 1996) are more likely to develop cardiac events in the future. A similar set of studies (e.g., Appels, 1990; Kop, Appels, Mendes de Leon, de Swart, & Bar, 1994) suggested that symptoms of exhaustion or fatigue, even in the absence of other clinical symptoms or depressive affect, are predictive of subsequent development or worsening of cardiovascular events or symptoms. This concept of a fatigue syndrome has been termed "vital exhaustion" (Appels, 1990) and its predictive value cannot be explained by the effects of illness on mood or energy level (Kop et al., 1994).

There are several mechanisms that may explain the link between depression and mortality in coronary patients. Carney, Freedland, et al. (1995) suggest that depressed cardiac patients are less likely to comply with medical therapeutic and exercise regimens. Amick and Ockene (1994) believe that a lack of compliance can often be attributed to an unsupportive social network. Others attributed depression in cardiac patients to the use of beta-blockers. However, over the first 30 months of the Beta-Blocker Heart Attack Trial, no difference was found between placebo and treatment groups in the percentage of patients who reported depressive episodes (Davis, Furberg, & Williams, 1987). Perhaps the most promising avenue of research has linked depression to reduced heart rate variability (a measure of cardiac autonomic function, specifically vagal tone in this instance) which is known to be a risk factor for sudden cardiac death (Carney, Saunders, et al., 1995). Research on mechanisms linking clinical depression to increased cardiac morbidity and mortality is ongoing and promises to be a fruitful area for further exploration. Rozanski et al. (1999) summarized many of the most important studies linking coronary artery disease and depression (see Table 15.1).

TABLE 15.1 Studies of Depression and Coronary Artery Disease

Study	No. of Subjects	F/U, y	Scales	End Points	Statistical Results
Healthy subjects					
Anda et al., 1993	2832	12.4	SS of generalized well-being schedule	CD, non-fatal IHD	RR for depressive sx = 1.5 (1.0–2.3)
					RR for severe hopelessness = 2.1 (1.1–3.9)
Arooma et al., 1994	5355	6.6	SS of GHQ	MI	RR for depressive sx = 3.5 (1.8–6.8)
			SS of PSE	MI, CHF, CVA,	
Vogt et al., 1994	2573	15	Investigator-tailored scale	ACM	*P* = NS for depressive sx
Everson et al., 1996	2428	6	SS of MMPI	CD; ACM	RR for severe hopelessness = 2.3 (1.1–3.9)
			Hopelessness scale		RR for moderate hopelessness = 1.6 (1.0–2.5)
Wassertheil-Smoller et al., 1996	4736	4.5	CES-D scale	ACM, CD, MI; CVA	*P* = NS for baseline depressive sx
					RR for increasing depressive sx = 1.3 (1.2–1.4)
Pratt et al., 1996	1551	13	DIS	MI	RR for MDE = 4.5 (1.7–12.4) RR for dysphoria = 2.1 (1.2–3.7)
Barefoot et al., 1996	730		OBD SS of MMPI	CD; MI	RR for depressive sx = 1.7 (1.2–2.3) (for MI)*
Ford et al., 1998	1190	37	Tailored scale	MI	RR for depressive sx = 2.1 (1.2–4.1)
Known disease					
Kennedy et al., 1987	88 pts; syncope or arrhythmia	1.5	Tailored scale	CD	*P* = 0.01 for depressive sx
Carney et al., 1988	52; CAD on cath	1.0	DIS	CD, MI, PTCA; CABG	RR for MDE = 2.5, *P* < 0.02†
Ahern et al., 1990	502, s/p MI and arrhythmia	1.0	BDI	ACM; CD	*P* < 0.05 for depressive sx
Frasure-Smith et al., 1995	222, s/p MI	1.5	DIS; BDI	CD	RR for MDE = 3.6 (1.3–10.1) RR for depressive sx = 7.8 (2.4–25.3)
Barefoot et al., 1996	1250; s/p MI	15.2	Zung Self-Rating Depression scale	CD	*P* = 0.002 for depressive sx
Denoillet et al., 1998	87; s/p MI & EF < 50%	7.9	Million Behavioral Health Inventory and BDI	CD; MI	RR for depressive sx = 4.3 (1.4–13.3)
Hermann et al., 1998	273, cardiopulmonary	1.9	HADS	ACM	RR for depressive sx = 2.6 (1.1–6.3)
Frasure-Smith et al., 1999	896, s/p MI	1.0	BDI	CD	RR for depressive sx = 3.2 (1.7–6.3)

F/U indicates follow-up; RR, risk ratio; pts, patients; cath, catheterization; s/p, status post; MI, myocardial infarction; EF, ejection fraction; SS, subscale; GHQ, General Health Questionnaire; PSE, Present State Examination; MMPI = Minnesota Multiphasic Personality Inventory; CES-D, Center for Epidemiological Studies–Depression; DIS, Mental Health Diagnostic Interview Schedule (*DSM-III* diagnosis of depression); OBD, obvious depression; BDI, Beck Diagnostic Interview (measures depressive symptoms); HADS, Hospital Anxiety and Depression Scale; CD, cardiac death; IHD, ischemic heart disease; CHF, congestive heart failure; CVA, cerebrovascular accident; ACM, all-cause mortality; Sx, symptom; and MDE, major depression episode.
*RR for cardiac death = 1.62, *P* < 0.03; †no CI reported.
Source: Reprinted with permission from Rozanski et al. (1999). *Circulation, 99,* 2192–2217.

Stress Reactivity

It was proposed that acute and chronic stress may lead to cardiac pathology via neural, endocrine, and cardiovascular pathways (Krantz, Kop, Gabbay, et al., 1996). Research has long shown that individuals physiologically respond differently to stress and that these responses (termed reactivity) to emotional stress may play a role in the development of cardiovascular diseases and/or high blood pressure (see Krantz & Manuck, 1984; Manuck, 1994). Reactivity is measured by assessing the cardiovascular and/or hormonal changes in response to stress as compared to resting levels of physiological variables. Individuals vary greatly in the magnitude of physiological responses to stress, with some people ("hot reactors") demonstrating sizable increases in response to challenging tasks, while others show little or no changes from resting levels. For example, some evidence indicates that behaviors associated with hostile Type A individuals are accompanied by similar kinds of cardiovascular and neuroendocrine responses thought to link psychosocial stress to cardiovascular disease (Contrada & Krantz, 1988; Krantz & Durel, 1983; Matthews, 1982). Researchers have explored the possibility that excessive reactivity to stress may itself be a risk factor or marker of risk for coronary disease. One study followed initially healthy men for 23 years and found the magnitude of their diastolic blood pressure reactions to a cold pressor test (immersing the hand in cold water) predicted later heart disease to a greater degree than standard risk factors assessed in the study (Keys et al., 1971). However, a later study (Coresh, Klag, Mead, Liang, & Whelton, 1992) failed to replicate these results. More recently, we observed that, among cardiac patients, high diastolic blood responders to stress were more likely to suffer cardiac events over a 3.5 year follow-up period (Krantz et al., 1999).

Treatment of Coronary Heart Disease

Medical and surgical treatment for coronary heart disease has made great strides in the past 30 years. Among the major developments include a variety of effective cardiac medications and procedures (e.g., coronary angioplasty). Nevertheless, evidence suggests that behavioral interventions can further improve medical and psychological outcomes in CAD. In this section, we review medical and surgical management approaches, followed by a discussion of behavioral and lifestyle treatments.

Medical and Surgical Treatment

Current guidelines for medical treatment of CHD include aspirin, which reduces clotting of platelets in the arteries, beta-blockers and calcium channel blockers, which act to reduce ischemia and may help to prevent myocardial infarction and sudden death, long acting nitrates, to dilate arteries in order to reduce angina, and lipid lowering drugs, which lower dangerous cholesterol levels. A now common medical procedure aimed to open up blocked coronary arteries, percutaneous transluminal coronary angiography (PTCA), involves threading a catheter-borne balloon up to the heart via the groin. The balloon is inflated at the site of blockage. By the same method, stents (coiled wires that provide structural support to an artery) are placed at the blockages or rotating blades break up plaque. The surgical treatment for CHD is coronary artery bypass graphing (CABG), during which the heart is revascularized by bypassing diseased arteries with veins from the leg or with an artery from the chest. Studies like the Veteran's Administration Cooperative Study (VA Study), the Coronary Artery Surgery Study (CASS), and the European Coronary Surgery Study (ECSS) compared the efficacy of these treatments and found that for patients that have three or more vessels or the important left main vessel diseased have a greater 10-year survival if surgically treated with CABG. Those patients without left main coronary involvement and less than three vessels diseased show no difference in prognosis between medical and surgical therapy, although surgery provides more symptom relief and better quality of life (Gibbons et al., 1999).

Exercise and Behavioral Components of Cardiac Rehabilitation

Cardiac rehabilitation, or risk factor intervention, aims to extend survival, improve quality of life, decrease the need for interventional procedures, and reduce incidence of myocardial infarction. Combined with medical and surgical treatment, comprehensive cardiac rehabilitation is shown to improve outcomes for coronary heart disease patients including the elderly and women (Eagle et al., 1999). The American Heart Association's recommendations for comprehensive risk reduction involve complete cessation of smoking, lipid management through drug treatment, and a diet low in saturated fats, physical activity a minimum of 30 minutes three times a week, weight management, blood pressure control through diet, reduced alcohol intake, sodium restriction, and estrogen replacement therapy for postmenopausal women (Smith et al., 1995). Evidence supports that these more moderate lifestyle changes correlate with less disease progression (Gibbons et al., 1999).

Exercise training is often the core of a cardiac rehabilitation program, since physical inactivity is an independent risk factor for CHD. Aerobic exercise increases exercise tolerance, helps in weight loss, lowers blood pressure, controls glucose levels in diabetics, raises HDL cholesterol, and lowers LDL cholesterol and triglycerides. Additionally, psychological factors including anxiety and depression improve for cardiac patients who undergo rehabilitation and physically fit individuals also have attenuated hemodynamic and neuroendocrine responses to behavioral stressors (Blumenthal & Wei, 1993; Lavie & Milani, 1997). Because recent evidence suggests that stress management and pyschosocial treatments have beneficial effects on morbidity and quality of life, these interventions are reviewed in detail in the following section.

Psychosocial Treatment Approaches/Implementation of Lifestyle Changes

Modifying Hostility and Type A Behavior

A number of intervention studies have attempted to modify Type A behavior in an attempt to reduce cardiovascular disease risk. Most early studies reported that elements of Type A behavior can be decreased in subjects who are motivated to change (Allan & Scheidt, 1996; Suinn, 1982). Nunes, Frank, and Kornfeld (1987) performed a meta-analysis of relevant literature and found that treatment of the Type A behavior pattern using a combination of treatment techniques reduced coronary events by about 50%. This finding should be taken cautiously, however, for it was based on a limited number of studies conducted prior to 1987.

The Recurrent Coronary Prevention Project (RCPP) (Friedman et al., 1986) was the first and most ambitious intervention trial to solely study whether Type A behavior could be modified, and how this modification might impact one's risk of cardiovascular morbidity and mortality. The study looked at a variety of Type A behaviors, including anger, impatience, aggressiveness, and irritability. Over 1,000 patients were assigned to one of three groups: a cardiology counseling treatment group, a combined cardiology counseling and Type A behavior modification group, or a nontreatment control group. The cardiology counseling included training on how to comply with drug, dietary, and exercise regimens as dictated by the participant's physician, counseling on non-Type A psychological problems resulting from the coronary experience, and education about all aspects of cardiovascular disease. Type A counseling included drills to modify various Type A behaviors, discussions on values and beliefs that may cause the behavior pattern, relaxation and stress reduction training to decrease physiological arousal, and changes in work and home demands.

After 4.5 years, the final results showed a larger decrease in global Type A behaviors as well as in its components in the Type-A counseling group. Also, rate of recurrent MI was significantly lower in the Type-A counseling group than in either the cardiology counseling or control groups (Friedman et al., 1986). However, recent evidence points to the fact that much of the reduced cardiac recurrences in the Type A counseling group may be attributed to multiple causes, including increased number of treatment contacts and increased social support (Mendes de Leon, Powell, & Kaplan, 1991).

Hostility is a specific component of Type A behavior that is a significant psychosocial risk factor for cardiovascular disease development. Girdon, Davidson, and Bata (1999) studied the effects of a hostility-reduction intervention on patients with coronary heart disease. Twenty-two highly hostile male coronary patients were randomly assigned to either a hostility intervention group or an information-control group. Those in the intervention group were observed at immediate and two-month follow-ups to be less hostile than controls, as assessed using self-report and structured interviews, and to have significantly lower diastolic blood pressures. Further investigations promise to provide insight into the role of hostility reduction in relation to cardiovascular disease.

Interventions to Increase Social Support and Reduce Life Stress

The Ischemic Heart Disease Life Stress Monitoring Program (Frasure-Smith & Prince, 1987, 1989) was based on prior studies that indicated that periods of increased life stress may precede recurrences of MI (e.g., Rahe & Lind, 1971; Wolff, 1952). Post-MI patients were either assigned to a treatment group ($n = 229$), which included life stress monitoring and intervention, or a control group ($n = 224$), which received only routine medical follow-up care. Patients in the treatment group were contacted by phone on a monthly basis and asked to rate 20 symptoms of distress, including insomnia and feelings of depression. If stress levels surpassed a critical level (more than 4 of the 20 symptoms), a project nurse made a home visit to attempt to help the patient assess the cause of the distress and to help the patient cope with the stressors. Over a one-year period, nearly half of the treatment group needed an intervention and received on average five to six hours of counseling, education on heart disease, and emotional and social support. Results showed that during the year of the project there was a 50% reduction in cardiac deaths, a reduction that continued for six months beyond the project's completion. Over seven years following the study, there were fewer MI recurrences among patients in the treatment group (Frasure-Smith & Prince, 1989).

The success of the Ischemic Heart Disease Life Stress Monitoring Program could at least partly be attributed to the social and emotional support given to the patients that helped ameliorate depression and feelings of distress, thereby reducing physiological arousal and its negative effects on the cardiovascular system. Specific aspects of the treatment program, including its individualized interventions and treatment based on an individual's stress score, may have also contributed to the programs success. However, these promising findings unfortunately do not hold up after additional study. Frasure-Smith et al. (1997) conducted the Montreal Heart Attack Readjustment Trial (M-HART), a randomized, controlled study of 1,376 post-MI patients assigned to either an intervention group, which received home-nursing visits and monthly telephone monitoring to help deal with stress, or a control group which received usual care. After one year, the program was found to have no overall survival impact. In fact, women in the intervention group had a higher cardiac and all-cause mortality rate than women in the control group (Figure 15.2). There was no evidence of either harm or benefit for men and overall the programs impact on depression and anxiety among survivors was small.

Despite the contradictory findings of these two studies, relatively few clinical studies have been designed specifically to reduce depressive symptoms or increase social support in patients with coronary disease. Based on strong epidemiological evidence that depression and social support are linked to coronary patients, the National Heart, Lung, and Blood Institute (NHLBI) has recently launched the Enhancing Recovery in CHD Patients (ENRICHD) study. The trial is studying 3,000 acute MI patients with depression or perceived low social support at eight different sites over the sampling for women and minorities. Patients were randomly assigned to a psychosocial intervention group, with individual and group therapy tailored to each patient's needs, or a control group that received only usual care. This is the first large, multicenter clinical trial to study the effects of psychosocial interventions on reinfarction and death in acute MI patients who are depressed or have low social support. These findings could pave the way for greater clinical acceptance of psychosocial factors in the treatment and rehabilitation of cardiac patients (The ENRICHD Investigators, 2000).

Long-Term Lifestyle Changes

The Lifestyle Heart Trial, which assessed whether coronary patients could be motivated to and benefit from making and sustaining comprehensive lifestyle changes, is one of the most important intervention studies conducted to date. Ornish and colleagues (1990) randomized 48 patients with moderate to severe coronary heart disease into two groups: an intensive lifestyle change group ($n = 28$) and a control group ($n = 20$). The intensive lifestyle change patients were given a lifestyle-modification program consisting of several components:

1. A 10%-fat vegetarian diet.
2. Stress management training and group support including yoga and mediation in group settings twice a week and individual practice for an hour each day.
3. Smoking cessation.
4. A program to moderate levels of aerobic exercise.

Control group patients were not asked to make lifestyle changes other than those recommended by their cardiologists. The intervention lasted one year and the extent of progression of coronary disease was assessed by comparing coronary angiograms obtained at study onset and at one year.

Study results (Ornish et al., 1990) showed that after one year, experimental group participants were able to make and maintain lifestyle changes with beneficial results, including a 37% reduction in low-density lipoprotein (LDL) cholesterol levels, a 91% reduction in anginal episodes, and a slight reduction in the extent of stenosis (or blockage) in coronary arteries. Controls had very different results, showing only a 6% decrease in LDL cholesterol levels, a 165% increase in reported anginal episodes, and a less significant reduction in the extent of stenosis in coronary arteries. Overall, 82% of participants in the lifestyle intervention group had an average change toward regression of disease. Interestingly, there was a relationship between the extent of adherence to the lifestyle change program and the measured degree of regression of disease, with the most compliant study subjects showing the most improvement in disease status (Figure 15.3).

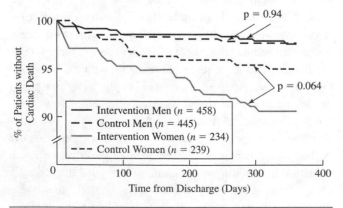

Figure 15.2 Cumulative survival during 365 days after discharge in Intervention and control groups in the M-HART program. Reprinted with permission from Frasure-Smith et al. (1997). *Lancet, 350,* 473–479.

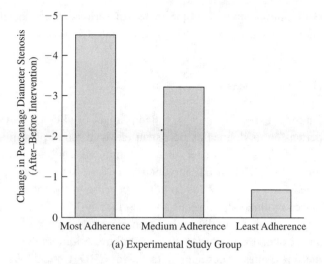

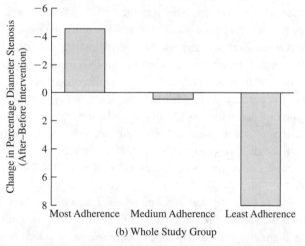

Figure 15.3 Disease regression measured in the (a) experimental study group and (b) whole study group by Ornish et al. Reprinted with permission from Ornish et al. (1990). *Lancet, 336,* 129–133.

After such encouraging findings, Ornish and colleagues extended the study follow-up for four additional years to determine whether participants could adhere to the intensive lifestyle changes and to assess what impact this adherence might have on their disease status (Ornish et al., 1998). The researchers found that on average there was more reduction and continued improvement after five years than after just one year in the intervention patients. However, control group patients showed a continued progression in average percent diameter stenosis over the five years despite the fact that over half of them were prescribed lipid-lowering medications throughout that period. None of the lifestyle change group was prescribed lipid-lowering medications, yet on average, they showed better results than even those in the control group who were taking the medications. The possible

additional benefits these medications might have conferred on the experimental group had they been taken are unknown. The control group experienced twice as many cardiac events per patient as the intervention group did. In addition, the researchers again found that there was a dose-response relationship between adherence to the lifestyle change program and reduction in percent diameter stenosis in coronary arteries.

Another important long-term lifestyle study is the Nurses' Health Study, which followed 85,941 healthy women (no cardiovascular disease or cancer) from 1980 through 1994, monitoring their medical history, lifestyle variables including smoking and diet, and disease development of any kind (Hu, Stampfer, Manson, et al., 2000). These observations were then used to determine what effect lifestyle and other risk factors had on the incidence of CHD. The study found that coronary disease declined by 31% from the two-year period 1980 to 1982 to the two-year period 1992 to 1994. Smoking also declined by 41% from 1980 to 1992, and there was a 175% increase in the use of hormone therapy for postmenopausal women. These variables combined to explain a 21% decline in the incidence of coronary disease over the duration of the study. It was also found that 3% of the study population who had none of the biggest risk factors (smoking, overweight, lack of exercise, and poor diet) had an 83% lower risk of coronary events than the rest of the women (Stampfer et al., 2000). Overall, 82% of coronary events in the study could be attributed to lack of adherence to a low-risk lifestyle as defined in the study.

Blumenthal and colleagues examined the extent to which mental-stress induced ischemia could be modified by exercise stress management and evaluated the impact of these interventions on clinical outcomes. A group of 107 patients with CAD and documented ischemia during either mental stress or ambulatory electrocardiographic monitoring were randomly assigned to a stress management group, an exercise training group, or a normal care control group and titrated from anti-ischemic medications. Myocardial ischemia was reassessed following four months of participation and patients were contacted for up to five years to document subsequent cardiac events. It was found that the stress management group had the lowest risk of experiencing a cardiac event during follow-up, followed by the exercise group, and then the control group. In addition, stress management was also associated with reduced ischemia induced by laboratory mental stress. These data reinforce the notion that behavioral interventions offer additional benefit above and beyond usual cardiac care in patients with documented myocardial ischemia (Figure 15.4) (Blumenthal et al., 1997).

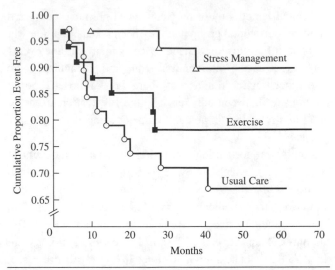

Figure 15.4 Cumulative time-to-event curves for exercise, stress management, and usual care groups. After adjusting for age, baseline left ventricular ejection fraction, and history of myocardial infarction, stress management was associated with a significantly lower risk of an adverse cardiac event compared with usual care. Exercise was also associated with a lower relative risk compared with usual care, but this difference was not statistically significant. The asterisk indicates significantly different from usual care at $P < .05$. *Source:* Reprinted with permission from Blumenthal et al. (1997). *Archives of Internal Medicine, 157,* 2213–2223.

Summary

Evidence has shown that there are several promising behavioral and psychosocial interventions to aid in the treatment and prevention of coronary disease in high-risk individuals. Those described included: cognitive-behavioral interventions directed at lessening and hostility and Type A behavior (RCPP); a tailored program (Ischemic Heart Disease Life Stress Monitoring Program), which provided social support and counseling aimed at reducing life stress; a lifestyle-modification program consisting of a low-fat vegetarian diet, group and individual stress management training, smoking cessation, and moderate levels of aerobic exercise (Lifestyle Heart Trial); and a long-term follow-up study of over 85,000 women which confirmed beliefs that lifestyle choices influence cardiac health. Meta-analyzes of 2,024 patients who received psychosocial treatment and 1,156 control subjects demonstrated that treatment group showed greater reductions in psychological distress, systolic blood pressure, heart rate, and cholesterol levels, while the control subjects showed greater mortality and cardiac recurrences during a two-year follow-up (Linden, Stossel, & Maurice, 1996). The data in this area suggest that it is vital to include psychosocial treatment components in cardiac rehabilitation, and that it is essential to identify the most effective and specific type of psychosocial treatment for each individual. Rozanski et al.

(1999) have summarized the impact of various psychosocial intervention trials on cardiac events (Table 15.2).

HYPERTENSION

Essential hypertension, also called primary or idiopathic hypertension, is defined as persistent elevated blood pressure, systolic pressure greater that 140 mm Hg and diastolic greater than 90 mm Hg, in which there is no single identifiable cause. It is a serious condition because of the burden it places on the body's organs and vascular system. There is a strong positive correlation between elevated blood pressure and stroke, renal failure, and heart failure. Additionally, it is the single most important risk factor for CHD (Cutler, 1996). Essential hypertension accounts for 95% of all hypertension cases. It is estimated that 24% of the adult population in the United States is hypertensive or is taking hypertensive medications (Carretero & Oparil, 2000a). This proportion changes with ethnicity, gender, age, and socioeconomic status. The percentage of African Americans with hypertension is the highest in the world. Additionally, they develop hypertension at an earlier age creating greater complications from the disease (Klag et al., 1997). American Indians and Hispanics have the same or lower rates than non-Hispanic Whites (Hall et al., 1997). More men than women have hypertension until menopause, when the numbers become equal and blood pressure rises with age, creating a greater prevalence in the elderly. Socioeconomic status, frequently an indicator of lifestyle attributes, is inversely related to the prevalence of hypertension (Carretero & Oparil, 2000a). The National Health and Nutrition Examination Survey (NHANES III) found that despite an increase in awareness from 51% in the 1970s to 73% in the 1990s and an increase in the number of people being treated for hypertension, the rate of those with controlled hypertension has *not* improved. Furthermore, the rates of complications from hypertension have risen (Burt et al., 1995).

Genetic and Environmental Interactions

Among the known factors that increase blood pressure are genetics, obesity, high alcohol intake, aging, sedentary lifestyle, stress, high sodium intake, and low intake of calcium and potassium (INTERSALT CO-operative Research Group, 1988; Severs & Poutler, 1989). Thus, essential hypertension appears to be caused by an interaction between genes and an environment that includes one or more or these risk factors. Research involving animal subjects and human twin subjects has shown a genetic link. It has proven that blood

TABLE 15.2 Studies of the Impact of Psychosocial Trials on Cardiac Events

Study	Type of Patients	Number of Patients Control Group	Number of Patients Intervention Group	F/U, y	Type of Intervention	Reduction in Psychosocial Factors?	Cardiac End Points	Reduction in Events?
Rahe et al., 1979	s/p MI	22	39	3	Group education and support	Yes (for overwork; time urgency)	CD/MI	Yes ($P < 0.05$)
Stern et al., 1983	s/p MI	20	35	1	Group counseling	Yes (for depression)	ACM; MI	No
Friedman et al., 1984	s/p MI	270	592	4.5	TABP modification and group counseling	Yes (for TABP)	CD/MI	Yes ($P < 0.005$)
Horlick et al., 1984	s/p MI	33	83	0.5	Hospital-based education program (6 wk)	No (for anxiety; depression)	CD	No
Patel et al., 1985	≥ 2 RF	93	99	4	Breathing, muscle relaxation, meditation	Not assessed	Angina; MI-1; CD	Small sample
Maeland et al., 1987	s/p MI	1115	137	3.3	Educational program	No (for anxiety; depression)	ACM	No*
Dixhoorn et al., 1987	s/p MI	46	42	2.5	Physiological relaxation (e.g., breathing, exercise)	Not assessed	CD; MI; UAP; CABG	Yes ($P = 0.05$)
Frasure-Smith et al., 1989	s/p MI	229	232	5	Home-based nursing intervention	Yes (for GHQ)	MI; CD	Yes ($P = 0.04$ for MI†)
Thompson et al., 1990	60 s/p MI	30	30	0.5	Group counseling	Yes (for anxiety and depression)	ACM	Small sample
Nelson et al., 1994	s/p MI	20	20	0.5	Physiologic stress Management (e.g., breathing)	Yes (for ability to handle "stress")	MI; ACM	Small sample
Burell et al., 1994	s/p MI	24	23	2	TABP modification	Yes (for TABP)	CD/MI	Small sample
Jones et al., 1996	s/p MI	1155	1159	1	Group sessions × 7 wks for stress management and counseling	No (for anxiety; depression)	ACM; CD	No
Blumenthal et al., 1997	CAD with EII	40	33	5	Structured group instruction with multiple stress reduction components	Yes (for GHQ scores and hostility)	CD, MI, PTCA, CABG	Yes RR = 0.26 (0.07–0.90)
Frasure-Smith et al., 1997	s/p MI	684	692	1	Home-based nursing intervention, to decrease transient increase in distress	No (for anxiety; depression)	CD	No

RF indicates risk factors; EII, exercise-induced ischemia; TABP, Type A behavior pattern; MI-1, undocumented myocardial infarction; and UAP, unstable angina pectoris.
*At 6 months of follow-up, short-term lower anxiety and death rate ($P < 0.05$) in intervention group.
†At 1 year (length of intervention), $P = 0.07$ for CD reduction in intervention group.
Source: Reprinted with permission from Rozanski et al. (1999). *Circulation, 99,* 2192–2217.

pressure levels are correlated among family members and more importantly they are correlated higher in blood related relatives versus adopted family members (Ward, 1990). Although research shows us the importance of genetics, the proportion of high blood pressure caused by genetics alone is difficult to determine because some risk factors, for example, obesity and alcohol, are both environmentally and genetically influenced.

Population studies also reveal a higher incidence in various cultures and socioeconomic groups that cannot be explained by genetics alone (Henry & Cassel, 1969). For example, African Americans have the highest proportion of hypertension than any other group in the United States, but hypertension prevalence among poor African Americans is higher than among those in the middle class (Harburg et al., 1973).

Role of Stress and Behavior

Many psychological and sociocultural studies have identified potential risk factors related to behavior that might play a role in the development of hypertension. The increased risk of hypertension for African Americans in the United States and among persons of lower socioeconomic status has been attributed to several factors, including dietary differences, exercise habits, and the social and physical characteristics of the environment (Kreiger & Sidney, 1996). Some studies have hypothesized that recurrent exposure to highly stressful environments (e.g., urban high-crime settings) that require constant vigilance and mobilization of coping resources may raise blood pressure (Gutmann & Benson, 1971; Henry & Cassel, 1969). One study of Detroit residents has explored the role stress plays in hypertension (Harburg et al., 1973).

Four areas of Detroit were categorized as "high stress" or "low stress" based on socioeconomic status, crime rates, population density, residential mobility, and marital breakup rates. Researchers found that blood pressure levels were highest among African American high-stress males, while Caucasian areas and African American low-stress areas had comparable blood pressure levels. Krieger and Sidney's (1996) data support this finding and suggest that racism may be linked to higher blood pressure in African Americans. However, the simple notion that social stress and cultural change are causally linked to hypertension has also been criticized as being inconsistent with other data available (Syme & Torfs, 1978).

Other research has shown that individuals in highly stressful occupations, such as air traffic controllers, have over four times the prevalence of hypertension than age-matched peers in other less stressful occupations (Cobb & Rose, 1973). Pickering et al. (1996) found an association between high job strain (using Karasek's previously described definition) and ambulatory blood pressure in blue-collar workers. This study was limited however to males who consumed alcohol. As with other cardiovascular disorders, hypertension may occur more frequently in occupations that are demanding yet offer little opportunity or flexibility to deal with those stressful demands (Karasek, Russel, & Theorell, 1982).

Personality and Essential Hypertension

Early clinical studies observed that many patients with chronic hypertension exhibited certain personality traits (e.g., Aymann, 1933). Over the years, interest has risen in finding which personality traits may play a role in the development of hypertension. Many traits have been associated with and/or prospectively predictive of hypertension, including suppressed anger and hostility (Dunbar, 1943; Johnson, Gentry, & Julius, 1992), neuroticism and anxiety (Markovitz, Matthews, Kannel, Cobb, & D'Agostino, 1993), and submissiveness (Esler et al., 1977). There has been speculation, however, over the validity of many of these early findings, for many of the studies used selected or convenience samples and had other methodological flaws. In addition, hypertension may not be a heterogeneous disease, but a number of disorders with differing pathophysiology that progress over years (Weiner & Sapira, 1987).

Recently, there has been growing research into the role that the psychological trait of defensiveness might play in hypertension development. Rutledge and Linden (2000) studied 127 initially normotensive male and female adults and looked for a variety of hypertension risk factors. Three years later, participants were measured for hypertension and

defensiveness. Twenty percent of patients who were initially found to be highly defensive had developed hypertension, while only 4.5% of those with low defensiveness developed the condition. Statistical adjustment for many general risk factors (including smoking, exercise levels, alcohol consumption, and body fat) revealed that membership in the highly defensive group was associated with more than a sevenfold risk of developing hypertension over the three-year period.

Various researchers differ in their views of the association between personality trait differences/emotions and hypertension. Early investigators (Alexander, 1939; Dunbar, 1943) and some more recent researchers (Jern, 1987) have hypothesized a causal role for personality traits in the development of hypertension. Some researchers (Esler et al., 1977; Weder & Julius, 1987) have postulated mechanisms by which certain personality traits elicit excessive central and sympathetic nervous system arousal, predisposing one to hypertension. Another possibility is that the differences reported on psychological tests between hypertensives and normotensives are the result of the label and medical attention accompanied by the diagnosis of hypertension. In support of this latter notion, Irvine, Garner, Olmsted, and Logan (1989) found that hypertensives who were aware of their condition scored significantly higher than normotensives and even hypertensives who were not aware of their condition on measures of state and trait anxiety, neuroticism, and self-reported Type-A behavior. However, Markovitz et al. (1993) reported a prospective relationship between anxiety in apparently normal individuals and the subsequent development of hypertension—an association that labeling could not create.

Treatment of Essential Hypertension

The goal in treating hypertension, according to guidelines set forth by consensus committees including the Joint National Committee on Prevention, Detection, Evaluation, and Treatment of High Blood Pressure (JNC, 1997) and the World Health Organization-International Society of Hypertension (WHO-ISH, 1999) is to reduce the risk for cardiovascular diseases and therefore reduce morbidity and mortality. JNC IV treatment guidelines begin with vigorous lifestyle changes for those individuals who present with moderate hypertension but no CVD risk and no organ damage (i.e., renal failure) as a result of hypertension. Lifestyle changes include weight loss, increased physical activity, moderation of alcohol consumption, dietary modifications, cessation of smoking, and stress reduction (Carretero & Oparil, 2000b). These lifestyle changes will be discussed in further detail. If blood pressure control is not achieved in this population or in those with severe hypertension and those with cardiovascular disease, CVD risk factors, and/or organ damage, pharmacological therapy should be initiated in conjunction with lifestyle changes. The JNC IV (1997) recommends that pharmacological therapy include diuretics and/or beta-blockers. Other drugs are controversially used, including ACE inhibitors and calcium channel blockers. Pharmaceutical treatments of hypertension continues to be an active area of research and more clinical trials are needed to prove these drugs ability to decrease CVD morbidity and mortality (Carretero & Oparil, 2000b).

Weight Loss and Dietary Changes

The reduction of weight, as little as 10 pounds, lowers blood pressure in the majority of overweight hypertensive patients (Trials of Hypertension Prevention Collaborative Research Group, 1997; Whelton, Applegate, & Ettinger, 1996). Additionally, this weight reduction enhances the efficacy of hypertension medications (Neaton et al., 1993). In addition, the direct effects on blood pressure weight loss has a beneficial effect on risk factors for other cardiovascular diseases and may enhance patients overall sense of well-being. The ability of weight loss to decrease comorbidities as well as lower blood pressure makes it the most effective nonpharmacological treatment for hypertension. Appetite suppressant drugs are contradicted in this population because of the cardiotoxicity associated with their use. Weight loss should be achieved with moderate calorie restriction and increased physical activity (Carretero & Oparil, 2000b).

High sodium intake has traditionally been associated with high blood pressure. While this hypothesis is supported by clinical trials, individual response to sodium varies. Restricted sodium diets are more effective at lowering blood pressure in certain individuals and specific populations, including African American and older patients (Weinberger, 1996). High potassium levels and high calcium levels, preferably from food sources, are recommended to help control blood pressure (Allender et al., 1996). Recently, the effects of the overall diet of an individual are being appreciated. The Dietary Approaches to Stop Hypertension Study (DASH) demonstrated significant reductions in blood pressure in moderately hypertensive subjects, regardless of age, gender, race, weight, family history, physical activity level, or socioeconomic status, when placed on a diet rich in fruits, vegetables, and low-fat dairy products compared to those control subjects maintained on a "usual American diet" (Colin et al., 2000). The food in the DASH trial contained a variety of combinations of vitamins, minerals, fiber, and other nutrients that could have alone or in combination created the dramatic results in the study.

Exercise Training

Thirty minutes of moderately intense aerobic physical activity at least three times per week has been shown to lower blood pressure in hypertensive and normotensive individuals and is advised by the National Institute of Health (1996) and the Centers for Disease Control (Pate et al., 1995). The additional benefits of physical activity include weight loss, improved sense of well-being, and reduced risk of cardiovascular disease. The Nurse's Health Study saw substantial reduction in stroke, caused by high blood pressure, associated with regularly performed moderately intense aerobic activity (Hu, Stampfer, Colditz, et al., 2000). Isometric exercise, such as lifting weight is not advised because it may increase blood pressure. The effect of exercise independent of weight loss is not determined and remains an active area of research.

Stress Management, Biofeedback, and Cognitive Interventions

Early studies suggested that techniques such as biofeedback and stress management could be used to alleviate the stress-induced components of high blood pressure, thereby reducing blood pressure in hypertensive patients. Several studies have reported that small but significant decreases in blood pressure can be achieved in hypertensives after a series of biofeedback or relaxation training sessions (including yoga and meditation) (see Dubbert, 1995; Eisenberg et al., 1993; Johnston et al., 1993). Patel and colleagues (Patel, Marmot, & Terry, 1981; Patel et al., 1985) found a positive effect by assessing the effect of eight weekly group sessions of training in breathing techniques, deep muscle relaxation, mediation, and stress management. Subjects were also told to partake in relaxation, and mediation for 15 to 20 minutes daily, and also to relax during daily stressful events. Subjects who received this relaxation training showed decreases in both systolic and diastolic blood pressure (approximately 7mgHg for both) over a four-year follow-up period, as compared with a control group who did not receive the training. A comparative study of the various behavioral techniques showed none superior to the others, with each independently producing modest declines in blood pressure (Shapiro, Schwartz, Ferguson, Redmond, & Weiss, 1977). Some studies have shown benefits from meditation and stress management in relation to hypertension. Nakao et al. (1997) assigned patients to either a biofeedback group or a control group that would later undergo the biofeedback treatment. The researchers found that those who had the four sessions of biofeedback had less of a response to mental stressors and had generally lower pressures at rest than those in the control group whose blood pressures remained unchanged from pretrial. Also, those in the control group who later underwent the biofeedback benefitted from the treatment, with decreases in overall blood pressure reading during rest and smaller responses to mental stressors. The researchers propose that biofeedback may be especially beneficial to those who have marked increases in blood pressure to stress. These techniques are appealing because they seem to have produced reductions in blood pressure without the use of medications and without any known side effects.

However, despite some promising findings, the results of other studies and meta-analyzes of an extensive body of research have revealed that the effects of stress management on hypertension appear to be minimal, and may be attributable to nonspecific effects or habituation to repeated blood pressure measurements over the course of the trials (Dubbert, 1995; Eisenberg et al., 1993; Jacob, Chesney, Williams, & Ding, 1991). In a very tightly controlled study, Johnston et al. (1993) studied the effects of stress management on resting and ambulatory blood pressure and on left ventricular mass (a clinically significant consequence of hypertension). Ninety-six individuals with mild hypertension underwent an extensive baseline evaluation to habituate them to blood pressure measurement. Each was then assigned to either 10 weeks of stress management and relaxation training or to 10 weeks of a nonaerobic stretching condition control. The study indicates that blood pressures fell during the habituation period, but blood pressures remained unchanged during the ambulatory and resting phases of treatment. However, patients had smaller blood pressure increases during a stressful interview if they had received the stress management training. Thus, the balance of research indicates that stress management appears not to be effective in lowering resting blood pressure (Dubbert, 1995; Eisenberg et al., 1993; Johnston et al., 1993).

Adherence to Treatment

As hypertension is frequently an asymptomatic condition that requires treatment including modification in lifestyle and/or expensive medications with side effects (e.g., fatigue, impotence, frequent urination), nonadherence to treatment is a common problem. Dunbar-Jacob, Wyer, and Dunning (1991) found fewer than 33% to 66% of patients were complying with their treatment plans. To improve medication adherence, the JNC VI recommends health care providers consider the cost of the medications. Newer drugs are usually more expensive than the older and more reliable diuretics and beta-blockers. Also, adherence is improved with once-a-day drugs. Making and maintaining lifestyle changes is often difficult because long-time habits need to be changed. The

utilization of a team health care approach, community resources (doctors, nurses, nutritionist, physical therapists), and family to provide long-term assistance in education and support is beneficial (JNC VI, 1997).

Summary

Behavioral factors that are important in the development of essential hypertension include obesity, lack of physical exercise, stress, and personality traits such as anger and anxiety. However, the effectiveness of so-called "cognitive" behavioral intervention techniques, such as stress management and biofeedback, in lowering blood pressure have been rather minimal, and many believe, clinically insignificant. Behavioral interventions such as weight loss and dietary changes, which confer direct physiological changes, have proven to be effective adjuncts to pharmacological interventions for treating hypertension. Finally, patient nonadherence to antihypertensive medication regimens is a prevalent and very significant problem that warrants further investigation.

CONCLUSION

There are many environmental, behavioral, and physiological variables that interact in the development of cardiovascular disorders. Many of the standard CHD risk factors have important behavioral components, and increasing evidence suggests important psychosocial risk factors for CHD, including occupational stress, hostility, and physiologic reactivity to stress. In cardiac patients, the presence of acute stress, low social support, lack of economic resources, and psychological depression also appear to be important psychosocial risk factors. The identification of psychosocial risk factors for coronary disease have led to several promising behavioral and psychosocial interventions to aid in the treatment and prevention of coronary disease in high risk individuals.

There also appear to be important biobehavioral influences in the development and treatment of essential hypertension. These include obesity, dietary salt intake, and stress. Evidence also indicates that genetic and environmental factors interact in the development of hypertension. However, the modest effects of cognitive stress-reducing techniques such as relaxation training, biofeedback, and meditation in lowering blood pressure have proven disappointing. Nevertheless, the important necessity for the involvement of health psychologists in the treatment of essential hypertension is underscored by the potential efficacy of weight loss, dietary modification, and exercise conditioning, as well as the need to ensure that patients adhere to medication regimens in order for pharmacologic interventions that have been shown to reduce subsequent morbidity to be effective (Krantz & Lundgren, 1998, p. 211).

It is imperative that future research in the fields of coronary heart disease and hypertension continues to focus on the roles of stress and psychosocial parameters as risk factors for these diseases. In addition, future research studies must advance our understanding of the mechanisms by which biobehavioral factors impact CHD and hypertension. A greater understanding of these physiological and behavioral mechanisms will enable health care professionals to better prevent and manage cardiac disorders, improving the quality of life for millions of people worldwide.

REFERENCES

Ahern, D. K., Gorkin, L., Anderson, J. L., Tierney, C., Hallstrom, A., Ewart, C., et al. (1990). Biobehavioral variables and mortality or cardiac arrest in the Cardiac Arrhythmia Pilot Study (CAPS). *American Journal of Cardiology, 66,* 59–62.

Alexander, F. (1939). Emotional factors in essential hypertension. *Psychosomatic Medicine, 1,* 173–179.

Allan, R., & Scheidt, S. (1996). Empirical basis for cardiac psychology. In R. Allan & S. Scheidt (Eds.), *Heart and mind: The practice of cardiac psychology* (pp. 63–124). Washington, DC. American Psychological Association.

Allender, P. S., Cutler, J. A., Follman, D., Cappucio, F. P., Pryer, J., & Elliott, P. (1996). Dietary calcium and blood pressure: A meta-analysis of randomized clinical trials. *Annals of Internal Medicine, 124,* 825–831.

American Heart Association. (1997). *1998 heart and stroke statistical update.* Dallas: Author.

American Heart Association. (1999). *Coronary heart disease and angina.* Dallas: Author.

American Medical Association, Council on Ethical and Judicial Affairs. (1991). Gender disparities in clinical decision making. *Journal of the American Medical Association, 266,* 559–562.

American Psychiatric Association. (1994). *Diagnostic and statistical manual of mental disorders* (4th ed.). Washington, DC: American Psychiatric Association.

Amick, T. L., & Ockene, J. K. (1994). The role of social support in the modification of risk factors for cardiovascular disease. In S. A. Shumaker & S. M. Czajkowski (Eds.), *Social support and cardiovascular disease: Plenum series in behavioral psychophysiology and medicine* (pp. 259–280). New York: Plenum Press.

Anda, R., Williamson, D., Jones, D., Macera, C., Eaker, E., Glasman, A., et al. (1993). Depressed affect, hopelessness, and the risk of ischemic heart disease in a cohort of U.S. adults. *Epidemiology, 4,* 285–294.

Appels, A. (1990). Mental precursors of myocardial infarction. *British Journal of Psychiatry, 156,* 465–471.

Arooma, A., Raitasalo, R., Reunanen, A., Impivaara, O., Heliovaara, M., Knekt, P., et al. (1994). Depression and cardiovascular diseases. *Acta Psychiatric Scandanavia, 377(Supp.),* 77–82.

Aymann, D. (1933). The personality type of patients with arteriolar essential hypertension. *American Journal of Medical Science, 186,* 213.

Barefoot, J. C., Dahlstrom, W. G., & Williams, R. B. (1983). Hostility, CHD incidence and total mortality: A 25 year follow-up study of 255 physicians. *Psychosomatic Medicine, 45,* 59–63.

Barefoot, J. C., Helms, M. J., & Mark, D. B. (1996). Depression and long-term mortality risk in patients with coronary artery disease. *American Journal of Cardiology, 78,* 613–617.

Barefoot, J. C., & Lipkus, I. M. (1994). The assessment of anger and hostility. In A. W. Siegman & T. W. Smith (Eds.), *Anger, hostility, and the heart* (pp. 43–66). Hillsdale, NJ: Erlbaum.

Barefoot, J. C., Peterson, B. L., Dahlstrom, W. G., Siegler, I. C., Anderson, N. B., & Williams, R. B., Jr. (1991). Hostility patterns and health implications: Correlates of Cook-Medley scores in national survey. *Health Psychology, 10,* 18–24.

Barefoot, J. C., & Schroll, M. (1996). Symptoms of depression, acute myocardial infarction, and total mortality in a community sample. *Circulation, 93,* 1976–1980.

Baum, A., Gatchel, R., & Krantz, D. S. (1997). *An introduction to health psychology* (3rd ed.). New York: McGraw-Hill.

Berkman, L. F., Leo-Summers, L., & Horwitz, R. I. (1992). Emotional support and survival after myocardial infarction: A prospective, population-based study of the elderly. *Annals of Internal Medicine, 117,* 1003–1009.

Blazer, D. G. (1982). Social support and mortality in an elderly community population. *American Journal of Epidemiology, 115,* 684–694.

Blumenthal, J. A., Jiang, W., Babyak, M. A., Krantz, D. S., Frid, D. J., Coleman, R. E., et al. (1997). Stress management and exercise training in cardiac patients with myocardial ischemia: Effects on prognosis and evaluation of mechanisms. *Archives of Internal Medicine, 157,* 2213–2223.

Blumenthal, J. A., & Wei, J. (1993). Psychobehavioral treatment in cardiac rehabilitation. *Cardiology Clinics, 11,* 323–331.

Blustein, J., & Weitzman, B. C. (1995). Access to hospitals with high-technology cardiac services: How is race important? *American Journal of Public Health, 85,* 345–351.

Bosma, H., Peter, R., Siegrist, J., & Marmot, M. (1998). Two alternative job stress models and the risk of coronary heart disease. *American Journal of Public Health, 88,* 68–74.

Burrell, G., Ohman, A., Sundin, O., Strom, G., Ramund, B., Cullhed, I., et al. (1994). Modification of the Type A behavior pattern in post-myocardial infarction patients: A route to cardiac rehabilitation. *International Journal of Behavioral Medicine, 1,* 32–54.

Burt, V. L., Whelton, P., Roccella, E. J., Brown, C., Cutler, J. A., Higgins, M., et al. (1995). Prevalence of hypertension in the

United States adult population: Results from the third National Health and Nutrition Examination Survey, 1988–1991. *Hypertension, 25*, 305–316.

Carlisle, D. M., Leake, B. D., & Shapiro, M. F. (1997). Racial and ethnic disparities in the use of cardiovascular procedures: Associations with type of health insurance. *American Journal of Public Health, 87*, 263–267.

Carney, R. M., Freedland, K. E., Rich, M. W., & Jaffe, A. S. (1995). Depression as a risk factor for cardiac events in established coronary heart disease: A review of possible mechanisms. *Annals of Behavioral Medicine, 17*(2), 142–149.

Carney, R. M., Rich, M. W., Freedland, K. E., Saini, J., Tevelde, A., Simeone, C., et al. (1988). Major depressive disorder predicts cardiac events in patients with coronary artery disease. *Psychosomatic Medicine, 50*, 627–633.

Carney, R. M., Rich, M. W., Tevelde, A., Saini, J., Clark, K., & Jaffe, A. S. (1987). Major depressive disorder in coronary artery disease. *American Journal of Cardiology, 60*, 1273–1275.

Carney, R. M., Saunders, R. D., Freedland, K. E., Stein, P., Rich, M. W., & Jaffe, A. S. (1995). Association of depression with reduced heart rate variability in coronary artery disease. *American Journal of Cardiology, 76*, 562–564.

Carretero, O. A., & Oparil, S. (2000a). Essential hypertension: Part I: definition and etiology. *Circulation, 101*, 329–341.

Carretero, O. A., & Oparil, S. (2000b). Essential hypertension: Part II: treatment. *Circulation, 101*, 446–458.

Center for Disease Control. (1999). The burden of cardiovascular diseases, cancer, and diabetes. *Chronic Diseases and their risk factors: The nation's leading causes of death* (pp. 6–10). Washington, DC: U.S. Department of Health and Human Services.

Cobb, S., & Rose, R. M. (1973). Hypertension, peptic ulcer, and diabetes in air traffic controllers. *Journal of the American Medical Association, 224*, 489–492.

Cohen, S., & Wills, T. A. (1985). Stress, social support and the buffering hypothesis: A critical review. *Psychological Bulletin, 98*, 310–357.

Colin, P. R., Chow, D., Miller, E. R., III, Svetkey, L. P., Lin, P. H., Harsha, D. W., et al. (2000). The effect of dietary patterns on blood pressure control in hypertensive patients: Results from the DASH trial. *American Journal of Hypertension, 13*, 949–955.

Contrada, R. J., & Krantz, D. S. (1988). Stress, reactivity and Type A behavior: Current status and future directions. *Annals of Behavioral Medicine, 10*, 64–70.

Cook, W. W., & Medley, D. M. (1954). Proposed hostility and pharisaic virtue scales for the MMPI. *Journal of Applied Psychology, 38*, 414–418.

Coresh, J., Klag, M. J., Mead, L. A., Liang, K. Y., & Whelton, P. K. (1992). Vascular reactivity in young adults and cardiovascular disease. A prospective study. *Circulation, 19*, 218–223.

Cottington, E. M., Matthews, K. A., Talbott, E., & Kuller, L. H. (1980). Environmental events preceding sudden death in women. *Psychosomatic Medicine, 42*, 567–574.

Cutler, J. A. (1996). High blood pressure and end organ damage. *Journal of Hypertension, 14*, S3–S6.

Daumit, G. L., Hermann, J. A., Coresh, J., & Powe, N. R. (1999). Use of cardiovascular procedures among black persons and white persons: A 7-year nationwide study in patients with renal disease. *Annals of Internal Medicine, 130*, 173–182.

Davis, B. R., Furberg, C., & Williams, C. B. (1987). Survival analysis of adverse effects data in the Beta-Blocker Heart Attack Trial. *Clinical and Pharmacological Therapy, 41*, 611–615.

Dembroski, T. M., MacDougall, J. M., Costa, P. T., Jr., & Grandits, G. A. (1989). Components of hostility as predictors of sudden death and myocardial infarction in the Multiple Risk Factor Intervention Trial. *Psychosomatic Medicine, 51*, 514–522.

Denoillet, J., & Brutsaert, D. L. (1998). Personality, disease severity, and the risk of long term cardiac events in patients with a decreased ejection fraction after myocardial infarction. *Circulation, 97*, 167–173.

Dixhoorn, J. V., Duivenvoorden, H. J., Staal, J. A., Pool, S. P., & Verhage, F. (1987). Cardiac events after myocardial infarction: Possible effect of relaxation therapy. *European Heart Journal, 8*, 1210–1214.

Douglas, P. (1997). Coronary artery disease in women. In E. Braunwald (Ed.), *Heart disease: A textbook of cardiovascular medicine* (5th ed., pp. 1704–1714). Philadelphia: Saunders.

Dubbert, P. M. (1995). Behavioral (life style) modification in the prevention and treatment of hypertension. *Clinical Psychology Review, 15*(3), 187–216.

Dunbar, R. (1943). *Psychosomatic diagnosis.* New York: Harper & Row.

Dunbar-Jacob, J., Dwyer, K., & Dunning, E. J. (1991). Compliance with antihypertensive regimen: a review of the research in the 1980s. *Behavior Medicine, 13*, 31–39.

Dzau, V. J. (1994). Pathobiology of atherosclerosis and plaque complication. *American Heart Journal, 128*, 1300–1309.

Eagle, K. A., Guyton, R. A., Davidoff, R., Ewy, G. A., Fonger, J., Gardner, T. J., et al. (1999). ACC/AHA guidelines for coronary artery bypass graft surgery: Executive summary and recommendations: A report of the American College of Cardiology, American Heart Association Task Force on Guidelines Committee for Coronary Artery Bypass Surgery. *Circulation, 100*, 1464–1480.

Eaker, E. D., Pinsky, J., & Castelli, W. P. (1992). Myocardial infarction and coronary death among women: Psychosocial predictors from 20-year follow-up of women in the Framingham Study. *American Journal of Epidemiology, 135*, 854–864.

Egolf, B., Lasker, J., Wolf, S., & Potvin, L. (1992). The Roseto effect: A 50-year comparison of mortality rates. *American Journal of Public Health, 82*, 1089–1092.

Eisenberg, D. M., Delbanco, T. L., Berkey, S. C., Kkaptchuk, T. J., Kupelnick, B., Kuhl, J., et al. (1993). Cognitive behavioral techniques for hypertension: Are they effective? *Annals of Internal Medicine, 188*, 964–972.

Enhancing Recovery in Coronary Heart Disease Investigators. (2000). Enhancing Recovery in Coronary Heart Disease Patients (ENRICHD): Study design and methods. *American Heart Journal, 139,* 1–9.

Eriksson, J. G., Forsen, T., Tuomilehto, J., Winter, P. D., Osmond, C., & Barker, I. (1999). Catch-up growth in childhood and death from coronary heart disease: Longitudinal study. *British Medical Journal, 318,* 427–431.

Esler, M., Julius, S., Zweifler, A., Randall, O., Harburg, E., & Gardiner, H. (1977). Mild high renin essential hypertension. A neurogenic human hypertension? *New England Journal of Medicine, 287,* 1209.

Everson, S. A., Goldberg, D. E., Kaplan, G. A., Cohen, R. D., Pukkala, E., Tuomilehto, J., et al. (1996). Hopelessness and risk of mortality and incidence of myocardial infarction and cancer. *Psychosomatic Medicine, 58,* 113–121.

Fava, M., Abraham, M., Pava, J., Shuster, J., & Rosenbaum, J. (1996). Cardiovascular risk factors in depression: The role of anxiety and anger. *Psychosomatics, 37,* 31–37.

Ferguson, J. A., Adams, T. A., & Weinberger, M. (1998). Racial differences in cardiac catheterization use and appropriateness. *American Journal of Medical Science, 315*(5), 302–306.

Follick, M. J., Ahern, D. K., Gorkin, L., Niaura, R. S., Herd, J. A., Ewart, C., et al. (1990). Relation of psychosocial and stress reactivity variables to ventricular arrhythmias in the Cardiac Arrhythmia Pilot Study (CAPS). *American Journal of Cardiology, 66,* 63–67.

Ford, D. E., Mead, L. A., Chang, P. F., Cooper-Patrick, L., Wang, N., & Klag, M. J. (1998). Depression is a risk factor for coronary artery disease in men. *Archives of Internal Medicine, 158,* 1422–1426.

Frasure-Smith, N., Lesperance, F., Juneau, M., Talajic, M., & Bourassa, M. G. (1999). Gender, depression, and one-year prognosis after myocardial infarction. *Psychosomatic Medicine, 61,* 26–37.

Frasure-Smith, N., Lesperance, F., Prince, R. H., Verrier, P., Garber, R. A., Juneau, M., et al. (1997). Randomised trial of home-based psychological nursing intervention for patients recovering from myocardial infarction. *Lancet, 350,* 473–479.

Frasure-Smith, N., Lesperance, F., & Talajic, M. (1993). Depression following myocardial infarction: Impact on 6-month survival. *Journal of the American Medical Association, 270,* 1819–1825.

Frasure-Smith, N., Lesperance, F., & Talajic, M. (1995). Depression and 18-month prognosis after myocardial infarction. *Circulation, 91,* 999–1005.

Frasure-Smith, N., & Prince, R. H. (1987). The Ischemic Heart Disease Life Stress Monitoring Program: Possible therapeutic mechanisms. *Psychology and Health, 1*(3), 273–285.

Friedman, M., & Rosenman, R. H. (1959). Association of specific overt behavior pattern with blood and cardiovascular findings. *Journal of the American Medical Association, 169,* 1286–1296.

Friedman, M., & Rosenman, R. H. (1974). *Type A behavior and your heart.* New York: Knopf.

Friedman, M., Thoresen, C. E., Gill, J. J., Powell, L. H., Ulmer, D., Thompson, L., et al. (1984). Alteration of Type A behavior in cardiac recurrences in postmyocardial infarction patients. *American Heart Journal, 108,* 237–248.

Friedman, M., Thorese, C., Gill, J., Ulmer, D., Powell, L., Price, V., et al. (1986). Alteration of Type A behavior and its effects on cardiac recurrences in post myocardial infarction patients: Summary results of the recurrent coronary prevention project. *American Heart Journal, 112,* 653–665.

Gabbay, F. H., Krantz, D. S., Kop, W. J., Hedges, S. M., Klein, J., Gottdiener, J. S., et al. (1996). Triggers of myocardial ischemia during daily life in patients with coronary artery disease: Physical and mental activities, anger and smoking. *Journal of the American College of Cardiology, 27,* 585–592.

Gibbons, R. J., Chatterjee, M. B., Daley, J., Douglas, J. S., Fihn, S. D., Gardin, J. M., et al. (1999). ACC/AHA/ACP–guidelines for the management of patients with chronic stable angina: Executive summary and recommendations: A report of the American College of Cardiologists/American Heart Association Task Force on Practical Guidelines Committee on Management of Patients with Chronic Stable Angina. *Circulation, 99,* 2829–2848.

Gidron, Y., Davidson, K., & Bata, I. (1999). The short-term effects of a hostility-reduction intervention on male coronary heart disease patients. *Health Psychology, 18,* 416–420.

Goldberg, K. C., Hartz, A. J., Jacobsen, S. J., Krakauer, H., & Rimm, A. A. (1992). Racial and community factors influencing coronary artery bypass graft surgery rates for all 1986 Medicare patients. *Journal of the American Medical Association, 267,* 1473–1477.

Goldman, L., & Cook, E. F. (1984). The decline in ischemic heart disease mortality rates. *Annals of Internal Medicine, 101,* 825–836.

Goldman, L., & Cook, E. F. (1988). Reasons for the decline in coronary heart disease mortality: Medical interventions versus lifestyle changes. In M. W. Higgins & R. V. Luepker (Eds.), *The influence in medical care* (pp. 67–75). New York: Oxford University Press.

Grundy, S. M., Pasternak, R., Greenland, P., Smith, S., & Fuster, V. (1999). Assessment of cardiovascular risk by use of the multi-risk factor assessment equation. *Circulation, 100,* 1481–1492.

Gullette, E. C., Blumenthal, J. A., Babyak, M., Jiang, W., Waugh, R. A., Frid, D. J., et al. (1997). Effects of mental stress on myocardial ischemia during daily life. *Journal of the American Medical Association, 277,* 1521–1526.

Gutmann, M. C., & Benson, H. (1971). Interaction of environmental factors and systemic arterial blood pressure: A review. *Medicine, 50*(6), 543–553.

Hall, W. D., Ferrario, C. M., Moore, M. A., Hall, J. E., Flack, J. M., Cooper, W., et al. (1997). Hypertension-related morbidity and mortality in the southeastern United States. *American Journal of Medical Science, 313,* 195–206.

Hannan, E. L., Kilburn, H., O'Donnell, J. F., Lukacik, G., & Shields, E. P. (1991). Interracial access to selected cardiac procedures for patients hospitalized with coronary artery disease in New York State. *Medical Care, 29*, 430–441.

Hans, M., Carney, R. M., Freedland, K. E., & Skala, J. (1996). Depression in patients with coronary heart disease: A 12-month follow-up. *General Hospital Psychiatry, 18*, 61–65.

Harburg, E., Erfurt, J. D., Haunstein, L. S., Chape, C., Schull, W. J., & Schork, M. A. (1973). Socioecologic stress, suppressed hostility, skin color and Black-White male blood pressure: Detroit. *Psychosomatic Medicine, 35*, 276–296.

Haynes, S. G., Feinleib, M., & Kannel, W. B. (1980). The relationship of psychosocial factors to coronary heart disease in the Framingham Study. III: Eight-year incidence of coronary heart disease. *American Journal of Epidemiology, 3*, 37–58.

Haywood, L. J. (1984). Coronary heart disease mortality/morbidity and risk in Blacks. I: Clinical manifestations and diagnostic criteria: The experience with the Beta Blocker Heart Attack Trail. *American Heart Journal, 108*, 787–793.

Hennekens, C. H. (1998). Risk factors for coronary heart disease in women. *Cardiology Clinics, 16*, 1–8.

Henry, J. P., & Cassel, J. C. (1969). Psychosocial factors in essential hypertension: Recent epidemiologic and animal experimental data. *American Journal of Epidemiology, 90*, 171–200.

Herrmann, C., Brand-Driehorst, S., Kaminsky, B., Leibing, E., Staats, H., & Ruger, U. (1998). Diagnosis groups and depressed mood as predictors of 22-month mortality in medical patients. *Psychosomatic Medicine, 60*, 570–577.

Higgins, M., & Thom, T. (1993). Cardiovascular disease in women as a public health problem. In N. K. Wenger, L. Speroff, & B. Packard (Eds.), *Cardiovascular health and disease in women* (pp. 15–19). Greenwich, CT: LeJacq Communications.

Hlatky, M. A., Lam, L. C., Lee, K. L., Clapp-Channing, N. E., Williams, R. B., Pryor, D. B., et al. (1995). Job strain and the prevalence and outcome of coronary artery disease. *Circulation, 92*, 327–333.

Horlick, L., Cameron, H. R., Firor, W., Bhalerao, U., & Baltzan, R. (1984). The effects of education and group discussion in the post myocardial infarction patients. *Journal of Psychosomatic Research, 28*, 485–492.

Howell, R. H., Gottdiener, J. S., Kop, W. J., Papademetriou, V., Lu, D. Y., Bower, A., et al. (1997). Acute mental stress as a trigger of coronary vasocontriction: Relation to hemodynamic responses and coronary risk factors [Abstract]. *Circulation, 94*, 94–95.

Hu, F. B., Stampfer, M. J., Colditz, G. A., Ascherio, A., Rexrode, K. M., Willett, W. C., et al. (2000). Physical activity and risk of stroke in women. *Journal of the American Medical Association, 283*, 920–1015.

Hu, F. B., Stampfer, M. J., Manson, J. E., Grodstein, F., Colditz, G. A., Speizer, F. E., et al. (2000). Trends in the incidence of coronary heart disease and changes in diet and lifestyle in women. *New England Journal of Medicine, 343*, 530–537.

Hu, F. B., Stampfer, M. J., Manson, J. E., Rimm, E., Colditz, G. A., Rosner, B. A., et al. (1997). Dietary fat intake and the risk of coronary heart disease in women. *New England Journal of Medicine, 337*, 1491–1499.

INTERSALT Co-Operative Research Group. (1988). Sodium, potassium, body mass, alcohol and blood pressure, the INTERSALT study. *Journal of Hypertension, 6*, S584–S586.

Irvine, M. J., Garner, D. M., Olmsted, M. P., & Logan, A. G. (1989). Personality differences between hypertensive and normotensive individuals: Influence of knowledge of hypertension status. *Psychosomatic Medicine, 51*, 537–549.

Jacob, R. G., Chesney, M. A., Williams, D. M., & Ding, Y. (1991). Relaxation therapy for hypertension: Design effects and treatment effects. *Annals of Behavioral Medicine, 13*, 5–17.

Jern, S. (1987). Specificity of personality factors found in hypertension. In S. Julius & D. R. Bassett (Eds.), *Handbook of hypertension: Behavioral factors in hypertension* (Vol. 9, pp. 150–161). Amsterdam: Elsevier.

Johnson, E. H., Gentry, W. D., & Julius, S. (1992). *Personality, elevated blood pressure, and essential hypertension.* Washington, DC: Hemisphere.

Johnston, D. W., Gold, A., Kentish, J., Smith, D., Vallance, P., Shah, D., et al. (1993). Effects of stress management on blood pressure in mild primary hypertension. *British Medical Journal, 306*, 963–966.

Joint National Committee on Prevention, Detection, Evaluation, and Treatment of High Blood Pressure. (1997). The sixth report of the Joint National Committee on Prevention, Detection, and Treatment of High Blood Pressure. *Journal of the American Medical Association, 157*, 2413–2446.

Jones, D. A., & West, R. R. (1996). Psychological rehabilitation after myocardial infarction: A multicenter randomized controlled trial. *British Medical Journal, 313*, 1517–1521.

Julius, S., & Bassett, D. R. (1987). *Behavioral factors in hypertension: Handbook of hypertension* (Vol. 9). Amsterdam: Elsevier.

Kaprio, J., Koskenvuo, M., & Rita, H. (1987). Mortality after bereavement: A prospective study of 95,647 persons. *American Journal of Public Health, 77*, 283–287.

Karasek, R. A., Baker, D., Marxer, F., Ahlbom, A., & Theorell, T. (1981). Job decision latitude, job demands, and cardiovascular disease: A prospective study of Swedish men. *American Journal of Public Health, 71*, 694–705.

Karasek, R. A., Russel, R. S., & Theorell, T. (1982). Physiology of stress and regeneration in job related cardiovascular illness. *Journal of Human Stress, 8*, 29–42.

Karasek, R. A., & Theorell, T. G. (1990). *Healthy work, stress, productivity, and the reconstruction of working life.* New York: Basic Books.

Kawachi, I., Sparrow, D., Spiro, A., III, Vokonas, P., & Weiss, S. C. (1996). A prospective study of anger and coronary heart disease: The Normative Aging Study. *Circulation, 94*, 2090–2095.

Kennedy, G. J., Hofer, M. A., Choen, D., Shindledecker, R., & Fisher, J. D. (1987). Significance of depression and cognitive impairment in patients undergoing programmed stimulation of cardiac arrhythmias. *Psychosomatic Medicine, 49,* 410–421.

Keys, A., Taylor, H. L., Blackburn, H., Brozek, J., Anderson, J., & Simonson, E. (1971). Mortality and coronary heart disease among men studied for 23 years. *Archives of Internal Medicine, 128,* 201–214.

Klag, M. J., Whelton, P. K., Randall, B. L., Neaton, L. D., Brancoti, F. L., & Stamler, J. (1997). End-stage renal disease in African-Americans and women: 16 year MRFIT findings. *Journal of the American Medical Association, 227,* 1293–1298.

Kop, W. J. (1999). Chronic and acute psychological risk factors for clinical manifestations of coronary artery disease. *Psychosomatic Medicine, 61,* 476–487.

Kop, W. J., Appels, A. P., Mendes de Leon, C. F., de Swart, H. B., & Bar, F. W. (1994). Vital exhaustion predicts new cardiac events after successful coronary angioplasty. *Psychosomatic Medicine, 56,* 281–287.

Krantz, D. S., & Durel, L. A. (1983). Psychobiological substrates of the Type A behavior pattern. *Health Psychology, 2,* 393–411.

Krantz, D. S., Grunberg, N. E., & Baum, A. (1985). Health psychology. *Annual Review of Psychology, 36,* 349–383.

Krantz, D. S., Kop, W. J., Gabbay, F. H., Rozanski, A., Barnard, M., Klein, J., et al. (1996). Circadian variation of ambulatory myocardial ischemia: Triggering by daily activities and evidence for an endogenous circadian component. *Circulation, 93,* 1364–1371.

Krantz, D. S., Kop, W. J., Santiago, H. T., & Gottdiener, J. S. (1996). Mental stress as a trigger of myocardial ischemia and infarction. *Cardiology Clinic, 14,* 271–287.

Krantz, D. S., & Lundgren, N. R. (1998). Cardiovascular disorders. In A. S. Bellack & M. Hersen (Eds.), *Comprehensive clinical psychology* (pp. 189–216). New York: Pergamon Press.

Krantz, D. S., & Manuck, S. B. (1984). Acute psychophysiologic reactivity and ride of cardiovascular disease: A review and methodologic critique. *Psychological Bulletin, 96,* 435–464.

Krantz, D. S., Santiago, H. T., Kop, W. J., Bairey Merz, C. N., Rozanski, A., & Gottdiener, J. S. (1999). Prognostic value of mental stress testing in coronary artery disease. *American Journal of Cardiology, 84,* 1292–1297.

Krieger, N., & Sidney, S. (1996). Racial discrimination and blood pressure: The CARDIA study of young black and white adults. *American Journal of Public Health, 86,* 1370–1378.

Lampert, R., Jain, D., Burg, M. M., Batsford, W. P., & McPherson, C. A. (2000). Destabilizing effects of mental stress on ventricular arrhythmias in patients with implantable cardioverter-defibrillators. *Circulation, 101,* 158–164.

Laouri, M., Kravitz, R. L., French, W. J., Yang, I., Milliken, J. C., Hilborne, L., et al. (1997). Underuse of coronary revascularization procedures: Application of a clinical method. *Journal of the American College of Cardiology, 29,* 891–897.

LaRosa, J. C., Hunninghake, D., Bush, D., Criqui, M. A., Getz, G. S., Gotto, A. M., Jr., et al. (1990). The cholesterol facts: A summary of evidence relating dietary fats, serum cholesterol and coronary heart disease: A joint statement of the American Heart Association and the National Heart, Lung, and Blood Institute. *Circulation, 81,* 1721–1733.

Lavie, C. J., & Milani, R. V. (1997). Exercise training and weight reduction on coronary risk factors, behavioral characteristics and quality of life in obese coronary patients. *American Journal of Cardiology, 79,* 397–399.

Leor, J., Poole, W. K., & Kloner, R. A. (1996). Sudden cardiac death triggered by an earthquake. *New England Journal of Medicine, 334,* 413–419.

Linden, W., Stossel, C., & Maurice, J. (1996). Psychosocial interventions for patients with coronary artery disease: A meta-analysis. *Archives of Internal Medicine, 156,* 745–752.

Lown, B. (1987). Sudden cardiac death: Biobehavioral perspective. *Circulation, 76*(Suppl. 1), 186–196.

Luepker, R. V., Rosamond, W. D., Murphy, R., Sprafka, J. M., Folsom, A. R., McGovern, P. G., et al. (1993). Socioeconomic status and coronary heart disease risk factor trends: The Minnesota Heart Survey. *Circulation, 88*(5, Pt. 1), 2172–2179.

Maeland, J. G., & Havic, O. E. (1987). The effects of in-hospital educational program for myocardial infarction patients. *Scandinavian Journal of Rehabilitation Medicine, 19,* 57–65.

Malinow, M. R., Bostrum, A. G., & Krauss, R. M. (1999). Homocysteine, diet, and cardiovascular disease: A statement for healthcare professionals from the Nutrition Committee American Heart Association. *Circulation, 99,* 178–182.

Manson, J. E. (1994). Postmenopausal hormone therapy and atherosclerotic disease. *American Heart Journal, 128*(Pt. 2), 1337–1343.

Manuck, S. B. (1994). Cardiovascular reactivity in cardiovascular disease: Once more unto the breach. *International Journal of Behavioral Medicine, 1,* 4–31.

Markovitz, J. H., Matthews, K. A., Kannel, W. B., Cobb, J. L., & D'Agostino, R. B. (1993). Psychological predictors of hypertension in the Framingham Study. *Journal of the American Medical Association, 270,* 2439–2443.

Marmot, M. G., & Syme, S. L. (1976). Acculturation and coronary heart disease in Japanese Americans. *American Journal of Epidemiology, 104,* 225–247.

Matthews, K. A. (1982). Psychological perspectives on the Type A behavior pattern. *Psychological Bulletin, 91,* 293–323.

Matthews, K. A., Glass, D. C., Rosenman, R. H., & Bortner, R. W. (1977). Competitive drive pattern A and coronary heart disease: A further analysis of some data from the Western Collaborative Group Study. *Journal of Chronic Diseases, 30,* 489–498.

Matthews, K. A., & Haynes, S. G. (1986). Type A behavior pattern and coronary disease risk: Update and critical evaluation. *American Journal of Epidemiology, 123,* 923–960.

Meisel, S. R., Kutz, I., Dayan, K. I., Pauzner, H., Chetboun, I., Arbel, Y., et al. (1991). Effect of Iraqi missile war on incidence of acute myocardial infarction and sudden death in Israeli civilians. *Lancet, 338,* 660–661.

Mendes de Leon, C. F., Powell, L. H., & Kaplan, B. H. (1991). Change in coronary-prone behaviors in the Recurrent Coronary Prevention Project. *Psychosomatic Medicine, 53,* 407–419.

Miller, T. Q., Smith, T. W., Turner, C. W., Guijarro, M. L., & Hallet, A. J. (1996). A meta-analytic review of research on hostility and physical health. *Psychological Bulletin, 119,* 322–348.

Mittleman, M. A., Maclure, M., Sherwood, J. B., Mulry, R. P., Tofler, G., Jacobs, S. C., et al. (1995). Triggering of acute myocardial infarction onset by episodes of anger. *Circulation, 92,* 1720–1725.

Myers, R. H., & Dewar, H. A. (1975). Circumstances surrounding sudden deaths from coronary artery disease with coroner's necropsies. *British Heart Journal, 37,* 1133–1143.

Nakao, M., Nomura, S., Shimosawa, T., Yoshiuchi, K., Kumano, H., Kuboki, T., et al. (1997). Clinical effects of blood pressure biofeedback treatment on hypertension by auto-shaping. *Psychosomatic Medicine, 59,* 331–338.

National Heart, Lung, and Blood Institute. (1994). *Report of the Task Force on Research in Epidemiology and Prevention of Cardiovascular Diseases.* Washington, DC: U.S. Department of Health and Human Services.

National Institute of Health Consensus Development Panel on Physical Activity and Cardiovascular Health. (1996). Physical activity and cardiovascular health. *Journal of the American Medical Association, 276,* 402–407.

Neaton, J. D., Grimm, R. H., Prineas, R. J., Stamler, J., Grandits, G. A., Elmer, P. J., et al. (1993). Treatment of mild hypertension study: Final results. *Journal of the American Medical Association, 270,* 241–246.

Nelson, D. V., Baer, P. E., Cleveland, S. E., Revel, K. F., & Montero, A. C. (1994). Six-months follow-up of stress management training versus cardiac education during hospitalization for acute myocardial infarction. *Journal of Cardiopulmonary Rehabilitation, 14,* 384–390.

Nunes, E. V., Frank, K. A., & Kornfeld, D. S. (1987). Psychologic treatment for the Type A behavior pattern and for coronary heart disease: A meta-analysis of the literature. *Psychosomatic Medicine, 49,* 159–173.

Oberman, A., & Cutter, G. (1984). Issues in the natural history and treatment of coronary heart disease in Black populations: Surgical treatment. *American Heart Journal, 108,* 688–694.

Ockene, I. S., & Ockene, J. K. (1992). *Prevention of coronary heart disease.* Boston: Little, Brown.

Ornish, D., Brown, S. E., Scherwitz, L. W., Billings, J. H., Armstrong, W. T., Ports, T. A., et al. (1990). Can lifestyle changes reverse coronary heart disease? *Lancet, 336,* 129–133.

Ornish, D., Scherwitz, L. W., Billings, J. H., Gould, K. L., Merritt, T. A., Sparler, S., et al. (1998). Intensive lifestyle changes for reversal of coronary heart disease. *Journal of the American Medical Association, 280,* 2001–2007.

Paffenbarger, R. S., Jung, D. C., Leung, R. W., & Hyde, R. T. (1991). Physical activity and hypertension: An epidemiological view. *Annals of Internal Medicine, 23,* 319–327.

Pate, R., Pratt, M., Blair, S. N., Haskell, W. L., Macera, C. A., Bouchard, C., et al. (1995). Physical activity and public health: A recommendation from the Centers for Disease Control and Prevention and the American College of Sports Medicine. *Journal of the American Medical Association, 273,* 402–407.

Patel, C., Marmot, M. G., & Terry, D. J. (1981). Controlled trial of biofeedback-aided behavioral methods in reducing mild hypertension. *British Medical Journal, 282*(6281), 2005–2008.

Patel, C., Marmot, M. G., Terry, D. J., Carruthers, M., Hunt, B., & Patel, M. (1985). Trial of relaxation in reducing coronary risk: Four year follow up. *British Medical Journal, 290,* 1103–1106.

Patterson, S. M., Gottdiener, J. S., Hecht, G., Vargot, S., & Krantz, D. S. (1993). Effects of acute mental stress on serum lipids: Mediating effects of plasma volume. *Psychosomatic Medicine, 55,* 525–532.

Peniston, R. L., Lu, D. Y., Papademetriou, V., & Fletcher, R. D. (2000). Severity of coronary artery disease in black and white male veterans and the likelihood of revascularization. *American Heart Journal, 139,* 840–847.

Peter, R., & Siegrist, J. (2000). Psychosocial work environment and the risk of coronary heart disease. *International Archives of Occupational and Environmental Health, 73*(Suppl.), S41–S45.

Peterson, E. D., Wright, S. M., Daley, J., & Thibault, G. E. (1994). Racial variation in cardiac procedure use and survival following myocardial infarction in the Department of Veterans Affairs. *Journal of the American Medical Association, 271,* 1175–1180.

Pickering, T. G. (1996). Job strain and the prevalence and outcome of coronary artery disease. *Circulation, 94,* 1138–1139.

Pickering, T. G., Devereux, R. B., James, G. D., Gerin, W., Landsbergis, P., Schnall, P. L., et al. (1996). Environmental influences on blood pressure and the role of job strain. *Journal of Hypertension, 14*(Suppl. 1), A54.

Pohjola-Sintonen, S., Rissaness, A., Liskola, P., & Luomanmaki, K. (1998). Family history as a risk factor of coronary heart disease in patients. *European Heart Journal, 225,* 1998–2003.

Pratt, L. A., Ford, D. E., Crum, R. M., Armenian, H. K., Gallo, J. J., & Eaton, W. W. (1996). Depression, psychotropic medication, and risk of myocardial infarction. *Circulation, 94,* 3123–3129.

Rahe, R. H., & Lind, E. (1971). Psychosocial factors and myocardial infarction. II: An outpatient study in Sweden. *Journal of Psychosomatic Research, 15,* 33–39.

Rahe, R. H., Ward, H. W., & Hayes, V. (1979). Brief group therapy in myocardial infarction rehabilitation: three- to four-year follow-up of a controlled trial. *Psychosomatic Medicine, 41,* 229–242.

Rosenman, R. H., Brand, R. J., Jenkins, C. D., Friedman, M., Straus, R., & Wurm, M. (1975). Coronary heart disease in the Western Collaborative Group Study: Final follow-up experience of 8½ years. *Journal of the American Medical Association, 233,* 872–877.

Rozanski, A., Blumenthal, J. A., & Kaplan, J. (1999). Impact of psychological factors on the pathogenesis of cardiovascular disease and implications for therapy. *Circulation, 99,* 2192–2217.

Ruberman, W., Weinblatt, E., Goldberg, J. D., & Chaudhary, B. S. (1984). Psychosocial influences on mortality after myocardial infarction. *New England Journal of Medicine, 311,* 552–559.

Rutledge, T., & Linden, W. (2000). Defensiveness status predicts 3-year incidence of hypertension. *Journal of Hypertension, 18,* 153–159.

Saliba, S. J. (2000). Prevention of coronary artery disease. *Primary Care, 27,* 120–136.

Schecter, A. D., Goldschmidt-Clermont, P. J., McKee, G., Hoffeld, D., Myers, M., Velez, R., et al. (1996). Influence of gender, race, and education on patient preferences and receipt of cardiac catheterizations among coronary care unit patients. *American Journal of Cardiology, 78,* 996–1001.

Schleifer, S. J., Keller, S. E., Bond, R. N., Cohen, J., & Stein, M. (1989). Major depressive disorder and immunity. *Archives of General Psychiatry, 46,* 81–87.

Schleifer, S. J., Macari-Hinson, M. M., & Coyle, D. A. (1989). The nature and course of depression following myocardial infarction. *Archives of Internal Medicine, 149,* 1785–1789.

Schulman, K. A., Berlin, J. A., Harless, W., Kerner, J. F., Sistrunk, S., Gersh, B. J., et al. (1999). The effect of race and sex on physicians' recommendations for cardiac catheterization. *New England Journal of Medicine, 340,* 618–626.

Severs, P. S., & Poutler, N. R. (1989). A hypothesis for the pathogenesis of essential hypertension: The initiating factors. *Journal of Hypertension, 7,* S9–S12.

Shapiro, A. P., Schwartz, G. E., Ferguson, D. C. E., Redmond, D. P., & Weiss, S. M. (1977). Behavioral methods in the treatment of hypertension. I: Review of their clinical status. *Annals of Internal Medicine, 86,* 626–636.

Sheifer, S. E., Escarce, J. J., & Schulman, K. A. (2000). Race and sex differences in the management of coronary artery disease. *American Heart Journal, 139,* 848–857.

Shekelle, R. B., Gale, M., Ostfeld, A. M., & Paul, O. (1983). Hostility, risk of coronary heart disease, and mortality. *Psychosomatic Medicine, 45,* 109–114.

Shekelle, R. B., Hulley, S. B., & Neaton, J. (1985). The MRFIT behavior pattern study. II: Type A behavior pattern and risk of coronary death in MRFIT. *American Journal of Epidemiology, 122,* 559–570.

Shumaker, S. A., & Czajkowski, S. M (Eds.). (1994). *Social support and cardiovascular disease* (Plenum series in behavioral psychophysiology and medicine). New York: Plenum Press.

Siegler, I. C. (1994). Hostility and risk: Demographic and lifestyle variables. In A. W. Siegman & T. W. Smith (Eds.), *Anger, hostility, and the heart* (pp. 199–214). Hillsdale, NJ: Erlbaum.

Siegman, A. W. (1994). From Type A to hostility to anger: Reflections on the history of coronary-prone behavior. In A. W. Siegman & T. W. Smith (Eds.), *Anger, hostility, and the heart* (pp. 1–21). Hillsdale, NJ: Erlbaum.

Siegrist, J., Peter, R., Junge, A., Cremer, P., & Seidel, D. (1990). Low status control, high effort at work and ischemic heart disease: Prospective evidence from blue-collar men. *Social Science Medicine, 31,* 1127–1134.

Smith, S. C., Blair, S. N., Criquim, M. H., Fletcher, G. F., Fuster, V., Gersh, B. J., et al. (1995). Preventing heart attack and death in patients with coronary disease. *Circulation, 92,* 2–4.

Stampfer, M. J., Hu, F. B., Manson, S. E., Rimm, E. B., & Willett, W. C. (2000). Primary prevention of coronary heart disease in women through diet and lifestyle. *New England Journal of Medicine, 343,* 16–22.

Stern, M. J., Gorman, P. A., & Kaslow, L. (1983). The group counseling v. exercise therapy study. *Archives of Internal Medicine, 143,* 1719–1725.

Stone, P. H., Thompson, B., Anderson, H. V., Kronenberg, M. W., Gibson, R. S., Rogers, W. J., et al. (1996). Influence of race, sex, and age on management of unstable angina and non-Q-wave myocardial infarction: The TIMI III registry. *Journal of the American Medical Association, 275,* 1104–1112.

Stoney, C. M., & Engebretson, T. O. (1994). Anger and hostility: Potential mediators of the gender difference in coronary heart disease. In A. W. Siegman & T. W. Smith (Eds.), *Anger, hostility, and the heart.* Hillsdale, NJ; Erlbaum.

Suinn, R. M. (1982). Intervention with type A behaviors. *Journal of Consulting and Clinical Psychology, 50*(6), 933–949.

Sutton-Tyrrell, K., Lassila, H. C., Meilahn, E., Bunker, C., Matthews, K. A., & Kuller, L. H. (1998). Carotid atherosclerosis in premenopausal and postmenopausal women and its association with risk factors measured after menopause. *Stroke, 29,* 1116–1121.

Syme, S. L., & Torfs, C. P. (1978). Epidemiologic research in hypertension: A critical appraisal. *Journal of Human Stress, 4,* 43–47.

Taylor, A. J., Meyers, G. S., Morse, R. W., & Pearson, C. E. (1997). Can characteristics of a health care system mitigate ethnic bias in access to cardiovascular procedures? Experience from the Military Health Services System. *Journal of the American College of Cardiology, 30,* 901–907.

Theorell, T., Tsutsumi, A., Hallqist, J., Reuterwall, C., Hogstedt, C., Fredlund, P., et al. (1998). Decision latitude, job strain, and myocardial infarction: A study of working men in Stockholm. *American Journal of Public Health, 88,* 382–388.

Thompson, D. R., & Meddis, R. (1990). A prospective evaluation of in-hospital counseling for first time myocardial infarction men. *Journal of Psychosomatic Research, 34,* 237–248.

Thomson, G. E. (1997). Discrimination in health care [Editorial]. *Annals of Internal Medicine, 126,* 910–912.

Trials of Hypertension Prevention Collaborative Research Group. (1997). Effects of weight loss and sodium restriction on blood pressure and hypertension incidence in overweight people with high-normal blood pressure: The Trials of Hypertension, Phase II. *Archives of Internal Medicine, 157,* 657–667.

Tunstall-Pedoe, H. (2000). Estimation of contribution of changes in coronary care to improving survival, event rates, and coronary heart disease mortality across the WHO MONICA Project populations. *Lancet, 355,* 688–700.

Verrier, R. L., & Mittleman, M. A. (1996). Life-threatening cardiovascular consequences of anger in patients with coronary heart disease. *Cardiology Clinics, 14,* 289–307.

Vogt, T., Pope, C., Mullooly, J., & Hollis, J. (1994). Mental health status as a predictor of morbidity and mortality: A 15-year follow-up of members of a health maintenance organization. *American Journal of Public Health, 84,* 227–231.

Ward, R. (1990). Familial aggregation and genetic epidemiology of blood pressure. In J. H. Laragh & B. M. Brenner (Eds.), *Hypertension pathophysiology, diagnosis and management* (pp. 81–100). New York: Raven Press.

Wassertheil-Smoller, S., Applegate, W. B., Berge, K., Chang, C. J., Davis, B. R., Grimm, R., et al. (1996). Change in depression as a precursor of cardiovascular events. *Archives of Internal Medicine, 156,* 553–561.

Weder, A. B., & Julius, S. (1985). Behavior, blood pressure variability and hypertension. *Psychosomatic Medicine, 47,* 406–414.

Weinberger, M. H. (1996). Salt sensitivity of blood pressure in human. *Hypertension, 27,* 487–490.

Weiner, H., & Sapira, J. D. (1987). Hypertension: A challenge to behavioral research. In S. Julius & D. R. Bassett (Eds.), *Handbook of hypertension: Behavioral factors in hypertension* (Vol. 9, pp. 59–74). Amsterdam: Elsevier.

Wells, J. A. (1985). Chronic life situations and life change events. In A. M. Ostfeld & E. D. Eaker (Eds.), *Measuring psychosocial variables in epidemiologic studies of cardiovascular disease* (NIH Publication No. 85–2270). Washington, DC: U.S. Department of Health and Human Services.

Wenneker, M. B., & Epstein, A. M. (1989). Racial inequalities in the use of procedures for patients with ischemic heart disease in Massachusetts. *Journal of the American Medical Association, 261,* 253–257.

Whelton, P. K., Applegate, W. B., & Ettinger, W. H. (1996). Efficacy of weight loss and reduced sodium intake in the Trial of Non-pharmacological Interventions in the Elderly (TONE). *Circulation, 94,* I-178.

Whittle, J., Conigliaro, J., Good, C. B., & Joswiak, M. (1997). Do patient preferences contribute to racial differences in cardiovascular procedure use? *Journal of General Internal Medicine, 12,* 267–273.

Whittle, J., Conigliaro, J., Good, C. B., & Lofgren, R. P. (1993). Racial differences in the use of invasive cardiovascular procedures in the Department of Veterans Affairs medical system. *New England Journal of Medicine, 329,* 621–627.

Williams, J. E., Paton, C. C., Siegler, I. C., Eigenbrodt, M. L., Nieto, F. J., & Tyroler, H. A. (2000). Anger proneness predicts coronary heart disease risk: Prospective analysis from the Atherosclerosis Risk in Communities (ARIC) Study. *Circulation, 101,* 2034–2039.

Williams, R. B., Barefoot, J. C., Califf, R. M., Haney, T. L., Saunders, W. B., Pryor, D. B., et al. (1992). Prognostic importance of social and economic resources among medically treated patients with angiographically documented coronary artery disease. *Journal of the American Medical Association, 267,* 520–524.

Wilson, P. W. (1994). Established risk factors and coronary artery disease: The Framingham Study. *American Journal of Hypertension, 7,* 7S-12S.

Wilson, P. W., D'Agostino, R. B., Levy, D., Belanger, A. M., Silbershatz, H., & Kannel, W. B. (1998). Prediction of coronary heart disease using risk factor categories. *Circulation, 97,* 1837–1847.

Winkleby, M. A., Fortmann, S. P., & Barrett, D. C. (1990). Social class disparities in risk of factors of disease: Eight year prevalence patterns by level of education. *Preventative Medicine, 19,* 1–12.

Wolff, H. G. (1952). *Stress and disease.* Springfield, IL: Charles C. Thomas.

World Health Organization. (1999). International Society of the Guidelines for Management of Hypertension. Guidelines Subcommittee. *Journal of Hypertension, 17,* 151–183.

Wulsin, L. R., Vaillant, G. E., & Wells, V. E. (1999). A systematic review of the mortality of depression. *Psychosomatic Medicine, 61,* 6–17.

CHAPTER 16

Chronic Fatigue Syndrome

LEONARD A. JASON AND RENEE R. TAYLOR

This chapter explores chronic fatigue syndrome (CFS), an illness that is not easily explained, and the societal response to it. In addition, it offers research strategies to address stigmatization caused by biases and unexamined assumptions. In the area of CFS, key decisions regarding the name, case definition, epidemiology, and treatment were made many years ago within a sociopolitical context in which CFS was assumed to be a psychologically based problem (Friedberg & Jason, 1998). In part, some of the decisions may have been due to the predominance of female patients with this illness, whose medical complaints have historically been discredited by the predominantly male establishment (Richman & Jason, 2001; Richman, Jason, Taylor, & Jahn, 2000). Many physicians and other professionals have continued to believe that most individuals with this syndrome have a psychiatric illness. Many CFS activists have argued that the current diagnostic label contributes to the invalidation and stigmatization process. Due to the controversy surrounding the diagnostic label, etiology, and diagnostic criteria of CFS, people with the illness frequently face disbelieving attitudes from their doctors, family, and/or friends; and many experience profound losses in their support systems (Jason et al., 1997).

Financial support for this study was provided by NIAID grant number AI36295.

CASE DEFINITION

The original case definition of CFS (Holmes et al., 1988) defined CFS as a new onset of persistent or relapsing, debilitating fatigue "severe enough to reduce or impair average daily activity below 50% of the patient's premorbid activity level for a period of at least six months." In addition, a patient must meet one of the following minor criteria requirements: (a) 8 or more of 11 minor symptoms (e.g., sore throat, painful lymph nodes, unexplained generalized muscle weakness) must be reported; or (b) at least 6 of the 11 minor symptom criteria must be reported and at least 2 of 3 physical signs must be documented by a physician on two occasions. However, the requirement for a high number of nonspecific symptoms in the original case definition of CFS, in conjunction with misuse and biased scoring of certain types of psychiatric measures, has been associated with erroneous estimates of the extent of comorbidity between CFS and psychiatric disorders.

The syndrome called CFS did not emerge spontaneously in the mid-1980s. Chronic fatigue has been described clinically for more than 150 years, and the term *neurasthenia* (fatigue as an illness in the absence of disease), which was coined in 1869 by George Beard, was one of the most prevalent diagnoses in the late 1800s (Wessely, Hotopf, & Sharpe, 1998). However, by the early part of the twentieth century, the diagnosis *neurasthenia* was used infrequently, and those with a diagnosis of severe fatigue were often considered by medical personnel to have either a depressive illness or another psychiatric condition.

In an influential review article, David, Wessely, and Pelosi (1991) concluded that depression occurs in about 50% of CFS cases; and anxiety and other disorders (i.e., somatization, minor depression, phobia, anxiety disorders) occur in about 25% of cases. These findings have led some to conclude that CFS is solely a psychiatric disorder. A key problem with the original CFS criteria was that it required eight or more minor symptoms, which involve many unexplained somatic complaints. However, the requirement of a high number of unexplained somatic complaints can inadvertently select individuals with psychiatric problems (Straus, 1992). Katon and Russo (1992) classified 285 chronic fatigue patients into four groups, with each group having a higher number of unexplained somatic symptoms. Patients with the highest numbers of unexplained physical symptoms had very high rates of psychiatric disorders. Patients in the group with the lowest number of unexplained symptoms displayed a prevalence of psychiatric symptoms similar to that reported for other clinic populations with chronic medical illnesses. The diagnostic criteria for CFS inadvertently selected subgroups of patients with high levels of psychiatric diagnoses.

The Diagnostic Interview Schedule (DIS; Robins, Helzer, Cottler, & Goldring, 1989), a structured psychiatric instrument designed for use in community surveys (Robins & Regier, 1991), has frequently been used to assess psychiatric comorbidity in CFS samples. However, this instrument was not designed for use with medically ill populations. If a respondent mentions that a symptom on the DIS (e.g., pains in arms or legs) is due to a medical problem that was diagnosed by a physician, DIS scoring rules indicate this symptom should not be counted as a psychiatric problem. If the physician attributed the patient's symptoms to nerves, unknown factors, or a psychiatric disorder, the patient would automatically receive a score counting toward a psychiatric diagnosis, regardless of whether the patient agreed with the physician. Also, if several physicians diagnosed a patient as having a medical disorder, but only one attributed the symptom to a psychiatric disorder, the item would be scored to count toward a psychiatric diagnosis. Many physicians still do not accept CFS as a legitimate medical disorder, so it is possible that many patients would have had at least one physician who diagnosed their medical complaints as being a psychiatric disorder, thus increasing the likelihood that people with CFS would receive a psychiatric disorder diagnosis when assessed with this instrument.

By contrast, the Structured Clinical Interview for the *DSM-IV* (SCID; Spitzer, Williams, Gibbons, & First, 1995) uses open-ended questions and all potential sources of information to encourage a thorough description of the problems by the interviewee. Use of the SCID is also limited to highly trained clinicians more able to recognize the subtle distinctions between CFS and psychiatric disorders. A study by Taylor and Jason (1998) involved the administration of both the DIS and the SCID to a sample of patients with CFS. Of individuals diagnosed with CFS, 50% received a current Axis I psychiatric diagnosis when using the DIS, but only 22% received a current diagnosis when using the SCID. These findings suggest that high or low psychiatric rates in CFS samples may be a function of whether symptoms are attributed to psychiatric or nonpsychiatric causation.

In 1994, a new CFS definition was published (Fukuda et al., 1994). This new case definition requires a person to experience chronic fatigue of new or definite onset that is not substantially alleviated by rest; that is not the result of ongoing exertion; and that results in substantial reductions in occupational, social, and personal activities. Unlike the Holmes et al. (1988) criteria (as specified by the Schluederberg et al., 1992 revision), anxiety disorders, somatoform disorders, and nonpsychotic or nonmelancholic depression existing prior to CFS onset do not constitute exclusionary conditions under the Fukuda et al. (1994) definition. In addition, the criteria require the concurrent occurrence of at least four of eight minor symptoms (sore throat, muscle pain, etc.), as compared with eight or more required by the Holmes et al. (1988) criteria. Jason, Torres-Harding, Taylor, and Carrico (2001) compared the Fukuda and Holmes criteria and found that the Holmes criteria did select a group of patients with higher symptomatology and functional impairment.

The Fukuda et al. (1994) criteria do not explicitly exclude people who have purely psychosocial stress or many psychiatric reasons for their fatigue. However, this broadening of the CFS definition raises questions regarding the extent to which patients with purely psychiatric explanations are erroneously included within the CFS rubric. Some individuals with CFS might have had psychiatric problems before and/or after CFS onset, and yet other individuals may have only primary psychiatric disorders with prominent somatic features. Including the latter type of patients in the current CFS case definition could seriously complicate the interpretation of epidemiologic and treatment studies. Major depressive disorder is an example of a primary psychiatric disorder that has some overlapping symptoms with CFS.

Fatigue, sleep disturbances, and poor concentration occur in both depression and CFS. It is important to differentiate those with a principal diagnosis of major depressive disorder from those with CFS only. This is particularly important because it is possible that some patients with major depressive disorder also have chronic fatigue and four minor symptoms that can occur with depression (i.e., unrefreshing sleep, joint pain, muscle pain, impairment in concentration). Fatigue and these four minor symptoms also are defining criteria for CFS. Is it possible that some patients with a primary affective disorder could be misdiagnosed as having CFS? Some CFS investigators would not see this as a problem because they believe that high rates of psychiatric comorbidity indicate that CFS is mainly a psychiatric disorder and that distinctions between the two phenomena are superficial and merely a matter of nomenclature.

However, several CFS symptoms, including prolonged fatigue after physical exertion, night sweats, sore throats, and swollen lymph nodes are not commonly found in depression. In addition, while fatigue is the principal feature of CFS, fatigue does not assume equal prominence in depression (Friedberg & Jason, 1998; Komaroff et al., 1996). Also, illness onset with CFS is often sudden, occurring over a few hours or days, whereas primary depression generally shows a more gradual onset. In summary, CFS and depression are two distinct disorders, although they share a number of common symptoms. Most importantly, the erroneous inclusion of people with primary psychiatric conditions in CFS samples will have detrimental consequences for the interpretation of both epidemiologic and treatment efficacy findings.

The reliability of current CFS criteria (Fukuda et al., 1994) needs to be improved. To accomplish this important task, it is relevant to examine the significant improvements made in the reliability of clinical diagnoses in the fields of psychology and psychiatry over the past 50 years. In the 1950s, researchers in the field of diagnostic reliability recognized that one of the key factors contributing to the problem of low interrater reliability in psychiatric diagnosis was the inability of two or more examiners to achieve a consensus on the symptoms or behaviors that characterized a specific diagnosis (Matarazzo, 1983). This is not unlike the current state of affairs regarding diagnostic criteria for CFS. Because a diagnosis or classification can be no more accurate than the classifier's knowledge and understanding of what he or she is classifying, it was determined that the first step to improving diagnostic reliability was the development of operationally explicit and objectively denotable criteria (Feighner et al., 1972).

By the 1970s, researchers in the field of diagnostics also recognized that the provision of operationally explicit, objectively denotable criteria was not enough to ensure that clinicians would know how to elicit the necessary information from a clinical interview to permit them to apply it to the reliable criteria (J. Endicott & Spitzer, 1977). These concerns led to the development of a series of structured interview schedules. Structured interview schedules ensure that clinicians in the same or in different settings conduct clinical interviews using standardized questions that maximize the accuracy of clinical diagnosis (J. Endicott & Spitzer, 1977). Thus, structured interview schedules serve to remove unreliability introduced by differences in the way clinicians elicit clinical information. Together, the provision of operationally explicit, objectively denotable criteria and standardized interviews were found to significantly improve the reliability of clinical diagnosis for a number of psychological and psychiatric conditions (Leckliter & Matarazzo, 1994). It is possible that similar strategies might be used to enhance the reliability of CFS criteria.

Diagnostic and epidemiological research requires diagnostic categories that are both reliable and valid (Cantwell, 1996). The criteria used in different case definitions must be clearly operationalized. Field tests must be conducted to determine the reliability and validity of these nosologies. In the determination of psychiatric diagnosis, considerable improvements were made to the *DSM-IV* (American Psychiatric Association [APA], 1994) when committees were appointed to make recommendations concerning different features of the overall diagnostic system (Leckliter & Matarazzo, 1994). These recommendations were implemented in nationwide field trials to establish diagnostic reliability. This approach might be used to bring greater precision to the case definition of CFS.

Several investigators have tried to validate or confirm approaches for the classification of fatigue using statistical methods (Haley, Kurt, & Hom, 1997; Hall, Sanders, & Repologle, 1994), or by attempting to distinguish psychological from physical fatigue (Katerndahl, 1993). Others have tried to clinically confirm the CFS criteria established by the Centers for Disease Control (CDC; Komaroff et al., 1996). Nisenbaum, Reyes, Mawle, and Reeves (1998) found that three correlated factors (fatigue-mood-cognition symptoms, flu-type symptoms, and visual impairment symptoms) explained a set of additional correlations between fatigue lasting for six or more months and 14 interrelated symptoms. No factor explained observed correlations among fatigue lasting for one to five months and other symptoms. Findings like these are of great interest because they indicate that only fatigue lasting six or more months (with selected symptoms) overlaps with published criteria to define CFS.

In another study, Friedberg, Dechene, McKenzie, and Fontanetta (2000) found three factors (cognitive problems, flu-like symptoms, and neurologic symptoms) in a sample of patients with CFS, and those with longer duration had a larger number of cognitive difficulties. Hadzi-Pavlovic et al. (2000) used latent class analysis to classify patients with CFS into three classes: those with multiple severe symptoms, those with lower rates of cognitive symptoms and higher rates of pain, and those with a less severe form of multiple symptoms (those in the last category were younger and had a shorter duration of the illness).

Disagreement continues about which symptoms should be included in the CFS case definition. For example, Komaroff and associates (1996) compared patients meeting the major criteria of the original U.S. CFS case definition (Holmes et al., 1988) with healthy controls and groups with multiple sclerosis and depression. They concluded that eliminating muscle weakness, arthralgias, and sleep disturbance, and adding anorexia and nausea would strengthen the case definition. Jason, Torres-Harding, Carrico, et al. (2002) compared individuals with CFS, melancholic depression, and controls, and in contrast to the Komaroff study, muscle weakness and arthralgias were reported in over half of participants with CFS and uniquely differentiated this group from controls. Jason, Torres-Harding, Carrico, et al. (2002) also found that anorexia and nausea occurred with relatively low frequency, and neither uniquely differentiated those with CFS from controls.

Others have provided experimental evidence for the importance of the CFS criteria (Hartz, Kuhn, Levine, & London, 1998). These authors (1998) examined persons with CFS and compared them to those with other fatigue-related conditions and those with no symptoms of fatigue. They concluded that persons with fatigue could be classified by the degree to which they matched the case definition of CFS (Fukuda et al., 1994). They also suggested including criteria such as frequent fever and chills, muscle weakness, and sensitivity to alcohol. Jason, Torres-Harding, Carrico, et al. (2002) found that muscle weakness and sensitivity to alcohol uniquely differentiated the CFS group from controls. They also found a symptom currently not part of the Fukuda criteria—shortness of breath. It did differentiate the groups and might play a role in neurally mediated hypotension, which has been connected to CFS (Poole, Herrell, Ashton, Goldberg, & Buchwald, 2000).

A study by Jason, Taylor, Kennedy, Jordan, Huang, et al. (2001) evaluated dimensions of chronic fatigue in a stratified random community-based sample of households within ethnically diverse neighborhoods. Factor analysis of items contained in a CFS Screening Questionnaire provided support for the existence of four distinct components of chronic fatigue. These were lack of energy (fatigue intensity), physical exertion (fatigue exacerbated by physical exertion), cognitive problems (difficulties with short-term memory, concentration, and information processing), and fatigue and rest (rest or sleep is not restorative). Results of these analyses were of theoretical importance because two of the primary dimensions of fatigue that emerged within the CFS-like group, postexertional fatigue and cognitive problems, corresponded closely with major definitional criteria for CFS (Dowsett, Goudsmit, Macintyre, & Shepherd, 1994; Lloyd, Hickie, Boughton, Spencer, & Wakefield, 1990). Postexertional fatigue is part of the major criteria for Myalgic Encephalomyelitis (ME; the British term for CFS) in Great Britain (Dowsett et al., 1994), and cognitive problems are part of the major criteria for the Australian definition of CFS (Lloyd et al., 1990). Postexertional fatigue and cognitive problems appear to represent primary dimensions of CFS.

A cluster analysis of the data just mentioned was performed to define a typology of chronic fatigue symptomatology (Jason & Taylor, in press). With respect to CFS, findings suggest that a majority of individuals with moderate to severe symptoms can be accurately classified into two important subgroups: one distinguished by severe postexertional fatigue and fatigue that is alleviated by rest; and one distinguished by severe overall symptomatology, severe postexertional fatigue, and fatigue that is not alleviated by rest. One key characteristic distinguishing the two clusters that contained almost all participants with CFS from the cluster containing only one CFS participant was markedly high severity of postexertional fatigue. This symptom has been designated as a major criteria for the London definition of Myalgic Encephalomyelitis (Dowsett et al., 1994), but as one of the minor criteria for the U.S. definition of CFS (Fukuda et al., 1994).

Results from this investigation highlight the relative importance of this symptom as a diagnostic marker for CFS and point to the potential utility in designating postexertional fatigue as a major criteria for CFS in future attempts to define this syndrome. A second key characteristic, fatigue in relation to rest, distinguished individuals in two clusters that contained individuals with CFS, but those in one cluster differed most significantly from those in the second cluster with respect to whether their fatigue was alleviated by rest. One of the major criteria for the current U.S. definition of CFS (Fukuda et al., 1994) is that fatigue is not substantially alleviated by rest. Findings from this investigation suggest that this criteria may be more accurately designated as one of the minor criteria for CFS so that it does not artificially exclude those with CFS who may experience some symptom relief with rest. A third result deserving attention involves the finding for more severe cognitive problems in the clusters with patients with CFS versus the cluster with only one patient with CFS. This finding highlights the importance of cognitive problems to the experience of CFS and supports the designation of cognitive problems as a major criteria for CFS in the London (Dowsett et al., 1994) and Australian (Lloyd et al., 1990) criteria.

SOCIODEMOGRAPHICS

Several studies have highlighted commonalities among individuals with CFS, including greater likelihood of being female, Caucasian, and of higher socioeconomic status (Reyes et al., 1997; Gunn, Connell, & Randall, 1993). However, community-based studies involving representative samples of ethnically and socioeconomically diverse populations indicate that the prevalence of CFS is actually higher for Latinos and African Americans than for Caucasians (Jason, Richman, Rademaker, et al., 1999), and higher for individuals of lower socioeconomic status than for those of higher socioeconomic status (Wessely, Chalder, Hirsch, Wallace, & Wright, 1997). Ethnic group differences found in a community sample of patients with CFS indicate that individuals classified as minorities experience significantly more severe symptomatology including sore throats, postexertional malaise, headaches, and unrefreshing sleep than Caucasians, and they additionally report poorer general health status (Jason, Taylor, Kennedy, Jordan, et al., 2000). In addition, Latinos who are female, older, and of higher SES report the highest relative severity of fatigue (Song, Jason, & Taylor, 1999). Higher rates of CFS among low-income groups and ethnic minorities may be attributed to psychosocial stress, behavioral risk factors, poor nutrition, inadequate health care, more hazardous occupations, or environmental exposures (Jason, Richman, et al., 1999).

CFS continues to be found to be more prevalent among women than men (Jason, Richman, et al., 1999), and there is some evidence of gender-related differences in the impact of CFS as well as in its prevalence. Among a sample of individuals with CFS, women were found to have a higher frequency of fibromyalgia, tender/enlarged lymph nodes, and lower scores on physical functioning. Men had higher frequency of pharyngeal inflammation and a higher lifetime prevalence of alcoholism (Buchwald, Pearlman, Kith, & Schmaling, 1994). Jason, Taylor, Kennedy, Jordan, and associates (2000) found that women with CFS had significantly poorer physical functioning, more bodily pain, poorer emotional role functioning, significantly more severe muscle pain, and significantly more impairment of work activities than men with CFS in a community-based sample. Findings for increased symptom severity and poorer functional outcomes among women may involve certain predisposing vulnerabilities that may be more likely to occur in women than in men. These could include biological factors such as reproductive correlates (Harlow, Signorello, Hall, Dailey, & Komaroff, 1998) and biopsychosocial factors such as stress-associated immune modulation (Glaser & Kiecolt-Glaser, 1998).

Some research has suggested that occupational circumstances may play a role in CFS. In particular, Jason and associates (1998) have found estimates of prevalence of CFS to be higher among a sample of nurses than in the general population, indicating that nurses may be a high-risk group for this illness. If CFS affects members of various professions at different rates or in different ways, this may reveal new information regarding the etiology and characteristics of the illness. In a recent epidemiologic study of CFS in a community sample (Jason, Taylor, Kennedy, Song, et al., 2000), health care workers comprised over 15% of the group of individuals with CFS, which is significantly higher than the composition of health care workers in the general U.S. population. Similarly, Coulter (1988) found that 40% of the members of a large U.S. patients' organization for individuals with CFS were associated with the health care professions, and Ramsay (1986) identified an overrepresentation of doctors among individuals with CFS.

Findings such as these suggest that certain occupational stressors, such as exposure to viruses, stressful shift work that is disruptive to circadian rhythms, and excessive work load may compromise the immune system and put health care workers at greater risk of infection or illness (Akerstedt, Torsvall, & Gillberg, 1985; Jason & Wagner, 1998; Leese et al., 1996). Hypothetical explanations highlighting the role of disrupted circadian rhythms are, in part, supported by biological findings among a sample of nurses working five consecutive night shifts (Leese et al., 1996). Disruptions in pituitary-adrenal responses to CRH found in that sample were highly consistent with the neuroendocrine abnormalities typically found in individuals with CFS (Leese et al., 1996). However, these findings must be interpreted in light of other studies that have not found an overrepresentation of professionals among individuals with CFS (Euba, Chalder, Deale, & Wessely, 1996).

EPIDEMIOLOGY

The first widely publicized study of CFS epidemiology was initiated by the CDC in the late 1980s (Gunn et al., 1993). Investigators requested physicians in four cities to identify patients with a specified set of fatigue-related symptoms. Prevalence rates of CFS were found to range from 4.0 to 8.7 individuals per 100,000 cases (Reyes et al., 1997). The majority of CFS cases were White upper-middle-class women. This epidemiological study conducted by the CDC, as well as others (Lloyd et al., 1990), derived its sample from physician referrals in hospital and community-based clinics. These studies, and others like them, underrepresented low-income and under-served minorities shown to manifest higher levels of chronic illness while also being less likely to have access to the health care system, and thus less likely to be counted in prevalence rates derived from treatment sources. These studies also underestimated the prevalence of CFS in the general population because they depended on diagnoses by health care providers who discounted the existence of the illness and would thus fail to diagnose it (Richman, Flaherty, & Rospenda, 1994).

In 1991, Jason and Wagner (1998) directly surveyed nurses, and 202 nurses (6%) out of a sample of 3,400 indicated that they had experienced debilitating fatigue for six months or longer. In 1992, these nurses were recontacted and interviewed by phone. Based on those interviews, a high-risk group of 82 who either reported having CFS or had most of the symptoms of CFS was selected. These nurses were interviewed using a structured psychiatric test, and their medical records and other collected information were evaluated by a Physician Review Team. Thirty-seven nurses met case criteria for current CFS, yielding a prevalence rate of 1.088% (1,088 per 100,000; Jason & Wagner, 1998). Because nurses are a high-risk population for CFS (e.g., nurses' work is stressful and schedules often disrupt circadian rhythms), it may not be possible to generalize these data to the entire population.

In 1993, Jason and colleagues (1995) screened a random community sample ($n = 1,031$) for the presence of CFS. Sixty-four percent of the fatigued group indicated that they had no current medical doctor overseeing their illness. The individuals who reported having CFS or who had many of the symptoms of CFS were examined by a physician and interviewed by a psychiatrist to determine whether they could be diagnosed with CFS. The DePaul University research team diagnosed two patients with current CFS (0.2% of the sample, or a CFS prevalence rate of 200 per 100,000), a number higher than we would have expected, given rates from past epidemiological studies.

The CDC conducted a community-based survey in San Francisco (Steele et al., 1998). Using telephone interviewing between June 1 and December 1, 1994, these investigators surveyed 8,004 (87%) of 9,155 households, providing data on 16,970 adult and minor residents. Based on this population-based telephone survey, the authors estimated the prevalence of CFS-like illness to be between .076 and .233% (76 and 233 per 100,000). Unfortunately, this study involved only self-reported data. In the absence of medical and psychiatric examinations, it was not possible to estimate the prevalence of actual CFS cases from this study.

Another prevalence study involved a random sample of 4,000 individuals in a health maintenance organization roster in the Seattle area (Buchwald et al., 1995). Seventy-seven percent ($n = 3,066$) of the individuals surveyed responded. Three individuals were determined to have CFS, for a prevalence rate of .075% (75 per 100,000). If the rates among non-respondents and nonparticipants were similar to the rates among study participants, the prevalence rate would rise to .267% (267 cases per 100,000). A limitation in this study is that only individuals with access to health care were represented.

In Great Britain, Pawlikowska et al. (1994) sought responses from 15,283 people recorded in the general practice register as having mild fatigue. Based on this sample, Wessely et al. (1995) later ascertained the presence of CFS in 1,199 people who presented to the physician with symptoms of infections and 1,167 for other reasons. Using health and fatigue questionnaires (Wessely et al., 1997), it was determined that 2.6% of the sample had CFS according to the Fukuda et al. (1994) criteria. These rates are within the range of prevalence of several mood disorders. (Mood disorders are the most prevalent psychiatric illness after anxiety disorders: For major depressive episode, the one-month prevalence is 2.2% and lifetime prevalence is 5.8%; Regier et al., 1988.) These CFS prevalence rates are considerably higher than those reported in other recent epidemiological studies.

In a subsequent study by Euba et al. (1996), those individuals with a CFS diagnosis in the community sample described previously were compared with people diagnosed in a hospital unit specializing in CFS. Whereas 74% of the community sample had a psychiatric diagnosis before the onset of their fatigue, only 21% of the hospital sample had a previous diagnosis. The community sample had significantly worse mental health scores and were more likely to be impaired in their work. Fifty-nine percent believed that their illness might be due to psychological or psychosocial causes (compared with 7% for the hospital sample). Wessely et al. (1997) did indicate that, of the 2.6% with CFS in the community sample, only 0.5% had no psychological disorder. In another study of CFS and psychiatric symptoms (Wessely, Chalder, Hirsch, Wallace, & Wright, 1996), 36 individuals were diagnosed as having CFS from a cohort of 1,985 primary care patients. Among the CFS subgroup, only 64% had sleep disturbances and 63% had postexertional malaise. These percentages are rather low, given that both symptoms are critical features of CFS. Wessely and colleagues' finding of an increased prevalence of CFS reflects the use of the new Fukuda et al. (1994) case definition and possibly indicates the inclusion of pure psychiatric cases in the category of CFS disorders. Thus, using a broad or narrow definition of CFS has an important influence on CFS prevalence estimates and the related issue of psychiatric co-morbidity.

Lawrie and Pelosi (1995) found a prevalence rate of 560 per 100,000 among a sample of 1,000 patients. The respondents were resurveyed one year later, and a random sample were interviewed again 18 to 22 months later (Lawrie, Manders, Geddes, & Pelosi, 1997). After controlling for confounding variables, only premorbid fatigue score was a significant predictor for developing chronic fatigue. (Emotional morbidity and physical attribution for fatigue were not risk factors.) Of the new chronic fatigue cases, 75% of those who had consulted a general practitioner for fatigue were probable psychiatric cases, whereas only 17% of those who had not consulted a general practitioner were psychiatric cases. Two cases of CFS were identified among the new chronic fatigue cases, and two cases of patients who had been ill at the time of the first prevalence study were found. (The cases were equally divided between the sexes.) The two incident cases described having recovered within a year (only one had a psychiatric diagnosis), whereas the two more long-standing prevalent cases had psychiatric diagnoses and neither had recovered 18 months later. At that follow-up, Lawrie et al. (1997) estimated the annual incidence of CFS to be 370 per 100,000 and the prevalence to be 740 per 100,000.

From 1995 until 1998, Jason, Richman, and colleagues (1999) attempted to contact a stratified sample of 28,673 households in Chicago by telephone. Of that sample, 18,675 individuals were screened for CFS symptomatology. The sample was stratified to ensure a representative sample of the diverse ethnic and socioeconomic groups comprising the Chicago general population. Based on the initial screening, participants with significant fatigue and CFS symptoms were selected to receive a psychological evaluation and medical examination. Approximately .4% of the sample was determined to have CFS, and rates of CFS were higher among Latino and African American respondents when compared to White respondents (Jason, Richman, et al., 1999). These data suggested that there might be as many as 800,000 adults in the United States with this syndrome, suggesting that it is one of the more common chronic health conditions. Data were also collected for youth, and the findings indicated a CFS prevalence of .06%, or 60 cases per 100,000 (Jordan et al., 2001).

Finally, Reyes, Nisenbaum, Stewart, and Reeves (1998) reported on the first phase of a CDC population-based prevalence study of fatigue-related disorders. The CDC used telephone calls to contact their sample of 34,018 households in Sedgewick County (Wichita), Kansas (87.8% of their sample was White). The rate of CFS was estimated at about 240 per 100,000. The CDC has now recommended that all future epidemiologic research involve randomly selected, community-based samples.

ETIOLOGY

People with CFS appear to have two basic problems with immune function: immune activitation as demonstrated by elevations of activated T lymphocytes, including cytotoxic T cells and elevations of circulating cytokines; and poor cellular function, with low natural killer cell cytotoxicity and frequent immunoglobulin deficiencies (most often IgG1 and IgG3) (Evengard, Schacterle, & Komaroff, 1999; Patarca, Fletcher, & Klimas, 1993; Patarca-Montero, Mark, Fletcher, & Klimas, 2000). Landay, Jessop, Lennette, and Levy (1991) were the first group of researchers to find that the CD8 CD11b suppressor cell population was reduced in patients with CFS, while the activation markers (CD38 and HLA-DR) had increased. This suggests that decreased suppressor cells lead to a hyperimmune response.

A variety of physical and psychological stressors can cause corticotropin-releasing hormone (CRH) to be released from the paraventricular nucleus of the hypothalamus. CRH causes adrenocorticotropin (ACTH) to be released from the anterior pituitary, and ACTH in turn stimulates cortisol release from the adrenal cortex. A frequently cited biological study by Demitrack et al. (1993) found low levels of cortisol in CFS patients, which might be due to a deficit in CRH. Deficits in cortisol have been linked to lethargy and fatigue, and this deficit might be contributing to the overactive immune system. In a summary of the literature, Scott and Dinan (1999) mentioned that patients with CFS have a reduced adrenal secretory reserve and their adrenal gland size is smaller compared to healthy subjects, whereas in major depression, enlarged adrenal glands are found. Neurotransmitters, including serotonin (5HT), are also involved in the release of CRH. Serotonin, according to Scott and Dinan, might play a role in the genesis of CFS, as altered 5HT neurotransmission seen in patients with CFS may account for disturbed sleep, muscle pain, gastrointestinal problems, and mood alterations. Scott and Dinan mention that vasopressin (VP) also acts in a synergistic fashion with CRH in stimulating ACTH release, and low VP levels have been found in subjects with postviral fatigue syndrome. Wessely (1993), however, states that it is simplistic to view CFS as a deficiency in CRH, but some abnormality in CRH metabolism possibly underlies both depression and CFS.

Another important biologically based explanation involves the 2'-5'A antiviral pathway, which causes the production of

RNase-L. Viral infections and interferon that is induced by viral infections increase levels of RNase-L, and this RNase-L selectively degrades viral RNA. Patients with CFS have higher levels of RNase-L (an 80 kDa polypeptide) than patients with any other disease, according to Suhadolnik et al. (1997), who has also found a novel low-molecular-weight (37 kDa) binding protein in a subset of individuals with CFS who are severely disabled by their disease. A European team (De Meirleir et al., 2000) has also found increased levels of 80 kDa and 37 kDa RNase-L in patients with CFS. The ratio of 37 kDa protein to the normal 80 kDa protein was high in 72% of patients with CFS and only 1% in healthy controls and none in depression and fibromyalgia control patients. Herst et al. (2001) treated two patients with CFS who were HHV-6 positive and had a high ratio of 37/80 kDa activity. Three to four months after Ampligen treatment, their RNase-L cell low molecular weight protein dropped and no HHV-6 infection was detectable, suggesting that these two biomarkers might be used in monitoring patients' response to treatment. Gow et al. (2001), however, did not find any evidence of upregulation of the antiviral pathway in a group with CFS and healthy controls, but a group with a group of patients with infections evidenced upregulation.

Another group of researchers (Bou-Holaigah, Rowe, Kan, & Calkins, 1995) found that 22 of 23 patients with CFS had an abnormal response consistent with neurally mediated hypotension. This condition occurs when the central nervous system misinterprets the body's needs when it is in an upright position. Then it sends a message to the heart to slow down and lower the blood pressure, responses that are directly opposite the responses the body needs. Other investigators, however, have not found neurally mediated hypotension to play a major role in CFS (Poole et al., 2000). In another study (Streeten & Bell, 2000), the majority of patients had striking decreases in circulating blood volume. It appears that the blood vessels in patients with CFS are constricted dramatically, and efforts to restore normal volume have met with limited success.

Other investigators have noted cardiac dysfunction (Lerner, Lawrie, & Dworkin, 1993), EEG abnormalities (Donati, Fagioli, Komaroff, & Duffy, 1994), abnormalities in cerebral white matter (Natelson, Cohen, Brassloff, & Lee, 1993), decreases in blood flow in certain areas of the brain (Schwartz et al., 1994), autonomic nervous system dysfunction (Freeman & Komaroff, 1997), frequent HHV-6 reactivation (Ablashi et al., 2000), and multiple mycoplasmal infections (Nicolson et al., 1999). However, such laboratory findings are inconsistent, which may be a function of combining distinctive groups of patients into a large heterogeneous group rather than analyzing them within subtypes. One

reason for medical skepticism concerning CFS is that many studies examining cellular immune response abnormalities in people with CFS have not been consistently reproduced (Krupp, Mendelson, & Friedman, 1991).

In reality, rarely is there a perfect biological test for an illness. With CFS, there does appear to be mounting evidence of brain and immune system abnormalities (Komaroff, 2000a). It is possible that low levels of circulating cortisol suggest a condition of mild adrenal insufficiency. In individuals with CFS, this condition could stimulate immune activation, which could contribute to brain dysfunction (Komaroff, 2000b). Although no virus has been identified as the cause of CFS, the immune pattern seems to be fighting a virus, as evidenced by the RNase-L pathway. Increasing evidence also points to neurological findings including hyperintense signals on MRI scans, reductions in cerebral blood flow on SPECT scans (Lange, Wang, DeLuca, & Natelson, 1998), and autonomic dysfunction (primarily orthostatic intolerance and neurally mediated hypotension; Schondorf & Freeman, 1999).

The onset of CFS is often linked with the recent presence of an infection. CFS has been reported following acute mononucleosis (a viral infection), Lyme disease (a bacterial infection), and Q fever (an infection with a different type of infectious agent; Komaroff, 2000b). Activation by macrophages due to a virus or bacteria produces a release of interleukin 1, which causes an alteration in the electrical activity of the brain; it also causes a number of behavioral changes (e.g., decreases in activity and social interaction, somnolence) designed to reduce unnecessary energy expenditure, so that available energy stores can be used to fight the infection (Maier, Watkins, & Fleshner, 1994). These cytokines might induce a state of chronic activation, which leads to a depletion of the stress hormone axis, and to other neuropsychiatric and neuroendocrine features associated with CFS (Saphier, 1994).

Some individuals might be at higher risk of developing this chronic activation due to genetic vulnerabilities, or to constitutional or psychological factors. Individuals with CFS might have hyperactive premorbid lifestyles, and this high "action-proneness" might be a predisposing factor for developing CFS (Van Houdenhove, Onghena, Neerinckx, & Hellin, 1995). Individuals who are chronically stressed have a persistent lack of cortisol, and this might also contribute to CFS (Heim, Ehlert, & Hellhammer, 2000). In addition, stress might be a conditioned stimulus that leads to an impaired immune response (Cohen, Moynihan, & Ader, 1994). In addition, environmental factors might play a role in the etiology of CFS: People with CFS have significantly higher levels of chlorinated hydrocarbons than do control subjects (Dunstan et al., 1995).

Zalcman, Savina, and Wise (1999) have found that immunogenic stimuli can alter brain circuitry, changing the brain's sensitivity to seemingly unrelated subsequent stimuli. Elenkov, Wilder, Chrousos, and Vizi (2000) review evidence that norepinephrine and epinephrine inhibit the production of type 1/proinflammatory cytokines whereas they stimulate the production of type 2/anti-inflammatory cytokines thereby causing a selective suppression of Th1 responses and cellular immunity and a Th2 shift toward dominance of humoral immunity. Gellhorn (1970) has further postulated that, under prolonged stimulation of the limbic-hypothalamic-pituitary axis, a lowered threshold for activation can occur. Once this system is charged, either by high-intensity stimulation or by chronically repeated low-intensity stimulation, it can sustain a high level of arousal (Gellhorn, 1968). Girdano, Everly, and Dusek (1990) suggest that the excessive arousal can lead to an increase in the dendrites of the limbic system, which can further increase limbic stimulation. The limbic system is growing more excitatory postsynaptic receptors, and its inhibitory presynaptic receptors are decreasing. People with CFS might be experiencing excitatory neurotoxicity. Two receptors residing on the cell surface membranes of neurons are the GABA, which inhibit neuronal firing; and the NMDA, which excite neuronal firing. The GABA and NMDA receptors should be balanced, but after an injury, NMDA fires more than GABA.

Almost every drug that down-regulates NMDA receptor firing (benzodiazipine therapy, magnesium, Nimotop, melatonin, calcium channel blockers) has been helpful for people with CFS (Goldstein, 1990). Brouwer and Packer (1994) have conducted research indicating that people with CFS might have "unstable cortical excitability associated with sustained muscle activity resulting in varied magnitudes of descending volleys" (p. 1212). Natelson et al. (1996) found that low-dose treatment with a monamine oxidase inhibitor produced a significant pattern of improvement in CFS patients, thus providing additional support for the hypothesis that CFS might involve a state of reduced central sympathetic drive via increased firing of the locus coeruleus. Snorrason, Geirsson, and Stefansson (1996) found that 70% of CFS patients reported at least a 30% improvement when treated with galanthamine hydrobromide, a selective inhibitor of acetycholinesterase; galanthamine increases plasma levels of cortisol.

Acetylcholine is a primary neurotransmitter of the parasympathetic nervous system, and it is widely distributed throughout the brain and spinal cord. Chaudhuri, Majeed, Dinan, and Behan (1997) believe that CFS entails a depletion of this acetylcholine and increased sensitivity of the postsynaptic acetylcholine receptors. Chaudhuri et al. studied

growth hormone levels in patients with CFS, healthy controls, and those with chronic exposure to organophosphate. (Workers who are chronically exposed to organophosphates show neurobehavioral symptoms similar to those of people with CFS.) One hour after these participants were given pyridostigmine, a substance that increases the amount of acetylcholine (which functions to increase the amount of growth hormone), both patient groups had a larger amount of growth factor released in comparison to healthy controls, suggesting that a similar mechanism might be at work in patients with CFS and in those with chronic organophosphate exposure. Acetylcholine hypersensitivity at the hypothalamic level is the most likely explanation of these findings.

There might be various pathways into such disregulation, with a viral infection representing just one possible route. This might be the reason that Wessely et al. (1995) found that some people with CFS had viral infections and some had other medical illnesses before they developed CFS. Jason, Taylor, and Carrico (2001) did find more patients reported an onset of CFS during January, a time when viral infections occur with the greatest frequency. In addition, it is possible that viral infection can occur in the absence of inflammation; in these cases, the virus evades the host immune system and allows the functions of the cell to continue (e.g., there is evidence of persistent cytomegalovirus infection in the pancreatic cells of people with diabetes; Wessely, 1993).

Exacerbation of symptoms might trigger maladaptive appraisals and coping strategies, which may perpetuate symptomatic episodes via affective, neuroendocrine, and immunologic pathways (Antoni et al., 1994). In addition, both high experienced overload and low attractiveness of external stimulation is related to fatigue (Rijk, Schreurs, & Bensing, 1999). Some medical illnesses (e.g., multiple sclerosis, hyperthyroidism) have been shown to elicit psychological disorders; and changes in mood, fatigue, and malaise are commonly associated with infection (Ray, 1991). In addition, depression can be a reaction to physical illness; for example, depression and anxiety are common in patients with cancer and heart disease. Ray believes that depression that accompanies a prolonged illness may be better conceptualized as demoralization rather than as psychiatric illness, particularly in ambiguous illnesses in which patients have difficulty gaining recognition of the legitimacy of their illness.

Many investigators have emphasized cognitive and behavioral factors in the etiology and maintenance of CFS (Vercoulen et al., 1998). However, the stereotype that patients with CFS are perfectionistic and have negative attitudes toward psychiatry has not been supported (Wood & Wessely, 1999). Functional somatic syndromes are characterized by diffuse, poorly defined symptoms that cause significant subjective distress and disability, cannot be corroborated by consistent documentation of organic pathology, and are highly prevalent even in healthy, nonpatient groups. Some argue that syndromes such as CFS, fibromyalgia, and irritable bowel syndrome may be better understood in terms of a unitary model of functional somatic distress, rather than as separate diagnostic entities (Barsky & Borus, 1999).

A recent study by Taylor, Jason, and Schoeny (2001) evaluated the diagnostic validity of conditions that have been labeled as functional somatic syndromes. Latent variable models of functional somatic distress were estimated from the responses of 213 community members to a medical questionnaire. Medical questionnaire items that closely conformed to formal diagnostic criteria for the conditions were used in model estimation. Results of confirmatory factor analysis supported diagnostic distinctions between five syndromes (fibromyalgia [FMS], CFS, somatic depression, somatic anxiety, and irritable bowel syndrome). Discrete diagnostic categories of fibromyalgia and CFS were then tested using logistic regression analysis, in which the outcome involved independent diagnosis of these conditions based on physician evaluation. The diagnostic validity of the latent constructs of FMS and CFS emerging from this five-factor model were cross-validated using findings from an independent physician evaluation.

In support of findings for distinctions among these syndrome constructs, Hickie, Koschera, Hadzi-Pavlovic, Bennett, and Lloyd (1999) found that chronic fatigue is a persistent diagnosis over time, and that longitudinal patterns of comorbidity of fatigue with psychological distress did not suggest a causal relationship or common vulnerability factor. Similar findings of a study by Van Der Linden and associates (1999) supported the existence of a pure, independent fatigue state over time, and this pure fatigue state did not predict subsequent psychiatric disorder. Morriss and associates (1999) also found that depression was not associated with the reporting of pain, FMS and IBS, and medically unexplained symptoms in individuals with CFS.

Rather than conceptualizing CFS solely as a disease of the body or the mind, a biopsychosocial perspective provides a transactional model, one that suggests that complex interactions between multiple biological and psychological factors influence the onset of CFS and pathways to further illness or recovery. The biopsychosocial model (Friedberg & Jason, 1998) contends that there might be multiple pathways leading to the cause and maintenance of the neurobiologic dysregulations and other symptoms experienced by individuals with CFS. Depending on the individual, these pathways may include unique biological, genetic, neurological, psychological, and socioenvironmental contributions. N. Endicott (1999), for

example, has found that patients with CFS have parents with increased prevalence of cancer and autoimmune disorders when compared to control patients' families. Recent twin studies of complex genetic and environmental relationships between psychological distress, fatigue, and immune system functioning suggest that these models need to acknowledge the increasing importance of the individual's genotype (Hickie, Bennett, Lloyd, Heath, & Martin, 1999). One strength of a biopsychosocial understanding of CFS is that it may serve as a means of bridging the theoretical gap between mind versus body explanations of these illnesses.

Similarly, a psychoneuroimmunological model (Jason et al., 1995) can provide another comprehensive heuristic framework for understanding this complex illness. Psychoneuroimmunology presents an alternative to current research-induced dichotomous conceptualizations as solely diseases of the body or the mind. A psychoneuroimmunological model suggests that an ongoing connection exists between nervous, endocrine, and immune systems within the body. Consequently, conditions of stress, depression, anxiety, loss of control, learned helplessness, loneliness, bereavement, or highly inhibited power motivation may interfere with adequate immune functioning. Psychological and environmental factors may serve to influence immunosuppression, including dysphoric responses (e.g., depressive affect, unhappiness, anxiety), immunosuppressive behaviors (e.g., dietary patterns, sleep habits, licit and illicit drug use), adverse life experiences (e.g., ongoing strains in interpersonal relationships), and preexisting vulnerabilities (e.g., the absence of interpersonal resources and coping patterns to forestall the impact of negative life experiences). In summary, psychoneuroimmunology provides a transactional model, which accounts for complex interactions between multiple biological and psychological factors that influence both the onset of these syndromes and pathways to further illness or recovery.

SUBTYPES

Individuals with CFS have been found to differ with respect to characteristics such as gender, ethnicity, and socioeconomic status, symptom severity, functional disability, psychiatric comorbidity, and coping styles (Friedberg & Jason, 1998). As a result of this heterogeneity, findings emerging from studies in a number of areas are, at best, discrepant, and at worst, contradictory. Heterogeneity among participant groups can also contribute to a lack of observable abnormalities in some laboratory studies. One central, methodological explanation for observations of discrepant findings across studies involves issues related to sampling and participant se-lection. A majority of investigations have employed nonran-dom, medically referred samples. Different types of illnesses are probably now contained within the CFS construct, which makes it even more difficult to identify commonalities in all people with this diagnosis. As an example, See and Tilles (1996) found that, with alpha interferon treatment, quality-of-life scores improved significantly only for those with NK cell dysfunction, suggesting that this subgroup of CFS patients might have benefited from the enhancement of cytokine production that was produced by the interferon-stimulated NK cells and that this might have led to restora-tion of normal immune function.

Findings from many empirical investigations of CFS sug-gest that subtypes of patients can be distinguished with re-spect to the mode of illness onset (whether gradual or sudden; DeLuca, Johnson, Ellis, & Natelson, 1997; Komaroff, 1988, 1994; Levine, 1997; Reyes et al., 1999). However, contro-versy exists as to whether prognosis of individuals with CFS is affected by the experience of sudden versus gradual onset. Reyes and associates (1999) examined symptoms experi-enced at illness onset for individuals with either sudden or gradual onset of CFS and found that those with sudden onset reported significantly more symptoms at onset than those with gradual onset, and symptoms were more likely to be of infectious nature, including fever, sore throat, chills, and ten-der lymph nodes. This is consistent with other research (Komaroff, 1988, 1994), which has suggested that sudden onset of CFS may be indicative of viral/infectious illness. Over time, however, symptom patterns among individuals in the Reyes et al. (1999) sample became more similar for those with sudden and gradual onset, and probability of recovery was not affected by mode of onset. In support of this finding, an examination of the fluctuation of symptoms and outcome of CFS over time (Hill, Tiersky, Scavalla, & Natelson, 1999) found that mode of illness onset was not predictive of positive or negative illness outcomes. Contrary to these findings, how-ever, Levine (1997) has found that individuals with sudden onset have a better prognosis than those with gradual onset.

In a random community sample, Jason, Taylor, Kennedy, Song, et al. (2000) found that individuals with sudden CFS onset were significantly more likely to experience more se-vere sore throat pain and more severe fatigue following exer-cise. One possible explanation for increased severity of these two symptoms in the sudden onset group may involve an in-creased likelihood of viral etiology in this subgroup of partic-ipants. Individuals with sudden onset were also more likely to experience lifetime psychiatric diagnosis.

The presence of a stressful life event preceding or precipitating onset of CFS is another factor that has been investigated and may differentiate subgroups of patients with CFS (Ray, Jeffries, & Weir, 1995; Salit, 1997; Theorell, Blomkvist, Lindh, & Evangard, 1999). Some evidence indi-cates that individuals with CFS have experienced a higher frequency of negative life events in the time directly preced-ing the onset than matched controls (Salit, 1997; Theorell et al., 1999). In a community-based sample, Jason, Taylor, Kennedy, Song, and associates (2000) found that individuals who were experiencing unusually severe stress at the time of CFS onset reported lower levels of vitality and lower emotional role functioning. Taylor and Jason (2001) found prevalence rates of sexual and physical abuse history among individuals with CFS were comparable to those found in indi-viduals with other conditions involving chronic fatigue, in-cluding medically based conditions. In addition, relative to those with CFS who report such history, most individuals with CFS did not report histories of interpersonal abuse. Other researchers (Ray et al., 1995) have found that the pres-ence of positive life events causing moderate or major life change are associated with lower fatigue and impairment scores in individuals with CFS, while negative life events do not impact these outcomes.

Findings from a number of empirical investigations of CFS conducted in England, the United States, and Australia suggest that two subtypes of patients can be distinguished in terms of symptom severity, functional level, and psychiatric status (Friedberg & Jason, 1998; Hickie et al., 1995; Manu, Lane, & Matthews, 1988). In a sample of patients with CFS analyzed by Hickie and associates (1995), distinctive sub-types emerged: (a) a "somatization-like" group, including those who have a higher prevalence of CFS symptoms and atypical symptoms, greater disability attributed to CFS and psychiatric symptoms, and a greater percentage unem-ployed and; (b) a "CFS" group, including those individuals with lower prevalence of CFS and atypical symptoms, less disability attributed to CFS and psychiatric symptoms, and a greater percentage employed.

In a U.S. sample, Manu and associates (1988) found a bi-modal distribution of symptoms among 100 chronic fatigue patients, including 21 patients with 10 to 15 symptoms and 79 patients with 0 to 9 symptoms. In two follow-up studies of patients with CFS, persistent symptoms and disability at the follow-up were associated with eight or more medically unexplained symptoms at time one (Bombardier & Buch-wald, 1995; Clark et al., 1995). A comparison group of non-CFS chronic fatigue patients exhibited fewer symptoms and higher functioning (Bombardier & Buchwald, 1995).

Lange et al. (1999) found no MRI differences between those with CFS and healthy controls; however, when the CFS group was divided into those with and without a psychiatric disorder occurring since their CFS diagnosis, 66.7% of those without psychiatric comorbidity had MRI abnormalities versus only 22.2% with psychiatric comorbidity. The CFS without psychiatric diagnosis group had the highest frequency of lesions, and these lesions were most often found in the frontal lobes.

Several investigators have also argued for the presence of important subgroups of patients including the presence versus absence of a premorbid psychiatric condition and gradual versus sudden onset of the illness (DeLuca et al., 1997). Johnson, DeLuca, and Natelson (1999) also suggest that there might be two groups of CFS patients, one with sudden onset, nonpsychiatric, and serious cognitive impairments, and the other with slow onset, psychiatric comorbidity, and mild cognitive impairment. However, in a community-based sample, higher frequency of symptoms was not associated with a greater number of psychiatric diagnoses (Jason, Taylor, Kennedy, Jordan, et al., 2001), but sudden onset of illness was associated with psychiatric comorbidity (Jason, Taylor, Kennedy, Song, et al., 2000). In addition, when patients with and without a premorbid psychiatric diagnosis were compared, there were no significant differences on sociodemographic variables, measures of fatigue and symptom severity, disability, stress, and coping (Jason, Taylor, Kennedy, Song, et al., 2001). Possible differences between these findings and those of DeLuca and associates (1997) may be attributed to different ways in which the participants were recruited. In the Jason, Taylor, Kennedy, Jordan, et al. (2001); Jason, Taylor, Kennedy, Song, et al. (2000); and Jason, Taylor, Kennedy, Song, et al. (2001) studies, participants with CFS were recruited using randomized, community-based telephone sampling. In the DeLuca et al. (1997) study, participants with CFS were self-referred based on media reports about a CFS treatment center and also recruited by physician referral.

Patients diagnosed with CFS and fibromyalgia have been found to be substantially more disabled than patients with either condition alone (Bombardier & Buchwald, 1996). Jason, Taylor, Kennedy, Song, et al. (2001) also found that those with CFS and comorbid FM compared to those with only CFS had increased symptoms and functional impairment. Jason, Taylor, and Kennedy (2000) found in a community sample of individuals with CFS that 15.6% also had FM, 40.6% had multiple chemical sensitivities (MCS), and 3.15% had FM and MCS, whereas only 40.6% had pure CFS. Future studies should subclassify patients according to whether they are pure types or have FM and or MCS.

It is possible that CFS is experienced differently by individuals depending on the particular illness phase. Fennell (1995) has proposed a four-phase model for understanding the phases individuals undergo when coping with CFS: In Phase 1 of the CFS illness, the individual moves into a crisis mode after illness onset, wherein he or she experiences the traumatic aspects of a new illness. In Phase 2, the person with CFS continues to experience chaos and dissembling, followed by the eventual stabilization of the individual's symptoms. In Phase 3, the person with CFS moves into the resolution mode, as he or she works to accept the chronicity and ambiguity of this chronic illness and create meaning out of the illness experience. Finally, in Phase 4, the person with CFS achieves integration, wherein he or she is able to integrate the pre- and post-illness self-concepts.

Jason, Fennell, and associates (1999) examined the factor structure of the Fennell Phase Inventory using a sample of 400 participants, who self-reported that a physician diagnosed them with CFS on a mail-in questionnaire. A three-factor solution emerged, yielding a crisis score, a stabilization score, and an integration score for each individual. A cluster analysis was then conducted using the three mean factor scores for each individual, and four clusters emerged. These clusters matched the four phases predicted by Fennell (Jason, Fennell, Taylor, Fricano, & Halpert, 2000).

In another study (Jason, Fricano, et al., 2000), 65 patients diagnosed with CFS by a physician were recruited and administered the Fennell Phase Inventory and other measures assessing CFS-related symptoms, disability, and coping. Each of the 65 patients was classified as one of four predefined clusters measuring a crisis phase, a stabilization phase, a resolution phase, and an integration phase. Results confirmed Fennell's model, revealing significant differences between the clusters in terms of levels of disability and modes of coping. Results suggest that the Fennell Phase Inventory accurately differentiates phases of adaptation to illness experienced by individuals with CFS. Phase models might help researchers better deal with the mass of conflicting research studies in the field of CFS. If patients experience these phases in qualitatively different ways, their responses on standardized questionnaires could be dramatically different, depending on the phase of their illness. If a researcher collapses the responses of patients in different phases, the findings might be obscured because the patients are experiencing fundamentally different processes.

Even the construct of fatigue must be better differentiated into various dimensions (e.g., postexercise symptoms, flare-up symptoms, remission symptoms, allergy fatigue; Dechene, Friedberg, MacKenzie, & Fontanetta, 1994). Until better-differentiated subgroups are developed, it will be exceedingly difficult to identify characteristics common to all people with the diagnosis of CFS (Friedberg & Jason, 1998).

PROGNOSIS

Knowledge about the course and long-term prognosis of CFS has been increasing. Duration of illness has been mentioned as a possible predictor of recovery by several investigators. Recovery rates for individuals in the Reyes et al. (1999) sample were impacted by duration of illness at time of enrollment in the study, with individuals with shorter duration of illness at time of enrollment being more likely to report recovery. Consistent with the findings of Reyes et al. (1999), other researchers (Clark et al., 1995; Ray, Jeffries, & Weir, 1997) determined that persistent illness and poorer outcomes could be predicted by longer duration of CFS symptoms. Wilson and associates (1994), however, did not find duration of illness to be a predictor of outcome, and Hill and associates (1999) found that neither duration of illness nor mode of onset predicted illness outcome.

In a community sample, Jason, Taylor, Kennedy, Song, et al. (2000) found that individuals with a shorter duration of illness perceived their health as better and had a more optimistic outlook regarding recovery than those with longer illness duration. In contrast to these differences in overall perceptions of health, however, analyses of outcome measures revealed that the severity of most CFS symptoms remained stable throughout the course of the illness, regardless of duration. Taken together, these two findings may indicate that individuals with shorter illness duration, though just as ill as those with longer duration, are more likely to be optimistic about overall self-perceived health and prognosis.

Follow-up studies generally suggest that illness attribution and coping styles are important predictors of long-term outcome in CFS. Wilson and associates (1994) conducted a three-year follow-up study of patients previously enrolled in a placebo-controlled treatment study. These researchers found that many remain functionally impaired over time. Psychological factors were found to be important determinants of outcome such that participants who cope with distress by somatization (presenting physical rather than psychological symptoms) and discount the possible modulating role of psychosocial factors are more likely to have an unfavorable outcome. Russo and colleagues (1998) followed tertiary care clinic patients with chronic fatigue for two and a half years and found that patients whose psychiatric disorders and physical examination signs were still present at follow-up were more likely to have persistent fatigue and work disability. Clark and associates (1995) also followed tertiary care clinic patients and found that the factors that predicted persistent illness in chronic fatigue patients included having more than eight medically unexplained physical symptoms, a lifetime history of dysthymia, a duration of chronic fatigue that was more than one and a half years, less than 16 years of formal education, and age over 38 years. Sharpe, Hawton, Seagroatt, and Pasvol (1992) conducted a follow-up of tertiary care patients six weeks to four years after initial clinic visit and similarly found that longer illness duration, belief in a viral cause of the illness, limiting exercise, changing or leaving employment, belonging to a self-help organization, and current emotional disorder predicted greater functional impairment.

Bombardier and Buchwald (1995) compared functional outcomes in patients with chronic fatigue and CFS and found that individuals who met the Holmes et al. (1988) definition of CFS had poorer prognosis than individuals who did not meet CFS criteria. Similar to the Clark et al. (1995) study, the coexistence of dysthymia predicted poorer outcome across groups. Kroenke, Wood, Mangelsdorff, Meier, and Powell (1988) conducted a one-year follow-up and found that a minority (28%) of CFS patients improved. Consistent with findings of other studies, older patients and individuals with higher scores on a measure of functional impairment had a poorer prognosis at follow-up. Vercoulen and associates (1996) found that improvement in CFS was related to a sense of control over symptoms and to not attributing the illness to physical causes.

Reyes et al. (1999) found that those who recovered from CFS were similar demographically to those who remained ill. Taylor, Jason, and Curie (2001) examined predictors of increased fatigue severity and predictors of continued chronic fatigue status at a follow-up within a random community-based sample of individuals previously evaluated in a prevalence study of chronic fatigue and CFS. Findings revealed that baseline fatigue severity was the only variable that predicted increased fatigue severity at the follow-up in the overall sample of individuals with and without chronic fatigue. In the smaller sample of individuals with chronic fatigue, baseline fatigue severity, worsening of fatigue with physical exertion, and feeling worse for 24 hours or more after exercise significantly predicted continued chronic fatigue status (versus improvement) at follow-up. Camacho and Jason (1998) compared individuals who had recovered from CFS versus those that had not. Analyses show no significant differences between groups on measures of optimism, stress, and social support, although a few significant differences were noted on measures of fatigue and coping. Not surprisingly, those who had recovered from CFS had less fatigue and spent less time focusing on symptoms than those who had not recovered. Those who had recovered in comparison to healthy controls more often used positive reinterpretation and growth strategies and thus may have, in some ways, benefited from the experience of being ill. The findings are consistent with what would be expected for persons dealing with a chronic illness.

Despite growing knowledge about long-term predictors of CFS outcome, uncertainty remains regarding the course of CFS and how the syndrome impacts quality of life over time. A review of prospective outcome studies in CFS patients (Joyce, Hotopf, & Wessely, 1997) reveals that a majority of patients report some improvement one and a half years to four years after initial medical evaluation, although substantial recovery occurs in less than 10% of cases. Also, one-fourth to one-third of CFS patients report worsening illness over time. The summary article by Joyce et al. (1997) concluded that psychiatric disorder and patient belief in a physical cause for their symptoms were predictors of poor outcome in every study. However, as Hedrick (1997) noted, "Some studies found no prospective relationships; others found relationships on only one or a few of numerous factors; and different factors were found to be significant in different studies. More importantly, the strength of such relationships is often so low to be of little significance in either understanding the etiology of CFS or guiding its treatment" (p. 724).

TREATMENT

Pharmacological and Alternative Treatments

Pharmacological (e.g., Prozac, Serzone, Klonopin, Ampligen) and alternative treatments (SAM-e, NADH, massage, acupuncture, malic acid, and magnesium) represent two avenues that may lead to alleviation of the severity of some, but not all, of the symptoms of CFS (Taylor, Friedberg, & Jason, 2001).

The most well-known treatment involves Ampligen, an immune system modulator. Ampligen significantly improved functional status and reduced symptoms in severely disabled CFS patients in a double blind placebo controlled study (Strayer et al., 1994). A subsequent clinical study of Ampligen (Strayer, Carter, Strauss, Brodsky, & Suhadolnik, 1995) in 15 severely disabled CFS patients found sustained improvements over a 48-week period in functional status, cognitive function, and exercise tolerance. Also, reductions were found in human herpesvirus-6, a herpesvirus that may play a role in CFS pathogenesis (Strayer et al., 1995). The treatment is recommended for those patients with sudden onset of symptoms who have cognitive deficits. However, it is a highly controversial drug that has also been anecdotally reported to be associated with highly negative long-term physical health consequences (Kansky, 2000). Potential benefits reported by patients with sudden illness onset, significant limitations in performing activities of daily living, and cognitive impairment include significant increases in energy and the ability to perform activities of daily living, reduction in pain, return of immune system functioning to normal range, and significant improvement in cognitive functioning. It is important to note that this drug is still in an experimental phase, and the exact percentage of patients who will benefit substantially, if at all in the long term, is yet to be determined. In short-term studies, use of Ampligen has been found to produce the following side effects, which tend to occur during the first three months of treatment: initial worsening of nausea, dizziness, headaches, and pain. Ampligen is available in the United States and Brussels on an experimental basis only and is extremely expensive. One year of treatment currently costs over $14,500. Thus, not all individuals with CFS will have access to this medication (Taylor, Friedberg, & Jason, 2001).

There have also been several rather controversial trials of providing hydrocortisone, based on the hypothesis that hypercortisolism is a contributing factor to CFS. A study by McKenzie et al. (1998) found that a dosage of 25 to 35 mg resulted in only minimal therapeutic improvements while causing substantial adrenal suppression. In contrast, a study by Cleare et al. (1999), which used a lower dose (5 mg or 10 mg daily of hydrocortisone) led to significant reductions in self-rated fatigue and disability in patients with CFS, and there was no compensatory suppression of endogenous cortisol production. More research needs to be conducted in this area.

Use of most pharmacological and alternative treatments with individuals with CFS has not yet been adequately and systematically studied (Reid, Chalder, Cleare, Hotopf, & Wessely, 2000), and preliminary studies have demonstrated varying degrees of efficacy depending on the specific symptom of the condition being treated. It should be cautioned that pharmocological and alternative treatments were not designed specifically to treat CFS and should be best considered as palliative in treating isolated symptoms only (e.g., pain, sleep, headache, and possibly fatigue and cognitive problems in some circumstances). Ongoing consultation with and careful monitoring by a physician or alternative medicine specialist highly experienced in the treatment of these conditions are strongly recommended before beginning therapy with any of these agents.

Regardless of the medication described, very few pharmocological agents have been well-established as effective (Reid et al., 2000), and what works well for one person may not be tolerated by, or may be ineffective for, another person. Reports by patients of hypersensitivity or negative reactions to even small doses of the medications described herein (particularly antidepressants) are not unusual among individuals with these conditions (Friedberg, 1996; Verrillo & Gellman, 1997). Some suggest that physicians who prescribe medications for patients with CFS should start at lower than normal dosages and increase slowly only if the drug is well tolerated (Taylor, Friedberg, & Jason, 2001).

Nonpharmacological Interventions

Cognitive behavior therapy (CBT) with graded exercise constitutes a popular form of treatment for CFS. This approach to psychotherapy challenges patients' attributions of CFS symptoms as resulting from physical disease, such as viral or immunological problems (Sharpe et al., 1996). Rather, it encourages patients to attribute their symptoms to social and psychological factors. According to this approach, individuals with CFS are encouraged to engage in gradual and consistent increases in activity and to try strategies other than activity avoidance as modes for managing their symptoms. Other components of this treatment include modifying excessive perfectionism and self-criticism and maintaining an active problem-solving approach in coping with interpersonal and occupational difficulties. Results of short-term studies that have employed cognitive behavior therapy with graded exercise suggest that this form of treatment is more effective in improving physical functioning than relaxation training (Deale, Chalder, Marks, & Wessely, 1997). Another study also using this form of cognitive behavior therapy (Sharpe et al., 1996) also reported significant effects. However, in a four-year follow-up differences decreased between the cognitive-behavior therapy and a control group (Sharpe, 1998).

In an effort to generalize these findings to less specialized settings using newly trained therapists, Prins et al. (2001) found that CBT was more effective than guided support groups, but there was a lower percentage of improved patients than the other CBT trials that had used highly skilled therapists. Powell, Bentall, Nye, and Edwards (2001) compared four conditions: two CBT treatment sessions plus two telephone follow-up calls, a similar intervention plus an additional seven follow-up calls, and a third intervention that included the prior interventions plus an additional seven face-to-face sessions. No significant differences were found between the three treatment conditions (69% achieved a satisfactory outcome in physical functioning), but patients receiving any of the treatments did significantly better than a control group receiving standardized medical care. (Among controls, only 6% achieved a satisfactory outcome.) Fulcher and White (1997) compared graded aerobic exercise to

flexibility/relaxation training, and those in the exercise group were more likely to rate themselves improved than those in the flexibility/relaxation group (52% versus 27%), but there was a high drop-out rate (29%). In addition, in a recent trial comparing CBT to counseling, the CBT group did not improve compared to CFS patients in the counseling group with respect to fatigue and social functioning (Ridsdale et al., 2001).

Other approaches to psychotherapy, including cognitive coping skills therapy (Friedberg & Krupp, 1994) and envelope theory (Jason, Melrose, et al., 1999), offer alternative ways of treating CFS patients. Cognitive coping skills therapy, for example, focuses on the identification of symptom relapse triggers and encourages activity moderation to minimize setbacks. This therapy also emphasizes cognitive and behavioral coping skills, stress reduction techniques, and social support in an attempt to promote self-regulation and management of CFS symptoms. Unlike some forms of cognitive behavioral therapy (Sharpe et al., 1996), cognitive coping skills therapy does not challenge or question patients' beliefs in a medical cause for CFS. Instead, practitioners using this approach are encouraged to respond to patients' symptom accounts with complete empathy and validation for the illness.

Envelope theory (Jason, Melrose, et al., 1999) assumes a similar perspective and does not challenge patients' beliefs in a medical cause for CFS. Instead, envelope theory recommends that patients with CFS pace their activity according to their available energy resources. In this approach, the phrase, "staying within the envelope," is used to designate a comfortable range of energy expenditure in which an individual avoids both overexertion and underexertion, maintaining an optimal level of activity over time. If a comfortable level of activity is maintained over time, the functional and health status of individuals with CFS will slowly improve, and individuals with CFS will find themselves able to engage in increasing levels of activity. Jason, Melrose, and associates (1999), King, Jason, Frankenberry, and Jordan (1997), and Pesek, Jason, and Taylor (2000) presented data on the use of this theory during interventions involving repeated self-ratings of perceived and expended energy over time. Findings indicated that when the participants' perceived and expended energy levels were maintained within proximity (within the envelope), the participants experienced decreases in fatigue over time. Advocates of this approach do not challenge a patient's belief in the medical cause of CFS, but rather point to positive medical benefits of exercise. If the HPA axis is implicated in the etiology of CFS, exercise is one of the more potent activators of the HPA, and employment of gradual increases in activity might activate the HPA, thereby increasing cortisol and alleviating symptoms (Scott & Dinan, 1999). In addition, a negative relationship between fitness and impairment appears to exist (Bazelmans, Bleijenberg, van der Meer, & Folgering, 2001).

Cognitive behavioral interventions have many features similar to stress-management trials, and both types of interventions deal with cognitive restructuring, coping skills, provision of psychological support, and illness education. It is still unclear whether these types of interventions influence the immune system (see a recent meta-analysis by Miller & Cohen, 2001). Miller and Cohen have proposed that patients evaluate stressful experiences as significant threats and exceeding coping resources, and this might elicit negative emotional responses. They also cited studies suggesting that these negative emotional responses cause distressed patients to engage in behaviors (e.g., tobacco use, decreasing physical activity, altering sleep patterns) that conceivably modify immune responses. In addition, negative emotional states might also activate the sympathetic division, whose fibers descend from the brain to lymphoid tissues (bone marrow, thymus, spleen, etc.), and these fibers could release substances that influence immune responses. Distress also can activate the HPA axis, and hormonal products from these systems can dysregulate the immune system. Psychological interventions might modify the way stressful circumstances are appraised and diminish the way negative emotional responses influence immune dysregulation. Relaxation, emotional-regulation training, and learning more adaptive coping responses might also decrease negative emotions.

As mentioned previously, over the past few years, research conducted in Europe by three independent groups has suggested that cognitive behavior therapy is an effective treatment approach for those with CFS. While cognitive behavior therapy has been applied to several medical problems from pain to fibromyalgia, its application to CFS has been more controversial. This is due in part to several of the components of cognitive behavior therapy, as practiced by the British investigators, that involve the following notions: Resting is not helpful, increasing levels of exercising is critical, and patients need to be convinced that the disorder does not have a viral or medical etiology. Because the findings of the British studies have been disseminated widely, it is not uncommon for medical practitioners today to encourage patients with CFS to begin an exercise program and for patients to be challenged about their beliefs about the medical etiology of their disorder. Many patient groups have been critical of these cognitive behavioral studies because they have been used to dispute either the severity or biological nature of their illness. The studies conducted to date on this topic have had serious methodological problems including, for example, heterogeneous patient groups that may have encompassed subjects manifesting purely psychiatric disorders. Considerable data indicates that cognitive behavioral interventions are very effective for individuals with depression; therefore, it remains unclear as to which population or subgroups of patients actually benefit from this type of treatment.

Medical Utilization

Because most prior research has consisted of medically referred samples, it has been unclear what medical services have been used by the population of individuals with CFS and what proportion of individuals suffering from CFS have gone untreated or have been treated for other illnesses. In a study of individuals with chronic fatigue, CFS, and fibromyalgia from a university-based chronic fatigue clinic (Bombardier & Buchwald, 1996), individuals were found to access health care services, both allopathic and alternative, at a rate higher than the average, possibly indicating simultaneous and uncoordinated use of services. This may be indicative of the lack of diagnostic or treatment satisfaction among individuals seeking care for fatiguing illnesses such as CFS. Related to this finding, Lane, Matthews, and Manu (1990) found that in individuals accessing physical examinations and laboratory investigations for a chief complaint of fatigue, diagnostic information was produced in only 2% of physical examinations and 5% of laboratory investigations. These investigations indicate that perhaps due to the nature of fatigue-related physical complaints, individuals with fatigue in general and CFS in particular are subject to inaccurate diagnoses and dissatisfaction with health care practitioners.

In a recent community-based study of CFS, Jason, Taylor, Kennedy, Song, et al. (2000) found that the majority of individuals diagnosed with CFS had consulted a physician regarding their fatigue (65.6%), but only 10% to 15% of them had been previously diagnosed with CFS. This is important for two reasons. First, over one-third of people with CFS have never been seen by a physician for their fatigue. This finding may be attributable, in part, to limited social and economic resources among many of the individuals with CFS in our sample (Jason, Richman, et al., 1999) and a resulting decreased tendency for those individuals to seek appropriate medical care. Second, of those who had been seen by a physician, very few had been appropriately diagnosed with CFS. This suggests that there may be inadequacies in medical awareness of diagnostic criteria and/or biases in medical perceptions of fatigue-related illness that prevent individuals from receiving appropriate diagnosis and treatment.

Findings for high levels of dissatisfaction with traditional medical care among individuals with CFS (Anderson &

Ferrans, 1997; David et al., 1991; Friedberg & Jason, 1998; Twemlow, Bradshaw, Coyne, & Lerma, 1997) may, in large part, be explained by this observed tendency among medical professionals to not recognize and to underdiagnose CFS. For example, a study by Anderson and Ferrans (1997) found that 77% of individuals with CFS reported past negative experiences with health care providers, and 35% indicated that they no longer sought treatment because of minimal benefits. In addition to these issues, the contrasting findings for a low frequency of CFS diagnoses despite a relatively high rate of consultation for fatigue-related problems (65.6%) may explain some of the previous findings of clinic-based studies (Bombardier & Buchwald, 1996; Twemlow et al., 1997) for higher rates of medical utilization among individuals with CFS. Individuals possessing social and economic resources often have to be persistent to obtain appropriate diagnoses and treatment. This persistence may manifest in high rates of medical utilization because these individuals know that they need medical care, but medical professionals are unable to provide an appropriate diagnosis or treatment.

Treatment Attributions

Taylor, Jason, Kennedy, and Friedberg (2001) evaluated whether differing orientations toward treating CFS influence attributions about the illness. A group of mental health professionals was randomly assigned to one of three conditions. All groups read the same case study of a person diagnosed with CFS, with the only difference between groups being in the type of treatment described. The three treatment conditions were cognitive-behavior therapy with graded activity, cognitive coping skills therapy, and intravenous ampligen infusion. Participants then answered a questionnaire assessing their attributions about certain aspects of the illness, including its cause, severity, prognosis, and the effectiveness of the proposed treatment. Findings indicated that participants who read the case study proposing treatment with Ampligen were more likely to report that the patient was correctly diagnosed with CFS and to perceive the patient as more disabled than those whose case study described cognitive-behavioral therapy with graded activity as the treatment.

Describing the use of Ampligen as a treatment for CFS seems to have influenced people to perceive the patient as more disabled than if another type of treatment was used. This supports the hypothesis that the use of a more medical-sounding treatment influences perceptions that the illness may be more medically legitimate and disabling. The finding that individuals in this condition also believed the patient was more likely to have been correctly diagnosed may indicate that accurate perceptions of CFS are more likely to be generated when a more medical-sounding treatment is proposed. Results and conclusions of this study do not imply that physicians should not recommend cognitive-behavior therapy interventions in treating individuals with CFS. However, they do highlight the salience of physician opinion and orientation toward CFS in influencing the attributions of other health care providers, such as mental health practitioners.

Results point to the potentially negative impact of psychologically based recommendations upon the attitudes and attributions about CFS of associated mental health practitioners, particularly in the absence of recommendations for medical forms of intervention. It is possible that such attributions can influence the level of empathy and validation for CFS symptoms among mental health practitioners, two components of psychotherapy that are highly important to treatment efficacy (Friedberg & Jason, 1998). Future research is necessary to demonstrate the role of attributions about CFS in influencing the strength of the therapeutic relationship and the overall effectiveness of psychotherapy with this illness population.

STIGMA

CFS is a serious and complex illness that affects many different body systems, and it is characterized by incapacitating fatigue (experienced as profound exhaustion and extremely poor stamina), neurocognitive problems, and other somatic symptoms (Jason et al., 1997). The actual term CFS was adopted in 1988 in the original case definition published in the *Annals of Internal Medicine* (Holmes et al., 1988). The authors, many of whom were connected with the CDC, selected this diagnostic label based on the limited knowledge about the illness and the fact that the most common symptom among patients was debilitating, prolonged fatigue. Unfortunately, the patient community has felt that this label trivializes the seriousness of this illness because fatigue is commonly experienced by many people in our society. In addition, CFS is frequently confused as solely chronic fatigue, a symptom of many illnesses. Thus, the name places too great an emphasis on the single symptom of fatigue (Hoh, 1997).

Although it was expected that the name CFS would eventually be replaced, this term became the most commonly used label and has remained for several years. Another label, Myalgic Encephalomyelitis, is a medically based term used to characterize CFS in the United Kingdom and proposed for use in the United States by various patient groups. Some patients have suggested changing the label to an eponym, a name given to characterize an illness by associating it with a well-known person who either had the illness or discovered it.

Florence Nightingale Disease has been suggested as a possible eponym for CFS, since Florence Nightingale, a nurse well known for improving public health during the Crimean War, became very ill following the war and spent the remainder of her life confined to bed and sofa due to chronic fatigue. It is possible that people with CFS would be taken more seriously if labeled with a medical diagnosis like Myalgic Encephalomyelitis or by an eponym.

Social stigma as defined by Gilbert, Fiske, and Lindzey (1998) involves having an attribute that conveys a devalued social identity in a particular context. More specifically, the problem of stigma does not reside in the stigmatized attribute, or in the person who possesses the attribute, but in the unfortunate circumstance of possessing an attribute that, in a given social context, leads to devaluation. For persons with CFS, the effects of stigmatization can be palpable. A source of this stigma arises from the fact that many people with this syndrome have symptoms that vary from person to person and fluctuate in severity. Thus, specific symptoms may come and go, complicating treatment and the person's ability to cope with the illness. In addition, most symptoms are not visibly apparent, which makes it difficult for others to understand the vast array of debilitating symptoms that patients have.

Shlaes, Jason, and Ferrari (1999) developed the CFS Attitude Test (CAT), as one way of assessing stigma, discrimination, and attitudes toward individuals with CFS. Using this newly developed scale, they found a relationship between beliefs about the degree to which people with CFS are responsible for their illness, beliefs about the relevance of CFS as a valid illness, and beliefs about the personality traits of people with CFS. If someone believes that people with CFS are responsible for their illness, it is likely that they will also believe that people with CFS have negative personality characteristics, such as being compulsive or overly driven.

Name changes that have been made for other illnesses have reduced stigma. For example, gay related infectious disease had less scientific information available when the name was changed to AIDS than is available for CFS. Multiple Sclerosis (MS) is a neurological disease with many symptoms similar to CFS (Richman et al., 2000). MS was previously believed to be caused by stress linked with oedipal fixations. When the name of the disorder changed from hysterical paralysis (a name functioning to discredit the legitimate medical complaints of predominantly female patients; see Richman & Jason, 2001), to MS, when no more scientific information was available than we currently have for CFS, less stigma was associated with this illness. Psychiatric assumptions, however, were not put to rest until after empirical research failed to show any consistent personality patterns in MS (Murray, 1995).

There has been considerable controversy over the term CFS during the past decade. In general, patients feel that this label tends to minimize the seriousness of the illness. During the summer of 1997, the chronic fatigue and immune dysfunction syndrome (CFIDS) Association of America conducted a survey of its members to determine their opinion about changing the diagnostic label. Eighty-five percent of respondents indicated they wanted the name changed (Name-Change Survey Results, 1997). Another survey of 182 respondents by the editor of a newsletter indicated that 92% wanted the CFS name changed (Burns, 1998). Many medical personnel and research scientists feel that if the name were changed, it would be best to have a scientific basis for the change. Unfortunately, few data have been collected to help guide the process of revising the name.

In a study by the research team headed by the first author (Jason, Taylor, Plioplys, Stepanek, & Shlaes, in press), 105 medical trainees were randomly assigned to one of three conditions, each featuring one of three different types of diagnostic labels for CFS. The same case study of a patient with classic symptoms of CFS was described across conditions. The only difference between the three conditions involved the name given for the illness that was described in the case study. For one-third of the trainees, the patient was described as having CFS. For another third of the trainees, the patient was described as having an illness known as Florence Nightingale Disease (FN), and for the final third of the trainees, the patient was described as having Myalgic Encephalopathy (ME). Findings indicated that those with a diagnosis of Myalgic Encephalopathy were considered less likely to improve over time, and less likely to qualify as candidates for organ donation. These attributions may, in part, be due to the medical terminology contained in the Myalgic Encephalopathy label, which may lead individuals to think that the illness is more severe and as more likely to have biological underpinnings.

This study also found that some medical trainees continue to attribute CFS to nonorganic factors and may not recognize the significance of associated physical symptoms. For example, almost half of the entire sample of trainees indicated that it was likely or very likely that CFS is stress-related, and 37% felt that the patient was suffering primarily from depression. In addition, symptoms of cognitive impairment and pain were not considered to be severe by 90% of respondents. Thus, although both stress and depression can play a role in exacerbating the course of many illnesses, including CFS, the medical trainees' tendency to attribute the illness solely to these factors and to grant little recognition to the severity of the patient's cognitive problems and pain suggests that many medical trainees may continue to hold stigmatizing beliefs about the cause and nature of CFS that correspond with the current cultural predisposition toward holding people more directly responsible for their own health. A second explanation for these findings may involve a general lack of education about CFS among medical trainees (13% of advanced medical students indicated that they had never heard of CFS, only 21% of them had ever read an article about CFS, and only 15% had ever known someone diagnosed with CFS).

There is a clear need for a better understanding of how we might conceptualize the benefits and limitations of possible names for this syndrome. As the process of changing the name of the illness begins, an advisory committee to study the renaming of CFS has been organized, called the Name Change Working Group of the U.S. Department of Health and Human Services. Continued data-based investigations, such as the study described, are needed to ensure that any new recommendation for naming this illness appropriately conveys its severity and does not continue to stigmatize patients.

FUTURE DIRECTIONS

When a new disease syndrome emerges, such as CFS, studies on attributions, diagnostic criteria, epidemiology, subtyping, and treatment approaches can help shape public policy decisions (Jason, Taylor, Plioplys, et al., in press). Beliefs about the medical legitimacy of the illness may influence federal and state resources allocated for research, prevention, and intervention (Friedberg & Jason, 1998). Scientists have key roles to play in investigating issues of attribution as they relate to new disease syndromes such as CFS. For example, the diagnostic label given to this illness, CFS, has been perceived, particularly by patient groups, as functioning to minimize its severity and the devastating consequences of CFS. It is unfortunate that many medical personnel continue to believe that CFS is a psychiatric disorder. To promote positive change, scientists should participate in conducting more rigorously designed research leading to more accurate diagnosis, characterization, and treatment of this disorder.

Throughout this chapter, the threats to reliability and validity of research resulting from the use of alternative criteria for diagnosing CFS cases have been emphasized. If inappropriate use of the case definition leads to the inclusion of individuals who have a purely psychiatric condition, this heterogeneity of patients with CFS and psychiatric conditions will present difficulties in interpreting the results of epidemiologic and treatment studies. Inevitably, there is some risk that samples of individuals with chronic fatigue and some somatic symptoms include those with solely psychiatric

diagnoses, those with solely CFS diagnoses, and some with CFS and psychiatric comorbidity. Therefore, these three groups need to be differentiated and analyzed separately as opposed to being collapsed into one category.

In addition, diagnostic criteria should be empirically derived and specify which diagnostic instruments are appropriate to use, what informants to use, and how to rate for presence and severity of the criteria. Future definitions of CFS should include specific guidelines pertaining to the importance of symptom severity in the diagnostic procedure. Given the high variability in symptom severity among persons with CFS, a standardized procedure for determining whether a particular symptom is severe enough to qualify as one of the four minor CFS symptoms should be employed. Presently, there are no guidelines for physicians to follow when determining whether a symptom is severe enough to qualify as meeting the diagnostic criteria. If CFS is to be diagnosed reliably across health care professionals, we recommend the establishment of discrete cutoff points. Without such standardization, symptom variability will remain a function of the assessment procedure and etiological factors. If health care professionals are to improve their understanding of the complexities of this disease and their ability to identify distinct subtypes of CFS patients, the current U.S. case definition (Fukuda et al., 1994) may need to be revised to clarify the significance of symptom severity in diagnostic and assessment procedures (Jason, King, et al., 1999).

Fatigue, arbitrarily defined as more than one month in duration, is common in the general population, occurring in between 19% and 28% of the population (Kroenke et al., 1988). However, severe fatigue is less common, with several studies suggesting that about 5% of a community sample would have significant fatigue for six months or more (Jason et al., 1995). Among this 5% with chronic fatigue, a key question involves the percentage likely to be diagnosed with CFS, and rates range from 2.6% to less than .1% (Friedberg & Jason, 1998). A broad or narrow definition will have important influences on both CFS epidemiologic and treatment studies (Jason et al., 1997). Different CFS criteria clearly account for some of this variability. In addition, some investigators believe that while CFS is probably a heterogeneous disorder, it is still possible to differentiate those having this discrete disorder from other psychiatric conditions that also encompass fatigue (Friedberg & Jason, 1998).

Over the past 10 years, a series of key decisions were made concerning the criteria for diagnosing CFS and the selection of psychiatric instruments, which could alternatively score CFS symptoms as reflective of medical or psychiatric problems. Many of these decisions were formulated within a societal and political context in which CFS was assumed to be a psychological problem. Many physicians and researchers believed that CFS was similar to neurasthenia, and that CFS would eventually have a similar fate once people recognized that most patients with this disease were really suffering from a psychiatric illness. Psychiatrists and physicians have also regarded fatigue as one of the least important presenting symptoms. These biases have been filtered to the media, which has portrayed CFS in simplistic and stereotypic ways.

Some progress has occurred with regard to the improved reliability and validity of results emerging from CFS research. At the same time, problems remain, which constitute important challenges for social science researchers. In the area of CFS epidemiology, critiques of sample selection biases in earlier studies (Richman et al., 1994) have lead to more recent research addressing the true prevalence of CFS in community samples, which is not biased by help-seeking behaviors or by access to the health care system (Jason et al. 1995; Jason, Richman, et al., 1999). However, a broadened interpretation of CFS appears to have complicated estimates of CFS prevalence by confounding the diagnosis of CFS with diagnoses of other illnesses, which have overlapping symptoms but which may not constitute CFS at all, or with conditions that are often comorbid with CFS. Moreover, beyond the need to obtain accurate epidemiologic estimates of CFS prevalence for public health policy formulation, reliable and valid diagnoses are crucial for determinations of CFS treatment efficacy. We believe that it is crucial for CFS research to move beyond fuzzy recapitulations of the neurasthenia concept and clearly delineate precise criteria for diagnosing pure CFS versus CFS that is comorbid with psychiatric disorders. It is also necessary to better differentiate CFS from other disorders that share some CFS symptoms but are not true CFS cases.

Approaches to treatment must be comprehensive, addressing a variety of care needs. Much attention of researchers has focused on the potential benefits of cognitive behavioral interventions. As mentioned, the long-term outcomes of this type of intervention are still unclear, but interventions that challenge basic patient illness beliefs might solidify already-negative attitudes of medical personnel toward people with this syndrome. Moreover, future research findings may legitimate patient beliefs regarding the organic nature of their illness, similar to the historical evolution of the social construction of multiple sclerosis from a psychological to an organically based illness (Richman & Jason, 2001). In addition to more psychologically based interventions, there is a clear need for advocacy, in which the general public and the medical community become better educated about the problems and difficulties associated with CFS. Some patients with CFS may need assistance from others to complete daily living tasks. Living arrangements that include "healthy" individuals or housing may be needed by people with CFS, because weakness from this illness might prevent them from accomplishing necessary chores. Interventions are needed that focus on enriching the sense of community, and such interventions may prevent isolation, depression, and preoccupation with the illness among patients with CFS (Jason, Kolak, et al., 2001). Unfortunately, there are few funding opportunities for these more innovative types of social and community interventions. Given that this syndrome is one of the more common chronic health conditions (Jason, Richman, et al., 1999) and the documented personal and familial costs associated with this condition (Friedberg & Jason, 1998), there is a clear need for public policy officials to devote more resources to developing a better infrastructure of support for individuals with CFS (Taylor, Friedberg, & Jason, 2001).

REFERENCES

Ablashi, D. V., Eastman, H. B., Owen, C. B., Roman, M. M., Fridman, J., Zabriskie, J. B., et al. (2000). Frequent HHV-6 reactivation in multiple sclerosis (MS) and chronic fatigue syndrome (CFS) patients. *Journal of Clinical Virology, 16*(3), 179–191.

Akerstedt, T., Torsvall, L., & Gillberg, M. (1985). Sleepiness and shift work: Field studies. *Sleep 5,* S95–S106.

American Psychiatric Association. (1994). *Diagnostic and statistical manual of mental disorders* (4th ed.). Washington, DC: Author.

Anderson, J. S., & Ferrans, C. E. (1997). The quality of life of persons with chronic fatigue syndrome. *Journal of Nervous and Mental Diseases, 185*(6), 359–367.

Antoni, M. H., Brickman, A., Lutgendorf, S., Klimas, N. G., Imia-Fins, A., Ironson, G., et al. (1994). Psychosocial correlates of illness burden in chronic fatigue syndrome. *Clinical Infectious Diseases, 18*(Suppl. 1), S73–S78.

Barsky, A. J., & Borus, J. F. (1999). Functional somatic syndromes. *Annals of Internal Medicine, 130,* 910–921.

Bazelmans, E., Bleijenberg, G., van der Meer, J. W. M., & Folgering, H. (2001). Is physical deconditioning a perpetuating factor in chronic fatigue syndrome? A controlled study on maximal exercise performance and relations with fatigue, impairment and physical activity. *Psychological Medicine, 31,* 107–114.

Bombardier, C. H., & Buchwald, D. (1995). Outcome and prognosis of patients with chronic fatigue and chronic fatigue syndrome. *Archives of Internal Medicine, 155,* 2105–2110.

Bombardier, C. H., & Buchwald, D. (1996). Chronic fatigue, chronic fatigue syndrome, and fibromyalgia: Disability and health care use. *Medical Care, 34*(9), 924–930.

Bou-Holaigah, I., Rowe, P. C., Kan, J., & Calkins, H. (1995). The relationship between neurally mediated hypotension and the chronic fatigue syndrome. *Journal of the American Medical Association, 274*(12), 961–967.

Brouwer, B., & Packer, T. (1994). Corticospinal excitability in patients diagnosed with chronic fatigue syndrome. *Muscle and Nerve, 17,* 1210–1212.

Buchwald, D., Pearlman, T., Kith, P., & Schmaling, K. (1994). Gender differences in patients with chronic fatigue syndrome. *Journal of General Internal Medicine, 9,* 387–401.

Buchwald, D., Umali, P., Umali, J., Kith, P., Pearlman, T., & Komaroff, A. L. (1995). Chronic fatigue and chronic fatigue syndrome: Prevalence in a Pacific Northwest Health Care System. *Annals of Internal Medicine, 123,* 81–88.

Burns, R. (1998). *Responses for CFS name survey two.* Available from: www.cais.net/cfs-news/responses-2.htm

Camacho, J., & Jason, L. A. (1998). Psychosocial factors show little relationship to chronic fatigue syndrome recovery. *Journal of Psychology and the Behavioral Sciences, 12,* 60–70.

Cantwell, D. P. (1996). Classification of child and adolescent psychopathology. *Journal of Child Psychology and Psychiatry, 37,* 3–12.

Chaudhuri, A., Majeed, T., Dinan, T., & Behan, P. O. (1997). Chronic fatigue syndrome: A disorder of central cholinergic transmission. *Journal of Chronic Fatigue Syndrome, 3,* 3–16.

Clark, M. R., Katon, W., Russo, J., Kith, P., Sintay, M., & Buchwald, D. (1995). Chronic fatigue. Risk factors for symptom persistence in a two and one half year followup study. *American Journal of Medicine, 98,* 187–195.

Cleare, A. J., Heap, E., Malhi, G. S., Wessely, S., O'Keane, V., & Miell, J. (1999). Low-dose hydrocortisone in chronic fatigue syndrome: A randomized crossover trial. *Lancet, 353,* 455–458.

Cohen, N., Moynihan, J. A., & Ader, R. (1994). Pavlovian conditioning of the immune system. *International Archives of Allergy and Immunology, 105,* 101–106.

Coulter, P. (1988). Chronic fatigue syndrome: An old virus with a new diagnosis. *Journal of Community Health Nursing, 5,* 87–95.

David, A. S., Wessely, S., & Pelosi, A. J. (1991). Chronic fatigue syndrome: Signs of a new approach. *British Journal of Hospital Medicine, 45,* 158–163.

Deale, A., Chalder, T., Marks, I., & Wessely, S. (1997). Cognitive behaviour therapy for chronic fatigue syndrome: A randomized controlled trial. *American Journal of Psychiatry, 154,* 408–414.

Dechene, L., Friedberg, F., MacKenzie, M., & Fontanetta, R. (1994). *A new fatigue typology for chronic fatigue syndrome.* Unpublished manuscript, Fitchburg State College, Fitchburg, MA.

DeLuca, J., Johnson, S. K., Ellis, S. P., & Natelson, B. H. (1997). Sudden versus gradual onset of chronic fatigue syndrome differentiates individuals on cognitive and psychiatric measures. *Journal of Psychiatric Research, 31,* 83–90.

De Meirleir, K., Bisbal, C., Campine, I., De Becker, P., Salehzada, T., Demettre, E., et al. (2000). A 37 kDa 2–5A binding protein as a potential biochemical marker for chronic fatigue syndrome. *American Journal of Medicine, 108,* 99–105.

Demitrack, M. A. (1993). Neuroendocrine research strategies in chronic fatigue syndrome. In P. J. Goodnick & N. G. Klimas (Eds.), *Chronic fatigue and related immune deficiency syndromes* (pp. 45–66). Washington, DC: American Psychiatric Press.

Donati, F., Fagioli, L., Komaroff, A. L., & Duffy, F. H. (1994, October). *Quantified EEG findings in patients with chronic fatigue syndrome.* Paper presented at the American Association of Chronic Fatigue Syndrome Research Conference, Ft. Lauderdale, FL.

Dowsett, E. G., Goudsmit, E. M., Macintyre, A., & Shepherd, C. (1994). London criteria for Myalgic Encephalomyelitis. In *Report from the National Task Force on Chronic Fatigue Syndrome (CFS), Post Viral Fatigue Syndrome (PVFS), Myalgic Encephalomyelitis (ME)* (pp. 96–98). Bristol, England: Westcare.

Dunstan, R. H., Donohoe, M., Taylor, W., Roberts, T. K., Murdoch, R. N., Watkins, J. A., et al. (1995). A preliminary investigation of chlorinated hydrocarbons and chronic fatigue syndrome. *Medical Journal of Australia, 163,* 294–297.

Elenkov, I. J., Wilder, R. L., Chrousos, G. P., & Vizi, E. S. (2000). The sympathetic nerve–An integrative interface between two supersystems: The brain and the immune system. *Pharmacological Reviews, 52,* 595–638.

Endicott, J., & Spitzer, R. L. (1977, May). *A diagnostic interview: The schedule for affective disorders and schizophrenia.* Paper presented at the American Psychiatric Association, Toronto, Ontario, Canada.

Endicott, N. A. (1999). Chronic fatigue syndrome in private practice psychiatry: Family history of physical and mental health. *Journal of Psychosomatic Research, 47,* 343–354.

Euba, R., Chalder, T., Deale, A., & Wessely, S. (1996). A comparison of the characteristics of chronic fatigue syndrome in primary and tertiary care. *British Journal of Psychiatry, 168,* 121–126.

Evengard, B., Schacterle, R. S., & Komaroff, A. L. (1999). Chronic fatigue syndrome: New insights and old ignorance. *Journal of Internal Medicine, 246,* 455–469.

Feighner, J. P., Robins, E., Guze, S. B., Woodruff, R. A., Winokur, G., & Munoz, R. (1972). Diagnostic criteria for use in psychiatric research. *Archives of General Psychiatry, 26,* 57–63.

Fennell, P. A. (1995). The four progressive stages of the CFS experience: A coping tool for patients. *Journal of Chronic Fatigue Syndrome, 1,* 69–79.

Freeman, R., & Komaroff, A. L. (1997). Does the chronic fatigue syndrome involve autonomic nervous system? *American Journal of Medicine, 102,* 357–364.

Friedberg, F. (1996). Chronic fatigue syndrome: A new clinical application. Professional Psychology. *Research and Practice, 27,* 487–494.

Friedberg, F., Dechene, L., McKenzie, M., & Fontanetta, R. (2000). Symptom patterns in long-term chronic fatigue syndrome. *Journal of Psychosomatic Research, 48,* 59–68.

Friedberg, F., & Jason, L. A. (1998). *Understanding chronic fatigue syndrome: An empirical guide to assessment and treatment.* Washington, DC: American Psychological Association.

Friedberg, F., & Krupp, L. B. (1994). A comparison of cognitive behavioral treatment for chronic fatigue syndrome and primary depression. *Clinical Infectious Diseases, 18,* S105–S110.

Fukuda, K., Straus, S. E., Hickie, I., Sharpe, M. C., Dobbins, J. G., & Komaroff, A. (1994). The chronic fatigue syndrome: A comprehensive approach to its definition and study. *Annals of Internal Medicine, 121,* 953–959.

Fulcher, K. Y., & White, P. D. (1997). Randomised controlled trial of graded exercise in patients with the chronic fatigue syndrome. *British Medical Journal, 314,* 1647–1652.

Gellhorn, E. (1968). CNS tuning and its implications for neuropsychiatry. *Journal of Nervous and Mental Diseases, 147,* 148–162.

Gellhorn, E. (1970). The emotions and the ergotropic and trophotropic systems. *Psychologische Forschung, 34,* 48–94.

Gilbert, D. T., Fiske, S. T., & Lindzey, G. (1998). Social stigma. In *Handbook of social psychology* (Vol. 2). New York: Oxford University Press.

Girdano, D. A., Everly, G. S., Jr., & Dusek, D. E. (1990). *Controlling stress and tension: A holistic approach.* Englewood Cliffs, NJ: Prentice-Hall.

Glaser, R., & Kiecolt-Glaser, J. K. (1998). Stress-associated immune modulation: Relevance to viral infections and chronic fatigue syndrome. *American Journal of Medicine, 105,* 35–42.

Goldstein, J. A. (1990). *Chronic fatigue syndrome: The struggle for health.* Beverly Hills, CA: Chronic Fatigue Syndrome Institute.

Gow, J. W., Simpson, K., Behan, P. O., Chaudhuri, A., McKay, I. C., & Behan, W. M. H. (2001). Antiviral pathway activation in patients with chronic fatigue syndrome and acute infection. *Clinical Infectious Diseases, 33,* 2080–2081.

Gunn, W. J., Connell, D. B., & Randall, B. (1993). Epidemiology of chronic fatigue syndrome: The Centers-for-Disease-Control study. In B. R. Bock & J. Whelan (Eds.), *Chronic fatigue syndrome* (pp. 83–101). New York: Wiley.

Hadzi-Pavlovic, D., Hickie, I. B., Wilson, A. J., Davenport, T. A., Lloyd, A. R., & Wakefield, D. (2000). Screening for prolonged fatigue syndromes: Validation of the SOFA scale. *Social Psychiatry and Psychiatric Epidemiology, 35,* 471–479.

Haley, R. W., Kurt, T. L., & Hom, J. (1997). Is there a Gulf War syndrome? Searching for syndromes by factor analysis of symptoms. *Journal of the American Medical Association, 277,* 215–222.

Hall, D. G., Sanders, S. D., & Repologle, W. H. (1994). Fatigue: A new approach to an old problem. *Journal of the Mississippi State Medical Association,* 155–160.

Harlow, B. L., Signorello, L. B., Hall, J. E., Dailey, C., & Komaroff, A. L. (1998). Reproductive correlates of chronic fatigue syndrome. *American Journal of Medicine, 105,* 94S–99S.

Hartz, A. J., Kuhn, E. M., & Levine, P. H. (1998). Characteristics of fatigued persons associated with features of chronic fatigue syndrome. *Journal of Chronic Fatigue Syndrome, 4,* 71–97.

Hartz, A. J., Kuhn, E. M., Levine, P. H., & London, R. (1998, October). Prognostic factors for persons with chronic fatigue. In L. A. Jason & W. Reeves (Chair), *New insights into the epidemiology of CFS.* Symposium conducted at the American Association for Chronic Fatigue Syndrome Conference, Cambridge, MA.

Hedrick, T. E. (1997). Summary of risk factors for chronic fatigue syndrome is misleading [Letter to editor]. *Quarterly Journal of Medicine, 90,* 723–725.

Heim, C., Ehlert, U., & Hellhammer, D. H. (2000). The potential role of hypocortisolism in the pathophysiology of stress-related bodily disorders. *Psychoneuroendocrinology, 25*(1), 1–35.

Herst, C., Olsen, K., Strayer, D., Whitman, J., Peterson, W. D., & Ablashi, D. (2001, January). *Detection and correlation of 2'-5'-A binding proteins (37 kDa and 80 kDa) and HHV-6 infection in CFS patients and in vitro expression of these proteins in cells.* Poster presented at the meeting of American Association of Chronic Fatigue Syndrome, Seattle, WA.

Hickie, I., Bennett, B., Lloyd, A., Heath, A., & Martin, N. (1999). Complex genetic and environmental relationships between psychological distress, fatigue and immune functioning: A twin study. *Psychological Medicine, 29,* 267–277.

Hickie, I., Koschera, A., Hadzi-Pavlovic, D., Bennett, B., & Lloyd, A. (1999). The temporal stability and co-morbidity of prolonged fatigue: A longitudinal study in primary care. *Psychological Medicine, 29,* 855–861.

Hickie, I., Lloyd, A., Wilson, A., Hadzi-Pavlovic, D., Parker, G., Bird, K., et al. (1995). Can the chronic fatigue syndrome be defined by distinct clinical features? *Psychological Medicine, 25,* 925–935.

Hill, N. F., Tiersky, L. A., Scavalla, V. R., & Natelson, B. H. (1999). Fluctuation and outcome of chronic fatigue syndrome over time. *Journal of Chronic Fatigue Syndrome, 5*(3/4), 93–94.

Hoh, D. (1997). Rename it? Debate Centers on timing, choices for a new name. *CFIDS Chronicle, 10,* 7–9.

Holmes, G. P., Kaplan, J. E., Gantz, N. M., Komaroff, A. L., Schonberger, L. B., Strauss, S. S., et al. (1988). Chronic fatigue syndrome: A working case definition. *Annals of Internal Medicine, 108,* 387–389.

Jason, L. A., Fennell, P. A., Klein, S., Fricano, G., Halpert, J., & Taylor, R. R. (1999). An investigation of the different phases of the CFS illness. *Journal of Chronic Fatigue Syndrome, 5,* 35–54.

Jason, L. A., Fennell, P. A., Taylor, R. R., Fricano, G., & Halpert, J. (2000). An empirical verification of the Fennell phases of the CFS illness. *Journal of Chronic Fatigue Syndrome, 6,* 47–56.

Jason, L. A., Fricano, G., Taylor, R. R., Halpert, J., Fennell, P. A., Klein, S., et al. (2000). Chronic fatigue syndrome: An examination of the phases. *Journal of Clinical Psychology, 56,* 1497–1508.

Jason, L. A., King, C. P., Richman, J. A., Taylor, R. R., Torres, S. R., & Song, S. (1999). U.S. case definition of chronic fatigue syndrome: Diagnostic and theoretical issues. *Journal of Chronic Fatigue Syndrome, 5*(3/4), 3–33.

Jason, L. A., Kolak, A. M., Purnell, T., Cantillon, D., Camacho, J. M., Klein, S., et al. (2001). Collaborative ecological community interventions for people with chronic fatigue syndrome. *Journal of Prevention and Intervention in the Community, 21,* 35–52.

Jason, L. A., Melrose, H., Lerman, A., Burroughs, V., Lewis, K., King, C. P., et al. (1999). Managing chronic fatigue syndrome: A case study. *AAOHN Journal, 47,* 17–21.

Jason, L. A., Richman, J. A., Friedberg, F., Wagner, L., Taylor, R. R., & Jordan, K. M. (1997). Politics, science, and the emergence of a new disease: The case of chronic fatigue syndrome. *American Psychologist, 52,* 973–983.

Jason, L. A., Richman, J. A., Rademaker, A. W., Jordan, K. M., Plioplys, A. V., Taylor, R. R., et al. (1999). A community-based study of chronic fatigue syndrome. *Archives of Internal Medicine, 159,* 2129–2137.

Jason, L. A., & Taylor, R. R. (in press). Applying cluster analysis to define a typology of chronic fatigue syndrome in a medically-evaluated random community sample. *Psychology and Health.*

Jason, L. A., Taylor, R. R., & Carrico, A. W. (2001). A community based study of seasonal variation in the onset of chronic fatigue syndrome and idiopathic chronic fatigue. *Chronobiological International, 18,* 315–319.

Jason, L. A., Taylor, R. R., & Kennedy, C. L. (2000). Chronic fatigue syndrome, fibromyalgia, and multiple chemical sensitivities in a community-based sample of persons with chronic fatigue syndrome-like symptoms. *Psychosomatic Medicine, 62,* 655–663.

Jason, L. A., Taylor, R. R., Kennedy, C. L., Jordan, K., Huang, C., Song, S., et al. (in press). A factor analysis of chronic fatigue symptoms in a community-based study. *Social Psychiatry and Psychiatric Epidemiology.*

Jason, L. A., Taylor, R. R., Kennedy, C. L., Jordan, K., Song, S., Johnson, D., et al. (2000). Chronic fatigue syndrome: Sociodemographic subtypes in a community-based sample. *Evaluation and the Health Professions, 23,* 243–263.

Jason, L. A., Taylor, R. R., Kennedy, C. L., Jordan, K., Song, S., Johnson, D., et al. (in press). Chronic fatigue syndrome: Symptom subtypes in a community based sample. *Women & Health.*

Jason, L. A., Taylor, R. R., Kennedy, C. L., Song, S., Johnson, D., & Torres, S. (2000). Chronic fatigue syndrome: Occupation, medical utilization, and subtypes in a community based sample. *Journal of Nervous and Mental Diseases, 188,* 568–576.

Jason, L. A., Taylor, R. R., Kennedy, C. L., Song, S., Johnson, D., & Torres, S. (2001). Chronic fatigue syndrome: Comorbidity with fibromyalgia and psychiatric illness. *Medicine and Psychiatry, 4,* 29–34.

Jason, L. A., Taylor, R. R., Plioplys, S., Stepanek, Z., & Shlaes, J. (in press). Evaluating attributions for an illness based upon the name: Chronic fatigue syndrome, myalgic encephalopathy and Florence Nightingale disease. *American Journal of Community Psychology.*

Jason, L. A., Taylor, R. R., Wagner, L., Holden, J., Ferrari, J. R., Plioplys, A. V., et al. (1995). Estimating rates of chronic fatigue syndrome from a community based sample: A pilot study. *American Journal of Community Psychology, 23,* 557–568.

Jason, L. A., Torres-Harding, S. R., Carrico, A. W., & Taylor, R. R. (2002). Symptom occurrence with chronic fatigue syndrome. *Biological Psychology, 59,* 15–27.

Jason, L. A., Torres-Harding, S. R., Taylor, R. R., & Carrico, A. W. (2001). A comparison of the 1988 and 1994 diagnostic criteria for chronic fatigue syndrome. *Journal of Clinical Psychology in Medical Settings, 8,* 337–343.

Jason, L. A., & Wagner, L. I. (1998). Chronic fatigue syndrome among nurses. *American Journal of Nursing, 98*(5), 16B–16H.

Jason, L. A., Wagner, L. I., Rosenthal, S., Goodlatte, J., Lipkin, D., Papernik, M., et al. (1998). Estimating the prevalence of chronic fatigue syndrome among nurses. *American Journal of Medicine, 105*(3A), 91S–93S.

Johnson, S. K., DeLuca, J., & Natelson, B. (1999). Chronic fatigue syndrome: Reviewing the research findings. *Annals of Behavioral Medicine, 21,* 258–271.

Jordan, K. M., Mears, C. J., Katz, B. Z., Jason, L. A., Rademaker, A., Huang, C., et al. (2002). *Prevalence of pediatric chronic fatigue syndrome in a community-based sample.* Manuscript submitted for publication.

Joyce, J., Hotopf, M., & Wessely, S. (1997). The prognosis of chronic fatigue and chronic fatigue syndrome: A systematic review. *Quarterly Journal of Medicine, 90,* 223–233.

Kansky, G. (2000). Is Ampligen a death sentence? *National Forum, 3,* 14–15.

Katerndahl, D. A. (1993). Differentiation of physical and psychological fatigue. *Family Practice Research Journal, 13,* 81–91.

Katon, W., & Russo, J. (1992). Chronic fatigue syndrome criteria: A critique of the requirement for multiple physical complaints. *Archives of Internal Medicine, 152,* 1604–1609.

King, C. P., Jason, L. A., Frankenberry, E. L., & Jordan, K. M. (1997, fall). Think inside the envelope. *CFIDS Chronicle,* 10–14.

Komaroff, A. L. (1988). Chronic fatigue syndromes: Relationship to chronic viral infections. *Journal of Virology Research, 21,* 3–10.

Komaroff, A. L. (1994). Clinical presentation and evaluation of fatigue and chronic fatigue syndrome. In S. E. Straus (Ed.), *Chronic fatigue syndrome* (pp. 61–84). New York: Marcel Dekker.

Komaroff, A. L. (2000a). The biology of chronic fatigue syndrome. *American Journal of Medicine, 108,* 169–171.

Komaroff, A. L. (2000b). The physical basis of CFS. *CFIDS Research Review, 1*(2), 1–3, 11.

Komaroff, A. L., Fagioli, L. R., Geiger, A. M., Doolittle, T. H., Lee, J., Kornish, R. J., et al. (1996). An examination of the working case definition of chronic fatigue syndrome. *American Journal of Medicine, 100,* 56–64.

Kroenke, K., Wood, D., Mangelsdorff, D., Meier, N., & Powell, J. (1988). Chronic fatigue in primary care: Prevalence, patient characteristics and outcome. *Journal of the American Medical Association, 260,* 929–934.

Krupp, L. B., Mendelson, W. B., & Friedman, R. (1991). An overview of chronic fatigue syndrome. *Journal of Clinical Psychiatry, 52*(10), 403–410.

Landay, A. L., Jessop, C., Lennette, E. T., & Levy, J. A. (1991). Chronic fatigue syndrome: Clinical condition associated with immune activation. *Lancet, 338,* 707–712.

Lane, T. J., Matthews, D. A., & Manu, P. (1990). The low yield of physical examinations and laboratory investigations of patients with chronic fatigue. *American Journal of Medical Science, 299*(5), 313–318.

Lange, G., DeLuca, J., Maldjian, J. A., Lee, H., Tiersky, L. A., & Natelson, B. H. (1999). Brain MRI abnormalities exist in a subset of patients with chronic fatigue syndrome. *Journal of Neurological Sciences, 171,* 3–7.

Lange, G., Wang, S., DeLuca, J., & Natelson, B. H. (1998). Neuroimaging in chronic fatigue syndrome. *American Journal of Medicine, 105*(SA), 50S–53S.

Laurie, S. M., Manders, D. N., Geddes, J. R., & Pelosi, A. J. (1997). A population-based incidence study of chronic fatigue. *Psychological Medicine, 27,* 343–353.

Lawrie, S. M., & Pelosi, A. J. (1995). Chronic fatigue syndrome in the community. Prevalence and associations. *British Journal of Psychiatry, 166,* 793–797.

Leckliter, I. N., & Matarazzo, J. D. (1994). Diagnosis and classification. In V. B. Van Hasselt & M. Hersen (Eds.), *Advanced abnormal psychology* (pp. 3–18). New York: Plenum Press.

Leese, G., Chattington, P., Fraser, W., Vora, J., Edwards, R., & Williams, G. (1996). Short-term night-shift working mimics the pituitary-adrenocortical dysfunction in chronic fatigue syndrome. *Journal of Clinical Endocrinological Metabolism, 81*(5), 1867–1870.

Lerner, A. M., Lawrie, C., & Dworkin, H. S. (1993). Repetitively negative changing T waves at 24-h electrocardiographic monitors in patients with chronic fatigue syndrome. *Chest, 104,* 1417–1421.

Levine, P. H. (1997). Epidemiologic advances in chronic fatigue syndrome. *Journal of Psychiatric Research, 31*(1), 7–18.

Lloyd, A. R., Hickie, I., Boughton, C. R., Spencer, O., & Wakefield, D. (1990). Prevalence of chronic fatigue syndrome in an Australian population. *Medical Journal of Australia, 153,* 522–528.

Maier, S. F., Watkins, L. R., & Fleshner, M. (1994). Psychoneuroimmunology: The interface between behavior, brain, and immunity. *American Psychologist, 49,* 1004–1017.

Matarazzo, J. (1983). The reliability of psychiatric and psychological diagnosis. In J. Hooley, J. Neale, & G. Davidson (Eds.), *Readings in abnormal psychology* (pp. 36–65). New York: Wiley.

Manu, P., Lane, T. J., & Matthews, D. A. (1988). The frequency of the Chronic Fatigue Syndrome in patients with symptoms of persistent fatigue. *Annals of Internal Medicine, 109,* 554–556.

McKenzie, R., O'Fallon, A., Dale, J., Demitrack, M., Sharma, G., Deloria, M., et al. (1998). Low-dose hydrocortisone for treatment of chronic fatigue syndrome. *Journal of the American Medical Association, 280*(12), 1061–1066.

Miller, G. E., & Cohen, S. (2001). Psychological interventions and the immune system: A meta-analytic review and critique. *Health Psychology, 20,* 47–63.

Morriss, R. K., Ahmed, M., Wearden, A. J., Mullis, R., Strickland, P., Appleby, L., et al. (1999). The role of depression in pain, psychophysiological syndromes, and medically unexplained symptoms associated with chronic fatigue syndrome. *Journal of Affective Disorders, 55,* 143–148.

Murray, T. J. (1995). The psychosocial aspects of multiple sclerosis. *Neurologic Clinics, 13,* 197–223.

Name-Change Survey Results. (1997). Available from: www.cfids.org/chronicle/97summer/survey.html.

Natelson, B. H., Cheu, J., Pareja, J., Ellis, S. P., Policastro, T., & Findley, T. W. (1996). Randomized, double blind, controlled placebo-phase in trial of low dose phenelzine in the chronic fatigue syndrome. *Psychopharmacology, 124,* 226–230.

Natelson, B. H., Cohen, J. M., Brassloff, I., & Lee, H. J. (1993). A controlled study of brain magnetic resonance imaging in patients with fatiguing illnesses. *Journal of the Neurological Sciences, 120,* 213–217.

Nicolson, G. L., Nasralla, M. Y., Haier, J., Irwine, R., Nicolson, N. L., & Ngwenya, R. (1999). Mycoplasmal infections in chronic illnesses: Fibromyalgia and chronic fatigue syndromes, Gulf War illness, HIV-AIDS and rheumatoid arthritis. *Medical Sentinel, 4,* 172–175.

Nisenbaum, R., Reyes, M., Mawle, A. C., & Reeves, W. C. (1998). Factor analysis of unexplained severe fatigue and interrelated symptoms: Overlap with criteria for chronic fatigue syndrome. *American Journal of Epidemiology, 148,* 72–77.

Patarca, R., Fletcher, M. A., & Klimas, N. G. (1993). Immunological correlates of chronic fatigue syndrome. In P. J. Goodnick & N. G. Klimas (Eds.), *Chronic fatigue and related immune deficiency syndromes* (pp. 1–21). Washington, DC: American Psychiatric Press.

Patarca-Montero, R., Mark, T., Fletcher, M. A., & Klimas, N. G. (2000). Immunology of chronic fatigue syndrome. *Journal of Chronic Fatigue Syndrome, 6,* 69–107.

Pawlikowska, T., Chalder, T., Wessely, S., Wright, D., Hirsch, S., & Wallace, P. (1994). A population based study of fatigue and psychological distress. *British Medical Journal, 308,* 763–766.

Pesek, J. R., Jason, L. A., & Taylor, R. R. (2000). An empirical investigation of the envelope theory. *Journal of Human Behavior in the Social Environment, 3,* 59–77.

Poole, J., Herrell, R., Ashton, S., Goldberg, J., & Buchwald, D. (2000). Results of isoproterenol tilt table testing in monozygotic twins discordant for chronic fatigue syndrome. *Archives of Internal Medicine, 160,* 3461–3468.

Powell, P., Bentall, R. P., Nye, F. J., & Edwards, R. H. T. (2001). Randomized controlled trial of patient education to encourage exercise in chronic fatigue syndrome. *British Medical Journal, 322,* 1–5.

Prins, J. B., Bleijenberg, G., Bazelmans, E., Elving, L. D., de Boo, T. M., Severens, J. L., et al. (2001). Cognitive behaviour therapy for chronic fatigue syndrome: A multicenter randomized controlled trial. *Lancet, 357,* 841–847.

Ramsay, M. (1986). *Postviral fatigue syndrome: The saga of royal free disease.* London: Gower Medical.

Ray, C. (1991). Chronic fatigue syndrome: Conceptual and methodological ambiguities. *Psychological Medicine, 21,* 1–9.

Ray, C., Jeffries, S., & Weir, W. R. C. (1995). Life-events and the course of chronic fatigue syndrome. *British Journal of Medical Psychology, 68,* 323–331.

Ray, C., Jeffries, S., & Weir, W. R. C. (1997). Coping and other predictors of outcome in chronic fatigue syndrome: A 1-year follow-up. *Journal of Psychosomatic Research, 43*(4), 405–415.

Regier, D. A., Boyd, J. H., Burke, J. D., Jr., Rae, D. S., Myers, J. K., Kramer, M., et al. (1988). One-month prevalence of mental disorders in the United States: Based on five epidemiological catchment area sites. *Archives of General Psychiatry, 45,* 977–986.

Reid, S., Chalder, T., Cleare, A., Hotopf, M., & Wessely, S. (2000). Extracts from "clinical evidence": Chronic fatigue syndrome. *British Medical Journal, 320,* 292–296.

Reyes, M., Dobbins, J. G., Nisenbaum, R., Subedar, N., Randall, B., & Reeves, W. C. (1999). Chronic fatigue syndrome progression and self-defined recovery: Evidence from the CDC surveillance system. *Journal of Chronic Fatigue Syndrome, 5,* 17–27.

Reyes, M., Gary, H. E., Jr., Dobbins, J. G., Randall, B., Steele, L., Fukuda, K., et al. (1997, February 21). Descriptive epidemiology of chronic fatigue syndrome: CDC surveillance in four cities. *Morbidity and Mortality Weekly Report Surveillance Summaries, 46*(No. SS–2), 1–13.

Reyes, M., Nisenbaum, R., Stewart, G., & Reeves, W. C. (1998, October). Update: Wichita population-based study of fatiguing illness. In L. A. Jason & W. Reeves (Chair), *New insights into the epidemiology of CFS.* Symposium presented at the American Association for Chronic Fatigue Syndrome Conference, Cambridge, MA.

Richman, J. A., Flaherty, J. A., & Rospenda, K. M. (1994). Chronic fatigue syndrome: Have flawed assumptions derived from treatment-based studies? *American Journal of Public Health, 84,* 282–284.

Richman, J. A., & Jason, L. A. (2001). Gender biases underlying the social construction of illness states: The case of chronic fatigue syndrome. *Current Sociology, 49,* 15–29.

Richman, J. A., Jason, L. A., Taylor, R. R., & Jahn, S. C. (2000). Feminist perspectives on the social construction of illness states. *Health Care for Women International, 22,* 173–185.

Ridsdale, L., Godfrey, E., Chalder, T., Seed, P., King, M., Wallace, P., & Wessely, S. (2001). Chronic fatigue in general practice: Is counseling as good as cognitive behaviour therapy? A randomized trial. *British Journal of General Practice, 51,* 19–24.

Rijk, A. E., Schreurs, M. G., & Bensing, J. (1999). Complaints of fatigue: Related to too much as well as too little stimulation? *Journal of Behavioral Medicine, 22,* 549–573.

Robins, L., Helzer, J., Cottler, L., & Goldring, E. (1989). *National Institute of Mental Health Diagnostic Interview Schedule* (Version Three Revised, *DIS-III-R*). St. Louis, MO: Washington University School of Medicine, Department of Psychiatry.

Robins, L. N., & Regier, D. A. (1991). *Psychiatric disorders in America: The ECA study.* New York: Free Press.

Russo, J., Katon, W., Clark, M., Kith, P., Sintay, M., & Buchwald, D. (1998). Longitudinal changes associated with improvement in chronic fatigue patients. *Journal of Psychosomatic Research, 45,* 67–76.

Salit, I. E. (1997). Precipitating factors for the chronic fatigue syndrome. *Journal of Psychiatric Research, 31*(1), 59–65.

Saphier, D. (1994, October). *A role for interferon in the psychoneuroendocrinology of chronic fatigue syndrome.* Paper presented at the American Association of Chronic Fatigue Syndrome Research Conference, Ft. Lauderdale, FL.

Schluederberg, A., Straus, S. E., Peterson, P., Blumenthal, S., Komaroff, A. L., Spring, S. B., et al. (1992). Chronic fatigue syndrome research: Definition and medical outcome assessment. *Annals of Internal Medicine, 117,* 325–331.

Schondorf, R., & Freeman, R. C. (1999). The importance of orthostatic intolerance in chronic fatigue syndrome. *American Journal of Medical Sciences, 317,* 117–123.

Schwartz, R. B., Komaroff, A. L., Garada, B. M., Gleit, M., Doolittle, T. H., Bates, D. W., et al. (1994). SPECT imaging of the brain: Comparisons of findings in patients with chronic fatigue syndrome, AIDS dementia complex, and major unipolar depression. *American Journal of Radiology, 162,* 943–951.

Scott, L. V., & Dinan, T. G. (1999). The neuroendocrinology of chronic fatigue syndrome: Focus on the hypothalamic-pituitary-adrenal axis. *Functional Neurology, 14*(1), 3–11.

See, D. M., & Tilles, J. G. (1996). Alpha interferon treatment of patients with chronic fatigue syndrome. *Immunological Investigations, 25,* 153–164.

Sharpe, M. (1998). *Psychiatric morbidity and CFS: Summary of the state of our knowledge.* Paper presented at symposium conducted at the Fourth International Research, Clinical, and Patient Conference of the American Association for Chronic Fatigue Syndrome, Cambridge, MA.

Sharpe, M., Hawton, K., Seagroatt, V., & Pasvol, G. (1992). Follow up of patients presenting with fatigue to an infectious diseases clinic. *British Medical Journal, 305,* 147–152.

Sharpe, M., Hawton, K., Simkin, S., Surawy, C., Hackmann, A., Klimes, I., et al. (1996). Cognitive behaviour therapy for the chronic fatigue syndrome: A randomized controlled trial. *British Medical Journal, 312,* 22–26.

Shlaes, J. L., Jason, L. A., & Ferrari, J. (1999). The development of the chronic fatigue syndrome attitudes test: A psychometric analysis. *Evaluation and the Health Professions, 22,* 442–465.

Snorrason, E., Geirsson, A., & Stefansson, K. (1996). Trial of selective acetylcholinesterase inhibitor, galanthamine hydrobromide, in the treatment of chronic fatigue syndrome. *Journal of Chronic Fatigue Syndrome, 2,* 35–54.

Song, S., Jason, L. A., & Taylor, R. R. (1999). The relationship between ethnicity and fatigue in a community-based sample. *Journal of Gender, Culture, and Health, 4,* 255–268.

Spitzer, R. L., Williams, J. B. W., Gibbon, M., & First, M. B. (1995). *Structured clinical interview for DSM-IV—Non-patient edition* (SCID-NP, Version 2.0). Washington, DC: American Psychiatric Press.

Steele, L., Dobbins, J. G., Fukuda, K., Reyes, M., Randall, B., Koppelman, M., et al. (1998). The epidemiology of chronic fatigue in San Francisco. *American Journal of Medicine, 105*(3A), 83S–90S.

Straus, S. (1992). Defining the chronic fatigue syndrome. *Archives of Internal Medicine, 152,* 1559–1570.

Strayer, D. R., Carter, W. A., Brodsky, I., Cheney, P., Peterson, D., Salvato, P., et al. (1994). A controlled clinical trial with a specifically configured RNA drug, poly(I)poly (C$_{12}$U), in chronic fatigue syndrome. *Clinical Infectious Diseases, 18*(Suppl. 1), S88–S95.

Strayer, D. R., Carter, W. A., Strauss, K. I., Brodsky, I., & Suhadolnik, R. J. (1995). Long term improvements in patients with chronic fatigue syndrome treated with Ampligen. *Journal of Chronic Fatigue Syndrome, 1,* 35–53.

Streeten, D. H., & Bell, D. S. (2000). The roles of orthostatic hypotension, orthostatic tachycardia, and subnormal erythrocyte volume in the pathogenesis of the chronic fatigue syndrome. *American Journal of the Medical Science, 320,* 1–8.

Suhadolnik, R. J., Peterson, D. L., O'Brien, K., Cheney, P. R., Herst, C. V. T., & Reichenbach, N. L. (1997). Biochemical evidence for a novel low molecular weight 2–5A-dependent RNase-L in chronic fatigue syndrome. *Journal of Interferon and Cytokine Research, 7,* 377–385.

Taylor, R. R., Friedberg, F., & Jason, L. A. (2001). *A clinician's guide to controversial illnesses: Chronic fatigue syndrome, fibromyalgia, and multiple chemical sensitivities.* Sarasota, FL: Professional Resource Exchange.

Taylor, R. R., & Jason, L. A. (1998). Comparing the DIS with the SCID: Chronic fatigue syndrome and psychiatric comorbidity. *Psychology and Health: The International Review of Health Psychology, 13,* 1087–1104.

Taylor, R. R., & Jason, L. A. (2001). Sexual abuse, physical abuse, chronic fatigue, and chronic fatigue syndrome: A community-based study. *Journal of Nervous and Mental Diseases, 189,* 709–715.

Taylor, R. R., Jason, L. A., & Curie, C. J. (in press). The prognosis of chronic fatigue in a community-based sample. *Psychosomatic Medicine.*

Taylor, R. R., Jason, L. A., Kennedy, C. L., & Friedberg, F. (2001). Effect of physician-recommended treatment on mental health practitioners' attributions for chronic fatigue syndrome. *Rehabilitation Psychology, 46,* 165–177.

Taylor, R. R., Jason, L. A., & Schoeny, M. E. (2001). Evaluating latent variable models of functional somatic distress in a community-based sample. *Journal of Mental Health, 10,* 335–349.

Theorell, T., Blomkvist, V., Lindh, G., & Evengard, B. (1999). *Psychosomatic Medicine, 61*(3), 304–310.

Twemlow, S. W., Bradshaw, S. L., Jr., Coyne, L., & Lerma, B. H. (1997). Patterns of utilization of medical care and perceptions of the relationship between doctor and patient with chronic illness including chronic fatigue syndrome. *Psychological Reports, 80*(2), 643–658.

Van Der Linden, G., Chalder, T., Hickie, I., Koschera, A., Sham, P., & Wessely, S. (1999). Fatigue and psychiatric disorder: Different or the same? *Psychological Medicine, 29,* 863–868.

Van Houdenhove, B., Onghena, P., Neerinckx, E., & Hellin, J. (1995). Does high action-proneness make people more vulnerable to chronic fatigue syndrome? A controlled psychometric study. *Journal of Psychosomatic Research, 39,* 633–640.

Vercoulen, J. H., Swanink, C. M., Fennis, J. F., Galama, J. M., van der Meer, J. W., & Bleijenberg, G. (1996). Prognosis in chronic fatigue syndrome: A prospective study on the natural course. *Journal of Neurology, Neurosurgery, and Psychiatry, 60,* 489–494.

Vercoulen, J. H., Swanink, C. M., Galama, J. M., Fennis, J. F., Jongen, P. J., Hommes, O. R., et al. (1998). The persistence of fatigue in chronic fatigue syndrome and multiple sclerosis: Development of a model. *Journal of Psychosomatic Research, 45,* 507–517.

Verrillo, E. F., & Gellman, L. M. (1997). *Chronic fatigue syndrome: A treatment guide.* New York: St. Martin's Griffin.

Wessely, S. (1993). The neuropsychiatry of chronic fatigue syndrome. In B. R. Bock & J. Whelan (Eds.), *Chronic fatigue syndrome* (pp. 212–229). New York: Wiley.

Wessely, S., Chalder, T., Hirsch, S., Pawlikowska, T., Wallace, P., & Wright, D. J. M. (1995). Postinfectious fatigue: Prospective cohort study in primary care. *Lancet, 345,* 1333–1338.

Wessely, S., Chalder, T., Hirsch, S., Wallace, P., & Wright, D. (1996). Psychological symptoms, somatic symptoms, and psychiatric disorder in chronic fatigue and chronic fatigue syndrome: A prospective study in the primary care setting. *American Journal of Psychiatry, 153,* 1050–1059.

Wessely, S., Chalder, T., Hirsch, S., Wallace, P., & Wright, D. (1997). The prevalence and morbidity of chronic fatigue and chronic fatigue syndrome: A prospective primary care study. *American Journal of Public Health, 87,* 1449–1455.

Wessely, S., Hotopf, M., & Sharpe, M. (1998). Chronic fatigue and its syndromes. New York: Oxford University Press.

Wilson, A., Hickie, I., Lloyd, A., Hadzi-Pavlovic, D., Boughton, C., Dwyer, J., et al. (1994). Longitudinal study of outcome of chronic fatigue syndrome. *British Medical Journal, 308,* 756–759.

Wood, B., & Wessely, S. (1999). Personality and social attitudes in chronic fatigue syndrome. *Journal of Psychosomatic Research, 47,* 385–397.

Zalcman, S., Savina, I., & Wise, R. A. (1999). Interleukin-6 increases sensitivity to the locomotor-stimulating effects of amphetamine in rats. *Brain Research, 847,* 276–283.

CHAPTER 17

Irritable Bowel Syndrome

EDWARD B. BLANCHARD AND LAURIE KEEFER

In this chapter, we discuss definitional and epidemiological issues and summarize information on various psychosocial issues in IBS, describe and discuss recurrent abdominal pain (RAP), a possible developmental precursor of IBS; and review the literature on psychological treatments of IBS, focusing primarily on what is known from randomized, controlled trials.

DEFINITIONAL, EPIDEMIOLOGICAL, AND ASSESSMENT ISSUES

Irritable bowel syndrome (IBS), previously known as "spastic colon," is one of several functional disorders diagnosed by gastroenterologists (GI). Functional gastrointestinal (GI) disorders, in general, are "persistent clusters of GI symptoms which do not have their basis in identified structural or biochemical abnormalities" (Maunder, 1998). IBS falls into the subset of a functional *bowel* disorder, which also includes functional diarrhea, functional constipation, functional bloating, and unspecified functional bowel disorder (Drossman, Corrazziari, Talley, Thompson, & Whitehead, 2000).

Preparation of this manuscript was supported in part by a grant from NIDDK, DK-54211. Requests for further information should be addressed to either author at: Center for Stress and Anxiety Disorders, 1535 Western Avenue, Albany, NY 12203.

Irritable bowel syndrome has been defined and redefined by the GI community over the years, however, two diagnostic features have remained constant. First, IBS has always been a diagnosis of *exclusion,* that is, the diagnosis is only warranted after all other gastrointestinal diseases have been ruled out. Second, none of the definitions of IBS have relied on a definitive test, partly because the symptoms are both chronic and intermittent. Thus, diagnostic criteria have been based on self-report of symptoms and established patient symptom profiles (Goldberg & Davidson, 1997). As you will soon see, the definition of IBS has been finely tuned to better identify the IBS patient—yet, it is still highly recommended that a physical examination, sigmoidoscopy, and blood assays for complete blood count and erythrocyte sedimentation rate be conducted, as well as an examination of a stool sample for parasites and occult blood (Manning, Thompson, Heaton, & Morris, 1978; Talley et al., 1986) to rule out other disorders prior to making a diagnosis of IBS. We next trace the progression of the definitions of IBS, discuss the landmark studies supporting the definitions to date, and end with a description of the most recent Rome II criteria.

Clinical Criteria

Originally, IBS was diagnosed according to "Clinical Criteria" that included recurrent abdominal pain or extreme abdominal tenderness accompanied by disordered bowel habit (Latimer, 1983). These two symptoms needed to be present much of the time for at least three months in order to fulfill the criteria, and a series of medical tests were necessary to rule out inflammatory bowel disease (IBD), lactose intolerance/malabsorption, intestinal parasites, and other GI diseases (Latimer, 1983). There were two main problems with this criterion. First, the definition of IBS was residual, and, second, as we began to better understand the IBS patient and her symptoms, we realized that, in addition to abdominal pain and altered bowel habits, IBS patients often experience other problematic symptoms that were not considered in the "Clinical Criteria." These included bloating, flatulence, belching, and borborygmi (noticeable bowel sounds).

Manning Criteria

Later, as the GI community became more aware of the problems associated with a diagnosis by exclusion, Manning et al. (1978) attempted to refine the Clinical Criteria by administering a questionnaire to 109 patients complaining of abdominal pain, constipation, or diarrhea. The questionnaire addressed the frequency of 15 GI symptoms during the past year. About two years later, chart notes were reviewed to arrive at a definitive diagnosis for each of the patients. Seventy-nine cases were analyzed (32 patients with IBS, 33 patients with organic disease, and 14 patients with diverticular disease who were excluded). Manning and colleagues (1978) found that the four symptoms that best discriminated ($p < .01$ or better) between IBS and organic disease were: (a) looser stools at onset of pain; (b) more frequent bowel movements at onset of pain; (c) pain that eased after a bowel movement; and (d) visible distention (bloating). In addition, trends were observed for feelings of distention, mucus per rectum, and the feeling (often) of incomplete emptying. However, because there are no pathognomonic symptoms of IBS (symptoms which occur only in IBS and no other disorder), and there were many false positives (8/30; 26.7%) and false negatives (6/31; 19.4%), these discriminators could not be considered completely reliable for the diagnosis of IBS.

Next, Manning and colleagues (1978) attempted to determine whether the presence of *two or more* of the aforementioned symptoms improved the ability to discriminate between IBS and organic GI disease, finding that when one endorsed *three or more* symptoms, 27 of 32 (84%) IBS patients were correctly identified, and 25 of 33 (76%) with organic disease were correctly identified. However, this still leaves a false positive rate of 24% (those with organic disease being diagnosed with IBS), which is an uncomfortable margin of error. A larger study evaluating the Manning criteria reported similar results (Talley et al., 1986).

Rome Criteria

In the late 1980s, the international gastroenterology community again attempted to redefine the criteria for IBS. After the Thirteenth International Congress of Gastroenterology (held in Rome, Italy, in 1988), Drossman, Thompson, et al. (1990) produced the first published report that proposed what is known as the Rome Criteria. Later, Thompson, Creed, Drossman, Heaton, and Mazzacca (1992) further defined *all* functional bowel disorders, and included IBS as their most prominent example.

The Rome Criteria were developed using a factor analysis of 23 symptoms that included the former Manning and Clinical criteria. The first sample were 351 women visiting Planned Parenthood clinics and 149 women recruited from church women's societies (Whitehead, Crowell, Bosmajian, et al., 1990). A second sample consisted of university psychology students. Analysis of these two samples revealed that in females, (Whites and African Americans), clustering of the three primary symptoms (excluding bloating) occurred. Similarly, in males, clustering of all four symptoms occurred, with bloating loading least strongly (Taub, Cuevas, Cook, Crowell, & Whitehead, 1995). Thus, three symptoms were chosen to make up the first part of the Rome I criteria. These include at least three months of continuous or recurrent symptoms of:

1. Abdominal pain or discomfort which is:
   (a) Relieved with defecation,
   (b) Associated with a change in stool frequency, and/or
   (c) Associated with a change in consistency of stool.
2. Two or more of the following, at least a quarter of occasions or days:
   (a) Altered stool frequency (more than three bowel movements a day or fewer than three bowel movements a week),
   (b) Altered stool form (lumpy/hard or loose/watery),
   (c) Altered stool passage (straining, urgency, or feeling of incomplete evacuation),
   (d) Passage of mucous, and/or
   (e) Bloating or feeling of abdominal distention.
3. Absence of historical, physical, and medical findings of organic disease or pathology.

One of the criticisms of the Rome Criteria has been that the definition lacks symptoms such as urgency, abdominal pain, or diarrhea in the postprandial period (Camilleri & Choi, 1997). Another common concern is whether the criteria's requirement of both abdominal pain and chronic alteration of bowel habit is too strict for the diagnosis—some surveys have suggested that most investigators use a combination of abdominal pain and two or more of the Manning Criteria to diagnose IBS (Camilleri & Choi, 1997).

A revised version of the Rome Criteria, known as *Rome II,* has been published (Thompson et al., 1999), making the criteria less restrictive, and addressing some of the other concerns. No changes in the original pain symptoms were made, since factor analyses of nonpatients (Taub et al., 1995; Whitehead et al., 1990) continued to support its inclusion. However, the second part of the Rome I Criteria was eliminated from the definition, and is now considered part of the nonessential symptoms to be used when attempting to define subgroups and/or improve diagnostic accuracy (Drossman et al., 2000). In addition, the requirement of two out of three pain-related symptoms ensures that altered bowel habit is always present. The Rome II Criteria, as described in Drossman et al. (2000) are:

At least 12 weeks or more, which need not be consecutive, in the preceding 12 months of abdominal discomfort or pain that has two out of three features:

1. Relieved with defecation,
2. Onset associated with a change in frequency of stool, and/or
3. Onset associated with a change in form (appearance) of stool.

Symptoms that cumulatively support the diagnosis of Irritable Bowel Syndrome include:

- Abnormal stool frequency,
- Abnormal stool form (lumpy/hard or loose/watery stool),
- Abnormal stool passage (straining, urgency, or feeling of incomplete evacuation),
- Passage of mucous, and/or
- Bloating or feeling of abdominal distention.

As we can see, the term *abdominal discomfort* was added broadening the symptom description. Abdominal distention was eliminated from the necessary criteria, and stool consistency was replaced by "form" to conform with the Bristol Stool Scale (O'Donnell, Virjee, & Heaton, 1990).

Epidemiology

The difficulty in defining IBS limits our ability to accurately determine its prevalence. Currently, however, it is estimated that its prevalence falls somewhere between 11% and 22% among American adults (Dancey, Taghavi, & Fox, 1998; Drossman, Sandler, McKee, & Lovitz, 1982; Talley, Zinsmeister, VanDyke, & Melton, 1991), depending on which definition is used. These prevalence rates tend to be fairly consistent around the world (Thompson, 1994), although some surveys suggest that the prevalence of IBS is lower among Hispanics in Texas (Talley, Zinsmeister, & Melton, 1995) and Asians in California (Longstreth & Wolde-Tasadik 1993). The occurrence of IBS in the general population is substantial, especially if we compares it to the prevalence rates for other common diseases, such as asthma (5%), diabetes (3%), heart disease (9%), and hypertension (11%) in the United States (Wells, Hahn, & Whorwell, 1997).

IBS is the seventh most commonly diagnosed digestive disease in the United States (Wells et al., 1997), has been known to account for up to 50% of referrals to gastrointestinal specialists (Sandler, 1990; Wells et al., 1997), and is the most common diagnosis given by gastroenterologists (Wells et al., 1997). Women appear to be the most commonly afflicted—with gender ratios ranging from . . . , females to males (1.4 to 2.6:1) (Drossman et al., 1993; Talley et al., 1995) although, as Sandler points out in his epidemiological study, such a finding may be biased toward gender differences in health care utilization. For example, while female patients seeking help for IBS are overrepresented in Western countries, they represent only 20% to 30% of the IBS patients in India and Sri Lanka (Bordie, 1972; Kapoor, Nigam, Rastogi, Kumar, & Gupta, 1985).

It is estimated that, in the United States, IBS accounts for nearly *$8 billion a year* in medical costs (Talley et al., 1995), and that people with IBS are more likely to seek medical attention for nongastrointestinal complaints, and undergo surgical procedures (Longstreth & Wolde-Tasadik, 1993). People with IBS have also been shown to miss up to three times as many days of work as those without IBS (Drossman et al. 1993).

Empirical Evidence

There are two important epidemiological studies that best convey the magnitude of the problem. In 1995, Talley and colleagues surveyed 4,108 residents of Olmstead County, Minnesota, between the ages of 20 and 95. They used a previously validated self-report postal questionnaire (Talley, Phillips, Melton, Wiltgen, & Zinsmeister, 1989) that identified GI symptoms experienced over the past year and determined the presence of functional GI disorders. Follow-up reminders were sent at two, four, and seven weeks and a telephone call was made at 10 weeks, which yielded a response rate of 74%. Of the sample, 195 were excluded because of a history of psychosis or dementia, 252 were excluded because they lived in a nursing home, 236 were excluded because they had an organic medical disease or had undergone major abdominal surgery. Using the Manning criteria, the authors found that 17.7% of their sample had IBS, while another 56.6% experienced some GI symptoms. The sample was 41% male (1.44 to 1 ratio), with an average age of 53.

In another landmark study of functional GI disorders, Drossman and colleagues (1993) used the U.S. Householder Survey of Functional GI Disorders to ascertain the presence of one or more functional GI disorders in a stratified random sample of 8,250 U.S. householders. Return rate was 65.8% (51% female, 96% White). Overall, 69.3% (3,761) respondents reported one or more functional GI disorders, with IBS being diagnosed (Rome Criteria) in 11.2% (606) of individuals. Females outnumbered males again, 1.88 to 1. The survey further suggested that patients with IBS missed an average of 13.4 days of work or school in the past year because of their symptoms.

Clearly, IBS is a widespread problem that affects between 19 and 34 million Americans, costs almost $8 billion annually in medical care, and leads to more than 250 million lost work days each year. Thus, it continues to be important to research this population to gain a better understanding of the IBS patient.

Psychological Distress

While the etiology of IBS is not well understood, IBS has typically been portrayed as a psychosomatic disorder with some researchers implying that IBS patients are merely "neurotics" who focus on their GI symptoms (Latimer, 1983). It has been fairly well established in the IBS literature that the individuals who seek treatment for their IBS symptoms tend to be more psychologically distressed than the general population. Folks and Kinney (1992) suggest that up to 60% of a gastroenterologist's patients have psychological complaints. However, literature in this area is mixed. It has not always been the case that IBS patients appear more psychologically distressed than other patients with chronic illness. To better understand this issue, we must look at the psychological distress in IBS sufferers both dimensionally and categorically.

Dimensional Measures of Distress

Several studies report that IBS patients show more distress across a variety of psychological measures when they are compared to groups with organic GI disease (Schwarz et al., 1993; Talley et al., 1990, 1991; E. A. Walker, Roy-Byrne, &

Katon, 1990), and to healthy controls (Gomborone, Dewsnap, Libby, & Farthing, 1995; Latimer et al., 1981; Talley et al., 1990; Toner et al., 1998). However, this is not always the case.

In 1981, Latimer and colleagues compared IBS patients to patients with anxiety and mood disorders and found that there were no significant differences on the Eysenck Personality Inventory (EPI; Eysenck & Eysenck, 1968) dimensions of neuroticism or extraversion. In 1995, Gomborone et al. compared IBS patients to (a) patients with inflammatory bowel disease (IBD); (b) outpatients with major depression; and (c) healthy controls. The psychiatric outpatients showed significantly higher Beck Depression Inventory (BDI; Beck, Ward, Mendelson, Mock, & Erbaugh, 1961) scores than the IBS patients, who were significantly higher than either the IBD patients or healthy controls. Using Kellner's (1981) Illness Attitude Scale, both the IBS group and the depressed outpatients showed more worry about illness, death phobia, and greater effects of these symptoms than the other two groups, with the IBS patients exhibiting the highest levels of hypochondriacal beliefs and disease phobia.

In 1987, Blanchard and colleagues found that treatment-seeking IBS patients were significantly more depressed and anxious, as measured by the Hamilton Scales (Hamilton, 1959, 1960), than either IBD patients or healthy controls who did not differ. In 1990, Toner et al. found no differences in BDI scores between depressed outpatients and IBS patients. In another study, IBS patients were compared with tension and migraine headache sufferers (a group also purported to have elevated psychological distress) on measures of depression and anxiety (Blanchard et al., 1986). On the BDI, both tension and migraine sufferers scored higher than normal controls, while the IBS patients scored higher than all three groups. On the State-Trait Anxiety Inventory (STAI; Speilberger, 1983), similar findings emerged, except that no significant differences were revealed among the IBS and tension headache groups. IBS sufferers also scored higher than all three groups on the F scale of the Minnesota Multiphasic Personality Inventory (MMPI; Hathaway & McKinley, 1951). Only the IBS and migraine group differed on the Life Events Survey (LES; Sarason, Johnson, & Siegel, 1978). This comparison of IBS patients to chronic headache sufferers is extremely important because it suggests that a pattern exists between "neuroticism" and psychosomatic disorders, in general, rather than being specific to IBS.

Latimer et al. (1981) found that IBS patients scored significantly higher on the STAI-Trait and BDI when compared to normal controls. When we consider the Albany studies, conducted over the past 15 years at our Center, BDI mean scores are consistent with those of patients who are mildly depressed, ranging between 10.9 and 13.7, although there are certainly subgroups (about 25% of females and 30% of males) of patients falling in the normal range. Similarly, scores on the STAI-state (current anxiety) range between 40.1 and 55.7, and scores on the STAI-trait (general anxiety) range from 46.9 to 57.6, indicating mild to moderate anxiety.

Categorical Measures of Psychopathology

When we look at psychological distress categorically, IBS patients also tend to show increased levels of disturbance. Talley et al. (1992) reported that the majority of gastroenterology patients with IBS could receive at least one *DSM-III-R* diagnosis. In addition, when compared with other GI patients, non-GI patients, and healthy controls, more patients with IBS reported current Axis I psychopathology (Talley et al., 1993; Toner et al., 1990; Walker et al., 1990). Several independent researchers have estimated that between 50% and 100% of patients with IBS have diagnosable mental disorders (Folks & Kinney, 1992).

Most often, psychiatric disturbances fall within the mood disorder (prevalence of depression is estimated to be between 8% and 61%) and anxiety disorder spectrums (Lydiard, Fosset, Marsh, & Ballenger, 1993; prevalence between 4% and 60%). In one study of treatment-seeking IBS sufferers, 94% of the sample met lifetime criteria for one or more *DSM-III-R* Axis I disorder, and 26% met the criteria currently (Lydiard et al., 1993). However, the proportion of IBS samples with no Axis I diagnosis is variable, ranging from only 6% (Lydiard, 1992; E. A. Walker et al., 1990) to 66% (Blewett et al., 1996; Walker et al., 1990). We have noted in our own research that about 44% of our samples have been free of Axis I psychopathology (Blanchard, Scharff, Schwarz, Suls, & Barlow, 1990). However, when we look at patients with nonfunctional bowel problems, such as inflammatory bowel disease (a good comparison sample as it has similar symptoms and flare-ups), up to 87% of patients are free of Axis I psychopathology (Blanchard et al., 1990; Ford, Miller, Eastwood, & Eastwood, 1987). Individuals with psychiatric disorders often report more gastrointestinal distress than their nonpsychiatric counterparts (Lydiard et al., 1994; Tollefson, Luxenberg, Valentine, Dunsmore, & Tollefson, 1991).

Gender Differences in Psychological Distress

Recent research at our center (Blanchard, Keefer, Galovski, Taylor, & Turner, 2001) identified gender differences in levels of psychological distress among IBS treatment seekers, although findings were far from conclusive. We examined possible gender differences in psychological distress in a sample of 341 treatment-seeking IBS patients (238 females, 83 males). Structured psychiatric interviews were available on 250 participants. We found significantly higher scores for females than males on the BDI, STAI-Trait, and Scales 2 (depression) and 3 (hysteria) of the MMPI. However, there were no differences in percentage of the two samples meeting criteria for one or more Axis I psychiatric disorders, with 65.6% of the total sample meeting these criteria. Thus, we could conclude from this study that gender differences in psychological distress appear to be a function of whether we use dimensional or categorical measurement of psychological distress. This issue clearly needs to be addressed in future research, especially since many studies have used exclusively female populations in both assessment (e.g., Whitehead, Bosmajian, Zonderman, Costa, & Schuster, 1988) and treatment (e.g., Toner et al., 1998) studies.

Another question that has not been adequately addressed with respect to psychological distress in IBS populations is that of whether IBS is a psychosomatic disorder or a somatopsychic disorder. In other words, does psychiatric distress precede the diagnosis of IBS, or does IBS lead to psychiatric distress? Blanchard et al. (1986) found reductions in depression and anxiety among IBS patients whose GI symptoms were reduced as a result of treatment, whereas there were no such reductions when GI symptoms were not improved. Lydiard et al. (1993) attempted to answer this question using a sample of 35 patients with moderate to severe IBS. Approximately 40% of patients had a psychiatric disorder prior to the onset of IBS, and an additional 30% developed IBS and an Axis I disorder simultaneously (within the same year). Walker and colleagues (E. A. Walker, Gelfand, Gelfand, & Katon, 1996) also noted that 82% of their sample experienced psychiatric symptoms prior to the diagnosis of IBS. An answer to this question would provide useful insight into the experience and treatment of the IBS patient.

IBS Patient versus IBS Nonpatient

It has been suggested that, at most, only 40% of those people with IBS have seen a physician for their GI problems (Drossman et al., 1993). What differentiates those who seek treatment from those who do not? We have seen previously that IBS *patients,* people who seek help for their GI symptoms, tend to be more psychologically distressed than controls. However, there is some speculation that the same does not hold true for IBS *nonpatients,* or people with IBS who do not seek help for their symptoms. However, research in this area is mixed.

Drossman and colleagues (1988) compared 72 IBS patients with 82 IBS nonpatients and 84 normal controls (no GI complaints) using the MMPI and the McGill Pain Questionnaire (MPQ; Melzack, 1975). The IBS *patients* were significantly more distressed on measures of depression, somatization, and anxiety than their nonpatient counterparts. In addition, IBS patients complained of more severe and frequent pain. However, Drossman and colleagues (1988) results have not been replicated in later studies.

There is evidence that the two groups, in general, do *not* differ on measures of psychological distress. For example, one study (Whitehead, Burnett, Cook, & Taub, 1996) divided a large group of college undergraduates into (a) students who met Manning Criteria for IBS and had seen a physician for their symptoms in the past year ($n = 84$); (b) students who met Manning Criteria for IBS but did not see a physician in the past year ($n = 165$); and (c) Nonsymptomatic controls ($n = 122$). All groups completed the NEO Personality Inventory (Costa & McCrae, 1985) as a measure of neuroticism, the Global Symptom Index (GSI) from the SCL-90 (Derogatis, Lipman, & Covi, 1973) as a measure of overall psychological distress, and the Short Form-36 (Ware, 1993), a measure of quality of life.

First, the IBS patients and nonpatients did not differ from one another on measures of neuroticism, overall psychological distress, or on the mental health subscale of the SF-36. However, both groups yielded scores significantly higher than the normal controls. However, the IBS patients appeared to be more poorly functioning than the IBS nonpatients, when subscales of the SF-36 were examined.

Another study used Rome Criteria to identify IBS patients and IBS nonpatients in a sample of 905 college students (Gick & Thompson, 1997). The STAI (Speilberger, 1983) was administered to a portion of these participants, who were matched on gender, and a group of non-GI disordered controls. The two IBS groups were more trait anxious than the controls, but did not differ from one another.

It is hard to draw firm conclusions from these various studies because the measures and samples used are not the same across studies. Many IBS patients do tend to present with some sort of psychological distress, and for that reason, psychological treatment may be beneficial. However, there is some speculation that the severity of symptoms may be the underlying factor among differences between patients and nonpatients. This remains an important research question.

The Role of Life Stress

For many people, gastrointestinal symptoms develop during moments of stress and anxiety (Maunder, 1998). While the etiology of IBS remains unknown and understudied, psychosocial stress is thought to play a key role in the onset,

maintenance, and severity of GI symptoms. Many health care clinicians and IBS patients believe that stress exacerbates their symptoms (Dancey & Backhouse, 1993; Dancey, Whitehouse, Painter, & Backhouse, 1995), and many even report that stress *causes* their symptoms (Drossman et al., 1982). IBS has conventionally been considered a good example of a psychosomatic disorder, in which stress leads to somatic complaints (Whitehead, 1994). In a study comparing IBS sufferers with continuous symptoms to IBS sufferers who have symptom-free periods, Corney and Stanton (1990) found that over half in the latter group attributed the recurrence of symptoms to stressful experiences. More than half of the patients in both groups linked the initial onset of GI symptoms to a specific stressful situation. Unfortunately, these studies relied on retrospective data.

Historically, researchers have struggled with the particular question of whether (a) stress leads to the symptoms (psychosomatic hypothesis) or (b) the *presence* of GI symptoms creates stress for the IBS patient (somatopsychic hypothesis). There are two main ways to look at the role of stress in the IBS patient's life. First, we can examine the presence of major life events as they relate to symptoms using:

1. The Social Readjustment Rating Scale (SRRS; Holmes & Rahe, 1967), in which major life events in the preceding year are weighted relative to their stressfulness, and

2. The Life Experiences Survey (LES; Sarason et al., 1978), in which the individual's appraisal of the stressful situation is taken into account.

Another way of examining the role of stress in the onset and maintenance of IBS is to look at the build-up of smaller, everyday stressful events. In this case, the Daily Hassles and Uplifts Scale (Kanner, Coyne, Schaefer, & Lazarus, 1981), which acknowledges the stressfulness of minor annoyances in everyday life, and the Daily Stress Inventory (Brantley & Jones, 1989), a weekly form that patients rate the occurrence and impact of 57 stressful events on a daily basis, are useful.

Major Life Events and GI Distress

With respect to research on the occurrence of major life events, there are few consistent results. When IBS patients were compared to healthy controls, four studies found a greater number of stressful life events in the IBS sample (Blanchard et al., 1986; Drossman et al., 1988; Mendeloff, Monk, Siegel, & Lillienfeld, 1970; Whitehead, Crowell, Robinson, Heller, & Schuster, 1992). On the contrary, two studies (Levy, Cain, Jarrett, & Heitkemper, 1997; Schwarz et al., 1993) did not find these same differences.

If we compare IBS patients to IBS nonpatients (those with symptoms who do not seek treatment), Drossman and colleagues (1988) found more negative life events and greater weighted scores for the IBS nonpatients. Levy and colleagues (1997) found no such differences. E. J. Bennett and colleagues (1998) found a significant relation between the number of functional GI symptoms (IBS, functional dyspepsia, etc.) and the number of endured chronic life stressors.

Finally, in 1986, we found higher scores on the Holmes and Rahe (1967) Social Readjustment Rating Scale (SRRS) for IBS patients than healthy controls (see Blanchard et al., 1986), but in 1993, we found no differences on the same scale when IBS patients were compared to healthy controls (Schwarz et al., 1993).

Minor Life Stressors and GI Distress

We have begun to look at the role that everyday annoyances play in the lives of IBS patients. Unfortunately, the literature in this area is even less complete. IBS patients have not been compared to other groups in any of the following studies.

In an effort to track symptoms and stress levels, Suls, Wan, and Blanchard (1994) used a prospective daily diary and performed an elegant analysis that controlled for prior symptom levels. They ultimately concluded that daily stress levels *did not* increase IBS symptoms. Dancey and colleagues (1995) found similar results, such that an increase in severity of stress did not occur prior to an increase in IBS symptom severity. However, they did find that an increase in IBS symptom severity was likely to *precede* an increase in patient report of common hassles. Note that neither of these studies supports the notion that stress *causes* GI distress; rather, most of the evidence thus far is consistent with a concurrent relation between stress and GI distress. In addition, to our knowledge, no study has included GI flare-ups as a life stressor, limiting our understanding of what may be evidence supporting the somatopsychic hypothesis mentioned earlier.

While stress is likely to play some role in the experience of GI symptoms, it is unlikely to be the only etiological explanation of IBS.

Role of Sexual and Physical Abuse in IBS

There is an abundance of literature examining the psychological (Beitchman, Zucker, Hood, 1992; Greenwald, Leitenberg, Cado, 1990) and somatic (Lechner, Vogel, Garcia-Shelton, Leichter, & Steibel, 1993; Leserman, Toomey, & Drossman, 1995) correlates of past abuse in a variety of pain and other chronic disorders. Studies have demonstrated that somatization, dissociation, and amplification of symptoms are common coping methods seen in women who have experienced childhood abuse (Wyllie & Kay, 1993). Leserman and colleagues (1996) reported that, in general, women with a sexual abuse history reported more pain, more somatic symptoms, more disability days, more lifetime surgeries, more psychological distress, and worse functional disability than healthy controls. Similarly, women with penetration experiences (actual or attempted intercourse or objects in the vagina) had more medical symptoms and higher somatization scores than less severely abused counterparts (Springs & Friedrich, 1992). Some investigators have interpreted such findings to mean that childhood abuse may lead to deficits in help-seeking, and a tendency to gain attention through the "safe domain" of physical symptoms (Wilkie & Schmidt, 1998). From a physiologic standpoint, trauma to the genital region may "downregulate" the sensation of visceral nociceptors, increasing sensitivity to both abdominal and pelvic pain (Mayer & Gebhart, 1994).

Drossman and colleagues (Drossman, Leserman, et al., 1990) have researched the occurrence of early abuse in the IBS population and have suggested that female patients with functional GI disorders report higher levels of early sexual and physical abuse than comparable female patients with a variety of organic GI disorders. In this study, 31% of 206 female GI clinic attendees diagnosed with functional GI disorders reported rape or incest as compared to 18% of those with organic diagnoses. In both Europe and the United States, other studies found similar results, with frequencies between 30% and 56% (Delvaux, Denis, Allemand, & French Club of Digestive Motility, 1997; Scarinci, McDonald-Haile, Bradley, & Richter, 1994; Talley et al., 1995; E. A. Walker, Katon, Roy-Byrne, Jemelka, & Russo, 1993). Rape (penetration), multiple abuse experiences, and perceived life-threatening abuse were associated with the poorest health status (Leserman et al., 1996). Walker et al. found a greater frequency of history of sexual abuse among IBS patients (54%) than patients with IBD (5%). In the previously described Olmstead County Survey study, Talley and colleagues (1994) also found a significantly greater sexual abuse history among patients with IBS (43.1%) than in the other groups (19.4%), and a higher incidence of any abuse (sexual or physical) among IBS patients (50%) when compared to non-IBS individuals (23.3%).

Drossman, Talley, Olden, and Barreiro (1995) have suggested that there is a pathway linking childhood abuse and adult functional GI disorders. Basically, they propose that IBS patients are physiologically predisposed to manifest GI symptoms, especially if they are psychologically distressed. When the trauma experienced during childhood abuse is added to the picture, the beginnings of GI symptoms emerge (more specifically, complaints of abdominal pain). When these somatic symptoms are reinforced via attention and nurturance, a process of symptom amplification and illness behavior lead to the development of an IBS patient. It is unlikely that early abuse forms a direct pathway to IBS—given that not all people who are abused develop IBS, and not all IBS patients have been abused. However, abuse may be associated with the communication of psychological distress through somatic symptoms (Drossman et al., 1995; Drossman, 1997).

As with almost all other research with IBS, the results are not always consistent when it comes to abuse. Talley, Fett, and Zinsmeister (1995) found no significant differences on total physical and sexual abuse among those with functional GI disorders and those with organic GI disorders. Drossman and colleagues (1997) also failed to find significant differences between functional and organic GI patients on presence of sexual or physical abuse.

However, we must keep in mind that high frequencies of sexual and physical abuse may not be unique to the irritable bowel syndrome. Rather, abuse rates approaching 50% have been reported by patients with other types of chronic or recurrent pain disorders, including headaches, fibromyalgia, and chronic pelvic pain (Laws, 1993; Leserman et al., 1995). For now, members of the GI community accept that there is a high incidence of early abuse in the histories of GI patients, both those with functional and organic disease.

Without a doubt, the presence of abuse and IBS make the symptoms more refractory to treatment than usual, and may also increase the likelihood of psychological disturbance (Drossman et al., 2000). Further, Drossman et al. (2000) states that

> Abuse or associated difficulties may: 1) lower the threshold of gastrointestinal symptom experience or increase intestinal motility; 2) modify the person's appraisal of bodily symptoms (i.e., increase medical help seeking) through inability to control the symptoms; and 3) lead to unwarranted feelings of guilt and responsibility, making spontaneous disclosure unlikely (p. 178).

It is also important to clarify the role that abuse plays in the experience of GI distress especially when one is considering the psychopathology often seen in treatment-seeking IBS patients. In an attempt to discern whether IBS patients who have been abused are the same group of IBS patients with diagnosable psychopathology, we examined a population of 71 (57 female, 14 male) IBS patients seeking psychological treatment at our center (Blanchard, Keefer, Payne, Turner, & Galovski, 2002). While we found expected levels of childhood sexual and physical abuse (57.7%) and expected levels of current Axis I psychiatric disorders (54.9%) in the sample, contrary to our expectations, there were *no* significant associations between early abuse and current psychiatric disorder in

this population (Blanchard et al., 2002). These findings suggest that those individuals with psychological distress are not exactly the same group with a history of abuse. These findings have important implications with respect to treatment.

General Comments

We have summarized the literature to date on IBS, with a specific focus on psychosocial factors of assessment. When diagnosing and assessing IBS, it is important to consider, in addition to definitional and epidemiological issues, the possible role of psychological distress, treatment-seeking factors, and the role of stress and early abuse in the manifestation of IBS symptoms. Such factors may be important to address in treatment, which we will discuss later in this chapter. Now, we turn to a possible developmental precursor to IBS—recurrent abdominal pain.

RECURRENT ABDOMINAL PAIN IN CHILDREN

While many patients describe GI distress dating back to their childhood, IBS is not usually a diagnosis associated with children and younger adolescents. There is, however, a functional GI disorder that does occur in childhood that may have some bearing on a future diagnosis of IBS—recurrent abdominal pain (RAP). Apley and Naish (1958) proposed the most commonly used definition of RAP: three episodes of pain occurring within three months that are severe enough to affect a child's activities and for which an organic explanation cannot be found.

Prevalence

RAP may be the most common recurrent pain problem of childhood. It is usually recognized in children older than 6 years (Wyllie & Kay, 1993). Faull and Nicol (1986) found a prevalence of almost 25% in an epidemiological study of 439 5- and 6-year-olds in northern England. A much earlier study (Apley & Naish, 1958) reported a prevalence rate of 11% among 1,000 children from primary and secondary schools. Typically, the peak age for RAP is between 11 and 12 years of age (Stickler & Murphy, 1979). With respect to gender, results are mixed. Faull and Nicol (1986) found equivalent prevalence among 5- and 6-year-olds, but Apley and Naish (1958) and Stickler and Murphy (1979) reported a higher incidence among girls, much like that of adulthood IBS.

RAP sufferers miss several school days per year (Bury, 1987; Robinson, Alverez, & Dodge, 1990) and make frequent visits to the pediatrician. P. A. McGrath (1990) estimates that at least 25% of pediatric emergency room visits for abdominal pain are due to RAP.

One particularly interesting question associated with RAP is that of its relationship with adulthood IBS. Do children with RAP go on to develop IBS as an adult? Christensen and Mortensen (1975) report that 47% of patients at follow-up warranted a diagnosis of what was then called "irritable colon." L. S. Walker, Guite, Duke, Barnard, and Greene (1998) used Manning Criteria to diagnose IBS in a five-year follow-up of RAP patients, and found that 35% of females and 32% of males met such criteria. We can cautiously conclude, then, that while RAP tends to remit in childhood in most cases, about one-third of children with RAP will go on to meet criteria for IBS as adults.

Etiology

Like irritable bowel syndrome, RAP is considered a disorder of gastrointestinal motility. Also, like IBS, a definitive "cause" has not been determined. However, some theories have been proposed. First, there is the model of dysfunctional GI motility. In this model, pain can be caused by distention and spasm of the distal colon, with bombardment of stimuli leading to the perception of pain (Davidson, 1986). This model also accounts for a familial tendency to a hypersensitive gut that may be exacerbated by stress and food (Davidson, 1986).

Another model proposes that RAP is a disorder of the autonomic nervous system (ANS). This model implies that there is a deficit in the child's ANS that makes it difficult for him to recover from stress (Page-Goertz, 1988). Unfortunately, there have been no studies to confirm this theory (see Barr, 1983; Fueuerstein, Barr, Francoeur, Hade, & Rafman, 1982).

The final model proposes a psychogenic cause for recurrent abdominal pain. A study by Robinson and colleagues (1990) used the Children's Life Events Inventory (Monaghan, Robinson, & Dodge, 1979) to show that children with RAP did not differ from controls in the total life events scores two years prior to the pain, but that in the 12 months directly preceding pain onset, RAP children scored markedly higher. These findings suggest that such events (including parental divorce and separation) may be important triggers in predisposed children (Robinson et al., 1990). A discussion of psychological distress and RAP follows in the next section.

Finally, Levine and Rappaport (1984) suggest that a multitude of factors "cause" abdominal pain, including lifestyle and habit (i.e., daily routines, diet, elimination patterns, school/family routine), temperament/learned responses (i.e., behavioral style, personality, affect, learned coping skills), milieu/critical events (i.e., characteristics of the child's surroundings, positive or negative stressful events), and a somatic predisposition to pain localized in the abdomen (i.e., dietary intolerance, constipation, underlying dysfunction/disorder). Similarly, Compas and Thomsen (1999) conceptualize RAP as a problem of psychological stress, individual differences in reaction to stress, and maladaptive coping. They maintain that the way children cope with such stress greatly influences the severity, frequency, and duration of RAP episodes; a disruption in the process of self-regulation and stress reactivity may precipitate abdominal pain.

Psychosocial Factors and RAP

As is the case in the IBS literature, RAP researchers have failed to agree regarding the possibility of there being differences between organic and nonorganic pediatric GI patients on a variety of psychosocial measures. Children with RAP have often been described as anxious and perfectionistic (Liebman, 1978). Typically, studies have compared children with functional GI disorders to children with organic GI diseases on the occurrence of stressful life events, anxiety, depression, behavior problems, and general family functioning. Walker, Garber, and Greene (1993) report that RAP patients had higher levels of emotional and somatic symptoms and came from families with a higher incidence of illness and encouragement of illness behavior than well children, but did not differ with respect to negative life events, competence levels, or family functioning. When compared to child psychiatric patients, RAP patients exhibited fewer emotional and behavioral problems, and tended to have better family functioning and higher levels of social competence, despite having more somatic complaints. Finally, RAP patients did not differ from organic abdominal pain patients on either emotional or organic symptoms; as discussed previously, similar findings have been described in the adult literature.

Some studies have found that RAP patients experienced significantly more negative life events than well controls and general medical patients (J. Greene, Walker, Hickson, & Thompson, 1985; Hodges, Kline, Barbero, & Flanery, 1984; Robinson et al., 1990), while others claim that there are no such differences (Hodges et al., 1984; Risser, Mullins, Butler, & West, 1987; L. S. Walker et al., 1993; Wasserman, Whitington, & Rivara, 1988). Further, some studies have shown that RAP patients actually experience *fewer* negative life events than other behaviorally disordered groups (J. Greene et al., 1985; L. S. Walker et al., 1993).

Depression

Typically, differences in depression levels appear only when comparing RAP children to well samples (Hodges, Kline,

Barbero, & Flanery, 1985; Walker & Greene, 1989; L. S. Walker et al., 1993). In a particularly thorough study of RAP patients, patients with organic peptic disease and well children, RAP children and the organic group scored significantly higher than well children on the Child Depression Inventory (CDI; Kovacs, 1980/1981) but the RAP and organic groups did not differ from each other (Walker et al., 1993). When RAP children are compared to children with organic abdominal pain, there are usually no differences between groups on levels of depression, as measured by the CDI (Garber, Zeman, & Walker, 1990; Hodges, Kline, Barbero, & Flanery, 1985; L. S. Walker & Greene, 1989). The exception to this finding is a study done by Gold, Issenman, Roberts, and Watt (2000), who found significant differences in CDI scores between children with a functional GI disorder and children with IBD. However, neither group scored in the clinically significant range on the CDI so it is difficult to conclude that depression is an underlying factor in the development of RAP.

Anxiety

Studies have consistently found that, when compared to control children, children with RAP do tend to report more anxiety on measures such as the Child Behavior Checklist (CBCL; Achenbach & Edelbrock, 1983) and Child Assessment Schedule [CAS: Hodges, Kline, & Fitch, 1981, 1990; (Garber et al., 1990; Hodges, Kline, Barbero, & Woodruff, 1985; Hodges, Kline, Barbero, & Flanery, 1985; Robinson et al., 1990)]. Again, however, it appears that they do not differ from children with organic explanations for their symptoms (Garber et al., 1990; L. S. Walker & Greene, 1989), at least to a clinically significant degree (L. S. Walker et al., 1993). This may suggest that anxiety may be specifically associated with having abdominal pain.

Somatization

When compared to their organic GI counterparts, children with functional RAP had significantly higher scores on the somatic complaints scale of the CBCL, and were more likely to have relatives with Somatization Disorder (Routh & Ernst, 1984). Results in a study done by E. A. Walker and colleagues (Walker, Gelfand, Gelfand, & Katon, 1996) were similar, with RAP children reporting higher levels of somatization symptoms than children with organically based pain and well controls at both initial assessment and three month follow-up.

We should keep in mind, however, that anxiety, depression, and somatization symptoms tend to be higher in patients with organic diseases in general (P. J. McGrath, Goodman,

Firestone, Shipman, & Peters, 1983; Raymer, Weininger, & Hamilton, 1984; Routh & Ernst, 1984; L. S. Walker & Greene, 1989). We are therefore unable to determine the role that recurrent abdominal pain itself may play in such psychological symptoms. However, psychological interventions, as in IBS, seem to be moderately effective.

Treatment of RAP

Apley and Naish (1958) recommend that children presenting with abdominal pain receive: (a) a careful and thorough medical work-up to rule out organic causes of pain, (b) reassurance that there is no organic or structural reason for the pain, and (c) support for both parent and child as they deal with the functional problem. This approach is fairly effective about half of the time (Apley & Hale, 1973; Stickler & Murphy, 1979). In the rest of the cases, however, it is important to examine other treatment options. Early interventions included operant approaches (see Miller & Kratochwill 1979; Sank & Biglan, 1974) and fiber treatments (see Christensen, 1986; Feldman, McGrath, Hodgson, Ritter, & Shipman, 1985). However, results in these areas were mixed. The majority of research into treatments for RAP has involved cognitive-behavioral approaches.

On the first line of defense, brief targeted therapy delivered in primary health care settings has had some effect on a range of problems associated with RAP. In one study, brief targeted therapy consisted of individualized interventions based on behavioral concerns and symptoms defined during the assessment process, and included techniques such as self-monitoring, relaxation training, limited reinforcement of illness behavior, dietary fiber supplementation, and participation in routine activities. In this study, 16 children with RAP underwent the brief targeted therapy and were evaluated on a variety of outcome measures, including medical care utilization, school records (absences and nurses visits), and symptom ratings. Treated children were compared to 16 untreated children. After treatment, most parents rated their children's pain symptoms as improved. Children undergoing treatment also missed significantly fewer days of school (Finney, Lemanek, Cataldo, Katz, & Fuqua, 1989).

Sanders et al. (1989) found that an eight-session CBT program that included self-monitoring of pain, operant behavioral training for parents distraction techniques, relaxation training, imagery for pain control, and self-control techniques such as self-instruction in coping statements was superior to a symptom-monitoring control condition. At posttreatment, six of eight (75%) treated children were pain free, and by three-month follow-up, seven of eight (87.5%) were pain free, as opposed to 37.5% of the controls. In a replication of this study, Sanders, Shepherd, Cleghorn, and Woolford (1994) compared the same CBT program to standard pediatric care with a sample of 44 children with RAP. The latter treatment included reassurance that the child's pain was real but that no organic disease was present. Results continued to show a significant advantage for the CBT (80% symptom reduction vs. 40% symptom reduction) over the reassurance condition over time—at six months, two-thirds of the CBT group were pain free, as opposed to less than one-third in the standard care condition.

To look at the individual components of CBT, we (Scharff, 1995) conducted a study that compared a parent-training approach with a stress management approach. In the parent-training condition, parents received education about RAP and psychosomatic symptoms, and learned behavior modification techniques described in *Living with Children* (Patterson, 1976). The treatment focused specifically on parents' ignoring mild pain behaviors and encouraging active behaviors in their child; the program was modified to meet individual needs. Essentially, parents were instructed to have their child lie down in a quiet, dark room with no distractions whenever they complained of pain. School attendance was required unless the child was vomiting or developed a fever.

In the stress-management condition, children were taught progressive relaxation and deep breathing exercises, and also learned cognitive distraction techniques for acute pain. Positive imagery and positive coping self-statements (Michenbaum, 1977) were also used. After treatment, patients monitored their symptoms for two weeks, and if there was no full remittance, they were crossed over to the other condition.

Outcome was determined by pain ratings kept by the child; ratings were made daily using a 0 to 4 scale ("no pain" to "very bad pain"). Parents also rated twice a day the frequency of pain behaviors. Both children and parents kept pain records for six weeks prior to treatment, throughout treatment, and for two weeks at posttreatment and three-month follow-up. Significant reductions were observed in both child pain ratings (from 1.2 to 0.2, $p < .001$) and parent ratings of frequency of pain behavior intervals (from 40% to 8%, $p < .001$) from the second baseline to the end of the second treatment. Results were maintained at follow-up. There was a trend for child pain ratings to decrease more when stress management was the first treatment received. The average degree of improvement for the child ratings was 86% and 82% for the parent ratings of pain behaviors. Overall, all 10 children were 62% improved or greater with 9 or 10 showing 75% reduction in their child pain diary ratings. With respect to parent ratings, all children were 61% improved or greater with 6 of 10 showing reductions of 75% or greater.

Thus, there appears to be a slight advantage to the stress management training.

What is it about RAP that predisposes a child to develop IBS as an adult? Some possible explanations include: (a) hypersensitivity to abdominal pain as a child continues into generalized GI tract sensitivity as an adult; (b) an anxious child grows up to be an anxious adult who is more likely to develop IBS; or (c) early learning about GI symptoms, the sick role and health care seeking predisposes him or her to be sensitive to GI symptoms and seek health care as an adult.

General Comments

We have addressed RAP as a possible developmental precursor to IBS, which has been understudied. Research in this area has begun to address questions similar to that in the IBS literature, including the role of stressful events and psychological distress in the onset and maintenance of symptoms. Treatment of RAP has been limited to a few behavioral interventions, but seems to show much promise. It is possible, that as we develop a more complete understanding of the psychosocial factors influencing the experience of RAP, we will be able to offer more specific interventions. Next, we look at psychological interventions as they apply to IBS.

PSYCHOLOGICAL TREATMENT OF IBS

Since 1983, three broad approaches to psychological treatment of IBS have been evaluated in randomized, controlled trials (RCTs): brief psychodynamic psychotherapy, hypnotherapy, and various combinations of cognitive and behavioral therapies. We describe each treatment approach briefly and summarize the outcome and follow-up results.

Brief Psychodynamic Psychotherapy

While the descriptive term, "brief psychodynamic . . . ," may seem a bit of a contradiction, it is accurate. The treatments were delivered over a three-month span and consisted of 10 sessions in one instance and only 7 in the other. Thus, the time span and number of sessions are not what we normally associate with psychodynamic psychotherapy. The therapy is psychodynamic to the extent that it seeks "insight" (Svedlund, Sjodin, Ottosson, & Dotevall, 1983) and "exploration of patients' feelings about their illness" (Guthrie, Creed, Dawson, & Tomenson, 1991).

In the first study (which we believe is the first RCT of psychological treatment for IBS), Svedlund et al. (1983) randomly assigned 101 IBS patients, all of whom were receiving conventional medical care, to either individual psychotherapy ($n = 50$) or the control condition ($n = 51$). Patients were assessed by blinded assessors at pretreatment, three months after treatment began (posttreatment), and at a 12-month follow-up.

The assessor ratings showed significantly greater improvement for the treated patients than the controls in reduction of abdominal pain and reduction of other somatic symptoms at the end of treatment. At the one-year follow-up, the assessor ratings showed treatment was superior to the control condition on reduction of abdominal pain and somatic symptoms, and on improvement in bowel dysfunction. Both groups were rated significantly less anxious and depressed at end of treatment and at follow-up.

In the second RCT of psychodynamic psychotherapy (Guthrie et al., 1991), IBS patients who failed to respond to routine medical care were randomly assigned to individual psychodynamic psychotherapy plus home practice of relaxation ($n = 53$) or a wait list condition ($n = 49$). Evaluation was by means of blinded assessor ratings and patient symptom diaries. After the posttreatment evaluation, 33 of the controls were crossed over to treatment while 10 who had improved were merely followed.

The assessor ratings showed greater improvement at end of treatment for the psychotherapy group versus the symptom monitoring controls on abdominal pain and diarrhea as well as on reductions in anxiety and depression; the patients ratings showed the same GI symptom results plus greater in bloating. The one-year follow-up data were based solely on patient global ratings. They showed that, of patients treated initially, 68% rated themselves as "better" or "much better." Among the treated controls, 64% gave similar ratings.

Although we cannot directly compare the content of the treatments, it seems clear that they are similar and have led to significantly greater improvement than controls on abdominal pain and bowel functioning. They thus yield comparable positive results which appear to hold up well over a one-year follow-up.

Hypnotherapy

The first RCT of hypnotherapy for IBS (Whorwell, Prior, & Faragher, 1984) appeared shortly after the Svedlund et al. (1983) trial described earlier. The hypnotherapy treatment was aimed at general relaxation and gaining control of intestinal motility along with some attention to ego strengthening. Patients also received an audiotape for daily home practice of autohypnosis. In the first study, 30 IBS patients who had been refractory to standard medical care were randomized to seven hypnotherapy sessions over three months ($n = 15$) or to supportive psychotherapy (seven sessions by the same therapist) and continued medical care ($n = 15$).

Evaluation was by means of patient symptom diary and blinded assessor ratings.

Results showed dramatic improvement in abdominal pain, bloating, dysfunctional bowel habit, and general well-being for the hypnotherapy condition; all patients were clinically improved. Active treatment was superior to the control on all measures. An 18-month follow-up (Whorwell, Prior, & Colgan, 1987) of the treated sample revealed very good maintenance of improvement. Two patients had minor relapses at about one year and responded to a single session of hypnotherapy.

The results were essentially replicated (Houghton, Heyman, & Whorwell, 1996) in a comparison of 25 cases treated with hypnotherapy to 25 other cases awaiting treatment. The protocol was now described as 12 sessions. Treated patients improved more than controls on abdominal pain, bowel dysfunction, bloating, and general sense of well-being. Importantly, those patients treated with hypnotherapy missed fewer work days ($X = 2$) than the controls ($X = 17$).

An independent replication of these results was reported by Harvey, Hinton, Gunary, and Barry (1989) who compared individually administered hypnotherapy to group hypnotherapy. There were equivalent significant improvements in both conditions with 61% of participants improved or symptom free at three months posttreatment.

In our center, Galovski and Blanchard (1998) also replicated Whorwell's results (using his hypnotherapy protocol) in a comparison of immediate treatment to symptom monitoring and delayed treatment. A composite symptom reduction score, based on patient GI symptom diaries, was significantly greater (52%) for treated patients versus controls (-32% [symptom worsening]). For the whole treated sample, there were significant reductions in abdominal pain, constipation, and trait anxiety.

With the continued positive results from Whorwell's clinic plus two independent replications, including one in the United States, it seems clear that hypnotherapy is a highly viable treatment for IBS.

Cognitive and Behavioral Treatments

The most active research approach to the psychological treatment of IBS by far has been the evaluation of various cognitive and behavioral treatments. Most studies have used a combination of treatment procedures in multicomponent treatment packages; however, a few have used only a single component such as relaxation training. Our own work, with the exception of the hypnotherapy study of Galovski and Blanchard (1998) described earlier, can be subsumed under this approach. This research, including our studies from Albany, is summarized chronologically in Table 17.1.

TABLE 17.1   Controlled Trials of Cognitive and Behavioral Treatments for IBS

Authors	Conditions	Sample Size	Differential Results
Bennett and Wilkinson, 1985	Education, PMR, change self-talk.	12	CBT reduction on trait anxiety; both groups reduced pain, bloating, diarrhea.
	Medical Care (3 drugs).	12	
Neff and Blanchard, 1987	Education, PMR, biofeedback, change self-talk, and coping.	10	CBT improved more on symptom composite than SM.
	Symptom monitoring.	9	
Lynch and Zamble, 1989	PMR, Cognitive Therapy, assertiveness training.	11	CBT improved more than SM on pain, constipation, trait anxiety.
	Symptom monitoring.	10	
Corney et al., 1991	Education, Cognitive Therapy, operant procedures.	22	CBT had less avoidance of food and tasks than regular medical care.
	Regular medical care.	20	
Shaw et al., 1991	Education, relaxation, and application.	18	CBT showed greater improvement on patient global ratings.
	Drug-Colpermin.	17	
Blanchard et al., 1992			
Study 1	Education, PMR, biofeedback, change in self-talk and coping.	10	Both treated groups improved more on symptom composite than SM; No difference between CBT and attention placebo.
	Psuedo-meditation and EEG alpha suppression biofeedback.	10	
	Symptom monitoring.	10	
Study 2	CBT.	31	Both treated groups improved more on symptom composite than SM; No difference between CBT and placebo.
	Placebo.	30	
	Symptom monitoring.	31	
van Dulmen et al., 1996	Group: Education, PMR, change in coping and cognitions.	27	CBT improved more than wait-list on pain.
	Wait-list.	20	
Toner et al., 1998	Group: Education, pain management, assertiveness training, cognitive therapy.	101 Total	CBT showed more reduction on BDI and on bloating than regular medical care. No difference between two group treatments.
	Group: Psycho-education.		
Heymann-Monnikes et al., 2000	CBT + Standard Medical Care (Education, PMR, Cognitive Therapy and Coping, Assertiveness Training).	12	CBT + SMC showed greater reduction in IBS symptoms, other GI symptoms, and psychological symptoms, than SMC alone.
	Standard medical care.	12	
Relaxation Alone			
Blanchard et al., 1993	PMR and application.	8	Relaxation improved more on symptom composite than SM.
	Symptom monitoring.	8	
Keefer and Blanchard, 2001	Meditative relaxation.	6	Relaxation improved more on symptom composite than SM.
	Symptom monitoring.	7	

(continued)

TABLE 17.1 (*Continued*)

Authors	Conditions	Sample Size	Differential Results
Cognitive Therapy Alone			
Greene and Blanchard, 1994	Cognitive Therapy.	10	Cognitive Therapy improved
	Symptom monitoring.	10	more on symptom composite than SM, also on BDI and Trait anxiety.
Payne and Blanchard, 1995	Cognitive Therapy.	12	Cognitive Therapy improved
	Group: Psycho-education support.	12	more on symptom
	Symptom monitoring.	10	composite than psycho-education and SM, also on BDI and Trait anxiety.
Vollmer and Blanchard, 1998	Group Cognitive Therapy.	11	Both cognitive therapy
	Individual Cognitive Therapy.	11	improved more than SM on
	Symptom monitoring.	10	symptom composite; no difference between cognitive therapy conditions.

Note: PMR = Progressive Muscle Relaxation; SM = Symptom Monitoring.

Included are synoptic descriptions of treatment conditions, sample sizes, and a summary of significant between group effects at the end of treatment and at follow-up.

There are a total of 15 RCTs involving cognitive and behavioral treatments presented in Table 17.1. Most are small trials, involving 12 or fewer patients per condition. Only two trials had 30 patients per condition (Blanchard et al., 1992, Study 2; Toner et al., 1998) while two others had between 20 and 30 per condition. The two larger trials found some advantage for CBT combinations over symptom monitoring controls but neither found the CBT combination superior to a psychological treatment control.

Of the 10 trials with combinations of cognitive and behavioral treatments, most include an education component (9 of 10) and a relaxation training (8 of 10) component (usually in the form of progressive muscle relaxation, PMR). Almost all included some attempt at directly modifying cognitive aspects of functioning, such as self-talk, cognitions, and schemas, or coping strategies.

Work from our center has begun the task of dismantling these CBT combinations. We have described two small trials comparing a pure relaxation condition (PMR in Blanchard & Andrasik, 1985; use of Benson's ([1975] relaxation response meditation in Keefer & Blanchard, 2001); both found relaxation superior to symptom monitoring.

We also summarize in Table 17.1, three small RCTs evaluating purely cognitive therapy alone. In all three, cognitive therapy was superior to symptom monitoring. More importantly, in *the only RCT to show an advantage for cognitive or behavioral treatment in comparison to a credible placebo,*

Payne and Blanchard (1995) showed that cognitive therapy was superior to psychoeducational support groups.

Our center has reported on one-, two-, and four-year follow-ups of IBS patients treated with CBT. In the longest follow-up (Schwarz, Taylor, Scharff, & Blanchard, 1990), we found 50% of treated patients still much improved (as verified by daily GI symptom diary). Other long-term follow-ups such as van Dulmen et al. (1996) and Shaw et al. (1991) have likewise reported good maintenance of GI symptom reduction.

It is clear that combinations of cognitive and behavioral treatment techniques, adapted to an IBS population, are superior to symptom monitoring and to some extent routine medical care. Moreover, the improvements have been shown to endure over follow-ups ranging from one to four years (Blanchard, Schwarz, & Neff, 1988).

Three studies from Albany, all using the same cognitive therapy protocol (B. Greene & Blanchard, 1994) have yielded consistently strong results across three different therapists and with three separate cohorts of IBS sufferers. Payne and Blanchard (1995) have shown the cognitive therapy superior to a highly credible psychological control condition. We recommend this approach at present.

General Comments

We have addressed the current psychological treatment literature as it applies to IBS. Many different forms of psychological treatment, including brief psychodynamic psychotherapy, hypnotherapy, and cognitive and behavioral treatments, alone and combined, seem to be moderately effective in treating IBS symptoms and superior to symptom monitoring alone. Currently, cognitive therapy appears to be the most highly recommended approach, as it has been tested against a credible placebo condition, in addition to symptom monitoring (Payne & Blanchard, 1995). Clearly, more randomized, controlled treatment studies that compare multiple treatments for IBS are needed.

CONCLUSIONS AND FUTURE DIRECTIONS

IBS is a complex health problem that needs to be understood within a biopsychosocial paradigm. This chapter offers several interesting insights into the diagnosis, classification, and treatment of IBS. First we addressed definitional and epidemiological aspects of IBS and introduced general psychosocial issues related to IBS. We then summarized the somewhat limited research on recurrent abdominal pain, a childhood functional GI problem that may be a developmental precursor to IBS. Finally, we reviewed the literature on psychosocial treatments of IBS, with a special emphasis on information gained from randomized, controlled treatment trials. While the psychosocial literature on IBS may have greatly benefited those with IBS and those who care for them, much more research needs to be done.

Diagnosing IBS has long been problematic for gastroenterologists and primary care physicians alike. Currently, IBS is diagnosed clinically when other potential causes have been ruled out. However, recent changes in criteria, including the Rome I and Rome II Criteria, have begun to address symptoms unique to IBS patients that may aid in a diagnosis without unnecessary and invasive tests. Unfortunately, diagnostic accuracy is far from perfect, and many gastroenterologists continue to rely on invasive procedures to rule out more life-threatening problems such as cancers and inflammatory bowel disease. Further research into identifying inclusive criteria for IBS is crucial for the effective assessment and management of these patients. Similarly, a better understanding of differences among IBS subtypes (diarrhea predominant, constipation predominant, mixed type) may also be beneficial.

While IBS prevalence rates seem to be fairly consistent around the world (Thompson, 1994), there do seem to be some cultural differences in both symptom reporting and treatment seeking. A better understanding of these differences may lead to a more contextual understanding of the development and maintenance of IBS symptoms. It is unclear as to why women seem to outnumber men in IBS treatment seeking in Western countries. Research as to whether these differences are related to variations in health care utilization, gender differences in the experience of pain and other GI symptoms, or other social/developmental factors would be valuable.

Another direction for future research involves a better understanding of differences between those who seek treatment for their symptoms (patients) and those who do not (nonpatients). Literature thus far has been mixed, with some studies suggesting that there are differences between groups on various measures of psychological distress (Drossman et al., 1993), and others suggesting that there are no such differences (Gick & Thompson, 1997; Whitehead et al., 1996). It is possible that differences among groups are a result of differences in symptom severity and/or role impairment associated with the recurrence of symptoms. This possibility has yet to be investigated.

As discussed numerous times in this chapter, it is important to address the somatopsychic hypothesis of IBS. In other words, which came first, the IBS or the psychopathology? Careful temporal tracking of psychological symptoms is important at this level. It may be that IBS is a causal factor in the development of anxiety and depression—certainly, GI symptoms have been known to keep people housebound. On the other hand, IBS symptoms may be an additional manifestation of psychopathological conditions. Understanding the potential causal relation between GI symptoms and psychopathology has important implications for the effective management of IBS patients.

Another important issue that has been somewhat neglected in the IBS literature is that of the role of stress in GI symptoms. While the majority of patients will link the onset and maintenance of their symptoms to stressful events, previous research has been unable to determine the exact relationship between either major life events or daily life hassles and GI symptoms. While some research has linked same-day hassles with same-day GI symptoms, there is currently little support for the notion that stressful events today lead to increased IBS symptoms tomorrow. It is possible that newer statistical methods may help us answer these questions more directly. Further, it is important to explore the role that GI symptoms, and even more specifically, GI flare-ups, play in the total experience of stress and the cycle of symptoms.

In addition, little is known about the role Axis II personality disorders may play in the onset and maintenance of GI symptoms. There are very few data that estimate the prevalence of such personality disorders in IBS treatment-seeking population. However, given the high rate of sexual and physical abuse, it is possible that a high level of such disorders exist. Assessing for personality disorders may have important treatment implications as well. For example, is treatment less effective when chronic and persistent psychopathology affects an individual's general role functioning?

While it has been fairly well established that there are high rates of prior abuse in the IBS population, it is unclear as to how such abuse relates to the experience of symptoms and distress levels seen in IBS populations. For example, does the abuse form a direct pathway to the onset and maintenance of GI symptoms? Or does abuse lead to psychopathology, which in turn leads to IBS? This is an important differentiation to make, as it is likely to influence the direction of psychosocial treatments for IBS.

While the IBS literature has many gaps and limitations, the literature on recurrent abdominal pain in children is even more scarce. Clearly, continued research on the appropriate diagnosis, prevalence, and relationship to IBS is necessary to effectively treat, and perhaps prevent problems in adulthood. Further, better differentiation between children with RAP and children with other GI symptom complaints is necessary for accurate assessment and treatment of such children. Finally, an understanding of possible maintaining factors in childhood may provide a more comprehensive model of functional GI problems in both childhood and later in life.

In addition to gaps in our understanding of IBS patients, it is important to address limitations of the treatment literature. Essentially, there are three (or probably four) psychological approaches to the treatment of IBS that have demonstrated efficacy in RCTs and for which follow-ups of at least a year demonstrate durability of improvement: brief psychodynamic psychotherapy, hypnotherapy, and cognitive behavioral therapy combinations. Purely cognitive therapy should also be on this list. Despite the variety of psychosocial treatments that have been shown to be effective in the treatment of IBS patients, very little is known about *why* such treatments work. One hypothesis is that a reduction in psychological distress can influence the manifestation of such symptoms. On the contrary, however, it is possible that a reduction in symptoms leads to reductions in psychological distress. This could be addressed within the drug treatment literature as well— what happens to Axis I disorders when drug (or psychological) treatment is effective in reducing GI symptoms?

Another limitation of the current psychosocial treatment literature is the lack of large, randomized treatment trials that compare two or more of the effective treatments for IBS, both with respect to effective drug treatments and established psychosocial treatments. It is possible that all of the established treatments for IBS are comparable to each other, and that our focus should turn to appropriate ways to match patients to appropriate treatments, or to determine the necessary combination of treatments to best manage GI symptoms. Research of two kinds could address these limitations: (a) controlled comparisons of the efficacious treatments. (The latter will need to be a very large, multi|minus|center trial; even then, it may be difficult to find a "winner" since all approaches yield very good outcome); and (b) research that attempts to match IBS patient characteristics to treatment. Finally, efforts to expand the work of Heymann-Monnikes et al. (2000), who is seeking to find the optimal blend of psychological treatment and drug treatment would be much appreciated.

REFERENCES

Achenbach, T. M., & Edelbrock, C. (1983). *Manual for the Child Behavior Checklist and Revised Child Behavior Profile.* Burlington: University of Vermont.

Apley, J., & Hale, B. (1973). Children with recurrent abdominal pain: How do they grow up? *British Medical Journal, 3,* 7–9.

Apley, J., & Naish, N. (1958). Recurrent abdominal pains: A field study of 1,000 school children. *Archives of Disease in Childhood, 33,* 165–170.

Barr, R. G. (1983). Recurrent abdominal pain. In M. E. A. Levine (Ed.), *Developmental behavioral pediatrics* (pp. 521–528). Philadelphia: Saunders.

Beck, A. T., Ward, C. H., Mendelson, M., Mock, J., & Erbaugh, J. (1961). An inventory for measuring depression. *Archives of General Psychiatry, 5,* 561–571.

Beitchman, J. H., Zucker, K. J., Hood, J. E., daCosta, G. A., Akman, D., & Cassavia, E. (1992). A review of the long-term effects of child sexual abuse. *Child Abuse and Neglect, 16,* 101–118.

Bennett, E. J., Piesse, C., Palmer, K., Badcock, C. A., Tennant, C. C., & Kellow, J. E. (1998). Functional gastrointestinal disorders: Psychological, social and somatic features. *Gut, 42,* 414–420.

Bennett, P., & Wilkinson, S. (1985). Comparison of psychological and medical treatment of the irritable bowel syndrome. *British Journal of Clinical Psychology, 24,* 215–216.

Benson, H. (1975). *The relaxation response.* New York: Morrow.

Blanchard, E. B., & Andrasik, F. (1985). *Management of chronic headache: A psychological approach.* Elmsford, NY: Pergamon Press.

Blanchard, E. B., Andrasik, F., Appelbaum, K. A., Evans, D. D., Myers, P., & Barron, K. D. (1986). Three studies of the psychological changes in chronic headache patients associated with biofeedback and relaxation therapies. *Psychosomatic Medicine, 48,* 73–83.

Blanchard, E. B., Greene, B., Scharff, L., & Schwarz-McMorris, S. P. (1993). Relaxation training as a treatment for irritable bowel syndrome. *Biofeedback and Self-Regulation, 18,* 125–132.

Blanchard, E. B., Keefer, L., Galovski, T. E., Taylor, A. E., & Turner, S. M. (2001). Gender differences in psychological distress among patients with irritable bowel syndrome. *Psychosomatic Research, 50,* 271–275.

Blanchard, E. B., Keefer, L., Payne, A., Turner, S., & Galovski, T. E. (2002). The differential impact of sexual abuse in patients with irritable bowel syndrome. *Behavior Research and Therapy, 40,* 289–298.

Blanchard, E. B., Scharff, L., Schwarz, S., Suls, J. M., & Barlow, D. H. (1990). The role of anxiety and depression in the irritable bowel syndrome. *Behavior Research and Therapy, 28*(5), 401–405.

Blanchard, E. B., Schwarz, S. P., & Neff, D. F. (1988). Two year follow-up of behavioral treatment of irritable bowel syndrome. *Behavior Therapy, 19,* 67–73.

Blanchard, E. B., Schwarz, S. P., Suls, J. M., Gerardi, M. A., Scharff, L., Greene, B., et al. (1992). Two controlled evaluations of multicomponent psychological treatment of irritable bowel syndrome. *Behaviour Research and Therapy, 30,* 175–189.

Blewett, A., Allison, M., Calcraft, B., Moore, R., Jenkins, P., & Sullivan, G. (1996). Psychiatric disorder and outcome in irritable bowel syndrome. *Psychosomatics, 37*(2), 155–160.

Bordie, A. K. (1972). Functional disorders of the colon. *Journal of the Indian Medical Association, 58,* 451–456.

Brantley, P. J., & Jones, G. N. (1989). *Daily Stress Inventory.* Odessa, FL: Psychological Assessment Resources.

Bury, R. G. (1987). A study of 111 children with recurrent abdominal pain. *Australian Pediatric Journal, 23,* 117–119.

Camilleri, M., & Choi, M. G. (1997). Review article: Irritable bowel syndrome. *Aliment Pharmacological Therapy, 11,* 3–15.

Christensen, M. F. (1986). Recurrent abdominal pain and dietary fiber. *American Journal of Diseases in Children, 140,* 738–739.

Christensen, M. F., & Mortensen, O. (1975). Long-term prognosis in children with recurrent abdominal pain. *Archives of Disease in Childhood, 50,* 110–114.

Compas, B. E., & Thomsen, A. H. (1999). Coping and responses to stress among children with recurrent abdominal pain. *Journal of Developmental and Behavioral Pediatrics, 20*(5), 323–324.

Corney, R. H., & Stanton, R. (1990). Physical symptom severity, psychological and social dysfunction in a series of outpatients with irritable bowel syndrome. *Journal of Psychosomatic Research, 34*(5), 483–490.

Corney, R. H., Stanton, R., Newell, R., Clare, A., & Fairclough, P. (1991). Behavioural psychotherapy in the treatment of irritable bowel syndrome. *Journal of Psychosomatic Research, 35,* 461–469.

Costa, J. P. T., & McCrae, R. R. (1985). *The NEO Personality Inventory manual.* Odessa, FL: Psychological Assessment Resources.

Dancey, C. P., & Backhouse, S. (1993). Towards a better understanding of patients with irritable bowel syndrome. *Journal of Advances in Nursing, 18*(9), 1443–1450.

Dancey, C. P., Taghavi, M., & Fox, R. J. (1998). The relationship between daily stress and symptoms of irritable bowel syndrome. *Journal of Psychosomatic Research, 44*(5), 537–545.

Dancey, C. P., Whitehouse, A., Painter, J., & Backhouse, S. (1995). The relationship between hassles, uplifts and irritable bowel syndrome: A preliminary study. *Journal of Psychosomatic Research, 39*(7), 827–832.

Davidson, M. (1986). Recurrent abdominal pain: Look to dyskenesia as the culprit. *Contemporary Pediatrics, 3,* 16.

Delvaux, M., Denis, P., Allemand, H., & the French Club of Digestive Motility. (1997). Sexual and physical abuses are more frequently reported by IBS patients than by patients with organic digestive diseases or controls: Results of a multi-center inquiry. *European Journal of Gastroenterological & Hepatology, 9,* 345–352.

Derogatis, L. R., Lipman, R. S., & Covi, L. (1973). SCL-90: An outpatient psychiatric rating scale: Preliminary Scale. *Psychopharmacology, 37,* 385–389.

Drossman, D. A. (1997). Irritable bowel syndrome and sexual/physical abuse history. *European Journal of Gastroenterology & Hepatology, 9,* 327–330.

Drossman, D. A., Corrazziari, E., Talley, N. J., Thompson, W. G., & Whitehead, W. E. (Eds.). (2000). *The functional gastrointestinal disorders* (2nd ed.). McLean, VA: Degnon.

Drossman, D. A., Leserman, J., Nachman, G., Li, Z. M., Gluck, H., Toomey, T. C., et al. (1990). Sexual and physical abuse in women with functional or organic gastrointestinal disorders. *Annals of Internal Medicine, 113*(11), 828–833.

Drossman, D. A., Li, Z., Andruzzi, E., Temple, R. D., Talley, N. J., Thompson, W. G., et al. (1993). U.S. Householder Survey of Functional Gastrointestinal disorders: Prevalence, sociodemography, and health impact. *Digestive Diseases and Sciences, 38,* 1569–1580.

Drossman, D. A., Li, Z., Toner, B. B., Diamant, N. E., Creed, F. H., Thompson, D., et al. (1995). Functional bowel disorders: A multicenter comparison of health status and development of illness severity index. *Digestive Diseases and Sciences, 40,* 1–9.

Drossman, D. A., McKee, D. C., Sandler, R. S., Mitchell, C. M., Lowman, B. C., & Burger, A. L. (1988). Psychosocial factors in the irritable bowel syndrome: A multivariate study of patients and non-patients with irritable bowel syndrome. *Gastroenterology, 95,* 701–708.

Drossman, D. A., Sandler, R. S., McKee, D. C., & Lovitz, A. J. (1982). Bowel patterns among subjects not seeking health care: Use of a questionnaire to identify a population with bowel dysfunction. *Gastroenterology, 83*(3), 529–534.

Drossman, D. A., Talley, N. J., Olden, K. W., & Barreiro, M. A. (1995). Sexual and physical abuse and gastrointestinal illness: Review and recommendations. *Annals of Internal Medicine, 123*(10), 782–794.

Drossman, D. A., Thompson, W. G., Talley, N. J., Funch-Jensen, P., Jannsens, J., & Whitehead, W. E. (1990). Identification of subgroups of functional gastrointestinal disorders. *Gastroenterology International, 3,* 159–174.

Eysenck, H. J., & Eysenck, S. B. G. (1968). *Eysenck Personality Inventory.* San Diego, CA: Educational Testing Service.

Faull, C., & Nicol, A. R. (1986). Abdominal pain in six-year olds: An epidemiological study in a new town. *Journal of Child Psychology and Psychiatry and Allied Disciplines, 27,* 251–260.

Feldman, W., McGrath, P., Hodgson, C., Ritter, H., & Shipman, R. T. (1985). The use of dietary fiber in the management of simple, childhood, idiopathic, recurrent abdominal pain. *American Journal of Diseases of Childhood, 139,* 1216–1218.

Finney, J. W., Lemanek, K. L., Cataldo, M. F., Katz, H. P., & Fuqua, R. W. (1989). Pediatric psychology in primary health care: Brief targeted therapy for recurrent abdominal pain. *Behavior Therapy, 20,* 283–291.

Folks, D. G., & Kinney, F. C. (1992). The role of psychological factors in gastrointestinal conditions. *Psychosomatics, 33*(3), 257–267.

Ford, M. J., Miller, P. M., Eastwood, J., & Eastwood, M. A. (1987). Life events, psychiatric illness and the irritable bowel syndrome. *Gut, 28,* 160–165.

Fueuerstein, M., Barr, R. G., Francoeur, T. E., Hade, M., & Rafman, S. (1982). Potential biobehavioral mechanisms of recurrent abdominal pain in children. *Pain, 13,* 287.

Galovski, T. E., & Blanchard, E. B. (1998). The treatment of irritable bowel syndrome with hypnotherapy. *Applied Psychophysiology and Biofeedback, 23,* 219–232.

Garber, J., Zeman, J., & Walker, L. S. (1990). Recurrent abdominal pain in children: Psychiatric diagnoses and parental psychopathology. *Journal of the American Academy of Child and Adolescent Psychiatry, 29,* 648–656.

Gick, M. L., & Thompson, W. G. (1997). Negative affect and the seeking of medical care in university students with irritable bowel syndrome: A preliminary study. *Journal of Psychosomatic Research, 43*(5), 535–540.

Gold, N., Issenman, R., Roberts, J., & Watt, S. (2000). Well-adjusted children: An alternate view of children with inflammatory bowel disease and functional gastrointestinal complaints. *Inflammatory Bowel Disease, 6*(1), 1–7.

Goldberg, J., & Davidson, P. (1997). A biopsychosocial understanding of irritable bowel syndrome: A review. *Canadian Journal of Psychiatry, 42,* 835–839.

Gomborone, J., Dewsnap, P., Libby, G., & Farthing, M. (1995). Abnormal illness attitudes in patients with irritable bowel syndrome. *Journal of Psychosomatic Research, 39,* 227–230.

Greene, B., & Blanchard, E. B. (1994). Cognitive therapy for irritable bowel syndrome. *Journal of Consulting and Clinical Psychology, 62,* 576–582.

Greene, J. W., Walker, L. S., Hickson, G., & Thompson, J. (1985). Stressful life events and somatic complaints in adolescents. *Pediatrics, 75,* 19–22.

Greenwald, E., Leitenberg, H., Cado, S., & Tarran, M. J. (1990). Childhood sexual abuse: Long-term effects on psychological and sexual functioning in a nonclinical and nonstudent sample of adult women. *Child Abuse and Neglect, 14,* 503–513.

Guthrie, E., Creed, F., Dawson, D., & Tomenson, B. (1991). A controlled trial of psychological treatment for the irritable bowel syndrome. *Gastroenterology, 100,* 450–457.

Hamilton, M. A. (1959). The assessment of anxiety states by rating. *British Journal of Medical Psychology, 32,* 50–55.

Hamilton, M. A. (1960). A rating scale for depression. *Journal of Neurology, Neurosurgery, and Psychiatry, 23,* 56–61.

Harvey, R. F., Hinton, R. A., Gunary, R. M., & Barry, R. E. (1989). Individual and group hypnotherapy in treatment of refractory irritable bowel syndrome. *Lancet, 1*(8635), 424–425.

Hathaway, S. R., & McKinley, J. C. (1951). *Minnesota Multiphasic Personality Inventory: Manual* (revised). San Antonio, TX: Psychological Corporation.

Heymann-Monnikes, I., Arnold, R., Florin, I., Herda, C., Melfsen, S., & Monnikes, H. (2000). The combination of medical treatment plus multicomponent behavioral therapy is superior to medical treatment alone in the therapy of irritable bowel syndrome. *American Journal of Gastroenterology, 95,* 981–994.

Hodges, K., Kline, J. J., Barbero, G., & Flanery, R. (1984). Life events occurring in families of children with recurrent abdominal pain. *Journal of Psychosomatic Research, 28,* 185–187.

Hodges, K., Kline, J. J., Barbero, G., & Flanery, R. (1985). Depressive symptoms in children with recurrent abdominal pain and in their families. *Journal of Pediatrics, 107,* 622–626.

Hodges, K., Kline, J. J., Barbero, G., & Woodruff, C. (1985). Anxiety in children with recurrent abdominal pain and their parents. *Psychosomatics, 26,* 859–866.

Hodges, K., Kline, J. J., & Fitch, P. (1981). The child assessment schedule: A diagnostic interview for research and clinical use. *Catalog of Selected Documents in Psychology, 11,* 56.

Holmes, T. H., & Rahe, R. H. (1967). The Social Readjustment Rating Scale. *Journal of Psychosomatic Research, 11,* 213–218.

Houghton, L. A., Heyman, D. J., & Whorwell, P. J. (1996). Symptomatology, quality of life and economic features of irritable bowel syndrome: The effect of hypnotherapy. *Alimentary Pharmacology and Therapeutics, 10,* 91–95.

Kanner, A. D., Coyne, J. C., Schaefer, C., & Lazarus, R. S. (1981). Comparison of two modes of stress management: Minor daily hassles and uplifts versus major life events. *Journal of Behavioral Medicine, 4,* 1–39.

Kapoor, K. K., Nigam, P., Rastogi, C. K., Kumar, A., & Gupta, A. K. (1985). Clinical profile of the irritable bowel syndrome. *Indian Journal of Gastroenterology, 4,* 15–16.

Keefer, L., & Blanchard, E. B. (2001). The effects of relaxation response meditation on the symptoms of irritable bowel syndrome: Results of a controlled treatment study. *Behaviour Research and Therapy, 39,* 801–811.

Kellner, R. (1981). *Manual of the IAS (Illness Attitudes Scale).* Albuquerque: University of New Mexico.

Kovacs, M. (1980–1981). Rating scales to assess depression in school-aged children. *Acta Paedo Psychiatrica, 46,* 305–315.

Latimer, P. R. (1983). *Functional gastrointestinal disorders: A behavioral medicine approach.* New York: Springer.

Latimer, P. R., Sarna, S., Campbell, D., Latimer, M., Waterfall, W., & Daniel, E. E. (1981). Colonic motor and myoelectrical activity: A comparative study of normal subjects, psychoneurotic patients and patients with irritable bowel syndrome. *Gastroenterology, 80,* 893–901.

Laws, A. (1993). Does a history of sexual abuse in childhood play a role in women's medical problems? A review. *Journal of Women's Health, 2,* 165–172.

Lechner, M. E., Vogel, M. E., Garcia-Shelton, L. M., Leichter, J. L., & Steibel, K. R. (1993). Self-reported medical problems of adult female survivors of childhood sexual abuse. *Journal of Family Practice, 36,* 633–638.

Leserman, J., Drossman, D. A., Zhiming, L., Toomey, T. C., Nachman, G., & Glogau, L. (1996). Sexual and physical abuse history in gastroenterology practice: How types of abuse impact health status. *Psychosomatic Medicine, 58,* 4–15.

Leserman, J., Toomey, T. C., & Drossman, D. A. (1995). Medical consequences in women of sexual and physical abuse. *Humane Medicine, 11,* 23–28.

Levine, M. D., & Rappaport, L. A. (1984). Recurrent abdominal pain in school children: The loneliness of the long-distance physician. *Pediatric Clinical of North America, 31*(5), 969–991.

Levy, R. L., Cain, K. C., Jarrett, M., & Heitkemper, M. M. (1997). The relationship between daily life stress and gastrointestinal symptoms in women with irritable bowel syndrome. *Journal of Behavioral Medicine, 20*(2), 177–193.

Liebman, W. M. (1978). Recurrent abdominal pain in children: A retrospective survey of 119 patients. *Clinical Pediatrics, 17,* 149–153.

Longstreth, G. F., & Wolde-Tasadik, G. (1993). Irritable bowel-type symptoms in HMO examinees: Prevalence, demographics and clinical correlates. *Digestive Diseases Science, 40,* 2647–2655.

Lydiard, R. B. (1992). Anxiety and the irritable bowel syndrome. *Psychiatric Annals, 22,* 612–618.

Lydiard, R. B., Fosset, M. D., Marsh, W., & Ballenger, J. C. (1993). Prevalence of psychiatric disorders in patients with irritable bowel syndrome. *Psychosomatics, 34*(3), 229–233.

Lydiard, R. B., Greenwald, S., Weissman, M. M., Johnson, J., Drossman, D. A., & Ballenger, J. C. (1994). Panic disorder and gastrointestinal symptoms: Findings from the NIMH Epidemiologic Catchment Area Project. *American Journal of Psychiatry, 151,* 64–70.

Lynch, P. N., & Zamble, E. (1989). A controlled behavioral treatment study of irritable bowel syndrome. *Behavior Therapy, 20,* 509–523.

Manning, A. P., Thompson, W. G., Heaton, K. W., & Morris, A. F. (1978). Toward a positive diagnosis of the irritable bowel. *British Medical Journal, 2,* 653–654.

Maunder, R. G. (1998). Panic disorder associated with gastrointestinal disease: Review and hypotheses. *Journal of Psychosomatic Research, 44*(1), 91–105.

Mayer, E. A., & Gebhart, G. F. (1994). Basic Books and clinical aspects of visceral hyperalgesia. *Gastroenterology, 107,* 271–293.

McGrath, P. A. (1990). *Pain in children: Nature, assessment, and treatment.* New York: Guilford Press.

McGrath, P. J., Goodman, J. T., Firestone, P., Shipman, R., & Peters, S. (1983). Recurrent abdominal pain: A psychogenic disorder? *Archives of Disease in Childhood, 58,* 888–890.

Melzack, R. (1975). McGill Pain Questionnaire: Major properties and scoring methods. *Pain, 1,* 277–299.

Mendeloff, A. I., Monk, M., Siegel, C. I., & Lillienfeld, A. (1970). Illness experience and life stresses in patients with irritable colon and ulcerative colitis. *New England Journal of Medicine, 282,* 14–17.

Michenbaum, D. (1977). *Cognitive behavior modification: An integrative approach.* New York: Plenum Press.

Miller, A. J., & Kratochwill, T. R. (1979). Reduction in frequent stomachache complaints by time out. *Behavior Therapy, 10,* 211–218.

Monaghan, J., Robinson, J. O., & Dodge, J. (1979). A children's life events inventory. *Journal of Psychosomatic Research, 23,* 63–68.

Neff, D. F., & Blanchard, E. B. (1987). A multi-component treatment for irritable bowel syndrome. *Behavior Therapy, 18,* 70–83.

O'Donnell, L. J. D., Virjee, J., & Heaton, K. W. (1990). Detection of pseudodiarrhea by simple clinical assessment of intestinal transit rate. *British Medical Journal, 300,* 439–440.

Page-Goertz, S. (1988). Recurrent abdominal pain in children. *Issues in Comprehensive Pediatric Nursing, 11,* 179–191.

Patterson, G. R. (1976). *Living with children.* Champaign, IL: Research Press.

Payne, A., & Blanchard, E. B. (1995). A controlled comparison of cognitive therapy and self-help support groups in the treatment of irritable bowel syndrome. *Journal of Consulting and Clinical Psychology, 63,* 779–786.

Raymer, D., Weininger, O., & Hamilton, J. R. (1984, February 25). Psychological problems in children with abdominal pain. *Lancet, 1*(8374), 439–440.

Risser, W. L., Mullins, D., Butler, P. M., & West, M. S. (1987). Diagnosing psychiatric disorders in adolescent females with abdominal pain. *Journal of Adolescent Health Care, 8,* 431–435.

Robinson, J. O., Alverez, J. H., & Dodge, J. A. (1990). Life events and family history in children with recurrent abdominal pain. *Journal of Psychosomatic Research, 34*(2), 171–181.

Routh, D. K., & Ernst, A. R. (1984). Somatization disorder in relatives of children and adolescents with functional abdominal pain. *Journal of Pediatric Psychology, 9,* 427–437.

Sanders, M. R., Rebgetz, M., Morrison, M., Bor, W., Gordon, A., Dadds, M., et al. (1989). Cognitive-behavioral treatment of recurrent nonspecific abdominal pain in children: An analysis of generalization, maintenance, and side effects. *Journal of Consulting and Clinical Psychology, 57*(2), 294–300.

Sanders, M. R., Shepherd, R. W., Cleghorn, G., & Woolford, H. (1994). The treatment of recurrent abdominal pain in children: A controlled comparison of cognitive-behavioral family. *Journal of Consulting and Clinical Psychology, 62,* 306–314.

Sandler, R. S. (1990). Epidemiology of irritable bowel syndrome in the United States. *Gastroenterology, 99*(2), 409–415.

Sank, L. I., & Biglan, A. (1974). Operant treatment of a case of recurrent abdominal pain in a 10-year-old boy. *Behavior Therapy, 5,* 677–681.

Sarason, I. G., Johnson, J. H., & Siegel, J. M. (1978). Assessing the impact of life changes: Development of the Life Experiences Survey. *Journal of Consulting and Clinical Psychology, 46,* 932–946.

Scarinci, I. C., McDonald-Haile, J. M., Bradley, L. A., & Richter, J. E. (1994). Altered pain perception and psychosocial features among women with gastrointestinal disorders and history of abuse: A preliminary model. *American Journal of Medicine, 97,* 108–118.

Scharff, L. (1995). *Psychological treatment of children with abdominal pain.* Unpublished manuscript, University at Albany-SUNY.

Schwarz, S. P., Blanchard, E. B., Berreman, C. F., Scharff, L., Taylor, A. E., Greene, B. R., et al. (1993). Psychological aspects of irritable bowel syndrome: Comparisons with inflammatory bowel disease and nonpatient controls. *Behavior Research and Therapy, 31*(3), 297–304.

Schwarz, S. P., Taylor, A. E., Scharff, L., & Blanchard, E. B. (1990). A four-year follow-up of behaviorally treated irritable bowel syndrome patients. *Behaviour Research and Therapy, 28,* 331–335.

Shaw, G., Srivastava, E. D., Sadlier, M., Swann, P., James, J. Y., & Rhodes, J. (1991). Stress management for irritable bowel syndrome: A controlled trial. *Digestion, 50,* 36–42.

Speilberger, C. D. (1983). *Manual for the State-Trait Anxiety Inventory-STAI (Form y).* Palo Alto, CA: Consulting Psychologists Press.

Springs, F. E., & Friedrich, W. N. (1992). Health risk behaviors and medical sequelae of childhood sexual abuse. *Mayo Clinic Procedures, 67,* 527–532.

Stickler, G. B., & Murphy, D. B. (1979). Recurrent abdominal pain. *American Journal of Diseases in Childhood, 133,* 486–489.

Suls, J., Wan, C. K., & Blanchard, E. B. (1994). A multilevel data-analytic approach for evaluation of relationships between daily life stressors and symptomatology: Patients with irritable bowel syndrome. *Health Psychology, 13*(2), 103–113.

Svedlund, J., Sjodin, I., Ottosson, J.-O., & Dotevall, G. (1983). Controlled study of psychotherapy in irritable bowel syndrome. *Lancet, 2*(8350), 589–592.

Talley, N. J., Fett, S. L., & Zinsmeister, A. R. (1995). Self-reported abuse and gastrointestinal disease in outpatients: Association with irritable bowel-type symptoms. *American Journal of Gastroenterology, 90*(3), 335–337.

Talley, N. J., Fett, S. L., Zinsmeister, A. R., & Melton, L. J., III. (1994). Gastrointestinal tract symptoms and self-reported abuse: A population-based study. *Gastroenterology, 107,* 1040–1049.

Talley, N. J., Gabriel, S. E., Harmsen, W. S., Zinsmeister, A. R., & Evans, R. W. (1995). Medical costs in community subjects with irritable bowel syndrome. *Gastroenterology, 109,* 1736–1741.

Talley, N. J., Helgeson, F., & Zinsmeister, A. R., (1992). Are sexual and physical abuse linked to functional gastrointestinal disorders? (Abstract). *Gastroenterology, 102,* 52.

Talley, N. J., Phillips, S. F., Bruce, B., Twomey, C. K., Zinsmeister, A. R., & Melton, L. J., III. (1990). Relation among personality and symptoms in a non-ulcer dyspepsia and the irritable bowel syndrome. *Gastroenterology, 99,* 327–333.

Talley, N. J., Phillips, S. F., Melton, L. J., Mulvihill, C., Wiltgen, C., & Zinsmeister, A. R. (1986). Diagnostic value of the Manning criteria in the irritable bowel syndrome. *Gut, 31,* 77–81.

Talley, N. J., Phillips, S. F., Melton, L. J., Wiltgen, C., & Zinsmeister, A. R. (1989). A patient questionnaire to identify bowel disease. *Annals of Internal Medicine, 111,* 671–674.

Talley, N. J., Weaver, A. L., Zinsmeister, A. R., & Melton, L. J., III. (1992). Onset and disappearance of gastrointestinal symptoms and functional gastrointestinal disorders. *American Journal of Epidemiology, 136,* 165–177.

Talley, N. J., Zinsmeister, A. R., & Melton, L. J. (1995). Irritable bowel syndrome in a community: Symptom subgroups, risk factors, and health care utilization. *American Journal of Epidemiology, 142*(1), 76–83.

Talley, N. J., Zinsmeister, A. R., & Melton, L. J., III. (1992). Irritable bowel syndrome in a community: Symptom subgroups, risk factors and health care utilization. *American Journal of Epidemiology, 142,* 76–83.

Talley, N. J., Zinsmeister, A. R., VanDyke, C., & Melton, L. J. (1991). Epidemiology of colonic symptoms and the irritable bowel syndrome. *Gastroenterology, 101,* 927–934.

Taub, E., Cuevas, J. L., Cook, E. W., Crowell, M., & Whitehead, W. E. (1995). Irritable bowel syndrome defined by factor analysis. *Digestive Disease Sciences, 40,* 2647–2655.

Thompson, W. G. (1994). Irritable bowel syndrome: Strategy for the family physician. *Canadian Family Physician, 40,* 307–310, 313–316.

Thompson, W. G., Creed, F., Drossman, D. A., Heaton, K. W., & Mazzacca, G. (1992). Functional bowel disease and functional abdominal pain. *Gastroenterology, 5,* 75–91.

Thompson, W. G., Longstreth, G. F., Drossman, D. A., Heaton, K. W., Irvine, E. J., & Muller-Lissner, S. A. (1999). Functional bowel disorders and functional abdominal pain. *Gut, 45*(Suppl. 2), II43–II47.

Tollefson, G. D., Luxenberg, M., Valentine, R., Dunsmore, G., & Tollefson, S. L. (1991). An open label trial of alprazolam in comorbid irritable bowel syndrome and generalized anxiety disorder. *Journal of Clinical Psychiatry, 52*(12), 502–508.

Toner, B. B., Garfinkel, P. E., Jeejeebhoy, K. N., Scher, H., Shulhan, D., & Gasbarro, I. D. (1990). Self-schema in irritable bowel syndrome and depression. *Psychosomatic Medicine, 52,* 149–155.

Toner, B. B., Segal, Z. V., Emmott, S., Myran, D., Ali, A., DiGasbarro, I., et al. (1998). Cognitive-behavioral group therapy for patients with irritable bowel syndrome. *International Journal of Group Psychotherapy, 48*(2), 215–245.

van Dulmen, A. M., Fennis, J. F. M., & Bleijenberg, G. (1996). Cognitive-behavioral group therapy for irritable bowel syndrome: Effects and long-term follow-up. *Psychosomatic Medicine, 58,* 508–514.

Vollmer, A., & Blanchard, E. B. (1998). Controlled comparison of individual versus group cognitive therapy for irritable bowel syndrome. *Behavior Therapy, 29,* 19–33.

Walker, E. A., Gelfand, A. N., Gelfand, M. D., & Katon, W. J. (1996). Psychiatric diagnoses, sexual and physical victimization, and disability in patients with irritable bowel syndrome or inflammatory bowel disease. *Psychological Medicine, 25*(6), 1259–1267.

Walker, E. A., Katon, W. J., Roy-Byrne, P. P., Jemelka, R. P., & Russo, J. (1993). Histories of sexual victimization in patients with irritable bowel syndrome or inflammatory bowel disease. *American Journal of Psychiatry, 150,* 1502–1506.

Walker, E. A., Roy-Byrne, P. P., & Katon, W. J. (1990). Irritable bowel syndrome and psychiatric illness. *American Journal of Psychiatry, 147,* 565–572.

Walker, L. S., Garber, J., & Greene, J. W. (1993). Psychosocial correlates of recurrent childhood pain: A comparison of pediatric patients with recurrent abdominal pain, organic illness, and psychiatric disorders. *Journal of Abnormal Psychology, 102,* 248–258.

Walker, L. S., & Greene, J. W. (1989). Children with recurrent abdominal pain and their parents: More somatic complaints, anxiety and depression than other patient families? *Journal of Pediatric Psychology, 14*(2), 231–243.

Walker, L. S., Guite, J. W., Duke, M., Barnard, J. A., & Greene, J. W. (1998). Recurrent abdominal pain: A potential precursor of irritable bowel syndrome in adolescents and young adults. *Journal of Pediatrics, 132,* 228–237.

Ware, J. E. (1993). *SF-36 Health Survey: Manual and interpretation guide.* Boston: New England Medical Center, Health Institute.

Wasserman, A. L., Whitington, P. F., & Rivara, F. P. (1988). Psychogenic basis for abdominal pain in children and adolescents. *Journal of the American Academy of Child and Adolescent Psychiatry, 27*(2), 179–184.

Wells, N. E. J., Hahn, B. A., & Whorwell, P. J. (1997). Clinical economics review: Irritable bowel syndrome. *Aliment Pharmacological Therapy, 11,* 1019–1030.

Whitehead, W. E. (1994). Assessing the effects of stress on physical symptoms. *Health Psychology, 13,* 99–102.

Whitehead, W. E., Bosmajian, L., Zonderman, A. B., Costa, P. T., Jr., & Schuster, M. M. (1988). Symptoms of psychological distress associated with irritable bowel syndrome. *Gastroenterology, 95,* 709–714.

Whitehead, W. E., Burnett, C. K., Cook, E. W., & Taub, E. (1996). Impact of irritable bowel syndrome on quality of life. *Digestive Diseases and Sciences, 41*(11), 2248–2253.

Whitehead, W. E., Crowell, M. D., Bosmajian, L., Zonderman, A., Costa, P. T., Jr., Benjamin, C., et al. (1990). Existence of irritable bowel syndrome supported by factor analysis of symptoms in two community samples. *Gastroenterology, 98,* 336–340.

Whitehead, W. E., Crowell, M. D., Robinson, J. C., Heller, B. R., & Schuster, M. M. (1992). Effects of stressful life events on bowel symptoms: Subjects with irritable bowel syndrome compared with subjects without bowel dysfunction. *Gut, 33,* 825–830.

Whorwell, P. J., Prior, A., & Colgan, S. M. (1987). Hypnotherapy in severe irritable bowel syndrome: Further experience. *Gut, 28,* 423–425.

Whorwell, P. J., Prior, A., & Faragher, E. B. (1984). Controlled trial of hypnotherapy in the treatment of severe refractory irritable bowel syndrome. *Lancet, 2*(8414), 1232–1234.

Wilkie, A., & Schmidt, U. (1998). Gynecological pain. In E. A. Blechman & K. D. Brownell (Ed.), *Behavioral medicine and women: A comprehensive handbook* (pp. 463–469). New York: Guilford Press.

Wyllie, R., & Kay, M. (1993). Causes of recurrent abdominal pain. *Clinical Pediatrics, 32*(6), 369–371.

CHAPTER 18

Spinal Cord Injury

TIMOTHY R. ELLIOTT AND PATRICIA RIVERA

Few injuries have as profound and long-lasting consequences as spinal cord injury (SCI). Loss of sensation, impaired mobility, and bladder, bowel, and sexual function are the primary areas of functioning affected by the occurrence of an SCI, but the economic, social, and psychological ramifications must also be considered. With advancements in medical treatments, an increasing availability of assistive technologies, and removal of societal and environmental barriers, many persons with SCI are healthy individuals who can participate actively and productively in society.

In this chapter, we review the major aspects of spinal cord injury and current information about the condition and its concomitants. We then provide a model of adjustment and present evidence concerning the major components of the model. We conclude with an overview of intervention strategies and issues in health and public policy that affect persons with SCI.

NEUROLOGICAL CATEGORIES AND CLASSIFICATION OF SPINAL CORD INJURY

The spine is made up of 33 vertebrae, or bones that are connected by ligaments and separated by disk-shaped cartilage. There are 7 cervical, 12 thoracic, 5 lumbar vertebra, and the sacrum (or tail bone). The spinal cord runs through the hollow center of each vertebra, from the base of the brain to the second lumbar vertebra and is the communication relay from the brain to the peripheral nervous system. The nerves within the spinal cord are known as *upper motor neurons* (UMN) while the nerves that branch out of the spinal cord are known as *lower motor neurons* (LMN). Lower motor neurons carry information related to movement from the spinal cord to the muscles and relay sensory information such as pressure and temperature back to the brain via the spinal cord. As

This chapter was supported in part by the National Institute on Disability and Rehabilitation Research Grant #H133B980016A, and the National Center for Medical Rehabilitation Research, National Institute of Child Health and Human Development, National Institutes of Health, Grant #T32 HD07420. The contents of this article are solely the authors' responsibility and do not necessarily represent the official views of the funding agencies.

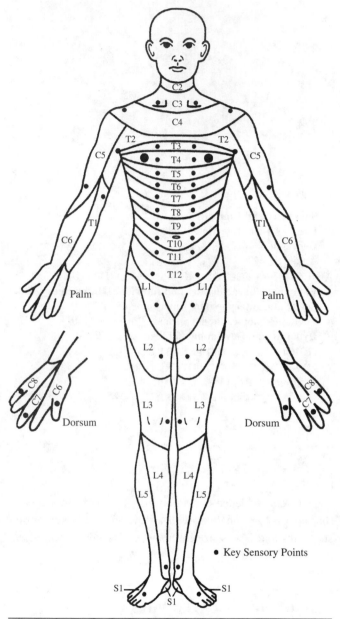

Figure 18.1   Levels of injury and corresponding motor and sensory impairments in the body.

function. A complete injury results in the total absence of all-voluntary movement or sensation below the level of injury. An incomplete injury allows for the retention of some sensation or movement below the level of injury. Thus, diagnosis describes the level of the vertebral fracture as well as the extent of the neurological deficit (e.g., a complete lesion at the fifth cervical vertebrae will be described as "C5, complete").

Levels of Injury and Functional Goals

The levels of injury to the spinal cord have been divided into ten general regions in which functional abilities cluster in persons with complete lesions. Damage to the spinal cord in the cervical region results in the greatest functional variability. Individuals with injuries to the cervical, or C region of the spinal cord between levels C1 and C3, are most likely to depend on ventilator assistance for breathing (see Figure 18.2). Implantation of a phrenic nerve pacemaker may be an option for mechanical assistance in breathing. For individuals with C1 to C3 SCIs, talking may be difficult, very limited, or impossible. Movement of the head and neck is limited, and functional goals for these individuals focus on communication and wheelchair mobility. Assistive technologies, such as a computer for speech or typing, and sip-and-puff chairs and switches, increase function and independence.

Head and neck control increases somewhat for individuals with a C3 or C4 SCI. Ventilator assistance is usually required at the initial stages of rehabilitation but prolonged use is not likely. With the relative increase in motor movement and the use of adaptive equipment at this level of injury, some individuals may have limited independence in feeding and control over environmental variables such as adjustable beds and wheelchair tilting to assist in pressure relief.

Individuals with a C5 level of injury typically have head, neck, and shoulder control. These persons can bend their elbows and turn their palms up (see Figure 18.1). Functional goals include independence with eating, drinking, face washing, toothbrushing, face shaving, and hair care, when set up with specialized equipment. Although many persons with C5 SCI may have the strength to push a manual wheelchair, a power wheelchair with hand controls is typically used for daily activities to prevent fatigue and secondary injuries such as strained muscles or stress fractures. Individuals can also manage their own health care by doing self-assist coughs and pressure reliefs by leaning forward or side-to-side. Driving may be possible with adaptive equipment.

An individual with C6 level of injury can often attain complete independence. This level of injury permits shoulder

displayed in Figure 18.1, the sensation provided by the LMNs corresponds directly to the level at the spinal cord and specific areas of the body known as dermatomes (Hammond, Umlauf, Matteson, & Perduta-Fujiniti, 1992).

Following SCI, paralysis ensues and is described as either *paraplegia* or *tetraplegia*. *Paraplegia* refers to paralysis affecting the lower part of the trunk and legs. *Tetraplegia* involves the lower and upper parts of the body including the arms and hands. The degree of neurological impairment experienced is described as either complete or incomplete depending on the degree of loss of motor and/or sensory

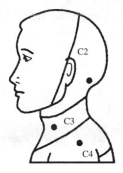

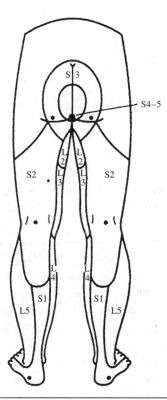

Figure 18.2 Levels of injury and corresponding motor and sensory impairments in the neck and legs.

shrug, elbow bends, palm turns, and extension of wrists (see Figure 18.1). Adaptive equipment allows for greater ease and independence in feeding, bathing, grooming, personal hygiene, and dressing. Some individuals may independently perform bladder and bowel care. While the use of a manual wheelchair is typical for daily activities, some use power wheelchairs for greater ease of independence. Additionally, individuals with this level of injury can independently perform light housekeeping duties, transfer, do pressure reliefs, turn in bed, and drive using adaptive equipment.

At a C7 level of injury, an individual may have similar movement as a person with C6 injury, along with the ability to straighten the elbows. Functional goals for an individual with C7 level include use of a manual wheelchair as a primary means of mobility, greater ease in performing household work and transferring, ability to do wheelchair pushups for pressure reliefs, and the need for fewer adaptive aids in independent daily living. Injuries at the C8 and the first thoracic, or T1, levels are similar (see Figure 18.1). The added movements at these levels of injury include development of strength and precision of fingers that result in a more natural hand function. Functional goals include independent living without the use of assistive devices.

At level T2 and below, an individual has normal motor function in the head, neck, shoulders, arms, hands, and fingers. Depending on the exact level, functional goals for injuries between T2 and T6 include increasing the use of ribs and chest muscles, or trunk control. For injuries at the levels between T7 and T12, there is additional abdominal control. Functional goals for individuals within these six levels of injury may include improving cough effectiveness and increasing ability to perform unsupported seated activities. Individuals with injuries between levels T2 and T12 are often capable of very limited walking. However, there is a high level of energy expenditure associated with this activity and the stress placed on the upper body results in no functional advantage, resulting in high reliance on a wheelchair for mobility.

With the help of specialized leg and ankle braces, walking may be a realistic goal for people with injuries at the level of L1-L5 (see Figure 18.1). Individuals with lower levels of injury will walk with greater ease than those persons with higher lumbar injuries. The functional goals of individuals with injuries from S1 through S5 include the ability to walk with fewer or no supportive devices. Depending on the level of injury, there are also various degrees of return of voluntary bladder, bowel, and sexual functions.

EPIDEMIOLOGY OF SPINAL CORD INJURY

In 1968, professionals and consumers testified before the U.S. Congress about the lack of informed and coordinated medical and psychosocial services available to persons with spinal cord injury. This situation existed, in part, because SCI is a relatively low-incidence but costly and high-impact disability that had been difficult to study in a programmatic fashion. Federal funds were eventually granted in 1970 to Good Samaritan Hospital in Phoenix, Arizona, to establish the first national model system of care to persons with SCI. To foster systematic research that could inform clinical care, a coordinated collaborative database (the National Spinal Cord Injury Data Research Center, NSCIDRC) was established in 1975 at the Arizona site to gather and archive demographic and medical information from the SCI Model Systems. Transferred in 1983 to the University of Alabama at Birmingham, the NSCIDRC has yielded more than 1,000 published research reports (Stover, Hall, DeLisa, & Donovan, 1995). Initially, the SCI model systems project emphasized collection of demographic and medical information pertinent to the clinical management of SCI and associated complications. Much of the literature concerning SCI has emanated from this database or from centers that have participated in the model systems project.

According to the National Spinal Cord Injury Statistical Center, there are approximately 10,000 new SCIs per year, and it is estimated that between 183,000 and 230,000 persons live with SCI in the United States (Stover, Whiteneck, & DeLisa, 1995). Over the years, studies from the archived database have revealed a reduction in the incidence of complete cord lesions (which are associated with more neurological impairment) among persons admitted for care, and an increase in the number of persons with incomplete lesions (indicating some sparing of neurological function below the lesion site). This trend is attributed, in part, to improved emergency service techniques at these sites that minimize further damage to the cord (Stover, Hall, et al., 1995).

Secondary complications (particularly the development of pressure-related skin sores) compromise personal health and quality of life, and are associated with increased costs to the person, the health care delivery system, and society. Treatment at a model system center has been associated with a decreased likelihood of a severe pressure ulcer during acute care and at long-term follow-up (Stover, Whiteneck, et al., 1995). This trend may be due to improved assessment, intervention, education, and health promotion methods. Decreased rehospitalizations and improved survival rates have been observed among persons with SCI who were treated in these centers (Stover, Hall, et al., 1995).

Age

SCI occurs mainly in persons between the ages of 16 and 30 years. Almost 80% of all SCIs documented by the NSCIDRC were among individuals 16 to 45 years of age, with an average age of 30.7 years. Women tend to be somewhat older at the time of injury, with a mean age of 32.2 years compared to men whose average age is 30.3 years. A trend identified by the NSCIDRC is the increase in individuals over the age of 61 years at the time of injury. This finding likely reflects the increase in the median age of the national population.

Gender

Men have a higher observed incidence of SCI in the NSCIDRC data set (82.2%). General population-based samples reflect a range of 69% to 81% of SCI's occurring in males vs. females. However, while this disproportionate representation of men may reflect the greater likelihood of high-risk activities among men in general, it is comparable to those figures reflecting unintentional mortality rates in the population at large (Go, DeVivo, & Richards, 1995).

Ethnicity

The NSCIDRC reports a change in the ethnic distribution of persons with SCI since 1990. During this period, the percentage of Caucasians with SCI in the model systems database dropped to 58.1% from 77.5% observed between 1973 and 1978. Similarly, a 1.6% decrease in SCI among American Indians was observed. A more disturbing trend is seen during the same time period, with spinal cord injuries to African Americans, Hispanics, and Asians increasing from 13.5% to 28%, 5.7% to 8.4%, and .8% to 2.1%, respectively. It is possible that the geographic locations of the model systems may contribute to an overrepresentation of the ethnic minorities with SCIs compared to the general population. Differences in ethnic distribution of persons with SCI and the population at large may also be explained by the proportionate decrease in the Caucasian population along with the concomitant increase in African American, Asian, and Hispanic populations. Finally, referral patterns to the model systems centers may also account for some of the observed variations.

Educational and Occupational Status

Because the median age of the SCI population is 26 years, it is encouraging to see that approximately 59% of these individuals have received a high school education. The observed tendency toward increased age at time of injury increases the likelihood of possession of a high school diploma or its equivalent, which can affect postinjury employment. Almost 80% of persons with SCI are employed at the time of their injury. Unfortunately, 14.3% are unemployed and are likely to remain that way despite a much lower national unemployment average. Interestingly, but perhaps not surprisingly, level of education is inversely related to likelihood of injury due to violence.

Marital Status

Given the relatively young age at which most individuals incur an SCI, most (53.5%) have never married at the time of their injury. There is an increased rate of divorce among persons with SCI in comparison with the general population (DeVivo & Fine, 1985; DeVivo, Hawkins, Richards, & Go, 1995), and the dissolution of the marriage tends to occur within a year following injury onset.

Etiology of Injury

Motor vehicle accidents, falls, and gunshot wounds are the three leading causes of SCI in the United States (Nobunaga, Go, & Karunas, 1999). Gender differentiates the next two causes, with diving and motorcycle accidents rounding out the top five causes in men, while medical procedures and diving accidents are the next leading causes of SCI in women. While increased age reduces the chance of SCI due to sporting accidents or violent acts, it is a large contributor to spinal cord injuries resulting from falls.

While motor vehicle accidents continue to be the primary cause of SCI in individuals up to age 45 years, injuries resulting from violence, primarily in the form of gunshot wounds, showed a startling increase of 64% in the 25-year period from 1973 to 1998. A slight decrease in violence-related SCI has been noted for the period from 1989 to 1998. Ethnicity-related differences in SCI etiology exist. Violence accounts for 7% to 8% of SCIs in Caucasians and Native Americans, 46% in African Americans, 43.8% in Hispanics, and 22% in Asians. Research is needed to determine whether ethnic classification functions as a proxy for other variables that may be involved.

Sexuality and Reproductive Health

Based on the type of injury incurred, sexual response—like sensation, movement, and other body functions—will be affected in a predictable manner (see Figure 18.1). Thus, it is important to determine the level, degree of injury, and whether the injury affected the upper or lower motor neuron system. When addressing issues of sexual function, it is important to identify the aspect of the sexual response on which to focus: erectile dysfunction, ejaculation, lubrication, or orgasm.

When diagnosing erectile dysfunction, it is important to determine whether reflexogenic or psychogenic erections are attainable. Reflexogenic erections occur as a result of stimulation in the genital area. Psychogenic erections result from cognitive stimulation. Men with complete UMN injuries typically retain the ability to achieve reflexogenic erections while those with incomplete UMN injuries retain abilities for both reflexogenic and psychogenic erections. Men with incomplete LMN injuries often have the ability to achieve psychogenic erections with a partially preserved ability for reflexogenic erections.

Ejaculation is a complex process that involves coordination of the sympathetic, parasympathetic, and somatic nervous systems affected by SCI. Retrograde ejaculation, a common consequence of SCI, occurs when semen is directed into the bladder as a result of lack of closure at the neck of the bladder. Use of pharmacological agents, vibratory stimulation, electroejaculation, and direct aspiration of seminal fluid are techniques employed to obtain sperm from men with SCI who would like to father children. Men report experiencing orgasm as similar, weaker, or different, and 38% of men with complete SCI report the ability to achieve orgasms (Alexander, Sipski, & Findley, 1993).

Although sexual desire decreases after SCI, most men continue to express interest in sexual activity. It is important to recognize that preservation of sensation is not necessary for sexual excitement and that stimulation above the level of injury tends to become hypersensitive and erogenous, contributing to the experience. Although most individuals with SCI resume sexual activity within a year of injury, there is a concomitant decrease in frequency of events, as well as a decreased sense of satisfaction, which (Berkman, Weissman, & Frielich, 1978) may be a result of decreased availability of partners. While 99% of men identify penile-vaginal intercourse as their favorite preinjury sexual activity, this figure drops to 16% postinjury. Oral sex, kissing, and hugging become preferred activities following SCI.

Information regarding female sexual response has been based largely on self-report. Vaginal lubrication is comparable to male erection and complete UMN injuries retain the ability for reflexogenic but not psychogenic lubrication (Sipski, Alexander, & Rosen, 1995). Women with incomplete UMN SCIs maintain the capacity to achieve reflexogenic and possibly psychogenic lubrication. About 25% of women with complete LMN SCIs experience psychogenic lubrication, and about 95% of women with incomplete LMN SCIs can continue experiencing both forms of lubrication. Sipski et al. (1995) support the belief that women with incomplete UMN SCIs can achieve psychogenic lubrication based on pinprick sensation at T11–12 dermatomes (see Figure 18.1), and women with incomplete UMN SCIs affecting sacral segments can retain reflexogenic lubrication.

About half of all women with SCI report the ability to achieve orgasm (Charlifue, Gerhart, Menter, Whiteneck, & Manley, 1992). Whipple, Gerdes, and Komisaruk (1996) report that women with complete SCI experience orgasm in response to genital and nongenital stimulation. Changes in heart rate, blood pressure, and arousal were monitored in 16 women with complete SCI and 5 able-bodied women. Despite having complete SCIs, the women retained the ability to achieve orgasm and registered physiologic and subjective changes similar to those of the able-bodied women.

Post-SCI amenorrhea is a common occurrence (Charlifue et al., 1992, Comarr, 1966) and can last an average of five months. With the resumption of the ovulatory menstrual cycle, a woman's ability to conceive also returns. However, Charlifue et al. found that the greater the level of impairment, the likelihood of having children decreased. This finding may possibly be due to women's recognition of the difficulty associated with caring for a child.

Medical problems associated with pregnancy in women with SCI include urinary tract infection (UTI) secondary to incomplete emptying of the bladder, spasticity, decubiti, increased risk of respiratory distress, and autonomic dysreflexia, which is the most life-threatening complication. Autonomic dysreflexia and preeclampsia must be distinguished to provide appropriate treatment. Complications associated with the loss of sensation include an absence of awareness of labor. However, women with SCI can be taught to recognize sympathetic nervous system symptoms as indicators of labor. There do not appear to be increased risks of preterm or rapid labor, nor of mode of delivery in this population (Baker & Cardenas, 1996).

Aging and Physiologic Changes

The history of spinal cord injury survival in this country provides a good illustration of the process of aging with SCI. In the 1940s, the only survivors of spinal cord trauma were individuals with low- to mid-level paraplegia. Survival was the primary medical goal, and subsequent lifetime institutionalization was the norm. The discovery and widespread use of antibiotic agents such as streptomycin and tetracycline to augment the efficacy of penicillin increased the survival rate of individuals with high-level paraplegia in the 1950s. At this time, rehabilitation goals for these persons were modified to include deinstitutionalization and return home with supervision. In the 1960s, the odds of survival increased for individuals who incurred low-level tetraplegia. The active social movement of the time sought rehabilitation goals of community reintegration and increased independence. In the 1970s, standards of care for emergency medical services were established. Regulation respiratory procedures greatly increased survival for individuals with mid- and high-level tetraplegia. In addition to the improved technology, activism and the creation of independent living centers with home-based support

services resulted in the creation of "super paras," who managed to supercede functional goals and expectations. High-energy expenditure, increased risk of injury, and mechanical overuse were some of the long-term consequences of this overachieving lifestyle. The past two decades have seen an increase in incomplete SCIs along with the recognition of aging-related issues. As survivors approach 40 years post-SCI, age-related complications such as orthopedic problems, neurologic complications, infections, obesity, and psychosocial difficulties are being recognized and addressed (Hohmann, 1982; Trieschmann, 1987).

A disturbing trend reported by the NSCIDRC is an increase in persons 61 years of age and older who are incurring SCIs. Many of these individuals have preexisting medical conditions that place them at higher risk for falls. Early data from this population reveal that these individuals are more likely to suffer cervical injuries that result in tetraplegia, have a greater likelihood of experiencing secondary complications during their acute and rehabilitation hospitalizations, and have an increased probability of requiring skilled nursing home placement following rehabilitation. Finally, this older cohort of persons with SCI is evidencing a greater number of rehospitalizations post-SCI compared to younger persons with SCI.

The process of aging affects the body systems of a person with SCI in much the same way as it will someone without an SCI. However, the difference lies in the way the aging-related physiologic changes affect functional ability for a person with SCI. For example, with time, the skin and subcutaneous tissue becomes thinner and less elastic. For individuals with SCI, this change increases susceptibility to tearing and/or bruising during transfers. The slowed healing process associated with aging-related immune functioning increases the likelihood of opportunistic infections and the potential development of decubitus ulcers (i.e., pressure sores). Endocrinological adjustments may lead to an increase in serum cholesterol levels and decreased glucose tolerance. Endocrine-associated complications include coronary artery disease, poor circulation, slow healing wounds, amputation, and blindness. Decreased range of motion and flexibility and increased incidence of contractures differentially affect the musculoskeletal system and, thus, the mobility of the individual with SCI. Osteoporosis, osteoarthritis, and the concomitant stiffening of joint and connective tissues increase risk of injury from mechanical stress. Fractures from spasticity and falls also increase with age.

Mortality

Current data indicate that 26% of all SCI deaths are attributable to heart disease and pulmonary emboli. Lifestyle factors including lack of aerobic exercise, smoking, diet high in saturated fats, high blood pressure, obesity, and stress are all known contributors to heart disease. Additionally, though not yet proven, it is believed that moderate exercise in persons with SCI may yield positive cardiovascular benefits that may ameliorate cardiovascular disease associated with aging.

Following SCI, muscle fibers change from slow aerobic to fast anaerobic. This change affects contraction and relaxation speed. Concomitantly, there is a reduction in endurance and an increase in fatigue that may, in turn, contribute to sedentariness. It is believed that ischemic heart disease will contribute to morbidity/mortality with increasing age of persons with SCI. Although electrocardiogram tests are not currently a routine part of physical exams for individuals with SCI, it is suggested that education and training regarding known risk factors and preventive measures be provided to reduce cardiovascular disease in this population.

SECONDARY COMPLICATIONS FOLLOWING SPINAL CORD INJURY

Other conditions that occur among persons who have SCI can stem from the physical and neurological impairments secondary to the cord injury, but may also be mediated by behavioral and social pathways. Among these complications are pain, pressure sores, contractures and spasticity, urinary tract infections, and psychological disorders of depression and anxiety. Other complications that merit attention but require more medical interventions can be reviewed elsewhere (e.g., deep vein thrombosis, heterotropic ossification; Cardenas, Burns, & Chan, 2000).

Pain

The incidence and prevalence estimates of pain following SCI vary considerably for several reasons including (a) the use of different measures of pain with samples from acute and community settings, and (b) the absence of operational definitions of pain following SCI. As a result, prevalence estimates of pain range from 18% to 91% (Anson & Shepard, 1996; Johnson, Gerhart, McCray, Menconi, & Whiteneck, 1998; Siddall, Taylor, McClelland, Rutklowki, & Cousins, 1999). Pain after SCI has been conceptualized into four different categories: musculoskeletal, visceral, neuropathic, and other (Siddall, Taylor, & Cousins, 1997). Research indicates that neuropathic pain is probably the most frequently reported pain condition and is more likely to be severe and resistant to treatment (Levi, Hultling, & Seiger, 1995; Siddall et al., 1999; Yezierski, 1996). Neuropathic pain is often described as "burning, stabbing, shooting, or electrical," and it may occur at the level of lesion or below

(Siddall et al., 1997). The mechanisms of pain below the site of lesion are not well understood, but research suggests that there are psychophysiological indicators of such pain. Research using single photon emission computed tomography (Ness et al., 1998) has recorded observed changes in cerebral flow, and these changes corresponded with the individual's pain reports.

Pressure Sores

Pressure sores result from restriction of blood flow to the skin, depletion of oxygen, and gradual erosion of tissue. Immobilization, paralysis, and loss of neuronal innervation and sensory input following SCI interact to set the stage for this sequence of events to which persons are at risk for the remainder of their lives. Skin is susceptible to persistent applications of even moderate pressure with a direct relationship between tissue damage, intensity, and duration of pressure (Yarkony, 1994). Atrophy, repeated trauma, scarring and/or secondary bacterial infection, shearing force, reduced transcutaneous oxygen tension, and friction are also major etiologic factors (Mawson et al., 1993; Yarkony, 1994). Metabolic and local factors thought to contribute to pressure ulcers include increased moisture, hypoalbuminemia, vitamin C deficiency, anemia, lean body build, muscle atrophy, older age, fever, and poor personal hygiene (Mawson et al., 1993; Yarkony, 1994). Sites most prone to development of pressure ulcers are bony prominences such as sacrum, ischium, heels, ankles, and trochanter. Untreated or improperly treated pressure ulcers that do not heal place persons at risk for potentially life-threatening complications.

Pressure ulcers are one of the most common, costly, and debilitating secondary complications in persons with SCI. Persons who develop severe pressure sores often require expensive and intensive medical intervention for repair, rehabilitation, and management of the skin ulcer (over $17,000 per person, excluding physician fees; Johnson, Brooks, & Whiteneck, 1996). Unquantified indirect costs include frustration; inconvenience; interference with rehabilitation, education, and vocational activities; and separation from the family unit with its impact on psychological and social development and successful reintegration into the community (Yarkony, 1994).

About 50% to 80% of persons with SCI will develop a pressure ulcer at some time in their lives (Mawson et al., 1993; Yarkony, 1994). Incidence ranges from 22% to 59% during acute care/rehabilitation and from 20% to 30% during one to five years postinjury (Stover, Whiteneck, et al., 1995; Yarkony, 1994). Pressure sores are considered preventable complications, as individuals who develop these sores are often noncompliant with recommended self-care regimens, engage in a variety of health compromising behaviors, and lack active coping skills (Yarkony, 1994). Yarkony stressed the importance of considering the multifactorial etiology and a person's general medical condition, nutrition, and social situation to achieve successful healing and prevent recurrence. The emphasis of most studies has been on prevention, stressing frequent repositioning, use of special beds, mattresses, and wheelchair cushions. The need for surgical closure tends to increase with the chronicity of the sore.

Spasticity and Contractures

Spasticity is a UMN disorder that refers to spasms, deep tendon reflexes, and clonus that occurs among persons with SCI (Cardenas et al., 2000). When untreated and recurring, the individual may experience weakness, fatigue, and loss of dexterity over time. Urinary tract infections and pressure sores can increase spasticity. Often spasticity is treated with pharmacological agents such as baclofen or diazepam if the spasms interfere with sleep, positioning, balance, skin integrity, or if the spasms are painful.

Contractures may occur when patients and/or caregivers do not provide adequate and continuous range of motion exercises. In their severe form, contractures cause permanent limitation to joint movement and may require surgical intervention. They can compromise sitting position and lead to additional complications such as pressure sores and compromised general quality of life because mobility, transfers, bowel and bladder care, and so on, are adversely affected.

Urinary Tract Infections

Even though the incidence of renal failure, secondary to chronic or recurrent UTI, in persons with SCI has decreased markedly due to advances in diagnostic, preventive, and therapeutic measures, UTI and its sequelae continue to be a major problem regardless of bladder-emptying method. Bladder management goals after SCI are to establish and maintain unrestricted urine flow from the kidneys and maintain urine sterility and bladder continence, thereby preserving renal function. Neurologic damage that affects control of bladder function, coupled with the need for catheters to facilitate emptying, results in impairment of normal anatomic and physiologic defense mechanisms responsible for eliminating bacteria and maintaining urinary tract sterility. Normally, the physical barrier of the urethra, urine flow, and toxic or anti-adherence effects mediated by the bladder mucosa limit spread and multiplication of bacteria in the urinary tract (Stover, Lloyd, Waites, & Jackson, 1991). However, in the neurogenic bladder, stagnant residual urine allows bacteria to accumulate. Mucosal ischemia associated with obstructed high-pressure voiding and poor bladder wall compliance may also facilitate tissue invasion. Vesicoureteral reflux caused by elevated bladder pressures facilitates access of urinary pathogens to the kidneys, leading to serious complications such as pyelonephritis, septicemia, and renal failure (Stover et al., 1991).

Other UTI risk factors include structural abnormalities, fluid intake, neurologic level, prior colonization of genital skin by pathogenic bacteria, age, limited access to health care providers, insurance coverage, social support systems, and being female (National Institute on Disability and Rehabilitation Research Consensus Statement, 1992; Stover et al., 1991). Psychological variables, personal hygiene, care of urinary drainage appliances, and drug abuse are the focus of investigation as they relate to development of UTI and pressure ulcers following severe physical disability stemming from the probability that inattention to self-care is one logical reason these complications occur.

Depression

Depression has received more attention from clinicians and researchers than any other psychological issue among persons with SCI (Elliott & Frank, 1996). For many years, clinical lore maintained that depression was to be expected soon after the onset of injury, and it was construed as a critical element in most stage models of adjustment, typically signaling rational acceptance of the permanence of the injury. (For a critique of these models, see Frank, Elliott, Corcoran, & Wonderlich, 1987.) Empirical study has broadened our understanding of depression considerably. Studies relying on *DSM-III* (American Psychiatric Association [APA], 1980) criteria using small samples of recently injured persons and conservative diagnostic interview techniques have found the rate of major depressive episodes to range from 22.7% to over 30% (Frank, Kashani, Wonderlich, Lising, & Visot, 1985; Fullerton, Harvey, Klein, & Howell, 1981). Lower rates have been observed in studies using less stringent interview methods (13.7%; Judd & Brown, 1992), and with self-report measures based on *DSM-III-R* (APA, 1987) criteria with a sample varying in time since the onset of injury (11%; Frank et al., 1992). Other data indicate that among newly injured persons who met criteria for major and minor depressive disorders, many may remit within three months of injury onset (Kishi, Robinson, & Forrester, 1994). Generally, many report decreasing problems with depressive symptomology over the first year of SCI (Richards, 1986).

The bulk of this research has relied on self-report measures of depressive behavior that do not assess unique symptoms of diagnosable depressive syndromes. These instruments yield useful information, but care should be taken in extrapolating from this work. It is probable that these instruments assess an underlying distress that may not distinguish depressive behavior from related problems with anxiety. Studies using these instruments have shown that depressive behavior is associated with increased expenditures, longer rehabilitation stays, and decreased self-reported quality of life (Elliott & Frank, 1996).

Depression is often associated with suicidal ideation, impaired quality of life, and requests for terminating life. Research has shown that persons with severe SCIs—ventilator- and nonventilator-dependent individuals with tetraplegia—report a high self-esteem and quality of life that extends up to decades postinjury (Crewe & Krause, 1990; Hall et al., 1999). An individual's request for termination of life support often occurs in a medical setting and tends to be met with paternalistic assumptions that health care professionals are best prepared to determine the patient's well-being. This concept is in opposition to the principle of autonomy that endorses informed consent and self-governance and is guaranteed by the Bill of Rights. However, competency must be established to exercise informed consent. Psychologists are often called on to evaluate a person's ability to (a) understand relevant information, (b) communicate available choices, (c) understand the implications of such choices, and (d) demonstrate logical decision-making processes.

Persons with high-level tetraplegia, who are ventilator-dependent, are more likely to request termination of life support than any other level of SCI. Individuals with high-level tetraplegia are at risk of cognitive deficits due to anoxia and may require neuropsychological testing to determine whether the impairment significantly affects their level of competency.

Anxiety

Problems with anxiety and related disorders have been observed among persons with SCI. In some situations, individuals will develop specific anxieties about social and personal problems that might cause considerable discomfort or embarrassment (e.g., bowel accidents in public places or during moments of intimacy; Dunn, 1977). In extreme cases, these anxieties may exacerbate and result in social isolation or specific phobias. In other cases, anxiety about general appearance and acceptance can compromise social interactions. Persons with recent-onset SCI may have significantly higher levels of anxiety than comparison groups, and these differences may be evident two years later (Craig, Hancock, & Dickson, 1994; Hancock, Craig, Dickson, Chang, & Martin, 1993).

When people incur SCI in acts of violence or in accidents that have traumatizing qualities, posttraumatic stress disorder (PTSD) may be observed. Radnitz and colleagues have shown that a significant minority of military service veterans with SCI met criteria for current PTSD (11% to 15%); 28% to 34% met criteria for lifetime incidence. In their research, 3.2% met criteria for a general anxiety disorder (Radnitz et al., 1995, 1996). Subsequent research suggests that persons with high-level tetraplegia report less intense PTSD symptoms than persons with paraplegia (Radnitz et al., 1998).

ADJUSTMENT FOLLOWING SPINAL CORD INJURY

Adjustment following SCI is a dynamic and fluid process in which characteristics of the person and the injury, their social and interpersonal world, the environment in general, and the historical and temporal context interact to influence physical and psychological health (see Figure 18.3). Rehabilitation psychology has long embraced the Lewinian field-theory perspective to understand behavior within the $B = f(P, E)$ equation (D. Dunn, 2000). However, aspects of this equation may receive different emphasis from individuals, depending on their perspective. Many physicians place greater emphasis on the nature and concomitants of the SCI, as is evident in the extant literature. Psychologists and other rehabilitation professionals tend to place greater weight on the person (Wright & Fletcher, 1982). Consumers and their advocates are much more sensitive to the demands and issues centered in the environment in which any behavior is framed (Olkin, 1999).

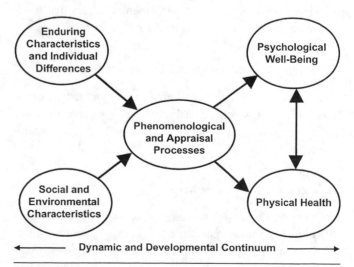

Figure 18.3 Model for understanding adjustment following spinal cord injury.

These groups represent essential stakeholders in any program of care and service, and the critical distinctions between these areas of emphasis ultimately reflect their opinions regarding future service and intervention. Thus, medical professionals are concerned about continued support for medical advancements, treatments, and management of SCI; consumers and advocates are invested in rectifying social barriers that impede full access and integration, and support the availability and provision of assistive technologies to enhance independence and quality of life.

In our model, we recognize that different elements influence adjustment at any time, and we argue that these characteristics depend to a great extent on the unique, phenomenological appraisals of the individual living with SCI. As depicted in Figure 18.3, adjustment is conceptualized into several broad-based domains, each of which has considerable influence on two areas of adjustment. The primary components involve individual characteristics and the immediate social and interpersonal environment (see left side of Figure 18.3). These influence the phenomenological and appraisal processes that constitute elements of positive growth and, in turn, predict psychological and physical health outcomes (see far right side of Figure 18.3). These components are framed within the developmental continuum that flow left to right, and is shown at the bottom of the figure. The dynamic continuum encompasses changes in any of the aforementioned five areas as people age, as technologies advance, as relationships shift, and as health and public policies evolve. This continuum reflects the ongoing process of growth, adaptation, and development in the person and the environment, and in corresponding alterations in interactions between these entities. Thus, in our model, we adopt a collectivistic approach in which behavior results from the combined interactions of individual, situational, and environmental factors that function in an integrated and fluid manner.

Enduring Characteristics and Individual Differences

Enduring characteristics are defined as demographic characteristics, disability-related characteristics (e.g., level of injury and pain), predisability behavioral patterns, and personality characteristics.

Demographic Characteristics

Few researchers have taken a priori theoretical perspectives in examining ethnic, gender, age, or socioeconomic status (SES) differences as they relate to adjustment following disability (Elliott & Uswatte, 2000; Fine & Asch, 1988). Most demographic characteristics are included in clinical studies for descriptive purposes only, and their relation is usually examined within the context of maladjustment. Demographic variables have been inconsistently related to outcome variables, although more sophisticated statistical models have provided more useful information in more recent years. In particular, study of intraindividual changes using growth curve analyses reveals intriguing differences in terms of gender, age, and education among persons in initial inpatient SCI rehabilitation that warrant further scrutiny (Warschausky, Kay, & Kewman, 2001). It should be noted that the socially defined constructs of ethnicity, gender, SES, and age share considerable overlap with the social/environment component of our model.

Older individuals who incur SCI may have a more difficult time adjusting in the first year of SCI and may engage in fewer activities than younger persons (Elliott & Richards, 1999). Life satisfaction seems to have a curvilinear relationship with age among young adults: Those in late adolescence and in their late twenties seem to have lower life satisfaction, particularly if they are not working (Putzke, Richards, & Dowler, 2000a). Stressful life events may have different effects on persons with SCI as a function of their age, which in turn may reflect different developmental tasks across the lifespan (Frank, Elliott, Buckelew, & Haut, 1988). Surveys indicate that younger persons with SCI are more interested in topics that concern sexuality, fertility, family planning, muscle function test, and nerve conductance, and are less interested in information concerning pain, bowel and bladder management, and pressure sore prevention than older persons with SCI (Hart, Rintala, & Fuhrer, 1996).

Several trends have been observed in regard to gender differences. Women report an overall higher life satisfaction than men (Dijkers, 1999). Men evidence more problems with pneumonia and other pulmonary/respiratory complications than women (Burns, Putzke, Richards, & Jackson, 2000). Postmenapausal women may experience significant deterioration in bone mineral density, contributing to problems with osteoporosis (Weeks, 2001).

Descriptive studies imply that persons from ethnic minority groups may face more difficulties in their adjustment. Some studies indicate that these persons may have higher levels of distress and lower life satisfaction than Caucasians, and certain secondary complications may be more frequent as well (Elliott & Uswatte, 2000). However, these data are tenuous for several reasons. The relations between ethnicity and any outcome variable may be mediated in part by a host of variables including education, access to health care, socioeconomic status, sponsorship, transportation, living arrangements, and trust between consumer and health care provider. Without appreciating the sociocultural and community context of ethnicity, simple associations between ethnicity and outcome are open to misinterpretation and speculation.

Disability-Related Characteristics

Level and completeness of the SCI do not reliably predict subsequent adjustment, although some occasional differences may be observed. SCI alone does not adversely affect emotional experiences, for example. People with SCI report many intense emotional experiences regardless of the level of autonomic feedback, and their ratings of positive and negative emotions are unequivocal to those provided by comparison groups (Chwalisz, Diener, & Gallagher, 1988). Changes in the physical condition itself, however, can influence routine activities, available resources, and ongoing behavioral patterns, thereby affecting adjustment.

For many years, clinical lore maintained that the passage of time was associated with eventual acceptance of the injury and lowered distress (see Frank, Elliott, Corcoran, & Wonderlich, 1987). Such notions were typically used to describe initial reactions to the injury, but empirical scrutiny has revealed inconsistent and uninformative relationships between indicators of time passage and adjustment. However, more recent research suggests that persons who have lived longer with SCI may have higher life satisfaction than those who have been injured for shorter periods of time, once other important variables such as education and employment are taken into account (Dijkers, 1999). Qualitative research indicates that regaining the ability to walk and having a focused interest in cure research are particular concerns for persons in the first year of injury that are not shared by persons who have been injured for several years (Elliott & Shewchuk, in press). Generally, individuals who have lived with SCI for longer periods of time seem to be more interested in community and health issues. Problems with bowel and bladder management are shared by persons with both recent and long-term SCI (Elliott & Shewchuk, in press; Rogers & Kennedy, 2000). These differences may reflect adaptation that occurs as a person lives with SCI and resumes interest in personal, social, and vocational roles and activities.

For years, people with SCI have reported that chronic, unresolved pain is especially distressing to them. Indeed, pain may constitute one of the most difficult obstacles faced by persons with SCI (Paralyzed Veterans of America, 1988). Pain can often be observed soon after injury onset, and reports of pain in the rehabilitation setting can be significantly predictive of distress two years later (Craig et al., 1994). Over time, pain is predictive of increases in depressive behavior, indicating a causal relationship (Cairns, Adkins, & Scott, 1996). Extreme pain is associated with increased rates

of rehospitalization, lower life satisfaction, poor physical and mental health, and more problems with mobility and social integration (Putzke, Richards, & Dowler, 2000b). It is understandable, then, that chronic, persistent pain can compromise acceptance and adjustment (Summers, Rapoff, Varghese, Porter, & Palmer, 1991).

Predisability Behavioral Patterns

People who engaged in health-compromising behaviors and had problems in interpersonal adjustment prior to SCI often have difficulty coming to terms with disability. These factors are often suspected variables in those who sustain SCI through acts of violence. Although many of these persons are victimized by acts of crime, others have been willing participants in a lifestyle characterized by violence or they have lived in areas where violence was a commonplace event. Violent onset of SCI has been associated with a higher rate of pressure sore occurrence in some studies (Waters & Adkins, 1997; Zafonte & Dijkers, 1999) but not in others (Putzke, Richards, & DeVivo, 2001); persons who are injured by gunshot may be likely to develop chronic pain (Richards, Stover, & Jaworski, 1990). These issues may stem from a confluence of societal and economic variables and may not be easily attributed to any single specific demographic or disability-related characteristic.

There is also some concern that people who incur SCI in high-impact incidents occasionally sustain brain injuries (BI) with subsequent neuropsychological consequences. In fact, almost half of those who acquire SCI in this fashion may experience loss of consciousness or posttraumatic amnesia (Dowler et al., 1997). Others may experience anoxia during surgical procedures or during cardiopulmonary arrest (Davidoff, Roth, & Richards, 1992). At times, a brain injury will be obvious, either due to the nature of the wound, or as evidenced by the immediate and pronounced sequelae (e.g., prolonged loss of consciousness, coma). However, in situations in which mild or moderate BI is suspected, diagnosis is more difficult and research has not consistently demonstrated how BI adversely affects adjustment, although there is some evidence that some persons with BI do experience adjustment difficulties over time (Davidoff et al., 1992).

This literature has been plagued by inconsistent means of diagnosing mild and moderate BI and the failure to account for possible pre-SCI brain injuries that may have occurred. Behaviors attributed to suspected mild BI may be related to other long-standing behavioral patterns that predate the SCI. Longitudinal research has not found meaningful differences over time between persons with and without loss of consciousness at injury onset, nor were differences found by level of injury or completeness of lesion (Richards, Brown, Hagglund, Bua, & Reeder, 1988).

Some persons have complicated histories of alcohol and substance abuse that may likely have contributed to the SCI and influence their later adjustment. These persons are at risk for developing secondary complications (e.g., urinary tract infections, pressure sores) that might be prevented in part by behavioral self-care regimens (Elliott, Kurylo, Chen, & Hicken, in press; Hawkins & Heinemann, 1998). Alcohol abuse has also been associated with higher levels of depression and life stress, and ratings of poor health among persons with SCI (Tate, 1993; Young, Rintala, Rossi, Hart, & Fuhrer, 1995). Persons who have previous histories of abusive alcohol ingestion often revert to their preinjury levels of intake soon after their return to the community (Heinemann, Keen, Donohue, & Schnoll, 1988); others may be susceptible to pressure sore development even if they abstain from alcohol (Heinemann & Hawkins, 1995). Individuals who consider alcohol and other substances as a means for coping with problems tend to report more problems with depression and anxiety a year following SCI than persons who do not report such ideation (Kennedy et al., 2000). Individuals with significant alcohol histories also appear to be at a higher rate for suicide among persons with SCI (Charlifue & Gerhart, 1991).

Persons with substance abuse histories prior to SCI may have a decreased investment in their health or a preoccupation with activities that might compromise their personal health. Persons with significant alcohol histories have been found to spend less time in rehabilitation therapies (Heinemann, Goranson, Ginsberg, & Schnoll, 1989), and they evidence impaired self-care behaviors up to 18 months following SCI onset (Bombardier & Rimmel, 1998). Evidence of inadequate coping in the Kennedy et al. study (2000) may indicate deficits in effective coping resources requisite for successful adjustment following SCI.

Preinjury Psychopathology

Early research using clinical personality measures found that persons with SCI report more impulsive characteristics than those with other chronic health conditions (Bourestrom & Howard, 1965); similar differences were found between persons incurring SCI in high-impact incidents and those who incurred SCI via other means (Fordyce, 1964). For many years, there has been some concern that persons who adventitiously acquire SCI may have more sensation-seeking tendencies than people in general (Kunce & Worley, 1966; Rohe & Krause, 1999), and these behaviors may be related to pressure sore development (Richards, 1981). Although elevations in excitement-seeking and impulsivity may reflect

characteristics of young men generally (who traditionally are at greatest risk for SCI; Trieschmann, 1980), research using a matched control design has found a greater degree of sensation seeking and criminality among persons with SCI than among others with similar demographics and from the same locale (Mawson et al., 1996).

Other work has examined the rate of individuals who meet operational criteria for personality disorder characteristics (Temple & Elliott, 2000). Although a high rate was found among persons with recent-onset SCI and among those receiving surgical repair for severe pressure sores, the instrument used was known to be reactive to existing mood states. Higher elevations on summary scales were predictive of lower acceptance of disability after controlling for depressive behavior reported at admission.

Personality Characteristics

Many psychological constructs have been related to adjustment following disability. For example, persons who have an internal locus of control often report less distress than those with more external expectancies (Frank, Umlauf, et al., 1987). Persons with a disability who have effective social problem-solving skills and who have positive orientations toward solving problems, as compared with their counterparts who lack these skills, are more assertive, psychosocially mobile, accepting of their disability, and less depressed (Elliott, 1999; Elliott, Godshall, Herrick, Witty, & Spruell, 1991). There is also evidence that people with SCI who develop pressure sores may lack effective problem-solving skills (Herrick, Elliott, & Crow, 1994).

Persons who are hopeful and optimistic may selectively attend to certain aspects of their situation following the onset of SCI (Elliott, Witty, Herrick, & Hoffman, 1991). Higher levels of hope and goal-directed energy are associated with less distress, greater use of more confident and sociable coping styles, and higher self-reported functional abilities (Elliott, Witty, et al., 1991). People who have greater tendencies to use denial and who have greater psychological defensiveness are less distressed, less angry, and have fewer handicaps throughout the first year of acquired disability (Elliott & Richards, 1999). These differences are also observed among those who have been injured for longer periods of time (Rosenbaum & Raz, 1977).

Early anecdotal models of adjustment following SCI borrowed liberally from Freudian notions of acceptance and loss (Grzesiak & Hicock, 1994). Empirical research has not been kind to the basic tenets of these models, due in part to the poor operationalization and ambiguous definitions of key constructs. Current research suggests that Kohutian conceptualizations of the self—expressed as goal instability and measured with a psychometrically sound instrument—may offer some explanations about adjustment following SCI. In a series of studies, a greater goal orientation was associated with less depression, greater acceptance of disability, and increased life satisfaction one year later among persons with recent-onset physical disability. Goal orientation was also associated with less perceived social stigma and increased mobility among community-residing persons (Elliott, Uswatte, Lewis, & Palmatier, 2000). We have known for years that persons who have many as compared to few goals evidence more optimal adjustment (Kemp & Vash, 1971). Goal-directed behavior may be indicative of a greater proclivity for optimal adjustment.

Other personality traits are predictive of adjustment as well. Krause and Rohe (1998) found that elements of neuroticism and extraversion were associated with life satisfaction among community-residing persons with spinal cord injuries. Specifically, a greater proclivity for depression was predictive of less life satisfaction. Similarly, Rivera and Elliott (2000) found that lower neuroticism and higher agreeableness were predictive of greater acceptance of disability among persons with a spinal cord injury after controlling for level of injury, completeness of injury, depression, and demographic variables. Men with SCI have significantly higher excitement-seeking facet scores, lower conscientiousness factor, and lower assertiveness and activity facet scores than normative samples on a measure of the five factor model of personality (Rohe & Krause, 1999). Because this sample ($n = 105$) averaged 17.9 years postinjury, it seems that excitement-seeking tendencies may not necessarily be a function of younger age among persons with recent onset SCI. Stable personality traits appear to be significant correlates of depression and acceptance of disability in persons with acquired SCI. Evidence indicates that nonpathological personality traits are not adversely affected by long-term SCI (Hollick et al., 2001).

Social and Interpersonal Environment

Following SCI, people face a complicated social and interpersonal landscape that can have direct effects on their health and adjustment. Married persons are often more involved in productive activity outside the home (Krause, 1990) and report greater life satisfaction than single persons with SCI (Putzke, Elliott, & Richards, 2001). However, persons in distressed marriages report fewer activities alone and with their spouse, and report greater dissatisfaction and more negative communications (Urey & Henggeler, 1987). The onset of SCI compels family members to directly confront issues of

trust, mortality, and values, and those who adapt often forge deeper commitments and restructure the meaning of marriage or kinship (Olkin, 1999). Some family members report a greater sense of closeness after SCI, with a greater emphasis on shared family values and personal relationships (Crewe, 1993).

Social support has been associated with well-being among persons with SCI (Rintala, Young, Hart, Clearman, & Fuhrer, 1992). The fluid nature of social support may reflect the various types of assistance (e.g., informational, emotional) required to complement specific coping efforts (McColl, Lei, & Skinner, 1995). Elements of social support can have positive and negative effects on other aspects of adjustment. For example, assertive persons may be able to marshal available social support in certain situations; however, this direct style also may alienate others in the social support system (Elliott, Herrick, et al., 1991). Others who have more proactive problem-solving styles may benefit from other types of support such as formal service provision (Elliott, Herrick, & Witty, 1992). Social support that provides a sense of intimacy and attachment is associated with more satisfactory leisure activities (Elliott & Shewchuk, 1995), and satisfaction with recreational activities is a major component of overall life satisfaction following SCI (Kinney & Coyle, 1992).

Family members who are forced to assume caregiving roles have an impact on the psychological and physical adjustments of persons with disabilities. Caregiver tendencies to solve problems carelessly and impulsively were significantly predictive of lower acceptance of disability among patients who were leaving a rehabilitation hospital (Elliott, Shewchuk, & Richards, 1999). A year following discharge, caregiver impulsivity carelessness toward solving problems measured during initial rehabilitation correctly classified 87.88% of those persons with and without a sore. It is conceivable that the persons with SCI were aware of their caregivers' problem-solving styles and these issues complicated their ability to adjust optimally. A significant percentage of family members meet clinical criteria for a depressive episode when they assume caregiving duties for a person who has incurred a SCI (Elliott & Shewchuk, in press). Family caregivers may face increasing problems with their physical health and well-being in the initial year of caregiving, particularly if they have a negative orientation toward solving problems (Elliott, Shewchuk, & Richards, 2001) and as their sources of emotional support dwindle throughout the year (Shewchuk, Richards, & Elliott, 1998).

The social environment can yield considerable stress because persons with disabilities are impeded from being integrated, and mobility is limited in society at large. Factors ranging from architectural barriers, transportation difficulties, and negative social stereotypes restrict mobility, hinder social integration, and impair independence (Targett, Wilson, Wehman, & McKinley, 1998). Perceived independence, personal transportation, and individual living arrangements are strong predictors of good self-concepts among community-residing persons with SCI (Green, Pratt, & Grigsby, 1984). Independent living and community residence has pronounced benefits. After matching study participants on major demographic characteristics, Putzke and Richards (2001) found that persons living in nursing homes reported lower life satisfaction and greater handicap in terms of decreased mobility, physical independence, and economic self-sufficiency than community-residing peers. Not surprisingly, greater social integration, employment, and increased mobility are associated with greater life satisfaction (Crisp, 1992; Dijkers, 1999; Richards et al., 1999).

Despite the obvious benefits, some persons with SCI may become very uncomfortable in anticipation of increased interactions with able-bodied persons and the resumption of social roles (M. Dunn, 1977). And while contact with others can augment coping in the first year of injury (Rogers & Kennedy, 2000), professionals, peers, and individuals in general may have negative reactions and make derogatory assumptions about persons with SCI if they express pessimism and distressed mood in social interactions (Elliott & Frank, 1990; Elliott, Yoder, & Umlauf, 1990).

Phenomenological and Appraisal Processes

In contemporary views of adjustment, an emphasis is placed on the importance of appraisals in understanding individual experiences. The appraisal component is the centerpiece of our model because its processes have considerable influence on subsequent adjustment. We believe that elements of positive growth are first evident in how people evaluate and interpret their situation and circumstances. Following SCI, people vary in their perception of life events and the degree to which these events are stressful, and these perceptions are directly associated with subsequent distress (Crisp, 1992; Frank & Elliott, 1987). Individuals actively process aspects of their situations to find positive meanings and side benefits (D. Dunn, 2000). Many people try to accept, positively reinterpret, and seek personal growth soon after the onset of SCI (Kennedy et al., 2000). Appraisal processes also may help to explain why persons with SCI who are distressed exhibit many different coping behaviors, whereas those who are less distressed reported fewer coping efforts and a greater sense of internal locus of control (Frank, Umlauf, et al., 1987). This may also account for the beneficial sequelae of acceptance coping and cognitive restructuring on the adjustments of persons with spinal cord injuries who return to their communities (Hanson, Buckelew, Hewett, & O'Neal, 1993; Kennedy, Lowe, Grey, & Short, 1995).

Specific beliefs about the disability (e.g., "I will walk again") and attributions of responsibility and blame are unstable over time and are not consistently related to objective and subjective indices of adjustment (Elliott & Richards, 1999; Hanson et al., 1993; Reidy & Caplan, 1994; Richards, Elliott, Shewchuk, & Fine, 1997; Schulz & Decker, 1985). People who ruminate about their perceived victimization, however, may do so at the expense of finding meaning and direction in their circumstances (Davis, Lehman, Wortman, Silver, & Thompson, 1995), and at the expense of therapeutic activities beneficial to their adjustment (A. Moore, Bombardier, Brown, & Patterson, 1994). Adaptive personality and interpersonal characteristics predispose some individuals toward more functional cognitive appraisals, and people lacking in these personal and social resources will be more likely to exhibit difficulties in accepting their condition and their circumstances.

Thus, it is probable that individuals who are more goal oriented, hopeful, effective in solving problems, and in supportive relationships will focus on positive aspects of their situation, report fewer problems with their environment, come to terms with their condition, and evidence less distress over time (Elliott, 1999; Elliott et al., 2000; Elliott, Godshall, et al., 1991; Elliott, Witty, et al., 1991). Individuals with these personal and social characteristics will be more likely to recognize, marshal, and use resources and support in their social environment to maximize their adjustment.

Dynamic and Developmental Processes

Changes in a person's belief system, interpersonal environment, and physical health may occur over time. Advances in medical therapies, assistive technologies, and public and health policy can facilitate adjustment. Social advocacy led to the passage of the Rehabilitation Act of 1973 and the Americans with Disabilities Act of 1990. More recently, actor Christopher Reeve has advocated successfully for increased public awareness about, and federal and private funding for, curative and quality-of-life research. Today's advocacy movement demands consideration for the relationship between individuals and their physical, social, and cultural environments.

Physical disability does not occur or exist in a vacuum. Changes in the interpersonal environment or in public and health policy can have dramatic effects on quality of life following SCI. Many of these changes are essentially outside the realm of personal volition, and opportunities may not be available to some individuals because of restricted access, lower socioeconomic status, or disabling aspects of the environment (e.g., lack of public transportation, limited funds in state Medicaid, vocational rehabilitation, or independent living programs). Health care providers and insurance payors vary considerably in their sensitivity to, and provision for, assistive devices that enhance quality of life and facilitate social integration.

Similarly, people with SCI face issues that emerge as they age. Children who incur SCI encounter many developmental challenges that must be navigated with ample support from family members, educational institutions, and service providers (Apple, 2000). These issues are readily apparent in the different interests observed between younger adults with SCI and others older who have lived with SCI for some time (Hart et al., 1996), and in the different stressors reported by older and younger adults who sustain SCI (Frank et al., 1988). The concerns and problems experienced by persons soon after injury are notably different from those who have lived with SCI for some time. Soon after injury, individuals may be more concerned with restorative therapies and possible curative approaches, but those living with SCI for years may be more interested in remedying social and interpersonal barriers and in addressing health problems associated with aging (Elliott & Shewchuk, 2000).

All of these changes represent developmental processes that can be understood within the context of our model. It is critical that we recognize the dynamic interplay between these evolving processes over time so that we can best understand adjustment following SCI. Therefore, studies of adjustment should be conducted with tools that are sensitive to the phenomenological experiences and to differences in individual trajectories of adaptation over time.

PSYCHOLOGICAL INTERVENTIONS

Decreasing financial support for psychosocial programs directed at persons with disabilities in the last decade has necessitated a shift in intervention policies from meeting institutional goals to focusing on the opinions, goals, and aspirations of the person with SCI (Frank, 1997). When these personal goals and aims are addressed, interventions are more likely to be effective (Glueckauf & Quittner, 1992). Wright (1983) recommended that services to people with disabilities be designed to eliminate societal barriers, increase accommodations, improve medical and psychosocial services where indicated, develop and provide assistive devices and technologies, and aid in the learning of new skills. Community-based services should (a) have a consumer-driven focus,

(b) be broad in income eligibility, (c) offer flexible service options including respite for caregivers, and (d) follow a family systems model. For example, programs such as interpersonal and social skills training, and innovative interventions such as aerobic exercise training, have been associated with increased abilities, a sense of well-being, and acceptance of disability among persons with SCI (Coyle & Santiago, 1995; M. Dunn, Van Horn, & Herman, 1981; Glueckauf & Quittner, 1992; Morgan & Leung, 1980). Cognitive-behavioral interventions designed to enhance coping effectiveness may have beneficial effects on people's ability to positively reappraise their situations and to increase their sense of hope, with corresponding improvements in psychological adjustment (King & Kennedy, 1999).

Strategies that include family members as an integral part of the rehabilitation process may be particularly effective (L. Moore, 1989); moreover, these approaches may be couched within cognitive-behavioral frameworks and delivered in innovative, home-based programs (Kurylo, Elliott, & Shewchuk, 2001). Assistive devices designed for improving sexual relations among couples—including vacuum devices, injections, and medications such as Viagra—have been found to increase sexual activity and improve satisfaction with sexual relationships among men with SCI (Richards, Lloyd, James, & Brown, 1992). Biofeedback—once considered a promising intervention for regulating certain physiological functions after SCI, particularly in applications with persons who have higher cord lesions—deserves greater empirical scrutiny and methodological rigor (Brucker & Bulaeva, 1996). There is also some indication that neuropathic pain may be responsive to pharmacological treatment (e.g., gabapentin; Ness et al., 1998).

Formal vocational rehabilitation intervention programs that support a return to career-related activities—broadly defined to include support for independent living, assistive devices, and meaningful social activities—remain important despite the constant threat of decreasing federal and state funding. Being employed is associated with a higher quality of life after SCI (Dowler, Richards, Putzke, Gordon, & Tate, 2001), and there are several factors that are related to employability following SCI (Krause et al., 1999). Behavioral expertise can be vital in making reasonable and logical allocations for these services and programs, but behavioral and social scientists have often overlooked the direct impact of public and health policy on the well-being of persons with physical disability (Elliott & Frank, 2000). Psychological and behavioral expertise is needed to inform policymakers about the unique needs of persons with SCI; however, this will require greater collaboration and partnership with consumer and advocacy groups and a subsequent appreciation for their views and opinions (Olkin, 1999).

Determining and appreciating these needs can be a tricky enterprise, particularly when working with other colleagues in multidisciplinary endeavors. In one example, a multidisciplinary panel working with a consumer group published clinical guidelines for assessing and treating depression among persons with SCI. This panel evaluated the scientific evidence and rated antidepressant therapy more favorably (and devoted more page space to these treatments) than behavioral approaches, despite the absence of any clinical trial of antidepressant therapy among persons with SCI (Consortium for Spinal Cord Medicine, 1998). Although other guidelines have been more favorable to behavioral issues and approaches among persons with SCI (e.g., the pressure sore guidelines, Consortium for Spinal Cord Medicine, 2000), this situation illustrates the need for the judicious representation of behavioral expertise in a sensitive, yet informed, manner at the different levels of policy formation.

ADVANCEMENTS AND FUTURE DIRECTIONS

Increased federal and private funding for curative and corrective research in SCI has resulted in several productive research programs. Advancements in these areas may soon have a substantial impact on persons living with SCI. Transplant research examining the use of stem and glial cells has demonstrated that nerve conduction and regeneration can occur in animal models (Imaizumi, Lankford, & Kocsis, 2000; Kocsis, 1999). Other projects have demonstrated that spinal nerve fiber regeneration may be facilitated with the implantation of electronic circuits (Borgens et al., 1999). Studies of electronic circuit implants will soon be conducted on individuals volunteering for clinical trials.

Similarly, there are considerable advancements in our understanding of chronic pain following SCI. Most clinical models of pain in this area have adopted an operant behavioral perspective (e.g., Umlauf, 1992). Research relying on animal models of pain following SCI has indicated that exitotoxic and ischemic damage to spinal gray and white matter are implicated in the development of persistent pain, and pharmacological approaches may be the best therapeutic strategies for preventing and alleviating pain sensations following SCI (Yezierski, 1996).

It is instructive to note that persons living with SCI have long expressed a desire for curative research and for assistance in alleviating persistent pain. These concerns were not necessarily ignored over the years, but many researchers and clinicians have attended to other problems that were deemed mutually important by policymakers, professionals, and consumer groups. A health care agenda that incorporates a greater consumer perspective, however, may ultimately be more cost-effective and satisfying to all stakeholders. Persons with SCI and their family members are interested in receiving continued rehabilitation therapies in the home (Elliott & Shewchuk, 2000). Travel to outpatient clinics may be difficult for some individuals, and research has found that distance to the clinic and transportation problems impede attendance in outpatient therapies (Canupp, Waites, DeVivo, & Richards, 1997). Professionals can work together to develop neighborhood centers in rural, underserved areas or use technology such as telecommunication devices to deliver a variety of cost-effective services and therapies to participants at home (Temkin & Jones, 1999).

Other technologies and assistive devices can have immense effects on positive growth (Scherer, 2000). Virtual reality technologies can be used to help individuals learn specific coping skills (e.g., coping with persistent pain; Hoffman, Doctor, Patterson, Carrougher, & Furness, 2000) and attain greater mobility and independence (e.g., learning driving skills; Schultheis & Rizzo, 2001). These technologies will eventually prove to be efficacious and, accordingly, should be subsidized by health care programs.

Behavioral researchers are urged to use measures and analyses that are less pathological in intent and more respectful and sensitive to the unique phenomenological experiences, interpretations, and concerns of people living with SCI. Consumer advocates have long criticized the biased approaches many behavioral researchers have toward persons with physical disabilities (Olkin, 1999). Many consumers view behavioral research with skepticism. It is imperative that tools are used that are at once reliable, valid, and theoretically relevant, and yet are sensitive and respectful to persons with SCI. Moreover, to achieve a truly consumer-driven service delivery, behavioral scientists will need to use qualitative measurement and research devices with greater precision and sophistication. This will ensure a more accurate representation of these individuals and their experience into research projects and in program development, which will in turn facilitate a greater partnership between these consumers and psychologists who wish to serve them.

REFERENCES

Alexander, C. J., Sipski, M. L., & Findley, T. (1993). Sexual activities, desire, and satisfaction in males pre- and post-spinal cord injury. *Archives of Sexual Behavior, 22,* 217–228.

Anson, C. A., & Shepard, C. (1996). Incidence of secondary complications in spinal cord injury. *International Journal of Rehabilitation Research, 19,* 55–66.

Apple, D. (Ed.). (2000, Summer). The Howard H. Steel conference on pediatric spinal cord injury, December 3–5, 1999. *Topics in Spinal Cord Injury Rehabilitation, 6*(Suppl.), 1–254.

Baker, E. R., & Cardenas, C. C. (1996). Pregnancy in spinal cord injured women. *Archives of Physical Medicine and Rehabilitation, 77,* 501–507.

Berkman, A. H., Weissman, R., & Frielich, M. H. (1978). Sexual adjustment in spinal cord injured veterans living in the community. *Archives of Physical Medicine and Rehabilitation, 59,* 29–33.

Bombardier, C., & Rimmel, C. (1998). Alcohol use and readiness to change after spinal cord injury. *Archives of Physical Medicine and Rehabilitation, 79,* 1110–1115.

Borgens, R., Toombs, J., Breur, G., Widmer, W., Waters, D., Harbath, A., et al. (1999). An imposed oscillating electrical field improves the recovery of function in neurologically complete paraplegic dogs. *Journal of Neurotrauma, 16,* 639–657.

Bourestrom, N., & Howard, M. (1965). Personality characteristics of three disability groups. *Archives of Physical Medicine and Rehabilitation, 46,* 626–632.

Brucker, B., & Bulaeva, N. V. (1996). Biofeedback effect on electromyography responses in patients with spinal cord injury. *Archives of Physical Medicine and Rehabilitation, 77,* 133–137.

Burns, A. S., Putzke, J. D., Richards, J. S., & Jackson, J. B. (2000). Gender and its impact on post-acute secondary medical complications following spinal cord injury. *Topics in Spinal Cord Injury, 6*(1), 66–75.

Cairns, D. M., Adkins, R. H., & Scott, M. D. (1996). Pain and depression in acute traumatic spinal cord injury: Origins of chronic problematic pain? *Archives of Physical Medicine and Rehabilitation, 77,* 329–335.

Canupp, K. C., Waites, K., DeVivo, M. J., & Richards, J. S. (1997). Predicting compliance with annual followup evaluations in persons with spinal cord injuries. *Spinal Cord, 35,* 314–319.

Cardenas, D. D., Burns, S. P., & Chan, L. (2000). Rehabilitation of spinal cord injury. In M. Grabois, S. J. Garrison, K. A. Hart, & L. D. Lehmkuhl (Eds.), *Physical medicine and rehabilitation: The complete approach* (pp. 1305–1324). Franklin, NY: Blackwell Science.

Charlifue, S., & Gerhart, K. (1991). Behavioral and demographic predictors of suicide after spinal cord injury. *Archives of Physical Medicine and Rehabilitation, 72,* 488–492.

Charlifue, S., Gerhart, K., Menter, R., Whiteneck, G., & Manley, M. (1992). Sexual issues of women with spinal cord injuries. *Paraplegia, 30,* 192–199.

Chwalisz, K., Diener, E., & Gallagher, D. (1988). Autonomic arousal feedback and emotional experience: Evidence from the spinal cord injured. *Journal of Personality and Social Psychology, 54,* 820–828.

Comarr, A. E. (1966). Observations of menstruation and pregnancy among female spinal cord injury patients. *Paraplegia, 3,* 263–272.

Consortium for Spinal Cord Medicine. (1998). *Depression following spinal cord injury: A clinical practice guideline for primary care physicians.* Washington, DC: Paralyzed Veterans of America.

Consortium for Spinal Cord Medicine. (2000). *Pressure ulcer prevention and treatment following spinal cord injury: A clinical practice guideline for health-care professionals.* Washington, DC: Paralyzed Veterans of America.

Coyle, C. P., & Santiago, M. C. (1995). Aerobic exercise training and depressive symptomology in adults with physical disabilities. *Archives of Physical Medicine and Rehabilitation, 76,* 647–652.

Craig, A. R., Hancock, K., & Dickson, H. (1994). Spinal cord injury: A search for determinants of depression two years after the event. *British Journal of Clinical Psychology, 33,* 221–230.

Crewe, N. (1993). Spousal relationships and disability. In F. P. Haseltine, S. Cole, & D. Gray (Eds.), *Reproductive issues for persons with physical disabilities* (pp. 141–151). Baltimore: Brookes.

Crewe, N., & Krause, J. S. (1990). An eleven year follow-up of adjustment to spinal cord injury. *Rehabilitation Psychology, 35,* 205–210.

Crisp, R. (1992). The long-term adjustment of 60 persons with spinal cord injury. *Australian Psychologist, 27,* 43–47.

Davidoff, G., Roth, E., & Richards, J. S. (1992). Cognitive deficits in spinal cord injury: Epidemiology and outcome. *Archives of Physical Medicine and Rehabilitation, 73,* 275–284.

Davis, C., Lehman, D., Wortman, C., Silver, R., & Thompson, S. (1995). The undoing of traumatic life events. *Personality and Social Psychology Bulletin, 21,* 109–124.

DeVivo, M. J., & Fine, P. R. (1985). Spinal cord injury: Its short-term impact on marital status. *Archives of Physical Medicine and Rehabilitation, 66,* 501–504.

DeVivo, M. J., Hawkins, L. N., Richards, J. S., & Go, B. (1995). Outcomes of post-spinal cord injury marriages. *Archives of Physical Medicine and Rehabilitation, 76,* 130–138.

Dijkers, M. P. (1999). Correlates of life satisfaction among persons with spinal cord injury. *Archives of Physical Medicine and Rehabilitation, 80,* 867–876.

Dowler, R., Herrington, D., Haaland, K., Swanda, R., Fee, F., & Fielder, K. (1997). Profiles of cognitive functioning and chronic spinal cord injury and the role of moderating variables. *Journal of the International Neuropsychological Society, 3,* 464–472.

Dowler, R., Richards, J. S., Putzke, J., Gordon, W., & Tate, D. (2001). The impact of demographic and medical factors on satisfaction with life post-spinal cord injury: A normative study. *Journal of Spinal Cord Medicine, 24,* 87–91.

Dunn, D. S. (2000). Matters of perspective: Some social psychological issues in disability and rehabilitation. In R. G. Frank & T. Elliott (Eds.), *Handbook of rehabilitation psychology* (pp. 565–584). Washington, DC: American Psychological Association.

Dunn, M. (1977). Social discomfort in the patient with SCI. *Archives of Physical Medicine and Rehabilitation, 58,* 257–260.

Dunn, M., Van Horn, E., & Herman, S. (1981). Social skills and spinal cord injury: A comparison of three training procedures. *Behavior Therapy, 12,* 153–164.

Elliott, T. (1999). Social problem solving abilities and adjustment to recent-onset physical disability. *Rehabilitation Psychology, 44,* 315–352.

Elliott, T., & Frank, R. G. (1990). Social and interpersonal reactions to depression and disability. *Rehabilitation Psychology, 35,* 135–147.

Elliott, T., & Frank, R. G. (1996). Depression following spinal cord injury. *Archives of Physical Medicine and Rehabilitation, 77*, 816–823.

Elliott, T., & Frank, R. G. (2000). Drawing new horizons for rehabilitation psychology. In R. G. Frank & T. Elliott (Eds.), *Handbook of rehabilitation psychology* (pp. 645–653). Washington, DC: American Psychological Association.

Elliott, T., Godshall, F., Herrick, S., Witty, T., & Spruell, M. (1991). Problem-solving appraisal and psychological adjustment following spinal cord injury. *Cognitive Therapy and Research, 15*, 387–398.

Elliott, T., Herrick, S., Patti, A., Witty, T., Godshall, F., & Spruell, M. (1991). Assertiveness, social support, and psychological adjustment of persons with spinal cord injury. *Behaviour Research and Therapy, 29*, 485–493.

Elliott, T., Herrick, S., & Witty, T. (1992). Problem solving appraisal and the effects of social support among college students and persons with physical disabilities. *Journal of Counseling Psychology, 39*, 219–226.

Elliott, T., Kurylo, M., Chen, Y., & Hicken, B. (in press). Alcohol abuse history and adjustment following spinal cord injury. *Rehabilitation Psychology*.

Elliott, T., & Richards, J. S. (1999). Living with the facts, negotiating the terms: Unrealistic beliefs, denial and adjustment in the first year of acquired disability. *Journal of Personal and Interpersonal Loss, 4*, 361–381.

Elliott, T., & Shewchuk, R. (1995). Social support and leisure activities following severe physical disability: Testing the mediating effects of depression. *Basic and Applied Social Psychology, 16*, 471–487.

Elliott, T., & Shewchuk, R. (in press). Social problem solving abilities and distress among family members assuming a caregiving role. *British Journal of Health Psychology*.

Elliott, T., & Shewchuk, R. (in press). Using the nominal group technique to identify the problems experienced by persons who live with severe physical disability. *Journal of Clinical Psychology in Medical Settings*.

Elliott, T., Shewchuk, R., & Richards, J. S. (1999). Caregiver social problem solving abilities and family member adjustment to recent-onset physical disability. *Rehabilitation Psychology, 44*, 104–123.

Elliott, T., Shewchuk, R., & Richards, J. S. (2001). Family caregiver social problem solving abilities and adjustment during the initial year of the caregiver role. *Journal of Counseling Psychology, 48*, 223–232.

Elliott, T., & Uswatte, G. (2000). Ethnic and minority issues in physical medicine and rehabilitation. In M. Grabois, S. J. Garrison, K. A. Hart, & L. D. Lehmkuhl (Eds.), *Physical medicine and rehabilitation: The complete approach* (pp. 1820–1828). Franklin, NY: Blackwell Science.

Elliott, T., Uswatte, G., Lewis, L., & Palmatier, A. (2000). Goal instability and adjustment to physical disability. *Journal of Counseling Psychology, 47*, 251–265.

Elliott, T., Witty, T., Herrick, S., & Hoffman, J. (1991). Negotiating reality after physical loss: Hope, depression, and disability. *Journal of Personality and Social Psychology, 61*, 608–613.

Elliott, T., Yoder, B., & Umlauf, R. (1990). Nurse and patient reactions to social displays of depression. *Rehabilitation Psychology, 35*, 195–204.

Fine, M., & Asch, A. (1988). Disability beyond stigma: Social interaction, discrimination, and activism. *Journal of Social Issues, 44*, 3–21.

Fordyce, W. E. (1964). Personality characteristics in men with spinal cord injury as related to manner of onset of disability. *Archives of Physical Medicine and Rehabilitation, 45*, 321–325.

Frank, R. G. (1997). Lessons from the great battle: Health care reform 1992–1994. *Archives of Physical Medicine and Rehabilitation, 78*, 120–124.

Frank, R. G., Chaney, J., Shutty, M., Clay, D., Beck, N., Kay, D., et al. (1992). Dysphoria: A major factor of depression in persons with disability or chronic illness. *Psychiatry Research, 43*, 231–241.

Frank, R. G., & Elliott, T. (1987). Life stress and psychological adjustment to spinal cord injury. *Archives of Physical Medicine and Rehabilitation, 68*, 344–347.

Frank, R. G., Elliott, T., Buckelew, S. A., & Haut, A. (1988). Age as a factor in the psychologic adjustment to spinal cord injury. *American Journal of Physical Medicine and Rehabilitation, 67*, 128–131.

Frank, R. G., Elliott, T., Corcoran, J., & Wonderlich, S. A. (1987). Depression after spinal cord injury: Is it necessary? *Clinical Psychology Review, 7*, 611–630.

Frank, R. G., Kashani, J., Wonderlich, S. A., Lising, A., & Visot, L. (1985). Depression and adrenal function in spinal cord injury. *American Journal of Psychiatry, 142*, 252–253.

Frank, R. G., Umlauf, R. L., Wonderlich, S. A., Ashkanazi, G., Buckelew, S. A., & Elliott, T. (1987). Coping differences among persons with spinal cord injury: A cluster analytic approach. *Journal of Consulting and Clinical Psychology, 55*, 727–731.

Fullerton, D., Harvey, R., Klein, M., & Howell, T. (1981). Psychiatric disorders in patients with spinal cord injury. *Archives of General Psychiatry, 32*, 369–371.

Glueckauf, R. L., & Quittner, A. L. (1992). Assertiveness training for disabled adults in wheelchairs: Self-report, role-play, and activity pattern outcomes. *Journal of Consulting and Clinical Psychology, 60*, 419–425.

Go, B. K., DeVivo, M. J., & Richards, J. S. (1995). The epidemiology of spinal cord injury. In S. L. Stover, J. A. DeLisa, & G. G. Whiteneck (Eds.), *Spinal cord injury: Clinical outcomes from the model systems* (pp. 21–55). Gaithersburg, MD: Aspen.

Green, A., Pratt, C., & Grigsby, T. (1984). Self-concept among persons with long-term spinal cord injury. *Archives of Physical Medicine and Rehabilitation, 65*, 751–754.

Grzesiak, R. C., & Hicock, D. A. (1994). A brief history of psychotherapy in physical disability. *American Journal of Psychotherapy, 48*, 240–250.

Hall, K., Knudsen, S., Wright, J., Charlifue, S., Graves, D., & Werner, P. (1999). Follow-up study of individuals with high tetraplegia (C1–C4) 14 to 24 years postinjury. *Archives of Physical Medicine and Rehabilitation, 80,* 1507–1513.

Hammond, M. C., Umlauf, R., Matteson, B., & Perduta-Fujiniti, S. (1992). *Yes, you can!* Walsdorf, MD: Paralyzed Veterans of America.

Hancock, F. M., Craig, A. R., Dickson, H., Chang, E., & Martin, J. (1993). Anxiety and depression over the first year of spinal cord injury: A longitudinal study. *Paraplegia, 31,* 349–357.

Hanson, S., Buckelew, S. P., Hewett, J., & O'Neal, G. (1993). The relationship between coping and adjustment after spinal cord injury: A 5-year follow-up study. *Rehabilitation Psychology, 38,* 41–51.

Hart, K., Rintala, D., & Fuhrer, M. (1996). Educational interests of individuals with SCI living in the community: Medical, sexuality, and wellness topics. *Rehabilitation Nursing, 21,* 82–90.

Hawkins, D. A., & Heinemann, A. W. (1998). Substance abuse and medical complications following spinal cord injury. *Rehabilitation Psychology, 43,* 219–231.

Heinemann, A. W., Goranson, N., Ginsberg, K., & Schnoll, S. (1989). Alcohol use and activity patterns following spinal cord injury. *Rehabilitation Psychology, 40,* 125–141.

Heinemann, A. W., & Hawkins, D. (1995). Substance abuse and medical complications following spinal cord injury. *Rehabilitation Psychology, 40,* 125–140.

Heinemann, A. W., Keen, N., Donohue, R., & Schnoll, S. (1988). Alcohol use by persons with recent spinal cord injuries. *Archives of Physical Medicine and Rehabilitation, 69,* 619–624.

Herrick, S., Elliott, T., & Crow, F. (1994). Self-appraised problem solving skills and the prediction of secondary complications among persons with spinal cord injury. *Journal of Clinical Psychology in Medical Settings, 1,* 269–283.

Hoffman, H. G., Doctor, J., Patterson, D., Carrougher, G., & Furness, T. (2000). Use of virtual reality for adjunctive treatment of adolescent burn pain during wound care: A case report. *Pain, 85,* 305–309.

Hohmann, G. (1982, April 30). *The challenge of gerontology in spinal cord injury* [Fifth annual John S. Young Lectureship]. Englewood, CO: Craig Hospital.

Hollick, C., Radnitz, C. L., Silverman, J., Tirch, D., Birstein, S., & Bauman, W. (2001). Does spinal cord injury affect personality? A study of monozygotic twins. *Rehabilitation Psychology, 46,* 58–67.

Imaizumi, T., Lankford, K., & Kocsis, J. D. (2000). Transplantation of olfactory ensheathing cells or Schwann cells restores rapid and secure conduction across the transected spinal cord. *Brain Research, 854,* 70–78.

Johnson, R. L., Brookes, C. A., & Whiteneck, G. G. (1996). Costs of traumatic spinal cord injury in a population-based registry. *Spinal Cord, 34,* 470–480.

Johnson, R. L., Gerhart, K., McCray, J., Menconi, J., & Whiteneck, G. (1998). Secondary conditions following spinal cord injury in a population based sample. *Spinal Cord, 36,* 45–50.

Judd, F. K., & Brown, D. J. (1992). Psychiatric consultation in a spinal injuries unit. *Australian New Zealand Journal of Psychiatry, 26,* 218–222.

Kemp, B. J., & Vash, C. L. (1971). Productivity after injury in a sample of spinal cord injured persons: A pilot study. *Journal of Chronic Disease, 24,* 259–275.

Kennedy, P., Lowe, R., Grey, N., & Short, E. (1995). Traumatic spinal cord injury and psychological impact: A cross-sectional analysis of coping strategies. *British Journal of Clinical Psychology, 34,* 627–639.

Kennedy, P., Marsh, N., Lowe, R., Grey, N., Short, E., & Rogers, B. (2000). A longitudinal analysis of psychological impact and coping strategies following spinal cord injury. *British Journal of Health Psychology, 5,* 157–172.

King, C., & Kennedy, P. (1999). Coping effectiveness training for people with spinal cord injury: Preliminary results of a controlled trial. *British Journal of Clinical Psychology, 38,* 5–14.

Kinney, W. B., & Coyle, C. (1992). Predicting life satisfaction among adults with physical disabilities. *Archives of Physical Medicine and Rehabilitation, 73,* 863–869.

Kishi, Y., Robinson, R. G., & Forrester, A. W. (1994). Prospective longitudinal study of depression following spinal cord injury. *Journal of Neuropsychiatry and Clinical Neuroscience, 6,* 237–244.

Kocsis, J. D. (1999). Restoration of function by glial cell transplantation into the demyelinated spinal cord. *Journal of Neurotrauma, 16,* 695–703.

Krause, J. S. (1990). The relationship between productivity and adjustment following spinal cord injury. *Rehabilitation Counseling Bulletin, 33*(3), 188–199.

Krause, J. S., Kewman, D., DeVivo, M., Maynard, F., Coker, J., Roach, M., et al. (1999). Employment after spinal cord injury: An analysis of cases from the model spinal cord injury systems. *Archives of Physical Medicine and Rehabilitation, 80,* 1492–1500.

Krause, J. S., & Rohe, D. (1998). Personality and life adjustment after spinal cord injury: An exploratory study. *Rehabilitation Psychology, 43,* 118–130.

Kunce, J., & Worley, B. (1966). Interest patterns, accidents, and disability. *Journal of Clinical Psychology, 22,* 105–107.

Kurylo, M., Elliott, T., & Shewchuk, R. (2001). FOCUS on the family caregiver: A problem-solving training intervention. *Journal of Counseling and Development, 79,* 275–281.

Levi, R., Hulting, C., & Seiger, A. (1995). The Stockholm Spinal Cord Injury Study. 2: Associations between clinical patient characteristics and post-acute medical problems. *Paraplegia, 33,* 585–594.

Mawson, A. R., Biundo, J., Clemmer, D., Jacobs, K., Ktasanes, V., & Rice, J. (1996). Sensation-seeking, criminality, and spinal cord injury: A case-control study. *American Journal of Epidemiology, 144,* 463–472.

Mawson, A. R., Siddiqui, F., Connolly, B., Sharp, J., Summer, W., & Biundo, J. (1993). Sacral transcutaneous oxygen tension levels in the spinal cord injured: Risk factors for pressure ulcers? *Archives of Physical Medicine and Rehabilitation, 74,* 745–751.

McColl, M. A., Lei, H., & Skinner, H. (1995). Structural relationships between social support and coping. *Social Science and Medicine, 41,* 395–407.

Moore, A., Bombardier, C. H., Brown, P., & Patterson, D. (1994). Coping and emotional attributions following spinal cord injury. *International Journal of Rehabilitation Research, 17,* 39–48.

Moore, L. I. (1989). *Behavioral changes in male spinal cord injured following two types of psychosocial rehabilitation experience.* Unpublished doctoral dissertation, St. Louis University, St. Louis, MO.

Morgan, B., & Leung, P. (1980). Effects of assertion training on acceptance of disability by physically disabled university students. *Journal of Counseling Psychology, 27,* 209–212.

National Institute on Disability and Rehabilitation Research Consensus Statement. (1992). The prevention and management of urinary tract infections among people with spinal cord injuries. *Journal of the American Paraplegia Society, 15,* 194–204.

Ness, T. J., San Pedro, E. C., Richards, J. S., Kezar, L., Liu, H., & Mountz, J. (1998). A case of spinal cord injury-related pain with baseline rCBF brain SPECT imaging and beneficial response to gabapentin. *Pain, 78,* 139–143.

Nobunaga, A. I., Go, B. K., & Karunas, R. (1999). Recent demographic and injury trends in people served by the model spinal cord injury care systems. *Archives of Physical Medicine and Rehabilitation, 80,* 1372–1382.

Olkin, R. (1999). *What psychotherapists should know about disability.* New York: Guilford Press.

Paralyzed Veterans of America. (1988). *Final report: The PVA needs assessment survey.* Washington, DC: Author.

Putzke, J. D., Elliott, T. R., & Richards, J. S. (2001). Marital status and adjustment one year post spinal cord injury. *Journal of Clinical Psychology in Medical Settings, 8,* 101–107.

Putzke, J. D., & Richards, J. S. (2001). Nursing home residence: Quality of life among individuals with spinal cord injury. *American Journal of Physical Medicine and Rehabilitation, 80,* 404–409.

Putzke, J. D., Richards, J. S., & DeVivo, M. J. (2001). Gunshot versus nongunshot spinal cord injury: Acute care and rehabilitation outcomes. *American Journal in Physical Medicine and Rehabilitation, 80,* 366–370.

Putzke, J. D., Richards, J. S., & Dowler, R. N. (2000a, Summer). Quality of life following spinal cord injury: Developmental issues in late adolescence and young adulthood. *Topics in Spinal Cord Injury, 6*(Suppl.), 155–169.

Putzke, J. D., Richards, J. S., & Dowler, R. N. (2000b). The impact of pain in spinal cord injury: A case control study. *Rehabilitation Psychology, 45,* 386–401.

Radnitz, C., Hsu, L., Tirch, D., Willard, J., Lillian, L., Walczak, S., et al. (1998). A comparison of posttraumatic stress disorder in veterans with and without spinal cord injury. *Journal of Abnormal Psychology, 107,* 676–680.

Radnitz, C., Schlein, I., Walczak, S., Broderick, C. P., Binks, M., Tirch, D., et al. (1995). The prevalence of posttraumatic stress disorder in spinal cord injury. *Spinal Cord Injury Psychosocial Process, 8*(4), 145–149.

Radnitz, C. L., Broderick, C. P., Perez-Strumolo, L., Tirch, D., Festa, J., Schlein, I., et al. (1996). The prevalence of psychiatric disorders in veterans with spinal cord injury: A controlled comparison. *Journal of Nervous and Mental Diseases, 184,* 431–433.

Reidy, K., & Caplan, B. (1994). Causal factors in spinal cord injury: Patients evolving perceptions and association with depression. *Archives of Physical Medicine and Rehabilitation, 75,* 837–842.

Richards, J. S. (1981). Pressure ulcers in spinal cord injury: Psychosocial correlates. *Spinal Cord Injury Digest, 3,* 11–18.

Richards, J. S. (1986). Psychological adjustment to spinal cord injury during first postdischarge year. *Archives of Physical Medicine and Rehabilitation, 67,* 362–366.

Richards, J. S., Bombardier, C., Tate, D., Dijkers, M., Gordon, W., Shewchuk, R., et al. (1999). Access to the environment and life satisfaction after spinal cord injury. *Archives of Physical Medicine and Rehabilitation, 80,* 1501–1506.

Richards, J. S., Brown, L., Hagglund, K., Bua, G., & Reeder, K. (1988). Spinal cord injury and concomitant traumatic brain injury: Results of a longitudinal investigation. *American Journal of Physical Medicine and Rehabilitation, 67,* 211–216.

Richards, J. S., Elliott, T., Shewchuk, R., & Fine, P. R. (1997). Attribution of responsibility for onset of spinal cord injury and psychosocial outcomes in the first year post-injury. *Rehabilitation Psychology, 42,* 115–124.

Richards, J. S., Lloyd, L. K., James, J. W., & Brown, J. (1992). Treatment of erectile dysfunction secondary to spinal cord injury: Sexual and psychosocial impact on couples. *Rehabilitation Psychology, 37,* 205–213.

Richards, J. S., Stover, S., & Jaworski, T. (1990). Effect of bullet removal on subsequent pain in persons with spinal cord injury secondary to gunshot wound. *Journal of Neurosurgery, 73,* 401–404.

Rintala, D., Young, J., Hart, K., Clearman, R., & Fuhrer, M. (1992). Social support and the well-being of persons with spinal cord injury living in the community. *Archives of Physical Medicine and Rehabilitation, 37,* 155–163.

Rivera, P., & Elliott, T. (2000, September). *Personality style as a predictor of adjustment to disability following spinal cord injury.* Paper presented at the annual conference of the American Association of Spinal Cord Injury Psychologists and Social Workers, Las Vegas, NV.

Rogers, B., & Kennedy, P. (2000). A qualitative analysis of reported coping in a community sample of people with spinal cord injuries: The first year post discharge. *Spinal Cord Injury Psychosocial Process, 13*(3), 41, 44–49, 63.

Rohe, D. E., & Krause, J. S. (1999). The five-factor model of personality: Findings in males with spinal cord injury. *Assessment, 6,* 203–213.

Rosenbaum, M., & Raz, D. (1977). Denial, locus of control and depression among physically disabled and nondisabled men. *Journal of Clinical Psychology, 33,* 672–676.

Scherer, M. J. (2000). *Living in the state of stuck: How technology impacts the lives of people with disabilities* (3rd ed.). Cambridge, MA: Brookline Books.

Schultheis, M. T., & Rizzo, A. A. (2001). The application of virtual reality technology for rehabilitation. *Rehabilitation Psychology, 46,* 296–311.

Schulz, R., & Decker, S. (1985). Long-term adjustment to physical disability: The role of social support, perceived control, and self-blame. *Journal of Personality and Social Psychology, 48,* 1162–1172.

Shewchuk, R., Richards, J. S., & Elliott, T. (1998). Dynamic processes in health outcomes among caregivers of patients with spinal cord injuries. *Health Psychology, 17,* 125–129.

Siddall, P. J., Taylor, D. A., & Cousins, M. J. (1997). Classification of pain following spinal cord injury. *Spinal Cord, 35,* 69–75.

Siddall, P. J., Taylor, D. A., McClelland, J., Rutklowski, S. B., & Cousins, M. J. (1999). Pain report and the relationship of pain to physical factors. I: The first 6 months following spinal cord injury. *Pain, 81,* 187–197.

Sipski, M. L., Alexander, C. J., & Rosen, R. (1995). Physiological parameters associated with psychogenic sexual arousal in women with complete spinal cord injuries. *Archives of Physical Medicine and Rehabilitation, 76,* 811–818.

Stover, S. L., Hall, K., DeLisa, J., & Donovan, W. (1995). System benefits. In S. L. Stover, J. DeLisa, & G. Whiteneck (Eds.), *Spinal cord injury: Clinical outcomes from the model systems* (pp. 317–326). Gaithersburg, MD: Aspen Press.

Stover, S. L., Lloyd, L., Waites, K., & Jackson, A. (1991). Neurogenic urinary tract infection. *Neurologic Clinics, 9,* 741–755.

Stover, S. L., Whiteneck, G. G., & DeLisa, J. A. (1995). *Spinal cord injury: Clinical outcomes from the model systems.* Gaithersburg, MD: Aspen Press.

Summers, J. D., Rapoff, M. A., Varghese, G., Porter, K., & Palmer, R. (1991). Psychosocial factors in chronic spinal cord injury pain. *Pain, 47,* 183–189.

Targett, P., Wilson, K., Wehman, P., & McKinley, W. O. (1998). Community needs assessment survey of people with spinal cord injury: An early follow-up study. *Journal of Vocational Rehabilitation, 10*(2), 169–177.

Tate, D. (1993). Alcohol use among spinal cord injured patients. *American Journal of Physical Medicine and Rehabilitation, 72,* 192–195.

Temkin, A. J., & Jones, M. L. (1999). Electronic medicine: Experience and implications for treatment of Spinal Cord Injury [Special issue]. *Topics in Spinal Cord Injury Rehabilitation, 5*(3), 1–74.

Temple, R., & Elliott, T. (2000). Personality disorder characteristics and adjustment following spinal cord injury. *Topics in Spinal Cord Injury Rehabilitation, 6*(1), 54–65.

Trieschmann, R. (1980). *Spinal cord injuries: Psychological, social and vocational adjustment.* New York: Pergamon Press.

Trieschmann, R. (1987). *Aging with a disability.* New York: Demos Press.

Umlauf, R. L. (1992). Psychological interventions for chronic pain following spinal cord injury. *Clinical Journal of Pain, 8,* 111–118.

Urey, J. R., & Henggeler, S. (1987). Marital adjustment following spinal cord injury. *Archives of Physical Medicine and Rehabilitation, 68,* 69–74.

Warschausky, S., Kay, J., & Kewman, D. (2001). Hierarchical linear modeling of FIM instrument growth curve characteristics after spinal cord injury. *Archives of Physical Medicine and Rehabilitation, 82,* 329–334.

Waters, R. L., & Adkins, R. (1997). Firearm versus motor vehicle related spinal cord injury: Preinjury factors, injury characteristics, and initial outcome comparisons among ethically diverse groups. *Archives of Physical Medicine and Rehabilitation, 78,* 15–155.

Weeks, C. (2001). Women, spinal cord injury, and osteoporosis. *Topics in Spinal Cord Injury Rehabilitation, 7*(1), 53–63.

Whipple, B., Gerdes, C. A., & Komisaruk, B. R. (1996). Sexual responses to self-stimulation in women with complete Spinal Cord Injury. *Journal of Sex Research, 33,* 231–240.

Wright, B. A. (1983). *Physical disability: A psychosocial approach.* New York: Harper & Row.

Wright, B. A., & Fletcher, B. (1982). Uncovering hidden resources: A challenge in assessment. *Professional Psychology, 13,* 229–235.

Yarkony, G. M. (1994). Pressure ulcers: A review. *Archives of Physical Medicine and Rehabilitation, 75,* 908–917.

Yezierski, R. P. (1996). Pain following spinal cord injury: The clinical problem and experimental studies. *Pain, 68,* 185–194.

Young, M., Rintala, D., Rossi, C., Hart, K., & Fuhrer, M. J. (1995). Alcohol and marijuana use in a community-based sample of persons with spinal cord injury. *Archives of Physical Medicine and Rehabilitation, 76,* 525–532.

Zafonte, R. D., & Dijkers, M. P. (1999). Medical and functional sequelae of spinal cord injury caused by violence: Findings from the model systems. *Topics in Spinal Cord Injury Rehabilitation, 4,* 36–50.

PART FOUR

HEALTH PSYCHOLOGY ACROSS THE LIFE SPAN

CHAPTER 19

Child Health Psychology

LAMIA P. BARAKAT, ALICIA KUNIN-BATSON, AND ANNE E. KAZAK

The field of child health psychology is broad, multifaceted, and multidisciplinary in nature. Encompassing the well-being of infants, children, adolescents, and young adults, it includes an emphasis on health (e.g., absence of disease, prevention) as well as illnesses and injuries (major and minor, acute and chronic). Child health psychologists collaborate with pediatricians, nurses, social workers, psychiatrists, and other health care providers to design and implement interventions aimed at reducing distress, promoting adjustment, and maintaining health. Child health psychologists may also be involved in public policy initiatives to promote health. The field of child health psychology draws from other specialized areas of psychology, including developmental, clinical, clinical-child, health, social, and family psychology. Comprehensive integration across these multiple disciplines and emphases is beyond the scope of any one chapter. In this summary of child health psychology, we integrate the diverse child health psychology intervention literature within the parameters of four focused assumptions and three levels of intervention that we believe are crucial to advancing the health and well-being of children and their families now and in the future.

BASIC ASSUMPTIONS

Assumption 1

Children's health and illness must be viewed contextually; the family is a central organizing framework for understanding child health. All aspects of child health psychology rest on the assumption that children live within a social context in which care will be provided and that children's growth and development within this context are paramount considerations. Social ecology (Bronfenbrenner, 1979) provides a helpful framework for understanding the context of child development; as applied in pediatric psychology by our group, it guides understanding of the interactions among childhood illness, the individual child, and systems internal (parent, siblings, extended family) and external (school, neighborhood, parent workplace, health care setting) to the family.

In social ecology, the ill child is at the center of a series of concentric circles (Figure 19.1). The child's circle is nested within a larger circle that includes members of the family system (mothers, fathers, siblings, extended family) and the illness (type, course, prognosis, chronicity, etc.). The family is central to the social context of the child for many reasons,

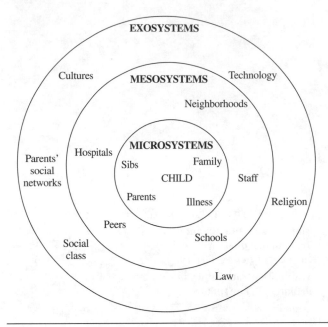

Figure 19.1 Social ecology theory.

including the fact that most children cannot consent for medical care independently. The theory highlights reciprocity and change in the course of development and rests on relationships and opportunities that unfold in the interactions of the child and his or her social ecology. Development also implies change over time and reinforces the importance of viewing the experience of children and families as fluid, undergoing many transitions over time.

At the time of a child's health crisis, other circles and systems within the social ecology are added, activated, or changed. The family remains the primary system, but school, peer groups, neighbors, and work systems are critically important and impacted. Additionally, families must make initial, essential treatment decisions while under stress and in the midst of forming new partnerships with health care providers. Health care systems may have been relatively insignificant in the life of some families prior to the onset of an illness (e.g., a three-year-old with leukemia who had primarily well child care previously). Other families may have involved histories with health care (e.g., another ill child or other family member/s with chronic illness) and now forge new relationships with memories of prior experiences coloring these collaborations.

Not only are relationships embedded in the social ecology, but beliefs of the child, family, and health care providers are as well. These beliefs are influenced tremendously by cultures' and subcultures' views on illness and pain. At diagnosis, children have beliefs about going to the hospital ("The needle is going to hurt," "I don't want my parents to leave me.") as do their parents ("Who can I trust?" "We will get all

the answers from the doctors.") Children and families have beliefs about childhood illnesses ("This cannot really be diabetes. I feel fine," "Cancer is a death sentence," "Cancer can be cured," "We are being punished," "Pain is not a big problem," "Be strong. Don't ask for help," "Pray.") Health care providers have beliefs about patients, families, illnesses, treatments, and outcomes ("This is a 'good' family," "These people are crazy," "This treatment will work. If it doesn't, we have another. And another.")

Thus, social ecology theory provides a useful framework not only for understanding illness but also for guiding interventions that promote competence and positive developmental outcomes. Although the importance of viewing the child within the context of the family is widely accepted, many interventions do not systematically include families. The majority of interventions (and prevention efforts) have focused on the child in isolation. Moreover, few interventions for children with chronic illness have targeted the outer circles, beyond but in interaction with the child and family.

Assumption 2

Pediatric psychology provides an umbrella under which child health can be summarized and integrated. While not the only professional framework to inform the field of child health, pediatric psychology offers a perspective consistent with the themes of this chapter. From the masthead of the *Journal of Pediatric Psychology* (*JPP*), pediatric psychology is defined as follows:

> Pediatric psychology is an interdisciplinary field addressing physical, cognitive, social and emotional functioning and development as they relate to health and illness issues in children, adolescents, and families . . . exploring the interrelationship between psychological and physical well-being of children, adolescents and families, including: psychosocial and developmental factors contributing to the etiology, course, treatment and outcome of pediatric conditions; assessment and treatment of behavioral and emotional concomitants of disease, illness, and developmental disorder; the role of psychology in health care settings; behavioral aspects of pediatric medicine; the promotions of health and health-related behaviors; the prevention of illness and injury among children and youth; and issues related to the training of pediatric psychologists.

Building on the theme of a marriage between pediatrics and psychology (Kagan, 1965), Wright (1967) wrote that the offspring of such a marriage would be the psychological pediatrician and the pediatric psychologist. Although clinical psychologists had been working with pediatricians for some time, these visionary writings set the stage for the birth of a specialty of pediatric psychology (Routh, 1975). Through efforts of psychologists who identified themselves as interested in pediatric psychology, the Society of Pediatric Psychology was founded in 1969. The Society achieved division status (54) within the American Psychological Association in 2000. Wright propounded that the success of the field would rest, in part, on the construction of a new body of knowledge in pediatric psychology. In this chapter, we present examples of how an impressive body of knowledge in child health has been amassed and increasingly used in practice.

Assumption 3

Competence and stress-and-coping paradigms, rather than deficits and psychopathology, define our understanding of child health psychology. The commonalities in orientations and approaches between child health psychologists and pediatricians include a solid developmental orientation and emphasis on normal child development, interests in treating and advocating for improvements in the health care available to children and families, and prevention. These aims are congruent with stress-and-coping models that are prominent in child health psychology and reflect the drive to understand competence (resilience) in concert with risks associated with childhood illness.

Childhood illness is often conceptualized as a stressor or trauma with the potential to impact children's short- and long-term functioning. The stressor may be associated with the illness itself (e.g., pain in sickle cell disease [SCD] and recurrent headache) or with the required treatment (e.g., bone marrow aspirations in childhood cancer, blood glucose testing, insulin injections, and dietary restrictions in insulin-dependent diabetes mellitus [IDDM], or surgery in solid organ transplantation). In addition, some childhood illnesses and their treatments lead to long-term medical problems after the children are considered "cured," including late effects of cancer treatment, cognitive deficits associated with brain tumors, and rejection in solid organ and bone marrow transplantation.

Early research in child health psychology (pre-1980) approached children with illness (generally mental retardation or chronic physical handicaps) by asking the question, "How do these families differ from 'normal' families?" The answer expected was that children with illness and their families would show increased evidence of distress, including psychopathology (e.g., depression, adjustment difficulties, marital discord and divorce). Some of the early literature supported this view, although closer examination of the research methodologies indicated that many samples were not representative and were based on families referred for psychological consultation and/or treatment.

Asking the same general question but with samples carefully recruited to reflect the complete spectrum of child and family functioning, a different picture began to emerge in the mid- to-late 1980s. Along with groups from other laboratories, our earlier teams found relatively few consistent differences between families with and without children with myelomeningocele, phenylketonuria, and mental retardation (Barakat & Linney, 1992; Kazak, 1988; Kazak & Marvin, 1984; Kazak, Reber, & Carter, 1988; Kazak, Reber, & Snitzer, 1988; Kazak & Wilcox, 1984).

Based on our work and that of others, some key findings when comparing families with and without children with a chronic pediatric illness are:

1. As a group, mothers of children with chronic illness show evidence of increased distress but not psychopathology.
2. Fathers, who continue to be neglected in research (Seagull, 2000), experience less distress than mothers, but show ongoing psychological reactions to their child's illness and its impact on the family.
3. In nonclinical representative samples, it is a myth that marriages necessarily falter and dissolve in the course of childhood illness. Some marriages improve.
4. Children with an illness and their siblings evidence the complete range of emotional, social, and behavioral concerns as other children, although children whose illness and/or treatment are linked to central nervous system damage have more difficulty adjusting over time.
5. There are differences in parents' social networks in families with and without ill children that suggest heightened social isolation and its associated physical and mental health implications.

Recognizing these vulnerabilities while focusing on competence has been a helpful pathway in guiding child health psychology through the 1990s and into the 2000s. Child health psychologists have turned to describing and testing stress-and-coping models for understanding what leads to successful adaptation in childhood chronic illness and what interferes with or impedes such adaptation. Through these models, demographic (child age and gender), disease/functionality (severity, course, brain involvement), intrapersonal (temperament, coping strategies, health beliefs), and interpersonal variables (family functioning, social support) have been proposed to impact child functioning (Rolland, 1990; see Wallander & Thompson, 1995, for a summary). A survey of findings provides support for the basic assumption that illness, child, and family factors impact the psychosocial functioning of children with chronic illness and their families.

The work of Bleil, Ramesh, Miller, and Wood (2000) reflects research in pediatric psychology that builds on these interrelationships. They reported on a cross-sectional study of children with asthma in which two competing hypotheses were tested; one hypothesis asserted that quality of the parent-child relationship would moderate the association of illness-related functional status with child depression, and the other hypothesis stated that parent-child relatedness would mediate the functional status and depression association. Using questionnaire data from 55 children and their caregivers, Bleil et al. found support for the mediator model with mothers suggesting that functional status does not directly influence depression in children with asthma nor does the mother-child relationship buffer or exacerbate the influence of functional status. Instead, it seems that functional status impacts the mother-child relationship in ways that influence the development of depressive symptoms. There were no significant results involving the father-child relationship. These data are of substantive value because they suggest specific targets for intervention (parent-child relationships) when working to improve children's well-being.

The importance of examining adaptation through prospective studies has been recognized. Kupst and colleagues' (1995) examination of the adaptation of children diagnosed with cancer and their families stands out as one of the first and longest prospective studies following families up to 10 years postdiagnosis. Their work showed the importance of parental coping in adaptation. Our own work with childhood cancer (Kazak & Barakat, 1997) supports the association of parenting stress and children's quality of life during treatment with well-being of children and their parents posttreatment. Clay and associates used growth modeling statistical procedures to examine data from a prospective study of adaptation in 16 children with juvenile rheumatoid arthritis (JRA), 40 children with IDDM, and 56 healthy children (Clay, Wood, Frank, Hagglund, & Johnson, 1995). These statistical procedures allowed for analysis of adaptation from a developmental perspective and for comparison of three models of adjustment. They found substantial individual variation in adaptation over time with parental adjustment and family functioning linked to changes in adaptation. Findings from these studies point to the importance of interventions aimed at parent-child relatedness in addressing psychological functioning. They also demonstrate the rationale for the increased focus in pediatric psychology research on testing interventions based on this broad and solid foundation of descriptive research.

Assumption 4

Outcome studies are important in establishing psychological interventions within child health. A large body of descriptive and explicative research has illustrated an increased risk of child and family adjustment difficulties in childhood chronic illnesses. These studies also describe the inherent competence of children and families and further suggest that intervention is likely to be helpful in mitigating distress and promoting adjustment. Pediatric psychologists are eager to apply interventions with established effectiveness to problems that children and families face around health and illness-related issues. Changes in health care and increased demands for showing the effectiveness of treatments have accelerated efforts to communicate more widely about effective treatments. Surprisingly few treatments have been investigated in a scientifically rigorous manner. However, many child health interventions help children and families. Similar to debates within clinical psychology, more broadly, the ways in which treatments are evaluated, promoted, and potentially translated into practice guidelines are viewed with a mixture of welcome and caution. As a first step in evaluating these interventions, the criteria for "empirically supported treatments" in psychology have been applied to pediatric psychology through a series of review papers in the *Journal of Pediatric Psychology* (1999, 2000, 2001).

The basic standards used to establish empirically supported treatments in clinical psychology, developed by a taskforce within Division 12 (Clinical Psychology) of the American Psychological Association, guided the identification of effective treatments in pediatric psychology (see Chambless & Hollon, 1998). Following the Division 12 guidelines, a *well-established treatment* must have been evaluated in "at least two good between group design experiments" that showed that the treatment was superior to a placebo or alternate treatment or equivalent to an already established treatment in studies with adequate statistical power (sample size of 30 per group). A series of nine or more well-designed case studies, in which the treatment is contrasted with another treatment, is also acceptable. Treatment manuals and a complete description of the sample were also required. Finally, to be deemed well-established, the findings must have been reported by two different laboratories. A *probably efficacious treatment* requires two experiments that show that the treatment was more effective than a waitlist control group or one or more experiments meeting the well-established criteria, but without replication by independent research teams.

The movement to establish criteria for effective treatments is critical to demonstrate that psychological interventions are powerful and meet relatively rigorous scientific scrutiny of their merit. Nonetheless, setting standards for effective treatments has generated discussion of the short- and long-term implications of categorizing treatment approaches by effectiveness, particularly in areas in which intervention research

TABLE 19.1 Summary of Special Series on Empirically Supported Treatments in the Journal of Pediatric Psychology

Pediatric Health Condition	Well-Established Treatments	Probably Efficacious Treatments	Promising Interventions	Citation and Notes
Headache	• Relaxation. • Self-hypnosis.	• Thermal biofeedback.	• Relaxation + Biofeedback. • Integration of CBT.	Holden, Delchmann, and Levy, 1999 $N = 13$ studies
Recurrent abdominal pain		• CBT.	• Fiber (constipation present).	Janicke and Finney, 1999 $N = 9$ studies Operant procedures did not meet minimal EST criteria.
Procedural pain	• Cognitive-behavioral therapy, encompassing different specific techniques.			Powers, 1999 $N = 13$ studies
Disease-related pain			• Cognitive-behavioral therapy.	Walco, Sterling, Conte, and Engel, 1999 Reviewed pediatric chronic illness literature.
Nocturnal enuresis	• Urine alarm. • "Dry-Bed Training."		• Hypnosis. • Cognitive-behavioral therapy, contingency management.	Mellon and M. McGrath, 2000 $N = 39$ studies
Constipation and encopresis		• Medical intervention (with and without fiber) + positive reinforcement. • Biofeedback + medical intervention. • Relaxation + reinforcers.	• Medical intervention plus positive reinforcement in small group format.	M. McGrath, Mellon, and Murphy, 2000 $N = 20$ studies
Severe feeding problems	• Contingency management (positive reinforcement, ignoring).		• Extinction. • Swallow induction.	Kerwin, 1999 $N = 32$ studies
Obesity	• Multicomponent behavioral intervention (for 8–12 year olds).		• For adolescents, behavioral diet regulation.	Jelalian and Saelens, 1999 $N = 42$ studies
Disease-related symptoms in asthma, cancer, diabetes	• EMG biofeedback for emotionally triggered asthma. • Imagery for children receiving chemotherapy.	• Relaxation for asthma. • Distraction with relaxation for chemotherapy.		McQuaid and Nassau, 1999
Bedtime refusals Night wakings	• Extinction. • Parent education.	• Graduated extinction. • Scheduled awakenings.	• Positive routines.	Mindell, 1999 $N = 41$ studies

Source: Journal of Pediatric Psychology: Special Series on Empirically Supported Treatments in Pediatric Psychology, 24(2, 3, 4, 6), 25(4), 26(5).

is expanding. In pediatric psychology, interventions typically target small samples with low base-rate occurrences of specific health conditions. In addition, pediatric intervention research is often conducted in health care settings as a primary site. That is, rather than move intervention studies from effectiveness trials (in the laboratory) to efficacy studies (in actual clinical settings), as in psychotherapy outcome research, pediatric psychologists are conducting all phases of intervention research in the "real world" of the pediatric inpatient or outpatient setting. This is inevitable and consistent with other medical/pediatric clinical trials, albeit different from psychotherapy outcome trials that formed the basis of the Division 12 guidelines. In an effort to acknowledge these differences, the criteria for effective treatments in pediatric psychology were modified (Spirito, 1999). Rather than a

treatment manual, treatments may rely on a specific protocol. In cases of relatively rare chronic illnesses, the sample size criteria were relaxed. Finally, a category called *promising interventions* was established, requiring at least one well-controlled group design and an additional less rigorous study with positive findings.

The findings extracted from the review papers published in the *Journal of Pediatric Psychology* are presented in Table 19.1. These papers address the following diseases and conditions: procedure-related pain; disease-related pain; recurrent headache; recurrent abdominal pain (RAP); disease-related symptoms in asthma, diabetes, and cancer; feeding problems; obesity; nighttime enuresis; encopresis and constipation; and sleep difficulties. A general conclusion is that many scientifically supported treatment approaches are offered by pediatric psychologists across a broad array of illnesses and symptoms. Well-established treatments are reported for headaches, procedural pain, enuresis, feeding problems, obesity, asthma, chemotherapy-related distress, and pediatric sleep problems. These interventions focus heavily on behavioral approaches. For example, one of the most highly established areas of intervention is procedural pain where combinations of cognitive-behavioral therapies (CBT; e.g., relaxation, imagery, distraction, self hypnosis) are well-established. Targets of CBT also lend themselves to measurement (e.g., observations of child behavior before, during, and after an intervention), which has helped establish their effectiveness and assured them a prominent place among the variety of approaches a psychologist may use in treating children and their families.

Even with well-established treatments, however, there is a need to continue to pursue research regarding other potentially effective treatments. Division 12 guidelines for empirically supported treatments should not be taken as blanket endorsement of an approach as necessarily better (or preferred) over other approaches. As shown in Table 19.1, a variety of treatments, largely similar to the well-established treatments, meet criteria for *probably efficacious* or *promising*. Most of the reviews in the *Journal of Pediatric Psychology* series include a relatively small number of published reports. The studies often rely on maternal reports for treatment outcomes. We are early in the process of testing child health psychology interventions. Given the wide range of child health concerns (and advances in medical and associated technology) that impact diverse populations with complex family contexts, it is essential that intervention outcome research continue, exploring the efficacy and effectiveness of other treatment modalities and new creative intervention partnerships.

LEVELS OF RISK AND RELATED PSYCHOLOGICAL INTERVENTIONS

The application of psychological practice across a wide range of child health domains suggests the need for a broad framework for understanding psychological child health interventions. Often, psychological practice in child health is associated with more severe and/or longstanding adjustment problems. That is, a threshold exists for when a child with diabetes, recurrent headache, or cancer is referred to a psychologist (either internal or external to the health care setting) for treatment of a disease or treatment-related concern. Other approaches (e.g., behavioral and cognitive-behavioral interventions) have application when treatment is clinically indicated but are also helpful in reducing the likelihood of

ongoing psychological distress under conditions of established duress (e.g., medical procedures). Alternatively, in the realm of primary prevention, for example, psychologists have contributed to the literature on injury prevention (e.g., seat belts and bicycle helmets). The existing literature (or descriptions of practice) is largely devoid of frameworks (rather than specific theoretical approaches) that might guide the systematic provision of effective intervention to children and families. Intermediary frameworks are needed to apply well-established and promising treatments, based on cognitive-behavioral, family systems, or other theories, in a clinically relevant manner. If psychological practice is to continue to be increasingly integrated into child health care, such "blueprints" for the provision of effective and cost-efficient psychological interventions to pediatric populations will be critical.

The model that we present provides an organization for illustrating examples of child health psychology research and practice. Based on prevention guidelines from the National Institute of Mental Health (NIMH), it has been applied to pediatric psychology practice at The Children's Hospital of Philadelphia (CHOP). The model evolved at CHOP in the mid- to late 1990s from a series of conversations among physicians, psychologists, and hospital administrators about models for providing psychological services at an academic pediatric health care hospital and system. It is a competence-based framework, which allows for the integration of research and clinical practice in child health psychology.

Existing models of psychological services in child health were threatened nationally during the 1990s when managed care shifted the focus of psychological care and created threats to the sustenance of mental health care generally. Psychological interventions in child health psychology that were based on fee-for-service payment or on contracts with public and private health insurance companies (and Health Maintenance Organizations [HMOs]) were threatened. At the same time, funding from the National Institutes of Health was limited.

These constraining forces were counterbalanced by the astuteness of the prediction of a "new morbidity" in pediatrics (Haggerty, Roghmann, & Pless, 1975). More children with diseases that were often fatal (e.g., cancer, cardiac disease, low birth weight infants) were surviving longer, but with attendant serious and/or chronic health problems. The psychological implications of intensive long-term care of an ill infant, child, or adolescent for families were becoming more evident. At the same time, the associations between behavior and health outcomes were more apparent. Finally, in the health care setting, the provision of increasingly highly technological care within shorter hospital stays highlighted the challenges and complexity of providing care in the face of psychological distress and dysfunction in the child patient and/or the family. The child health psychology literature has contributed directly to all of these concerns. What appeared to be missing were models for explaining how research and clinical care could be linked in a comprehensive, effective, yet cost-effective, approach.

Any target patient group, whether broad (e.g., all patients at a children's hospital, all patients followed in an outpatient pediatric practice) or narrow (e.g., patients seen by a subspecialty clinic such as oncology, cardiology, adolescent medicine) includes individuals representing a range of psychological functioning. We have conceptualized three general categories to describe children's and families' responses to child health crises. We further link these categories to proposed levels of psychological care. These correspond to NIMH prevention categories of universal, selective, and indicated care, which is illustrated under each description and graphically shown in Figure 19.2.

Universal Interventions

Most families maintain well-being by coping adaptively with the disruption and distress associated with childhood chronic illnesses. For example, in childhood cancer, psychological adjustment improves over the first 12 to 18 months after diagnosis, irrespective of whether an intervention is provided (Kazak, Penati, Brophy, & Himelstein, 1998), and psychological adjustment of children treated with heart transplantation improves after the first year posttransplant (Todaro, Fennell, Sears, Rodrigue, & Roche, 2000). These children and families were most likely functioning within normal

limits prior to the health crisis, and their underlying psychological resilience help to assure recovery from the stressors associated with childhood illness and treatment. To draw a parallel with the preventive, public health model, like having fluoride in drinking water, these families receive the most general types of psychosocial support available in the hospital, clinic, and community setting and function well with that level of intervention. This group represents the largest of the three proposed groups affected by pediatric health problems.

In this chapter, the interventions we discuss under universal interventions may also be described as preventive efforts targeting a population of children who are not necessarily at high risk for illness or psychological problems. Although all interventions in child health require the collaboration of psychologists with families, pediatricians, teachers, and others, universal interventions are defined by interdisciplinary collaborations and are most successful when implemented on multiple levels from the individual and family to the community and to policy initiatives.

Selective Interventions

Selective interventions target children at moderate risk for psychological difficulties. These children may be at risk due to stressful aspects of the treatment regimens required for their illnesses or because of intense, recurring pain associated with their illnesses. Children with cancer, for example, experience repeated painful procedures in their treatment regimens. Children with SCD and children with recurrent headache experience pain as part of the illness process. Adherence is of concern for all children requiring medical

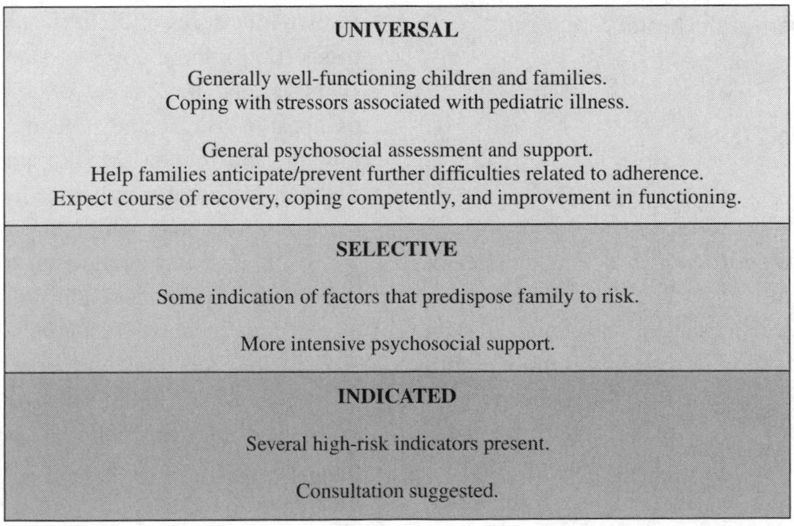

UNIVERSAL

Generally well-functioning children and families.
Coping with stressors associated with pediatric illness.

General psychosocial assessment and support.
Help families anticipate/prevent further difficulties related to adherence.
Expect course of recovery, coping competently, and improvement in functioning.

SELECTIVE

Some indication of factors that predispose family to risk.

More intensive psychosocial support.

INDICATED

Several high-risk indicators present.

Consultation suggested.

Figure 19.2 Levels of risk and implications for intervention approaches. *Source:* Adapted from: Priorities for Prevention Research at NIMH: A National Advisory Mental Health Council Workgroup on Mental Disorders Prevention Research, 1998.

treatment but particularly for children with intensive regimens such as children with IDDM and children with asthma. Family factors may also place some families at risk for sustained distress. For example, child behavior problems, marital strain, or financial considerations that predate a child's health concern may result in parental expression of intense and sustained levels of anxiety, exceeding that usually seen in parents of patients. These families may also be at risk for problems with adherence (e.g., assuring that a child with behavior problems takes medication regularly, transportation difficulties that result in irregular attendance at outpatient visits) and are likely to benefit from more intensive interventions.

Indicated Interventions

Some children and families show more obvious psychological difficulties and are at high risk because of the illness itself or the presence of stress, intrapersonal, and social risk factors. These families may have preexisting psychological difficulties (or psychopathology), be in the midst of divorce, have recent life changes that tax their coping abilities, and so on. They may also have a long-term history of difficulty managing a pediatric illness (e.g., maintaining desirable blood glucose erratically in a child with diabetes, repeated hospitalizations for pain in a child with sickle cell disease). In this chapter, we focus our discussion around life-threatening illnesses with treatments and long-term effects of sufficient severity that intervention is indicated in most cases. These illnesses involve cognitive functioning, traumatic brain injury and brain tumors specifically, and illnesses leading to solid organ or bone marrow transplantation. While smallest in number, these families tend to use a high level of hospital resources and necessitate intensive and sustained intervention, often from multiple members of the health care team.

UNIVERSAL INTERVENTIONS

Interventions in Primary Care Settings

Pediatricians in primary care settings routinely address caregivers' questions and concerns regarding their children's development and behavior. Pediatricians are also charged with the dual tasks of caring for ill children and promoting children's health. Because of their expertise, child health psychologists are uniquely positioned to shed light on these pediatric primary care issues. Collaborations among psychologists and pediatricians in primary care settings have a long history, but few reports of the integration of psychologists in the primary care setting are found in the literature. A notable exception is Schroeder (1999), who outlined a long-standing collaboration between pediatric psychologists and pediatricians focused on assessment and intervention with a host of issues from developmental concerns to pathological conditions, from adherence to prevention. This model of collaboration incorporated early intervention through telephone consultation and recommendations. These collaborations, although not without their difficulties and pitfalls, may have satisfactory outcomes from pediatrician, psychologist, and family perspectives.

Kanoy and Schroeder (1985), in a prospective study, reported on the effectiveness of brief interventions with parents, provided by telephone or in person through a primary care practice. They found that parental education regarding appropriate expectations for developmental concerns and suggestions of specific behavioral interventions to address negative behaviors and socialization problems were viewed as most effective by parents. However, concerns of parents lingered over the one-year follow-up, particularly in the area of sibling and peer problems, suggesting that ongoing interaction with families was needed for maintenance of improvements. We focus the rest of our discussion of primary care settings on prevention efforts in primary care through immunizations.

Immunizations

Efforts in the past 15 years to immunize children have led to a dramatic reduction in previously common and serious infectious childhood illnesses such as polio, tetanus, and diphtheria. However, the number of immunizations developed, along with the repeated administration required, place financial, logistical, and emotional burdens on families and on the health care system. It is recommended that, by age 2, children receive four doses of diphtheria and tetanus toxoids and pertussis (DTP), three doses of Haemophilus influenzae type b (Hib) vaccine, three doses of poliovirus vaccine, three doses of hepatitis B vaccine, one dose of vaccine for measles, mumps, and rubella (MMR), and the more recently added doses of vaccine for pneumococcal meningitis and for varicella (chicken pox; National Vaccine Advisory Committee, 1999). Infants may require up to four immunization injections at one appointment. Only about 60% of children receive all the immunizations recommended by age 2; almost 1 million children need one more dose of vaccine by age 2 to reach full immunization (National Vaccine Advisory Committee). Following a measles outbreak in the early 1990s, there was renewed effort to address gaps in the systems that support immunization of young children (Freed, Bordley, & Defriese, 1993). Although a comprehensive and efficient immunization delivery system has not yet been developed, immunization rates for young children have increased, and most children are immunized by the time they enter school.

Parental attitudes are not a barrier to immunization. Rather, the primary barrier to immunization is poverty and factors associated with poverty (National Vaccine Advisory Committee). Studies have shown that families adhere to immunization recommendations when barriers are reduced (Melman, Nguyen, Ehrlich, Schorr, & Anbar, 1999; The National Vaccine Advisory Committee, 1999). For example, state implemented, federal entitlement programs and state legislation mandating coverage of immunizations by insurance companies have improved the availability of vaccine while standards for immunization practice has facilitated delivery of immunization (Freed et al., 1993; National Vaccine Advisory Committee).

A subcommittee on immunization coverage of the National Vaccine Advisory Committee summarized the literature on immunization efforts and made recommendations for further improving immunization rates (National Vaccine Advisory Committee). The task force found that attempting to immunize in emergency rooms and relying on educating parents were not sufficient interventions to increase immunization rates. Instead, improvement requires addressing barriers on these multiple systems levels. As an example of research into the effectiveness of interventions to increase immunization rates, Sinn, Morrow, and Finch (1999) reported on the development of an immunization task force committee as a quality improvement initiative. They reviewed immunization rates and practices after three assessments and suggested innovations designed to improve immunization rates. Over a two-year period, mean practice immunization rates improved significantly to 69.7% from 50.9% at baseline, and age at immunization decreased. The increased rates were attributed to improved record keeping and tracking and screening for immunization at every office visit. In another intervention, Goldstein, Lauderdale, Glushak, Walter, and Daum (1999) reported on the effectiveness of a community-based outreach program in a Chicago public housing development. In this three-year intervention, they found that door-to-door canvassing by trained emergency technicians was effective in ascertaining immunization status of children, enrolling them in an immunization program, improving rates of immunization, and increasing the percentage of children with up-to-date immunization coverage (from 37% to 50%). Support for tracking and outreach as effective and cost-efficient procedures for improving immunization was found in a randomized, controlled study conducted in nine primary care sites (Rodewald et al., 1999).

Efforts to improve childhood immunization are most effective on a systems level, impacting health care delivery and public policy. Child health psychologists have an important role to play in guiding the development of interventions such as these, particularly concerning suggestions for overcoming barriers, improving communication between primary care provider and parents, and developing user-friendly reminder systems. The emerging area of immunization for sexually transmitted diseases will require child health psychologists to consider individually focused interventions due to the interaction of adolescent developmental considerations with family and health care priorities (see Fortenberry & Zimet, 1999; Webb, Zimet, Mays, & Fortenberry, 1999; Zimet, Mays, & Fortenberry, 2000).

Prevention of Unintentional Injuries

Injuries are the major causes of death and disability for children. As a result of injuries, approximately 22,000 children and adolescents die each year; seven to eight times more are permanently disabled and require continued care. Injuries account for 15% of medical spending in pediatrics (Miller, Romano, & Spicer, 2000). The most common and costly causes of unintentional injuries are falls, motor vehicle accidents (pedestrian, bicyclist, or occupant), poisonings, fire, and burns (Kronenfeld & Glik, 1995; Miller et al., 2000). Factors that place children at risk for unintentional injuries are best characterized as related to one's behavior (e.g., age, gender, temperament, estimation of physical ability) or to one's environment (e.g., low socioeconomic status and unsafe physical environment; Finney et al., 1993; Miller et al., 2000). The term *accident* implies fate, luck, or uncontrollable forces; therefore, the term *injury*, which allows for empirical consideration of contributing factors and preventive interventions, is preferred. The focus of this section is on unintentional injuries, in contrast to intentional injuries or those that result from physical abuse, neglect, and sexual abuse. Child health psychologists are called on to rule out, assess, and address child maltreatment, which affects an estimated 437,500 children per year in the United States (Knutson & DeVet, 1995). However, the scope of this literature is too broad to adequately review in this chapter (see Belsky, 1993; Edgeworth & Carr, 2000; Reece, 2000; Wolfe, 1991, for information).

Prevention efforts, targeting increased safe behaviors, decreased risky behaviors, and increased safety of the environment have generally been shown to be cost effective (Miller et al., 2000). Education of the parent and having the parent make rules will not be enough to reduce the risk of injury for children in part because having information does not necessarily lead to changes in injury-related behaviors (Finney et al., 1993). Even if behaviors are modified and attempts to apply rules are made, rules cannot be generated for all of the unusual and unexpected accidents that lead to injury in children (Hillier & Morrongiello, 1998; Peterson & Saldana, 1996). Therefore, successful prevention efforts are aimed at both active behavior change and environmental change (Finney et al., 1993) and are implemented on multiple levels: individual/family, community, and population/policy.

Although the concept of the "accident-prone" child has been retired due to a lack of empirical support (Rivara & Mueller, 1987), studies suggest that some child characteristics are associated with increased risk for injury. First, the types of accidents and injuries that occur depend on child age due to development of motor skills and cognitive abilities. Infants are more likely to die of asphyxiation; preschool-age children, from falls; school-age children, from pedestrian accidents, drowning, or fire; and adolescents, from motor vehicle accidents (Rivara & Mueller, 1987). Second, statistics show that males are more likely to be involved in accidents and experience injuries than females, specifically injuries involving gross motor skills and a mechanical transfer of energy (fractures for males versus poisonings equally for males and females; Rivara & Mueller, 1987). In terms of psychological characteristics, Schwebel and Plumert (1999) showed prospectively that children who are high on extroversion and low on inhibitory control when they are preschoolers tend to overestimate their physical abilities and to experience more injuries as they grow older (school age). Children low on extroversion and high on inhibitory control underestimated their abilities and had fewer injuries. Finally, factors that reduce families' abilities to supervise children, including stressful life events and poverty, increase the likelihood of injury (Kronenfeld & Glik, 1995).

Prevention aimed at environmental change has impacted significantly the health and safety of children. Helping families make home environments more secure for their children by using education, modeling, and feedback has shown measured success (see Roberts, Fanurik, & Layfield, 1987). Additionally, community standards for safe surface areas in playgrounds, policies regarding toy safety, and the use of childproof caps on medications illustrate environmental changes that have reduced accidents and injuries among children (Finney et al., 1993).

A notable example of moderate success in prevention efforts aimed at behavior change is the use of child restraints to reduce morbidity and mortality associated with motor vehicle accidents (Klassen, MacKay, Moher, Walker, & Jones, 2000). On a policy level, by 1985 all U.S. states had passed laws mandating child restraint use, and there is evidence that infant and child seatbelt laws have significantly reduced morbidity and mortality associated with automobile accidents

(Rock, 1996). On the community level, prevention has targeted primarily the child under the assumption that the child will monitor restraint use in the family and that families are more likely to use seatbelts if their children do not resist (Klassen et al., 2000). In one program, a school-based educational program (kindergarten through second grade) was linked with public education on television, in radio, and in newspapers (Hazinski, Eddy, & Morris, 1995). The study's authors reported that motor vehicle restraint use improved significantly only in low-income schools with high adherence to the program. There was less impact in high-income schools where use of restraints was higher at baseline. In another study, preschool-age children who received stickers if they arrived at daycare in a restraint showed significantly higher motor vehicle restraint use (Roberts & Layfield, 1987). However, there remains room for improvement as child restraints are often used incorrectly, rates of restraint use are reduced over time without continual reinforcement (Roberts & Layfield, 1987), and nearly 15% of infants and 40% of toddlers are still not regularly restrained (Klassen et al., 2000). Psychologists are challenged to develop programs that will impact larger portions of the population by better understanding the factors that lead to behavior change and the mechanisms in action between risk factors and injuries (Finney et al., 1993).

SELECTIVE INTERVENTIONS

Management of Pain and Distress

The biobehavioral model of pediatric pain (Varni, Blount, Waldron, & Smith, 1995) serves as a useful framework for guiding the development of interventions for procedure-related and disease-related pain and for understanding the targets of the intervention studies reviewed next. The core of this model places pain (perception and behaviors) in the context of precipitants and intervening variables on the one hand and functional status outcomes on the other. The precipitant may be unpredictable disease-related pain, as in vaso-occlusive crises in SCD or headache pain, or predictable pain from procedures such as bone marrow aspirations in childhood cancer and needle sticks for blood tests, insertion of IV for provision of fluids, antibiotic, or blood transfusion in SCD. The intervening variables are cognitive appraisal of pain and of one's ability to impact pain, coping strategies for handling pain and painful procedures, and perceived social support. Finally, pain perception and pain behaviors impact and are impacted by functional status outcomes including school attendance, depression and anxiety symptoms, behavior problems, and interpersonal relations.

Flowing from the biobehavioral model, Varni and his colleagues (1995) recommend that interventions move beyond narrowly focused strategies aimed at decreasing reports of pain. To enhance effectiveness, interventions must target pain perception, pain behaviors, and the intervening variables (Varni, 1999; Varni et al., 1995). Modifying pain perception involves self-regulatory mechanisms such as self-hypnosis, meditative breathing, progressive muscle relaxation, and guided imagery. Manne (1999) emphasizes the need to address cognitive appraisal of painful procedures as part of interventions for procedure-related pain by helping children and their parents to perceive the procedure as less threatening. Furthermore, by targeting intervening variables such as coping strategies, children and their parents may be supported in managing adaptively aspects of treatment or of the illness, thereby improving functional status outcomes as well as reducing pain perception. Coping strategies such as seeking social support, active behavioral distraction, problem solving, and self-instruction or self-talk may be most adaptive for children with chronic medical conditions.

To this point, the role of the family in pain perception and behaviors and in functional status outcomes has not been clearly delineated. While many disease-related pain interventions invite family participation (e.g., Dinges et al., 1997), the family's role is not addressed directly. Models for intervening in procedure-related pain are useful because they integrate family. Varni et al. (1995) summarize this literature by noting that parent appraisals of the illness and of pain, parent coping, and family functioning will influence parent interactions with their children during painful procedures (and painful crises) as expressed through parent distress and anxiety-promoting behaviors. These parent behaviors will, in turn, impact children's coping and children's pain perception and behaviors. As such, parent or family factors must be addressed as an integral element of effective interventions.

Interventions for Procedure-Related Pain

Childhood cancer is life threatening and experienced by children and their parents with fear, horror, and helplessness (Kazak, Stuber, Barakat, & Meeske, 1996; Smith, Redd, Peyser, & Vogl, 1999). It is not a discrete trauma but is repetitive (diagnosis and treatments) and chronic (in the form of follow-up visits, medical late effects, and the risk of recurrence or second cancers; Nir, 1985; Smith et al., 1999; Stuber, Kazak, Meeske, & Barakat, 1998). Given this traumatic experience, short- and long-term responses to childhood cancer can be understood as trauma responses. Studies have found that mothers and fathers of survivors of childhood cancer report significantly more symptoms of posttraumatic stress than parents of healthy children dealing with moderately severe stressors (Barakat et al., 1997; Kazak et al., 1997). Young adult survivors, but not child or adolescent survivors, report significant symptoms of posttraumatic stress (Barakat et al., 1997; Rourke, Stuber, Hobbie, & Kazak, 1999; see Butler, Rizzi, & Handwerger, 1996, for an exception). Currently, interventions focus on reducing the traumatic nature of cancer and its treatment during the treatment phase in addition to providing support as families move off treatment and into the survivor phase (Kazak et al., 1999).

Children with cancer must endure repeated invasive and painful medical procedures such as bone marrow aspirates, biopsies, and lumbar punctures, as these are integral components of cancer diagnosis and treatment. Studies have shown that children with cancer consider painful procedures as the most unpleasant and feared aspect of cancer treatment (Fowler-Kerry, 1990). The associated pain and distress does not appear to decrease with repeated procedures and may worsen if pain is not adequately managed. For example, a child who has been sensitized by a previous painful procedure that was not successfully managed may have anticipatory anxiety to the point of noncompliance or refusal to cooperate with future procedures (Miser, 1993). Our research has shown that child survivors of cancer report that getting shots and needles are among the most recalled and upsetting aspects of cancer (Kazak et al., 1996). Parents, too, report that seeing their child in pain results in fear, horror, and helplessness (Kazak et al., 1996). Thus, the optimal approach to procedure-related pain in children with cancer is critical for the well-being of the child and family and may have long-term implications for adjustment. This presents a compelling clinical and research goal that requires interdisciplinary collaboration.

In clinical practice, a number of different psychological treatments are used for children undergoing painful medical procedures (e.g., hypnosis, biofeedback), but the constellation of treatments commonly referred to as cognitive-behavioral therapy has been the most widely studied (e.g., Chen, Joseph, & Zeltzer, 2000; Powers, 1999). In his review of literature, Powers (1999) illustrated that cognitive-behavioral interventions are a well-established treatment for reducing behavioral distress and anxiety in children undergoing painful medical procedures. Typical components of a cognitive-behavioral treatment package often include breathing exercises, distraction, imagery, positive self-statements, modeling, behavioral rehearsal/role play, and positive reinforcement for using coping skills or lying still. Active direction from a "coach" (e.g., psychologist, medical staff, nurse, or parent) is another common component of CBT. As these approaches are well-known and described in detail elsewhere, we have provided brief descriptions of these techniques in Table 19.2.

TABLE 19.2   Cognitive and Behavioral Interventions for Procedural Pain

Technique	Description
Preparation	Providing step-by-step procedural information (what will be done) and sensory information (what it may feel like) to help the child develop realistic expectations for the procedure.
Desensitization	Gradually exposing the child, in hierarchical fashion, to stimuli associated with the procedure (through imagery or in vivo exposure).
Positive self-statements	Coaching children to use simple statements (which focus on self-efficacy and realistic appraisal of the situation) that they can repeat to themselves just before or during the procedure.
Reframing beliefs Changing memories	Helping the child to realistically appraise the situation and his/her own ability to cope with it to increase self-efficacy and reduce anticipatory anxiety.
Imagery	Child focuses intensely on a vivid pleasant mental image (with auditory, visual, and kinesthetic components), which is guided by the therapist. Like distraction, it takes the child's focus away from the procedure.
Relaxation	A combination of progressive muscle relaxation and deep, controlled breathing is often used to reduce physiological arousal and anxiety before and during procedures.
Modeling/ Behavioral rehearsal	Observation of another child or an adult undergoing a mock procedure while demonstrating positive coping behaviors (e.g., a video). The child can then practice these strategies by rehearsing with the therapist, staff, or parent.
Distraction	Engaging the child in cognitive activities or behaviors that divert attention from the painful procedure. Blowing bubbles, watching a video, listening to a story, or counting may be appropriate depending on the developmental level of the child.
Positive reinforcement	Specific labeled praise ("I like how well you stayed still") and tangible rewards (e.g., stickers) after completing a painful procedure.

Successful interventions for procedure-related pain and anxiety must be individualized to the child's developmental level, the invasiveness and duration of the procedure, the child's medical status, and the context in which the procedure occurs (Anderson, Zeltzer, & Fanurik, 1993). The developmental level of the child is important in determining understanding of the pain experience and response to specific intervention techniques. Many of the cognitive and behavioral techniques described earlier are useful for children from preschool through adolescence, but must be tailored to the interests and abilities of the individual child. For 2- to 3-year-old children, pop-up books or simple electronic toys that make animal noises, say a sentence, or play a tune when the child touches the picture may be effective distractions (Dahlquist, 1999). A 9-year-old may find a computer game or video distracting from a painful procedure, whereas an older adolescent may be able to use cognitive distractors (e.g., imagery, counting ceiling tiles, or focusing on a particular object in the room). Relaxation techniques can also be tailored to the child's level of development. Young children can be taught to take deep breaths during a procedure and to focus on inhaling and exhaling each breath slowly using bubble blowers or noise makers. Older children and adolescents may benefit from techniques such as progressive muscle relaxation (Anderson et al., 1993).

Children do not use distraction and other pain management techniques without guidance and prompting by adults (Dahlquist et al., 1986). Parents, however, are often anxious not only about their child's distress, but also about their own ability to comfort their child through the medical procedure. Parents, as well as health care providers, may also be unaware of how they are responding when the child is distressed and of the impact their reactions have on the child. During painful medical procedures, anxious and distressed parents can appear angry at their child for crying, scolding the child or threatening punishment if he or she does not cooperate (Anderson et al., 1993; Dahlquist, 1999). Others plead with their child, repeating the same vague commands over and over in a misguided attempt to soothe their child (e.g., "Please relax"). Several studies have shown that adult criticism, vague commands, apology, agitation, and reassuring statements do not appear to be helpful for children undergoing painful medical procedures and may actually contribute to increased distress (Dahlquist, Power, & Carlson, 1995; Dahlquist, Power, Cox, & Fernbach, 1994). Thus, an important target for interventions is to decrease the amount of anxiety and distress experienced by parents and communicated to the child.

In the past decade, researchers have begun to recognize the influence of parents' behaviors and beliefs on child distress and anxiety and have attempted to measure these directly. Successful interventions that rely on relationships among the child, family, and staff have been developed. Parent and staff report of child behavioral distress/cooperation have been used as measures of treatment outcome (e.g., Manne et al., 1990; Powers, Blount, Bachanas, Cotter, & Swan, 1993). These studies include observations of child coping behaviors (e.g., breathing, imagery) and parent/staff coping-promoting behaviors (e.g., prompting the child to use certain coping strategies, distracting the child with talk/activities), which generally have been found to improve with the use of cognitive-behavioral interventions.

Researchers have also begun to investigate the impact of children's prior experiences and temperament on treatment efficacy. Chen, Craske, Katz, Schwartz, and Zeltzer (2000) evaluated the relationship between pain sensitivity and children's distress during lumbar punctures to determine whether pain sensitivity moderates children's responses to a brief cognitive-behavioral intervention. This study is unique and important because it examined temperament as a predictor of children's response to an intervention for acute procedural distress. Among children who received no intervention, those with high pain sensitivity showed greater increases in staff-rated distress, systolic blood pressure, and parent anxiety over time. Children with higher pain sensitivity who received intervention showed greater decreases in these variables than children with lower pain sensitivity. That is, intervention was most efficacious for those who were most pain-sensitive. Their results also suggest that providing pain-vulnerable children with intervention helps reduce parent anxiety.

For psychological interventions for procedural pain to be effectively implemented, the broader context of the attitudes and roles of the multidisciplinary treatment team must be considered. Effective interventions require the active engagement of a triad, composed of the patient, parents/family, and medical staff. Like parents, staff may also experience anxiety and self-doubt when they are unable to successfully manage a child's pain during a procedure (Dahlquist, 1999). Their anxiety may interfere with their ability to execute a delicate procedure and contribute to the child's and parents' emotional distress. Thus, helping staff members manage their own anxiety is also critical.

Many variables impact the extent to which psychological interventions for procedure-related pain are integrated into standard medical care. At the most basic level, the medical team must have a clear understanding of psychological interventions and how they work to make the environment conducive to using the intervention (Dahlquist, 1999). This may entail appreciating how the relationships between the interventionist, patient, and family must be structured and maintained for a successful outcome (e.g., rapport building and review of prior procedures may take some time at the outset of the procedure). Fanurik, Koh, Schmidtz, and Brown (1997) have suggested that the integration of pharmacological and psychological techniques can maximize the advantages of both approaches and minimize the disadvantage of either approach used alone. They argue that when psychological methods are introduced early in anticipation of a child's distress, pharmacologic intervention can sometimes be delayed or even avoided. Similarly, psychological interventions may reduce short- and long-term fear responses and teach children and families generalizable coping techniques. In

contrast, most pharmacologic approaches target primarily pain reduction. The few studies that have examined the efficacy of combined interventions have found them to have advantages over pharmacotherapy (Kazak et al., 1996; Kazak et al., 1998) or CBT alone (Jay, Elliott, Woody, & Siegel, 1991). Despite the established efficacy of both psychological and pharmacologic treatment approaches, there remains a puzzling lack of integration and application of these treatments in practice (Zeltzer et al., 1990), and little discussion in the pediatric literature as to how to design and implement integrated approaches.

Interventions for Disease-Related Pain

Sickle Cell Disease. The incidence of SCD in the United States is 1 in every 400 to 500 live births for the African American population for which sickle cell disease is most prevalent (Hurtig, Koepke, & Park, 1989; Morgan & Jackson, 1986). SCD is a group of hematological disorders that are inherited, chronic, and interfere with hemoglobin production. Complications of SCD include recurrent episodes of severe pain in the lower extremities, back, abdomen, and chest referred to as vaso-occlusive crises, pneumococcal infections, anemic episodes, retarded growth, splenic changes, and strokes (Hurtig et al., 1989). Treatment may involve administration of analgesic medication on an inpatient or outpatient basis to control pain, prophylactic antibiotics to reduce susceptibility to infections, folic acid supplementation to help red cell production, regular follow-up and early identification and treatment of symptoms, and blood transfusion. On average, school-age children with SCD experience at least one to two pain episodes a month and one to two hospital admissions and/or one emergency department visits a year (Hurtig & White, 1986).

The unpredictable nature of SCD and its treatment, including frequent hospitalizations and school absenteeism, potentially threaten quality of life and disrupt psychosocial development (Lemanek, Buckloh, Woods, & Butler, 1995). Additionally, peer relationships may be affected by changes in physical appearance of children with SCD, who are usually smaller in size, or by their inability to engage in normal physical activities because of fatigue (Morgan & Jackson, 1986). Research on the adjustment of children with SCD shows conflicting results (e.g., Brown, Kaslow, et al., 1993; Lemanek, Horwitz, & Ohene-Frempong, 1994), but generally suggests that these children may be at risk for problems in psychosocial functioning. Children with SCD have displayed less body satisfaction (Morgan & Jackson, 1986), less interaction with peers (Kumar, Powars, Allen, & Haywood, 1976), doubts about their ability to become independent

(Hurtig & Viera, 1986), and depression related to a perceived loss of control (Brown, Armstrong, & Eckman, 1993). Adolescents with SCD seem to be especially vulnerable to disturbances in behavior, social adjustment, and dissatisfaction with body image (Brown, Kaslow, et al., 1993; Gil, Williams, Thompson, & Kinney, 1991; Lemanek et al., 1995).

Intermittent, unpredictable, and, at times, extreme pain related to vaso-occlusive crises and impacting quality of life is the most common symptom of SCD. As a result, pain management, both in the hospital and at home, is a focal issue for children with SCD, their families, and their health care providers. There is a solid medical literature to guide pharmacological approaches to pain management in children with SCD (see Embury, Hebbel, Mohandas, & Steinberg, 1994). However, there are few well-controlled studies examining nonpharmacological approaches to pain management, particularly for children with SCD. Similar to the literature on procedure-related pain, CBT has the most empirical support in the management of disease-related pain but the literature on disease-related pain is less developed than that concerning procedure-related pain.

Gil and her colleagues (2001) compared the efficacy of a coping skills intervention with standard care to address painful episodes in children with SCD ($n = 46$). The intervention comprised one session of face-to-face instruction in relaxation, imagery, and self-talk followed by daily practice supported by an audiotape. Results at the end of the intervention supported the coping skills training in terms of reducing pain sensitivity and negative thinking. However, at one-month follow-up, only effects for increased coping attempts remained, and there were no between-group differences on measures of pain and health care contact. Other studies have shown an impact of cognitive-behavioral interventions on pain in SCD. In a study conducted by Dinges et al. (1997), standard treatment for SCD-related pain was compared with standard treatment plus self-hypnosis training. Thirty-seven children, adolescents, and adults with SCD participated in a group-based training in self-hypnosis over an 18-month period. Family members were invited to participate in the groups. From results based primarily on daily pain diaries completed by the participants, the frequency of pain episodes was reduced and the number of pain-free days was increased. Medication use decreased for those who had more days free of pain as a result of the intervention. The intervention seemed most effective for milder pain episodes. There was no effect on absenteeism from work or school. In an earlier study, Cozzi, Tryon, and Sedlacek (1987) reported on the effectiveness of relaxation training, assisted by biofeedback and administered by audiotape. Results with a small sample of eight children and adolescents with SCD found improvement in only self-reports of pain-related symptoms but not in more objective measures of pain such as emergency department visits or hospitalizations. No follow-up data were collected.

The studies reviewed here, and those using samples of adults with SCD (e.g., Zeltzer, Dash, & Holland, 1979), provide qualified support for the effectiveness of cognitive-behavioral approaches in reducing SCD-related pain and improving quality of life, as is the case for such interventions in other pediatric groups (Walco, Sterling, Conte, & Engel, 1999). Replication of these findings with pediatric samples using standardized interventions and control groups is necessary (Walco et al., 1999). Furthermore, issues specific to SCD, such as cognitive functioning and anxiety and depression, must be considered to assess utility for painful episodes (Gil et al., 2001). In summary, "evidence for the generalization, maintenance, practicality, and cost-effectiveness of these interventions will be an important future goal" (Manne, 1999, p. 148).

Recurrent Headache.   Recurrent headache in children involves discrete and unpredictable pain episodes that may significantly impact psychosocial functioning. About 25 of every 1,000 school-age children experience recurrent headache; more than 1 million children experience migraine specifically (Holden, Rawlins, & Gladstein, 1998). Diagnosis of headache, which has typically been made as migraine (autonomic nervous system symptoms) or tension headaches (muscular tension), may also be conceptualized on a continuum as children and adolescents often experience more than one type of headache (Holden, Deichmann, & Levy, 1999). Assessment and diagnosis of recurrent headache is made through history-taking and carefully selected laboratory tests. As in the case of pediatric pain more generally, a pain diary can be a useful tool in the assessment of headache (McGrath & Larsson, 1997). Precise diagnosis is hampered by a lack of clear underlying physiology and the lack of reliability of children's reports.

Individual and family factors must be considered in designing interventions for children with recurrent headache given evidence that psychosocial factors play a role in their onset, maintenance, and exacerbation. Holden et al. (1998) reported that gender and perceived control influence how adolescents cope with recurrent headache. Active coping was used by males who perceived control over their headaches and by females who did not perceive control. Problem solving, seeking medical help, using social support, cognitive restructuring, and relaxation were viewed as most helpful. Labbe (1999) pointed to research showing the impact of family context; parental modeling of coping with headache is an important issue as may be positive reinforcement children receive for reports of headache pain.

There is compelling evidence to support CBT, targeting the antecedents and consequences of recurrent headache, as effective. Specifically, Holden et al. (1999) concluded that the use of relaxation/self-hypnosis is a well-established and efficacious treatment (see Tables 19.1 and 19.2). Studies typically use imagery-based or progressive muscle relaxation and encourage children and adolescents to engage in relaxation at the onset of headache symptoms. The focus of this research has been on promoting the use of the intervention, through practice at home, without the aid of a psychologist/coach. Furthermore, implementation of treatment in nonclinic-based sites (in schools) and in self-administered formats has been successful. For instance, McGrath et al. (1992) developed an intervention in which children and adolescents with migraine headaches were trained in coping and in relaxation techniques; one group self-administered the intervention and one group received the training with an interventionist. Compared to an education-only control group, both intervention groups show improvement in headache pain.

In the case of recurrent headache, the literature suggests that cognitive-behavioral interventions are more effective than pharmacological interventions (Hermann, Kim, & Blanchard, 1995). However, the combined effects of CBT with pharmacotherapy have not been well studied (Holden, Deichmann, & Levy, 1999). In practice, cognitive-behavioral interventions are employed with children with recurrent headache less often than they merit. It has been recommended that the research reviewed here be disseminated widely; physicians and parents need to be informed of the effectiveness shown for CBT for pediatric pain (McGrath, 1999).

Treatment Adherence

Nonadherence to prescribed treatment for acute and chronic conditions is estimated to be about 50% in pediatric populations (La Greca & Schuman, 1995). Nonadherence also occurs in the context of life-threatening conditions and in spite of potentially serious short- and long-term consequences in terms of development of illness symptoms, hospitalizations and missed school days, and permanent disability. The factors associated with treatment adherence are complex and various but key individual, family, and contextual factors that promote adherence are being elucidated. Christiaanse, Lavigne, and Lerner (1989) contend that treatment adherence may be viewed as one aspect of adjustment to chronic illness. The association between factors related to adjustment and those related to adherence (Christiaanse et al., 1989) has been supported in the general pediatric literature. Child factors of younger age (Korsch, Fine, & Negrete, 1978; La Greca, 1990), use of adaptive coping strategies (Jacobson et al., 1990), and adequate adjustment (Christiaanse et al., 1989; Korsch et al., 1978) have been related to greater treatment adherence in various pediatric samples. Parent problem-solving skills (Fehrenbach & Peterson, 1989) and family functioning (Christiaanse et al., 1989) have also been positively related to treatment adherence.

Illness severity has not been reported as a predictor of adherence while disease chronicity and treatment complexity have (La Greca & Schuman, 1995). IDDM requires a complex and intensive treatment regimen (Johnson, 1998); therefore, it has drawn the attention of child health psychologists. The goal of treatment for IDDM is to give insulin in a manner that approaches normal pancreatic function (Johnson, 1998). This goal is accomplished through blood glucose monitoring and insulin provision over the course of the day. Dietary restrictions and exercise are used to stabilize blood glucose levels. This regimen requires knowledge, the ability to make judgments regarding insulin requirements, technical skill in terms of injections, and commitment. Hypoglycemia and hyperglycemia are possible short-term complications. Long-term complications of IDDM, particularly if poorly controlled, include blindness, heart disease, renal disease, and amputations.

Building an alliance among patient, parents, and health care providers plays a role in improving adherence behaviors (Gavin, Wamboldt, Sorokin, Levy, & Wamboldt, 1999). The term *treatment adherence* has replaced the older term, *compliance,* because *adherence* connotes the active and willful role of the patient and family in administering treatment and making decisions regarding illness management—it presumes the need for a partnership. Gavin et al. (1999) examined the association of treatment alliance with adherence ratings and asthma outcome measured one year after initial assessment in a study of 30 adolescents with asthma and their families. Childhood asthma is a major cause of school absenteeism and hospitalization. The treatment regimen for asthma is composed of medication management and prevention through manipulation of environmental triggers. Poverty and barriers to health care complicate treatment adherence (Creer, 1998). In the Gavin et al. (1999) study, physician report of treatment alliance was associated with measures of treatment adherence and asthma outcome for these adolescents. Treatment alliance was not associated with demographic characteristics of the sample or adolescent psychological functioning but was associated with parent self-esteem and family functioning.

A number of models have been presented to explain nonadherence and identify targets for intervention. The health belief model has received attention in the literature with mixed results. In this model, perceived susceptibility to illness or illness symptoms, perceived severity of symptoms, and costs (perceived barriers) versus benefits of engaging in treatment interact to predict adherence (Janz & Becker, 1984). Bond, Aiken, and Somerville (1992) illustrate the complexity and inconsistency of findings regarding the health belief model. They applied the model to adolescents with IDDM, adding perceived cues (onset or change in illness symptoms) to engage in adherence behaviors. They reported that perceived cues were most associated with adherence such that when symptoms were experienced, adolescents with IDDM were more likely to seek medical help. Benefits-costs were also associated with adherence. For threat (perceived susceptibility and severity), adherence was highest in the case of low threat and high benefits-costs but metabolic control was highest in the case of high threat and high cues.

Research examining the effectiveness of interventions to improve treatment adherence is complicated by a proliferation of indirect and direct approaches to measuring adherence and related questions regarding the reliability and validity of the measures used (La Greca & Schuman, 1995). Indirect measures are patient and parent reports of adherence behaviors or patient, parent, and physician ratings of adherence. These measures tend to overestimate adherence. Direct or objective measures of adherence such as observation of patient engagement in procedures, drug assays, and pill counts have been subjected to criticism due to observer bias and individual differences in metabolism. An additional complication is the lack of one-to-one correspondence between following prescribed treatment and positive medical outcome; that is, as the health beliefs model suggests, why engage in complicated, time-consuming, and sometimes painful treatments when the payoff in terms of illness symptoms is unclear? This not only contributes to a lack of adherence but also makes physical health an unreliable outcome measure for interventions targeting adherence. It has been suggested that multiple measures of adherence, direct and indirect, be employed and that patients' specific adherence behaviors be compared to treatment prescribed specifically to them (not a general treatment regimen for the condition under study; La Greca & Schuman, 1995).

Research with pediatric samples supports the effectiveness of education for parents and children, that is, improving knowledge and skills in carrying out treatment for chronic pediatric illnesses (Delamater et al., 1990). Coping skills training or training in approaches to problem solving has also been effective in work with children with chronic illness because it allows the patient to address his or her unique barriers to adherence (Delamater et al., 1990; Satin, La Greca, Zigo, & Skyler, 1989). Satin et al. (1989) studied adolescents with IDDM who participated in multiple family groups only or multiple family groups and simulation of treatment requirements by parents. Multiple family groups concentrated on problem-solving barriers to adherence. A control group received no intervention. Findings showed that compared to the control group, both treatment groups had better metabolic control and maternal reports of adherence for up to six months.

Concrete measures, such as increased medical supervision, token reinforcement, and parental praise for keeping appointments (Finney, Lemanek, Brophy, & Cataldo, 1990; Greenan-Fowler, Powell, & Varni, 1987), are effective in improving adherence. Da Costa, Rapoff, Lemanek, and Goldstein (1997) reported the outcome of an intervention program involving parent and child education and token reinforcement for taking medication using a case study, a withdrawal design with two children with moderate to severe asthma. Results indicated that use of token reinforcement was helpful in improving medication adherence; however, maintenance was problematic once the reinforcement was withdrawn, and the impact on pulmonary function was not clear.

To summarize, multicomponent intervention programs appear to be most effective in improving adherence to prescribed treatments because they can target each family's barriers to adherence (La Greca & Schuman, 1995). However, it is difficult to determine which components of these programs lead to their effectiveness. It is recommended that the effectiveness of interventions with particular patients and their families be assessed in prospective studies that employ primarily objective measures of adherence.

INDICATED INTERVENTIONS

Traumatic Brain Injury in Children

Traumatic brain injury (TBI) is the leading cause of death and permanent disability in children and adolescents (Guyer & Ellers, 1990), affecting between 185 and 230 per 100,000 children under 15 years of age (Kraus, 1995). TBI is not evenly distributed in the population. That is, some children and adolescents appear to be at increased risk for injury, including those with behavior and/or learning problems, high risk taking, or disadvantaged families who monitored their behavior less prior to injury (Kraus, Rock, & Hamyari, 1990; Ylvisaker, 1998). In turn, these risk factors impact the availability of supports necessary after the injury.

The impact of TBI on society is profound in terms of financial cost, family stress, disruption in school, and the potential it presents for long-term difficulties into adulthood. As with other injuries and illnesses that occur in childhood, TBI disrupts the normal course of development. Tasks previously mastered must be relearned before the child can move forward (Sherwin & O'Shanick, 1998). The manner in which this disruption occurs varies as a function of pre- and postinjury factors, including the child's age, premorbid ability, achievement and personality, the nature and severity of the injury, and the quality of early medical intervention, ongoing rehabilitation and educational services, and family, friends, and community resources (Ylvisaker, 1998). These factors combine in many different ways, resulting in a broad range of clinical presentations.

Despite the varying clinical pictures of children with TBI, researchers have attempted to identify common neurocognitive characteristics among these children. Visuomotor and visuospatial functions have been consistently described as areas of weakness (e.g., Chadwick, Rutter, Shaffer, & Shrout, 1981; Winogron, Knights, & Bawden, 1984). Decreased arousal and alertness are common in the early phase of recovery, and difficulties with attention (e.g., distractibility, poor attentional control, difficulty shifting attention) may persist (Dennis, Wilkinson, Koski, & Humphreys, 1995). Problems with encoding and retrieving new information are also commonly observed (Levin, Ewing-Cobbs, & Eisenberg, 1995). Executive functions (i.e., organizing, self-monitoring, reasoning, and judgment) are often significantly impaired, resulting in social, behavioral, and affect-regulation difficulties as well as academic struggles. Children with TBI often experience difficulties in everyday activities that require them to apply and/or generalize previously learned information in a new way, retain information over time, and focus or monitor attentional effort over time (Ewing-Cobbs, Levin, & Fletcher, 1998). These weaknesses may not readily be apparent without observation of behaviors and cognitive functioning within the naturalistic context of the child's classroom. This type of collaborative, multidisciplinary assessment is essential to highlight the impact of the child's injury on daily functioning and plan for an effective rehabilitation program (Ylvisaker, 1998).

In most clinical settings, rehabilitation programs for severe TBI in children involve a multidisciplinary team of professionals (physicians, nurses, occupational therapists, psychologists, speech and language psychologists, social workers, and teachers), each working to enhance functioning. Empirical studies examining the effectiveness of rehabilitation with this population are sparse. In general, the literature consists mostly of descriptive case studies that are not designed to evaluate efficacy. Published studies lack control groups of children matched on injury variables and preinjury demographic variables, and children have not been randomized to receive the intervention (Michaud, 1995). Additionally, many rehabilitative approaches are borrowed from adult models and applied to children, with little attention to the vast differences between children and adults in brain development, cognitive processes, and the role of the family in recovery (Ylvisaker & Szekeres, 1998). Early rehabilitation programs focused on improving discrete cognitive processes via hierarchically graded retraining exercises or by promoting compensation for specific cognitive weaknesses by teaching specific strategies in an office-bound setting. While techniques such as these often result in performance gains on rehabilitation-specific tasks, they seldom transfer to functional activities in the child's life (e.g., Frazen, Roberts, Schmits, Verduyn, & Manshdi, 1996), and the extent to which these gains are maintained over time is unclear. This has led to a call for greater inclusion of functional tasks into rehabilitation programs to bridge the gap between skills being taught and "real-life functioning" (Gordon & Hibbard, 1992, p. 364).

More recently, Ylvisaker (1998) proposed a framework for cognitive rehabilitation, which emphasizes an integrated, nonhierarchical, contextual approach that promotes enhanced cognition as well as improved performance of functional activities. Unlike traditional adult models, this framework stresses the importance of collaboration with "everyday people" (e.g., teachers, family members) as key members of the child's rehabilitation team (Ylvisaker & Feeney, 1998, p. 9). This model acknowledges the competence of family members, teachers, and others who have contact with the child daily, and looks to them to provide valuable insights into the child's strengths, weaknesses, and motivation. Rehabilitation efforts are focused toward meaningful, pragmatic aspects of the child's functioning such as enhancing school performance (by improving planning, organization, and memory functioning), prevention behavior problems (via contingency management), and decreasing social isolation (by increasing social contacts and improving social relations). Ylvisaker argues that provision of rehabilitation services in multiple settings encourages generalization and promotes maintenance of gains. Embedding training in functional tasks from the outset, rather than beginning with retraining exercises that have less application to real-world settings, is also presumed to facilitate generalization. Involving and training nonprofessionals in the rehabilitation program is particularly important with managed care health insurance, which has often reduced the intensity and duration of services provided.

Finally, in planning a comprehensive intervention program for children with TBI, it is important to remember that the child's social ecology is impacted (Waaland, 1998). Children may be painfully aware that school and learning are now much more difficult than prior to their injury. They may feel abandoned by friends and unable to be involved in activities they enjoyed previously because of physical or cognitive limitations. Parents are confronted with how to manage the multiple needs of their previously healthy child. Family members may each have very different beliefs about the child's current behaviors/abilities and potential for recovery. Siblings too may feel confused, neglected, and may blame themselves for their sibling's injury. It is particularly important to be aware of family beliefs and reactions to the child's injury, as family environment (e.g., family stress, burden) has been shown to have an impact on psychosocial and behavioral outcomes (Taylor et al., 1995). This underscores the importance of involving and supporting whole families throughout the rehabilitation process.

Pediatric Brain Tumors

With increasing numbers of survivors of pediatric brain tumors, attention has turned to the impact of these diseases and treatments on quality of life. Increased survival has been linked to medical, cognitive, and psychological sequelae; children who survive pediatric brain tumors are more frequently at risk for significant late effects from the tumor and the treatment than other childhood cancer survivors (Ris & Noll, 1994).

Children with brain tumors are at risk for cognitive impairment due to the nature and location of the disease process and of frequently used irradiation treatment. Ris and Noll (1994) noted that most studies of neuropsychological functioning after brain tumor diagnosis and treatment contain samples that include various tumor types located in different brain areas, making generalizations regarding cognitive deficits difficult. Nevertheless, there are some consistencies; research suggests that children with supratentorial tumors are at greater risk for intellectual impairment than infratentorial tumors (Mulhern, Crisco, & Kun, 1983; Mulhern & Kun, 1985), and that the pattern of deficits for children with brain tumors resembles the pattern found in children with nonverbal learning disabilities (Buono et al., 1998).

Children who are treated for brain tumors exhibit lower social competence, fewer and more negative peer relationships, and more problematic social adjustment than healthy children (Foley, Barakat, Herman-Liu, Radcliffe, & Molloy, 2000; Mulhern, Hancock, Fairclough, & Kun, 1992; Vannatta, Garstein, Short, & Noll, 1998). Furthermore, studies have shown an association between special education placement and poor social adjustment in childhood cancer survivors (Deasy-Spinetta, Spinetta, & Oxman, 1989; Kazak & Meadows, 1989).

Research on interventions to address the apparent social skills deficits that underlie problems in social adaptation of children with brain tumors is limited. The limited data on brain tumor survivors suggests that social skills training may be helpful for some survivors (Die-Trill et al., 1996). In addition, there is a published report of the successful use of social skills training with survivors of childhood cancer (Varni, Katz, Colegrove, & Dolgin, 1993), but children with brain tumors were not included in the sample. The authors evaluated individual social skills training as a supplement to a standard school reintegration program for children with cancer. Using a random sample of 64 children between the ages of 5 and 13 years old, they found that those children who received the social skills training reported higher perceived peer and teacher social support at a nine-month follow-up compared to baseline levels. Furthermore, parents of these children reported decreased internalizing and externalizing behavior problems and an increase in social competence. By contrast, the standard treatment group did not report any significant change in social or behavioral functioning. The literature on the effectiveness of social skills training with samples similar to children with brain tumor, such as children with learning disabilities, is promising (Schneider, 1992); social skills training programs have been widely used with this population for more than 20 years (Kavale & Forness, 1996). Schneider (1992) reported that social skills programs were more successful when used with socially withdrawn children who are much like brain tumor survivors.

One of the authors (LPB) is involved in a pilot study testing a manual-based, social skills training intervention for 8- to 13-year-old children treated for brain tumors and assessing the association of neuropsychological functioning with social skills and with children's ability to benefit from the intervention. The training took place in six weekly groups of five to eight children and had a closely linked parent component. Targeted social skills were nonverbal social skills, starting, maintaining, and finishing conversations, giving compliments, empathy and conflict resolution, and cooperation. In each session, homework was reviewed first while parents were present, then specific skills were presented, examples demonstrated, and role-plays undertaken. Children were given weekly homework assignments. The parent component involved education and information regarding the targeted social skills, problem-solving barriers to practicing social skills, and discussions of the impact of the brain tumor on the child and on the family. Initial feedback from families was positive, and attendance was consistent. Preliminary findings support an association of neuropsychological functioning with social skills (Carey, 2000) and improved social skills and social functioning from baseline to a nine-month follow-up assessment. The findings suggest that further research to test social skills training in an empirically rigorous manner is required.

Transplantation

In the past 15 years, transplantation has become the treatment of choice for children with end stage disease due largely to the availability of effective immunosuppressive agents. Solid organ transplants (such as kidney, cardiovascular, and liver) and stem cell transplants are the most common pediatric transplants in children and adolescents. Multiple organ transplants remain experimental in children and adolescents. Three-year survival rates vary by type of transplant and age of the child (younger children have poorer survival rates), but the rates vary between 70% and 90% (Stuber & Canning, 1998).

Children treated with transplantation show psychological difficulties similar to those reported for other children with chronic illnesses. For instance, DeBolt, Stewart, Kennard, Petrik, and Andrews (1995) used standardized measures of child and family functioning to compare 41 children and adolescents at least four years post-liver transplant with published norms for chronically ill and medically well children. Although the functioning of the transplant patients was similar to that of children with chronic illness, children with transplants showed lower social competence and more functional difficulties than the medically well children. The impact of the transplant on family functioning was less significant than with other children with chronic illness. Age at hospitalization, years posttransplant, and other demographic factors were not associated with child and family functioning. Similar findings were reported in a study of children and their families awaiting heart or heart-lung transplantation at two points six months apart, with the exception that family and marital stress were significant (Serrano-Ikkos, Lask, & Whitehead, 1997). In a review of the literature on cognitive and psychological functioning of children who have undergone heart transplant, Todaro and colleagues (2000) found that children with complicated transplants (such as those who experience infection or rejection) are at risk for problematic cognitive functioning, and children in the first year posttransplant may be at risk for psychological difficulties. However, children's distress reduces over time and children without complications do not show problematic cognitive outcomes. Subclinical levels of distress have been reported for parents of children undergoing transplantation especially prior to admission, compared to during and after the transplant (Heiney, Neuberg, Myers, & Bergman, 1994; Streisand, Rodrique, Houck, Graham-Pole, & Berlant, 2000).

The psychological transplantation literature is sparse, reflecting insufficient standardization of assessment strategies and few empirical studies of interventions. From the extant literature, assessment and intervention in organ and bone marrow transplants are approached on multiple levels (patient, family, and health care context) and over three phases of transplant: pretransplant, during the transplant, and posttransplant (Stuber & Canning, 1998). Unlike adult transplant, assessment pretransplant usually does not serve as a gatekeeper to transplant in pediatrics but as a method for anticipating problems with adjustment to the transplant and adherence with burdensome hospitalization and medical interventions during and after. Specifically, pretransplant assessment focuses on child and parent psychological adjustment, the child's cognitive functioning as it impacts ability to understand and to adhere to treatment, the availability of social support during the hospitalization, understanding of the transplant and commitment to the procedure by both the child and at least one parent, and current and past treatment adherence issues (Shaw & Taussig, 1999).

Interventions pretransplant are aimed at preparing the child and family for the stress of transplant hospitalization by addressing misunderstandings about the procedure, by treating problems in adjustment, and by teaching the child and the family adaptive coping strategies and cognitive-behavioral approaches to pain management. In addition, pretransplant interventions aim to improve outcome by building strong alliances between families and the medical team and bolstering family and community supports. Streisand et al. (2000) reported a pilot intervention aimed at improving the coping responses of parents of children undergoing bone marrow transplantation. A stress-inoculation approach, with cognitive and behavioral components, was implemented in a randomized, controlled, one-session design. The authors reported that parents who participated in the intervention showed more adaptive coping efforts, suggesting that the intervention was successful in teaching parents stress-reduction techniques. However, the change in coping did not result in less distress for intervention parents when compared to parents receiving standard transplant care.

During the transplant, which involves an extensive period of hospitalization, psychological and physical aspects of the transplant are the foci of assessment and intervention. Most commonly, pain management, reduction of the fear, anger, and anxiety associated with pain and prolonged hospitalization, addressing withdrawal often exhibited by children, and addressing strains in the relationship of staff to families are helpful in this phase (Slater, 1994; Stuber & Canning, 1998).

Transplantation is associated with long-term medical complications including rejection of the organ or bone marrow, secondary infection, and effects of long-term use of immuno-suppressive agents (Sormanti, Dungan, & Rieker, 1994). Moreover, limitations on quality of life remain due to continued medical complications (Zamberlan, 1992), and concerns about prognosis, parental adjustment, and finances continue (Sormanti et al., 1994). Future directions for research in transplantation include the prospective assessment of stress and adjustment in children and their parents. This information may be used in the development and systematic evaluation of interventions particularly focused on implementation early in the transplant process (Streisand et al., 2000).

CONCLUSIONS

We have integrated the literature on interventions in child health psychology developing four assumptions and within the framework of levels of intervention, universal, selective, and indicated. Although a number of well-established interventions have been identified, systematic intervention research to establish the effectiveness of interventions for the broad range of child health issues is in its beginning stages. Reflecting on the surprising lack of published intervention studies in pediatric psychology, Drotar (1997) discusses several barriers that have limited this literature. The inherent difficulties in conducting intervention trials, combined with increasing pressures for pediatric psychologists to focus on provision of direct services to patients and families, can be significant impediments. At the same time, as Drotar notes, there are several avenues by which research on child health interventions can partner with, and enhance, the overall quality of care provided to children and families. For example, there is increased acknowledgment of the importance of psychosocial well-being and function as an outcome of pediatric treatments. While research and clinical practice have often been viewed as separate activities by child health psychologists, more attention to the acceptability (social validity) of psychological interventions, to patients, families, and staff, may lead to increased interest and support for our efforts to provide treatments with empirically supported outcomes.

Future directions for intervention research in child health psychology have been delineated throughout this chapter. We focus on three goals here. First is the integration of psychological and pediatric interventions and outcomes. In procedural pain, for example, evaluation of approaches combining pharmacological and psychological interventions (e.g., sedative, anxiolytic, or pain medication plus CBT) has proven helpful. Work related to treatment adherence must consider medical variables to maximize resolution of these problems.

Second, some of the most effective treatments in Table 19.1 rely on combined approaches; therefore, it will be important to understand what elements of the intervention are contributing to its effectiveness. This may allow for greater precision in the development of interventions and for refinement of interventions that may facilitate their acceptability to patients, families, and health care providers. Alternatively, it allows us to step back and view the field of child health intervention more broadly. For example, what general characteristics of interventions are important and how can we maximize these more generic contributors? It is critical that we be able to say that an intervention was delivered in the manner that it was intended, or that the interventionist was adherent to the treatment manual or protocol and competent in the implementation. Establishing this type of validation for the delivery of interventions is crucial (Moncher & Prinz, 1991).

Finally, research on issues that cut across disease groups may be facilitated using family systems theory and intervention. The child health psychology literature is generally organized by medical disease groups, attendant to the National Institutes of Health's organization by disease-defined Institutes. Yet, as Table 19.1 indicates, the generally effective methods are highly consistent across diseases. It appears that there are commonalities to the types of experiences that children with various chronic illnesses and their families have (e.g., disruption, fear, ongoing needs for care, worries about other children) although there are specific aspects of particular diseases and treatments that may be common to some but not all illnesses (e.g., dietary requirements, cognitive impairments, restrictions in mobility).

In conclusion, child health psychology is a growing field in which psychological knowledge is applied to address the concerns of pediatric health and illness. A broad, contextual orientation provides a framework for integrating research and clinical practice to support children, families, and health care providers as they confront challenges related to children's well-being. The field is diverse; the current primary challenge of child health psychology is the development and evaluation of effective interventions with sufficient flexibility to address the entire range of diseases, treatments, and related child and family adjustment.

REFERENCES

Anderson, C., Zeltzer, L., & Fanurik, D. (1993). Procedural pain. In N. L. Schechter, C. B. Berde, & M. Yaster (Eds.), *Pain in infants, children and adolescents* (pp. 435–458). Baltimore: Williams & Wilkins.

Barakat, L. P., Kazak, A. E., Meadows, A. T., Casey, R., Meeske, K., & Stuber, M. L. (1997). Families surviving childhood cancer: A comparison of posttraumatic stress symptoms with families of health children. *Journal of Pediatric Psychology, 22,* 843–859.

Barakat, L. P., & Linney, J. A. (1992). Children with physical handicaps and their mothers: The interrelation of social support, maternal adjustment and child adjustment. *Journal of Pediatric Psychology, 17,* 725–739.

Belsky, J. (1993). Etiology of child maltreatment: A developmental-ecological analysis. *Psychological Bulletin, 114,* 413–434.

Bleil, M. E., Ramesh, S., Miller, B. C., & Wood, B. L. (2000). The influence of parent-child relatedness on depressive symptoms in children with asthma: Tests of moderator and mediator models. *Journal of Pediatric Psychology, 25,* 481–491.

Bond, G. G., Aiken, L. S., & Somerville, S. C. (1992). The health belief model and adolescents with insulin-dependent diabetes mellitus. *Health Psychology, 11,* 190–198.

Bronfenbrenner, U. (1979). *The ecology of human development.* Cambridge, MA: Harvard University Press.

Brown, R. T., Armstrong, F. D., & Eckman, J. R. (1993). Neurocognitive aspects of pediatric sickle cell disease. *Journal of Learning Disabilities, 26,* 33–45.

Brown, R. T., Kaslow, N. J., Doepke, K., Buchanan, I., Eckman, J., Baldwin, K., et al. (1993). Psychosocial and family functioning in children with sickle cell syndrome and their mothers. *Journal of the American Academy of Child and Adolescent Psychiatry, 32,* 545–553.

Buono, L. A., Morris, M. K., Morris, R. D., Krawiecki, N., Norris, F. H., Foster, M. A., et al. (1998). Evidence for the syndrome of nonverbal learning disabilities in children with brain tumors. *Child Neuropsychology, 4,* 144–157.

Butler, R. W., Rizzi, L. P., & Handwerger, B. A. (1996). Brief report: The assessment of posttraumatic stress disorder in pediatric cancer patients and survivors. *Journal of Pediatric Psychology, 21,* 499–504.

Carey, M. (2001, April). Neuropsychological functioning and social functioning in children treated for brain tumors: Evidence of nonverbal learning disabilities. *Dissertation Abstracts International, 61*(9-B), 4974.

Chadwick, O., Rutter, M., Shaffer, D., & Shrout, P. E. (1981). A prospective study of children with head injuries. IV: Specific cognitive deficits. *Journal of Clinical Neuropsychology, 3,* 101–110.

Chambless, D. L., & Hollon, S. D. (1998). Defining empirically supported therapies. *Journal of Consulting and Clinical Psychology, 66,* 7–18.

Chen, E., Craske, M. G., Katz, E., Schwartz, E., & Zeltzer, L. (2000). Pain sensitive temperament: Does it predict procedural distress and response to psychological treatment among children with cancer? *Journal of Pediatric Psychology, 25,* 269–278.

Chen, E., Joseph, M., & Zeltzer, L. (2000). Behavioral and cognitive interventions in the treatment of pain in children. *Pediatric Clinics of North America, 47,* 513–525.

Christiaanse, M. E., Lavigne, J. V., & Lerner, C. V. (1989). Psychosocial aspects of compliance in children and adolescents with asthma. *Journal of Developmental and Behavioral Pediatrics, 10,* 75–80.

Clay, D. L., Wood, P. K., Frank, R. G., Hagglund, K. J., & Johnson, J. C. (1995). Examining systematic differences in adaptation to chronic illness: A growth modeling approach. *Rehabilitation Psychology, 40,* 61–70.

Cozzi, L., Tryon, W. W., & Sedlacek, K. (1987). The effectiveness of biofeedback-assisted relaxation in modifying sickle cell crises. *Biofeedback and Self-Regulation, 12,* 51–61.

Creer, T. (1998). Childhood asthma. In T. H. Ollendick & M. Hersen (Eds.), *Handbook of child psychopathology* (3rd ed., pp. 395–415). New York: Plenum Press.

Da Costa, I. G., Rapoff, M. A., Lemanek, K., & Goldstein, G. L. (1997). Improving adherence to medication regimens for children with asthma and its effect on clinical outcome. *Journal of Applied Behavior Analysis, 30,* 687–691.

Dahlquist, L. M. (1999). *Pediatric pain management.* New York: Kluwer Academic/Plenum Press.

Dahlquist, L. M., Gil, K., Armstrong, F. D., DeLawyer, D. D., Greene, P., & Wuori, D. (1986). Preparing children for medical examinations: The importance of previous medical experience. *Health Psychology, 5,* 249–259.

Dahlquist, L. M., Power, T., & Carlson, L. (1995). Physician and parent behavior during invasive cancer procedures: Relationship to child behavioral distress. *Journal of Pediatric Psychology, 20,* 477–490.

Dahlquist, L. M., Power, T., Cox, C., & Fernbach, D. (1994). Parenting and child distress during cancer procedures: A multidimensional assessment. *Children's Health Care, 23,* 149–166.

Deasy-Spinetta, P., Spinetta, J., & Oxman, J. (1989). The relationship between learning deficits and social adaptation in children with leukemia. *Journal of Psychosocial Oncology, 6,* 109–121.

DeBolt, A. J., Stewart, S. M., Kennard, B. D., Petrik, K., & Andrews, W. S. (1995). A survey of psychosocial adaptation in long-term survivors of pediatric liver transplants. *Children's Health Care, 24,* 79–96.

Delamater, A. M., Bubb, J., Davis, S. G., Smith, J. A., Schmidt, L., White, N. H., et al. (1990). Randomized prospective study of self-management training with newly diagnosed diabetic children. *Diabetes Care, 13,* 492–498.

Dennis, M., Wilkinson, M., Koski, L., & Humphreys, R. P. (1995). Attention deficits in the long term after childhood head injury. In S. H. Broman & M. E. Michel (Eds.), *Traumatic head injury in children* (pp. 165–187). New York: Oxford University Press.

Die-Trill, M., Bromberg, J., LaVally, B., Portales, L. A., SanFeliz, A., & Patenaude, A. F. (1996). Development of social skills in boys with brain tumors: A group approach. *Journal of Psychosocial Oncology, 14,* 23–41.

Dinges, D. P., Whitehouse, W. G., Carota-Orne, E., Bloom, P. B., Carlin, M. M., Bauer, N. K., et al. (1997). Self-hypnosis training as an adjunctive treatment in the management of pain associated with sickle cell disease. *International Journal of Clinical and Experimental Hypnosis, 65,* 417–432.

Drotar, D. (1997). Intervention research: Pushing back the frontiers of pediatric psychology. *Journal of Pediatric Psychology, 22,* 593–606.

Edgeworth, J., & Carr, A. (2000). Child abuse. In A. Carr (Ed.), *What works with children and adolescents?: A critical review of psychological interventions with children, adolescents and their families* (pp. 17–48). Florence, KY: Taylor & Francis/Routledge.

Embury, S. H., Hebbel, R. P., Mohandas, N., & Steinberg, M. H. (Eds.). (1994). *Sickle cell disease: Basic Books principles and clinical practice.* New York: Raven Press.

Ewing-Cobbs, L., Levin, H. S., & Fletcher, J. M. (1998). Neuropsychological sequelae after pediatric traumatic brain injury: Advances since 1985. In M. Ylvisaker (Ed.), *Traumatic brain injury rehabilitation: Children and adolescents* (pp. 11–26). Boston: Butterworth-Heinemann.

Fanurik, D., Koh, J., Schmidtz, M., & Brown, R. (1997). Pharmacobehavioral intervention: Integrating pharmacologic and behavioral techniques for pediatric medical procedures. *Children's Health Care, 26,* 31–46.

Fehrenbach, A. M. B., & Peterson, L. (1989). Parental problem-solving skills, stress, and dietary compliance in phenylketonuria. *Journal of Consulting and Clinical Psychology, 57,* 237–241.

Finney, J. W., Christophersen, E. R., Friman, P. C., Kalnins, I. V., Maddux, J. E., Peterson, L., et al. (1993). Society of Pediatric Psychology Task Force Report: Pediatric psychology and injury control. *Journal of Pediatric Psychology, 18,* 499–526.

Finney, J. W., Lemanek, K. L., Brophy, C. J., & Cataldo, M. F. (1990). Pediatric appointment keeping: Improving adherence in a primary care allergy clinic. *Journal of Pediatric Psychology, 15,* 571–579.

Foley, B., Barakat, L. P., Herman-Liu, A., Radcliffe, J., & Molloy, P. (2000). The impact of childhood hypothalamic/chiasmatic brain tumors on child adjustment and family functioning. *Children's Health Care, 29,* 209–223.

Fortenberry, J. D., & Zimet, G. D. (1999). Received social support for sexually transmitted disease-related care-seeking among adolescents. *Journal of Adolescent Health, 25,* 174–178.

Fowler-Kerry, S. (1990). Adolescent oncology survivors' recollection of pain. In D. C. Tyler & E. J. Krane (Eds.), *Pediatric pain: Advances in pain research and therapy* (Vol. 15, pp. 365–372). New York: Raven Press.

Frazen, K. M., Roberts, M. A., Schmits, D., Verduyn, W., & Manshdi, F. (1996). Cognitive remediation in pediatric traumatic brain injury. *Child Neuropsychology, 2,* 176–184.

Freed, G. L., Bordley, W. C., & Defriese, G. H. (1993). Childhood immunization programs: An analysis of policy issues. *Milbank Quarterly, 71,* 65–96.

Gavin, L. A., Wamboldt, M. Z., Sorokin, N., Levy, S. Y., & Wamboldt, F. S. (1999). Treatment alliance and its association with family functioning, adherence, and medical outcome in adolescents with severe, chronic asthma. *Journal of Pediatric Psychology, 24,* 355–365.

Gil, K. M., Anthony, K. K., Carson, J. W., Redding-Lallinger, R., Daeschner, C. W., & Ware, R. E. (2001). Daily coping practice predicts treatment effects in children with sickle cell disease. *Journal of Pediatric Psychology, 26,* 163–174.

Gil, K. M., Williams, D. A., Thompson, R. J., & Kinney, T. R. (1991). Sickle cell disease in children and adolescents: The relation of child and parent pain coping strategies to adjustment. *Journal of Pediatric Psychology, 16,* 643–663.

Goldstein, K. P., Lauderdale, D. S., Glushak, C., Walter, J., & Daum, R. S. (1999). Immunization outreach in an inner-city housing development: Reminder-recall on foot. *Pediatrics, 104,* e69.

Greenan-Fowler, E., Powell, C., & Varni, J. W. (1987). Behavioral treatment of adherence to therapeutic exercise by children with hemophilia. *Archives of Physical Medicine and Rehabilitation, 68,* 846–849.

Gordon, W. A., & Hibbard, M. R. (1992). Critical issues in cognitive remediation. *Neuropsychology, 6,* 361–370.

Guyer, B., & Ellers, B. (1990). Childhood injuries in the United States: Mortality, morbidity, and cost. *American Journal of Diseases of Children, 144,* 649–652.

Haggerty, R., Roghmann, K., & Pless, I. (1975). *Child health and the community.* New York: Wiley.

Hazinski, M. F., Eddy, V. A., & Morris, J. A. J. (1995). Children's traffic safety program: Influence of early elementary school safety education on family seat belt use. *Journal of Trauma, 39,* 1063–1068.

Heiney, S. P., Neuberg, R. W., Myers, D., & Bergman, L. H. (1994). The aftermath of bone marrow transplantation for parents of pediatric patients: A post-traumatic stress disorder. *Oncology Nursing Forum, 21,* 843–847.

Hermann, C., Kim, M., & Blanchard, E. B. (1995). Behavioral and prophylactic pharmacological interventions studies of pediatric migraine: An exploratory meta-analysis. *Pain, 60,* 239–256.

Hillier, L. M., & Morrongiello, B. A. (1998). Age and gender differences in school-age children's appraisals of injury risk. *Journal of Pediatric Psychology, 23,* 229–238.

Holden, E. W., Deichmann, M. M., & Levy, J. D. (1999). Empirically supported treatments in pediatric psychology: Recurrent pediatric headache. *Journal of Pediatric Psychology, 24,* 91–109.

Holden, E. W., Rawlins, C., & Gladstein, J. (1998). Children's coping with recurrent headache. *Journal of Clinical Psychology in Medical Settings, 5,* 147–158.

Hurtig, A. L., Koepke, D., & Park, K. B. (1989). Relation between severity of chronic illness and adjustment in children and adolescents with sickle cell anemia. *Journal of Pediatric Psychology, 14,* 117–132.

Hurtig, A. L., & Viera, C. T. (1986). *Sickle cell disease: Psychological and psychosocial Issues.* Chicago: University of Illinois Press.

Hurtig, A. L., & White, L. S. (1986). Psychosocial adjustment in children and adolescents with sickle cell disease. *Journal of Pediatric Psychology, 11,* 411–427.

Jacobson, A. M., Hauser, S. T., Lavori, P., Wolfsdorf, J. I., Herskowitz, R. D., Milley, J. E., et al. (1990). Adherence among children and adolescents with insulin-dependent diabetes mellitus over a four-year longitudinal follow-up: I. The influence of patient coping and adjustment. *Journal of Pediatric Psychology, 15,* 511–526.

Janicke, D., & Finney, J. (1999). Empirically supported treatments in pediatric psychology: Recurrent abdominal pain. *Journal of Pediatric Psychology, 24,* 115–127.

Janz, N. K., & Becker, M. H. (1984). The health belief model: A decade later. *Health Education Quarterly, 11,* 1–47.

Jay, S., Elliott, C., Woody, P., & Siegel, S. (1991). An investigation of cognitive-behavioral therapy combined with oral valium for children undergoing medical procedures. *Health Psychology, 10,* 317–322.

Jelalian, E., & Saelens, B. (1999). Empirically supported treatments in pediatric psychology: Pediatric obesity. *Journal of Pediatric Psychology, 25,* 223–248.

Johnson, S. B. (1998). Juvenile diabetes. In T. H. Ollendick & M. Hersen (Eds.), *Handbook of child psychopathology* (3rd ed., pp. 417–434). New York: Plenum Press.

Kagan, J. (1965). The new marriage: Pediatrics and psychology. *American Journal of Diseases of Childhood, 110,* 272–278.

Kanoy, K. W., & Schroeder, C. S. (1985). Suggestions to parents about common behavior problems in a pediatric primary care office. *Journal of Pediatric Psychology, 10,* 15–30.

Kavale, K., & Forness, S. (1996). Social skills deficits and learning disabilities: A meta-analysis. *Journal of Learning Disabilities, 29,* 226–237.

Kazak, A. E. (1988). Stress and social networks in families with older institutionalized retarded children. *Journal of Social and Clinical Psychology, 6,* 448–461.

Kazak, A. E., & Barakat, L. P. (1997). Parenting stress and quality of life during treatment for childhood leukemia predicts child and parent adjustment after treatment ends. *Journal of Pediatric Psychology, 22,* 749–758.

Kazak, A. E., Barakat, L. P., Meeske, K., Christakis, D., Meadows, A. T., Casey, R., et al. (1997). Post traumatic stress, family functioning, and social support in survivors of childhood leukemia and their mothers and fathers. *Journal of Consulting and Clinical Psychology, 65,* 120–129.

Kazak, A. E., Blackall, G., Boyer, B., Brophy, P., Buzaglo, J., Penati, B., et al. (1996). Implementing a pediatric leukemia intervention for procedural pain: The impact on staff. *Families, Systems and Health, 14,* 43–56.

Kazak, A. E., & Marvin, R. (1984). Differences, difficulties, and adaptation: Stress and social networks in families with a handicapped child. *Family Relations, 33,* 67–77.

Kazak, A. E., & Meadows, A. T. (1989). Families of young adolescents who have survived cancer: Social-emotional adjustment, adaptability, and social support. *Journal of Pediatric Psychology, 14,* 175–191.

Kazak, A. E., Penati, B., Brophy, P., & Himelstein, B. (1998). Pharmacologic and psychologic interventions for procedural pain. *Pediatrics, 102,* 59–66.

Kazak, A. E., Reber, M., & Carter, A. (1988). Structural and qualitative aspects of social networks in families with young chronically ill children. *Journal of Pediatric Psychology, 13,* 171–182.

Kazak, A. E., Reber, M., & Snitzer, L. (1988). Childhood chronic disease and family functioning: A study of phenylketonuria. *Pediatrics, 81,* 224–230.

Kazak, A. E., Simms, S., Barakat, L. P., Hobbie, W., Foley, B., Golomb, V., et al. (1999). Surviving Cancer Competently Intervention Program (SCCIP): A cognitive-behavioral and family therapy intervention for adolescent survivors of childhood cancer and their families. *Family Process, 38,* 175–191.

Kazak, A. E., Stuber, M. L., Barakat, L. P., & Meeske, K. (1996). Assessing posttraumatic stress related to medical illness and treatment: The Impact of Traumatic Stressors Interview Schedule (ITSIS). *Families, Systems, and Health, 14,* 365–380.

Kazak, A. E., & Wilcox, B. (1984). The structure and function of social support networks in families with a handicapped child. *American Journal of Community Psychology, 12,* 645–661.

Kerwin, M. (1999). Empirically supported treatments in pediatric psychology: Severe feeding problems. *Journal of Pediatric Psychology, 24,* 193–214.

Klassen, T. P., MacKay, J. M., Moher, D., Walker, A., & Jones, A. L. (2000). Community-based injury prevention interventions. *Future of Children, 10,* 83–110.

Knutson, J. F., & DeVet, K. A. (1995). Physical abuse, sexual abuse, and neglect. In M. C. Roberts (Ed.), *Handbook of pediatric psychology* (2nd ed., pp. 589–616). New York: Guilford Press.

Korsch, B. M., Fine, R. N., & Negrete, V. F. (1978). Noncompliance in children with renal transplants. *Pediatrics, 61,* 872–876.

Kraus, J. F. (1995). Epidemiological features of brain injury in children: Occurrence, children at risk, causes and manner of injury, severity, and outcomes. In S. H. Broman & M. E. Michel (Eds.), *Traumatic head injury in children* (pp. 22–39). New York: Oxford University Press.

Kraus, J. F., Rock, A., & Hamyari, P. (1990). Brain injuries among children, adolescents, and young adults. *American Journal of Diseases of Children, 144,* 684–691.

Kronenfeld, J. J., & Glik, D. C. (1995). Unintentional injury: A major health problem for young children and youth. *Journal of Family and Economic Issues, 16,* 365–393.

Kumar, S., Powars, D., Allen, J., & Haywood, L. J. (1976). Anxiety, self-concept, and personal and social adjustments in children with sickle cell anemia. *Journal of Pediatrics, 88,* 858–863.

Kupst, M. J., Natta, M. B., Richardson, C. C., Schulman, J. L., Lavigne, J. V., & Das, L. (1995). Family coping with pediatric leukemia: Ten years after treatment. *Journal of Pediatric Psychology, 20,* 601–617.

Labbe, E. E. (1999). Commentary: Salient aspects of research in pediatric headache and future directions. *Journal of Pediatric Psychology, 24,* 113–114.

La Greca, A. M. (1990). Issues in adherence with pediatric regimens. *Journal of Pediatric Psychology, 15,* 423–436.

La Greca, A. M., & Schuman, W. B. (1995). Adherence to prescribed medical regimens. In M. C. Roberts (Ed.), *Handbook of pediatric psychology* (2nd ed., pp. 55–83). New York: Guilford Press.

Lemanek, K. L., Buckloh, L. M., Woods, G., & Butler, R. (1995). Diseases of the circulatory system: Sickle cell disease and hemophilia. In M. C. Roberts (Ed.), *Handbook of pediatric psychology* (2nd ed., pp. 286–309). New York: Guilford Press.

Lemanek, K. L., Horwitz, W., & Ohene-Frempong, K. (1994). A multiperspective investigation of social competence in children with sickle cell disease. *Journal of Pediatric Psychology, 19,* 443–456.

Levin, H. S., Ewing-Cobbs, L., & Eisenberg, H. M. (1995). Neurobehavioral outcome of pediatric closed head injury. In S. H. Broman & M. E. Michel (Eds.), *Traumatic head injury in children* (pp. 70–94). New York: Oxford University Press.

Manne, S. L. (1999). Commentary: Well-established treatments for procedure-related pain: Issues for future research and policy implications. *Journal of Pediatric Psychology, 24,* 147.

Manne, S. L., Redd, W. H., Jacobsen, P. B., Gorfinkle, K., Schorr, O., & Rapkin, B. (1990). Behavioral intervention to reduce child and parent distress during venipuncture. *Journal of Consulting and Clinical Psychology, 58,* 565–572.

McGrath, M., Mellon, M., & Murphy, L. (2000). Empirically supported treatments in pediatric psychology: Constipation and encopresis. *Journal of Pediatric Psychology, 25,* 225–254.

McGrath, P. J. (1999). Commentary: Recurrent headaches: Making what works available to those who need it. *Journal of Pediatric Psychology, 24,* 111–112.

McGrath, P. J., Humphreys, P., Keene, D., Goodman, J. T., Lascelles, M. A., Cunningham, S. J., et al. (1992). The efficacy and efficiency of a self-administered treatment for adolescent migraine. *Pain, 49,* 321–324.

McGrath, P. J., & Larsson, B. (1997). Headache in children and adolescents. *Child and Adolescent Psychiatric Clinics of North America, 6,* 843–861.

McQuaid, E., & Nassau, J. (1999). Empirically supported treatments of disease-related symptoms in pediatric psychology: Asthma, diabetes, and cancer. *Journal of Pediatric Psychology, 24,* 305–328.

Mellon, M., & McGrath, M. (2000). Empirically supported treatments in pediatric psychology: Nocturnal enuresis. *Journal of Pediatric Psychology, 25,* 193–214.

Melman, S. T., Nguyen, T. T., Ehrlich, E., Schorr, M., & Anbar, R. D. (1999). Parental compliance with multiple immunization injections. *Archives of Pediatric and Adolescent Medicine, 153,* 1289–1291.

Michaud, L. (1995). Evaluating efficacy of rehabilitation after pediatric traumatic brain injury. In S. H. Broman & M. E. Michel (Eds.), *Traumatic head injury in children* (pp. 247–257). New York: Oxford University Press.

Miller, T. R., Romano, E. O., & Spicer, R. S. (2000). The cost of childhood unintentional injuries and the value of prevention. *Future of Children, 10,* 137–163.

Mindell, J. (1999). Empirically supported treatments in pediatric psychology: Bedtime refusal and night wakings in young children. *Journal of Pediatric Psychology, 24,* 465–481.

Miser, A. (1993). Management of pain associated with childhood cancer. In N. L. Schechter, C. B. Berde, & M. Yaster (Eds.), *Pain in infants, children and adolescents* (pp. 411–434). Baltimore: Williams & Wilkins.

Moncher, F. J., & Prinz, R. J. (1991). Treatment fidelity in outcome studies. *Clinical Psychology Review, 11,* 247–266.

Morgan, S. A., & Jackson, J. (1986). Psychological and social concomitants of sickle cell anemia in adolescents. *Journal of Pediatric Psychology, 11,* 429–440.

Mulhern, R. K., Crisco, J. J., & Kun, L. E. (1983). Neuropsychological sequelae of childhood brain tumors: A review. *Journal of Clinical Child Psychology, 12,* 66–73.

Mulhern, R. K., Hancock, J., Fairclough, D., & Kun, L. E. (1992). Neuropsychological status of children treated for brain tumors: A critical review and integrative analysis. *Medical and Pediatric Oncology, 20,* 181–192.

Mulhern, R. K., & Kun, L. E. (1985). Neuropsychologic function in children with brain tumors. III: Interval changes in the six months following treatment. *Medical and Pediatric Oncology, 13,* 318–324.

The National Vaccine Advisory Committee. (1999). Strategies to sustain success in childhood immunizations. *Journal of the American Medical Association, 282,* 363–370.

Nir, Y. (1985). Post-traumatic stress disorder in children with cancer. In S. Eth & R. Pynoos (Eds.), *Post traumatic stress disorders in children* (pp. 121–132). Washington, DC: American Psychiatric Press.

Peterson, L., & Saldana, L. (1996). Accelerating children's risk for injury: Mother's decisions regarding common safety rules. *Journal of Behavioral Medicine, 19,* 317–331.

Powers, S. W. (1999). Empirically supported treatments in pediatric psychology: Procedure-related pain. *Journal of Pediatric Psychology, 24,* 131–145.

Powers, S. W., Blount, R. L., Bachanas, P. J., Cotter, M. W., & Swan, S. C. (1993). Helping preschool leukemia patients and their parents cope during injections. *Journal of Pediatric Psychology, 18,* 681–695.

Reece, R. M. (Ed.). (2000). *Treatment of child abuse: Common ground for mental health, medical, and legal practitioners.* Baltimore: Johns Hopkins University Press.

Ris, M. D., & Noll, R. B. (1994). Long-term neurobehavioral outcome in pediatric brain tumor patients: Review and methodological critique. *Journal of Clinical and Experimental Neuropsychology, 16,* 21–42.

Rivara, F. P., & Mueller, B. A. (1987). The epidemiology and causes of childhood injuries. *Journal of Social Issues, 43,* 13–31.

Roberts, M. C., Fanurik, D., & Layfield, D. A. (1987). Behavioral approaches to prevention of childhood injuries. *Journal of Social Issues, 43,* 105–118.

Roberts, M. C., & Layfield, D. A. (1987). Promoting child passenger safety: A comparison of two positive methods. *Journal of Pediatric Psychology, 12,* 257–271.

Rock, S. M. (1996). Impact of the Illinois Child Passenger Protection Act: A retrospective look. *Accident Analysis and Prevention, 28,* 487–492.

Rodewald, L. E., Szilagyi, P. G., Humiston, S. G., Barth, R., Kraus, R., & Raubertas, R. F. (1999). A randomized study of tracking with outreach and provider prompting to improve immunization coverage and primary care. *Pediatrics, 103,* 31–38.

Rolland, J. S. (1990). Anticipatory loss: A family systems developmental framework. *Family Process, 29,* 229–244.

Rourke, M. T., Stuber, M. L., Hobbie, W. L., & Kazak, A. E. (1999). Posttraumatic stress disorder: Understanding the psychosocial impact of surviving childhood cancer into young adulthood. *Journal of Pediatric Oncology Nursing, 16,* 126–135.

Routh, D. K. (1975). The short history of pediatric psychology. *Journal of Clinical Child Psychology, 4,* 6–8.

Satin, W., La Greca, A. M., Zigo, M. A., & Skyler, J. S. (1989). Diabetes in adolescence: Effects of multifamily group intervention and parent simulation of diabetes. *Journal of Pediatric Psychology, 14,* 259–276.

Schneider, B. H. (1992). Didactic methods for enhancing children's peer relations: A quantitative review. *Clinical Psychology Review, 12,* 363–382.

Schroeder, C. S. (1999). Commentary: A view from the past and a look to the future. *Journal of Pediatric Psychology, 24,* 447–452.

Schwebel, D. C., & Plumert, J. M. (1999). Longitudinal and concurrent relations among temperament, ability estimation, and injury proneness. *Child Development, 70,* 700–712.

Seagull, E. (2000). Beyond mothers and children: Finding the family in pediatric psychology. *Journal of Pediatric Psychology, 25,* 161–169.

Serrano-Ikkos, E., Lask, B., & Whitehead, B. (1997). Psychosocial morbidity in children, and their families, awaiting heart or heart-lung transplantation. *Journal of Psychosomatic Research, 42,* 253–260.

Shaw, R. J., & Taussig, H. N. (1999). Pediatric psychiatric pretransplant evaluation. *Clinical Child Psychology and Psychiatry, 4,* 353–365.

Sherwin, E. D., & O'Shanick, G. J. (1998). From denial to poster child: Growing past the injury. In M. Ylvisaker (Ed.), *Traumatic brain injury rehabilitation: Children and adolescents* (pp. 331–344). Boston: Butterworth-Heinemann.

Sinn, J. S., Morrow, A. L., & Finch, A. B. (1999). Improving immunization rates in private pediatric practices through physician leadership. *Archives of Pediatric and Adolescent Medicine, 153,* 597–603.

Slater, J. A. (1994). Psychiatric aspects of organ transplantation in children and adolescents. *Child and Adolescent Psychiatric Clinics of North America, 3,* 557–598.

Smith, M. Y., Redd, W. H., Peyser, C., & Vogl, D. (1999). Posttraumatic stress disorder in cancer: A review. *Psycho-Oncology, 8,* 521–537.

Sormanti, M., Dungan, S., & Rieker, P. P. (1994). Pediatric bone marrow transplantation: Psychosocial issues for parents after a child's hospitalization. *Journal of Psychosocial Oncology, 12,* 23–42.

Spirito, A. (1999). Introduction to the special series on empirically supported treatments in pediatric psychology. *Journal of Pediatric Psychology, 24,* 87–90.

Streisand, R., Rodrigue, J. R., Houck, C., Graham-Pole, J., & Berlant, N. (2000). Parents of children undergoing bone marrow transplantation: Documenting stress and piloting a psychological intervention program. *Journal of Pediatric Psychology, 25,* 331–337.

Stuber, M. L., & Canning, R. D. (1998). Organ transplantation. In R. T. Ammerman & J. V. Campo (Eds.), *Handbook of pediatric psychology and psychiatry* (Vol. 2, pp. 369–382). Boston: Allyn & Bacon.

Stuber, M. L., Kazak, A. E., Meeske, K., & Barakat, L. P. (1998). Is posttraumatic stress a viable model for understanding responses to childhood cancer? *Child and Adolescent Psychiatric Clinics of North America, 7,* 169–182.

Taylor, H. G., Drotar, D., Wade, S., Yeates, K., Stancin, T., & Klein, S. (1995). Recovery from traumatic brain injury in children: The importance of the family. In S. H. Broman & M. E. Michel (Eds.), *Traumatic head injury in children* (pp. 188–216). New York: Oxford University Press.

Todaro, J. F., Fennell, E. B., Sears, S. F., Rodrigue, J. R., & Roche, A. K. (2000). Review: Cognitive and psychological outcomes in pediatric heart transplantation. *Journal of Pediatric Psychology, 25,* 567–576.

Vannatta, K., Garstein, M. A., Short, A., & Noll, R. B. (1998). A controlled study of peer relationships of children surviving brain tumors: Teacher, peer, and self-ratings. *Journal of Pediatric Psychology, 23,* 279–287.

Varni, J. W. (1999). Commentary: Brief response to Walco et al. *Journal of Pediatric Psychology, 24,* 171.

Varni, J. W., Blount, R. L., Waldron, S. A., & Smith, A. J. (1995). Management of pain and distress. In M. C. Roberts (Ed.), *Handbook of pediatric psychology* (2nd ed., pp. 105–123). New York: Guilford Press.

Varni, J. W., Katz, E. R., Colegrove, R., & Dolgin, M. (1993). The impact of social skills training on the adjustment of children with newly diagnosed cancer. *Journal of Pediatric Psychology, 18,* 751–767.

Waaland, P. K. (1998). Families of children with traumatic brain injury. In M. Ylvisaker (Ed.), *Traumatic brain injury rehabilitation: Children and adolescents* (pp. 345–368). Boston: Butterworth-Heinemann.

Walco, G., Sterling, C., Conte, P., & Engel, R. (1999). Empirically supported treatments in pediatric psychology: Disease-related pain. *Journal of Pediatric Psychology, 24,* 155–167.

Wallander, J. L., & Thompson, R. J., Jr. (1995). Psychosocial adjustment of children with chronic physical conditions. In M. C. Roberts (Ed.), *Handbook of pediatric psychology* (2nd ed., pp. 124–141). New York: Guilford Press.

Webb, P. M., Zimet, G. D., Mays, R., & Fortenberry, J. D. (1999). HIV immunization: Acceptability and anticipated effects on sexual behavior among adolescents. *Journal of Adolescent Health, 25,* 320–322.

Winogron, H. W., Knights, R. M., & Bawden, H. N. (1984). Neuropsychological deficits following head injury in children. *Journal of Clinical Neuropsychology, 6,* 269–278.

Wolfe, D. A. (1991). *Preventing physical and emotional abuse of children.* New York: Guilford Press.

Wright, L. (1967). The pediatric psychologist: A role model. *American Psychologist, 22,* 323–325.

Ylvisaker, M. (1998). Traumatic brain injury in children and adolescents: Introduction. In M. Ylvisaker (Ed.), *Traumatic brain injury rehabilitation: Children and adolescents* (pp. 1–10). Boston: Butterworth-Heinemann.

Ylvisaker, M., & Feeney, T. J. (1998). Everyday people as supports: Developing competences through collaborations. In M. Ylvisaker (Ed.), *Traumatic brain injury rehabilitation: Children and adolescents* (pp. 429–464). Boston: Butterworth-Heinemann.

Ylvisaker, M., & Szekeres, S. F. (1998). A framework for cognitive rehabilitation. In M. Ylvisaker (Ed.), *Traumatic brain injury rehabilitation: Children and adolescents* (pp. 429–464). Boston: Butterworth-Heinemann.

Zamberlan, K. E. W. (1992). Quality of life in school-age children following liver transplantation. *Maternal-Child Nursing Journal, 20,* 167–229.

Zeltzer, L., Altman, A., Cohen, D., LeBaron, S., Munuksela, L., & Schechter, N. (1990). Report of the subcommittee on the management of pain associated with procedures in children with cancer. *Pediatrics, 86,* 826–831.

Zeltzer, L. K., Dash, J., & Holland, J. P. (1979). Hypnotically-induced pain control in sickle cell anemia. *Pediatrics, 64,* 533–546.

Zimet, G. D., Mays, R. M., & Fortenberry, J. D. (2000). Vaccines against sexually transmitted infections: Promise and problems of the magic bullets for prevention and control. *Sexually Transmitted Diseases, 27,* 49–52.

CHAPTER 20

Adolescent Health

SHERIDAN PHILLIPS

Adolescent health is a broad, multidisciplinary field encompassing, at a minimum, clinical and developmental psychology, education, environmental design, law, nursing, nutrition, pediatrics, psychiatry, and social work. The sheer amount of information relevant to promoting adolescent health poses various challenges. Clinically, good patient care requires collaborative efforts among different disciplines, with an overlap of core knowledge that is shared, as well as appreciation for the specialized expertise of each professional. Similarly, designing training programs necessitates setting priorities for knowledge and skills for one discipline while drawing from others as well. Advancing our knowledge of adolescent development and care, and disseminating such information, ideally involves familiarity with findings and journals in many fields.

One chapter cannot do justice to this broad array of areas. We focus on those unique aspects of adolescence that have particular salience for teenagers' health and health care. Many aspects of health are therefore omitted. For example, while the treatment of psychiatric disorders is clearly important in adolescence, these mental health needs are not unique to this developmental stage. Similarly, some adolescents require treatment for cancer, heart disease, and a variety of other physical disorders, but such problems are more prevalent at other ages. This chapter reviews aspects of physical and psychosocial development specific to adolescence and their interaction with health care, including major sources of morbidity and mortality, salient areas of health care, and special services for adolescents.

ADOLESCENT DEVELOPMENT AND HEALTH

Physical Development

The onset of puberty in males is typically signaled by subtle testicular changes at about 11.5 years of age, concomitant with the start of their growth spurt. The average duration of puberty is three years, but it can range from two to five years. The growth spurt peaks relatively late at about 14 years, when changes in the genitals and pubic hair are very evident. (For further information regarding physical development, see McAnarney, Kreipe, Orr, & Comerci, 1992; Neinstein, 1996a.)

Pubertal development begins earlier in females, with the start of their growth spurt at about 8.7 years, followed by the first sign of breast development (breast budding) one year later. Their growth spurt peaks at 11.6 years, well before significant changes in breast and pubic hair and before menarche at about 12.3 years. Major changes in body size and composition therefore occur much earlier in girls than boys, with girls reaching their growth peak at about the same chronological age as boys begin their adolescent growth spurt.

Even among normal adolescents, the timing and duration of puberty vary tremendously and are thus poorly correlated with chronological age. This prompted the development of a rating scale for sexual maturity (Tanner, 1962), based on pubic hair and breasts for females and pubic hair and genitalia in males. For both sexes, the scale ranges from Stage 1 (completely prepubertal) to Stage 5 (adult secondary sexual characteristics). Adolescent medicine specialists have promoted the routine use of Tanner staging. Clinically, a 12-year-old girl at Stage 1 will have very different concerns and health risks than 12-year-old girls at Stage 4 or 5.

Tanner staging is also valuable for research purposes. For example, a study of panic attacks among sixth- and seventh-grade girls reported striking differences in the incidence of panic attacks as a function of sexual maturity, but no differences due to chronological age (Hayward, Killen, & Hammer, 1992). Traditionally, Tanner stage is rated by physicians and based on physical examination. Fortunately, Litt and her colleagues (Duke, Litt, & Gross, 1980) found that teenagers can rate themselves with considerable accuracy, and this method has been employed in more recent research. While accuracy appears to be more problematic with abnormal samples (e.g., adolescents with growth retardation), self-ratings seem to be acceptably reliable and valid with normal populations (see Finkelstein et al., 1999).

It is impossible to overemphasize the extent of physical change that occurs during the relatively brief period of puberty. Major endocrine changes are associated with the onset of puberty, with three distinct changes in the hypothalamic-pituitary unit and (typically) increased secretion of sex hormones from the adrenal gland. Other changes occur in insulin secretion, growth hormone, and somatomedins. While it seems evident that substantial increases in hormonal levels (especially testosterone) would be related to increased sexual urges and to aggression, the effects on behavior are not yet well understood. What is clear is that teenagers experience major biochemical and skeletal changes during puberty.

During childhood (age 5 to 10 years), the average child grows 5 cm to 6 cm per year. In contrast, during the average adolescent growth spurt (24 to 36 months), girls grow 23 cm to 28 cm, and boys grow 26 cm to 28 cm taller—a growth rate of 10 cm to 11 cm per year, twice that of childhood. For both genders, pubertal growth accounts for 20% to 25% of final adult height. Weight growth is even more dramatic, accounting for about 50% of ideal adult body weight.

Other physical changes accompany rapid increase in height and weight. Adolescents grow in a concentric fashion, with their extremities (heads, hands, and feet) reaching adult size first, followed by their limbs and finally their torsos. This accounts for the "gangly" appearance of many teenagers, who seem to be "all arms and legs." Teenagers also experience significant changes in body composition. Percentage of body fat changes from about 15% in prepubertal girls (comparable to that of prepubertal boys) to 27% by Tanner Stage 4, along with pelvic remodeling and the emergence of breasts and hips. In contrast, lean body mass increases in boys to about 90% at maturity, largely reflecting increased muscle mass. During puberty, boys also experience a sevenfold increase in the size of the testes, epididymis, and prostate, while the phallus usually doubles in size. Given these significant changes in body size and shape, adolescent medicine clinicians joke that young teenagers are obsessed with their hair because it is the only part of their bodies that they recognize from one month to the next. Indeed, it is remarkable that adolescents are able to remain sufficiently coordinated to be able to play a variety of sports.

Spermarche, the onset of seminal emission, appears to be an early pubertal event for boys (median age 13.4 years) although there is considerable variation (range 11.7 to 15.3). It precedes peak height velocity in most boys and may occur with no evidence of pubic hair development. Some sperm are usually present in the ejaculate by Tanner Stage 3 but fertility is generally not reliable until Tanner Stage 4.

Menarche, the onset of a girl's monthly period, has been studied much more extensively than spermarche, presumably because it is a discrete and salient event unlike the more subtle sexual development of boys. American girls experience menarche at about 12.3 years (with normal variation from 9 to 17 years). A secular trend has been observed over the last century, with a gradual decrease in the age of menarche both in the United States and in European countries. This decrease is hypothesized to reflect improved nutrition and appears to have leveled out with little decrease from 1960 to the present.

For individual girls, the age of menarche is a function of factors such as race, socioeconomic status, heredity, nutrition, culture, and body composition. For example, menarche tends to occur at a later age in rural families, in larger families, and at higher altitudes. Also, amenorrhea (the absence or cessation of periods) is commonly found among girls who are underweight and/or have an unusually low percentage of body fat, such as athletes or ballerinas who train intensively.

Despite the apparent stability of the age of menarche, however, there have been reports that the onset of secondary sexual characteristics is occurring at an earlier age for many American girls. After observing breast development in a number of young female patients (age 7 to 9 years), a pediatrician launched a large study of 17,000 girls. This investigation confirmed the clinical observation, and it does appear probable that American girls are developing secondary sexual characteristics at an earlier age than they did in the 1960s, even through the age of menarche remains unchanged (Herman-Giddens et al., 1997). This finding has prompted intense speculation regarding the reason for the change, with the most popular culprit hypothesized to be the increased fat in the American diet: It may be that even mild obesity is providing the trigger for very early sexual development. Alternative hypotheses focus on environmental changes, including increased hormones in milk and other animal products (see Lemonick, 2000). Whatever its origin, this physical trend prompts concern among both parents and health professionals regarding the potential impact on girls' psychosocial development.

Psychosocial Development

The developmental period of life that we term *adolescence* is somewhat elastic in its boundaries, but generally includes children from 12 to 20 years of age. It is bounded by biology at one end (the onset of puberty) and by social and legal conventions at the other end (the age when one is considered an adult). For individual children, the perception that they have entered adolescence may be triggered by their own pubertal changes or by changes evident in their peers, hence the lack of a clear-cut boundary. The end point is also unclear, with American children being considered sufficiently adult to drive at age 16, vote at age 18, and drink only at age 21 (depending on the state where they live). Transition times also vary in health care settings, with pediatric services typically including age 12 to 20 (except for college health) while psychiatric services designed for adolescents are generally unavailable after their eighteenth birthday.

Adolescents have a number of developmental tasks to accomplish during this relatively brief period of life (see Table 20.1). They must learn to function as independent adults, separate from their families, while not severing ties to the family. They also become increasingly oriented to others outside the family as they develop significant relationships with other adults (e.g., teachers, coaches) and with peers of both sexes. Their self-image is consolidated and incorporates their sexual identity (e.g., What does it mean to be a woman? How am I the same as, and different from, a man?). Self-image includes body image, which many believe is crystallized during adolescence. A host of new sensations and feelings emerge, and adolescents must come to terms with their sex drives and determine how to manage them. The transition from concrete operations to formal operations not only paves the way for learning higher order mathematics and other abstract concepts, but also provides adolescents with

new tools and interests as they increasingly contemplate their own lives and the human condition. Finally, adolescents need to develop a plan for their future, establishing a direction, goals, and appropriate training for a career.

This is a daunting list of tasks to accomplish in eight years, reinforcing the traditional, psychoanalytic view of adolescence as a tumultuous, troubled time of life. Yet, a considerable amount of more recent data (Offer, Ostrov, & Howard, 1981) reports that about 75% to 80% of teenagers experience adolescence as a positive and pleasant period of life. How do adolescents manage this, with so many developmental tasks to accomplish?

One reason is that many of these tasks are not begun de novo in adolescence. For example, children have been gaining increased independence throughout childhood as they learn to feed and dress themselves, choose preferred activities, stay overnight at a friend's house, and go away to camp. In a study of 483 children and adolescents, Larson and Richards (1991) reported that the amount of time children spend with their families decreases from about 50% at Grade 5 to about 25% at Grade 9. While this is a considerable decrease, it is not an all-to-none change. Similarly, many aspects of self-image have been developed by the end of childhood, and preadolescents can identify their assets and weaknesses. The task in adolescence is to refine this self-image and to incorporate sexual identity. Finally, development continues past the age of 20 as the completion of adolescent tasks continues in young adulthood.

Another reason adolescents manage their developmental tasks with relative ease is that they focus on different issues at different times, reducing the number that they must address simultaneously. As Table 20.2 shows, developmental theorists divide adolescence into different periods: preadolescence and early, middle, and late adolescence. Note that boys' progress

TABLE 20.1 Developmental Tasks of Adolescence

Gain independence from family.
Expand relationships outside home:
    Other adults.
    Same-sex peers.
    Opposite-sex peers.
Have realistic self-image.
Handle sexual drives.
Concrete to abstract thought.
Develop value system.
Make realistic plan for social and economic stability.

TABLE 20.2 Focus of Development at Different Stages of Adolescence

Age	Grade	Developmental Focus
Preadolescence:		
Females: 9–11 years	5–7	Same-sex peers
Males: 10–12 years		
Early adolescence:		
Females: 11–13 years	6–8	Independence
Males: 12–14 years		Same-sex peers
		Body image
		Abstract thought
Middle adolescence:		
Females: 13–16 years	7–10	Opposite-sex peers
Males: 14–17 years		Sexual drives
		Sexual identity
		Morality
Late adolescence:		
Females: 16–20 years	11–	Vocational plans
Males: 17–20 years	College	Intimacy

through these phases lags behind that of girls, just as with physical development.

One major focus during *early adolescence* is the desire for increased independence from family, combined with a rapid rise in the importance of peers. Need for conformity with peers peaks in preadolescence and early adolescence, followed by a gradual decline through late adolescence. Such conformity includes dress, hairstyle, music, and language. Abrupt changes in these areas can startle parents as they see their child turn into someone they barely recognize. Yet this new orientation toward peers (versus family) does not represent a total transformation. Young teenagers certainly respond to peer influence, especially that of same-sex peers, in areas where they (probably correctly) perceive that their parents will not be knowledgeable about what constitutes "cool" clothing, "in" music, and appropriate patterns of interaction with same- and opposite-sex peers. However, they typically respond to parental influence regarding educational plans and aspirations, moral and social values, and understanding the adult world. For example, one large-scale study of two groups of boys (blue-collar versus upper middle class) in Chicago revealed that each group's values and expectations were more similar to those of their parents than they were to their peers in the other socioeconomic group (Youniss & Smollar, 1989).

Another major focus during early adolescence is body image, hardly surprising given the massive physical changes that occur during this time. Young teenagers evidence intense interest in and often dissatisfaction with specific parts of their bodies. A classic study (Douvan & Adelson, 1966) asked seventh graders what one aspect of themselves or their lives they would change if they could, and 59% selected a specific body part. This suggests that disease, illness, trauma, or even deviations in normal development, which have obvious physical consequences, will pose even more psychological challenges for young adolescents than for older teenagers. Another implication is that it is particularly important for young adolescents to receive detailed feedback during routine physical examinations, reassuring them that their physical development is proceeding normally and encouraging them to express concerns and questions that almost certainly are present but which they often are too embarrassed to raise spontaneously.

The developmental focus shifts in *mid-adolescence* because most teenagers begin to date between the ages of 13 to 15, with the onset of dating being influenced by gender and social status. With increasing interaction with the opposite sex, teenagers concentrate on sexual identity, dating behavior, communication skills, and rules for interaction with peers of both sexes. These early relationships are often brief and shallow, with physical appearance and skills playing a major role in choice of partner.

The transition to abstract thought, which has typically occurred during early adolescence, paves the way for new cognitive activity in mid-adolescence. It is generally during this time that adolescents display increased interest in abstract concepts and even thinking per se; one teenager informed the author that "I'm thinking about the fact that I'm thinking about the fact that I'm thinking." Morality, justice, and fairness become a focus, both regarding teenagers themselves (and those who inhabit their world) and society in general. Teenagers in mid-adolescence thus often devote time and thought to rules and laws (school and national), social structure, and systems of government.

To address the first major task of *late adolescence,* teenagers begin to focus seriously on career plans, which often are unstable until the age of 16. By 17, most adolescents have at least established an initial direction for their future career and made plans to implement appropriate education and training to achieve these goals. However, completing such training and alteration in career goals often continues throughout young adulthood.

The second major task of late adolescence is development of intimacy in personal relationships, especially with an opposite-sex partner. Older teenagers focus on different aspects of dating, moving beyond external appearance, as they develop true sharing and caring. Establishing a personal support system of friends, partner, and meaningful adults (e.g., teacher or boss) is as important as economics in allowing teenagers to function separately from their families. The developmental task of independence from family is thus frequently not fully completed until well after adolescence.

Interaction of Physical and Psychosocial Development

Timing of Puberty

The onset of puberty occurs at a mean age of 11.2 years for girls and 11.6 years for boys with evident physical changes at mean ages of 12.2 years and 12.9 years. Because of the tremendous variability present among normally developing adolescents, however, visual evidence of puberty (Tanner Stage 3) can range from age 10.1 to 14.3 (girls) and 10.8 to 15 (boys). These age ranges are within two standard deviations from the mean and considered medically normal. Extreme delay or precocity (2 standard deviations above or below the mean) requires medical evaluation to determine potential hypothalamic, pituitary, or gonadal dysfunction; undiagnosed chronic illness; or chromosomal abnormality (see "Special Conditions" in a following section). However, even teenagers who do not meet medical criteria for abnormality may appear very different from the majority of their peers: girls who still have completely prepubertal bodies at the age of 13 or who are fully developed before the age of 12, and boys who are still prepubertal at 15 or appear fully adult by the age of 12.5 (references are to Tanner Stage 1 versus Tanner Stage 5; see "Physical Development").

Adolescents who are in the lowest 10% to 15% and the highest 10% to 15% of this distribution are considered to be early versus late maturers, normal variations of development that most likely reflect their genetic inheritance. A series of classic studies beginning in the 1950s (see Conger & Galambos, 1997) found that early maturation provided a psychosocial advantage for boys, who more often took leadership roles and were perceived by teachers and peers as more mature and responsible than boys maturing "on time." In contrast, late maturing boys were more likely to act "the class clown," were perceived as being more immature and self-conscious by teachers and peers, and were less likely to be popular or to be leaders. Nottelmann et al. (1987) confirmed that adolescent adjustment problems were more common for late-maturing boys, and Crockett and Petersen (1987) report a linear relationship between timing of puberty and self-esteem.

These differences are hypothesized to reflect the fact that early maturing boys are taller, heavier, and more muscular, all of which are advantageous for sports (an asset highly prized by peers at this age) and makes them closer in size to girls of the same age. Also, their more adult appearance presumably encourages adults and peers to treat them differently, giving them more responsibility and turning more to them for assistance. Analogously, late-maturing boys cannot "throw their weight around," both literally and figuratively, to the same extent.

In a longitudinal follow-up, which continued through age 38, men who had matured early retained their psychosocial advantage (Livson & Peskin, 1980). As adults, early maturing males were found to be more responsible, cooperative, sociable, and self-contained (although late maturers were not totally without assets, being more insightful and creatively playful). It is important to note that this advantageous effect was maintained despite the fact that, on the average, late-maturing boys eventually attain greater adult height than early maturing boys because they continue to grow at a childhood rate before beginning their growth spurt; little additional growth occurs after the conclusion of the growth spurt. Greater height clearly provides a psychosocial advantage for American males and yet the advantage of early maturation appears to outweigh the advantage of greater height in adulthood for late maturers.

The evidence regarding female development is mixed, with some reports that both extremes are disadvantageous,

especially for early maturing girls (Susman et al., 1985), while other studies report no substantial effects for girls (Nottelmann et al., 1987). Simmons, Blyth, and McKinney (1983) report that pubertal status appears problematic when it places a girl in a different or deviant position from her peers. The impact of early or late puberty may well vary as a function of a girl's socioeconomic status and the degree of tolerance and acceptance of her appearance within her social environment.

From a psychosocial standpoint, early physical maturation is advantageous for American boys whereas the ideal for girls is to mature exactly at the average time and rate. However, adolescents cannot design the nature of their pubertal development, leaving late-maturing boys (especially) and early maturing girls at potential risk for adjustment problems and difficulties with peer status and body image. In addition to appearing unusually immature, late-maturing boys have a disadvantage in addressing their developmental tasks: It is difficult to incorporate one's new sexuality in self-image or body image until one has developed some degree of sexual maturity, or learn to handle sexual drives before they are experienced. These developmental issues are delayed and thus add to the number of tasks that must be addressed simultaneously at a later chronological age. Late maturers do not have the same option as other teenagers to focus sequentially on different developmental tasks and thus face an additional challenge.

In the absence of data to guide intervention, clinical experience suggests that even brief therapy can be helpful for late-maturing boys. Goals for treatment include (a) developing skills that are valued by peers (e.g., sports that are less dependent on size, computer skills, and video games), (b) participating in organized activities (e.g., Scouts) where leadership responsibilities (based on abilities rather than appearance) are conferred by adults, and (c) enhancing social skills, especially with peers. With early-maturing girls, publicity regarding the increasing incidence of early development (Lemonick, 2000) has prompted increased attention to the plight of girls with clear outward evidence of sexual maturity at ages 6, 7, and 8. Endocrinologists are increasingly more reluctant to slow development with hormone therapy, as they did previously with girls under 8, leaving young girls with bodies that are considered normal medically but which are obviously very different from their peers. In this case, goals for therapy include (a) parents remaining alert to potential sexual harassment and abuse, (b) promoting the choice of clothing, books, music, and activities that are appropriate for a girl's chronological age, (c) developing skills and talents that are unrelated to physical appearance, (d) enhancing social skills with female peers, and (e) strengthening relationships with family and female friends.

Body Image

Considerable evidence indicates that American girls in general are less satisfied with their bodies than are boys (with weight satisfaction being the largest gap) and that boys' satisfaction increases with age while girls' does not. In fact, gender differences in depression were virtually eliminated by controlling for negative body image and low self-esteem in a study of White high school students (Allgood-Merten, Lewinsohn, & Hops, 1990). In general, body image affects overall self-image and self-esteem, especially for girls. A report by the American Association of University Women (AAUW, 1992) found that confidence in "the way I look" was the most important contributor to self-worth among White schoolgirls whereas boys more often based self-worth on their abilities.

Results of a multiethnic study of 877 adolescents in Los Angeles (Siegel, Yancey, Aneshengel, & Schuler, 1999) suggest that body image and even the impact of pubertal timing vary considerably as a function of both gender and ethnicity. Asian American boys and girls reported similar levels of body satisfaction whereas boys were more satisfied than girls for all other ethnic groups of teenagers. Overall, African American girls had the most positive body image and, in sharp contrast to the other ethnic groups, were not dissatisfied with their bodies if they perceived themselves as being early maturers. As with African American boys, African American girls were least satisfied with their bodies if they perceived themselves as late developers. Given that boys' body image improves with age, that Asian American girls appear less concerned about physical appearance than girls in other ethnic groups, and that African American girls have a relatively positive body image, the authors conclude that the most problematic teenagers are White and Hispanic girls, both of whom evidence dissatisfaction with their body image, which becomes increasingly negative with age.

Special Conditions

Gynecomastia is a benign increase in male breast tissue associated with puberty, not the fatty tissue often seen with obese patients. It is found in about 20% of 10.5-year old boys, with a peak prevalence of 65% at age 14 (mean age of onset is 13.2). About 4% of boys will have severe gynecomastia, with very evident, protruding breasts, that persists into adulthood. Gynecomastia is thought to result from an imbalance between circulating estrogens and androgens, thus representing a normal concomitant of hormonal change during puberty. The condition usually resolves in 12 to 18 months but can last for more than two years.

Given that more than half of adolescent boys experience this condition, and at a developmental stage when concerns about their bodies and relationships with their peers are at a lifetime peak, it is remarkable that so little data are available regarding psychological impact and treatment. Clinical experience indicates that many young adolescent boys are seriously concerned about their breast development and its implications for their sexual development and identity, often prompting them to avoid sports or other activities that require them to remove their shirts. At a minimum, explanation and reassurance is required. Medical intervention is limited, largely due to concern about side effects, but Tamoxifen (especially) and Testolactone may provide relief for adolescents with significant psychological sequelae. Surgery is another useful option for boys with moderate to severe gynecomastia or in cases where the condition has not resolved after an extended period of time. Surgery may not be an option, however, for many boys because it is considered to be cosmetic surgery and not generally covered by health insurance.

Abnormal maturational delay is defined statistically as those 5% of teenagers who fall at least two standard deviations above the mean onset of puberty. Physical examination and laboratory tests are employed to screen for a variety of disorders that may cause delay: hormonal deficiencies (including growth hormone), chromosomal abnormalities, and chronic illness (e.g., cystic fibrosis, sickle cell anemia, heart disease, or inflammatory bowel disease), which may be undiagnosed. In some cases, medical intervention can promote catch-up growth and sexual development but the effects are irreversible in most cases. However, 90% to 95% of delayed puberty represents constitutional delay rather than an underlying disease or abnormality.

Neinstein and Kaufman (1996) report (anecdotally) that it is, not surprisingly, most often male adolescents who complain about delayed puberty. Treatment with hormones often can increase growth velocity without excessive bone age advancement, but potential side effects, such as the possible attenuation of mature height, must be considered. It is not only psychological sequelae that are of concern. Adult men with a history of constitutionally delayed puberty have decreased radial and spinal bone mineral density, suggesting that the timing of sexual maturation may determine peak bone mineral density (Finkelstein, Neer, & Biller, 1992).

Delayed menstruation (primary amenorrhea) is defined as the absence of spontaneous uterine bleeding and secondary sex characteristics by age 14 to 15, or by 16 to 16.5 regardless of the presence of secondary sex characteristics. Such delay can represent underlying disease or abnormalities, or constitutional delay, but it can also result from drug use (e.g., heroin), stress, weight loss (e.g., with anorexia), or intense exercise. Serious female athletes have substantially higher rates of amenorrhea—up to 18% of recreational runners, 50% of competitive runners, and 79% of ballet dancers (note that dancers both diet and exercise strenuously). Among predisposing factors are training intensity, weight loss, changes in percentage of body fat, and younger age of onset of intense training (Neinstein, 1996b).

Amenorrhea is of concern primarily because loss in bone mineral density (BMD) can begin soon after amenorrhea develops. For example, female athletes have low levels of estrogen and thus are at higher risk for osteoporosis and stress fractures (Neinstein, 1996b). The vast majority of bone mineralization in adolescent girls is completed by age 15 to 16, and loss of bone density can have significant long-term consequences. For example, most adolescents who recover from anorexia nervosa before age 15 can have normal total body BMD, but regional BMD (lumbar spine and femoral neck) may remain low; the longer the weight loss persists, the less likely it is that BMD will return to normal (Hergenroeder, 1995).

Amenorrhea is usually reversible with weight gain or, for athletes, lessening the intensity of exercise. At a minimum, amenorrheic girls should be treated with increased calcium intake and lifestyle intervention. There is substantial controversy regarding the use of hormone-replacement therapy, which is generally considered for girls who do not gain weight or reduce activity after six months. Who should be treated and the extent of benefit for BMD are questions that remain unresolved (Neinstein, 1996b). The optimal intervention would be behavioral rather than medical. This physical disorder is both prompted by attitudes and behavior, and treatable by changes in attitudes and behavior. However, while intervention with eating disorders has been studied extensively, there has been no systematic study of intervention with athletes, despite awareness that athletes are more likely to engage in various health risk behaviors than are nonathletes (Patel & Luckshead, 2000) and that competitive female athletes are at particular risk for loss of bone density.

Short stature is considered present when a child falls below the third percentile (Neinstein & Kaufman, 1996) or the fifth percentile (Delamater & Eidson, 1998) on the normal growth chart. Most instances represent normal variants, reflecting familial short stature and/or constitutional growth delay, while some cases are due to underlying pathology. A variety of behavioral and psychological problems has been reported for children and adolescents with short stature (Delamater & Eidson, 1998); not surprisingly, the effects of

stature are more evident in adolescence than in childhood. For example, a longitudinal study of 47 children with short stature (Holmes, Karlsson, & Thompson, 1985) reported an age-related decline in social competence that began in early adolescence; this appeared to be related to fewer friendships and social contacts. Allen, Warzak, Greger, Bernotas, and Huseman (1993) found increased behavior problems and decreased competence, compared with nonclinical norms, only for older children (age 12 and above); measures of personality, self-concept, anxiety, and social competence correlated significantly with the magnitude of the discrepancy in height, compared with normal peers. Sandberg, Brook, and Campos (1994) reported parent ratings of social competence and behavioral and emotional problems: Compared with both nonclinical norms and with girls of short stature, boys were less socially competent and evidenced more behavioral and emotional problems (particularly with regard to internalizing disorders). In the same study, boys' self-report indicated lower social competence and decreased self-concept in athletic and job competence; this was particularly evident for older boys. A study of 311 children and adolescents with short stature resulting from four different disorders and a fifth group representing normal variation (Steinhausen, Dorr, Kannenberg, & Malin, 2000) reported that behavioral problems were a function of short stature per se, with no significant differences found for diagnostic category.

Just as short stature is particularly problematic for boys, concern about excessive growth or *tall stature* appears to be most evident for girls. The differential diagnosis includes familial tall stature, excess growth hormone, anabolic steroid excess, hyperthyroidism, and various pathological syndromes. When there are no abnormal causes for tall stature, the decision regarding medical treatment is dependent on the patient's (and family's) perception of what height is "excessive." Treatment with estrogen will slow the rate of growth until skeletal growth (epiphyseal fusion) is completed and hormone supplements can be discontinued. Treatment is currently begun later than was previously recommended (Neinstein & Kaufman, 1996); intervention is delayed until a girl is at least age 9 or 10, puberty has begun, and she is at 5.5 feet tall.

Side effects of hormonal treatment of girls appear to be mild and no adverse long-term consequences have been reported. Because boys are rarely treated for tall stature, only one study (Zachman, Ferrandez, & Muurse, 1976) has reported the effects of treatment with testosterone. Side effects appeared more significant than those for girls, including weight gain, acne, edema, and decreased testicular volume; all appeared to resolve after therapy ended. There are no reports of psychosocial effects of excessive stature either for male or female adolescents.

Interaction between Developmental Issues and Health Care

Rising Importance of Peers and Increased Risk Taking

As children enter the developmental stage of adolescence, they become more responsive to peer attitudes and norms and also become increasingly independent, spending more time in circumstances without close parental supervision (sometimes without any adult supervision) and acquiring increased personal mobility. They also become larger and more powerful physically, more cognitively sophisticated, and often have more discretionary income. These factors, combined with biological changes, provide teenagers with increased motivation and ability to engage in behaviors that may have adverse consequences for their health.

A relatively small subset of adolescents are at very high risk for significant problems. For example, some psychiatric problems meet diagnostic criteria for the first time during adolescence; difficulties in childhood may be exacerbated by puberty and/or increasing age and social demands. This problematic subgroup consists of teenagers who constitute a significant danger to themselves (e.g., long-term street youth) or others (e.g., those arrested for major crimes before the age of 15). Most teenagers, however, are distributed along a continuum of risk that ranges from higher to lower; it would be difficult to find adolescents who have not engaged in any risky behavior throughout adolescence.

Some risks are so common that they virtually define adolescence. For example, it is expected that all teenagers will begin to drive, typically doing so independently by the age of 16. Yet motor vehicle deaths are the leading cause of death among adolescents, and both deaths and crashes are four times more likely to occur with drivers between 16 and 19 years of age, compared with drivers 25 to 69 years old (Patel, Greydanus, & Rowlett, 2000). Similarly, sexual activity is the norm, with at least 50% of 15-year-olds having begun sexual activity (R. Brown, 2000) and about 82% of 18- to 20-year-olds having had sexual intercourse (Neinstein & MacKenzie, 1996). Substance use is also very prevalent, with 26% of high school seniors reporting current use of illegal drugs (excluding alcohol and tobacco) and 48% reporting previous or current use, 25% reporting daily cigarette smoking, and 32% reporting problem drinking (consuming five or more drinks in a row at least once in the past two weeks). Note that these statistics do not include teenagers who have dropped out of school (Comerci & Schwebel, 2000). The drop-out rate is about 25% nationally but 50% to 80% in some inner cities (Scales, 1988). Finally, 49% of adolescent boys and 28% of adolescent girls reported having been in at least one physical fight in the past year (Neinstein & Mackenzie, 1996). In summary, from a normative perspective, adolescence per se is a risky business.

Increasing evidence suggests that multiple types of risk-taking behavior are associated (Irwin, 1990). Alcohol and other substance use is a factor in violence, motor vehicle accidents, and risky sex. Some behaviors appear to occur in clusters, such as sensation seeking in sports and self-reported criminality (Patel & Luckstead, 2000). Most teenagers age 12 to 17 do not engage in multiple forms of risk taking, but there is a dramatic increase with age. Approximately one-third of 14- to 17-year-olds does so versus one-half of 18- to 20-year-olds, with males and out-of-school teens being substantially more likely to display multiple high-risk behaviors (Brener & Collins, 1998). The line of demarcation is not always clear, with a continuum of risk often existing even for the same behavior. For example, some high school students (23% of males and 15% of females) and college students (12% of males and 7% of females) report rarely or never using seat belts (see Patel et al., 2000), but only 34% of teenagers report *consistent* use of seat belts (see Neinstein, 1996c).

Morbidity and Mortality

Of the 10 leading causes of death among American adolescents and youth (age 12 to 24), four are behavioral in origin: unintentional injury/accidents, homicide, HIV, and suicide. The leading cause of death in this age group is unintentional injury, primarily from motor vehicle crashes. Accidents, suicide, and homicide cause more than 80% of deaths of 15- to 24-year olds. Death rates and causes vary as a function of gender and race. Overall, adolescent males have twice the death rate of adolescent females. African American youth (age 15 to 24) are twice as likely to die as White youth and are more than three times more likely to die than Asian American youth. Further, African American youth are most likely to die as a result of homicide and legal intervention, whereas accidents are the primary cause of death for all other major racial groups. The homicide rate for African American males (15 to 24) is nine times that for White males, and the Hispanic rate is 3.5 times that for White males (for all statistics, see Neinstein 1996c).

Even if unintentional injury does not result in death, it is a major source of morbidity (e.g., injury is the leading cause of loss of productive years of life). Adolescents have the highest injury rate of all age groups, with the highest rates for older adolescents, males, Whites, and Midwestern residents (Fraser, 1995). Automobile crashes are the leading cause of both fatal and nonfatal unintentional injuries, but significant mortality and morbidity also result from motorcycles, bicycles, skateboards, and all-terrain vehicles, as well as firearms, drowning, poisoning, sports, and home fires. The frequency and extent of accidental injury is exacerbated by alcohol and other substance use and failure to use seat belts or helmets, and ameliorated by nighttime curfews and mandatory seatbelt laws (see Neinstein, 1996c; Patel et al., 2000).

The New Morbidity

The physical results of injury-risking behavior, illegal substance use, unprotected sex, fighting, homicide, and suicide have been termed "the new morbidity" (Haggerty, 1986). In the second half of the twentieth century, these behaviorally based threats to health eclipsed the previous causes of pediatric mortality and morbidity as medical advances eradicated many childhood diseases. Unfortunately, improvements in health care have not led to better health status among American teenagers; adolescents are the only age group in the United States whose mortality rate has actually increased over the past 30 years (Gans, 1990). Increased recognition of the new morbidity prompted major changes in pediatrics.

A national survey of pediatricians conducted by the American Academy of Pediatrics clearly indicated that they felt inadequately trained to assess and address behavioral issues. The report of this Task Force in 1978 spurred significant changes in pediatric education and the development of a new specialty, behavioral pediatrics (American Academy of Pediatrics, 1978). As part of this same national change, adolescent medicine began a transformation from a traditional, biologically focused practice of medical care for adolescents to a multidisciplinary approach to promoting adolescent health (Phillips, Moscicki, Kaufman, & Moore, 1998). Funding from private foundations and the Department of Health, Education, and Welfare provided the financial support to recruit additional pediatric faculty members from the field of psychology, as well as to provide faculty positions for nurses, nutritionists, and social workers. The influx of these professionals, while not an enormous number, significantly changed training in adolescent medicine and, especially, contributed disproportionately to knowledge and dissemination of information about adolescent health (Cromer & Stager, 2000; Phillips et al., 1998).

The Adolescent as a Patient

The adolescent is in transition, having left the world of childhood but not yet having achieved adult status, either developmentally or legally. This fact has numerous implications for the structure of health care for teenagers. One of the earliest issues addressed by adolescent medicine practitioners was the advisability of establishing an inpatient ward specifically designed for teenagers rather than housing adolescents on children's or adult wards (McAnarney, 1992). Similarly, primary care practitioners were advised to avoid decorating their waiting rooms and offices with bunny pictures and to include reading material appropriate for teenagers, possibly also setting different times for office visits by children versus adolescents. More thorny practice issues include how and when to see the teenager alone and with his parent(s), confidentiality and its limitations, and fees.

The issue of billing illustrates problems engendered by the adolescent's "in-between" status. If parents are paying the bills, to what extent is it possible to maintain confidentiality regarding diagnosis or the content and purpose of care? Is the provider's primary responsibility to the teenager or to his parents? For what conditions is the teenager considered to be an emancipated minor, legally entitling him or her to seek care without parental knowledge or consent? If the family is not involved, how can the adolescent pay for professional fees and medication? The issue of payment is particularly problematic for teenagers because they almost always require more professional time than children, whose parents typically assume responsibility for reporting symptoms, understanding treatment recommendations, and managing care, or adults, who have generally learned how to be patients. For example, consider the financial implications of the average Medicaid reimbursement rate for the following services: $37 for a 30-minute counseling visit, $47 for a preventive visit, and $18 for a hepatitis B immunization (English, Kaplan, & Morreale, 2000). Given these difficulties, it is hardly surprising that adolescent services often struggle financially and that funding is a significant barrier to good adolescent health care (Hein, 1993).

The Health Care Provider

The onset of adolescence signals the beginning of a new relationship between the patient and health care provider, with a host of new issues that ideally should be assessed and addressed. The American Medical Association (AMA) published guidelines in 1994 for health screening in adolescence (Guidelines for Adolescent Preventive Services, or GAPS). The GAPS recommendations suggest annual preventive visits with additional counseling for parents twice during adolescence and comprehensive physical examinations at least three times between the ages of 11 and 21. For the general population, screening is recommended to include height, weight, blood pressure, and problem drinking and, for females, a Pap test, chlamydia screen, and Rubella serology. Routine intervention includes immunizations, chemoprophylaxis (multivitamin with folic acid for females), and counseling regarding injury prevention, substance use, sexual behavior, diet and exercise, and dental health. Additional interventions are suggested for a variety of high-risk populations.

Given the content of much of the GAPS, it is obvious that the care provider must be able to establish a trusting and credible relationship with the teenager if assessment and counseling are to be at all effective. Adolescent providers thus have to not only learn the nature of health risks and potential risk-reduction strategies, but also acquire skills in interviewing, establishing rapport, and recommending behavioral changes. Textbooks in adolescent medicine, therefore, include a long list of tips for interacting with teenagers and specific techniques to enhance the accuracy of information they receive about illicit or illegal behavior (for example, see Neinstein, 1996a).

Physicians do have some inherent advantages in this process. They have literally seen the teenager naked and can begin to establish their credibility and usefulness by reassuring teenagers that their physical development is progressing normally (or explain normal variations) and probe for common concerns in this area. Skilled physicians can build on the unique nature of their relationship with a teenager in a way that most mental health providers cannot.

It is especially important that all clinicians who treat adolescents develop knowledge and skills regarding behavior and development because the majority of American teenagers will receive only screening and counseling, if at all, from a primary care provider rather than from a mental health professional or an adolescent medicine specialist (Silber, 1983). The ability to detect, address, and potentially refer behavioral problems is thus a key component of primary care. Yet, there are consistent reports that pediatricians fail to detect psychopathology, identifying, at most half of their patients with mental health needs (e.g., Costello et al., 1988). Unfortunately, current training for primary care providers falls short in adolescent health care and may fare even worse in the future as managed care weakens the financial stability of adolescent divisions in teaching hospitals.

Compliance with Medical Regimens

Adolescence can signal a new era of noncompliance, even with health routines that have been well-established in childhood. While noncompliance is certainly a problem for all age groups and for a variety of acute and chronic conditions, it has been of particular concern in chronic diseases such as diabetes, asthma, and juvenile rheumatoid arthritis because of the potential for significant and irreversible consequences. As a corollary, evidence regarding diabetes suggests that intensive management yields even better short-term effects and reduces long-term complications beyond those considered to be the norm with conventional diabetes management (see Ruggiero & Javorsky, 1999).

Considerable evidence suggests that adolescence is associated with poorer compliance than childhood (Manne, 1998). For example, compared with children, diabetics ages 16 to 19 years administer their injections less regularly, exercise less frequently, eat too few carbohydrates and too many fats, eat less frequently, and test their glucose levels less often (Delameter et al., 1989; Johnson, Freund, Silverstein, Hansen, & Malone, 1990). The average age when children first show a pattern of serious and persistent noncompliance with diabetes management is 14.8 years (Kovacs, Goldston, Obrosky, & Iyengar, 1992). Noncompliance is such a common problem with adolescents that it has been suggested that adolescence per se is a contraindication for receipt of organ transplantation (see discussion in Stuber & Canning, 1998).

Age differences in compliance vary as a function of the treatment regimen under study (e.g., very young children experience more problems with oral medications; Phipps & DeCuir-Whalley, 1990). Adolescent noncompliance appears most likely when the regimen is related to independence (either rebelling against parental nagging or reflecting reduced parental supervision), undesirable side effects (e.g., cosmetic side effects of steroids), or the need for peer conformity. Some of these challenges are most evident with diabetes because adherence requires eating foods different from what their peers eat and at different times from their peers, refraining from drinking alcohol, and giving oneself injections (which can be readily misinterpreted by both peers and adults as significant drug abuse). It is no wonder, then, that some teenagers try to hide their disease status (Johnson, Silverstein, Rosenbloom, Carter, & Cunningham, 1986). Finally, pubertal changes per se may exacerbate problems with metabolic control during adolescence (see Ruggiero & Javorsky, 1999), further complicating good management.

Relatively little systematic intervention has specifically targeted adolescent noncompliance with disease management. Three studies of social skill training (with peers and/or parents) reported mixed, albeit promising, results with diabetic adolescents, as did one study of family interventions, a study of anxiety management training, and a single-case study of biofeedback training (see Manne, 1998). Most other chronic-disease interventions have focused on children or a mixed group of adolescents and children. There have also been many and varied interventions with adolescents that have targeted noncompliance with regimens such as dental care and treatment of addictions and eating disorders, with appointment-keeping, and with prevention efforts focused on smoking, drug and alcohol use, exercise, nutrition, and sexually transmitted disease. A comprehensive review of noncompliance and adherence is beyond the scope of this chapter.

Much of the research on noncompliance has focused on patient characteristics such as gender, age, socioeconomic status, family characteristics, knowledge, skills, attitudes, health beliefs, and health status. However, the demands of the treatment regimen, the structure of health care, and the nature of the patient-provider relationship are also key factors in promoting compliance (see Manne, 1998; Phillips, 1997b; Ruggiero & Javorsky, 1999). While not yet demonstrated empirically, it would be reasonable to expect interaction effects among these variables, with specific aspects of the regimen, delivery system, and patient-provider relationship exerting greater influence on compliance among teenagers than for patients in other age groups.

Vulnerability to Abuse

Maltreatment of children and adolescents includes physical, emotional, and sexual abuse and neglect. Overall rates of maltreatment are lower in adolescence than in childhood; Burgdoff (1980) reports estimates that adolescents represent 23% to 47% of all reported cases. However, differences between age groups vary as a function of the type of abuse and appear related to adolescents' increasing independence and physical power, increasing contact with persons beyond their immediate families, and sexual development. Compared with children, adolescents are less likely to experience physical abuse and more likely to experience emotional abuse (Burgdoff, 1980), although the picture is complicated by the unreliability of estimates regarding how much abuse has been ongoing versus that with onset in adolescence. In general, adolescents are more likely than children to be abused by acquaintances and strangers rather than by family members (Christoffel, 1990; Crittenden & Craig, 1990). Gender differences are difficult to summarize because overall maltreatment rates for females increase in adolescence, with twice as many females maltreated than males, while male teenagers are more likely than female teenagers to be the victims of physical abuse and homicide.

For those adolescents who are maltreated by their families, family risk factors appear to be different from those seen for maltreated children. While socioeconomic status is negatively correlated with maltreatment risk during childhood, there is little relationship in adolescence: The families of adolescents have higher incomes and parents have more

education, compared with maltreated children (National Center of Child Abuse and Neglect, 1988). However, families of maltreated adolescents are more likely to include stepparents, even after controlling for the effect of older families, and it has been noted that stepparent-adolescent interaction is especially problematic when the adolescent demonstrates any developmental pathology (Burgess & Garbarino, 1983).

The psychosocial sequelae of maltreatment in adolescence are similar to those of childhood maltreatment, although it has been suggested that the processes involved may be different (Garbarino, Schellenbach, & Sebes, 1986). Compared with community controls, abused teenagers displayed significantly higher rates of diagnosed psychopathology even after controlling for parental psychopathology, family structure, and gender; this included major depression, dysthymia, conduct disorder, drug use and abuse, and cigarette use (Kaplan, 1994). A separate study using the Child Behavior Checklist and Youth Self-Report Form reported significantly more behavior problems (especially externalizing problems) among maltreated teenagers than among teenagers who were not maltreated (Garbarino et al., 1986).

The clearest instance of increased vulnerability for adolescents is seen with sexual abuse, particularly rape (the following discussion refers to forcible rape without consent, not statutory rape). Adolescents are twice as likely as adults to be victims of rape (Finkelhor & Dziuba-Leatherman, 1994), with half of all rape victims in the United States being under the age of 18; the peak age for victimization is 16 to 19 (Neinstein, Juliani, Shapiro, & Warf, 1996). These statistics presumably reflect the fact that teenagers are both physically attractive and more vulnerable to deception and coercion than adults. Compared with rape victims over the age of 20, adolescent victims have been assaulted more often by an acquaintance or relative (77% versus 56%) and have delayed medical evaluation (Peipert & Domalgalski, 1994). While 96% of victims of reported rapes are female, it is important to note that male teenagers also are victims of rape and that male rape may be even more underreported than female rape (Finkelhor & Dziuba-Leatherman, 1994). The rapist also tends to be young, with the peak age being 16 to 20 and 66% of all rapists being between the ages of 16 and 24 (Neinstein, Juliani, et al., 1996).

A rare study of 122 adolescent rape victims (Mann, 1981) judged the impact of the rape to be severe more often for parents (80%) than for the teenagers themselves (37%). Rather disturbingly, 80% of the teenagers reported having problems with their parents after the rape, and only 20% described their parents as supportive and understanding. More parents (67%) expressed anger at the assailant than did the teenagers (45%), and 41% of parents expressed anger at the victim. While teenagers were most often concerned about their safety and feelings of guilt and shame, parents were most often concerned about retaliation and especially the sexual sequelae; parental concern included immediate effects such as fear of pregnancy (79%), physical damage such as infertility (67%), and fear of sexually transmitted disease (52%), and long-term effects such as increased risk of future sexual activity (66%). This latter fear is not unfounded because there is a definite relationship between the onset of sexual activity at a younger age and a history of rape as the first sexual act; girls who begin their sexual careers at ages 13 and 14 are four to five times more likely to have had sex forced on them initially than are girls whose sexual activity began at age 16 or 17 (Harlap et al., 1991).

Health Care and Physical Appearance

Given the preoccupation with physical appearance and increased orientation to peers that emerge during adolescence, it would be logical to expect that any aspect of health care that relates to physical appearance would have even greater salience for teenagers than for children or adults. For example, it is no surprise that anorexia and bulimia almost always have their onset during adolescence. Yet, remarkably little research has focused on this aspect of health care.

Childhood obesity has psychosocial consequences—rejection by peers, psychological distress, dissatisfaction with one's body, and low self-esteem (Wadden & Stunkard, 1985). Because the incidence of obesity increases during adolescence, the psychosocial effects will affect more teenagers numerically and may even have more pronounced psychological impact. Measures of chronic stress, based on adolescents' reports of daily hassles, include items on skin problems and being overweight (see Repetti, McGrath, & Ishikawa, 1999). A study of burn victims reported that problems with peer relationships intensified during adolescence (Sawyer, Minde, & Zuker, 1982). The disfiguring aspects of burns suggest that this would be a particularly important area of research, yet a review by Tarnowski and Brown (1999) states, "To a large extent, the psychological aspects of pediatric burns has been a neglected topic."

A less serious, yet more common, example is acne. Acne is the most common skin disease, and possibly the most common health concern, experienced by teenagers; 85% of adolescents have some degree of acne. Prevalence and severity increases with pubertal development and peaks between ages 14 to 17 years in girls and 16 to 19 years in boys; acne varies from a short, mild course to a severe disease lasting 10 to 15 years (Pakula & Neinstein, 1996). Virtually all acne is treatable,

albeit not eradicable, given the advent of new medications such as Accutane and surgical options (see Pakula & Neinstein, 1996). Clinical experience indicates that acne is of some concern to most teenagers and a significant obstacle to peer interaction (especially with opposite-sex peers) for some, yet little information is available regarding its psychosocial impact.

The psychological impact of physical conditions would appear to be most relevant when such information might guide decisions about treatment and insurance coverage. For example, when does acne cease being just a common hassle and become a significant obstacle to social development? Similarly, under what circumstances is plastic surgery indicated, and when should families with limited financial resources receive assistance in obtaining surgery, which is typically considered purely cosmetic? Currently, such decisions represent a judgment call by clinicians and especially by families. Cost may be a significant deterrent because health insurance rarely covers cosmetic procedures. Data regarding the social and psychological benefits of cosmetic treatment would be very useful in making decisions about adolescents' health care. Even if costly treatment was not feasible, research could suggest strategies to assist teenagers in overcoming the social effects of acne or other conditions related to physical appearance.

Effects of Illness on Development

Large-scale studies of children with chronic illness and physical handicaps indicate that they are twice as likely to evidence behavioral and emotional disorders as their nondisabled peers, with internalizing disorders being more prevalent than externalizing disorders; sensory conditions (e.g., deafness) and neurological conditions (e.g., seizure disorders) increase risk more than other chronic illnesses (e.g., cancer or cystic fibrosis; see Quittner & DiGirolamo, 1998). Some difficulties are the direct result of the disabling condition, such as associated neurological problems and hyposexuality in epilepsy. Most problems, however, represent the indirect effect of disease on development because of its impact on parental and peer attitudes. Parental worry can lead to altered expectations and excessive restrictions on the child's activities and lifestyle, with family reactions ranging from overprotection to rejection, resulting in a variety of developmental problems such as low self-esteem, lack of social skills, guilt, or adopting a sick role (see Aldenkamp & Mulder, 1999).

Such effects are also found with adolescents, whose functioning is impacted negatively by having a disability, although family connectedness has been identified as having an even greater effect on emotional well-being (Wolman,

Resnick, & Harris, 1994). Specific effects on development also reflect the type of disorder, including chronicity, course, visibility, side effects of medication, amount of disruption of control, and prognosis. A highly visible disease with significant cosmetic effects, such as psoriasis, may cause more emotional distress and peer rejection than an illness such as Hodgkin's disease. Disorders or trauma that affect mobility and independence (e.g., amputation or seizure disorders) can have particular impact on adolescents' need for self-mastery, with resulting risks for psychological and social development (Neinstein & Zeltzer, 1996). Teenagers with chronic conditions often experience repeated and extended hospital stays, and various strategies have been suggested to structure the adolescent ward and its management to be appropriate for adolescents' stage of development and their concerns (Neinstein & Zeltzer, 1996).

Health Promotion

Because so much of morbidity and mortality in adolescence is preventable, promoting health via prevention has become an increasingly important focus, especially in the past decade. Anticipatory guidance for teenagers and parents is a prominent component of the AMA's GAPS recommendations for primary care. Specific interventions have included public service spots on television, largely addressing substance use and staying in school, and a host of special school and/or community programs designed to reduce the risk of pregnancy, violence, and substance abuse.

Current prevention efforts employ a dual strategy, attempting to reduce risk factors and also enhance protective factors. The concept of resilience has provided a framework for understanding how children can thrive even in adverse circumstances. Considerable evidence has identified consistent protective factors that cut across racial, gender, and economic groups. One key characteristic of resilient young people is having a close relationship with at least one caring, competent, reliable adult who promotes prosocial behavior; optimally, this sense of connectedness to adults is enhanced by opportunities to develop social skills and other skills, which engender self-confidence and self-esteem (see Resnick, 2000). Attempts to promote such adult relationships have focused on strengthening family functioning and communication as well as on the development of extrafamilial relationships through adult mentoring programs and community service.

Another important aspect of health promotion is advocacy, both for individuals and at the state/national level. Advocacy efforts range from increased funding for health care (English et al., 2000) to legal intervention. Advocacy for

laws requiring infant car seats and bicycle helmets have reduced childhood injuries. Analogously, efforts to reduce the toll of automobile accidents on adolescents have assessed the effectiveness of current strategies and explored promising new ones. Research indicates that traditional driver education has not been effective whereas a graduated driver licensing system and nighttime curfews have decreased accidents, injuries, and fatalities for teenage drivers. The most successful measures to date have been mandatory seatbelt use, minimum drinking age laws, and drunk driving laws, while other promising interventions—ignition interlock devices, administrative alcohol laws, random screening programs, and education regarding vehicle crash-worthiness—are under study (see Patel et al., 2000).

SALIENT AREAS OF ADOLESCENT HEALTH

Health care for teenagers and prevention efforts have focused on the major contributors to morbidity and mortality (trauma, substance misuse, and risky sex) as well as on problems that typically emerge during adolescence (anorexia and bulimia). Such efforts have resulted in more widespread development of shock trauma centers to reduce the impact of severe trauma and the burgeoning field of sports medicine. For example, there is now considerable evidence that athletes engage in more health-risk behaviors than nonathletes (e.g., less seat belt and helmet use, more alcohol and physical fights) and a subset of thrill-seekers are at very high risk for trauma. More recently, there has been increased attention to the other major contributor to trauma—violence (see Pratt & Greydanus, 2000). Finally, substance use and misuse is of concern per se but also as a contributor to other risky behaviors.

Many threats to adolescent health are thus interrelated, and increasing evidence suggests that multiple types of risk-taking behaviors co-occur in clusters (Irwin, 1990). A comprehensive review of these salient areas of adolescent health is beyond the scope of this chapter (see DiClemente, Hanson, & Ponton, 1996). However, a brief review of risky sexual behavior is presented in the following section.

Sexual Activity and Health Consequences

Sexual activity among American teenagers has increased dramatically over the past 40 years, largely because sexual intercourse is now initiated at a younger age (see Phillips, 1997a). Among young people ages 18 to 21, 82% reported having had sexual intercourse in a 1991 survey (see Neinstein, 1996c). Precise prevalences of sexual activity among younger teenagers are difficult to obtain because much of the available national data is obtained from high school students and thus does not include young adolescents or teenagers who are not in school. There is evidence that out-of-school teenagers are considerably more likely to have had intercourse than those still in school (70% versus 45%) as well as engage in other risky behaviors (see Neinstein, 1996c). As a rough estimate, half of girls and almost two-thirds of boys will have had sexual intercourse by the age of 15 (see R. Brown, 2000). Urban rates tend to be higher, with as many as 24% of teenagers ages 12 to 13 having had sexual intercourse (see R. Brown, 2000).

This change in sexual activity is clearly a national phenomenon, with a downward shift in age evident across all subgroups of the adolescent population. Nevertheless, there are variations among individuals and subgroups of teenagers, reflecting such factors as maternal educational level, age of menarche, intelligence, attitudes toward achievement and religion, extent of peer influence, and parenting style. In general, earlier sexual activity is correlated with other risk behaviors although less so for African American adolescents (see R. Brown, 2000).

The earlier onset of sexual intercourse has resulted in a very large number of teenagers who are sexually active and thus vulnerable to adverse health effects from sexually transmitted disease and unintended pregnancy. In addition to intercourse, the downward shift in age includes many sexual activities that are traditionally precursors to intercourse (e.g., heavy petting) or substitutes for intercourse (see Phillips, 1997a). Reported sexual practices of virginal high schoolers, males and females, included fellatio with ejaculation (11% and 8%), cunnilingus (9% and 12%), and anal intercourse (1% and .4%; see R. Brown, 2000). While avoiding the risk of pregnancy, such extra-intercourse sexual activity still presents the risk of sexually transmitted disease.

Sexually Transmitted Disease

The increased number of teenagers becoming sexually active at younger ages prompts concern regarding sexually transmitted disease (STD) not only because there is a longer time for potential exposure but also because of the cumulative effect on number of sexual partners. For example, of women who were sexually active by age 15, 25% reported 10 or more lifetime sexual partners, in contrast to 6% of those who delayed sexual activity until age 20 (see Cates & Berman, 1999). Also, teenagers may be more vulnerable to infection if they are exposed, both because they are less likely to use protection consistently and because their immune and reproductive systems are less well-developed than those of adults (e.g., cervical

ectopy in adolescents leaves more vulnerable tissue exposed; R. Brown, 2000). Significant sequelae of STDs include pelvic inflammatory disease, lowered fertility, sterility, congenital syphilis, and life-threatening disorders such as ectopic pregnancy, pelvic abscesses, cancer, and death from AIDS (R. Brown, 2000; Cates & Berman, 1999; Glazer, Goldfarb, & James, 1998).

STDs are difficult to control because of their exponential spread and because those who are infected (especially women) are often asymptomatic and hence can unwittingly transmit the infection. This results in prevalence rates among young people that are considered to be of epidemic proportions. Rough estimates indicate that three million adolescents (1 in 4 sexually active teenagers) acquire an STD every year (R. Brown, 2000). Accurate prevalence rates are difficult to obtain because only gonorrhea, syphilis, and AIDS are required to be reported to the Centers for Disease Control, and many cases are not reported despite the requirement. Because of its prevalence and the reporting requirement, gonorrhea is often used as a marker of STD patterns in general, although other STDs are more common (e.g., chlamydia is four times as prevalent) and include currently incurable diseases such as genital herpes and genital warts.

Overall, the incidence of gonorrhea decreased in the United States from 1975 through 1996, with a more recent increase of 9% from 1997 to 1999 (D. Brown, 2000). The decrease was slower for adolescents than for older age groups, resulting in the second-highest rates of gonorrhea occurring in the 15- to 19-year age group (20 to 24 being the highest; see Cates & Berman, 1999). In 1999, the highest rate of gonorrhea of all ages and racial groups was that of African American teenagers, with rates being particularly high in mid-Atlantic and southern cities (D. Brown, 2000). Further, rates have remained stable or increased for African American teenagers, in contrast to the general decline seen for White and Hispanic teenagers and for older African Americans. The effect of these trends has been to widen the racial gap for teenagers with regard to gonorrhea (and presumably most other STDs). Rates among African American teenagers (male and female) were 12 times and 9 times as high as those among White teenagers in 1981; by 1991, the rates were 44 times and 15 times as high (see Cates & Berman, 1999). In 1999, the highest rate of gonorrhea of all ages and racial groups was that of African American teenagers, with rates being particularly high in mid-Atlantic and southern cities (D. Brown, 2000).

The racial difference among teenagers probably reflects various factors, including (a) greater success with prevention messages in White communities, (b) public STD clinics being overwhelmed and underfunded, (c) publicly funded control efforts shifting from gonorrhea to chlamydia and syphilis, and (d) STD risk behaviors being fueled by illicit drugs (see Cates & Berman, 1999). These factors probably also affect patterns of HIV transmission in the United States, where it is rapidly becoming a disease of the young and the non-White population. While only 1% of all reported AIDS cases represent teenagers (ages 13 to 19), 20% of cases represent young adults (ages 20 to 29). With a mean incubation period of seven to ten years from HIV infection to AIDS, it is obvious that most of the young adults with AIDS acquired the disease as teenagers (Belzer & Neinstein, 1996). Persons of color are markedly overrepresented, comprising 55% of all cases among young people ages 13 to 24 (see Belzer & Neinstein, 1996). Finally, most AIDS cases are still occurring in the male population, but women, adolescents, and children are now the groups with the fastest growth of new infections in the United States. As heterosexual transmission increasingly becomes the major form of transmission (as it is in most of the world), adolescents will become increasingly affected (see Glazer et al., 1998).

STD prevention efforts that have emphasized abstinence and/or delaying the start of sexual activity have met with extremely limited success (see R. Brown, 2000; Cates & Berman, 1999). A general increase in public awareness seems to have had some effect on condom use, with use at last intercourse reported to range from 27% to 66% in studies of adolescents, rates that are at least twice as high as those in the 1970s, although less than half the teenagers who used condoms reported doing so all the time (see Cates & Berman, 1999). Specific interventions tailored to promote safe sexual practices suggest that it may be easier to reduce some risky behaviors than others. A group of adolescents hospitalized for psychiatric problems responded to an intensive AIDS education program by reporting that they were more likely to discontinue unprotected sex and sex with homosexual men than they were to discontinue injecting drugs or sharing needles (Ponton, DiClemente, & McKenna, 1991). Metzler, Biglan, Noell, Ary, and Ochs (2000) provided behavioral intervention to adolescents recruited in public STD clinics, who (at 6-month follow-up) reported no increase in condom use but some reduction (particularly for nonminority males) in other risk behaviors: number of sexual partners, nonmonogamous partners, sex with strangers, and use of marijuana before or during sex. They note that the relatively few interventions with some success addressed attitudes, decision making, risk recognition, and coping skills in addition to education. An entirely different strategy is prevention via vaccination, currently being employed for hepatitis B. Unfortunately, the highest risk populations of teenagers have been those least likely to have received vaccination (Cates & Berman, 1999).

Pregnancy

In the past 20 years, there has been an increase in contraception use at first intercourse, from 48% in 1982, to 65% in 1988, to 78% in 1995, largely the result of increased condom use, especially by non-Hispanic White teenagers (see R. Brown, 2000; Phillips, 1997a). However, almost one-quarter of young women remain unprotected at first intercourse. A larger number are unprotected subsequently because most young women (60%) delay seeking medical contraceptive services for at least a year after beginning sexual activity, and even those who do use contraception do not all do so consistently or correctly (see Neinstein, Rabinovitz, et al., 1996; Phillips, 1997a).

Effective contraception requires acceptance of one's sexuality; acknowledgment of risk; access to contraceptives; planning ahead; ability to communicate with one's partner; taking active measures on *each* occasion to prevent only *possible* future consequences; acceptance of side effects; coping with attitudes of peers, partners, family, and the larger community; and the perception of a positive future that will be threatened by pregnancy (see Phillips, 1997a). Even adults have difficulties in many of these areas and, given their developmental stage, consistent contraception poses particular challenges for adolescents. These obstacles to contraception result in more than one million pregnancies annually among teenage girls, the overwhelming majority being unintentional; approximately half of teenage pregnancies end in abortion and about half in live births (see Neinstein, Rabinovitz, et al., 1996).

Abortion is almost always considered to be a negative event, although remarkably little is known about the decision-making process. The early literature on psychological sequelae of abortion focused on psychopathological responses, largely based on case studies or findings from self-selected groups. More recent empirical studies of American women undergoing legal abortions suggest that the experience does not pose major psychological hazards for most women (see Adler et al., 1992), with feelings of relief and happiness being reported more frequently and with more intensity than feelings of guilt and sadness. While most women appear to cope well after an abortion, some do experience significant distress and other negative outcomes. This appears more likely for women who are younger, nulliparous, unmarried, and whose culture or religion prohibits abortion; other factors include delaying abortion until the second trimester, viewing pregnancy as highly meaningful, perceived social support by parents and partner, and expectations regarding coping well with abortion (see Phillips, 1997a). These data suggest that abortion may be an even more significant event for teenagers than for older women. The advent of RU-486, approved by the Food and Drug Administration, could reduce the difficulty and negative impact of abortion (see Phillips, 1997a).

Live births are of concern due to a variety of physical and psychosocial risks for the infant and mother (Neinstein, Rabinovitz, et al., 1996; Phillips, 1997a). One of these is the risk of teenage parenthood, which is highly likely given that adoption has become an unpopular choice for White teenagers (3% elect adoption) and has historically been uncommon among African American teenagers (less than 1% elect adoption); teenage parents (especially mothers) are likely to complete less education, be socioeconomically disadvantaged, be unmarried in adulthood, and have more children (see Neinstein, Rabinovitz, et al., 1996).

As with STD prevention, pregnancy prevention efforts that have emphasized abstinence or brief education have generally had limited success (R. Brown, 2000; Harlap, Kost, & Forest, 1991; Metzler et al., 2000). Some programs have had some success in postponing sexual activity among young teenagers. For example, the Postponing Sexual Involvement (PSI) program was developed for eighth graders in 16 middle schools in Atlanta and reported some effect on delaying sexual activity past the eighth grade, although not changing the behavior of girls who were already sexually active (Friedman, 1998). A randomized-control evaluation of a program for seventh and eighth graders in Washington, D.C. used elements of the PSI intervention and found no change in attitude toward abstinence and no effects for males except greater knowledge of birth control method efficacy, compared with a control group; girls did more often report virginity and birth-control use at last intercourse (for nonvirgins; Aarons et al., 2000). In general, however, abstinence-focused and brief educational programs have had little impact on reducing pregnancy rates (U.S. Congress, OTA, 1991).

Because STDs and pregnancy are the result of similar risky behaviors, formal interventions that have had some success and recommendations for clinical intervention with individuals share many of the same features: targeting specific behaviors, skills training, attitude change, and tailoring intervention to the individual teenager's future goals (R. Brown, 2000; Cates & Berman, 1999; Metzler et al., 2000; Phillips, 1997a). Effective and consistent use of protection may be at least as much a function of access to methods and a sympathetic staff as it is due to gains in knowledge (Zabin, Hirsch, & Smith, 1986). The good news is that the adolescent birth rate has declined, with a 12% drop from 1991 to 1996; this was especially pronounced for African American teenagers (a 21% decrease) while Hispanic teenagers' rates have not decreased and their birth rate is now the highest of any ethnic group in the United States (R. Brown, 2000).

SPECIAL SERVICES FOR ADOLESCENTS

Legal Consultation

While the legal aspects of health care are relevant for all age groups, they are particularly important for adolescents, given their unique "in-between" status. Care providers must become familiar with general constitutional principles, federal statutes, and the statutes of their own states. The most relevant issues relate to consent, confidentiality, and payment.

Adolescent providers confront a host of difficult circumstances in which these issues are commingled. For example, it is common for parents to request a drug screen for their teenager without his or her knowledge, and the parents are paying the bill. Who controls the medical record varies from state to state, with some denying disclosure to parents if the minor objects and some permitting noncontingent access by the parents. Patient-physician privilege can prevent physician disclosure in court in most but not all states (and may not extend to nonphysicians), but medical records can be subpoenaed. Most states permit minors to consent to treatment for contraception and pregnancy, communicable diseases, substance abuse, and emotional problems without parental notification, but provisions for abortion are highly variable and controversial; in some cases, the teenager may request a "judicial bypass" by the court to avoid parental notification.

Successfully navigating the challenges posed by most teenagers' legal status requires, at a minimum, that education of adolescent health providers include the legal requirements and guidelines that apply to diagnosis, treatment, counseling, record keeping, and court testimony. The availability of good legal counsel for providers is also a necessity. Finally, many providers find that patient advocacy is facilitated by learning about inexpensive legal resources that can be accessed by their adolescent patients.

School-Based Health Services

One obstacle to good adolescent health care is the need to learn about and access services in hospitals and clinics, with attendant problems with transportation, payment, and potential parental knowledge. Efforts to facilitate care prompted a movement to expand health services available in schools. Prior to 1980, school health typically consisted of, at best, a nurse in a "health room" and a school psychologist who provided psychoeducational assessment in multiple schools, with an extremely limited role for each professional; more extensive services were generally provided only for special education services (see Weist, 1997). Given increased recognition of the "new morbidity" and the need for preventive services and intervention, the obvious advantages of providing services in the school fueled an expansion of school-based programs in the 1980s and 1990s.

In addition to geographic ease of access, school-based services offer many advantages both to the individual patient and the student population in general. For example, a teenager can discreetly request treatment for a cold, feared pregnancy, or suicidal thoughts in the same general setting. Also, the overall school environment can be improved through special prevention programs and other collaborative efforts between health and educational staff. The obvious advantages of this approach led to amazing growth, with 607 school-based health centers being established by 1994; these are located in 41 states and the District of Columbia, with the majority located in high schools (46%) or middle schools (16%) (see Weist, 1997).

Mental health services have been increasingly incorporated as a needed component of comprehensive care. For example, there were mental health programs in three Baltimore schools in 1987 and in 60 schools by 1995; 80% of the Baltimore students referred for services had had no prior mental health services despite significant presenting problems (see Weist, 1997). School-based health programs are thus a very important aspect of national efforts to improve teenagers' health, although they confront a variety of ongoing challenges ranging from funding problems to integration with community services and are still very far from being able to meet the national need (Weist, 1997).

School-based health has come to refer to health services placed in elementary, middle, and high schools. Another component of school-based health, however, has been in existence for 50 years or more: college health services. Virtually every college and university in the United States provide health services on campus for their students, and these services frequently include mental health. College health providers are also adolescent health providers and are well-represented among the membership of the Society for Adolescent Medicine (SAM). The line of demarcation between adolescents and young adults is so unclear that SAM has adopted the formal position that "adolescent medicine" covers the ages of 10 to 25 (SAM, 1995).

FUTURE DIRECTIONS

Empirical investigation of adolescent health has expanded and changed considerably over the past two decades. For example, Cromer and Stager (2000) analyzed articles published in the *Journal of Adolescent Health Care* 1980 to 1998, reporting an increase in annual numbers of articles (69 to 169), decreased proportion of medical topics (61% to 38%), and increased proportion of psychosocial issues (23% to 50%). This change reflects increased awareness of "the new morbidity" and recognition of the relevance of psychosocial considerations to health risks, health promotion, and intervention. Also evident was the increasing participation of nonphysicians from nonpediatric disciplines such as psychology, public health, and nutrition. These changes were accompanied by a shift in research design from retrospective reviews to cross-sectional and longitudinal studies, although the percentage of experimental designs has remained low (never more than 5%).

This increased scholarly activity has prompted numerous national reports summarizing current knowledge and identifying future directions for research. Members of the National Adolescent Health Information Center (Millstein et al., 2000) have summarized recommendations from 53 national documents published between 1986 and 1997. They identified four major content areas as targets for future research: adolescent development, social and environmental contexts, health-related behaviors, and physical and mental disorders. In each area, priorities focused on specific applications to health. For example, additional research on adolescent cognition is needed to address teenagers' health beliefs and attitudes and decision making regarding health behaviors.

In addition to content areas, Millstein et al. (2000) identified four cross-cutting themes that should be prioritized in future research: applying a developmental perspective to investigation of adolescent health, focusing on health rather than treatment of illness, recognizing the diversity of the adolescent population, and investigating multiple models of influence. For example, studies of causal influences should consider the interrelationships among biological, psychological, and social aspects of development; their effects on behavior and health; and the multiple sources of social and environmental influences on adolescent development and health.

Millstein et al. (2000) note that implementing these research priorities will necessitate the requisite human resources and adequate funding. They recommend establishing a task force on training needs to identify gaps in training and propose training initiatives. Since children and adolescents currently receive less than 3% of national research funds, Millstein et al.

(2000) also recommend establishing a task force on funding to increase available funds and identify those areas of high priority that are now most underfunded. As with other areas of research, implementing this research agenda will require strengthening the links between research and practice. Making the results truly useful will necessitate closer and stronger integration of research and policy.

SUMMARY

Social changes in the past half century have both expanded the concept of adolescence and markedly altered the threats to adolescent health. Biological changes in pubertal maturation have lowered the age at which adolescence begins, and economic and educational demands have expanded the upper limits of adolescence. Increased access to weapons, contraception, illegal substances, and motor vehicles, combined with changing social attitudes and reduced adult supervision (due to divorce and the increased proportion of working parents) have worsened the overall health status of contemporary American teenagers, compared with those in the 1950s and with Americans in all other age groups.

At least 80% of morbidity and mortality in adolescence is behaviorally based and thus preventable or at least reducible. Improving adolescent health will require increased knowledge of effective prevention and treatment strategies, better dissemination of such information, and the willingness to make legislative and funding changes to enhance protective factors and reduce injury or risks. Health is more than the absence of disease; it includes the enjoyment of oneself and of life, together with the ready acceptance of personal and social responsibilities. Raising healthy adolescents will ultimately yield healthier and better adjusted adults.

REFERENCES

Aarons, S. J., Jenkins, R. R., Raine, T. R., El-Khorazaty, M. N., Woodward, K. M., Williams, R. L., et al. (2000). Postponing sexual intercourse among urban junior high school students: A randomized controlled evaluation. *Journal of Adolescent Health, 27,* 236–247.

Adler, N. E., David, H. P., Major, B. N., Roth, S. H., Russo, N. F., & Wyatt, G. E. (1992). Psychological factors in abortion: A review. *American Psychologist, 47,* 1194–1204.

Aldenkamp, A. P., & Mulder, O. G. (1999). Psychosocial consequences of epilepsy. In A. J. Goreczny & M. Hersen (Eds.), *Handbook of pediatric and adolescent health psychology* (pp. 105–114). Boston: Allyn & Bacon.

Allen, K. D., Warzak, W. J., Greger, N. G., Bernotas, T. D., & Huseman, C. A. (1993). Psychosocial adjustment of children with isolated growth hormone deficiency. *Children's Health Care, 22,* 61–72.

Allgood-Merten, B., Lewinsohn, P. M., & Hops, H. (1990). Sex differences and adolescent depression. *Journal of Abnormal Psychology, 99,* 55–63.

American Academy of Pediatrics. (1978). *A report by the Task Force on Pediatric Education.* Elk Grove, IL: American Academy of Pediatrics.

American Association of University Women. (1992). *How schools shortchange girls: The AAUW report: A study of major findings on girls in education* (p. 116). Washington, DC: American Association of University Women Educational Foundation.

American Medical Association. (1994). *AMA Guidelines for Adolescent Preventive Services (GAPS): Recommendations and rationale.* Baltimore: Williams & Wilkins.

Belzer, M. E., & Neinstein, L. S. (1996). HIV infections and AIDS. In L. S. Neinstein (Ed.), *Adolescent medicine: A practical guide* (3rd ed., pp. 513–544). Baltimore: Williams & Wilkins.

Brener, N. D., & Collins, J. L. (1998). Co-occurrence of high-risk behaviors among adolescents in the United States. *Journal of Adolescent Health, 22,* 209–213.

Brown, D. (2000, December 6). Gonorrhea decline reverses: Cases up 9%. *The Washington Post,* p. A3.

Brown, R. T. (2000). Adolescent sexuality at the dawn of the 21st century. In V. C. Strasburger & D. E. Greydanus (Eds.), At-risk adolescents: An update for the new century. *Adolescent Medicine State of the Art Reviews, 11,* pp. 19–34.

Burgdoff, K. (1980, December). *Recognition and reporting of child maltreatment: Findings from the National Incidence and Severity of Child Abuse and Neglect Study.* Washington, DC: National Center on Child Abuse and Neglect.

Burgess, R. L., & Garbarino, J. (1983). Doing what comes naturally? An evolutionary perspective on child abuse. In D. Finkelhor, R. Gelles, G. Hotaling, & M. Straus (Eds.), *The dark side of families* (pp. 38–60). Beverly Hills, CA: Sage.

Cates, W., Jr., & Berman, S. M. (1999). Prevention of sexually transmitted diseases other than human immunodeficiency virus. In A. J. Goreczny & M. Hersen (Eds.), *Handbook of pediatric and adolescent health psychology* (pp. 361–370). Boston: Allyn & Bacon.

Christoffel, K. K. (1990). Violent death and injury in U.S. children and adolescents. *American Journal of Diseases of Children, 144,* 697–706.

Comerci, G. D., & Schwebel, R. (2000). Substance abuse: An overview. In V. C. Strasburger & D. E. Greydanus (Eds.), At-risk adolescents: An update for the new century. *Adolescent Medicine State of the Art Reviews, 11,* pp. 79–101.

Conger, J. J., & Galambos, N. L. (1997). *Adolescence and youth* (5th ed., pp. 71–74). New York: Addison Wesley Longman.

Costello, E. J., Edelbrock, C., Costello, A. J., Dulcan, M. K., Burns, B. J., & Brent, D. (1988). Psychopathology in pediatric primary care: The new hidden morbidity. *Pediatrics, 82,* 415–424.

Crittenden, P. M., & Craig, S. E. (1990). Developmental trends in the nature of child homicide. *Journal of Interpersonal Violence, 5,* 202–216.

Crockett, L. J., & Petersen, A. C. (1987). Pubertal status and psychosocial development: Findings from the early adolescent study. In R. M. Lerner & T. T. Roch (Eds.), *Biological and psychosocial interactions in early adolescence: A life-span perspective* (pp. 173–188). Hillsdale, NJ: Erlbaum.

Cromer, B. A., & Stager, M. M. (2000). Research articles published in the *Journal of Adolescent Health*: A two-decade comparison. *Journal of Adolescent Health, 27,* 306–313.

Delamater, A., Davis, S., Bubb, J., Santiago, J., Smith, J., & White, N. (1989). Self monitoring of blood glucose by adolescents with diabetes: Technical skills and utilization of data. *Diabetes Educator, 15,* 56–61.

Delamater, A. M., & Edison, M. (1998). Endocrine disorders. In R. T. Ammerman & J. V. Campo (Eds.), *Handbook of pediatric psychology and psychiatry* (Vol. 2, pp. 244–265). Boston: Allyn & Bacon.

DiClemente, R. J., Hanson, W., & Ponton, L. (Eds.). (1996). *Handbook of adolescent health risk behavior.* New York: Plenum Press.

Douvan, E. A., & Adelson, J. (1966). *The adolescent experience.* New York: Wiley.

Duke, P. M., Litt, I. F., & Gross, R. T. (1980). Adolescent self-assessment of sexual maturation. *Pediatrics, 66,* 918–920.

English, A., Kaplan, D., & Morreale, M. (2000). Financing adolescent health care: The role of Medicaid and CHIP. In V. C. Strasburger & D. E. Greydanus (Eds.), At-risk adolescents: An update for the new century. *Adolescent Medicine State of the Art Reviews, 11,* pp. 165–182.

Finkelhor, D., & Dziuba-Leatherman, J. (1994). Victimization of children. *American Psychologist, 49,* 173–183.

Finkelstein, J. S., Neer, R. M., & Biller, B. M. K. (1992). Osteopenia in men with a history of delayed puberty. *New England Journal of Medicine, 326,* 600–606.

Finkelstein, J. W., D'Arcangelo, R., Susman, E. J., Chinchilli, V. M., Kunselman, S. J., Schwab, J., et al. (1999). Self-assessment of physical sexual maturation in boys and girls with delayed puberty. *Journal of Adolescent Health, 25,* 379–381.

Fraser, J. J., Jr. (1995). Nonfatal injuries in adolescents: United States, 1998. *Journal of Adolescent Health, 16,* 146.

Friedman, L. (1998). Postponing sexual involvement. In A. Henderson & S. Champlin (Eds.), *Promoting teen health: Linking schools. health organizations, and community* (pp. 228–232). Thousand Oaks, CA: Sage.

Gans, J. E. (1990). *America's adolescents: How healthy are they? U.S. Congress, OTA, Adolescent Health* (pp. 1–108). Chicago: American Medical Association.

Garbarino, J., Schellenbach, C., & Sebes, J. (1986). *Troubled youth, troubled families.* New York: Aldine.

Glazer, J. P., Goldfarb, J., & James, R. S. (1998). Infectious diseases. In R. T. Ammerman & J. V. Campo (Eds.), *Handbook of pediatric psychology and psychiatry: Disease, injury, and illness* (Vol. 2, pp. 347–368). Boston: Allyn & Bacon.

Haggerty, R. (1986). The changing nature of pediatrics. In N. A. Krasnegor, J. D. Arateh, & M. F. Cataldo (Eds.), *Child health behavior: A behavioral pediatrics perspective* (pp. 9–16). New York: Wiley.

Harlap, S., Kost, K., & Forest, J. D. (1991). *Preventing pregnancy, protecting health: A new look at birth control choices in the United States.* New York: Allen Guttmacher Institute.

Hayward, C., Killen, J. D., & Hammer, L. D. (1992). Pubertal stage and panic attack history in sixth and seventh grade girls. *American Journal of Psychiatry, 149,* 1239–1243.

Hein, K. (1993). Evolution or revolution: Reforming health care for adolescents in America. *Journal of Adolescent Health, 14,* 520–523.

Hergenroeder, A. C. (1995). Bone mineralization, hypothalmic amenorrhea, and sex steroid therapy in female adolescents and young adults. *Journal of Pediatrics, 126,* 683–688.

Herman-Giddens, M. E., Slora, E. J., Wasserman, R. C., Bourdony, C. J., Bhapkar, M. V., Koch, G. G., et al. (1997). Secondary sexual characteristics and menses in young girls seen in office practice: A study from the Pediatric Research in Office Settings Network. *Pediatrics, 99,* 505–512.

Holmes, C., Karlsson, J., & Thompson, R. (1985). Social and school competencies in children with short stature: Longitudinal patterns. *Developmental and Behavioral Pediatrics, 6,* 263–267.

Irwin, C. E., Jr. (1990). The theoretical concept of at-risk adolescents. *Adolescent Medicine State of the Art Reviews, 1,* 1–17.

Johnson, S. B., Freund, A., Silverstein, J., Hansen, C., & Malone, J. (1990). Adherence-health status relationships in childhood diabetes. *Health Psychology, 9,* 606–631.

Johnson, S. B., Silverstein, J., Rosenbloom, A., Carter, R., & Cunningham, W. (1986). Assessing daily management in childhood diabetes. *Health Psychology, 5,* 545–564.

Kaplan, S. J. (1994). *Adolescent abuse: Overview of recent research findings.* Paper presented at the annual meetings of the American Psychiatric Association, Washington, DC.

Kovacs, M., Goldston, D., Obrosky, S., & Iyengar, S. (1992). Prevalence and predictors of pervasive noncompliance with medical treatment among youths with insulin-dependent diabetes mellitus. *Journal of the American Academy of Child and Adolescent Psychiatry, 31,* 1112–1119.

Larson, R., & Richards, M. H. (1991). Daily companionship in late childhood and early adolescence: Changing developmental contexts. *Child Development, 62,* 284–300.

Lemonick, M. D. (2000, October 30). Teens before their time. *Time,* 66–74.

Livson, N., & Peskin, H. (1980). Perspectives on adolescence from longitudinal research. In J. Adelson (Ed.), *Handbook of adolescent psychology* (pp. 47–98). New York: Wiley.

Mann, E. B. (1981). Self-reported stresses of adolescent rape victims. *Journal of Adolescent Health Care, 2,* 29–37.

Manne, S. L. (1998). Treatment adherence and compliance. In R. T. Ammerman & J. V. Campo (Eds.), *Handbook of pediatric psychology and psychiatry: Disease, injury, and illness* (Vol. 2, pp. 103–132). Boston: Allyn & Bacon.

McAnarney, E. R. (1992). Adolescent general inpatient unit. In E. R. McAnarney, R. E. Kreipe, D. P. Orr, & G. D. Comerci (Eds.), *Textbook of adolescent medicine* (pp. 161–162). Philadelphia: Saunders.

McAnarney, E. R., Kreipe, R. E., Orr, D. P., & Comerci, G. D. (Eds.). (1992). *Textbook of adolescent medicine.* Philadelphia: Saunders.

Metzler, C. W., Biglan, A., Noell, J., Ary, D. V., & Ochs, L. (2000). A randomized controlled trial of a behavioral intervention to reduce high-risk sexual behavior among adolescents. *Behavior Therapy, 31,* 27–54.

Millstein, S. G., Ozer, E. J., Ozer, E. M., Brindis, C. D., Knopf, D. K., & Irwin, C. E., Jr. (2000). *Research priorities in adolescent health: An analysis and synthesis of research recommendations, executive summary.* San Francisco: University of California, National Adolescent Health Information Center.

National Center of Child Abuse and Neglect. (1988). *Study findings: Study of National Incidence and Prevalence of Child Abuse and Neglect.* Washington, DC: U.S. Department of Health and Human Services.

Neinstein, L. S. (Ed.). (1996a). *Adolescent health care: A practical guide* (3rd ed., pp. 3–39). Baltimore: Williams & Wilkins.

Neinstein, L. S. (1996b). Amenorrhea. In L. S. Neinstein (Ed.), *Adolescent health care: A practical guide* (3rd ed., pp. 783–795). Baltimore: Williams & Wilkins.

Neinstein, L. S. (1996c). Vital statistics and injuries. In L. S. Neinstein (Ed.), *Adolescent health care: A practical guide* (3rd ed., pp. 110–138). Baltimore: Williams & Wilkins.

Neinstein, L. S., Juliani, M. A., Shapiro, J., & Warf, C. (1996). Rape and sexual abuse. In L. S. Neinstein (Ed.), *Adolescent health care: A practical guide* (3rd ed., pp. 1143–1172). Baltimore: Williams & Wilkins.

Neinstein, L. S., & Kaufman, F. R. (1996). Abnormal growth and development. In L. S. Neinstein (Ed.), *Adolescent health care: A practical guide* (3rd ed., pp. 165–193). Baltimore: Williams & Wilkins.

Neinstein, L. S., & MacKenzie, R. (1996). High-risk and out-of-control behavior. In L. S. Neinstein (Ed.), *Adolescent health care: A practical guide* (3rd ed., pp. 1094–1106). Baltimore: Williams & Wilkins.

Neinstein, L. S., Rabinovitz, S. J., & Schneir, A. (1996). Teenage pregnancy. In L. S. Neinstein (Ed.), *Adolescent health care: A practical guide* (3rd ed., pp. 656–676). Baltimore: Williams & Wilkins.

Neinstein, L. S., & Zeltzer, L. K. (1996). Chronic illness in the adolescent. In L. S. Neinstein (Ed.), *Adolescent health care: A practical guide* (3rd ed., pp. 1173–1195). Baltimore: Williams & Wilkins.

Nottelmann, E. D., Susman, E. J., Inoff-Germain, G., Cutler, G. B., Loriaux, D. L., & Chrousos, G. P. (1987). Developmental process in early adolescence: Relationships between adolescent adjustment problems and chronologic age, pubertal stage, and puberty-related serum hormone levels. *Journal of Pediatrics, 110,* 473–480.

Offer, D., Ostrov, E., & Howard, K. I. (1981). *The adolescent: A psychological self-portrait.* New York: Basic Books.

Pakula, A. S., & Neinstein, L. S. (1996). Acne. In L. S. Neinstein (Ed.), *Adolescent health care: A practical guide* (3rd ed., pp. 349–359). Baltimore: Williams & Wilkins.

Patel, D. R., Greydanus, D. E., & Rowlett, J. D. (2000). Romance with the automobile in the 20th century: Implications for adolescents in a new millennium. In V. C. Strasburger & D. E. Greydanus (Eds.), At-risk adolescents: An update for the new century. *Adolescent Medicine State of the Art Reviews, 11,* pp. 127–140.

Patel, D. R., & Luckstead, E. F. (2000). Sport participation, risk taking, and health risk behaviors. In V. C. Strasburger & D. E. Greydanus (Eds.), At-risk adolescents: An update for the new century. *Adolescent Medicine State of the Art Reviews, 11,* pp. 141–156.

Peipert, J. F., & Domagalski, L. R. (1994). Epidemiology of adolescent sexual assault. *Obstetrics and Gynecology, 84,* 867–873.

Phillips, S. (1997a). Adolescent sexuality, contraception, and abortion. In J. D. Noshpitz (Series Ed.) & L. T. Flaherty & R. M. Sarles (Vol. Eds.), *Handbook of child and adolescent psychiatry. Vol 3: Adolescence: Development and syndromes* (pp. 181–191). New York: Wiley.

Phillips, S. (1997b). Compliance with medical regimes. In J. D. Noshpitz (Series Ed.) & L. T. Flaherty & R. M. Sarles (Vol. Eds.), *Handbook of child and adolescent psychiatry. Vol 3: Adolescence: Development and syndromes* (pp. 407–412). New York: Wiley.

Phillips, S. A., Moscicki, A. B., Kaufman, M., & Moore, E. (1998). The composition of SAM: Development of diversity. *Journal of Adolescent Health, 23,* 162–165.

Phipps, S., & DeCuir-Whalley, S. (1990). Adherence issues in pediatric bone marrow transplantation. *Journal of Pediatric Psychology, 15,* 459–476.

Ponton, L. E., DiClemente, R. J., & McKenna, S. (1991). An AIDS education and prevention program for hospitalized adolescents. *Journal of the American Academy of Child and Adolescent Psychiatry, 91,* 729–734.

Pratt, H. D., & Greydanus, D. E. (2000). Adolescent violence: Concepts for a new millennium. In V. C. Strasburger & D. E. Greydanus (Eds.), At-risk adolescents: An update for the new century. *Adolescent Medicine State of the Art Reviews, 11,* pp. 103–126.

Quittner, A. L., & DiGirolamo, A. M. (1998). Family adaptation to childhood disability and illness. In R. T. Ammerman & J. V. Campo (Eds.), *Handbook of pediatric psychology and psychiatry: Disease, injury, and illness* (Vol. 2, pp. 70–102). Boston: Allyn & Bacon.

Repetti, R. L., McGrath, E. P., & Ishikawa, S. S. (1999). Daily stress and coping in childhood and adolescence. In A. J. Goreczny & M. Hersen (Eds.), *Handbook of pediatric and adolescent health psychology* (pp. 343–360). Boston: Allyn & Bacon.

Resnick, M. D. (2000). Protective factors, resiliency, and healthy youth development. In V. C. Strasburger & D. E. Greydanus (Eds.), At-risk adolescents: An update for the new century. *Adolescent Medicine State of the Art Reviews, 11,* pp. 157–164.

Ruggiero, L., & Javorsky, D. J. (1999). Diabetes self-management in children. In A. J. Goreczny & M. Hersen (Eds.), *Handbook of pediatric and adolescent health psychology* (pp. 49–70). Boston: Allyn & Bacon.

Sandberg, D., Brook, A., & Campos, S. (1994). Short stature: A psychosocial burden requiring a growth hormone therapy? *Pediatrics, 94,* 832–840.

Sawyer, M. G., Minde, K., & Zuker, R. (1982). The burned child: Scarred for life? *Burns, 9,* 201–213.

Scales, P. (1988, Fall). Helping adolescents create their futures. *Florida Educator,* 4–9.

Siegel, J. M., Yancey, A. K., Aneshengel, C. S., & Schuler, R. (1999). Body image, perceived pubertal timing, and adolescent mental health. *Journal of Adolescent Health, 25,* 155 165.

Silber, T. J. (1983). Adolescent medicine: Origins, segmenting, synthesis. *Journal of Adolescent Health Care, 4,* 136–140.

Simmons, R. G., Blyth, D. A., & McKinney, K. L. (1983). The social and psychological effects of puberty on White females. In J. Brooks-Gunn & A. C. Peterson (Eds.), *Girls at puberty: Biological and psychosocial perspectives* (pp. 229–272). New York: Plenum Press.

Society for Adolescent Medicine. (1995). A position statement of the SAM. *Journal of Adolescent Health, 16,* 413–416.

Steinhausen, H., Dorr, H. G., Kannenberg, R., & Malin, Z. (2000). The behavior profile of children and adolescents with short stature. *Developmental and Behavioral Pediatrics, 21,* 423–428.

Stuber, M. L., & Canning, R. D. (1998). Organ transplantation. In R. T. Ammerman & J. V. Campo (Eds.), *Handbook of pediatric psychology and psychiatry: Disease, injury, and illness* (Vol. 2, pp. 369–382). Boston: Allyn & Bacon.

Susman, E. J., Nottelmann, E. D., Inoff-Germain, G., Dorn, L. D., Cutler, G. B., Jr., Loriaux, D. L., et al. (1985). The relation of relative hormonal levels and physical development and social-emotional behavior in young adolescents. *Journal of Youth and Adolescence, 14,* 245–264.

Tanner, J. M. (1962). *Growth at adolescence* (2nd ed.). Springfield, IL: Charles C Thomas.

Tarnowski, K. J., & Brown, R. T. (1999). Burn injuries. In A. J. Goreczny & M. Hersen (Eds.), *Handbook of pediatric and adolescent health psychology* (p. 117). Boston: Allyn & Bacon.

U.S. Congress, Office of Technology Assessment. (1991, November). Background and the effectiveness of selected prevention and treatment services. *Adolescent health* (Vol. 2). Washington, DC: U.S. Congress.

Wadden, T. A., & Stunkard, A. J. (1985). Social and psychological consequences of obesity. *Annals of Internal Medicine, 103,* 1062–1067.

Weist, M. D. (1997). Expanded school mental health services: A national movement in progress. In T. Ollendick & R. J. Prinz (Eds.), *Advances in clinical child psychology* (Vol. 19, pp. 319–352). New York: Plenum Press.

Wolman, C., Resnick, M. D., & Harris, L. J. (1994). Emotional well-being among adolescents with and without chronic conditions. *Journal of Adolescent Health, 15,* 199–206.

Youniss, J., & Smollar, J. (1989). Adolescents: Interpersonal relationships in social contexts. In T. J. Berndt & G. W. Ladd (Eds.), *Peer relationships in child development* (pp. 300–316). New York: Wiley.

Zabin, L. S., Hirsch, M. B., & Smith, E. A. (1986). Evaluation of a pregnancy-prevention program for urban teenagers. *Family Planning Perspectives, 18,* 119–126.

Zachman, M., Ferrandez, A., & Muurse, G. (1976). Testosterone treatment of excessively tall boys. *Journal of Pediatrics, 88,* 116–121.

CHAPTER 21

Adult Development and Aging

ILENE C. SIEGLER, HAYDEN B. BOSWORTH, AND MERRILL F. ELIAS

Aging and age have always been constructs that play central roles in health psychology. Health psychologists study individuals with specific physical illnesses and seek to understand how the aging process might modify the impact of these diseases on behavior. Age has potential interactions with all of the important causal and mediating variables in

health psychology and is a major risk factor for most chronic diseases.

There is a long history of concern with health in the psychology of adult development and aging. In each of the *Handbooks of Aging,* there has been a "health psychology" chapter (Deeg, Kardaun, & Fozard, 1996; Eisdorfer & Wilkie, 1977; M. Elias, Elias, & Elias, 1990; Siegler & Costa, 1985). Collectively, these Handbooks provide excellent reviews of the relevant literature that need not be repeated here. In this chapter, we deal with psychological studies of adults that evaluate the impact of aging on cardiovascular disease and cancer with attention to the role of cognition, personality, and social functioning—that is, the health psychology of aging in the context of known diseases. We start with an overview of important aging concepts and issues. We then turn to the study of hypertension because it is especially useful in illustrating the issues that separate the effects of aging from the effects of disease on associated cognitive factors. We then turn to a review of methodological issues in the field, summarize work in personality and social factors on disease, and point out some

Dr. Siegler's work is supported by Grants R01 AG12458, R01 AG-19605, and P01 AG17553 from the National Institute on Aging; R01 HL55356 from the National Heart, Lung, and Blood Institute; and P01 CA72099 from the National Cancer Institute.

Dr. Bosworth's work is supported by Grant P01 CA72099 from the National Cancer Institute and from the Department of Veterans Affairs, Veterans Health Administration, HSR&D Service, Program 824 Funds.

Dr. Elias' work is supported by Grants R01 HL67358 and R01 HL65117 from the National Heart Lung and Blood Institute, R01 AG16495 and R01 AG08122 from the National Institute on Aging, and R01 NS17950 from the National Institute of Neurological Diseases and Stroke.

We would like to thank Mike Robbins for his help with the chapter.

emerging areas in developmental health psychology with particular attention to problems associated with cancers.

WHAT HEALTH PSYCHOLOGISTS NEED TO KNOW ABOUT AGING

When we consider the age group 65 to 69, 83% have no disability and only 3% are in nursing homes; at ages 85 to 89, 45% have no disability and 15% are in nursing homes; by age 100, 18% have no disability and 48% are in nursing homes (Siegler, Bosworth, & Poon, in press). Thus, the age of the study sample has consequences for both research design and the conclusions that can be drawn.

What Do We Know from a Person's Age?

All we know for sure from a person's age is the year of birth (birth cohort) and the historical time period of the person's development. This information has implications for the intersection of lifecycle with sociohistorical events and varies with gender, race, social class, and physical location. Studies have often focused on cohort and aging effects, but there has been a lack of focus on period effects that may explain observed age differences when examining the relationship between health, behavior, and aging. A *period effect* or is a societal or cultural change that may occur between two measurements that present plausible alternative explanations for the outcome of a study (Baltes, Reese, & Nesselroade, 1988). This is particularly true for medical advances and changes in treatments. For example, in the field of cardiology, advances with surgery (i.e., stents) and new medications have increased survival following a myocardial infarction, but the increased number of persons surviving has resulted in increased numbers of people with congestive heart failure. The introduction of the prostate-specific antigen (PSA) test in 1987 accounts for age-related changes in the detection of prostate cancer. At older ages, age does not provide the developmental benchmark that it does early in the lifecycle. With increased age, there is also increased interindividual differences such that the difference between two 10-year-olds will be significantly less than the difference between two 80-year-olds. Increased environmental exposure can influence development in later life as can be seen when looking at studies involving older twins (see McClearn & Heller, 2000).

Disease Prevalence in Aging

Disease prevalence has generally risen in the older noninstitutionalized population (Crimmins & Saito, 2000). The largest increases have been in heart disease and cancer, two major causes of old-age mortality. Although prevalence has increased, there has been a decline in mortality from heart disease from the late 1960s through the present. Recently, cancer mortality has also declined. The increased prevalence of heart disease and cancer most likely results from mortality declines and longer survival for people with these diseases (Crimmins & Saito, 2000).

Older persons are more likely to have multiple disorders. In 1987, 90 million Americans were living with chronic conditions; 39 million of these were living with more than one chronic condition. More than 45% of noninstitutionalized Americans have one or more chronic conditions (Hoffman, Rice, & Sung, 1996). Among adults age 65 years and older, the five most prevalent physician-diagnosed diseases were hypertension (57%), diabetes (20%), coronary artery disease (15%), cancer (9%), and cardiovascular disease (9%; Fillenbaum, Pieper, Cohen, Cornoni-Huntley, & Guralnik, 2000). While the prevalence of diseases is increasing, the rates of disability are declining (Manton & Gu, 2001)—these declines may be due to a better risk profile earlier in the lifecycle. Future projections (Singer & Manton, 1998) suggest that this decline will continue.

Age-Related Changes in Functioning

Older persons are likely to have more sensory deficits. Hearing impairment is the third most common chronic condition of older people, second only to arthritis and hypertension (Fowles, 1994). More than 30% of noninstitutionalized individuals age 65 and older report problems with hearing, and 10% report problems with vision (USDHHS, 1994). Other studies have found visual loss present in 13% of those 65 years and older and in 27% of those more than 85 years of age (Havlik, 1986).

Not all physiological functions decline with age and not all decline at the same rate. Age-related changes occur commonly in pulse pressure, creatinine clearance, glucose tolerance, body fat composition, and pulmonary vital capacity. All of these may alter the effect of particular risk factors on cardiovascular outcomes as well as survivorship after disease onset, and they may not all be accounted for in various population studies (Kaplan, Haan, & Wallace, 1999). Overall, independent of disease status, the older the organism, the longer it will take to recover from a measured stress (Siegler, 1989).

Defining Normal Aging

How do we differentiate aging and disease? This is one of the most conceptually important questions in health psychology. The definition is made difficult by the increasingly close interrelationship between disease and aging. With advancing age, there is an increasing recognition of new diseases, and discovery of treatments and cures for old diseases. The definition is fundamental to the study of interactions between aging and disease.

Despite the attention this issue has received, there is still no definitive answer to what is disease, what is primary aging, and which, if any, diseases are irreversible. The fact that the diseases, once thought to be intrinsic to the aging processes, are being identified every day serves to place us on shifting sand. Today's primary aging variable is tomorrow's secondary aging variable. J. G. Evans of Oxford University states this most eloquently: "In fact to draw a distinction between disease and normal aging is to attempt to separate the undefined from the indefinable" (Evans, 1988, p. 40). Despite the difficulty in making distinctions between primary and secondary aging caused by progress in diagnostics and treatment, it is necessary to make this distinction for each patient and to do so explicitly. The "age variable" in any experiment or analysis is an empty variable unless operationally defined or indexed.

Not only are there research implications with respect to our conceptions of primary and secondary aging, but there are also significant implications for treatment. Evans (1988) summarizes these issues and argues that the distinction between normal aging and disease has arisen from clinical medicine because of its tradition of thinking dichotomously, that is, if one must treat or not treat, it then becomes important to think in terms of disease or nondisease. Most importantly, he argues that the disease and nondisease model is inappropriate for clinical practice with the elderly because it precludes nontraditional interventions and allows physicians to dismiss potential medical problems as the natural consequence of aging. Siegler and Costa (1985) point out that patients may seek treatment if they do not dismiss changes in health and behavior as an inevitable consequence of aging. In a classic study, Dye and Sassenrath (1979) reported that health care professionals classified as "normal aging" any condition associated with the onset of old age, even though that condition could be treated or reversed.

INTERACTIONS WITH OTHER DISCIPLINES

Both aging and disease are dynamic processes, and the study of these processes is inherently multidisciplinary involving particularly geriatric medicine and epidemiology.

Geriatric Medicine

It is important to review the literature of geriatric medicine. Very good summaries on the impact of age on basic mechanisms of the immune system (Murasko & Bernstein, 1999; Roth & Yen, 1999), cardiovascular system (Lakatta, 1999), and endocrine system (Gruenwald & Matsumoto, 1999;

Matthews & Cauley, 1999; Tenover, 1999), as well as major diseases of aging that are studied in health psychology—especially coronary heart disease (Wei, 1999), hypertension (Applegate, 1999), diabetes (Halter, 1999), and Alzheimer's disease (AD; Kawas, 1999), can be found in Hazzard et al.'s text (1999) on geriatric medicine. The 126 chapters of this compendium provide an excellent source for the clinical care of the aged and should be extremely useful for health psychologists when working in an area with older persons as research subjects or patients.

Geriatric medicine includes the full range of variation seen at the end of the lifecycle. For some, life span continuation is the norm, and the typical health psychology orientation by disease makes sense. For others, homeostasis has broken down (see Siegler, 1989), and death appears to result from nonspecific mechanisms (see Nuland, 1995), making the search for behavioral correlates difficult.

Epidemiology and Preventive Medicine

Familiarity with the epidemiological literature and training in epidemiology, at some level, is very important for behavioral scientists who work in aging and healthy psychology. You need not be an epidemiologist to be sufficiently well-versed in epidemiological methods to bring these tools into your practice. Basic familiarity with epidemiological designs, methodological issues, and definitions provides useful tools for research to health and psychologists and facilitates cross-disciplinary communication. Epidemiological terms, also sometimes used widely in medical research, are used incorrectly by psychologists. The term *incidence* (new cases over some period of time) is often confused with *prevalence* (number of cases at a designated time). Descriptions of designs (e.g., case study, prospective cohort, retrospective cohort) are often used incorrectly in the psychological literature. Psychologists should become familiar with these terms. A number of texts offer this background (Fletcher, Fletcher, & Wagner, 1988; Hennekens, Buring, & Mayerent, 1987; Sackett, Haynes, Guyatt, & Tugwell, 1991). Rothman's work (1986, 1988) offers an advanced exposure to methodological issues such as subject selection, power calculation, and logistic regression analysis (Hosmer & Lemeshow, 1998), while Larsen and Shadlen (1999) provide an excellent chapter on who should interpret screening diagnostics tests in individual cases.

COGNITION AND NEUROPSYCHOLOGY

Research on cardiovascular disease and aging represents a well-studied topic in health-aging research and serves as a model for conceptual and methodological problems associated with the broader literature on disease, aging, and cognition.

Cardiovascular Disease, Aging, and Cognitive Functioning

Familiarity with the literature on cardiovascular disease or with risk factors for cardiovascular disease such as hypertension, obesity, diabetes, cigarette smoking, and high cholesterol and cognitive function is a prerequisite for understanding research in the area of cardiovascular disease and behavior. (See the review by Waldstein & Elias, 2001.) Hypertension, diabetes, smoking, and obesity have been associated with poorer cognitive functioning, although total cholesterol and alcohol consumption have been associated both with better and poorer cognition depending on "dose relationships" and the specific cognitive measures employed (see P. Elias, Elias, D'Agostino, Silbershatz, & Wolf, 1999; Muldoon, Flory, & Ryan, 2001).

Because of the significant volume of research on cardiovascular disease variables, we focus on studies of older populations and of interactions of disease factors with age (cross-sectional) or aging (longitudinal). We restrict our review to hypertension because it has received the greatest amount of attention and because it serves as a model, or general paradigm, for studies of the cumulative impact of aging and disease, or risk for disease, on cognitive functioning.

Hypertension and Age: Main Effects

It is well-known that age and aging are associated with declines in cognitive functioning. It is also clear that hypertension and increments in systolic and diastolic blood pressure (DBP) are associated with lower levels of cognitive functioning across all ages. Hypertension affects almost all areas of the cerebral vasculature. A wide range of abilities are adversely affected, including psychomotor speed, visual constructive ability, learning memory, selective attention, fluid ability, and executive function (M. Elias & Robbins, 1991a; Waldstein, 1995; Waldstein & Katzel, 2001). The most recent summaries of hypothetical variables relating high blood pressure and cognitive performance in explanatory models have been provided in papers by Waldstein (1995) and Waldstein and Katzel (2001). These mechanisms include genetic and environmental factors, psychosocial variables, mood states and traits, and a long list of biological factors including cerebral metabolism, blood flow, changes in endothelial dysfunction, cellular dysfunction, neurochemical dysfunction, white matter disease, silent infarction, brain atrophy, and atherosclerosis. An important aspect of these models is that they posit different mechanisms that cause blood pressure to impact cognitive function. Although much of the evidence for the validity of these models is indirect, they are consistent with what is known about the physiological and structural consequence of sustained hypertension and hypertension in youth. Less comprehensive, but nevertheless important, models for explaining why other cardiovascular risk factors and disease affect cognitive functioning may be seen in the various chapters of the Waldstein and Elias (2001) text. In the following section, we focus on the literature on hypertension.

Hypertension in Old Age

Comprehensive reviews of the aging-hypertension literature are available (M. Elias, Elias, D'Agostino, & Wolf, 2000; Waldstein, 2000). Studies with very large prospective community samples show that blood pressure level in middle age predicts cognitive functioning in old age (M. Elias, Wolf, D'Agostino, Cobb, & White, 1993; Launer, Masaki, Petrovitch, Foley, & Havlik, 1995). These reviews summarize the many studies indicating that the cognitive functioning of older and very old persons is affected by hypertension and the mounting evidence that high blood pressure in middle age (M. Elias et al., 1993; Launer et al., 1995; Swan, Carmelli, & LaRue, 1995) is a predictor of lowered levels of cognitive functioning in old age, and that this is true even when subjects are being treated with antihypertensive drugs (M. Elias et al., 1993). Hypertension and blood pressure, as well as diabetes mellitus and other risk factors, are also predictors of Alzheimer's disease (Guo, Viitanen, Fratiglioni, & Winblad, 1996), although it is not yet clear if high blood pressure is a cause or consequence of Alzheimer's disease. Additional studies with controls for blood pressure-related comorbidities are needed. It also appears that a drop in blood pressure from middle- to old age may be a predictor of lower levels of performance in old age (Swan, Carmelli, & LaRue, 1998), but this work needs to be replicated in studies that employ multiple waves of longitudinal testing.

Early Longitudinal Data

The emphasis on hypertension by aging interactions appears to have been influenced by Busse's (1969) definition of *primary aging* as changes inherent to the aging process that are irreversible and *secondary aging* as caused by disease that are positively correlated with age but usually reversible (M. Elias et al., 1990). The narrower translation of this model, such that it speaks to hypertension and primary aging, has been defined as the "classic age by hypertension model"

(P. Elias, D'Agostino, Elias, & Wolf, 1995). The classic age by hypertension model predicts that the combination of age and hypertension will produced accelerated decline in cognitive function over time relative to the decline observed in the absence of hypertension.

A study comparing 10-year change in cognitive functioning on the Wechsler Adult Intelligence Scale (WAIS) for 60- to 79-year-old Duke Longitudinal Study (DLS) participants produced the first data consistent with the classic aging by hypertension model. The DLS started in 1955 with respondents ages 60 to 103 and followed them for 11 repeated measures until 1976 (see Busse et al., 1985; Siegler, 1983). Wilkie and Eisdorfer (1971) reported that study participants, defined as clearly hypertensive (diastolic BP > 106 mmHg) and 60 to 79 years of age at entry into the study, exhibited over a decade significant decline in cognitive functioning relative to a normotensive cohort (diastolic BP range = 65 to 95 mmHg) and a borderline hypertensive cohort (96 to 105 mmHg) of comparable age.

It is sobering to note that no severely hypertensive individuals survived long enough to participate in the same study between 70 and 79 years of age. However, both the normotensive and borderline hypertensive individuals exhibited statistically significant decline in WAIS performance scores over a 10-year period while the "moderately hypertensive" participants exhibited significantly more decline over 10 years than the normotensive participants.

This finding was consistent with the classic aging times disease interaction model and served as a major stimulus to other studies, although it involved a very small sample of subjects and did not involve controls for antihypertension drugs and hypertension-related disease, which could have accounted for the higher rate of cognitive decline for the hypertensive subjects.

Cross-Sectional Data

There have been several reports of interactions of age and hypertension for samples of adults less than 40 to 50 years of age, but findings were opposite those predicted by the classic age by hypertension model. In two studies, differences in test performance between middle-aged hypertensive and normotensive individuals have been *smaller* than the differences between young adult hypertensive and normotensive individuals. This was true for a wide range of measures of attention, memory, executive functions, and psychomotor abilities (Waldstein, 1995). However, the range of ages employed in these studies makes a difference with respect to interactions. Wilkie and Eisdorfer (1971) found significant negative correlations between diastolic blood pressure and every subtest in

the Wechsler Adult Intelligence test in a 70- to 79-year-old cohort, but no significant correlations for 60- to 79-year-old cohort. However, no evidence of age times blood pressure interactions was obtained in a large-sample cross-sectional study involving three age cohorts of 1,695 men and women (55 to 64, 65 to 74, and 75 to 88 years) participating in the Framingham Heart Study (P. Elias et al., 1995).

Models advanced by Waldstein (1995) and Waldstein and Katzel (2001) show that there are a number of physiological and morphological changes in the brain in the presence of young adult hypertension that could explain lowered cognitive functioning. However, in terms of the cumulative effects of blood pressure on the brain, it is difficult to explain why hypertension in old age should not be associated with disproportionately accelerated change in cognitive function. Structural and functional changes in the brain seen with hypertension are progressive and cumulative and generally irreversible once they occur.

Waldstein (1995) advanced a U-shaped age by hypertension interaction model to explain the observation, based on aggregating data from all cross-sectional studies, that young and elder individuals are more adversely affected by hypertension than middle-aged subjects. This model fits the cross-sectional data in a general way, but the data are inconsistent with contemporary longitudinal studies.

M. Elias et al. (1990) have provided a "signal-to-noise-ratio explanation" of poorer test performance in association with youth and old age. The argument is that apparently disproportionate effects of hypertension on cognitive test performance in youth affects the cohort against which they are compared. In youth, hypertension occurs more against a background of relatively good health than it does in middle or advanced age. The prevalence hypertension-related pathophysiology and comorbidity increase with age. Thus, as an individual ages, hypertension becomes a risk factor seen against a background of multiple disease and other risk factors (e.g., diabetes, high cholesterol, high homocysteine levels, B12 deficiency; M. Elias, Elias, Robbins, Wolf, & D'Agostino, 2001). While these confounds can be adjusted out statistically, this can be the case only if subclinical diseases could be recognized and diagnosed. This objective is impossible to reach without great cost. One possibility may be to follow the same individuals over time.

In fact, difficulties in explaining cross-sectional results may be due to methodological rather than conceptual (model building) deficiencies. Cross-sectional studies are associated with a number of methodological challenges relating to the fact that the same individuals are not followed over time. This problem is particularly acute in case control studies. Sample bias due to self-selection for studies (M. Elias,

Robbins, & Schultz, 1987) and survival effects represent two major problems encountered in cross-sectional studies (M. Elias et al., 1990; Waldstein 1995, 2001). Consequently, there is general agreement that longitudinal studies provide the best paradigm for examining relations between hypertension, or any other cardiovascular disease risk factor, and cognitive functioning.

Contemporary Longitudinal Studies

Findings of greater cognitive decline over a four-year test/retest period (Tzourio, Dufouil, Ducimetière, & Alpérovitch, 1999) and a six-year longitudinal period (Knopman et al., 2001) for middle-aged and elderly subjects are consistent with the earlier findings (Wilkie & Eisdorfer, 1971), although both studies involved only two measurements—baseline and follow-up. The study by Knopman et al. (2001) involved an impressively large sample of subjects ($n = 10,963$) and risk factors other than hypertension. Diabetes and incident stroke, as well as hypertension, were related to greater decline over the six-year study period. However, neither of these studies followed subjects over a significant period of time, and neither involved a cognitive test battery or a measure of general intellectual functioning.

To meet these criteria, we need to turn to data published from the Maine-Syracuse Longitudinal Study of Hypertension and Cognitive Functioning, which has followed subjects over a 25-year period (1975 to 2001). This study involved an extremely comprehensive battery of tests, including the original version of the WAIS, as well as significant numbers of tests from the Halstead-Reitan Battery and the Wechsler Memory Scale. The mean length of time between waves is five years. The first wave of longitudinal data collection with the first cohort took place in Syracuse, New York, in 1981 and 1982. Since then, four additional longitudinal-study cohorts have entered the study. This is essentially a time-lagged, cross-sectional, and prospective longitudinal design (Dwyer & Feinleib, 1992). Longitudinal analyses make use of the data from serial examinations. Cross-sectional analyses are made possible by pooling data for an examination across cohorts. Secular trends may be examined by comparing subjects who entered the study at different times.

Multiple studies have evolved from this 25-year project. Several studies illustrate the use of contemporary longitudinal data analysis methods designed to deal with the problem of selective attrition, to control for potential confounds related to comorbidity and hypertension-related diseases, and to use all available data even though not every subject in the study has completed the same number of longitudinal examinations.

M. Elias, Robbins, Elias, and Streeten (1998b) employed 140 relatively healthy men and women taken from a larger sample of individuals who had completed the WAIS. Sample size was significantly reduced because they restricted the sample to persons who (a) completed the WAIS; (b) were between 40 and 70 years of age at baseline; (c) free from stroke, dementia, secondary forms of hypertension, and co-existing diseases; and (d) free from treatment with antihypertensive medications at baseline (M. Elias, Robbins, Elias, & Streeten, 1998a), using a method of analysis that both accounts for attrition and allows estimation of missing longitudinal data (Willett, 1988).

An important feature of this longitudinal analysis is that it allows estimates of decline in performance for a given number of years (e.g., 10 or 20). It does not require that all subjects complete every longitudinal examination as long as at least two examinations are completed at some point in the longitudinal study. One significant benefit of this analysis is that it adjusts for longitudinal attrition because data for dropouts are not discarded from the analysis. This data has been collected for persons who were enrolled in the study from periods ranging from 5 to 20 years. In this study, the predictors of decline on the WAIS were (a) ever-never hypertensive status; (b) blood pressure over all examinations (diastolic or systolic); and (c) most importantly, blood pressure at baseline (examination). Crystallized ability (verbal abilities) was unrelated to the blood pressure predictor measures, but a measure of speed (digit symbol substitution) and a composite measure of fluid ability (visualisation-performance) were.

Figure 21.1 shows the estimated decline in a fluid ability composite score (picture arrangement + object assembly + picture completion + block design) per 20 years of longitudinal study participation for persons defined as always-normotensive or ever-hypertensive. Expressed in percent of correct scores and adjusted for covariates (age, education, occupation, anxiety, depression, cigarette smoking, alcohol consumption), the estimated decline over 20 years was 12.1% greater for persons who were hypertensive at any examination versus those who were never hypertensive. For both the fluid V-P composite (shown in Figure 21.1) and speed (digit symbol substitution scores), persons who were hypertensive at baseline exhibited greater longitudinal decline. This finding with fluid V-O was observed for each of the BP predictor variables including untreated diastolic and systolic blood pressure values at baseline. The higher the BP, the greater the longitudinal decline in cognitive functioning. All-exam (averaged) DBP was also associated

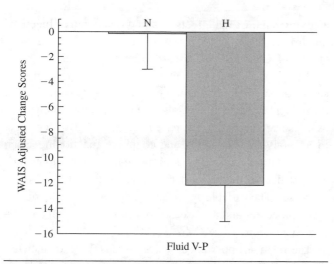

Figure 21.1   Change in estimated mean Adjusted Fluid V-P (Visualization-Performance) scores over twenty years for Hypertensive (H) and Normotensive (N) cohorts participating in the Maine-Syracuse Longitudinal Study of Cognitive Function. Change scores are adjusted for age, education, occupation, gender, and treatment with antihypertensive medication. Adapted for this chapter from tabled data presented in Elias, M. F., Robbins, M. A., Elias, P. K., and Streeten, D. H. P. (1998). A longitudinal study of blood pressure in relation to performance on the Wechsler Adult Intelligence Scale. *Health Psychology, 17,* 486–493, with permission of the authors.

with decline in psychomotor speed (Digit Symbol Substitution). None of the BP predictors were significantly related to the crystallized-verbal composite score. Age at entry into the study (at baseline) was significantly associated with longitudinal decline and was positively correlated with blood pressure. However, all significant associations between blood pressure predictors and cognitive performance scores remained statistically significant when adjusted for the age at entry into the study (baseline). Most importantly, there were consistent reductions in the strength and magnitude of associations between age and cognitive functioning when the various measures of blood pressure were introduced into the model following age and the other covariates. For example, introducing the control for systolic blood pressure averaged over all examinations reduced associations between age and the fluid ability composite measure by 50%. This finding is consistent with a cross-sectional report by Madden and Blumenthal (1998) that age-related variance in a measure of selective attention was reduced by approximately 58% when systolic and diastolic blood pressure were controlled.

These findings have been replicated more recently with a larger sample of men and women and are consistent with the results of a 15-year study of neuropsychological test performance (M. Elias et al., 1998b). The higher the blood pressure, the greater was the rate of decline per year of longitudinal study participation. From this work, we conclude that hypertension and increments in systolic or diastolic blood pressure are related to more accelerated rates of decline in cognitive functioning.

Future Research

While interactions of age and hypertension, and to a lesser extent, diabetes, insulin resistance, stroke, and coronary bypass surgery (Newman, Stygall, & Kong, 2001; C. Ryan, 2001) have received major attention in the cognitive function literature, there are many cardiovascular disease (CVD) risk factors (with positive or negative effects on cognitive function) that have not been studied sufficiently with regard to age. These include cigarette smoking, cholesterol, obesity, left ventricular hypertrophy, family history of premature coronary heart disease (CHD), low blood levels of folate and vitamin B12, and elevated homocysteine levels. These areas also offer excellent research opportunities: low blood pressure, menopause, estrogen, estrogen replacement, and oral contraceptive devices. A review of this literature (M. Elias et al., 2001) indicates that each of these risk factors has been related to lowered cognitive functioning in geriatric populations and many with AD and brain morphology, but also with lowered cognitive performance in elderly individuals. M. Elias et al. (2001) point out that particularly promising research opportunities exist with respect to Apolipoprotein e4. Apolipoprotein e4 (APOE-4) allele is not only a risk factor for AD but also for cognitive decline within generally normal limits (Riley et al., 2000) and in the absence of dementia (Small, Basun, & Bachman, 1998). It is particularly important to have studies that examine the impact of cardiovascular risk factors on cognitive functioning in the presence of the APOE-4 allele and that they do so in the context of designs that consider aging (longitudinal change in cognitive functioning) or age cohort differences. Many studies have had the opportunity to do this via a large sample of men and women varying widely in age but have neglected to do so. It is particularly important to undertake these studies as well as give more attention to women's health issues. For example, Rosenberg et al. (1985) reported that female smokers who use oral contraceptives are at 20 times the risk of coronary heart disease than female nonsmokers who do not use oral contraceptives. We are unaware of any studies relating the cumulative risk of smoking and oral contraception to cognitive functioning in the context of aging research.

It is now well-known that hard-driving aggressiveness, hostility, depression, anxiety, anger, social isolation, low social support, low socioeconomic status, marital stress, and job stress (Muir, 1998; Williams et al., 1997) represent social psychological risk factors for cardiovascular disease, and that the lethal mechanisms include increases in BP, blood cholesterol (Muir, 1998), and sympathetic and cardiovascular responses (Williams, 1994). We need a systematic series of studies that examine the cumulative impact of both biological-cardiovascular and psychosocial-cardiovascular risk factors on cognitive performance, and the impact of aging on cognitive functioning.

METHODOLOGICAL CONSIDERATIONS WHEN STUDYING AGING

The distinction between a risk factor for cardiovascular disease and disease itself is difficult and often academic (M. Elias et al., 2001). Cardiovascular diseases are risk factors for other diseases. Clinically defined hypertension is a good example. Several overlapping definitions of the term *risk factor* emerged early in the course of the Framingham Heart Study (Kannel, Dawber, Kagan, Revortskie, & Stokes, 1961; Kannel & Sytkowski, 1987): (a) a correlate of cardiovascular disease, (b) a characteristic of an individual that predisposes that individual to cardiovascular disease; and (c) a factor that emerges as a cause of a cardiovascular disease. Because associations between risk and cardiovascular disease are more easily demonstrated than causal relationships, the first and second definitions have been employed more frequently in the literature dealing with vascular risk factors for cognitive decline. There is general agreement that variables such as blood pressure, hypertension, diabetes, obesity, cigarette smoking, and total cholesterol, among others, are risk factors for disease.

However, a major conceptual problem is created because age is itself a risk factor for cardiovascular disease. This has implications for three of the most frequently employed analyses in the health psychology of aging: (a) examine interactions of age cohort status (or change over time, aging), and a cardiovascular risk factor; (b) via regression or covariance analyses, subtract the effects of aging on cognitive functioning from effects of CVD risk or disease; (c) subtract the effects of CVD risk or disease from the effects of aging. M. Elias et al. (1990) note that failure to render age a nonsignificant predictor of cognitive functioning by adjusting out the influence of one or several risk factors is frequently cited as evidence that risk for disease is unimportant with respect to relations between aging and cognitive functioning. Such conclusions reflect a naive assumption that age or aging variables reflect little more than primary aging (nondisease) processes. The variable age in any study reflects both primary aging processes and all diseases and risk factors that are correlated with age.

The relative importance of age, versus Type II diabetes, diastolic BP, and cigarette smoking as risk factors for poor cognitive functioning is illustrated by data from the Framingham Heart Study (M. Elias et al., 1998b, 2001). Beginning in 1950, all participants were screened for cardiovascular risk factors and events every two years. All subjects were free of history of definite completed stroke and Type I diabetes. All were ages 55 to 85 at the time of neuropsychological testing. A summary of the level of independent risk of lowered cognitive functioning is shown in Table 21.1.

Thus, every five years of age produces an increased risk of 67% of declines in learning and memory, 61% in the composite score, 44% on similarities, and 19% on attention/ concentration. This age risk, controlling for the very well-measured disease and risk information, is the largest factor. Whether one considers diabetes and hypertension as risk factors or comorbid conditions, they do have increasing effects on cognitive decline.

In another set of analyses based on this same archival data set, M. Elias et al. (2001) employed a risk factor scale that reflected the cumulative impact of multiple risk factors on cognitive functioning. These investigators designed a simple risk factor scale that was used to determine the combined impact of multiple cardiovascular risk factors, excluding aging. Subjects were given a score (e.g., 0, 1, 2), depending on the number of

TABLE 21.1 Adjusted Odds Ratios of Performing At or Below the 25th Percentile on the Framingham Neuropsychological Test Measurements (covariates included education, occupation, gender, alcohol consumption, previous history of cardiovascular disease, and antihypertensive treatment)

Neuropsychological Test	Type II Diabetes (per 5 years)	Diastolic BP (per 10 mm HG)	Cigarettes/day (per 5 cigs.)	Age in Years (per 5 years)
Composite score	1.21	1.30	1.04	1.61
Learning and memory	1.22	1.25	1.03	1.67
Similarities	1.19	1.01	1.09	1.44
Attention/concentration	1.00	1.15	0.98	1.19

BP exams 4–15; Diabetes exams 1–15; cigarettes/day at time of neuropsychological assessment; age ranged from 55 to 88 at time of neuropsychological testing.

cardiovascular risk factors present during neuropsychological testing. For an overall composite score involving all of the neuropsychological tests, there was a 23% (odds ratio = 1.23) increase in risk for poor cognitive functioning (performance at or below the 25 percentile) *per risk factor* beyond zero risk factors. In a secondary analysis, a long-term risk factor scale was derived from cardiovascular risk data collected over 18 to 20 years. For this scale, there was an estimated 31% increase (odds ratio = 1.31) in risk for poor cognitive functioning per risk factor. The largest increase in risk (39%) was associated with learning and immediate memory.

Unfortunately, no studies have asked the question as to whether cumulative risk, as determined by multiple risk factor scale, is exacerbated or diminished with increasing age. Moreover, studies adjusting the impact of age on cognitive functioning for risk factors have not used a multiple risk factor scale reflecting the long-term and cumulative impact of risk. Such studies are needed. While the examples have been given with data from cardiovascular disease and cognition, the principles apply generally in aging and health psychology.

Epidemiologic Concerns

The need for more sophisticated models that take into account relations between risk factors, aging, and disease is apparent. But testing these models constitutes a major challenge. Design problems created by the dynamic character of both disease and aging are evident. An excellent and well-written summary of these designs and issues may be found in Hennekens et al. (1987) and Collins and Horn (1991).

Understanding these issues is particularly important to two critical decisions in the design of health-aging studies: (a) selection of exclusionary variables; and (b) identification of confounders, necessary to model specification. These problems are common to all research areas but acutely important in health-aging research for two reasons: (a) the coexistence of chronic diseases increases with advancing age and diseases interact in complex ways, and (b) the duration of exposure to risk factor and disease is correlated with age (Kaplan et al., 1999). These correlations are particularly problematic in covariance analyses involving the adjustment of risk factors for the impact of comorbidities and in designs in which disease effects are adjusted for age, or vice versa. Covariance assumptions are often not met in circumstances in which they are most needed. Pedhauser and Schmelkin's (1991) discussion of covariance issues and solutions is most valuable. Hennekens et al.'s (1987) chapter on confounding and bias in public health research is very useful. Sackett et al. (1991) offers an excellent discussion of issues surrounding subject selection.

Kaplan et al. (1999) provide a good review of the particular odd things about aging when considering epidemiologic research. The review is very valuable with respect to design decisions such as whom to exclude, what confounders are important conceptually, how to handle comorbidity (by exclusion or by statistical adjustment), and issues of subject selection, sample bias, and survival. This discussion begins with complex and mixed findings in studies where cardiovascular disease risk factors are related to cardiovascular disease outcomes. It is widely assumed that the association between CVD risk factors and CVD events and outcomes grows weaker with advancing age, but the literature does not support this conclusion (Kaplan et al., 1999). A pattern of declining associations between CVD risk factors and cardiovascular disease has been reported in some large population studies (Psaty et al., 1990; Whisnant, Wiebers, O'Fallon, Sicks, & Frye, 1996). Increasing strength of associations (Benefante, Reed, & Frank, 1992; Keil, Sutherland, Knapp, & Gazes, 1992) and mixed results have been observed in others.

Kaplan et al. (1999) point out very complex and dynamic associations among the following variables: (a) CVD risk factors, (b) comorbid conditions, (c) subject selection and attrition, (d) mortality, (e) subclinical disease, (f) clinical disease detection, (g) treatment, (h) clinical events, (i) metabolic and physiologic changes, and (j) "aging senescence." These 10 variables provide a practical checklist for data design and analysis. They all change with age and interact with each other. Each of these changes (or modifications) correlate with age, aging, and the passage of time. They affect, and are affected by, manifestation of diseases, accuracy of self-report and recall of exposures to risk, selection bias, accuracy of measurement, changing diagnostic and assay methods, attrition and differential rates of attrition from longitudinal studies, selective survival, and the validity of covariance analyses.

A particular problem is the need to use proxy variables and data from informants other than the study participant. Efforts to avoid this problem often lead to exclusion of some subject populations (e.g., institutionalized individuals) and result in their underrepresentation in study samples.

The problem of dropout in longitudinal designs has been discussed in our review of the hypertension-cognitive functioning literature. Especially problematic for longitudinal studies of cognitive functioning is that persons who perform more poorly at one time are less likely to return for repeat testing than those who perform well (M. Elias & Robbins, 1991b).

Longitudinal Analysis Methods

The recognition of problems, such as selective attrition and the need to estimate missing data, has moved sophisticated investigators beyond the use of repeated measurements analysis of variance as a method of analyzing cross-sectional and longitudinal data. The importance of designs with both components is emphasized in the contemporary literature. Health psychologists who wish to study aging should consider this important contemporary approach to analysis of longitudinal and cross-sectional data. Repeated measurement analyses of variance results are still popular, although it provides no built-in method for correcting for attrition. It is common to find plots of changes in means over time. Such plots obscure intra-individual differences, and often no single subject in the study shows a trend similar to the trend in means over time. Reporting of changes in means over time obscures inter-individual differences in rate of change and often presents an inaccurate picture of change over time. It is possible to find that not a single subject in the study exhibits a trend similar to the mean change over time. For an excellent example of how longitudinal data should be presented, see McArdle and Hamagami (1991). A simple but useful method for adjusting for attrition is seen in the work of M. Elias et al. (1998a) on blood pressure.

There are methods of combined cross-sectional and longitudinal data analysis that allow statistical adjustment for attrition, *missing data, and data imputation.* All investigators using longitudinal designs (i.e., studies with multiple wave of longitudinal data not simply time 1 versus time 2 difference scores) should take full advantage of these methods. Many contemporary methods for longitudinal analyses are reviewed in Collins and Horn (1991). Illustrations of problems of attrition in studies of disease are provided in M. Elias & Robbins's text (1991b), as well as topics of great importance, such as missing data, ordinal methods of assessing change, time series applications, intra-individual differences in intra-individual change, latent growth curve modeling, and modeling incomplete cross-sectional and longitudinal data using dynamic structural equation modeling. A very creative application of survival analysis to longitudinal studies of behavior is found in Willett & Singer's work (1991). Solutions to attrition and missing data, as well as the pitfalls of analysis of variance approaches to change over time and the descriptive data that accompany these methods, are described in these texts. An excellent example in AD research is the analysis by Wilson, Gilley, Bennett, Beckett, and Evans (2000), in which a large community-based population with AD was followed and changes in cognition documented (see also Siegler, Bosworth, & Poon, in press). It is becoming increasingly clear that rates of health change vary dramatically among individuals; and as new, sophisticated analyses become more accepted, researchers will be able to document changes across individuals.

PERSONALITY AND SOCIAL FACTORS

Personality and social factors are involved in disease etiology, although there appear to be multiple mechanisms (Contrada & Guyll, 2001; Contrada, Leventhal, & O'Leary, 1990; Smith & Gallo, 2001). There is evidence that personality characteristics, such as hostility, operate through risky behaviors (Scherwitz et al., 1992; Siegler, Peterson, Barefoot, & Williams, 1992) as well as through reactivity (Williams, 1994), at least in terms of cardiovascular disease (Rozanski, Blumenthal, & Kaplan, 1999). The evidence is less consistent for hypertension (B. Jonas, Franks, & Ingram, 1997; S. Jonas & Lambo, 2000; Levenstein, Kaplan, & Smith, 2000; Spiro, Aldwin, Ward, & Mroczek, 1995), stroke (Everson, Roberts, Goldberg, & Kaplan, 1998), diabetes (Niaura et al., 2000), and cancer (Contrada & Guyll, 2001; Everson et al., 1996; I. Schapiro et al., 2001). Evidence is accumulating that depression and social support have a significant impact on the course of coronary heart disease (Barefoot & Schroll, 1996; Williams & Chesney, 1993) such that a clinical trial called Enhancing Recovery in Coronary Heart Disease (ENRICHD) to reduce the impact of depression among myocardial infarction patients is underway (ENRICHD investigators, 2000).

Most of these studies are conducted on middle-age and older persons; therefore, there is no doubt that these relationships hold over the adult age span. To date, there has been little interest in understanding how and why age is such a powerful risk factor for disease and how it interacts with psychosocial indicators; but this is starting to change.

Williams (2001) has reviewed the literature on these questions and concludes that after the age of 25, hostility does appear to be related to CHD incidence. It is also true that the same characteristic that leads to an increased probability of disease such as a heart attack, if survived, may also be related to increased survival after the heart attack. A good example is the Type A behavior pattern. Williams et al. (1988) showed that under the age of 55, Type A predicted CHD; but after age 55, it was associated with lower rates of CHD. Kop (1997) has proposed a theory to explain the stronger impact of psychosocial risk on CHD at younger ages, but there is insufficient empirical evidence at present to verify his conclusions. In particular, the National Heart, Lung, and Blood Institute (NHLBI; 2000) considers age a risk factor for heart disease at age 45 in men and age 55 in women. This makes the understanding of the role of psychosocial factors in CHD before these ages extremely important.

Research on hostility shows that hostility is operative across the lifecycle from age 18 to age 100 and that hostility varies by age, race, gender, and socioeconomic status (see Siegler, 1994, for review). Barefoot et al. (1987) showed that suspiciousness as measured by the Cattell 16-PF also predicted all cause mortality for older men and women while P. Martin et al. (1992) reported survival for centenarians was enhanced for those high on suspiciousness—a measure of hostility and a reversal similar to the Type A findings reported by Williams et al. (1988) earlier in the lifecycle.

Exciting new findings from the Nun Study (Danner, Snowdon, & Friesen, 2001; Snowdon, 2001) suggest that positive emotions measured in late adolescence are related to long-term survival.

Does Disease Cause Personality Change in Adulthood?

It seems a truism to say it depends on the disease, but that appears to be the case. Siegler (2000) reviewed the evidence for rated personality change in AD patients. In studies in the United States and the United Kingdom, AD patients are rated as more vulnerable (N6) and less conscientious (C) as would be expected. When the same technique was used to describe patients with other brain disorders, the pattern of change was specific to diagnosis, thus, it would appear that where behavior change is a symptom of the disorder, it is specific to the disorder.

Siegler and colleagues (1991, 1994) looked at the role of premorbid personality in the facets of the NEO-PI. It was clear that rank order stability is maintained on the facets of personality that are not the hallmark of the disease. The Spearman correlations are highly significant (r's range from $-.397$, $p = .02$ to $-.776$, $p = .0001$) for all domains and facets of the NEO-PI except for N6—vulnerability ($r = -.046, p = .80$), and C—conscientiousness ($r = -.001$, $p = .999$), which are hallmarks of a dementing disorder.

A study of sources of personality change in the University of North Carolina (UNC) Alumni Heart Study Cohort found that divorce versus remarriage and *not the development of a disease during midlife* (from ages 42 to 50) was associated with change in personality (Costa, Herbst, McCrae, & Siegler, 2000). Thus, disease is not an engine of personality change unless there are major structural alternations in brain functioning during midlife. Studies that depend on self-reports of disease or self-rated health tend to report personality change, but these findings may be related to the appraisal process.

The overall general stability of personality is also important in the study of personality disorders (Costa, McCrae, & Siegler, 1999). This is an area assumed to have no relevance to later life, as personality disorders were thought to age out. Research in this area (Costa & Widiger, 1994) indicates that this is not true, and indeed, the persistence of disordered personality patterns can often be mistaken for the disruption of

Alzheimer's disease (Costa, 2000; Siegler, Bastian, Steffens, Bosworth, & Costa, in press).

Role of Behavioral Risk Factors

CHD, cancer, disability, and total mortality are all increased by "bad habits" and hostility is related to these bad habits. Some data from our ongoing UNC Alumni Heart Study help tell this story. Siegler et al. (1992) reported on the ability of hostility to predict risk. This was measured at college enrollment, and the study continued as the subjects aged into their early forties. Hostility was significantly associated with caffeine use, ratio of total/HDL cholesterol, amount of alcohol, and body mass index in the predicted direction—higher hostility, higher risk—and to exercise in the opposite direction—higher hostility, more exercise—controlling for age and gender. As a follow-up to that paper, Siegler and colleagues examined the association between the same college hostility measure and risky behaviors measured during the following 10 years of data collection from 1989 to 1999. In this analysis, high-risk behavior is set at a level generally accepted in the literature. In this college-educated cohort, high hostility in college still predicts excess risk during midlife for both men and women if they are current smokers, have high depressive and alcoholism symptoms, and appraisals of their current life situation are negative. Those not still predicted by college hostility were all significantly predicted by hostility when remeasured at age 42 by and change in hostility from age 19 to age 42 (Siegler et al., 2002). Furthermore, this paper indicated that college hostility, adult hostility, raw change in hostility, and residualized change in hostility were all differentially associated with risk, indicating the complexity of developmental patterns relating psychosocial factors to disease risk indicators. This is particularly important from an aging point of view because these same risk indicators (smoking, obesity, sedentary behavior) predict Medicare costs (Daviglus et al., 1989) and disability (Vita, Terry, Hubert, & Fries, 1998). Early predictors of these risk indicators can help ensure a healthy life span, and interventions aimed at hostility modification might have significant dividends and a role to play in primary prevention of CHD in both men and women earlier in the life span (Stampfer, Hu, Manson, Rimm, & Willett, 2000). Understanding the role of genetic polymorphisms related to neurotransmitter function is another way to understand the potential associations of personality, risky behavior, and disease risk (Williams et al., 2001).

There is increasing interest in health promotion and disease prevention in older persons, and interest in successful aging shifts the focus to those older persons who are doing well as opposed to the usual focus on the "four D's" (disease, disability, death, and dementia). Many of the factors that health psychologists study are related to becoming a "successful ager" and, as we have discussed, modifying risky behaviors can contribute to that process.

Social Support

This relationship has been well-documented. Adequate social support reduces morbidity (Bosworth & Schaie, 1997; Vogt, Mullooly, Ernst, Pope, & Hollis, 1992), mortality (Berkman & Syme, 1979; Fratiglioni, Wang, Erickson, Maytan, & Winblad, 2000; Strawbridge, Cohen, Shema, & Kaplan, 1996; Williams et al., 1992), physical functioning (Kaplan, Strawbridge, Camacho, & Cohen, 1993), and marital status (K. Martin et al., 1995; Tucker, Friedman, Wingard, & Schwartz, 1996), which has differential impact for men than for women (Tucker, Schwartz, Clark, & Friedman, 1999). One possible mechanism by which social support may lead to successful outcomes is friends and relatives encouraging less risky behaviors and encouraging healthy behaviors (Umberson, 1987). A second mechanism may consist of the person's social network providing necessary information or encouragement for seeking preventive health care services such as a prostate cancer screening and treatment (Berkman, 1995). Third, the social network may provide the patient with information from other people who have direct or indirect experience with a problem or medical condition.

Self-Rated Health

Self-rated health has been found to be a predictor of mortality (Bosworth et al., 1999; Idler & Benyamini, 1997) and morbidity (Bosworth & Schaie, 1997). While self-rated health captures scores of summary information about health status, it does not represent the specific disease status of an individual. What is still not understood is the meaning of self-rated health as a covariate and how it influences aging research findings (see Siegler, Bosworth, & Poon, in press).

Objective assessment of health (physician examination combined with objective diagnostic methods) represents the gold standard. On the other hand, objective data collection is often either impractical, unethical, or both, given cost-benefit considerations and the possibility of risk to the study participant. Moreover, important data may be lost if we insist on objective measurement of disease; that is, retrospective data, archival data, and data collection that achieves large samples and/or representative samples but does not permit direct subject contact. Self-report is necessary where self-assessment is central to the research question; in studies, we are directly concerned with how subjects rate themselves in relation to

objective measurements. It has been argued that self-report is a questionable practice when new data collection is possible and when the objective is to identify and define a few targeted diseases with high levels of sensitivity and specificity (M. Elias et al., 1990), unless of course, subject risk is unacceptably high in relation to benefits.

Because self-report may be the focus of health-aging research or a necessary evil, it is important to understand its limitations. Costa and McCrae (1985) point out that the employment of self-ratings as "proxy measures of objective health status" is common and that investigators often justify this approach based on statistically significant correlations between physician-rated health and self-ratings, even though those correlations are modest. A series of classic studies has shown that self-report of disease and disease itself are not veridical and can be influenced by neuroticism and many other social-psychological factors, including disease (e.g., Costa & McCrae, 1985). We can not ignore information that can be gained from archival data, retrospective studies, or large sample mail or phone survey data because objective assessment of disease is not possible. However, the investigator is charged with the responsibility of establishing the validity of the self-report measuring techniques used. Where possible, however, the ascertainment of the reliability of self-report data via medical case records, follow-up with physicians and other informants, and treatment history is highly desirable.

NEW DEVELOPMENTS IN GENETICS AND AGING

How and where do aging and health psychology researchers learn to use the exploding new information, and where do we have data already applied to aging problems? While genes are fixed at birth, they can have different effects at different ages and interact with environments differentially at different ages, and furthermore, behave differentially in different populations. There are age-related changes in heritability, that is, in the amount of variance in a population due to genetic variance. In addition to age related changes in heritability, it is quite possible that different genes or different combinations of genes are operative at one part of the lifecycle and inoperative at another.

McClearn and Heller (2000) discuss intersections of genetics and aging. Psychologists look to genetics for the sources of individual differences in rates and patterns of aging. They illustrate their discussion with findings from the Swedish Adoption/Twin Study of Aging that has the advantage of twins raised apart by unconfounding genetic and environmental similarity in comparing twins raised together and raised separately. Greater resemblance in twins raised together implicates shared environmental influences. The twins were born between 1886 and 1958. Longitudinal data were collected by mail and in personal interviews every three years. McClearn and Heller developed a battery of sophisticated statistical methods for analysis of their data that allows them to estimate parameters in adjacent age bands of respondents that include estimates of relative genetic, environmental, and shared variance from the ages of 36 to 76. They present data on three measures of lipids—serum cholesterol, HDL cholesterol, and triglycerides—taken at in-person visits. While we may have thought this complex enough—data show that relative proportions of genetic, shared rearing environment, and nonshared rearing environment change with age differentially for the health-related variables studied—this is particularly striking for the three indicators of cholesterol measured at in-person testing. The complex patterns show important age relationships that had not been even dreamed of before.

Ewbank (2000) reviewed the extraordinary progress in genetics during the past 10 years and puts it in context. While written for demographers, the data is useful for psychologists as well. Demographers are more advanced in their thinking about the role of behavioral and social variables on survival and the role that age plays in such models. One gene has figured prominently in the study of Alzheimer's disease: apolipoprotein E. It has three different common polymorphisms—e2, e3, and e4—and individuals can have one of six combinations. The e3/e3 is the most common and is found in 60% to 70% of most populations. The e3/4 and the e4/4 are associated with increased risk of both AD and CHD, and the e2/2 and e2/3 are associated with a reduced risk of AD. In particular, the detailed discussion of the apolipoprotein E gene, which has implications for both Alzheimer's disease and ischemic heart disease, is particularly useful, along with a paper by Corder et al. (2000) indicating that APOE determines survival time in those over age 85 due to cardiovascular disease, not due to dementia. For a complete discussion of the genetic factors in Alzheimer's disease, see Roses and Saunders (2001).

The genetics revolution is also changing what we thought we knew about cognitive changes in survival, distance from death, and terminal drop. See Bosworth & Siegler (in press) for a detailed discussion of these issues.

RESEARCH OPPORTUNITIES IN HEALTH PSYCHOLOGY AND AGING

Aside from the traditional understanding of the role of aging on disease and the role of disease on aging, there are some opportunities for research in health psychology that will benefit from a consideration of aging or are better studied from an aging point of view. These include stress and aging, decision making, adherence to treatments for chronic disease, coping with disease, and gender differences in health. Health psychology also has important contributions to make to studies of cancer and aging.

Stress and Aging

Psychosocial factors and stress are key health psychology concerns (see Baum & Posluszny, 1999). An excellent venue to study the relationship between stress and aging has been caregiving. Work by Vitaliano et al. (in press) and by Robinson-Whelen, Kiecolt-Glaser, and Glaser (2000) has been important in using this approach to study the physiological as well as the psychological consequences of caregiving.

Decision Making

Decisions about health may be compromised by cognitive changes (see Peters, Finucane, MacGregor, & Slovic, 2000), thus research on decision making that takes these cognitive changes into consideration is needed. Even without cognitive changes, older persons may be more dependent on children and spouses in making decisions about health care screening and treatment options.

Adherence and Chronic Disease

Health psychology can play an important role among the elderly in terms of behavioral interventions. It is known that risk-reduction programs are efficacious (see Burke, Dunbar-Jacobs, & Hill, 1997, for a summary). However, the extent to which these programs are effective in the individual may depend on adherence. Nonadherence crosses treatment regimens, age and gender groups, and socioeconomic strata. Adherence is a significant problem. It is estimated that 50% of individuals discontinue participation in cardiac rehabilitation programs in the first year, 16% to 50% of hypertension patients discontinue their medication in the first year of treatment (Flack, Novikov, & Ferrario, 1996; Jones, Gorkin, Lian, Staffa, & Fletcher, 1995; Juncos, 1990), and 20% to 80% of patients who have antidepressant medications prescribed fail to adhere to the prescription at one month (DiMatteo, Lepper, & Croghan, 2000). Nonadherence rates for hormonal replacement medication over one to two years range from 27% to 61% (Brett & Madans, 1997; Chung, Lau, Cheung, & Haines, 1998; Faulkner, Young, Hutchins, & McCollam, 1998; Hemminki & Topo, 1997; Oddens & Boulet, 1997; P. Ryan, Harrison, Blake, & Fogelman, 1992). Since the beneficial effects of risk reduction on many chronic diseases and problems are not realized immediately, long-term adherence is essential for the strategies to be effective (Burke et al., 1997). Age does not affect adherence directly. However, changes in cognitive functioning and multiple prescriptions may make adherence more difficult with increasing age.

Aging and Coping with Disease

A growing body of literature indicates that older chronic patients are likely to cope better with chronic diseases than their younger counterparts. Younger cancer patients, for example, are more likely to be distressed than older patients (Van't Spijker, Trijsburg, & Duivenvoorden, 1997). Possible explanations are that older adults with diseases are less distressed than younger adults because they experience less violation of cognitive schemas, they engage in more positive downward social comparisons, and they perceive less attendant blockage to central goals. It is also possible that this age difference is an epiphenomenon of younger adults' propensity to report greater distress in general. Finally, Neugarten (1976) points out that the onset of chronic illness in old age is more usual in that part of the lifecycle and therefore possibly less disruptive. We found support for this last point in a study of 4,278 cardiac catheterization patients. We observed that physical function and physical role function were lower with age, whereas mental health, emotional role function, and vitality were higher with age (Bosworth et al., 2000).

Geropsychology

In this chapter, we have not reviewed the literature with the elderly as a clinical treatment population in detail. Geropsychology has been an area of concern for a long time—excellent review chapters have been collected for the past 20 years (e.g., Gatz, 1989; Nordhus, VandenBos, Berg, & Fromholt, 1988; Qualls & Abeles, 2000; Storandt, Siegler, & Elias, 1978). The research base needed to develop appropriate treatments at the intersections of physical disease, and aging is part of the content of behavioral medicine that health psychologists need to know (see Siegler, Bastian, et al., in press). An excellent set of chapters can be found in Smith and Kendall (in press) in their special issue updating the clinical aspects of behavioral medicine.

Gender, Health, and Aging

Menopause presents women with choices about hormone replacement therapy that are determined not only by menopausal symptoms but also by long-term possible prevention of CHD, osteoporosis, and Alzheimer's disease (Matthews, Wing, Kuller, Meilahn, & Owens, 2000; Siegler et al., 2002). Conversely, there is not a clear marker of midlife in men. Like estrogens, androgen levels decrease with age and have a broad range of effects on sexual organs and metabolic processes. Androgen deficiency in men older than 65 leads to a decrease in muscle mass, osteoporosis, decrease in sexual activity, and changes in mood and cognitive function, leading us to speculate that there may be at least two phases of chronic diseases related to androgen levels in men. Whether men over 65 would benefit from androgen replacement therapy is not known (Tenover, 1999). Any potential benefits from this therapy would need to be weighed against the possible adverse effects on the prostate and cardiovascular system. Thus, considering men and women separately may be useful (Siegler, Bastian, & Bosworth, 2001). In fact, research on timing of menopause suggests that ovarian aging may be a marker of an overall biological clock (Robine, Kirkwood, & Allard, 2001; Snowdon, 2001).

An additional reason to examine the relationship between health, disease, and aging separately for gender is that, at all ages, women are more likely than men to have acute and chronic conditions. The problem is not that they receive less health care. In fact, women are more likely to be insured and more likely to go to the doctor. Men have higher rates of certain diseases, notably heart disease, stroke, lung cancer, and liver disease, but women have more of nearly all other chronic conditions, including hypertension, arthritis, osteoporosis, eating disorders, diabetes, depression, and reproductive diseases (Merrill & Verbrugge, 1999). Before 70 years of age, women have a worse prognosis than men following acute myocardial infarction (AMI; Vaccarino, Krumholz, Yarzebski, Gore, & Goldberg, 2001). Studies in men suggest that psychosocial factors are important determinants of cardiovascular health (Kaplan et al., 1993; Orth-Gomer, Unden, & Edwards, 1988; Williams & Littman, 1996). In particular, work stress has been associated with increased coronary heart disease (CHD) incidence and poorer prognosis in men (Schnall & Landsbergis, 1994). Among women in this age group, psychosocial stress in relation to CHD has been studied rarely (Eaker, 1998). However, it appears that work stress is not as relevant to women whereas marital stress has been found to be a significant increased risk of recurrent CHD and poorer response in a middle-age sample of women (Orth-Gomer et al., 2000).

Cancer and Aging

Compared to the work on cardiovascular disease, there has been less work in cancer. This is a major opportunity for health psychologists interested in the intersection of aging and health.

Cancer Prevention and Aging

In general, there appears to be an increase in cancer screening with age to around 70 followed by a decline. For example, data from the 1990 National Cancer Institute (NCI) Mammography Attitudes and Usage Survey indicated that 40% of women in their forties reported having an annual mammogram, compared to only 18% of women over the age of 70. Therefore, the situation for older women seems especially perilous; not only do they have a greater risk of developing breast cancer, but it seems they have less chance of having the cancer detected. These patterns are unfortunate given that the incidence of cancer increases with age.

Cancer Diagnosis and Aging

Researchers have found that psychological impact of cancer diagnosis is inversely associated with age for at least both prostate and breast cancer patients (Cordova et al., 1995; McBride, Clipp, Peterson, Lipkus, & Demark-Wahnefried, 2000). Cancer diagnosis may have less psychological impact for older patients, because illness may be regarded as a natural part of aging and, thus, an "on-time" event. Younger age at diagnosis may also be indicative of greater family risk of cancer, which may increase the psychological impact of the diagnosis.

Cancer Progression, Recurrence, and Aging

A wide range of psychosocial factors has been associated with the course of established cancer, though this literature is replete with inconsistencies (Fox, 1998). Some studies have suggested, for example, that breast cancer patients' reactions to the stress of diagnosis characterized by a "fighting spirit" predicted the course of disease (e.g., Greer, Morris, Pettingale, & Haybittle, 1990). One study, however, reported that among 578 women with breast cancer, an increased risk of relapse or death over a five-year period was associated with greater helplessness/hopelessness but was unrelated to stoicism, denial, or fighting spirit (Watson, Haviland, Greer, Davidson, & Bliss, 1999). These inconsistencies may be because of the heterogeneity in the samples of patients studied (e.g., mixed cancer types and stages), psychosocial variables assessed, psychosocial interventions tests, and the study designs, control variables, and analytic procedures used (Garssen & Goodkin, 1999). Cancer recurrence is devastating, and the magnitude of distress is even greater than that found with the initial diagnosis.

Cancer Treatment and Aging

Breast cancer is of particular concern to older women because age is positively correlated with increased incidence and mortality. Women ages 65 to 69 have an annual incidence rate of 350 per 100,000, and for women age 85 years or older, the incidence climbs to 412 per 100,000. Over half of all breast cancer deaths occur in women who are over 65 years old (Morbidity and Mortality Weekly Report, 1996).

Postmenopausal breast cancer patients frequently have one or more preexisting comorbid conditions at the time of diagnosis (e.g., heart disease, chronic obstructive pulmonary disease, hypertension, diabetes, arthritis; Yancik et al., 2001). Thus, the prediagnostic health status of cancer patients in middle and later age groups may affect tumor prognosis and treatment decisions. Studies have shown that age and comorbidity strongly influence therapeutic decisions and are associated with less aggressive cancer therapy (Newschaffer, Penberthy, & Desch, 1996; Silliman, Guadagnoli, Weitberg, & Mor, 1989; Silliman, Troyan, Guadagnoli, Kaplan, & Greenfield, 1997). Furthermore, much of the data on cancer treatment efficacy comes from clinical trial investigations that tend to exclude breast cancer patients age 70 years and older who are likely to have preexisting diseases and other health limitations (Hutchins, Unger, Crowley, Coltman, & Albain, 1999).

Elderly women are offered axillary node dissection, chemotherapy, and reconstruction significantly less often than their younger counterparts (Chu et al., 1987; Newschaffer et al., 1996; Samet, Hunt, Key, Humble, & Goodwin, 1986; Silliman et al., 1989). The 1990 National Institute of Health (NIH) Consensus Development Conference on the treatment of early-stage breast cancer concluded that axillary node dissection was preferred treatment for all women with Stage 1 and Stage II disease regardless of age, although few trials included women over age (NIH Consensus Conference: Treatment of Early Stage Breast Cancer, 1991). Only 62% of a large sample of breast cancer survivors age 65 years and older met guidelines for annual mammography, and women at greatest risk for disease recurrence (those treated with breast-conserving surgery) were least likely to receive follow-up mammography (M. Schapiro, McAuuliffe, & Nattinger, 2000).

Cancer, Aging, and Survivorship

While much research has been conducted examining the relationship between coronary artery disease and age, much less has been reported of the interaction between cancer and aging and subsequent survivorship. The term *survivor* typically refers to individuals surviving at least five years, as the probability of late recurrences declines significantly after that time for most sites. Survival of persons diagnosed with cancer is improving. Today, almost 60% of adults diagnosed with cancer will be alive in five years. For those diagnosed with early stage or localized prostate, breast, or colon cancer, five-year survival is even higher (92%, 77%, and 65%, respectively). Currently in the United States, more than 10 million persons have survived a diagnosis of cancer, approximately 8 million of whom have survived five or more years (Hewitt, Breen, & Devesa, 1999). Some of the success in treating these cancers is attributable to the growing use of effective screening methods and, hence, diagnosis of earlier, more treatable forms of the disease. More effective adjuvant treatments have also contributed to better prognoses.

While more patients are living longer after being treated for cancer, and with the increased number of older adults, an area of research that has received limited attention is cancer survivorship. Concurrent with an increased vulnerability to cancer, increasing age also confers high risks for a number of other health problems (Guralnik, 1996; Yancik et al., 2001). Despite the broad impact of survivorship throughout the lives of patients and their families and caregivers, relatively little research has been directed at problems of survivorship beyond the immediate posttreatment phase.

Lingering emotional distress from the "trauma" of cancer diagnosis, treatment, and the life threat associated with the cancer is similar to distress experienced by individuals who have experienced other traumatic events (e.g., physical assault, natural disasters; Alter et al., 1996). The residual distress associated with the diagnosis and treatment of a life-threatening disease like cancer is now included as one of the circumstances that may precipitate posttraumatic stress disorder (PTSD). Although it is unlikely that a PTSD diagnosis would be made for the "average" cancer patient, Cordova and colleagues (1995) documented PTSD rates in a breast cancer sample ranging from 5% to 10% and suggested that this may be comparable, if not an underestimate, to other cancer survivor populations. Van't Spijker et al. (1997) conducted a meta-analytic review of 58 studies performed from 1980 to 1994 of psychological sequelae of cancer diagnosis. Focusing on studies that included validated instruments, the authors found that from 0% to 46% of patients qualified for depressive disorder; and from 0.9% to 49% qualified for anxiety disorder across the various studies. Compared to published reference norms for the general population, cancer patients were significantly more depressed. Despite the increased risk of distress, longitudinal data indicate that if the cancer is controlled, by one-year posttreatment, the severe distress of diagnosis will have dissipated for most patients (Andersen, Anderson, & deProsse 1989; Brown, 1987).

One life area that undergoes disruption for cancer survivors is sexuality. All cancer patients with solid tumors (approximately 85% of adult patients) and many treated for hematologic malignancies are vulnerable to sexual dysfunction. Across sites, estimates range from 10% (e.g., breast cancer patients treated with lumpectomy), 70% to 90% (e.g., women with vulva cancer treated with modified radical vulvectomy) to 100% (e.g., men with prostate cancer treated with radical prostatectomy), with the distribution skewed toward greater levels of disruption; among the hematologic malignancies, estimates are in the range of 20% (Andersen & Lamb, 1995).

Once cancer treatment ends, cancer survivors need to be carefully followed for potential late effects of disease. Because of their treatments, many are at increased risk of developing secondary tumors. For example, within 25 years of diagnosis of childhood cancer in Britain, about 4% of survivors develop a secondary primary cancer—about six times the expected number of cancers (Hawkins, Draper, & Kingston, 1987). This excess risk among survivors is attributable to the carcinogenic effects of treatments for the original childhood cancer as well as to genetic predisposition (Harnish et al., 2001). Treatment is also related to other chronic conditions, such as osteoporosis, diabetes, and cardiovascular diseases. Most cardiovascular disease, for example, is the result of a direct effect by radiation and chemotherapeutic agents, but injury to other organs can contribute indirectly.

There is limited information about the health behaviors of patients beyond the active cancer treatment period. Demark-Wahnefried, Peterson, McBride, Lipkus, and Clipp (2000) found that 55% of their sample of 978 survivors ate fewer than five daily servings of fruits and vegetables. Prostate cancer survivors ate even fewer servings than breast cancer survivors. Over 30% indicated they did not adhere to a low-fat diet, with prostate cancer patients again indicating worse practice than breast cancer survivors in this area. Also, 42% of survivors did not engage in routine exercise and 8% were current smokers. In this study, receptivity of the survivors to interventions to promote lifestyle changes was stated to be high.

FUTURE DIRECTIONS

A major contribution of health psychology to the study of aging is to deal with diseases and how they impact individuals as they age and to incorporate the best of epidemiology into our work. This should lead to the appearance of more health psychology-aging papers in medical and epidemiological journals, where they will be read by physicians and persons working in epidemiology and other areas of public health, and a more informed use of behavioral outcome measures in medical research.

Aging is a natural part of the lifecycle and the number of older persons is growing. In terms of the literature, a very significant portion of the work in health psychology, except that limited to conditions in childhood and adolescence, deals with adult development and aging. In dealing with the multiple medical conditions common in geriatric medicine (Hazzard, Blass, Ettinger, Halter, & Ouslander, 1999), the issue is health status and not age, per se. Moreover, there are childhood and adolescence antecedents to adult behaviors shown across many fields. Kuh and Ben-Shlomo (1997) provide an excellent set of chapters that speak to true life span theory and data related to physical health conditions, particularly with the studies such as the 1946 cohort study in Britain, which has related childhood characteristics to adult health status at midlife (Wadsworth, 1991) with superb data. In sum, with the aging of our population, the opportunities for health psychologists to make significant contributions to research, clinical care, and the quality of life for older persons is limitless.

REFERENCES

Alter, C., Pelcovitz, D., Axelrod, A., Goldenberg, B., Harris, H., Meyers, B., et al. (1996). Identification of PTSD in cancer survivors. *Psychosomatics, 37,* 137–143.

Andersen, B., Anderson, B., & deProsse, C. (1989). Controlled prospective longitudinal study of women with cancer. II: Psychological outcomes. *Journal of Consulting and Clinical Psychology, 57,* 692–697.

Andersen, B., & Lamb, M. A. (1995). Sexuality and cancer. In D. F. A. Holleb & G. P. Murphy (Ed.), *Clinical oncology* (2nd ed., pp. 699–713). Atlanta, GA: American Cancer Society.

Applegate, W. B. (1999). Hypertension. In W. R. Hazzard, J. P. Blass, W. H. Ettinger, J. B. Halter, & J. G. Ouslander (Eds.), *Principles of geriatric medicine and gerontology* (pp. 713–720). New York: McGraw-Hill.

Baltes, P. B., Reese, H. W., & Nesselroade, J. R. (1988). *Introduction to research methods: Life-span developmental psychology.* Hillsdale, NJ: Erlbaum.

Barefoot, J. C., Siegler, I. C., Nowlin, J. B., Peterson, B. L., Haney, T. L., & Williams, R. B. (1987). Suspiciousness, health and mortality: A follow-up study of 500 older adults. *Psychosomatic Medicine, 49,* 450–457.

Barefoot, J. C., & Schroll, M. (1996). Symptoms of depression, acute myocardial infarction, and total mortality in a community sample. *Circulation, 93,* 1976–1980.

Baum, A., & Posluszny, D. M. (1999). Health psychology: Mapping biobehavioral contributions to health and illness. *Annual Review of Psychology, 50,* 137–163.

Benefante, R., Reed, D., & Frank, J. (1992). Do coronary heart disease risk factors measured in the elderly have the same predictive roles as in the middle aged: Comparisons of relative and attributable risks. *Annals of Epidemiology, 2,* 273–282.

Berkman, L. F. (1995). Role of social relations in health promotion. *Psychosomatic Medicine, 57,* 245–254.

Berkman, L. F., & Syme, S. L. (1979). Social networks, host resistance, and mortality: A nine-year follow-up study of Alameda county residents. *American Journal of Epidemiology, 109,* 186–204.

Bosworth, H. B., & Schaie, K. W. (1997). The relationship of social environment, social networks, and health outcomes in the Seattle Longitudinal Study: Two analytical approaches. *Journals of Gerontology: Series B, Psychological Sciences and Social Science, 52*(5), 197–205.

Bosworth, H. B., & Siegler, I. C. (in press). Terminal change: An updated review of longitudinal studies. *Experimental Aging Research.*

Bosworth, H. B., Siegler, I. C., Brummett, B. H., Barefoot, J. C., Williams, R. B., Clapp-Channing, N., et al. (1999). Self-rated health as a predictor of mortality in a sample of coronary artery disease patients. *Medical Care, 37*(12), 1226–1236.

Bosworth, H. B., Siegler, I. C., Olsen, M. K., Barefoot, J. C., Brummett, B. H., Haney, T. L., et al. (2000). Social support and quality of life in patients with coronary artery disease. *Quality of Life Research, 9*(7), 829–839.

Brett, K., & Madans, J. H. (1997). Use of postmenopausal hormone replacement therapy: Estimates from a nationally representative cohort study. *American Journal of Epidemiology, 145,* 536

Brown, J. (1987). Psychological response to mastectomy. *Cancer, 59,* 189–196.

Burke, L., Dunbar-Jacobs, J. M., & Hill, M. N. (1997). Compliance with cardiovascular disease prevention strategies: A review of the research. *Annals of Behavioral Medicine, 19,* 239–263.

Busse, E. W. (1969). Theories of aging. In E. W. Busse & E. Pfeiffer (Eds.), *Behavior and adaptation in later life* (pp. 11–32). Boston: Little, Brown.

Busse, E. W., Maddox, G. L., Buckley, C. E., Burger, P. C., George, L. K., Marsh, G. R., et al. (1985). *The Duke longitudinal studies of normal aging: 1955–1980.* New York: Springer.

Chu, J., Diehr, P., Feight, P., Glaelke, G., Begg, C., Glicksman, A., et al. (1987). The effect of age on the care of women with breast cancer in community hospitals. *Journal of Gerontology, 42,* 185–190.

Chung, T. H., Lau, T. K., Cheung, L. P., & Haines, C. J. (1998). Compliance with hormone replacement therapy in Chinese women in Hong Kong. *Maturitas, 28*(3), 235–242.

Collins, L. M., & Horn, J. L. (Eds.). (1991). *Best methods for analysis of change: Recent advances, unanswered questions, future directions.* Washington, DC: American Psychological Association.

Contrada, R. L., & Guyll, M. (2001). On who gets sick and why: The role of personality and stress. In A. Baum, T. R. Revenson, & J. E. Singer (Eds.), *Handbook of health psychology* (pp. 59–84). Hillsdale, NJ: Erlbaum.

Contrada, R. L., Leventhal, H. L., & O'Leary, A. (1990). Personality and health. In L. A. Pervin (Ed.), *Handbook of personality* (pp. 638–669). New York: Guilford Press.

Corder, E. H., Basun, H., Fratiglioni, L., Guo, A., Lannfelt, L., Viitanen, M., et al. (2000). Inherited frailty: ApoE Alleles determine survival after a diagnosis of heart disease or stroke at ages 85+. *Annals of the New York Academy of Sciences, 908,* 295–298.

Cordova, M. J., Andrkowski, M. A., Kenady, D. E., McGrath, P. C., Sloan, D. A., & Redd, W. H. (1995). Frequency and correlates of posttraumatic-stress-disorder-like symptoms after treatment for breast cancer. *Journal of Consulting and Clinical Psychology, 63,* 981–986.

Costa, P. T., Jr. (2000). *Cutting edge research in personality: The importance of personality disorders to understanding normal aging.* Baltimore: National Institute on Aging.

Costa, P. T., Jr., Herbst, J. H., McCrae, R. R., & Siegler, I. C. (2000). Personality at midlife: Stability, intrinsic motivation and responses to life events. *Assessment, 7,* 365–378.

Costa, P. T., Jr., McCrae, R. R., & Siegler, I. C. (1999). Continuity and change over the adult life cycle: Personality and personality disorders. In C. R. Cloninger (Ed.), *Personality and psychopathology* (pp. 129–153). Washington, DC: American Psychiatric Press.

Costa, P. T., Jr., & Widiger, T. (1994). *Personality disorders and the five-factor model of personality.* Washington, DC: American Psychological Association.

Costa, P. T., Jr., & McCrae, R. R. (1985). Hypochondriasis, neuroticism and aging: When are somatic complaints unfounded? *American Psychologist, 40,* 19–28.

Crimmins, E., & Saito, Y. (2000). Change in the prevalence of diseases among older Americans: 1984–1994. *Demographic Research, 3*(9). Available from http://www.history-journals.de/hjg-eartic-j0064.html.

Danner, D. D., Snowdon, D. A., & Friesen, W. V. (2001). Positive emotions in early life and longevity: Findings from the Nun Study. *Journal of Personality and Social Psychology, 80,* 804–813.

Daviglus, M. L., Liu, K., Greenland, P., Dyer, A. R., Garside, D. B., Manheim, L., et al. (1989). Benefit of a favorable cardiovascular risk-factor profile in middle age with respect to Medicare costs. *New England Journal of Medicine, 339,* 1122–1129.

Deeg, D. H. J., Kardaun, J. W. P. F., & Fozard, J. L. (1996). Health, behavior and aging. In J. E. Birren & K. W. Schaie (Eds.), *Handbook of the psychology of aging* (4th ed., pp. 129–149). San Diego, CA: Academic Press.

Demark-Wahnefried, W., Peterson, B., McBride, C., Lipkus, I., & Clipp, E. (2000). Current health behaviors and readiness to pursue life-style changes among men and women diagnosed with early stage prostate and breast carcinomas. *Cancer, 88,* 674–684.

DiMatteo, M., Lepper, H. S., & Croghan, T. W. (2000). Depression is a risk factor for noncompliance with medical treatment: Meta-analysis of the effects of anxiety and depression on patient adherence. *Archives of Internal Medicine, 160*(14), 2101–2107.

Dwyer, J. H., & Feinleib, M. (1992). Introduction to statistical models for longitudinal observation. In J. H. Dwyer, M. Feinleib, P. Lippert, & H. Hoffmeister (Eds.), *Statistical models for longitudinal studies of health* (pp. 3–48). New York: Oxford University Press.

Dye, C., & Sassenrath, D. (1979). Identification of normal aging and disease-related processes by health care professionals. *Journal of the American Geriatrics Society, 27,* 472–475.

Eaker, E. D. (1998). Psychosocial risk factors for coronary heart disease in women. *Cardiology Clinics, 16*(1), 103–111.

Eisdorfer, C., & Wilkie, F. W. (1977). Stress, disease, aging and behavior. In J. E. Birren & K. W. Schaie (Eds.), *Handbook of the psychology of aging* (pp. 251–275). New York: Van Nostrand-Reinhold.

Elias, M. F., Elias, J. W., & Elias, P. K. (1990). Biological and health influences on behavior. In J. E. Birren & K. W. Schaie (Eds.), *Handbook of the psychology of aging* (3rd ed., pp. 79–102). San Diego, CA: Academic Press.

Elias, M. F., Elias, P. K., D'Agostino, R. B., & Wolf, P. A. (2000). Comparative effects of age and blood pressure on neuropsychological test performance. In S. Manuck, J. R. Jennings, B. S. Rabin, & A. Baum (Eds.), *Behavior, health and aging* (pp. 199–223). Hillsdale, NJ: Erlbaum.

Elias, M. F., Elias, P. K., Robbins, M. A., Wolf, P. A., & D'Agostino, R. B. (2001). Cardiovascular risk factors and cognitive functioning: An epidemiological perspective. In S. R. Waldstein & M. F. Elias (Eds.), *Neuropsychology of cardiovascular disease* (pp. 84–104). Mahwah, NJ: Erlbaum.

Elias, M. F., & Robbins, M. A. (1991a). Cardiovascular disease, hypertension and cognitive function. In A. P. Shapiro & A. Baum (Eds.), *Behavioral aspects of cardiovascular disease* (pp. 249–285). Hillsdale, NJ: Erlbaum.

Elias, M. F., & Robbins, M. A. (1991b). Where have all the subjects gone? Longitudinal studies of disease and cognitive function. In L. M. Collins & J. L. Horn (Eds.), *Best methods for the analysis of change: Recent advances, unanswered questions, future directions* (pp. 264–275). Washington, DC: American Psychological Association.

Elias, M. F., Robbins, M. A., Elias, P. K., & Streeten, D. H. P. (1998a). A longitudinal study of blood pressure in relation to performance on the Wechsler Adult Intelligence Scale. *Health Psychology, 17,* 486–493.

Elias, M. F., Robbins, M. A., Elias, P. K., & Streeten, D. H. P. (1998b). Cognitive ability declines as a function of blood pressure level. *Circulation, 98*(Suppl.), I-860.

Elias, M. F., Robbins, M. A., & Schultz, N. (1987). Influence of essential hypertension on intellectual performance: Causation or speculation. In J. W. Elias & P. H. Marshall (Eds.), *Cardiovascular disease and behavior* (pp. 107–149). Washington, DC: Hemisphere.

Elias, M. F., Wolf, P. A., D'Agostino, R. B., Cobb, J., & White, L. R. (1993). Untreated blood pressure is inversely related to cognitive functioning: The Framingham Study. *American Journal of Epidemiology, 138,* 353–364.

Elias, P. K., D'Agostino, R. B., Elias, M. F., & Wolf, P. A. (1995). Blood pressure, hypertension, and age as risk factors for poor cognitive performance. *Experimental Aging Research, 21,* 393–417.

Elias, P. K., Elias, M. F., D'Agostino, R. B., Silbershatz, H., & Wolf, P. A. (1999). Alcohol consumption and cognitive performance in the Framingham Heart Study. *American Journal of Epidemiology, 150,* 580–589.

Enhancing Recovery in Coronary Heart Disease Investigators. (2000). Enhancing Recovery in Coronary Heart Disease Patients (ENRICHD): Study design and methods. *American Heart Journal, 139,* 1–9.

Evans, J. G. (1988). Aging and disease. In D. Evered & J. Whelan (Eds.), *Research and the aging population* (pp. 38–57). New York: Wiley.

Everson, S., Roberts, R., Goldberg, D., & Kaplan, G. (1998). Depressive symptoms and increased risk of stroke mortality over a 29-year period. *Archives of Internal Medicine, 158,* 1133–1138.

Everson, S. A., Goldberg, D. E., Kaplan, G. A., Cohen, R. D., Pukkala, E., Tuomilehto, J., et al. (1996). Hopelessness and risk of mortality and incidence of myocardial infarction and cancer. *Psychosomatic Medicine, 58,* 113–121.

Ewbank, D. (2000). Demography and the age of genomics: A first look at the prospects. In C. E. Finch, J. W. Vaupel, & K. Kinsella (Eds.), *Cells and Surveys* (pp. 64–109). Washington, DC: National Academy Press.

Faulkner, D. L., Young, C., Hutchins, D., & McCollam, J. S. (1998). Patient noncompliance with hormone replacement therapy: A nationwide estimate using a large prescription claims database. *Menopause, 5*(4), 226–229.

Fillenbaum, G. G., Pieper, C. F., Cohen, H. J., Cornoni-Huntley, J. C., & Guralnik, J. M. (2000). Comorbidity of five chronic health conditions in elderly community residents: Determinants and impact on mortality. *Journal of Gerontology: Series A, Biological Sciences and Medical Science, 55*(2), M84–M89.

Flack, J., Novikov, S. V., & Ferrario, C. M. (1996). Benefits of adherence to antihypertensive drug therapy. *European Society of Cardiology, 17*(Suppl. A), 16–20.

Fletcher, R. H., Fletcher, S., & Wagner, E. H. (1988). *Clinical epidemiology: The essentials* (2nd ed.). Boston: Little, Brown.

Fowles, D. (1994). *A profile of older Americans.* Washington, DC: U.S. Department of Health and Human Services, Program Resources Department, American Association of Retired Persons (AARP) and Administration on Aging (AoA).

Fox, B. H. (1998). A hypothesis about Spiegel et al.'s 1989 paper on Psychosocial intervention and breast cancer survival. *Psycho-Oncology, 7*(5), 361–370.

Fratiglioni, L., Wang, H.-X., Ericsson, K., Maytan, M., & Winblad, B. (2000). Influence of social network on occurrence of dementia: A community based longitudinal study. *Lancet, 355,* 1315–1319.

Garssen, B., & Goodkin, K. (1999). On the role of immunological factors as mediators between psychosocial factors and cancer progression. *Psychiatry Research, 85*(1), 51–61.

Gatz, M. (1989). Clinical psychology and aging. In M. Storandt & G. R. VandenBos (Eds.), *The adult years: Continuity and change* (pp. 83–114). Washington, DC: American Psychological Association.

Greer, S., Morris, T., Pettingale, K. W., & Haybittle, J. L. (1990). Psychological response to breast cancer and 15-year outcome. *Lancet, 335*(8680), 49–50.

Gruenwald, D. A., & Matsumoto, A. M. (1999). Aging of the endocrine system. In W. R. Hazzard, J. P. Blass, W. H. Ettinger, J. B. Halter, & J. G. Ouslander (Eds.), *Principles of geriatric medicine and gerontology* (pp. 949–965). New York: McGraw-Hill.

Guo, Z., Viitanen, M., Fratiglioni, L., & Winblad, B. (1996). Low blood pressure and dementia in elderly people: The Kungsholmen project. *British Medical Journal, 312,* 805–808.

Guralnik, J. (1996). Assessing the impact of comorbidity in the older population. *Annals of Epidemiology, 6,* 376–380.

Halter, J. B. (1999). Diabetes mellitus. In W. R. Hazzard, J. P. Blass, W. H. Ettinger, J. B. Halter, & J. G. Ouslander (Eds.), *Principles of geriatric medicine and gerontology* (pp. 991–1011). New York: McGraw-Hill.

Hamish, B., Blacklay, A., Eiser, C., Davies, H., Hawkins, M., Levitt, G. A., et al. (2001). Developing strategies for long term follow up of survivors of childhood cancer. *British Medical Journal, 323,* 271–274.

Havlik, R. (1986). *Aging in the eighties: Impaired senses for sound and light in persons age 65 years and over.* NCHS, Advance Data, Vital, and Health Statistics of the National Center for Health Statistics, No. 125.

Hawkins, M. M., Draper, G. J., & Kingston, J. E. (1987). Incidence of second primary tumours among childhood cancer survivors. *British Journal of Cancer, 56,* 339–347.

Hazzard, W. R., Blass, J. P., Ettinger, W. H., Halter, J. B., & Ouslander, J. G. (1999). *Principles of geriatric medicine and gerontology.* New York: McGraw-Hill.

Hemminki, E., & Topo, P. (1997). Prescribing of hormone therapy in menopause and postmenopause. *Journal of Psychosomatic Obstretics Gynecology, 18,* 145.

Hennekens, C. H., Buring, J. E., & Mayerent, S. L. (1987). *Epidemiology in medicine.* Boston: Little, Brown.

Hewitt, M., Breen, N., & Devesa, S. (1999). Cancer prevalence and survivorship issues: Analyses of the 1992 National Health Interview Survey. *Journal of the National Cancer Institute, 91,* 1480–1486.

Hoffman, C., Rice, D., & Sung, H. (1996). Persons with chronic conditions: Their prevalence and costs. *Journal of the American Medical Association, 276,* 1473–1479.

Hosmer, D. W., & Lemeshow, S. (1998). *Applied logistic regression.* New York: Wiley.

Hutchins, L., Unger, J. M., Crowley, J. J., Coltman, C. A., & Albain, K. S. (1999). Under-representation of patients 65 years of age or older in cancer treatment trials. *New England Journal of Medicine, 341,* 2061–2067.

Idler, E. L., & Benyamini, Y. (1997). Self-rated health and mortality: A review of twenty-seven community studies. *Journal of Health and Social Behavior, 38,* 21–37.

Jonas, B. S., Franks, P., & Ingram, D. D. (1997). Are symptoms of anxiety and depression risk factors for hypertension? Longitudinal evidence from the National Health and Nutrition Examination Survey. I: Epidemiologic follow-up study. *Archives of Family Medicine, 6*(1), 43–49.

Jonas, S. J., & Lambo, J. F. (2000). Negative affect as a prospective risk factor for hypertension. *Psychosomatic Medicine, 62,* 188–196.

Jones, J., Gorkin, L., Lian, J. F., Staffa, J. A., & Fletcher, A. P. (1995). Discontinuation of and changes in treatment after start of new courses of antihypertensive drugs: A study of the United Kingdom population. *British Medical Journal, 311,* 293–295.

Juncos, L. (1990). Patient compliance and angiotension converting enzyme inhibitors in hypertension. *Journal of Cardiovascular Pharmacology, 15,* S22–S25.

Kannel, W. B., Dawber, T. R., Kagan, A., Revortskie, N., & Stokes, J., III. (1961). Factors of risk in the development of coronary heart disease—six-year follow-up experience: The Framingham Study. *Annals of Internal Medicine, 55,* 33–50.

Kannel, W. B., & Sytkowski, P. A. (1987). Atherosclerosis risk factors. *Pharmacology and Therapeutics, 32,* 207–235.

Kaplan, G. A., Haan, M., & Wallace, R. B. (1999). Understanding changing risk factor associations with increasing age in adults. *Annual Review of Public Health, 20,* 89–108.

Kaplan, G. A., Strawbridge, W. J., Camacho, T., & Cohen, R. D. (1993). Factors associated with change in physical functioning in the elderly: A six-year prospective study. *Journal of Aging and Health, 5,* 140–153.

Kawas, C. H. (1999). Alzheimer's disease. In W. R. Hazzard, J. P. Blass, W. H. Ettinger, J. B. Halter, & J. G. Ouslander (Eds.), *Principles of geriatric medicine and gerontology* (pp. 1257–1269). New York: McGraw-Hill.

Keil, J. E., Sutherland, S. E., Knapp, R. G., & Gazes, P. C. (1992). Serum cholesterol—risk factor for coronary disease mortality in younger and older Blacks and Whites: The Charleston Heart Study, 1960–1988. *Annals of Epidemiology, 2,* 93–99.

Knopman, D., Boland, L. L., Mosely, T., Howard, G., Liao, D., Szklo, M., et al. (2001). Cardiovascular risk factors and cognitive decline in middle-aged adults. *Neurology, 56,* 42–48.

Kop, W. J. (1997). Acute and chronic psychological risk factors for coronary artery syndromes: Moderating effects of coronary artery severity. *Journal of Psychosomatic Research, 43*(2), 167–181.

Kuh, D., & Ben-Shlomo, Y. (Eds.). (1997). *A life-course approach to chronic disease epidemiology.* Oxford, England: Oxford University Press.

Lakatta, E. G. (1999). Circulatory function in young and older humans in health. In W. R. Hazzard, J. P. Blass, W. H. Ettinger, J. B. Halter, & J. G. Ouslander (Eds.), *Principles of geriatric medicine and gerontology* (pp. 645–660). New York: McGraw-Hill.

Larsen, E. B., & Shadlen, M.-F. (1999). Diagnostic tests. In W. R. Hazzard, J. P. Blass, W. H. Ettinger, J. B. Halter, & J. G. Ouslander (Eds.), *Principles of geriatric medicine and gerontology* (pp. 275–286). New York: McGraw-Hill.

Launer, L. J., Masaki, K., Petrovitch, H., Foley, D., & Havlik, R. J. (1995). The association between midlife blood pressure levels and late-life cognitive function. *Journal of the American Medical Association, 274,* 1846–1851.

Levenstein, S. L., Kaplan, G. A., & Smith, M. W. (2000). Psychosocial predictors of hypertension in men and women: Prospective analyses from the Alameda County study. *Psychosomatic Medicine, 62,* 111.

Madden, D. J., & Blumenthal, J. A. (1998). Interaction of hypertension and age visual selective attention performance. *Health Psychology, 17,* 76–83.

Manton, K. G., & Gu, X. (2001). Changes in the prevalence of chronic disability in the United States Black and nonblack population above age 65 from 1982 to 1989. *Proceedings of the National Academy of Sciences, 98,* 4770–4775.

Martin, L. R., Friedman, H. S., Tucker, J. S., Schwartz, J. E., Criqui, M. H., Wingard, D. L., et al. (1995). An archival prospective study of mental health and longevity. *Health Psychology, 14,* 381–387.

Martin, P., Poon, L., Clayton, G., Lee, H. S., Fulks J. S., & Johnson, M. A. (1992). Personality, life events and coping in the oldest-old. *International Journal of Aging and Human Development, 34,* 19–30.

Matthews, K. A., & Cauley, J. A. (1999). Menopause and midlife health changes. In W. R. Hazzard, J. P. Blass, W. H. Ettinger, J. B. Halter, & J. G. Ouslander (Eds.), *Principles of geriatric medicine and gerontology* (pp. 179–189). New York: McGraw-Hill.

Matthews, K. A., Wing, R. R., Kuller, L. H., Meilahn, E. N., & Owens, J. F. (2000). Menopause as a turning point in midlife. In S. B. Manuck, R. Jennings, B. S. Rabin, & A. Baum (Eds.), *Behavior, health and aging* (pp. 43–56). Mahwah, NJ: Erlbaum.

McArdle, J. J., & Hamagami, F. (1991). Modeling incomplete longitudinal and cross-sectional data using latent growth structural equation models. In L. M. Collins & J. L. Horn (Eds.), *Best methods for the analysis of change: Recent advances, unanswered questions, future directions* (pp. 275–303). Washington, DC: American Psychological Association.

McBride, C. M., Clipp, E., Peterson, B. L., Lipkus, I. M., & Demark-Wahnefried, W. (2000). Psychological impact of diagnosis and risk reduction among cancer survivors [in process citation]. *Psycho-Oncology, 9*(5), 418–427.

McClearn, G. E., & Heller, D. A. (2000). Genetics and aging. In S. B. Manuck, R. Jennings, B. S. Rabin, & A. Baum (Eds.), *Behavior, health and aging* (pp. 1–14). Mahwah, NJ: Erlbaum.

Merrill, S. S., & Verbrugge, L. M. (1999). Health and disease at midlife. In S. L. Willis & J. R. Reid (Eds.), *Life in the middle: Psychological and social development in middle age* (pp. 77–103). San Diego, CA: Academic Press.

Morbidity and Mortality Weekly Report. (1996). Breast cancer incidence and mortality—United States, 1992. *Morbidity and Mortality Weekly Report, 45*(39), 833–837.

Muir, J. (1998). Personality and psychological environment. In M. Lawrence, A. Neil, D. Mant, & G. Fowler (Eds.), *Prevention of cardiovascular disease* (pp. 93–105). Oxford, England: Oxford University Press.

Muldoon, M. F., Flory, J. D., & Ryan, C. M. (2001). Serum cholesterol, the brain, and cognitive functioning. In S. R. Waldstein & M. F. Elias (Eds.), *Neuropsychology of cardiovascular disease* (pp. 37–60). Mahwah, NJ: Erlbaum.

Murasko, D. M. K. A., & Bernstein, E. D. (1999). Immunology of aging. In W. R. Hazzard, J. P. Blass, W. H. Ettinger, J. B. Halter, & J. G. Ouslander (Eds.), *Principles of geriatric medicine and gerontology* (pp. 97–116). New York: McGraw-Hill.

National Heart, Lung, and Blood Institute. (2000). Available from www.nhlbi.nih.gov/guidelines/cholesterol/etp3-rpt.pdf. Retrieval date 2/26/01, pp. 11–23, Table 11.4-2.

National Heart, Lung, and Blood Institute. (2001, May). *Detection, evaluation and treatment of high blood cholesterol in adults [Adult treatment panel III]* (NIH Publication No. 01–3670). Bethesda, MD: National Institutes of Health.

National Institute of Health. (1991). Consensus conference: Treatment of early-stage breast cancer. *Journal of the American Medical Association, 26,* 391–395.

Neugarten, B. (1976). Adaptation and the life cycle. *Counseling Psychologist, 6,* 16–20.

Newman, S., Stygall, J., & Kong, R. (2001). Neuropsychological consequences of coronary artery bypass surgery. In S. R. Waldstein & M. F. Elias (Eds.), *Neuropsychology of cardiovascular disease* (pp. 189–218). Mahwah, NJ: Erlbaum.

Newschaffer, C., Penberthy, L., & Desch, C. F. (1996). The effect of age and comorbidity in the treatment of elderly women with non-metastatic breast cancer. *Archives of Internal Medicine, 156,* 85–90.

Niaura, R., Banks, S. M., Ward, K. D., Stoney, C. M., Spiro, A., Aldwin, C. M., et al. (2000). Hostility and the metabolic syndrome in older males: The normative aging study. *Psychosomatic Medicine, 62,* 7–16.

Nordhus, I. H., VandenBos, G. R., Berg, S., & Fromholt, P. (1998). *Clinical geropsychology.* Washington, DC: American Psychological Association.

Nuland, S. B. (1995). *How we die: Reflections of life's final chapter.* New York: Random House.

Oddens, B. J., & Boulet, M. J. (1997). Hormone replacement therapy among Danish women aged 45–65 years: Prevalence, determinants, and compliance. *British Journal of Obstetrics and Gynecology, 104*(Suppl. 16), 1–3.

Orth-Gomer, K., Unden, A. L., & Edwards, M. E. (1988). Social isolation and mortality in ischemic heart disease. *Acta Medica Scandinavica, 224,* 205–215.

Orth-Gomer, K., Wamala, S. P., Horsten, M., Schenk-Gustafsson, K., Schneiderman, N., & Mittleman, M. A. (2000). Marital stress worsens prognosis in women with coronary heart disease: The Stockholm Female Coronary Risk Study. *Journal of the American Medical Association, 284,* 3008–3014.

Pedhauser, E. J., & Schmelkin, L. P. (1991). *Measurement, design and analysis: An integrated approach.* Hillsdale, NJ: Erlbaum.

Peters, E., Finucane, M. L., MacGregor, D. G., & Slovic, P. (2000). The bearable lightness of aging: Judgment and decision processes in older adults. In P. C. Stern & L. L. Carstensen (Eds.), *The aging mind* (pp. 144–165). Washington, DC: National Academy Press.

Qualls, S. H., & Abeles, N. (Eds.). (2000). *Psychology and the aging revolution.* Washington, DC: American Psychological Association.

Riley, K. P., Snowdon, D. A., Saunders, A. M., Roses, A. D., Mortimer, J. A., & Nanayakkara, N. (2000). Cognitive function and Apolipoprotein E in very old adults: Findings from the Nun Study. *Journal of Gerontology: Series B, Psychological Sciences and Social Sciences, 55,* S69–S75.

Robine, J.-M., Kirkwood, T. B. L., & Allard, M. (2001). *Sex and longevity: Sexuality, gender, reproduction parenthood.* Berlin, Germany: Springer Verlag.

Robinson-Whelen, S., Kiecolt-Glaser, J. K., & Glaser, R. (2000). Effects of chronic stress on immune function and health in the elderly. In S. B. Manuck, R. J. Jennings, B. S. Rabin, & A. Baum (Eds.), *Behavior, aging and health* (pp. 69–82). Mahwah, NJ: Erlbaum.

Rosenberg, L., Kaufman, D. W., Helmrich, S. P., Miller, D. R., Stolley, P. D., & Shapiro, S. (1985). Myocardial infarction and cigarette smoking in women younger than 50 years of age. *Journal of the American Medical Association, 253,* 2965–2969.

Roses, A. D., & Saunders, A. M. (2001). Alzheimer's disease: Genetic factors. In G. L. Maddox (Editor-in-Chief), S. W. Sussman (Managing Ed.), R. C. Atchley, J. G. Evans, R. B. Hudson, R. A. Kane, et al. (Eds.), *Encyclopedia of aging* (pp. 63–65). New York: Springer.

Roth, J., & Yen, C.-J. (1999). The role of intracellular communication in diseases of old age. In W. R. Hazzard, J. P. Blass, W. H. Ettinger, J. B. Halter, & J. G. Ouslander (Eds.), *Principles of geriatric medicine and gerontology* (pp. 45–59). New York: McGraw-Hill.

Rothman, K. J. (1986). *Modern epidemiology.* Boston: Little, Brown.

Rothman, K. J. (Ed.). (1988). *Causal inference.* Chestnut Hill, MA: Epidemiology Resources.

Rozanski, A., Blumenthal, J. A., & Kaplan, J. (1999). Impact of psychological factors on the pathogenesis of cardiovascular disease and implications for therapy. *Circulation, 99,* 2192–2217.

Ryan, C. M. (2001). Diabetes-associated cognitive dysfunction. In S. R. Waldstein & M. F. Elias (Eds.), *Neuropsychology of cardiovascular disease* (pp. 61–82). Mahwah, NJ: Erlbaum.

Ryan, P., Harrison, R., Blake, G. M., & Fogelman, I. (1992). Compliance with hormone replacement therapy (HRT) after screening for post menopausal osteoporosis. *British Journal of Obstetrics and Gynecology, 99,* 325–328.

Sackett, D. L., Haynes, R. B., Guyatt, G. H., & Tugwell, P. (1991). *Clinical epidemiology: A basic science for clinical medicine* (2nd ed.). Boston: Little, Brown.

Samet, J., Hunt, W. C., Key, C., Humble, C. G., & Goodwin, J. S. (1986). Choice of cancer therapy varies with age of patient. *Journal of the American Medical Association, 255,* 2285–3390.

Schapiro, I. R., Ross-Petersen, L., Saelan, H., Garde, K., Olsen, J. H., & Johansen, C. (2001). Extroversion and neuroticism and the associated risk of cancer: A Danish cohort study. *American Journal of Epidemiology, 153,* 757–763.

Schapiro, M., McAuuliffe, T. L., & Nattinger, A. B. (2000). Underutilization of mammography in older breast cancer survivors. *Medical Care, 38,* 281–289.

Scherwitz, L. W., Perkins, L. L., Chesney, M. A., Hughes, G. H., Sidney, S., & Manolio, T. A. (1992). Hostility and health behaviors in young adults: The CARDIA study. *American Journal of Epidemiology, 36,* 136–145.

Schnall, P., & Landsbergis, P. A. (1994). Job strain and cardiovascular disease. *Annual Review of Public Health, 15,* 381–411.

Siegler, I. C. (1983). Psychological aspects of the Duke Longitudinal Studies. In K. W. Schaie (Ed.), *Longitudinal studies of adult psychological development* (pp. 136–190). New York: Guilford Press.

Siegler, I. C. (1989). Developmental health psychology. In M. Storandt & G. R. VandenBos (Eds.), *The adult years: Continuity and change* (pp. 119–142). Washington, DC: American Psychological Association.

Siegler, I. C. (1994). Hostility and risk: Demographic and lifestyle factors. In A. W. Siegman & T. W. Smith (Eds.), *Anger, hostility and the heart* (pp. 199–214). Hillsdale, NJ: Erlbaum.

Siegler, I. C. (2000). Aging research and health: A status report. In S. H. Qualls & N. Abeles (Eds.), *Psychology and the aging revolution* (pp. 207–218). Washington, DC: American Psychological Association.

Siegler, I. C., Bastian, L. A., & Bosworth, H. B. (2001). Health, behavior and aging. In A. Baum, T. R. Revenson, & J. E. Singer (Eds.), *Handbook of health psychology* (pp. 469–476). Hillsdale, NJ: Erlbaum.

Siegler, I. C., Bastian, L. A., Steffens, D. C., Bosworth, H. B., & Costa, P. T. (in press). Behavioral medicine and aging: Middle age, aging and the oldest-old. *Journal of Consulting and Clinical Psychology.*

Siegler, I. C., Bosworth, H. B., & Poon, L. W. (in press). Disease, health and aging. In R. M. Lerner, M. A. Easterbrooks, & J. Mistri (Eds.), *Comprehensive handbook of psychology: Developmental psychology* (Vol. 6). New York: Wiley.

Siegler, I. C., Brummett, B. H., Barefoot, J. C., Williams, R. B., Feaganes, J. R., Dahlstrom, W. G., et al. (2002). *Age, hostility change high risk behaviors during midlife.* Manuscript submitted for publication.

Siegler, I. C., & Costa, P. T. (1985). Health behavior relationships. In J. E. Birren & K. W. Schaie (Eds.), *Handbook of the psychology of aging* (2nd ed., pp. 144–166). New York: Van Nostrand-Reinhold.

Siegler, I. C., Peterson, B. L., Barefoot, J. C., & Williams, R. B. (1992). Hostility during late adolescence predicts coronary risk factors at mid-life. *American Journal of Epidemiology, 136,* 146–154.

Siegler, I. C., Welsh, K. A., Dawson, D. V., Fillenbaum, G. G., Earl, N. L., Kaplan, E. B., et al. (1991). Ratings of personality change in patients evaluated for memory disorders. *Alzheimer's Disease and Associated Disorders, 5*(4), 240–250.

Silliman, R., Guadagnoli, E., Weitberg, A. B., & Mor, V. (1989). Age as a predictor of diagnostic and initial treatment intensity in newly diagnosed breast cancer patients. *Journal of Gerontology, 44,* 46–50.

Silliman, R., Troyan, S. L., Guadagnoli, E., Kaplan, S. H., & Greenfield, S. (1997). The impact of age, marital status, and physician-patient interactions on the care of older women with breast carcinoma. *Cancer, 80*(7), 1326–1334.

Singer, B. H., & Manton, K. G. (1998). The effects of health changes on projection of health service needs for the elderly population of the United States. *Proceedings National Academy of Sciences, 95,* 15618–15622.

Small, B., Basun, H., & Bachman, L. (1998). Three-year changes in cognitive performance as a function of Apolipoprotein E genotype: Evidence from very old adults without dementia. *Psychology and Aging, 13,* 80–87.

Smith, T. W., & Gallo, L. C. (2001). Personality traits as risk factors for physical illness. In A. Baum, T. Revenson, & J. Singer (Eds.), *Handbook of health psychology* (pp. 139–173). Hillsdale, NJ: Erlbaum.

Smith, T. W., & Kendall, P. C. (in press). Behavioral medicine and clinical health psychology. *Journal of Consulting and Clinical Psychology.*

Snowdon, D. (2001). *Aging with grace.* New York: Bantam Books.

Spiro, A., Aldwin, C., Ward, K. D., & Mroczek, D. K. (1995). Personality and incidence of hypertension among older men: Longitudinal findings from the Normative Aging Study. *Health Psychology, 14,* 563–569.

Stampfer, M. J., Hu, F. B., Manson, J. E., Rimm, E. B., & Willett, W. C. (2000). Primary prevention of coronary heart disease in women through diet and lifestyle. *New England Journal of Medicine, 343,* 16–22.

Storandt, M., Siegler, I. C., & Elias, M. F. (1978). *The clinical psychology of aging.* New York: Plenum Press.

Strawbridge, W. J., Cohen, R. D., Shema, S. J., & Kaplan, G. A. (1996). Successful aging: Predictors and associated activities. *American Journal of Epidemiology, 144*(2), 135–141.

Swan, G. E., Carmelli, D., & LaRue, A. (1995). Performance on the digit symbol substitution test and 5-year mortality on the Western Collaborative Group Study. *American Journal of Epidemiology, 141,* 32–40.

Swan, G. E., Carmelli, D., & LaRue, A. (1998). Systolic blood pressure tracking over 25 to 30 years and cognitive performance in older adults. *Stroke, 29,* 2334–2340.

Tenover, J. L. (1999). Trophic factors and male hormone replacement. In W. R. Hazzard, J. P. Blass, W. H. Ettinger, J. B. Halter, & J. G. Ouslander (Eds.), *Principles of geriatric medicine and gerontology* (pp. 1029–1040). New York: McGraw-Hill.

Tucker, J. S., Friedman, H. S., Wingard, D. L., & Schwartz, J. E. (1996). Martial history at midlife as a predictor of longevity: Alternate explanations to the protective effect of marriage. *Health Psychology, 15,* 94–101.

Tucker, J. S., Schwartz, J. E., Clark, K. M., & Friedman, H. S. (1999). Age-related changes in the associations of social network ties with mortality risk. *Psychology and Aging, 14,* 564–571.

Tzourio, C., Dufouil, C., Ducimetière, P., & Alpérovitch, A. (1999). Cognitive decline in individuals with high blood pressure: A longitudinal study in the elderly. *Neurology, 53,* 1948–1952.

Umberson, D. (1987). Family status and health behaviors: Social control as a dimension of social integration. *Journal of Health and Social behavior, 28,* 306–319.

U.S. Department of Health and Human Services. (1994). *Vital and health statistics: Current estimates from the National Health Interview Survey, 1993* [Series 10: Data from the National Health Survey, No. 190, DHHS Publication PHS 95–1518]. Hyattsville, MD: Author.

Vaccarino, V., Krumholz, H. M., Yarzebski, J., Gore, J. M., & Goldberg, R. J. (2001). Sex differences in 2-year mortality after hospital discharge for myocardial infarction. *Annals of Internal Medicine, 134*(3), 173–181.

Van't Spijker, A., Trijsburg, R. W., & Duivenvoorden, H. J. (1997). Psychological sequalae of cancer diagnosis: A meta-analytical review of 58 studies after 1980. *Psychosomatic Medicine, 59,* 280–293.

Vita, A. J., Terry, R. B., Hubert, H. B., & Fries, J. F. (1998). Aging, health risks and cumulative disability. *New England Journal of Medicine, 338,* 1035–1041.

Vitaliano, P. P., Scanlan, J. M., Zhang, J., Savage, M. V., Hirsch, I. B., & Siegler, I. C. (in press). A path model of chronic stress, the metabolic syndrome, and CHD. *Psychosomatic Medicine.*

Vogt, T. M., Mullooly, J. P., Ernst, D., Pope, C. R., & Hollis, J. F. (1992). Social networks as predictors of ischemic heart disease, cancer, stroke, and hypertension: Incidence, survival, and mortality. *Journal of Clinical Epidemiology, 45,* 659–666.

Wadsworth, M. E. J. (1991). *The imprint of time.* Oxford, England: Clarendon Press.

Waldstein, S. R. (1995). Hypertension and neuropsychological function: A lifespan perspective. *Experimental Aging Research, 21,* 321–352.

Waldstein, S. R. (2000). Health effects on cognitive aging. In P. C. Stern & L. L. Carstensen (Eds.), *The aging mind* (pp. 189–217). Washington, DC: National Academy Press.

Waldstein, S. R., & Elias, M. F. (Eds.). (2001). *Neuropsychology of cardiovascular disease.* Mahwah, NJ: Erlbaum.

Waldstein, S. R., & Katzel, L. I. (2001). Hypertension and cognitive functioning. In S. R. Waldstein & M. F. Elias (Eds.), *Neuropsychology of cardiovascular disease* (pp. 15–36). Mahwah, NJ: Erlbaum.

Watson, M., Haviland, J. S., Greer, S., Davidson, J., & Bliss, J. M. (1999). Influence of psychological response on survival in breast cancer: A population-based cohort study. *Lancet, 354*(9187), 1331–1336.

Wei, J. Y. (1999). Coronary heart disease. In W. R. Hazzard, J. P. Blass, W. H. Ettinger, J. B. Halter, & J. G. Ouslander (Eds.), *Principles of geriatric medicine and gerontology* (pp. 661–668). New York: McGraw-Hill.

Whisnant, J. P., Wiebers, D. O., O'Fallon, W. M., Sicks, J. D., & Frye, R. L. (1996). A population-based model of risk factors for ischemic stroke: Rochester, Minnesota. *Neurology, 47,* 1420–1428.

Wilkie, F. L., & Eisdorfer, C. (1971). Intelligence and blood pressure in the aged. *Science, 172,* 959–962.

Willett, J. B. (1988). Questions and answers in the measurement of change. In E. Z. Rothkopf (Ed.), *Review of research in education* (Vol. 15, pp. 345–422). Washington, DC: American Educational Research Association.

Willett, J. B., & Singer, J. D. (1991). How long did it take? Using survival analysis in educational and psychological research. In L. M. Collins & J. L. Horn (Eds.), *Best methods for the analysis of change: Recent advances, unanswered questions, future directions* (pp. 243–250). Washington, DC: American Psychological Association.

Williams, R. B. (1994). Basic Books biological mechanisms. In A. W. Siegman & T. W. Smith (Eds.), *Anger, hostility and the heart* (pp. 117–125). Hillsdale, NJ: Erlbaum.

Williams, R. B. (2001). Hostility (and other psychosocial risk factors): Effects on health and the potential for successful behavioral approaches to prevention and treatment. In A. Baum, T. R. Revenson, & J. E. Singer (Eds.), *Handbook of psychology and health* (pp. 661–668). Hillsdale, NJ: Erlbaum.

Williams, R. B., Barefoot, J. C., Blumenthal, J. A., Helms, M. J., Luecken, L., Pieper, C. F., et al. (1997). Psychosocial correlates of job strain in a sample of working women. *Archives of General Psychiatry, 54,* 543–548.

Williams, R. B., Barefoot, J. C., Califf, R. M., Haney, T. L., Saunders, W. B., Pryor, D. B., et al. (1992). Prognostic importance of social and economic resources among medically treated patients with angiographically documented coronary artery disease. *Journal of the American Medical Association, 267,* 520–524.

Williams, R. B., Barefoot, J. C., Haney, T. L. Harrell, F. E., Blumenthal, J. A., Pryor, D. B., et al. (1988). Type A behavior and angiographically documented coronary atherosclerosis in a sample of 2,289 patients. *Psychosomatic Medicine, 50,* 139–152.

Williams, R. B., & Chesney, M. A. (1993). Psychosocial factors and prognosis in established coronary artery disease. *Journal of the American Medical Association, 270,* 1860–1861.

Williams, R. B., & Littman, A. B. (1996). Psychosocial factors: Role in cardiac risk and treatment strategies. *Cardiology Clinics, 14,* 97–104.

Williams, R. B., Marchuk, D. A., Gadde, K. M., Barefoot, J. C., Cleary, G. L., Grichnik, K., et al. (2001). Central nervous system serotonin function and biological response to stress. *Psychosomatic Medicine, 63,* 300–305.

Wilson, R. S., Gilley D. W., Bennett, D. A., Beckett, L. A., & Evans, D. A. (2000). Person-specific paths of cognitive decline in Alzheimer's disease and their relation to age. *Psychology and Aging, 15,* 18–28.

Yancik, R., Wesley, M. N., Ries, L. A., Havlik, R. J., Edwards, B. K., & Yates, J. W. (2001). Effect of age and co-morbidity in postmenopausal breast cancer patients aged 55 years and older. *Journal of the American Medical Association, 285,* 885–892.

PART FIVE

SPECIAL TOPICS

CHAPTER 22

Women's Health Psychology

PAMELA A. GELLER, MARIA C. GRAF, AND FAITH DYSON-WASHINGTON

Women represent approximately 52% of the U.S. population (U.S. Census Bureau, 1999), yet only in the 1990s did women's health begin to gain recognition as an important area of research. Prior to 1990, limited medical research attended to the many health issues important to women, and women were consistently underrepresented in clinical trials. According to the American Medical Association's Council on Ethical and Judicial Affairs (1991), research focused on men because "a woman's menstrual cycle may often constitute a separate variable affecting test results," thereby requiring researchers to apportion funds and develop a plan to monitor women's hormone levels throughout the experimental process. Researchers also were hesitant to conduct studies on women in their childbearing years for fear of affecting fertility (American Medical Association [AMA], 1991). The research that was completed with women stemmed from a biomedical perspective and largely focused on diseases that affect fertility and reproduction. As a result, women traditionally have received diagnoses and treatment based largely on research conducted on men, as in the case of coronary heart disease, which is discussed later in this chapter.

According to Haynes and Hatch (2000), several occurrences fueled the emergence of action in women's health in the past decade. First, a report from the General Accounting Office (GAO) highlighted the National Institutes of Health's (NIH) failure to include women in research (Nadel, 1990). Then, in response to the GAO report, the Office of Research on Women's Health (ORWH), a national entity, was created. Pinn (1994) remarked that the ORWH functions for three major purposes:

(1) to strengthen, develop and increase research into diseases, (2) to ensure that women are appropriately represented in research studies, and (3) to direct initiatives to increase the number of women in biomedical careers.

Finally, the NIH Revitalization Act of 1993 was passed, which mandated that women and minorities be included in federally funded research, including clinical trials.

Whereas there had been a biomedical focus, researchers and clinicians now recognize the importance of addressing women's health issues from a more comprehensive perspective that involves biological, psychological, and sociological aspects of women's lives. Such a biopsychosocial framework involves the complex interaction of biological, physiological, economic, political, environmental, psychological, cultural, and familial components (American Psychological Association, 1996).

This chapter provides a brief but comprehensive introduction to pertinent issues in women's health to increase awareness of the needs of women among researchers and health practitioners and suggests areas in need of further attention. In general, we suggest that further exploration of gender differences in symptom presentation, diagnosis, prognosis, risk factors, treatment effectiveness, and psychosocial factors for various disease entities is needed to enhance appropriate prevention and intervention strategies for women and their families.

We begin with an overview of the top five causes of death among women (i.e., coronary heart disease, cancer [lung and breast], stroke, chronic obstructive pulmonary disease, and HIV/AIDS); the leading cause of injury to women (i.e., domestic violence); and chronic diseases common in women (i.e., arthritis, fibromyalgia, and osteoporosis). We next discuss certain mental health conditions prevalent among women (i.e., depressive disorders, anxiety disorders, eating disorders) and substance use in women. As comprehensive definitions of women's health recognize the importance of the association between mental and physical health in that many physical illnesses can be risk factors for certain mental illnesses and vice versa, we include information on this relationship when available. After a brief discussion of issues relevant to women in mental health treatment, other issues related to health care are discussed (i.e., health insurance and relationships with health care providers). A section highlighting stressful conditions related to pregnancy (i.e., miscarriage, infertility, postpartum reactions, and peripartum cardiomyopathy) is then presented. Later in the chapter, we discuss social and cultural influences on women's health focusing on the relationship between socioeconomic status, multiple roles, sex roles, and socialization as they relate to the incidence of psychological and physiological illness in women. We conclude with a discussion of the current status of women in health care and psychology, and future directions in the field of women's health.

PHYSICAL HEALTH ISSUES

There are numerous physical health issues women confront throughout their life span. Mortality statistics indicate that women live longer than men, while morbidity statistics suggest women are less healthy. Therefore, although women are living longer than men, women often experience a dramatic decline in health during these additional years. Presenting issues related to prevalence, gender and ethnic-racial group differences, risk factors, and treatment, this section focuses on the five leading causes of death and the leading cause of injury among women, as well as chronic physical health conditions that are more prevalent among women. With the exception of breast cancer research, comprehensive investigation of gender differences in the diagnosis, treatment, and prevention of the top five causes of death among women has been sparse. Additional research in the area of physical health that includes gender as a variable is sorely needed.

Coronary Heart Disease

Coronary heart disease (CHD) is the leading cause of death for both men and women in the United States (Centers for Disease Control and Prevention [CDC], 1999). CHD is characterized by a narrowing of the coronary arteries usually due to atherosclerosis (thickening of the arteries), which can prevent oxygen and nutrients from entering the heart. Myocardial infarction (heart attack) occurs when oxygen and/or blood cannot enter the heart. It has been estimated that in the United States approximately 7.1 million men and 6.8 million women have a history of myocardial infarction and/or angina pectoris (chest pain due to lack of blood and oxygen entering the heart; Bittner, 2000). Although prevalence rates are similar for men and women, more women actually die from CHD each year than men. Study of mortality rates indicates that 42% of women who have a myocardial infarction die within one year compared to 24% of men (American Heart Association [AHA], 1999). Mortality rates among women with CHD increase as women get older, and CHD is most common among postmenopausal women over the age of 60 years (Stoney, 1998). Regardless of age, however, African American women have a higher risk of developing CHD than European American women, and those African American women younger than age 75 are more likely to die from CHD than their European American counterparts (see Newton, Lacroix, & Buist, 2000, for a review). Possible reasons for this health disparity are limited access to medical resources and a higher prevalence of risk factors among African American women (Holm & Scherubel, 1997).

CHD risk factors for men and women include cigarette smoking, family history of CHD, high blood pressure, high cholesterol, diabetes, physical inactivity, poor diet, and obesity (Bittner, 2000; Newton et al., 2000). These risks factors often are interrelated. For example, diabetes often is associated with high blood pressure, high cholesterol, and obesity (see Newton et al., 2000). Women tend to develop heart disease 10 years later in life on average than do men and are more likely to have chronic, comorbid risk factors (e.g., diabetes and hypertension), which can make diagnosis, detection, and treatment of heart disease extremely difficult (Office on Women's Health [OWH], 2000). Studies conducted with men have indicated that modification of risk factors (e.g., lipid levels, blood pressure, smoking) helps decrease mortality and morbidity (Ness, 2000). Although alteration of these risk factors in women would yield the same results, research in this area remains sparse and therefore inconclusive.

Heart attack symptoms in women often differ from those in men, resulting in women not seeking medical attention promptly or having their symptoms misdiagnosed (Malacrida et al., 1998). The results of the Worcester Heart Study, a large population-based investigation, found that women more commonly experience neck, back, jaw pain, and nausea than men, whereas chest and arm pain are experienced at similar rates (Goldberg et al., 1998). Further research is needed to examine gender differences in symptom presentation to prevent the delay of a CHD diagnosis in women to the later stages of the disease when prognosis is poor, or from having the disease go completely undetected.

Research has indicated that sex and ethnic racial status can determine the course of treatment for patients with CHD. For example, Schulman et al. (1999) found that the sex and ethnic racial status of a patient influenced whether a physician referred patients with chest pain for cardiac catheterization. In this study, different actors portrayed patients with identical histories, and researchers controlled for personality characteristics. Regardless of patients' clinical presentation, these physicians were less likely to recommend cardiac catheterization for women; this was particularly true for African American women.

Likewise, Steingart et al. (1991) found that physicians tend to be less aggressive in their management approach to CHD in women than in men. Women with CHD were less likely to undergo cardiac catheterization and coronary bypass surgery than men. The results could not be accounted for by coronary risk factors or cardiovascular medications, two reasons a physician may use a less aggressive approach. Women reported more cardiac disability than men but were less likely to undergo aggressive procedures to address their symptoms or improve functioning. Similarly, women who are hospitalized for CHD undergo fewer diagnostic and therapeutic procedures than men (Ayanian & Epstein 1991; D'Hoore, Sicotte, & Tilquin, 1994). Ayanian and Epstein found that hospitalized men with diagnosed or suspected CHD were more likely to undergo coronary angiography and revascularization procedures even when they adjusted for possible clinical and demographic confounding variables. However, researchers are careful to note that further research should be done in this area to explore the reasons for this underutilization because it is possible that certain procedures may not be appropriate for women.

In summary, women with CHD often display different symptomatology than men with CHD, which may help explain why women delay seeking treatment. Subsequently, prevention efforts should focus on educating women and health care practitioners about the typical symptoms of CHD among females to facilitate women in seeking prompt medical attention when CHD symptoms arise. In addition, prevention efforts should focus on publicizing risk factors for CHD in women and developing strategies to reduce and manage risk factors, especially among African American women, who have the highest risk of developing CHD and the worst prognosis after myocardial infarction. Furthermore, studies indicate physicians are less likely to perform aggressive coronary techniques (e.g., cardiac catheterization and coronary bypass surgery) on women than men, and further research is warranted to assess whether this underutilization is appropriate. Although CHD mortality rates are higher for women than men, practically all studies on risk factors, interventions, and treatments have focused on men. Like other areas of medical research, women have been excluded or underrepresented in cardiovascular research "because they are either of childbearing age or are elderly with coexisting illness" (Sechzer, Denmark, & Rabinowitz, 1994). Because women often experience greater disability after myocardial infarction, it is imperative that future research efforts include women in sufficient numbers to examine gender differences in symptom presentation, risk factors, and treatment options. These factors can help inform the development of psychosocial interventions. For example, clinical health psychologists may be consulted to help with patient adherence to diet, exercise regimen, and stress management to help promote healthy functioning in women with CHD.

Cancer

Lung Cancer

According to the American Cancer Society (ACS; 2000), cancer is the second leading killer of American women, with lung cancer being the leading cause of cancer death among women in the United States. Lung cancer has the third highest incidence rate for women (after breast and colon cancers; Anderson, Golden-Kreutz, & DiLillo, 2001). It is estimated that 157,400 deaths will occur from lung cancer in 2001

(90,100 men and 67,300 women) and an estimated 169,500 new cases will occur (90,700 among men and 78,800 among women). According to B. Miller et al. (1996), incidence rates for lung cancer are higher for Alaska Native women, African American women, Non-Hispanic White women, and Hawaiian women (i.e., 43 to 51 per 100,000); lower for Vietnamese and Chinese women (i.e., 25 to 31 per 100,000); and the lowest for Hispanic, Filipinos, Korean, and Japanese women (i.e., 15 to 20 per 100,000). Risk factors for lung cancer include age, cigarette smoking, asbestos exposure, occupational exposure (e.g., due to mining), air pollution, and genetic predisposition. Because of increased smoking rates among American women, deaths from lung cancer now surpass those from breast cancer (ACS, 2000).

There is a great need to examine cigarette smoking in women as a function of coping, stress reduction, and the alleviation of depression and anxiety, and as a strategy employed to suppress appetite. Prevention strategies should continue to focus educational efforts about the risk of lung cancer associated with cigarette smoking on women, especially on younger women where the onset of smoking occurs. Moreover, health psychologists should continue to assist in the development of smoking cessation programs designed to address concerns specific to women, such as weight gain associated with smoking cessation.

Breast Cancer

Breast cancer is the second leading cause of cancer death among American women from all age groups and remains the leading cause of cancer death among women ages 15 to 54 (ACS, 2000). It is estimated that 192,200 new cases of breast cancer will occur (1,500 men) and 40,600 individuals will die from breast cancer in 2001 (40,200 women and 400 men). While European American women have a higher age-adjusted incidence rate of breast cancer, African American women are almost 30% more likely to die from breast cancer than European American women. Positive news is that the mortality rates for breast cancer declined during 1990 to 1997, with the largest decreases among younger women.

Risk factors for breast cancer include current age, age at menarche, age at menopause, age at first full-term pregnancy, family history, obesity, and physical inactivity (ACS, 2000; Ursin, Spicer, & Bernstein, 2000). Risk for breast cancer increases with age, with 77% of women being over the age of 50 at the time of diagnosis (ACS, 2000). Likewise, women with a first-degree relative with breast cancer are twice as likely to develop breast cancer. Women who start menstruating before age 12, reach menopause at a late age (i.e., 55 years or later), experience a first pregnancy after the

age of 30, or have no children, have a slightly higher risk of developing breast cancer (ACS, 2000). Last, obesity and physical inactivity are associated with greater risk of developing breast cancer. Studies have indicated that protective factors against breast cancer include exercise, maintaining ideal body weight, breastfeeding, reduced alcohol consumption, and avoidance of long-term hormone replacement therapy (see Kerlikowske, 2000, for a review).

In part because of the efforts of women's health advocacy groups, breast cancer research is one of the few areas pertinent to women's health that has received a tremendous amount of attention. In the past decade, there has been a proliferation of breast cancer studies, with a particular focus on treatment choices and "psychosocial interventions" and outcomes (Rowland, 1998). In other words, research has focused not only on medical treatment options, but also on the psychological and sociological effects of the disease (e.g., coping skills and importance of social support). In addition, numerous educational programs stress the importance of routine screening, and attempts have been made to make mammography accessible to all women. Consequently, women with breast cancer are being diagnosed in the earlier stages of the disease when the chance for recovery is 70% or greater (Rowland, 1998). Health care providers also have increased the use of "breast-sparing approaches" and adjunctive treatment such as chemotherapy, radiotherapy, and hormonal therapy. As a result, women are provided with treatment choices, and fewer have to undergo the more aggressive treatments that can greatly impact women's body perception and self-identity (e.g., mastectomy). In addition to increasing awareness of breast cancer and treatment options, health psychologists can help women diagnosed with the disease and their families adjust to what can be traumatic effects of surgery, as well as manage side effects associated with nonsurgical intervention, such as anticipatory nausea, hair loss, and fatigue.

Stroke

Stroke, the third leading cause of death for American men and women, occurs as a result of a blocked or ruptured artery. The brain is then deprived of needed oxygen and brain cells begin to die. Stroke occurs at a higher rate among African American and Latina women compared to European American women (CDC, 1999). Risk factors for men and women include high blood pressure, cigarette smoking, diabetes, and high cholesterol (Wolf, 1990), but biological sex is a determinant in the prevalence of these risk factors and in the etiology of stroke. Arboix and colleagues (2001) noted that limited research is available examining gender-related differences in "risk factors, clinical presentation and mortality rates" of stroke patients. Therefore, they conducted a study to examine differences in vascular risk factors, clinical manifestation, and progression of the disease among men and women. The findings demonstrated major gender differences: Women have different predictive risk factors for stroke than men, including obesity, congestive heart failure, atrial fibrillation, hypertension, limb weakness, and age. The results also indicate that women suffer more severe strokes resulting in higher in-hospital mortality, higher neurological deficits, and longer hospitalization.

Similar to coronary heart disease, research on gender differences in stroke is limited because stroke research either excludes women or includes them in insufficient numbers to evaluate gender effects (Brey & Kittner, 2000). There is a need for research to examine gender differences in terms of risk factors, prevention, intervention, and psychosocial effects. Last, this is an area in which health psychologists can help women adjust to the physical and neurocognitive sequelae of stroke (e.g., physical limitations, memory loss, speech deficits).

Chronic Obstructive Pulmonary Disease

Chronic Obstructive Pulmonary Disease (COPD) includes chronic bronchitis, emphysema, and asthmatic bronchitis, which are conditions that obstruct airflow from the lungs. COPD is the fourth leading cause of death among women in the United States (CDC, 1999). Although prevalence rates traditionally have been higher among men than women, COPD rates have almost doubled over the past 20 years, with the most rapid increases occurring in women age 75 and older (OWH, 2000). The rise in COPD rates in women is attributed to increased smoking among women (Wise, 1997).

Researchers are beginning to explore possible gender differences in the diagnosis and prognosis of the disease. Silverman and colleagues (2000) reported that women may have a higher risk of developing severe COPD and that this finding may be due to gender differences in genetic predisposition. Moreover, Chapman, Tashkin, and Pye (2001) reported that COPD is underdiagnosed in women (i.e., doctors are more likely to diagnosis men with COPD than women), which may have implications for treatment and prognosis if the disease is detected at a more advanced stage in women. Additional research in this area is needed to identify effective diagnostic testing, examine risk factors, and develop prevention strategies appropriate for both men and women. Again, as in lung cancer, health psychologists have the ability to assist with COPD prevention by developing and facilitating effective smoking cessation programs.

HIV/AIDS

Human immunodeficiency virus (HIV) causes acquired immune deficiency syndrome (AIDS), which is the fifth leading cause of death among American women between the ages of 25 and 44 years, and the third leading cause of death among African American women in this age group (CDC, 1998). There have been dramatic increases in rates of HIV/AIDS around the world since the first reported occurrence, with rates increasing more rapidly among women than men (Richardson, 1998).

Women most commonly acquire the HIV infection through heterosexual contact and intravenous drug use (Richardson, 1998). Although women who practice intravenous drug use have a higher risk of contracting HIV because they are more likely to share a needle with a partner (Morokoff, Harlow, & Quina, 1995), a woman changing her own behaviors to reduce her risk does not always result in a decrease in mortality or morbidity since women often are affected by the risk behaviors of their partners. This is particularly true for women who are in controlling and abusive relationships (Kamb & Wortley, 2000), which seems especially relevant given the findings that two-thirds of HIV-positive women (as well as two-thirds of women at risk for HIV infection) experience domestic violence during their lifetimes (M. Cohen et al., 2000).

Research on gender differences in risk factors, as well as research addressing gender differences in treatment, prevention, and psychosocial effects (e.g., caregiving, social support, stigmatization, depression), is growing. Such research is helping to inform clinicians and health care providers of the unique effects of HIV/AIDS on women and the needs of women living with HIV/AIDS (e.g., family planning), and could assist in the development of improved prevention and psychosocial treatment protocols for women and their families. Prevention intervention efforts should include components that educate women about possible risk behaviors of their partners and their impact on the contraction of HIV and sexually transmitted diseases (STDs). A recently developed prevention intervention protocol targeting women with chronic mental illness aims to increase the use of female-controlled methods of STD/HIV prevention to give women more control in limiting their risk of infection through heterosexual contact (Collins, Geller, Miller, Toro, & Susser, 2001). See the chapter by Carey and Vanable in this volume for additional information on HIV/AIDS.

Domestic Violence

Domestic violence, or battering, is the number one cause of injury for women ages 15 to 44 in the United States (Novella,

Rosenberg, Saltzman, & Shosky, 1992). Attacks by husbands on wives account for more injuries requiring medical treatment than rapes, muggings, and auto accidents combined (Alpert, Freund, Park, Patel, & Sovak, 1992; Bachman, 1994). Typically defined as a pattern of controlling and violent behaviors that an individual exhibits toward a present or former intimate partner (El-Bayoumi, Borum, & Haywood, 1998), domestic violence encompasses physical, psychological and sexual abuse, and isolation and economic control. More reliable tracking systems for monitoring violence against women need to be instituted, but estimates suggest that between two million and four million women are abused each year, with a woman being battered every nine seconds in the United States. Men and women can be victims of domestic violence; however, 95% of reported victims are heterosexual women (Bachman, 1994). Domestic violence occurs among all ethnic, racial, and socioeconomic groups.

Victims of domestic violence often present themselves in a variety of health care settings including emergency departments, primary care, gynecological services, and dental offices. Studies have indicated that between 7% and 30% of all visits by women to an emergency room result from domestic violence (Plichta, 1992). Women who are victims of violence seek treatment for injuries sustained as a result of being physically abused (e.g., bruises, lacerations, fractures, and dental injuries; M. Dutton, Haywood, & El-Bayoumi, 1997; Stewart & Robinson, 1995), as well as for many other health issues, including headaches, gastrointestinal problems, gynecological concerns, and pulmonary problems (El-Bayoumi et al., 1998). Moreover, victims of domestic violence are more likely than nonvictims to present with such somatic and mental health problems as chronic pain syndrome, stomach ulcers, irritable bowel syndrome, insomnia, depression, anxiety, posttraumatic stress disorder, dissociative disorders, eating disorders, and substance abuse (M. Dutton et al., 1997; El-Bayoumi et al., 1998; Golding, 1999; Stewart & Robinson, 1995). Mental health symptoms can persist for years after the abuse ends and many studies have linked history of abuse with an elevated risk of suicide (Golding, 1999).

Intervention strategies should continue to focus on the implementation of domestic violence screening instruments in various health care settings including emergency rooms, primary care, and gynecological services (e.g., Alpert et al., 1992). By increasing awareness and educating staff in these settings about domestic violence, appropriate referrals can be made and supportive interventions can be applied. Psychologists and health care providers should be educated about the high incidence of domestic violence among women and be trained in appropriate screening and intervention strategies to help protect women and their families, such as setting up safety plans before the woman leaves the treatment setting.

Chronic Health Conditions

This section presents a brief overview of chronic illnesses that are more prevalent among women. These diseases are persistent, debilitating, and frequently related to a myriad of psychosocial effects (e.g., depression, unemployment, inability to care for children). Controversy as to whether these conditions are medically based or psychological in nature often interferes with diagnosis and treatment planning. Although attention is increasing as to importance, further research is needed to explore etiology, risk factors, treatment options, and psychosocial effects of these chronic health conditions.

Arthritis

According to the CDC (1999), arthritis is the most chronic health condition reported by women. Rheumatoid arthritis is the most common cause of chronic inflammatory arthritis, causing inflammation in the lining of joints and/or other internal organs (Arthritis Foundation, 2001). Arthritis affects approximately 1% to 2% of the population; 75% of those affected are women (Belilos & Carsons, 1998). Although the onset of the disease usually occurs in middle age (typically between 20 and 40 years), its incidence continues to increase with age (Hochberg, 1990). American women report that arthritis limits their ability to perform basic daily activities, with rates of disability higher among certain groups of Native American women relative to European American women (Del Puente, Knowler, & Bennett, 1989). The etiology of rheumatoid arthritis remains unknown, although there may be a genetic predisposition to develop the disease. Treatment consists of reducing swelling, relieving pain, and reducing inflammation (Arthritis Foundation, 2001; see chapter by Burke, Zautra, Davis, and Schultz in this volume for additional information).

The fact that rheumatoid arthritis has its onset in middle age raises questions as to how the disease affects such things as pregnancy and breastfeeding. Subsequently, research is beginning to explore the relationship between rheumatoid arthritis and fertility (for a review, see Dugowson, 2000). Further research should explore the etiology and psychosocial factors of the disease. Finally, there is a need for health psychologists to facilitate the development of pain management strategies (e.g., relaxation training, medication adherence, exercise) and strategies for coping with decreased physical mobility.

Fibromyalgia

Fibromyalgia is characterized by a widespread pain syndrome and decreased pain threshold. Women represent 80% to 90% of patients with this disease (Belilos & Carsons, 1998), and approximately 2% of American women have the disease (Hawley & Wolfe, 2000). Symptoms include diffuse aches and pains, sleep disturbance, fatigue, headaches, irritable bowel syndrome, and psychological distress. Patients with this disorder often have difficulty pinpointing the location of their pain. Diagnosis can be difficult since no single test is available to determine the presence of the disease. Therefore, diagnosis often is made after testing for other disorders reveals negative findings, or after patients are misdiagnosed because symptoms are similar to another disorder such as chronic fatigue syndrome. In addition to improving underlying sleep disorders, the treatment of fibromyalgia has focused on the use of antidepressants, muscle relaxants, and exercise programs. Treatment efforts have been largely unsuccessful because the use of antidepressants, exercise programs, and cognitive behavioral therapy has shown only short-term improvement or mild effectiveness (see Hawley & Wolfe, 2000, for a review).

The diagnosis and treatment of fibromyalgia have been controversial because some researchers and health care providers believe the disorder is primarily psychological as opposed to physical. However, not all patients with fibromyalgia have comorbid psychiatric symptomatology or disorders. Furthermore, because the diagnosis of fibromyalgia is based solely on self-reported complaints of pain, women with this disorder may experience minimization or trivialization of their symptoms by health care providers. An interdisciplinary team approach is recommended to address the multiple problems and offer treatment options. Further research is warranted into ethnic-racial differences, etiology, diagnosis, and treatment of this disease. Health psychologists can assist in screening for mental health disorders in this population, as well as in teaching women to recognize the relationship between physical and psychological symptoms, use relaxation techniques in response to pain, and manage stressors and psychosocial difficulties related to their symptoms.

Osteoporosis

Osteoporosis is a debilitating disease characterized by the loss of bone mass, which often leads to bone fractures. The most common fractures occur in the hip, spine, or wrist and can cause severe disability or death. The disease occurs in older women four times more often than in men of comparable age (Wisocki, 1998). According to the National Osteoporosis Foundation (2001), 28 million Americans age 50 and older have osteoporosis or are at risk of developing the disease, which accounts for more than 1.5 million fractures annually. Additional research is needed to clarify rates according to ethnic-racial status.

The risk factors for osteoporosis include being female, having a small frame, older age, and family history. Research also indicates that caffeine intake, alcohol intake, cigarette smoking, and lack of exercise can be associated with lower bone mass resulting in higher risk of fracture (Kaplan-Machlis & Bors, 2000). Prevention and treatment efforts often focus on decreasing the risk of fracture, but prevention efforts educating women about the importance of calcium intake in the prevention of osteoporosis may be the most productive in decreasing women's mortality. To be effective, prevention needs to begin at an early age for girls. Health psychologists may be able to assist with osteoporosis prevention through the development of effective national awareness programs for women and children.

MENTAL HEALTH ISSUES

This section presents a brief overview of issues related to prevalence, gender differences, and risk factors for the categories of mental disorders most prevalent among women— depressive disorders, anxiety disorders, and eating disorders. Given the fact that women with substance use disorders are more likely to experience severe physical and mental health effects, we also present relevant data on nicotine and alcohol use. Further research addressing gender differences, the etiology of these disorders, and prevention strategies for these mental health problems in women is needed.

Depressive Disorders

Depression is a serious health problem for women; in fact, it has been reported as the leading cause of disability for women worldwide (C. Murray & Lopez, 1996). Major epidemiological studies such as the Epidemiological Catchment Area (ECA) Study and the National Comorbidity Survey (NCS) indicate that women are twice as likely to be affected by major depressive disorder and dysthymia than are men (Kessler et al., 1994; Robins, Locke, & Regier, 1991). According to the NCS, lifetime prevalence rates for a major depressive episode are 21.3% for women and 12.7% for men. Lifetime prevalence rates for dysthymia are 8.0% for women and 4.8% for men. Although gender differences begin to emerge with the onset of puberty, the average age of onset of major depression is approximately 25 years, with the highest prevalence rates for women between 18 and 44 years (Kessler, McGonagle, Swartz, Blazer, & Nelson, 1993). Pregnancy and postpartum are also high-risk times for depression, with postpartum depression occurring in about 10% to 16% of women in the first six months after they have given birth (Llewellyn, Stowe, & Nemeroff, 1997). Kathol, Broadhead, and Kroenke (1997) report that depression is more prevalent among primary care patients with certain mental disorders (e.g., 30% of patients with an anxiety disorder, 15% to 25% of patients with substance abuse disorders, 28% of patients with schizophrenia, 30% to 40% of patients with dementia and 75% of individuals with obsessive-compulsive disorder). Likewise, Rouchell, Pounds, and Tierney (1999), indicate that prevalence rates for depression are higher for individuals with certain physical illnesses (e.g., 16% to 19% of individuals with CHD, 20% to 38% of individuals with cancer, 27% of individuals with stroke, and 30% of individuals with HIV/AIDS). These statistics highlight the importance of examining the interaction between mental and physical health to increase the quality of women's lives.

Risk factors for the occurrence of an episode of major depression include family history of psychiatric illness, adverse childhood experiences, personality characteristics, isolation, and stressful life events (see Kessler, 2000, for a review). For women, such stressful life events can be associated with marital and reproductive status (e.g., divorce, death of a spouse, birth, and miscarriage). Women who assume a caretaker role for an ill spouse, parent, or child are also at higher risk for major depression (Kessler & McLeod, 1984; McCormick, 1995; Rosenthal, Sulman, & Marshall, 1993). However, many studies do not control for history of depression and inappropriately conclude that certain risk factors are associated with the onset of a depressive episode when, in actuality, history of depression accounts for the association (Kessler, 2000). The etiology of depression in women remains a conundrum in the research community. Studies that have examined gender differences in reporting symptoms conclude that reporting differences does not account for the higher rates of depression in women (see Kessler, 2000). As discussed later in this chapter, many theories (e.g., multiple roles theory) have been presented to explain why women are twice as likely as men to suffer from major depression. However, research is still needed in this area to explore risk factors for the onset of depression, its chronicity, and relapse to inform prevention interventions and treatment implementation. Finally, the prevalence of depression is high among women with specific physical illnesses. This highlights the importance of health psychologists routinely screening for depression, particularly among those diagnosed with the top five disease killers of women.

Anxiety Disorders

Anxiety disorders, characterized by panic attacks, worrying, and fear, are the most common of all mental disorders. Neugebauer, Dohrenwend, and Dohrenwend (1980) reported higher rates of anxiety in women than men in the 18 studies they reviewed, with an average female-to-male ratio of 2.9. The NCS estimates that the lifetime prevalence rate for all anxiety disorders is 19.2% for men and 30.5% for women (Kessler et al., 1994). In examination of specific anxiety disorders, women demonstrated lifetime prevalence rates of 10.4% for posttraumatic stress disorder as compared to 5.0% for men (Kessler, Sonnega, & Bromet, 1995), and 6.6% for generalized anxiety disorder (GAD) compared to 3.6% for men (Kessler et al., 1994). Women are also twice as likely as men to develop panic disorder and simple phobia (Kessler et al., 1994; Robins et al., 1984).

Not only are women more prone to experience anxiety disorders, but also they are more likely to have a comorbid anxiety condition or other psychiatric disorders. Pigott (1999) reported that women with panic disorder often have an additional diagnosis of GAD, simple phobia, or alcohol abuse. Similarly, anxiety disorders frequently are comorbid with depression (see C. Brown & Schulberg, 1997). Research has identified physical disorders that often mimic symptoms of anxiety, including cardiac conditions, pulmonary conditions, and gastrointestinal conditions (see Henry, 2000); however, less attention has been given to the actual co-occurrence of anxiety and various physical illnesses.

As with depression, theories have been postulated as to why women experience higher rates of anxiety disorders, and gender-specific risk factors have been suggested. However, research examining gender differences in the etiology of anxiety is sparse. Research has not yet offered an explanation as to why women experience anxiety disorders more often than men. Further investigation is warranted to create effective prevention, intervention, and treatment strategies. Health psychologists also can assist with routine screening for anxiety in medical settings to provide insight into the comorbidity of anxiety with various physical illnesses.

Eating Disorders

This section addresses the three primary eating disorders of anorexia nervosa (AN), bulimia nervosa (BN), and binge eating disorder (BED). It has been reported that females constitute more than 90% of reported AN and BN cases (American Psychiatric Association, 1994) with lifetime prevalence rates estimated to be approximately 0.5% for AN, 1% to 3% for BN, and 0.7% to 4% for BED in community samples (American Psychiatric Association, 2000).

The impact of eating disorders on women's health involves both physical and psychological consequences. One of the most common physical effects on women is primary or secondary amenorrhea (i.e., absence of menstruation)—a symptom required to receive a *Diagnostic and Statistical Manual of Mental Disorders, Fourth Edition* (*DSM-IV;* American Psychiatric Association, 1994), diagnosis of AN. Although absence of menses is not a core requirement for BN, about one-third of bulimic women report amenorrhea (Mitchell, Seim, Colon, & Pomeroy, 1987). This hormone disturbance reduces, but does not eliminate, the chance for reproduction; however, there is fetal risk associated with pregnancy in the presence of AN (Goldbloom & Kennedy, 1995). Later in this chapter, we discuss the psychological impact of infertility on women; consequently, it is important to consider that women with eating disorders present twice as often as women in the general population for treatment at infertility clinics (Stewart, 1992). Women with eating disorders are at increased risk for osteoporosis (Goldbloom & Kennedy, 1995) and for developing stress fractures and other bone-related problems because of low bone-mineral density associated with amenorrhea (Putukian, 1994). Vomiting or purging, a frequent symptom of eating disorders, has been associated with various medical problems, including salivary gland hypotrophy (Mitchell, 1995) and electrolyte imbalance with 50% of bulimic women experiencing electrolyte abnormality. Cardiovascular problems such as bradycardia and hypotension (Stewart, 1992), as well as cardiomyopathy (Mitchell, 1995), are common in AN and BN. It is equally important to examine the physical health problems associated with being obese, a common symptom in women with BED, as obesity has been associated with type 2 diabetes mellitus (noninsulin dependent), hypertension, stroke, cardiovascular disease, gallbladder disease, cancer, and arthritis (Pike & Striegel-Moore, 1997; Pi-Sunyer, 1995).

Eating disorders also have been linked to increased risk for comorbid psychological disorders. Pike and Striegel-Moore (1997) suggest that rates of depression in individuals with eating disorders (including AN, BN, and BED) are higher than those in the general population. Approximately 45% of those with AN have a lifetime history of an affective disorder (Santonastaso, Pantano, Panarotto, & Silvestri, 1991), as do 43% to 88% of those with BN (Kendler et al., 1991) and 32% to 50% of those with BED (Yanovski, Nelson, Dubbert, &

Spitzer, 1993). Cooper (1995) reported that approximately half of those individuals seen in a clinic for an eating disorder also have a lifetime history of major depressive disorder. Eating disorders have been linked to anxiety disorders, with obsessive-compulsive disorder disproportionately found among those with eating disorders (Kaye, Weltzin, & Hsu, 1993). Eating disorders also have been linked to personality disorders, with 30% to 50% of bulimic individuals having a personality disorder—the majority of these in the *DSM-IV* Cluster B category (i.e., antisocial, borderline, histrionic, and narcissistic; Sokol & Gray, 1998). Eating disorders have a strong sociocultural component as women face unique pressures to be thin, exacerbating the numerous detrimental effects on women's physical and psychological health documented in this section.

Substance Use

Cigarette Smoking

Approximately 22 million women in the United States (22.6%) smoke cigarettes (Husten & Malarcher, 2000). Cigarette smoking kills approximately 152,000 women each year because of resulting cardiovascular disease, cancer, and respiratory diseases (CDC, 1997). More specifically, cigarette smoking accounts for an estimated 85% of CHD deaths and 79% of COPD deaths among women ages 45 to 49 years (CDC, 1997; Davis & Novotny, 1989). Cigarette smoking is also associated with increased risk of stroke, infertility, and low birth weight infants. Cigarette smoking among women typically starts in adolescence. Various risk factors have been linked to the initial smoking behaviors among adolescent girls such as peer pressure, depression, drug abuse, poor academic achievement, familial smoking behaviors, and the belief that smoking helps control weight gain (see Husten & Malarcher, 2000). Because smoking results in a variety of physical health problems and is the "leading preventable cause of death among women in the United States" (Husten & Malarcher, 2000), prevention efforts should focus on educating women of all ages about the health consequences of smoking, especially in populations where prevalence rates are particularly high (e.g., among women who live below the poverty level and women who have less than 12 years of education (Adler & Coriell, 1997).

Alcohol

A national study in the United States revealed that approximately four million women above the age of 18 years could be considered "alcoholic" or "problem drinkers"—with 58%

of these women between the ages of 18 and 29 years (B. Grant, Hartford, Dawson, Chou, & Pickering, 1994). Lifetime prevalence rates for *DSM-IV* alcohol use disorders (i.e., abuse and/or dependence) are 25.54% for males and 11.36% for females (B. Grant & Harford, 1995). Rates of disorders decrease with age, and African American women have lower rates across all age groups relative to non-African American women. Although fewer women than men abuse alcohol, mortality rates for women who abuse alcohol are higher than among women in the general population and higher than those of men who abuse alcohol (Greenfield, 1996). Risk factors for alcohol dependence vary over a woman's lifespan and include, but are not limited to, family history of substance abuse, dysfunctional and unstable family environment, peer pressure, divorce, and retirement (see Stoffelmayr, Wadland, & Guthrie, 2000). Alcohol use itself is a risk factor for a variety of health problems such as alcohol-related organ damage, adverse birth outcomes, and physical trauma related to motor vehicle accidents, as well as for social problems such as unprotected sex resulting in STD/HIV infection and unplanned pregnancies.

Studies have demonstrated that there are gender differences in alcohol use responses. For example, alcohol consumption leads to higher blood alcohol levels in women than in men. Therefore, given the same amount of alcohol, women become more intoxicated than men (El-Guebaly, 1995). Also, women tend to abuse alcohol later in life than men, but women deteriorate more rapidly and develop alcohol-related symptoms faster than men. This phenomenon, known as "telescoping," is often associated with the development of liver, cardiovascular, and gastrointestinal diseases (Lex, 1992). Furthermore, women who are heavy drinkers are more susceptible to depression (four times more than men who are heavy drinkers), menstrual problems, infertility, and early menopause (see Stoffelmayr et al., 2000). Women's drinking patterns can be influenced by their social relationships. For example, married women who abuse substances are more likely to have a spouse that abuses a substance than are married men who abuse substances (T. Brown, Kokin, Seraganian, & Shields, 1995). Research efforts should continue to explore gender differences in etiology (particularly related to psychosocial factors), risk factors, treatment outcomes, and prevention programs. Specific issues to be examined include use of alcohol as a coping strategy and the role of alcohol in stress management, depression, and domestic violence, for example.

Issues Relevant to Treatment of Mental Disorders

Although women are more likely to suffer from depressive, anxiety, and eating disorders, most do not seek treatment.

Women seek treatment for mental disorders more often than men (Zerbe, 1999), but only one-third to one-fourth of women with depression actually seek professional help or treatment (Kessler, 2000). Women are also unlikely to pursue treatment for a substance abuse disorder (Mondanaro, 1989). When women do seek help, it is usually from their primary care physicians rather than from a mental health specialist (Glied, 1997; Narrow, Regier, Rae, Manderscheid, & Locke, 1993). Primary care physicians typically provide pharmacological treatment for affective disorders (e.g., antidepressants). Therefore, for the interdisciplinary intervention needed to treat such mental disorders, it is important for clinical health psychologists to have a presence in primary care settings—either as a referral source for adjunctive psychotherapy or as part of a multidisciplinary treatment team in the primary care setting itself. Treatment outcomes are likely to be enhanced when the various treatment team members (e.g., physicians, mental health care providers) communicate and coordinate their efforts. Moreover, interdisciplinary treatment that incorporates a biopsychosocial approach can facilitate adherence to antidepressant medication protocols, improve satisfaction with care, and help offset medical costs (Katon, 1995).

Although women commonly receive psychotropic medications, research has not investigated the interaction between such medications and a woman's menstrual cycle even though menstrual cycle, pregnancy, and the postpartum period can influence the course of mood and anxiety disorders (Leibenluft, 1999). Moreover, drug and treatment trials were researched primarily on men. This has left many questions of how medications interact with female hormones. As a result, the American Medical Association (1991) notes that research on the use of antidepressants originally was conducted on men and cautions that antidepressants may work differently for women than men, citing the fact that effectiveness of some antidepressants can vary over the course of a woman's menstrual cycle. It has also been noted that women experience more adverse side effects when taking antidepressants. Specifically, women are less likely to tolerate the side effects of weight gain or drowsiness and often stop treatment when these side effects occur (Kessler, 2000). Medical research should continue to investigate the interaction of psychotropic medications with the menstrual cycle, pregnancy, and lactation, as well as identify side effects specific to women so that such treatment barriers can be addressed.

HEALTH CARE

Women are major consumers of the health care industry in a variety of ways. According to Smith Barney Research (1997),

"Women make three-fourths of the health care decisions in American households and spend almost two of every three health care dollars." It has also been noted that more than 61% of visits to physicians are made by women, 59% of prescription drugs are purchased by women, and 75% of nursing home residents over the age of 75 are women. These statistics suggest that women continue to make a large proportion of health care decisions for their family as they have historically, especially regarding their children and elderly relatives (Office of Women's Health, 2000). Women typically visit their doctors on a regular basis and use preventive services twice as much as men, but, unfortunately, women spend more money out-of-pocket for needed medical care (Commonwealth Fund, 1994).

Health Insurance

Managed care is a significant source of women's health care. Women usually have some type of insurance coverage; however, they are more likely to be covered by public insurance, specifically Medicaid (Clancy, 2000). Furthermore, women are substantially more likely than men to have minimal or no coverage because they represent the majority of part-time and service employees (Commonwealth Fund, 1994). Women of color and women with low incomes have the highest risk of being uninsured (OWH, 2000). As expected, women without health insurance go without needed medical care, especially vital preventive services including mammograms and Pap smears (Commonwealth Fund, 1994). Insurance also influences use of various health care services and treatment options. For example, women in HMOs are more likely to receive medications than psychotherapy compared to women with fee-for-service payment plans (Glied, 1997). The lack of health care coverage also may help explain why many diseases go undetected in women.

Relationships with Health Care Providers

Women frequently receive services from more than one physician because reproductive services are traditionally isolated from other health services (Clancy, 2000). As a result, many women have difficulty navigating the health care system to receive appropriate medical care. According to the OWH, research indicates that women are often unsatisfied with their health care provider or the level of communication with their provider, and several studies have indicated that health care providers treat women differently from men. They also noted that, "Health providers may give women less thorough evaluations, minimize their symptoms, provide fewer interventions, and give less explanations in response to questions" (OWH, 2000).

Studies indicate that the use of preventive care services is related to the age and sex of the physician, with younger physicians and female physicians more likely to provide preventive services (Clancy, 2000). More specifically, female physicians are more likely to provide Pap smears and recommend mammography to their patients than male physicians (Franks & Clancy, 1993; Lurie et al., 1993). In a study conducted by Lurie, Margolis, McGovern, Mink, and Slater (1997), physicians and patients were surveyed to see why higher rates of breast and cervical cancer screening occur among female physicians. The results indicated that higher rates of screening occur because women prefer female physicians and that female physicians are more concerned about prevention issues. Female physicians spent more time per visit with patients than male physicians and were more concerned about prevention issues (e.g., smoking, sexual practices, seatbelt use, and cancer screening). Furthermore, female physicians reported feeling more comfortable performing breast exams and Pap smears, as well as taking a sexual history from women.

Studies have also revealed that male and female physicians communicate differently with patients. Roter, Lipkin, and Korsgaard (1991) analyzed 537 audiotapes of medical visits to evaluate gender differences in communication between physicians and patients. Female physicians talked 40% longer than male physicians during the history-taking segment of the visit. Likewise, patients of female physicians talked 58% more during the history-taking segment of the visit. Female physicians spent more time with patients, and patients of female physicians asked more questions and gave more relevant health-related information. Hall, Irish, Roter, Ehrlich, and Miller (1994) conducted a similar study to analyze the relationship between gender and physician/patient communication in a primary care setting. Physicians and patients were videotaped during medical visits. The findings revealed that female physicians talked more and asked more questions than male physicians, and engaged in more positive, nonverbal behavior (e.g., smiling and nodding) than male physicians. Patients of female physicians communicated more and gave more medical information.

In summary, women are the primary consumers of the health care industry yet often are underinsured and unsatisfied with their health care relationships. These issues can affect women's mortality and morbidity in numerous ways (e.g., underutilization of preventive and medical services, inadequate communication with health care providers, and limited availability of treatment options). As a result, efforts should be made to ensure that women have adequate access to quality health care, and health providers should be educated about practical communication strategies when interacting with female patients.

STRESSFUL CONDITIONS RELATED TO PREGNANCY

Our culture typically associates pregnancy and childbirth with positive emotions and with motherhood; however, this is not the case for all pregnancies or for all women. This section addresses a different aspect of these reproductive events, specifically focusing on stressful conditions related to pregnancy. Whereas postpartum depression has received a great deal of attention in the literature, other postpartum reactions and issues relating to infertility have received less, and psychosocial factors related to such phenomenon as miscarriage and peripartum cardiomyopathy have received even less.

Miscarriage

Miscarriage involves the spontaneous termination of an intrauterine pregnancy with the conceptus dead on expulsion, with most studies defining miscarriage as the unintended termination of pregnancy before 27 completed weeks of gestation (Neugebauer et al., 1992). Miscarriage occurs in 10% to 20% of clinically recognized pregnancies (Kline et al., 1995), but risk varies substantially by age (e.g., 9% for women aged 20 to 24 years, but 75% for women over age 45 years; Nybo Andersen, Wohlfahrt, Christens, Olsen, & Melbye, 2000). Stillbirth, defined as late fetal death with a fetus weighing more than 500 grams, is not uncommon with a risk of 0.4 to 1.2 per 1,000 in singleton pregnancies (Yudkin & Redman, 2000) and with a higher risk in multiple pregnancies. Risk factors established or suspected in one or more studies can be broadly classified as environmental (e.g., caffeine, nicotine, and other drug use; toxins; electromagnetic fields; stressful life events), or biological (e.g., genetic, including chromosomal abnormalities; endocrinologic; anatomic; immunologic; microbiologic; see Klier, Geller, & Ritsher, 2002, for a review).

For many women, miscarriage constitutes an unanticipated, traumatic experience that can be associated with considerable physical pain and discomfort and may pose a serious threat to the life of the woman (Saraiya et al., 1999). Physiologically, miscarriage marks the end of a pregnancy, and psychologically, may produce fears and doubts about procreative competence. Psychological reactions to reproductive loss vary, but often include sadness, distress, guilt, and fear (e.g., Borg & Lasker, 1981). In contrast to the large body of research on risk for reproductive failure, studies concerning psychological distress in the aftermath of the loss event are more limited, and investigations employing appropriate comparison groups are sparse (Klier et al., 2002). However, research including such comparison groups has established that miscarriage is a risk factor for depressive reactions ranging from depressive symptoms (Janssen, Cuisinier, Hoogduin, & de Graauw, 1996; Neugebauer et al., 1992; Thapar & Thapar, 1992) to minor and major depressive disorder (Klier, Geller, & Neugebauer, 2000; Neugebauer et al., 1997). Specifically, miscarrying women's risk for an episode of minor depression in the six months after loss is 5.2-fold, and for major depression, 2.5-fold, that of otherwise comparable community women. History of major depression is a risk factor for a recurrent episode, but length of gestation at time of loss or attitude toward the pregnancy do not seem to play a role (Klier et al., 2000; Neugebauer et al., 1997). Studies that investigated the development of anxiety symptoms following loss found mixed results, although those with comparison groups suggest that anxiety levels may be substantial after miscarriage (Beutel, Deckardt, Von Rad, & Weiner, 1995; Lee & Slade, 1996; Thapar & Thapar, 1992). In a study of anxiety disorders that employed a cohort design, Geller, Klier, and Neugebauer (2001) reported that miscarriage increases risk for a recurrent episode of obsessive compulsive disorder (OCD), but not for panic disorder or specific phobia. Risk for posttraumatic stress disorder (PTSD) may also be increased following reproductive loss (Engelhard, van den Hout, & Arntz, 2001).

Clinical attention in the early weeks after miscarriage may help to offset more serious psychological and psychiatric consequences of the loss. Psychological symptoms may also occur in pregnancies subsequent to a miscarriage, and health care and mental health professionals should attend to these concerns as well. Not only is it important to attend to the psychological sequelae of miscarriage in women, but also to psychosocial factors such as women's relationships with their partners and children, as well as attachment to future children (Hughes, Turton, Hopper, McGauley, & Fonagy, 2001; Klier et al., 2002). In addition, since miscarriage involves a loss that often remains unknown to all but a woman's most intimate confidants and her health care providers, the grieving process may be compounded by limited social support and the challenge of managing feelings associated with the loss of a *potential* child. After multiple miscarriages, women may decide to undergo evaluation and treatment for secondary infertility, which, as discussed next, may challenge coping resources to an even further degree. There is a great need for the development and evaluation of postloss mental health intervention. To develop appropriate clinical screening methods and treatment protocols for these women, further empirical evaluation of the psychosocial and mental health consequences of miscarriage is necessary using larger sample sizes, comparison cohorts, and more intensive monitoring of clinical outcomes.

Infertility

Infertility, defined as the inability to conceive a pregnancy after one year of unprotected coitus or the inability to carry a pregnancy to a live birth, has been termed a "crisis" of our time (Cooper-Hilbert, 1998). Whether the infertility is primary (i.e., no pregnancies despite attempts) or secondary (i.e., at least one past pregnancy, regardless of outcome), 10% to 15% of couples in industrialized nations experience infertility; approximately half of these couples will eventually achieve pregnancy (Goldman, Missmer, & Barbier, 2000). Worldwide estimates indicate that approximately 8% of couples (50 to 80 million people) experienced infertility, with sub-Saharan countries displaying the highest prevalence (30% to 50% of women; see review in Goldman et al., 2000). In the United States, infertility is increasing at a dramatic rate across all age groups (but particularly among women aged 35 to 44 years), with numbers projected to reach 5.4 to 7.7 million by 2025, up from approximately 5 to 6.3 million currently (Stephen & Chandra, 1997). These increasing rates have been attributed to a variety of factors, such as delayed childbearing; undetected pelvic inflammatory disease due to increased incidence of sexually transmitted diseases (STDs) including chlamydia and gonorrhea; use of substances such as caffeine, nicotine, and alcohol; chronic stress (i.e., neuroendocrines such as catecholamines, prolactin, and adrenal steroids can impact reproduction); and exposure to work and environmental health hazards (Cooper-Hilbert, 1998; see review in Goldman et al., 2000). Although a single cause of infertility is rarely found, 35% to 40% of infertility cases can be attributed to male factors (e.g., abnormal sperm count or mobility, adult mumps, hormonal imbalances, injury to reproductive organs, retrograde ejaculation, testicular failure, use of certain drugs, varicose veins in the scrotum), 35% to 40% to female factors (e.g., aging or depleted oocyte reserve, anovulation, body mass index, cervical problems, endocrine disorders, endometriosis, intrauterine device use, structural abnormalities of the uterus), and 20% to factors from both members of the couple (Cooper-Hilbert, 1998; see review in Goldman et al., 2000).

This "infertility epidemic" results in a variety of psychosocial issues relevant to the work of health care and mental health professionals. When confronted with infertility, women often experience myriad affective responses, such as initial shock and denial, disappointment, and anger

(at themselves, their partners, and other women with children, for example), helplessness and perceived loss of control, and guilt or self-blame—particularly those who believe their infertility problems may be due to past behaviors such as contraceptive choice, induced abortions, or STDs (Cooper-Hilbert, 1998; Downey & McKinney, 1992). In a prospective study, Downey and McKinney found that 11% of infertile women met criteria for major depression relative to 4% of a fertile population.

There are gender differences associated with reactions to fertility status (Greil, 1997), with women's sense of self-identity more deeply affected than men's due to socialized pressures (Whiteford & Gonzalez, 1995). Society places pressure on women, regardless of socioeconomic status (SES), ethnic-racial status, and religion, to view motherhood as her primary adult role. Violating these societal norms and expectations has both social and personal consequences: Stigma associated with childlessness that involves social definitions of women as selfish, unfeminine, unnatural, and inadequate—ideas that many women incorporate into their own self-schema (Lee, 1998; Whiteford & Gonzalez, 1995). Fertile women who choose motherhood but are in unconventional relationships, such as lesbian women or women without partners, are often subjected to similar social stigma and may be viewed as deviant (Lee, 1998).

Although visits to all physicians for fertility-related concerns have increased as treatment options become more sophisticated and information is more available, the proportion of couples who seek medical advisement or treatment remain relatively low (approximately 31% to 48%), with younger women, European American women, women with higher SES, and couples with primary infertility more likely to seek services (see Goldman et al., 2000). Further research addressing factors associated with access and barriers to treatment is needed.

Infertility intervention options available to women include hormones, artificial insemination, a range of variations on in-vitro fertilization (IVF), and ovum donation. As both infertility and its treatments may proceed for an indeterminate amount of time, impose pressure and stress, and challenge couple's coping resources, daily living, interpersonal relationships, and overall quality of life can be impacted. There also may be physical pain and other health risks associated with the often intrusive, reproductive procedures. Each time a woman does not conceive or cannot carry the fetus to term following treatment, couples must confront possible distress, grief, and despair related to multiple losses, and sense of failure (Greil, 1997). Given the strong stigma associated with childlessness, many women continue to endure intense treatments despite continued failure to be absolutely certain they have done everything they can to confirm that they are truly infertile. Women such as these report relief when they finally stop treatment (Lee, 1998). Furthermore, couples undergoing infertility treatment can be faced with financial hardship because of the high cost of ongoing treatment.

For many women, treatment subsequent to the infertility procedures ultimately may involve efforts to promote acceptance of their infertility and exploration of alternatives to childbirth (e.g., surrogate motherhood, adoption, remaining childless). However, these options bring their own unique set of challenges, stressors, and stigma. It is vital for health and mental health providers to recognize and appreciate the enduring and pervasive consequences of infertility for those who remain childless by chance as opposed to choice (Cooper-Hilbert, 1998; Lee, 1998). To understand the nature of these reactions and psychosocial consequences, there is a great need for further research—especially research employing appropriate comparison groups.

Postpartum Reactions

Although the frequency of many psychiatric disorders is increased in the postpartum period, three puerperal conditions—postpartum dysphoria, depression, and psychosis—have been described most commonly, with the increased onset most evident within 30 days following childbirth (e.g., Llewellyn et al., 1997; O'Hara & Swain, 1996). Postpartum dysphoria, which has also been referred to as "baby blues" or postpartum blues, is a mild and transient condition involving tearfulness and depressed mood that peaks at about the fifth day postpartum and, in large part, has been attributed to normal hormonal fluctuations following childbirth (O'Hara, Schlechter, Lewis, & Varner, 1991). Postpartum dysphoria appears to be independent of specific sociocultural or environmental factors and consistent across cultures (Kumar, 1994). Estimates suggest that 26% to 85% of all mothers experience postpartum blues, the wide range due to differing assessment techniques across studies (O'Hara et al., 1991). Postpartum dysphoria, which usually resolves within ten days without treatment, has yet to be established as an entity clearly distinct from normal experience.

Postpartum depression is more severe and persistent than postpartum dysphoria, with symptoms resembling those of other forms of major depressive disorder. This condition occurs in 10% to 16% of women in the first six months after they have given birth, with onset usually within two weeks of childbirth (Llewellyn et al., 1997; O'Hara & Swain, 1996). Community-based surveys—many of which used the Edinburgh Postnatal Depression Scale—indicate that rates of postpartum depression seem to be relatively consistent across countries, although estimates tended to vary when other assessment tools were employed and depending on how the time frame of the postpartum period was defined (see Lee, 1998). In addition to significant physiological changes following delivery, major adjustment is required because of changing social and personal circumstances, especially with the birth of the first child. Although psychosocial stressors and hormonal shifts have been suspected of playing a role in the development of postpartum depression, prior psychiatric history is a significant and well-documented risk factor: 20% to 30% of women with a history of major depression prior to conception develop postpartum depression, and a prior episode of postpartum depression or depression during a previous pregnancy increases a women's risk following subsequent pregnancies (50% to 62%; Llewellyn et al., 1997; O'Hara & Swain, 1996). During pregnancy, 10% to 16% of women meet the diagnostic criteria for major depression (Llewellyn et al., 1997). Psychosocial factors implicated include life events (e.g., marital discord), limited social support of an appropriate nature, and personality factors (Kumar, 1994; O'Hara et al., 1991; O'Hara & Swain, 1996). Unrealistic societal stereotypes that bias women to expect that motherhood and maternal-infant bonding come immediately and easily, and are natural phenomenon that are always positive and fulfilling, may also have implications for the development of postpartum depression (Kumar, 1994; Lee, 1998).

The most severe, albeit rare, of the three postpartum conditions is postpartum psychosis, which occurs in one to two of every 1,000 deliveries and across all societies as far back as 150 years (Kendell, Chalmers, & Platz, 1987; Kumar, 1994). Symptoms are similar to those of schizophrenia, but the content of hallucinations and delusions often involves themes associated with pregnancy, childbirth, or the baby, and suicidal and infanticidal ideation can be present. Symptoms similar to an organic brain syndrome (e.g., confusion, attentional deficits, clouding of the senses) have also been noted. More than 50% of women with this disorder also meet criteria for postpartum depression (Kendell et al., 1987). The primary risk factors include a family history, but particularly a personal history, of psychiatric illness (e.g., bipolar disorder), with women who experience postpartum psychosis at elevated risk for later episodes. It appears that a diathesis (biological predisposition) stress (childbirth) model may best explain postpartum psychosis at this point, because research generally has not confirmed an association between this disorder and purely biological factors or social factors (e.g., prior life events, social support or marital discord; see Lee, 1998). Although the onset of postpartum psychosis ordinarily is rapid, occurring in the first 48 to 72 hours to two weeks post-delivery, risk remains high for several months (Kendell et al., 1987); therefore, women with a psychiatric history should be monitored closely. The prognosis for postpartum psychosis is much more positive than for other psychotic disorders, yet the experience, which often involves inpatient psychiatric treatment, can be devastating for women and their families.

For all the postpartum reactions discussed previously, health psychologists and other care providers can play a vital role in helping women and their families adjust and focus on their strengths and resources to facilitate coping at a time when childbirth results in unanticipated stressors. Additional work is needed to add to the growing body of literature reporting increased onset and/or exacerbation of anxiety disorders, such as panic disorder and obsessive compulsive disorder, during pregnancy and postpartum (e.g., L. Cohen et al., 1996; Shear & Mammen, 1995; Williams & Koran, 1997). Postpartum psychiatric disorders and resulting mother-infant bonding problems in the postpartum period have consequences not only for the woman, but also for the developing child in terms of cognitive deficits, and emotional and behavioral disturbances, for example (e.g., Martins & Gaffan, 2000; L. Murray & Cooper, 1997; Sinclair & Murray, 1998). Research and clinical attention to screen for, and address, these issues is growing (e.g., Brockington et al., 2001). Prevention efforts are needed not only to educate those women with a history of depression and anxiety about postpartum reactions and possible consequences so that coping strategies can be enhanced and activated ideally prior to birth, but also to encourage women to adopt more realistic expectations about pregnancy, motherhood, and infant-mother attachment.

Peripartum Cardiomyopathy

Pertipartum cardiomyopathy (PPCM) is a rare, life-threatening congestive heart failure of unknown cause that occurs most often in the last trimester of pregnancy or the first six months postpartum. It has been estimated that PPCM occurs in one of every 3,000 to 4,000 pregnancies with approximately 1,000 to 1,300 women in the United States affected each year (Ventura, Peters, Martin, & Maurer, 1997). While the criteria for diagnosing PPCM varies slightly because of the rarity of the disorder, the criteria most commonly referred to was established by Demakis and Rahimtoola (1971). These criteria require the development of cardiac failure during pregnancy or after delivery as specified previously in the absence of prior demonstrable heart disease and determinable etiology for the cardiac failure. In recent years, modern diagnostic echocardiography has provided evidence of left ventricular systolic dysfunction, which has helped differentiate PPCM from shared pregnancy-related symptoms that can mimic heart failure. Some of the common symptoms shared between PPCM and pregnancy include pedal edema, dyspnea, fatigue, weight gain, chest and abdominal discomfort, and cough.

The identified risk factors for PPCM include multiparity, advanced maternal age, multifetal pregnancy, preeclampsia, gestational hypertension, and African American race (Pearson et al., 2000). It is unclear if racial status is an independent risk factor or a result of an interaction of race and hypertension. While the etiology of PPCM remains unknown, current evidence suggests PPCM is a type of myocarditis (inflammation of the muscular tissue of the heart) with proposed causes such as abnormal immune responses to pregnancy, maladaptive responses to the hemodynamic stresses of pregnancy, stress-activated cytokines, and prolonged tocolysis (Pearson, et al., 2000). In some women, PPCM resolves completely after delivery; however, there is a high mortality rate for women who do not experience a resolution of symptoms within six months following delivery (C. Brown & Bertolet, 1998), with mortality rates in the United States ranging from 25% to 50% (Lampert & Lang, 1995). Women with PPCM appear to be at high risk for pregnancy complications or mortality should they become pregnant again (C. Brown & Bertolet, 1998; Lampert & Lang, 1995).

Because of the limited understanding of the medical etiology of PPCM, the majority of research has focused on the medical aspects, failing to address psychosocial factors related to PPCM and its impact. The sudden and unexpected nature of PPCM compounds the stress for women and their families, who are also adjusting to the physical and emotional demands normally imposed by pregnancy and the birth of a child. In one of few studies examining psychosocial factors relating to PPCM, Geller, Striepe, Lewis, and Petrucci (1996) studied a sample of women with PPCM admitted to a heart transplant unit for evaluation. Factors such as stressful life events (e.g., history of abuse or unstable relationships; history of miscarriage or cesarean section), health-related behaviors (e.g., substance use; nutritional/dietary concerns), social support, and coping style were assessed (Geller, Striepe, & Petrucci, 1994). In addition to the stressors of pregnancy and the diagnosis of PPCM, these psychosocial factors could potentially exacerbate the physical symptoms or contribute to treatment-related issues, such as noncompliance, comorbid psychological or substance abuse disorders, and adjustment to lifestyle changes imposed by the illness. Studies employing appropriate comparison cohorts are needed to further evaluate these psychosocial factors.

SOCIAL AND CULTURAL INFLUENCES ON WOMEN'S HEALTH

Earlier in this chapter, we discussed the advances and shortcomings in the research and health care of women. It is important that strides continue to be made to better understand how women's expression of disease symptoms, potential warning signs, and risk factors for both psychological and physical disorders may differ from those documented by research conducted on men. However, it is equally important that researchers and health care professionals understand and appreciate women's health on a sociocultural level. Lee (1998, p. 3) made the point that the study of "women's health" has primarily focused on the study of women's illness, with little focus on understanding women from a social standpoint. Lee suggests that women's health should not be limited to the prevention and treatment of illness, but it should encompass the complex social factors that play into being a woman. The focus of this section is to examine the influence of socioeconomic status, multiple roles, and gender socialization on the psychological and physical health of women.

Socioeconomic Status and Women

Socioeconomic status (SES) refers to "a composite measure that typically incorporates economic status, measured by income; social status, measured by education; and work status, measured by occupation" (D. Dutton & Levine, 1989). The relationship between SES and health is quite relevant for women because 35.6% of female-headed households fell below the federal poverty level, according to the U.S. Bureau of the Census (1995). Gender differences in SES can be largely explained from a social standpoint. Comparing median annual income, women earn 73.8% of what men earn, with women earning a median salary of $23,710 and men earning $32,144 (U.S. Department of Labor, 1997a). Such gender differences may be explained in large part by the fact that the majority of employed women continue to hold jobs in traditional female occupations (e.g., 45% of employed females work in clerical or service occupations, 22% work in sales, and secretary was the leading occupation for women in both 1981 and 1996), allowing little opportunity for career advancement that may lead to comparable salary increases. Many of these female-dominated occupations also put women at increased risk for physical injury, specifically, carpal tunnel syndrome, where 71% of those injured or forced to miss work have been women (U.S. Bureau of Labor Statistics, 1991; U.S. Department of Labor, 1997a, 1998).

While gender alone places women at increased risk for poverty and, consequently, poor health, ethnicity also has an association with SES. Annual salary differences according to ethnic racial status indicate that European American women earn $2,687 more than African American women and $5,495 more than Hispanic women (U.S. Department of Labor, 1997a). In the United States, 51% of female-headed households run by Hispanic women, 44% run by African American women, and 27% run by European American women, were below the poverty level (U.S. Bureau of the Census, 1997), indicating minority women are further at risk for poverty.

Adler, Boyce, Chesney, Folkman, and Syme (1993) found a linear relationship between SES and health. Specifically, they reported that those in the highest SES bracket had the lowest morbidity and mortality rates, with these rates steadily increasing as SES level decreases (Adler & Coriell, 1997). The following sections examine the association between SES and both physical and mental health.

Physical Health and SES

Research addressing the association between SES and health consistently find the poor, unemployed, and poorly educated to have increased mortality and morbidity for the great majority of diseases and health conditions (Illsley & Baker, 1991). One explanation involves the link between poor health behaviors that may be risk factors for various physical illnesses and low SES (Adler et al., 1993). For example, in a review of specific health risks for women, Rimer, McBride, and Crump (2001) reported that approximately 25% of women currently smoke cigarettes, 20% have high cholesterol (greater than 240 mg/dl), 35% are obese, and 73% do not exercise regularly.

Women from lower SES backgrounds may face a greater number of challenges in the pursuit of a healthy lifestyle. Some of the challenges associated with financial adversity and increased risk for physical health problems include limited access to or high cost of healthful foods (e.g., fresh fruits and vegetables) resulting in consumption of less expensive, high-fat foods that are low in nutritional value (Adler & Coriell, 1997); lack of, or inadequate, health insurance coverage that subsequently results in limited access to health care services (National Center for Health Statistics, 1996); and increased likelihood of residing in poorer neighborhoods, resulting in greater exposure to environmental stressors (e.g., violence, crime, pollution; B. Miller & Downs, 2000; Silbergeld, 2000). These challenges have implications for families because women traditionally are responsible for grocery shopping and food preparation, as well as for making health care decisions and taking children to health care appointments. With respect to the high percentage of impoverished households headed by females, it is important to address the influence of SES on the lifestyle and health of the entire family.

Low SES has been linked to increased morbidity and mortality rates in the majority of the specific physical illnesses we reviewed earlier in this chapter. For some conditions, this association has been linked with health risk behaviors. For example, Winkleby, Fortmann, and Barrett (1990) found that orientation. Such support may offset negative health consequences. However, since males maintain the majority of key supervisor positions at this time, these findings indicate that women continue to be at a disadvantage in terms of organizational advancement.

Women's Role as Spouse and as Caregiver

Although most women ultimately marry, age at first marriage is increasing (Barnett & Hyde, 2001), divorce remains a stable entity, and many individuals choose to cohabitate with an intimate partner. As a result, there are a large number of unmarried, as well as married, individuals in the workforce. The research literature addressing multiple roles, however, has tended to focus on women in traditional heterosexual marriages.

When examining women's role as support provider to their husbands, Waldron and Jacobs (1989) found European American women who were married or employed, or both married and employed, had favorable health trends, as opposed to European American women who were not married or employed. Interestingly, for European American women, marriage had beneficial effects for those who were not working, while employment had significant health benefits for those who were not married. For African American women, it was found that employment had positive effects on health, but only for those with children at home. Furthermore, African American women who did not work and stayed home with their children showed negative health trends.

While research has demonstrated positive health outcomes related to the marriage (i.e., wife) role, Preston (1995) studied married and unmarried individuals and found married women to be in the poorest physical and mental health and the most vulnerable to stress. A significant main effect of social support on health also was reported, with a positive correlation between social support and health for married men, and a negative correlation for married women. In other words, married men benefited, in terms of health, from social support while married women who received more social support indicated poorer health.

Women's role as caregiver, both lay and professional, has been a primary focus in the research examining multiple roles because the caregiving role is held by the great majority of women. Multiple roles do not merely imply juggling work and household tasks, because women are also the predominant caregivers and support providers to elderly parents, in-laws, husbands, and other family members (Preston, 1995; Walker, Pratt, & Eddy, 1995). Women with this additional role constitute the "sandwich generation." Such women are at increased risk for health problems as they experience the stress and time constraint of providing care to elderly friends, parents, or other family members while simultaneously providing care to their own children, supporting their partners, and functioning as employees in the workplace.

In comparison with population norms and noncaregiver controls, caregivers reported higher levels of both depressive symptoms and clinical depression and anxiety (Schulz, O'Brien, Bookwala, & Fleissner, 1995; Schulz, Visintainer, & Williamson, 1990). In a review of the empirical research on psychiatric morbidity and gender differences in caregivers, Yee and Schulz (2000) found that female caregivers tended to report higher rates of depression and anxiety and lower levels of life satisfaction than male caregivers. The authors suggest these increased rates of depression are largely attributable to the caregiver role because the rates reported by female caregivers were higher than female noncaregivers in the community. This is supported by results finding significant increases in psychological distress as women adjust to the caregiver role, as well as in women who are continuing to provide care to a disabled or ill person (Pavalko & Woodbury, 2000). In addition to psychiatric morbidity, women may also be at increased risk for physical illness because of caregiving, as women caregivers were less likely than men to engage in preventative health behaviors, such as exercise, rest, taking time off when sick, and remembering to take medications (Burton, Newsom, Schulz, Hirsch, & German, 1997). It may be that having a few roles serves as a buffer against such mental health outcomes as depression, but occupying additional roles—particularly in combination with the caregiver role—counterbalances the positive effects reaped from other roles (e.g., employment), further contributing to role strain (Cleary & Mechanic, 1983). The effects of caregiving on women are not limited to lay caregivers; over 90% of paid caregivers are also women (Leutz, Capitman, MacAdam, & Abrahams, 1992).

Women Occupying Multiple Roles: Who Benefits and Who Suffers?

Researchers have attempted to investigate different factors that may increase a woman's risk for role overload or serve as a buffer for experiencing distress related to multiple roles. A major factor that appears to help limit women's struggles with finding a healthy balance between work and home life and enhance the benefits of multiple roles involves social support from family and friends (Marshall & Barnett, 1991, 1993). For example, women who do not feel they have their husband's support or approval concerning their employment role will experience increased role strain (Elman & Gilbert, 1984). Marks (1977) suggested that role commitment is a

those with less education (used as proxy measure of social class), had more risk factors for CHD (e.g., cigarette smoking, hypertension, body mass index [BMI], and total cholesterol level). Lower SES not only serves as a risk factor for incidence of CHD in women, but also for mortality (Brezinka & Kittel, 1996). Lung cancer has the highest cancer mortality rate in women in the United States and has the third highest incidence rate for women (after breast and colon cancers; Anderson et al., 2001). This has been attributed to cigarette smoking; prevalence of smoking is highest among those women who are less educated and who live in poverty (Adler & Coriell, 1997). Environmental hazards such as air pollution, asbestos, and radon, which are found more in urban areas and lower status occupations, also are risk factors for lung cancer (Moy & Christiani, 2000). Although European American women have a higher incidence of breast cancer than African American women, black women have a 17% lower five-year survival rate (National Cancer Institute, 1995). These ethnic-racial differences have been explained in part by the confound of ethnic-racial status and SES in the United States, such that women of lower SES have lower mammography utilization rates (Champion, 1992) and report less knowledge about breast cancer (A. Miller & Champion, 1997). Gay and Underwood (1991) reported that the women at highest risk for contracting HIV are those with lower education levels, lack of employment opportunities (sometimes resulting in sex industry work such as prostitution), and difficulty receiving adequate health care services—factors all associated with poverty.

Mental Health and SES

Lower SES has been linked not only to physical health problems, but also to increased rates of psychopathology and mental disorders. In a review of 20 prevalence studies, Neugebauer et al. (1980) found that 17 of these studies reported higher rates of psychopathology in the lowest socioeconomic class than in the highest class. These findings were supported by multiple studies using data from the ECA study (Holzer et al., 1986; Regier et al., 1993; Robins et al., 1991). Regier et al. found individuals from the lowest SES level to have a 2.6 greater relative risk for overall psychopathology than those in the highest SES level in terms of one-month prevalence rates. In comparing rates of specific disorders between the lowest and highest social levels, there is an 8.1 greater risk for schizophrenia, 2.9 for obsessive-compulsive disorder, and 2.5 for alcoholism in those from lower SES levels, indicating significantly higher rates of overall psychopathology, as well as increased risk for specific psychological disorders in low socioeconomic groups. In support of

these results, Holzer et al. examined six-month prevalence rates and found similar results, again revealing higher rates of psychological disorders in low compared to high socioeconomic levels.

In examination of gender differences and psychopathology, women from lower socioeconomic backgrounds reported higher levels of depressive symptoms (Hirschfeld & Cross, 1982), with a review by Neugebauer et al. (1980) reporting an average female-to-male depression ratio of 3.0. This suggests women are at increased risk for depression, with augmented risk for women from lower socioeconomic backgrounds. As discussed earlier, women also have increased rates of anxiety disorders relative to men (Kessler et al., 1994, 1995; Neugebauer et al., 1980). In summary, the results of these epidemiological studies suggest that women and individuals from low socioeconomic backgrounds are at increased risk for major depression, anxiety, and other psychiatric disorders (Kohn, Dohrenwend, & Mirotznik, 1998).

Multiple Roles: Risk or Protective Factor?

Theories regarding women in the workplace began to emerge in the 1950s with the growing numbers of women entering the workforce. Since then, there continue to be changes and developments in the quantity and quality of women's involvement in the workplace and at home, which makes the modification of these initial theories necessary although the underlying issues may be similar (Barnett & Hyde, 2001). Although women have always been responsible for a variety of tasks (e.g., managing household chores; providing care to their children, elderly parents, or relatives), entering the workforce initiated significant changes in women's life roles. Employed women now constitute 48% of the U.S. labor force (Bond, Galinsky, & Swanberg, 1998), with 54% of women with children under the age of one year and 70.8% of women with children under the age of 18 years working outside the home (U.S. Department of Labor, 1997b). As the number of working mothers in the work force, and the number of hours women work outside the home, continue to rise, the number of women who occupy multiple roles, as well as the number of roles held by women, will increase.

Society places unique demands on women to find a balance between meeting the role expectations of an employee, earning an income to support their family, and pursuing a career on the one hand, and juggling the social roles of being a wife, mother, caretaker, and supportive friend, on the other. The debate as to whether occupying multiple roles serves as a risk or protective factor in the physical and psychological health of women continues to be a widely researched and important issue. The research on multiple roles presents contradictory findings, likely representing the current clash between more traditional views that multiple roles have a negative impact on a woman's health and relatively recent findings that suggest multiple roles can result in positive health effects.

The two primary theories that serve as a basis for a great majority of the research examining multiple roles are the *scarcity hypothesis* (Goode, 1960) and the *enhancement* or *expansion hypothesis* (Marks, 1977; Sieber, 1974). Whereas the scarcity hypothesis suggests that the more roles occupied by a woman, the more likely she is to deplete her limited resources, resulting in negative consequences for her health and well-being (Goode, 1960), the enhancement hypothesis suggests that multiple roles result in greater access to resources (i.e., social support, financial rewards) and increased likelihood for role balance (Marks, 1977; Sieber, 1974). These two main theories differ in their perspective on the relationship between multiple roles and women's health: The scarcity hypothesis portends that multiple roles produce deleterious mental and physical health effects, stress, and cause conflict in balancing roles related to work and family, while the enhancement hypothesis suggests that engaging in multiple roles is protective and provides positive physical and psychological health benefits for many women. To illustrate the opposing views offered by these two theories, we present a summary of empirical research relevant to women's roles as employee and caregiver, and the respective health advantages and disadvantages associated with each.

The Employment Role

Approximately half of the current U.S. labor force consists of women, and although not equally represented in top-level and more traditional male positions, women hold a wide range of jobs that expose them to stress and health risks (Bond, Galinsky, & Swanberg, 1998). Burke (1988) identified long work hours, stressful job conditions, high work demands, the number and ages of children at home, and lack of social support as factors that contribute to the strain women experience with work-family conflicts. Likely the most researched and notable cause of this strain is that women continue to take on the primary responsibilities for household chores and childcare, even though the majority also are employed outside the home (Marshall & Barnett, 1995). Furthermore, the contributions of men tend to include tasks such as playing with the children while women tend to assume more time-pressured tasks, such as housecleaning, preparing meals, and driving children to appointments (Thompson & Walker, 1989).

Women seem to experience work-family conflict differently than men do, not only because of the nature of women's roles, but also because of the attitude with which they view the roles. Gunter and Gunter (1990) examined gender differences in perceptions of domestic, household chores (i.e., cleaning, cooking, taking care of children) and found that women view these chores as a personal responsibility, whereas men tend to view such tasks as "helping out." Along these lines, men and women have different attitudes regarding what is the most important resource to provide to the family. Men feel that providing financially for their family is the single most important responsibility, while women feel it is equally important to provide childcare and complete household-related chores in addition to contributing to family financial resources (Perry-Jenkins, 1993; Perry-Jenkins & Crouter, 1990). Women, therefore, have added pressure and time constraints because of a sense of personal responsibility to complete the bulk of household chores and childcare, in addition to attending to their role as a caregiver, spouse, or partner, and meeting the actual and self-imposed demands of their role as an employee.

Work-related challenges, such as work-family conflict, limited coworker support, gender bias, and restricted opportunity for career advancement, have not only direct financial and occupational consequences for women, but also impact on women's stress levels. In a study by Northwestern National Life (1992), employed women reported nearly double the levels of stress-related illnesses and job burnout than employed men. Another study found 60% of female workers reported job stress as their primary problem (Reich & Nussbaum, 1994). Although women are gaining representation in all fields, the majority of female-dominated occupations (e.g., those involving customer service and the provision of care) are associated with such common stressors as lack of job security, poor relationships with co-workers and supervisors, and monotonous tasks (Hurrell & Murphy, 1992). Stressors are not limited to women working in less prestigious, lower paying jobs. Women in professional occupations also combat stress as their competency may pose a threat to men—both in the professional and personal environment. For example, single women may feel that a successful career may jeopardize their prospects for marriage (Post, 1987). Professional women in particular may experience difficulty forming interdependent, intimate relationships because reliance on independence and self-sufficiency serve as key components in their achievement of professional success (Post, 1982).

Although employment for women has been seen as imposing demands on personal and social resources contributing to the challenge of balancing work and family life,

employment has also been found to have positive effects on both the psychological and physical health of a woman. For example, Lennon (1998) examined the relationship between housework and depressive symptoms in employed women and homemakers. Differences were found in the amount of time these two groups devoted to housework, with employed women averaging 25 hours per week and homemakers averaging 38.5 hours. When employment hours outside the home are added to housework hours, employed women averaged 64.7 hours per week. Without accounting for specific work conditions, hours, and fairness, there were no significant differences in reports of depressive symptoms between employed wives and homemakers. However, when hours, work conditions, and fairness were taken into account, employed wives averaged significantly fewer depressive symptoms than homemakers. These results suggest that employment may balance the negative aspects of housework, resulting in improved mental health.

To challenge the hypothesis that employment is the catalyst that causes role overload, role conflict, and distress, Barnett, Davidson, and Marshall (1991) examined the interplay of women's work and family roles and the effect the employment role has on the family role. Among employed women, they found that helping others buffered the negative effects of concern about role overload resulting in reduced health problems (e.g., fatigue, headache, stomach, and back pain), and that salary satisfaction also buffered negative health effects for employed mothers. The finding that employment offering women the chance to help others served as a buffer against role overload distress and poor physical health symptoms is especially relevant because a high percentage of women's employment involves service provision and caregiving. No evidence was found that work overload caused conflict in the family role or increased physical health risks. Furthermore, in a review of positive aspects of multiple roles, Barnett and Hyde (2001) indicated the work-related factors of added income, social support, opportunity to experience success, and increased self-complexity all contribute to improved mental and physical health. These results suggest that the employment role does not always result in negative health effects for women.

In addition to the social systems of family, friends, and community, women also belong to social systems in the workplace. Given the increased number of women who work outside the home, workplace stress and support are issues of increasing importance to women. These issues appear to influence physical health directly. For example, Hibbard and Pope (1985) reported that women who felt more supported by their coworkers and more included in their workplace spent fewer days in the hospital over the course of one year. Repetti

(1993) concluded that individuals who percei

tionships with supervisors and coworkers as n

and high in conflict appear to be at increased ri

illnesses and physical symptoms (e.g., headach

Therefore, the quality and function of work relatio

pear to play a role in women's health.

Still, gender differences have been reported in the

workplace support on health and well-being. In an ir

tion of the amount and effects of social support, jol

and tedium experienced by men and women (Ge

Hobfoll, 1994), women reported greater life tediun

men, and men reported the receipt of more household

tance than women. Despite the fact that the men and w

in this study reported receiving similar amounts of sup

from their coworkers and supervisors, men benefited m

from these support sources, particularly coworker suppe

The researchers offer the possibility that men benefit mo

from their work relationships because they may interact wit

their colleagues on a more informal level, which House

(1981) suggests may be most effective in the prevention of

work stress and its negative consequences. Because individu-

alistic characteristics are so highly valued in the workplace,

and because men are more inclined to engage in this individ-

ualistic orientation, support may be provided more genuinely

among men and may be more effective since it can involve

mutual exchange and spontaneous acts, rather than role-

required behavior (House, 1981). Men, therefore, may

benefit more than women in terms of workplace health

consequences.

Another potential factor serving as a key obstacle in women's obtainment of the necessary social support in the workplace may be subtle gender bias, which can result in overt stereotyping and sexual harrassment (Gutek, 2001). If women want to retain people's approval, they must demonstrate qualities of female gender role (i.e., warmth, expressiveness), whereas if they want to succeed professionally in a traditional work setting, they must act according to the male model of managerial success, by being assertive and competitive (Bhatnagar, 1988; J. Grant, 1987). These conflicting expectations may contribute to women's lack of work support, as behaving aggressively may alienate and anger potential supporters (Lane & Hobfoll, 1992). Examining existing gender bias in the workplace, Geller and Hobfoll (1993) found that each gender preferred to mentor and offer support to his or her own gender, a seeming historical change in women's socialization. Because of increased awareness and sensitivity to problems such as work-family conflict and the glass ceiling, women may be recognizing a need for increased camaraderie, consequently, developing increased understanding and acceptance of women adopting a more individualistic

second factor that may increase women's distress when dealing with multiple roles because those individuals who are highly committed to a single role (i.e., job, parenthood) are more likely to experience role strain than individuals who are equally committed to multiple roles.

The disparity in research findings regarding the health effects of multiple roles highlights the need for clinicians and researchers to further investigate the possible negative effects that can be garnered by women who occupy multiple roles, specifically with regard to physical and psychological health. More research addressing additional personal and social resources that can offset negative sequelae, as well as other possible risk and protective factors, is warranted in individuals from diverse social groups (e.g., marital status, sexual preference, SES), occupations, and ethnic-racial backgrounds. Future research on multiple roles needs to focus not only on the individual, but also on the effect socially constructed gender roles have in shaping society's perception of different roles, as well as the degree to which these gender roles shape the attitudes and behaviors of women.

Sex Roles, Socialization, and Women's Health

This section examines the ways the female sex role and socialization process may contribute directly or indirectly to women's health. The etiology of the disorders and stressors discussed suggests the role of society largely explains the higher prevalence of these disorders among women.

Gender is a salient social category that helps individuals and society understand and perceive the world (Beall, 1993). Unlike biological sex, gender is influenced by the society in which the individual lives, as different cultures have different gender stereotypes that influence the way men and women are perceived. Gender schema theory (Bem, 1981) proposes that society classify the behaviors and attitudes of women and men into "feminine" and "masculine" traits, and that one's self-concept is assimilated to his or her gender schema. In most cultures, the distinction between male and female is clear, and individuals are expected to behave in a way that is appropriate to their respective sex role. In Western cultures, the traditional female sex role has been characterized by traits of warmth and expressiveness while the traditional male sex role suggests traits of dominance and instrumentality. The influence of this female sex role has numerous direct and indirect consequences on the psychological and physical health of women. For example, the female sex role and socialization process largely impact women's desire to be thin and may be a contributing factor to high rates of eating disorders. American society tends to equate thinness with attractiveness, especially for individuals in higher socioeconomic brackets (Sokol & Gray, 1998). Women are judged by

their physical appearances more often than men (Sobal, 1995), and it has been suggested that body weight and shape are the primary factors in determining a woman's attractiveness and desirability (Polivy & McFarlane, 1998). In reality, the average woman is not able to achieve these standards, which results in feelings of low self-esteem, body dissatisfaction, and excessive dieting (Heffernan, 1998). As discussed earlier, the impact of societal expectations on mental and physical health is also evident for women experiencing infertility as well as postpartum depression.

Coping and Women's Expression of Illness

Several suggestions involving socialization have been offered to explain gender discrepancy in morbidity and mortality. An older idea is that the "sick role" is more in line with women's sex role stereotype of being a homemaker than to men's role of provider, and that this allows greater acceptance and opportunity for women to seek medical attention for their illnesses (Nathanson, 1975). It also has been suggested that sickness is a socially acceptable way for women to be relieved of their household, caregiving, and employment responsibilities (Toner, 1994). An alternative explanation is that women's higher morbidity rates result from the stress women experience occupying multiple roles (i.e., wife, mother, paid employee), which in turn leads to higher rates of illness (Reifman, Biernat, & Lang, 1991).

Equally important is how women cope with illness. In a study of couples where one partner had been diagnosed with cancer, Baider and colleagues (1996) attempted to further understand gender differences in coping with psychological distress. Their evaluation of 101 couples revealed that the wives of male spouses with cancer reported significantly higher levels of anxiety than did female patients or their sick partners. Interestingly, the distress experienced by female patients was accounted for by degree of difficulty in the domestic environment, extended family relations, and their husband's psychological distress, with education having a protective effect. However, distress among male patients primarily was accounted for by the degree of difficulty in the domestic environment. It is noteworthy that the psychological distress experienced by the male patient contributed to the distress experienced by the female spouse; however, the psychological distress of the female patient did not contribute to the male spouse's distress. These results suggest that the health behaviors and coping styles used by women may be explained by the female social role that encourages women to focus on emotional support, nurturance, and caring for others, as well as care for oneself, while the male social role encourages concern with instrumentality and problem solving. Nezu and

Nezu (1987) found that level of masculinity, not biological sex, predicted distress levels and effective use of problem-solving coping skills in undergraduate students and that coping skills may mediate the relationship between sex roles and distress. Similarly, Friedman, Nezu, Nezu, Trunzo, & Graf (1999) found problem-solving skills and masculinity, regardless of biological sex, to be significant predictors of psychological distress in persons with cancer, whereas femininity was not predictive of these factors. Results such as these suggest that social roles or sex roles may better explain differences in coping style, thoughts, and behaviors because studies examining biological sex differences in coping have been inconclusive (Dunkel-Schetter, Feinstein, Taylor, & Falke, 1992).

These results have implications for women in both research and clinical settings. With respect to social context, women are stereotypically categorized as being high in femininity and expected to model the traditional female sex role. Those in the field of medicine and mental health must remain cautious of classifying patients according to their biological sex exclusively. By considering the sex role orientation of the individual (rather than making assumptions based on biological sex), researchers and mental health and health care professionals can reduce clinical biases that can potentially hamper treatment, among other variables.

CONCLUSIONS AND FUTURE DIRECTIONS IN WOMEN'S HEALTH

This chapter addresses several of the physical and psychological health problems faced by women, as well as social factors that may contribute to women's health problems. Despite advances in the field, women's health remains an area deserving increased attention. It is important for clinicians and researchers who work in the field of women's health to continue to serve as ambassadors for increased research funding, health education, and outreach to women from all ethnic-racial and cultural groups, and for the achievement of equal status for women in academia. Those working in the field of women's health must look at past achievements and successes as a guide for future goals, opportunities, and continued progress. This section provides a summary of the current status of women's health, as well as some possible challenges and opportunities we may confront in the future.

Health Care

Historically, health care has been a male-dominated profession, with men serving as the primary providers and administrators in the field. This has changed significantly as the 13.4% of women graduating from medical school in 1975 increased to 40% in 1997 (Bertakis, 1998). Despite this significant increase in women's medical school enrollment, more women drop out of medical school than men, with attrition rates for women steadily increasing over time (Fitzpatrick & Wright, 1995). Future research must examine not only rates of attrition, but also potential factors contributing to higher medical school drop-out for women across the nation (e.g., financial burden, role strain) and possible solutions.

As a result of women entering and graduating from medical school in greater numbers, more women currently serve as faculty members in academic medicine than ever before. This is positive in terms of the interaction between female physicians and female medical students with respect to mentorship, the availability of female physicians for training both male and female medical students, and possible augmented exposure to women's health issues, as well as greater research and clinical opportunities available in the area of women's health because of increased numbers of women in the field. However, while great strides have been made in the number of women entering academic medicine, the rate of women faculty who are awarded tenure and achieve senior ranks or high administrative ranks has not advanced at the rate expected given the influx of women in academia (Morahan et al., 2001). In a review of the literature, Carnes et al. (2001) reported that lack of role models and mentors, feelings of isolation, gender discrimination, and lack of support for family-related responsibilities that most commonly fall on women serve as potential reasons women do not achieve academic leadership positions. Traditionally, such positions are obtained through research and the acquisition of grant funding, areas in which improvement for women is needed. In the future, women's health is an area of research that may allow female psychologists, physicians, and scientists to advance to academic positions, at the same time promoting the clinical and research knowledge of women's health.

Psychology

The entrance and advancement of women in the field of psychology has been dramatic as women earned 66% of the PhD degrees in psychology awarded in 1999. The rate of women earning PhD degrees has increased 8% since 1990, at which time 58% of new PhD degrees were awarded to women. The majority of these degrees were awarded to European American women (84%), followed by Hispanic women (6%), African American women (5%), Asian women (4%), and women of Native American descent (1%). Over the past decade, the percentage of PhD degrees awarded to women of color increased from 12% to 17%, indicating increasing diversity among women in the profession of psychology (Kohout, 2001). The growing number of women entering psychology overall, in addition to increases in women of color, no doubt will influence research agendas and clinical attention in the area of women's health.

The growing number of women earning PhDs in psychology has coincided with a 49% increase in the number of grants submitted by women and a 92% increase in the number of grants awarded to women in psychology from 1988 to 1997. Since the 1970s, the percentage of articles with female first authors published in psychology journals, including top-tiered journals, has dramatically increased. In the field of health psychology, for example, 19% of the articles published in the *Journal of Behavioral Medicine* were first authored by women when the journal was first published in 1978, compared to 48% in 1990. Women also are becoming increasingly represented in editorial roles, with a female currently serving as editor for 32% of the APA's journals as compared to 5% in the early 1980s. There is a similar trend for associate editor positions (currently 37% female) as well as consulting editor and reviewer positions (currently 34% female) in APA journals (Kite et al., 2001).

Despite these advances, women in psychology face many of the same challenges as women employed in health care. One primary challenge that exists is the obtainment of senior faculty positions in academia. While women constitute 39% of the full-time faculty at four-year academic institutions, 30% of women achieve tenure compared to 53% of men (American Psychological Association, 2000). The reasons for this discrepancy must be evaluated and remediated.

Mentorship

The increasing number of women in health care and psychology has a direct impact on the personal and professional development of women pursuing undergraduate and advanced degrees. While female mentors at senior levels may be difficult to find in academia, those female graduate students who have the opportunity to work with female mentors benefit professionally as well as personally (Schlegel, 2000). As discussed throughout this chapter, women experience stressors that are unique to those experienced by men. Having a female mentor can help the female student navigate these stressors and find an adaptive balance between her role as a professional and being a woman with many other life roles.

Research

Scant research prior to the 1990s included female samples exclusively. This approach failed women because it was assumed that either women's physiological systems were the same as males, or female hormones would confound research, resulting in a strictly male sample. Despite the development of organizations, such as the Office of Research on Women's Health in 1990 and the NIH Revitalization Act of 1993 that required research supported by federal funds to include women and individuals from diverse ethnic-racial groups, advancements still are needed in women's health research.

Future research must strive to increase the inclusion of women in clinical research trials and to focus on female samples when appropriate. Studies designed to further assess risk factors and disease symptoms that may differ significantly from those of men, or those factors and symptoms that may be exclusively found in women, must be conducted. For example, as discussed earlier in this chapter, women continue to be assessed for and diagnosed with heart disease based on criteria researched on men. This has drawbacks in that symptoms considered atypical for men may be what are typical for women, and without this knowledge, appropriate care for women may be limited. In addition to further research focusing on gender differences in risk factors, illness presentation and course, and pharmacology and other treatments, more attention and increased funding must be dedicated to disorders that occur primarily in women, such as lupus and rheumatoid arthritis. Furthermore, women cannot be categorized as a homogenous population. For example, although morbidity and mortality statistics provide evidence for ethnic-racial disparity for various health conditions, adequate research illuminating risk and other relevant factors is lacking. Despite statistics that show African American women living in the United States have the fastest growing rates of HIV infection, as well as poorer cancer-related health outcomes relative to European American women, research has failed to reach out to women of color and gain their participation in clinical trials (Killien et al., 2000). Women's health research must include representative samples of all women, including neglected or hard-to-reach populations, such as women of color, lesbians, women from lower socioeconomic backgrounds, and the elderly. Cross-cultural investigations that include women from various countries also are warranted.

Why Women's Health? Why Now?

The need for research and clinical attention to women's health issues has always been present. However, only in the past few decades have women's health care needs, research, and social and cultural issues been deemed important health topics in both the clinical and research setting. Because women are living longer than ever, the need for empirically based research findings, clinical care, and a more comprehensive understanding of women's health is greater than ever. In 1940, there were 211,000 women over the age of 85 living in the United States. Today, in the United States alone, there are over 2.9 million women over the age of 85—many of whom have multiple chronic diseases that impact the physical and psychological health (Guralnik, 2000). Earlier in this chapter, we discussed the three leading causes of death for American women: CHD, cancer, and stroke. With respect to elderly women, nearly 70% of total deaths can be attributed to these three conditions (Guralnik, 2000). Research focusing on health behaviors and lifestyle factors relevant to disease development, course, outcome, and quality of life is necessary to develop and disseminate prevention programs, promote psychosocial intervention, and facilitate coping efforts. Attention to such behaviors as cigarette smoking, alcohol consumption, exercise, diet, and seeking routine Pap smears and mammograms can influence not only illness prevention, but also outcome.

Prevention and treatment issues are equally important for psychological health, as well as physical health. Elderly women commonly experience the death of spouses and friends, the diagnosis of medical conditions, and the social stereotypes of growing old in a society that glorifies youth, all of which contribute to health and well-being. Problems experienced by the elderly influence women of all ages because 72% of care given to the elderly is provided by women, including daughters (29%), wives (23%), and other women who serve as lay or professional caregivers (20%; Siegler, 1998), placing the female caregiver at risk for both physical and psychological health concerns as reviewed earlier in this chapter.

Because women live longer than men, with a great majority of elderly women living alone, health education must create interventions and outreach programs that accommodate elderly women who serve as their own primary caretakers, as well as younger caretakers who may have a difficult time leaving the house because of child care or household responsibilities. In addressing this concern, the Centers of Excellence in Women's Health (CoE) have turned to the World Wide Web as a way to reach women. The CoE have adopted online health information sites relevant to women patient support groups and is developing other plans to expand these Internet services (Crandall, Zitzelberger, Rosenberg, Winner, & Holaday, 2001). Because women continue to make the majority of the family health care decisions, the Internet serves as a convenient and informative way for women to access resources and acquire education related to women's health. Caution is warranted, of course, as not all Internet sites relevant to women's health issues provide comprehensive or accurate information.

Several U.S.-based programs and organizations are cornerstones in the field of women's health, including the American Medical Women's Association, Division 35 of the American Psychological Association (i.e., Society for the Psychology of Women), the Office of Research on Women's Health, the Society for Women's Health Research, and the Women's Health Initiative (WHI). In an effort to unite the multiple aspects and professions included in the field of women's health, the National Centers of Excellence in Women's Health (CoE) were developed in 1996 with the goal of promoting women's health by bringing together those associated with research, clinical care, health education and outreach, and medical training, and increasing the number of women in academic medicine (Morahan et al., 2001). There are currently 15 CoE in academic health centers (Gwinner, Strauss, Milliken, & Donoghue, 2000), with women serving as directors for 13 of these centers (Carnes et al., 2001). It is programs such as these that allow both the physical and psychological care of women to transcend the standards and practices of the past.

The future of the field of women's health largely depends on organizations such as these not only to further the advancement of knowledge in women's health issues, but also to offer interdisciplinary support to women across the applied fields of medicine, health care, and psychology, and their corresponding academic departments. The field of women's health holds many exciting opportunities and potential advancements for all women.

REFERENCES

Adler, N. E., Boyce, T., Chesney, M. A., Folkman, S., & Syme, S. L. (1993). Socioeconomic inequalities in health: No easy solution. *Journal of the American Medical Association, 269,* 3140–3145.

Adler, N. E., & Coriell, M. (1997). Socioeconomic status and women's health. In S. J. Gallant, G. Puryear Keita, & R. Royak-Schaler (Eds.), *Health care for women: Psychological, social, and behavioral influences* (pp. 11–23). Washington, DC: American Psychological Association.

Alpert, E. J., Freund, K. M., Park, C. C., Patel, J. C., & Sovak, M. A. (1992). *Partner violence: How to recognize and treat victims of abuse. A guide for physicians.* Waltham: Massachusetts Medical Society.

American Cancer Society. (2000). *2000 cancer facts and figures.* Retrieved June 4, 2001, from www.cancer.org/statistics /biostats/biowo.htm

American Heart Association. (1999). *Biostatistical fact sheet.* Retrieved May 8, 2001, from www.americanheart.org/statistics /biostats/biowo.htm

American Medical Association. (1991). Gender disparities in clinical decision making. *Journal of the American Medical Association, 266*(4), 559–562.

American Psychiatric Association. (1994). *Diagnostic and statistical manual of mental disorders* (4th ed.). Washington, DC: Author.

American Psychiatric Association. (2000). *Diagnostic and statistical manual of mental disorders* (4th ed., text rev.). Washington, DC: Author.

American Psychological Association. (1996). *Research agenda for psychosocial and behavioral factors in women's health.* Washington, DC: Author.

American Psychological Association. (2000). *Women in academe: Two steps forward, one step back.* Washington, DC: Author.

Anderson, B. L., Golden-Kreutz, D. M., & DiLillo, V. (2001). Cancer. In A. Baum, T. A. Revenson, & J. E. Singer (Eds.), *Handbook of health psychology* (pp. 709–725). Mahwah, NJ: Erlbaum.

Arboix, A., Oliveres, M., Garcia-Eroles, L., Maragall, C., Massons, J., & Targa, C. (2001). Acute cerebrovascular disease in women. *European Neurology, 45,* 199–205.

Arthritis Foundation. (2001). *Rheumatoid arthritis.* Retrieved May 8, 2001, from www.arthritis.org/conditions/DiseaseCenter /ra.asp# What % 20 Is % 20 It.

Ayanian, J. Z., & Epstein, A. M. (1991). Differences in the use of procedures between women and men hospitalized for coronary heart disease. *New England Journal of Medicine, 325*(4), 221–225.

Bachman, R. (1994). *Violence against women: A national crime victimization survey report.* Washington, DC: U.S. Department of Justice.

Baider, L., Kaufman, B., Peretz, T., Manor, O., Ever-Hadani, P., & Kaplan De-Nour, A. (1996). Mutuality of fate: Adaptation and psychological distress in cancer patients and their partners. In L. Baider, C. L. Cooper, & A. Kaplan De-Nour (Eds.), *Cancer and the family* (pp. 173–186). Chichester, England: Wiley.

Barnett, R. C., Davidson, H., & Marshall, N. L. (1991). Physical symptoms and the interplay of work and family roles. *Health Psychology, 10,* 94–101.

Barnett, R. C., & Hyde, J. S. (2001). Women, men, work, and family. *American Psychologist, 56*(10), 781–796.

Beall, A. E. (1993). A social constructionist view of gender . In A. E. Beall & R. J. Sternberg (Eds.), *The psychology of gender* (pp. 127–147). New York: Guilford Press.

Belilos, E., & Carsons, S. (1998). Rheumatologic disorders in women. *Medical Clinics of North America, 82*(1), 77–101.

Bem, S. L. (1981). Gender schema theory: A cognitive account of sex typing. *Psychological Review, 88,* 354–364.

Bertakis, K. D. (1998). Physician gender and physician-patient interaction. In E. A. Blechman & K. D. Brownell (Eds.), *Behavioral medicine and women: A comprehensive handbook* (pp. 849–853). New York: Guilford Press.

Beutel, M., Deckardt, R., Von Rad, M., & Weiner H. (1995). Grief and depression after miscarriage: Their separation, antecedents, and course. *Psychosomatic Medicine, 57*(6), 517–526.

Bhatnagar, D. (1988). Professional women in organizations: New paradigms for research and action. *Sex Roles, 18,* 343–355.

Bittner, V. (2000, Spring). Heart disease in women. *Clinical Reviews, 62*–66.

Bond, J. T., Galinsky, E., & Swanberg, J. E. (1998). *The 1997 national study of the changing workforce.* New York: Families and Work Institute.

Borg, S., & Lasker, J. (1981). *When pregnancy fails: Families coping with miscarriage, stillbirth, and infant death.* Boston: Beacon Press.

Brey, R. L., & Kittner, S. J. (2000). Cerebrovascular disease in women. In M. B. Goldman & M. C. Hatch (Eds.), *Women and health* (pp. 797–810). San Diego, CA: Academic Press.

Brezinka, V., & Kittel, F. (1996). Psychosocial factors of coronary heart disease in women: A review. *Social Science Medicine, 42*(10), 1351–1365.

Brockington, I. F., Oates, J., George, S., Turner, D., Vostanis, P., Sullivan, M., et al. (2001). A screening questionnaire for mother-infant bonding disorders. *Archives of Women's Mental Health, 3,* 133–140.

Brown, C. S., & Bertolet, B. D. (1998). Peripartum cardiomyopathy: A comprehensive review. *American Journal of Obstetrics and Gynecology, 178*(2), 409–414.

Brown, C. S., & Schulberg, H. C. (1997). Depression and anxiety disorders: Diagnosis and treatment in primary care practice. In S. J. Gallant, G. P. Keita, & R. Royak-Schaler (Eds.), *Health care for women: Psychological, social, and behavioral influences* (pp. 237–256). Washington, DC: American Psychological Association.

Brown, T. G., Kokin, M., Seraganian, P., & Shields, N. (1995). The role of spouses of substance abusers in treatment. *Journal of Psychoactive Drugs, 27*(3), 223–229.

Burke, R. J. (1988). Some antecedents and consequences of work-family conflict. *Journal of Social Behavior and Personality, 3,* 287–302.

Burton, L. C., Newsom, J. T., Schulz, R., Hirsch, C. H., & German, P. S. (1997). Preventative health behaviors among spousal caregivers. *Preventative Medicine, 26,* 162–169.

Carnes, M., Vandenbosche, G., Agatisa, P. K., Hirshfield, A., Dan, A., Shaver, J. L. F., et al. (2001). Using women's health research to develop women leaders in academic health sciences: The national centers of excellence in women's health. *Journal of Women's Health and Gender-Based Medicine, 10*(1), 39–47.

Centers for Disease Control and Prevention. (1997). Smoking-attributable mortality and years of potential life lost-United States, 1984. *Morbidity and Mortality Weekly Report, 46,* 444–451.

Centers for Disease Control and Prevention. (1998). Diagnosis and reporting of HIV and AIDS in the States with the integrated HIV and AIDS surveillance. *Morbidity and Morality Weekly Report, 47*(15), 309–314.

Centers for Disease Control and Prevention. (1999). *Health, United States with health and aging chartbook.* Hyattsville, MD: Public Health Services. Available from www.cdc.gov/nchswww /products/pubs/pubd/hus/hus.htm

Champion, V. L. (1992). Compliance with guidelines for mammography screening. *Cancer Detection and Prevention, 16,* 253–258.

Chapman, K. R., Tashkin, D. P., & Pye, D. J. (2001). Gender bias in the diagnosis of COPD. *Chest, 119*(6), 1691–1695.

Clancy, M. C. (2000). Gender issues in women's health care. In M. B. Goldman & M. C. Hatch (Eds.), *Women and health* (pp. 50–54). San Diego, CA: Academic Press.

Cleary, P. D., & Mechanic, D. (1983). Sex differences in psychological distress among married people. *Journal of Health and Social Behavior, 24,* 111–121.

Cohen, L. S., Sichel, D. S., Faraone, S. V., Robertson, L. M., Dimmock, J. A., & Rosenbaum, J. F. (1996). Course of panic disorder during pregnancy and the puerperium: A preliminary study. *Biological Psychiatry, 39,* 950–954.

Cohen, M., Deamant, C., Barkan, S., Richardson, J., Young, M., Holman, S., et al. (2000). Domestic violence and childhood sexual abuse in HIV-infected women and women at risk for HIV. *American Journal of Public Health, 90,* 560–565.

Collins, P. Y., Geller, P. A., Miller, S., Toro, P., & Susser, E. (2001). Ourselves, our bodies, our realities: An HIV prevention intervention for women with severe mental illness. *Journal of Urban Health, 78*(1), 162–175.

Commonwealth Fund Commission on Women's Health. (1994). *Health care reform: What is at stake for women? Policy report of the Commonwealth Fund Commission on Women's Health.* New York: Author.

Cooper, P. J. (1995). Eating disorders and their relationship to mood and anxiety disorders. In K. D. Brownell & C. G. Fairburn (Eds.), *Eating disorders and obesity: A comprehensive handbook* (pp. 159–164). New York: Guilford Press.

Cooper-Hilbert, B. (1998). *Infertility and involuntary childlessness: Helping couples cope.* New York: Norton.

Crandall, C., Zitzelberger, T., Rosenberg, M., Winner, C., & Holaday, L. (2001). Information technology and the National Centers of Excellence in Women's Health. *Journal of Women's Health and Gender-Based Medicine, 10*(1), 49–55.

Davis, R. M., & Novotny, T. E. (1989). The epidemiology of cigarette smoking and its impact on chronic obstructive pulmonary disease. *American Review of Respiratory Disease, 140,* S82–S84.

Del Puente, A., Knowler, W. C., & Bennett, P. H. (1989). High incidence and prevalence of rheumatoid arthritis in Pima Indians. *American Journal of Epidemiology, 129,* 1170–1178.

Demakis, J. G., & Rahimtoola, S. H. (1971). Peripartum cardiomyopathy. *Circulation, 44,* 964–968.

D'Hoore, W., Sicotte, C., & Tilquin, C. (1994). Sex bias in the management of coronary artery disease in Quebec. *American Journal of Public Health, 84*(6), 1013–1015.

Downey, J., & McKinney, M. (1992). The psychiatric status of women presenting for infertility evaluation. *American Journal of Orthopsychiatry, 62,* 196–205.

Dugowson, C. E. (2000). Rheumatoid arthritis. In M. B. Goldman & M. C. Hatch (Eds.), *Women and health* (pp. 674–685). San Diego, CA: Academic Press.

Dunkel-Schetter, C., Feinstein, L. G., Taylor, S. E., & Falke, R. L. (1992). Patterns of coping with cancer. *Health Psychology, 11*(2), 79–87.

Dutton, D. B., & Levine, S. (1989). Overview, methodological critique, and reformulation. In J. P. Bunker, D. S. Gomby, & B. H. Kehrer (Eds.), *Pathways to health* (pp. 29–69). Menlo Park, CA: Henry J. Kaiser Family Foundation.

Dutton, M. A., Haywood, Y., & El-Bayoumi, G. (1997). Impact of violence on women's health. In S. J. Gallant, G. P. Keita, & R. Royak-Schaler (Eds.), *Health care for women: Psychological, social, and behavioral influences* (pp. 41–56). Washington, DC: American Psychological Association.

El-Bayoumi, G., Borum, M. L., & Haywood, Y. (1998). Domestic violence in women. *Medical Clinics of North America, 82*(2), 391–401.

El-Guebaly, N. (1995). Alcohol and polysubstance abuse among women. *Canadian Journal of Psychiatry, 40*(2), 73–79.

Elman, M. R., & Gilbert, L. A. (1984). Coping strategies for role conflict in married professional women with children. *Family Relations, 33,* 317–337.

Engelhard, I. M., van den Hout, M. A., & Arntz, A. (2001). Posttraumatic stress disorder after pregnancy loss. *General Hospital Psychiatry, 23,* 62–66.

Fitzpatrick, K. M., & Wright, M. P. (1995). Gender differences in medical school attrition rates. *Journal of the American Medical Women's Association, 50*(6), 204–206.

Franks, P., & Clancy C. M. (1993). Physician gender bias in clinical decision making: Screening for cancer in primary care. *Medical Care, 31,* 213–218.

Friedman, S. H., Nezu, A. M., Nezu, C. M., Trunzo, J., & Graf, M. C. (1999, November). *Sex roles, problem solving, and psychological distress in persons with cancer.* Poster presented at the 33rd convention of the Association for Advancement of Behavior Therapy, Toronto, Ontario, Canada.

Gay, J., & Underwood, U. (1991). Women in danger: A call for action. *The world's women 1970–1990. Trends and statistics.* United Nations: National Council for International Health.

Geller, P. A., & Hobfoll, S. E. (1993). Gender differences in preference to offer social support to assertive men and women. *Sex Roles, 28,* 419–432.

Geller, P. A., & Hobfoll, S. E. (1994). Gender differences in job stress, tedium, and social support in the workplace. *Journal of Personal and Social Relationships, 11,* 555–572.

Geller, P. A., Klier, C. M., & Neugebauer, R. (2001). Anxiety disorders following miscarriage. *Journal of Clinical Psychiatry, 62*(6), 432–438.

Geller, P. A., Striepe, M. I., Lewis, J., III, & Petrucci, R. J. (1996, September). *Women on heart transplant units: The importance of psychosocial factors among women with cardiovascular disease.* Paper presented at the American Psychological Association Psychosocial and Behavioral Factors in Women's Health: Research, Prevention, Treatment and Service Delivery in Clinical and Community Settings conference, Washington, DC.

Geller, P. A., Striepe, M. I., & Petrucci, R. J. (1994, October). *Psychosocial factors in peripartum cardiomyopathy.* Poster presented at the third biennial conference on Psychiatric, Psychosocial, and Ethical Issues in Organ Transplantation, Richmond, VA.

Glied, S. (1997). The treatment of women with mental health disorders under HMO and fee-for-service insurance. *Women and Health, 26*(2), 1–16.

Goldberg, R. J., O'Donnell, C., Yarzebski, J., Bigelow, C., Savageau, J., & Gore, J. M. (1998). Sex differences in symptom presentation associated with acute myocardial infarction: A population-based perspective. *American Heart Journal, 136*(2), 189–195.

Goldbloom, D. S., & Kennedy, S. H. (1995). Medical complications of anorexia nervosa. In K. D. Brownell & C. G. Fairburn (Eds.), *Eating disorders and obesity: A comprehensive handbook* (pp. 266–270). New York: Guilford Press.

Golding, J. M. (1999). Intimate partner violence as a risk factor for mental disorders: A meta-analysis. *Journal of Family Violence, 14*(2), 99–132.

Goldman, M. B., Missmer, S. A., & Barbier, R. L. (2000). Infertility. In M. B. Goldman & M. C. Hatch (Eds.), *Women and health* (pp. 196–214). San Diego, CA: Academic Press.

Goode, W. (1960). A theory of strain. *American Sociological Review, 25,* 483–496.

Grant, B. F., & Hartford, T. C. (1995). Comorbidity between *DSM-IV* alcohol use disorders and major depression: Results of a national survey. *Drug and Alcohol Dependence, 39,* 197–206.

Grant, B. F., Hartford, T. C., Dawson, D. A., Chou, S. P., & Pickering, R. P. (1994). Prevalence of *DSM-IV* alcohol abuse and dependence: United States, 1992. *Alcohol Health and Research World, 18,* 243–248.

Grant, J. (1987). Women as managers: What they can offer to organizations. *Organization Dynamics, 16*(3), 56–63.

Greenfield, S. F. (1996). Women and substance use disorders. In M. F. Jensvold, J. A. Hamilton, & U. Halbreich (Eds.), *Psychopharmacology and women: Sex, gender, and hormones* (pp. 299–321). Washington, DC: American Psychiatric Press.

Greil, A. L. (1997). Infertility and psychological distress: A critical review of the literature. *Social Science and Medicine, 45,* 1679–1704.

Gunter, N. C., & Gunter, B. G. (1990). Domestic division of labor among working couples: Does androgyny make a differences? *Psychology of Women Quarterly, 14,* 355–370.

Guralnik, J. M. (2000). Aging. In M. B. Goldman & M. C. Hatch (Eds.), *Women and health* (pp. 1143–1145). San Diego, CA: Academic Press.

Gutek, B. (2001). Women and paid work. *Psychology of Women Quarterly, 25,* 379–393.

Gwinner, V. M., Strauss, J. F., Milliken, N., & Donoghue, G. D. (2000). Implementing a new model of integrated women's health in academic health centers: Lessons learned the National Centers of Excellence in Women's Health. *Journal of Women's Health and Gender-Based Medicine, 9*(9), 979–985.

Hall, J. A., Irish, J. T., Roter, D. L., Ehrlich, C. M., & Miller, L. H. (1994). Gender in medical encounters: An analysis of physician and patient communication in a primary care setting. *Health Psychology, 13*(5), 384–392.

Hawley, D. J., & Wolfe, F. (2000). Fibromyalgia. In M. B. Goldman & M. C. Hatch (Eds.), *Women and health* (pp. 1068–1083). San Diego, CA: Academic Press.

Haynes, S. G., & Hatch, M. C. (2000). State of the art methods for women's health research. In M. B. Goldman & M. C. Hatch (Eds.), *Women and Health* (pp. 37–49). San Diego, CA: Academic Press.

Heffernan, K. (1998). Bulimia nervosa. In E. A. Blechman & K. D. Brownell (Eds.), *Behavioral medicine and women: A comprehensive handbook* (pp. 358–363). New York: Guilford Press.

Henry, J. G. A. (2000). Depression and anxiety. In M. A. Smith & L. A. Shimp (Eds.), *20 common problems in women's health care* (pp. 263–301). New York: McGraw-Hill.

Hibbard, J. H., & Pope, C. R. (1985). Employment status, employment characteristics and women's health. *Women and Health, 10,* 59–77.

Hirschfeld, R. M. A., & Cross, C. K. (1982). Epidemiology of affective disorders: Psychosocial risk factors. *Archives of General Psychiatry, 39,* 35–46.

Hochberg, M. C. (1990). Changes in the incidence and prevalence of rheumatoid arthritis in England and Wales, 1970–1982. *Seminar Arthritis Rheumatoid, 19,* 294–302.

Holm, K., & Scherubel, J. (1997). Coronary heart disease. In K. M. Allen & J. M. Phillips (Eds.), *Women's health across the lifespan* (pp. 125–143). Philadelphia: Lippincott.

Holzer, C. E., Shea, B. M., Swanson, J. W., Leaf, P. J., Myers, J. K., George, L., et al. (1986). The increased risk for specific psychiatric disorders among persons of low socioeconomic status: Evidence from the Epidemiologic Catchment Area surveys. *American Journal of Social Psychiatry, 6,* 259–271.

House, J. S. (1981). *Work stress and social support.* Reading, MA: Addison-Wesley.

Hughes, P., Turton, P., Hopper, E., McGauley, G. A., & Fonagy, P. (2001). Disorganised attachment behaviour among infants born subsequent to stillbirth. *Journal of Child Psychology and Psychiatry and Allied Disciplines, 42*(6), 791–801.

Hurrell, J. J., Jr., & Murphy, L. R. (1992). Psychological job stress. In W. N. Rom (Ed.), *Environmental and occupational medicine* (2nd ed., pp. 675–684). Boston: Little, Brown.

Husten, C. G., & Malarcher, A. M. (2000). Cigarette smoking: Trends, determinants, and health effects. In M. B. Goldman & M. C. Hatch (Eds.), *Women and health* (pp. 563–577). San Diego, CA: Academic Press.

Illsley, R., & Baker, D. (1991). Contextual variation in the meaning of health inequality. *Social Science and Medicine, 32,* 359–365.

Janssen, H. J., Cuisinier, M. C., Hoogduin, K. A., & de Graauw, K. P. (1996). Controlled prospective study on the mental health of women following pregnancy loss. *American Journal of Psychiatry, 153*(2), 226–230.

Kamb, M. L., & Wortley, P. M. (2000). Human immunodeficiency virus and AIDS in women. In M. B. Goldman & M. C. Hatch (Eds.), *Women and health* (pp. 336–351). San Diego, CA: Academic Press.

Kaplan-Machlis, B., & Bors, K. P. (2000). In M. A. Smith & L. A. Shimp (Eds.), *20 common problems in women's health care* (pp. 631–664). New York: McGraw-Hill.

Kathol, R. G., Broadhead, W. E., & Kroenke, K. (1997). Depression. In L. S. Goldman, T. N. Wise, & D. S. Brody (Eds.), *Psychiatry for primary care physicians* (pp. 73–96). Chicago: American Medical Association.

Katon, W. (1995). Collaborative care: Patient satisfaction, outcomes, and medical cost-offset. *Family Systems Medicine, 13*(3/4), 351–365.

Kaye, W. H., Weltzin, T. E., & Hsu, L. K. G. (1993). Relationship between anorexia nervosa and obsessive and compulsive behaviors. *Psychiatric Annals, 23,* 365–373.

Kendell, R. E., Chalmers, J. C., & Platz, C. (1987). Epidemiology of puerperal psychoses. *British Journal of Psychiatry, 150,* 662–673.

Kendler, K. S., Maclean, C., Neale, M., Kessler, R., Heath, A., & Eaves, L. (1991). The genetic epidemiology of bulimia nervosa. *American Journal of Psychiatry, 148,* 1627–1637.

Kerlikowske, K. (2000). Breast cancer screening. In M. B. Goldman & M. C. Hatch (Eds.), *Women and health* (pp. 895–905). San Diego, CA: Academic Press.

Kessler, R. C. (2000). Gender and mood disorders. In M. B. Goldman & M. C. Hatch (Eds.), *Women and health* (pp. 997–1009). San Diego, CA: Academic Press.

Kessler, R. C., McGonagle, K. A., Swartz, M. S., Blazer, D. G., & Nelson, C. B. (1993). Sex and depression in the National Comorbidity Survey. I: Lifetime prevalence, chronicity and recurrence. *Journal of Affective Disorders, 29,* 85–96.

Kessler, R. C., McGonagle, K. A., Zhao, S., Nelson, C. B., Hughes, M., Eshleman, S., et al. (1994). Lifetime and 12-month prevalence of *DSM-III-R* psychiatric disorders in the United States:

Results from the National Comorbidity Survey. *Archives of General Psychiatry, 51,* 8–19.

Kessler, R. C., & McLeod, J. D. (1984). Sex differences in vulnerability to undesirable life events. *American Social Review, 49,* 620–631.

Kessler, R. C., Sonnega, A., & Bromet, E. (1995). Post-traumatic stress disorder in the National Comorbidity Survey. *Archives of General Psychiatry, 52,* 1048–1060.

Killien, M., Bigby, J. A., Champion, V., Fernandez-Repollet, E., Jackson, R. D., Kagawa-Singer, M., et al. (2000). Involving minority and underrepresented women in clinical trials: The National Centers of Excellence in Women's Health. *Journal of Women's Health and Gender-Based Medicine, 9*(10), 1061–1070.

Kite, M. E., Russo, N. F., Brehm, S. S., Fouad, N. A., Hall, C. C. I., Hyde, J. S., et al. (2001). Women psychologists in academe: Mixed progress, unwarranted complacency. *American Psychologist, 56*(12), 1080–1098.

Klier, C. M., Geller, P. A., & Neugebauer, R. (2000). Minor depressive disorder in the context of miscarriage. *Journal of Affective Disorders, 59*(1), 13–21.

Klier, C. M., Geller, P. A., & Ritsher, J. (2002). *Affective disorders in the aftermath of miscarriage: A critical review.* Manuscript submitted for publication.

Kline, J., Levin, B., Kinney, A., Stein, Z., Susser, M., & Warburton, D. (1995). Cigarette smoking and spontaneous abortion of known karyotype: Precise data but uncertain inferences. *American Journal of Epidemiology, 141,* 417–427.

Kohn, R., Dohrenwend, B. P., & Mirotznik, J. (1998). Epidemiological findings on selected psychiatric disorders in the general population. In B. P. Dohrenwend (Ed.), *Adversity, stress, and psychopathology* (pp. 235–284). New York: Oxford University Press.

Kohout, J. (2001). Who's earning those psychology degrees? *American Psychological Association Monitor, 32*(2), 42.

Kumar, R. (1994). Postnatal mental illness: A transcultural perspective. *Social Psychiatry and Psychiatric Epidemiology, 29,* 250–264.

Lampert, M. B., & Lang, R. M. (1995). Peripartum cardiomyopathy. *American Heart Journal, 130,* 860–870.

Lane, C., & Hobfoll, S. E. (1992). How loss affects anger and alienates potential support. *Journal of Clinical and Consulting Psychology, 60,* 935–942.

Lee, C. (1998). *Women's health: Psychological and social perspectives.* London: Sage.

Lee, C., & Slade, P. (1996). Miscarriage as a traumatic event: A review of the literature and new implications for intervention. *Journal of Psychosomatic Research, 40,* 235–244.

Leibenluft, E. (1999). Foreword. In E. Leibenluft (Ed.), *Gender differences in mood and anxiety disorders* (pp. xiii–xxii). Washington, DC: American Psychiatric Press.

Lennon, M. C. (1998). Domestic arrangements and depressive symptoms: An examination of housework conditions. In B. P. Dohrenwend (Ed.), *Adversity, stress, and psychopathology* (pp. 409–421). New York: Oxford University Press.

Leutz, W. N., Capitman, J. A., MacAdam, M., & Abrahams, R. (1992). *Care for frail elders: Developing community solutions.* Westport, CT: Auburn House.

Lex, B. W. (1992). Alcohol problems in special populations. In J. H. Mendelson & N. K. Mello (Eds.), *Medical diagnosis and treatment of alcoholism* (pp. 71–154). Saint Louis, MO: McGraw-Hill.

Llewellyn, A. M., Stowe, Z. N., & Nemeroff, C. B. (1997). Depression during pregnancy and the puerperium. *Journal of Clinical Psychiatry, 58*(15), 26–32.

Lurie, N., Margolis, K. L., McGovern, P. G., Mink, P. J., & Slater, J. S. (1997). Why do patients of female physicians have higher rates of breast and cervical cancer screening? *Journal of General Internal Medicine, 12,* 34–43.

Lurie, N., Slater, J., McGovern, P., Ekstrum, J., Quam, I., & Margolis, K. (1993). Preventive care for women: Does the sex of the physician matter? *New England Journal of Medicine, 329,* 478–482.

Malacrida, R., Genoni, M., Maggioni, A. P., Spataro, V., Parish, S., Palmer, A., et al. (1998). A comparison of the early outcome of acute myocardial infarction in women and men. *New England Journal of Medicine, 338*(1), 8–14.

Marks, S. R. (1977). Multiple roles and role strain: Some notes on human energy, time and commitment. *American Sociological Review, 41,* 921–936.

Marshall, N. L., & Barnett, R. C. (1991). Race and class and multiple role strains and gains among women employed in the service sector. *Women and Health, 17,* 1–19.

Marshall, N. L., & Barnett, R. C. (1993). Work-family strains and gains among two earner couples. *Journal of Community Psychology, 21,* 64–78.

Marshall, N. L., & Barnett, R. C. (1995, August). *Child care, division of labor and parental well-being among two earner couples.* Paper presented at the meeting of the American Sociological Association, Washington, DC.

Martins, C., & Gaffan, E. A. (2000). Effects of early maternal depression on patterns of infant-mother attachment: A meta-analytic investigation. *Journal of Child Psychology and Psychiatry, 41,* 737–746.

McCormick, L. H. (1995). Depression in mothers of children with attention deficit hyperactivity disorder. *Family Medicine, 27*(3), 176–179.

Miller, A. M., & Champion, V. L. (1997). Attitudes about breast cancer and mammography: Racial, income, and educational differences. *Women and Health, 26*(1), 41–63.

Miller, B. A., & Downs, W. R. (2000). Violence against women. In M. B. Goldman & M. C. Hatch (Eds.), *Women and health* (pp. 529–540). San Diego, CA: Academic Press.

Miller, B. A., Kolonel, L. N., Bernstein, L., Young, J. L., Jr., Swanson, G. M., West, D., et al. (Eds.). (1996). *Racial/ethnic patterns of cancer in the United States 1988–1992* (NIH Publication No. 96–4104). Bethesda, MD: National Cancer Institute.

Mitchell, J., Seim, H., Colon, E., & Pomeroy, C. (1987). Medical complications and medical management of bulimia. *Annals of Internal Medicine, 107,* 71–77.

Mitchell, J. E. (1995). Medical complications of bulimia nervosa. In K. D. Brownell & C. G. Fairburn (Eds.), *Eating disorders and obesity: A comprehensive handbook* (pp. 271–275). New York: Guilford Press.

Mondanaro, J. (1989). *Chemically dependent women: Assessment and treatment.* Lexington, MA: Lexington Books.

Morahan, P. S., Voytko, M. L., Abbuhl, S., Means, L. J., Wara, D. W., Thorson, J., et al. (2001). Ensuring the success of women faculty at AMC's: Lessons learned from the National Centers of Excellence in Women's Health. *Academic Medicine, 76,* 19–31.

Morokoff, P. J., Harlow, L. L., & Quina, K. (1995). Determinants of prenatal care use in Hawaii: Implications for health promotion. *American Journal of Preventive Medicine, 11*(2), 79–85.

Moy, E. V., & Christiani, D. C. (2000). Environmental exposures and cancer. In M. B. Goldman & M. C. Hatch (Eds.), *Women and health* (pp. 634–648). San Diego, CA: Academic Press.

Murray, C. J. L., & Lopez, A. D. (1996). Alternative visions of the future: Projecting mortality and disability, 1990–2020. In C. J. L. Murray & A. D. Lopez (Eds.), *The global burden of disease: A comprehensive assessment of mortality and disability from diseases, injuries, and risk factors in 1990 and projected to 2020* (pp. 325–395). Boston: Harvard University Press.

Murray, L., & Cooper, P. J. (Eds.). (1997). *Postpartum depression and child development.* London: Guilford Press.

Nadel, M. V. (1990). *National Institutes of Health: Problems implementing policy on women in study population* (U.S. General Accounting Office). Washington, DC: Author.

Narrow, W., Regier, D., Rae, D., Manderscheid, R. W., & Locke, B. Z. (1993). Use of services by persons with mental and addictive disorders. *Archives of General Psychiatry, 50,* 95–107.

Nathanson, C. A. (1975). Illness and the feminine role: A theoretical review. *Social Science and Medicine, 9,* 57–62.

National Cancer Institute. (1995). *Cancer facts.* Washington, DC: Author.

National Center for Health Statistics. (1996). *Health, United States, 1995.* Hyattsville, MD: Public Health Services.

National Osteoporosis Foundation. (2001). *Disease statistics fast facts.* Retrieved June 6, 2001, from www.nof.org/index.html

Ness, R. (2000). Cardiovascular disease and cardiovascular risk in women. In M. B. Goldman & M. C. Hatch (Eds.), *Women and health* (pp. 753–755). San Diego, CA: Academic Press.

Neugebauer, R., Dohrenwend, B. P., & Dohrenwend, B. S. (1980). Formulation of hypotheses about the true prevalence of functional psychiatric disorders among adults in the United States. In B. P. Dohrenwend, B. S. Dohrenwend, M. S. Gould, B. Link, R. Neugebauer, & R. Wunsch-Hitzig (Eds.), *Mental illness in the United States* (pp. 45–94). New York: Praeger.

Neugebauer, R., Kline, J., O'Connor, P., Shrout, P., Johnson, J., Skodol, A., et al. (1992). Depressive symptoms in women in the six months after miscarriage. *American Journal of Obstetrics and Gynecology, 166*(1, Pt. 1), 104–109.

Neugebauer, R., Kline, J., Shrout, P., Skodol, A., O'Connor, P., Geller, P. A., et al. (1997). Major depressive disorder in the 6 months after miscarriage. *Journal of the American Medical Association, 277*(5), 383–388.

Newton, K. M., Lacroix, A. Z., & Buist, D. S. (2000). Overview of risk factors for cardiovascular disease. In M. B. Goldman & M. C. Hatch (Eds.), *Women and health* (pp. 757–770). San Diego, CA: Academic Press.

Nezu, A. M., & Nezu, C. M. (1987). Psychological distress, problem solving, and coping reactions: Sex role differences. *Sex Roles, 16*(3/4), 205–214.

Northwestern National Life. (1992). *Employee burnout: Causes and cures.* Minneapolis, MN: Author.

Novella, A., Rosenberg, M., Saltzman, L., & Shosky, J. (1992). From the Surgeon General, U.S. public health service. *Journal of the American Medical Association, 267,* 3132.

Nybo Andersen, A. M., Wohlfahrt, J., Christens, P., Olsen, J., & Melbye, M. (2000). Maternal age and fetal loss: Population based register linkage study. *British Medical Journal, 320,* 1708–1712.

Office on Women's Health. (2000, May). *Women's health issues: An overview.* Retrieved March 2001, from www.4woman.gov/owh /pub/womhealth%20issues/index.htm

O'Hara, M. W., Schlechte, J. A., Lewis, D. A., & Varner, M. W. (1991). Controlled prospective study of postpartum mood disorders: Psychological, environmental and hormonal variables. *Journal of Abnormal Psychology, 100,* 63–73.

O'Hara, M. W., & Swain, A. M. (1996). Rates and risk of postpartum depression—a meta-analysis. *International Review of Psychiatry, 8,* 37–54.

Pavalko, E. K., & Woodbury, S. (2000). Social roles as process: Caregiving careers and women's health. *Journal of Health and Social Behavior, 41,* 91–105.

Pearson, G. D., Veille, J. C., Rahimtoola, S., Hsia, J., Celia, M., Hosenpud, J. D., et al. (2000). Peripartum cardiomyopathy: National heart, lung, and blood institute and office of rare diseases (National Institutes of Health) workshop recommendations and review. *Journal of the American Medical Association, 283*(9), 1183–1188.

Perry-Jenkins, M. (1993). Family roles and responsibilities: What has changed and what has remained the same. In J. Frankel (Ed.), *The employed mother and the family context* (pp. 245–259). New York: Springer.

Perry-Jenkins, M., & Crouter, A. C. (1990). Men's provider-role attitudes: Implications for household work and marital satisfaction. *Journal of Family Issues, 11,* 136–156.

Pigott, T. A. (1999). Gender differences in the epidemiology and treatment of anxiety disorders. *Journal of Clinical Psychiatry, 60*(Suppl. 18), 4–15.

Pike, K. M., & Striegel-Moore, R. H. (1997). Disordered eating and eating disorders. In S. J. Gallant, G. Puryear Keita, & R. Royak-Schaler (Eds.), *Health care for women: Psychological, social, and behavioral influences* (pp. 97–114). Washington, DC: American Psychological Association.

Pinn, V. W. (1994). The role of the NIH's Office of Research on Women's Health. *Academic Medicine, 69*(9), 698–702.

Pi-Sunyer, F. X. (1995). Medical complications of obesity. In K. D. Brownell & C. G. Fairburn (Eds.), *Eating disorders and obesity: A comprehensive handbook* (pp. 401–405). New York: Guilford Press.

Plichta, S. (1992). The effects of women abuse on health care utilization and health status: A literature review. *Jacobs Institute for Women's Health, 2*(3), 154–163.

Polivy, J., & McFarlane, T. L. (1998). Dieting, exercise, and body weight. In E. A. Blechman & K. D. Brownell (Eds.), *Behavioral medicine and women: A comprehensive handbook* (pp. 369–373). New York: Guilford Press.

Post, R. D. (1982). Dependency conflicts in high achieving women: Toward an integration. *Psychotherapy: Theory, Research, and Practice, 19,* 82–87.

Post, R. D. (1987, August). *Self sabotage among successful women.* Paper presented at the annual meeting of the American Psychological Association, New York.

Preston, D. B. (1995). Marital status, gender roles, stress, and health in the elderly. *Health Care for Women International, 16,* 149–165.

Putukian, M. (1994). The female triad: Eating disorders, amenorrhea, and osteoporosis. *Medical Clinics of North America, 78,* 345–356.

Regier, D. A., Farmer, M. E., Rae, D. S., Myers, J. K., Kramer, M., Robins, L. N., et al. (1993). One-month prevalence of mental disorders in the United States and sociodemographic characteristics: The Epidemiologic Catchment Area study. *Acta Psychiatrica Scandinavica, 88,* 35–47.

Reich, R. B., & Nussbaum, K. (1994). *Working women count! A report to the nation.* Washington, DC: U.S. Department of Labor, Women's Bureau.

Reifman, A., Biernat, M., & Lang, E. L. (1991). Stress, social support, and health in married professional women with small children. *Psychology of Women Quarterly, 15,* 431–435.

Repetti, R. L. (1993). The effects of workload and the social environment at work on health. In L. Goldberger & S. Breznitz (Eds.), *Handbook of stress: Theoretical and clinical aspects* (pp. 368–385). New York: Free Press.

Richardson, J. L. (1998). HIV infection. In E. A. Blechman & K. D. Brownell (Eds.), *Behavioral medicine and women: A comprehensive handbook* (pp. 659–663). New York: Guilford Press.

Rimer, B. K., McBride, C. M., & Crump, C. (2001). Women's health promotion. In A. Baum, T. R. Revenson, & J. E. Singer (Eds.), *Handbook of health psychology* (pp. 519–539). Mahwah, NJ: Erlbaum.

Robins, L., Helzer, J., Weismann, M., Orvaschel, H., Gruenberg, E., Burke, J. D., et al. (1984). Lifetime prevalence of specific psychiatric disorders in three sites. *Archives of General Psychiatry, 41*, 949–958.

Robins, L. N., Locke, B. Z., & Regier, D. A. (1991). An overview of psychiatric disorders in America. In L. N. Robins & D. A. Regier (Eds.), *Psychiatric disorders in America: The Epidemiological Catchment Area study* (pp. 258–290). New York: Free Press.

Rosenthal, C. J., Sulman, J., & Marshall, V. X. (1993). Depressive symptoms in family caregivers of long stay patients. *Gerontologist, 33*, 249–257.

Roter, D., Lipkin, M., Jr., & Korsgaard, A. (1991). Sex differences in patients' and physicians' communication during primary care medical visits. *Medical Care, 29*, 1083–1093.

Rouchell, A. M., Pounds, R., & Tierney, J. G. (1999). Depression. In J. R. Rundell & M. G. Wise (Eds.), *Textbook of consultation-liaison psychiatry* (pp. 121–147). Washington, DC: American Psychiatric Press.

Rowland, J. H. (1998). Breast cancer: Psychological aspects. In E. A. Blechman & K. D. Brownell (Eds.), *Behavioral medicine and women: A comprehensive handbook* (pp. 577–587). New York: Guilford Press.

Santonastaso, P., Pantano, M., Panarotto, L., & Silvestri, A. (1991). A follow-up study on anorexia nervosa: Clinical features and diagnostic outcome. *European Psychiatry, 6*, 177–185.

Saraiya, M., Green, C. A., Berg, C. J., Hopkins, F. W., Koonin, L. M., & Atrash, H. K. (1999). Spontaneous abortion: Related death among women in the United States, 1981–1991. *Obstetrics and Gynecology, 94*(2), 172–176.

Schlegel, M. (2000). Women mentoring women. *Monitor on Psychology, 31*(10), 33–36.

Schulman, K. A., Berlin, J. A., Harless, W., Kerner, J. F., Sistrunk, S., Gersh, B. J., et al. (1999). The effect of race and sex on physician's recommendations for cardiac catheterization. *New England Journal of Medicine, 340*(8), 618–625.

Schulz, R., O'Brien, A. T., Bookwala, J., & Fleissner, K. (1995). Psychiatric and physical morbidity effects of dementia caregiving: Prevalence, correlates, and causes. *Gerontologist, 35*, 771–791.

Schulz, R., Visintainer, P., & Williamson, G. M. (1990). Psychiatric and physical morbidity effects of caregiving. *Journal of Gerontology: Psychological Sciences, 45*, 181–191.

Sechzer, J. A., Denmark, F. L., & Rabinowitz, V. C. (1994, March). *Sex and gender as variables in cardiovascular research.* Paper presented at the Conference on Psychosocial and Behavioral Factors in Women's Health: Creating an agenda for the 21st century, program of the American Psychological Association, Washington, DC.

Shear, K. M., & Mammen, O. (1995). Anxiety disorder in pregnant and postpartum women. *Psychopharmacological Bulletin, 31*, 693–703.

Sieber, S. D. (1974). Towards a theory of role accumulation. *American Sociological Review, 39*, 567–578.

Siegler, I. C. (1998). Alzheimer's disease: Impact on women. In E. A. Blechman & K. D. Brownell (Eds.), *Behavioral medicine and women: A comprehensive handbook* (pp. 551–553). New York: Guilford Press.

Silbergeld, E. K. (2000). The environment and women's health: An overview. In M. B. Goldman & M. C. Hatch (Eds.), *Women and health* (pp. 601–606). San Diego, CA: Academic Press.

Silverman, E. K., Weiss, S. T., Drazen, J. M., Chapman, H. A., Carey, V., Campbell, E. J., et al. (2000). Gender-related differences in severe early onset chronic obstructive pulmonary disease. *American Journal of Respiratory and Critical Care Medicine, 162*, 2152–2158.

Sinclair, D., & Murray, L. (1998). Effects of postnatal depression on children's adjustment to school. *British Journal of Psychiatry, 172*, 58–63.

Smith Barney Research. (1997, April). *The new women's movement: Women's healthcare.* Available from women's health facts and links, The Society for the Advancement of Women's Health Research, womens-health.org/factsheet.html

Sobal, J. (1995). Social influences on body weight. In K. D. Brownell & C. G. Fairburn (Eds.), *Eating disorders and obesity: A comprehensive handbook* (pp. 73–82). New York: Guilford Press.

Sokol, M. S., & Gray, N. S. (1998). Anorexia nervosa. In E. A. Blechman & K. D. Brownell (Eds.), *Behavioral medicine and women: A comprehensive handbook* (pp. 350–357). New York: Guilford Press.

Steingart, R. M., Packer, M., Hamm, P., Coglianese, M. E., Gersh, B., Geltman, E. M., et al. (1991). Sex differences in the management of coronary artery disease. *New England Journal of Medicine, 325*(4), 226–230.

Stephen, E. H., & Chandra, A. (1997). Updated projections of infertility in the United States: 1995–2025. *Fertility and Sterilization, 70*, 30–34.

Stewart, D. (1992). Reproductive functions in eating disorders. *Annals of Medicine, 24*, 287–291.

Stewart, D. E., & Robinson, G. E. (1995). Violence against women. In J. M. Oldham & M. B. Riba (Eds.), *Review of psychiatry* (pp. 261–282). Washington, DC: American Psychiatric Press.

Stoffelmayr, B., Wadland, W. C., & Guthrie, S. K. (2000). Substance abuse. In M. A. Smith & L. A. Shimp (Eds.), *20 common problems in women's health care* (pp. 225–262). New York: McGraw-Hill.

Stoney, C. M. (1998). Coronary heart disease. In E. A. Blechman & K. D. Brownell (Eds.), *Behavioral medicine and women: A comprehensive handbook* (pp. 609–614). New York: Guilford Press.

Thapar, A. K., & Thapar, A. (1992). Psychological sequelae of miscarriage: A controlled study using the general health questionnaire and the hospital anxiety and depression scale. *British Journal of General Practice, 42*(356), 94–96.

Thompson, L., & Walker, A. J. (1989). Gender in families: Women and men in marriage, work, and parenthood. *Journal of Marriage and the Family, 51,* 845–871.

Toner, B. B. (1994). Cognitive-behavioral treatment of functional somatic syndromes: Integrating gender issues. *Cognitive and Behavioral Practice, 1,* 157–178.

Ursin, G., Spicer, D. V., & Bernstein, L. (2000). Breast cancer epidemiology, treatment, and prevention. In M. B. Goldman & M. C. Hatch (Eds.), *Women and health* (pp. 871–883). San Diego, CA: Academic Press.

U.S. Bureau of the Census. (1995). Income, poverty and valuation of noncash benefits: 1993. *Current population reports* (Series P-60, 198). Washington, DC: U.S. Government Printing Office.

U.S. Bureau of the Census. (1997). Poverty in the United States: 1996. *Current population reports* (Series P-60, 198). Washington, DC: U.S. Government Printing Office.

U.S. Bureau of the Census. (1999). *United States population estimates, by age, sex, race, and Hispanic origin, 1990 to 1997.* Available from www.census.gov/population/estimates/nation

U.S. Bureau of Labor Statistics. (1991, January). *Employment and earnings.* Washington, DC: U.S. Government Printing Office.

U.S. Bureau of Labor Statistics. (1997a). *Employment and earnings.* Washington, DC: U.S Government Printing Office.

U.S. Bureau of Labor Statistics. (1997b). *Employment characteristics of families: 1996.* Washington, DC: U.S. Government Printing Office.

U.S. Bureau of Labor Statistics. (1998). *Occupational injuries and illnesses: Counts, rates, and characteristics, 1995* [Bulletin 2493]. Washington, DC: U.S. Government Printing Office.

Ventura, S. J., Peters, K. D., Martin, J. A., & Maurer, J. D. (1997). Births and deaths: United States, 1996. *Monthly Vital Statistics Report, 46*(1), 1–40.

Waldron, I., & Jacobs, J. A. (1989). Effects of multiple roles on women's health: Evidence from a national longitudinal study. *Women and Health, 15,* 3–19.

Walker, A. J., Pratt, C. C., & Eddy, L. (1995). Informal caregiving to aging family members. *Family Relations, 44,* 402–411.

Whiteford, L. M., & Gonzalez, L. (1995). Stigma: The hidden burden of infertility. *Social Science in Medicine, 40,* 27–36.

Williams, K. E., & Koran, L. M. (1997). Obsessive-compulsive disorder in pregnancy, the puerperium, and the premenstruum. *Journal of Clinical Psychiatry, 58,* 330–334.

Winkleby, M. A., Fortmann, S. P., & Barrett, D. C. (1990). Social class disparities in risk factors for disease: Eight-year prevalence patterns by level of education. *Preventative Medicine, 19,* 1–12.

Wise, R. A. (1997). Changing smoking patterns and mortality from chronic obstructive pulmonary disease. *Preventive Medicine, 26,* 418–421.

Wisocki, P. A. (1998). Arthritis and osteoporosis. In E. A. Blechman & K. D. Brownell (Eds.), *Behavioral medicine and women: A comprehensive handbook* (pp. 562–565). New York: Guilford Press.

Wolf, P. A. (1990). An overview of the epidemiology of stroke. *Stroke, 21*(Suppl. 2), 4–6.

Yanovski, S. Z., Nelson, J. E., Dubbert, B. K., & Spitzer, R. L. (1993). Binge eating disorder is associated with psychiatric co-morbidity in the obese. *American Journal of Psychiatry, 150*(10), 1472–1479.

Yee, J. L., & Schulz, R. (2000). Gender differences in psychiatric morbidity among female caregivers: A review and analysis. *Gerontologist, 40,* 147–164.

Yudkin, P., & Redman, C. (2000). Prospective risk of stillbirth: Impending fetal death must be identified and pre-empted. *British Medical Journal, 320,* 444.

Zerbe, K. J. (1999). *Women's mental health in primary care.* Philadelphia: Saunders.

CHAPTER 23

Cultural Aspects of Health Psychology

KEITH E. WHITFIELD, GERDI WEIDNER, RODNEY CLARK, AND NORMAN B. ANDERSON

The composition of the United States is quickly becoming more demographically diverse, particularly in the number of people of color (e.g., Macera, Armstead, & Anderson, 2000). In addition, employment patterns among women have changed drastically since the 1950s. For example, the participation of U.S. women in the workforce has risen from 34% in 1950 to 60% in 1997 (Wagener et al., 1997). What implications does this social and economic diversity have for research in health psychology? It offers new and unique opportunities to examine how sociodemographic characteristics, health, and behavior are interconnected and creates new challenges for the improvement of health. For example, we might examine how differences in diet related to acculturation impact the incidence of chronic illnesses, such as cardiovascular disease (CVD), among Hispanics who migrate to this country, compared to CVD rates in their country of origin. In some cases, this means reexamining how well-studied biobehavioral relationships that contribute to increased incidence of disease may operate differently in certain people who may be adversely affected or protected due to social or contextual forces.

The National Institutes of Health (NIH) has responded to the growing research on sociodemographic factors that influence health. In 1990, the Office for Research on Minority Health was created by the director of the NIH. The mission of this office is to identify and supporting research opportunities to close the gap in health status of underserved populations, promote the inclusion of minorities in clinical trials, enhance the capacity of the minority community to address health problems, increase collaborative research and research training between minority and majority institutions, and improve the competitiveness and increase the numbers of well-trained minority scientists applying for NIH funding. Similarly, in 1990, the Office of Research on Women's Health was established in the NIH. Its mandate is to strengthen and enhance research focused on diseases and conditions that affect women and to ensure that women are adequately represented in research studies. In February 1998, President Clinton committed the United States to the elimination of health disparities in racial and ethnic minority populations by the year 2010. This "call to arms" requires a better understanding of the current status of health among minorities as well as identifying how social and economic classifications influence the treatment of disease and implementing programs to promote health behaviors. Responsive to these initiatives, this chapter provides a selective overview of health psychology research on sociodemographically diverse populations, with a focus on ethnicity, gender, and socioeconomic status (see chapter on aging by Siegler, Bosworth, & Elias in this volume). Last, we provide suggestions for future directions.

RACE/ETHNICITY

There are similarities and differences across ethnic groups in relation to the prevalence of health, disease, and health behaviors. To this end, we review reports on mortality and morbidity, major behavioral risk factors, and major biobehavioral risk factors among African Americans, Asian Americans, Latinos, and Native Americans separately. We conclude this section with a brief review of behavioral treatment and prevention programs.

African Americans

Morbidity and Mortality

One of the most striking demographic characteristics in health statistics continues to be the difference between African Americans and Caucasians. The age- and gender-adjusted death rate from all causes is 60% higher in African Americans than in Caucasians (U.S. Department of Health and Human Services [DHHS], 1995a). This difference in death rates for African Americans persists until age 85 (DHHS, 1995b), resulting in a life expectancy gap of 8.2 years for men and 5.9 years for women (DHHS, 1995a).

One of the major factors in this life expectancy gap is mortality from circulatory diseases. For example, heart disease continues to be the leading cause of death in the United States (Gardner, Rosenberg, & Wilson, 1996; National Heart Lung and Blood Institute [NHLBI], 1985; Peters, Kochanek, Murphy, 1998). Trends suggest that while heart disease is decreasing among Caucasian men, it may be increasing in African American men (Hames & Greenlund, 1996). Similarly, African Americans experience higher age-adjusted morbidity and mortality rates than Caucasians not only for coronary heart disease but also for stroke (NHLBI, 1985). For example, the NHLBI examined the 1980 age-adjusted stroke mortality rates by state and found 11 states with stroke death rates that were more than 10% higher than the U.S. average. These states included Alabama, Arkansas, Georgia, Indiana, Kentucky, Louisiana, Mississippi, North Carolina, South Carolina, Tennessee, and Virginia. The NHLBI and others have designated these 11 states as the "Stroke Belt." These "Stroke Belt" states also correspond with some of the highest populations of older African American adults.

Deaths associated with CVD arise from a myriad of risk factors including elevated blood pressure, cigarette smoking, hypercholesterolimia, excess body weight, sedentary lifestyle, and diabetes, all of which are influenced to varying degrees by behavioral factors (e.g., Manson et al., 1991; Powell, Thompson, Caspersen, Kendrick, 1987; Stamler,

Stamler, & Neaton, 1993; Willet et al., 1995; Winkleby, Kraemer, Ahn, & Varady, 1998). The clustering (comorbidity) of coronary heart disease risk factors in African Americans appears to play an important role in excess mortality from coronary heart disease observed in African Americans (Potts & Thomas, 1999).

Major Behavioral Risk and Protective Factors

Tobacco Use.   In the general population, tobacco consumption slowed down when the deleterious health effects of cigarette smoking were made public in the 1950s. Cigarette smoking prevalence reaches a peak between the ages of 20 and 40 years among both men and women and then decreases in later adulthood; but across all ages, smoking prevalence is higher among males than among females. Smoking is more prevalent among African Americans than Caucasians (Escobedo, & Peddicord, 1996; Garfinkel, 1997). Even among minority groups, African Americans experience the most significant health burden (*Mortality and Morbidity Weekly Report [MMWR]*, 1998; "Response to Increases," 1998).

Diet.   The age-adjusted prevalence of overweight adults continues to be higher for African American women (53%) than for Caucasian women (34%; National Center for Health Statistics [NCHS], 2000). The prevalence of obesity among African American women has reached epidemic proportions (Flynn & Fitzgibbon, 1998). A number of studies attribute the high rate of obesity in women in part to differences in body images, suggesting that African American women subscribe to the belief that overweight bodies are more attractive, but the results are still not completely clear because of divergent methodologies (see Flynn & Fitzgibbon, 1998). Nutritional status, which contributes to obesity, among minority populations may be adversely affected by a number of factors associated either directly or indirectly with aging (Buchowski & Sun, 1996).

Physical Activity.   In minority samples, physical activity has been linked to decreased risk for diabetes (D. Clark, 1997; Manson, Rimm, and Stampfler, et al., 1991; Ransdell & Wells, 1998), CVD (Yanek et al., 1998), and blood pressure regulation (e.g., Agurs-Collins, Kumanyika, Ten Have, & Adams-Campbell, 1997). Conversely, there is evidence to suggest that African Americans do not exercise at the same rates as Caucasians (Sallis, Zakarian, Hovell, & Hofstetter, 1996; Young, Miller, Wilder, Yanek, Becker, 1998). Women of color, women over 40, and women without a college education have been shown to participate the least in a study of leisure time physical activity (Ransdell & Wells, 1998). This may be due, in part, to differences in body perception and visual cues suggesting the need to regulate weight. For example, in a study by Neff, Sargent, McKeown, Jackson, and Valois (1997), Caucasian adolescents were more likely to perceive themselves as being overweight as compared to African American adolescents. This difference in perception could translate into unhealthy weight management practices during adulthood that impact long-term consequences for health (Neff, Sargent, McKeown, Jackson, & Valois, 1997).

Sexual Behavior. Young African Americans are emerging as a group at significant risk for contracting human immunodeficiency virus (HIV; Maxwell, Bastani, & Warda, 1999). Data from the National Health and Social Life Survey (NHSLS) showed that African Americans were almost five times more likely to be infected by sexually transmitted diseases (STDs) than the other racial/ethnic group (Laumann & Youm, 1999). In another study, Cummings, Battle, Barker, and Krasnovsky (1999) found that 64% of African American women surveyed did not express AIDS-related worry. Their results indicated that African American women were not protecting themselves by using condoms or by careful partner selection.

Alcohol Abuse. Alcohol-related problems are strong predictors of intimate partner violence among African Americans (Cunradi, Caetano, Clark, & Schafer, 1999). Using data from two nationwide probability samples of U.S. households between 1984 and 1995, Caetano and Clark (1999) found that the rates of frequent heavy drinking and alcohol-related problems have remained especially high among African American and Hispanic men. In a study by Black, Rabins, and McGuire (1998), African Americans with a current or past alcohol disorder were 7.5 times more likely than others to die during a 28-month follow-up period.

Social Support. Social factors such as social support (e.g., Cohen, & Syme, 1985; Dressler, Dos-Santos, Viteri, 1986; House, Landis, & Umberson, 1988; Strogatz & James, 1986; Williams, 1992) and religious participation (Livingston, Levine, & Moore, 1991) have been found to be important predictors of health outcomes. Health is also adversely influenced by psychological factors such as hostility (Barefoot et al., 1991), anger (e.g., Kubzansky, Kawachi, & Sparrow, 1999), perceived stress (Dohrenwend, 1973; McLeod, & Kessler, 1990), and stress coping styles (S. James, Hartnett, & Kalsbeek, 1983). Some previous research suggests associations between health and social support in African Americans (e.g., J. Jackson, 1988; J. Jackson, Antonucci, & Gibson, 1990; S. James, 1984). From

this research, three conclusions can be drawn: (a) Social disorganization is related to elevated stroke mortality rates, (b) individuals in cohesive families are at reduced risk for elevated blood pressure, and (c) social ties and support play a positive role in reducing elevated blood pressure (J. Jackson et al., 1990; S. James, 1984).

Major Biobehavioral Risk Factors

The most studied biobehavioral risk factor for poor health among African Americans is cardiovascular reactivity. Research by V. Clark, Moore, and Adams (1998) showed that both low and high density lipoprotein cholesterol (LDL, HDL) were significant predictors of blood pressure responses in a sample of African American college students. They also found a positive correlation between total serum cholesterol and LDL, and stroke volume, contractile force, and blood pressure reactivity. These findings suggest that cardiovascular reactivity to stress may be a new risk factor for heart and vascular diseases. (V. Clark et al., 1998).

Research suggests that neighborhoods and socioeconomic status (SES) act as risk factors for stress reactivity for African Americans. Lower family SES and lower neighborhood SES have been found to produce greater cardiovascular reactivity to laboratory stressors in African Americans (Gump, Matthews, & Raikkonen, 1999; R. Jackson, Treiber, Turner, Davis, & Strong, 1999).

Asian Americans/Pacific Islanders

Morbidity and Mortality

Heart disease and cancer are leading causes of death for Asians and Pacific Islanders (APIs). Hoyert and Kung (1997) found a great variation in the leading causes of deaths by age among the API subgroups, which included Samoan, Hawaiian, Asian Indian, Korean, and Japanese. They also found that age-adjusted death rates were the greatest and life expectancy was the lowest for Samoan and Hawaiian populations (Hoyert & Kung, 1997).

Prevalence of diabetes has been found to be high among Hawaiians, which suggests that other Asian and Pacific Island populations may share similar susceptibility to diabetes (Grandinetti et al., 1998).

Major Behavioral Risk and Protective Factors

Tobacco Use. Relatively little is known about Asian American tobacco and alcohol use patterns. The little that is known suggests that Chinese use less tobacco than other cultures. For example, a study by Thridandam, Fong, Jang, Louie, and Forst (1998) indicates that the prevalence of both tobacco and alcohol use is lower for San Francisco's Chinese population than for the general population.

Diet. There are complicated scenarios related to diet and acculturation among Asian Americans. For example, acculturation has been found to affect dietary patterns of Korean Americans. Korean Americans who were more acculturated ate more "American foods" such as oranges, low-fat milk, bagels, tomatoes, and bread mostly during breakfast meals (S. Lee, Sobal, & Frongillo, 1999). In contrast, there may be lost health benefits for Asian Americans who opt to change to American-style diets rather than more traditional Asian diets. For example, there is evidence that Japanese diets may reduce the prevalence of diabetes (Huang et al., 1996) and that soy intake among Asians may be related to a reduction in the risk of breast cancer (Wu, 1998).

Physical Activity. As in other minority groups, there is evidence that physical activity serves as a protective factor against chronic illness among Asian Americans. Research on Japanese American men who participated in the Honolulu Heart Program study suggests that physical activity is associated inversely with incident diabetes, coronary heart disease morbidity, and mortality (Burchfiel et al., 1995a, 1995b; Rodriguez et al., 1994).

Sexual Behavior. Nationally, the incidence of AIDS is increasing at a higher rate among Asian and Pacific Islander American men who have sex with men than among Caucasians (Choi, Yep, Kumekawa, 1998). It has been reported that the rate of new AIDS cases among API men who have sex with men increased by 55% from 1989 (4.0%) to 1995 (6.2%; Sy, Chng, Choi, & Wong, 1998). However, most of the discussions have focused on the relatively low prevalence of APIs with AIDS in the United States (Sy et al., 1998). Underestimating the risk of HIV may increase unsafe sex practices and subsequently increase AIDS cases in this population.

Alcohol Abuse. Cheung (1993) suggests that a review of the literature finds consistently low levels of alcohol consumption and drinking problems among the Chinese in America. Previous research has attempted to explain these low levels using two theories: (a) The physiological explanation attributes the light alcohol use among the Chinese to their high propensity to flush, which protects them from heavy drinking or; (b) a cultural explanation that suggests Chinese cultural values emphasize moderation and self-restraint,

which discourages drinking to the point of drunkenness. Cheung's (1993) review of the existing research shows that neither theory seems to provide an adequate explanation of the current empirical findings.

Social Support. The role of social support as a factor in health among minorities is also evident among Asian Americans. In an examination of the nature of social support for Asian American and Caucasian women following breast cancer treatment, Wellisch et al. (1999) found differences in the size, mode, and perceived adequacy of social support that favored Caucasians. This is not to imply social support does not promote health among Asian Americans but that social support does not appear to be as prevalent for Asian Americans as for Caucasians.

Major Biobehavioral Risk Factors

The impact of stress on health is also a biobehavioral risk factor in American Asians. Research suggests that most newly arrived Amerasians experience acculturative stress in areas of spoken English, employment, and limited formal education (Nwadiora & McAdoo, 1996). The impact of this stress on biomedical indicators of health has yet to be examined empirically.

Latino(a) Americans

Morbidity and Mortality

While most of the research on ethnic minorities and CVD risk factors has focused on African Americans, some studies suggest that there are also higher prevalence rates of excess weight, diabetes, untreated hypertension, cigarette smoking, and low-density lipoprotein cholesterol in Mexican Americans compared to Caucasians (Kuczmarski, Flegal, Cambell, & Johnson, 1994; Sundquist & Winkleby, 1999). Studies have also shown that the incidence and rate of CVD mortality are higher for Hispanic women compared to Caucasians (Kautz, Bradshaw, & Fonner, 1981). When age differences are taken into account, Mexican-American men and women also have elevated blood pressure rates compared to Caucasians (NCHS, 2000).

As in other populations, Latinos/Latinas experience higher age-adjusted stroke rates compared to Caucasians (e.g., Karter et al., 1998). Sacco et al. (1998) found that Hispanics had a twofold increase in stroke incidence compared with Caucasians. Furthermore, Haan and Weldon (1996) found that among community-dwelling elderly Hispanics and Caucasians, Hispanics experienced greater levels of disability from stroke, which they attribute to lower socioeconomic status, and higher prevalence of other disabling conditions.

Major Behavioral Risk and Protective Factors

Tobacco Use. Research on self-reported nicotine dependence shows that Hispanics were less likely than Caucasians to smoke on a daily basis, to smoke at least 15 cigarettes a day, and, among daily smokers, to smoke within 30 minutes of awakening (Navarro, 1996). Interestingly, acculturation appears to play an important role in the incidence of smoking among Hispanics. Navarro (1996) also found that Hispanics from households in which English was a second language (less acculturated), were less likely to be daily smokers and to smoke more than 15 cigarettes a day than those who were acculturated (those from households in which English was the primary language).

Diet. In relation to eating habits, Hispanics have been found to be more likely than Caucasians to report inadequate intake of vegetables, problems with teeth or dentures that limited the kinds and amounts of food eaten, difficulty preparing meals, and lack of money needed to buy food (Marshall, 1999). Hispanic women also report more nutritional risk factors than Hispanic men; however, other indicators suggest that Hispanic men may be at higher risk of nutritional deficiency (Marshall, 1999).

Physical Activity. While research clearly demonstrates physical activity is inversely related to the development of chronic illnesses, the data on the level of physical activity among Hispanics is mixed. Some evidence suggests that Hispanics are more physically active than other ethnic groups. For example, in a telephone study of African American, Hispanic, American Indian/Alaskan Native, and Caucasian women age 40 and older, Hispanic women were more likely to have high physical activity scores than the other racial/ethnic groups investigated (Eyler et al., 1999). However, the larger body of evidence suggests that Hispanics do not differ from the low levels reported in other ethnic groups. For example, data from National Health and Nutrition Examination Survey (NHANES) show rates of inactivity are greater for women, older persons, non-Hispanic blacks, and Mexican Americans (Crespo, Keteyian, Heath, & Sempos, 1996).

Sexual Behavior. There appear to be increasing trends of HIV/AIDS among Hispanic populations. The trends seem to be accounted for by unprotected sex, unprotected sex with injected drug users, reporting heterosexual contact with an HIV-infected partner whose risk was not specified, and an increase

in the cases among foreign-born Hispanics (e.g., Diaz & Klevens, 1997; Klevens, Diaz, Fleming, Mays, & Frey, 1999; Neal, Fleming, Green, & Ward, 1997). Of all modes of exposure to HIV, heterosexual contact has increased the most rapidly (Neal et al., 1997). African Americans and Hispanics account for three-fourths of all AIDS cases that could be attributed to heterosexual contact between 1988 and 1995 (Neal et al., 1997).

Culture and acculturation appear to be important factors in HIV/AIDS among Hispanics. There appears to be differences in behavioral risks for HIV/AIDS among Hispanics, depending on the subgroup and cultural factors of subgroups. For example, Diaz and Klevens (1997) found in a sample of Latinos that Puerto Rican men were more likely to have injected drugs than men from Central America. In contrast, they also found that male-male sex was the most common mode of exposure to HIV, except among Puerto Ricans. Results from research by Hines and Caetano (1998) indicate that less acculturated Hispanic men and women were more likely to engage in risky sexual behavior than those who were more acculturated.

Alcohol Abuse. In general, Hispanics continue to be more at risk than Caucasians for developing a number of alcohol-related problems (Caetano, 1997). Prevalence rates of past heavy drinking among Mexican American and Puerto Rican males are approximately three times higher than rates reported for non-Hispanic male populations (D. Lee, Markides, & Ray, 1997). Research on trends in frequent heavy drinking and alcohol-related problems in Hispanics shows relatively stable patterns for women but increased rates for men over the same period (Caetano & Clark, 1998). Research on alcohol use among Hispanics indicates that less acculturated men drank more than those who were more acculturated, but among women the opposite was true (Hines & Caetano, 1998).

Social Support. Although low levels of social support have been related to CVD mortality among African Americans, little is known about the role of social support among Mexican Americans. In the Corpus Christi Heart Project (Farmer et al., 1996), survival following myocardial infarction was greater for those with high or medium social support than for those with low social support. Specifically for Mexican Americans, the relative risk of mortality was 3.38 (95% Confidence Intervals (CI), 1.73–6.62) for those with low social support (Farmer et al., 1996). Furthermore, informal social support networks, such as extended families and civic clubs, were seen as more helpful for African Americans and Hispanics as compared with Caucasians in assisting cancer patients with continuing treatment (Guidry, Aday, Zhang, & Winn, 1997).

Major Biobehavioral Risk Factors

There is emerging evidence that acculturative stress among Hispanics may impact health. Ontiveros, Miller, Markides, and Espino (1999) found that higher levels of education and language acculturation among Mexican Americans were risk factors for having a stroke. They interpret their finding to suggest that Mexican Americans who are less acculturated are more healthy and that acculturation may increase stroke morbidity and mortality. Goslar et al. (1997) found that among Mexican American women, there was a relationship between acculturation and higher systolic and diastolic blood pressure that was independent of diet, body composition, and physical activity.

Native Americans

Morbidity and Mortality

American Indians (AI)/Alaskan Natives (AN) represent greater than 1% of the total U.S. population (272 million persons) and are culturally diverse; 557 of the many tribes are federally recognized ("HIV/AIDS among American Indians," 1998). Mortality data reveal excess overall mortality among AI/AN, as well as excesses for specific causes of death, including accidents, diabetes, liver disease, pneumonia/influenza, suicide, homicide, and tuberculosis (Mahoney & Michalek, 1998). For example, in an analysis of data from NHANES II, age-specific prevalence of diabetes in Alaskan Eskimos was similar to that found in U.S. Caucasians but were the highest reported to date (Ebbesson et al., 1998). In contrast, there is almost a "deficit" of deaths noted for heart disease, cancer, and HIV infections in this population.

Major Behavioral Risk and Protective Factors

Poor socioeconomic conditions, lack of education, and cultural barriers contribute to the enduring poor health status of AI/AN. While health care is free to many in this population, it is limited, inadequately funded, or has a limited focus on preventative care (Joe, 1996). For example, only 50% of AIs/ANs have had their cholesterol checked in the past two years (NCHS, 2000).

Tobacco Use.   Unusually high rates of smokeless tobacco have been found in some Native American populations (Spangler et al., 1999). Kimball, Goldberg, and Oberle (1996) found that cigarette smoking was more prevalent among American Indian men and women than it was in the general population in the same geographic area. Of the American Indians interviewed, 43% of men and 54% of women reported that they currently smoked (Kimball et al., 1996). However, on closer examination of their smoking habits, they tended to smoke much less heavily than smokers in the general population.

Diet.   As in other ethnic groups, diet has been implicated as a primary risk factor in the development of chronic diseases among American Indian tribes. There is concern that the dietary transition from traditional foods to more market (store-bought) foods among indigenous populations will bring about a rise in diet-related chronic disease (Whiting & Mackenzie, 1998). Foods like bacon, sausage, and fried bread and potatoes are high-fat foods frequently consumed by Native Americans (Ballew et al., 1997; Harnack, Story, & Rock, 1999). As in many other ethnic groups, research has found low levels of consumption of fruits and vegetables (Ballew et al., 1997; Harnack et al., 1999). The lack of fruit and vegetable consumption is thought to be due to barriers such as cost, availability, and quality (Harnack et al., 1999).

Physical Activity.   As with the other risk factors for chronic illness among Native Americans, the significant heterogeneity and unique aspects of individual tribes produce variability in the results on physical activity reported in the current literature. However, most of the previous research suggests that Native Americans do not participate in physical activity at levels sufficient to protect against the development of cardiovascular disease risk factors, obesity, and noninsulin-dependent diabetes mellitus (NIDDM; Adler, Boyko, Schraer, & Murphy, 1996; de Groot & van Staveren, 1995; Harnack, Story, & Rock, 1999; Yurgalevitch et al.). This lack of physical activity has been ascribed to a change from traditional activities and lifestyle that require greater energy expenditure (Adler et al., 1996; Ravussin, Valencia, Esparza, Bennett, & Schulz, 1994).

Sexual Behavior.   There is relatively little literature on sexual behavior, sexually transmitted diseases, and HIV/AIDS among AI/AN populations. Less than 1% of the AIDS cases reported to the Centers for Disease Control (CDC) from 1981 through December 1997 (1,783 or 0.3%) occurred in AI/AN populations ("HIV/AIDS among American Indians," 1998). While the number of AIDS cases is low among this population, there is concern that the future could bring significant increases in prevalence. The primary sources of increases in the number of AIDS cases are predicted to occur from increases in nontraditional lifestyles and sexual partnerships composed of Native American women and Caucasian men who are injection drug users (Fenaughty et al., 1998).

Alcohol Abuse.   Contact with European Americans has caused dramatic increases in the use and changes in the function of alcoholic beverages among AI/AN societies (Abbott, 1996). Acute heavy drinking has been found to be prevalent among Native Americans. In a study by Kimball et al. (1996) of Northwest Indians, 40% of men and 33% of women reported acute heavy drinking for the previous month. Although much has been made about high rates of alcoholism among Native Americans, the rate of alcohol metabolism has been shown to be the same as in Caucasians (Gill, Eagle Elk, Liu, & Deitrich, 1999). In addition, there is evidence that older urban American Indians are not different from other older people with respect to consumption of alcohol (J. Barker & Kramer, 1996). Why then is there such prevalence of alcoholism among Native Americans? Further research is necessary to address the issues of Native Americans to gather a clearer picture for the creation and implementation of culturally sensitive and effective prevention programs.

Social Support.   Similar to findings in other ethnic minorities, available research seems to suggest social support is related to health among AI/AN populations. A study of Navajo Indians' family support (family characteristics and the amount of family support the patient perceived) at the time of hospitalization showed greater perceived support was associated with longer length of stay (R. Williams, Boyce, & Wright, 1993). These results provide support for the notion that social systems gain importance not from structure but from their function (R. Williams, Boyce, & Wright, 1993). The context in which Native Americans live also contributes to the amount of social support. Frederickes and Kipnis (1996) found that urban Native Americans reported receiving less social support than rural Native Americans. Social support research on Native Americans shows social support is related to health behaviors. Spangler, Bell, Dignan, and Michielutte (1997) found that cigarette smoking was related to separated or divorce status and low church participation. In contrast, they also found that smokeless tobacco use was associated with widowed marital status and having a high number of friends.

Major Biobehavioral Risk Factors

One of the major challenges for Native Americans is to balance their cultural values with the larger American societal values. The difficult interpersonal struggle to create this balance causes some to commit suicide. Suicide rates have been found to positively correlate with acculturation stress and negatively with traditional integration (e.g., Lester, 1999).

Behavioral Treatment and Prevention Approaches for Ethnic Minorities

Many protective factors are associated with the reduction of health problems. There is growing evidence that behavioral interventions could significantly reduce the mortality and morbidity burden experienced by minority populations. Reducing morbidity through health promotion and disease prevention could both improve the quality of life and lessen the burden on the health care system. The challenge is to create interventions that include information about nutrition and promote physical activity in culturally appropriate ways (see Buchowski & Sun, 1996).

In an effort to reduce chronic illness among ethnic minorities, behavioral treatment and prevention programs are being developed. There are difficulties common to all interventions: language, culture, and interactions between ethnicity and SES. Difficulties due to language differences include the translation of materials in another language while maintaining the meaning and significance of the message being communicated. Differences in culture preclude being able to simply apply successful treatment and prevention programs across minority groups. The interaction between ethnicity and SES has been addressed by attempting to account for acculturation but may also drive the need for ethnic by SES group-specific programs.

Smoking Interventions

Successful smoking cessation exists but little is known about the psychosocial factors that influence smoking cessation among ethnic minorities (e.g., Nevid, Javier, & Moulton, 1996). While information alone is not enough to produce a behavioral change as complex as quitting smoking, many researchers believe that culturally appropriate messages about the health consequences of smoking is a critical motivating factor in a smoking cessation program (e.g., Marin et al., 1990; Vander, Cummings, & Coates, 1990), and these programs need strategies that reflect ethnoculturally specific features (Parker et al., 1996).

There are numerous areas of investigation and changes to be made to create culturally appropriate smoking interventions. These changes include, but are not limited to: (a) directing efforts toward promoting cessation through proven behavioral and pharmacological approaches, (b) making new smoking prevention and cessation programs tailored for minorities by focusing on smoking as a family-wide issue, (c) identifying sources of cultural stress and adding stress-reduction techniques to smoking cessation programs, (d) focusing on group-specific attitudes and expectancies about quitting smoking, and

(e) addressing the effect of acculturation in shaping attitudes and expectancies (particularly among Hispanics; Ahluwalia, Resnicow, & Clark, 1998; DHHS, 1998; Klonoff & Landrine, 1999).

Physical Activity Interventions

A review of the literature suggests that there are relatively few studies of physical activity interventions for minorities (Stone, McKenzie, Welk, & Booth, 1998). Of these results, several document programs that significantly increase the aerobic fitness with a moderate exercise training regimen and are culturally appropriate (for review, see Duey et al., 1998). In studies of barriers to physical activity among minorities, the most common environmental barriers included safety, availability, cost, transportation, child care, lack of time, health concerns, lack of motivation, and an exercise environment that includes Blacks (Carter-Nolan, Adams-Campbell, & Williams, 1996; Eyler et al., 1998; Jones & Nies, 1996). The social dimension of the planned activity may be as important as the selection of activities. Research in this area suggests that community-based exercise programs that are specific to African Americans are needed (Jones & Nies, 1996). So, the challenge is to create culturally appropriate physical activity programs (D. Clark, 1997). Data from adolescents suggest that there is need for specificity in the selection of physical activities (Sallis et al., 1996). For example, swimming is not seen as a viable activity among African Americans because of the effect of water and chlorine on their hair.

A review of the literature on physical activity in African Americans suggests that greater attention is needed in the development of culturally appropriate instruments. These instruments should include well-defined, inoffensive terminology, and increase the recall of unstructured and intermittent physical activities (Tortolero, Masse, Fulton, Torres, & Kohl, 1999).

Dietary Interventions

Given the high rates of obesity among minority populations, particularly minority women, and the consequences for chronic illness, dietary interventions are critical to improving the health of ethnic minorities. A realistic diet plan should be based on individual needs, economic status, availability of food, likes and dislikes, lifestyle, and family dynamics (Kaul & Nidiry, 1999). Two critical components to successful dietary intervention among minority populations are individualized diets and sensitivity to food preferences (Kaul & Nidiry, 1999). In addition to nutrition education, the development of exercise and behavior modification related to food intake must also be taught in dietary interventions.

GENDER

One universal inequity that cuts across both ethnic and socioeconomic class lines is the gender gap in life expectancy. On average, men die seven years earlier than women (National Vital Statistics Reports, 1999). Almost all of the 10 leading causes of death for the entire population in 1997 show men to be at greater risk than women. That is, the male-to-female ratios of age-adjusted death rates exceeded 1.3 for the number one killer, diseases of the heart (ratio = 1.8), followed by malignant neoplasms (ratio = 1.4), chronic obstructive pulmonary diseases and allied conditions (ratio = 1.5), accidents (ratio = 2.4), pneumonia and influenza (ratio = 1.5), suicides (ratio = 4.2), kidney diseases (ratio = 1.5), and chronic liver disease and cirrhosis (ratio = 2.3; National Vital Statistics Reports, 1999). These causes of mortality accounted for 70.7% of deaths among men and women in the United States in 1997. It should be noted that very large male-to-female ratios were recorded for homicide and HIV infection (3.8 and 3.5, respectively). However, deaths due to these causes ranked 13 and 14 among the leading 15 causes of death for the population in 1997, each accounting for only 0.7% of total deaths (National Vital Statistics Reports, 1999). Several factors might account for the gender gap in life expectancy. These can be grouped into four categories: biological, behavioral, psychosocial, and biobehavioral.

Biological Factors

In her now-classic papers dealing with the question, "Why do women live longer than men?" Waldron concludes that "physiological differences have not been shown to make any substantial contribution to higher male death rates" (Waldron & Johnston, 1976, p. 23; also see Waldron, 1976). This conclusion has not changed much over the past decades. Although men's greater vulnerability to infectious diseases (attributed in part to lower levels of serum level of immunoglobulin M [IgM]) is a probable contributor to the greater male mortality in several of the leading causes of death, gender differences in IgM are present only between the ages of 5 and 65 (Reddy, Fleming, & Adesso, 1992). However, males still have higher rates of infectious diseases than females before and after these age markers (Reddy et al., 1992). Even the role of estrogens in the protection from heart disease among women has been questioned (Barrett-Connor, 1997; Barrett-Connor & Stuenkel, 1999). Furthermore, international data on coronary heart disease (CHD) mortality from 46 communities in 24 countries show that although CHD mortality rates in women are less than male rates, male-to-female ratios vary widely, ranging from 10 to

1 in Iceland to 10 to 6 in Beijing, China (Jackson et al., 1998). The fact that the differences between countries are larger than the difference between the sexes suggests that "male anatomy is not destiny," at least in regard to CHD. Additionally, the epidemic of cardiovascular disease among Eastern European men has widened the gender gap in life expectancy over a very brief time span, suggesting that nongenetic factors play a role (Weidner, 1998; Weidner & Mueller, 2000).

Behavioral Factors

Behavioral factors are involved in many of the major causes of death. Specifically, cigarette smoking has been linked to heart disease, lung cancer (the major form of malignant neoplasms), chronic obstructive pulmonary disease, and pneumonia. Excessive alcohol consumption increases the risk for a number of diseases—foremost, heart and liver disease. Alcohol, along with lack of seat belt use, also plays a major role in motor vehicle accidents. Other "accidental deaths," such as homicide and suicide, often involve firearms. Overeating, unhealthy diets, and lack of exercise (resulting in obesity) contribute to almost all chronic diseases. In regard to obesity, it appears that adverse health effects are primarily associated with abdominal fat accumulation (Lapidus et al., 1988; Larsson et al., 1988).

Examining gender differences in these behaviors (with the exception of overeating and exercise) favors women (Reddy et al., 1992; Waldron, 1995). With regard to overeating (quantity), the sexes appear to be similar. However, one consequence of overeating, fat distribution, favors women; men have a tendency to accumulate fat in the abdominal region (becoming "apple-shaped"), whereas most women accumulate fat in a "pear-shaped" fashion. There seems to be some evidence that men's diets have a higher ratio of saturated- to polyunsaturated fat and men have lower vitamin C intake than women (Connor et al., in press; Waldron, 1995). This ratio could contribute to men's elevated risk for CHD and cancers. The only gender difference favoring men consistently appears to be exercise. However, this may be due to the use of questionnaires designed for men, which focus on sports and neglect physical activities associated with housework (Barrett-Connor, 1997).

Furthermore, stress may play a greater role for health-damaging behaviors among men than among women. For example, job strain appears to be associated with increases in health-damaging behaviors (e.g., cigarette smoking, excessive alcohol and coffee consumption, lack of exercise) among men, but not among women (Weidner, Boughal, Connor, Pieper, & Mendell, 1997). Thus, considering the major be-

haviors involved in many causes of death, women clearly fare better than men.

Of the leading causes of death, the most information is available for heart disease, which still ranks number one as the cause of death in the United States, accounting for 31.4% of total deaths in 1997 (National Vital Statistics Reports, 1999). To what extent gender differences in health behaviors contribute to the observed gender difference in many of the leading causes of death remains unclear. The study by Jackson and colleagues (Jackson et al., 1998) sheds some light on this question, at least in regard to the leading cause of death, CHD. Based on their analyses of five major coronary risk factors (elevated blood pressure, elevated cholesterol, low HDL cholesterol, cigarette smoking, and obesity), the authors conclude that 40% of the variation in the gender ratios of CHD mortality in 24 countries could be explained by gender differences in these five risk factors. While these results underscore the importance of these factors for heart disease and suggest that interventions aimed at reducing levels of these risk factors in men would narrow the gender gap in CHD mortality, they also point to other factors that contribute to the gender gap.

Psychosocial Factors

Although "other" factors have not been investigated as much as behavioral factors, evidence of adverse health effects is accumulating for several psychosocial characteristics: Hostility/anger, depression or vital exhaustion, lack of social support, and work stress all have prospectively been linked to premature mortality from all causes, although most studies focus on heart disease mortality (Barefoot, Larsen, von der Lieth, & Schroll, 1995; Cohen & Herbert, 1996; Hemingway & Marmot, 1999; House et al., 1988; Miller, Smith, Turner, Guijarro, & Haller, 1996; Rozanski, Blumenthal, & Kaplan, 1999; Schnall, Landsbergis, & Baker, 1994; Shumaker & Czajkowski, 1994; Uchino, Cacioppo, & Kiecolt-Glaser, 1996; Weidner & Mueller, 2000).

Gender-specific associations of personality attributes (Type A behavior, hostility), negative emotions (particularly depression), and social support to heart disease have been summarized previously (Orth-Gomer & Chesney, 1997; Schwarzer & Rieckman, in press; Weidner, 1995; Weidner & Mueller, 2000). Not only is the relationship of these risk factors to heart disease stronger in men than in women (e.g., Wulsin et al., 1999), but also women appear to be at an advantage when considering individual risk factor levels: They score lower on coronary-prone behaviors such as Type A and hostility than men. Both of these attributes are characteristics of the male ("macho") gender role, which has been linked to behavioral risk factors, such as smoking, excessive alcohol consumption, and lack of seat belt use (Waldron, 1997), as well as decreased motivation to learn stress management skills (Sieverding, in press).

Additionally, women not only report more social support than men, but also have more sources of social support, thus decreasing their dependency on a single source. For example, studies of middle-age people in Massachusetts found that men were more than twice as likely as women to name their spouse (or their partner) as their primary provider of social support (65.5% versus 26.4%). Furthermore, 24.2% of men (but only 6.1% of women) said this was their only source of support (New England Research Institutes, 1997). These data may, in part, explain why men's health is more seriously affected by partner loss through separation, divorce, or widowhood (Miller & Wortman, in press).

At first glance, gender differences in negative emotions appear to favor men. In most studies, women report more negative emotions such as depression than men (although this is not consistently found in populations where women and men have similar roles, such as college students; Nolen-Hoeksema & Girgus, 1994). Although women may report more depression, they may be coping more effectively than men. Generally, men are more likely to use avoidant coping strategies, such as denial and distraction, whereas women are more likely to employ vigilant coping strategies, paying attention to the stressor and its psychological and somatic consequences (Weidner & Collins, 1993). Which style is more adaptive depends largely on the situation. Most stressful experiences consist of uncontrollable daily hassles, which are short-lived and typically of no great consequence. Here avoidant strategies would be more adaptive ("What I cannot control and what can't hurt me is best to be ignored"). Thus, men's strategies are likely to pay off for these types of events, contributing to their lesser experience (or report) of emotional discomfort or distress. But what if disaster hits? How do people cope with uncontrollable events requiring long-term adaptation, such as divorce, loss of a loved one, job loss, sudden financial crisis, and economic uncertainty? Here it may be women's greater vigilance that is more adaptive: preparing for the crisis, seeking help, advice, and so on. Consistent with this reasoning are data from the Hungarian population that show that women tend to accept their negative mood as a disorder to be treated, whereas men are more likely to engage in self-destructive behavior, such as excessive alcohol consumption (Kopp, Skrabski, & Székely, in press).

Similarly, research on how people cope with disasters (e.g., hurricanes and tornadoes) supports the notion of men's maladaptive coping: Increases in alcohol consumption and depression were related to personal disaster exposure among men, whereas no such direct relationship was evident among women (Solomon, Smith, Robins, & Fishbach, 1987; Solomon, in press). Furthermore, socioeconomic deprivation appears to be more closely related to depression in men than in women (Kopp et al., 1988). Thus, men's psychosocial risk factor profile appears to further contribute to their enhanced health risk.

Biobehavioral Factors

Support for the notions that psychosocial and behavioral factors affect and are affected by biological processes that directly influence health and illness has been increasing during the past decade (Baum & Posluszny, 1999). For example, exposure to stress can lead to enhanced cardiovascular arousal that has been shown to predict cardiovascular disease, at least in men (for review, see Weidner & Messina, 1998). In laboratory studies, men appear to be hyperreactive (e.g., they show exaggerated cardiovascular reactivity) to a wider range of environmental stressors than women. On the other hand, there is some evidence that men benefit more from social support (i.e., decreased cortisol response to stress) provided by their partner than do women (Kirschbaum, Klauer, Filipp, & Hellhammer, 1995; also see Orth-Gomer & Chesney, 1997). This finding is consistent with (and may even explain) the fact that marriage has much greater health benefits for men than for women.

Psychosocial factors, such as stress, affect not only cardiovascular and endocrine responses, but also reactions of the immune system. While there is consistent evidence to suggest gender differences in immune function (e.g., women have higher antibody levels, higher rates of graft rejection, higher rates of autoimmune diseases, lesser vulnerability to infectious diseases), few studies have found gender differences in stress-related immune changes (Glaser & Kiecolt-Glaser, 1996).

Last, health behaviors such as smoking and alcohol consumption may have different biological consequences for men than for women. For example, men metabolize nicotine more rapidly than women and may require higher nicotine intake to maintain similar plasma nicotine levels (Waldron, 1997). Similarly, the cardioprotective effects of moderate alcohol consumption on high-density lipoprotein cholesterol levels appear to occur at higher doses of alcohol in men than in women (Weidner et al., 1991).

Gender, Treatment, and Prevention Approaches

Gender differences in behavioral, psychosocial, and biobehavioral risk factors are likely contributors to the gender gap in several major causes of death. Although our understanding of the mechanisms linking these factors to increased health risk is still incomplete, it should be pointed out that diseases can be prevented or effectively treated long before causative mechanisms are understood. For example, the cessation of tobacco chewing to prevent oral cancer was discovered in 1915. However, it was not until 1974 that NI-nitrosornicotine was discovered as the causal agent of oral cancer (Wynder, 1998). Thus, it comes as no surprise that, without a complete understanding of the mechanisms, several behavioral interventions designed to improve health have been quite successful. Generally, most behavioral interventions are conducted with male participants, leading several authors to caution against generalizing results obtained from male samples. The need for gender-specific interventions may be most obvious for those focusing on social support and work stress. For example, social support interventions often seek to elicit the support from a person's partner. This strategy may be effective for men, who tend to see their spouses as their primary source of social support, but not for women, whose primary source of social support consists of friends and family members (New England Research Institutes, 1997). Thus, soliciting social support from one's partner may not be the best strategy for women and could even lead to exacerbated stress responses, as suggested by Kirschbaum et al.'s (1995) findings.

Similarly, interventions designed to reduce work stress that have been shown to be effective with men may not generalize to women, because women's work situations differ from those of men. Because of the unequal division of labor at home, married women who are employed full time have a greater total workload than men. Thus, compared to men in similar positions, women are more stressed by their greater unpaid work load (as indicated, for example, by higher norepinephrine levels; Lundberg & Frankenhaeuser, 1999). Furthermore, there is evidence that the same job positions are more stressful for women than for men. In a sample of employed men and women in high-ranking positions, Lundberg and Frankenhaeuser report the largest gender difference in response to the question, "Do you have to perform better than a colleague of the opposite sex to have the same chance of promotion?" Most of the women, but none of the men, agreed with this statement (Lundberg & Frankenhaeuser, 1999).

With regard to treatment, gender-specific approaches also appear to be indicated. For example, it has been suggested that female heart disease patients may be able to reverse coronary atherosclerosis by making fewer lifestyle changes than male heart disease patients (Ornish et al., 1990). However, large-scale clinical trials including women and men representing more sociodemograpically diverse populations are needed to evaluate the effectiveness of behavioral treatments. One promising attempt toward this end is the behavioral intervention entitled "Enhancing Recovery in Coronary Heart Disease" (ENRICHD) Patients Study. This study is a major multicenter, randomized clinical trial that is currently testing the effects of a psychosocial intervention, aimed at decreasing depression and increasing social support, on reinfarction and mortality in 3,000 post-Miocardial Infarction (MI) patients at high psychosocial risk (i.e., depressed and/or socially isolated patients). The study, in which 50% of the patients will be women, will be completed in 2001 and will provide valuable information on the role of emotions in heart disease among both women and men from more sociodemographically diverse backgrounds.

In summary, behavioral interventions designed to increase social support, decrease negative emotions, and improve lifestyle behaviors and coping skills in both women and men are clearly indicated. However, given the many situational differences between men's and women's lives, the design of gender-specific interventions may be required to yield effective outcomes.

SOCIOECONOMIC STATUS

The health of the United States population has improved appreciably during the past two centuries. Concomitant with these improvements, however, clinically significant differences in health outcomes by socioeconomic status (SES) have persisted (Liao, McGee, Kaufman, Cao, & Cooper, 1999; Pappas, Queen, Hadden, & Fisher, 1993). Although the voluminous research literature examining the relationship between SES and health outcomes precludes a detailed analysis of the topic here, a number of reviews have examined this body of literature and are suggested for further reading (N. Anderson & Armstead, 1995; Krieger, Rowley, Herman, Avery, & Phillips, 1993; Krieger, Williams, & Moss, 1997; Marmot & Feeney, 1997; Marmot, Kogevinas, & Elston, 1987; West, 1997; D. Williams & Collins, 1995). This section briefly (a) reviews how SES has been assessed and the methodological limitations associated with the assessment of SES; (b) discusses the association between SES and health status; (c) examines the interactions among ethnicity, SES, and health; (d) explores the relationships between SES and biobehavioral/psychosocial risk and protective factors, as well as SES and behavioral prevention and treatment approaches; and (e) concludes with suggestions for future research on mechanism linking SES and health.

Assessment of SES

At least three factors currently retard our understanding of the relationship between SES and health status. First, opposed to research that explicitly focuses on the potential sources of SES differences, the overwhelming majority of studies designed to delineate the determinants of health tend to statistically control for the effects associated with SES. From a clinical perspective, the observation that SES groups differ with respect to a number of health indices, although informative, does not lead logically to the more proximal variables that are related to biobehavioral processes, which may be more amenable to prevention and treatment strategies. Second, the assessment of SES has historically been rather crude. The most frequently used proxies for SES include income, education, and occupation, with income showing the strongest relationship to health (Stronks, van de Mheen, Van Den Bos, & Mackenbach, 1997). It is important to note that within SES groupings (whether assessed by income, education, or occupation), the major U.S. ethnic groups are differentially distributed, with African Americans and Hispanics being disproportionately represented in the lowest SES groups, and Asian or Pacific Islanders being disproportionately represented in the highest SES groups (NCHS, 1998; D. Williams, 1996). Third, in most empirical investigations, SES is measured cross-sectionally. This methodological limitation is particularly noteworthy, given that an emerging body of literature suggests that changes in socioeconomic status (Hart, Smith, & Blane, 1998; Lynch, Kaplan, & Shema, 1997; McDonough, Duncan, Williams, & House, 1997) and early life experiences (D. Barker, 1995; Peck, 1994; Rahkonen, Lahelma, & Huuhka, 1997) are predictive of health outcomes.

SES and Health Status

The medical expenditures associated with negative health outcomes are exceedingly high in the United States. For example, the estimated medical costs associated with treating *only* three of the major chronic diseases (heart disease, lung cancer, and diabetes mellitus) were $131 billion in 1995 (NCHS, 1998). Research delineating factors related to negative health outcomes has the potential of better informing prevention and intervention efforts, and as a result, reduces health care costs. Socioeconomic status is one such factor that has been explored extensively by research scientists.

The observation that individuals with fewer social and economic resources generally have more negative health outcomes than their more "resourceful" counterparts is reported to be at least 2,000 years old (Lloyd, 1983; Sigerist, 1956). With the exception of some cancers (Gold, 1995; Kelsey & Bernstein, 1996) and heart disease mortality during the first half of the twentieth century (Marmot, Shipley, & Rose, 1984), more contemporary studies continue to document inverse relationships between SES and morbidity and mortality. This SES-health gradient has been observed across ethnic, gender, and age groups for all-cause and disease-specific mortality and an array of chronic diseases, communicable diseases, and injuries (Breen & Figueroa, 1996; Cantwell, McKenna, McCray, & Onorato, 1998; Gissler, Rahkonen, Jarvelin, & Hemminki, 1998; JNC, 1993; Litonjua, Carey, Weiss, & Gold, 1999; Liu, Wang, Waterbor, Weiss, & Soong, 1998; NCHS, 1998; Ogle, Swanson, Woods, & Azzouz, 2000; Robert & House, 1996). These data indicate that persons of lower SES are disproportionately burdened by negative health outcomes.

Interactions of Ethnicity, SES, and Health

Because African Americans and Hispanics have lower median household incomes, educational attainments, and occupational positions, as well as poorer outcomes for a number of medical ailments (NCHS, 1998; U.S. Department of Health and Human Services, 1985), it was once believed that if SES were controlled (via stratification or statistically), the between-ethnic group health disparities would be eliminated. That is, if poorer health is secondary to a relative lack of resources for nutritional needs, access to, and use of, quality health care and adequate housing (controlling for SES) should "even the playing field," thereby eliminating between-group disparities. Although intuitively appealing, an emerging body of literature suggests that adjustments for SES may substantially reduce or eliminate these disparities for some (Cantwell et al., 1998; Litonjua et al., 1999) but not all health outcomes (Kington & Smith, 1997; Lillie-Blanton & Laveist, 1996; NCHS, 1998; Schoenbaum & Waidmann, 1997; Schoendorf, Hogue, Kleinman, & Rowley, 1992; D. Williams, 1996).

A number of hypotheses have been presented to explain the persistence of these between-group disparities (N. Anderson & Armstead, 1995; Kington & Nickens, 1999; D. Williams, 1996). For example, R. Clark, Anderson, Clark, and Williams (1999) proposed two reasons to help explain findings that the prevalence of hypertension and all-cause mortality are higher for African Americans than European Americans at comparable educational levels (Pappas et al., 1993). First, within-SES group "protection" may not be comparable across ethnic groups (N. Anderson & Armstead, 1995; D. Williams & Collins, 1995). As such, attempts to compare African Americans and European Americans at any given educational level, for instance, would not take into account the observation that African Americans earn significantly less than their European American counterparts at every level of education attainment (NCHS, 1998). Second, if African Americans disproportionately perceive their environments as threatening, harmful, or challenging as a result of ethnically specific stimuli (Clark, Tyroler, & Heiss, 2000; S. James, 1993; Krieger, 1990; Outlaw, 1993; Sears, 1991; Thompson, 1996; D. Williams, Yu, Jackson, & Anderson, 1997), they may be required to expend an inordinate amount of "energy" to cope with the psychological and physiological stress responses that follow these perceptions, relative to European Americans. Over time, the cumulative psychological and physiological effects associated with these added stressors have the potential to account for, in part, between- and within-group health disparities.

SES and Behavioral Risk Factors

The major chronic diseases and disease-specific mortality have common behavioral risk factors that are interrelated in complex ways. For example, smoking is related to heart disease and lung cancer; dietary intake (e.g., saturated fat, cholesterol intake, and sodium intake) and physical inactivity are related to obesity and hypertension; obesity is related to hypertension, heart disease, and diabetes; physical inactivity is related to hypertension; and hypertension is related to heart disease and cerebrovascular disease (JNC, 1993; NCHS, 1998). Research suggests that smoking, obesity, dietary intake, and hypertension are inversely related to SES (Harrell & Gore, 1998; King, Polednak, Bendel et al., 1999; Lowry, Kann, Collins, & Kolbe, 1996; Luepker et al., 1993; Winkleby, Robinson, Sundquist, & Kraemer, 1999), and that statistically adjusting for known behavioral risk factors does not eliminate the SES-health gradient (Lantz et al., 1998; Smith, Shipley, & Rose, 1990).

Research has also identified factors that appear to decrease the probability of disease occurrence. These protective factors (e.g., physical activity and health knowledge) have been shown to be positively associated with SES (Jeffrey & French, 1996; Luepker et al., 1993). Additional research is needed to delineate why higher disease risk profiles are overrepresented among persons low in SES (Elman & Myers, 1999; Harrell & Gore, 1998; W. James, Nelson, Ralph, & Leather, 1997).

SES and Psychosocial Risk Factors

In addition to these more traditional biobehavioral risk and protective factors, the examination of psychosocial factors may lead to a more informed understanding of the relationship between SES factors and health outcomes (N. Anderson & Armstead, 1995; Taylor, Repetti, & Seeman, 1997). That is, given the plausible mechanistic links between psychosocial

factors and some physical health outcomes and processes (N. Anderson, McNeilly, & Myers, 1991; Barefoot, Dahlstrom, & Williams, 1983; Burchfield, 1985; Cacioppo, 1994; R. Clark et al., 1999; Everson, Goldberg, Kaplan, Julkunen, & Solonen, 1998), coupled with the observation that known and measured risk factors do not account for all of the variability in SES-health differentials (Lantz et al., 1998; D. Williams, 1996), it is possible that psychosocial factors mitigate the relationship between SES and health outcomes. These psychosocial factors include anger expression, perceptions of unfair treatment (e.g., racism and sexism), cynical hostility, coping styles, and locus of control. For example, S. James, Strogatz, Wing, and Ramsey (1987) found that the active-coping style of "John Henryism" interacted with SES to increase the risk of hypertension for African American, but not European American, males. That is, African American males who were low in active coping and low in SES were nearly three times more likely to be hypertensive, compared to African American males who were high in active coping and high in SES. Subsequent studies have failed to find support for the John Henryism: The ability to assess the degree to which people feel they can control their environment SES interaction in females and more affluent samples (S. James, Keenan, Strogatz, Browning, & Garrett, 1992; Wiist & Flack, 1992).

SES and Prevention and Intervention Approaches

Persons of low SES, regardless of ethnic group, are more likely to have no health insurance coverage, no physician contact, greater unmet needs for health care, and more avoidable hospitalizations, compared to persons of medium and high SES (NCHS, 1998). Because access to health care is generally needed to take advantage of prevention and intervention services, it is reasonable to postulate that SES will be inversely related to the availability and use of these services. Also, to the extent that these services are positively related to health outcomes (Alexander et al., 1999; Fortmann, Williams, Hulley, Maccoby, & Farquhar, 1982; JNC, 1993), persons of low SES would be expected to have the poorest outcomes.

Relative to persons of higher SES, persons of lower SES are less likely to report ever receiving or being up-to-date on prevention services such as cholesterol screening, Pap smear, stress test, mammography, and breast examination (Davis, Ahn, Fortmann, & Farquhar, 1998; Haywood et al., 1993; NCHS, 1998; Solberg, Brekke, & Kottke, 1997), but not blood pressure screening or "needed" services (Solberg et al., 1997). The positive relationship between the receipt of services and SES has also been observed for intervention services such as hormone therapy (Marks & Shinberg, 1998), but not informal care (Tennstedt & Chang, 1998). Research does suggest, however, that the relative lack of services for some persons of low SES may be influenced by the assertiveness of the patient (Krupat et al., 1999).

FUTURE RESEARCH DIRECTIONS

With changes in the racial/ethnic composition of the United States, trends in health technology, and a greater appreciation for the need to study health in women, ethnic minorities, and economically underserved populations, there are an endless number of directions for future research. In summary, emerging areas of research on the relationship and impact of race/ethnicity, gender, and SES on health, disease, and health behaviors require a systems perspective for continued advancements in the field.

Investigations that explore mechanisms linking SES and health could benefit from addressing questions such as: What is the relationship between SES, psychosocial factors, and health outcomes? Is SES a social hierarchy that will inherently have toxic biopsychosocial effects? How are SES and allostatic load related? Research is needed to elucidate the relationship between SES and psychological traits/responses and coping resources. Laboratory and ambulatory monitoring studies would be instrumental in identifying the physiological (e.g., cardiovascular, immune, and adrenocortical) responses associated with perceptions of chronic interpersonal and environmental stressors, between and within SES groups. In addition, cross-cultural studies are needed to delineate biological, psychological, behavioral, and social correlates of health among persons in societies with varying degrees of social and economic orderings. We also suggest examining the effect health promotion programs have on mitigating the relationship between SES and health outcomes and processes to further our understanding of how to overcome the impact of economic variability on health.

Considerations in the Study of Ethnicity, SES, Gender, and Health

Much of the research on ethnicity, SES, gender, and health involves statistical analyses that compare group means. One central assumption in these types of analyses is homogeneity of variance. Meeting this assumption may be very difficult in cross-cultural comparisons of health indices across ethnic groups. Ethnic minorities possess unique attributes by virtue of their language, lifestyle, socioeconomic status, and historical experiences. These attributes create different degrees of variability within groups that may violate assumptions of homogeneity of variance.

If assumptions of homogeneity of variance can be met, the misinterpretation of cross-cultural data on health and health behaviors is another potential difficulty and concern for research on ethnicity. Cauce, Coronado, and Watson (1998) describe three models typically used in conceptualizing and interpreting results from cross-cultural research, which exemplify this issue. These models are the (a) Cultural Deviance Model, (b) Cultural Equivalence Model, and (c) Cultural Variant Model.

The Cultural Deviant Model characterizes differences or deviations between groups as deviant and inferior. The Cultural Equivalence Model is an improvement over the Cultural Deviance Model in that it proposes that superior socioeconomic status (SES) provides advantages, which create superior performance. The Cultural Deviance Model attributes advantages or superior performance to culture. Putting the onus on culture blames a group for not having the same ideals, resources, attitudes, and beliefs as the majority culture. Placing culpability on SES shifts the responsibility to social structures that are inherently unbalanced in their distribution of resources. The Cultural Variant Model describes differences as adaptations to external forces, exemplifying resilience in the face of oppression. Differences are explained not in relation to a majority/superior group but as culturally rooted internal explanations. The third model by definition allows an appreciation for between-group differences, and challenges us to explore within-group heterogeneity.

Including race as a between-subject variable assesses the variability due to the categorization of subjects by race. However, it does not assess the possible dynamic effect of ethnicity on the variables in the model being tested. Race implies only a biological differentiation while ignoring other possible sources of variability in cross-cultural comparisons, such as lifestyle, beliefs about aging, language, and historical experiences. Race then is not an adequate proxy for the synergistic effects present in studies designed to address ethnic diversity. To this end, an important point in developing research questions is that *factors that account for between-group variability do not necessarily account for within-group variability* (Whitfield & Baker-Thomas, 1999). One strategy for overcoming the performance bias in comparisons of different cultural groups is to study each group as its own heterogenous population *first* and investigate the appropriateness of the measure and its items for each population under study. Then examine the mean and, perhaps more importantly, variances and error variances between groups. Another approach is to use an acculturation measure as a covariate in between-group analyses. In this way, health behaviors devoid of the impact of culture can be examined appropriately.

CONCLUSION

Science is currently in the process of understanding the unique patterns in health that economic status, culture/ethnicity/race, and gender form. Considerable work needs to be done to understand the biobehavioral mechanisms that interact in synergistic ways to affect health, particularly in ethnic minorities. Further research, specifically longitudinal research, is needed to depict the complexities of health among ethnic minorities.

While the president's initiative to eliminate health disparities will be difficult to attain, it is a necessary and critical goal given the unequal burden of disease and access to health care. The challenges are not only in the reduction of incidence of disease but also in the conceptual, methodological, and epistemological basis of the study of health and disease. Researchers with a health psychology perspective are essential in understanding the complicated, sometimes chaotic (meant as describing complex systems) ways that health and disease manifest in minority populations and across gender and socioeconomic status.

Francis Collins, director of the National Human Genome Research Institute (NHGRI) of the NIH, announced in June 2000 that they had developed a "working draft" of the human genome. This historic event places science on the doorstep of limitless possibilities in the struggle to understand diseases and how to treat them. Knowing the sequence of the genome is only the beginning. Equally important will be our knowledge of how the environment influences health, disease, and health behaviors. Previous research on the significant impact that sociodemographic factors play in contributing to disease processes is perhaps our best indicator that science must avoid the reductionistic view, which assumes that knowing and manipulating the genome will cure all our ills. We must understand how genes and environmental influences work in concert to produce positive and negative health consequences. Much of what produces differences in health and disease in ethnic minorities are behaviors that are interwoven in the fabric of being, which we call culture. The challenge is to ascertain the underlying effect of genes in complex environments on health and learn how to create programs and interventions that take account for both. We may also find that polymorphisms that occur in genotypes found to be responsible for damaging or protective factors related to disease and health are created, modified, or triggered by cultural and context factors.

The introduction to the 1991 special issue on "Gender, Stress, and Health" in *Health Psychology* (Vol. 10, No. 2, p. 84) written by Baum and Greenberg concludes: "Research on health and behavior should consider men and women—not because it is discriminatory not to do so—but because it is good science. The study of women and men, of young and old, of African Americans and Caucasians, Asians, Hispanics, and Native Americans will all help to reveal psychosocial and biological mechanisms that are critical to understanding mortality, morbidity, and quality of life."

REFERENCES

Abbott, P. J. (1996). American Indian and Alaska native aboriginal use of alcohol in the United States. *American Indian and Alaska Native Mental Health Research, 7*(2), 1–13.

Adler, A. I., Boyko, E. J., Schraer, C. D., & Murphy, N. J. (1996). The negative association between traditional physical activities and the prevalence of glucose intolerance in Alaska Natives. *Diabetic Medicine, 13*(6), 555–560.

Agurs-Collins, T. D., Kumanyika, S. K., Ten Have, T. R., & Adams-Campbell, L. L. (1997). A randomized controlled trial of weight reduction and exercise for diabetes management in older African-American subjects. *Diabetes Care, 20*(10), 1503–1511.

Ahluwalia, J. S., Resnicow, K., & Clark, W. S. (1998). Knowledge about smoking, reasons for smoking, and reasons for wishing to quit in inner-city African Americans. *Ethnicity and Disease, 8*(3), 385–393.

Alexander, F. E., Anderson, T. J., Brown, H. K., Forrest, A. P., Hepburn, W., Kirkpatrick, A. E., et al. (1999). 14 years of follow-up from the Edinburgh randomized trial of breast-cancer screening. *Lancet, 353,* 1903–1908.

Anderson, N. B., & Armstead, C. A. (1995). Toward understanding the association of socioeconomic status and health: A new challenge for the biopsychosocial approach. *Psychosomatic Medicine, 57,* 213–225.

Anderson, N. B., McNeilly, M., & Myers, H. (1991). Autonomic reactivity and hypertension in Blacks: A review and proposed model. *Ethnicity and Disease, 1,* 154–170.

Ballew, C., White, L. L., Strauss, K. F., Benson, L. J., Mendlein, J. M., & Mokdad, A. H. (1997). Intake of nutrients and food sources of nutrients among the Navajo: Findings from the Navajo Health and Nutrition Survey. *Journal of Nutrition, 127*(Suppl. 10), 2085S–2093S.

Barefoot, J. C., Dahlstrom, W. G., & Williams, R. B. (1983). Hostility, CHD incidence and total mortality: A 25-year follow-up study of 225 physicians. *Psychosomatic Medicine, 45,* 59–63.

Barefoot, J. C., Larsen, S., von der Lieth, L., & Schroll, M. (1995). Hostility, incidence of acute myocardial infarction and mortality in a sample of older Danish men and women. *American Journal of Epidemiology, 142*(5), 477–484.

Barefoot, J. C., Peterson, B. L., Dahlstrom, W. G., Siegler, I. C., Anderson, N. B., & Williams, R. B., Jr. (1991). Hostility patterns and health implications: Correlates of Cook-Medley Hostility Scale scores in a national survey. *Health Psychology, 10*(1), 18–24.

Barker, D. J. P. (1995). *Mothers, babies, and disease in later.* London: British Medical Journal.

Barker, J. C., & Kramer, B. J. (1996). Alcohol consumption among older urban American Indians. *Journal of Studies on Alcohol, 57*(2), 119–124.

Barrett-Connor, E. (1997). Sex differences in coronary heart disease: Why are women so superior? The 1995 Ancel Keys Lecture. *Circulation, 95,* 252–264.

Barrett-Connor, E., & Stuenkel, C. (1999). Hormones and heart disease in women: Heart and estrogen/progestin replacement study in perspective. *Journal of Clinical Endocrinology and Metabolism, 84,* 1848–1853.

Baum, A., & Posluszny, D. M. (1999). Health psychology: mapping biobehavioral contributions to health and illness. *Annual Review of Psychology, 50,* 137–163.

Black, B. S., Rabins, P. V., & McGuire, M. H. (1998). Alcohol use disorder is a risk factor for mortality among older public housing residents. *International Psychogeriatrics, 10*(3), 309–327.

Breen, N., & Figueroa, J. B. (1996). Stage of breast and cervical cancer diagnosis in disadvantaged neighborhoods: A prevention policy perspective. *American Journal of Preventive Medicine, 12,* 319–326.

Buchowski, M. S., & Sun, M. (1996). Nutrition in minority elders: Current problems and future directions. *Journal of Health Care for the Poor and Underserved, 7*(3), 184–209.

Burchfiel, C. M., Curb, J. D., Rodriguez, B. L., Yano, K., Hwang, L. J., Fong, K. O., et al. (1995). Incidence and predictors of diabetes in Japanese-American men: The Honolulu Heart Program. *Annals of Epidemiology, 5*(1), 33–43.

Burchfiel, C. M., Sharp, D. S., Curb, J. D., Rodriguez, B. L., Hwang, L. J., Marcus, E. B., et al. (1995). Physical activity and incidence of diabetes: The Honolulu Heart Program. *American Journal of Epidemiology, 141*(4), 360–368.

Burchfield, S. R. (1985). Stress: An integrative framework. In S. R. Burchfield (Ed.), *Stress: Psychological and physiological interactions* (pp. 381–394). New York: Hemisphere.

Cacioppo, J. (1994). Social neuroscience: Autonomic, neuroendocrine, and immune responses to stress. *Psychophysiology, 31,* 113–128.

Caetano, R. (1997). Prevalence, incidence and stability of drinking problems among Whites, Blacks and Hispanics: 1984–1992. *Journal of Studies on Alcohol, 58*(6), 565–572.

Caetano, R., & Clark, C. L. (1998). Trends in alcohol-related problems among Whites, Blacks, and Hispanics: 1984–1995. *Alcoholism: Clinical and Experimental Research, 22*(2), 534–538.

Cantwell, M. F., McKenna, M. T., McCray, E., & Onorato, I. M. (1998). Tuberculosis and race/ethnicity in the United States:

Impact of socioeconomic status. *American Journal of Respiratory and Critical Care Medicine, 157,* 1016–1020.

Carter-Nolan, P. L., Adams-Campbell, L. L., & Williams, J. (1996). Recruitment strategies for Black women at risk for noninsulin-dependent diabetes mellitus into exercise protocols: A qualitative assessment. *Journal of the National Medical Association, 88*(9), 558–562.

Cauce, A. M., Coronado, N., & Watson, J. (1998). Conceptual, methodological, and statistical issues in culturally competent research. In M. Hernandez & M. R. Isaacs (Eds.), *Promoting cultural competence in children's mental health services* (pp. 305–331). Baltimore: Brookes.

Cheung, Y. W. (1993). Beyond liver and culture: A review of theories and research in drinking among Chinese in North America. *International Journal of the Addictions, 28*(14), 1497–1513.

Choi, K. H., Yep, G. A., & Kumekawa, E. (1998). HIV prevention among Asian and Pacific Islander American men who have sex with men: A critical review of theoretical models and directions for future research. *AIDS Education and Prevention, 10*(Suppl. 3), 19–30.

Clark, D. O. (1997). Physical activity efficacy and effectiveness among older adults and minorities. *Diabetes Care, 20*(7), 1176–1182.

Clark, R., Anderson, N. B., Clark, V. R., & Williams, D. R. (1999). Racism as a stressor for African Americans: A biopsychosocial model. *American Psychologist, 54,* 806–815.

Clark, R., Tyroler, H. A., & Heiss, G. (2000). Orthostatic blood pressure responses as a function of ethnicity and socioeconomic status: The ARIC Study. *Annals of the New York Academy of Sciences, 896,* 316–317.

Clark, V. R., Moore, C. L., & Adams, J. H. (1998). Cholesterol concentrations and cardiovascular reactivity to stress in African American college volunteers. *Journal of Behavioral Medicine, 21*(5), 505–515.

Cohen, S., & Herbert, T. B. (1996). Health psychology: Psychological factors and physical disease from the perspective of human psychoneuroimmunology. *Annual Review of Psychology, 47,* 113–142.

Cohen, S., & Syme, S. L. (1985). *Social support and health.* San Francisco: Academic Press.

Comuzzie, A. G., & Allison, D. B. (1998). The search for human obesity genes. *Science, 280*(5368), 1374–1377.

Crespo, C. J., Keteyian, S. J., Heath, G. W., & Sempos, C. T. (1996). Leisure-time physical activity among U.S. adults: Results from the third National Health and Nutrition Examination Survey. *Archives of Internal Medicine, 156*(1), 93–98.

Cummings, G. L., Battle, R. S., Barker, J. C., & Krasnovsky, F. M. (1999). Are African American women worried about getting AIDS? A qualitative analysis. *AIDS Education and Prevention, 11*(4), 331–342.

Cunradi, C. B., Caetano, R., Clark, C. L., & Schafer, J. (1999). Alcohol-related problems and intimate partner violence among

White, Black, and Hispanic couples in the U.S. *Alcoholism: Clinical and Experimental Research, 23*(9), 1492–1501.

Davis, S. K., Ahn, D. K., Fortmann, S. P., & Farquhar, J. W. (1998). Determinants of cholesterol screening and treatment patterns: Insights for decision-makers. *American Journal of Preventive Medicine, 15,* 178–186.

de Groot, L. C., & van Staveren, W. A. (1995). Reduced physical activity and its association with obesity. *Nutrition Reviews, 53*(1), 11–13.

Diaz, T., & Klevens, M. (1997). Differences by ancestry in sociodemographics and risk behaviors among Latinos with AIDS: The supplement to HIV and AIDS Surveillance Project Group. *Ethnicity and Disease, 7*(3), 200–206.

Dohrenwend, B. S. (1973). Life events as stressors: A methodological inquiry. *Journal of Health and Social Behavior, 14*(2), 167–175.

Dressler, W. W., Dos-Santos, J. E., & Viteri, F. E. (1986). Blood pressure, ethnicity, and psychosocial resources. *Psychosomatic Medicine, 48,* 509–519.

Duey, W. J., O'Brien, W. L., Crutchfield, A. B., Brown, L. A., Williford, H. N., & Sharff-Olson, M. (1998). Effects of exercise training on aerobic fitness in African-American females. *Ethnicity and Disease, 8*(3), 306–311.

Ebbesson, S. O., Schraer, C. D., Risica, P. M., Adler, A. I., Ebbesson, L., Mayer, A. M., et al. (1998). Diabetes and impaired glucose tolerance in three Alaskan Eskimo populations: The Alaska-Siberia Project. *Diabetes Care, 21*(4), 563–569.

Elman, C., & Myers, G. C. (1999). Geographic morbidity differentials in the late nineteenth-century United States. *Demography, 36,* 429–443.

Escobedo, L. G., & Peddicord, J. P. (1996). Smoking prevalence in U.S. birth cohorts: The influence of gender and education. *American Journal of Public Health, 86*(2), 231–236.

Everson, S. A., Goldberg, D. E., Kaplan, G. A., Julkunen, J., & Solonen, J. T. (1998). Anger expression and incident hypertension. *Psychosomatic Medicine, 60,* 730–735.

Eyler, A. A., Baker, E., Cromer, L., King, A. C., Brownson, R. C., & Donatelle, R. J. (1998). Physical activity and minority women: A qualitative study. *Health Education and Behavior, 25*(5), 640–652.

Eyler, A. A., Brownson, R. C., Donatelle, R. J., King, A. C., Brown, D., & Sallis, J. F. (1999). Physical activity social support and middle- and older-aged minority women: Results from a U.S. survey. *Social Science and Medicine, 49*(6), 781–789.

Farmer, I. P., Meyer, P. S., Ramsey, D. J., Goff, D. C., Wear, M. L., Labarthe, D. R., et al. (1996). Higher levels of social support predict greater survival following acute myocardial infarction: The Corpus Christi Heart Project. *Behavioral Medicine, 22*(2), 59–66.

Fenaughty, A. M., Fisher, D. G., Cagle, H. H., Stevens, S., Baldwin, J. A., & Booth, R. (1998). Sex partners of Native American drug users. *Journal of Acquired Immune Deficiency Syndromes, 17*(3), 275–282.

Flynn, K. J., & Fitzgibbon, M. (1998). Body images and obesity risk among Black females: A review of the literature. *Annals of Behavioral Medicine, 20*(1), 13–24.

Fortmann, S. P., Williams, P. T., Hulley, S. B., Maccoby, N., & Farquhar, J. W. (1982). Does dietary health education reach only the privileged? The Stanford Three Community Study. *Circulation, 66*(1), 77–82.

Gardner, P., Rosenberg, H. M., & Wilson, R. W. (1996). Leading causes of death by age, sex, race, and Hispanic origin: United States, 1992. *Vital and Health Statistics, 29,* 1–94. (Series 20: Data from the National Vital Statistics System)

Garfinkel, L. (1997). Trends in cigarette smoking in the United States. *Preventive Medicine, 26*(4), 447–450.

Gill, K., Eagle Elk, M., Liu, Y., & Deitrich, R. A. (1999). An examination of ALDH2 genotypes, alcohol metabolism and the flushing response in Native Americans. *Journal of Studies on Alcohol, 60*(2), 149–158.

Gissler, M., Rahkonen, O., Jarvelin, M. R., & Hemminki, E. (1998). Social class differences in health until the age of seven years among the Finnish 1987 birth cohort. *Social Science and Medicine, 46,* 1543–1552.

Glaser, R., & Kiecolt-Glaser, J. K. (1996). Marital conflict and endocrine function: Are men really more physiologically affected than women? *Journal of Consulting and Clinical Psychology, 64,* 324–332.

Gold, E. B. (1995). Epidemiology of and risk factors for pancreatic cancer. *Surgical Clinics of North America, 75,* 819–843.

Goslar, P. W., Macera, C. A., Castellanos, L. G., Hussey, J. R., Sy, F. S., & Sharpe, P. A. (1997). Blood pressure in Hispanic women: The role of diet, acculturation, and physical activity. *Ethnicity and Disease, 72*(2), 106–113.

Grandinetti, A., Chang, H. K., Mau, M. K., Curb, J. D., Kinney, E. K., Sagum, R., et al. (1998). Prevalence of glucose intolerance among Native Hawaiians in two rural communities: Native Hawaiian Health Research (NHHR) Project. *Diabetes Care 21*(4), 549–554.

Guidry, J. J., Aday, L. A., Zhang, D., & Winn, R. J. (1997). The role of informal and formal social support networks for patients with cancer. *Cancer Practice, 5*(4), 241–246.

Gump, B. B., Matthews, K. A., & Raikkonen, K. (1999). Modeling relationships among socioeconomic status, hostility, cardiovascular reactivity, and left ventricular mass in African American and White children. *Health Psychology, 18*(2), 140–150.

Haan, M. N., & Weldon, M. (1996). The influence of diabetes, hypertension, and stroke on ethnic differences in physical and cognitive functioning in an ethnically diverse older population. *Annals of Epidemiology, 6*(5), 392–398.

Hahn, R. A., Heath, G. W., & Chang, M. H. (1998). Cardiovascular disease risk factors and preventive practices among adults—

United States, 1994: A behavioral risk factor atlas. Behavioral Risk Factor Surveillance System State Coordinators. *Morbidity and Mortality Weekly Report, 47*(5), 35–69.

Hames, C. G., & Greenlund, K. J. (1996). Ethnicity and cardiovascular disease: The Evans County Heart Study. *American Journal of the Medical Sciences, 311*(3), 130–134.

Harnack, L., Story, M., & Rock, B. H. (1999). Diet and physical activity patterns of Lakota Indian adults. *Journal of the American Dietetic Association, 99*(7), 829–835.

Harrell, J. S., & Gore, S. V. (1998). Cardiovascular risk factors and socioeconomic status in African American and Caucasian women. *Research on Nurses Health, 21*(4), 285–295.

Hart, C. L., Smith, G. D., & Blane, D. (1998). Inequalities in mortality by social class measured at 3 stages of life course. *American Journal of Public Health, 88,* 471–474.

Haywood, L. J., Ell, K., deGuman, M., Norris, S., Blumfield, D., & Sobel, E. (1993). Chest pain admissions: Characteristics of Black, Latino, and White patients in low- and mid-socioeconomic strata. *Journal of the National Medical Association, 85,* 749–757.

Hemingway, H., & Marmot, M. (1999). Psychosocial factors in the aetiology and prognosis of coronary heart disease: Systematic review of prospective cohort studies. *British Medical Journal, 318,* 1460–1467.

Hines, A. M., & Caetano, R. (1998). Alcohol and AIDS-related sexual behavior among Hispanics: Acculturation and gender differences. *AIDS Education and Prevention, 10*(6), 533–547.

HIV/AIDS among American Indians and Alaskan Natives—United States, 1981–1997. (1998). *Morbidity and Mortality Weekly Report, 47*(8), 154–160.

House, J. S., Landis, K. R., & Umberson, D. (1988). Social relationships and health. *Science, 241,* 540–545.

Hoyert, D. L., & Kung, H. C. (1997). Asian or Pacific islander mortality, selected states, 1992. *Monthly Vital Statistics Report, 46*(1), 1–63.

Huang, B., Rodriguez, B. L., Burchfiel, C. M., Chyou, P. H., Curb, J. D., & Yano, K . (1996). Acculturation and prevalence of diabetes among Japanese-American men in Hawaii. *American Journal of Epidemiology, 144*(7), 674–681.

Jackson, J. J. (1988). Social determinants of the health of aging Black populations in the United States. In J. Jackson (Ed.), *The Black American elderly: Research on physical and psychosocial health* (pp. 69–98). New York: Springer.

Jackson, J. S., Antonucci, T. C., & Gibson, R. C. (1990). Cultural, racial, and ethnic minority influences on aging. In J. E. Birren & K. W. Schaie (Eds.), *Handbook of the psychology of aging* (pp. 103–123). San Diego, CA: Academic Press.

Jackson, R., Chambless, L., Higgins, M., Kuulasmaa, K., Wijnberg, L., & Williams, D. (1998). Gender differences in ischemic heart disease and risk factors in 46 communities: An ecologic analysis. *Cardiovascular Risk Factors, 7,* 43–54.

Jackson, R. W., Treiber, F. A., Turner, J. R., Davis, H., & Strong, W. B. (1999). Effects of race, sex, and socioeconomic status upon cardiovascular stress responsivity and recovery in youth. *International Journal of Psychophysiology, 31*(2), 111–119.

James, S. A. (1984). Socioeconomic influences on coronary heart disease in Black populations. *American Heart Journal, 108*(3, Pt. 2), 669–672.

James, S. A. (1993). Racial and ethnic differences in infant mortality and low birth weight: A psychosocial critique. *Annals of Epidemiology, 3,* 130–136.

James, S. A., Hartnett, S. A., & Kalsbeck, W. (1983). John Henryism and blood pressure differences among Black men. *Journal of Behavioral Medicine, 6,* 259–278.

James, S. A., Keenan, N. L., Strogatz, D. S., Browning, S. R., & Garrett, J. M. (1992). Socioeconomic status, John Henryism, and blood pressure in Black adults. *American Journal of Epidemiology, 135,* 59.

James, S. A., Strogatz, D. S., Wing, S. B., & Ramsey, D. L. (1987). Socioeconomic status, John Henryism, and hypertension in Blacks and Whites. *American Journal of Epidemiology, 126,* 664–673.

James, W. P., Nelson, M., Ralph, A., & Leather, S. (1997). Socioeconomic determinants of health: The contribution of nutrition to inequalities in health. *British Medical Journal, 314,* 1545–1549.

Jeffery, R. W., & French, S. A. (1996). Socioeconomic status and weight control practices among 20- to 45-year-old women. *American Journal of Public Health, 86*(7), 1005–1010.

Joe, J. R. (1996). The health of American Indian and Alaska Native women. *Journal of the American Medical Women's Association, 51*(4), 141–145.

Joint National Committee on Detection, Evaluation, and Treatment of High Blood Pressure. (1993). The fifth report of the Joint National Committee on Detection, Evaluation, and Treatment of High Blood Pressure. *Archives of Internal Medicine, 153,* 154–183.

Jones, M., & Nies, M. A. (1996). The relationship of perceived benefits of and barriers to reported exercise in older African American women. *Public Health Nursing, 13*(2), 151–158.

Karter, A. J., Gazzaniga, J. M., Cohen, R. D., Casper, M. L., Davis, B. D., & Kaplan, G. A. (1998). Ischemic heart disease and stroke mortality in African-American, Hispanic, and non-Hispanic White men and women, 1985 to 1991. *Western Journal of Medicine, 169*(3), 139–145.

Kaul, L., & Nidiry, J. J. (1999). Management of obesity in low-income African Americans. *Journal of the National Medical Association, 91*(3), 139–143.

Kautz, J. A., Bradshaw, B. S., & Fonner, E., Jr. (1981). Trends in cardiovascular mortality in Spanish-surnamed, other White and Black persons in Texas, 1970–1975. *Circulation, 64,* 730–735.

Kelsey, J. L., & Bernstein, L. (1996). Epidemiology and prevention of breast cancer. *Annual Review of Public Health, 17,* 47–67.

Kimball, E. H., Goldberg, H. I., & Oberle, M. W. (1996). The prevalence of selected risk factors for chronic disease among American Indians in Washington state. *Public Health Reports, 111*(3), 264–271.

King, G., Polednak, A. P., Bendel, R., & Hovey, D. (1999). Cigarette smoking among native and foreign-born African Americans. *Annuals of Epidemiology, 9*(4), 236–244.

Kington, R., & Nickens, H. (1999, March). *The health of African Americans: Recent trends, current patterns, future directions.* Presentation at the Midwest Consortium for Black Studies Conference, University of Michigan, Ann Arbor.

Kington, R. S., & Smith, J. P. (1997). Socioeconomic status and racial and ethnic differences in functional status associated with chronic diseases. *American Journal of Public Health, 87,* 805–810.

Kirschbaum, C., Klauer, T., Filipp, S.-H., & Hellhammer, D. H. (1995). Sex-specific effects of social support on cortisol and subjective responses to acute psychological stress. *Psychosomatic Medicine, 57,* 23–31.

Klevens, R. M., Diaz, T., Fleming, P. L., Mays, M. A., & Frey, R. (1999). Trends in AIDS among Hispanics in the United States, 1991–1996. *American Journal of Public Health, 89*(7), 1104–1106.

Klonoff, E. A., & Landrine, H. (1999). Acculturation and cigarette smoking among African Americans: Replication and implications for prevention and cessation programs, *Journal of Behavioral Medicine, 22*(2), 195–204.

Kopp, M. S., Skrabski, A., & Szedmak, S. (1998). Inequality and self-rated morbidity in a changing society. *Social Science and Medicine.*

Kopp, M. S., Skrabski, A., & Székely, A. (in press). Risk factors and inequality in relation to morbidity and mortality in a changing society. In G. Weidner, M. Kopp, & M. Kristenson (Eds.), *Heart Disease: Environment, Stress and Gender*, NATO Science Series, Series I: Life and Behavioural Sciences, Volume: 327. Amsterdam: IOS Press.

Krieger, N. (1990). Racial and gender discrimination: Risk factors for high blood pressure? *Social Science and Medicine, 12,* 1273–1281.

Krieger, N., Rowley, D. L., Herman, A. A., Avery, B., & Phillips, M. T. (1993). Racism, sexism, and social class: Implications for studies of health, disease, and well-being. *American Journal of Preventive Medicine, 9,* 82–122.

Krieger, N., Williams, D. R., & Moss, N. E. (1997). Measuring social class in U.S. public health research: Concepts, methodologies, and guidelines. *Annual Review of Public Health, 18,* 341–378.

Krupat, E., Irish, J. T., Kasten, L. E., Freund, K. M., Burns, R. B., Moskowitz, M. A., et al. (1999). Patient assertiveness and physician decision-making among older breast cancer patients. *Social Science and Medicine, 49,* 449–457.

Kubzansky, L. D., Kawachi, I., & Sparrow, D. (1999). Socioeconomic status, hostility, and risk factor clustering in the Normative Aging Study: Any help from the concept of allostatic load? *Annals of Behavioral Medicine, 21*(4), 330–338.

Kuczmarski, R. J., Flegal, K. M., Cambell, S. M., & Johnson, C. L. (1994). Increasing prevalenced of overweight among U.S. adults: The National Health and Nutrition Examination Surveys, 1960–1991. *Journal of the American Medical Association, 272,* 205–211.

Lantz, P. M., House, J. S., Lepkowski, J. M., Williams, D. R., Mero, R. P., & Chen, J. (1998). Socioeconomic factors, health behavior, and mortality results from a nationally representative prospective study of U.S. adults. *Journal of the American Medical Association, 279,* 1703–1708.

Lapidus, L., & Bengtsson, C. (1988). Regional obesity as a health hazard in women: a prospective study. *Acta Med Scandinavica Suppl, 723,* 53–59.

Larsson, B. (1988). Regional obesity as a health hazard in men: Prospective studies. *Acta Med Scandinavica Suppl, 723,* 45–51.

Laumann, E. O., & Youm, Y. (1999). Racial/ethnic group differences in the prevalence of sexually transmitted diseases in the United States: A network explanation. *Sexually Transmitted Diseases, 26*(5), 250–261.

Lee, D. J., Markides, K. S., & Ray, L. A. (1997). Epidemiology of self-reported past heavy drinking in Hispanic adults. *Ethnicity and Health, 2*(1/2), 77–88.

Lee, S. K., Sobal, J., & Frongillo, E. A., Jr. (1999). Acculturation and dietary practices among Korean Americans. *Journal of the American Dietetic Association, 99*(9), 1084–1089.

Lester, D. (1999). Native American suicide rates, acculturation stress and traditional integration. *Psychological Reports, 84*(2), 398.

Liao, Y., McGee, D. L., Kaufman, J. S., Cao, G., & Cooper, R. S. (1999). Socioeconomic status and morbidity in the last years of life. *American Journal of Public Health, 89,* 569–572.

Lillie-Blanton, M., & Laveist, T. (1996). Race/ethnicity, the social environment, and health. *Social Science and Medicine, 43,* 83–91.

Litonjua, A. A., Carey, V. J., Wciss, S. T., & Gold, D. R. (1999). Race, socioeconomic factors, and area of residence are associated with asthma prevalence. *Pediatric Pulmonology, 28,* 394–401.

Liu, T., Wang, X., Waterbor, J. W., Weiss, H. L., & Soong, S. J. (1998). Relationships between socioeconomic status and race-specific cervical cancer incidence in the United States, 1973–1992. *Journal of Health Care for the Poor and Underserved, 9,* 420–432.

Livingston, R. L., Levine, D., & Moore, R. (1991). Social integration and Black intra-racial variation in Blood pressure. *Ethnicity and Disease, 1,* 135–151.

Lloyd, G. E. R. (1983). *Hippocratic writings.* London: Penguin Books.

Lowry, R., Kann, L., Collins, J. L., & Kolbe, L. J. (1996). The effect of socioeconomic status on chronic disease risk behaviors among U.S. adolescents. *Journal of the American Medical Association, 276,* 792–797.

Luepker, R. V., Rosamond, W. D., Murphy, R., Sprafka, J. M., Folsom, A. R., McGovern, P. G., et al. (1993). Socioeconomic status and coronary heart disease risk factor trends: The Minnesota Heart Survey. *Circulation, 88,* 2172–2179.

Lundberg, U., & Frankenhaeuser, M. (1999). Stress and workload of men and women in high-ranking positions. *Journal of Occupational Health Psychology, 4,* 1–10.

Lynch, J. W., Kaplan, G. A., & Shema, S. J. (1997). Cumulative impact of sustained economic hardship on physical, cognitive, psychological, and social functioning. *New England Journal of Medicine, 337,* 1889–1895.

Macera, C. A., Armstead, C. A., & Anderson, N. B. (2000). Sociocultural influences on health. In A. Baum, T. Revenson, & J. Singer, *Handbook of health psychology* (pp. 427–440). Mahwah, NJ: Erlbaum.

Mahoney, M. C., & Michalek, A. M. (1998). Health status of American Indians/Alaska Natives: General patterns of mortality. *Family Medicine, 30*(3), 190–195.

Manson, J. E., Colditz, G. A., Stampfer, M. J., Willett, W. C., Krolewski, A. S., Rosner, B., et al. (1991). A prospective study of maturity-onset diabetes mellitus and risk of coronary heart disease and stroke in women. *Archives of Internal Medicine, 151*(6), 1141–1147.

Marin, B. V., Marin, G., Perez-Stable, E. J., Otero-Sabogal, R., & Sabogal, F. (1990). Cultural differences in attitudes toward smoking: Developing messages using the theory of reasoned action. *Journal of Applied Social Psychology, 20*(6, Pt. 1), 478–493.

Marks, N. F., & Shinberg, D. S. (1998). Socioeconomic status differences in hormone therapy. *American Journal of Epidemiology, 148,* 581–593.

Marmot, M., & Feeney, A. (1997). General explanations for social inequalities in health. *IARC Scientific Publications, 138,* 207–228.

Marmot, M. G., Kogevinas, M., & Elston, M. A. (1987). Social/economic status and disease. *Annual Review of Public Health, 8,* 111–135.

Marmot, M. G., Shipley, M. J., & Rose, G. (1984). Inequalities in death—Specific explanations of a general pattern? *Lancet, 1*(8384), 1003–1006.

Marshall, J. A., Lopez, T. K., Shetterly, S. M., Morgenstern, N. E., Baer, K., Swenson, C., et al. (1999). Indicators of nutritional risk in a rural elderly Hispanic and non-Hispanic White population: San Luis Valley Health and Aging Study. *Journal of the American Dietetic Association, 99*(3), 315–322.

Maxwell, A. E., Bastani, R., & Warda, U. S. (1999). Condom use in young Blacks and Hispanics in public STD clinics. *Sexually Transmitted Diseases, 26*(8), 463–471.

McDonough, P., Duncan, G. J., Williams, D., & House, J. (1997). Income dynamics and adult mortality in the United States, 1972 through 1989. *American Journal of Public Health, 87,* 476–483.

McLeon, J. D., & Kessler, R. C. (1990). Socioeconomic status differences in vulnerability to undesirable life events. *Journal of Health and Social Behavior, 3*(2), 162–172.

Menon, S. C., Pandey, D. K., & Morgenstern, L. B. (1998). Critical factors determining access to acute stroke care. *Neurology, 51*(2), 427–432.

Miller, E., & Wortman, C. B. (in press). Gender differences in mortality and morbidity following a major stressor: The case of conjugal bereavement. In G. Weidner, M. Kopp, & M. Kristenson (Eds.), *Heart Disease: Environment, Stress and Gender*, NATO Science Series, Series I: Life and Behavioural Sciences, Volume: 327. Amsterdam: IOS Press.

Miller, T. Q., Smith, T. W., Turner, C. W., Guijarro, M. L., & Haller, A. J. (1996). A meta-analytic review of research on hostility and physical health. *Psychological Bulletin, 119*(2), 322–348.

Morbidity and Mortality Weekly Report. (1998). Tobacco use among U.S. racial/ethnic minority groups, African Americans, American Indians and Alaska Natives, Asian Americans and Pacific Islanders, Hispanics: A report of the surgeon general. *Centers for Disease Control, 47,* 1–16.

National Center for Health Statistics. (1998). *Health, United States, 1998 with socioeconomic status and health chart book.* Hyattsville, MD: U.S. Government Printing Office.

National Center for Health Statistics. (2000, June 30). Health people 2000 review, 1998–1999. *National Vital Statistics Reports, 47,* 5. (Series 19: Data from the National Vital Statistics System)

National Heart Lung and Blood Institute. (1985). Hypertension prevalence and the status of awareness treatment and control in the U.S.: Final report of the subcommittee on definition and prevalence of the 1984 Joint National Committee. *Hypertension, 7,* 457–468.

Navarro, A. M. (1996). Cigarette smoking among adult Latinos: The California Tobacco Baseline Survey. *Annals of Behavioral Medicine, 18*(4), 238–245.

Neal, J. J., Fleming, P. L., Green, T. A., & Ward, J. W. (1997). Trends in heterosexually acquired AIDS in the United States, 1988 through 1995. *Journal of Acquired Immune Deficiency Syndromes, 14*(5), 465–474.

Neff, L. J., Sargent, R. G., McKeown, R. E., Jackson, K. L., & Valois, R. F. (1997). Black-White differences in body size perceptions and weight management practices among adolescent females. *Journal of Adolescent Health, 20*(6), 459–465.

Nevid, J. S. Javier, R. A., & Moulton, J. L., III. (1996). Factors predicting participant attrition in a community-based, culturally specific smoking-cessation program for Hispanic smokers. *Health Psychology, 15*(3), 226–229.

New England Research Institutes. (1997, Spring/Summer). Gender differences in social supports: Data from the Massachusetts

Male Aging Study and the Massachusetts Women's Health Study. *Network, 12.*

Nolen-Hoeksema, S., & Girgus, J. S. (1994). The emergence of gender differences in depression during adolescence. *Psychological Bulletin, 115,* 424–443.

Nwadiora, E., & McAdoo, H. (1996). Acculturative stress among Amerasian refugees: Gender and racial differences. *Adolescence, 31*(122), 477–487.

Ogle, K. S., Swanson, G. M., Woods, S. N., & Azzouz, F. (2000). Cancer and comorbidity: Redefining chronic diseases. *Cancer, 88,* 653–663.

Ontiveros, J., Miller, T. Q., Markides, K. S., & Espino, D. V. (1999). Physical and psychosocial consequences of stroke in elderly Mexican Americans. *Ethnicity and Disease, 9*(2), 212–217.

Ornish, D., Brown, S. E., Scherwitz, L. W., Billings, J. H., Armstrong, W. T., Ports, T. A., et al. (1990). Can lifestyle changes reverse coronary heart disease? The Lifestyle Heart Trial. *Lancet, 336,* 129–133.

Orth-Gomer, K., & Chesney, M. A. (1997). Social stress/strain and heart disease in women. In D. G. Julian & N. K. Wenger (Eds.), *Women and heart disease* (pp. 407–420). London: Martin Dunitz.

Outlaw, F. H. (1993). Stress and coping: The influence of racism on the cognitive appraisal processing of African Americans. *Issues in Mental Health Nursing, 14,* 399–409.

Pappas, G., Queen, S., Hadden, W., & Fisher, G. (1993). The increasing disparity and mortality between socioeconomic groups in the United States, 1960 and 1986. *New England Journal of Medicine, 329,* 103–109.

Parker, V. C., Sussman, S., Crippens, D. L. Scholl, D., & Elder, P. (1996). Qualitative development of smoking prevention programming for minority youth. *Addictive Behaviors, 21*(4), 521–525.

Peck, M. N. (1994). The importance of childhood socio-economic group for adult health. *Social Science and Medicine, 39,* 553–562.

Peters, K. D., Kochanek, K. D., & Murphy, S. L. (1998). Deaths: Final data for 1996. *National Vital Statistics Reports, 47*(9), 1–100.

Potts, J. L., & Thomas, J. (1999). Traditional coronary risk factors in African Americans. *American Journal of the Medical Sciences, 317*(3), 189–192.

Powell, K. E., Thompson, P. D., Caspersen, C. J., & Kendrick, J. S. (1987). Physical activity and the incidence of coronary heart disease. *Annual Review of Public Health, 8,* 253–287.

Rahkonen, O., Lahelma, E., & Huuhka, M. (1997). Past or present? Childhood living conditions and current socioeconomic status as determinants of adult health. *Social Science and Medicine, 44,* 327–336.

Ransdell, L. B., & Wells, C. L. (1998). Physical activity in urban White, African American, and Mexican American women. *Medicine and Science in Sports and Exercise, 30*(11), 1608–1615.

Ravussin, E., Valencia, M. E., Esparza, J., Bennett, P. H., & Schulz, L. O. (1994). Effects of a traditional lifestyle on obesity in Pima Indians. *Diabetes Care, 17*(9), 1067–1074.

Reddy, D. M., Fleming, R., & Adesso, V. J. (1992). Gender and health. In S. Maes, H. Leventhal, & M. Johnston (Eds.), *International review of health psychology* (Vol. 1, pp. 117–132). Chichester, England: Wiley.

Response to increases in cigarette prices by race/ethnicity, income, and age groups—United States, 1976–1993. (1998). *Morbidity and Mortality Weekly Report, 47*(29), 605–609.

Robert, S., & House, J. S. (1996). SES differentials in health by age and alternative indicators of SES. *Journal of Aging and Health, 8,* 359–388.

Rodriguez, B. L., Curb, J. D., Burchfiel, C. M., Abbott, R. D., Petrovitch, H., Masaki, K., et al. (1994). Physical activity and 23-year incidence of coronary heart disease morbidity and mortality among middle-aged men: The Honolulu Heart Program. *Circulation, 89*(6), 2540–2544.

Rozanski, A., Blumenthal, J. A., & Kaplan, J. (1999). Impact of psychological factors on the pathogenesis of cardiovascular disease and implications for therapy. *Circulation, 99,* 2192–2217.

Sacco, R. L., Boden-Albala, B., Gan, R., Chen, X., Kargman, D. E., Shea, S., et al. (1998). Stroke incidence among White, Black, and Hispanic residents of an urban community: The Northern Manhattan Stroke Study. *American Journal of Epidemiology, 147*(3), 259–268.

Sallis, J. F., Zakarian, J. M., Hovell, M. F., & Hofstetter, C. R. (1996). Ethnic, socioeconomic, and sex differences in physical activity among adolescents. *Journal of Clinical Epidemiology, 49*(2), 125–134.

Schnall, P. L., Landsbergis, P. A., & Baker, D. (1994). Job strain and cardiovascular disease. *Annual Review of Public Health, 15,* 381–411.

Schoenbaum, M., & Waidmann, T. (1997). Race, socioeconomic status, and health: Accounting for race differences in health. *Journals of Gerontology: Series B, Psychological Sciences and Social Sciences, 52,* 61–73.

Schoendorf, K. C., Hogue, C. J. R., Kleinman, J., & Rowley, D. (1992). Mortality among infants of Black as compared with White college-educated parents. *New England Journal of Medicine, 326,* 1522–1526.

Schwarzer, R., & Rieckmann, N. (in press). Social support, cardiovascular disease, and mortality. In G. Weidner, M. Kopp, & M. Kristenson (Eds.), *Heart Disease: Environment, Stress and Gender*, NATO Science Series, Series I: Life and Behavioural Sciences, Volume: 327. Amsterdam: IOS Press.

Sears, D. O. (1991). Symbolic racism. In P. A. Katz & D. A. Taylor (Eds.), *Eliminating racism: Profiles in controversy* (pp. 53–84). New York: Plenum Press.

Shumaker, S. A., & Czajkowski, S. M. (1994). *Social support and cardiovascular disease.* New York: Plenum Press.

Sieverding, M. (in press). Gender and health-related attitudes: The role of a "macho" self-concept. In G. Weidner, M. Kopp, & M. Kristenson (Eds.), *Heart disease: Environment, stress and gender* (Vol. 327). Amsterdam: IOS Press. (NATO Science Series, Series I: Life and behavioural sciences)

Sigerist, H. E. (1956). Galen's hygiene. In H. E. Sigerist (Ed.), *Landmarks in the history of hygiene* (pp. 1–19). London: Oxford University Press.

Smith, D. G., Shipley, R., & Rose, G. (1990). Magnitude and causes of socioeconomic differentials in mortality: Further evidence from the Whitehall Study. *Journal of Epidemiology and Community Health, 44,* 265–270.

Solberg, L. I., Brekke, M. L., & Kottke, T. E. (1997). Are physicians less likely to recommend preventive services to low-SES patients? *Preventive Medicine, 26,* 350–357.

Solomon, S. D., Smith, E. M., Robins, L. N., & Fishbach, R. L. (1987). Social involvement as a mediator of disaster-induced stress. *Journal of Applied Social Psychology, 17,* 1092–1112.

Spangler, J. G., Bell, R. A., Dignan, M. B., & Michielutte, R. (1997). Prevalence and predictors of tobacco use among Lumbee Indian women in Robeson County, North Carolina. *Journal of Community Health, 22*(2), 115–125.

Spangler, J. G., Bell, R. A., Knick, S., Michielutte, R., Dignan, M. B., & Summerson, J. H. (1999). Epidemiology of tobacco use among Lumbee Indians in North Carolina. *Journal of Cancer Education, 14*(1), 34–40.

Stamler, J., Stamler, R., & Neaton, J. D. (1993). Blood pressure, systolic and diastolic and cardiovascular risks. *Archives of Internal Medicine, 153,* 598–615.

Stone, E. J., McKenzie, T. L., Welk, G. J., & Booth, M. L. (1998). Effects of physical activity interventions in youth: Review and synthesis. *American Journal of Preventive Medicine, 15*(4), 298–315.

Strogatz, D. S., & James, S. A. (1986). Social support and hypertension among Blacks and Whites in a rural southern community. *American Journal of Epidemiology, 124,* 949–956.

Stronks, K., van de Mheen, H., Van Den Bos, J., & Mackenbach, J. P. (1997). The interrelationship between income, health and employment status. *International Journal of Epidemiology, 26,* 592–600.

Sundquist, J., & Winkleby, M. A. (1999). Cardiovascular risk factors in Mexican American adults: A transcultural analysis of NHANES III, 1988–1994. *American Journal of Public Health, 89*(5), 723–730.

Sy, F. S., Chng, C. L., Choi, S. T., & Wong, F. Y. (1998). Epidemiology of HIV and AIDS among Asian and Pacific Islander Americans. *AIDS Education and Prevention, 10*(Suppl. 3), 4–18.

Taylor, S. E., Repetti, R. L., & Seeman, T. (1997). Health psychology: What is an unhealthy environment and how does it get under the skin? *Annual Review of Psychology, 48,* 411–447.

Tennstedt, S., & Chang, B. H. (1998). The relative contribution of ethnicity versus socioeconomic status in explaining differences in disability and receipt of informal care. *Journals of Gerontology: Series B, Psychological Sciences and Social Sciences, 53,* 61–70.

Thompson, V. L. S. (1996). Perceived experiences of racism as stressful life events. *Community Mental Health Journal, 32,* 223–233.

Thridandam, M., Fong, W., Jang, M., Louie, L., & Forst, M. (1998). A tobacco and alcohol use profile of San Francisco's Chinese community. *Journal of Drug Education, 28*(4), 377–393.

Tortolero, S. R., Masse, L. C., Fulton, J. E., Torres, I., & Kohl, H. W., III. (1999). Assessing physical activity among minority women: Focus group results. *Women's Health Issues, 9*(3), 135–142.

Uchino, B. N., Cacioppo, J. T., & Kiecolt-Glaser, J. K. (1996). Relationship between social support and physiological processes: A review with emphasis on underlying mechanisms and implications for health. *Psychological Bulletin, 119,* 488–531.

U.S. Department of Health and Human Services. (1985). *Report of the Secretary's task force on Black and minority health.* Washington, DC: U.S. Government Printing Office.

U.S. Department of Health and Human Services. (1995a). *Health in the United States, 1994* (DHHS Publication No. PHS 95–1232). Hyattsville, MD: Author.

U.S. Department of Health and Human Services. (1995b). *Vital and health services: Trends in the health of older Americans United States, 1994* (Series 3: Analytic and Epidemiological Studies, No. 30, DHHS Publication No. PHS 95–1414). Hyattsville, MD: Author.

Vander, M. R., Cummings, S. R., & Coates, T. J. (1990). Ethnicity and smoking: Differences in White, Black, Hispanic, and Asian medical patients who smoke. *American Journal of Preventive Medicine, 6*(4), 194–199.

Wagener, D. K., Walstedt, J., Jenkins, L., Burnett, C., Lalich, N., & Fingerhut, M. (1997). Women: Work and health. *Vital and Health Statistics, 31,* 1–91. (Series 3: Analytical and Epidemiological)

Waldron, I. (1976). Why do women live longer than men? Part I. *Journal of Human Stress, 2,* 2–13.

Waldron, I. (1995). Contributions of changing gender differences in behavior and social roles to changing gender differences in mortality. In D. Sabo & D. F. Gordon (Eds.), *Men's health and illness* (pp. 22–45). Thousand Oaks, CA: Sage.

Waldron, I. (1997). Changing gender roles and gender differences in health behavior. In D. S. Gochman (Ed.), *Handbook of health research. I: Personal and social determinants.* New York: Plenum Press.

Waldron, I., & Johnston, S. (1976). Why do women live longer than men? Part II. *Journal of Human Stress, 3,* 19–29.

Weidner, G. (1995). Personality and heart disease in women: Past research and future directions. *Zeitschrift fuer Gesundheitspsychologie (Journal for Health Psychology), 1,* 4–23.

Weidner, G. (1998). Gender gap in health decline in Eastern Europe. *Nature, 395,* 835.

Weidner, G., Boughal, T., Connor, S. L., Pieper, C., & Mendell, N. R. (1997). The relationship of job strain to standard coronary risk factors in women and men of the Family Heart Study. *Health Psychology, 16,* 239–247.

Weidner, G., & Collins, R. L. (1993). Gender, coping, and health. In H. W. Krohne (Ed.), *Attention and avoidance* (pp. 241–265). Seattle, WA: Hogrefe & Huber.

Weidner, G., Connor, S. L., Chesney, M. A., Burns, J. W., Connor, W. E., Matarazzo, J. D., et al. (1991). Sex differences in high density lipoprotein cholesterol among low-level alcohol consumers. *Circulation, 83,* 176–180.

Weidner, G., & Messina, C. R. (1998). Cardiovascular reactivity to mental stress and cardiovascular disease. In K. Orth-Gomer, M. A. Chesney, & N. Wenger (Eds.), *Women, stress, and heart disease* (pp. 219–236). Hillsdale, NJ: Erlbaum.

Weidner, G., & Mueller, H. (2000). Emotions and heart disease. In M. B. Goldman & M. C. Hatch (Eds.), *Women and health* (pp. 789–796). San Diego, CA: Academic Press.

Wellisch, D., Kagawa-Singer, M., Reid, S. L., Lin, Y. J., Nishikawa-Lee, S., & Wellisch, M. (1999). An exploratory study of social support: A cross-cultural comparison of Chinese-, Japanese-, and Anglo-American breast cancer patients. *Psycho-Oncology, 8*(3), 207–219.

West, P. (1997). Health inequalities in the early years: Is there equalisation in youth? *Social Science and Medicine, 44,* 833–858.

Whitfield, K. E., & Baker-Thomas, T. A. (1999). Individual differences in aging among African-Americans. *International Journal of Aging and Human Development, 48*(1), 73–79.

Whiting, S. J., & Mackenzie, M. L. (1998). Assessing the changing diet of indigenous peoples. *Nutrition Reviews, 56*(8), 248–250.

Wiist, W. H., & Flack, J. M. (1992). A test of the John Henryism hypothesis: Cholesterol and blood pressure. *Journal of Behavioral Medicine, 15,* 15–29.

Willett, W. C., Manson, J. E., Stampfer, M. J., Colditz, G. A., Rosner, B., Speizer, F. E., et al. (1995). Weight, weight change, and coronary heart disease in women: Risk within the "normal" weight range. *Journal of the American Medical Association, 273*(6), 461–465.

Williams, D. R. (1992). Social structure and the health behaviors of Blacks. In K. W. Schaie, D. Blazer, & J. S. House (Eds.), *Aging, health behaviors, and health outcomes* (pp. 59–64). Hillsdale, NJ: Erlbaum.

Williams, D. R. (1996). Race/ethnicity and socioeconomic status: Measurement and methodological issues. *International Journal of Health Services, 26,* 483–505.

Williams, D. R., & Collins, C. (1995). Socioeconomic and racial differences in health. *Annual Review of Sociology, 21,* 349–386.

Williams, D. R., Yu, Y., Jackson, J., & Anderson, N. (1997). Racial differences in physical and mental health: Socioeconomic status, stress and discrimination. *Journal of Health Psychology, 2,* 335–351.

Williams, R., Boyce, W. T., & Wright, A. L. (1993). The relationship of family structure and perceived family support to length of hospital stay. *Family Practice Research Journal, 13*(2), 185–193.

Winkleby, M. A., Kraemer, H. C., Ahn, D. K., & Varady, A. N. (1998). Ethnic and socioeconomic differences in cardiovascular disease risk factors: Findings for women from the third National Health and Nutrition Examination Survey, 1988–1994. *Journal of the American Medical Association, 280*(4), 356–362.

Winkleby, M. A., Robinson, T. N., Sundquist, J., & Kraemer, H. C. (1999). Ethnic variation in cardiovascular disease risk factors among children and young adults: Findings from the third National Health and Nutrition Examination Survey, 1988–1994. *Journal of the American Medical Association, 281,* 1006–1013.

Wu, A. H., Ziegler, R. G., Nomura, A. M., West, D. W., Kolonel, L. N., Horn-Ross, P. L., et al. (1998). Soy intake and risk of breast cancer in Asians and Asian Americans. *Journal of Clinical Nutrition, 68*(Suppl. 6), 1437S–1443S.

Wynder, E. L. (1998). Tobacco as a cause of lung cancer: Some reflections. *American Journal of Epidemiology, 148,* 1133–1134.

Yanek, L. R., Moy, T. F., Blumenthal, R. S., Raqueno, J. V., Yook, R. M., Hill, M. N., et al. (1998). Hypertension among siblings of persons with premature coronary heart disease. *Hypertension, 32,* 123–128.

Young, D. R., Miller, K. W., Wilder, L. B., Yanek, L. R., & Becker, D. M. (1998). Physical activity patterns of urban African Americans. *Journal of Community Health, 23*(2), 99–112.

Yurgalevitch, S. M., Kriska, A. M., Welty, T. K., Go, O., Robbins, D. C., & Howard, B. V. (1998). Physical activity and lipids and lipoproteins in American Indians ages 45–74. *Medicine and Science in Sports & Exercise, 30*(4), 543–549.

CHAPTER 24

Occupational Health Psychology

JAMES CAMPBELL QUICK, LOIS E. TETRICK, JOYCE ADKINS, AND CHARLES KLUNDER

Raymond, Wood, and Patrick (1990) used the term *occupational health psychology* (OHP) to describe the emerging interdisciplinary specialty at the crossroads of health psychology and public health in the organizational context of work environments. OHP applies several specialties in psychology to organizational settings for the improvement of the quality of work life, the protection and safety of workers, and promotion of healthy work environments. Healthy work

The authors have drawn on several aspects of their work and previous publications developed for the American Psychological Association and the National Institute for Occupational Safety and Health in the preparation of this review chapter on occupational health psychology. We thank Robert Brown for editing the "Special Section: Occupational Health Psychology," in *Professional Psychology: Research and Practice,* with articles by Sauter and Hurrell (1999), Quick (1999b), Adkins (1999), and Schneider, Camara, Tetrick, and Stenberg (1999). Support for this work came in part through a faculty development leave (2000–2001) to the first author from the University of Texas at Arlington. We thank Donna Ross for preparing the manuscript and Joanne Gavin for technical support. The opinions expressed are those of the authors and do not necessarily reflect the views of the University of Texas, the United States Air Force, the Department of Defense, or the United States Government.

environments are ones where people feel good, achieve high performance, and have high levels of well-being, which is consistent with the happy/productive worker thesis (Quick & Tetrick, in press; Staw, 1986; T. Wright & Cropanzano, 1997).

OHP is founded on strong traditions both throughout Europe and in the United States. In keeping with those traditions, Murphy and Cooper (2000) present a model along with international cases of healthy work organizations. The broad interdisciplinary framework of OHP has arisen in the United States because of the need for closer integration between psychology, related behavioral sciences, and occupational medicine to address the growing health and productivity costs of distress at work (Sauter, Murphy, & Hurrell, 1990). While psychology and the behavioral sciences play important roles in areas of occupational safety and health, such as ergonomics, behavioral toxicology, behavioral safety, and employee assistance, OHP is expanding the boundaries of established disciplines and integrating related domains of scientific knowledge and professional practice.

The first section of the chapter provides a brief historical overview of OHP. The next section reviews the ecological dimensions of OHP. The third section presents a framework for preventive health management, and the fourth section presents an organizational health center model followed by an OHP training model. A case of organizational transition is presented next, followed by a discussion of future directions.

THE HISTORY OF OCCUPATIONAL HEALTH PSYCHOLOGY

Sauter and Hurrell (1999), Quick (1999a), and Quick, Camara, et al. (1997) provide brief historical reviews of OHP from its origins in the early twentieth century through the close of the century. Many of the foundational concepts in OHP emerge from research on the stress concept from its framing by Walter B. Cannon in the early 1900s through its elaboration in the 1990s. Quick, Quick, Nelson, and Hurrell (1997) provide a comprehensive and historical view of this body of knowledge. More recently, Barling and Griffiths (in press) provide a detailed discussion of the history of occupational health psychology. Their discussion of the historical roots dates to the mid-nineteenth century (circa 1845) and covers the detailed descriptions by Friedrich Engels of the physical and psychological health problems suffered by workers from many different trades. At the outset of the Industrial Revolution in England, Engels believed the origins of these problems to be in the organization of work and its associated social and environmental conditions.

In addition to the occupational health and organizational stress initiatives described in these sources, there were initiatives early in the American twentieth century that drew attention to the importance of broader concerns with psychological well-being and mental health. Adolf Meyer at Johns Hopkins and William James at Harvard advanced the cause of mental health, commonly known as mental hygiene, early in the 1900s throughout America (Winters, 1952). Their attention initially focused on the burden of suffering associated with depression and then broadened more generally to psychological well-being and mental health. The first use of the term *preventive management* was in Henry Elkind's (1931) collected volume on mental hygiene in industry, which applied psychiatry and the mental hygiene national agenda to workplace issues of industrial relations, human nature in organizations, management, and leadership.

Donald Laird (1929), as director of the Colgate Psychological Laboratory and with support from members of the Central New York Section of the Taylor Society, developed a series of essays applying psychological concepts and ideas to industrial contexts at companies such as Ford Motor Company and Remington-Rand Company. He advanced the thesis that every executive could become his or her own psychologist by enhancing personal development, reducing fatigue, and improving morale. In addition, Laird founded the *Industrial Psychology Monthly*. During this time, James brought Hugo Münsterberg from Europe to head the Harvard Psychological Laboratory. Münsterberg later became president of the American Psychological Association and concerned himself early in the century with industrial accidents and human safety (Offermann & Gowing, 1990). A more contemporary figure, Richard Lowman (1993), sets forth a clinically useful taxonomy of psychological work-related dysfunctions as a guide to disentangle personality disorders, psychopathology, and dysfunctions with their roots in the workplace.

ECOLOGICAL DIMENSIONS OF OCCUPATIONAL HEALTH PSYCHOLOGY

With roots in both the profession of psychology and the public health notions of prevention, OHP has as a central concern the design, creation, and maintenance of healthy work environments. As early as 1961, Abraham Maslow was calling for the definition and creation of healthy work environments. Healthy work environments may be characterized by high productivity, high employee satisfaction, good safety records, low frequencies of disability claims and union grievances, low absenteeism, low turnover, and the absence of violence. Here we suggest that one framework for OHP uses three key ecological dimensions as the basis for action: the work environment, the individual, and the work-family interface. Each ecological dimension includes several key concepts of concern to OHP. After discussing each of these dimensions separately, we address the concept of goodness-of-fit.

The Work Environment

The health of a work environment may be influenced by a broad range of occupational, psychological, organizational, and work design demands or stressors (Cooper & Marshall, 1976; Hurrell & Murphy, 1992; Murphy & Cooper, 2000). While not limited to the following elements, these include (a) factors intrinsic to the job and its context, such as workload, pace, control, and the physical environment; (b) factors related to the individual's role in the organization, such as role conflict, ambiguity, and person-role conflict; (c) factors concerned with individual career development, such as job security and advancement potential; (d) factors associated with the individual's relationships at work, such as social support, participative management, and supervisory support; and (e) factors related to organizational characteristics (e.g., communication, culture, and structure).

Professionals in OHP may develop a specific focus in this broad spectrum. For example, Theorell and Karasek (1996), Karasek (1979), Gardell (1987), and Sauter, Hurrell, and Cooper (1989) emphasize the concept of worker control, self-determination, or job decision latitude as an important work environment design parameter that impacts employee strain (distress) and health. Beyond the concept of control, Landy, Quick, and Kasl (1994) address uncertainty and conflict as other key concepts in the design of healthy work environments. At the organizational systems level, the climate and the culture of the organization is an important OHP concept (Rosen, 1986). For example, Chaparral Steel Company and Southwest Airlines exhibit healthy organizational climates and work cultures that place people at the center, treating them as human resource assets rather than labor cost liabilities. In the case of Chaparral Steel, four pieces of evidence support this conclusion: (a) more than 90% of the workforce's participation in corporate sponsored continuing education; (b) over 65% of the workforce's stock ownership in the company; (c) an employee turnover rate of less than 2% per quarter; and (d) an extraordinary labor productivity of 1.38 man hours per ton or 1,100 tons of steel per man year. While highly productive, Chaparral Steel cares equally for its people through a safe, secure working environment. Chaparral Steel is ranked second in workers' compensation experience ratings (0.36 compared to an industry average of 0.91) by the United States National Council on Compensation Insurance. Chaparral's lost time frequency for the 20-year period of 1975 to 1995 is also significantly better (range = <1 to 4) than the steel industry average (range 6 to 15).

Gordon Forward has been an advocate for a new industrial revolution from manufacturing (made by hand) to mentofacturing (made by the mind), based on a paradigm shift to a work environment that emphasizes learning, human development, risk-taking, and technology transfer (Forward, Beach, Gray, & Quick, 1991). The values at the center of Chaparral's work culture are (a) trust and responsibility, (b) risk and curiosity, (c) knowledge and expertise, (d) networking and information exchange, and (e) humor and humility. These values emphasize human strength, capability, and competence. Chaparral Steel managers like to say that they manage by "adultery" because they treat employees like adults and expect them to act and behave responsibly. The German industrial engineer Luczek (1992) has advocated anthropocentric, "good work design," for well over a decade. Anthropocentric work design places the individual at the center of the work design process. In addition to the product sector of the economy, organizations in the service sector of the economy espouse similar values in their organizational cultures. Southwest Airlines is an example of a service organization with a healthy work culture, whose core values center around humor, altruism, and people. In the early 1990s, Southwest's productivity per employee was significantly better than the U.S. airline industry average while its labor-management relations have been better than many of its sister airlines where conflict and acrimony have, at times, resulted in organizational demise (Quick, 1992).

The Individual

A broad range of individual characteristics similarly influences the health of a work environment. These characteristics include career stage, age, coping style, negative affectivity, self-esteem, health-status, and self-reliance. Beyond designing work environments that are person-oriented and healthy, OHP is concerned with individuals in their own right. Some of the specific concepts related to individual behavior important to OHP include emotion, anger, workaholism, and gender difference predispositions. For example, anger has been found to have a lethal role in individuals' lives and to exacerbate the experience of distress and strain (Spielberger, Krasner, & Solomon, 1988; L. Wright, 1988). Some normative data on trait anger precipitated by the work environment, apart from state anger, has found that individuals who score above the 75th percentile are at risk of psychological and interpersonal problems, while individuals who score above the 90th percentile run the additional risk of medical problems (Spielberger, 1991). Played out in the workplace, anger can have psychologically and physically destructive effects as well as adverse organizational impacts such as reduced productivity and impaired teamwork.

Gender, one important diversity difference in organizations, is an individual characteristic that has important implications for OHP. For example, men and women experience stress and strain differently. Nelson, Quick, and Hitt (1989) found significant differences in distress between men and women in the personnel profession while at the same time finding only one difference in their experience of work-related demands. Specifically, women reported that they experienced significantly more stress associated with organizational politics. Research further suggests social support may be a more potent buffer for women and white-collar men and perceptions of control a more potent buffer for blue-collar men (Johnson & Hall, 1988).

Von Dusch (1868) was the first to call attention to excessive involvement in work; *workaholism* is the contemporary label for this individual behavior. It is a third individual factor that may have destructive organizational impacts and has been a concern in the domain of work stress for more than a decade (McLean, 1979). While healthy work behavior results in a wide range of positive outcomes for individuals and organizations, patterns of overcommitment to work (i.e., workaholism) may have adverse effects on the individual as well as on the workplace and the family (Lowman, 1993). Porter (1996) shows how workaholism is a form of addictive behavior that distorts interpersonal relationships and interferes with organizational operations. Thus, workaholism, anger and emotion, and gender are three examples in a broad spectrum of important individual differences in the domain of OHP.

The Work-Family Interface

People live in multiple life arenas and work environment demands are not the only ones that impact their health. Numerous work-family interface factors such as shift work, flextime, leave policy, day care, elder care, overtime, and dual career issues are highly relevant to the occupational health of people at work. While it may make conceptual sense to partition these various elements of a person's life into different roles, it is difficult to avoid spillover effects or interactions (Lobel, 1991; Whittington, Paulus, & Quick, in press). An important area in a person's nonwork life is the family, and the work-family interface has been found to be important in understanding a person's health at work as well as at home (Piotrkowski, 1979). As workforces become more diverse and as a greater number of women enter the workforce, work-family interaction increases. This may be especially true for two-career family systems. Hence, gender mixes with the work-family interface and may create conflict and adverse health-related outcomes for family members (Frone, Russell, & Barnes, 1996). While the negative effects of conflict are more common, work-family interface can actually have positive effects as well (Frone, in press).

Goodness-of-Fit

In OHP, healthy work environments must also give consideration to the issue of goodness-of-fit among the three basic design dimensions of the work environment, the individual, and the work-family interface. The concept of goodness-of-fit is an extension of the person-environment fit theory (Edwards, 1996). This approach suggests that badness-of-fit is the problem, not that there is always an inherent problem in the work environment, the person, or the family system. Therefore, dysfunction results from a lack of goodness-of-fit (i.e., badness-of-fit), or compatibility, between the various design elements. While the research may suggest, in general, that more control at work is healthier, that less anger in an individual is healthier, and that fewer work-family conflicts are better, there is variance along each of these design dimensions.

Thus, there are individuals who prefer more control than others do and some jobs in which a certain amount of competitive anger may fuel productive outcomes. Hence, the best of circumstances occurs when the individual fits well with the work environment and when there is a fit between both the individual and the work environment with the family system.

PREVENTIVE HEALTH MANAGEMENT

The Occupational Safety and Health Act of 1974 established that employees in the United States should have a safe and healthy work environment. Similar legislation has been enacted in The Netherlands, Sweden, and the European Union (Kompier, 1996). This legislation resulted from the view that the work environment presents risk factors to the safety and health of workers. Certainly the statistics on the number of individuals who are treated for occupational injuries yearly or who die from injuries that occurred on the job support this view (Sauter & Hurrell, 1999). However, it is now recognized that the work environment can also enhance the health and safety of individuals (Sauter et al., 1990). Since work is a central aspect of many people's lives (Cox, 1997), it is not surprising that the workplace has grown to be viewed as a focal place for health promotion (Gebhardt & Crump, 1990), as well as for injury and illness prevention.

OHP emerged as a discipline that viewed the work environment not only as a risk factor but also as a health enhancer, and it takes a public health perspective (Rosenstock, 1997; Sauter & Hurrell, 1999). OHP's primary concern is developing and maintaining the health and well-being of employees and their families. Thus, the primary focus is on the prevention of injuries and illnesses and the enhancement of health, rather than the treatment of injuries and illnesses, by creating safe and healthy working environments (Quick, Camara, et al., 1997; Sauter, Hurrell, Fox, Tetrick, & Barling, 1999). These ideas come from concepts in preventive medicine and public health, originally developed and applied to stem the onset and spread of disease epidemics (Wallace, Last, & Doebbeling, 1998).

The public health model classifies interventions into three categories: primary interventions, secondary interventions, and tertiary interventions (Schmidt, 1994). Primary interventions follow a population prevention strategy (Rose, 1992) and are applied to all people, including those who may not be at risk. They are frequently used in health promotion and health education campaigns where the message is sent to everyone despite their current risk status. In the field of OHP, an example of a primary intervention is providing all managers training in improving their relationships with their subordinates. Many of those managers may already have very good relationships with their subordinates; thus, their subordinates are not at risk of stress-related problems due to poor supervision. Secondary interventions focus on people who are believed to be at risk for injury or illness. An example of a secondary intervention might be the initiation of frequent breaks for data-entry operators who are known to be at risk for musculoskeletal distress from prolonged use of keyboards. Tertiary interventions target people who are experiencing symptoms of illness or injury and attempt to restore them to health. Examples of tertiary interventions might be individual counseling to reduce anxiety or establishing a return-to-work plan for an injured worker.

OHP concentrates on primary prevention interventions although it may include secondary interventions in which known risk factors in the work environment are eliminated. The previous examples describe interventions conducted at the individual level. However, it is possible that interventions can target workgroups, teams, departments, and organizations. Cooper and Cartwright (1994) have suggested that healthy organizations will reduce the need for secondary or tertiary interventions. However, when primary prevention is not feasible or effective, occupational health psychologists must be able to recognize situations where individual employees may need tertiary treatments (Quick, 1999b). Given the vast array of potential risk factors in the work environment and the interdependencies among individuals in the work environment, OHP is truly multidisciplinary in nature and training models need to reflect this.

ORGANIZATIONAL HEALTH

This section discusses the evolution of the concept of organizational health; develops the scientist-practitioner model; reviews the public health functions of assessment, surveillance, and evaluation; and concludes with a case illustration of the organizational health center concept as a practice model. OHP seeks to promote the systemic health of organizations. The discipline has evolved in concept and application over the last decade of the twentieth century. Whereas health, well-being, and especially work-related health were once viewed solely as a personal concern and responsibility of the individual worker, the focus has shifted to a more ecological or systems view in which organizations and leaders bear increasing responsibility. This shift has expanded the worldview of occupational health to include a transactional relationship between workers and the workplace, with an equal emphasis on the psychosocial context and the physical work environment. Individuals function in a mutually interdependent relationship with the work structure and process.

The concept of organizational health has grown from this perspective: Organizational health is inherently systemic. To promote organizational health requires the joint achievement of both individual well-being and organizational effectiveness. Because organizations are dynamic, multidimensional systems (Katz & Kahn, 1966), disease, or dysfunction in any element in the organization disrupts the balance in the system and negatively impacts other elements. Similarly, intervention at any one point in the system influences all other elements.

Like individual health, organizational health is not a state of being or a fixed characteristic of the organization; it is a process that requires continuous management. Organizations operate in a state of continuous change and flux. Only organizations that are able to flex with short-term change and adapt to long-term cycles of growth and transformation are able to achieve, maintain, and enhance levels of organizational health. In keeping with the fluidity of the process, organizational health runs along a continuum, from high levels of effectiveness to organizational disease (Adkins, Quick, & Moe, 2000). Promoting organizational health involves more than the reduction of illness and injury of workers or the minimization of organization distress. OHP seeks to promote optimal functioning of the organizational system rather than focusing only on deficit-based change.

Optimizing organizational health requires a broad, problem-solving perspective to assess and intervene in this multifaceted, fluid organizational system. OHP moves away from a narrowly specialized field of vision into a more integrative, collaborative model, looking across disciplinary lines to find the most effective methodologies to apply in the organizational context. No one professional domain can hold all the knowledge necessary across such a broad landscape. Thus, occupational health psychologists often find themselves in the role of integrating agent, bringing together interdisciplinary teams to provide knowledge and insight into all facets of the system. They also work collaboratively in the workplace, forming positive relationships with both management and labor to build capacity in the social capital of the organization.

Thus, effective organizational health programs, from proactive prevention through tertiary intervention, consider the processes, structure, systems, and culture of the organizational client as well as individual differences of the workers. Promoting individual health and well-being in the workplace is expected to lead to or support organizational effectiveness. Programs, such as worksite health promotion (Terborg, 1986) and worksite stress management interventions (Ivancevich, Matteson, Freedman, & Phillips, 1990), boast the benefits to both the individual and the organization of proactively developing healthy workers and minimizing the potentially negative impact of stressful working conditions. Outcome and evaluation studies confirming the value of worksite support programs have been riddled with methodological flaws and theoretical insufficiencies (Donaldson, 1995; Elkin & Rosch, 1990; Murphy, 1988). Yet, results from increasingly rigorous studies lend evidence to substantiate the positive benefit to organizations in such areas as reduced absenteeism and turnover, increased productivity, reduced health care utilization, and reduced workers' compensation costs (Cooper, Sloan, & Williams, 1988; Landy et al., 1994; Moran, Wolff, & Green, 1995; Pellitier, 1991).

Nevertheless, the health of the organization is more than simply the collective health of the individual workers. Practices and policies targeted by individually focused worksite health programs comprise only a part of the matrix of OHP services. The need to promote organizational health through intervention in the organizational domain, identifying and removing psychosocial hazards, and reducing behavioral risk has been advocated as critical to the advancement of occupational health and safety goals on a national and organizational level (Sauter & Hurrell, 1999). In addition, the organizational system takes on characteristics separate from individual health, making assessment, intervention, research, and surveillance at a systems level a valid point of entry into the occupational health process. The transactional-ecological perspective of organizational health (Adkins, 1998; Barone, 1995; Lazarus, 1995) as an interdependent system helps to maintain a dual focus on both the individual and the organization that is fundamental to OHP.

Scientist-Practitioner Model

As an interdisciplinary field, OHP draws on the theory, principles, and history of component disciplines. It is, by nature and development, firmly entrenched in the scientist-practitioner model—a model that relies on the application of scientific principles and methodology to professional practice. Practitioners have the potential to influence the affective, cognitive, behavioral, and physical well-being of clients, whether those clients are individuals, families, groups, or entire organizations. Because of the potential for harm to arise from that influence, ethical standards require that practice principles have a reasonable expectation of efficacy and a low probability of negative effects. Practices founded in scientific theory and solid empirical evidence provide at least a minimal level of assurance. Scientist-practitioners rely on available empirical evidence to guide established practices as well as to develop new practices and to ensure those actions not only do no harm but also have a high potential for successful outcomes. Further, they apply

the scientific method of problem solving to issues encountered when standard practices are not clearly available.

The implementation of scientifically derived practice standards is equally as important in working with organizations as in working with individuals. OHP practitioners are involved with large groups of people who may experience stress and strain associated with their work. The realities of organizational turbulence and chaotic change experienced by organizations worldwide require that stress and its relationship with the organizational environment be taken into consideration in both current operations and future planning (Gowing, Kraft, & Quick, 1998). Large-scale practices and policy development related to occupational stress prevention and management magnify the potential for positive impact as well as harmful effects. The responsibility to ensure that practices and policies are efficacious is ever present and increases with the level and breadth of potential influence. Likewise, practices that are detrimental to the effective functioning of the organization eventually affect individual well-being (Quick, Murphy, & Hurrell, 1992). Low productivity and high costs associated with organizational disease create threats to job security and potential deleterious effects of job loss (DeFrank & Ivancevich, 1986; Levi et al., 1984). It is therefore incumbent on practitioners to ensure that their programs provide value for their cost and ultimately improve the bottom line of the organization.

Apart from ethical standards, both public and private organizations are increasingly focused on data-driven, results-based programs and practices. A competitive, global environment demands attention to the costs and benefits of each business unit. Private and government agencies are likewise held to performance standards and cost controls. OHP practitioners have both professional and business stakes in the outcome of the programs and policies they recommend and implement. To survive in this context, OHP practitioners and programs must demonstrate quantitative or qualitative measures of value to the organization.

Assessment, Surveillance, and Evaluation

Occupational health psychologists engage in a range of roles and functions encompassing research, teaching, and practice (Adkins, 1999). Quantitative and qualitative information is the foundation for policy and practice decisions as well as a means for marketing principles and programs to organizational clients. OHP is, in fact, a data-driven discipline. The need for valid and reliable information on which to make policy and program decisions cuts across OHP data-based functions, domains of intervention, and factors associated with the organizational health process, as indicated in Figure 24.1.

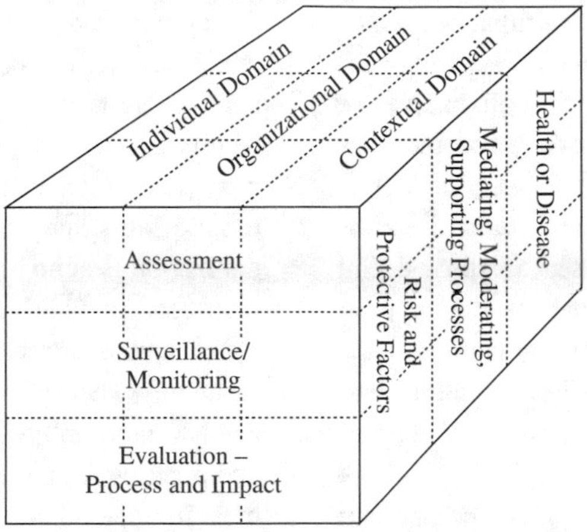

The Organizational Health Center

Mission Statement

. . . maximizing human potential and productivity through optimal health—physical, behavioral, and organizational.

We believe our most valuable resource is people. Therefore, in partnership with organizational and community agencies, we form an integrated, multi-disciplinary team, presenting a single face to the human services and behavioral analysis user. We provide innovative and responsive support to the quality of work life process through measurable, long-range plans that emphasize current and future needs. We provide training and consultation in effective and efficient business practices that empower our people to excel. Through our efforts we strive to magnify productivity, pride, and well being for our people and our organization.

Statement of Purpose

- To enhance both productivity and well-being.
- To focus on prevention and organizational intervention.
- To focus on the workplace as the area of intervention.
- To provide a total, integrated workforce service

Founding Goals

- To improve working conditions through organizational intervention.
- To provide information, education, and technical training.
- To enrich health and support services for all workers.
- To monitor psychosocial risk factors and disorders in the workplace.

Program Components

- *Services Coordination*—Integrating Agent.
- *Organizational Consultation and Development*—Organizational Assessments, Team Development, Labor-Management Partnerships, Leadership Development, Executive Coaching.
- *Information Broker*—Communications Clearinghouse.
- *Specialized Program Management*—Workplace Violence, Suicide Prevention, Conflict Resolution.
- *Worksite Support*—Employee Assistance, Workplace Health Promotion, Peer Counselors, Behavioral Consultation.
- *Research, Surveillance, and Evaluation*—Needs assessment, program evaluation, integrated metrics.

Figure 24.1   Occupational Health Psychology Data-based Dimensions.

The process of risk identification and assessment is fundamental to developing countermeasures to mitigate and manage those risks. Following implementation, methods for evaluating effectiveness and outcomes of policies and practices ensure that programs are implemented with fidelity, meet their intended objectives, and ultimately produce their intended results or impact (Adkins & Weiss, in press). At all times, continuous monitoring or surveillance of hazards, risks, and capabilities enables control of and planned intervention into emerging negative processes at work. All three measurement strategies can be applied across OHP domains and along the entire continuum of organizational health.

The basis for propelling psychosocial risks and the consequent illnesses and injuries into the mainstream of occupational health and safety came from the component roots in public health, epidemiology, and medical surveillance (Quick, Quick, Nelson, & Hurrell, 1997; Sauter & Hurrell, 1999).

Information collected from large-scale national and international surveys, such as the multiyear quality of employment surveys first initiated in 1969 (Quinn & Staines, 1978) and the 1985 National Health Interview Survey (Shilling & Brackbill, 1987), as well as epidemiological studies conducted through the National Institute for Occupational Safety and Health (NIOSH; Caplan, Cobb, French, Harrison, & Pinneau, 1975), prompted the recognition of psychosocial risk factors as among the leading causes of occupational illness and injury (Sauter & Hurrell, 1999). Similar lines of research placed psychological disorders among the top ten illnesses associated with job-related causes, including stress and other psychosocial hazards. (Millar, 1984; Sauter et al., 1990).

The processes associated with, and the importance of, assessment and evaluation arise from clinical and organizational psychology and organization development. While epidemiological data can be used to estimate problems in the workplace, context-unique assessments of occupational environments have generally relied on self-report, employee-opinion questionnaires (Griffin, Hart, & Wilson-Evered, 2000; Kraut, 1996). Similar but more expansive methods provide for in-depth organizational assessment procedures, often identified in the rubric of organizational evaluations, diagnosis, or audits (Cartwright, Cooper, & Murphy, 1995; Levinson, 2002). These methodologies generally add qualitative information obtained from interviews with individuals and groups, supplemented with behavioral observations and organizational records to add depth to the more general opinion surveys.

Outcome measures are taken from all OHP component disciplines and cover a wide array of both individual and organizational indices. Self-report measures used in outcome evaluations are often collected in conjunction with opinion surveys during assessment procedures. Collection of objective measures of organizational variables, such as productivity measures, has varied in use and effectiveness. At the organizational level, measures used to indicate organizational health or the impact of intervention programs have included corporate financial status (Casio, 1998) and production output, as well as employee-related measures of work withdrawal and job satisfaction. Experience sampling techniques, which collect information in real time through the use of diaries or electronic records taken at random across a period of time, have been increasingly used to overcome the problems associated with retrospective self-report measures (Weiss, 2001). At the individual level, illness and accident rates, morbidity and mortality rates, unscheduled absences, and various measures of physical, psychological, or emotional distress have been widely used.

Despite the important role of a data-based foundation in OHP growth and development, measurement and methodological problems have plagued the field of OHP as has been the case generally in occupational stress research (Koop, 1992). Methodologies and instruments used to measure organizational health and its related processes are generally inconsistent across studies, with new researchers using their own favorite techniques or measures or, more likely, developing a unique measure for each new purpose. A number of standardized measurement instruments have been designed to measure job stress, individual and organizational strain or distress, individual coping (e.g., Cooper et al., 1988; Hurrell & McLaney, 1988; Moos, 1981; Osipow & Spokane, 1992; Speilberger, 1994), human factors (Kohler & Kamp, 1992; Reason, 1997), behavioral risk (Yandrick, 1996), and organizational climate (James & James, 1989). Yet, the inconsistent use of standardized instruments across studies examining similar constructs continues to limit the ability of both

researchers and practitioners to make comparisons across occupations, across industries, across international boundaries, and across time. In addition, the ability to generalize the results of intervention strategies that use a wide variety of constructs and measures is limited. Effective surveillance and monitoring strategies are needed to determine where the organization is at any time and to control the process of movement toward positive health states, as well as to evaluate the effectiveness and outcomes of prevention and intervention strategies. Theory-linking variables and processes are also in need of substantive development. Theory-driven evaluation and practice is increasingly recognized as vital to developing meaningful explanations for the results of intervention as well as for bolstering the probability of replication of program results across occupations, industries, and organizations (Adkins & Weiss, in press).

Thus, promoting organizational health requires developing effective organizational health assessment methodologies. Methods for assessing and monitoring psychosocial risk factors, as well as for measuring and tracking outcomes from interventions designed to eliminate the risks or to reduce or mitigate the impact of those risk factors on individual well-being and organizational effectiveness, provide metrics vital to both practitioners and researchers. Assessing psychosocial strengths and weaknesses associated with both the organizational environment and the individuals in that environment can target resources at high-risk, high-leverage variables. By repeating the process following a period of intervention, managers and change agents can track outcomes and refine intervention targets as changes occur. Basic and applied research into these processes form a foundation for the on-going development of OHP practice guidelines.

Organizational Health Centers: A Practice Model

The scientist-practitioner model has provided a solid foundation for the development of organizational health centers (OHC). It is through practice that organizations and individual workers find benefit in the developing OHP knowledge and technology. OHCs represent the practical application of OHP theory and principles to the workplace.

The American Psychological Association (APA) and National Institute for Occupational Safety and Health (NIOSH) proposed a national strategy for the prevention of work-related psychological disorders (Sauter et al., 1990) and to address workplace psychosocial risk factors and stress contributing to occupational illness and injury rates. This strategy included a blueprint of four objectives: (a) to improve working conditions through organizational modification to reduce potential psychosocial risks and produce a health-engendering work environment, (b) to enhance information, education, and training for the workforce at all levels, (c) to enrich psychological health services for workers, and (d) to improve surveillance and monitoring of risk factors and associated psychological disorders.

The strategy set the stage for a new era in occupational health and safety. However, without application, the strategy would be of little value (Millar, 1984, 1992). OHCs put these goals into practice through an integrated, multidisciplinary service designed to apply behavioral science technology to a workplace setting in an attempt to enhance both organizational effectiveness and individual employee well-being.

Practices associated with an OHC can be provided either internally in a consulting function or from an external consulting position. Regardless of ownership, the positioning of the OHC function is critical. The operation of an OHC is most effective when the principal consultant serves in a position similar to a chief psychological officer (CPO), reporting directly to the upper management of the organization, generally the chief executive officer (CEO) or chief operating officer (COO), or to the management function of the business unit being served. It is also important for the practitioner to be viewed as a neutral party whose interests lie in improving the overall health of the organization rather than being allied with either management, labor, or associated with any politically charged faction in the organization. Therefore, the OHC is ideally positioned at the executive level but serves an impartial consulting role.

OHCs are founded not only on the scientist-practitioner model, but also the practices are rooted in a business culture. While OHP sits at the crossroads of psychology, public health, and business, programs and policies take place in an organizational context. The language and focus must therefore take on a business frame of reference. Effective integration of organizational health processes requires integration of the goals and objectives of the OHC with the goals and objectives of the organization it serves. One of the obstacles to creating lasting change in organizations is building management support and ownership for the programs and values underlying them (Beer & Walton, 1990). Meshing the OHC program goals with the overall corporate goals and strategies offers a method to maximize corporate ownership and build processes with lasting impact.

A prototype OHC was founded at the Sacramento Air Logistics Center at McClellan Air Force Base, California, in 1993 (Adkins, 1999). The OHC function was initiated in response to concerns about the potential impact of occupational stress on productivity and workforce health in a large industrial military installation. The initial program produced positive outcomes after the first year of implementation, leading to the establishment of additional centers at other defense installations as well as implementation of individual program components at other levels in the defense organization. Similar centers have been established in civilian venues under various names. Some programs operate as a complete, multidisciplinary system while others provide customized programs depending on the needs and configuration of the organizational client. Although OHCs operate differently across venues, we discuss seven critical, common functions:

1. Data-based programming.
2. Integrating agent.
3. Organizational consulting.
4. Information broker.
5. Targeted training and prevention.
6. Worksite support.
7. Surveillance, monitoring, and evaluation.

Data-Based Programming

Initiation of an OHC begins with a baseline. Resources are targeted at high-leverage activities and groups based on recognized and assessed issues. While expected problem occurrence rates can be estimated through established general epidemiological incidence and prevalence studies, a baseline specific to the organization is needed to more accurately direct action. In the Sacramento OHC, an organizational health risk appraisal (OHRA) process was designed for overall needs assessment and evaluation in the context of an overall organizational health promotion program. Similar to an individual health risk appraisal, the OHRA was based on a self-report questionnaire designed to identify psychosocial risk factors for the organization taken as an entity. Baseline data such as these provide a broad understanding of the organization to allow for targeting and timing of intervention strategies, as well as a means of monitoring risk factors over time and across interventions. In addition, at the time of baseline data collection, decisions are needed regarding the organizational metrics available and appropriate to use in ongoing surveillance. These measures should be specific, collected reliably and continuously, relevant to the organization, and available over time. The vision of the OHC and its function often drives the selection of metrics.

Integrating Agent

The work of the OHC requires an interdisciplinary perspective either through dedicated staff or a matrix team using available internal talent and external consultants. In addition, the OHC serves an integrating function by bringing together the multiple support services in the organization to form a multidisciplinary team. Change management or stress management teams have been shown to be effective tools for building organizational health (Murphy, 1988). By including management and labor representatives on the team, decisions made can be implemented into action more readily.

Organizational Consulting

OHC staff work with individuals, work teams or units, and the larger organization. The baseline provides overall organizational data for initial planning. However, much of the real work is conducted at a work unit level. OHC staff consult with individual work units, conducting evaluations and interventions into the specific dynamics and issues arising in the work team. Organization development processes, both technostructural and process consulting (Beer & Walton, 1990; Schein, 1988), are used in business units experiencing problems, those at high risk for problems, as well as those desiring to enhance functioning. The Sacramento OHC used an organizational health assessment (OHA) process to diagnosis work unit problems and aid management and labor representatives in developing a plan for intervention. Using that information, work unit impact teams were convened to implement the change process. Repeat OHAs at the end of six months and one year provided outcome information on which to base decisions on change program continuation or modification. Team development and management-coaching strategies conducted for all business units complemented the more intensive organizational intervention strategies.

At a broader, organizational level, the Sacramento OHC facilitated development of a labor-management partnership council as a proactive problem-solving body (Schwartz & Adkins, 1996). A partnership council brought together labor and management leaders prior to organizational changes so that consensus could be achieved in advance rather than conflicts resolved after the fact. The successful functioning of the council reduced grievances and unfair labor practice complaints. In many ways, the partnership council also served as a board of directors for the OHC, further integrating organizational health programs into the business culture and providing a powerful champion for OHC-recommended policies and practices.

Information Broker

Information flow in organizations is notoriously inefficient and ineffective, but essential for development of a sense of control for individual workers. OHC staff facilitate the flow of information and find ways to ensure that accurate information is conveyed and that systems and methods of communication function effectively.

Targeted Training and Prevention

OHC program development is not intended to overstep the domains of other human resources and personnel support services. On the contrary, targeted areas include situations that fall across disciplinary lines or that may be neglected by current functions in the organization. Common examples include suicide prevention, workplace violence prevention, conflict mediation, and training of the general workforce, as well as support personnel in occupational stress, organizational change, and organizational health.

Worksite Support

Supervisory and social support, both peer and family, have demonstrated utility in reducing the negative impact of both occupational and personal stress. The OHC functions to bring enhanced support services to the workforce, increasing availability and evaluating the effectiveness of available services in meeting the needs of a changing workforce. Support is provided through employee assistance programs, workplace health promotion, worksite stress management, peer counseling, and occupational health and safety, including occupational mental health services.

Surveillance, Monitoring, and Evaluation

OHC programs and policies are extracted from the literature available and targeted using epidemiological estimates, baseline information, and organizational assessment data. Process and outcome measures demonstrate the value of ongoing programs and advocate an improved work environment. Bringing together metrics from across all levels of assessment, surveillance, and evaluation and across disciplinary lines in the organization enables a comprehensive look at organizational health and effective ongoing planning for improved organizational wellness.

The Sacramento OHC incorporated assessment, formative, and summative evaluation strategies at the work unit and overall organizational levels. Needs assessments focused on organizational risk factors and individual vulnerabilities, as well as protective factors or capacity at both levels. The state of strain or signs and symptoms of ill health were also evaluated and monitored. Outcome measures at a corporate level included health care utilization rates, workers' compensation costs, and productive years lost to behaviorally related illness and injury. The first year of operations found positive trends in all measures. Over the course of that year, the OHC staff made more than 10,000 individual employee contacts and conducted over 250 organizational consultations. Customer satisfaction in every case was rated as excellent. Outcome data indicated a 4% reduction in workers' compensation claims following a doubling of claims experience the previous five years and exceeding the organizationally set goal of a 3% savings, a 58% reduction in behaviorally related mortality, and a 12% reduction in lost productivity associated with health care utilization for job-related illness and injuries.

TRAINING IN OCCUPATIONAL HEALTH PSYCHOLOGY

The National Institute for Occupational Safety and Health defines OHP: "Occupational health psychology concerns the application of psychology to improving the quality of work-life and to protecting and promoting the safety, health and well-being of workers" (Sauter et al., 1999). This rather broad definition incorporates a large array of potential risk factors as well as numerous factors that could enhance safety and health in the workplace. Programs being developed in the United States and those that have been founded in The Netherlands, Sweden, and the United Kingdom have several common elements. The European programs typically focus on organizational risk factors for stress, illness, and injury and work redesign as the primary intervention. U.S. programs may be more varied at present because of their early stage of development. In this section, we present a model for training in OHP that we believe reflects the definition of OHP, the underlying philosophy of OHP, and incorporates many of the common elements of U.S. and European programs.

The definition of OHP includes two dimensions: the protection from harm and the promotion of health. This bifurcation mirrors the definition of health as the absence of illness versus health as something more than simply the absence of illness (Downie & Macnaughton, 1998; Raphael, 1998). Thus, it is important that training in OHP recognize the influence of organization of work factors in both the reduction of illness and injury and the enhancement of health and well-being.

Underlying the philosophy and development of OHP is the multidisciplinary approach to understanding the work environment, behavior of individuals in that environment, and the interaction between the work environment and their behavior that results in physical and psychological well-being. Ilgen (1990) recognized that disciplines and specialties within disciplines view problems and generate solutions based on their own perspectives. Understanding a complex phenomenon such as health in today's complex work environments requires not only knowledge of key content areas in psychology but also an awareness of other relevant content areas and disciplines. This awareness, coupled with leadership and communication skills, allows occupational health psychologists to bring together and lead a team with the necessary skills to address the complexity of the concerns without being blinded by their own disciplines.

In this framework, a training model for OHP that acknowledges content areas to be covered and skills to be developed can be visualized. The list of content areas is indeed long. If we consider the risk factors for occupational stress that have been compiled (e.g., the review by Kahn & Byosiere, 1992), there are multiple disciplines and specialties that can contribute to OHP. Industrial and organizational psychology, clinical psychology, life-span developmental psychology, and social psychology offer relevant knowledge as reflected in Volumes 5, 6, 8, and 12 of this Handbook. Topics that might be incorporated in a graduate level OHP seminar would typically include occupational stress and burnout, job and work design, social support, organizational health, health psychology, occupational safety and health hazards, job security, work-nonwork balance, and individual differences.

In addition, other disciplines can contribute to our understanding of organizational risk factors and individual behavior as they relate to health and safety. These include the biological and health sciences, economics, engineering, industrial relations, management, and law. Therefore, training in OHP should cut across academic departments. This may be accomplished by establishing collaborative arrangements with other departments or institutions so that students can take courses in safety engineering, occupational safety and health law, conflict resolution, epidemiology, and human resources management and policies.

Because the list of relevant topics is long, it is probably unrealistic to expect any individual to be an expert in all possible areas. Rather, individuals need to have sufficient awareness of other disciplines so that they can recognize the need to enlist team members with the appropriate knowledge. They also should develop leadership skills and team-building skills to manage the occupational safety and health function in organizations. These skills are probably best developed through internships and practica.

Formal training in OHP is just getting underway. Some academic education in stress and occupational health has been offered at the undergraduate level (e.g., at the United States Air Force Academy). Courses at the master's level have been offered at several schools (e.g., University of

California–San Francisco & Irvine, University of Hawaii, University of Houston, University of Nottingham, Oklahoma State University, The University of Texas at Arlington, and Xavier University). By 2001, universities that have incorporated courses in OHP and/or minors at the doctoral level include Bowling Green State University, Kansas State University, University of Minnesota, University of Houston, Tulane University, Clemson University, Portland State University, and University of California–Los Angeles. Schneider, Camara, Tetrick, and Stenberg (1999) discuss the role of postdoctoral educational, for example, funded for several years through the APA/NIOSH postdoctoral fellowships and the U.S. Air Force postdoctoral OHP fellowship at Harvard Medical School in 1998–1999. In addition, there now exists a European Academy of Occupational Health Psychology (www.ea-ohp.org).

A CASE STUDY

The preferred point of intervention from a public health standpoint is always primary prevention and, as applied in OHP, this generally translates to organizational intervention. The use of the term *clinical* is often associated with treatment and therapeutic settings, yet it has important applications for more diagnostic and intervention applications in organizations (van de Loo, 2000). Thus, this case application of OHP by a clinical psychologist in an organizational context draws heavily on the public health notions of surveillance and prevention, exemplifying the inherently interdisciplinary nature of OHP.

This section reviews the origins and role of an OHP program at a major military installation during the downsizing period preceding base realignment and closure, with the attendant risks and possible negative consequences associated with major industrial restructuring activities. With closure of a major facility, a multitude of anticipated coping problems may result from a significant change in routine and expected way of living. These problems include the potential for increased substance abuse, increased family and/or interpersonal violence, and increased potential for suicide (Adkins, 1998).

History and Role of Organizational Health Psychology at Kelly Air Force Base

An OHP program for Kelly Air Force Base (AFB) had been in a conceptual stage since 1994. At that time, the Base Realignment and Closure (BRAC) committee was evaluating military facilities for possible elimination as part of an ongoing military downsizing effort. This process had a negative influence on the overall productivity and morale of the base. With the July 1995 announcement that the base would be closed in July 2001, senior leadership on the base became increasingly concerned about the potential impact of the stress of transition and closure. By placing a full time, active duty Air Force psychologist on his executive staff, the installation commander endorsed a proactive approach. The psychologist was to oversee relevant aspects and integration of the necessary services required to manage the impending downsizing and closure, a major restructuring event that placed the well-being and mental health of the work population at risk.

More precisely defined, the organizational clinical psychologist directed all phases of an Air Force industrial operational program, managing the program to increase productivity and teamwork and to reduce psychosocial work hazards. The psychologist also (a) led systems-focused, comprehensive intervention programs, (b) coordinated base and community activities, (c) evaluated the workplace to identify pertinent negative stressors to be eliminated and positive factors to be retained or added, and (d) promoted positive organizational behavior as a key manager on the executive team.

Workforce Composition

The OHP position, initiated in March 1997, was filled by an active duty Air Force clinical psychologist. At that time, the 12,000-member San Antonio Air Logistics Center workforce represented the largest industrial complex in the southwestern United States. This workforce reflected the overall Hispanic demographic composition of the city of San Antonio. More than 60% of the Kelly employees were Hispanic. The Kelly population represented 48% of the total Air Force civilian Hispanic workforce and 14% of Department of Defense (DOD) Hispanic employees. It was the single largest group of civilian Hispanic personnel located at any one DOD facility or installation.

The average Kelly employee was a 47-year-old Hispanic male blue-collar WG-9 (wage grade) worker with 19 years of service. He was earning approximately $29,829 per year, plus additional personnel benefits, with generous overtime available. He was a high school graduate, a Vietnam combat veteran, whose father, and maybe even grandfather, had been a Kelly career employee. He was married and had a mid-sized family, which, based on local definitions, included four or five children.

The Hispanic culture and heritage is a deeply integrated aspect of local life and is reflected in most aspects of what individuals do and how they react to situations. As determined by individual and small group discussions, these cultural aspects played a significant role in the existent problems of transition, downsizing, and closure.

Cultural Issues and Dilemmas

Certain positive facets associated with the Hispanic culture, including deep family, emotional, and cultural roots, pervade most aspects of Hispanic life. It is not unusual to see three generations of a family, as well as their siblings, living in proximity. Decision making is based on an executive corporate management style with significant consideration given to the overall impact on the entire family structure. The close family cohesiveness provides for a very good support system, especially during times of turmoil and crisis. Members develop a great emotional dependency on the extended family network and respectfully take the advice of the family corporate council.

However, this significantly integrated family system can place great emotional strains on the individual who may entertain thoughts of change, especially geographic relocation. There is a tendency toward a generalized rigidity in this social system resulting from a perceived inability to leave the family network. These barriers to relocation may affect the individual, the spouse, or both. Even if the worker was willing to leave the area for continued Civil Service employment and benefits, the spouse would often refuse to accompany him to avoid breaking overall family and community ties, leading to increased strain and domestic discord. Therefore, the worker found himself facing additional dilemmas. He would have to face added increased conditional stressors, such as marital and family separation or divorce unless a compromise could be reached. The degree of compromise might appear to be rather one-sided. As an example, one perception among groups of workers at Kelly was the idea that a relocation to Tinker AFB in Oklahoma was better than the perceived option of relocation to Robins AFB in Georgia. This was because Tinker was considered to be within weekend commuting distance even though it was 488 miles away.

Course of Transition

During the transition process, the workforce experienced several cycles of upheaval and recovery. Initially, a pervasive sense of overt optimism helped carry many workers over the low points. This optimism had been reinforced by infrequent, yet significant, perceptions of potential salvation from job loss.

The initial downsizing focus was on the 1,400 workers of the aircraft maintenance branch. During the first major reduction in force (RIF), focus groups and individual contacts indicated a popular and consistent belief that Kelly would be removed from the base closure list by the executive branch of the government. This perception was maintained by the belief that Kelly was currently the oldest functioning Air Force base, had the largest and most modern structures for the maintenance of a prevalently used aircraft, and, not incidentally, had the largest Hispanic population in the DOD. The results did not support these beliefs.

Subsequently, Kelly workers turned their focus to a long-time Hispanic congressman who had proven his dedication to the San Antonio community in the past. On his retirement, the workers' expectations were then focused on their union representatives, who apparently had their own shortcomings and agendas. After each setback, Kelly workers remained steadfast and optimistically convinced that something good would happen.

The "something good" occurred just prior to the first known RIF. In February 1998, Boeing Corporation announced a plan to move its aircraft fleet maintenance and overhaul work to San Antonio. As part of the privatization initiative, Boeing representatives signed a 20-year lease for the aircraft facilities at Kelly. This agreement indicated that approximately 800 private industry jobs would become available by the summer of 1999. In small group and individual discussions, workers verbalized their understanding that the workforce outnumbered the proposed positions and that Boeing would be offering transfers to their current employees. However, in general, the majority of the Kelly workers individually believed that he or she would obtain one of the available openings.

As that reinforcing "something good" was happening, the initial RIF took place in the base's aircraft maintenance branch of approximately 1,400 workers. After the departure of 233 temporary employees, 29 retirees, and the 390 workers who opted for one of the two offered buy-out programs, only three permanent employees were involuntarily separated. This extremely low number did not cause any great alarm to the Kelly community. The remaining employees were shifted to other open positions in their occupational categories based on the employees' seniority. This bump and retreat process contributed to the underlying currents of stress and potential disorganization. As a worker was identified as having sufficient seniority to be retained, for the time being, he or she would retreat to another job location and bump another worker with less seniority. Frequently, the newcomer's presence would create significant turmoil. The existing work unit, which may have been together for some time, was now altered and one of the original members was dismissed. The newcomer was seen as the cause of the disorganization. He or she slowed production while learning the team's unique procedures taught by the group being disrupted and became a threatening symbol of what could happen to the others.

The propulsion directorate, with approximately 3,500 employees, was the next group to be scrutinized for reductions. Faced with a declining number of opportunities and openings, workers still maintained high levels of production. One stabilizing line of thought had been that the presence of Boeing would act as a catalyst for drawing a major engine company to the area. This was subsequently reinforced by an agreement with Lockheed Propulsion and Tinker AFB. This agreement kept some of the engine work in San Antonio; however, once again, the number of employees exceeded the number of possible jobs.

The results of the RIFs and the various separations appeared to have a rather negligible initial impact. The workers remained optimistic, and production rates and job performance remained high. However, the "whisper network," a term coined by the base chaplain, was beginning to indicate an increase in concerns, worries, and strains that resulted in an exacerbation of potential negative stress reactions. The existing network of base and community service providers was organized to address relevant issues and to attempt to buffer the impact of negative stressors.

Service-Oriented Networks

A number of service-oriented networks focused on the needs of Kelly personnel and assisted them in meeting their objectives for a successful transition. A nonexclusive number of key base and community agencies included the Kelly Action Information Board, the Integrated Delivery System team, the Chaplain Office, the Civilian Employee Transition Office, and the Kelly chapter of the United Way.

The Kelly Action Information Board

The Kelly Action Information Board (KAIB) was a cross-functional structure composed of a variety of necessary base and community organizations whose main purpose was to disseminate information and provide guidance to programs relevant to base closure. It was similar to the change management team as outlined by Adkins (1998). The KAIB was chaired by the installation vice commander, which reflected the degree of importance associated with the welfare of the Kelly community.

The Integrated Delivery System Team

The Integrated Delivery System (IDS) team was the main working group of the KAIB. Its purpose was to coordinate all

preventive, educational programs aimed at individual and family well-being and to ensure there were no redundancies or gaps in available programs and services. The OHP psychologist, as the designated representative of the installation commander, chaired the IDS. A major goal of the group was to facilitate the integration and implementation of all necessary services, resources, and support activities to meet the needs of the Kelly military and civilian population during the transition of base realignment and closure. It was highly preferred that IDS interventions be as proactive and preventive as possible. This required a sensor system that would provide an accurate assessment of workforce needs and perceptions. By assessing these perceptions, workforce concerns could be addressed at an earlier stage and healthier decision options could be offered and implemented. A major concern was in acquiring relevant, usable data from the workforce. Thus, IDS objectives were to determine the needs of individual subgroups, increase the awareness of available services, and define roles and responsibilities for those services.

Chaplains

The role of the chaplain's office in service delivery was indispensable. The chaplains were viewed by the workforce as individuals who could maintain confidence of shared information. Talking with a chaplain was viewed as acceptable in terms of self-disclosure when events become increasingly difficult. A great deal of relevant information was obtained through the whisper network, by which unofficial floor information was conveyed throughout the workforce. This network conveyed valid information as well as rumor. It revealed the perceptions of the workers and was essential in lending credibility to organizational offerings.

The Civilian Transition Office

The Civilian Transition Office (CTO), a department of the Civilian Personnel Office, provided various developmental workshops and services designed to help employees enhance their marketability as they transitioned from Kelly to other employment. The CTO also acted as a networking link to numerous outside sources and systems to provide awareness of opportunities available to the workforce. The CTO covered four functional areas: transition assistance program, career counseling, permanent change of station, and supervisor feedback surveys.

The Civilian Personnel Office held a view to the future and deliberately focused on the importance of the overall base mission. They very quickly obtained training grants, outlined timetables of events and outcome expectations, and provided detailed monthly newsletters, which earned them a high degree of credibility. The Civilian Personnel Office pro-vided education and training in many transition areas, including opportunities in self-employment. This training was successful in allowing individuals to begin their own businesses but was also successful in dissuading those whose probability of success was low.

The United Way

The United Way representatives for Kelly provided significant contributions to the transition process. The referral agent (RA) system was a vital link between the workers and necessary services they required. They were the eyes and ears of the base organizations. The objective of the RA system was to maintain an informal network of employee volunteer leaders to help transitioning coworkers and positively impact mission accomplishment. The RAs provided limited referral information with more complicated cases being referred to appropriate agencies. The RAs were informational points of contact. These volunteers worked in the very same settings as their peers and were well-known to their coworkers, enabling them to carry a considerable degree of credibility, which was often hard to come by on the working floor. They also provided quantitative data to management on workforce needs and stress levels. RAs provided assistance with a minimum disruption to production, conformed to federal and state confidentiality policies, and encouraged coworkers to take advantage of available transition services. They were not meant to counsel, solve problems, or make decisions. They did not discuss coworkers' interviews with others, and they did not intervene in potentially violent situations. Under the contractual agreement between Kelly and United Way, three base program managers were provided to oversee and support the RAs, provide monthly in-service training, and compile monthly service reports. The 11-person professional staff at the United Way conducted 20 hours of entry-level training to each RA, provided information and referral back-up during regular work hours, and provided a 24-hour counseling and crisis intervention helpline. United Way involvement provided a neutral, highly credible third party. This non-Air Force affiliation enabled them to reach employees in denial or distrustful of being identified to base services. This appealed to the employee's strong need for confidentiality based on unsubstantiated concern that identification might result in an early lay-off.

Barriers and Goals

Given the nature of the organizational transition, the OHP program relied on consistently produced, long-term results. Plans and projects were developed to provide appropriate

services and interventions in a timely manner. However, timeliness is relative to the perceptions of the community served. Events were not always predictable, and projects evolved slowly in this particular environment. The overall population required increased awareness and encouragement to become involved in making use of available services.

One significant barrier in achieving program results was acceptance. As with most organizational entities, Kelly was composed of a multitude of different subgroups. The initial objective was to elicit information from work groups. In general, individuals who were not members of labor were perceived as management, automatically providing a significant barrier to communication. At the very least, a nongroup member would be seen as an outsider. Superficial, polite conversation might take place, but it took considerable time to establish meaningful dialogues. This communication barrier hindered service gap identification, as the OHP was perceived as looking for problems. Persistence and a near-constant presence on the shop floor were means to overcome this resistance.

A number of the IDS group members were frequently involved in providing workshops and presentations for all levels of the Kelly community. These presentations focused on topics such as violence in the workplace, suicide awareness, and stress management. They were offered both at the worksite and at other base facilities at a variety of convenient times. The attendees were assured that these presentations were informal, and attendance was not officially documented. The informal setting and educational nature of the sessions encouraged involvement because workers did not have to acknowledge a problem but could participate just to obtain information.

Transition Life Advisor Program

One very important achievement of the OHP program was establishment of a Transition Life Advisor (TLA) Program. Based on the monthly report of service and information referrals made by the RAs, a group of significant problem areas—categorized as work related, mental health, medical, financial, protective services, substance abuse, and legal—emerged. RAs reported that a relatively constant group of individuals consistently sought information for the same problem areas. This appeared to support the idea that approximately 10% of any workforce needs some assistance at any given time. Of that group, approximately 25% to 30% (2.5% to 3% of the total workforce) are dealing with significant problems and are chronic, heavy users of the service system.

It became necessary to target service intervention to provide for the needs of this high-risk group. In the TLA

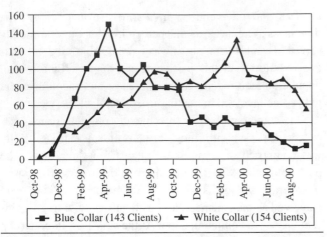

Figure 24.2 Fiscal years 1990 and 2000 "high risk" case management appointments.

Program, designed by Klunder and Scheibler, clinical social workers were hired and deployed to base organizations with the goal of identifying these individuals and attempting to assist them in the transition process. These consultants acted as case managers working with identified members, helping them set a path for transition, then ensuring their follow-up with the outlined recommendations. The consultants were available for crisis management as well as routine guidance and assistance. This also visibly demonstrated senior management concern for the employees and their families. Figure 24.2 shows utilization charts for services over the critical period of the transition.

However, a number of barriers had to be overcome. These seasoned professionals had to be age, gender, and ethnically similar to the populations they served. Given the cultural norms in the workforce, troubled individuals would have had considerable resistance in dealing with a young counselor. A more mature counselor would be seen as having a better understanding of life circumstances. The caseworkers were strategically embedded throughout the industrial complex with a priority to locations that were high on the RIF list. Their offices were located in the work areas, and they made daily rounds with frequent contact with the entire workforce in their buildings. They built collaborative networks with supervisors, union stewards, on-base providers, and workers to facilitate referrals and working relationships. They conducted aggressive outreach marketing activities to identify and acquire high-risk employees for services. They consulted with senior and mid-level management on individual worker and workforce stabilization issues. Even though the clinical director was the OHP psychologist, the TLAs were not identified as being management, which greatly facilitated their acceptance.

High-Risk Work Environment, Good Results

In the context of this high-risk work environment with dramatic change occurring daily, there was concern that serious problems, such as suicide and workplace violence, might become overtly manifest. This was a particular concern for the at-risk employee population. The at-risk employee population presented with very complicated personal and family problems, and with little or no identified plan of action to resolve them. Troubled employees with chronic performance problems were facing layoffs without a realistic transition plan. Individuals remained in denial despite RIFs, workforce movements, and building closures. Employees experienced job disidentification when they were moved to a variety of locations with the intent of helping them. Many workers developed or experienced exacerbation of existing physical problems. The base occupational medicine clinic indicated that more than 30% of the Kelly workforce did not have medical insurance. TLAs were able to fill a needed gap in support services, especially for uninsured workers, and therefore played a significant role in facilitating a smoother transition for the Kelly population.

Suicides

The three key results over the six-year closure process that have been examined were suicides, workplace violence, and labor grievance or complaint rates. The results are very affirming of the comprehensive OHP strategy for the health of this working population. While there was a degree of suicidal ideation and intent, as reported by TLAs, swift and direct intervention resulted in several saved lives. Only one suicide was completed within the base population during the six-year period, and that event occurred with a new employee who entered the workforce under psychiatric care. The event appeared to be totally unrelated to the work environment. During much of this period, the U.S. Air Force was very actively pursuing a suicide prevention program, which the Centers for Disease Control and Prevention credited with a five-year drop in suicide rates of 16 per 100,000 (1994) to 2.2 per 100,000 (1999), an over 80% decline. However, even in this high-risk environment, the Kelly results were well below the 1999 overall Air Force rates.

Workplace Violence

While there was some angry language, heated emotions, and minor pushing and shoving on occasion, there was never a serious physical altercation throughout the six-year period of the transition, re-alignment, and closure process.

Cost Savings

The TLA program has been credited with significant cost avoidance. The Kelly Equal Employment Opportunity (EEO) Office indicated that overall approximately 40% of initial complaints move to formal status. The minimum administrative and investigative costs associated with a formal complaint is $80,000 regardless of whether it is validated. Based on the highest risk and highest/severe risk complaints dealt with by the TLAs, EEO projections attribute an administrative saving of between $23.9 million and $33.7 million. These are processing costs and do not include an undetermined amount of potential outcome costs that may have been awarded to complainants.

The TLA team also presented a visible symbol of concern on management's part, which assisted workers in overcoming a sense of isolation and fostered group cohesiveness. There was a minimized loss of production time associated with incident intervention, resolution, and disposition as workers took greater responsibility for their actions and outcomes. Aside from the humanitarian concerns, there were also practical results. The Air Force did not incur violence or suicide liability exposure. Financial liability resulting from litigation with a victim, traumatized coworker, family member, or class action coalition was eliminated.

To Kelly employees, the TLA program provided comprehensive, readily accessible services to needy families as well as a confidential alternative to on-base services. To work supervisors, the program helped minimize worksite employee stress and lost production time. It allowed supervisors to focus on production priorities and provided an outlet for supervisor needs. To Kelly management, TLAs represented a visible sign of commitment to the workforce during heightened periods of turmoil, provided a preventive approach to minimizing suicide as well as interpersonal and family violence, and minimized administrative time and costs associated with incident intervention, resolution, and disposition.

FUTURE DIRECTIONS IN OCCUPATIONAL HEALTH PSYCHOLOGY

As a relatively young specialty in psychology, a key question to be answered is how will OHP continue to grow and evolve? We see four directions for OHP. First, we see more bridge building with other disciplines, especially engineering. However, we can see the need for bridges into disciplines such as finance, economics, information systems, and production operations as well. Second, we see a greater emphasis on an organizational balance between task mastery and interpersonal support in the workplace. Third, we see an integration of the professions addressing the human side of the enterprise. Finally, we see the need for systems to address the toxins and emotional pain all too endemic to organizational life.

Luczek's (1992) ideas of anthropocentric work design, which place the individual at the center of the design process, exemplify the bridge building between psychology and engineering. When it comes to the design of a wide variety of workplaces and tasks, those in OHP must make more extensive and concerted efforts to develop partnerships with the engineering disciplines. The design of bricks, mortar, workstations, and a wide variety of machines and mechanisms for technological leverage in organizations require the combined input of experts in materials and products as well as people and behavior. Frederick Taylor was the first engineer to delve into psychology and human behavior. We must follow his example by linking psychology with engineering as well as with other disciplines.

OHP needs to help managers and organizations better understand the need for balance between task mastery and interpersonal support in the workplace (Joplin, Nelson, & Quick, 1999). Humans have two instinctual drives that are somewhat intractable. One is the drive to explore and master the world, and the other is to feel safe and secure. The intensity and degree to which these drives operate across individuals and across life stages varies. In the adulthood years, these drives are often manifest in the language of love and work. While task mastery leads to productive activity and achievement, secure interpersonal attachments and support provide the platform for emotional, psychological, and physical health. Both needs must be addressed and balanced if organizations and the individuals in them are to maintain their health in the midst of effortful striving (Frese, 1997).

We briefly discussed the concept of a chief psychological officer in an organization earlier in the chapter. A key role for a chief psychological officer, or even chief people officer, in an organization is to provide an integrating function for the specialties on the human side of the enterprise. These specialties include human resource professionals, physicians and medical personnel, psychologists, safety professionals, security forces, and chaplains and spiritual advisors. Each expert offers a different type of expertise aimed at caring for people at work, as well as for the health of the organization. These experts need to be integrated and organized in functional role interrelatedness such that they are complimenting and supplementing each other as they provide the support and responses individuals at work need. In a complex work setting, it may not be clear whether a worker should call the security forces, a psychologist, or a personnelist.

Finally, Edgar Schien (Quick & Gavin, 2000) and Peter Frost (Frost & Robinson, 1999) are among those concerned with addressing the toxins and emotional pain all too often endemic to organizational life. While healthy organizational systems may have natural homeopathic agents and immune systems that metabolize these psychological toxins and emotional pain, OHP can take the lead in crafting mechanisms and systems to help manage these unhealthy energies that inevitably, yet unintentionally, emerge in many work organizations. Schein uses the term *organizational therapy,* and we need to evolve language and mechanisms for making this process more concrete and complimentary to the other leading edges of occupational health psychology.

REFERENCES

Adkins, J. A. (1998). Base closure: A case study in occupational stress and organizational decline. In M. K. Gowing, J. D. Kraft, & J. C. Quick (Eds.), *The new organizational reality: Downsizing, restructuring, and revitalization* (pp. 111–142). Washington, DC: American Psychological Association.

Adkins, J. A. (1999). Promoting organizational health: The evolving practice of occupational health psychology. *Professional Psychology: Research and Practice, 30,* 129–137.

Adkins, J. A., Quick, J. C., & Moe, K. O. (2000). Building world class performance in changing times. In L. R. Murphy & C. L. Cooper (Eds.), *Healthy and productive work: An international perspective* (pp. 107–132). Philadelphia: Taylor & Francis.

Adkins, J. A., & Weiss, H. (in press). Evaluating organizational health programs. In J. C. Quick & L. Tetrick (Eds.), *Handbook of occupational health psychology.* Washington, DC: American Psychological Association.

Barling, J., & Griffiths, A. (in press). A history of occupational health psychology. In J. C. Quick & L. Tetrick (Eds.), *Handbook of occupational health psychology.* Washington, DC: American Psychological Association.

Barone, D. (1995). Work stress conceived and researched transactionally. In R. Crandall & P. L. Perrewe (Eds.), *Occupational stress: A handbook* (pp. 29–37). Washington, DC: Taylor & Francis.

Beer, M., & Walton, E. (1990). Developing the competitive organization: Intervention and strategies. *American Psychologist, 45,* 154–161.

Caplan, R. D., Cobb, S., French, J. R. P., Jr., Harrison, R. V., & Pinneau, S. R., Jr. (1975). *Job demands and worker health: Main effects and occupational differences* (DHEW NIOSH Publication No. 75-160). Washington, DC: U.S. Government Printing Office.

Cartwright, S., Cooper, C. L., & Murphy, L. R. (1995). Diagnosing a healthy organization: A proactive approach to stress in the workplace. In L. R. Murphy, J. J. Hurrell, S. L. Sauter, & G. P. Keita (Eds.), *Job stress interventions* (pp. 217–234). Washington, DC: American Psychological Association.

Casio, W. F. (1998). Learning from outcomes: Financial experiences of 300 firms that have downsized. In M. Gowing, J. Kraft, & J. C. Quick (Eds.), *The new organizational reality* (pp. 55–70). Washington, DC: American Psychological Association.

Cooper, C. L., & Cartwright, S. (1994). Healthy mind, healthy organization: A proactive approach to occupational stress. *Human Relations, 47,* 455–471.

Cooper, C. L., & Marshall, J. (1976). Occupational sources of stress: A review of the literature relating to coronary heart disease and mental ill health. *Journal of Occupational Psychology, 49,* 11–28.

Cooper, C. L., Sloan, S. J., & Williams, S. (1988). *Occupational stress indicator management guide.* Oxford, England: NFER-Nelson.

Cox, T. (1997). Workplace health promotion. *Work and Stress, 11,* 1–5.

DeFrank, R. S., & Ivancevich, J. M. (1986). Job loss: An individual level review and model. *Journal of Vocational Behavior, 28,* 1–20.

Donaldson, S. I. (1995). Worksite health promotion: A theory-driven empirically based perspective. In L. R. Murphy, J. J. Hurrell, S. L. Sauter, & G. P. Keita (Eds.), *Job stress interventions* (pp. 73–90). Washington, DC: American Psychological Association.

Downie, R. S., & Macnaughton, R. J. (1998). Images of health. *Lancet, 351,* 823–825.

Edwards, J. R. (1996). An examination of competing versions of the person-environment fit approach to stress. *Academy of Management Journal, 39,* 292–339.

Elkin, A. J., & Rosch, P. J. (1990). Promoting mental health at the workplace: The prevention side of stress management. *Occupational Medicine: State of the Art Review, 5,* 739–754.

Elkind, H. B. (Ed.). (1931). *Preventive management: Mental hygiene in industry.* New York: B. C. Forbes.

Forward, G. E., Beach, D. E., Gray, D. A., & Quick, J. C. (1991). Mentofacturing: A vision for American industrial excellence. *Academy of Management Executive, 5, 32–44.*

Frese, M. (1997). Dynamic self-reliance: An important concept for work in the twenty-first century. In C. L. Cooper & S. E. Jackson (Eds.), *Creating tomorrow's organizations: A handbook for future research in organizational behavior* (pp. 399–416). Chichester, England: Wiley.

Frone, M. R. (in press). Work-nonwork balance. In J. C. Quick & L. Tetrick (Eds.), *Handbook of occupational health psychology.* Washington, DC: American Psychological Association.

Frone, M. R., Russell, M., & Barnes, G. M. (1996). Work-family conflict, gender, and health-related outcomes: A study of employed parents in two community samples. *Journal of Occupational Health Psychology, 1,* 57–69.

Frost, P., & Robinson, S. (1999). The toxic handler: Organizational hero—and casualty. *Harvard Business Review, 77,* 97–106.

Gardell, B. (1987). Efficiency and health hazards in mechanized work. In J. C. Quick, R. S. Bhagat, J. E. Dalton, & J. D. Quick (Eds.), *Work stress: Health care systems in the workplace* (pp. 50–71). New York: Praeger Scientific.

Gebhardt, D. L., & Crump, C. E. (1990). Employee fitness and wellness programs in the workplace. *American Psychologist, 45,* 262–272.

Gowing, M. K., Kraft, J. D., & Quick, J. C. (1998). *The new organizational reality.* Washington, DC: American Psychological Association.

Griffin, M. A., Hart, P. M., & Wilson-Evered, E. (2000). Using employee opinion surveys to improve organizational health. In L. R. Murphy & C. L. Cooper (Eds.), *Healthy and productive work* (pp. 15–36). Philadelphia: Taylor & Francis.

Hurrell, J. J., Jr., & McLaney, M. A. (1988). Exposure to job stress: A new psychometric instrument. *Scandinavian Journal of Work, Environment, and Health, 14,* 27–28.

Hurrell, J. J., Jr., & Murphy, L. R. (1992). Psychological job stress. In W. N. Rom (Ed.), *Environmental and occupational medicine* (pp. 675–684). New York: Little, Brown.

Ilgen, D. R. (1990). Health issues at work: Opportunities for industrial/organizational psychology. *American Psychologist, 45,* 273–283.

Ivancevich, J. M., Matteson, M. T., Freedman, S. M., & Phillips, J. S. (1990). Worksite stress management interventions. *American Psychologist, 45,* 223–239.

James, L. A., & James, L. R. (1989). Integrating work perceptions: Explorations into the measurement of measuring. *Journal of Applied Psychology, 74,* 739–751.

Johnson, J. V., & Hall, E. M. (1988). Job strain, workplace social support and cardiovascular disease: A cross-sectional study of a random sample of the Swedish working population. *American Journal of Public Health, 78,* 1336–1342.

Joplin, J. R. W., Nelson, D. L., & Quick, J. C. (1999). Attachment behavior and health: Relationships at work and home. *Journal of Organizational Behavior, 20,* 783–796.

Kahn, R. L., & Byosiere, P. (1992). Stress in organizations. In M. D. Dunnette & L. M. Houigh (Eds.), *Handbook of industrial and organizational psychology* (2nd ed., Vol. 3, pp. 571–650). Palo Alto, CA: Consulting Psychologists Press, Inc.

Karasek, R. A. (1979). Job demands job decision latitude, and mental strain: Implications for job redesign. *Administrative Science Quarterly, 24,* 285–308.

Katz, D., & Kahn, R. L. (1966). *The social psychology of organizing.* New York: Wiley.

Kohler, S., & Kamp, J. (1992). *American workers under pressure technical report.* St. Paul, MN: St. Paul Fire and Marine Insurance.

Kompier, M. A. J. (1996). Job design and well-being. In M. J. Schabracq, J. A. M. Winnubst, & C. L. Cooper (Eds.), *Handbook of work and health psychology* (pp. 349–368). Chichester, England: Wiley.

Koop, C. E. (1992). Opening remarks of the APA/NIOSH conference on Work and Well-Being. In G. P. Keita & S. L. Sauter (Eds.), *Work and well-being: An agenda for the 1990s* (pp. 3–4). Washington, DC: American Psychological Association.

Kraut, A. I. (Ed.). (1996). *Organizational surveys: Tools for assessment and change.* San Francisco: Jossey-Bass.

Laird, D. A. (1929). *Psychology and profits.* New York: B. C. Forbes.

Landy, F., Quick, J. C., & Kasl, S. (1994). Work, stress and well-being. *International Journal of Stress Management, 1*(1), 33–73.

Lazarus, R. S. (1995). Psychological stress in the workplace. In R. Crandall & P. L. Perrewe (Eds.), *Occupational stress: A handbook* (pp. 3–14). Washington, DC: Taylor & Francis.

Levi, L., Brennar, S. O., Hall, E. M., Hjelm, R., Saolvaara, H., Arnetz, B., et al. (1984). The psychological, social, and biochemical impacts of unemployment in Sweden. *International Journal of Mental Health, 13*(1/2), 18–34.

Levinson, H. (2002). *Organizational assessment: A manual.* Washington, DC: American Psychological Association.

Lobel, S. A. (1991). Allocation of investment in work and family roles: Alternative theories and implications for research. *Academy of Management Review, 16*(3), 507–521.

Lowman, R. L. (1993). *Counseling and psychotherapy of work dysfunctions.* Washington, DC: American Psychological Association.

Luczek, H. (1992). "Good work" design: An ergonomic, industrial engineering perspective. In J. C. Quick, L. R. Murphy, & J. J. Hurrell, Jr. (Eds.), *Stress and well-being at work* (pp. 96–112). Washington, DC: American Psychological Association.

McLean, A. (1979). *Work stress.* Reading, MA: Addison-Wesley.

Millar, J. D. (1984). The NIOSH-suggested list of the ten leading work-related diseases and injuries. *Journal of Occupational Medicine, 26,* 340–341.

Millar, J. D. (1992). Public enlightenment and mental health in the workplace. In G. P. Keita & S. L. Sauter (Eds.), *Work and well-being: An agenda for the 1990s* (pp. 5–8). Washington, DC: American Psychological Association.

Moos, R. H. (1981). *Work Environment Scale manual.* Palo Alto, CA: Consulting Psychologists Press.

Moran, S. K., Wolff, S. C., & Green, J. E. (1995). Workers' compensation and occupational stress: Gaining control. In L. R. Murphy, J. J. Hurrell, S. L. Sauter, & G. P. Keita (Eds.), *Job stress interventions* (pp. 355–369). Washington, DC: American Psychological Association.

Murphy, L. R. (1988). Workplace interventions for stress reduction and prevention. In C. L. Cooper & R. Payne (Eds.), *Causes, coping and consequences of stress at work* (pp. 301–339). New York: Wiley.

Murphy, L. R., & Cooper, C. L. (Eds.). (2000). *Healthy and productive work: An international perspective.* Philadelphia: Taylor & Francis.

Nelson, D. L., Quick, J. C., & Hitt, M. A. (1989). Men and women of the personnel profession: Some differences and similarities in their stress. *Stress Medicine, 5,* 145–152.

Offermann, L. R., & Gowing, M. K. (1990). Organizations of the future: Changes and challenges. *American Psychologist, 45,* 95–108.

Osipow, S. H., & Spokane, A. R. (1992). *Occupational Stress Inventory: Manual, research version.* Odessa, FL: Psychological Assessment Resources.

Pellitier, K. R. (1991). A review and analysis of the health and cost-effective outcome studies of comprehensive health promotion and disease prevention programs. *American Journal of Health Promotion, 5,* 311–315.

Piotrkowski, C. S. (1979). *Work and the family system.* New York: Free Press.

Porter, G. (1996). The organizational impact of workaholism: Suggestion for researching the negative outcomes of excessive work. *Journal of Occupational Health Psychology, 1,* 70–84.

Quick, J. C. (1992). Crafting an organizational culture: Herb's hand at Southwest Airlines. *Organizational Dynamics, 21,* 45–56.

Quick, J. C. (1999a). Occupational health psychology: Historical roots and future directions. *Health Psychology, 18,* 82–88.

Quick, J. C. (1999b). Occupational health psychology: The convergence of health and clinical psychology with public health and preventive medicine in an organizational context. *Professional Psychology: Research and Practice, 30,* 123–128.

Quick, J. C., Camara, W. J., Hurrell, J. J., Jr., Johnson, J. V., Piotrkowski, C. S., Sauter, S. L., et al. (1997). Introduction and historical overview. *Journal of Occupational Health Psychology, 2,* 3–6.

Quick, J. C., & Gavin, J. H. (2000). The next frontier: Edgar Schein on organizational therapy. *Academy of Management Executive, 14,* 30–44.

Quick, J. C., Murphy, L.R., & Hurrell, J. J., Jr. (1992). *Stress and well-being at work: Assessments and interventions for occupational mental health.* Washington, DC: American Psychological Association.

Quick, J. C., Quick, J. D., Nelson, D. L., & Hurrell, J. J., Jr. (1997). *Preventive stress management in organizations.* Washington, DC: American Psychological Association.

Quick, J. C., & Tetrick, L. (in press). *Handbook of occupational health psychology.* Washington, DC: American Psychological Association.

Quinn, R. P., & Staines, G. L. (1978). *The 1977 Quality of Employment Survey: Descriptive statistics, with comparison data from the 1969–70 and the 1972–73 survey.* Ann Arbor: University of Michigan Survey Research Center.

Raphael, D., Steinmetz, B., Renwick, R., Rootman, I., Brown, I., Sehdev, H., et al. (1999). The community quality of life project: A health promotion approach to understanding communities. *Health Promotion International, 14*(3), 197–209.

Raymond, J. S., Wood, D. W., & Patrick, W. D. (1990). Psychology training in work and health. *American Psychologist, 45*(10), 1159–1161.

Reason, N. (1997). *Managing the risks of organizational accidents.* Hampshire, UK: Ashgate.

Rose, G. (1992). *The strategy of preventive medicine.* Oxford, England: Oxford University Press.

Rosen, R. H. (1986). *Healthy companies.* New York: American Management Association.

Rosenstock, L. (1997). Work organization research at the National Institute for Occupational Safety and Health. *Journal of Occupational Health Psychology, 2,* 7–10.

Sauter, S. L., & Hurrell, J. J. (1999). Occupational health psychology: Origins, content, and direction. *Professional Psychology: Research and Practice, 30,* 117–122.

Sauter, S. L., Hurrell, J. J., Jr., & Cooper, C. L. (1989). *Job control and worker health.* Chichester, England: Wiley.

Sauter, S. L., Hurrell, J. J., Jr., Fox, H. R., Tetrick, L. E., & Barling, J. (1999). Occupational health psychology: An emerging discipline. *Industrial Health, 37,* 199–211.

Sauter, S. L., Murphy, L. R., & Hurrell, J. J., Jr. (1990). Prevention of work-related psychological distress: A national strategy proposed by the National Institute for Occupational Safety and Health. *American Psychologist, 45,* 1146–1158.

Schein, E. H. (1988). *Process consultation* (Rev. ed.), Reading, MA: Addison-Wesley.

Schmidt, L. R. (1994). A psychological look at public health: Contents and methodology. *International Review of Health Psychology, 3,* 3–36.

Schneider, D. L., Camara, W. J., Tetrick, L. E., & Stenberg, C. R. (1999). Training in occupational healthy psychology: Initial efforts and alternative models. *Professional Psychology: Research and Practice, 30,* 138–142.

Schwartz, D. F., & Adkins, J. A. (1997). In pursuit of partnership. In M. A. Rahim, R. T. Golembiewski, & C. C. Lundberg (Eds.), *Current topics in management* (Vol. 2, pp. 243–252). Greenwich, CT: JAI Press.

Shilling, S., & Brackbill, R. M. (1987). Occupational health and safety risks and potential health consequences perceived by U.S. workers. *Public Health Reports, 102,* 47–53.

Spielberger, C. D. (1991). *State-trait anger expression inventory: Revised research edition.* Odessa, FL: Psychological Assessment Resources.

Spielberger, C. D. (1994). *Professional manual for the job stress survey (JSS).* Odessa, FL: Psychological Assessment Resources.

Spielberger, C. D., Krasner, S. S., & Solomon, E. P. (1988). The experience, expression, and control of anger. In M. P. Janisse (Ed.), *Health psychology: Individual differences and stress* (pp. 89–108). New York: Springer Verlag.

Staw, B. M. (1986). Organizational psychology and the pursuit of the happy/productive worker. *California Management Review, 28*(4), 40–53.

Terborg, J. R. (1986). Health promotion at the worksite: A challenge for personnel and human resources management. *Research in Personnel and Human Resources Management, 4,* 225–267.

Theorell, T., & Karasek, R. (1996). Psychosocial work environment and coronary heart disease: The role of the individual's possibility to control working conditions. *Journal of Occupational Health Psychology, 1,* 9–26.

Wallace, R. B., Last, J. M., & Doebbeling, B. N. (Eds.). (1998). *Maxcy-Rosenau-Last: Public health and preventive medicine.* Stamford, CT: Appleton and Lange.

Weiss, H. M. (2001). *Experience sampling methods (ESM).* Panel presentation at the Society for Industrial-Organizational Psychology Conference, San Diego, CA.

Whittington, J. L., Paulus, P. B., & Quick, J. C. (in press). Management development, well-being and health in the twenty-first century. In M. J. Schabracq, J. Winnubst, & C. L. Cooper (Eds.), *Handbook of work and health psychology* (Rev ed.). Chichester, England: Wiley.

Winters, E. E. (Ed.). (1952). *The collected papers of Adolf Meyer: Mental hygiene* (Vol. 4). Baltimore: Johns Hopkins University Press.

Wright, L. (1988). The Type A behavior pattern and coronary artery disease. *American Psychologist, 43,* 2–14.

Wright, T. A., & Cropanzano, R. (1997). Well-being, satisfaction and job performance: Another look at the happy/productive worker thesis. In L. N. Dosier & J. B. Keys (Eds.), *Academy of management best paper proceedings* (pp. 364–368). Statesboro, GA: Georgia Southern University.

van de Loo, E. (2000). The clinical paradigm: Manfred Kets De Vries's reflection on organizational therapy. *European Management Journal, 18,* 2–22.

Von Dusch, T. (1868). *Lehrbuch der herzkrankheiten* [Textbook of heart disease]. Leipzig, Germany: Verlag von Wilhelm Engelman.

Yandrick, R. M. (1996). *Behavioral risk management.* San Francisco: Jossey-Bass.

CHAPTER 25

Complementary and Alternative Therapies

CHRISTINE MAGUTH NEZU, SOLAM TSANG, ELIZABETH R. LOMBARDO, AND KIM P. BARON

Complementary and alternative therapeutic approaches to the treatment of medical disorders share many fundamental concepts and philosophies with health psychology. The term *complementary and alternative therapy* is used to describe a set of treatments that serve as an adjunct to, or complement, standard medicine practices, but also serve as an alternative form of medical therapy. Many of these approaches promote a holistic view of medicine, positing that psychological or emotional experiences have a reciprocal relationship with physical experiences, with a growing body of research supporting this link (see Cohen & Herbert, 1996; Pelletier, 1992). A common perspective of many complementary and alternative treatment approaches is that healing is viewed as a process of becoming whole on many different levels (physical, emotional, social, spiritual) and often involves an increase in awareness and self-discovery. Complementary and alternative practitioners, similar to many health psychologists, aim to help patients achieve an increased understanding of how their bodies, health, and well-being are linked. They also aim to empower their patients to take a more active approach in health maintenance and decision making. In this chapter we (a) present a description of popular complementary and alternative approaches to medicine, their clinical applications, and a brief summary of supporting research; (b) present several common themes of these approaches from a health psychology perspective; and (c) provide suggestions

for the future regarding the integration of such treatments with psychological intervention.

One major criticism concerning complementary and alternative therapies that frequently emerges throughout this chapter is the difficulty in applying current scientific standards to these therapy approaches. This challenge is due partially to the idiographic treatment and case history methodologies employed by many complementary and alternative therapies, which contrast with the general diagnosis-based methodologies employed by the biomedical approach. Because health is often viewed as being related to multiple causes and influenced by multiple systems, conventional measurement and analyses are difficult to apply. Hence, results from existing research data tend to be inconsistent and inconclusive. Until therapies are subjected to rigorous methodologies, many of these healing approaches will not be considered credible cures in their own right. Nevertheless, complementary and alternative therapies have been increasingly accepted by the public. The various complementary and alternative approaches have originated from Western (e.g., homeopathy, osteopathy, chiropractic) and Eastern (e.g., Ayurveda, traditional Chinese medicine) cultures. Herbal remedies, lifestyle modifications, tactile therapies, movement therapies, and mind/body therapies are frequently used as treatment interventions for maintaining health across cultures.

WESTERN SYSTEMS OF HEALING

Homeopathy

Homeopathy, founded by Samuel Hahnemann, M.D. (1755–1843), is based on the Law of Similars, or "Let likes be cured by likes." It is a form of self-healing in which the substance (e.g., minerals, plant extracts, chemicals, or disease-producing germs) that creates illness symptoms in a healthy individual is used to cure those very symptoms when prescribed in microdoses. Symptoms are not thought to be part of the illness but part of a curative process (Spencer & Jacobs, 1999) because outward manifestations of illness represent an attempt of an organism to heal itself, with the corresponding remedy reinforcing that attempt in some way (Micozzi, 1996).

The homeopathic practitioner views illness as a disturbance of the vital force of an individual, manifesting itself as a totality of physical, mental, and emotional symptoms that is unique to each patient (Micozzi, 1996). Homeopathic remedies exist for psychological conditions such as depression, anxiety, and the wide range of distressed mental states. For example, minerals such as argentum nitricum and aurum metallicum have been prescribed for anxiety and depression, respectively (Lockie, 1989; Stanton, 1981). Plant derivatives such as ignatia, arnica, and equisetum have been prescribed for grief, shock, and for curing bedwetting in both children and adults, respectively (Lockie, 1989; Stanton, 1981). Typical homeopathic practice includes a thorough idiographic assessment of a patient's case history and presenting symptoms (e.g., physical, cognitive, and emotional) to find a homeopathic remedy that matches the individual rather than a specific illness, with the correct remedy or combination of remedies aimed at curing the patient's whole spectrum of symptoms.

One of the main advantages of homeopathic remedies is that they are relatively safe and have no side effects because of the infinitesimal amounts of the homeopathic substances. However, because homeopathy is highly individualized, it is a difficult and exacting art. A skilled homeopathic practitioner might try several remedies before any benefit is obtained. Furthermore, there remains a lack of understanding of dilute remedies' mechanism of action, as well as an inability to predict how a patient will respond to a certain remedy or which symptoms will be affected. These factors greatly hinder the study of treatment efficacy of homeopathic remedies.

Therapeutic Approaches

To minimize the potentially toxic effects of a medicinal substance, extremely minute doses are used. The preparation of the homeopathic remedy starts with an amount of the medicinal substance (e.g., herbal tincture) and serially diluting it either 10- or 100-fold with water a number of times, followed by vigorous shaking between each dilution (potentizing; Ernst, Rand, & Stevinson, 1998; Micozzi, 1999). The dosage must be tailored to fit the patient very much like the choice of the remedy itself. The general rule is to stop the administration of the remedy once the reaction is apparent, allowing the remedy to complete its course of action, and repeating only when the reaction has subsided.

The therapeutic goal of homeopathy is to find a substance that matches as many of the individual's symptoms as possible, including not only physical symptoms, but also the living experience of the patient, such as the full range of thoughts and feelings. Hence, both cognitive and emotional symptoms sometimes weigh heavily in choosing the remedy. The homeopathic diagnostic interview is composed of a physical examination, laboratory work, and the opportunity for the patient to tell his or her life story. This provides an opportunity for assessment of symptoms and as a means of catharsis. It makes the homeopathic interview a possible healing experience in its own right, leading critics to believe that effectiveness of homeopathic remedies may be a function of the placebo effect.

Clinical Applications

To date, there are significantly more descriptive studies in the literature than there are clinical trials. A meta-analysis of homeopathic clinical trials uncovered 105 controlled trials, of which 81 indicated positive results and 24 indicated a lack of positive results compared to placebo (Kleijnen, Knipschild, & ter Riet, 1991). Another meta-analysis extracted 89 of 185 homeopathic trials as having appropriate data for such an analysis (Linde et al., 1997). The results were also in support of homeopathy.

A number of studies in peer-reviewed journals report the apparent effectiveness of homeopathy for certain asthmatic and allergic conditions. In a randomized, double-blind, placebo-controlled clinical trial involving 28 patients with allergic asthma, homeopathy was found to produce significantly more symptom improvement than placebo (Reilly et al., 1994). Another study with a similar design involving 144 patients with symptoms of hay fever found a significant reduction in symptom intensity and use of histamines (50% less) in the homeopathy treatment group compared to the placebo group (Reilly, Taylor, McSharry, & Aitchison, 1986). The results from these studies suggest potential benefits of homeopathy as a complementary treatment for asthma, allergies, and other stress-related conditions.

The value of homeopathy as a treatment for depression is presently unknown because of the lack of substantiation by systematic research. Davidson, Morrison, Shore, and Davidson (1997) reported a case study of a 47-year-old woman whose depressive and anxious symptoms improved on fluoxetine (Prozac) and calcarea carbonica (a homeopathic remedy). The thorough review of homeopathy clinical trials by Kleijnen et al. (1991) and the meta-analysis by Linde et al. (1997) detected only one study related to depression. Although this study (Ernst et al., 1998) produced a result in favor of homeopathy, the study was of low methodological quality. Furthermore, two large reviews of the role of homeopathy in clinical medicine concluded that, except for the occasionally demonstrated benefit, there was little scientific evidence to support the use of homeopathy in the majority of clinical settings (Watkins, 1994).

Several problems exist in studying the efficacy of homeopathic treatments. To provide some scientific rigor, most conventional clinical research involves administering the same remedy to all patients, which contradicts the philosophy of the idiographic approach involved in homeopathic treatments. Furthermore, most homeopathic studies are case reports but do not include methodologies that include multiple baselines or a reversal to baseline methodology.

Osteopathy

Osteopathy, founded by Andrew Taylor Still, M.D. (1823–1917), is a complete system of prevention, diagnosis, and treatment based on a "whole person" approach. It posits that there is an interrelationship between the structure and function of the human body and that the body has the ability to self-regulate and self-heal. Specifically, when the body is in a normal structural relationship with adequate nutrition, it is capable of maintaining its own defenses against diseases and other pathologic conditions (Micozzi, 1996; C. M. Nezu, Nezu, Baron, & Roessler, 2000). However, when there are alterations in the structural relationships of the body parts, the body has difficulty resisting or recovering from illness. It has been proposed that structural difficulties in the body can cause numerous problems such as arthritis, headaches, emotional problems, breathing problems, heart problems, and digestive problems depending on which area in the musculoskeletal system is restricted or under stress (The Burton Goldberg Group, 1995). Recovery from these conditions is said to occur through normalization of body mechanics and the neuromusculoskeletal system via osteopathic manipulative treatment (OMT).

It is important to distinguish between the actual practices of osteopathic physicians from osteopathic manipulative treatments. Osteopathic training in the United States blends conventional medical practices and training in biomedical sciences with osteopathic manipulative treatment approaches as an integrated system of health care. Depending on the focus of the licensed osteopathic physicians, the actual practice of osteopathy may vary according to the area of specialty (Sirica, 1995).

Therapeutic Approaches

The diagnostic process in osteopathy emphasizes a close and personal relationship between the physician and patient because it is based on the premise that familiarity with a patient's personality and habits is essential to providing high-quality health care (Hruby, 1995). Because osteopathy evaluates the human body as an integral unit, treatment modalities are selected based on the patient's report of signs and symptoms, along with a comprehensive patient history and examination in which the structure and function of the musculoskeletal system provides important clues to dysfunction (Micozzi, 1996). OMT is a therapeutic means of correcting these dysfunctions and is often prescribed in conjunction with other clinical modalities, including education on nutrition, lifestyle, breathing techniques, relaxation techniques, and postural correction to reduce tension to the affected areas of the body (C. M. Nezu et al., 2000). Although osteopathy is considered a comprehensive system of healing, it is best known for its reliance on the diagnostic and therapeutic value of the musculoskeletal system and OMT, which is a distinguishing hallmark of the osteopathic profession. Different manipulative approaches available to the osteopathic physician include muscle energy, myofascial, counterstrain, and thrusting techniques (DiGiovanna & Schiowitz, 1991). Muscle energy techniques focus on directing muscles against a distinct counterforce such as increased tension or resistance. The goal is to mobilize joints by gently tensing and releasing specific muscles to produce relaxation. Myofascial techniques, also known as soft tissue techniques, focus on the continuous layer of connective tissue below the skin (i.e., fascia) that surrounds and bonds all of the body's internal organs. They are used to relax and release restrictions in the soft tissues of body. In counterstrain techniques, somatic dysfunction is believed to have a neuromuscular basis. These are functional and positional release methods used to relieve pain by placing the patient in a specific position to allow the body to relax and release muscular spasms that may have been caused by strain or injury. Thrusting techniques are small, high velocity forces applied by a practitioner in an effort to alleviate joint dysfunction (e.g., by altering the range of motion available at a joint).

Clinical Applications

Research to date focuses on the philosophy of osteopathic medicine and manipulation techniques and less on treatment outcome. Patients with HIV disease have been reported to use OMT for relaxation and pain management because of drug toxicity or disease progression (Micozzi, 1999). Treatment includes massage and myofascial release techniques to relax muscle tension, counterstrain techniques to relax and elongate muscle fiber for increased joint mobility and range of motion, muscle energy techniques to foster normalization of the musculoskeletal system, and visceral manipulation, which may potentiate normal physiologic function of individual organs.

Chiropractic

Chiropractic, derived from the Greek word meaning "done by hands," was founded by Daniel David Palmer in 1895 based on the premise that vertebral subluxation (a spinal misalignment causing abnormal nerve transmission) is the cause of virtually all disease and that chiropractic adjustment (a manual manipulation of the subluxated vertebrae) is its cure (Palmer, 1910). Similar to the fundamental principles of osteopathy and the foundation of the emerging holistic health or wellness paradigm, a chiropractic approach views human beings as possessing an innate healing potential. Like osteopathy, structure and function are believed to exist in intimate relation with one another. Hence, structural distortions of the spine are proposed to cause functional abnormalities, which may impede the communication and balance between the different branches of the nervous system (central, autonomic, and peripheral) that are required for health maintenance. This is believed to result in injury or stress, causing pain. Restoration and maintenance of proper bodily function involves realigning the spine to remove the pressure of bone impingement on spinal nerves to restore spinal joint mobility and nerve function. Whereas osteopaths provide manual therapy to a variety of areas in the body, chiropractors focus specifically on spinal maladjustments. A balanced, natural diet and exercise is also considered an important part of treatment for maintaining proper bodily function and optimal health.

Therapeutic Approaches

Of the patients seeking chiropractors, 90% present with neuromuscular problems such as back pain, neck pain, and headaches, conditions for which spinal manual therapy (SMT) is most effective (Plamondon, 1995). The central focus of chiropractic practice is to determine when and where SMT is appropriate, and what type of adjustment is most appropriate in a given situation. The most common form of chiropractic SMT is the high-velocity, low-amplitude thrust adjustment (HVLA), also known as osseous adjustment (Micozzi, 1996). It involves manual movement of a joint to the end point of its normal range of motion, followed by local pressure on bony prominences and then imparting a swift, specific, low-amplitude thrust for joint cavitation. Although patients often report significant functional improvements and healing effects following chiropractic adjustment, positive health changes have never been convincingly correlated with vertebral alignment (Micozzi, 1996; Winkel, Aufdemkampe, Matthijs, Meijer, & Phelps, 1996).

Clinical Applications

Several comprehensive reviews exist on clinical outcome studies in spinal manipulation. Shekelle, Adams, Chassin, Hurwitz, and Brook (1992) analyzed nine randomized, controlled trials that tested the effects of spinal manipulation against various conservative treatments for patients with acute low back pain (e.g., back pain that does not result from fractures, tumors, infections, and vascular, abdominal, or urinary diseases). All nine studies found spinal manipulation to be efficacious, leading the authors to conclude that spinal manipulation hastens recovery from uncomplicated low back pain. Findings from two other meta-analyses (Abenhaim & Bergeron, 1992; Anderson et al., 1992) provide some evidence of the short-term effectiveness of spinal manipulation in relieving acute and chronic back pain, although long-term effects of this treatment have not been adequately evaluated. Chiropractic treatment has also been demonstrated to be more effective in treating the pain from muscle tension headaches than the tricyclic antidepressant amitriptyline for long-term relief of pain (Boline, 1991). Patients maintained their levels of improvement after treatment was discontinued, while those taking medication returned to pretreatment status in an average of four weeks following its discontinuation. Further research is needed to address the question of long-term efficacy of spinal manipulation for different types of pain.

Other studies have focused on applying chiropractic manipulation to spinal cord injury patients (Fritz-Ritson, 1995; Woo, 1993), infantile colic (Klougart, Nilsson, & Jacobsen, 1989), and enuresis (Leboeuf et al., 1991; Reed, Beavers, Reddy, & Kern, 1994). The results generated from these studies are inconsistent and inconclusive because of limitations in research design. Further research is needed to determine the effectiveness of chiropractic manipulations in these populations.

EASTERN SYSTEMS OF HEALING

Ayurveda

Ayurveda, a Sanskrit word meaning "the science of life and longevity," is a major health system developed in India more than 5,000 years ago that emphasizes a preventive approach to health by focusing on an inner state of harmony and spiritual realization for self-healing. It focuses on the whole organism and its relation to the external world because human beings are viewed as minute representations of the universe and contain within them everything that makes up the surrounding world. The cosmos is believed to be composed of five basic elements (earth, air, fire, water, and space), which occur as the three doshas (*vata, pitta,* and *kapha*), or the basic bodily and mental human energy forces (Micozzi, 1996). Most people possess a combination of doshas, in which one dosha predominates. When the three doshas are in equilibrium, health is said to be maintained. When an imbalance occurs among them, body dysfunctions that lead to the manifestation of disease exist. The cause of the imbalance may originate in the body, outside the body, or from spiritual sources.

In addition to the doshas, Ayurveda principles indicate that an individual is influenced by three mental states based on the qualities of balance, energy, and inertia (Micozzi, 1996). The mind is said to be in equilibrium when it is in the state of balance. The mind is excessively active when it is in a state of energy and is inactive when it is in a state of inertia, with both states causing weakness in equilibrium. Hence, the body and the mind can interact to create a healthy and functional, or unhealthy and nonfunctional, condition. During the assessment phase, the Ayurvedic physician determines both the mental and physical conditions of the patient before proceeding with any form of diagnosis and treatment. Treatment aims to restore the balance of the doshas or to maintain the proper balance of energy flow (*prana;* C. M. Nezu et al., 2000). This can be achieved through a variety of methods such as meditation, exercise, diet, herbs, aromatherapy, oil massages, yoga, and medicated enemas (Spencer & Jacobs, 1999), with a main focus on lifestyle changes.

Although a centuries-old healing phenomena, Ayurveda was revived in recent decades by Maharishi Mahesh Yogi. This specific reformulation of Ayurveda is known as Maharishi Ayurveda (MAV). "MAV promotes the idea of consciousness as a primary importance in maintaining optimal health, and emphasizes meditation techniques as a way to develop integrated holistic functioning," according to Micozzi (1996, p. 243). The fundamental principles of MAV are similar to those of traditional Ayurveda. However, the ultimate basis of disease in MAV is associated with losing a person's sense of spiritual being. Prevention and cure is focused primarily on restoring the conscious connection to the person's spiritual core, enabling the full expression of the body's "inner intelligence."

Therapeutic Approaches

The two general courses of treatment in Ayurveda are prophylaxis and therapy (Micozzi, 1996). Prophylaxis is used to help a healthy person maintain health and prevent disease. Therapy is used to help an ill person restore health. When a person is diagnosed with an imbalance of the doshas, purification therapy, alleviation therapy, or a combination of these is prescribed. In purification therapy, a patient might be given a purgative, such as an enema, to eliminate the dosha that is thought to be causing the disease. Alleviation therapy uses the condiments honey, butter or ghee, and sesame or caster oil for the same purpose. Once the individual returns to health, continuous prophylaxis is recommended based on a variety of methods such as diet, meditation, herbal regimens, and regular therapeutic purification procedures.

In MAV, the most important technique in achieving overall well-being is transcendental meditation (TM), where "the mind transcends even the subtlest impulses of thought and settles down to the simplest state of awareness" (Micozzi, 1996, p. 246), a state known as transcendental consciousness. Although MAV views unfolding consciousness as the single most important strategy of both disease prevention and cure, lifestyle, behavioral, and emotional factors can also have a great impact. For example, traditional virtues such as respecting others, familial harmony, practicing nonviolence, pardoning others, and maintaining a positive emotional tone are understood to promote health for the individual's mind and body, as well as for the community and society.

Clinical Applications

Herbal remedy is an important component of Ayurvedic medicine. Laboratory and animal studies have found cytotoxicity in some traditional and MAV remedies (Sharma et al., 1991; Smit et al., 1995), suggesting potential effectiveness in cancer treatments. However, no randomized studies in humans have been conducted (Spencer & Jacobs, 1999). Some

Ayurvedic herbal mixtures have been found to have beneficial health effects. The herbal mixture *MA-631* may be used to prevent and treat atherosclerotic vascular disease (Hanna, Sharma, Kauffman, & Newman, 1994). Herbal mixtures *MAK-4* and *MAK-5* have been found to be effective in angina patients in significantly reducing angina frequency and systolic blood pressure, and in improving exercise tolerance (Dogra, Grover, Kumar, & Aneja, 1994).

The extant research surrounding TM appears to support its proposed beneficial effects on health, suggesting that TM may be an effective complementary intervention for patients suffering from a variety of psychological and physical problems. A Harvard study of elderly nursing home residents compared the practice of TM with two other types of meditation and relaxation techniques over a three-year period (Alexander, Langer, Newman, Chandler, & Davies, 1989). The study found that the TM group had the greatest reductions in stress and blood pressure, and the lowest mortality rate. A meta-analysis on the effect of meditation and trait anxiety conducted at the Stanford Research Institute found that TM is approximately twice as effective as other meditation techniques at reducing trait anxiety (Eppley, Abrams, & Shear, 1989). TM has also been found in several studies to retard biological aging (Glaser et al., 1992), to significantly reduce high blood pressure and cholesterol (Cooper & Aygen, 1978), and to help in giving up harmful habits such as cigarette smoking, heavy drinking, and illegal drug use by incorporating more healthy dietary and lifestyle changes (Alexander, Robinson, & Rainforth, 1994; Gelderloos, Walton, Orme-Johnson, & Alexander, 1991). These studies collectively suggest that practicing TM has beneficial effects on health.

Traditional Chinese Medicine

Similar to Ayurveda, traditional Chinese medicine (TCM) diagnostic and treatment strategies involve a search for imbalance and disharmony in each individual patient. The philosophy of TCM begins with *yin* (shady side) and *yang* (sunny side), which are opposing but complementary forces that exist in a dynamic equilibrium (The Burton Goldberg Group, 1995). Like Ayurveda, TCM focuses on interrelation and interdependence of the whole organism with the external world. In addition to being viewed in relation to their surroundings, yin and yang are also used to correlate the body and other phenomenon to the human experience of health and disease, and all health treatments are aimed at keeping yin and yang in balance.

Another concept that is crucial to understanding TCM is *qi*, often translated with the term *energy* or *life force*. While the Western definition of energy is the capacity to do work, *qi* implies that "the body is pervaded by subtle material and mobile influences that cause most physiological functions and maintain the health and vitality of the individual" (Micozzi, 1996, p. 195). According to TCM, this vital energy system exists in the body along pathways called *meridians* or channels. When energy is flowing at normal levels, the body is balanced and healthy, resistant to disease, and can activate its own healing efforts. When imbalances or blockages occur, physiological and pathological changes ensue. Practitioners of TCM believe that all illnesses result from a disturbance of *qi* within the body.

In TCM, there is no distinction between mind and body. TCM believes that an individual's emotional and physiological experiences are reciprocal. Hence, aspects of the human emotional experience are linked to specific physiological organs (e.g., anger is related to the liver, joy to the heart), and, thus, are causal factors in disease. There are three categories for the causes of disease: external causes (i.e., wind, cold, fire, dampness, summer heat, and dryness, collectively referred to as "the six environmental evils"), internal causes (i.e., joy, anger, anxiety, thought, sorrow, fear, and fright, collectively referred to as "the seven affects"), and causes that are neither external nor internal (e.g., dietary irregularities, excessive sexual activity, overexertion, or complete inactivity; Micozzi, 1996). Each of the causes of disease disrupts the balance of yin and yang in the body and disrupts the free movement of *qi*. Successful diagnosis and treatment are based on identifying the precise pattern of such imbalances. This is accomplished by taking a comprehensive medical history, which includes asking about the nature of the patient's complaints, the presence of any excessive activities such as sleeping or waking, diet, and sensations of "hot" and "cold." Treatment involves helping the person regain health by reestablishing a normal balance and flow in the energy system, so that the body may heal itself. All of the treatment modalities in TCM are designed to achieve this harmony. Healthy individuals also practice these treatment modalities prophylactically to maintain health and prevent disease.

Therapeutic Approaches

There are a number of therapeutic approaches in TCM, of which *Qigong* is the most powerful (Micozzi, 1996). *Qigong* is a form of exercise-stimulation therapy that proposes to improve health by redirecting mental focus, breathing, coordination, and relaxation to mobilize and regulate the movement of *qi* in the body to facilitate the body's own healing capacities (Spencer & Jacob, 1999). *Tai Chi Ch'uan* (also called tai chi) is a type of martial art that uses slow, purposeful motor-physical movements to achieve control and a more balanced physiological and psychological state. This technique is particularly popular among senior adults, and has been endorsed by the National Institute of Aging. Other TCM approaches include acupuncture, acupressure, massage (*Tui Na*), herbal medicine, and diet.

Acupuncture is employed to remove the obstruction causing the interruption of the flow of *qi,* or to redirect the flow of *qi* to where it is insufficient. Thin needles are inserted superficially on the skin throughout the body where meridian points are located (Spencer & Jacobs, 1999). To further enhance the movement of *qi,* acupuncture is often used in conjunction with heat (*moxibustion*) or electric current (*electroacupuncture*). Healing is proposed by restoration of a balance of *qi* flow within the body.

Acupressure uses the deep pressure of the fingers or hands to stimulate meridian points and *qi* flow. It is an effective self-care and preventative health care treatment for tension-related ailments (The Burton Goldberg Group, 1995). Acupressure is also prescribed to help decrease psychological distress by assisting persons to increase their body awareness and ability to cope with stress through release of built-up tension (Jacobs, 1996). *Tui Na* is a form of acupressure massage that uses techniques such as pushing, rolling, kneading, rubbing, grasping, percussion, and vibration to improve circulation and to stimulate stale blood and lymph from tissues (The Burton Goldberg Group, 1995). It is often used as an adjunct to acupuncture treatment, to increase the range of motion of a joint, or in populations where acupuncture is contraindicated (e.g., pediatric). A type of popular acupressure called *Shiatsu* (finger pressure) originated in Japan and uses applied pressure for 3 to 10 seconds in a rhythmic fashion. Shiatsu uses the same points as acupressure, but a practitioner of shiatsu refers to such points as *tsubo,* rather than meridian points. Shiatsu combines meridian point therapy with gentle stretching and both soft tissue and joint manipulation and relies on gravity, rather than muscular force, to operate.

Although *magnetic therapy* is not a TCM approach, it has recently gained popularity in the Chinese culture because of its self-help properties via the production of accessible devices such as magnetic bracelets and small magnets that can be easily adhered to the skin. The belief is that magnets can heal and enhance health by placing them either along a particular meridian or directly over the area of dysfunction to remove the obstruction of *qi* flow. Despite the increasing use of magnetic therapy as a form of self-help, empirical studies to support its proposed benefits are lacking (Dexter, 1997).

Chinese herbal medicine is an integral part of Chinese culture and medical practice. It includes not only plants, but also mineral and animal parts as listed in the traditional Chinese material medica (also Liu, 1988; Spencer & Jacobs, 1999). Prescribing rules exist for consideration of the compatibilities and incompatibilities of substances, the traditional pairing of substances, and their combination for specific symptoms (Liu, 1988). All of the formulas are organized in such a way as to support the *qi* that is desired for returning the body to a balanced and harmonious state.

Maintaining a balanced diet in TCM is extremely important in maintaining health and in preventing, or recovering from, diseases and other pathological conditions. Many of the foods that are used for therapy in TCM are also routinely prepared by families and are part of cultural practices. Special foods, as characterized by their yin and yang properties, may be prepared when seasons change or when a person is ill. These food preparations are aimed at keeping yin and yang in balance in the individual and preventing disturbance in *qi* flow.

Clinical Applications

Most of the research studies in the literature on TCM focus on meridian point therapies such as acupuncture, electroacupuncture, and acupressure. Thus far, the evidence on the efficacy of acupuncture in the management of chronic pain is controvertible. One well-controlled study by Vincent (1989) demonstrated the long-term effectiveness of acupuncture in the treatment of migraine headaches. There was a 43% reduction in past treatment pain scores and a 38% reduction in medication usage for the acupuncture group compared to the placebo group, and these results were maintained at four-month and one-year follow-up. Patel, Gutzwiller, Paccand, and Marazzi (1989) examined the effectiveness of acupuncture for chronic pain in a meta-analysis of 14 randomized, controlled trials comparing acupuncture with placebo or standard care. The pooled results suggest that acupuncture was effective in treating low back and chronic headache pain. However, a second meta-analysis of 51 trials (ter Riet, Kleijnen, & Knipschild, 1990) found that most of the studies were of mediocre or poor quality with the best studies yielding contradictory results, raising significant debate over effectiveness.

The benefits of acupuncture have also been explored in a variety of other conditions. For example, acupuncture was found to be effective in the management of symptoms associated with withdrawal from a variety of addictive substances such as cocaine (Culliton & Kiresuk, 1996). Jobst (1995) concluded that acupuncture produced favorable effects in the management of patients with bronchial asthma, chronic bronchitis, and chronic disabling breathlessness. Although there is no evidence that acupuncture is an effective treatment for cancer itself, there are claims that it may be effective in providing some relief from the side effects of cancer or the symptoms associated with conventional cancer treatments, such as pain control, and nausea and vomiting associated with chemotherapy (Vickers, 1996).

Some benefits of acupressure are supported in the scientific literature. For example, compared to sham acupressure, true acupressure was more effective in improving the quality of sleep in institutionalized residents (Chen, Lin, Wu, & Lin, 1999). In randomized controlled studies, acupressure treatment resulted in significantly less nausea and vomiting than placebo in persons undergoing laparoscopy (Harmon, Gardiner, Harrison, & Kelly, 1999) and caesarean sections (Harmon, Ryan, Kelly, & Bowen, 2000). Acupressure also resulted in less nausea than treatment as usual in a sample of women with breast cancer undergoing chemotherapy treatment (Dibble, Chapman, Mack, & Shih, 2000). However, not all published studies support the efficacy of acupressure. For example, acupressure was not effective at decreasing motion sickness in a double-blinded controlled study with a sample of male college students (Warwick-Evans, Masters, & Redstone, 1991).

There is some support for the use of electroacupuncture in the treatment of depression. Two randomized, controlled clinical trials compared the effects of electroacupuncture and amitriptyline hydrochloride in depressed patients (Luo, Jia, Wu, & Dai, 1990; Luo, Jia, & Zhan, 1985). Both studies found a significant reduction in clinician's ratings of depression scores after treatment for both groups; however, there were no significant differences between groups. Furthermore, a two- to four-year follow-up also found no significant differences between groups in the rate of depression recurrence, with electroacupuncture having fewer side effects than antidepressant medication. Additional well-designed studies are needed to further delineate the efficacy of meridian point therapies in the treatment of depression.

Clinical data for the efficacy of other TCM therapeutic approaches also exist. Ryu et al. (1996) studied the effects of *Qigong* and meditation on stress hormone levels in 20 subjects who were engaged in at least four months of *Qigong* training. The results supported the stress-relieving benefits of such training. However, the study lacked both a control group and random selection of treatment group participants. As such, well-controlled studies are warranted to reach more conclusive results. Although most studies on tai chi have limited generalizability because randomized trials with control groups were rarely used, positive cardiovascular changes (i.e., reductions in heart rate, blood pressure, and urinary catecholamines) have been demonstrated when comparing a participant's own pretest and posttest scores in performance

(Jin, 1992). Tai chi may also help in promoting cardiorespiratory functioning in elderly subjects (Lai & Lan, 1995), as well as enhancing positive mood (Jin, 1989, 1992). These results suggest that the practice of *Qigong* and tai chi may have stress-moderating functions.

OTHER COMMON HEALING APPROACHES

Herbal Remedies

Although frequently employed as part of the overall healing systems previously discussed, herbs have also been used as a sole treatment to promote healing and balance. In the past two decades, herbal remedies for psychiatric and medical care have been increasingly used and investigated scientifically. One survey suggests that in 1990, "Americans made an estimated 425 million visits to providers of unconventional therapy" (Eisenberg et al., 1993, p. 247). Another survey found that between 30% and 70% of patients in developed countries use complementary and alternative medicine (Linde et al., 1996). Overall, early studies suggest that phytotherapy, the use of active substances found in plants, can enhance psychotherapeutic and medical treatment. The phytotherapeutic substances, described next, have undergone some degree of scientific study.

Echinacea

Echinacea, also known as purple cornflower, is derived from the Greek word *echinos,* meaning "hedgehog" or "sea urchin," a name given to the plant because of its spiky seed heads (Gunning, 1999). The herb is popular among Native Americans and in Germany, and is represented by nine species found in the United States. Echinacea is classified by the plant species used, the part of the plant processed, the mode of processing, and the mode of application (Grimm & Muller, 1999). A majority of studies have investigated echinacea for the treatment of colds and upper respiratory infections (URIs), chronic arthritis, cancer, chronic fatigue syndrome, wounds and ulcers, and chronic pelvic infections (e.g., see Grimm & Muller, 1999). A review of 13 published and unpublished, randomized, placebo-controlled trials of echinacea in the treatment of URIs found echinacea to be more effective than placebo in eight out of nine treatment trials by decreasing the severity and duration of URI symptoms (Barrett, Vohmann, & Calabrese, 1999). Other studies (Grimm & Muller, 1999; Melchart, Walther, Linde, Brandmaier, & Lersch, 1998) have not found such positive effects.

The active ingredient of echinacea is unclear. Studies suggest that echinacea produces its effects via the immune system (Gunning, 1999), such as inducing cytokine production (Bruger, Torres, Warren, Caldwell, & Hughes, 1997) or enhancing cellular immune function of peripheral blood mononuclear cells (See, Broumand, Sahl, & Tilles, 1997). In their review, Barrett et al. (1999) highlight the difficulty in comparing the research studies because different species are studied and there are no universally accepted standardization procedures.

Garlic

Although commonly considered a food substance, garlic (*Allium sativum*) is a commonly prescribed supplemental herb for the treatment of high cholesterol. Allicin is considered the active compound found in the garlic bulb. Many of the studies investigate Kwai garlic powder tablets because it is standardized for alliin content (1.3% by weight). While Kleijnen, Knipschild, and ter Riet (1989) suggest that early studies on the efficacy of garlic were methodologically flawed, more recent studies suggest garlic is effective in treating hypercholesterolaemia. Two meta-analyses (Silagy & Neil, 1994; Warshafsky, Kamer, & Sivak, 1993) suggest that garlic reduces the high serum cholesterol levels considered to be a risk factor for coronary artery disease. Warshafsky et al. (1993) found 13 studies to meet their methodological criteria, and meta-analytic results suggested that garlic significantly lowered cholesterol levels by about 9% in the experimental groups as compared to placebo. The results of Silagy and Neil's (1994) meta-analysis of the 16 trials meeting their standards for methodological quality found that garlic lowered serum cholesterol over one to three months and did not produce significantly more adverse effects. While several authors (Isaacsohn et al., 1998; Jain, Vargas, Gotzkowsky, & McMahon, 1993) criticized these early meta-analytic findings, more recent, randomized, controlled trials have found garlic to reduce ratios of serum total cholesterol (Adler & Holub, 1997) and decrease low-density lipoprotein cholesterol in healthy men (Jain et al., 1993; Steiner, Khan, Holbert, & Lin, 1996).

Ginger

Zingiber officinale, commonly known as ginger, has been primarily investigated for its antiemetic effects. This research has been particularly important for individuals who suffer from motion sickness and from postoperative nausea, or who experience nausea and vomiting due to chemotherapy but are unable to take synthetic drugs because of side effects such as sedation and visual disturbances. Several early studies found ginger to be more effective than placebo in alleviat-

ing gastrointestinal symptoms of motion sickness (Mowrey & Clayson, 1982), reducing symptoms of seasickness (Grontved, Brask, Kambskard, & Hentzer, 1988), reducing nausea (Bone, Wilkinson, Young, McNeil, & Charlton, 1990) and reducing the request for antiemetics (Phillips, Ruggier, & Hutchinson, 1993) in postoperative patients. In addition, ginger has been studied for its antitumor effects (Koshimizu, Ohigashi, Tokudo, Kondo, & Yamaguchi, 1988). Vimala, Norhanom, and Yadav (1999) demonstrated that some, but not all, types of ginger inhibit Epstein Barr virus (EBV) activation without the cytotoxicity effects. The authors suggest that populations with a high risk of cancer are "encouraged" to take plants with ginger, yet they also acknowledge that such use will not completely eliminate the disease.

Ginkgo Biloba

Ginkgo biloba extract is derived from the maidenhair tree and has been studied primarily for its effect on the brain, dementia, and Alzheimer's disease. Active ingredients include Egb 761 (tapenoids), which have platelet-activating factor antagonistic properties, and gingkolides and flavanoids (Oken, Storzbach, & Kaye, 1998). Three of the most popular preparations used in controlled trials include Tebonin, Tanakan, and Rokan, all of which are different names for the extract Egb 761. Various products available to the public contain different amounts of ginkgo biloba extract. In their review of the literature, Itil and Martorano (1995) suggest ginkgo has been "proven effective" in the treatment of tinnitus, sudden hearing loss, retinal damage, arthritic symptoms, vertigo, water retention, circulatory dysfunction, and age-related dementia. Early studies demonstrated the efficacy of Egb 761 on reducing the negative effects of experimentally induced stress on rats (Hasenohrl et al., 1996; Porsolt, Martin, Lenegre, Fromage, & Drieu, 1990; Rapin, Lamproglou, Drieu, & Defeudis, 1994) over other depressive medications (Porsolt et al., 1990) and over placebo (Porsolt et al., 1990; Rapin et al., 1994; Rodriguez de Turco, Droy-Lefaix, & Bazan, 1993). For instance, Rapin et al. (1994) found Egb 761 to decrease plasma hormone levels such as epinephrine, norepinephrine, and corticosterone. Alternatively, in their critical review of 40 controlled trials on Ginkgo and cerebral insufficiency in humans, Kleijnen and Knipschild (1992) found that only eight trials met criteria of good methodology, with only one showing positive effects compared with placebo on symptoms such as difficulty concentrating, memory problems, confusion, lack of energy, tiredness, depressive mood, anxiety, dizziness, tinnitus, and headaches. Similarly, a more recent meta-analysis of more than 50 articles (Oken et al., 1998) found only four studies (Hofferberth,

1994; Kanowski, Hermann, Stephan, Wierich, & Horr, 1996; Le Bars et al., 1997; Wesnes et al., 1997) that met the authors' standards for strong research methodology. These authors concluded there to be a "small but significant effect" of ginkgo biloba extract on cognitive function, such as memory and attention, in patients with Alzheimer's disease (Oken et al., 1998). Likewise, studies have found ginkgo biloba to improve mild to moderate memory impairment in elderly patients (Rai, Shovlin, & Wesnes, 1991), memory and psychopathology (Hofferberth, 1994), as well as daily living and social behavior (Le Bars et al., 1997). Moreover, consistent with previous reviews, ginkgo biloba was found to have no significant adverse effects.

Ginseng

Ginseng, a popular herb in traditional Chinese medicine, is primarily used for its effects on anxiety, concentration, and physical stress. Yun (1996) found *Panax ginseng* C. A. Meyer (Korean ginseng) to prevent the development of cancer in mice by inhibiting the proliferation of tumors. He has also demonstrated a decrease in the risk of certain types of cancer in 1,987 pairs of humans when ginseng was ingested as a fresh extract or powder, as well as a decrease in the relative risk of cancer in a prospective population-based study of 4,634 adults. Ginseng has also demonstrated to improve quality of life among healthy volunteers (Wiklund, Karlberg, & Lund, 1994), as well as improve mood, vigor, well-being, and psychomotor performance in patients with noninsulin-dependent diabetes mellitus (Sotaniemi, Haapakoski, & Rautio, 1995).

Several studies investigating the mechanism of action through which ginseng works demonstrate antinociceptive effects of ginseng on stress-induced mice (H.-S. Kim, Oh, Rheu, & Kim, 1992; Takahashi, Tokuyama, & Kaneto, 1992). Other studies suggest ginseng may enhance nitric oxide synthesis (Gillis, 1997), promote cytokine induction (Sonoda et al., 1998), or enhance natural killer cell activity in healthy subjects and in patients with chronic fatigue and acquired immunologic syndromes (Gillis, 1997).

Kava

Kava, which means "bitter" in Polynesian, is derived from a black pepper plant in the South Pacific called Piper methysticum, or "intoxicating pepper." Kava has been traditionally ingested as a drink, but recently sold in capsule form in health food stores in the United States. Explorers' journals have documented the effects of kava for centuries: Kava has a numbing effect on the tongue when drunk, is tranquilizing

and relaxing, and has genitourinary antiseptic qualities (Anonymous, 1988). However, too much kava can cause adverse effects such as dermopathy (Norton & Ruze, 1994), a skin condition characterized by scaly skin, gastrointestinal distress, and sleepiness (Cerrato, 1998), or a semicomatose state when it interacts with alprozam (Almeida & Grimsley, 1996).

There are few randomized trials investigating the efficacy of kava on anxiety. The majority of trials that do exist are published in German. These studies have found kava extract to be superior to placebo and comparable to oxazepam and bromazepam (Volz & Keiser, 1997). A randomized, placebo-controlled study of 101 outpatients with various anxiety disorders according to the *Diagnostic and Statistical Manual of Mental Disorders, 3rd Edition, Revised* (*DSM-III-R;* American Psychiatric Association, 1987) criteria also found kava to be superior to placebo by reducing anxiety and causing fewer side effects (Volz & Keiser, 1997).

The psychopharmacology of kava remains unclear. Initial hypotheses suggested by investigators include: (a) Kava increases the number of binding sites of $GABA_A$ receptors (Jussofie, Schmitz, & Hiemke, 1994); (b) it modulates the serotonin-1A receptor activity (Walden, Von Wegerer, Winter, & Berger, 1997; Walden, Von Wegerer, Winter, Berger, & Grunze, 1997); (c) it serves as reversible MAO-B inhibitors (Uebelhack, Franke, & Schewe, 1998); or (d) it inhibits NA+ channels (Magura, Kopanitsa, Gleitz, Peters, & Krishtal, 1997).

St. Johns' Wort

St. Johns' wort (SJW) is an herbal product resulting from the flowering of the plant *Hypericum perforatum* L. The plant's oil has been used for centuries as a medicine to heal burns and improve mood. Over the past two decades, the pharmaceutical industries have attempted to develop extracts of SJW for more popular and standardized use. In Germany, SJW is the most widely prescribed treatment for depression, totaling more than 25% of prescribed antidepressants (Muller & Kasper, 1997).

Overall, the research suggests SJW to be efficacious in reducing depressive symptoms and to produce significantly fewer side effects as compared to popular antidepressants. Studies comparing SJW to placebo have found antidepressive efficacy as well as high tolerability for SJW among patients with mild depression (Hansgen, Vesper, & Plouch, 1994; Hubner, Lande, & Podzuweit, 1994; Sommer & Harrer, 1994). SJW has also demonstrated to be as effective as imipramine (Vorbach, Hubner, & Arnold, 1994), maprotiline (Harrer, Hubner, & Podzuweit, 1994), and amitryptiline

(Wheatley, 1997), yielding a slightly better side effect profile. Meta-analyses evaluating theses studies have found SJW to be between 1.5 to 3 times more likely to produce an antidepressant response as compared to placebo, and to be equivalent in efficacy to tricyclic antidepressants, (see H. L. Kim, Streltzer, & Goebert, 1999; Linde et al., 1996).

Research on the biological mechanisms through which SJW may exert its antidepressant effects suggests that similar to popular pharmaceutical antidepressants, SJW influences amine levels. The main difficulty in studying the biological mechanism of SJW pertains to the fact that several active constituents have been identified from *H. perforatum* (Nahrstedt & Butterweck, 1997) including hypericin (Muller, Rolli, Schafer, & Hafner, 1997), and hyperforin (Chatterjee, Bhattacharya, Wonnemann, Singer, & Muller, 1998; Laakmann, Schule, Baghai, & Kieser, 1998; Muller et al., 1997, 1998; Schellenberg, Sauer, & Dimpfel, 1998). Overall, research indicates that SJW may inhibit the synaptosomal reuptake of serotonin, dopamine, and norepinephrine (Muller et al., 1997, 1998; Muller & Rossol, 1994; Neary & Bu, 1999); upregulate postsynaptic serotonin receptors (Teufel-Mayer & Gleitz, 1997); and interfere with the central dopaminergic system (Butterweck, Wall, Lieflander-Wulf, Winterhoff, & Nahrstedt, 1997; Franklin et al., 1999).

Studies demonstrate that the main advantage to SJW is its more preferable side effect profile and tolerability to synthetic antidepressants. The most common adverse side effects included gastrointestinal symptoms (0.6%), allergic reactions (0.5%), tiredness (0.4%), and restlessness (0.3%) (Woelk, Burkard, & Grunwald, 1994). In addition, hypericum has been found to be safer with regard to cardiac function than tricyclic antidepressants (Czekalla, Gastpar, Hubner, & Jager, 1997). While SJW appears to be a safe herbal remedy for depression when taken alone, the major danger with SJW seems to lie in its potential for drug interactions.

Current limitations in the research include lack of "well characterized populations" (Cott, 1997); translation bias (Gaster & Holroyd, 2000); limited research on long-term efficacy, safety, and tolerance at various doses (Volz & Kieser, 1997); efficacy for severe depression (Gaster & Holroyd, 2000); and efficacy as compared to serotonin reuptake inhibitors.

Summary of Herbal Treatment Research

In addition to the herbal remedies highlighted, more than 20,000 herbs are available to the public over the counter. For a good review of herbal remedies frequently used in psychiatric practice, refer to Wong, Smith, and Boon (1998). Currently, the Dietary Supplement Health and Education Act (DSHEA) does not require manufacturers to provide data on the safety, purity, and efficacy of their products (Wagner, Wagner, & Hening, 1998). Moreover, the Food and Drug Administration (FDA) does not regulate their use or standardize their purity or content (Lantz, Buchalter, & Giambanco, 1999). Therefore, individuals are able to self-prescribe herbs without the guidance of a physician, which may lead to adverse side effects and drug interactions. For instance, Lantz et al. (1999) discussed several case studies of elderly patients who developed serotonin syndrome (e.g., central and peripheral serotonergic hyperstimulation) from taking SJW in conjunction with their prescribed antidepressant. It is important that clinicians appreciate the strength of these herbs and ask their patients about herbal use and educate them on the dangers of herbal and drug interactions. Lantz et al. also recommends that herbal remedies provide warning labels and that efficacy studies be subjected to "the same vigorous standards" as prescription medications as related to efficacy and safety.

While the research suggests efficacy of a variety of herbal remedies, further research in required. There is a need for studies with (a) larger sample sizes, (b) data assessing participants' ability to distinguish placebo from the herb, (c) better characterization of the active constituents and mechanisms of action, and (d) results on the effects of chronic dosing, side effects, and standardization of preparation.

Dietary, Nutrition, and Lifestyle Modification

Dietary modification has recently become a way for individuals to take an active role in their well-being and a way to prevent the onset of illness or reduce the negative consequences of disease. Medical practitioners commonly recommend dietary modification and lifestyle changes as a complement to traditional treatment, rather than as a sole alternative cure.

Very Low Fat Diets

In 1988, the National Cholesterol Education Program (NCEP) published guidelines for the treatment of high cholesterol in adults. The guidelines recommend dietary therapy for the lowering of LDL cholesterol (LDL-C). Specifically, they recommend an initial diet that includes an intake of total fat less than 30% of calories (National Cholesterol Education Program Expert Panel, 1998). Lichtenstein and Van Horn (1998) conducted a review of the literature on the efficacy of a very low fat diet, and reported that while there is "overwhelming evidence" that reductions in saturated fat, dietary cholesterol, and weight are effective in reducing total cholesterol, LDL-C levels, and cardiovascular risk, the long-term effects remain unclear.

Macrobiotic Diets

Macrobiotics stems from the Greek words *macro,* meaning large, and *bios,* meaning life. A macrobiotic diet is composed of whole grains and cereals, vegetables (including sea vegetables), fruits, beans, nuts, and seeds. A macrobiotic approach underscores social interactions, climate, geographic location, and diet as all-important lifestyle habits to promote well-being and longevity. George Ohsawa is considered to be the founder of the macrobiotic diet, and it was popularized in the United States by Michio Kushi. Two early studies support the theory that a vegetarian diet results in a significant reduction in blood pressure among patients with hypertension (Margetts, Beilin, Vandongen, & Armstrong, 1986; Rouse, Beilin, Armstrong, & Vandongen, 1983). The use of macrobiotic in treatment of other medical conditions (e.g., cancer) remains controversial and has not been scientifically tested.

Atkins' Diet

In 1972, Robert Atkins published the book *Dr. Atkins' Diet Revolution.* He proposed metabolic imbalance to be the cause of obesity and stated that many of today's diseases, including diabetes, hypoglycemia, and cardiac disease, are a result of "carbohydrate intolerance" (Atkins, 1972). Atkins proposed that carbohydrates prevent our bodies from ketogenesis, a process by which the body burns fat and turns it into fuel. There are no scientific studies investigating ketogenic diets for the previously mentioned diseases, and therefore, these diets may be based more on theory than on scientific evidence. However, ketogenic diets have been investigated for their efficacy in managing epilepsy and seizure disorder. One study found that 54% of a group of children with intractable seizures who remained on a ketogenic diet reported a decrease in the frequency of their seizures by more than 50% three months after initiating the diet (Vining et al., 1998). Despite such findings, there is continued controversy regarding its use. Roach (1998) argues that while there is "a clear biochemical rationale and a well-defined therapeutic objective" (p. 1404), he urges for more rigorous investigations on safety and efficacy.

Gerson Method

Nutrition has become increasingly used, though not necessarily empirically supported, by individuals diagnosed with cancer. Max Gerson was a German-born physician who believed that "degenerative" diseases such as cancer, arthritis, and multiple sclerosis are the result of extreme body toxicity. Therefore, he advocated a special diet in the treatment of cancer, which included "detoxification" of the body, a no-sodium, no-fat, high-potassium, and high-carbohydrate diet, as well as coffee enemas. There are few studies investigating the efficacy of the Gerson Method; however, those that exist are methodologically flawed. One study (Hildenbrand, Hildenbrand, Bradford, & Calvin, 1995) investigated the efficacy of Gerson's diet therapy with 153 patients diagnosed with melanoma and found the five-year survival rate to be 100% for individuals at Stage I and II, 72% for individuals at Stage IIIA, and 41% for individuals at Stage IVA. While there was no placebo control group in this study, five-year survival rates were significantly higher than the survival rates published in other studies.

It should be noted that the Gerson Method is highly controversial. The American Cancer Society (ACS) reported a lack of evidence of the efficacy of the Gerson Method and urged people with cancer not to seek treatment with the Gerson Method (ACS, 1990). The ACS publicly acknowledges that while the dietary measures may have preventive utility, there is no scientific evidence than any nutritionally related regimen is appropriate as a primary treatment for cancer (ACS, 1993).

Ornish Lifestyle Heart Trial

Dean Ornish is well-known for his work with patients with coronary artery disease through vegetarian diet, exercise, and stress management on coronary atherosclerosis. The Lifestyle Heart Trial (Ornish et al., 1990), a prospective, randomized, controlled trial of patients with coronary artery disease, demonstrated that this prescribed lifestyle modification resulted in regression on coronary atherosclerosis as evidenced by a decrease in diameter stenosis. The study, however, did not investigate the individual contributions of the various interventions (e.g., low-fat vegetarian diet, stopping smoking, stress management training, exercise) to the outcome measure. Later studies (Gould et al., 1995; Ornish et al., 1998) investigated a similar lifestyle change program in patients with coronary artery disease over five years and found that the size and severity of perfusion abnormalities on dipyridamole positron emission tomography images decreased (improved) after risk factor modification in the experimental group, compared with an increase (worsening) of size and severity in the control group.

Tactile Therapies

Tactile therapies are defined as interventions that center on soft tissue or energy mobilization techniques performed by a health care provider. Such methods can be divided into soft tissue therapies, energy mobilization, and meridian point therapy.

Soft Tissue Therapies

Encompassing a variety of treatment approaches, soft tissue therapies are geared toward decreasing dysfunction in muscles and fascia (i.e., the continuous subcutaneous layer of soft tissue throughout the body). Soft tissue therapies are purported to alleviate somatic organizational dysfunction, thus enhancing both psychological and physical health.

The goal of *massage* is to decrease muscular tension using strokes, kneading, and friction techniques. Proposed benefits of massage include both psychological and physiological relaxation, facilitated ease with breathing, enhanced immune function, reduced anxiety, increased vigor, lessened pain, and improved sleep (Wanning, 1993). Positive effects from massage have been demonstrated in both adult and child populations (Field, Ironson, et al., 1996; Field, Morrow, et al., 1992). In one study, participants with depression and adjustment disorders were randomly assigned to receive a back massage or watch relaxing videos for 30 minutes over a five-day period (Field, Morrow, et al., 1992). Results demonstrated decreased depressive symptoms, anxiety, and salivary cortisol, as well as enhanced sleeping, for the massage group only.

Aromatherapy, the use of fragrances to augment mood and activity, is often used in conjunction with massage. Aromatherapy uses specific essential oils from plants for therapeutic use. For example, lavender is believed to have calming and analgesic effects, while ginger is deemed to incite stimulating, warming sensations (Jacobs, 1996). In one study, 122 patients in an intensive care unit were randomly assigned to massage, massage with lavender oil, or rest (Dunn, Sleep, & Collett, 1995). Only patients receiving massage with lavender oil demonstrated significantly enhanced mood following intervention.

Aromatherapy can also be used via bathing, candles, and culinary manners. Assessing the effects of aromatherapy ventilated throughout a room, one nonrandomized study demonstrated that depressed patients used less antidepressant medication after being exposed to citrus oils (Komori, Fujiwara, Tanida, Nomura, & Yokoyama, 1995). There are few empirical studies on aromatherapy, and the majority of those conducted use poor control and lack statistical analyses (Martin, 1996). In a review article, Evans (1995) suggests that the paucity of psychometrically sound studies makes it difficult to differentiate the beneficial effects of aromatherapy from attention, social interaction, or the use of massage.

Reflexology is a soft tissue mobilization centered on the foot. This technique is based on the belief that distinct areas of the foot represent different parts of the body. By applying pressure to specific regions of the foot, the corresponding body structure can be stimulated, promoting a health response. For example, the head and sinus regions are mapped in the toes, and massage of the toes is believed to help alleviate headaches and sinus pressure. A quasi-experimental study of persons with lung or breast cancer demonstrated positive effects on anxiety and pain following reflexology (Stephenson, Weinrich, & Tavakoli, 2000).

Myofascial release and *Rolfing* are two additional types of soft tissue therapies, both of which are purported to decrease pain and enhance health. The purpose of myofascial release is to free restrictions in the myofascial caused by physical or psychological stress using gentle pushing techniques against the client's skin. This technique is used to treat musculoskeletal dysfunction, headaches, chronic pain, and temporomandibular pain (Ramsey, 1997). Rolfing also attempts to manipulate myofascial constraints, but, unlike myofascial release, it uses the forces of gravity and more vigorous pressure from the practitioner. It has been suggested that Rolfing permits increased muscular efficiency, decreases physiological stress on the body, and promotes neurological functioning (Jacobs, 1996); however, scientific studies to support these claims are not present in the literature.

Energy mobilization attempts to alleviate poor physical and psychological health that is said to result from disturbances in a person's forces of energy. For example, *therapeutic touch* (TT) involves techniques that are aimed at centering awareness and energy in the client. Despite its name, this procedure does not necessarily involve direct contact with the client and may consist of the clinician's hands being held over the areas of needed energy mobilization.

Some literature supports the efficacy of TT. For example, the effects of TT in reducing anxiety were assessed in a sample of psychiatric in-patients (Gagne & Toye, 1994). Patients were randomly assigned to TT, mimic TT, or relaxation therapy. Results demonstrated significant decreases in anxiety for the TT and relaxation groups, with the former exhibiting greater benefits than the latter. The group receiving mimic TT demonstrated no significant changes. An additional randomized study supports TT as being more effective than "calm touch" at decreasing the time necessary to soothe medically hospitalized children between the ages of two weeks to two years (Kramer, 1990). In a randomized study of elderly individuals with arthritis, both TT and progressive muscle relaxation interventions resulted in comparable and significant improvements in pain, tension, and mood (Peck, 1998). However, not all studies support the beneficial effects of

TT (e.g., Olson, et al., 1997). A literature review and meta-analysis highlights the poor methodology implemented in TT studies but calculated an average effect size of .39 for TT (Winstead-Fry & Kijek, 1999).

Reiki, another type of energy mobilization, means "universal life force energy." Whereas TT involves the mobilization of energy in the client's body, Reiki entails transferring or mobilizing energy from the clinician to the client. It is based on the concept that all living creatures possess energy and that the human body is programmed to heal itself. Practitioners of Reiki report positive effects of this technique on mood, psychological distress, pain, and functional abilities, but these results are based on patient case history reports.

A similar energy-based approach, *polarity therapy,* is based on the concept that the body holds an electromagnetic force, with a positive charge located cephalically and a negative charge situated toward the toes. The clinician's hands are believed to be conductors of energy. When they are placed in certain areas of the client's human energy field, the clinician attempts to facilitate energy movement in the client's body. This facilitation is believed to enhance energy flow and relaxation throughout the mind and body. Scientific studies regarding its efficacy are absent.

Movement Therapies

Movement therapies are complementary approaches to health that emphasize changes in the client's bodily positions. *Leisure activity* (e.g., casual walking) has been demonstrated to buffer anxiety in the face of stressors (Carmack, Boudreaux, Amaral-Melendez, Brantley, & de Moor, 1999). Active perimenopausal women reported less psychosomatic symptoms (e.g., irritability, headaches) and fewer sexual problems than those who were more sedentary (Li, Gulanick, Lanuza, & Penckofer, 1999).

Some literature exists supporting the psychological benefits of *aerobic exercise.* Correlational studies predominantly endorse positive psychological health in people who participate in aerobic exercise. One study assessing more than 3,400 participants found that those who engaged in exercise two or more times each week reported less depressive symptoms, anger, cynical distrust, and stress compared to those exercising less or not at all (Hassmen, Koivula, & Uutela, 2000). This former group also reported a greater sense of social integration and perceived health. Similarly, meta-analytic reviews revealed that those who exercise are significantly less likely to be depressed (Craft & Landers, 1998) and to report distress (Crews & Landers, 1987). However, other meta-analyses demonstrate little (i.e., only one-half standard deviation; North, McCullagh, & Tran, 1990) or no (e.g., Schlicht, 1994) difference in psychological distress between exercisers and nonexercisers.

Intervention studies provide stronger evidence for the psychological benefits of aerobic exercise regarding psychological distress. One study randomly assigned participants with dysphoric mood to cognitive therapy, aerobic exercise, or a combination of these two interventions over a 10-week period (Fremont & Craighead, 1987). Although no significant differences were noted between the groups, all three demonstrated significant decreases in depressive symptoms. Similarly, older patients with major depressive disorder were randomly assigned to aerobic exercise (3 times per week), antidepressant medication (sertraline hydrochloride), or both for 16 weeks (Blumenthal et al., 1999). Results demonstrated all three groups significantly improved on measures of depression, anxiety, self-esteem, life satisfaction, and dysfunctional attitudes from pre- to posttreatment, but no differences were noted between the groups following intervention. Those receiving antidepressant medications did, however, demonstrate quicker enhancement of mood compared to those participating in aerobic exercise only.

A meta-analytic study demonstrated the effects of rehabilitative exercise programs on anxiety and depression in patients with coronary disease (Kugler, Seelbach, & Kruskemper, 1994). Specifically, exercise resulted in moderate decreases in both anxiety and depressive symptoms and did not differ significantly from psychotherapy. Similarly, breast cancer survivors randomly assigned to exercise or exercise plus behavior modification demonstrated comparably significant decreases in depressive symptoms and anxiety (Segar et al., 1998). The waitlist control (WLC) group in this study did not initially exhibit such declines in distress. However, following the waiting period, those participants in the WLC who partook in the exercise program also exhibited significantly diminished anxiety and depressive symptoms. In addition to aerobic exercise, *resistance exercise* (e.g., weight lifting) has also demonstrated beneficial effects on health (Tsutumi et al., 1998).

Fox's (1999) review of the literature on exercise and mental health supports the following conclusions: Exercise (a) is an effective treatment for clinical depression; (b) decreases state and trait anxiety; (c) enhances self-perceptions and, perhaps, self-efficacy; (d) improves mood; and (e) may improve cognitive functioning, especially in older adults. Possible mechanisms of action may be in the physiological (e.g., release of endorphins), psychological (e.g., diversion, improved self-image), and/or social (e.g., social interactions, receiving attention) domains.

Yoga incorporates exercise, static poses, breathing, relaxation, and meditation (Jacobs, 1996). The purpose of yoga is to "center" the person's mind, body, and spirit. Specific hypothesized benefits include improving muscular and cardiovascular endurance, boosting the immune system, enhancing circulation, increasing muscular and cognitive flexibility, and relaxation. Yoga is often used as complementary therapy for medical disorders such as asthma, arthritis, HIV/AIDS, cancer, and coronary artery disease. While there are several different types of yoga, *Hatha yoga* is most frequently practiced in the West. Hatha yoga combines stretching, breathing, relaxation, and meditation (Wanning, 1993).

Research supports positive benefits of practicing yoga. Patients with epilepsy were randomly assigned to true yoga, sham yoga (i.e., similar but distinct postures), and a nontreatment control group (Panjwani, Gupta, Singh, Selvamurthy, & Rai, 1995). Decreases in galvanic skin response, as an indicator of sympathetic nervous system activity, were noted in the true yoga group only. Another study compared yoga, relaxation (i.e., progressive muscle relaxation), and visualization in a group of healthy adults (Wood, 1993). Participants practiced for six, 25- to 30-minute sessions over a two-week period. Following intervention, the yoga group reported increased mental and physical energy, alertness, and positive mood. These benefits were significantly greater than the other two groups. The relaxation group was more tired and sluggish compared with yoga, and the visualization group reported more sluggishness and less contentment compared to those performing yoga. Additionally, yoga has been integrated into cardiac rehabilitation programs (Ornish et al., 1998).

Additional movement therapies conjectured to enhance mind and body health include the Alexander technique and Feldenkrais. The *Alexander technique* is based on the concept that poor posture produces functional problems in the mind and body. Those practicing this technique strive to work with unconscious thoughts and to correct poor postures, especially centered on the head, neck, and back. One uncontrolled study investigated the effects of the Alexander technique on patients with Parkinson's disease (Stallibrass, 1997). Following a series of lessons (mean number = 12), participants demonstrated decreased depressive symptoms and increased functional abilities.

Similarly, *Feldenkrais' functional integration* is based on the premise that pain and decreased movement are caused by poor usage patterns. The goal of this movement therapy is to develop "freedom through awareness" via "re-educating" motor components by using slow, purposeful movements. As a result, the body and mind are hypothesized to relax, permitting ease with movement, thinking, and feeling. One randomized controlled study investigating Feldenkrais movement was identified (Johnson, Frederick, Kaufman, & Mountjoy, 1999). In this study, patients with multiple sclerosis participated in true or sham Feldenkrais sessions. Only those participants in the true Feldenkrais intervention reported less perceived stress and anxiety.

Expressive Therapies

Expressive therapies include techniques designed to increase the person's awareness and expression of emotions. *Written emotional disclosure* refers to writing about thoughts and feelings regarding a stressful or traumatic event. This type of expressive therapy has consistently demonstrated positive effects on psychological well-being, mood, and physiological and general functioning (Smyth, 1998). Specifically, written emotional disclosure has resulted in greater positive mood, less negative mood, decreased anxiety, fewer somatic complaints, and less frequent physician visits for both students and unemployed adults (Greenberg & Stone, 1992; Pennebaker, 1993; Pennebaker, Colder, & Sharp, 1990).

With regard to medical populations, patients with rheumatoid arthritis (RA) and asthma were randomly assigned to write about either stressful experiences or a neutral topic (Smyth, Stone, Hurewitz, & Kaell, 1999). Four months following intervention, those in the former group demonstrated significant health benefits not gleaned from the group writing about neutral events. Specifically, patients with RA demonstrated improvements in overall disease activity, while those with asthma demonstrated improved lung function. Furthermore, 47% of those writing about stressful events, compared to 9% in the other group, demonstrated clinically significant improvements. Positive mood and enhanced physical function were also noted in another study in a group of patients with RA (Kelley, Lumley, & Leisen, 1997). Similar to the previous study, only participants randomly assigned to disclose stressful events (this time via verbal means) gained psychological and physical benefits, while those randomly assigned to discuss a neutral topic showed no psychological or physical health benefits.

Dance movement therapy (DMT) attempts to promote expression and reduce tension through movement. It has been prescribed in the clinical literature to help treat children and adults with behavior problems or expressive difficulties. DMT is believed to help decrease negative effects of stress (e.g., tension, fatigue) by gaining a sense of control through (a) the spiritual aspect of dance, (b) moving (e.g., increased circulation), (c) distraction from stress, and (d) confronting stressors by projecting them in dance (Hana, 1995).

While there are intervention studies investigating the benefits of DMT for patients with a range of psychological symptoms (Brooks & Stark, 1989; Stewart, McMullen, & Rubin, 1994), most were conducted with poor methodological control.

Music therapy (MT) involves the active or passive use of music to enhance health and express emotions (Achterberg et al., 1994). It has been used with adults and children who exhibit cognitive and affective deficits. In addition, patients with physical disabilities and chronic mental illness were reported to benefit from MT (Achterberg et al., 1994). A review of the literature provides support for the use of MT to decrease anxiety associated with specific events (i.e., surgery and medical procedures) in some populations (i.e., cardiac patients and premature neonates; Snyder & Chlan, 1999; and patients with asthma; Lehrer et al., 1994). With regard to depression, one study observed the impact of elderly patients who were randomly assigned to either home-based MT, self-administered MT, or waitlist control (WLC) over an eight-week period (Hanser & Thompson, 1994). Results demonstrated both MT groups achieved a greater decrease in depression than those on the waitlist, and these benefits were maintained at a nine-month follow-up assessment.

Art therapy entails using drawing, painting, or sculpting to express oneself and increase self-awareness (Achterberg et al., 1994). Art therapy has been connected with mental health since the 1800s. Few empirical studies have been conducted investigating the efficacy of art therapy as a treatment for specific medical or psychological disorders. However, Anand and Anand (1997) discussed the benefits gleaned from art therapy in patients following laryngectomy. Specifically, art therapy reportedly served as an adjunct assessment and treatment tool for patients who experience depression, anxiety, grief, and concern regarding physical appearance.

Mind/Body Therapies

Complementary and alternative therapies categorized as *mind/body* interventions have often been derived from decades of psychological and behavioral science. They are discussed in other chapters of this volume with regard to their efficacy in treatment of psychological and physical syndromes, such as pain, that are associated with various medical disorders. These include many cognitive and behavioral interventions such as relaxation training, guided visualization, cognitive restructuring, behavior modification, self-instructional training, stress inoculation training, prob-

lem solving, anger management, and psychoeducation, as well as other psychological interventions such as hypnosis and supportive group counseling.

When employed to reduce psychological distress (e.g., anxiety and depression), to manage stress, or to treat a range of other behavioral disorders, many of these therapies are well-tested and thus considered standard approaches to treatment. For example, many clinical interventions falling under the rubric of cognitive-behavioral treatment have been documented through numerous studies, reviews, and texts as effective for a wide range of psychological and behavioral problems (Beutler, Harwood, & Caldwell, 2001). Many are listed as empirically validated techniques. Cognitive-behavioral therapies are markedly present among the list of empirically supported psychotherapies (Chambless & Hollon, 1998).

When the focus of such therapies is on the reduction of medical symptoms and disease, their use may be viewed as alternative or complementary, because they have not been traditionally prescribed or employed in a medical context. However, as many of the chapters in this volume indicate, mind/body strategies have shown promise as potentially effective strategies that can alter the occurrence, course, or management of medical syndromes. Additionally, their potential effectiveness regarding many medically unexplained symptoms has been suggested (A. M. Nezu, Nezu, & Lombardo, 2001). This is particularly relevant with regard to the large percentage of individuals who seek medical care each year from their primary care physicians, in which there exists no identifiable underlying medical disease that can explain the persistent experience of certain physical symptoms (A. M. Nezu et al., 2001). Recent reviews concerning other interventions such as hypnosis have also shown promise as both alternative and complementary interventions for medical disorders such as obesity, insomnia, hypertension, asthma, irritable bowel syndrome, and dermatological disorders (Nash, 2001).

Are all complementary and alternative therapies mind/body? As traditional psychological interventions are more frequently applied to both medical and psychological parameters of disease, and as other complementary and alternative treatments described earlier in this chapter gain wider public attention and acceptance, the dichotomous line between *medical* and *nonmedical* symptoms, disorders and treatments can be rapidly blurred. As such, the concept of mind/body therapies to maintain health and heal disease can be expanded to include almost all interventions based on the understanding that such conditions represent an interaction of physical, psychological, emotional, and spiritual factors. Most of the interventions described in this chapter are "mind/body" therapies.

COMMON THEMES

From a health psychology perspective, several important themes emerge that concern the shared characteristics of alternative and complementary treatments in the context of an expanded mind/body rubric. These include:

1. A biopsychosocial model, which incorporates biological, immunological, psychological, spiritual, interpersonal, and environmental variables, characterizes an underlying mind/body philosophy of most complementary and alternative approaches. Psychological wellness is viewed as a critical component of health regarding most of these therapeutic systems. Many psychological interventions, such as cognitive-behavioral therapy, group therapy, and hypnosis, may provide strategies that increase psychological well-being and decrease distress.

2. A holistic, individualized case assessment approach is a common method of diagnosis and treatment. Although each healing approach may vary in the methodology, such as use of the interview, physical exam techniques, or tests that are administered, there is a marked tendency to design treatment specific to the individual case formulation rather than rely on a standard prescription or dosage strategy.

3. The underlying philosophy on which many complementary and alternative interventions are based view health as a state of harmony and energy balance, wherein the physical, emotional, mental, and spiritual aspects of energy are all given significant weight and seen as interrelated.

4. Treatment efficacy is most often associated with stress-related disorders and those diseases that have been etiologically linked to cognition, behavior, and lifestyle. This covers a wide range of what have been historically considered medical disorders, such as cardiac problems, diabetes, immune functioning disorders, asthma, pain syndromes, and gastrointestinal disorders.

FUTURE DIRECTIONS

Integration of Psychological Interventions and Complementary and Alternative Therapies

Because psychological health is considered such an integral part of most complementary and alternative approaches, there is wide applicability for psychological interventions to be delivered in conjunction with these approaches as part of an overall health maintenance strategy. Particularly helpful in this regard would be the widespread provision of psychoeducation and promotion of a biopsychosocial model, so that patients can learn to view psychological interventions as part of a comprehensive treatment, rather than an indication that health providers have labeled them as "crazy" or diagnosed their problem as "all in their head." Additionally, psychological interventions specifically shown to be efficacious with comorbid symptoms of anxiety and depression, which occur with high prevalence in patients with diagnosed difficulties such as cancer or heart disease, can be integrated with ongoing treatment aimed at the cancer itself.

A Decision-Making Problem

Because of the wide choice of treatments available, individuals who are interested in pursuing a more holistic approach to their health and incorporating complementary and alternative approaches are faced with the daunting task of sorting through myriad information. Media and technology have made available to the general public both the access and marketing of information concerning a wide range of health choices possible. Thus, when faced with a disease diagnosis, people are in the position of choosing from competing philosophies, therapies, and providers. Such decisions are difficult enough—when compounded by the emotional impact of an illness, a person's decision making can be further impaired (A. M. Nezu, Nezu, Friedman, Faddis, & Houts, 1998). Training patients in decision making strategies, such as social problem-solving skills, as a way of coping with the many decisions they must confront may serve as a particularly useful intervention in this regard. *Problem solving*, defined by D'Zurilla and Nezu (2001), is a "self-directed cognitive-behavioral process by which a person attempts to identify and discover effective and adaptive solutions for specific problems encountered in everyday living" (p. 212). Findings from a variety of studies have provided support for problem-solving therapy as a potent intervention to reduce stress, increase quality of life, and perhaps most germane to this discussion, increase sense of self-efficacy and confidence in making decisions (A. M. Nezu et al., 1998). Training patients in such skills can increase the likelihood that patients will become active partners with their various health care providers, deriving maximum benefit from the range and combination of treatment alternatives available.

REFERENCES

Abenhaim, L., & Bergeron, A. M. (1992). Twenty years of randomized clinical trials of manipulative therapy for back pain: A review. *Clinical and Investigative Medicine, 15*(6), 527–535.

Achterberg, J., Dossey, L., Gordon, J. S., Hegedus, C., Herrmann, M. W., & Nelson, R. (1994). Mind-body interventions. In B. M. Berman & D. B. Larson (Co-Chairs), *Alternative medicine: Expanding medical horizons. A report to the National Institutes of Health on alternative medical systems and practices in the United States prepared under the auspices of the Workshop on Alternative Medicine (1992, Chantilly, VA)* (pp. 3–43). Washington, DC: U.S. Government Printing Office.

Adler, A. J., & Holub, B. J. (1997). Effect of garlic and fish-oil supplementation on serum lipid and lipoprotein concentrations in hypercholesterolemic men. *American Journal of Clinical Nutrition, 65,* 445–450.

Alexander, C. N., Langer, E. J., Newman, R. I., Chandler, H. M., & Davies, J. L. (1989). Transcendental meditation, mindfulness and longevity: An experimental study with the elderly. *Journal of Personality and Social Psychology, 57,* 950–964.

Alexander, C. N., Robinson, P., & Rainforth, M. (1994). Treating alcohol, nicotine, and drug abuse through transcendental meditation: A review and statistical meta-analysis. *Alcoholism Treatment Quarterly, 11,* 13–87.

Almeida, J. C., & Grimsley, E. W. (1996). Coma from the health food store: Interaction between kava and alprazolam. *Annals of Internal Medicine, 125*(11), 940–941.

American Cancer Society. (1990). Unproven methods of cancer management: Gerson method. *CA—A Cancer Journal for Clinicians, 40*(4), 252–256.

American Cancer Society. (1993). Questionable methods of cancer management: "Nutritional" therapies. *CA—A Cancer Journal for Clinicians, 43*(5), 309–319.

American Psychiatric Association. (1987). *Diagnostic and statistical manual of mental disorders* (3rd ed., rev.). Washington, DC: Author.

Anand, S. A., & Anand, V. K. (1997). Art therapy with laryngectomy patients. *Art Therapy, 14,* 109–117.

Anderson, R., Meeker, W., Wirick, B. E., Mootz, R. D., Kirk, D. H., & Adams, A. (1992). A meta-analysis of clinical trials of spinal manipulation. *Journal of Manipulative and Physiological Therapeutics, 15*(3), 181–194.

Anonymous. (1988). Kava. *Lancet, 2,* 258–259.

Atkins, R. C. (1972). *Dr. Atkins' diet revolution.* New York: Bantam Books.

Barrett, B., Vohmann, M., & Calabrese, C. (1999). Echinacea for upper respiratory infection. *Journal of Family Practice, 48*(8), 628–635.

Beutler, L. E., Harwood, M. T., & Caldwell, R. (2001). Cognitive-behavioral therapy and psychotherapy integration. In K. S. Dobson (Ed.), *Handbook of cognitive and behavioral therapies* (2nd ed., pp. 138–172). New York: Guilford Press.

Blumenthal, J. A., Babyak, M. A., Moore, K. A., Craighead, W. E., Herman, S., Khatri, P., et al. (1999). Effects of exercise training on older patients with major depression. *Archives of Internal Medicine, 159,* 2349–2356.

Boline, P. D. (1991). *Chiropractic treatment and pharmaceutical treatment for muscle contraction headaches: A randomized comparative clinical trial.* Proceedings from the 1991 Conference on Spinal Manipulation, Arlington, VA; Foundation for Chiropractic Education and Research.

Bone, M. E., Wilkinson, D. J., Young, J. R., McNeil, J., & Charlton, S. (1990). Ginger root—A new antiemetic: The effect of ginger root on postoperative nausea and vomiting after major gynaecological surgery. *Anaesthesia, 45,* 669–671.

Brooks, D., & Stark, A. (1989). The effect of dance/movement therapy on affect: A pilot study. *American Journal of Dance Therapy, 11,* 101–112.

Bruger, R. A., Torres, A. R., Warren, R. P., Caldwell, V. D., & Hughes, B. G. (1997). Echinacea-induced cytokine production by human macrophages. *International Journal of Immunopharmacology, 19*(7), 371–379.

The Burton Goldberg Group. (1995). *Alternative medicine.* Fife, WA: Future Medicine.

Butterweck, V., Wall, A., Lieflander-Wulf, U., Winterhoff, H., & Nahrstedt, A. (1997). Effects of the total extract and fractions of *hypericum perforatum* in animal assays for antidepressant activity. *Pharmacopsychiatry, 30*(Suppl. 2), 117–124.

Carmack, C. L., Boudreaux, E., Amaral-Melendez, M., Brantley, P. J., & de Moor, C. (1999). Aerobic fitness and leisure activity as moderators of the stress-illness relation. *Annals of Behavioral Medicine, 21,* 251–257.

Cerrato, P. L. (1988). Natural tranquilizers. *RN, 61*(12), 61–62.

Chambless, D., & Hollon, S. D. (1998). Defining empirically supported therapies. *Journal of Consulting and Clinical Psychology, 66,* 7–18.

Chatterjee, S. S., Bhattacharya, S. K., Wonnemann, M., Singer, A., & Muller, W. E. (1998). Hyperforin as a possible antidepressant component of hypericum extracts. *Life Sciences, 63*(6), 499–510.

Chen, M. L., Lin, L. C., Wu, S. C., & Lin, J. G. (1999). The effectiveness of acupressure in improving the quality of sleep of institutionalized residents. *Journals of Gerontology: Series A, Biological Sciences and Medical Sciences, 54,* M389–M394.

Cohen, S., & Herbert, T. B. (1996). Health psychology: Psychological factors and physical disease from the perspective of human psychoneuroimmunology. *Annual Review in Psychology, 47,* 113–142.

Cooper, M. J., & Aygen, M. M. (1978). Effect of transcendental meditation on serum cholesterol and blood pressure. *Harefuah, 95*(1), 1–2.

Cott, J. M. (1997). In vitro receptor binding and enzyme inhibition by *hypericum perforatum* extract. *Pharmacopsychiatry, 30*(Suppl. 2), 108–112.

Craft, L. L., & Landers, D. M. (1998). The effect of exercise on clinical depression and depression resulting from mental illness: A meta-analysis. *Journal of Sport and Exercise Psychology, 20,* 339–357.

Crews, D. J., & Landers, D. M. (1987). A meta analytic review of aerobic fitness and reactivity to psychosocial stressors. *Medicine and Science in Sports and Exercise, 19,* S114–S120.

Culliton, P. D., & Kiresuk, T. J. (1996). Overview of substance abuse acupuncture treatment research. *Journal of Alternative and Complementary Medicine, 2*(1), 149–159.

Czekalla, J., Gastpar, M., Hubner, W. D., & Jager, D. (1997). The effect of hypericum extract on cardiac conduction as seen in the electrocardiogram compared to that of imipramine. *Pharmacopsychiatry, 30*(Suppl. 2), 86–88.

Davidson, J. R. T., Morrison, R. M., Shore, J., & Davidson, R. T. (1997). Homeopathic treatment of depression and anxiety. *Alternative Therapies in Health and Medicine, 3*(1), 46–49.

Dexter, D. (1997). Magnetic therapy is ineffective for the treatment of snoring and obstructive sleep apnea syndrome. *Wisconsin Medical Journal, 96,* 35–37.

Dibble, S. L., Chapman, J., Mack, K. A., & Shih, A. S. (2000). Acupressure for nausea: Results of a pilot study. *Oncology Nursing Forum, 27,* 41–47.

DiGiovanna, E. L., & Schiowitz, S. (Eds.). (1991). *An osteopathic approach to diagnosis and treatment.* Philadelphia: Lippincott.

Dogra, J., Grover, N., Kumar, P., & Aneja, N. (1994). Indigenous free radical scavenger MAK 4 and 5 in angina pectoris: Is it only a placebo? *Journal of the Association of Physicians of India, 42*(6), 466–467.

Dunn, C., Sleep, J., & Collett, D. (1995). Sensing an improvement: An experimental study to evaluate the use of aromatherapy, massage, and periods of rest in an intensive care unit. *Journal of Advanced Nursing, 21,* 34–40.

D'Zurilla, T. J., & Nezu, A. M. (2001). Problem-solving therapies. In K. S. Dobson (Ed.), *Handbook of cognitive and behavioral therapies* (2nd ed., pp. 211–246). New York: Guilford Press.

Eisenberg, D. M., Kessler, R. C., Foster, C., Norlock, C., Calkins, D. R., & Delbanco, T. L. (1993). Unconventional medicine in the United States: Prevalence, costs, and patterns of use. *New England Journal of Medicine, 328*(4), 246–252.

Eppley, K. R., Abrams, A., & Shear, J. (1989). Differential effects of relaxation techniques on trait anxiety: A meta-analysis. *Journal of Clinical Psychology, 45,* 957–974.

Ernst, E., Rand, J. I., & Stevinson, C. (1998). Complementary therapies for depression. *Archives of General Psychiatry, 55,* 1026–1032.

Evans, B. (1995). An audit into the effects of aromatherapy massage and the cancer patient in palliative and terminal care. *Complementary Therapies in Medicine, 3,* 239–241.

Field, T., Ironson, G., Scafidi, F., Nawrocki, T., Goncalves, A., Burman, I., et al. (1996). Massage therapy reduces anxiety and enhances EED pattern of alertness and math computations. *International Journal of Neuroscience, 86,* 197–205.

Field, T., Morrow, C., Valdeon, C., Larson, S., Kuhn, C., & Schanberg, S. (1992). Massage reduces anxiety in child and adolescent psychiatric patients. *Journal of the American Academy of Child and Adolescent Psychiatry, 31,* 125–131.

Fox, K. R. (1999). The influence of physical activity on mental well-being. *Public Health Nutrition, 2,* 411–418.

Franklin, M., Chi, J., McGavin, C., Hockney, R., Reed, A., Campling, G., et al. (1999). Neuroendocrine evidence for dopaminergic actions of hypericum extract (LI 160) in healthy volunteers. *Biological Psychiatry, 46,* 581–584.

Fremont, J., & Craighead, L. W. (1987). Aerobic exercise and cognitive therapy in the treatment of dysphoric moods. *Cognitive Therapy and Research, 11,* 241–251.

Fritz-Ritson, D. (1995). Phasic exercises for cervical rehabilitation after "whiplash" trauma. *Journal of Manipulative and Physiological Therapeutics, 18*(1), 21–24.

Gagne, D., & Toye, R. C. (1994). The effects of therapeutic touch and relaxation therapy in reducing anxiety. *Archives of Psychiatric Nursing, 8,* 184–189.

Gaster, B., & Holroyd, J. (2000). St. John's wort for depression: A systematic review. *Archives of Internal Medicine, 160,* 152–156.

Gelderloos, P., Walton, K. G., Orme-Johnson, D. W., & Alexander, C. N. (1991). Effectiveness of the transcendental meditation program in preventing and treating substance misuse: A review. *International Journal of Addictions, 26,* 293–325.

Gillis, C. N. (1997). Panax ginseng pharmacology: A nitric oxide link? *Biochemical Pharmacology, 54,* 1–8.

Glaser, J. L., Brind, J. L., Vogelman, J. H., Elsner, M. J., Dillbeck, M. C., Wallace, R. K., et al. (1992). Elevated serum dehydroepiandrosterone sulfate levels in practitioners of the transcendental meditation (TM) and TM-Sidhi programs. *Journal of Behavioral Medicine, 15*(4), 327–341.

Gould, K. L., Ornish, D., Scherwitz, L., Brown, S., Edens, R. P., Hess, M. J., et al. (1995). Changes in myocardial perfusion abnormalities by positron emission tomography after long-term, intense risk factor modification. *Journal of the American Medical Association, 274*(11), 894–901.

Greenberg, M. A., & Stone, A. A. (1992). Writing about disclosed versus undisclosed traumas: Immediate and long-term effects on mood and health. *Journal of Personality and Social Psychology, 63,* 75–84.

Grimm, W., & Muller, H. H. (1999). A randomized controlled trial of the effect of fluid extract of *echinacea purpurea* on the incidence and severity of colds and respiratory infections. *American Journal of Medicine, 106,* 138–143.

Grontved, A., Brask, T., Kambskard, J., & Hentzer, E. (1988). Ginger root against seasickness. *Acta Otolaryngolica, 105,* 45–49.

Gunning, K. (1999). Echinacea in the treatment and prevention of upper respiratory tract infections. *Western Journal of Medicine, 171,* 198–200.

Hana, J. L. (1995). The power of dance: Health and healing. *Journal of Alternative and Complementary Medicine, 4,* 323–331.

Hanna, A. N., Sharma, H. M., Kauffman, E. M., & Newman, H. A. (1994). In vitro and in vivo inhibition of microsomal lipid peroxidation by MA-631. *Pharmacology, Biochemistry, and Behavior, 48,* 505–510.

Hanser, S. B., & Thompson, L. W. (1994). Effect of music therapy strategy on depressed older adults. *Journal of Gerontology, 49,* 265–269.

Hansgen, K. D., Vesper, J., & Plouch, M. (1994). Multicenter double blind study examining the antidepressant effectiveness of the hypericum extract LI 160. *Journal of Geriatric Psychiatry and Neurology, 7,* 15–18.

Harmon, D., Gardiner, R., Harrison, R., & Kelly, A. (1999). Acupressure and the prevention of nausea and vomiting after laparoscopy. *British Journal of Anaesthesia, 82,* 387–390.

Harmon, D., Ryan, M., Kelly, A., & Bowen, M. (2000). Acupressure and the prevention of nausea and vomiting during and after spinal anaesthesia for cesarean section. *British Journal of Anaesthesia, 84,* 463–467.

Harrer, G., Hubner, W. D., & Podzuweit, H. (1994). Effectiveness and tolerance of the hypericum extract LI 160 compared to maprotiline: A multicenter double-blind study. *Journal of Geriatric Psychiatry and Neurology, 7,* S24–S28.

Hasenohrl, R. U., Nichau, C. H., Frisch, C. H., De Souza Silva, M. A., Huston, J. P., Mattern, C. M., et al. (1996). Anxiolytic-like effect of combined extracts of zingiber officinale and ginkgo biloba in the elevated plus-maze. *Pharmacology, Biochemistry, and Behavior, 53*(2), 271–275.

Hassmen, P., Koivula, N., & Uutela, A. (2000). Physical exercise and psychological well-being: A population study in Finland. *Preventative Medicine, 30,* 17–25.

Hildenbrand, G. L., Hildenbrand, L. C., Bradford, K., & Calvin, S. W. (1995). Five-year survival rates of melanoma patients treated by diet therapy after the manner of Gerson: A retrospective review [Abstract]. *Alternative Therapies in Health and Medicine, 1*(4), 29–37.

Hofferberth, B. (1994). The efficacy of EGb 761 in patients with senile dementia of the Alzheimer type, a double-blind, placebo-controlled study on different levels of investigation. *Human Psychopharmacology, 9,* 215–222.

Hruby, R. J. (1995). Session II: Contemporary philosophy and practice of osteopathic medicine. In C. M. Sirica (Ed.), *Osteopathic medicine: Past, present, and future* (pp. 49–80). New York: Josiah Macy Jr. Foundation.

Hubner, W. D., Lande, S., & Podzuweit, H. (1994). Hypericum treatment of mild depressions with somatic symptoms. *Journal of Geriatric Psychiatry and Neurology, 7,* 12–14.

Isaacsohn, J. L., Moser, M., Stein, E. A., Dudley, K., Davey, J. A., Liskov, E., et al. (1998). Garlic powder and plasma lipids and lipoproteins. *Archives of Internal Medicine, 158,* 1189–1194.

Itil, T., & Martorano, D. (1995). Natural substances in psychiatry (ginkgo biloba in dementia). *Psychopharmacology Bulletin, 31*(1), 147–158.

Jacobs, J. (1996). *The encyclopedia of alternative medicine: A complete guide to complementary therapies.* Boston: Carlton Books Limited.

Jain, A. K., Vargas, R., Gotzkowsky, S., & McMahon, F. G. (1993). Can garlic reduce levels of serum lipids? A controlled clinical study. *American Journal of Medicine, 94,* 632–635.

Jin, P. (1989). Changes in heart rate, noradrenaline, cortisol, and mood during tai chi. *Journal of Psychosomatic Research, 33*(2), 197–206.

Jin, P. (1992). Efficacy of tai chi, brisk walking, meditation, and reading in reducing mental and emotional stress. *Journal of Psychosomatic Research, 36*(4), 361–370.

Jobst, K. A. (1995). A critical analysis of acupuncture in pulmonary disease: Efficacy and safety of the acupuncture needle. *Journal of Alternative and Complementary Medicine, 1*(1), 57–85.

Johnson, S. K., Frederick, J., Kaufman, M., & Mountjoy, B. (1999). A controlled investigation of bodywork in multiple sclerosis. *Journal of Alternative and Complementary Medicine, 5,* 237–243.

Jussofie, A., Schmitz, A., & Hiemke, C. (1994). Kavapyrone enriched extract from piper methysticum as modulator of the GABA binding site in different regions of rat brain. *Psychopharmacology, 116,* 469–474.

Kanowski, S., Hermann, W. M., Stephan, K., Wierich, W., & Horr, R. (1996). Proof of efficacy of ginkgo biloba special extract EGb 761 in outpatients suffering from mild to moderate primary degenerative dementia of the Alzheimer type or multi-infarct dementia. *Pharmacopsychiatry, 29,* 47–56.

Kelley, J. E., Lumley, M. A., & Leisen, J. C. C. (1997). Health effects of emotional disclosure in rheumatoid arthritis patients. *Health Psychology, 16,* 331–340.

Kim, H.-S., Oh, K.-W., Rheu, H.-M., & Kim, S.-H. (1992). Antagonism of U-50, 448H-induced antinociception by ginseng total saponins is dependent on serotonergic mechanisms. *Pharmacology, Biochemistry, and Behavior, 42,* 587–593.

Kim, H. L., Streltzer, J., & Goebert, D. (1999). St. John's wort for depression: A meta-analysis of well-defined clinical trials. *Journal of Nervous and Mental Diseases, 187*(9), 532–538.

Kleijnen, J., & Knipschild, P. (1992). Ginkgo biloba for cerebral insufficiency. *British Journal of Clinical Pharmacology, 34,* 352–358.

Kleijnen, J., Knipschild, P., & ter Riet, G. (1989). Garlic, onions and cardiovascular risk factors: A review of the evidence from human experiments with emphasis on commercially available preparations. *British Journal of Clinical Pharmacology, 28,* 535–544.

Kleijnen, J., Knipschild, P., & ter Riet, G. (1991). Clinical trials of homeopathy. *British Medical Journal, 302,* 316–323.

Klougart, N., Nilsson, N., & Jacobsen, J. (1989). Infantile colic treated by chiropractor. *Journal of Manipulative and Physiological Therapeutics, 12*(4), 281–288.

Komori, T., Fujiwara, R., Tanida, M., Nomura, J., & Yokoyama, M. M. (1995). Effects of citrus fragrance on immune function and depressive states. *Neuroimmunomodulation, 2,* 174–180.

Koshimizu, K., Ohigashi, H., Tokudo, H., Kondo, A., & Yamaguchi, K. (1988). Screening of edible plants against anti-tumor promoting activity. *Cancer Letters, 39,* 247–257.

Kramer, N. A. (1990). Comparison of therapeutic touch and causal touch in stress reduction of hospitalized children. *Pediatric Nursing, 16,* 483–485.

Kugler, J., Seelbach, H., & Kruskemper, G. M. (1994). Effects of rehabilitation exercise programmes in anxiety and depression in coronary patients: A meta-analysis. *British Journal of Clinical Psychology, 33,* 401–410.

Laakmann, G., Schule, C., Baghai, T., & Kieser, M. (1998). St. John's wort in mild to moderate depression: The relevance of hyperforin for the clinical efficacy. *Pharmacopsychiatry, 31*(Suppl. 1), 54–59.

Lai, J. S., & Lan, C. (1995). Two-year trends in cardiorespiratory function among older tai chi chuan practitioners and sedentary subjects. *Journal of American Geriatrics Society, 43,* 1222–1227.

Lantz, M. S., Buchalter, E., & Giambanco, V. (1999). St. John's work and antidepressant drug interactions in the elderly. *Journal of Geriatric Psychiatry and Neurology, 12,* 7–10.

Le Bars, P., Katz, M. M., Berman, N., Itil, T. M., Freedman, A. M., & Schatzberg, A. F. (1997). A placebo-controlled, double-blind, randomized trial of an extract of ginkgo biloba for dementia. *Journal of the American Medical Association, 278*(16), 1327–1332.

Leboeuf, C., Brown, P., Herman, A., Leembruggen, K., Walton, D., & Crisp, T. C. (1991). Chiropractic care of children with nocturnal enuresis: A prospective outcome study. *Journal of Manipulative and Physiological Therapeutics, 14*(2), 110–115.

Lehrer, P. M., Hochron, S. M., Mayne, T., Isenberg, S., Carlson, V., Lasoski, M., et al. (1994). Relaxation and music therapies for asthma among patients prestabilized on asthma medications. *Journal of Behavioral Medicine, 17,* 1–21.

Li, H. K., Gulanick, M., Lanuza, D., & Penckofer, S. (1999). The relationship between physical activity and perimenopause. *Health Care for Women International, 20,* 163–178.

Lichtenstein, A. H., & Van Horn, L. (1998). Very low fat diets. *Circulation, 98*(9), 935–939.

Linde, K., Claudius, N., Ramirez, G., Melchart, D., Eitel, F., Hedges, L. V., et al. (1997). Are the clinical effects of homeopathy placebo effects? A meta-analysis of placebo-controlled trials. *Lancet, 350,* 834–843.

Linde, K., Ramirez, G., Mulrow, C., Pauls, A., Weidenhammer, W., & Melchart, D. (1996). St. John's wort for depression: An overview and meta-analysis of randomized clinical trials. *British Medical Journal, 313,* 253–258.

Liu, Y. (1988). *The essential book of traditional Chinese medicine: Clinical practice* (Vol. 2). New York: Columbia University Press.

Luckle, A. (1989). *The family guide to homeopathy.* New York: Simon & Schuster.

Luo, H., Jia, Y., Wu, X., & Dai, W. (1990). Electro-acupuncture in the treatment of depressive psychosis. *International Journal of Clinical Acupuncture, 1,* 7–13.

Luo, H., Jia, Y., & Zhan, L. (1985). Electro-acupuncture in the treatment of depressive states. *Journal of Traditional Chinese Medicine, 5,* 3–8.

Magura, E. I., Kopanitsa, M. V., Gleitz, J., Peters, T., & Krishtal, O. A. (1997). Kava extract ingredients, (+)-methysticin and (+−)-kavain inhibit voltage-operated Na+-channels in rat CA1 hippocampal neurons. *Neuroscience, 81*(2), 345–351.

Margetts, B. M., Beilin, L. J., Vandongen, R., & Armstrong, B. K. (1986). Vegetarian diet in mild hypertension: A randomised controlled trial. *British Medical Journal, 293,* 1468–1471.

Martin, G. N. (1996). Olfactory remediation: Current evidence and possible applications. *Social Science and Medicine, 43,* 63–70.

Melchart, D., Walther, E., Linde, K., Brandmaier, R., & Lersch, C. (1998). Echinacea root extracts for the prevention of upper respiratory tract infections: A double-blind, placebo-controlled trial. *Archives of Family Medicine, 7,* 541–545.

Micozzi, M. S. (1996). *Fundamentals of complementary and alternative medicine.* New York: Churchill-Livingstone.

Micozzi, M. S. (1999). *Current review of complementary medicine.* Philadelphia: Current Medicine.

Mowrey, D. B., & Clayson, D. E. (1982). Motion sickness, ginger, and psychophysics. *Lancet, 1,* 655–657.

Muller W. E., & Kasper, S. (1997). Clinically used antidepressant drugs. *Pharmacopsychiatry, 30*(Suppl. 2), 71.

Muller, W. E., Rolli, M., Schafer, C., & Hafner, U. (1997). Effects of hypericum extract (LI 160) in biochemical models of antidepressant activity. *Pharmacopsychiatry, 30*(Suppl. 2), 102–107.

Muller, W. E., & Rossol, R. (1994). Effects of hypericum extract on the expression of serotonin receptors. *Journal of Geriatric Psychiatry and Neurology, 7*(Suppl. 1), S63–S64.

Muller, W. E., Singer, A., Wonnemann, M., Hafner, U., Rolli, M., & Schafer, C. (1998). Hyperforin represents the neurotransmitter reuptake inhibiting constituent of hypericum extract. *Pharmacopsychiatry, 31*(Suppl. 1), 16–21.

Nahrstedt, A., & Butterweck, V. (1997). Biologically active and other chemical constituents of the herb of *hypericum perforatum* L. *Pharmacopsychiatry, 30*(Suppl. 2), 129–134.

Nash, M. R. (2001). The truth and the hype of hypnosis, *Scientific American, 285,* 46–55.

National Cholesterol Education Program Expert Panel. (1988). Report of the National Cholesterol Education Program Expert Panel on detection, evaluation, and treatment of high blood cholesterol in adults. *Archives of Internal Medicine, 148,* 36–69.

Neary, J. T., & Bu, Y. (1999). Hypericum LI 160 inhibits uptake of serotonin and norepinephrine in astrocytes. *Brain Research, 816,* 358–363.

Nezu, A. M., Nezu, C. M., Friedman, S. H., Faddis, S., & Houts, P. S. (1998). *Helping cancer patients cope: A problem-solving approach.* Washington, DC: American Psychological Association.

Nezu, A. M., Nezu, C. M., & Lombardo, E. R. (2001). Cognitive-behavior therapy for medically unexplained symptoms: A critical review of the treatment literature, *Behavior Therapist, 32,* 537–583.

Nezu, C. M., Nezu, A. M., Baron, K. P., & Roessler, E. (2000). Alternative therapies. In G. Fink (Ed.), *Encyclopedia of stress* (Vol. 1, pp. 150–158). San Diego, CA: Academic Press.

North, T. C., McCullagh, P., & Tran, Z. V. (1990). Effect of exercise on depression. *Exercise and Sports Science Review, 18,* 379–415.

Norton, S. A., & Ruze, P. (1994). Kava dermopathy. *Journal of the American Academy of Dermatology, 31,* 89–97.

Oken, B. S., Storzbach, D. M., & Kaye, J. A. (1998). The efficacy of ginkgo biloba on cognitive function in Alzheimer disease. *Archives of Neurology, 55,* 1409–1415.

Olson, M., Sneed, N., LaVia, M., Virella, G., Bonadonna, R., & Michel, V. (1997). Stress-induced immunosuppression and therapeutic touch. *Alternative Therapies, 3,* 68–74.

Ornish, D., Brown, S., Scherwitz, L. W., Billings, J. H., Armstrong, W. T., Portis, T., et al. (1990). Can lifestyle changes reverse coronary hear disease: The lifestyle heart trial. *Lancet, 336,* 129–133.

Ornish, D., Scherwitz, L. W., Billings, J. H., Gould, K. L., Merritt, T. A., Sparler, S., et al. (1998). Intensive lifestyle changes for reversal of coronary heart disease. *Journal of the American Medical Association, 280*(23), 2001–2007.

Palmer, D. D. (1910). *Textbook of the science, art and philosophy of chiropractic.* Portland, OR: Portland Printing House.

Panjwani, U., Gupta, H. L., Singh, S. H., Selvamurthy, W., & Rai, U. C. (1995). Effect of Sahaja yoga practice on stress management in patients with epilepsy. *Indian Journal of Physiology and Pharmacology, 39,* 111–116.

Patel, M., Gutzwiller, F., Paccand, F., & Marazzi, A. (1989). A meta-analysis of acupuncture for chronic pain. *International Journal of Epidemiology, 18*(4), 900–906.

Peck, S. D. (1998). The efficacy of therapeutic touch from improving functional abilities in elders with degenerative arthritis. *Nursing Science Quarterly, 11,* 123–132.

Pelletier, K. R. (1992). Mind-body health: Research, clinical, and policy applications. *American Journal of Health Promotion, 6,* 345–358.

Pennebaker, J. W. (1993). Putting stress into words: Health, linguistic, and therapeutic implications. *Behavioral Research and Therapy, 31,* 539–548.

Pennebaker, J. W., Colder, M., & Sharp, L. K. (1990). Accelerating the coping process. *Journal of Personality and Social Psychology, 58,* 528–537.

Phillips, S., Ruggier, R., & Hutchinson, S. E. (1993). Zingiber officinale (Ginger)—An antiemetic for day case surgery. *Anaesthesia, 48,* 715–717.

Plamondon, R. L. (1995). Summary of 1994 ACA annual statistical study. *Journal of American Chiropractic Association, 32*(1), 57–63.

Porsolt, R. D., Martin, P., Lenegre, A., Fromage, S., & Drieu, K. (1990). Effects of an extract of ginkgo biloba (EGB 761) on "learned helplessness" and other models of stress in rodents. *Pharmacology, Biochemistry, and Behavior, 36,* 963–971.

Rai, G. S., Shovlin, C., & Wesnes, K. A. (1991). A double-blind, placebo controlled study of ginkgo biloba extracts (Tanakan) in elderly outpatients with mild to moderate memory impairment. *Current Medical Research and Opinion, 12*(6), 350–355.

Ramsey, S. M. (1997). Holistic manual therapy techniques. *Primary Care: Clinics in Office Practice, 24,* 759–786.

Rapin, J. R., Lamproglou, I., Drieu, K., & Defeudis, F. V. (1994). Demonstration of the "anti-stress" activity of an extract of ginkgo biloba (EGb 761) using a discrimination learning task. *General Pharmacology, 25*(5), 1009–1016.

Reed, W. R., Beavers, S., Reddy, S. K., & Kern, G. (1994). Chiropractic management of primary nocturnal enuresis. *Journal of Manipulative and Physiological Therapeutics, 17*(9), 596–600.

Reilly, D. T., Taylor, M. A., Beattie, N. G., Campbell, J. H., McSharry, C., Aitchison, T. C., et al. (1994). Is evidence for homeopathy reproducible? *Lancet, 344,* 1601–1606.

Reilly, D. T., Taylor, M. A., McSharry, C., & Aitchison, T. (1986). Is homeopathy a placebo response? Controlled trial of homeopathic potency, with pollen in hay fever as model. *Lancet, 2,* 881–886.

Roach, E. S. (1998). Alternative neurology: The ketogenic diet. *Archives of Neurology, 55*(1), 1403–1404.

Rodriguez de Turco, E. B., Droy-Lefaix, M. T., & Bazan, N. G. (1993). EGb 761 inhibits stress-induced polydipsia in rats. *Physiology and Behavior, 53,* 1001–1002.

Rouse, I. L., Beilin, L. J., Armstrong, B. K., & Vandongen, R. (1983). Blood-pressure-lowering effect of a vegetarian diet: Controlled trial in normotensive subjects. *Lancet, 1,* 5–10.

Ryu, H., Lee, H. S., Shin, Y. S., Chung, S. M., Lee, M. S., Kim, H. M., et al. (1996). Acute effect of qigong training on stress hormonal levels in man. *American Journal of Chinese Medicine, 24*(2), 193–198.

Schellenberg, R., Sauer, S., & Dimpfel, W. (1998). Pharmacodynamic effects of two different hypericum extracts in healthy volunteers measured by quantitative EEG. *Pharmacopsychiatry, 31*(Suppl. 1), 44–53.

Schlicht, W. (1994). Does physical exercise reduce anxious emotions? A meta-analysis. *Anxiety, Stress, and Coping: an International Journal, 6,* 275–288.

See, D. M., Broumand, N., Sahl, L., & Tilles, J. G. (1997). In vitro effects of echinacea and ginseng on natural killer and antibody-dependent cell cytotoxicity in healthy subjects and chronic fatigue syndrome or acquired immunodeficiency syndrome patients. *Immunopharmacology, 35,* 229–235.

Segar, M. L., Katch, V. L., Roth, R. S., Garcia, A. W., Portner, T. I., Glickman, S. G., et al. (1998). The effect of aerobic exercise on self-esteem and depressive and anxiety symptoms among breast cancer survivors. *Oncology Nursing Forum, 25,* 101–113.

Sharma, H. M., Dwivedi, C., Satter, B. C., Gudehithlu, C. P., Abou-Issa, H., Malarkey, W., et al. (1991). Antineoplastic properties of Maharishi-4 against DMBA-induced mammary tumors in rats. *Pharmacology, Biochemistry, and Behavior, 35,* 767–773.

Shekelle, P. G., Adams, A. H., Chassin, M. R., Hurwitz, E. L., & Brook, R. H. (1992). Spinal manipulation of low-back pain. *Annals of Internal Medicine, 117*(7), 590–598.

Silagy, C., & Neil, A. (1994). Garlic as a lipid lowering agent: A meta-analysis. *Journal of the Royal College of Physicians of London, 28*(1), 39–45.

Sirica, C. M. (Ed.). (1995). *Osteopathic medicine: Past, present, and future.* New York: Josiah Macy Jr. Foundation.

Smit, H. F., Woerdenbag, H. J., Singh, R. H., Meulenbeld, G. J., Labadie, R. P., & Zwaving, J. H. (1995). Ayurvedic herbal drugs with possible cytostatic activity. *Journal of Ethnopharmacology, 47*(2), 75–84.

Smyth, J. M. (1998). Written emotional expression: Effect sizes, outcome types, and moderating variables. *Journal of Consulting and Clinical Psychology, 66,* 174–184.

Smyth, J. M., Stone, A. A., Hurewitz, A., & Kaell, A. (1999). Effects of writing about stressful experiences on symptom reduction in patients with asthma or rheumatoid arthritis: A randomized trial. *Journal of the American Medical Association, 281,* 1304–1309.

Snyder, M., & Chlan, L. (1999). Music therapy. *Annual Review of Nursing Research, 17,* 3–25.

Sommer, H., & Harrer, G. (1994). Placebo-controlled double blind study examining the effectiveness of a hypericum preparation in 105 mildly depressed patients. *Journal of Geriatric Psychiatry and Neurology, 7*(Suppl. 1), 9–11.

Sonoda, Y., Kasahara, T., Mukaida, N., Shimizu, N., Tomoda, M., & Takeda, T. (1998). Stimulation of interleukin-8 production by acidic polysaccharides from the root of Panax ginseng. *Immunopharmacology, 38,* 287–294.

Sotaniemi, E. A., Haapakoski, E., & Rautio, A. (1995). Ginseng therapy in non-insulin-dependent diabetic patients. *Diabetes Care, 18*(10), 1373–1375.

Spencer, J. W., & Jacobs, J. J. (1999). *Complementary/alternative medicine: An evidence-based approach.* St. Louis, MO: Mosby.

Stallibrass, C. (1997). An evaluation of the Alexander Technique for the management of disability in Parkinson's disease: A preliminary study. *Clinical Rehabilitation, 11,* 8–12.

Stanton, H. E. (1981). Enuresis, homeopathy, and enhancement of the placebo effect. *American Journal of Clinical Hypnosis, 24*(1), 59–61.

Steiner, M., Khan, A. H., Holbert, D., & Lin, I.-S. (1996). A double-blind crossover study in moderately hypercholesterolemic men that compared the effect of aged garlic extract and placebo

administration on blood lipids. *American Journal of Clinical Nutrition, 64,* 866–870.

Stephenson, N. L., Weinrich, S. P., & Tavakoli, A. S. (2000). The effects of foot reflexology on anxiety and pain in patients with breast and lung cancer. *Oncology Nursing Forum, 27,* 67–72.

Stewart, N. J., McMullen, L. M., & Rubin, L. D. (1994). Movement therapy with depressed inpatients: A randomized multiple single-case design. *Archives of Psychiatric Nursing, 8,* 22–29.

Takahashi, M., Tokuyama, S., & Kaneto, H. (1992). Anti-stress effect of ginseng on the inhibition of the development of morphine tolerance in stressed mice. *Japanese Journal of Pharmacology, 59,* 399–404.

ter Riet, G., Kleijnen, J., & Knipschild, P. (1990). Acupuncture and chronic pain: A criteria-based meta-analysis. *Journal of Clinical Epidemiology, 43,* 1191–1199.

Teufel-Mayer, R., & Gleitz, J. (1997). Effects of long-term administration of hypericum extracts on the affinity and density of the central serotonergic 5-HT1 A and 5-HT2 A receptors. *Pharmacopsychiatry, 30*(Suppl. 2), 113–116.

Tsutumi, T., Don, B. M., Zaichkowsky, L. D., Takenaka, K., Oka, K., & Ohno, T. (1998). Comparison of high and moderate intensity of strength training on mood and anxiety in older adults. *Perceptual and Motor Skills, 87,* 1003–1011.

Uebelhack, R., Franke, L., & Schewe, H. J. (1998). Inhibition of platelet MAO-B by kava pyrone-enriched extract from piper methysticum forster (Kava-kava). *Pharmacopsychiatry, 31,* 187–192.

Vickers, A. J. (1996). Can acupuncture have specific effects on health? A systematic review of acupuncture antiemesis trials. *Journal of the Royal Society of Medicine, 89,* 303–311.

Vimala, S., Norhanom, A. W., & Yadav, M. (1999). Anti-tumor promoter activity in Malaysian ginger rhizobia used in traditional medicine. *British Journal of Cancer, 80*(1/2), 110–116.

Vincent, C. A. (1989). A controlled trial of the treatment of migraine acupuncture. *Clinical Journal of Pain, 5,* 305–312.

Vining, E. P. G., Freeman, J. M., Ballaban-Gil, K., Camfield, C. S., Camfield, P. R., Holmes, G. L., et al. (1998). A multicenter study of the efficacy of the ketogenic diet. *Archives of Neurology, 55*(11), 1433–1437.

Volz, H. P., & Keiser, M. (1997). Kava-kava extract WS 1490 versus placebo in anxiety disorders: A randomized placebo-controlled 25-week outpatient trial. *Pharmacopsychiatry, 30,* 1–5.

Vorbach, E. U., Hubner, W. D., & Arnold, K. H. (1994). Effectiveness and tolerance of the hypericum extract LI 160 in comparison with imipramine. *Journal of Geriatric Psychiatry and Neurology, 7*(Suppl. 1), S19–S23.

Wagner, J., Wagner, M. M., & Hening, W. A. (1998). Beyond benzodiazepines: Alternative pharmacologic agents for the treatment of insomnia. *Neuropsychiatry, 32,* 680–691.

Walden, J., Von Wegerer, J., Winter, U., & Berger, M. (1997). Actions of kavain and dihydromethysticin on ipsapirone-induced field potential changes in the hippocampus. *Human Psychopharmacology, 12,* 265–270.

Walden, J., Von Wegerer, J., Winter, U., Berger, M., & Grunze, H. (1997). Effects of kawain and dihydromethysticin on fieldpotential changes in the hippocampus. *Progress in Neuro-Psychopharmacology and Biological Psychiatry, 21,* 697–706.

Wanning, T. (1993). Healing and the mind/body arts. *American Association of Occupational Health Nurses Journal, 41,* 349–351.

Warshafsky, S., Kamer, R. S., & Sivak, S. L. (1993). Effect of garlic on total serum cholesterol. *Annals of Internal Medicine, 119,* 599–605.

Warwick-Evans, L. A., Masters, I. J., & Redstone, S. B. (1991). A double-blind placebo controlled evaluation of acupressure in the treatment of motion sickness. *Aviation Space and Environmental Medicine, 62,* 776–778.

Watkins, A. D. (1994). The role of alternative therapies in the treatment of allergic diseases. *Clinical and Experimental Allergy, 24*(9), 813–825.

Wesnes, K. A., Feleni, R. A., Hefting, N. R., Hoogsteen, G., Houben, J. J. G., Jenkins, E., et al. (1997). The cognitive, subjective, and physical effects of a ginkgo biloba/Panax ginseng combination in healthy volunteers with neurasthenic complaints. *Psychopharmacology Bulletin, 33*(4), 677–683.

Wheatley, D. (1997). LI 160, an extract of St. Johns' wort, versus amitriptyline in mildly to moderately depressed outpatients: A controlled 6-week clinical trial. *Pharmacopsychiatry, 30*(Suppl. 2), 77–80.

Wiklund, I., Karlberg, J., & Lund, B. (1994). A double-blind comparison of the effect on quality of life of a combination of vital substances including standardized ginseng G115 and placebo. *Current Therapeutic Research, 55*(1), 32–42.

Winkel, D., Aufdemkampe, G., Matthijs, O., Meijer, O. G., & Phelps, V. (1996). *Diagnosis and treatment of the spine.* Gaithersburg, MD: Aspen.

Winstead-Fry, P., & Kijek, J. (1999). An integrative review and meta-analysis of therapeutic touch research. *Alternative Therapies in Health and Medicine, 5,* 58–67.

Woelk, H., Burkard, G., & Grunwald, J. (1994). Benefits and risks of the hypericum extract LI 160: Drug monitoring study with 3250 patients. *Journal of Geriatric Psychiatry and Neurology, 7*(Suppl. 1), S34–S38.

Wong, A. H. C., Smith, M., & Boon, H. S. (1998). Herbal remedies in psychiatric practice. *Archives of General Psychiatry, 55,* 1033–1044.

Woo, C. C. (1993). Post-traumatic myelopathy following flopping high jump: A pilot case of spinal manipulation. *Journal of Manipulative and Physiological Therapeutics, 16*(5), 336–341.

Wood, C. (1993). Mood change and perceptions of vitality: A comparison of the effects of relaxation, visualization, and yoga. *Journal of the Royal Society of Medicine, 86,* 254–258.

Yun, T.-K. (1996). Experimental and epidemiological evidence of the cancer-preventive effects of Panax ginseng C. A. Meyer. *Nutrition Reviews, 54*(11), S71–S81.

Author Index

Author Index **627**